# The Case Approach to Financial Planning

## Bridging the Gap between Theory and Practice, Second Edition

John E. Grable • Derek D. Klock • Ruth H. Lytton

National Underwriter Academic Series

ISBN 978-1-936362-99-8

**THE NATIONAL UNDERWRITER COMPANY**

Copyright © 2008, 2013
The National Underwriter Company
5081 Olympic Blvd.
Erlanger, KY 41018

Second Edition

Printed in the United States of America

# ABOUT THE AUTHORS

## JOHN E. GRABLE, PH.D., CFP®

*Professor and Athletic Association Endowed Professor of Family Financial Planning, University of Georgia*

John Grable received his undergraduate degree in economics and business from the University of Nevada, MBA from Clarkson University, and Ph.D. from Virginia Tech. He teaches and conducts research in the CFP Board of Standards Inc. undergraduate and graduate program at the University of Georgia. Prior to entering the academic profession he worked as a pension/benefits administrator and later as a Registered Investment Advisor in an asset management firm. Dr. Grable served as the founding editor for the *Journal of Personal Finance*, a rigorous peer-reviewed research journal, and he is currently the co-editor of the *Journal of Financial Therapy*. His research interests include financial risk-tolerance assessment, financial planning help-seeking behavior, and financial therapy/counseling. He has been the recipient of several research and publication awards and grants, and is active in promoting the link between research and financial planning practice where he has published numerous refereed papers, co-authored two financial planning textbooks, and co-edited a financial planning and counseling scales book. Dr. Grable has served on the Board of Directors of the International Association of Registered Financial Consultants (IARFC), as Treasurer and President for the American Council on Consumer Interests (ACCI), and as Treasurer for the Financial Therapy Association. He also served on the Research Advisory Council of the Take Charge America Institute (TCAI) for Consumer Education and Research at the University of Arizona. He is the recipient of the prestigious Cato Award for Distinguished Journalism in the Field of Financial Services, the IARFC Founders Award, and the Dawley-Scholer Award for Faculty Excellence in Student Development, and the ACCI Mid-Career Award.

## DEREK D. KLOCK, M.B.A.

*Assistant Professor of Practice, Pamplin College of Business, Virginia Tech*

Derek Klock is an award-winning faculty member at Virginia Tech. During his six-year tenure with the Department of Finance he has won both departmental and university awards for his teaching and his career-advising efforts, including the Herakovich Undergraduate Teaching Excellence Award and the Virginia Tech Award for Excellence in Career Advising. Mr. Klock serves as the Coordinator of the Pamplin Finance CFP Program and also serves as the career advisor for the more than 500 undergraduate Finance majors. He is the co-advisor to the student-led, fixed-income, investment group BASIS that manages approximately $5 million for the Virginia Tech Foundation. He has developed print and digital financial education tools, including the co-development of personal financial planning educational software packages for top-ranking collegiate-level textbooks. He is also the co-author for two financial planning books. Mr. Klock serves the financial planning industry as a consultant to the *NextGen* initiative of *Investment News* and has previously served as a board member for the International Association of Registered Financial Consultants (IARFC) and as a reviewer for the *Journal of Personal Finance*. Mr. Klock received both his Bachelor's degree and MBA from Virginia Tech. Prior to returning to the Pamplin College of Business to pursue his MBA, he worked in the banking and brokerage industry for nearly five years. Since leaving banking, Mr. Klock has worked as an independent financial advisor and consultant. He has previously held the Virginia State Life and Health Agents License, and the NASD (now FINRA) Series 6, 7, and 63 registrations as well as the Registered Financial Consultant (RFC) designation. Mr. Klock also served the nation in the military where he was twice decorated for meritorious achievement during his service as a Drill Sergeant.

# RUTH H. LYTTON, PH.D.

*Professor, Financial Planning, Virginia Tech*

Ruth Lytton is the Director of the CFP Board of Standards, Inc.-Registered undergraduate programs at Virginia Tech. In addition to serving as program director, she provides student services (e.g., academic/career advising, internship supervision, and job placement coaching) and teaches several courses. Dr. Lytton has received various student association, university, and national professional association awards for her contributions as a teacher, researcher, and career/academic advisor, including the College of Human Resources Certificate of Teaching Excellence, the North American Colleges & Teachers of Agriculture (NACTA) Teaching Award of Merit, the College of Human Resources and Education Excellence in Undergraduate Student Advising Award, the Virginia Tech Award for Excellence in Career Advising, and the Association for Financial Counseling and Planning Education (AFCPE) Mary Ellen Edmondson Educator of the Year Award. Over her career, over 5,000 students have taken her introductory personal finance course. She is co-author of two financial planning books as well the student study guide, instructor's manual and other print and digital resources for multiple editions of a leading personal finance textbook. She is an academic member of the National Association of Personal Financial Advisors (NAPFA) and the Financial Planning Association (FPA). In 2009 she was awarded the John H. Cecil Lifetime Service Award from the Central Virginia Chapter of the Financial Planning Association (FPA). Dr. Lytton also serves as an Advisory Editor for the Social Science Research Network's (SSRN) *Journal in Behavioral & Experimental Finance*. She previously served as Editor of the *Journal of Personal Finance,*and currently serves on the Editorial Board. Dr. Lytton received her B.S., M.S., and Ph.D. from Virginia Tech. Honorary memberships include Phi Upsilon Omicron, Phi Sigma Society, Kappa Omicron Nu, Phi Kappa Phi, and Golden Key National Honor Society.

# ACKNOWLEDGMENTS

Creating a book of this magnitude is not without challenges. Several individuals have been instrumental in keeping the project on task. First and foremost, we will always be grateful to the editors at National Underwriter who showed unwavering confidence in the original casebook concept. Without their editorial leadership you would not be holding this book today. This edition of the book would not have been possible without the tireless work of our editor, Jane Garwood. Little did she know what she was tackling when she first met us. Her patience, diligence, encouragement, and editing talents made this revision come together. Thanks also go to Kathy Flanagan, Diana Rietz, Rick Kravitz, and Gerry Centrowitz for fully supporting this book from revision to publication. The anonymous reviewers who spent countless hours evaluating chapters prior to publication also deserve sincere thanks.

We are also thankful for the opportunity to have worked with undergraduate, graduate, and certificate financial planning students over the past several years. Through this daily work with students the idea of this case book was formulated. Every student who has passed through the financial planning programs at Kansas State University and Virginia Tech has had an impact on this book. We are immensely thankful for what you taught us, and how you challenged us to strive for better ways to explain and teach financial planning.

We would also like to say a special "thank you" to our families. Without your support this book would never have been completed.

# PREFACE

The profession of financial planning has expanded quickly since its inception in 1969. Then financial planning consisted of little more than a small consortium of financial services professionals interested in offering clients something in addition to insurance and mutual fund products. Increasingly, financial planning is a respected career captured in broad but dynamic statements such as "financial planners and wealth managers help individuals plan their financial futures."[1] Today, financial planning has reached the pinnacle of sought-after careers. In 2011, CNN Money ranked the financial adviser profession Number 3 in terms of job growth with a projected 10-year job growth rate of 30%.[2] In 2012 CareerCast.com ranked financial planner the Number 5 job in its top-10 list.[3] It is not surprising, then, that the Bureau of Labor Statistics predicts that employment opportunities for personal financial advisors will continue to grow much faster than average. It projects more than 32% growth in employment from 2010 through 2020; 14% is the average growth rate for all other occupations.[4]

One effect of the growth in financial planning is that the study of financial planning has taken root as an academic discipline on college campuses, offering both undergraduate and graduate education as well as professional certificates. The need for a case study methodology to help educate future financial planners has been ongoing since the first financial planning courses were developed. But the requirement that a financial plan development course be included in the curriculum for all students undertaking a CFP Board of Standards, Inc., registered program in 2012 cemented this need. With the growing demand for well-trained planners, the demand for cases today is more apparent than ever. *A Case Approach to Financial Planning: Bridging the Gap between Theory and Practice, Second Edition* was written to meet the need for a comprehensive case study methodology book.

Thus, this text was not designed to be a casebook, an advanced financial planning book, or a CFP® certification exam preparation book—although we believe it is, to some extent, a combination of all three. As a casebook, this text includes a comprehensive teaching case, 11 mini-cases, and numerous case examples in each chapter to which the topics, tools, and techniques of financial planning are applied. As an advanced financial planning book, it provides a review of basic—and in some chapters, more advanced—content, particularly as applied in select case examples. Finally, as a CFP® certification exam preparation book, it attempts to provide a review of relevant content matched to many of the 78 CFP Board topical areas. But *A Case Approach to Financial Planning, Second Edition* is the first and only book of its kind where the advanced concepts of developing an integrated financial plan are taught from the foundation of client situational analysis leading to actionable recommendations that can be critiqued and combined into a comprehensive financial plan, including an explanation of implementation and monitoring.

# PURPOSE

This book was written to illustrate how the systematic financial planning process developed by Lytton, Grable, and Klock in the *Process of Financial Planning, Second Edition*, published by National Underwriter, can be used to help clients achieve multiple financial goals and objectives through a financial plan. A second purpose of the book is to provide quality case studies to practice the case study methodology and help students gain confidence in identifying, applying, and integrating synergistic personal finance strategies into plans. Several objectives guided the development of the book, which offers:

- Review of the steps necessary to complete a current situation analysis in the core content areas of financial planning

- Summarized reviews of commonly used financial planning product and procedural strategies, including the advantages and disadvantages of each

- Review of the unique challenges of each core content area as applied to a special population or more narrowly defined financial planning audience

- A continuous case that can be used to practice current situation analysis and to write a comprehensive financial plan

- Chapter-based case studies that illustrate the use of specific strategies to meet client needs

- End-of-chapter mini-cases that apply core content planning knowledge from each chapter

- Several targeted financial planning cases that address and, in some situations, integrate specific financial planning knowledge

## UNDERLYING ASSUMPTIONS

When first conceptualized, *A Case Approach to Financial Planning* was unlike any other casebook of its kind. Little has changed today except that the demand for a case study methodology for developing a plan, cases for applying knowledge and practicing skills, and models for integrated, actionable financial planning recommendations continues to grow. This second edition has been refined to better meet the needs of students and instructors. Because of its unique focus, it is very important that readers fully understand the core assumptions of the book before reading chapters or completing case assignments. The following points comprise key underlying assumptions:

- This is a companion book to *The Process of Financial Planning, Second Edition* by Ruth Lytton, John Grable, and Derek Klock and published by The National Underwriter Company. Readers interested in knowing more about the systematic financial planning process and how it applies to developing and writing comprehensive financial plans ought to read *The Process of Financial Planning, Second Edition*. This text assumes that readers already have a foundation in the systematic process of financial planning; thus, only a limited review of the process is provided here.

- This text is intended for use in midlevel or capstone courses in financial planning programs at colleges and universities. It is appropriate for use at the undergraduate, graduate, and certificate levels. When used at the undergraduate level, it is assumed that the book will be used in the final course of a student's last semester or term. Although a review of key planning assumptions is provided in each core content chapter, this book is not—nor should it be considered—a replacement for a financial planning textbook in each core content area. *A Case Approach to Financial Planning, Second Edition,* as the name implies, is primarily a case book that illustrates a case methodology in the context of the systematic financial planning process.

- To successfully complete case assignments and questions, students are assumed to have already completed or be enrolled in classes in the six core areas of financial planning: Financial Situation Analysis, Tax Planning, Insurance (Risk Management) Planning, Investment Planning, Retirement Planning, and Estate Planning. This text offers a review of important concepts and strategies, but in no way are the core content chapters intended to provide a comprehensive overview of each financial planning topic.

- This book is not intended for use as a CFP® examination study guide. The comprehensive case, the chapter-specific cases, and the targeted cases are designed to help faculty and students assess minimum financial planning competencies. The cases presented can certainly help those who wish to sit for the comprehensive CFP® certification examination, but they are not intended for that purpose exclusively.

- *A Case Approach to Financial Planning, Second Edition* is intended to present timely and accurate information; however, the strategies, tools, and techniques presented are designed for educational purposes only. Although the authors and outside reviewers have reviewed the information, data analysis methods, recommendations, strategies, and other material, some material presented in the text could be affected by changes in tax law, court findings, or future interpretations of rules and regulations. Therefore, the accuracy and completeness of the information, data, and opinions in the book are in no way guaranteed. The authors specifically disclaim any personal, joint, or corporate (profit and nonprofit) liability for loss or risk incurred as a consequence of the content of the book.

## FEATURES

Underlying the development of this text and the various student learning experiences is Bloom's taxonomy of cognitive skills.[5] For example, *knowledge* and *comprehension* are covered through the traditional presentation and testing of financial planning concepts. *Application* and *analysis* are fostered through the discussion of planning strategies, where students are challenged to evaluate the advantages and disadvantages of each relative to the needs of the individual client situation. The book excels at building skills in *synthesis* and *evaluation*. It provides a repeatable methodology that students can practice with discrete content cases and across the comprehensive case to build the knowledge and skills for progressing through the systematic financial planning process. Designing an integrated, actionable plan matched to a client's situational factors and resources (i.e., cash flow, net worth, and employee benefits) requires competency across Bloom's taxonomy of cognitive skills. Furthermore, faculty and peer review of the potential efficacy of the plan and its presentation to clients present additional opportunities to use the taxonomy of cognitive skills to foster identification of best practices and professional judgment.

Readers will find this book unique in focus and approach. Several educational strategies to promote student focus, retention, and research are repeated in each chapter, including the following:

- Learning Objectives linked to end-of-chapter Learning Outcomes, new to the second edition.

- A list of Key Terms, shown in bold font and defined in the text, new to the second edition.

- An expanded list of supplementary Chapter Resources and Notes to promote self-study or additional research, including books, journal articles, and Web-based information.

- Expanded in-chapter examples showing both the formulas and the Texas Instrument BA II Plus calculator solutions, new to the second edition.

Additionally, the text and the Web site have several important pedagogical features to enhance student learning, discussed below.

## Chapter Overview

The book includes a review of the systematic financial planning process (Chapters 1 and 14), personal finance math calculations (Chapter 2), and the fundamental steps involved in the analysis of a client's current financial situation. The latter is the focus of Chapters 3 through 13, which also include the explanation of several product and procedural strategies unique to each core content planning area. One of the purposes of a financial planning case course is to provide a forum for students to develop and critique planning strategies matched to a client's needs. For many students, the capstone course is the only place in the curriculum where all six core content planning areas are reviewed and integrated in the context of a specific client situation. This text provides multiple commonly used financial planning strategies matched to each core content planning area for classroom review and discussion. In addition, a variety of case examples are presented in each chapter. The major parts of the book and the content in each part include:

**Part I—Review of the Systematic Process and Computational Skills for Developing a Financial Plan**

1. *The Systematic Financial Planning Process: Steps 1 to 3.* This chapter describes the general financial planning process and outline of the book. The systematic financial planning process, the basis of the case methodology, is also presented. The comprehensive Bedo financial planning case is introduced in an appendix to this chapter.

2. *Computations for Financial Planning.* This chapter provides a comprehensive review of key concepts related to time value of money and general personal finance calculations.

**Part II—Analyzing and Evaluating a Client's Financial Status to Plan for Client Earnings**

3. Cash Flow and Net Worth Planning. This chapter examines the process of analyzing and evaluating a client's current financial situation. It offers common financial planning strategies that planners often use to improve a client's cash flow and net worth position. The chapter concludes with an illustration of how particular financial situation strategies can be used to meet client goals and objectives.

4. Income Tax Planning. The purpose of this chapter is to review the basic steps involved in analyzing and evaluating a client's current tax planning situation. In addition, it presents several widely used tax planning strategies and an example of how they can be used to influence a client's financial situation.

**Part III—Analyzing and Evaluating a Client's Financial Status to Plan for Client Risk Protection**

5. *Life Insurance Planning.* This chapter reviews the basic steps involved in a financial planner's analysis and evaluation of a client's current life insurance situation. It also presents popular life insurance planning strategies and a demonstration of how strategies can be compared and adapted to meet client needs.

6. *Health Insurance Planning.* This chapter reviews the fundamental steps of a financial planner's analysis of a client's current health insurance situation. Common health insurance strategies and an example of how strategies can be shaped to meet client financial goals are presented.

7. *Disability Insurance Planning.* This chapter reviews the steps involved in conducting a disability insurance planning analysis, including several disability insurance planning strategies and an example of how certain strategies can be adapted to meet client needs.

8. *Long-term Care Insurance Planning.* This chapter examines the process underlying financial planners' analysis and evaluation of a client's long-term care insurance situation. It also discusses common product and procedural strategies used with clients. A long-term care policy selection process is illustrated.

9. *Property and Liability Insurance Planning.* This chapter considers issues related to maximizing a client's plan for protecting property and liability exposure. It reviews the fundamental steps in the analysis and evaluation of a client's current property and liability situation and presents examples of commonly used strategies and how they can be transformed into tools to protect client assets.

**Part IV—Analyzing and Evaluating a Client's Financial Status to Plan for the Growth and Distribution of Assets**

10. *Investment Planning.* In this chapter, important issues surrounding the analysis of a client's investment situation are explored. The investment planning process is reviewed and examples of how to develop strategies to meet client

needs are provided. How investment strategies can affect a client's financial goals is explained.

11. *Education Planning.* The steps typically followed when analyzing and evaluating a client's current educational funding situation are reviewed. A selection of education funding strategies demonstrating how some financial planners strategize when planning a client's education situation and an illustration of how strategies can be formed into tools to help achieve investment objectives are presented.

12. *Retirement Planning.* This chapter describes the analysis and evaluation of a client's current situation and reviews common retirement planning strategies that can be used to meet retirement objectives. Strategies to develop recommendations for retirement planning across the life cycle are also provided.

13. *Estate Planning.* Essential steps for conducting an estate planning analysis are reviewed. A brief outline of how planners estimate a client's gross and taxable estate is provided. Other important issues are presented, such as transferring assets, providing for survivors or other legacy needs, and planning for incapacitation and other end-of-life decisions. The chapter ends with a review of how certain estate planning strategies can be used in the financial planning process.

### Part V—Review of the Systematic Process

14. *The Financial Planning Process: Steps 4 to 6.* This chapter reviews important concepts related to recommendation development, and plan implementation and monitoring. Important considerations in ranking, integrating, and funding recommendations in the development of a comprehensive plan are explained and illustrated using systematic financial planning forms.

### Part VI—Financial Planning Case Studies

Thirteen cases followed by multiple-choice questions appear in Part VI. Although these cases are not as comprehensive as the continuous Bedo family case that appears in Chapters 3 through 13, the mini-cases help develop a student's ability to quickly evaluate a client's current financial situation, arrive at correct outputs from analysis and calculations, and then choose from appropriate financial planning strategies to develop actionable recommendations for a plan. A financial planning ethics case is also presented in the unique format of dialogue in a play. It is designed to test students' knowledge of securities rules and financial planning practice standards.

## Planning for Special Populations

New to the second edition of this text, Chapters 3 through 13 each include one or two features called *Planning for Special Populations*. These features reflect the CFP Board focus on planning for clients with special circumstances. These features also illustrate that one benefit of a systematic process is that it can and should be applied consistently, regardless of differing planning situation or clients. Each chapter features a different special population to illustrate to students that its planning needs may be similar to or very different from those of the broader population and that these unique planning needs can add complexities not previously considered.

## Chapter-based Case Studies and Quantitative /Analytical Mini-case Problems

Although successfully developing a financial plan for a client case is rewarding, the downside to case analysis is that the process can sometimes seem far removed from reality. This book attempts to bridge the gap between theory and practice by providing a short chapter-based case study at the end of chapters 3 through 14. These chapter-based case studies illustrate how financial planning strategies can be developed and shaped into tools and matched to a client's situational factors to meet specific financial planning goals and objectives.

End-of-chapter quantitative and analytical problems challenge students to practice calculation and critical thinking procedures. These skills are essential to the application, synthesis, and evaluation needed to artfully analyze a client's situation, identify and match workable strategies to the client's situation, and then to integrate these strategies into actionable recommendations for implementation.

All of these cases, as well as the continuous Bedo case, are designed to remind students that despite the focus on analytical skills and detailed factual knowledge, clients—real people—and their financial goals and dreams are truly the reason for financial planning. As noted earlier, financial planners help clients, people with whom planners may develop relationships that span decades and often even generations, *plan* their financial futures.

## Comprehensive Bedo Case

A significant feature of the text is the Tyler and Mia Bedo comprehensive case, which was designed to test a student's ability to evaluate a client's current financial situation, review strategies, develop recommendations, and integrate these recommendations into a comprehensive financial plan. Questions related specifically to the Bedo case are included at the end of Chapters 1 and 3 through 14. Use of the Financial Facilitator to analyze the Bedos' financial situation is recommended. After answering the questions for each chapter, it will be possible to write a comprehensive financial plan for the Bedos. New to the second edition is an added focus on oral, written, and graphic presentations in each core content chapter, as well as a presentation of the comprehensive plan developed in Chapter 14.

Two objectives guided the development of the case narrative. First, it was to be as comprehensive as possible, meaning that it is impossible to develop client alternatives for one section of the case without influencing other case sections. Second, the narrative was developed to support both simple and complex strategies and recommendations. This latter aspect of the case enables instructors to adapt the expectations to challenge students along the spectrum of financial planning knowledge and experience to provide unique client solutions.

## Integrated Spreadsheet, Financial Facilitator

An integrated Excel financial planning spreadsheet package called the *Financial Facilitator* is available at: http://pro.nuco.com/booksupplements/NUCollege-CaseBook2e. The spreadsheets are designed to "facilitate" analysis and free the student to creatively model and develop efficient and effective client-centered recommendations. Chapters 3 through 13 provide not only a review of the steps involved in analyzing a client's current financial position, but they also describe how to use the Financial Facilitator to expedite the client review. Many of the calculation questions presented in the cases can be solved using the Financial Facilitator; however, the spreadsheets are not necessary to complete the cases.

New to the second edition is an additional functionality that enables note-taking within the Financial Facilitator package. This functionality gives both students and instructors the ability to make comments, take notes, notate reminders, or make suggestions directly within the Excel file.

Financial Facilitator spreadsheets are not designed for use with clients or in professional practice. The authors specifically disclaim any personal, joint, or corporate (profit and nonprofit) liability for loss or risk incurred as a consequence of the use of the Financial Facilitator.

## Fillable Forms

The systematic financial planning process promotes the repeated use of planning forms and procedures to guide and document the planning process. Some financial planners, instructors, and students find the systematic tools and techniques useful for framing a protocol to "attack" the issues presented by a client's situation. Because the approach is methodical and repeatable, the forms are available on the Web site (http://pro.nuco.com/booksupplements/NUCollege-CaseBook2e) as fillable forms for students and instructors to download and complete. These exact duplicates of many of the forms and exhibits shown in the chapters can be completed electronically.

## Instructor's Resources

A number of resources are available on the Web site for instructors. PowerPoint presentations are provided for each chapter. Answers to select end-of-chapter questions and the 13 mini-case questions are provided in a separate *Instructor's Manual*, which provides insight into possible case answers while showing solutions using the Financial Facilitator spreadsheet when applicable. Also, to keep the Bedo case fresh for use in different classes, suggestions are presented regarding how to make changes to the case to reduce student sharing of information without having to identify a new case each time the class is taught.

## Tips for Case/Plan Development Success

The case study methodology presented in this book was developed and tested at Kansas State University and Virginia Tech over the past several years. The outcomes associated with these methods have been successful. During a 10-year period, teams of undergraduate students from Kansas State University and Virginia Tech used the tools and techniques presented in this book to compete in and win several Ameriprise Financial, Inc. (formerly American Express Financial Advisors) Financial Planning Invitational championships. Many students who have used these tools in their plan writing course, using the case methodology, have gone on to pursue successful careers in the fields of financial planning and financial services.

Four aspects of student success are tied directly to how well students do when working on the development of plans. First, successful students tend to have a strong proficiency in the use of personal finance calculators. Second, the best students have an interest in working with computer spreadsheets and confirming calculations obtained on their calculator with spreadsheets. Third, successful students do extremely well at applying critical thinking skills. Exploring issues, looking for the integration of concepts, and willingness to research and use reference materials are all indicators of success for those engaged in the case study method. Finally, the most successful students understand that developing a plan in response to a case situation—especially a comprehensive case—takes time. A commitment to taking the time to analyze a situation, develop strategies, craft workable client-centered recommendations, and work on ways to implement and monitor recommendations is critical to plan writing success.

## Notes

1.  Careers-in-Finance, *Careers in Financial Planning and Wealth Management*. Available at http://www.careers-in-finance.com/fp.htm.

2.  CNN Money, *Best Jobs in America*. Available at http://money.cnn.com/magazines/moneymag/best-jobs/2011/fast-growing-jobs/3.html.

3.  CareerCast.com, *The 10 Best Jobs of 2012*. Available at http://www.careercast.com/content/10-best-jobs-2012-5-financial-planner.

4.  Bureau of Labor Statistics, *Occupational Outlook Handbook, Personal Financial Advisors*. Available at http://www.bls.gov/ooh/business-and-financial/personal-financial-advisors.htm.

5.  B. S. Bloom, *Taxonomy of Educational Objectives, Handbook I: The Cognitive Domain* (New York: David McKay, 1956).

# ABBREVIATIONS COMMONLY USED IN FINANCIAL PLANNING

Alternative Minimum Tax—AMT

Assets Under Management—AUM

Accredited Investment Fiduciary®— AIF®

Certificate of Deposit—CD

Certified Financial Planner Board of Standards, Inc.—CFP Board

Certified Financial Planner® Certification Examination—CFP® exam

Certified Investment Management Analyst—CIMA

Certified Investment Management Consultant— CIMC (No longer awarded)

Certified Life Underwriter—CLU

Charitable Remainder Annuity Trust—CRAT

Charitable Remainder Unitrust—CRUT

Chartered Financial Analyst—CFA

Chartered Financial Consultant—ChFC

Chartered Investment Counselor—CIC

Chartered Life Underwriter—CLU

Consolidated Omnibus Budget Reconciliation Act of 1986—COBRA

Coverdell Education Savings Account—Coverdell ESA or CESA

Discretionary Cash Flow—DCF

Employee Retirement Income Security Act of 1974—ERISA

Enrolled Agent—EA

Errors and Omissions— E&O

Exchange Traded Fund—ETF

Financial Industry Regulatory Authority—FINRA

Financial Planning Association—FPA

Flexible Spending Account—FSA

Grantor Retained Annuity Trust—GRAT

Grantor Retained Unitrust—GRUT

Guaranteed Auto Protection Insurance—GAP Insurance

Health Insurance Portability and Accountability Act of 1996—HIPAA

Health Savings Account—HSA

High Deductible Health Plan—HDHP

Homeowners Policy—HO Policy

Incentive Stock Option—ISO

Individual Retirement Arrangement—IRA

Investment Advisor Representative—IAR

Investment Advisor Registration Depository —IARD

Investment Policy Statement—IPS

Internal Revenue Code—IRC

Internal Revenue Code Section 529—529 Plan

Internal Revenue Service—IRS

Irrevocable Life Insurance Trust—ILIT

Joint Tenancy with the Right of Survivorship—JTWROS

Long Term Care—LTC

Million Dollar Round Table—MDRT

National Association of Insurance Commissioners— NAIC

National Association of Personal Financial Advisors—NAPFA

North American Securities Administrators Association—NASAA

Payable on Death—POD

Personal Automobile Policy—PAP

Personal Financial Specialist—PFS

Qualified Personal Residence Trust— QPRT

Qualified Terminable Interest Property Trust—QTIP Trust

Real Estate Investment Trust—REIT

Registered Investment Advisor—RIA

Securities Investor Protection Corporation—SIPC

Self-Regulatory Organization—SRO

Transferable on Death—TOD

Uniform Gift to Minors Act Account—UGMA Account

Uniform Prudent Investor Act—UPIA

Uniform Transfers to Minors Act Account—UTMA Account

U.S. Securities and Exchange Commission—SEC

Variable Universal Life—VUL

# SUMMARY TABLE OF CONTENTS

### Part I: Overview of the Systematic Process and Computational Skills for Developing a Financial Plan

### Part II: Analyzing and Evaluating a Client's Financial Status to Plan for Client Earnings

### Part III: Analyzing and Evaluating a Client's Financial Status to Plan for Client Risk Protection

### Part IV: Analyzing and Evaluating a Client's Financial Status to Plan for the Growth and Distribution of Assets

### Part V: Review of the Systematic Process

**Part VI:** Financial Planning—Case Studies

---

The *Financial Factilitator* and all fillable forms needed to complete text activities can be found on the student website at: http://pro.nuco.com/booksupplements/NUCollege-CaseBook2e.

---

# DETAILED TABLE OF CONTENTS

**Part III:** Analyzing and Evaluating a Client's Financial Status to Plan for Client Risk Protection

**Part IV:** Analyzing and Evaluating a Client's Financial Status
to Plan for the Growth and Distribution of Assets

**Part V:** Review of the Systematic Process

# PART I: Overview of the Systematic Process and Computational Skills for Developing a Financial Plan

# The Systematic Financial Planning Process: Steps 1 to 3

## Learning Objectives

1. Describe how the financial planning process, as established by the CFP Board, serves as a framework for guiding financial planners and advisors.

2. Describe the benefits of utilizing a systematic process.

3. Summarize and explain the first three steps of the systematic financial planning process.

4. Identify what client data are needed to provide financial planning services and explain how the data are collected.

5. Describe the three substeps of Step 3, Analyze and Evaluate the Client's Financial Situation, and explain how they serve as a framework for the core content chapters.

6. Explain the purpose and use of a Planning Recommendation Form within the systematic financial planning process.

# Key Terms

| | |
|---|---|
| assumptions | life planning |
| attitudes | map |
| beliefs | money scripts |
| client intake form | objective |
| data collection questionnaire | procedural strategy |
| discovery | product strategy |
| financial planning | risk tolerance |
| financial planning process | systematic financial planning process |
| focused interview | targeted or modular plan |
| goal | time horizon |
| life cycle event | values |
| life transition | want |

**Figure 1.1** The Systematic Financial Planning Process

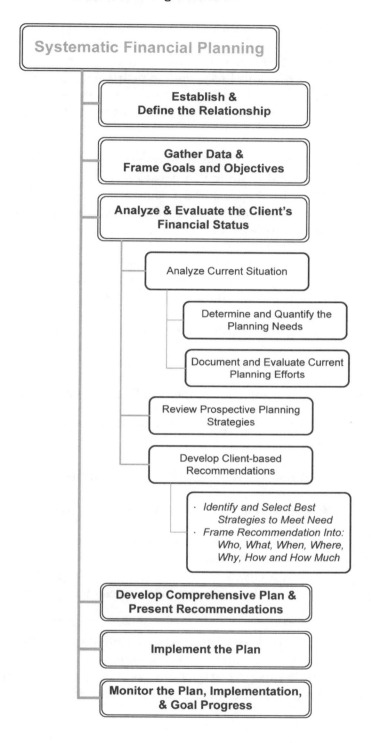

## DEFINING THE FINANCIAL PLANNING PROCESS

The growth of financial planning, both as a recognized profession and as an important aspect of the lives of individuals and families, has been remarkable. Starting with fewer than 50 Certified Financial Planner (CFP®) certificants in the early 1970s, the number of CFP® certificants has grown to nearly 66,000 in early 2012, and the number is steadily climbing.[1] Worldwide growth is outpacing growth in the United States. As the profession has expanded in recent years, the number of students studying financial planning has also grown.

Professional organizations and leading members of the financial planning community have defined financial planning in a variety of ways. One of the most recognized definitions, offered by the Certified Financial Planner Board of Standards, Inc. (CFP Board), defines financial planning as a process. According to the CFP Board, **"Financial planning** denotes the process of determining whether and how an individual can meet life goals through the proper management of financial resources. Financial planning integrates the financial planning process with the financial planning subject areas."[2] In its *Standards of Professional Conduct*, the CFP Board further explains the **financial planning process** as involving the following six steps:

1. Establishing and defining the client-planner relationship;

2. Gathering client data, including goals;

3. Analyzing and evaluating the client's financial status;

4. Developing and presenting financial planning recommendations and/or alternatives;

5. Implementing the financial planning recommendations; and

6. Monitoring the financial planning recommendations."[3]

The CFP Board identifies the subject areas of the financial planning process as typically including but not limited to the following: financial statement preparation and analysis (including cash flow analysis/planning and budgeting); insurance planning and risk management; employee benefits planning; investment planning; income tax planning; retirement planning; and estate planning.

The CFP Board also developed and promulgated the *Financial Planning Practice Standards*, a *Code of Ethics*, and *Rules of Conduct*—all of which have evolved with the profession to guide professional actions and benefit consumers. Specifically, the CFP Board noted that the Practice Standards are intended to:

- Assure that the practice of financial planning by CERTIFIED FINANCIAL PLANNER™ professionals is based on established norms of practice;

- Advance professionalism in financial planning; and

- Enhance the value of the financial planning process.[4]

The same commitment to establishing norms of practice, advancing professionalism, and promoting the value of the financial planning process led the authors to write *The Process of Financial Planning: Developing a Financial Plan, Second Edition.*[5] The underlying premise of that book is that financial planning can be improved, despite the variety of financial planning practice models, when a process is consistently and systematically applied. This is true of students learning the process as well as for planners practicing the process. Whether the advisor (1) produces a comprehensive plan; (2) works on a per-project basis focusing on analysis and advice; (3) writes a targeted, or modular plan; (4) provides financial planning analysis, but no plan, as a means to provide products; or (5) develops a plan as a means to establish product needs, the constant in all of these situations is the fundamental *process*. In fact, in some situations, writing a comprehensive plan may be beyond the scope of what a client needs or a planner provides. But the methodology applied should be consistent, regardless of whether or not a written "financial plan" is the primary deliverable.

A **systematic financial planning process** is needed to guide the analytic approach as well as the presentation, implementation, and monitoring of the financial planning results. A systematic approach is also needed to help students and novice planners develop the methods to effectively collect and utilize the necessary client information. *The Process of Financial Planning, Second Edition,* attempts to fill that need by developing a systematic, almost step-by-step financial planning process based on the general financial planning process promoted by the CFP Board and other organizations.[6] Although the systematic financial planning process is intended for use by comprehensive financial planners, the process is equally applicable for those who want to conduct a systematic and defensible analysis of client investment or investment-based insurance product suitability. Advisors who follow the process are assured that (1) a client's personal and financial objectives will be incorporated into the planning process; (2) client goals and objectives are met in an effective, efficient, and defensible way; and (3) the process can be easily documented.

This book, a companion to *The Process of Financial Planning, Second Edition,* applies the systematic six-step financial planning process shown in Figure 1.1:

- Chapter 1 provides a summary of the first three steps in the process.

- Chapter 2 presents a summary of important financial planning computations useful in the quantitative analysis of a financial situation.

- Chapters 3–13 provide comprehensive and in-depth coverage of Step 3, Analyze and Evaluate the Client's Financial Status applied to each of the core content planning areas.

- Chapter 14 provides a summary of the last three steps in the process.

It is important to identify accepted and effective methods for conducting Step 3, Analyze and Evaluate the Client's Financial Status if norms of practice are to gain widespread acceptance. The focus is on the core content planning areas that the CFP Board refers to as "financial planning subject areas."

Specifically, Chapters 3–13 proceed from assessing a client's financial situation through risk management assessment, investment planning, education planning, retirement planning, and estate planning. Each chapter systematically applies the three substeps of Step 3:

1. Analyze the current situation.

2. Review prospective planning strategies.

3. Develop client-based recommendations.

Together, Chapters 3–13 provide comprehensive and in-depth coverage of Step 3 in the financial planning process. The Financial Facilitator, described later in this chapter, "facilitates" analysis of the client's "financial" situation in each chapter while fostering discussion of the client data, analytical methods, and assumptions used. Each chapter presents practical examples of how analysis can lead to strategies that can be transformed into recommendations. In addition to providing an in-depth look at the substeps involved in analyzing and evaluating a client's financial status, these chapters provide a broad—but basic—summary of information for each topical area. In effect, the information provided is intended to be a review of the core concepts that every financial planner ought to know. Furthermore, in these chapters the systematic and repetitive approach builds a thorough grounding in the analytical methods and forms used. This approach and the forms are then applied in unique chapter-based case studies that appear in every chapter that addresses a core content planning area.

This book then applies the systematic six-step process through case analysis. Because financial planning students and practitioners must go beyond comprehension of isolated analytical methods to the application, analysis, synthesis, and evaluation levels of knowledge and skill to craft an integrated comprehensive financial plan, the case study methodology is an ideal way to practice. Consequently, the need for financial planning cases has increased. To that end, a comprehensive client case, the Bedo household, is introduced as an appendix to this chapter. This continuing case provides practice in analyzing and evaluating the Bedos' financial situation in each of the core financial planning content areas in Chapters 3–13. The end-of-chapter Bedo Case Analysis Questions lead the reader through the process. Product and procedural strategies at the end of each core content planning chapter can be used to answer case questions and help students build an arsenal of strategies for future use.

Finally, this book applies the systematic six-step process by summarizing Steps 4, 5, and 6 and applying them to the development of a comprehensive plan for the Bedo family. Chapter 14 describes the method by which client-specific recommendations are integrated and prioritized for formulation into a comprehensive financial plan that can then be implemented and monitored in response to a client's goals. Thus, this chapter offers the opportunity to integrate the Bedos' situation and financial planning needs in a comprehensive manner. Throughout the book the concept is emphasized that planning is a process, and a decision made in one core content area of a client's plan will undoubtedly influence other planning areas. The continuing Bedo case is designed to enhance communication skills, decision-making skills, and critical thinking skills, as well as problem structuring and problem-solving abilities—all of which must be demonstrated throughout the planning process, but which are particularly relevant in the last three steps of the systematic financial planning process.

Several multiple-choice mini-cases are provided in Part VI: Additional Financial Planning Case Studies. Each case is targeted to one or a few core financial planning content areas. Sometimes a client's objectives can be met most effectively through a **targeted or modular plan** in which recommendations are focused on one or a few specific client goals. These cases provide opportunities to practice the systematic planning process and explore some of the complexities involved when conducting modular planning.

Whether students or planners write comprehensive or targeted financial plans independently or depend on professional software packages, the craft of (1) analyzing a client's situation, (2) identifying strategies, and (3) developing recommendations can be improved by applying the case study approach. Becoming a proficient financial planner entails adequate time devoted to understanding and practicing the process. In the end, there is only one way to truly become more proficient at analyzing financial cases, fictional or real, and developing financial plans. The secret is deceptively simple: practice and apply the tools and techniques learned in the classroom to client situations. Over time the process will become so routine that it is followed reflexively, and the goals of establishing norms of practice, advancing professionalism, and promoting the value of the financial planning process will be achieved. Accomplishing these goals will benefit students and professionals individually, benefit the profession globally and—most importantly—ensure that clients are well served.

## AN OVERVIEW OF THE SYSTEMATIC FINANCIAL PLANNING PROCESS[7]

Too often students look for *one* correct answer when working on client cases. Unfortunately, financial planning does not always lend itself to a single correct response. As acknowledged by the CFP Board, there may be *multiple* solutions that enable a client to reach a goal. These answers flow from subjective professional judgment. Client situations can be addressed in multiple ways by different financial planners. Some recommendations might be equally effective and others dismissed as less likely to result in successful goal attainment or simply ill-conceived. Some strategies, although generally valid and workable, might not match a client's values or personality. It is important for students and practitioners to thoroughly review the methodology used to guide the progression from strategies and recommendations to a final plan.

The systematic approach to planning promotes the repeated use of planning forms and protocols to guide and document the planning process. Some financial planners will find systematic tools and techniques useful for framing a protocol to "attack" the issues presented by a client's situation. Others will conclude that such tools limit creativity and are cumbersome or repetitive. Because the approach is methodical and organized, systematic planning tools can help students and novice planners:

- Organize what may initially appear to be an overwhelming mass of data and analysis into a manageable format.

- Focus attention on critical planning needs.

- Focus attention on problems or issues that might require research or consultation with other professionals.

- Focus attention on issues or questions that require additional input from the client.

- Recognize the need for creative alternatives to meet the client's goals.

- Feel confident that relevant issues have not been overlooked.

Finally, it is important to note that the conceptualization of the systematic process as distinct and sequential steps is a conceptual representation of the *reality* of planning. In actual client work, and when done in the context of different business planning models, some activities might not occur exactly as described. Because of the recursive nature of the process, several steps can be ongoing and overlapping as the client progresses through the process on different goals and objectives. Also, as a result of monitoring the plan for changes needed in response to the client's situation; the success of the products or strategies recommended; or the current economic, market, or tax environment, it may be necessary to start the process over for some goals or objectives.

## Step 1: Establish and Define the Relationship

The process begins by establishing and defining the planner-client relationship. This step is complicated by the need to combine professional, disclosure, and contractual responsibilities with initiating a trusting and personal yet professional advisor-client relationship.  At this stage of the process a planner initiates the relationship with potential clients (by referral or marketing strategies), meets with prospective clients to discuss potential products and services, and formalizes the scope of the planner-client engagement. The relationship should begin by outlining the responsibilities of both planner and client and the extent of the contractual arrangement. Specifically, conflicts of interest, compensation arrangements, the length of the agreement period, and the products or services to be provided should be fully disclosed and agreed on. In short, Step 1 encompasses the regulatory, contractual, and professional expectations of the planner-client relationship.

Professional practice expectations and regulatory agencies determine the objectives of this step. For example, the Securities and Exchange Commission (SEC) and state regulatory agencies require that registered investment advisors (RIAs) distribute Part 2 of Form ADV, the Uniform Application for Investment Advisor Registration, to prospective clients before or at the time an agreement is executed. Similarly, a privacy statement and opt-out procedures for sharing information with nonaffiliated third parties must be provided before the agreement is executed. The privacy statement must be provided annually, and clients must be informed of material changes in ADV Part 2 and offered a copy annually. The most recent copy of an investment adviser's Form ADV is available at the Investment Advisor Public Disclosure Web site (typically referred to as the *IAPD Web site*), for either state- or SEC-registered advisors.

## Step 2: Gather Data and Frame Goals and Objectives

The second step in the systematic planning process involves collecting information and identifying client goals. Client information can be obtained through data collection questionnaires (completed by the client independently or in conjunction with the advisor), client-planner interviews, and original source documents provided by the client. Regardless of the method(s) utilized, however, the primary objective is for the planner to gather vital financial and personal information—quantitative *and* qualitative—that encourages discussion. Best planning practices suggest that clients should be encouraged to complete basic data forms independently, via hard copy or secure encrypted electronic access, whenever possible. This frees up advisor-client time to review the quantitative data to ensure full understanding by both parties, and it allows more time to explore the client's values, goals, dreams, attitudes, and beliefs.

The importance attributed to attitudes, beliefs, and values—in shaping both the client's relationship with money and the client's goals—has expanded this aspect of the data-gathering or discovery process, with clients. Klontz, Kahler, and Klontz suggest that **money scripts**, which they define as "unconscious beliefs people hold about money, often unexplored and only partially true [that] are formed in childhood,"[8] can have a significant effect on adult money behaviors. They offer exercises for exploring money scripts as well as issues related to money disorders (e.g., compulsive spending or hoarding) and problematic money behaviors (e.g., overspending or underspending). Although the definition and scope of **life planning** as actually practiced by advisors varies, the focus of financial life planning is to ground the financial plan in the client's life —past, present, and future. In short, financial life planning integrates financial planning and life planning. Exploring a client's attitudes, beliefs, and values can encompass the emotional, experiential, and spiritual issues that influence not only the use of money, but also the goals that frame a meaningful life for the client. Because of the scope of the questions and methods that might be employed in this holistic exploration, this portion of the data collection process has come to be called **discovery** or referred to as *discovery meetings*.

There are two very important outcomes from these initial meetings: (1) the establishment of trust between the parties; and (2) the exploration and collection of information to help the planner understand the client and the client's financial situation. Because of the significance of this step and the variety of approaches utilized in practice, the discussion focuses on the abstract and practical implications of four fundamental questions:

1. What client data are collected?

2. How does the planner use the data?

3. How are the data collected?

4. What does it mean to frame goals and objectives?

### What Data Are Collected?

Planners are challenged to gain enough information to fully understand the client, assess the situation, and generate a workable plan that is acceptable to the client, and to do so effectively and efficiently. And, as if that conundrum were not sufficiently challenging, consider that most people think talking about money is culturally unacceptable. For too many individuals, any talk of money is laden with emotional undertones that may reflect explicit memories (good or bad) or an implicit uneasiness that defies explanation. It is not hard to understand why many planners prefer the safety of products to the psyche of the client, but increasingly planners are considering both.

There are four situational factors that characterize clients and influence their money scripts. The first three factors also characterize planners —as both individuals and professionals. These factors are:

1. Temperament and personality

   Temperament is commonly explained by inherited cross-cultural traits that characterize mood or disposition. Behavioral, emotional, and attitudinal tendencies comprise personality. Together these dimensions profile individuals and offer insight into their relationships with others and with money. An extroverted client who is talkative, full of life, and spontaneous will likely have a very different view of retirement than the introvert who is organized, disciplined, and enjoys a quiet home life. A moody, anxious client who lacks organization and persistence might be easily distracted from financial goals; such clients could require more planner and staff time to collect needed data or need more motivation to implement recommendations.

2. Attitudes, beliefs, and behaviors

   Attitudes, beliefs, and behaviors are interrelated concepts in that attitudes and beliefs are thought to affect behavior. **Attitudes** may reflect an individual's views, opinions, desires, choices, purposes, or values. Although the concept of belief connotes different meanings, in psychology **beliefs** are recognized as a type of attitude because the belief reflects an interpretation, expectation, or claim about some aspect of life. Values represent strongly held attitudes and beliefs indicate an individual's perception of what is right or desirable. **Values** are said to reflect an individual's fundamental meaning or interpretation of life and as such are a significant influence on personal goals and choices.

   Although other attitudes related to financial well-being, economic trends, or market returns can be assessed, a client's financial risk tolerance is the attitude most frequently considered. Financial **risk tolerance** is defined as the maximum amount of risk a client is comfortable with in a financial situation. This attitude affects a wide range of financial decisions beyond the obvious applications of investments, retirement planning, or investment-based insurance, where questions of suitability are typical and assessment of risk tolerance is required. There is a *need to understand the client* for the purposes of client-centered financial planning as well as a *need to document the client's risk tolerance* for regulatory compliance. To accomplish this, some planners use scales included in financial planning software or provided by their broker-dealer or custodian, and others purchase psychometric tests from independent firms, such as FinaMetrica.[9]

   Considered in the context of portfolio management, risk tolerance centers on a client's reactions to, or level of comfort with, losses in investment value. But a client's risk tolerance can also affect decisions concerning type of mortgage, debt level, emergency fund, choice of insurance coverage, tax preparation approach, or estate planning strategy. A client with a high level of risk tolerance can be expected to take greater risks and act with less information than less risk-tolerant individuals who require that more certainty be associated with financial decisions.

3.  Financial knowledge and experience

    Financial knowledge and experience could represent the most extreme difference between planner and client; both parties bring different levels of knowledge and experience to the planning engagement. Some clients lack knowledge, and others may have the knowledge but lack confidence and want a planner to confirm that their "financial situation is ok." Professional responsibility and CFP Board *Rules of Conduct* constrain planners to offer services within the purview of their acknowledged expertise and suitable for a client's knowledge, experience, or capacity for loss. Some recommendations will almost certainly include products or services about which a client lacks experience or knowledge. In such cases, it becomes even more important to educate clients about the risks and benefits of the product or service.

4.  Socioeconomic descriptors

    Socioeconomic descriptors represent a broad range of factual or quantitative characteristics to describe clients. Categories of information include the demographic profile of a client's household, including relevant medical history or other factors that can influence client goals; financial data (income, assets, liabilities, insurance coverage, etc.); and a description of the client's lifestyle, or what might be referred to as social position or status. The latter category might include travel, hobbies, collectibles, leisure activities, personal property, or real estate that supports the client's lifestyle.

Gathering the client data needed for a thorough and defensible evaluation of a client's situation—whether for a single-issue analysis, to support a product sale, or to complete a comprehensive plan—may appear intrusive, but in fact it provides a foundation for the client's financial future. Throughout the planning process, the planner or planning team must demonstrate to the client genuine empathy, balanced with rigorous analytical skills and product knowledge. Furthermore, this information is the primary source of data for the analysis of each of the core content planning areas and is reconsidered throughout the planning process.

For example, a client's household situation, lifestyle, and occupation could suggest a need for additional life insurance based on the planner's attitudes, financial knowledge, and experience with other, similar clients. The client might have come to the planner with the goal of purchasing more life insurance. Or the client may never have considered this need, which was discovered only after the advisor analyzed the situation. But the client's attitudes about insurance and risk will influence the final purchase decision, as will the advisor's personality, assertiveness, or conscientiousness in educating and motivating the client regarding this need.

## How Does a Planner Use Data?

A client and planner enter the planning relationship with unique characteristics of temperament, personality, attitudes, beliefs, financial knowledge, and experience that shape the planning process. Without specific training or the input of a trained professional such as a psychologist or a financial therapist as a part of the planning team, a planner's experience may be the best guide for working with the range of temperaments, personalities, attitudes, knowledge, and experience that clients exhibit. The more a planner knows about a client, the greater the likelihood of developing a plan that will accommodate the client's unique situation. A planner's role is to collect and objectively process client data. However, three limitations must be acknowledged.

First, regardless of all efforts to function as objective, independent professionals, planners are constrained to some extent by personal temperament, personality, attitudes, beliefs, values, and financial knowledge and experience. These "filters" directly and indirectly affect the planning process. Although this may be equally true of other professionals, it is more apparent in financial planning because of the need to divulge extremely private information to craft a plan matched to a client's unique situation. Care must be taken to minimize the impact of personal feelings, interpretative judgments, subjective inferences, and opinions; all interpretations should be confirmed with the client.

Second, a planner is privy only to the information that a client is willing to share. Clients may knowingly withhold information from lack of trust or unknowingly because the information is thought to be irrelevant or was overlooked. Without a client's full disclosure, a planner will not be able to suggest optimal solutions. It is incumbent on planners to make every attempt to encourage clients to divulge as much relevant information as can be useful to the planning engagement.

Third, as professionals, advisors must fully acknowledge their own limitations of expertise, conflicts of interest, or other paradigms that could adversely affect or bias the client-planner relationship. The necessary steps should be taken to compensate for or overcome such issues in the professional relationship.

## How Are the Data Collected?

Several methods are used to collect client data both initially in Step 2 and during the ongoing planner-client relationship. Accuracy and security are primary concerns. As noted earlier, planners must strive for professional objectivity and extreme accuracy when collecting and recording client data. Care also must be taken to ensure, to the extent possible, that the client is candid and forthright because of the tendency not to disclose all information or to provide answers that are more socially acceptable or "what the planner expects." Planners must develop a secure system for collecting, organizing, and managing data throughout the planning process as well as safeguarding them in the future. Each of the three primary data collection methods is briefly considered.

1.  Supporting documents

    Original source documents can be used to verify information already provided by the client, or other documents can provide technical information beyond the scope of a client's knowledge. Clients can also authorize a planner to obtain from other financial service adviors or professionals, on their behalf, the private information needed to analyze the client's situation or develop recommendations. Care must be taken to safeguard these documents and the client's privacy and to return original documents quickly after electronic scanning or copying.

Planners and clients can use a form such as that shown in Exhibit 1.1 to track the flow of original documents between parties. The supporting documents column can also be duplicated and modified to verify or acknowledge the receipt—or later, the return—of documents. These forms can include a line for the signatures of planning staff or the client, respectively, to verify transfers. They can be completed for the household, and individual lines can be added in each category, as applicable, for spouses or partners, or an individual form can be completed for each individual.

**Exhibit 1.1** Client Supporting Document Tracking Form

| Date Requested from Client | Date Received from Client | Date Returned to Client | Supporting Document (for Client 1, Client 2, and joint accounts, as applicable) |
|---|---|---|---|
| | | | Latest bank statement(s) |
| | | | Latest investment account statement(s) |
| | | | Loan statement(s) (e.g., real estate 1, real estate 2, car 1, car 2, boat/motorcycle/ATV/R, student loan(s), etc.) |
| | | | Real estate deed, deed of trust, and HUD-1: summary of closing costs |
| | | | Latest credit card and/or department store credit statement(s) |
| | | | Federal and state tax returns for the last three years |
| | | | All insurance policies (e.g., life, disability, health, homeowners, automobile, umbrella, etc.) |
| | | | Any current budget or record of spending |
| | | | Most recent paycheck stub(s) |
| | | | Employee benefit statement(s) |
| | | | Employee retirement plan statement(s) |
| | | | Other retirement plan statement(s) |
| | | | Summary of the retirement plan description |
| | | | Wills, trusts, or other estate planning documents |
| | | | Other: |
| | | | Other: |

2.  The client intake form

Although not all financial planners actually use a formalized **client intake form** or **data collection questionnaire**, such forms afford several benefits. First, because data gathering can be somewhat subjective, it is a good policy to complete an objective data collection questionnaire with every client. To the extent it is completed with accuracy and candor, a well-designed form or questionnaire can capture a client's quantitative and, to a more limited extent, qualitative information. Second, the form can reduce professional liability claims from clients, family members, or legal entities. Planners who document client responses objectively and definitively are better prepared to defend themselves against claims of professional misconduct. Third, the consistent use of a standard form can help a planner pinpoint a client's financial strengths and weaknesses as well as attitudes or expectations that could affect the planner-client relationship. In summary, the use of a client data-gathering questionnaire provides a framework for summarizing a client's goals, attitudes, and financial profile, all of which are needed to write a comprehensive plan. More importantly, it opens up discussion of other issues, fears, or concerns beyond the obvious data collected on the form.

The client intake form discussed in the companion book, *The Process of Financial Planning, Second Edition,* and available on the Web site for this text, provides an example of the range of client information collected. Some planners use specialized data collection forms for targeted client situations, such as small business owners or retirement plan participants, whereas others use forms associated with professional software to facilitate data entry. Finally, for planners affiliated with product providers, a proprietary client data form may be required to ensure regulatory compliance.

3.  Guided planner-client interviews

The meaningful exploration of a client's financial situation and its many nuances does not typically occur solely through conversation. Planners who work with clients to jointly complete or review a client intake form have a purpose: to collect accurate, factual data. But to expand that preliminary exchange into the realm of goals, attitudes, values, dreams, concerns, fears surrounding money, or the role of money in a client's life could necessitate entering into a conversation with a purpose—an interview. A **focused interview** is an excellent way to explore another person's feelings, experiences, perceptions, attitudes, views, or knowledge. The concept of a semistandardized, or focused interview, is borrowed from social science research, where a set of questions guides the interview, but the order of the questions, their wording, and the follow-up probes and interviewer responses can be adapted by the interviewer. The interview is *focused* on learning about the client's **map**, as defined by feelings, experiences, views, or knowledge that define the individual, whereas a standardized interview would be formally structured, like the client intake form, to collect specific quantitative data.

Approaching the client meeting as an interview should not inadvertently change the tone or formality of the meeting, but it does take preparation. An issue-oriented, topical list or set of questions must be carefully planned to guide the interview. However, the advisor's questions and approach should still allow for adaptations regarding the level of language, word choice, or order of questioning to best match the client and the situation. Open-ended questions that are nonjudgmental and respect the sensitivity of the topic are most effective. Questions beginning with *why* should be avoided because they can cause defensiveness. The objective is to encourage a client to openly and freely share information, feelings, perceptions, or observations. Follow-up questions and verbal or nonverbal reinforcements should be used as necessary to encourage clients to elaborate.

Where do students or novice planners obtain targeted questions for discovery meetings? Specialized approaches, such as those promoted by George Kinder,[10] Mitch Anthony,[11] Roy Diliberto,[12] and Carol Anderson,[13] for example, offer planners training as well as interview questions and other assessment tools to help clients increase their understanding of financial and life planning. Kinder,[14] one of the founders of life planning, is recognized for the following questions (asked in this order) to help clients explore what he calls "a life worth living":

1. "If you had all the money you needed, what would you do with your life?"

2. "If you had only five to ten years to live, but would be in good health the entire time, what would your life look like?"

3. "If you knew you were going to die tomorrow, what did you miss? What did you not get to do? Who did you not get to be?"

Although some planners argue that these global questions are beyond the scope of financial planning, other advisors are embracing the integration of financial planning and life planning. Developing a focused interview matched to a planner's business model can: (1) increase the planner's confidence; (2) encourage more in-depth understanding of the topic and the client's perspectives and motives; and (3) build a trust-based planner-client relationship. The shift from a client relationship based on one or more separate *transactions* to one based on complete *transformation* could have a significant impact on the practice of financial planning.

### What Does It Mean to Frame Goals and Objectives?

Framing goals and objectives requires a planner, in consultation with a client, to identify results or accomplishments that should ensue from the planning process. Broadly defined, the goals should give meaning to a client's life and motivate the client to pursue the financial planning process. Depending on the issue considered, a goal can range from the abstract to the concrete. A **goal** is a more global statement of a client's personal or financial purpose, while an **objective** is a more discrete financial target that supports a goal. For example, a client may set the goal of a "comfortable retirement," but only through further discussions and clarification can a planner discern a definite objective, based on the client's proposed retirement lifestyle, of accumulating $2.65 million by age 55.

Although clients' goals can be framed or defined in limitless ways, goals basically emanate from (1) wants and needs, (2) life cycle events, and (3) life transitions. Wants and needs are differentiated by their significance in sustaining life, while **life cycle events** represent typical biological, socioeconomic, or sociocultural events that occur over a lifetime. Anthony defines goals as what the client would like to "have, do, or be" during life, whereas a **life transition** represents a "change or transition" currently faced or expected to occur in the near future.[15] Clients can identify a new goal, modify existing goals, or change the hierarchy of goals as the result of a perceived want or need, life cycle event, or life transition. These categories are not mutually exclusive, because a divorce may result from an unfulfilled personal need or be viewed as a life cycle event or a life transition.

Often, through the discovery process, a planner will uncover a goal that the client was either uncomfortable listing, thought was beyond accomplishment, or simply could not fully articulate. The communication required to fully identify, and frame goals can sometimes be challenging. Such insights increase a planner's understanding of a client and help the clieint and planner identify nuances and subtle priorities among the goals. Recognizing and examining these relationships provides a deeper understanding of the client's situation, and the outcomes attained are essential to preparing feasible, actionable, client-oriented recommendations. Goals and recommendations may be subject to further refinement based on the planner's own financial planning knowledge and experience as well as other descriptive factors.

Planners and clients should not look at a goal in isolation. Goals can be independent, interrelated, or interdependent. And the best solution for one goal may have a deleterious effect on another goal. For interrelated goals, the first goal might have to be fulfilled as a prerequisite to fulfilling the second goal. Goals are typically categorized by a **time horizon** for accomplishment. *Short-term* goals can be accomplished in less than two years, while it may require two to 10 years to accomplish an *intermediate-term* goal. *Long-term* goals, such as preparing for retirement, take more than 10 years and could actually require effort over several decades.

The idea of a personal goal hierarchy or ranking is commonly accepted, and some clients can easily prioritize their goals. But in cases where a client has several equally important but somewhat conflicting goals, ranking becomes significantly more problematic. Of course, the ranking of goals may not be an issue if sufficient funding is available; however, this is rarely the case. Because goals can be ranked does not necessarily mean that the highest-ranking goal should be dealt with first. Client goals and objectives and the corresponding recommendations developed can be moderated by a planner's professional judgment and knowledge of a client's situational factors.

---

**Data-gathering Tip: The Importance of Specifically Recording Client Goals**

It is always a good practice to put client information—no matter how it is provided— in a format for practical use. It is unlikely that a client will ever arrive in a planner's office with goals specifically outlined and ranked. Most clients have a general idea of what they would like to accomplish, but few can define their goals precisely during the initial discovery meeting. It takes energy, intuition, and persuasion to coax goals and objectives from a client. Recording a client's goals and objectives, as understood by the planner, is a good way to develop a checklist for further discussion. Furthermore, realistically framing, articulating, and ranking goals can occur only as the client's "dreams" are brought into perspective by the data-gathering and analytical skills of the planner. A thoughtful and honest interchange between client and planner is necessary to arrive at final goals for the plan—and everyone must realize that both goals and plan are subject to changing circumstances and the vagaries of the future.

---

## Step 3: Analyze and Evaluate the Client's Financial Status

Many view the step of analyzing and evaluating a client's financial situation as the essence of financial planning. The realities of a client's income and expenses, net worth, financial products owned, and financial strategies employed to date are scrutinized during this step in the process. From the narrowest view, this step is fact based and solution oriented. But central to this step is a perspective that goes beyond the present factual situation, to a larger and perhaps more multifaceted view of the client, as characterized by the situational factors and the client's financial future. Such exploration should have occurred in Step 2, and it should have identified issues that could influence the analysis and planning that occurs during this third step of the process.

It might take years of study and experience to fully comprehend the nuances and complexities of conducting a thorough analysis and evaluation of a client's situation. This process is a financial planning challenge built on known facts about the client, inferences gleaned from the planner-client relationship, and assumptions that should be mutually agreed on by planner and client. Too often at this step the "solution-focused" planner overemphasizes quantitative analysis to the detriment of the person for whom the plan is designed. It is essential that a planner consider a client's goals and related planning assumptions during this analysis. Only by knowing a client's specific goals and using the assumptions agreed on with the client can a financial planner anticipate, determine, and quantify planning needs. Then, in conjunction with the client, a course of action that offers the best risk-adjusted probability of success is identified.

As illustrated in Figure 1.1, Step 3 is a multilayered step comprising three substeps:

1. Analyze the current situation.

2. Review prospective planning strategies.

3. Develop client-based recommendations.

These steps can be summarized as: know your client, consider the universe of strategies for meeting the client's needs, and match the two to formulate the client-specific recommendations most likely to meet the client's goals. Each step is explained in further detail below.

## Analyze the Current Situation

Analysis of the client's current situation requires planners to review and distill all of the information collected about a client's situation in the context of the marketplace, including the tax, economic, political, and legal or regulatory environment. This analysis is designed to answer four questions for each core content area:

1. *What is the client's planning need?* Planning needs can range from a discrete financial question or issue involving one core content planning area to an extensive review of all of a client's financial matters. The determination, or *identification*, of the planning need is based on an advisor's professional judgment and familiarity with the client's situation. Both quantitative and qualitative data are considered to identify both known and unknown needs. For example, currently known or identified financial needs might cross several different core content planning areas. The review can also reveal other unknown or unrecognized needs that could affect the client now or in the future. A 45-year-old client might be strongly committed to purchasing a long-term care insurance policy—now or in the future—because of a foreseen need created by a family history of Alzheimer's disease. Planning needs may be identified by the client or the planner.

2. *What assumptions are relevant to the client's planning need?* **Assumptions** are inferences based on premises, reasoned conclusions, facts, or circumstantial evidence that affect a client's planning need and the quantification of that need. For example, historical stock market returns, recent inflationary increases in the cost of higher education, and average skilled nursing home costs are supported by factual data and can be included in the quantification of a client's need. These assumptions and many others reflect the current or projected marketplace, such as the tax, economic, political, and regulatory environments. Other assumptions reflect a client's personal situation (e.g., the assumed need for long-term care insurance, the likelihood of a child receiving college scholarships or fellowships, or life span projections). Assumptions must be fully disclosed, mutually agreed upon, and realistic.

3. *Can the client's planning need be quantified?* Technical expertise, computations, and other analytical tools should be used (where applicable) to objectively analyze and *quantify* a client's need. For some core content planning areas, such as estimating life insurance needs, several recognized approaches are available and supported by software applications. The quantification of other needs (e.g., the need for long-term care insurance protection) can be far harder to calculate and defend because of multiple seemingly unrelated factors, such as the client's projected net worth or the daily benefit amount for future medical care.

4.  *How is the planning need currently being met?* A planner must document planning efforts currently in place to meet identified needs or the absence of any efforts on the part of the client to address them. Then, a thorough and objective assessment of the products and strategies currently in use must be completed to project the likelihood of achieving the goal. Results of this evaluation can reveal needed changes or validate the client's approach and show that no changes are warranted. (For more information on standard benchmarks that can be used to evaluate insurance and investment products, see the companion book, *The Process of Financial Planning, Second Edition*.)

Although these four questions must be applied to each core content planning area, the data sources considered and the analytics completed can be quite different for each. Because of its importance and complexity, the substep Analyze the Current Situation and the other substeps are applied individually and systematically to each of the core content planning areas in Chapters 3–13.

At this juncture in the planning process, based on data gathered and analysis of the client's current situation, a planner will have an arsenal of useful information to process, as outlined below:

- Insights into the client's temperament, personality, motivations, risk tolerance, financial knowledge, experience, and perceived level of financial success to this point. The planner can begin to answer the key strategy, recommendation, and implementation questions of *who* and *why* as well as the questions *for whom, what,* and *how.*

- Clear, mutually agreed-upon definitions of client goals, planning objectives, and the desired outcomes of the planning process. The planner can begin to answer the questions of *why, what, when,* and *for whom.*

- For each of the core content planning areas—cash flow management, income taxes, risk management (e.g., life, health, disability, long-term care, property, and liability), investments, education or other special needs planning, retirement planning, and estate planning—the planner can begin to answer *why, what, when, where, how,* and *how much* based on the following results:

  - Quantitative data analyses built on mutually agreed-upon personal and economic assumptions and conducted independently and systematically for each of the core content planning areas;

  - Qualitative and household needs assessments to identify potential individual, lifestyle, life event, or other factors that could affect the client in any of the core content planning areas;

  - The planner's knowledge and professional insights regarding factors that might influence the client in any of the core content areas, including issues, problems, or concerns beyond the client's awareness;

  - The planner's and/or client's scan of the legislative, tax, political, economic, and regulatory environmental factors that could have an impact on the implementation of the plan, immediately or in the future; and

• The planner's consultation or collaboration with other professionals.

### Review Prospective Planning Strategies

Once an analysis of the situation is complete, the advisor should have a clear understanding of the issues to be addressed and thus be ready to proceed to the next substep, Review Prospective Planning Strategies. This substep in analyzing the client's situation focuses on the identification of possible strategies or alternatives available to meet the client's needs and goals. With the results of the quantitative and qualitative analysis complete, the planner can begin to fully answer the strategy, recommendation, and implementation questions of *why, when, where, how much, how*, and *by whom*.

Strategies reflect an advisor's technical competence and the universe of solutions that could apply to a client's situation. Simply put, strategies are the "Rolodex," or toolkit of answers that a planner must identify and then apply to the client's situation (or at least eliminate as an option) until the process yields a limited number of viable alternatives for each core content planning area. Strategies can be categorized as product or procedural. A **product strategy** reflects the use of a specific type of product or product feature to meet a planning goal or need. A **procedural strategy** emphasizes a process, service, or type of ownership rather than a product. Product and procedural strategies are identified for each of the core content planning areas discussed in Chapters 3–13.

Professional judgment, ethics, and practice standards constrain planners to offer services within the purview of their acknowledged expertise, to seek the collaboration of other professionals, or to refer clients to others. Planners can become accustomed to using certain strategies or products or focusing on particular patterns of information. It is becoming common practice to develop two to four alternative strategies related to each goal; equally common is the practice of planners falling back on using the same old strategies they have used for years. A planner may turn to these heuristics, or favored solutions, when working with a client. The biggest problem with this approach is that the financial planning profession (and more specifically its products and regulations) is changing almost constantly. These changes create additional opportunities for planners and clients, but they also create confusion.

Although commonly used strategies or products can increase a planner's efficiency and promote depth of knowledge in a diverse universe of products, they may or may not yield the best client outcome. Professional judgment and ethical practice standards recommend that advisors acknowledge any limitations, prejudices, or other relationships that could adversely affect or bias the planner-client relationship. Furthermore, advisors are encouraged to continually apply professional skepticism to compensate for or override such issues.

### Develop Client-based Recommendations

With strategies identified, a planner can make recommendations matched to the client. These strategies might need to be altered or combined as the planner weighs the advantages and disadvantages of each potential recommendation and considers the probable outcomes and effects on a client's situation. As the planner attempts to align recommendations with a client's goal(s), the total cost of the recommendations must be compared to the available cash flow or other assets available to fund the recommendations.

Consider the example of an investment recommendation to fund a future goal (e.g., retirement, education, a vacation home) based on the product strategy of an actively managed mutual fund. Facts and assumptions are at issue as the advisor considers increasing the anticipated rate of return (an assumption) in an attempt to limit or reduce the present value cost (a fact). Another relevant assumption, the client's risk tolerance for the goal, must be incorporated into the analysis. This assumption influences portfolio allocation and projected returns as well as the client's potential comfort with, and commitment to, the recommendation if risk tolerance is exceeded.

The process of separating, distilling, and integrating client situational factors, planner factors, and strategies results in the development of one or more client-based recommendations that define the scope of the planning engagement. This is true whether an advisor is developing a comprehensive plan or a modular plan that targets a single issue. The recommendations should offer the client cost-effective, adaptable alternatives. Contingent on the scope of the engagement and the degree of specificity implied in that arrangement, the recommendations should address these key questions:

- Who should implement the recommendation?

- What should be done?

- When should the recommendation be implemented?

- Where should the client (or other party) implement the recommendation?

- Why should the recommendation be implemented? Why is it important to the client's financial future?

- How should implementation take place?

- How much should be purchased, saved, or invested to implement the recommendation? Specifically, what is the cost of the recommendation?

The significance of considering each of these questions when developing recommendations should not be overlooked. The questions may seem too simplistic to be meaningful, or answering all seven may seem unnecessary. But routine use of this simple rubric for framing recommendations can be a powerful tool for two reasons. First, careful consideration of these questions helps an advisor reconsider the logic of each recommendation and its consistency with the client's goals and situation. Second, the rubric helps advisors meticulously consider and articulate funding and other implementation issues critical to sound plan development and motivated client action.

Exhibit 1.2, The Planning Recommendation Form, helps students or novice planners focus on the essential issues to include in an actionable recommendation. This useful planning tool, recommended in the systematic planning process, summarizes the answers to the seven critical recommendation questions of *who, what, when, where, why, how,* and *how much* into one simple format. When initially identifying possible recommendations, the form is useful for summarizing and projecting the costs and benefits of recommendations. As the plan develops, it may be necessary to combine, sort, and rank recommendations from other core content planning areas, and the forms can quickly be revised for each recommendation. Once finalized, the forms can be used to document information for planning staff or to communicate information to the client. Possibly one of the most beneficial uses of the form is to document the titling of assets and beneficiary designations. Examples of completed Planning Recommendation Forms for each of the core content planning areas appear in Chapters 3–13.

**Exhibit 1.2** Planning Recommendation Form

| | | | | | |
|---|---|---|---|---|---|
| **Financial Planning Content Area** | | | | | |
| **Client Goal** | | | | | |
| **Recommendation No.** | | **Priority (1–6)** lowest to highest: | | | |
| **Projected/Target Value ($)** | | | | | |
| **Product Profile** | | | | | |
| Type | | | | | |
| Duration | | | | | |
| Provider | | | | | |
| Funding Cost per Period ($) | | | | | |
| Maintenance Cost per Period ($) | | | | | |
| Current Income Tax Status | Tax-qualified | | | Taxable | |
| Projected Rate of Return | | | | | |
| Major Policy Provisions | | | | | |
| **Procedural Factors** | | | | | |
| Implementation by Whom | Planner | | | Client | |
| Implementation Date or Time Frame | | | | | |
| Implementation Procedure | | | | | |
| **Ownership Factors** | | | | | |
| Owner(s) | | | | | |
| Form of Ownership | | | | | |
| Insured(s) | | | | | |
| Custodial Account | Yes | | | No | |
| Custodian | | | | | |
| In Trust For (ITF) | Yes | | | No | |
| Transfer on Death (TOD) | Yes | | | No | |
| Beneficiary(ies) | | | | | |
| Contingent Beneficiary(ies) | | | | | |
| **Proposed Benefit** | | | | | |

## INTRODUCING THE FINANCIAL FACILITATOR

Analyzing a client's current financial situation and determining the impact of several recommendations on the client's financial future can be a technically challenging endeavor. Most planners use a variety of software programs and spreadsheets to help with these calculations. The Bedo continuing case provides practice in analyzing and evaluating the family's financial situation in each of the core content planning areas. To help with this analysis, the text includes the Financial Facilitator, a set of partially linked Excel™ spreadsheets designed to answer many of the analytical questions posed in Chapters 3–13, as well as additional cases in Part VI.

The Financial Facilitator spreadsheets, although not designed for use with clients or in professional practice, provide examples for applying assumptions and inputting client data.  Developed in a more transparent manner than most "professional" products, these spreadsheets should facilitate discussion of the various analytical methods, assumptions, and choices available. The Financial Facilitator includes spreadsheets for basic financial statement analysis, future cost of goals analysis, income tax analysis, education cost analysis, life and disability insurance needs analysis, retirement cost analysis, and estate tax analysis. Only the highlighted cells accept input. The "computation" cells are protected so that input mistakes do not destroy viability and computational accuracy.

Pictures of Financial Facilitator spreadsheets appear in Chapters 3–13 and are presented along with a discussion of the methodology used to complete the analysis. Graphics include a picture of the spreadsheet as well as comment boxes that explain what and/or how financial information should be input. Also, because the spreadsheets are linked, several graphics include information about the source or origin of a particular number, because it may have been entered on an earlier spreadsheet or calculated based on other input.

The case study methodology gives students practice in the art (creativity) and science (analysis) of generating client-centered recommendations. The remainder of this book is focused on the "science" of financial planning by building core content planning knowledge and analytical skills. The Financial Facilitator was designed to "facilitate" analysis of a client's "financial" situation. Using it should simplify this analysis and free the user to creatively develop efficient and effective client-centered recommendations that can be integrated into a comprehensive plan matched to a client's daily life.

## INTRODUCING THE COMPREHENSIVE CASE: TYLER AND MIA BEDO

The Bedos, a hypothetical household, are meant to represent the type of clients that might seek the help of a financial planner just starting out in the profession. The Bedos earn more income than the average American family and significantly more than the typical family living in Springfield, Missouri, where they reside.

Does the fact that the Bedos earn more than average make the case too easy? Having high relative income does not necessarily make the case any easier—it merely offers assets that must be successfully managed to accomplish multiple goals. However, having more income to work with provides greater opportunities to meet a client's long-term goals by allowing the development of more creative solutions. As a client's income increases, so does the range and complexity of solutions. This means that in terms of pure simplicity, it can sometimes be easier to work with clients who are aspiring to wealth because suggestions and alternatives tend, by default, to be constrained by available cash flow. Because higher-income clients may not be as income constrained, potential solutions are often riddled with the complexities inherent in multiple, interrelated options.

Furthermore, income and lifestyle are relative measures. Certainly, the Bedos earn a substantial amount of money for a young couple living in southwest Missouri. On the other hand, their income may be quite modest for meeting the cost of living and different lifestyle demands of a similar household in cities like Los Angeles, San Francisco, New York, Washington, or Boston. But the fact that a client earns a substantial income in no way means that all goals and objectives can be met. Clients tend to "live up" to their level of income regardless of how much they earn. In other words, high-income clients tend to spend much of their income, just as moderate-income clients tend to spend most of their income.

The case narrative was developed with two aims in mind. One goal was to make the case as comprehensive as possible, meaning that it is impossible to resolve issues in one core content planning area without influencing the Bedos' other issues and goals. When faced with developing recommendations, financial planners will encounter several interrelated issues and constraints, all of which influence each other. These interacting issues make the case relatively difficult to analyze, yet not too difficult to develop a plan to improve the Bedos' financial situation—both now and in the future. The second goal was to allow the Bedos' needs to be resolved using both simple and complex solutions. This aspect of the case approach provides greater opportunities to offer unique client proposals that may vary by advisor but still offer a viable option for meeting the Bedos' goals and objectives.

The Bedos are introduced in Appendix 1A. Specific questions to guide the analysis and development of appropriate strategies and recommendations are provided at the end of Chapters 3–14 as well as this chapter. By following the chapter structure and the systematic financial planning process, it is possible to analyze the case and write a financial plan.

# Learning Outcomes

1.  The financial planning process, as defined by the CFP Board, serves as a framework for guiding financial planners and advisors in their service to clients. The CFP Board defines financial planning, the six steps that comprise the planning process, and the seven content areas typically included in the scope of financial planning. However, the CFP Board asserts that, although financial planning typically includes the seven areas of financial statement preparation and analysis (including cash flow analysis/planning and budgeting); insurance planning and risk management; employee benefits planning; investment planning; income tax planning; retirement planning; and estate planning,  the process is not limited to these seven content areas. The CFP Board also established *Financial Planning Practice*

*Standards*, a *Code of Ethics*, and *Rules of Conduct* to further guide the profession. For more information see the *CFP Board's Standards of Professional Conduct* (http://www.cfp.net/Downloads/2010Standards.pdf).

2.  The systematic financial planning process promotes the repeated use of planning forms and protocols to guide and document the planning process. Because of its organized, consistent methodology, this approach can help students and novice planners organize and analyze client data into a manageable format; focus attention on critical planning needs; identify needs where additional client information or assistance from other professionals may be warranted; and discern routine and creative strategies for meeting client goals. Perhaps most important, repeated and consistent use of the systematic financial planning process can foster confidence that relevant issues have not been overlooked in thoroughly and competently planning for client needs.

3.  The first three steps of the process can be summarized as (1) establish the contractual relationship and the scope of services to be rendered, including the responsibilities of both planner and client; (2) collect the qualitative and quantitative data necessary to fully understand a client's situation and planning needs; and (3) analyze the data and the client's financial planning efforts as a foundation for crafting client-based recommendations.

4.  The breadth and depth of client information sought by a planner will vary with the scope of financial planning services provided. Qualitative data include information on a client's temperament, personality, attitudes, beliefs and behaviors, which influence financial decisions and help the planner better understand the client, the client's map of reality, and the client's money script. Examples of quantitative data are socioeconomic descriptors and other factual financial data. A client's financial knowledge and experience may reflect the interaction of both qualitative and quantitative information. Data are collected from original source documents (e.g., an income tax form) provided by the client, client intake forms or other questionnaires completed by the client, and focused interviews and other discovery meetings conducted by the planner.

5.  The three substeps of Step 3, Analyze and Evaluate the Client's Financial Situation, include (1) analyze the client situation; (2) review prospective planning product and procedural strategies; and (3) develop recommendations matched to the client and that clearly answer the questions *who, what, when, where, why, how*, and *how much* should be purchased, saved, or invested to implement the recommendation. The first substep, analysis of the client situation, proceeds through a progressive, almost linear series of steps that include (1) identification of the client's known and unknown planning needs; (2) identification of mutually agreed-upon assumptions relevant to the client's needs; (3) analysis, incorporating the assumptions, to project and quantify needs; and (4) identification and analysis of the potential success of planning efforts currently in place to meet the client's planning needs. Once this step is complete, a planner has sufficient information to review prospective strategies and select the most relevant to craft into client-based recommendations.

Because of its importance and the specific approach presented in the systematic planning process, this step is repeated for each of the core content planning areas in Chapters 3–13. Thus, repetition of this step serves as the framework for core content chapters.

6.  The Planning Recommendation Form helps students and novice planners focus on the essential issues to include in an actionable, client-based recommendation. The form summarizes in one simple format the answers to the seven critical recommendation questions of *who, what, when, where, why, how,* and *how much.* Additionally, the form requires that cost, benefit, and titling information be considered. As the plan develops, it may be necessary to combine, sort, and rank recommendations from across core content planning areas, and the forms from the different core content planning areas can be used to facilitate decision making. Once finalized, the forms can be used to document information for the planning staff or to communicate information to the client.

## Chapter Resources

Anthony, M. *Your Clients for Life: The Definitive Guide to Becoming a Successful Financial Planner.* Chicago, IL: Dearborn Financial Publishing, 2002.

*Assessing Your Financial Risk Tolerance* (http://www.rce.rutgers.edu/money/riskquiz/default. asp). Certified Financial Planner Board of Standards, Inc. (www.cfp.net).

Diliberto, R. T. *Financial Planning—The Next Step: A Practical Approach to Merging Your Clients' Money with Their Lives.* Denver, CO: FPA Press, 2006.

Financial Industry Regulatory Authority (FINRA) (www.finra.org).

FinaMetrica® (www.finametrica.com).

Financial Therapy Association (http://financialtherapyassociation.org/).

Investment Advisor Registration Depository (http://www.iard.com/).

Investment Advisor Public Disclosure Web site (http://www.adviserinfo.sec.gov/ (S(l2wrhvakmfteghqc1qtt0v5m))/IAPD/Content/IapdMain/iapd_SiteMap.aspx).

Kinder, G. *Seven Stages of Money Maturity: Understanding the Spirit and Value of Money in your Life.* New York: Dell Publishing, 2000.

Kinder, G., and S. Galvan. *Lighting the Torch: The Kinder Method™ of Life Planning.* Denver, CO: FPA Press, 2006.

Klontz, B., R. Kahler, and T. Klontz. *Facilitating Financial Health: Tools for Financial Planners, Coaches, and Therapists.* Cincinnati, OH: National Underwriter Company, 2008.

Klontz, B., and T. Klontz. *Mind over Money: Overcoming the Money Disorders That Threaten Our Financial Health.* New York: Crown Business, 2009.

Lytton, R., J. Grable, and D. Klock. *The Process of Financial Planning: Developing a Financial Plan,* 2nd Ed. Erlanger, KY: National Underwriter, 2012.

Money Quotient® Putting Money in the Context of Life™ (http://moneyquotient.org/).

The Kinder Institute of Life Planning (http://www.kinderinstitute.com/index.html).

The Financial Life Planning Institute (http://www.flpinc.com/.

U.S. Securities and Exchange Commission (www.sec.gov).

Your Mental Wealth™ (http://www.yourmentalwealth.com/).

The *Financial Factilitator* and all fillable forms needed to complete text activities can be found on the student website at: http://pro.nuco.com/booksupplements/NUCollege-CaseBook2e.

# Quantitative/Analytical Mini-case Problems

Later chapters include quantitative or analytical problems that challenge readers to practice the skills from specific core financial planning content areas—usually in the context of a short case situation. Although software applications can perform these functions in the typical financial planning office, it is important that planners have the skill to understand and test the assumptions and results provided.

# Comprehensive Bedo Case—Analysis Questions

The Bedo case is an integral part of learning and applying the financial planning process. This case and the other cases found throughout the book present clinical studies of real-life situations that financial planners might face. They are meant to confront—but also confine—the complexity and ambiguity of the practical world by focusing on the questions to ask, the assumptions to use, and the calculations to complete when analyzing a situation.

There should be a logical progression from the analysis of each of the core content areas to the identification of strategies consistent with the Bedos' client situational factors. Through integrative analysis of the client's situation and identification of potential strategies, client-specific recommendations and a plan will emerge. The identification of implementation and monitoring plans completes the financial planning process.

1.  Complete the Client Intake Form, available in the companion book, *The Process of Financial Planning, Second Edition,* and on the Web site for this book, for Tyler and Mia Bedo. For any client situational factor information that is not provided, make a defensible assumption to guide the planning process. For information that is unavailable, note how it would have been collected from the Bedos.

2.  As part of Step 1: Establish and Define the Relationship, develop a thorough but brief description of the systematic financial planning process to help the Bedos understand the services to be provided. Prepare this description (narrative, outline, etc.) for inclusion in the financial plan *or* for presentation to the client with or without the aid of PowerPoint slides or handouts.

3.  Within the scope of Step 1, what documents would have been presented to the Bedos? Why are they included in this step of the process? What purpose do the documents serve? For additional information, see the companion book, *The Process of Financial Planning, Second Edition,* or CFP *Board's Standards of Professional Conduct* (at http://www.cfp.net/Downloads/2010Standards.pdf).

4.  Develop a preliminary list of five to 10 financial strengths, weaknesses, opportunities, and threats (typically referred to as a *SWOT analysis*) for the Bedo household. During which step(s) of the systematic financial planning process might these be identified—in general or through more in-depth analysis?

5.  Why is a goal stated as "to live life with a relatively high level of financial satisfaction" not very useful in terms of a practical financial planning analysis?

6.  List and prioritize the Bedos' financial goals. Classify each as emanating from needs or wants, a life cycle event, or a life transition. Classify each as short-, intermediate-, or long-term.

7.  What needs, wants, life cycle events, or life transitions might influence the Bedos' financial plans over the next five years? The next 15 years? Why is it important to consider these issues, either independently as a planner or in discussion with the Bedos?

8.  What other information would be helpful to obtain from the Bedos as you move forward with developing a comprehensive financial plan?

9.  Make a list of additional information or original source documents that you would request from the Bedos. Be sure to review the Client Intake Form and the Client Supporting Document Tracking Form for ideas. What explanation would you provide regarding why the documents are needed?

10. Prepare and organize a list of general or critical core content planning area-specific assumptions for use when working on the case.

11. Answers to questions 6–10 may emerge from the Client Intake Form or an initial conversation with the Bedos regarding their reason(s) to seek financial planning. However, other questions, as

part of a focused interview or the discovery meetings, will likely be necessary to gain a broader understanding of the Bedos. Generate a list of questions based on a review of the financial planning literature or interviews with financial planners. (Note: This may be assigned as a small group or class project.)

12. Given the initial review of the Bedos' situation, what other professionals might be needed to help the planner develop the Bedos' plan? How are these decisions guided by the CFP Board for CFP® certificants? For additional information, see the companion book, *The Process of Financial Planning, Second Edition,* or *CFP Board's Standards of Professional Conduct* (at http://www.cfp.net/Downloads/2010Standards.pdf).

13. If you were to rewrite the case narrative, given the current state of the economy, how would you change the rate-of-return assumptions presented in the case? What other assumptions should be changed or updated?

14. Complete the following for the introductory sections of the Bedos' financial plan:

    a.  Draft the introductory cover letter to the client.

    b.  Prepare the client profile and draft a summary of goals and general or specific assumptions that will guide the planning process. (Note: The list of goals and assumptions will be reviewed and revised in each core content planning area for final inclusion in the plan.)

## Notes

1.  Certified Financial Planner Board of Standards, Inc., *CFP® Certificant Profile.* Available at http://www.cfp.net/media/profile.asp.

2.  Certified Financial Planner Board of Standards, Inc., *CFP Board's Standards of Professional Conduct.* Available at http://www.cfp.net/Downloads/2010Standards.pdf, p. 4.

3.  CFP Board, *Standards of Professional Conduct,* p. 5.

4.  CFP Board, *Standards of Professional Conduct,* p. 14.

5.  R. Lytton, J. Grable, and D. Klock, *The Process of Financial Planning: Developing a Financial Plan,* 2nd Ed. (Erlanger, KY: National Underwriter Company, 2012).

6.  CFP Board, *Standards of Professional Conduct,* pp. 13–27.

7.  This section of the chapter was summarized from the companion text by Lytton, Grable, & Klock, *The Process of Financial Planning: Developing a Financial Plan* (Cincinnati, OH: National Underwriter, 2012).

8.  B. Klontz, R. Kahler, and T. Klontz, *Facilitating Financial Health* (Erlanger, KY: National Underwriter, 2008): 14.

9.  A psychometrically designed risk tolerance scale commonly used in the United States and abroad is available from FinaMetrica® at www.finametrica.com.

10. G. Kinder, *Seven Stages of Money Maturity: Understanding the Spirit and Value of Money in Your Life* (New York: Dell, 1999).

11. M. Anthony, *Your Clients for Life: The Definitive Guide to Becoming a Successful Financial Planner* (Chicago: Dearborn Financial Publishing, 2002).

12. R. D. Diliberto, *Financial Planning—The Next Step, A Practical Guide to Merging Your Clients' Money with Their Lives* (Denver, CO: Financial Planning Association Press, 2006).

13. Carol Anderson, *MoneyQuotient® Putting Money into the Context of Life.* For more information see http://moneyquotient.org/.

14. "Interview: George Kinder & Life Planning," *NAPFA Advisor* (August 2003): 7–13.

15. M. Anthony, *Life Transitions Profile,* Financial Life Planning Institute. Available at www.financialifeplanning.com.

# Meet Your Clients

## INTRODUCING THE BEDO CASE STUDY

The purpose of this narrative is to provide you with the information needed to write a comprehensive financial plan for your clients, Tyler and Mia Bedo. By studying this case, you should have a relatively solid understanding of the types of personal and financial information that a planner needs to write a comprehensive financial plan. It will become increasingly important for you to have a clear understanding of the case facts.

As you read through the case, you should make a concerted effort to highlight and note any special assumptions presented. Strive to be inquisitive and to anticipate how certain case facts and assumptions might influence your choice of strategies, the development of interrelated recommendations, the implementation of recommendations, and future monitoring actions. Train yourself to identify the client's financial strengths and weaknesses. This list will help ensure that the Bedos' stated—and even unrecognized—financial goals and objectives have been addressed.

By the end of the planning process, you should be able to collaborate with the Bedos to prioritize their goals and objectives, determine the net impact of strategies on cash flow and net worth, and develop a clearly delineated implementation plan that will enable them to accomplish their primary financial aspirations. And in doing so, you will chart a course that could change the Bedos' financial lives and establish the foundation of a long-term planner-client relationship.

## THE BEDO FAMILY PROFILE

Recently, Tyler and Mia Bedo took time to start thinking about financial planning issues. They were prompted to do so by two events. First, Mia's close high school friend Brenda died of a heart attack. Brenda left a grieving husband and three children. She had no life insurance, and from what Mia could learn, Brenda's husband was having a hard time financially. This event was followed by an advertisement by a major financial planning firm that caught their attention. The advertisement encouraged viewers to start planning today for the future.

These two events started the Bedos thinking about the need for financial planning. As a result, they made a new year's resolution to seek the counsel and advice of a competent financial planner in January.

Today is the day the Bedos have come to see you, armed with a large amount of financial and personal information. The following narrative provides more detail about the Bedos' financial life.

## Personal and Family Information

Tyler Bedo
Age: 42
State of residence: Missouri
Citizen: U.S.
Health status: No known health issues
SS#: 555-55-5555

Mia Bedo
Age: 42
State of residence: Missouri
Citizen: U.S.
Health status: No known health issues
SS#: 555-55-4444

Dependent Children
Becky Bedo
Age: 5
Health status: No known health issues

Home Address
727 Success Lane
Springfield, MO

Employment

Tyler's:
Golden Tee Golf Association, Inc.
6282 Star Drive
Springfield, MO
Occupation: Sales consultant
Years employed: 12

Mia's:
The Family and Career Institute
5600 Cedar Lane Road, Suite #150
Springfield, MO
Occupation: Career counselor
Years employed: 3

## Overview of Family History

Tyler and Mia Bedo met during their undergraduate days at the University of Nevada in Reno. After graduation, they were married at a Lake Tahoe chapel. Shortly thereafter, they moved to Springfield, Missouri, so that Tyler could begin his career as a golf course sales consultant. The Bedos love Springfield and have no plans to leave the area.

This is Tyler and Mia's first marriage and, from what you've learned, they are happily married. Their first child, Becky, was born five years ago. At this point, they do not anticipate having any more children.

Becky is a bright and enthusiastic child. She is actively involved in sports. She particularly likes youth basketball and soccer. She and her mom are taking golf lessons together. She is currently taking piano lessons. Becky's future is one reason the Bedos were prompted to seek your financial advice. By talking with their friends and co-workers, they have learned that college can be expensive.

Because one of their goals is to fund as much of Becky's college as possible, they thought now could be the time to work through some college funding numbers with a professional. The good news is that the Bedos have already investigated some college costs. They have determined that four years of in-state tuition to a good public university today would cost about $10,000 per semester, including room and board.

Mia is the youngest child of a very large family. She has four brothers and three sisters. Her mother Jenny passed away when Mia was age 30. Her father Terrance passed away three years later. Both died of cancer. Mia's parents donated the majority of their estate to a church in California. Mia received a few items from the estate, including a gold nugget ring, three signed collector paintings, an antique china cabinet with a full eight-piece set of collector's china, and her mother's harp.

Tyler's child life was significantly different from Mia's. Tyler is the only child in his family. His parents, both age 65, are healthy and living in Springfield. His parents' wills currently list him as the sole beneficiary of their combined assets. However, the Bedos are not expecting an inheritance anytime soon, and they do not want to plan on receiving assets from Tyler's parents.

Neither Tyler nor Mia has had much experience working with other professional advisors. They have used the services of an enrolled agent at tax time. They are pleased with the service provided. They do not have a relationship with an attorney or any other financial planning professional. Until this point, they have relied on advice from friends and family regarding their financial situation.

## CASH FLOW PLANNING

### Income Discussion

Mia enjoys her job as a career counselor. She received her undergraduate degree in Family Studies but, because she was unable to find a job right after college, she decided to pursue a graduate degree in Family Counseling. Her first job as a counselor was with a small private practice in Springfield. She worked for the firm for four years before resigning to spend time with Becky.

When Becky was older, Mia took a part-time job with her current employer, The Family and Career Institute of Missouri. She is paid a monthly salary and anticipates receiving a 3.0% salary increase each year in the future.

Currently, Becky is enrolled in kindergarten on a half-day basis. Her grandmother picks her up from school and takes care of Becky until the early afternoon. They have no regular child care expenses. As soon as Becky begins school, Mia plans to devote more time to volunteer activities in the community.

Tyler is highly valued by his employer. He has a degree in golf course management and a Masters in Business Administration. Tyler works for Golden Tee Golf Association, Inc., a relatively small (29 employees) golf course management consulting firm.

Tyler's job requires him to travel monthly to golf courses associated with his firm and conduct onsite management and consulting services. He is also responsible for soliciting new golf course management contracts. He is very successful in his career and plans to stay with his current employer until he retires.

Tyler is currently paid a salary and bonus. He conservatively estimates that his salary will increase by 3.0% each year. His bonus—50% of his salary paid out semiannually—is very generous, and also very consistent.

Before meeting with you, the Bedos summarized their current yearly income in Table 1A.1.

**Table 1A.1** Income (Gross)

|  | Client | Amount | Frequency |
|---|---|---|---|
| Salary | Tyler | $2,633.33 | Biweekly |
| Salary | Mia | $2,708.00 | Monthly |
| Bonus | Tyler | $17,116.65 | Semiannually |

## Expense Summary

Unlike many clients, the Bedos have always kept a close eye on their income and expenses. The majority of their annual expenses are detailed in Tables 1A.2–1A.5.

**Table 1A.2** Income and Payroll Taxes

|  | Amount | Frequency |
|---|---|---|
| **Tyler** | | |
| Federal income tax withholding | $ 718.00 | Biweekly |
| State and local income tax withholding | $ 187.00 | Biweekly |
| FICA (Social Security and Medicare) tax withholding | $ 300.00 | Biweekly |
| **Mia** | | |
| Federal income tax withholding | $ 292.50 | Monthly |
| State and local income tax withholding | $117.00 | Monthly |
| FICA (Social Security and Medicare) tax withholding | $207.17 | Monthly |

**Note:** Late last year, the Golden Tee Golf Association, Inc. had a computer payroll problem. The firm responsible for tracking FICA withholding miscalculated the maximum cap on the Social Security portion of FICA. Tyler believes that the amount withheld for FICA may be incorrect.

Both Tyler and Mia are allowed to invest in a limited number of mutual funds within their 401(k) plans. These mutual funds are the same ones that your financial planning firm tracks on a regular basis. For a complete listing of the funds, refer to the rates-of-return section presented later in the case. Table 1A.3 lists the funds that Tyler and Mia are currently using to fund their retirement objectives.

**Table 1A.3** Retirement Plan Contributions

|  | Contribution Amount | Notes | Employer Contribution |
|---|---|---|---|
| **Tyler's Investment Choices** |  |  |  |
| Consumer Fund | 3% of base salary | 401(k) plan deductions are not taken from bonus payments (the employer does not match bonus payments) | 0% |
| Graham Fund | 3% of base salary | | 3% (100% match on the first 3%) |
| **Mia's Investment Choices** |  |  |  |
| Rocket Fund | 10% of salary | For future planning, 401(k) plan deductions are not taken from bonus payments (the employer does not match bonus payments) | 3% (50% match on the first 6%) |

The Bedos are diligent savers. Table 1A.4 shows how much they save each month. Note that at the current time, only annuity and money market account savings are allocated to a goal. Additional regular expenses are shown in Table 1A.5.

**Table 1A.4** Systematic Savings Outside of Qualified Retirement Plans

| Description | Amount | Frequency | Savings Purpose |
|---|---|---|---|
| Sagebrush Fund | $250 | Monthly | Any purpose |
| Haley G&I Fund | $250 | Monthly | Any purpose |
| Ruth Fund | $250 | Monthly | Any purpose |
| Individual conservative fixed-annuity contract | $250 | Monthly | Mia's retirement |
| Money market account | $150 | Monthly | Cash reserves |

**Table 1A.5** Expenses

| Housing | Periodic Amount | Frequency |
|---|---|---|
| Real estate taxes | $1,675 | Annually |
| Homeowners insurance | $700 | Annually |
| Utilities (e.g., electric, fuel, water, sewer) | $350 | Monthly |
| Other household (e.g., yard service, trash) | $100 | Quarterly |
| | | |
| **Food/Clothing/Transportation** | | |
| Food/groceries | $425 | Monthly |
| Clothing | $700 | Quarterly |
| Auto maintenance (e.g., oil, fuel) | $125 | Monthly |
| Auto insurance premiums | $1,000 | Semiannually |
| Missouri vehicle plate/tag tax | $450 | Annually |
| | | |
| **Loan Payments** | | |
| Mortgage loan payments | $1,088 | Monthly |
| Auto loan payments | $451 | Monthly |
| Charge account and credit card payments | $425 | Monthly |
| | | |
| **Other Committed Expenses** | | |
| Medical costs (copay) | $20 | Monthly |
| Prescriptions | $20 | Monthly |
| Dental and eye care expenses | $50 | Monthly |
| Life insurance premiums | $172 | Monthly |
| Medical (health) insurance premiums (pretax through a § 125 plan) | $300 | Monthly |
| Umbrella insurance premiums | $175 | Annually |
| Disability insurance premiums | $25 | Monthly |
| Other misc. insurance premiums | $25 | Monthly |
| Telephone (land line and cell) | $125 | Monthly |
| Bank charges | $10 | Monthly |
| Personal care (e.g., hair, dry cleaning) | $100 | Monthly |
| | | |
| **Discretionary Expenses** | | |
| Entertainment (e.g., movies, plays, shows) | $225 | Monthly |
| Satellite TV | $50 | Monthly |
| Dining out | $275 | Monthly |
| Recreation (e.g., boating, hiking) | $225 | Monthly |
| Travel (e.g., trips to Branson) | $3,000 | Annually |
| Savings for art and art gallery | $150 | Monthly |
| Gifts to charities: | | |
|     University alumni fund | $1,000 | Annually |
|     Church | $350 | Monthly |
|     United Way | $50 | Monthly |
| Holiday giving | $1,800 | Annually |
| Home improvements | $150 | Monthly |
| Dues (e.g., organizations, golf course, health clubs) | $150 | Monthly |
| Subscriptions (e.g., Time, Money) | $80 | Monthly |
| Housekeeping service | $80 | Monthly |
| Pet care expenses | $35 | Monthly |
| Tax preparation fees | $400 | Annually |

**Note:** Some expenses may not be accounted for in this table.

## Asset and Liability Summary

The Bedos live in a split-level, 2,250-square-foot home on a ¾-acre lot. It has a brick veneer on the first level and vinyl siding over the upper floor. It has a formal living room, dining room, and kitchen on the main floor; three bedrooms and two full baths on the upper floor; and a family room, laundry area, and a half-bath on the ground floor along with a two-car attached garage. Their home features a gas fireplace, a vaulted ceiling in the living and dining rooms, and a standing-seam metal roof. The metal roof is fairly new and was recommended to them because of the wind associated with violent spring thunderstorms that frequently develop tornadoes.

The Bedos have also provided you with a list of their assets and liabilities, with current market values. They have attempted to calculate all of their liabilities, but in a few cases they were unable to determine a pay-off value. They are hoping you can help them determine some of these key account balances. Assets and liabilities are shown in Tables 1A.6–1A.10

**Table 1A.6** Personal and Real Assets

| Description | Owner/Title | Current Value |
|---|---|---|
| Home | Joint | $250,000 |
| Furnishings | Joint | $45,000 |
| Four-door sedan (3 years old, Ford Taurus) | Joint | $20,000 |
| Minivan (5 years old, Nissan Quest) | Joint | $15,500 |
| Yard equipment (John Deere x500, plus other small equipment) | Joint | $8,000 |
| Jewelry and collectibles (Mia's ring, paintings, china cabinet w/china, and harp) | Joint | $10,000 |
| Phil Mickelson-signed Calloway Driver golf club | Joint | $5,000 |
| Golf clubs/other sporting equipment | Joint | $2,500 |
| Golf artwork (Linda Hartough reproductions, set of 5 lithographs) | Joint | $5,000 |
| Aluminum boat (2001 Alumacraft V16 Lunker LTD; w/ 50hp Mercury motor) | Joint | $5,800 |

**Table 1A.7** Monetary Assets

| Description / Purpose | Owner | Market Value | Current Yield |
|---|---|---|---|
| Savings account (cash reserve) | Joint | $10,000 | 3.00% |
| Checking account (cash reserve) | Joint | $3,500 | 0.00% |
| Money market account (cash reserve) | Joint | $10,000 | 3.00% |
| Checking account II (savings: art gallery/collection) | Joint | $5,000 | 0.00% |

**Table 1A.8** Investment Assets (Nonretirement)

| Description | Owner | Market Value | Current Yield |
|---|---|---|---|
| Miscellaneous EE bonds* | Joint | $25,000 | 3.50% Deferred |
| Haley G&I Fund** | Joint | $69,000 | 3.20% |
| Konza Fund** | Joint | $43,000 | 1.75% |
| Ruth Fund** | Joint | $13,000 | 4.00% |
| Sagebrush Fund** | Joint | $8,000 | 0.50% |

*The EE bonds were purchased 12 years ago by Tyler's parents as a gift for Tyler and Mia. The bonds will earn interest for the next 18 years and reach their $30,000 face value in another 5 years, as guaranteed by the U.S. Treasury.

**The Bedos' basis in these assets is equal to 50% of the assets' value

**Table 1A.9** Retirement Assets

| Description | Owner | Market Value | Rate of Return |
|---|---|---|---|
| Tyler's 401(k) | Tyler | | |
|     Consumer Fund | | $69,000 | 8.75% |
|        Graham Fund | | $134,000 | 4.10% |
| Tyler's traditional IRA | Tyler | | |
|     certificate of deposit | | $52,000 | 3.50% |
| Mia's 401(k) | Mia | | |
|     Rocket Fund | | $15,250 | 14.00% |
| Mia's Rollover IRA | Mia | | |
|     Ruth Fund | | $32,500 | 4.80% |
| Mia's traditional IRA | Mia | | |
|     certificate of deposit | | $52,000 | 3.50% |
| Conservative annuity | Mia | | |
|     Potsdam Fixed Annuity | | $125,000 | 5.00% |

**Table 1A.10** Other Liabilities

|  | Liability 1 | Liability 2 | Liability 3 | Liability 4 |
|---|---|---|---|---|
| Description | Mortgage | Sedan car loan | Visa credit card | MasterCard credit card |
| Loan detail | Springfield National Bank (joint liability) | Ford Motor credit (joint liability) | Springfield National Bank (joint liability) | University Bank (joint liability) |
| Loan type | Installment | Installment | Revolving | Revolving |
| Interest rate (APR) | 7.875% | 3.90% | 18.25% | 16.75% |
| Minimum payment calculation | Amortization | Amortization | Greater of 4% of monthly balance or $50 | Greater of monthly interest charge + 1.5% of balance or $50 |
| Minimum payment | $1,087.60 | $451.00 | $140.00 | $60.00 |
| Payment frequency | Monthly | Monthly | Monthly | Monthly |
| Original balance | $150,000* *The Bedos purchased this home with a special 100% financing loan option. | $24,549 | $3,500 (current balance) | $2,000 (current balance) |
| Number of payments made | 124 | 36 | NA | NA |
| Original term (months) | 360 | 60 | NA | NA |

# INSURANCE PLANNING

Tyler and Mia are also concerned about the negative outcomes associated with dramatic events like death or disability. Over the past several years, they have taken steps to purchase insurance to meet different life, health, and property contingencies. They are still uncertain whether these policies are best suited to their needs. Details about their insurance policies are presented below.

## Health Insurance Policies

Health insurance is provided for the entire family by a group health insurance policy offered through Tyler's work. The health provider, Peacock & Peacock, is a health maintenance organization. Tyler pays $300 a month in premiums for this coverage through his company's § 125 plan. The plan allows for pretax premium payments.

The policy has an annual deductible of $450 and a stop-loss of $3,000. Under the policy, doctors' visits cost $20 per appointment to the primary care physician and $40 per visit to specialists, and for emergency treatment a $100 copayment is required. Monthly prescriptions are $10 for generic brands and $25 for other brands. There is no copayment for hospitalization in semiprivate accommodations, and private rooms are provided when medically necessary. The original lifetime ceiling for services, per family member, was $2 million; however, with the passage of the Patient Protection and Affordable Care Act limits have been removed.

Over the past several years the Bedos have averaged about $50 per month in dental and eye care expenses, which they pay out of discretionary cash flow. A flexible spending account for health costs is available through Tyler's employer. They have not funded this account in the past because of uncertainty related to "use it or lose it" rules.

## Disability Policies

The Bedos are automatically covered for disability by their employers. Mia also pays for additional long-term disability coverage through her employer. Information about each policy is presented in Table 1A.11.

**Table 1A.11** Disability Policies

|  | Policy 1 | Policy 2 | Policy 3 | Policy 4 |
|---|---|---|---|---|
| Type of Policy | Group | Group | Group | Group |
| Insurance company | Mid-America Disability Assurance Corporation | All-World Life and Disability Company | Mid-America Disability Assurance Corporation | All-World Life and Disability Company |
| Rating | A.M. Best: A | A.M. Best: A | A.M. Best: A | A.M. Best: A- |
| Person insured | Tyler | Mia | Tyler | Mia |
| Wait periods (days) | 0 days | 0 days | 90 days | 90 days |
| Benefit period | 90 days | 90 days | To age 65 | To age 65 |
| Disability benefit | 100% of salary and bonus | 100% of salary and bonus | 60% of salary and bonus | 70% of salary and bonus |
| Definition | Own occupation | Own occupation | Own occupation | Modified own occupation |
| Benefit frequency | Biweekly | Monthly | Biweekly | Monthly |
| Premium amount | Company paid | Company paid | Company paid | $25 monthly (purchased through employer with pretax dollars) |
| Premium payment frequency | NA | NA | NA | Monthly |

## Life Insurance Policies

The Bedos currently have life insurance through their employers and through private policies. Their private policies were purchased several years ago from a friend who was selling life insurance. Information about their policies is shown in Table 1A.12.

**Table 1A.12** Life Insurance Policies

|  | Policy 1 | Policy 2 | Policy 3 | Policy 4 |
|---|---|---|---|---|
| Type of policy | Whole-life* | Whole-life* | Group term | Group term |
| Insurance company | Manhattan Insurance Company | Manhattan Insurance Company | Great Plains Assurance and Protection Corporation | Virginia Highland Life Insurance Company |
| Rating | A.M. Best: A | A.M. Best: A | A.M. Best: A | A.M. Best: A |
| Equivalent after-tax rate of return | 5.50% | 5.50% | 0% | 0% |
| Death benefit | $100,000 | $100,000 | 1 x salary (not including bonus) | 4 x salary (not including bonus) |
| Person insured | Tyler | Mia | Tyler | Mia |
| Owner | Tyler | Mia | Tyler | Mia |
| Beneficiary | Mia | Tyler | Mia | Tyler |
| Cash value | $8,750 | $8,350 | $0 | $0 |
| Premium amount | $92 | $80 | Company paid | Company paid |
| Payment frequency | Monthly | Monthly | NA | NA |

*At the beginning of last year, the cash value of their whole-life policies equaled $7,850 for Tyler and $7,500 for Mia. They both received a dividend in the policy equal to $250.

## Automobile Insurance

Tyler and Mia have split-limit coverage of 100/300/50 on both of their cars, in addition to $100,000 of uninsured/underinsured motorist coverage. Automobile insurance is provided by Missouri Valley Insurance Corporation (A.M. Best Rating: A). Deductibles are $500 for comprehensive coverage and $500 for collision coverage. This insurance includes medical payments, car rental coverage, and towing.

## Homeowners Insurance

The Bedos currently have an HO-3 policy with a $100,000 liability limit that provides replacement value on contents through an endorsement underwritten by Missouri National Insurance (A.M. Best rating: A). Their home is currently insured for $225,000. They do not know if their policy has an inflation endorsement. The deductible is $500. The premium is $700 per year.

Three years ago, their insurance agent recommended that they purchase a $500,000 umbrella insurance policy. The premium for the policy is $175 per year.

# INVESTMENT PLANNING

Before meeting with you, Tyler and Mia completed a confidential risk tolerance questionnaire downloaded from an Internet Web site. The results from the risk quiz suggested that both Tyler and Mia have a moderate to lower level of financial risk tolerance.

Tyler and Mia are interested in ideas that could improve their current returns without taking excessive risk. However, Tyler has made it very clear that he is extremely apprehensive about investing and feels that he tends to be risk averse. Mia, on the other hand, feels comfortable taking additional risks if she is confident that she can earn higher returns.

# RETIREMENT PLANNING

Tyler and Mia have expressed a strong desire to retire at age 62. They both feel that they have other talents and dreams that they would like to pursue during retirement. Tyler loves golfing, gardening, and traveling. His dream is to teach aspiring young golfers on a volunteer basis during retirement.

Mia loves to paint, attend art shows, and occasionally golf. With the demands of her job, motherhood, and volunteer activities, she has had little time for any of these activities. Her plan in retirement is to build a small addition to their home and fill it with art. If built today, the addition would cost $20,000.

Mia would then like to open a small art gallery in downtown Springfield. She estimates that the cost of the gallery would be $80,000 if opened today. If she is successful as an art gallery owner, she plans to donate any net revenue from the art gallery to local youth groups to enhance creative learning.

In addition, Mia would like to improve her golf game so that Tyler would enjoy playing more golf with her.

Neither Tyler nor Mia have a strong desire to travel in retirement. Tyler travels enough now, and he would prefer to enjoy life in southwest Missouri during retirement. They do, however, plan on taking an occasional trip, especially to go and see their daughter if she is not living in Springfield.

Tyler and Mia feel that with these occasional trips, they will need approximately 85% of their current earned before-tax income (in today's dollars) when they retire. They believe they will receive Social Security benefits, and they want to take their benefits at the earliest opportunity. Also, they have a strong desire to leave an estate as large as possible for Becky's benefit at their death. Therefore, they would very much like to minimize the depletion of their retirement assets.

## ESTATE PLANNING

Tyler and Mia have wills that they created when Becky was two years old. They used a will kit purchased at an office supply store because they did not have much time—they were about to begin a 14-day vacation in Europe when it occurred to them that they should have a will. They have not looked at their wills since.

In their wills, Mia's oldest sister Barbara—who is single and living in Oregon—was named Becky's guardian. The Bedos' wills leave all assets to each other in case of death.

Tyler and Mia want to make sure that they do not pay unnecessary estate taxes. They have also been reading magazine articles about probate. Mia is particularly concerned about maintaining privacy and making Becky's life less complicated in the event that she or Tyler was to die.

## ADDITIONAL INFORMATION AND ASSUMPTIONS

### Working Assumptions

Your firm has established expected rate-of-return and portfolio risk objectives for all investment portfolios and has concluded that these rate-of-return expectations (shown in Table 1A.13) represent the maximum returns that should be used in financial planning models.

**Table 1A.13** Expected Rates of Return

| | Expected Before-tax Total Rate of Return* | Estimated Target After-tax Total Rate of Return** | Maximum Portfolio Risk | |
| --- | --- | --- | --- | --- |
| | | | Beta (indexed to S&P 500) | Standard Deviation |
| Conservative | 5.25% | 3.7% | < 0.40 | < 7.0 |
| Moderately conservative | 7.75% | 5.4% | < 0.80 | < 9.0 |
| Moderately aggressive | 10.00% | 7.0% | 0.80 < 1.00 | < 13.0 |
| Aggressive | 12.14% | 8.5% | > 1.00 | > 13.0 |

*Note that these returns include capital appreciation, dividends, and interest received.

** Assumes a combined federal and state tax rate of 30%.

Your financial planning firm uses a screening technique to select and track mutual funds that can be used in client portfolios. Your firm currently uses 11 equity funds, six bond funds, one money market fund, and one variable-annuity product. Tyler and Mia, after consulting with you, have agreed to use these investments, as you recommend, to meet their financial planning goals and objectives. (These are the same investments available in their 401(k) plans.) Detailed information on each investment product is presented in Tables 1A.14 and 1A.15.

**Table 1A.14** Equity Funds

| Fund | Investment Style | Before-tax Rate of Return | Standard Deviation | Correlation with Equity Market | Yield |
|---|---|---|---|---|---|
| Value Fund | Large cap | 9.00% | 12.00% | 0.95 | 3.00% |
| Growth Fund | Large cap | 10.20% | 15.00% | 0.90 | 2.00% |
| Eastside Fund | Mid-cap | 8.40% | 10.00% | 0.92 | 2.00% |
| Konza Fund | Mid-cap | 9.20% | 13.00% | 0.91 | 1.75% |
| Sagebrush Fund | Small cap | 11.20% | 21.00% | 0.80 | 0.50% |
| Rocket Fund | Small cap | 14.00% | 22.00% | 0.75 | 0.00% |
| Consumer Fund | Small cap | 8.75% | 11.00% | 0.99 | 2.50% |
| Acquisitions Fund | Mid-cap | 7.50% | 5.20% | 0.20 | 4.00% |
| International Fund | International (EAFE Index) | 10.00% | 11.20% | 0.50 | 2.00% |
| Haley G&I Fund | Large cap | 8.00% | 10.00% | 0.90 | 3.20% |
| Graham Fund | Real Estate and Precious Metals | 4.10% | 12.00% | 0.10 | 2.00% |

**Table 1A.15** Bond Funds

| Fund | Investment Style | Before-tax Rate of Return | Standard Deviation | Correlation with Bond Market | Yield |
|---|---|---|---|---|---|
| Ruth Fund | Government bond | 4.80% | 4.90% | 0.85 | 4.00% |
| Cardinal Fund | Corporate bond | 5.20% | 5.10% | 0.90 | 4.80% |
| Clock Fund | Corporate bond | 6.00% | 6.20% | 0.98 | 5.40% |
| Ely Fund | Government bond | 6.10% | 6.05% | 0.92 | 6.00% |
| Companion Fund | High yield | 7.00% | 13.00% | 0.80 | 6.10% |
| States Fund | Government bond | 5.70% | 6.00% | 0.75 | 4.00% |
| Barrister Fund | Money market | 3.00% | 0.00% | 0.00 | 3.00% |

Other investments available for use when working with the Bedos include:

- The Potsdam Fixed Annuity (current guaranteed yield of 5.0%). Contract was purchased eight years ago and the guaranteed yield period will expire in two years.

- The Bostonian Variable Annuity includes a guaranteed investment contract that currently yields 5.0% and allows investments in all of the funds listed in the preceding tables. The cash and cash equivalent assets listed in the following table are also available.

Additionally, your financial planning firm finds it useful to create custom benchmarks by which to measure the performance of each client's portfolio. General information about the various segments of the market are shown in Tables 1A.16 and 1A.17

**Table 1A.16** Market Indexes

| Index | Before-tax Rate of Return* | Standard Deviation | Yield* |
|---|---|---|---|
| Treasury bills | 3.00% | 5.00% | 3.00% |
| Treasury coupon bonds | 5.00% | 6.00% | 5.50% |
| Treasury zero-coupon bond "strips" | 6.00% | 6.50% | 0.00% |
| Investment-grade corporate coupon bonds | 7.00% | 7.00% | 7.00% |
| Investment-grade corp. zero-coupon bonds | 7.50% | 8.00% | 0.00% |
| High-yield corporate bonds | 9.00% | 12.00% | 9.00% |
| International bonds | 10.00% | 15.00% | 10.00% |
| U.S. large-cap equity | 10.00% | 18.00% | 2.25% |
| U.S. small-cap equity | 12.00% | +20.00% | <1.00% |
| Developed international equity | 15.00% | +25.00% | ≈0.00% |

\* More representative of long-term averages than current market conditions

**Table 1A.17** Cash and Cash Equivalents

| Asset | Yield* |
|---|---|
| Savings accounts | 2.00% |
| Money market accounts | 3.00% |
| Money market mutual funds | 3.00% |
| Missouri municipal money market account | 2.30% |
| One-year certificates of deposit | 3.50% |

\* More representative of long-term averages than current market conditions

## Universal Assumptions

- The universal inflation rate is expected to average 3.0% per annum.

- The prime interest rate is currently 3.25%, but is expected to increase in the future.

- Life expectancy for Tyler and Mia is age 95.

- They would like to assume a 30.0% combined state and federal tax bracket until retirement and a 25.0% combined state and federal marginal tax bracket during retirement.

# SPECIFIC GOALS AND OBJECTIVES

Tyler and Mia's primary goal is to live life with a relatively high level of financial satisfaction. They want to be self-sufficient in retirement. As such, their primary objective is to retire at age 62, if possible. Their secondary objective is to provide 100% of Becky's college education.

As suggested earlier, Mia would like to turn her love of collecting art into a small business during retirement by renting a retail outlet and selling art supplies and collectibles. They are also interested in maintaining the privacy of their financial affairs. Finally, they would like to ensure Becky's financial welfare if they die.

# ISSUES

# Cash Reserve Issues

- Their cash reserve goal is six months of total dedicated and discretionary expenses, not including taxes paid. In case of an emergency, Mia is willing to use her accumulated art gallery savings as long as the money remains in a bank, checking, or money market account. They would like to achieve this goal within two years.

- They are comfortable assuming a yield of 3.0% before taxes on their savings and money market accounts. Their checking accounts do not earn interest.

- The Bedos are comfortable assuming that their EE savings bonds will grow at a 3.50% tax-deferred rate and not mature for at least another 10 years.

- For simplified tax-planning purposes, dividends are considered nonqualified and do not qualify for reduced tax rates.

- The Bedos do not want to pay off their car loan at this time. They anticipate always having some form of auto loan in the future.

- Any mortgage refinancing will incur 3.0% of the mortgage as a closing cost. The Bedos would like to see an analysis showing the impact of both including closing costs in the mortgage and paying closing costs from assets.

- Their home is expected to appreciate by approximately 4.0% annually over the long-term.

- The Bedos would also like to assume that any interest earned from savings is reinvested rather than spent on household expenses, and that all dividends and capital gains from other investment assets are also reinvested.

## Tax Issues

- The Bedos spent several hours the previous day calculating their state income tax liability. They believe that the amount of state tax withholding closely matches their estimated state tax due for the year, but they would like you to double-check their figures.

- For the purposes of this case, the Bedos are in the 5.0% Missouri tax bracket; they qualify for one state deduction worth $1,000 and two state exemptions valued at $900 each. The state calculation is based on federal adjusted gross income.

## Disability Insurance Coverage Issues

After careful thought, the Bedos are willing to assume the following:

- They will receive no Social Security disability benefits.

- They plan to continue to save for other financial planning goals in the event of a disability.

- Any cash settlements received will be invested using a moderately conservative asset allocation approach.

## Long-term Care Issues

The following assumptions should be used only to address long-term care insurance planning issues.

- For planning purposes the Bedos would like to assume that annual nursing home expenses in in their area are currently $49,000.

- The average age for entering as assisted living facility is 75, with an assumed average length of stay of 2.5 years.

- The average age for those entering a nursing home is 83, with an assumed average stay of 1.5 years.

- Long-term care expenses have been increasing at 5.0% per year.

- In the event that either client enters a nursing home, household expenses are expected to be approximately $115,000 per year (in today's dollars).

- Assets for use in funding long-term care expenses will grow at a modest 5.5% after-tax rate of return.

## Asset Management Issues

- Mia's annuity is invested 100% in the Potsdam Fixed Annuity earning 5% (no other investment alternatives are available within the annuity). She originally purchased the annuity when she was 27 years of age. The annuity has a 10-year declining withdrawal penalty.

- Both traditional IRAs are in one-year certificates of deposit maturing in a few months. The CDs yield 3.50% annually. The renewable rate is also 3.5%.

- Mia's rollover IRA is currently invested in the Ruth Fund.

- Tyler's 401(k) has a 100% employer match, up to 3% of the amount he contributes. The entire match is going to the Graham fund.

- Mia is contributing 10% to the Rocket Fund in her 401(k) plan. Her employer is matching 50% of her contributions, up to 6% of contributions.

- In the event that an investment asset is sold, the Bedos would prefer to assume (for tax purposes) that their basis in all after-tax investments is equal to 50% of the fair market value of these assets, and that all investment gains are subject to ordinary income tax rates.

- The Bedos would also like to assume that any interest earned from savings is reinvested rather than spent on household expenses, and that all dividends and capital gains from other investment assets are also reinvested.

## Education Issues

The following assumptions should be used only to address education planning issues.

- In-state tuition at a good private university for four years will cost $10,000 per semester, including room and board (in today's dollars).

- Tuition costs are increasing at 5.0% per year.

- Tyler and Mia are willing to invest in a moderately aggressive portfolio for this goal, before Becky begins college and during her college years.

- The Bedos want all college savings to be accumulated before Becky begins college and therefore plan to stop saving for college expenses once Becky begins college.

- No assets are currently targeted for college savings needs.

- They would prefer to invest in a tax-advantaged investment to pay for college, if possible.

## Premature Death Issues

The following assumptions should be used only to address life insurance planning issues.

- Assets available at Tyler's death include his IRA and 401(k) plan.

- Assets available at Mia's death include her IRA, her 401(k) plan, the annuity, and her IRA rollover account.

- The clients will need $115,000 in before-tax yearly income to fund total household expenses at the death of either Tyler or Mia.

- The Bedos are willing to allocate $100,000 of their nonretirement investment assets toward survivor needs.

- In case of death, the surviving spouse will invest any cash settlements in a moderately conservative portfolio before and after retirement; the Bedos want this assumption to supersede all other rate-of-return assumptions used in other calculations.

- Tyler and Mia would like to prefund their retirement and education objectives, even if one of them dies.

- For insurance planning purposes, the surviving spouse will need approximately $115,000 per year (in today's dollars) when the spouse retires.

- They feel that the following allocations will meet their final expense needs: $20,000 for final debts (e.g., credit card, auto loans, etc., but not the mortgage); $1,500 for final illness costs; $9,000 for funerals; $13,500 for estate administration costs; $10,000 for other short-term needs; and $25,000 for a spousal adjustment period.

- In the event that either Tyler or Mia dies prematurely, each would like all liabilities, including the home mortgage, to be paid off.

- Social Security benefits, in the event of Tyler's death, are as follows:

    - $23,448 yearly to Mia after age 67

    - $17,580 additional yearly to Mia until Becky turns age 18

    - $17,580 yearly to Becky until age 18

    - $16,765 yearly to Mia from age 60 to age 67 (This is a 28.5% reduction in benefits based on age-67 survivor benefits.)

- Social Security benefits, in the event of Mia's death, are as follows:

  - $26,400 yearly to Tyler after age 67

  - $9,552 additional yearly to Tyler until Becky turns age 18

  - $9,552 yearly to Becky until age 18

  - $0 to Tyler from age 60 to 67

- In the event of either spouse's death, the other spouse plans to stop working at age 60 and begin taking early retirement survivor benefits (if available).

- For conservative planning purposes, the Bedos do not plan to use interest or dividends as an income source when planning insurance needs.

- The capital retention replacement ratio is assumed to be 100%.

## Retirement Issues

The following assumptions should be used only to address retirement planning issues.

- Mia would like to build a small addition to their home and fill it with art. If built today, the addition would cost $20,000.

- Mia would then also like to open a small art gallery. She estimates the cost of the gallery would be $80,000 if opened today.

- The Bedos are willing to invest in a moderately aggressive portfolio to fund the art gallery and house addition. Currently, assets and savings for these goals are invested very conservatively in a bank account.

- They will need approximately 85% of their current earned before-tax income (in today's dollars) when they retire.

- They are willing to reallocate retirement assets and savings to earn a before-tax moderately conservative rate of return prior to retirement. The Bedos are willing to increase their rate of return through a reallocation of their retirement assets to meet these return assumptions. At the current time, however, the Bedos are earning less, given the allocation of their current portfolio. It is necessary to calculate their current rate of return to determine their retirement income need.

- Once retired, the Bedos would like to assume a before-tax conservative rate of return.

- The Bedos would like to assume a 25% federal marginal tax bracket while in retirement.

- Normal retirement age is age 67 for Tyler and Mia.

- The Bedos want to retire at age 62, but it is more important that they do not deplete their assets over their lifetime.

- They are unwilling to reduce their projected life expectancy unless absolutely required to achieve their age-at-retirement objective.

- They are willing to reallocate assets and savings to meet their retirement objective.

- They believe that their incomes will increase at the rate of inflation into the future.

- The Bedos plan to increase contributions to their retirement accounts by 3.0% each year.

- The primary insurance amount in today's dollars at age 67 for Tyler is $2,200 and $1,300 for Mia.

## Estate Planning Issues

The following assumptions should be used only to address estate planning issues.

- The assumed appreciation rate on their gross estate, debt, loans, and other financial position items is 4.0%.

- Funeral and administration expenses are assumed to be $9,000 for each person. These expenses will grow 4.0% annually. Executor fees are anticipated to be approximately $13,500 each.

# Computations for Financial Planning

## Learning Objectives

1. Define, calculate, and apply the three different methods to calculate holding-period returns for an investment.

2. Define, calculate, and apply the two different methods to calculate average annual returns for an investment and to explain the error between the two methods.

3. Demonstrate how to calculate a weighted average return for a multi-asset portfolio.

4. Define, calculate, and explain the use of different interest rates (real, nominal, serial, tax-exempt, and taxable) in different financial planning situations.

5. Explain the difference in the required rate of return and the risk-free rate as applied in time value of money calculations.

6. Understand the significance of time value of money calculations used by financial planners to move money across time for analysis and comparisons.

7. Define, calculate, and explain the use of different interest rates (effective annual rate, nominal or annual percentage rate, effective periodic rate) in time value of money calculations, as well as the methods for adjusting between nominal and effective interest rates.

8. Define, calculate, and explain the application of the future value of a single-sum formula and the present value of a single-sum formula to different financial planning scenarios.

9. Define, calculate, and explain the application of the future value of an annuity formula and the present value of an annuity formula, differentiating by beginning (annuity "due") or end-of-period payments, to different financial planning scenarios.

10. Demonstrate and explain when to use the formulas for the future value of a geometrically varying "growing" annuity and the present value of a geometrically varying "growing" annuity to different financial planning scenarios.

## Learning Objectives

11. Demonstrate and explain the use of net present value and internal rate of return calculations to evaluate an investment.

12. Demonstrate and explain the use of time value of money calculations to determine the outstanding balance, the amount paid to date, or the total amount of interest paid over a period of time (e.g., annually) for an amortized loan.

## Key Terms

| | |
|---|---|
| amortization schedule | holding-period return |
| annual percentage rate (APR) | inflation |
| annuity | internal rate of return |
| annuity due | net present value |
| bias | nominal (or simple) rate |
| compound annualized growth rate (cagr) | present value |
| compound interest | present value of an annuity |
| double discounting | rate of return |
| effective annual rate (ear) | required rate of return |
| effective periodic rate (epr) | rule of 72 |
| future value | serial interest rate |
| future value of an annuity | standard deviation |
| geometric average | time value of money |
| geometrically varying annuity | weighted average |

**Figure 2.1** The Systematic Financial Planning Process

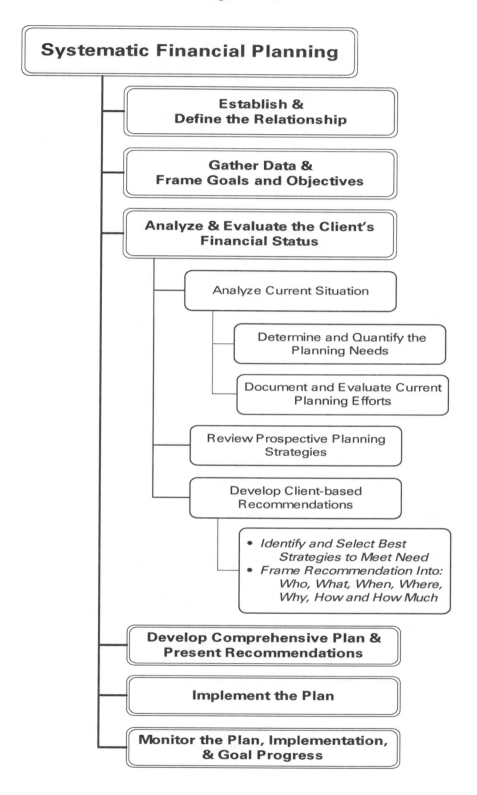

## FINANCIAL COMPUTATION: THE BASICS

Almost all aspects of personal financial planning involve mathematical calculations. The good news is that the math is not extremely complex. Furthermore, sophisticated calculators and software programs are available to do most of the work. The most important caveat with financial planning calculations is that outputs depend entirely upon the quality of inputs.

The formulas needed for the majority of the calculations are relatively easy to memorize. Applying the correct formula and related inputs within a calculation usually causes the most difficulty. More important than the formulas themselves is a fundamental understanding of the logic, or reasoning, required to identify the correct mathematical formula for a particular purpose.

Once the logic is correct, there may be multiple ways to derive the correct solution to a financial planning question. For example, one financial planner may choose to adjust a **future value** calculation for taxes at the end of period, while another will adjust a savings need at the beginning to account for taxes. Both planners should arrive at the same answer. This can sometimes be confusing to students versed in hard sciences, where one method is preferred and is often the only way to calculate an outcome.

What is important, then, is for planners to choose the method that they are comfortable with and practice that method until the process becomes second nature. Then, it is equally important to ensure accuracy—in both the input of the data and the supporting assumptions on which a calculation is based.

The purpose of this chapter is to briefly review some of the most important calculations made in personal financial planning. After reading this chapter, readers should understand rates of return and time value of money formulas and how to set up equations for later use in a spreadsheet application or financial calculator. It is assumed that much of the content of this chapter is a review. However, a thorough grounding in personal financial math is fundamental to financial planning.

## HISTORICAL RATE-OF-RETURN CALCULATIONS

One of the most elementary of all personal finance calculations is **determining the total return** earned on an investment. Financial planners use this calculation to determine how much profit has been earned on an investment during a certain period of time. **Rate of return** describes the relationship between profit or loss relative to the amount saved or invested. For example, an investor deposits $1,000 into an account, the account has a stated rate of return of 6%, and the investor leaves that money in the account for one year. What will be the account balance at the end of the investment period? How much of the account balance is principal and how much is interest? How much will the account be worth in real terms if **inflation**—the general increase in the price of goods and services over time—averaged 4% over the same time period? How much money will be available after paying taxes on the earnings? All of these questions are answered by using various rate of return calculations.

To calculate return on an investment, all sources of income must be identified. The two most common sources of return are *income* and *capital gain*. In general, income is derived from periodic payments received by the investor, either in cash or as deposits to the account during the investment period. Examples include stock dividends, bond interest payments, mutual fund dividends, or savings account interest payments. Capital gains (or losses), on the other hand, are generally received or realized when the investment period ends because the investment is sold, liquidates, or matures. If the security is sold for more (or less) than the purchase price, the investor will realize a capital gain (or loss).

These two sources of cash inflow serve as the basis for the nominal return on investment. A nominal value, in its simplest form, means an *unadjusted* value. It can be thought of as the gross return. The most common adjustment made to a nominal value is an inflation adjustment; however, nominal values can be adjusted for many other reasons. Later in the chapter, nominal values will be the basis of adjustments for inflation (real returns), taxes (after-tax returns), compounding frequencies (effective returns), and others. When calculating total returns or future values, it is as important to understand the interrelationship between the nominal and adjusted rate as it is to be able to accurately calculate the nominal rate of return.

## Holding-period Based Returns

### Holding-period Return

A simple method of calculating nominal returns involves determining an investor's **holding-period return** (HPR). The formula considers a beginning and ending value for the investment, income earned during the holding period, and transaction costs. The income received could be dividends from an equity (or stock) investment, or the income could be coupon "interest" payments from a debt (or bond) investment.

$$HPR = \frac{Income + (Ending\ Value - Beginning\ Value) - Transaction\ Costs}{Beginning\ Value}$$

*Example:* Bob purchased one share of stock for $45 per share, received two dividend payments of $1 each that were not reinvested, and paid a transaction fee of $5. Bob then sold the stock for $55. What was Bob's holding-period return?

$$HPR = \frac{\sum Div + (End - Beg) - Costs}{Beg}$$

$$HPR = \frac{(1+1) + (55 - 45) - 5}{45} = \frac{2 + 10 - 5}{45} = 15.6\%$$

Another common modification to nominal rates of return is an adjustment for taxes paid at the state and federal levels. However, calculating tax-adjusted returns can be complex. First, a planner needs to know what type of income was generated as a result of the return. Second, the planner must know what tax rate applies to each type of return. For example, interest income, dividends (qualified or nonqualified), and capital gains may be taxed at different rates, and the rates may also vary depending on the holding period for the investment (e.g., short-term or long-term capital gains). Different investments may be taxed at different rates.

To accurately calculate the tax-adjusted rate of return, the HPR must be offset by any tax liability generated as a result of owning the investment. The following adjustment can be used for historical return calculations.

$$Tax\ Adjusted\ HPR\ =\ \frac{(Income - Income\ Tax) + (Capital\ Gains - Cap\ Gains\ Tax) - (Costs\ adjusted\ for\ Taxes)}{Beginning\ Value}$$

Obviously, this equation can be used only for historical calculations because the actual amount of tax liability must be determined prior to calculating the return. However, to estimate the after-tax rate of return for projection purposes, where taxation occurs annually, a financial advisor could also use the following equation.

$$r_t = R \times (1 - t)$$

Where:

$r_t$ = tax-adjusted return

R = nominal return

t = investor's marginal tax bracket

*Example:* Expanding on the previous example, assume Bob owned the stock in a non-tax-qualified account and dividends and capital gains were taxed at a short-term tax rate of 15%. His after-tax rate of return would be 13.26%, as shown below.

$$r_t = 15.6\% \times (1 - 0.15) = 13.26\%$$

## Dollar-weighted Return

The problem with the holding-period return is that the formula does not account for the timing of subsequent cash flows into or out of the account. A very basic formula that corrects for the timing of subsequent cash flows is the dollar-weighted return formula, shown below:

$$Dollar\ Weighted\ Rate\ of\ Return\ =\ \frac{Inc + \left[End - \left(Beg + D - W\right)\right] - Costs}{Beg + D_t - W_t}$$

Where:

Inc = income

End = ending value

Beg = beginning value

D = deposit amount

W    =    withdrawal amount

Costs =    transaction costs

$D_t$    =    $D \times (1 - \text{timing of deposit})$

$W_t$    =    $W \times (1 - \text{timing of withdrawal})$

*Example:* Altering the preceding example, assume that one year after Bob made his initial one-share purchase he bought an additional two shares of stock at $48 ($48 x 2 = $96). Further, assume that he sold one share at $45 at the end of the second year and liquidated the account after three years at $50 per share ($50 x 2 = $100). He still receives semiannual dividends of $1 per share ($12 total) and the total transaction cost is still $5. What is Bob's dollar-weighted rate of return?

$$\text{Dollar-Weighted HPR} = \frac{\$12 + \left[\$100 - (\$45 + \$96 - \$45)\right] - \$5}{\$45 + \left[\$96\left(1 - \frac{12}{36}\right)\right] - \left[\$45\left(1 - \frac{24}{36}\right)\right]}$$

$$= \frac{\$12 + \$4 - \$5}{\$45 + \$64 - \$15} = 11.7\%$$

## Time-weighted Return

An alternative to dollar-weighted returns is a time-weighted return. This method of calculation ignores the actual value of the investment during each time period.

*Example:* Once again, use Bob's situation, but this time solve for the time-weighted return. From the previous example, it is known that the stock was initially purchased for $45 per share and was valued as follows:

End-of-year 1 = $48

End-of-year 2 = $45

End-of-year 3 = $50

Using the holding-period return formula results in the following annual rates of return:

$$Year\ 1 \quad = \frac{\$2 + (\$48 - \$45)}{\$45} = 11.1\%$$

$$Year\ 2 \quad = \frac{\$2 + (\$45 - \$48)}{\$48} = -2.1\%$$

$$Year\ 3 \quad = \frac{\$2 + (\$50 - \$45)}{\$45} = 15.6\%$$

$$Average = \frac{11.1\% - 2.1\% + 15.6\%}{3} = 8.2\%$$

Thus, the average of the three annual returns results in a time-weighted return of 8.2%. Note that the dividend was the same for all three periods because the time-weighted return ignores the number of shares (dollar amount) owned in each period.

So, which measure is superior? It depends on asset control. Investors who control their own investments (both the timing and amount of purchases) would want to use the dollar-weighted average. In this case, the more money invested when a stock is performing well, the more money the investor will have in the end. However, a person who does not control the timing and amount of the investment, such as a portfolio manager, would want to measure performance using the time-weighted measure. It would be inappropriate to measure a manager's success or failure based on a measure over which the manager does not have complete control.

## Average Annual Returns

Average annual returns are some of the most-quoted statistics in finance. They are easy to calculate, relatively simple to interpret, and —for the most part—intuitive. However, the most common usage for these statistics is to use them to predict future results because forecasters want to believe that, given a long enough time horizon, the future tends to resemble the past. But most calculations of historic returns tend to have a **bias** or partial perspective when used to project future or terminal values. A downward bias means that the average used to project the future value tends to underestimate the actual outcome, and an upward bias results in overestimation. Such bias occurs because cumulative return is a nonlinear function of average return.

The following discussion of arithmetic average (mean) and geometric average (mean) not only presents the calculation of the two statistics but also addresses two issues inherent in using either average as a means to project future results: standard deviation and time horizon. Both of these factors play a role in the bias created when projecting terminal values.

### Arithmetic and Geometric Means—Calculation and Deterministic Forecasting

Although holding-period-based returns are very simple to use and calculate, most returns are quoted on an average annual basis, because annual returns are more intuitive for investors to understand and are often required by regulators. A financial planner can use a number of different methods to measure average rates of return. The simplest method is to calculate the arithmetic mean, which is a linear interpretation of past performance.

$$Average\ Return\ (AR) = \frac{r_1 + r_2 + r_3 + ... + r_n}{n}$$

Where:

r = return for period

n = number of periods

*Example:* Consider a client who makes 8%, 2%, and –5% in each of three years, respectively. The average of these returns is 1.67%.

$$AR = \frac{8\% + 2\% - 5\%}{3} = 1.67\%$$

The arithmetic mean, although quick to calculate and easy to explain, is often a poor representation of actual performance due to the variability (measured by **standard deviation**) of returns. Therefore, it can be said that the higher the standard deviation of returns, even over a short time period, the greater the potential upward bias of the projection. The resultant overestimation of future values is even more problematic when short-term arithmetic averages are used for long-term forecasting.

For longer forecasting periods, or for forecasting using a more highly varied return, the **geometric average** is more appropriate because this mean is computed for a geometric series and therefore takes on more of the characteristics found in long-term averages and corrects for the upward bias. In other words, future values by their very nature are the result of geometric series rather than linear series. The rule is that, unless the variation of returns is zero, then the geometric average will always be lower than the arithmetic return. How much less depends on the variation (standard deviation) of returns. **Standard deviation** is the average difference between an individual outcome (in this case the investment return) and the average, or expected, outcome for the applicable group. Standard deviation will be discussed in more depth later.

Consider a $100 stock that rises 50% in one year and falls 50% the next. The arithmetic mean return is zero. However, when the return is tracked, it is apparent that in the first year the final price was $150. Then the 50% drop resulted in a final value of $75. The total return is obviously less than zero—it is a negative 25% total return, and a negative 13.4% geometric return. For this reason, the geometric mean is recommended for forecasting future values. The geometric mean is often referred to as geomean, the annualized return or the **compound annualized growth rate (CAGR)**. The formula for calculating a geometric average is as follows:

*Geometric Mean Return =*

$$\left[(1 + r_1) \times (1 + r_2) \times (1 + r_3) \times ... \times (1 + r_n)\right]^{1/n} - 1$$

Where:

r = return for period

n = number of periods

*Example:* Tonya purchased an investment seven years ago. According to the annual report, the investment earned the rates of return shown in the table below. She wants to know what return she could project for the next seven years by calculating the annualized return.

| Year | Rate of Return |
| --- | --- |
| 1 | 9% |
| 2 | –8% |
| 3 | 2% |
| 4 | 12% |
| 5 | 18% |
| 6 | –7% |
| 7 | 4% |

$$Geomean = \left[(1+0.09)\times(1-0.08)\times(1+0.02)\times(1+0.12)\times(1+0.18)\times(1-0.07)\times(1+0.04)\right]^{\frac{1}{7}} - 1$$

$$Geomean = 3.90\%$$

Now compare this result to the simple linear average.

$$Arithmetic\,Mean = \frac{9\%-8\%+2\%+12\%+18\%-7\%+4\%}{7}$$

$$Arithmetic\,Mean = 4.29\%$$

Clearly the arithmetic average overstates expected return—upward bias. For example, seven years ago a client asked for the future value of $500,000 in seven years. Using the arithmetic average of 4.29% would result in a projected value of $670,916.82; however, the account only grew to $653,550.03. Using the arithmetic average to project the future value would have resulted in an overstatement of the actual account value by $17,366.79. This may seem like an insignificant amount given the very fluid nature of financial markets and the subjective nature of projections. But what if the client had $2,000,000 and asked for a 25-year projection. In this case the difference between the arithmetic projection and the geometric projection is more than half a million dollars and most likely would undermine the planner/client relationship.

Using a geometric average will result in a more precise measure of the client's true return when projecting account values into the future. The arithmetic mean can be useful in certain circumstances or for a quick estimate, but for actual reporting and forecasting, the geometric mean is generally preferred. However, this method too is not without flaws. A future value calculated using the geometric average is likely to have a slight downward bias; meaning that the actual future value achieved is likely to be slightly greater than the future value projected using the geometric average. The amount of underestimation will depend on the ratio of the sampled estimation period compared to the forecasted period. The closer the ratio is to one, the less likely the downward bias.[1]

So the estimation rule for time is that (1) for forecasting periods that are much shorter than the sample period from which the averages were calculated, the true average tends to be closer to the arithmetic mean; and (2) for forecasting periods that are much closer in length to the sample period, the true average will be closer to the geometric mean.

### Arithmetic vs. Geometric: Margin for Error

Again, when comparing the arithmetic mean and the geometric mean, it is interesting to note that as the standard deviation of the returns approaches zero, the difference between the arithmetic mean and the geometric mean also approaches zero. This is because the arithmetic mean and the geometric mean are equal if the return is fixed, meaning that the exact same outcome (return) occurs in each period, resulting in a standard deviation of zero. However, the inverse is also true. As the standard deviation of outcomes increases, the difference between the arithmetic mean and the geometric mean also increases.

Consider the S&P 500 total returns in Table 2.1. The difference between the two means is quite large, 1.90% (10.10% – 8.20%), because the standard deviation is nearly 20%. As this example illustrates, the relationship between the two statistics becomes quite apparent and very important.

**Table 2.1** S&P 500 Returns (1990–2009)

| Year | Annual Return | Year | Annual Return |
|---|---|---|---|
| 1990 | -3.10% | 2000 | -9.10% |
| 1991 | 30.46% | 2001 | -11.89% |
| 1992 | 7.62% | 2002 | -22.10% |
| 1993 | 10.08% | 2003 | 28.68% |
| 1994 | 1.32% | 2004 | 10.88% |
| 1995 | 37.58% | 2005 | 4.91% |
| 1996 | 22.96% | 2006 | 15.80% |
| 1997 | 33.36% | 2007 | 5.49% |
| 1998 | 28.58% | 2008 | -37.00% |
| 1999 | 21.04% | 2009 | 26.46% |
| Arithmetic Average | 10.10% | Geometric Average | 8.21% |
| Variance | 3.89% | Standard Deviation | 19.73% |

*Example:* A client has an account balance of $50,000. The client assumes that since the average annual return of the stock market has been 10% over the last 20 years, the next 20 years should result in the same return. Even if history were to repeat itself, the client still should not use the 10% average annual return but should use the 8.2% geometric average return. By using the incorrect average return for projecting the value of the account in 20 years, the client would overstate the account balance by nearly $95,000. Using the incorrect 10% return results in an account balance of $336,375.00; using the correct 8.2% return results in an account balance of $241,832.81.

One of the biggest issues about calculating geometric averages is that individual periodic returns are needed to construct the geometric series, but usually the literature and Web sites provide only multi-period average returns (e.g., 3-year, 5-year, 10-year). However, if the standard deviation is also available for the corresponding period, then the geomean can be estimated. The following formula can be used to back into the geomean if a return series is unavailable.

$$Geometric\ Mean = Arithmetic\ Mean - \tfrac{1}{2}\ Variance$$

Using the preceding example where the arithmetic average is 10.10% and the variance is 3.89%, the geomean can quickly be estimated as:

$$Geometric\ Mean = 10.10\% - \tfrac{1}{2} * 3.89\% = 8.155\%$$

## WEIGHTED AVERAGE RETURN

### Multi-asset Portfolio Returns

Sometimes it is necessary to calculate a weighted average return for different assets or values. A **weighted average** is calculated by multiplying an investment return by the proportion of the investment, stated as a percentage of the total portfolio, and then summing the total for all of the investments. For example, Table 2.2 provides rate of return data from seven mutual funds. The amount invested in each fund is also provided. These data are used to determine that this portfolio had a weighted average rate of return of 5.64%.

**Table 2.2** Hypothetical Portfolio Values and Returns

| Fund | Objective | Value (A) | Percent of Portfolio (B) | RoR (C) | Weighted Return (D) |
|---|---|---|---|---|---|
| Calculation | | | (A /E) | | (B x C) |
| Fund A | Moderately Aggressive | $75,000 | 15.79% | 8.00% | 1.26% |
| Fund B | Moderately Conservative | $100,000 | 21.05% | 9.00% | 1.89% |
| Fund C | CD | $94,000 | 19.79% | 3.00% | 0.59% |
| Fund D | Aggressive | $14,000 | 2.95% | 10.00% | 0.29% |
| Fund E | Conservative | $35,000 | 7.37% | 3.00% | 0.22% |
| Fund F | CD | $45,000 | 9.47% | 2.00% | 0.19% |
| Fund G | Conservative | $112,000 | 23.58% | 5.00% | 1.18% |
| Total | | $475,000 (E) | 100.00% | | 5.64% |

## Scenario-based Return Forecasting

As stated earlier, most often forecasts are based on the belief that the future will closely resemble the past. But as the last decade has taught us, sometimes it is the long past. Therefore, deterministic modeling based on historical averages can sometimes be highly misrepresentative of the near-term future. In this case, it might be better to account for multiple potential outcomes, where each outcome is assigned a probability of occurrence. Using the same methodology as for weighted average return, where the weights each represent a percentage of the whole portfolio, a planner could reassign the weights to the probability of occurrence, as shown in Table 2.3. Then each outcome is assigned a corresponding potential return.

**Table 2.3** Scenario-based Potential Returns

| Potential Economic Outcome | Probability of Occurrence (A) | Corresponding Return (B) | Weighted Return (A x B) |
|---|---|---|---|
| Super-normal growth | 15.0% | 20.00% | 3.00% |
| Normal growth | 55.0% | 12.00% | 6.60% |
| Stagnation | 5.0% | 3.00% | 0.15% |
| Recession | 20.0% | -8.00% | −1.60% |
| Depression | 5.0% | -25.00% | −1.25% |
| | 100.00% | | 6.90% |

# TYPES AND FORMS OF INTEREST RATES

## Real vs. Nominal Rates

Nearly all interest rates quoted in newspapers, magazines, and annual reports are **nominal rates**, meaning that the rate has not been adjusted to account for inflation. Nominal rates are used when the actual dollar amount of an investment is important. By contrast, the real rate of return is the return "left over" after adjusting for inflation. This provides a more accurate representation of purchasing power, which is an important consideration for long-term investments. A client may be interested in having a portfolio value of $1 million when she turns 65, but she needs to recognize that the purchasing power of that portfolio will be far less than what $1 million provides today. This is why adjusting returns to account for inflation is of paramount importance.

Two equations are used to account for the effects of inflation: one if the nominal rate of return is continuously compounded and another if the nominal rate is discretely or *not continuously compounded*. If the nominal rate of return is continuously compounded, it is appropriate to subtract the inflation rate from the nominal rate to determine an approximation of the real rate.

$$r = R - i$$

Where:

r  = real rate

R = nominal rate

i  = inflation rate

*Example:* The nominal annual rate of return on Mary's portfolio is 9% and the annual inflation rate is 4%. In this case, the nominal rate of return is continuously compounded. What is her real rate of return?

$$r = 9\% - 4\% = 5\%$$

However, if the nominal rate is not continuously compounded, a different equation, often referred to as the *Fisher Equation*, should be used to take into account the effects of this compounding difference. The result of this calculation is sometimes referred to as a **serial interest rate**.

$$r = \frac{(1 + R)}{(1 + i)} - 1$$

Where:

r  = real rate

R = nominal rate

i  = inflation rate

*Example:* The nominal annual rate of return on Mary's portfolio is 9% and the annual inflation rate is 4%. In this case, the nominal rate of return is not continuously compounded. The real rate of return is no longer 5%, but slightly less than 5%.

$$r = \frac{(1.09)}{(1.04)} - 1 = 4.81\%$$

This calculation should be used whenever a client faces inflation risk when making an investment. These are particularly important formulas when determining the present value of an inflation-adjusted dollar amount—as would be the case anytime a planner or client is calculating future values, but stating the results in today's dollars.

## Tax-exempt vs. Taxable Rates

In addition to the difference between nominal and real rates of return is the difference between taxable and tax-exempt rates of return. The effect of taxes must always be considered, because a client cannot keep what the government gets. In the earlier discussion of holding-period return, the concept of *tax impact* was briefly introduced. For the most part, exact after-tax returns cannot be determined until the end of the investing period. However, applying a client's marginal tax brackets to a return calculation can at least offer a reasonable estimate of future tax impact on a projected return.

*Example:* A client is in the 25% marginal tax bracket, and the expected return on an investment is 7%. By applying the following formula, a financial advisor can determine how much of the return will actually benefit the client. In other words, how many of the dollars earned will be kept?

$$r' = R \times (1 - t)$$

Where:

$r'$ = after-tax rate

$R$ = nominal rate

$t$ = Fed tax rate

$$r' = 0.07 \times (1 - 0.25) = 5.25\%$$

In this case the investor's after-tax return would be 5.25%. Therefore, it can be estimated that if that client invested $1,000 in a taxable account and the account returned 7% per year, or $70, then the client would keep $52.50 of those dollars and would pay $17.50 in taxes. This formula can also be expanded to include the state tax impact on nominal returns.

In many states, state income taxes are levied against gains that remain after federal tax liability has been applied; in such states, the state tax rate cannot simply be added to the federal tax rate in the preceding formula. The state tax rate is, in essence, reduced by the client's federal tax bracket. This is accomplished by using the same formula as above, except that the nominal rate in the formula is replaced by the state tax rate.

$$s' = s \times (1 \ t)$$

Where:

$s'$ = applicable state tax rate

$s$ = state tax rate

$t$ = Federal tax rate

Now the combined after-tax rate can be determined by combining both of the preceding equations.

$$r' = R \times [1 - (t + (s \times (1 - t)))] \quad \text{or} \quad r' = R \times [1 - (t + s')]$$

This may seem like a lot of manipulation for some fairly simple projections; however, this may be useful in determining the **taxable equivalent yield** (TEY). A TEY is the investor's implied required rate of return on a taxable investment with identical risk/reward characteristics. In other words, if an investor could earn 6% on a tax-free investment, the TEY would need to be higher to compensate the investor equally on an after-tax basis. The formula to determine exactly how much higher is simply a variation of the preceding formulas.

The following formula is used to determine the TEY on a taxable investment that can then be compared with a federal tax-free investment (e.g., an out-of-state municipal bond) using the federal marginal tax bracket (FMTB).

$$TEY = \frac{Bond\ Yield}{(1 - FMTB)}$$

However, this formula accounts only for federal taxes and it applies only to certain situations, including: (1) the purchase of out-of-state municipal bonds; (2) the comparison of in-state municipal bonds to Treasury bonds, because neither bond is subject to state taxes; or (3) when the client's state of residence does not levy a state income tax. But outside of these situations, the impact of both federal and state taxes should be considered. To include the impact of state taxes, the formula would need to be slightly altered to include the state marginal tax bracket (SMTB).

$$TEY = \frac{Bond\ Yield}{1 - [FMTB + (SMTB \times (1 - FMTB))]}$$

*Example:* A client desires a fixed-income investment and has narrowed the list of choices to two bonds: (1) an in-state municipal bond with an annual coupon rate of 6%; and (2) a corporate bond with an annual coupon rate of 8%. The investor is in the 25% federal tax bracket and the 5% state tax bracket. Which bond would be the better bond to purchase?

On the surface, it would seem that the corporate bond that pays $80 per $1,000 invested would be the better choice. However, the client would have to pay taxes on the $80, leaving the client with less than $80 after taxes. The other choice is the municipal bond that pays only $60, but the client would, under most circumstances, not owe any federal or state taxes on that amount.

By using the TEY formula, the client can determine the required yield on a taxable investment that would provide equal compensation. In other words, this is the yield that is required to "net" the client the same amount of "spendable" dollars after paying the tax liability on the earnings.

$$TEY = \frac{0.06}{1 - [0.25 + (0.05 \times (1 - 0.25))]} = \frac{0.06}{0.7125} = 0.08421\ or\ 8.421\%$$

By completing the preceding formula, the advisor can determine that a taxable return would have to be 8.421% for the client to maintain the same net return. Therefore, the client would be better off purchasing the in-state municipal bond.

## Risk and Returns

Inflation risk, default risk, interest rate risk, reinvestment risk, political risk, exchange rate risk, and others must be analyzed and either removed, mitigated, or compensated for. To be compensated for these risks, an investor has to receive a rate of return high enough to adjust for the risk—the investor's **required rate of return**. This rate is greater than the risk-free rate that simply compensates the investor for delaying consumption and is used as the basis for time value of money calculations.

# TIME VALUE OF MONEY

It has been said that a financial plan is the foundation of a client's financial future. If that is the case, then the time value of money is the cornerstone of that foundation. The concept of the **time value of money** (TVM) has two primary purposes: (1) to allow money to be moved around in time while accurately reflecting its true value or purchasing power; and (2) to solve for complex spending and savings scenarios, such as college or retirement funding. The TVM formulas can answer such questions as: What will be the value of a client's savings in 10 years? How much does a client need to save today to fund something in the future? What will be the impact of inflation on a client's standard of living?

The underlying assumption behind all TVM calculations is that generally it is more beneficial to receive a dollar today than later. Someone who waits to receive a dollar rather than taking it today must be compensated for waiting. That person would be willing to spend less than a dollar today in order to receive a dollar in the future.

## Effective and Nominal Rates

**Compound interest** is simply the idea that interest earned in a prior period is reinvested and therefore earns additional interest in subsequent periods. Referred to by Albert Einstein as the "eighth wonder of the world," this mechanism adds a level of complexity when calculating present or future values, which substantiates the less well-known component of his quote: "He who understands it, earns it...he who doesn't, pays it."

The simplest example is that if a $100 investment earns a *simple* 10% per year, then the account will pay the owner $10 the first year, the tenth year, every year. But, if that same account reinvests or *compounds* the interest, the account would earn more interest in each subsequent year. So while the first year still returns $10, the tenth year returns $23.58 based on a prior year value of $235.79.

For TVM calculations, it is assumed that all accounts will compound the interest; therefore, the interest rate, or the investor's required rate of return, is the variable that compounds or discounts the cash flows. **Compound interest** takes into account both principal and the interest earned on the principal. This is the variable that keeps values equal across time. When using the TVM formulas, it is critical that the interest rate used be an *effective rate*—one that considers the effects of compounding when compounding occurs more than once a year. In other words, this is the actual *accrued* annual interest rate.

If the rate is not an effective rate, then it is a nominal rate, often referred to as an *annual percentage rate* (APR). The nominal rate may be used in a financial calculator because the calculator can automatically adjust for the compounding period (payment frequency). It generally may not be used in mathematical formulas unless adjustments are made to the formulas. The following formula is used to adjust a nominal rate to an effective rate.

$$Effective\,Annual\,Rate = \left(1 + \frac{APR}{m}\right)^{m} - 1$$

Where:

APR  =  annual percentage rate or the nominal rate

m  =  number of compounding periods per year

The **effective annual rate** (EAR) is the rate that, under annual compounding, would produce the same future value at the end of one year as produced by more frequent compounding. If compounding occurs on an annual basis, the effective annual rate and the nominal rate are the same. If compounding occurs more frequently, the effective annual rate is greater than the nominal rate.

In addition to the effective annual rate, there is also an **effective periodic rate** (EPR). The EPR, or iPER, is the rate charged by a lender or paid by a borrower each period. It can be a semiannual, quarterly, monthly, or daily rate; in fact it can be any time interval, for example, every 10 years.

*Example:* What is the EAR in a bank account that has an APR of 6%, but the interest is compounded quarterly?

$$EAR = \left(1 + \frac{APR}{m}\right)^m - 1$$

$$= \left(1 + \frac{0.06}{4}\right)^4 - 1$$

$$= 1.015^4 - 1$$

$$= 1.0714 - 1 = 0.0614 \text{ or } 6.14\%$$

*Example:* What is the effective monthly interest rate on a mortgage with a stated APR of 8%? This would be the rate necessary to determine the monthly interest charges on a simple-interest mortgage with a monthly payment.

$$EPR = \frac{APR}{m}$$

$$EPR = \frac{0.08}{12} = 0.0667 \text{ or } 0.667\%$$

Table 2.4 illustrates common variations of the equations used to adjust between nominal and effective interest rates.

**Table 2.4** Adjusting Between Nominal and Effective Interest Rates

| Type of Interest Rate Known | Type of Interest Rate Desired | Formula Needed |
|---|---|---|
| EAR | EPR | $(1 + EAR)^{1/m} - 1 = EPR$ |
| EAR | APR | $\left[(1 + EAR)^{1/m} - 1\right] \times m = APR$ |
| EPR | EAR | $(1 + EPR)^m - 1 = EAR$ |
| EPR | APR | $EPR \times m = APR$ |
| APR | EPR | $\dfrac{APR}{m} = EPR$ |
| APR | EAR | $\left[1 + \left(\dfrac{APR}{m}\right)\right]^m - 1 = EAR$ |

In all cases, m is the number of compounding periods per year.

One of the most important concepts to understand when manipulating the rates of return in TVM equations is that the compounding frequency of the effective rate must match the payment frequency. In other words, the rate used must match the compounding frequency to how often cash flows, or payments, occur. For example, if a payment is occurring monthly, then the effective rate needs to be adjusted so that it is also compounded monthly. This adjustment does not affect the actual interest earned; it simply adjusts how the rate is interpreted within the equation.

Payments are the periodic inflows or outflows that occur during a valuation period, and they are used only with annuity equations. For a cash flow to be considered a *payment*, it must happen more than once and occur on a fixed periodic basis (e.g., monthly, semiannually, annually). Because the frequency of the payment and the interest rate must match and the payment frequency is independent, the interest rate must be adjusted to match the payment frequency.

*Example:* A client is planning to save for retirement by contributing to an employer-sponsored 401(k) plan on a semimonthly (twice per month) basis. However, the account reports and compounds at a monthly rate of 0.721%. For the TVM equation to be accurate, the rate must reflect the semimonthly compounding period.

To make this conversion, two of the effective rate equations must be used. First convert the monthly effective rate into an EAR.

$$EAR = (1 + EPR)^m - 1$$

$$EAR = (1 + 0.00721)^{12} - 1 \text{ (M = 12 because the account compounds monthly)}$$

$$EAR = 9.00\%$$

Now the EAR must be converted back into a semimonthly effective rate.

$$EPR = (1 + EAR)^{\frac{1}{m}} - 1$$

$$EPR = (1 + 0.09)^{\frac{1}{24}} - 1 \text{ (M = 24 due to semimonthly payment frequency)}$$

$$EPR = 0.360\%$$

This new EPR can be used in the formula to determine what the required savings amount is, the future value of the account, or whatever else the advisor may be calculating.

## Basic Time Value of Money Calculations

Every TVM calculation involves at least three of six possible variables, including:

1.  FV—A single cash flow or series of cash flows (FVA) that occur at any point(s) in time after the present.

2.  PMT—A series of equal* and uninterrupted cash flows that occur for multiple consecutive periods (*payments may not be equal, but related, in the case of growing annuities).

3.  PV—The value today of a single cash flow or of a series of cash flows (PVA) that will occur in the future. Please note, however, that present values can exist at any point in time so long as the cash flows are being discounted.

4.  I/Y—The rate of return required by an investor to forgo consumption in the current time period. This is often referred to as the *discount rate* and can be used interchangeably with **internal rate of return** (IRR), because this rate equates future benefits with current costs.

5.  N—The number of periods (and payments, if an annuity) across which cash flows are being discounted or compounded. Typically $N$ is used to denote years and $M$ is used to denote periods or payments per year, but often the variable $N$ is used to represent the total number of periods regardless of the duration of the period.

6.  G—The growth rate or inflation rate at which a payment increases or decreases over the annuity period. Growth rates apply only to annuities, which are often then referred to as *geometrically varying*, *graduated*, or *growing annuities*.

Understanding not only the definitions of each variable but the impact of changing each variable is paramount to truly understanding the TVM. Review Table 2.5 to ensure that you are familiar with how changing one variable in an equation affects results.

**Table 2.5** Relationships between Inputs and Outcomes in Time Value of Money

| Variable Change (All Others Constant) | Impact On | | | |
|---|---|---|---|---|
| | Present Value | Future Value | Present Value of Annuity | Future Value of Annuity |
| Increase I/Y | Decrease | Increase | Decrease | Increase |
| Decrease I/Y | Increase | Decrease | Increase | Decrease |
| Increase N | Decrease | Increase | Increase* | Increase |
| Decrease N | Increase | Decrease | Increase | Decrease |
| Increase PMT | N/A | N/A | Increase | Increase |
| Decrease PMT | N/A | N/A | Decrease | Decrease |
| Increase G | N/A | N/A | Increase | Increase |
| Decrease G | N/A | N/A | Decrease | Decrease |

*This may counter intuition, but as the number of payments increase, total value decreases.

## Future Value of a Single Sum

One of the most common questions in all of finance is, "How much will a sum invested today be worth in the future?" To answer this question, a financial planner should use a basic future value formula. The future value of a single sum formula is as follows:

$$FV_n = PV (1 + i)^n$$

*Example:* Assume that Jack made a $10,000 deposit into a three-year certificate of deposit that paid an annual interest rate of 5%. How much will Jack accumulate when the certificate of deposit matures? To answer this question, simply insert the facts into the formula as follows.

$$FV_3 = \$10,000(1 + 0.05)^3 = \$11,576.25$$

This type of simple calculation can also quickly be done on a financial calculator. The following table shows the corresponding key strokes to determine the future value of a lump sum.

| Input | Keystroke | Result |
|-------|-----------|--------|
| 0 | [PMT] | PMT = 0.00 |
| 10000 [+/–] | [PV] | PV = –10,000.00 |
| 5 | [I/Y] | I/Y = 5.00 |
| 3 | [N] | N = 3.00 |
| [CPT] | [FV] | FV = 11,576.25 |

**Note:** The PV is input as a negative because an investment is an assumed outflow.

The preceding example can also be used to explore the effects of different compounding periods. Table 2.6 solves the same client question but assumes various compounding frequencies. It is interesting to note that a continued increase in compounding frequency decreases the marginal effect.

**Table 2.6** Effects of Compounding Frequency on Future Value

| Compounding Frequency | Effective Periodic Rate | Effective Annual Rate | Formula | Future Value |
|-----------------------|-------------------------|-----------------------|---------|--------------|
| Annual | 0.05/1 = 0.0500 | 0.05000 | $10{,}000*(1.0500^{3*1})$ | $11,576.25 |
| Semiannual | 0.05/2 = 0.0250 | 0.05063 | $10{,}000*(1.0250^{3*2})$ | $11,596.93 |
| Bimonthly | 0.05/6 = 0.0083 | 0.05105 | $10{,}000*(1.0083^{3*6})$ | $11,611.12 |
| Monthly | 0.05/12 = 0.0042 | 0.05116 | $10{,}000*(1.0042^{3*12})$ | $11,614.72 |
| Weekly | 0.05/52 = 0.0010 | 0.05125 | $10{,}000*(1.0010^{3*52})$ | $11,617.51 |

**Note:** EPRs and EARs are rounded for display but are not rounded for calculation.

---

**Financial Computation Tip: Rule of 72**

A quick estimate for calculating the future value of a single sum is the rule of 72, which can be used whenever a client wishes to know approximately how long it will take to double an investment. To answer such a question, 72 is divided by the interest or discount rate earned. So, for example, it will take approximately eight years to double an investment that earns 9% annually (72/9 = 8).

A planner can also use this shorthand tool to determine the rate of return needed to double a client's initial investment. For example, if a client has six years to meet a goal that requires the doubling of an asset's value, what rate of return must be achieved? In this case, the client must earn 12% on average over the six-year period (72/6 = 12).

However, caution must be used, because this is only an estimate. With low interest rates, this estimate works just fine. However, when higher interest rates are used, this method produces a less accurate estimate. This should be fairly obvious, because an interest rate of 72% would not result in a one-year doubling of value.

---

## Present Value of a Single Sum

**Present value** is used to determine the value of a future asset in today's dollars. The present value of a single sum formula follows:

$$PV_n = \frac{FV}{(1+i)^n}$$

*Example:* Assume that Melissa needs to accumulate $50,000 in 10 years. She is confident that she can earn an annual effective rate of 8% per year in her portfolio. How much does Melissa need to deposit into the account today to achieve her goal? The present value of a single sum formula can be used to solve this question. The answer to Melissa's question is easily found by entering the known variables into the formula, as shown in the following.

$$PV_n = \frac{\$50,000}{(1+0.08)^{10}} = \$23,159.67$$

| Input | Keystroke | Result |
|---|---|---|
| 0 | [PMT] | PMT = 0.00 |
| 50000 [+/–] | [FV] | FV = 50,000.00 |
| 8 | [I/Y] | I/Y = 8.00 |
| 10 | [N] | N = 10.00 |
| [CPT] | [PV] | PV = –23,159.67 |

**Note:** In this case the present value answer is given as a negative, because this is the amount Melissa would have to part with today.

Both future value of a lump sum and present value of a lump sum calculations assume that a client is dealing with a single lump sum of money being invested or received. However, sometimes a client needs to know the future or present value of a series of equal payments rather than a lump sum. A series of equal payments or receipts is known as an *annuity*. For a series of payments to be considered an annuity, the series must adhere to three rules: (1) The payments must be equal in amount; (2) the payments must continue on a fixed frequency (e.g., monthly, annually, weekly); and (3) the required rate of return must remain constant over the entire period of the annuity payments. If the series of payments adheres to all three of these rules, then the payments may be treated as an annuity to calculate the amount of the payments.

The annuity equation is set up to perform two calculations simultaneously. First, it discounts (or compounds) each cash flow payment to a common point in time—most often the current time. Second, it summates the now discounted (or compounded) payments. So quite frequently the annuity equation is represented as either:

$$FVA_n = \sum_{n=1}^{t} CF_n (1+i)^n \quad \text{or} \quad PVA_n = \sum_{n=1}^{t} \frac{CF_n}{(1+i)^n}$$

These forms of the equations show how each payment will be discounted (or compounded), then the sum of the number of payments to occur is totaled.

## Future Value of an Annuity

The **future value of an** ordinary **annuity** values a series of uninterrupted payments as of when the last payment occurs. That is to say, if an annuity paid 20 annual installments starting at time 1 and ending at time 20, then the future value formula would provide a value for the series of payments at time 20. The typical representation of the formula for the future value of an ordinary annuity follows:

$$FVA_n = \frac{PMT}{i}\left[(1+i)^n - 1\right]$$

*Example:* Thomas would like to know how much he will accumulate if he invests $5,000 per year in a Roth IRA for 20 years earning an annual 9% interest. Answering Thomas's question is easy using the future value of an ordinary annuity formula and a financial calculator.

$$FVA_{20} = \frac{\$5,000}{0.09}\left[(1.09)^{20} - 1\right] = \$255,800.60$$

| Input | Keystroke | Result |
|---|---|---|
| 5000 | [PMT] | PMT = –5000.00 |
| 0 | [PV] | PV = 0.00 |
| 9 | [I/Y] | I/Y = 9.00 |
| 20 | [N] | N = 20.00 |
| [CPT] | [FV] | FV = 255,800.60 |

**Note:** In this case the payment is given as a negative because this is the amount that Thomas would have to pay each year.

## Present Value of an Annuity

The **present value of an annuity** is used to determine the value of a series of equal, uninterrupted payments as of the beginning of the period in which the first payment occurs. Therefore, if an annuity pays annual payments beginning at time 1 and lasting for four years, the present value equation would return a value at the beginning of period 1 or time 0. The present value of an ordinary annuity formula follows:

$$PVA_n = \frac{PMT}{i}\left[1 - \frac{1}{(1+i)^n}\right]$$

*Example:* Consider Erik and Erin, who want to make an immediate lump sum deposit into an account earning an annual rate of 5% to fund four years of college expenses beginning at the end of this year. Current college costs are assumed to be $15,000 per year and are not expected to change. How much do they need in the account today? To gauge the true amount needed, the present value of an annuity formula should be used as follows.

$$PVA_0 = \frac{\$15,000}{0.05}\left[1 - \frac{1}{(1.05)^4}\right] = \$53,189.26$$

| Input | Keystroke | Result |
|---|---|---|
| 15000 | [PMT] | PMT = 15,000.00 |
| 0 | [FV] | FV = 0.00 |
| 5 | [I/Y] | I/Y = 5.00 |
| 4 | [N] | N = 4.00 |
| [CPT] | [PV] | PVA = –53,189.26 |

**Note:** In this case the present is given as a negative because this is the amount Erik and Erin would have to pay today.

In other words, Erik and Erin need to deposit $53,189.26 into an account today, earning 5% per year, to fund college costs of $15,000 per year for four years with the first payment occurring one year from today.

### Using the Financial Calculator to Solve Annuities with Nonannual Payments

Using the formulas to solve annuities with nonannual payments is as simple as it is for lump sums. Simply change your interest rate into the corresponding EPR form and solve for the answer. However, using the financial calculator is a bit more involved in that you have to manually change some of the basic calculator settings.

To adjust your calculator for nonannual payments, you must press the [2nd] key, then press the [I/Y] key. This allows access to the payments-per-year setting. Once "P/Y = M" (where M is the number of payments per year) is displayed, you must type the number of payments desired (e.g., 12 for monthly payments) and then press [Enter.] You may now exit the settings by pressing the [2nd] key and then the [CPT] key.

To enable this functionality when solving, you must now get in the habit of entering N as the number of years the payment is occurring rather than as the total number of payments that occur. So instead of entering the total number of payments and then pressing the [N] key, you must first get the calculator to multiply the N you entered with the M you previously set. To do this, press the [2nd] key and then the [N] key. Now that the calculator has multiplied N by M, press the [N] key a second time. What is now displayed is the total number of payments.

Another result of changing this setting is that when you changed the payments per year the calculator also adjusted the compounding period per year to correspond. The benefit is that the calculator will now calculate the appropriate EPR behind the scenes; therefore, you can input the APR as usual.

*Example:* Reconsider Erik and Erin, who still want to make an immediate lump sum deposit into an account earning an annual rate of 5% to fund four years of college expenses beginning at the end of this year. However, now it is assumed that college costs are paid $7,500 per semester (six months apart) and are not expected to change. How much do they need in the account today?

First you must calculate the appropriate EPR for semiannual payments.

$$EPR = \frac{APR}{m} = \frac{0.05}{2} = 0.025$$

Now, using the EPR, solve for the present value normally.

$$PVA_0 = \frac{\$7,500}{0.025}\left[1 - \frac{1}{(1.025)^8}\right] = \$53,776.03$$

| Input | Keystroke | Result |
|---|---|---|
| 7500 | [PMT] | PMT = 7,500.00 |
| 0 | [FV] | FV = 0.00 |
| 5 (as APR) | [I/Y] | I/Y = 5.00* |
| 4 | [2nd] [N] [N] | N = 8.00 |
| [CPT] | [PV] | PVA = –53,776.03 |

*After adjusting the M to two periods per year, the APR will still display on the calculator screen although the EPR is actually being used for the calculation.

## Present Value of a "Delayed" Annuity

Remember the rule that the present value of an annuity values the payments as of the beginning of the period in which the first payment occurred? Well, what happens when a financial planner needs to know the present value of the cost of college as of a child's fifth birthday, rather than simply at the beginning of college? Again consider Erik and Erin, who are planning for future education expenses, perhaps for a younger child. In the previous example, it was assumed that the first tuition payment occurred at the end of the first year. But what would happen if that tuition payment was not due for 10 years?

Again the clients would need to know how much they need to save by the beginning of college, but they now have 10 years for an account to accumulate the required amount before the first tuition payment. The formula to solve for this type of equation is a combination of two of the previous formulas: the present value of an annuity and the present value of a single sum. The two equations are:

$$PVA_n = \frac{PMT}{i}\left[1 - \frac{1}{(1+i)^n}\right] \quad \text{and} \quad PV_n = \frac{FV}{(1+i)^n}$$

The solution to this situation begins in the same way as the previous example, by solving for the present value of the annuity for the four years of college. However, in the first example this answer was as of today ($T_0$); now, it is as of 10 years from today ($T_{10}$).[2] Therefore, the value would have to be discounted a second time—back to today. This is referred to as **double discounting**, because the first equation discounted the four payments to the beginning of the payment period, and the second equation discounted that result back to today. Functionally, the first answer, which was solved for as a present value, becomes a future value when solving for the second answer. These equations may be combined into one equation that handles both steps. The equation on the left is then substituted into the numerator of the equation on the right, as shown below:

$$PVA_n = \frac{PMT}{i}\left[1 - \frac{1}{(1+i)^n}\right] \quad \longrightarrow \quad PV_o = \frac{PVA_n}{(1+i)^d}$$

Where:

n = number of payments

d = number of periods delayed

Completely combining the two equations results in the following:

$$PV_0 = \frac{\dfrac{PMT}{i}\left[1 - \dfrac{1}{(1+i)^n}\right]}{(1+i)^d}$$

*Example:* To return once again to Eric and Erin, the advisor would solve for the present value of the annuity at year 10, which is \$53,189.26, and then discount that result back to today. The final need can then be determined to be \$32,653.59, as shown in the following equation.

$$PV_d = \frac{\dfrac{\$15,000}{0.05}\left[1 - \dfrac{1}{(1.05)^4}\right]}{(1.05)^{10}}$$

$$PV_d = \frac{\$53,189.26}{1.62889} = \$32,653.59$$

In essence, in the second discounting (during periods 1–10) the equation is backing out the interest earned between today ($T_0$) and the beginning of the year in which the first payment occurs ($T_{10}$).

This is also the first instance where it may be simpler to use the equations than to use the TVM keys on the calculator. This is because the calculator cannot handle both steps of the equation simultaneously. Instead, it is a two-step solution:

| Input | Keystroke | Result |
|---|---|---|
| 15000 | [PMT] | PMT = 15,000.00 |
| 0 | [FV] | FV = 0.00 |
| 5 | [I/Y] | I/Y = 5.00 |
| 4 | [N] | N = 4.00 |
| [CPT] | [PV] | $PVA_{10}$ = –53,189.26 |

| Input | Keystroke | Result |
|---|---|---|
| 53,189.26 | [FV] | FV = 53,189.26 |
| 5 | [I/Y] | I/Y = 5.00* |
| 10 | [N] | N = 10.00 |
| [CPT] | [PV] | $PV_0$ = –32,653.59 |
| [CPT] | [PV] | $PVA_{10}$ = –53,189.26 |

*The present value of the annuity at time 10 in step one becomes the future value of the lump sum in step two.

This type of combined equation can be used anytime a stream of payments begins after the first period. In such a case, it is appropriate to discount the cash flow twice: once to bring the stream back to the beginning of the year in which the first payment occurs, $T_n$; and once again to bring that result back to the present time, $T_0$.

## Future Value of a Geometrically Varying "Growing" Annuity

Up to this point, the assumption has been that the dollar amount of each payment received or paid during an annuity is fixed. To differentiate, this assumption is sometimes referred to as a *fixed, constant-dollar, or level-payment* annuity. However, there is an alternative, namely that the client's payment will change from year to year by a constant percentage. (Note: The rate of change must always be at a constant percentage amount and *not* a constant dollar amount.) This could be due to a number of factors (e.g., changes in salary, changes in disposable income), but the most common reason for a changing payment is inflation.

Such annuities are actually much more common than they may seem. In fact, most payments (e.g., college, retirement, Social Security) will change over time by some rate of inflation. The issue is that rates of inflation are not constant, so to be able to treat a series of payments as an annuity one must make an assumption about what the average rate of change will be. For example, actual annual inflation is almost never 4%, but this is one of the most common assumptions about inflation—that it will average 4%. This simplifying assumption is what makes the use of the growing annuity equations so powerful.

If a client wants a payment, either in or out of an annuity, to keep pace with inflation, then a growth rate must be applied. The growth rate may be positive or—though it apparently contradicts its name—negative, but it cannot be equal to the rate of return. If the growth rate is zero, then the fixed annuity equation should be used. Growing annuities apply to either present value or future value situations. The equation for the future value of a growing annuity follows:

$$FVGA_n = \frac{PMT_1}{(i-g)}\left[(1+i)^n - (1+g)^n\right]$$

Where:

$i$ = interest rate ($i \neq 0$)

$g$ = growth rate of payment ($i \neq g$)

The growing annuity equation performs three calculations simultaneously. First, it changes the payment at a constant rate. Second, it compounds each payment to a common point in time. Third, it summates the now compounded payments. Therefore, breaking the annuity equation into its component parts would look like this:

$$FVGA_n = PMT_1(1+g)^{n-n}(1+r)^{n-1} + PMT_1(1+g)^{n-(n-1)}(1+r)^{n-2} + \ldots + PMT_1(1+g)^{n-1}(1+r)^{n-n}$$

Consider a client who participates in a 401(k) or 403(b) plan. Usually, defined contribution plan salary reductions are based on a percentage of an employee's annual income. So if the income increases by 3% annually it follows that the retirement plan contribution will also increase by the same percentage. A basic future value of annuity formula cannot account for this assumption. A **geometrically varying annuity** formula must be used to determine a future value whenever a payment is expected to increase at a fixed geometric rate.

*Example*: Assume that Thomas will make annual payments[3] into a 401(k) for 20 years, earning an effective annual rate of 9%. He will begin with a $3,000 contribution, which is 5% of his income. But every year thereafter, he will increase his deposit by 3% to reflect the expected increase in his salary. Using this assumption, how much will Thomas accumulate at the end of 20 years?

$$FVGA_n = \frac{\$3,000}{(0.09-0.03)}\left[(1.09)^{20} - (1.03)^{20}\right]$$

$$FVGA_n = \$50,000 * 3.7983 = \$189,914.98$$

In this case, the fact that Thomas's subsequent deposits into the 401(k) grow by 3% annually means that he will have approximately $189,915 in the account at the end of 20 years. When using growing annuities, it is often beneficial—or at least interesting—to compare the results of a growing annuity and a fixed annuity, keeping all of the variables besides the growth rate fixed.

$$FVGA_n = \frac{\$3,000}{(0.09-0.00)}\left[(1.09)^{20} - (1.00)^{20}\right]$$

$$FVGA_n = \frac{\$3,000}{0.09}\left[(1.09)^{20} - 1\right]$$

$$FVGA_n = \frac{\$13,813.23}{0.09} = \$153,480.36$$

Solving the previous example, but without growing the payment by 3% per year, can be done using the same formula and entering a zero for the growth rate, or it can be solved using the fixed annuity equation shown below.

By removing the growth rate, the value in Thomas's account at the end of 20 years is $36,435 ($189,915 x $153,480) less if he chooses not to increase his annual payment. Therefore, increasing payments over a long-term planning horizon can have a significant impact on meeting a client's financial goals.

It is also important to note that when using a growing annuity equation, the payment used in the calculation will be the first payment. Similarly, when using the equation to solve for the payment amount, the equation solves for the first payment (PMT1). It is important to understand that this distinction is relevant because the value increases or decreases across the series of payments in a growing annuity, whereas in a fixed annuity all of the payments are the same so no differentiation is needed. All other payments must be derived by using PMT1 and then increasing payments by the growth rate. Therefore PMT2 equals PMT1*(1 + g)1 and so on.

### Present Value of a Geometrically Varying "Growing" Annuity

An equation that is very similar in form and function to the present value of a fixed annuity is the present value of a growing annuity. Just as for the future value of a growing annuity above, a growth rate must be included. For instance, a client may also desire to know the amount that must be saved, or available, at the beginning of a withdrawal period if the desired withdrawal amount changes over time. This is a highly likely scenario because of the effects of inflation on purchasing power. In this situation, the client wants to know the present value of a growing annuity.

$$PVGA_n = \frac{PMT_1}{(i-g)}\left[1 - \frac{(1+g)^n}{(1+i)^n}\right]$$

Again, the growing annuity equation does three calculations simultaneously. In this case it (1) changes the payment at a constant rate; (2) discounts each payment to a common point in time; and (3) sumates the now discounted payments. So breaking the present value of a growing annuity equation into its component parts would look like this:

$$PVGA_n = \frac{PMT_1(1+g)^{n-(n-0)}}{(1+r)^{n-(n-1)}} + \frac{PMT_1(1+g)^{n-(n-1)}}{(1+r)^{n-(n-2)}} + ... + \frac{PMT_1(1+g)^{n-1}}{(1+r)^{n-(n-n)}}$$

*Example:* Middle-aged clients, Joshua and Rebecca Rosenbaum, want to know how much they need to have saved by retirement to withdraw $80,000 in the first year and to have that amount increase by 4% per year. They assume that they can earn an EAR of 8.5% throughout their 25 years of retirement.

$$PVGA_n = \frac{\$80,000}{(0.085-0.04)}\left[1 - \frac{(1.04)^{25}}{(1.085)^{25}}\right]$$

$$PVGA_n = \$1,777,777.78[0.65319] = \$1,161,228.92$$

In this case the Rosenbaums must save $1,161,228.92 by the time they retire to meet their withdrawal goal. However, similar to the previous comparison done with the future value of a growing annuity, they need to save only $818,735.26 if they choose not to increase their annual withdrawal by 4%. Note again that assuming the growth rate is zero allows the fixed-payment annuity equation to be used.

$$PVGA_n = \frac{\$80,000}{(0.085-0.00)}\left[1 - \frac{(1.00)^{25}}{(1.085)^{25}}\right]$$

$$PVGA_n = \frac{\$80,000}{0.085}\left[1 - \frac{1}{(1.085)^{25}}\right]$$

$$PVGA_n = \frac{\$69,592.50}{0.085} = \$818,735.26$$

## Serial Interest Rates

Another method for solving growing annuity equations is to calculate the **serial rate**. In fact, if a financial calculator is to be used, the serial rate would be required. The serial rate is calculated using the same equation used to determine the real rate.

$$Serial\ Rate = \left[\frac{(1+i)}{(1+g)}\right] - 1$$

Where:

i  = interest rate

g = growth rate of payment (could be the inflation rate)

*Example:* Consider the first step to the previous retirement savings example, where Joshua and Rebecca are determining how much they need to save by retirement to fund a growing stream of retirement payments. Using assumptions identical to those above, the problem may also be solved using the fixed-annuity equation by substituting the serial rate for $i$. First solve for the serial rate.

$$Serial\ Rate = \left[\frac{(1.085)}{(1.04)}\right] - 1 = 4.327\%$$

The serial rate should then be inserted into the adjusted present value of a fixed annuity formula as follows:

$$PVA_n = \frac{PMT/(1+g)}{i}\left[1 - \frac{1}{(1+i)^n}\right]$$

$$PVA_n = \frac{\$80,000/1.04}{0.04327}\left[1 - \frac{1}{(1.04327)^{25}}\right]$$

$$PVA_n = \$1,777,746.17[0.65320] = \$1,161,219.63$$

The difference from the earlier calculation is caused by rounding. If the serial rate 4.327% were not rounded, $PVA_n$ would equal $1,161,228.91.

Even more interesting to note is the small adjustment that was made to the present value formula. Notice how the payment is adjusted down by the factor of $(1 + g)$. You may be asking yourself why this is necessary. It is necessary because the serial rate cannot distinguish when the payment needs to grow (e.g., from time 1 to time 2) and when it does not (e.g., from time 0 to time 1). Refer again to the present value of a growing annuity formula, this time simplified with $N = 5$.

$$PVGA_n = \frac{PMT_1(1+g)^{5-(5-0)}}{(1+i)^{5-(5-1)}} + \frac{PMT_1(1+g)^{5-(5-1)}}{(1+i)^{5-(5-2)}} + ... + \frac{PMT_1(1+g)^{5-1}}{(1+i)^{5-(5-5)}}$$

$$PVGA_n = \frac{PMT_1(1+g)^0}{(1+i)^1} + \frac{PMT_1(1+g)^1}{(1+i)^2} + ... + \frac{PMT_1(1+g)^4}{(1+i)^5}$$

It clearly shows that the relationship between the number of periods of growth and the number of periods of discounting is off by one period. This is because payment 1 is given in terms of time 1 and not time 0. Said another way, the first payment does not grow, but it is still discounted. The serial rate is constant for all time periods, so an adjustment must be made to allow the serial rate to both grow and discount the first payment; this adjustment is made by forcibly reducing the value of the first payment to its time 0 equivalent.

The use of the serial rate is also required when using the financial calculator to solve growing annuity calculations, but the calculator does not provide a separate input for "G." Again, consider the Rosenbaums' need to save for retirement.

| Input | Keystroke | Result |
|---|---|---|
| 80000/1.04 | [PMT] | PMT = 76,923.08 |
| 0 | [FV] | FV = 0.00 |
| 4.327 | [I/Y] | I/Y = 4.327 |
| 25 | [N] | N = 25.00 |
| [CPT] | [PV] | PVA = -1,161,219.64 |

**Note:** The initial payment is adjusted by the factor of $(1 + g)$ to resolve the serial rate issue previously discussed.

---

### What about Using the Financial Calculator for the Future-Value of Growing Annuities?

This situation presents an interesting challenge. Refer to Table 2.5 Did you notice that, for the present value of an annuity, a change in G has the opposite effect as a change in I/Y? Therefore, a lower rate to account for a higher payment is reasonable.

So when calculating the serial rate, increases in G functionally serve to decrease I/Y.

This all makes sense, because intuition tells us that if you increase the payment going into (or from) an annuity, the value of the annuity should increase—as it does when I/Y decreases. But when you look at changes to the future value of the annuity, the impacts are no longer reversed; increases in G have the same impact as increases in I/Y.

However, serial rate still declines as G increases.

So the serial rate cannot be used to directly solve for future values of growing annuities. Instead, the serial rate is used to determine the present value of the growing annuity, and the second step is to calculate the future value of that lump sum using the original interest rate.

---

Revisiting the prior problem, what if the Rosenbaums needed to determine the future value of their retirement annuity? (Not that this is a realistic issue, because knowing the future value of a prior payment stream at death is not very useful, but it serves for demonstration purposes). This now becomes a two-step solution.

| Input | Keystroke | Result |
|---|---|---|
| 80000/1.04 | [PMT] | PMT = 76,923.08 |
| 0 | [FV] | FV = 0.00 |
| 4.327 | [I/Y] | I/Y = 4.327 |
| 25 | [N] | N = 25.00 |
| [CPT] | [PV] | PVA = –1,161,219.64 |

| Input | Keystroke | Result |
|---|---|---|
| 0 | [PMT] | PMT = 0.00 |
| –1,161,219.64 | [PV] | PV = –1,161,219.64 |
| 8.5 | [I/Y] | I/Y = 8.50* |
| 25 | [N] | N = 25.00 |
| [CPT] | [FV] | FV = 8,926,019.42 |

*The nominal rate is used to determine the compound future rate.

## Annuity "Due" (Payments Occuring at the Beginning of Each Period)

So far, all of the examples have assumed that each payment has occurred at the end of each time period, "in arrears." This is not always the case. For example, tuition is normally paid at the beginning of each semester, "in advance." The term *annuity due* is used whenever the present value of an "in advance" payment is needed. This obviously affects the value or cost of college in that each payment is now taken out six months earlier, meaning six months of interest will not be earned. The only way to make up for this is to save more money. So it stands to reason that the present value of an annuity due will need to be greater than that of an ordinary annuity. How much greater? It will need to be approximately one period of interest greater for each payment, because not only the first payment is removed six months early; *every* payment is removed six months early. Therefore, the present value of every payment will have to increase.

$$PV\ Ordinary\ Annuity = \frac{PMT_1}{(1+i)^1} + \frac{PMT_2}{(1+i)^2} + \ldots + \frac{PMT_n}{(1+i)^n}\ or\ \frac{PMT}{i}\left[1 - \frac{1}{(1+i)^n}\right]$$

$$PV\ Annuity\ Due = \frac{PMT_1(1+i)^1}{(1+i)^1} + \frac{PMT_2(1+i)^1}{(1+i)^2} + \ldots + \frac{PMT_n(1+i)^1}{(1+i)^n}$$

Simplifying the numerator by removing the (1 + r) adjustment from each leaves:

$$PV\ Annuity\ Due = \left[\frac{PMT_1}{(1+i)^1} + \frac{PMT_2}{(1+i)^2} + \ldots + \frac{PMT_n}{(1+i)^n}\right](1+i)\ or\ \frac{PMT}{i}\left[1 - \frac{1}{(1+i)^n}\right](1+i)$$

The difference in value between an ordinary annuity and an annuity due is simply a factor of $(1 + i)$. Reworking the problem of Erik and Erin, who want to fund four years of college expenses starting at the *beginning* of this year, is as simple as this:

$$PVA_0 = \frac{\$15,000}{0.05}\left[1 - \frac{1}{(1.05)^4}\right](1.05) = \$53,189.26(1.05) = \$55,848.72$$

And this adjustment also works for calculating the future value of an annuity. Even if it is a growing annuity, the adjustment remains the same. The factor $(1 + i)$ always works!

## Present Value of a Growing Perpetuity—The Simplest Solution

Although not very common, there are certain instances when a payment will either be made or received forever. This equation could be used in several retirement planning scenarios when a client wants to be very conservative, because the equation assumes that the principal of the investment is never liquidated; it continues in "perpetuity."

*Example:* A client wants to make sure that he leaves a legacy for his wife and children, but he also wants to ensure a comfortable retirement. He requires an annual rate of return of 7.0%. He wants an initial annual payment of $100,000 that will keep pace with expected inflation of 3.5%. How much does the client need to save by the beginning of the withdrawal period?

$$PVP = \frac{PMT}{(i - g)}$$

$$PVP = \frac{\$100,000}{(0.070 - 0.035)} = \frac{\$100,000}{0.035}$$

$$PVP = 2,857,142.86$$

Therefore, for the client to ensure that he will not outlive his money nor lose purchasing power to inflation, he needs to have nearly $2.9 million saved.

An interesting thing about perpetuities is that their present values are not significantly larger than long annuities. See Table 2.7 for a summary of present values for different terms.

**Table 2.7** Comparison of Present Values by Term Length

| Periodic Payment | Discount Rate | Periods | Present Value |
|---|---|---|---|
| $1,000 | 7% | 20 | $10,594 |
| $1,000 | 7% | 35 | $12,948 |
| $1,000 | 7% | 50 | $13,801 |
| $1,000 | 7% | 65 | $14,110 |
| $1,000 | 7% | Infinite | $14,286 |

## Mixed-stream Calculations

The **net present value** (NPV) method of calculation can be used when a series of payments, either made by the client or received by the client, fluctuates on a per-period basis. The traditional present value of annuity calculation assumes that payments remain fixed, or if they do change, that the rate of growth is fixed. NPV is defined as the present value of a stream of earnings less the present value of contributions. The formula for NPV is:

NPV = PV of Cash Inflows – PV of Cash Outflows

Where:

NPV = net present value

PV   = present value

NPV compares benefits and cost. Therefore, the rule for NPV is that if the present value of benefits *exceeds* the present value of costs (NPV > 0), then the investment should be accepted; if the present value of benefits *does not exceed* the present value of costs (NPV < 0), then the investment should be rejected. The following formula illustrates that a present value cost is subtracted from the discounted future value benefits of a particular investment opportunity.

$$NPV = \frac{PMT_1}{(1+r)^1} + \frac{PMT_2}{(1+r)^2} + ... + \frac{PMT_n}{(1+r)^n} + \frac{FV_n}{(1+r)^n} - PV$$

A simple example can be used to illustrate the NPV method.

*Example:* Assume that a client is considering an investment of $5,000. Currently, the client is making 11% on the $5,000 in an alternative investment. The client anticipates that the investment will make payments back to him as shown below:

| | |
|---|---|
| Year 1: | $1,500 |
| Year 2: | $1,000 |
| Year 3: | $500 |
| Year 4: | $500 |
| Year 5: | $4,000 |

Should the client make the investment? A quick way to answer this question might be to compute NPV using the cash flow tables in a financial calculator (shown in the next section). However, the formula may also be used to find a solution.

$$NPV = \frac{\$1,500}{(1.11)^1} + \frac{\$1,000}{(1.11)^2} + \frac{\$500}{(1.11)^3} + \frac{\$500}{(1.11)^4} + \frac{\$4,000}{(1.11)^5} - \$5,000$$

$$NPV = \$1,351.35 + \$811.62 + \$365.60 + \$329.37 + \$2,373.81 - \$5,000$$

$$NPV = \$5,231.75 - \$5,000 = \$231.75$$

When using the NPV method, it is critical to understand what the answer is saying. When the NPV is positive, it means that the internal rate of return (IRR) is greater than the required rate and therefore the investment should be accepted. If the NPV is negative, it means that the IRR is less than the required rate and therefore the investment should be rejected. If the IRR equals the required rate, then the investment should be accepted because the required rate is achieved.

## Net Present Value and Internal Rate of Return—Solving for I/Y

What if you know both how much a client is willing to spend today (PV) and the values of the future cash flows (FV)? This raises a different question: what is the IRR? The IRR and its close cousin NPV are more sophisticated methods that determine whether or not an investment is expected to meet a client's required rate of return.

The IRR measures the discount rate at which the present value of cash inflows (returns or benefits) equals the present value of cash outflows (investments or costs). It takes into account the TVM by considering the amount and timing of cash inflows and outflows over the life of an investment. Calculating the IRR is done through a trial-and-error process. IRR can be calculated manually by doing multiple iterations of NPV with different interest rates until NPV is equal to zero. The trial-and-error calculation can also be automated by using the IRR function in a spreadsheet program or using the cash flow tables in a financial calculator.

A similar rule applies to IRR, given that NPV and IRR are related: If the IRR of an investment exceeds the required rate of return, then accept the investment; if IRR does not exceed the required rate of return, reject the investment.

Again, the IRR measures the present value of a series of cash flows in relation to an initial (and possibly subsequent) investment amount. The formula for calculating IRR is used when both the value of each subsequent cash flow and the present value are known:

$$PV = \frac{PMT_1}{(1+r)^1} + \frac{PMT_2}{(1+r)^2} + ... + \frac{PMT_n}{(1+r)^n} + \frac{FV_n}{(1+r)^n}$$

Where:

PV   = present value

FV   = future value

PMT  = periodic payment

r    = internal rate of return

However, as mentioned earlier, it would take multiple iterations—not to mention mountains of algebra—to determine the rate that would result in the NPV being equal to zero. Therefore, using the formula for calculating IRR can be tiresome. Fortunately, IRRs can be determined relatively easily using a financial calculator. There are two main methods for determining the IRR: (1) using the TVM keys if future cash flows can be considered as an annuity; or (2) using the cash flow tables if the future cash flows are uneven, often called *mixed sum*.

## Using TVM Keys to Solve for IRR

Using the TVM key to solve for IRR is as simple as using the TVM key to solve for any other unknown. Simply enter the known variables and solve for those remaining.

*Example:* Assume that John invests $500 today in an investment that will pay him $50 per year for 10 years. At the end of the investment period, John receives $1,000. What rate of return did he make? Entering these data into a BA II Plus calculator, as shown below, results in an IRR equal to 14.94%.

| Input | Keystroke | Result |
| --- | --- | --- |
| 100 | [PMT] | PMT = 100.00 |
| –1000 | [PV] | PV = –1,000 |
| 10 | [N] | N = 15.00 |
| 2000 | [FV] | FV = 2000 |
| [CPT] | [I/Y] | I/Y = 14.94% |

Although the method for calculating IRR looks innocuous enough, its application can become quite tedious, especially when the periodic payments fluctuate every period. However, a financial calculator can also be used if the periodic cash flows are not fixed.

## Using Cash Flow Tables to Solve for IRR

By using the built-in cash flow tables or registers, individual cash flows may be entered separately.  To enter the cash flow tables in the BA II Plus calculator, press the [CF] key. Always begin by clearing the register of any previous work by pressing the [2nd] key and then the [CLR WORK] key in succession. It is important to remember a major difference between using the TVM keys and the CF tables: in order to enter the value into the table, the [enter] key must always be pressed after entering the desired value.

*Example:* Assume that Shameka is considering an investment that requires a $5,000 payment today. The required rate of return, based on her next best investment choice, is 11% in a mutual fund. If she anticipates receiving the following payments, should she make the investment?

| | |
|---|---|
| Year 1: | $1,500 |
| Year 2: | $1,000 |
| Year 3: | $500 |
| Year 4: | $500 |
| Year 5: | $4,000 |

Calculating the IRR of these individual cash flows is possible using the following formula; however, it would require a great deal of time and some more difficult algebra.

$$\$5,000 = \frac{\$1,500}{(1+r)^1} + \frac{\$1,000}{(1+r)^2} + \frac{\$500}{(1+r)^3} + \frac{\$500}{(1+r)^4} + \frac{\$4,000}{(1+r)^5}$$

Instead, it is much easier to let the financial calculator handle the algebra and use the cash flow tables as demonstrated below. There are always two sets of entries for the cash flow tables: the amount of each cash flow, and the number of consecutive times the cash flow happens, known as the *frequency* of the cash flow. Once all of the cash flows are entered into the cash flow table, IRR is computed by pressing the [IRR] key and then pressing the [CPT] key.

| Input | Keystroke | Result |
|---|---|---|
| | [CF] | Turn-on tables |
| [2nd] | [CLR WORK] | Clear register |
| −5000 | [ENTER] | CF0 = −5,000,00 |
| [↓] 1500 | [ENTER] | CF1 = 1,500.00 |
| [↓] 1* | [ENTER] | F01 = 1.00 |
| [↓] 1000 | [ENTER] | CF2 = 1,000.00 |
| [↓] 1 | [ENTER] | F02 = 1.00 |
| [↓] 500 | [ENTER] | CF3 = 500.00 |
| [↓] 2 | [ENTER] | F03 = 2.00 |
| [↓] 4000 | [ENTER] | CF4 = 4,000.00 |
| [↓] 1 | [ENTER] | F04 = 1.00 |
| [IRR] | [CPT] | IRR = 12.55% |

*One is the default entry for the frequency of the cash flow.

In this case, the IRR is 12.55%, which is greater than her next best alternative of 11%. Therefore, applying the decision rule previously discussed, she would accept this investment alternative.

To solve for NPV, however, an estimated rate of return must be entered. After the [NPV] key is pressed, the calculator will ask for the required rate of return—in this case, 11%—her next best alternative. Once the return is entered, pressing the down arrow key again will display the NPV, which will be computed when the [CPT] key is pressed. For this example, the NPV is $231.74.

| Input | Keystroke | Result |
|-------|-----------|--------|
| [NPV] 7 | [ENTER] | I/Y = 11.00% |
| [↓] | [CPT] | NPV = $231.74 |

**Note:** One is the default entry for the frequency of the cash flow.

Basically this means that if Shameka's required return is 11%, she should be willing to pay up to $231.74 more ($5,231.74) for the agreed-upon cash flows. So both the IRR and NPV methods of computing the value of cash flows produced the same decision— to accept the investment.

## Loans and Amortization Schedules—An Exercise in Calculating Payment

One of the most common uses for TVM formulas is when a client or planner is working with an amortized loan, which is a liability where the payment is normally fixed and set to repay the obligation over a fixed period of time. Every payment for the loan is composed of principal and interest and, as the loan is paid back, the percentage of each payment attributable to interest declines. This happens because a simple interest loan (which represents the majority of loan structures to individuals) recalculates the interest expense each period based on the remaining outstanding balance. Therefore, as the outstanding balance declines, so does the periodic interest expense.

A prevalent method of presenting this information to a client is with an amortization table. An **amortization schedule** can be created for any loan that has a fixed rate of interest and a known number of payment periods. Although an outstanding loan balance can be calculated using a financial calculator or present value of an annuity formula, it is sometimes more helpful to create an amortization schedule using a computer spreadsheet. A spreadsheet can more easily display different loan payoff amounts at different times. It can also be used to illustrate how a change in interest rates or duration can change a client's cash flow situation. Table 2.8 provides an example of how an amortization schedule can be created in a computer spreadsheet.

**Table 2.8** Partial Amortization Spreadsheet Calculations

| Inputs | Interest Rate | 7% annual [AFR] (0.583% monthly EFR) | | | |
|---|---|---|---|---|---|
| | Present Value | $100,000 | | | |
| | Term | 30 years (360 months) | | | |

| A Month | B Beginning Balance | C Total Monthly Payment | D Monthly Interest Payment | E Monthly Principal Payment | F Ending Balance |
|---|---|---|---|---|---|
| | | | (B x EPR) | (C – D) | (B – E) |
| 1 | $100,000.00 | $665.30 | $583.33 | $81.97 | $99,918.03 |
| 2 | $99,918.03 | $665.30 | $582.85 | $82.45 | $99,835.58 |
| | | | | | |
| 359 | $1,319.05 | $665.30 | $7.69 | $657.61 | $661.44 |
| 360 | $661.44 | $665.30 | $3.86 | $661.44 | $0.00 |

However, another method may be more useful and much quicker when trying to determine the outstanding balance of a loan. This method uses the previously discussed present value of an annuity (PVA) formula. It stands to reason, because the original payment for the loan could be determined with the PVA formula, that the same formula could be applied to that payment to determine the outstanding balance. The key is to change the *n* (number) in the equation to reflect the number of payments *remaining*.

*Example:* Recall the sample loan from Table 2.8. The table illustrates how the loan is amortized, but in this example it does not show the outstanding balance at all points in time. If the client wanted to pay off this loan after the 120th payment (in conjunction with the 121st payment), the client would need to know the outstanding balance at that time. To provide the client with the necessary information, the planner would simply solve for the PVA with the PMT equaling $665.30, the periodic interest rate equaling 0.583%, and the number of payments remaining equal to 240 (360 total payments x 120 payments previously paid).

$$PVA_n = \frac{PMT}{i}\left[1 - \frac{1}{(1+i)^n}\right]$$

$$PVA_{120} = \frac{\$665.30}{0.00583}\left[1 - \frac{1}{1.00583^{240}}\right]$$

$$PVA_{120} = \$114,116.64[0.75220] = \$85,838.54$$

Although it hardly seems to make sense that more than 85% of the loan remains outstanding, this is a common occurrence because the progression of a geometric function is not linear over time. In other words, the loan balance does not decline in a straight line.

Another useful application based on the TVM formulas is to determine how much money has already been paid on a loan. This is necessary information when determining the total amount of interest paid, because the difference between the total amount of payments and the change in the outstanding balance is the total interest paid to date. The following formula is used to determine the total amount paid to date on a loan.

*Total Payments = PMT Amount x Number of PMTs*

*Example:* Revising the previous example, it has already been determined that the client has reduced the outstanding balance of the loan by $14,161.46 ($100,000 − $85,838.54); however, this does not show how much the client has paid in total. Nor does it tell how much interest the client paid over the first 10 years of the loan. To determine the total paid, the monthly payment is multiplied by the number of payments made, as shown below.

*Total Payments = $665.30 x 120 = $79,836.00*

To determine the total amount of interest paid, the change in outstanding balance is subtracted from the total amount of payments. In this example, the total interest paid to date is determined to be $65,674.54.

*Total Payments = Total of PMT − Change in Balance*

*Total Interest = $79,836.00 − $14,161.46 = $65,674.54*

## CHAPTER SUMMARY

Although many consider financial planning an art, as can be seen throughout this chapter, there is also a lot of science. Understanding the general mathematic calculations behind everyday planning activities is of paramount importance. For without accurate calculations and appropriate representation, a great ability to communicate will not matter. Every planning discussion has two parts: the message and the tone. Which is more important, the ability to verbally induce clients to start investing in a 401(k) account, or the ability to calculate the required monthly payment they need to invest every month to meet their retirement goals?

# Learning Outcomes

1.  Holding-period return, or the total return for a defined period of time, is typically calculated as a ratio of how much money was earned from an investment to the original investment amount. The simple ratio is normally the total change in value divided by the amount invested. Also considered total returns are (1) dollar-weighted returns that adjust for the timing of intermediate cash flows so returns are more accurately represented by the total dollars invested over time; and (2) time-weighted returns that do not consider whether more or less money was invested, but instead consider the length of time the investment lasted.

2.  Average annual returns can be computed using a linear series average, known as the *arithmetic average*, or computed using a geometric series average, known as the **geometric average**. Both are accurate representations of past performance, but they should not be used without consideration for the purposes of projecting future value. Because of the variability of returns over time, the geometric average is more accurate for projecting long-term values.

3.  The weighted-average return calculation is used in the same manner to determine the return for a multi-asset portfolio as it is for a return based on any other weighting criteria. The weight is determined based on the relative amount of the asset owned compared to the total value of the portfolio.

4.  Interest rates show a relative measure of output given a certain input; however, the output may need to be adjusted for one or more of several factors. Most frequently, interest rates are adjusted for inflation or taxes. Inflation-adjusted (real) or growth-adjusted (serial) interest rates consider losses or gains in purchasing power, so the results are based on purchasing power parity. Tax-adjusted interest rates are useful because different investments have different tax treatments. To be comparable on a tax-neutral basis, an adjustment must be made to compare tax-exempt to taxable investment returns.

5.  Typically there is some uncertainty about the outcome, or future value, of an investment; and the amount of return that is required by a potential investor is in no small part based on the level of uncertainty. Therefore, although investors are willing to invest money at a risk-free rate if they are only delaying consumption without accepting any risk, they want compensation for the risk in the form of a higher return. Types of risk for which an investor would seek compensation include, but are not limited to, inflation risk, interest rate risk, and default risk.

6.  The TVM may be the most central tenet in all of economics and finance, and it is predicated on the idea the people would rather consume today than wait. Put another way, a dollar spent (or received) today is more valuable than it is tomorrow. To determine how much more (or less) valuable it is depends on the rate of return required and the length of time until the dollar is realized. Proper use of the TVM formulas allows for a proper comparison of money spent (or received) at different points in time by aligning the two dollar amounts.

7.  The primary difference between nominal rates and effective rates is that effective rates adjust for nonannual compounding periods. Most interest rates are stated in nominal terms, such as 7% APR, but without reference to the underlying compounding period. Effective rates are actual (or realized) rates of return after the adjustment for nonannual compounding. Although effective rates can be given in any compounding frequency (e.g., monthly, semiannually, etc.), most often the rates are converted into the EAR form because it is the most intuitive method for stating rates.

8.  The future or present value of a single sum formula is most often applied when a direct comparison needs to be made about a single exchange—one inflow and one outflow. An example of this would be making a single investment in a bank CD. The future value formula tells an investor how much the CD will be worth when it matures, whereas the present value formula can be used to determine how much the client needs to invest today to achieve a particular goal upon maturity. In the former case, value today was known, and in the latter, the goal was known.

9.  The future or present value of an annuity formula is used to determine the future or present value, respectively, of a stream of equal payments, projecting the value into the future or discounting the stream of payments back to a current time period. An example of this would be making a series of payments to an IRA. The future value formula tells an investor how much the IRA will be worth at some future date. In contrast, if an investor were promised a series of payments in the future, such as from a fixed annuity, the present value of an annuity formula could be used to determine how much the promised series of payments is actually worth today. Accuracy depends on determining the correct number of compounding periods by adjusting the calculation to reflect whether payments occur at the beginning or end of the year (i.e., an annuity due or an ordinary annuity).

10. The future or present value of a geometrically varying or "growing" annuity formula is used to determine the future or present value, respectively, of a stream of annually increasing payments, projecting the value into the future or discounting the stream of payments back to a current time period.  An example of this would be making a series of payments to a 529 college savings plan where the investor plans to increase the payment amount by 5% annually. The future value of an annuity formula, adapted for the annual "growth" of the payment, tells the investor how much will be available to fund college at a future date. Alternatively, if the investor wants to provide the future college student a series of allowance payments that increases by 4% annually, the present value of a geometrically varying or "growing" annuity formula may be used to determine how much the investor needs to have available when the student begins college. Accuracy depends on determining the correct number of compounding periods by adjusting the calculation to reflect whether payments occur at the beginning or end of the year (i.e., an annuity due or an ordinary annuity).

11. The trial-and-error method for determining the IRR can easily be replaced by using the TVM keys of a calculator to solve for the IRR of even cash flows (i.e., an annuity) or by using the calculator cash flow tables (registers) for uneven cash flows.

12. A spreadsheet may be the easiest approach to quickly display how changes in the interest rate or term of a loan affect other loan information. But the present value of an annuity formula can quickly provide the outstanding loan balance, which can then be calculated for different points in time and compared to the sum of the total payments to determine the total interest paid over the loan period.

## Chapter Resources

Texas Instruments BAII Plus Reference Manual (http://education.ti.com/guidebooks/financial/baiiplus/BAIIPLUSGuidebook_EN.pdf).


The *Financial Factilitator* and all fillable forms needed to complete text activities can be found on the student website at: http://pro.nuco.com/booksupplements/NUCollege-CaseBook2e.

# Quantitative/Analytical Mini-case Problems

1.  Holding-Period Returns

    a.  Last year Marla purchased 100 shares of stock for $8 per share. She paid a flat $75 to purchase the shares. Since making her purchase, she has received $200 in dividends. Marla is concerned that the stock price will fall below its current FMV of $7. Calculate her holding-period return if she sells today and pays a $75 commission.

    b.  Swarn bought 200 shares of a stock for $36 per share. He paid $245 in trading commissions. He has received dividends in the amounts of $98, $156, and $300 over the last three years, respectively. Assuming that Swarn is in the 15% marginal tax bracket for capital gains and dividends, what is his holding-period return if he sells all of the shares at $40 each with a $245 trading commission? What is Swarn's tax-adjusted holding period rate of return?

2.  Dollar-Weighted Returns

    a.  Brad purchased 10 shares of stock for $10 per share. He paid a $5 commission. One year later, he purchased another 10 shares at $9 per share. Again, he paid a $5 commission. In the second year, his disappoint got the best of him  and he sold 10 shares at $7 per share, paying another $5 commission. At the end of third year, Brad liquidated his holdings, paying $5 in commissions at $8 per share. What was his dollar-weighted rate of return?

    b.  Buckley purchased a collectible stamp for $600. He was thrilled to learn that the stamp price had moved up, so one year later he purchased another stamp for $700. At the end of the second year, he sold one of the stamps for $800. He held his original stamp for the third year. Buckley then sold his stamp at the end of the fourth year for $1,000. What was Buckley's dollar-weighted rate of return?

3.  Time-weighted Returns

    a.  Camerin purchased one ounce of gold for $1,400. The following year, the price of gold shot up to $1,800, but in the third year prices fell back to $1,500. What was Camerin's time-weighted return?

    b.  Marybeth purchased one share of stock for $92. At the end of year 1, the stock was worth $95. At the end of year 2, the stock was worth $100; and at the end of year 3, the stock was worth $92. What was Marybeth's time-weighted return? How does this compare to her holding period rate of return?

4.   Mean Returns

   a.   Maurice purchased a coin collection several years ago. Each year he has had the collection appraised by a reputable coin dealer. Maurice has calculated the yearly percentage gain or loss based on the appraisal, as shown below:

| | |
|---|---|
| Year 1: | 10% |
| Year 2: | 5% |
| Year 3: | 9% |
| Year 4: | -5% |
| Year 5: | 2% |
| Year 6: | -3% |
| Year 7: | 12% |

   What is the average (mean) return of the coin collection over the seven-year period?

   Use the rate of return data provided by Maurice to calculate the geometric mean return. How does this compare to the mean return?

5.   Weighted Average Returns

   a.   Sherman is a novice investor. The following table shows his portfolio holdings and market values for each holding. Please calculate Sherman's weighted average return for his portfolio.

| | Market Value | Rate of Return |
|---|---|---|
| Junk Bond Fund | $ 13,000.00 | 7.50% |
| Gold Fund | $ 19,500.00 | 12.00% |
| Small Cap Fund | $ 36,000.00 | 3.40% |
| Index Fund | $ 9,800.00 | 6.20% |
| CD | $ 41,000.00 | 1.00% |

   b.   Sonya and Josh own several pieces of expensive jewelry. The following table summarizes their most important gem assets:

| | Market Value | Purchase Price |
|---|---|---|
| Diamond Ring | $ 12,000.00 | $ 7,250.00 |
| Sapphire Necklace | $ 23,000.00 | $ 18,875.00 |
| Emerald Pendant | $ 19,500.00 | $ 19,000.00 |
| Ruby Brooch | $ 21,200.00 | $ 23,000.00 |
| TOTAL | $ 75,700.00 | $ 68,125.00 |

   Use this information to calculate the holding-period return.

6.  Real and Nominal Rates

   a.  Consumer prices have been averaging 3.50% in South Korea. If So-Hyun can earn a nominal rate of return on her investment portfolio of 10.25%, what is her real rate of return, assuming continuous compounding?

   b.  Farrell wants to retire in six years. To have sufficient assets to fund retirement, Farrell needs to accumulate an additional $400,000 between today and retirement. As his advisor, you assume that inflation will average 5%. You are also confident that you can build a portfolio that will generate an 8% compounded annual after-tax return. What serial payment should Farrell invest at the end of the first year to fund this goal?

7.  Tax-exempt and Taxable Rates

   a.  Thomas Jones is in the 25% marginal federal tax bracket, the 4% marginal state tax bracket, and the 2% marginal city tax bracket. If he earns 9.25% on his portfolio, what is his after-tax rate of return?

   b.  Stephanie is considering purchasing a fixed-income investment. She has narrowed her list of bond choice to two AAA-rated investments. The first is a corporate bond that matures in seven years. The bond yields 6.35%. The second bond also matures in seven years; however, this bond is a municipal bond issued by the state in which Stephanie resides. The bond has a current coupon rate at 4.79%. Stephanie is in the 25% marginal federal tax bracket and the 3.50% marginal state tax bracket. Which bond should she invest in to maximize her after-tax rate of return?

8.  Effective Rate Conversion Problems

   a.  A client was earning an EAR of 7%. The client was contributing to the account on a monthly basis. What would be the appropriate EPR?

   b.  A client wants to compute the estimated future value of a bank account. The account pays a semiannual rate of 4% (EPR). The client is investing in the account on a biweekly basis. What is the appropriate EPR to be able to solve for an estimated future value for the client?

9.  Future Value Problems

   a.  Ted has $1,000. He can earn an annual effective rate of 5%. How much will he have in 10 years?

   b.  Lanisha currently earns $45,000 per year. She expects her salary to increase by 3.5% per year. She plans to work for another 20 years. How much will she earn in her final year of work?

10.  Present Value Problems

   a.  Tammy has determined that she will need $3 million when she retires in 45 years. The current interest rate is 7% (EAR). How much does she need today to fully fund this goal at that rate?

b. David and Iantha expect their 10-year-old daughter to get married someday. They estimate that her wedding would cost $30,000 today. Wedding costs will increase by 3% per year, and she will marry in 15 years. David and Iantha earn a pre-tax annual rate of 5%. They are in the 20% marginal tax bracket. What amount do they need to set aside today for their daughter's wedding?

11. Future Value of Annuity Problems

a. Sue wants to save $1,000,000 in 20 years. She estimates she can earn 8.5% on savings. She intends to make deposits at the beginning of every year in a series of equal payments starting today. How much does she need to save each year to reach her goal?

b. Merita has been offered a choice of either receiving $100,000 in 10 years or receiving $7,000 per year (at the end of each year) for the next 10 years. Which is the better option if her required annual rate of return is 7%?

12. Present Value of Annuity Problems

a. Mike needs to receive $40,000 per year (at the beginning of each year) from his investments for the next 30 years. His opportunity cost of money is 5%. How much does he need in an account today to generate this level of income if he fully depletes the account?

b. Roshanna has just won the lottery. Her required rate of return is 6%. Should she take the annual annuity payment of $125,000 for the next 20 years or an immediate lump-sum payout of $1.5 million?

13. Future Value of Growing Annuity Problems

a. Martha wants to start saving for college. She estimates that she will need $50,000 when she starts college four years from now. She plans to save $9,500 this year and increase deposits by 5% annually (payments at the end of each year). She can earn 7% on her savings. Will she meet her savings goal of $50,000 for college four years from now?

b. Todd is saving $3,000 annually into an account (payments at the end of each year). He plans to increase the annual level of savings by 5% each year. He can earn 9% annually. How much will he have in the account at the end of 20 years?

14. Present Value of Growing Annuity Problems

a. Mike wants to receive $40,000 per year pretax from his investments for the next 30 years. He is concerned about inflation, which he expects to average 3%. He can earn a pretax rate of 6% on his money. How much does he need in an account to generate $40,000 in annual inflation-adjusted income (payments at the end of each year)?

b. A client is doing some investment/retirement planning. She is attempting to determine how much of her estate she needs to set aside today to fully fund her retirement. She desires annual beginning-of-period withdrawals for the next 25 years. She would like inflation-adjusted withdrawals that start at $50,000 per year. Assume an annual post-tax rate of return of 7.5% and that inflation will increase at an annual effective rate of 3.5%. What amount does she need to dedicate to this goal?

15. Present Value of Delayed Annuity Problems

   a.  Jonas desires fixed annual income of $85,000 beginning 20 years from now and lasting for 20 years. He plans to deplete the account. His annual required return is 9.5%. How much does he need to invest today to achieve his goal?

   b.  An investor has two options: (1) $50,000 received at the end of this year, or (2) $10,000 received each year for 10 years but beginning 10 years from now. Assume the rate of return is 7%. Which option has the higher present value?

16. Present Value of Perpetuity Problems

   a.  An investment would provide end-of-year annual income of $2,000. The client's required rate of return is 12.5%. What price should the client be willing to pay for the investment?

   b.  Jose Marie and his wife, Ayna, want to ensure that they do not outlive their money. They want to make end-of-year withdrawals that start at $80,000 after tax and increase by 4% per year. They can earn an annual effective rate of 7.2% after tax. How much do they need to have invested to make withdrawals that last forever?

17. Internal Rate of Return

   a.  Ruth invested $16,000 in an exchange-traded fund six years ago. Dividends and earnings were automatically reinvested in new shares. Although Ruth considers herself to be a buy-and-hold investor, she nonetheless made a few trades during the time period, as follows:

   - $3,025 redemption at the end of the second year

   - $1,825 redemption at the end of the third year

   - $4,200 additional investment into the fund at the end of the fifth year

   - $19,885 received at the end of the sixth year, when Ruth redeemed the shares.

   What was Ruth's internal rate of return on the investment?

   b.  Lawrence Block is considering investing in a gold coin. The coin costs $47,500. He anticipates spending $1,000 to have the coin's value reevaluated by experts at the end of the first year. Lawrence believes that he can receive $3,500 in exhibitor fees by allowing a major museum to showcase his coin during the second year of ownership. He would like to sell the coin, but he will need to market and promote it first. He anticipates spending $2,000 by the end of the third year on the process. If he can receive $50,000 at the end of the fourth year, should Lawrence make this investment if he needs to earn 4.50% on it?

18. Net Present Value

a.  Derek invested $12,000 in a mutual fund five years ago. He received a dividend check for $1,000 after the first year. He received $750 after the second year. At the end of the third year, he received a check for $1,500. After the fourth year, he collected $750. His final dividend check of $1,000 was received at the end of the fifth year. Assume that Derek sold the mutual fund at the end of the fifth year for $18,000. What was Derek's internal rate of return on this investment?

b.  Kristy purchased shares of a mutual fund five years ago. She has since made the following additional transactions:

    •   End of year 2, invested additional $2,500 in the fund

    •   End of year 3, invested additional $9,000 in the fund

    •   End of year 5, redeemed all of her shares in the fund, receiving $16,000

    Kristy just told you she achieved an annual return of 9% in this investment. If Kristy is correct, what was her initial investment in the fund?

19. Loan Amortization Problems

a.  Willy and Ursha have just purchased a new car for $38,000. They financed $35,000 for five years at 6.75% (APR). What is the monthly payment and total interest expense?

b.  Assume an initial loan amount of $150,000, an APR of 6.5%, fixed monthly payments, and an amortization period of 20 years. What is the outstanding balance on the loan after 60 payments have been paid?

20. Kristin and Dan Peterson wonder how much they will need to save to fully fund four years of college for their daughter, Samantha, who is 12 years old today. She plans to attend college at age 18. They know that their first choice of college currently costs $13,000 per year. College costs are increasing 5% annually. They feel that it is possible to earn an effective annual rate of 8.3% (8% compounded monthly), both before and during college.

a.  How much will Samantha's first year of college cost?

b.  How much do the Peterson's need to fully fund college costs when Samantha begins college?

c.  How much do Kristin and Dan need to deposit in an account today to fully fund four years of expenses?

d.  How much will they need to save on a monthly basis starting at the end of this month to fully fund four years of expenses?

21. Tony has been eyeing a new car. Last weekend, he went to the dealership and noted that his dream car would cost $23,000 if purchased today. Tony currently has $9,000 saved. He does not want to go into debt to buy the car, so he has decided to save toward the purchase for three years. Tony estimates that inflation will average 4.5% per year. He earns 7% (EAR) on his savings.

    a.  How much will the car cost in exactly three years?

    b.  How much must he save per year (at end of each year) to purchase the car in three years?

22. John is an avid stamp collector. He has been noting the rapid rise in prices for stamps printed in the 19th century. Some of the best stamps from that time period have been increasing in value by 12% per year. John has the rare opportunity to purchase several impressive stamps from a reputable dealer.

    The dealer has offered to sell the stamps to John for $65,000 today. As an alternative, John can put down $10,000 toward the purchase today and buy the stamps outright for an additional $89,500 in four years. Assume an annual discount rate of 12%. Assuming John has the cash for either deal, which should he take?

# Comprehensive Bedo Case—Analysis Questions

There are no Bedo case questions for this chapter. The preceding quantitative/analytical mini-case problems can serve as a good review. TVM concepts will be applied to the Bedo case in many other chapters to quantify needs and funding.

## Notes

1. E. Jacquire, A. Kane, and A. Marcus, "Geometric or Arithmetic Mean: A Reconsideration," *Financial Analyst Journal* 59, no. 6 (2003): 46–53.

2. $T_0$ is always the present time, "today." Future points in time are then counted to, with the first period ($T_1$) being one period in the future. For example, 10 periods in the future would be designated as $T_{10}$. The period could be years, months, or any other definable period.

3. Annual payments are assumed because the growth rate is annual. Semimonthly or biweekly payments would be expected. However, the growing annuity equation assumes that the payment change frequency caused by applying the growth rate is the same as the payment frequency.

# PART II: Analyzing and Evaluating a Client's Financial Status to Plan for Client Earnings

# Cash Flow Planning

## Learning Objectives

1. Understand the importance of cash flow planning within the comprehensive financial planning framework.

2. Describe the cash flow planning process and how financial planners use it to understand a client's current financial situation and the cash flow management strategies needed.

3. Identify the client situational information necessary to complete a comprehensive cash flow analysis.

4. Demonstrate the ability to differentiate between dedicated and discretionary expenses in constructing and interpreting an income statement.

5. Demonstrate how to calculate and interpret an income statement and a balance sheet.

6. Demonstrate how to calculate and interpret the major financial ratios.

7. Understand the importance of and potential funding sources for an emergency fund.

8. Identify the types of major consumer debt and demonstrate the ability to analyze and make recommendations pertaining to a client's debt load.

9. Identify mortgage alternatives matched to the client situation, and demonstrate how to analyze and interpret the different options for an initial purchase or refinance.

10. Identify and recommend appropriate and reasonable cash flow management strategies matched to a client's situation.

# Key Terms

adjustable-rate mortgage

back-end mortgage qualification ratio

cash flow statement

cash-out refinance

credit usage ratio

current liabilities

current ratio

debt-to-income ratio

dedicated expenses

discount point

discretionary expenses

emergency fund ratio

financial assets

fixed expenses

front-end mortgage qualification ratio

home equity line of credit

income and expense statement

investment assets

IRC § 79 income

long-term debt coverage ratio

long-term liabilities

monetary assets

non-taxable income

real asset

savings ratio

debt ratio

taxable income

use assets

variable expense

**Figure 3. 1** Systematic Financial Planning Process for Cash Flow Planning

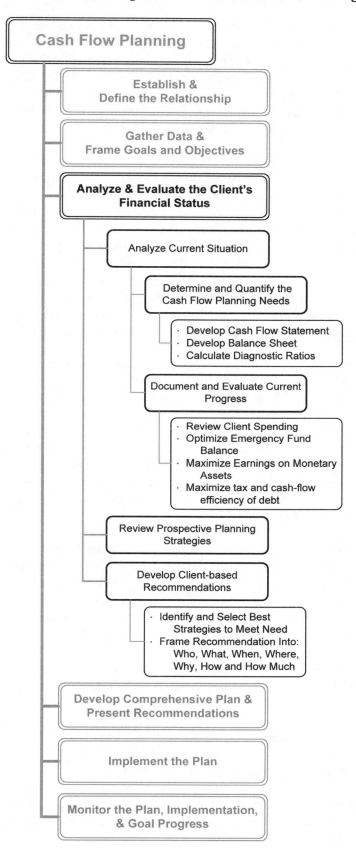

111

## FINANCIAL SITUATION ANALYSIS: THE BASICS

Helping clients achieve their lifetime financial goals starts with an assessment of their current financial situation. The calculation of a client's annual cash flow and current net worth coupled with diagnostic financial ratios provides a foundation for evaluating a client's financial strengths and weaknesses. The backbone of cash flow-based financial planning is discretionary cash flow; but calculating discretionary cash flow can be difficult because *discretionary* is simply the residual income after accounting for dedicated expenses—and *dedicated* has many qualifiers.

Income is typically divided in one of two ways: (1) based on source—earned or unearned (passive); or (2) based on tax consequence—taxable or nontaxable. Expenses, on the other hand, can be divided in many ways: (1) fixed vs. variable; (2) short-term vs. long-term; (3) one-time vs. recurring, to name only a few. However, one of the most planning-focused categories of expenses is to classify them as either dedicated or discretionary. In the strictest sense, **dedicated expenses** are cash flows required by contract or other similarly binding agreement. However, such a narrow definition could meet with some resistance, so a more agreeable definition of this category might include more client-defined life- and goal- "essential" items (e.g., insurance and savings). On the other hand, **discretionary expenses** are cash flows that the client completely controls and can change as necessary to meet other objectives.

From a financial planner's perspective, discretionary cash flow measures how much income remains at the end of the period after accounting for all expenses. A negative discretionary cash flow indicates that a client is spending more than is earned on a periodic basis. A positive discretionary cash flow suggests that a client has unallocated income that can be used to meet other goals and objectives. So this is the challenge. Cash flow planning can have two very different starting points for client/planner relationships where the client has adequate discretionary cash flow remaining after all expenses, and for those where the client does not. (Note: although it may be easy to think of this delineation in terms of high-net-worth/high-lifestyle clients versus others, that is not necessarily the case.)

When a client has adequate discretionary cash flow, the planner may not need to help the client discover more discretionary cash flow to fund additional or revised planning goals by reviewing the client's expenses. However, often planners will have to thoroughly review a client's current situation to free up additional discretionary money. Just because clients appear to be overspending their income doesn't necessarily mean that they do not have discretionary or potentially discretionary income available.

Some might define discretionary cash flow as income remaining at the end of a period after paying all *required* or *necessary* expenses. Otherwise, a client with voluntary or unnecessary excess spending could appear to have no discretionary cash flow when in fact the client chose to spend the available cash flow over which the client exercised discretion. Furthermore, discretionary cash flow is not the same as savings, although discretionary cash flow can be reduced because of a client's efforts to save or invest. Some clients save some or all income remaining at the end of a period, and other clients spend this discretionary cash flow either through planned or unplanned expenditures. So it is very important to clearly define what discretionary cash flow is and what a discretionary expense is. Nevertheless, discretionary cash flow can be spent by the client's choice.

More about these concepts appears throughout this chapter, but for general purposes, discretionary cash flow will be defined as money left over at the end of a planning period. Therefore, without positive cash flow, or the potential to generate positive cash flow—possibly via reductions in dedicated expenses or reallocation of discretionary expenses—it is difficult for clients to fund their financial goals.

The purpose of this chapter is to examine the process of analyzing and evaluating a client's current financial situation, as illustrated in Figure 3.1. The chapter also provides examples of common financial planning strategies to improve a client's cash flow and net worth position. It concludes with an illustration of how an advisor can identify particular financial situational strategies to develop client-specific recommendations.

## CASH FLOW MANAGEMENT AND THE FINANCIAL PLANNER

One of the primary roles of the financial planner, at the early stage of the financial planning process, is to assist the client in building a solid foundation for funding other goals and objectives identified throughout the planning process. Efforts may be needed to more appropriately align cash flow or household spending decisions with current and future financial objectives. Efforts to optimally fund an emergency fund or other cash reserves may be necessary. For those with sufficient **monetary assets**, defined as very liquid financial assets (e.g., cash, checking or savings accounts, certificates of deposit, or money market mutual funds), a review of accounts might be necessary to maximize earnings. Finally, it may be necessary to restructure consumer or mortgage debt to increase discretionary cash flow.

Cash flow and net worth planning is designed to increase discretionary cash flow, increase assets, and decrease liabilities, especially non-tax-efficient liabilities. Not all clients need all possible cash flow and net worth strategies. For example, higher-income or higher-net-worth clients might already be maximizing the use of tax-efficient debt. Some may also have a large or steadily increasing discretionary cash flow, regardless of current consumption. For such clients, it may be sufficient to simply confirm that they are on track with the foundational components of the financial planning process.

But a word of caution is warranted. Do not assume that a client's financial situation—regardless of net worth or income—is in order and then haphazardly proceed to other areas of the financial planning process. **The foundation of financial planning is grounded in the cash flow and net worth planning phase of the planning process.**

A thorough cash flow and net worth analysis should be conducted for every client seeking comprehensive financial planning services. Even if a client's situation is financially sound and no recommendations are made, this analysis ensures that the client has adequately addressed the needs commonly considered in cash flow and net worth management (e.g., managing cash flow, building emergency income sources, and managing secured and unsecured debt). This systematic approach assures the planner that a cash flow or net worth item that could become a significant issue later in the comprehensive analysis has not been ignored. A determination of these key factors can also help planners decide quickly whether a client offers the prospect of a long-term planning relationship. Insights gained from the development of a client financial profile can help planners detect the need for debt counseling as a prerequisite to financial planning. Furthermore, it is important that planners communicate to clients the importance of comprehensive and forthright sharing of all relevant financial information.

The basic nature of cash flow and net worth management calculations should not lull planners into sloppy mathematics. If the income and expense calculation is incorrect, mathematical discrepancies will flow through every section of the plan. If a planner over-estimates discretionary cash flow, then the cost of recommendations could exceed a client's funding capacity. If the net worth statement is inaccurate, both planner and client will have a distorted view of true "wealth." In many cases, miscalculation of net worth is caused by underestimating or overlooking liabilities, such as home mortgages, auto loans, and other outstanding debt. This type of error is easily compounded in other aspects of the plan by recommending inadequate property and liability insurance or life insurance coverage. The lesson is: calculate and check—and then double-check—the client's discretionary cash flow and net worth numbers.

---

### Planning for Special Populations: Cash Management for Recent Widows and Widowers

Regardless of age or the circumstances surrounding the death of a spouse or partner, addressing cash flow management issues can be both psychologically and financially empowering. Grieving spouses should be cautioned not to make major financial or lifestyle decisions too quickly. But an important first step is to assist them in developing a new income and expense statement and balance sheet. This strategy can encourage independence and responsibility in the new situation; help the survivor avoid financial problems by addressing necessary changes in spending, employment, or lifestyle; and most importantly, provide needed peace of mind.

Whether this is a new or ongoing professional relationship will determine the amount of effort required to build trust and collect information, but the following are three important considerations:

1.   Identifying other professionals (e.g., estate planning attorney, accountant or tax professional, investment managers, insurance providers, bankers, creditors) who are, or should be, working in collaboration with the planner and the client. A valued family friend or child can also be involved.

2.   Identifying all cash flows that could occur over a specified time period, for example, a year. Some of these may be glaringly obvious, while others couuld be overlooked if the planner does not systematically help the client identify income sources and expense needs. A comprehensive assessment can help discover benefits (i.e., Social Security, COBRA coverage, retirement or life insurance benefits, or other services) that might be available; service providers or additional expenses that need to be identified (e.g., a lawn service), and changes that must occur to ensure financial stability for the selected time period.

> 3. Identifying all assets and liabilities for the new net worth statement will establish the financial position. Retitling inherited or jointly held assets may be necessary, debts may have to be restructured, or assets may need to be liquidated. But these decisions cannot be made without an accurate assessment of cash flows and net worth.
>
> Helping to stabilize the situation by developing a new spending plan and net worth statement can increase the grieving spouse's feelings of control and reduce pressure to make major life changes.

## ANALYZE THE CLIENT'S CURRENT SITUATION

The primary purpose of a comprehensive financial planning review is to help clients reach financial goals and objectives. In its most basic sense, this cannot be achieved unless a client has the capacity to fund most of, or at least the most important of, the planner's goal-based recommendations. Although reducing spending, increasing savings, or restructuring liabilities could meet some needs, nearly all long-term financial goals are met through the planned allocation of discretionary cash flow and savings, a reallocation of other assets, or a reduction in liabilities. The latter may not be necessary, depending on the client's situation. For example, financial leverage can be an effective strategy, especially when net worth is sufficient, the debt is easily manageable, or the interest rate paid is less than the after-tax earnings on alternative investments. These interrelationships among net worth, cash flow, and other financial goals make this initial step of the financial planning process extremely important. Before improvements or changes can be considered, the current situation must be fully explored.

### Determine and Quantify the Client's Need for Cash Flow Planning

Analyzing a client's current financial situation is the first step in the systematic financial planning process and it serves two important purposes. First, the calculation of the income and expense statement, the net worth statement, and diagnostic financial ratios grounds the financial plan in the reality of the client's current financial profile. Second, these documents provide baseline data for comparison with periodically revised documents that can be used to track the financial planning process, goal accomplishment, and the evolution of new financial goals and objectives over the client's life cycle.

An income and expense or **cash flow statement** differs from a budget or spending plan. A budget is simply a *projection* of how much a client will earn and spend in any given period, whereas the income and expense statement reflects actual consumption. Although it is important for most clients to have a budget, when it comes time for serious planning, a complete income and expense statement should be used to generate recommendations. The amount of detail in the income and expense statement can vary with the financial complexity of the client.

It is equally important to understand the balance of assets owned and debt owed, because these factors play a role in increasing or decreasing a client's annual cash flow. A net worth statement, also commonly referred to as a *balance sheet*, provides a one-time picture of a client's assets and liabilities and is a key measure of a client's cumulative financial progress. The result of subtracting liabilities from assets is net worth, or *wealth*. Ideal financial planning clients, regardless of age, tend to have a positive and growing net worth, a prerequisite to achieving long-term financial success.

The numbers and financial documents generated provide the foundation for the financial planning process. For the perceptive planner, the same numbers can provide a window into a client's world. Planners who focus too much on the quantitative aspect of the financial situation miss a valuable opportunity to understand more fully what drives the finances in a client's household. Although it is important for the *planner-technician* to ensure the completeness and accuracy of the numbers, it is equally important for the *planner-counselor* to fully understand the story that the numbers can tell. For this reason, many planners have clients complete the data-gathering questionnaire, or client intake form, before the meeting. This helps redirect attention from the numbers to an exploration of the client's situational factors.

Planners can use this information to help clients see where their money is going, either before or after the planners' recommendations have been implemented. Exhibit 3.1 is representative of how a planner might choose to inform a client about the current cash flow situation while it (1) educates the client, (2) suggests a change in current financial management practices, and (3) graphically summarizes information. Referring the client to the more detailed information in an appendix gives the client a choice regarding how much information to consider, now or in the future.

The client's temperament and personality, attitudes and beliefs, and financial knowledge and experience are all likely evident in the income and expense and net worth statements. For example, a client's values and attitudes are often apparent from spending patterns, and risk tolerance and financial knowledge or experience can be inferred from the client's net worth statement. A client's reactions of embarrassment, guilt, or even defiance about past spending patterns, investments, or financial decisions can offer useful insights for the planner who is sensitive to the nuances of these messages. Other anxious clients, particularly those in or near retirement, could simply need reassurance that it is ok to spend and enjoy assets.

Although the client's socioeconomic descriptors might logically be the focus of the current financial situation analysis, students and novice planners are cautioned to maintain a balanced approach. A sincere willingness to understand a client's world can build trust and communicate a genuine concern for the client's financial future. Planners who skillfully document the numbers and explore the story behind the numbers build a strong foundation for the planner-client relationship. Furthermore, broadly exploring client situational factors increases opportunities to discuss future household changes that could positively or negatively influence a client's financial situation, employment, or lifestyle—changes that will affect the client's income, expenses, and net worth.

**Exhibit 3.1** Cash Flow Planning Example for the Vest Family

### Cash Flow Summary

Doug and Chris, an income and expense statement summarizes income earned and expenses incurred during a given period, in your case one year. Using this information, we can determine your level of discretionary cash flow. This statement helps us determine if you are earning more than you spend, and have surplus cash flow, or are spending more than you earn, and have a deficit. This statement is an integral part of your financial plan and helps us to determine how much money is available to allocate to your financial goals. A detailed income and expense statement can be found in the appendix on page A-12; however, the pie chart below illustrates how your income is currently allocated to various dedicated and discretionary expenses.

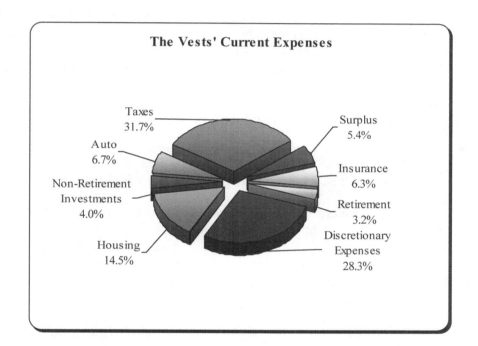

**The Vests' Current Expenses**

- Taxes 31.7%
- Surplus 5.4%
- Auto 6.7%
- Insurance 6.3%
- Non-Retirement Investments 4.0%
- Retirement 3.2%
- Discretionary Expenses 28.3%
- Housing 14.5%

We are delighted to see that you have a monthly surplus of $685, or $8,224 annually. To free up additional cash flow you may want to review your top five discretionary expenses (shown on the income and expense statement in the appendix) and consider possible reductions. This will enable you to realize your goals more quickly, but we also want to take care not to compromise your lifestyle.

Doug & Chris Vest                    Confidential Financial Plan

Before beginning the analysis of a client's financial situation, an advisor must determine a starting and ending date for the data collection period. An annual income and expense statement is typically recommended, because annualized statements limit confusion about the timing of income and expenses. If a monthly income and expense statement is used, for example, it becomes difficult to account for income earned on a biweekly basis or expenses incurred on a nonmonthly basis. Using income and expenses from the prior month or two and then extrapolating to an annual basis is a viable alternative, but it could lead to serious inaccuracies, depending on the client's recordkeeping. Annualized statements also provide a broad view of a client's assets and liabilities, which can be used to determine financial ratios.

In general, one of two 12-month statement alternatives can be used. First, and perhaps the easiest, is to reproduce a calendar year 12-month period. In this case, the cash flow and net worth statement would show a start date of January 1 and an end date of December 31 of the previous year. A second method is to reflect the 12 months preceding the month closest to the date of a client engagement. If a client were to engage financial planning services on May 8th, for example, the easiest approach would be to develop the income and expense statements from May 1st of the previous year through April 30th of the current year. The important thing to remember is that accuracy and consistency really count. Finally, because the net worth statement reflects a point in time, and not a period of time, the planner can choose any reasonable date close to the initiation of the planning process.

---

### Planning for Special Populations: Cash Management for the "Suddenly Wealthy"

It would be erroneous to assume that all high-net-worth (HNW) and ultra-high-net-worth (UHNW) clients lack the need for cash flow planning. It would be easy to say that these clients must be excellent at managing finances, and perhaps if the client was self-made, that assumption would be correct. However, if a client happened to achieve high net worth via a windfall, the client might have absolutely no idea how to manage cash flow.

When windfall money is mentioned many think of lottery winnings, but much more often financial windfalls come from inheritance or the sale of a business or the signing of a professional sports contract. (Although to the untrained such events could seem wonderful, financial planners must recognize that some windfalls come as the result of a loss—and in some cases, they create loss.) Advising a client who has just received a life-altering sum of money about cash flow management can be incredibly trying.  After all, who in the world goes broke after receiving millions of dollars?

The Internet is littered with stories of sudden millionaires who go from ignorance to bliss to broke in only a few years—and unsound financial advice or no financial advice is usually to blame. But building a simple income and expense statement and then using it as a platform for a reasonable budget will go a long way in preserving this wealth. Cash flow planning, although normally thought of as the basis for becoming wealthy, is also a cornerstone for remaining wealthy.

However, Susan Bradley, who has written a book and started an Institute centered on sudden wealth, suggests that a person who receives sudden wealth actually delay making any financial or other important decisions until after he or she feels comfortable and grounded in the new situation. This pause allows time for people to truly contemplate how they want their life to change rather than simply letting their life change. Life-altering sums of money are just that—life altering, not merely lifestyle altering. People have strange emotional reactions to receiving an out-sized amount of money at one time. Anxiety, guilt, resentment, fear, and isolation can all be emotional responses. So it may be that a financial planner must first become the planner-counselor before becoming the planner-technician. Although many resources may be available about what to *do* with a financial windfall, precious few deal with how to *cope* with one.

## Calculating an Income and Expense Statement

Developing an income and expense statement for a client is relatively straightforward, although again there are several different approaches to categorizing income and expenses. The approach presented here is both mechanically and philosophically different from some other approaches in that cash flows committed to client goals are identified as dedicated expenses. A more traditional approach, as mentioned at the beginning of the chapter, limits dedicated expenses to what are traditionally defined as contractual obligations. Granted, clients do have the discretion to stop allocations to short-term savings and long-term investments at any time and, in the process of working with a financial planner, may choose to do so in lieu of other financial goals. However, identifying these savings and investment expenses as equally important to debt service or insurance protection can change the way they a client views them.

Exhibits 3.2 through 3.5 are examples of Financial Facilitator worksheets that can be used to calculate a client's annual cash flow. Note that the income and expense statement has been divided into three separate worksheets. The first is the Annual Income Statement, shown in Exhibit 3.2 which categorizes a client's earned, unearned, and nontaxable income. Data from this worksheet flows directly into the Annual Dedicated Expense Statement, shown in Exhibit 3.3 This worksheet lists fixed annual expenses as well as savings and investments that the client has dedicated to funding. Subtracting dedicated expenses from income provides an indication of how much income remains to be spent on variable, or discretionary, expenses that are recorded on the Annual Discretionary Expense Statement (Exhibits 3.4 and 3.5). Details regarding each statement are presented below.

As shown in Exhibit 3.2, the Financial Facilitator provides an easy way to summarize a client's earned, unearned, and nontaxable income. Income is reported on an annual before-tax basis. Total potentially **taxable income** includes all sources of income that could be subject to federal and state taxation (e.g., wages, salaries, tips, bonuses, group benefit income, interest, dividends, tax refunds, and pensions). It is also important to include all sources of **nontaxable income** (e.g., gift, child support, qualified distributions for a Roth plan) to provide a complete accounting of all income sources available to the household.

**Exhibit 3.2** Annual Income Statement

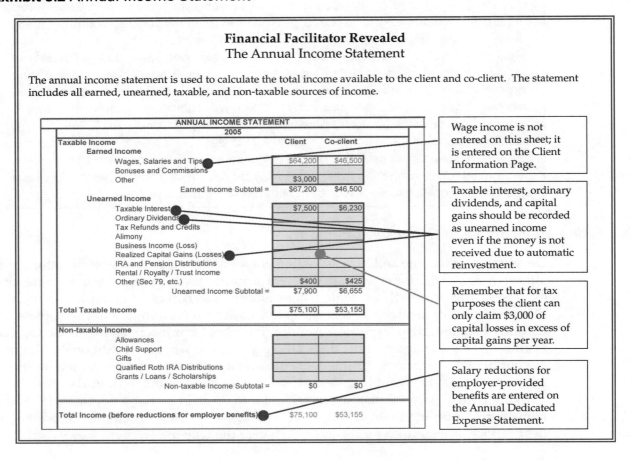

Financial Facilitator Revealed
The Annual Income Statement

The annual income statement is used to calculate the total income available to the client and co-client. The statement includes all earned, unearned, taxable, and non-taxable sources of income.

**IRC § 79 income** is an often-overlooked but commonly available source of unearned income. Certain employer-provided benefits, such as group term life insurance plans, can cause gross taxable income to be greater than salary or wages. Employer-related term insurance plans are sometimes known as IRC § 79 plans. The first $50,000 in employer-funded group term life insurance coverage is generally tax free to all participants; premiums paid by the employer for the benefit of the employee on amounts over $50,000 are subject to federal income tax. (A key employee in a discriminatory plan cannot exclude the first $50,000 of coverage and is required to use the actual cost if it is higher than the imputed income based on Table 3.1.) The taxable amount of the premium is calculated based on each participant's age and amount of insurance above $50,000 (if excludible) as shown in Table 3.1. The following table is used to calculate the amount of taxable income that must be added to income and reported on a Form W-2.

**Table 3.1** IRS Table I: Employer's Tax Guide to Fringe Benefits

| Age | Cost per Month per $1,000 of Term Insurance Coverage | Cost per Year per $1,000 of Term Insurance Coverage |
|---|---|---|
| Under 25 | $0.05 | $0.60 |
| 25–29 | 0.06 | 0.72 |
| 30–34 | 0.08 | 0.96 |
| 35–39 | 0.09 | 1.08 |
| 40–44 | 0.10 | 1.20 |
| 45–49 | 0.15 | 1.80 |
| 50–54 | 0.23 | 2.76 |
| 55–59 | 0.43 | 5.16 |
| 60–64 | 0.66 | 7.92 |
| 65–69 | 1.27 | 15.24 |
| 70 and above | 2.06 | 24.72 |

*Source*: IRS *Employer's Tax Guide to Fringe Benefits*, Publication 15-B, p. 14. Available at http://www.irs.gov/pub/irs-pdf/p15b.pdf.

*Example.* Assume that a client, age 42, earns $80,000 per year, and is insured for twice her annual salary ($80,000 × 2 = $160,000). The client may receive $50,000 in coverage tax free, but premiums paid by the employer for the remaining $110,000 of the policy are subject to tax. Therefore the client's reported taxable income will increase by $132 for the year, as shown below.

$$Taxable\ Income = \frac{Insurance\ in\ Excess\ of\ \$50,000}{\$1,000} \times Table\ Factor \times 12$$

$$Taxable\ Income = \frac{\$160,000 - \$50,000}{\$1,000} \times 0.10 \times 12 = \$132.00$$

This calculation was completed using the IRS Table I rates shown in Table 3.1. Taxes on the premium cannot be avoided by assigning the policy to another individual.

---

### Financial Situation Tip: § 79 Income and Expenses

To accurately calculate discretionary cash flow, all § 79 income should also be shown as an expense on the Dedicated Expense sheet. If this offsetting expense is not recorded, discretionary cash flow will be overestimated. § 79 imputed income, although taxable, is not available for clients to spend.

---

**Exhibit 3.3** illustrates the Financial Facilitator Annual Dedicated Expense Statement for recording a client's dedicated expenses. The term *dedicated expense* refers to everyday expenditures that a client has little control over, either because of a contractual commitment or a dedicated personal commitment to fund a goal. Primary categories of expenses include income tax, debt service, insurance premiums, and savings and investments. Note also that total potentially taxable income is reduced by pretax employer deductions, such as employer -sponsored health and disability insurance, as well as deductions for other pretax benefits and funded retirement plans. Care should be taken to determine whether disability insurance is, in fact, a pretax deduction; if so, any benefits subsequently received are then taxable. Mortgage, auto, and education loan payments as well as retirement contributions generally occur on a regular basis. Often, an employer or creditor deducts these obligations electronically. This approach can work equally well to facilitate funding goals that a client views as dedicated expenses.

**Exhibit 3.3** Annual Dedicated Expense Statement

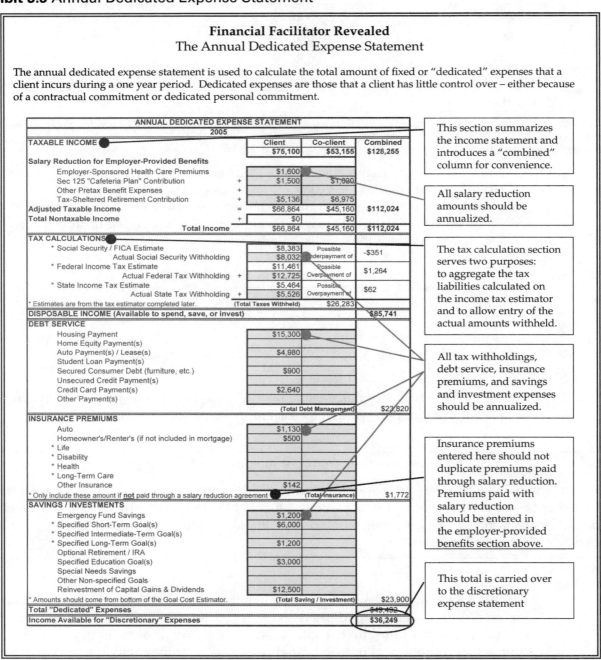

In summary, dedicated expenses are similar to what some financial planners call **fixed expenses**. Using the preceding definition to describe fixed expenses means that items such as regular savings and contributing to retirement plans are shown as an expense rather than as an addition to discretionary cash flow. Although a client can stop saving for a specific goal at any time, it is the act of saving on a regular basis and the personal commitment to that goal that makes savings activities a dedicated expense.

---

### Financial Situation Tip: Reinvested Dividends, Capital Gains, and Interest

When developing an income and expense statement, it is important to enter reinvested interest, dividends, and capital gains amounts from nonqualified accounts as income on the annual income statement and as a corresponding expense on the dedicated expenses statement. If this income is not reflected as an offsetting expense, discretionary cash flow will be overestimated and the corresponding investment balances will be underestimated. Although this income was not directly "received," the taxpayer chose to "spend" the income by reinvesting it. The tax implication of these transactions must not be overlooked.

However, for a qualified investment account (e.g., an IRA, variable universal life insurance, etc.), reinvested interest and dividends should not show up on the income and expense statement, because they are not reportable as income for tax purposes.

---

Discretionary expenses, as compared to dedicated expenses, are variable outlays that a client can control more directly, either by the choice to spend or the amount to spend. These expenses are recorded on the Annual Discretionary Expense Statement shown in Exhibits 3.4 and 3.5. Major categories of expenses include communication, entertainment, education, food, housing operation, household and personal care, medical, transportation, banking and investment, and miscellaneous. Discretionary, or daily living, expenses are variable and as such can vary month-to-month and year-to-year. Unlike a mortgage payment, for instance, expenses such as entertainment and dining, home improvements, and telephone expenses tend to fluctuate from one period to the next. Separating dedicated expenses from discretionary expenses is necessary to better understand where a client's income is being spent.

The term *discretionary expense* is interchangeable with **variable expense**, which is a term often used to describe everyday living expenses that clients can more easily control. It is important to note that not everyone will agree that the expenses shown in Exhibits 3.4 and 3.5 are truly discretionary. In many respects, the choice to call an expense *dedicated* (fixed) or *discretionary* (variable) is something a financial planner must make in consultation with the client to best represent the client's perception of the individual expense. For example, tuition expenses for a child to attend private or parochial school or the adjacent public school district are discretionary expenses that are not necessary given the availability of a local free public school. However, parents who choose to pay the education expenses, for whatever personal reason, would likely assert that the expense is not discretionary. What is really important is to account for all of a client's expenses, regardless of whether the expense is deemed dedicated or discretionary. The desired result is to calculate a client's level of discretionary cash flow, which is defined as income less dedicated and discretionary expenses.

**Exhibit 3.4** Annual Discretionary Expense Statement

The role of discretionary cash flow as the foundation of the financial planning process cannot be overestimated. For the purpose of the worksheets and the working definitions used in this book, discretionary cash flow is calculated by subtracting all of a client's dedicated and discretionary expenses from total income. The term *discretionary*, in this sense, refers to available income that can be used to fund goals and objectives.

**Exhibit 3.5** Annual Discretionary Expense Statement (Continued)

**Financial Facilitator Revealed**
The Annual Discretionary Expense Statement Section Two

| Banking and Investment | | | $881 |
|---|---|---|---|
| User Fees (safe deposit box, etc.) | $45 | | (sub-total) |
| Annual or Monthly Fees | $96 | | |
| IRA Maintenance Fees | $140 | | |
| Commissions | | | |
| Legal & Accounting Service Fees | $600 | | |
| Miscellaneous | | | $9,500 |
| Contributions (religious, charitable, etc.) | $6,000 | | (sub-total) |
| Travel | | | |
| Personal Vacations / Long Weekends | $2,500 | | |
| Business | | | |
| Tobacco / Gambling / Alcohol | | | |
| Child Support | | | |
| Alimony | | | |
| Pet Care and Supplies | | | |
| Postage / Shipping | | | |
| Gifts | $1,000 | | |
| Other | | | |
| Total "Discretionary" Expenses | $34,767 | $0 | $34,767 |

Total Annual Income Remaining = $1,482
Congratulations, you have income remaining for additional savings

Remember that some professional services and investment fees are tax deductible if the client itemizes.

Remember that charitable contributions could also have an impact on taxable income if the client itemizes deductions.

If this number is negative, reductions will be necessary if additional expenses or savings goals are to be met.

If a client's discretionary expenses are large, there might be opportunities to reduce them, which could result in an increase in discretionary cash flow. The larger the proportion of income spent on dedicated expenses, the smaller the opportunity to reduce expenses and increase discretionary cash flow. This is evident for contractual expenses such as debt or insurance, but the status of dedicated or fixed savings is less clear.

Such confusion arises out of the knowledge that clients often save or invest on a regular basis, following the philosophy of "save first." This type of savings appears on the income and expense statement as a dedicated expense, thereby reducing discretionary cash flow. Some planners prefer to add back dedicated saving amounts to discretionary cash flow to arrive at a total amount that could then be allocated to meet all planning needs or goals.

It may be preferable, however, simply to acknowledge that discretionary cash flow is only one source of available funds. A client, in consultation with a planner, could agree that savings amounts dedicated to a particular financial objective should continue or be discontinued, in lieu of funding other financial goals and objectives. Depending on the client's cash and credit management approach, it is possible to have zero or even negative discretionary cash flow, although "savings" expenses are substantial.

## Calculating Net Worth

A client's net worth is calculated by subtracting liabilities from assets using a balance sheet. Assets are typically recorded on a balance sheet in a hierarchical manner based on liquidity and are separated into two broad categories: financial assets and use assets. Loosely defined, **financial assets** can be spent or invested. **Use assets** support a client's lifestyle and could necessitate property or liability insurance protection.

Although exceptions occur when a use asset might also be a financial asset (e.g., art work, collectibles), these terms provide an easy preliminary method for categorization. Aside from these conventions, the categorization of assets may vary.

As shown in Exhibits 3.6 and 3.7, eight categories of assets are identified on the balance sheet. Exhibit 3.6 includes five categories of financial assets: monetary/liquid, investment, retirement, insurance, and education/special needs; Exhibit 3.7 lists the last three categories of tangible assets: real, personal/collectible, and use/lifestyle.

**Exhibit 3.6** Balance Sheet, Financial Assets

### Financial Facilitator Revealed
### The Balance Sheet, Financial Assets

The financial asset section of the balance sheet is a record of all monetary, investment, retirement, insurance, and education/special needs assets. Its purpose is to track account values and types, as well as ownership.

**BALANCE SHEET**
**2005**

**ASSETS**

| Name / Type of Holding | Allocation Classification | Value | Ownership | Tax-Shelter | Account Type |
|---|---|---|---|---|---|
| **Monetary / Liquid Assets** | | | | | |
| Checking | cash | $3,900 | joint | No | Non-Qual |
| Savings | cash | $6,525 | joint | No | Non-Qual |
| Money Market Account | cash | $18,000 | Client | No | Non-Qual |
| Money Market Account | cash | $5,000 | Co-client | No | Non-Qual |
| Certificate of Deposit | cash | $12,000 | Co-client | No | Non-Qual |
| **Investment Assets** | | | | | |
| Large cap stock | equity | $11,000 | joint | No | Non-Qual |
| Large cap stock | equity | $3,575 | joint | No | Non-Qual |
| Small cap stock | equity | $8,150 | Client | No | Non-Qual |
| Large cap ETF | equity | $3,325 | Co-client | No | Non-Qual |
| International ETF | international | $8,900 | Co-client | No | Non-Qual |
| Large cap stock | equity | $4,450 | Co-client | No | Non-Qual |
| ABC Fixed Annuity | cash | $21,000 | Client | Yes | Whole life |
| **Retirement Assets** | | | | | |
| Large cap mutual fund | equity | $101,000 | Client | Yes | 401(k) |
| Global equity mutual fund | international | $65,550 | Client | Yes | 401(k) |
| Corporate bond mutual fund | bond | $27,845 | Co-client | Yes | 401(k) |
| Mid cap mutual fund | equity | $32,500 | Co-client | Yes | Roth IRA |
| Real estate mutual fund | equity | $14,250 | Client | Yes | Trad IRA |
| Small company mutual fund | equity | $8,975 | Client | Yes | Trad IRA |
| Bostonian VUL large cap account | equity | $30,000 | Client | Yes | VUL |
| Bostonian VUL govt bond account | bond | $26,500 | Client | Yes | VUL |

| Insurance Assets | Face Value | Cash Value | Ownership | | Account Type |
|---|---|---|---|---|---|
| Employer life insurance | $128,400 | $0 | Client | | Term life |
| Employer life insurance | $93,000 | $0 | Co-client | | Term life |
| Individual permenent policy | $250,000 | $29,600 | Client | Yes | Universal life |

| Education / Special Funding Assets | Allocation Classification | Value | Ownership | Tax-Shelter | Account Type |
|---|---|---|---|---|---|
| Large cap value mutual fund | equity | $19,600 | trust/other | Yes | 529 Plan |
| Bond index mutual fund | bond | $12,400 | trust/other | Yes | 529 Plan |
| Large index mutual fund | equity | $13,250 | trust/other | Yes | 529 Plan |
| Government bond mutual fund | bond | $6,375 | trust/other | Yes | 529 Plan |

**Exhibit 3.7** Balance Sheet, Tangible Assets

---

**Financial Facilitator Revealed**
The Balance Sheet, Tangible Assets

The tangible asset section of the balance sheet is a record of all real, personal/collectible, and use/lifestyle assets. Its purpose is to track account values and ownership.

| Name / Type of Holding | Value | Ownership |
|---|---|---|
| **Real Assets** | | |
| Primary Residence | $275,000 | joint |
| Secondary Residence | | |
| Vacation Home | | |
| | | |
| | | |
| | | |
| **Personal/Collectible Assets** | | |
| Auto 1 | $23,515 | Client |
| Auto 2 | $17,229 | Co-client |
| Auto 3 | | |
| Watercraft (Boat/Jet-ski) | $4,100 | joint |
| | | |
| | | |
| | | |
| **Use/Lifestyle Assets** | | |
| Furniture | $30,000 | joint |
| Electronics | $12,000 | joint |
| | | |
| | | |
| | | |

---

Financial assets are further delineated by ownership, account type, or tax status of the account (e.g., taxable or tax-advantaged). Assets such as cash, checking accounts, money market mutual funds, and short-term certificates of deposit are summed to calculate total monetary, or liquid, assets available to the client. While **investment assets** can include some of the same financial products as monetary assets, these accounts are designated for longer-term goals, rather than the day-to-day operation of the household. Additional investment assets would include stocks, bonds, or mutual funds.

Retirement assets, which are typically delineated by special tax or ownership status, can include some of the same financial products as the preceding categories. However, separating these assets facilitates financial planning analyses.

Another category of assets that is typically tax-advantaged is savings for education, such as 529 Plan balances, Coverdell savings account balances, and other assets specifically devoted to funding education expenses. In cases where a client has special goals (e.g., funding a house addition or improvement, funding a vacation) or special needs (e.g., accumulating funds for long-term support of a dependent with special needs), these assets should also be clearly identified. Other special needs assets might include annuities or legal settlements. Because of special tax treatment and government regulations, life insurance cash value is also included as a separate category.

In terms of using the worksheets, the placement of an asset in one category or another is left to the discretion of each planner or client. For example, in Exhibit 3.6 the fixed annuity is shown as an investment asset. Another planner or client using the worksheet could just as easily have classified the product as an insurance asset. The same is true of the variable universal life insurance policies (VULs). In the example, the VULs are shown as retirement assets, whereas they could also have been classified as insurance assets. This difference is determined by how this client chooses to view the asset, basically arranging the assets by goal as well as by type.

A client's primary residence is an example of a **real asset**, which is defined as a physical asset, as compared to a financial asset. Other real assets include a second home, ownership interests in vacation property, and other direct real estate holdings. If a client owns collectibles, art, antiques, and other assets, these as well as other personal property such as autos, motorcycles, or boats (which are subject to personal property tax in many states) also are listed as personal/collectible assets. Finally, furniture, appliances, electronics, and all other assets that support daily life are listed as use/lifestyle assets. Carefully listing these three categories of use assets can help a planner spot property and liability insurance needs that may be necessary to fully protect the client. A classification system that is systematically used can also help reduce the work associated with calculating a client's estate tax liability. If all assets and liabilities are shown, with correct ownership listings, it may be easier to determine the gross estate.

Liabilities, or debts, are also listed in hierarchal order on The Balance Sheet, Liabilities and Net Worth worksheet (see Exhibit 3.8). **Current liabilities** include debts due within the month or other accounts that can be paid in full within the next 12 months. Although credit card debt is technically a liability, given the nature of revolving credit, credit cards may or may not be considered current bills. Clients who pay their credit card bills in full every month would have no outstanding credit card liability. This is true even if the bill has not been paid, because the actual expenses (e.g., restaurant bills, shopping charges, entertainment expenses) on the credit card statement are accounted for on the income and expense statement as routine expenses. As long as the bill is, or will be, paid monthly, it would be inappropriate to count the expenses as debt. In this case, the credit card is simply used as a cash management tool for easy payment.

Once all current liabilities have been recorded, **long-term liabilities** must be identified. Examples include mortgage debt, home equity debt, automobile loans, boat and recreational vehicle debt, education loans, life insurance loans, retirement plan loans, and other types of installment loans with durations of more than one year.

When calculating a client's balance sheet using the worksheet, it is important to enter the fair market value of each asset and the full, or outstanding, balance due for each liability. The subtraction of total liabilities from total assets yields net worth. Also, the balance sheet worksheet provides a column for denoting tax-sheltered assets and tax-advantaged liabilities. These classifications provide a useful, and quickly available, reference when considering debt restructuring, tax, or other issues throughout the planning process.

**Exhibit 3.8** Balance Sheet, Liabilities and Net Worth

**Financial Facilitator Revealed**
The Balance Sheet, Liabilities and Net Worth

The liabilities and net worth section of the balance sheet is a record of all current and long-term liabilities. Its purpose is to track account values, types, and ownership as well as summarize the net worth of the client.

LIABILITIES

| Name of Holding | Interest Rate | Amount | Ownership | Tax-Advantage | Account Type |
|---|---|---|---|---|---|
| **Current Liabilities** | | | | | |
| Credit Card | 16.45% | $4,075 | Client | No | Visa |
| Credit Card | 12.95% | $3,250 | Co-client | No | Visa |
| Credit Card | 9.99% | $0 | joint | No | Discover Card |
| Short-term Installment | | | | | |

| Name of Holding | Interest Rate | Amount | Ownership | Tax-Advantage | Account Type |
|---|---|---|---|---|---|
| **Long-term Liabilities** | | | | | |
| First Mortgage (Primary Residence) | 5.88% | $118,876 | joint | Yes | Mortgage |
| Second Mortgage / Home Equity | | | | | |
| Automobile 1 | 6.25% | $15,620 | Client | No | Auto |
| Automobile 2 | | | | | |
| Consumer Loan (Jet-ski) | 0.00% | $2,200 | joint | No | Other |

**Summary Net Worth Statement**

ASSETS

| | |
|---|---|
| Monetary / Liquid | $45,425 |
| Investment | $60,400 |
| Retirement | $306,620 |
| Insurance (cash value only) | $29,600 |
| Education / Special Needs | $51,625 |
| Real | $275,000 |
| Personal / Collectible | $44,844 |
| Use / Lifestyle | + $42,000 |
| Total | $855,514 |

LIABILITIES

| | |
|---|---|
| Current | $7,325 |
| Long-term | + $136,696 |
| Total | $144,021 |

| | |
|---|---|
| NET WORTH | $711,493 |

## Using Financial Ratios to Assess Financial Wellness

Once a client's income and expense and net worth statements have been completed, it is time to interpret the findings. Simply looking at the numbers on a statement generally tells a limited story. Financial ratios help the planner better understand a client's current financial position by providing a quantitative measure of financial health that can be compared to a benchmark. As such, ratios are used to diagnose problems or identify issues not immediately evident from the basic financial statements.

Financial ratios have long been the measures of financial health in the areas of corporate finance, and although the earliest household applications reference the 1960s, it was not until the 1980s and 1990s when much was done in researching the applicability of these ratios on the household level. Although there is still some disagreement over which are the most reliable ratios for predicting future economic health, it has become commonplace to apply a variety of ratios dealing with liquidity (have adequate income to cover expenses) and solvency (have adequate assets to cover liabilities) to household finance.[1]

Not all financial planners use financial ratios in practice, however. Some dislike the use of financial ratios because, by definition, ratios are predicated on benchmarks that fail to account for each client's unique situation. Further, there is no consensus regarding what makes a particular benchmark appropriate because most have not been validated by broad-based research.

Even so, a number of financial ratios are recognized as appropriate for establishing baseline information about clients. Care should be taken to interpret ratios within the broader context of a client's financial situation and not in isolation. These ratios are summarized in Table 3.2 and later described in more detail.

**Table 3.2** Commonly Used Financial Ratios

| Ratio | Formula | Benchmark |
|---|---|---|
| Current ratio | $\dfrac{\text{Monetary assets}}{\text{Current liabilities}}$ | > 1 |
| Emergency fund ratio | $\dfrac{\text{Monetary assets}}{\text{Monthly living expenses}}$ | 3–6 months |
| Savings ratio | $\dfrac{\text{Personal savings and employer contributions}}{\text{Annual gross income}}$ | > 10% |
| Debt ratio | $\dfrac{\text{Total liabilities}}{\text{Total assets}}$ | < 40% |
| Long-term debt coverage ratio | $\dfrac{\text{Annual gross income}}{\text{Total annual long-term debt payments}}$ | > 2.5 |
| Debt-to-income ratio | $\dfrac{\text{Annual consumer credit payment}}{\text{Annual after-tax income}}$ | < 15% |
| Credit usage ratio | $\dfrac{\text{Total credit used}}{\text{Total credit available}}$ | < 30% |
| "Front-end" mortgage qualification ratio | $\dfrac{\text{Annual mortgage (PITI) payment}}{\text{Annual gross income}}$ | < 28% |
| "Back-end" mortgage qualification ratio | $\dfrac{\text{Annual mortgage (PITI) and credit payment}}{\text{Annual gross income}}$ | < 36% |
| Rental expense ratio | $\dfrac{\text{Annual rent and renter's insurance premium}}{\text{Annual gross income}}$ | < 25% |

The **current ratio** is a measure of client liquidity. This ratio determines whether sufficient current monetary assets are available to pay off all outstanding short-term debts. The recommended benchmark for the current ratio is a number greater than one, which means that if all current liabilities were paid the client would still retain some monetary assets.

The **emergency fund ratio**, sometimes called the *month's living expenses covered ratio*, is very important because it indicates how long a client could live in a crisis situation without liquidating nonmonetary assets or being forced into an unfavorable employment situation. A benchmark of three to six months of expenses is recommended. However, in the wake of the 2008/9 financial crisis and resultant structural changes in employment, the average duration of unemployment has dramatically increased, so some planners are now suggesting that up to 12 months of living expenses be maintained in an emergency fund. The rationale for having a range rather than a single value is based on a number of factors in addition to general economic conditions, including job and income stability, the number of household earners and the relative economic contribution of each, types and amount of available credit, the current credit usage ratio, and the current savings ratio.

An alternative approach for calculating the emergency fund ratio uses monetary assets divided by monthly *emergency fund* expenses, rather than monthly *living* expenses. However, defining emergency fund expenses can be problematic. For example, this number can be computed by taking gross living expenses and subtracting federal, state, and FICA taxes paid, dedicated savings, and other expenses that are not essential to the maintenance of a household, assuming that the emergency is caused by loss of employment, disability, or a similar event.

Another approach focuses on fundamental living expenses that clients must continue, such as auto and home loans, insurance premiums, utilities, and other variable expenses (e.g., grocery costs, utilities, home repairs). These everyday living costs, although required to maintain a household, can be reduced.

In effect, emergency fund expenses represent the bare minimum level of expense a household must pay in case of a financial crisis. Common practice dictates that clients have liquid assets or other forms of designated accessible funding to provide three to six months of living expenses, regardless of the method used to calculate the emergency fund ratio. However, it is clear that these methods offer a more or less conservative measure that could be matched to an individual client situation.

One of the most important questions clients ask financial planners is, "Am I saving as much as I should?" The **savings ratio** can be used to answer this question. This ratio sums a client's personal savings and employer contributions to retirement plans, and divides by the client's annual gross income. A benchmark of 10% or more is recommended. In other words, at least 10% of gross earnings should be saved annually. (Note: This ratio is very subjective and should not be blindly applied. Rather, great care should be taken to match clients' total savings need to their total goal-funding need.)

Clients often wonder whether they have too much debt. The **debt ratio** provides a guideline to help answer this question. In effect, this ratio shows the percentage of total assets financed by borrowing. A benchmark of 40% is typically used for this ratio. In other words, the typical client should strive to have no more than four dollars in liabilities for every ten dollars in assets.

As is the case with most financial ratios, the interpretation of this benchmark is flexible, depending on a client's unique circumstances and stage in the life cycle. For example, clients in the early stage of their careers may not have much choice except to exceed the optimal percentage because of car loans, education loans, revolving credit accounts (for furniture and appliance purchases), and other household formation costs.

The **long-term debt coverage ratio** tells how many times a client can make debt payments, based on current income. This formula can be calculated in several ways. A common method involves dividing annual gross income by total annual long-term debt payments. Another method uses after-tax income as the numerator.

Examples of long-term debt payments include mortgage payments, automobile loan payments, student loan payments, and other debts that take more than one year to repay. If a client's monthly credit card payment is large enough that servicing the debt could take more than one year, this amount can also be included in the denominator of the formula.

A long-term debt coverage ratio of at least 2.5 is recommended. The inverse of this formula tells an interesting story. The inverse of a long-term debt coverage ratio of 2.5 is 0.40. This means that a client should allocate no more than 40% of income to cover long-term debt payments.

Related to the long-term debt coverage ratio is the **debt-to-income ratio,** which measures the percentage of take-home pay committed to consumer credit repayment, defined as all revolving and installment nonmortgage debts. A ratio of less than 10% of take-home, or disposable, income is optimal, although up to 15% is considered safe. Between 15% and 20% is considered a questionable practice, while consumer debt repayments in excess of 20% of take-home pay are usually considered a serious problem. Because automatic payments, optional salary deferral retirement plans, and other employee benefits can further reduce after-tax income, it is important that planners use care when calculating this ratio. However the interpretation is rather clear: when clients commit 15% to 20% (or more) of disposable, or take-home, pay to consumer debt repayment, usually little is left for meeting all other financial obligations.

The **credit usage ratio** is not only a factor in determining the adequacy of the emergency fund ratio, but it is also one of the key factors in determining credit score. High credit usage, such as balances above 50% of the credit limit, is usually considered negative. This is because creditors may think more credit is being used than can be repaid. (Note: For clients with very high credit scores, as little as 20% credit usage can have a minor negative impact.)

Lenders also use mortgage qualification ratios to measure repayment ability for mortgage qualification. Variations of debt-to-income ratios, in this case referred to as *mortgage qualification ratios*, are used to determine how much of a client's annual income would be used to pay for proposed monthly mortgage and existing nonmortgage, or consumer, debt payments. Two debt limit ratios are widely used.

The first is called the *28% Rule*, or what some refer to as the **front-end mortgage qualification ratio** or the *mortgage debt service ratio*. This ratio results from a comparison of the projected total mortgage payment for principal, interest, taxes, and insurance (PITI) to gross household income. To pass this ratio, PITI generally cannot exceed 28% of gross annual income.

The second qualification ratio is called the *36% Rule*, the **back-end mortgage qualification ratio**, or the *debt repayment ratio*. This rule states that a client should pay no more than 36% of gross income on the projected mortgage PITI plus other regular monthly consumer debt payments (e.g., credit card, student loan, auto).

These qualification ratios are currently applied throughout the mortgage industry for conventional loans, although the range may vary slightly by lender. Special loan programs or government-subsidized loan programs allow for more lenient ratios. Clients whose ratios exceed these benchmarks may not qualify for a mortgage or refinance option. If allowed, a lender can require a higher rate of interest or suggest using other available assets to reduce debt. One final but important note: for a client to qualify for a maximum mortgage, these two ratios implicitly limit other consumer debt payments to 8% of gross income. This corresponds closely to the original debt-to-income ratio that recommends a consumer credit payment limit of 10% of take-home income.

The rental expense ratio compares the cost of rent and renter's insurance to annual income. Renter's expenses are not too different from homeowner's expenses in that the rental income likely subsidizes principal, interest, taxes, and property insurance for the landlord, who also benefits from the equity in the property. Given this analogy to PITI, it is prudent to apply a slightly stricter benchmark to the rental expense ratio (< 25% to < 28% of gross income) similar to the front-end mortgage ratio. Although the cost of rent in major urban areas could make this benchmark unachievable, offsetting reductions in other expenses that are not part of the urban lifestyle can balance the increased housing costs.

## Document and Evaluate the Client's Current Financial Situation

A primary purpose for conducting a financial situation analysis is to determine, at the outset of a financial engagement, the financial strengths and weaknesses a client brings to the planning relationship. Ideal clients have a strong net worth position, with a large and growing investment asset base and declining liabilities. Although they may have debt, it will be primarily tax-efficient debt. On the income and expense side of their financial life, ideal clients will start the financial planning process with available and potentially expanding discretionary cash flow. These clients, from the moment the services of a financial planner are engaged, will be ready to begin implementing recommendations. In short, model clients have the cash flow and net worth to fully take advantage of available financial planning strategies and products.

Over the course of a planning career, a financial planner is likely to see all kinds of clients with diverse financial situations. Equally diverse may be clients' attitudes and willingness to work with a planner collaboratively to achieve financial goals and follow sound financial advice. Regardless of how the client-planner relationship evolves, it is important initially to communicate to clients that they are managing some of their financial affairs well and to compliment these successes, even if they are doing other things imprudently. The following discussion highlights some of the basic issues a planner should evaluate before moving forward in the planning process.

### Evaluate Income, Expenses, and Net Worth

Some planners initially consider where or how a client spends money. Others unquestionably accept spending patterns reported by a client. Certain benchmarks, usually developed in-house by the planner based on regional or national spending data, can be used to suggest that the client might be overspending or not effectively managing cash flow. Some planners—and clients—are reluctant to engage in a discussion of the client's lifestyle and spending patterns. Depending on the planner-client relationship and the amounts of income and discretionary cash flow available, the discussion may or may not be necessary.

For some clients with sufficient income to fund living expenses and identified goals, the discussion may be moot, regardless of the amount of income or net worth. Other clients, again regardless of the amount of income or net worth, may be overspenders who will resist the planner's efforts to address the topic. For these reasons, a review of spending may be perilous to the planner-client working relationship. Asking a client to reduce expenditures may be paramount to asking a chocoholic to give up chocolate. It might be the right thing to do, but it still may be met with resistance.

On the other hand, engaging a client in this discussion can lead to increased client motivation to seriously review and weigh the benefits of the current lifestyle against the benefits of other short- or long-term goals. Discussing income and expense relationships can also be a simple and effective way to communicate a very important message: the client is ultimately responsible for both crafting and accomplishing the financial plan. In very simple terms, the planner can be a knowledgeable coach, but not a financial magician. Although a review of spending patterns may or may not yield a sufficient increase in discretionary cash flow for funding the planning needs identified, it can be a simple, beneficial, and insightful exercise for the advisor and the client.

The goal of maximizing earnings while maintaining access to monetary assets can also be addressed in a review of income, expenses, and net worth. An appraisal of account types and balances, as well as rates of returns being earned, can offer options not previously considered by the client. For example, it may be wise to move large balances in liquid low-earning accounts to other types of investments to provide a moderate increase in cash flow or earnings. Alternatively, such funds could be repositioned and used for funding goals or reducing debt without compromising the need for current spending or sufficient cash reserves.

In summary, whether a planner chooses to confront or ignore a client's spending patterns, the information gained from a thorough review of the supporting financial documents and diagnostic ratios can offer valuable insights. Increased discretionary cash flow is the optimal result; but the information gained could serve as a foundation for more fully understanding other client goals and objectives.

## Build an Emergency Savings Fund

The need for a client emergency fund equivalent to three to six months of expenses is almost an unchallenged assumption. Factors that can affect the number of months of needed expenses include job security and consistency of income (e.g., salary vs. commission), number of household earners, and availability of unused credit capacity.

What is less agreed upon is how a client should fund an account to weather a financial crisis. Obviously, the most common approach is to increase monetary assets. However, this is not the only option. In a low-interest-rate environment, it may be better to designate other assets as available for emergency income if needed, and instead invest some of the monetary assets more aggressively to earn a higher rate of return. If a client does not have sufficient monetary assets or chooses to reduce monetary assets, other assets or income sources should be designated.

As might be expected, one source can be designated as, or a combination of sources can be combined to create, an emergency savings fund, contingent on the individual client situation. The key factor is that the asset or source of emergency income be designated and the ramifications of this decision fully considered.

If a planner and client believe that some or all of the assets should be readily available to meet emergencies, highly liquid short-term savings alternatives typically are recommended. Monetary assets that pay the highest rate of interest should be chosen, all other factors held constant. Possible accounts include money market deposit accounts, money market mutual funds, Treasury bills, and other liquid assets.

Certificates of deposit (CDs) and other assets with a distribution penalty (e.g., EE and I Savings Bonds have a penalty in the first five years) can offer safety of principal and competitive returns, but they could lack needed liquidity unless a laddered approach is used. In a ladder approach, at least one month of living expenses would be held in a highly liquid account. Assets equivalent to two to three months of expenses would be held in other liquid assets, such as Treasury bills. Three-month CDs would then be used for the remaining assets. As the Treasury bills and CDs mature, the ladder would be restructured so that funds equal to at least three months of expenses were always available.

Some planners scoff at the idea of holding three to six months' living expenses in low-yielding assets. These risk-tolerant planners argue that certain types of bonds, stocks, or mutual funds can be used for emergency fund purposes. It should be noted, however, that these planners are in the minority. Should the assets have experienced a loss in value when needed for an emergency expense, an untimely sale, without the flexibility of waiting for the value to rebound could offset the possibility of a higher rate of return. Short-term bonds and bond mutual funds are recommended as a compromise position, offering a safer alternative than stocks or equity mutual funds and, perhaps, a slightly higher yield than traditional monetary assets.

Other planners assert that although an emergency fund is essential and some level of monetary assets should be maintained, the choice of assets designated can be flexible. In other words, the emergency account can be funded, as explained above, or the account can be "unfunded," such as with a credit source. For example, the cash value of a life insurance policy or other investment assets can be designated as a source of emergency income. Credit card and home equity lines of credit can be used as substitutes for, or supplements to, traditional monetary assets within an emergency fund. For clients who pay their credit cards in full each month, the credit line available might be thought of as an emergency fund.

Of more relevance for emergencies is a **home equity line of credit**. These open lines of credit are pre-established with a lending institution, but the client is under no obligation to use the loan. In fact, many institutions stipulate no costs to maintain an open, unused line of credit, so establishing one to have funds available when needed can be an easy solution. When the credit line is accessed, a payment schedule, similar to that for credit cards, is used to determine monthly debt payments.

There are potential disadvantages associated with this method of creating an emergency fund. First, the client's home is the collateral for the line of credit. Without careful use and repayment, this could put the home at risk. Second, this strategy might not work unless the line of credit is established prior to a financial emergency. This may not be an impediment if the home has adequate equity and the client's credit score and income support a quick establishment of the credit line. If this is a recommended strategy within a comprehensive financial plan, the client should be encouraged to implement the strategy sooner rather than later.

### Restructure Unsecured and Secured Consumer Debt

One of the best places to look to increase a client's level of discretionary cash flow is on the liability side of the net worth statement. The review of a client's type of debt, as well as the available and outstanding balances, may reveal the need for better debt management. Issues can stem from the client's attitudes about money, as well as the financial products selected.

For instance, a client could have difficulty spending assets in a savings account to reduce, or pay off, a high-interest revolving credit balance. The client could be indicating a common trait of mental accounting by perceptually accounting for savings and debt differently. Client attitudes and account preferences must be balanced against the mathematical logic of interest earned and interest paid.

Exploring these issues with a client requires patience as well as the time to provide some fundamental financial education. Two options for restructuring consumer credit to optimize cash flow include (1) paying off unsecured debt with assets paying little or no after-tax return, or (2) replacing unsecured non-tax-deductible debt with tax-efficient debt. Both strategies are considered in more detail below.

In almost all cases, efforts should be made to pay off high-interest non-tax-deductible debt using monetary assets earning low interest. The interest rate paid on credit card or other unsecured debt almost always exceeds interest earned on monetary assets. If a client still has short-term debt after reducing the balance with monetary assets, other short-term investment assets could be considered. The choice of which asset to use is contingent on the rate of return generated, although client preferences also must be considered. An EE Savings Bond, for instance, earning less than 3% compounded semiannually may be an appropriate asset to pay off a credit card charging 15% compounded monthly. The cost of the high-interest debt, compared to the after-tax rate of interest earned, offsets the advantage of holding monetary assets.

Sometimes clients will be apprehensive about liquidating savings because they will feel worse off, temporarily. Unless there is an immediate need for monetary assets and no alternatives can be identified, using these assets to reduce debt is typically a good idea. When viewed from a strict financial ratio perspective, liquidating assets could cause a client to fall below emergency fund benchmark levels. However, paying off short-term debt leads to an instant increase in monthly discretionary cash flow that can be used to fund other goals or to rebuild monetary assets, assuming a client makes a commitment to avoid incurring revolving debt.

In some instances, restructuring assets and liabilities is not feasible or possible. Some monetary or investment assets could have particular significance or family value that excludes them from consideration in cash flow management planning. The client could prefer another alternative, regardless of the mathematical rationale. For clients who cannot manage cash flow to pay credit cards in full monthly, it may be necessary to consider other remedial debt management strategies.

Clients also might have a marginal loss of income from reduced interest on investment earnings. But in most cases, this trade-off is an attractive one. There is no change in net worth because, although an asset was used, there was an offsetting reduction in a liability, leaving a net zero change. In sum, using low-yielding assets to repay debt can have a major impact on the financial situation, countered by a modest impact on a client's tax plan.

The costs and benefits of liquidating longer-term investment assets to pay off non-tax-deductible debt must be carefully considered. This strategy subjects a client to the verities of market conditions. A client who sells an investment at a depressed price will be less satisfied than a client who uses monetary assets, if available. A break-even sale, or one with a gain, can offer the client fiscal benefits as well as psychological benefits from the elimination of the debt.

However, it is important to consider the cost to the goal the assets supported, as well as the after-tax return on the assets compared to the interest rate on the non-tax-deductible debt. Selling an investment to pay off debt could cause an unexpected tax liability, as well as commissions. However, liquidating an investment asset to pay off debt may be prudent when the sale can generate a needed capital loss.

If credit cards and other high-interest debts cannot be eliminated with monetary assets, it could be appropriate to analyze the costs and benefits of replacing these liabilities with tax-efficient debt. Using a home equity loan or line of credit is one way to increase discretionary cash flow and obtain an itemized tax deduction, if applicable, and the client is not subject to the Alternative Minimum Tax. It might also be wise to use a client's home equity to pay off automobile debt or to make a future purchase.

It could, however, be more appropriate for a client to finance certain purchases (e.g., furniture, appliances, automobiles) using manufacturer low- or zero-percent financing. Although the interest may not be tax deductible, the after-tax cost of the loan may be lower than that offered by a home equity line of credit or loan. Multiple types of credit also increase the FICO credit score, which affects rates on all types of borrowing.

*Example*: A client plans to purchase a new car that costs $30,000. The car manufacturer is offering 0% financing for three years or $3,000 cash back. If the client is in the 28% marginal tax bracket, can borrow on a home equity loan at 5%, and has a required rate of return of 6% for investments, how should the client make the purchase?

At first glance, the 0% financing option looks attractive. However, two additional factors must be analyzed. One is that the client is comparing a tax-advantaged financing option (assuming the client is not subject to the Alternative Minimum Tax) to another that does not offer the same tax advantages. To make the two options similar, the client must determine the effective after-tax rate for the home equity loan using the following formula:

After-Tax Rate = Nominal Rate × (1 - Marginal Tax Bracket)

After-Tax Rate = 5.0% × (1 - 0.28) = 3.6%

Now that the two loans are using equivalent interest rates, the monthly payments should be calculated. In the dealer-financed option, if the initial loan amount is $30,000, the monthly payment is $833.33 ($30,000 ÷ 36 months).

In the home equity loan option, where the initial amount financed is $27,000 ($30,000 - $3,000 cash back), the monthly payment is only $792.35 when using the effective after-tax home equity loan rate of 3.6%.

$$\$27,000 = \frac{PMT}{0.003}\left[1 - \frac{1}{1.003^{36}}\right]$$
$$\$792.35 = PMT$$

The second consideration is the difference in the two payments that could be invested in another account earning the 6% required rate of return. Therefore, by calculating the present value of a 36-month annuity where the payments are $40.98 ($833.33 - $792.35), the client can determine that using the home equity loan results in a $1,347.05 lower present value cost.

$$PVA = \frac{\$40.98}{0.005}\left[1 - \frac{1}{1.005^{36}}\right]$$
$$PVA = \$1,347.05$$

### Mortgage Debt: Primary Mortgage and Home Equity Line of Credit (HELOC)

Gone are the days of 100% financing and no-documentation loans where homeowners could use their home equity like a piggy bank. In the aftermath of the 2008/9 financial crisis, lenders have returned to more stringent underwriting standards. To consider a real estate loan, a lender will in most cases require a homeowner to have at least 20% initial or remaining equity in the home, have sufficient income to meet the qualification ratios previously discussed, be able to substantiate all sources of income claimed on the loan application, and have a high credit score. For qualified homeowners, however, the resulting low-interest-rate environment has created a great opportunity.

Whenever mortgage rates are declining, clients should consider refinancing alternatives. Generally, refinancing makes sense for a client whenever the available mortgage rate is at least 1% to 2% less than the client's current mortgage rate. Depending on the client situation and the costs to refinance, savings could be worthwhile with as little as a 0.5% to 0.75% reduction in annual interest rate. In addition to rate and refinance costs, other factors to consider are estimated time in the house (i.e., the life of the loan), credit history, current income, and the current loan-to-value of the home.

Refinancing can offer valuable benefits matched to the individual client's financial situation. There are three primary reasons to refinance mortgage debt: (1) to reduce the payment amount; (2) to reduce the total amount of interest paid over the remaining life of a loan; and (3) to take available equity out of the house; although most often clients consider refinancing when interest rates have fallen sufficiently to make it cost-effective. The reduction in mortgage interest rate can reduce payments (depending on the loan term) and the total interest cost of the loan. Other clients could benefit from the option to increase the amount of the mortgage and to use the proceeds for other needs, or to pay off non-tax-advantaged debt. Refinancing can even benefit clients who can afford to pay off the mortgage but choose to retain financing or perhaps even extend the payoff period to allow other assets to remain invested, thereby targeting a higher rate of return than the cost of borrowing. Creativity with the mortgage factors of balance, term, and interest rate can help a client retain or increase financial flexibility and improve overall cash flow management.

Refinancing is typically not cost free, because it involves paying all closing costs (commonly estimated between 1% and 3% of the value of the mortgage to cover legal fees, bank fees, title search fees, and appraisal work) and any discount points associated with the new mortgage. However, many homeowners choose to borrow an extra amount to cover these costs, provided the value of the home allows this option. This alternative, used by many who refinance, marginally increases the monthly mortgage payment but allows the client to avoid funding closing costs from monetary assets or current income.

---

#### Financial Situation Tip: Home Affordable Refinance Program (HARP)

In 2009 the federal government enacted legislation and provided funding for HARP. This program, set to expire on December 31, 2013, allows homeowners with conventional mortgages backed by either Fannie Mae or Freddie Mac to refinance their existing balances at a lower rate to reduce their payments or change from a variable rate mortgage to a fixed-rate mortgage at greatly reduced out-of-pocket expense.

To qualify, the current mortgage must be (1) on an owner-occupied primary residence, (2) up-to-date with no late payments in the past 12 months, and (3) the homeowner must be able to afford the new payment

The program was established primarily to assist homeowners who owed more on their mortgages than the market value of their homes (known as being underwater); however, any qualifying homeowner can take advantage of the program. In fact, the greatest benefit of the program in the wake of the massive decline in property values is that for homeowners looking to convert an adjustable-rate mortgage to a fixed-rate mortgage there is no loan-to-value maximum —a criterion that would typically disqualify underwater borrowers.

Additional government-sponsored programs are available for borrowers in other circumstances. Most of these programs are currently scheduled to expire on December 31, 2012. For more information on these programs visit www.makinghomeaffordable.gov

---

Assuming the client can meet the mortgage qualification ratios, another option is to increase the balance of the new mortgage above the payoff on the existing mortgage. Known as a **cash-out refinance**, this option can be used to consolidate other debts into the new mortgage balance (e.g., car loans or credit card liabilities) or to generate funds for other goals or needs. Consolidating other debt can decrease the monthly total payment relative to the multiple payments and offer the benefit of converting non-tax-advantaged debt to tax-deductible debt, assuming the client is not subject to the Alternative Minimum Tax.

However, this strategy effectively extends the repayment for the consumer debt over the life of the mortgage—a disadvantage not to be overlooked—unless the mortgage rate is substantially lower than that of the consumer debt. Nevertheless, the consumer debt is refinanced over the life of the mortgage, typically 15 to 30 years, far beyond the useful life of most consumer durables or nondurables.

Finally, the client must be aware that home equity cannot be viewed as the ATM machine of the future. But increasing the mortgage balance can, in effect, increase monthly discretionary cash flow and provide funding for other client goals and planner recommendations.

Central to the refinance decision is the choice of mortgage duration that best corresponds with a client's overall financial goals. For instance, if a client would like to retire in 20 years, it might be wise to choose a 20-year mortgage, although the monthly payment will be higher than for a comparable 30-year mortgage. Conversely, the 30-year mortgage without a prepayment penalty could be a better alternative. The lower monthly mortgage payments associated with a 30-year mortgage allow greater financial flexibility now and the payments could, over the course of the loan, become relatively minor in inflation-adjusted terms. Those who favor a longer-maturity loan argue that a client can usually prepay a 30-year simple interest mortgage to, in effect, make it a shorter-term loan without sacrificing itemized interest deductions or financial flexibility.

An aversion to housing debt could make a long-term refinance option unattractive to some clients. They would prefer to make higher monthly mortgage payments to eliminate the debt in 15 years. Other planners and clients argue that using a 15-year mortgage does not take advantage of time value of money principles. Although interest rates with a 15-year mortgage are typically lower than for a longer-term loan, which means lower total interest costs, the impact of the higher monthly payments on cash flow management should not be overlooked. Once the debt is repaid, reallocating the mortgage payment for other goals could be an attractive benefit to some clients.

Arguments for the optimal mortgage term are open for debate when the original mortgage has a remaining term of more than 20 to 25 years. In most cases, it is best to refinance mortgages with a term of 20 years or less remaining with a similar maturity loan. The reason for this recommendation is that clients with 15 years or less remaining on a 30-year mortgage could also be closer to retirement. These clients may not be able, or willing, to make a mortgage payment, albeit a small one, in retirement. However, it may be prudent to recommend a 30-year mortgage regardless of a client's age, if (1) this is consistent with other financial plans (e.g., to live in the house for only a limited time prior to sale or relocation), and (2) the mortgage allows for prepayment.

Sometimes a simple 30- or 15-year mortgage option will not work for a client. The monthly principal and interest payment associated with these traditional loans could exceed a client's budget or severely restrict discretionary cash flow for meeting other goals. Perhaps the client does not plan to live in the house for more than five to seven years but would prefer to have lower fixed payments during that time.

These and other situations often call for the use of an adjustable-rate mortgage or some other form of mortgage loan. An **adjustable-rate mortgage** (ARM) is one in which the initial interest rate is typically lower than that on a traditional fixed-rate mortgage. Depending on the ARM contract, however, the interest rate on the loan can fluctuate in the future. Although adjustable rate mortgages typically offer an initial rate that is lower than the comparable fixed-rate alternative, this is not always the case. In times of interest rate uncertainty or a rising-rate environment, an ARM might have a higher initial rate, although that certainly decreases the favorability of the option.

Although certainly not as prevalent as during the height of the 2003–2007 real estate bubble, adjustable rate mortgages continue to offer flexibility to prospective homeowners who don't mind trading the risk of a variable interest rate for a lower rate. Although different financial institutions structure ARM products differently, it is important to note that all rate increases are subject to the restrictions established in the mortgage agreement. Although restrictions can vary, a 2/6 rate restriction is common with many lenders. This means that the rate can increase a maximum of 2% per year and no more than 6% over the life of the loan. Rate cap restrictions are always preferable to payment caps, which can result in negative amortization with significant rate increases. Some of the most popular forms of ARM products are described below.

- 10/1, 7/1, 5/1, or 3/1-year ARM: The interest rate and monthly payment remain fixed for 10, 7, 5, or 3 years, respectively. Beginning the subsequent year, the interest rate is adjusted annually for the remainder of the term, typically either 20 or 30 years.

- 5/5, 3/3, or 1-year ARM: The interest rate and monthly payment remain fixed for 5, 3, or 1 year(s), respectively. There are subsequent interest rate adjustments for each 5-, 3-, or 1-year period, respectively, until the loan is repaid.

- 7/23 or 5/25-year ARM: The interest rate and monthly payment remain fixed for 7 or 5 years, respectively. In the next year, the client can convert the mortgage into a traditional loan based on prevailing rates.

- 7-year Balloon: The interest rate and monthly payment remain fixed for 7 years. At the end of 7 years, the loan is due in full. Usually, the client must refinance at the prevailing rate and pay all closing costs for the new mortgage.

Clients who choose an ARM over a fixed-rate loan are, in some cases, speculating on the future. Some anticipate that increasing salary levels will offset potential mortgage payment increases. Others plan to refinance to lock in a lower rate if rates start to increase. Others reason that interest rates at the predetermined time of interest rate adjustment will be equal to or lower than when the loan originated.

When long-term rates begin to increase, clients should consider the benefits of a fixed-rate mortgage relative to their ARM. This is especially true if a client plans to live in the house for a long time. Finally, it is important that clients fully understand the short-term benefits and potentially long-term implications of an ARM on cash flow management. For clients who do not anticipate living in the house for many years, an ARM could be the best option.

### Renting: A "New" Cash Flow Management Tool

For the last nearly 70 years, home ownership has been the linchpin of the American Dream; unless you lived in cost-prohibitive areas of New York, California, or Hawaii; however, on the heels of the housing crisis the dream may be changing. After peaking at more than 69% in early 2005, the homeownership rate has declined to just over 66% in 2011.2 This change in homeownership desire and capability is part of the reason real estate prices have declined and stagnated. This is terrible news for current homeowners, but possibly great news for prospective homeowners—those who previously rented.

Although renting has advantages such as a low or no down payment, no market risk for the occupant, and possibly greater near-term affordability, many have historically believed that the disadvantages outweigh the advantages—so much so that renting was almost relegated to a second-class citizen status reserved for college students. Even young singles and families wanted their own home in which to live their lives. This all began to change in the mid-2000s. With the specter of negative equity, increasing payments due to adjustable-rate mortgages, and potential foreclosure, many prospective homeowners decided that renting was not only a viable but an attractive alternative.

This housing choice presents several additional opportunities for financial planning discussions. From a cash flow perspective renting may seem very different from owning, but one key similarity that is often overlooked is that rent is also an adjustable payment that should be planned for. A renter can see a change in rent every contract period; sometimes this adjustment can reduce the cost, but in most cases rent prices increase. In some cases, these increases can be dramatic.

Although it is easiest to consider the financial aspects of the housing decision, a financial planner should also recognize that it is also a lifestyle choice. Clients who have always lived in densely populated areas (e.g., New York City) or even clients who may originally be from another country (e.g., Japan, India, most of Europe) are accustomed to and potentially prefer renting.

## STRATEGIES

### Review Prospective Financial Situation Strategies

Few Americans today are free from credit card debt; estimates suggest that only about a third of users pay the monthly balance in full. A large proportion of Americans would have a very difficult time funding three months of emergency expenses. Fewer still are financially savvy enough to know how to increase their discretionary cash flow.

This does not mean that the average American does not need financial planning, nor does it mean that the products and strategies available to model clients are out of reach for the average client. What it does mean, however, is that the planner and client must carefully rank and implement recommendations in a way that will offer maximum benefit. Furthermore, it is important to keep the balance between cash flow and net worth in mind. Clients with a high debt balance, such as student loan debt incurred by a professional, must be considered in light of earnings potential and long-term prospects for asset growth.

Once a client's core financial strengths and weaknesses have been identified, the financial planning process turns to a review of the strategies available to improve management of the financial situation.

### Identify Prospective Cash Flow Management Strategies

Any number of financial planning techniques can be used to increase discretionary cash flow, increase assets, or reduce and possibly eliminate non-tax-efficient liabilities. The choice of strategies will depend entirely on the situation being addressed. Although this is true of all planning decisions, the fundamental connection between cash flow and net worth management and a client's lifestyle cannot be overlooked. The following product and procedural strategies represent just a few approaches that could be used when working with clients.

### Product Strategy 1: Refinance Mortgage with a Fixed-Rate, Fixed-Term Loan

**Advantage**: This strategy offers clients one of the best ways to decrease expenditures for housing while increasing annual discretionary cash flow, assuming the term of the new loan is equal to or greater than the loan being replaced. A break-even analysis comparing monthly savings to total refinancing costs will indicate how long it will take to break even on a refinance decision.

**Disadvantage**: Disadvantages include the expenses associated with closing and the possibility that replacing a mortgage with a mortgage of a shorter duration will increase annual expenses. Interest for itemized deductions could decrease, resulting in a marginal increase in tax liability. A complete break-even analysis should be completed to determine the payback period and cost effectiveness of any refinance strategy.

### Product Strategy 2: Obtain, or Refinance with, an Adjustable-rate Mortgage (ARM)

**Advantage:** This strategy is effective when a client must significantly reduce housing expenses to increase annual discretionary cash flow. The strategy works best in a declining-interest-rate environment, unless the adjustable-rate mortgage offers conversion to a fixed rate. The strategy can also work well if the sale of a client's house is planned during the initial fixed-rate period of the ARM.

**Disadvantage:** Using an adjustable-rate mortgage could subject a client to fluctuations in interest rates in the future. If rates increase, a client's annual housing expenses will likely increase as the mortgage payment rises. This strategy also presents clients with refinancing risks—if rates do increase, a client could be forced to lock in a new mortgage with a higher interest rate.

### Product Strategy 3: Use an Interest-only Mortgage

**Advantage:** Interest-only mortgages, as the name implies, allow a client to make monthly mortgage payments consisting entirely of interest for a predetermined number of years, after which the payments include both principal and interest. This strategy can reduce a monthly mortgage payment by as much as 50% when compared to a conventional mortgage.

This is an effective strategy for clients who need to decrease housing expenditures as one method to increase discretionary cash flow. It is also a potentially effective strategy for the disciplined client who believes earnings on the money invested elsewhere will exceed the mortgage rate. Interest-only mortgages are also attractive for those who know that they will live in the house for only a short period of time. In some high-priced housing markets, an interest-only mortgage can be an effective way to finance a house that would be unaffordable with a traditional mortgage.

**Disadvantage:** This strategy is based on the premise that future housing prices will steadily appreciate, which, as we have recently learned, is not always the case. Clients who use this approach are assuming that the future home value will be substantially greater than the mortgage amount, so that future equity will be sufficient to reduce the outstanding mortgage. If housing prices do not increase as predicted, an interest-only mortgage can leave a client with a large outstanding balance, even after paying mortgage payments for many years.

### Product Strategy 4: Consolidate Debts with a Home Equity Loan

**Advantage:** This strategy offers the benefit of converting non-tax-advantaged consumer debt into a home equity loan with a lower interest rate and tax-deductible interest (assuming that a client is not subject to the AMT, and that the non-acquisition-based debt does not exceed $100,000). Another reason to consider this strategy is that total loan payments could be lower than payments made individually on unconsolidated debt. This is true because, generally, home equity loans carry a longer duration and a lower interest rate than open-ended loans and collateralized loans typically used to purchase assets such as automobiles.

**Disadvantage:** Although this strategy can result in increased levels of discretionary cash flow, using a home equity loan to consolidate debt places the client's home at risk in case of default.

### Product Strategy 5: Establish a Home Equity Line of Credit as a Source of Emergency Funds

**Advantage:** This strategy is useful whenever assets designated for emergency savings are depleted for another purpose, or when a client's monetary assets are insufficient to meet the minimum of three to six months of emergency expenses. Essentially, the line of credit substitutes for actual assets. A home equity line of credit can typically be obtained with little or no closing costs, and there is no requirement that it be used.

**Disadvantage:** Anything purchased using a line of credit subjects the client's home equity to risk. However, this option offers several benefits over other types of consumer credit or lending sources. Spending of equity should be restricted to true emergency situations. Failure to meet qualification standards could restrict the use of this strategy or increase the associated costs.

### Procedural Strategy 1: Pay off Unsecured Debt with Assets Earning Lower Rates of Return

**Advantage:** This strategy is most appropriate for clients who currently have a revolving balance on their credit cards or other unsecured debt. Implementing this strategy decreases annual interest expenses, thereby increasing annual discretionary cash flow for funding other financial goals or objectives. In the event of an emergency where assets are needed immediately, the client could re-incur debt, if necessary, to cover expenses. This strategy applies to a wide range of client situations.

**Disadvantage:** Two potential disadvantages are associated with this strategy. First, some clients find it psychologically difficult to reduce the level of cash or cash equivalents in their portfolio. Suggesting this strategy could cause stress for a client struggling with the thought of being "cash poor" until the liquidated assets can be restored. Second, for clients who fail to control spending, paying off debt could lead to the accumulation of more debt and a further reduction in net worth.

### Procedural Strategy 2: Identify Client Expenses That Can Be Reduced

**Advantage:** This strategy could uncover hidden or excessive lifestyle expenses that a client does not consciously consider on a daily basis. The importance of other goals or objectives could override the short-term benefits of these expenses and encourage the client to curtail or eliminate these costs. This is a very sensitive discussion that must balance a planner's knowledge of expense categories relative to household income with a sincere appreciation of a client's values and spending motives. However, this strategy can effectively increase discretionary cash flow without the cost of incurring liabilities or selling assets.

**Disadvantage:** Typically, clients are committed to their lifestyle and the associated expenses. Asking a client to reduce or eliminate select expenses could cause a negative reaction. Nevertheless, a planner must clearly communicate the benefits (short- or long-term) of this strategy and give the client responsibility for the identification of acceptable spending changes.

### Procedural Strategy 3: Use the Cash Value of Life Insurance as an Emergency Source of Income

**Advantage:** The cash value portion of a life insurance policy can be designated and, if necessary, used as a source of emergency income. The cost of the loan is relatively inexpensive, and no qualification standards must be met.

**Disadvantage:** Taking a policy loan generally reduces the death benefit and the cash surrender value while the loan is outstanding. The loan also incurs interest expense. Depending on the policy, the return on the cash value could be reduced until the loan is fully repaid. Loans against the policy value reduce the amount of assets available for earnings used to offset future premium payments. Further, loans that go unserviced for too long (i.e., no regular payments being submitted) can cause a policy to lapse, which can create a taxable event that could generate a substantial embedded tax liability.

### Procedural Strategy 4: Use Financial Assets to De-lever Mortgage Debt

**Advantage:** Using financial assets to reduce the outstanding balance lowers the loan-to-value (LTV) ratio of the mortgage and could increase the options available for refinancing. Banks are more willing to finance real estate that has an LTV ratio of less than 80%. This means a homeowner could have a wider choice of mortgage options, including a shorter loan term, a fixed versus variable rate, and a lower interest rate. Using assets that have a lower expected rate of return than the after-tax interest rate on the mortgage would also optimize overall investment returns.

**Disadvantage:** Using financial assets to pay down mortgage debt can reduce financial flexibility in the event of an emergency or could have unintended consequences on the achievement of other financial goals. Additionally, using tax-sheltered assets would most likely trigger income tax and a tax penalty. Another consequence is that a lower mortgage balance would reduce the interest paid and therefore reduce itemized deductions.

## CHAPTER-BASED CASE STUDY

## A Client-based Financial Situation Recommendation Example

At times, refinancing a client's mortgage can offer one of the best ways to generate additional discretionary cash flow. Again, there are three primary reasons to refinance mortgage debt: (1) to reduce the payment amount and thereby increase discretionary cash flow; (2) to reduce the total amount of interest paid over the remaining life of the loan; and (3) to take available equity out of the property. Adjusting the balance, term, and interest rate of the mortgage offers the planner and client a number of options for creating financial flexibility and improved overall cash flow management—whether for an initial purchase or a refinance.

For those with available monetary assets, the option to pay loan discount points is another consideration. A **discount point** is 1% of the amount borrowed and is treated as prepaid interest on the loan. Mortgage lenders often allow a client to *buy down* the stated interest rate for the mortgage by paying *points*. The choice of prepaying interest with discount points should be based on a review of the following factors:

- *The break-even period relative to an assumption about how long the client expects to live in the house.* The break-even period can be calculated in a number of ways.

  The first and most common method determines the number of months required to recover the cost of paying points and closing costs by dividing these costs by the difference in monthly principal and interest payments. However, this method ignores the time value of money, in that it assumes that the value of a lower payment paid today and the value of that same lower payment made in five years are equal; of course they are not.

  The second, more accurate, method considers the present value of the future stream of savings resulting from the difference in loan payments over the time period required to recoup the cost of the discount points and closing costs. It also considers the loan balance remaining at the end of the projection period. Note that this break-even approach does not address whether a client will save money on total interest paid over the course of the loan. This calculation simply shows how long it will take to recoup total closing costs if a loan is refinanced.

  The third break-even method discussed takes the present value of the future stream of savings resulting from the difference in interest expense over the time period required to recoup the cost of the discount points and closing costs. This method could be preferable over the standard breakeven if the term of the loan is shortened, thus increasing the payment amount. An increased payment, while lessening the total interest cost, can increase the break-even period. In some cases, if the new payment is higher then the old payment, a traditional break-even point will never be reached. However, this method is the most cumbersome because the difference in interest payments is neither constant nor variable at a fixed rate. Therefore, the present value of the interest payment difference cannot be solved for using a present value of annuity or present value of a geometric series; it must be solved for using a summation formula in a spreadsheet.

  With all of these methods, the shorter the time period the client anticipates living in the house, the less attractive paying points and closing costs becomes. Financing closing expenses as part of the mortgage will exacerbate this by increasing the monthly payment and extending the break-even period.

- *The future value of the after-tax earnings on the monetary assets used to pay points relative to the future value of the interest savings between the two mortgages.* Stated another way, paying points and closing costs out of pocket is not cost effective if the after-tax rate of return on the investment exceeds the mortgage rate. In essence, that would be leveraging in reverse. Typically, a client would want to keep money in whichever asset was earning more (i.e., cost less).

- *The appropriate income tax treatment of any discount points paid as an itemized deduction on the client's income tax, which can vary from full deductibility for the current year to partial deductibility over the life of the mortgage.* Care must be taken to ensure the proper tax treatment of the points, but in almost all situations the points qualify as an itemized deduction and will potentially reduce taxable income, thus reducing tax liability.

An example with data is presented to help to clarify the information needed for the analysis.

## A Sample Recommendation: Refinance the Mortgage

Cheryl Cabell's parents often credit their comfortable retirement lifestyle to years of working closely with a financial planner. In fact, it was their planner's recommendation to give $12,000 to Cheryl and her husband, Tom that gave them the money necessary to seriously consider refinancing their mortgage. They were fully aware of the potential long-term savings, but their attitude about adding debt simply would not let them include the costs of the closing in the mortgage, so without sufficient savings to meet the closing costs, they postponed the refinance. The Cabells agreed to spend up to $5,500 on the mortgage refinance and to use the remainder of the gift to start § 529 college savings plans for their sons, ages 2 and 4.

Cheryl's parents were so pleased to hear about the plans for the gift that they also agreed to pay their planner's hourly fee to help Cheryl and Tom sort through their options. Given the planner's long-term relationship with Cheryl's parents and the independent recommendation to make a gift of the funds to reduce the estate value, no conflict of interest existed for the planner to help Cheryl and Tom with this isolated planning need.

Cheryl and Tom's current mortgage has a remaining balance of $150,000, has 273 remaining monthly payments, and carries an annual interest rate of 6.750%. As shown in Table 3.3, Cheryl, Tom, and their financial planner finally narrowed their choices to three fixed rate mortgages: (1) 30 years at 5.625% with two points; (2) 20 years at 5.500% with 2.125 points; and (3) 20 years at 5.875% with zero points.

Within their $5,500 closing cost limit, they also briefly considered a 3/1 ARM at a 3.750% rate and a monthly principal and interest payment of $695. However, the Cabells' general risk aversion, fear of rate increases (a 6% cap), and because Tom and Cheryl plan to stay in their home for many years, they were uncomfortable with this option, although the monthly cash flow increase of $382 was very attractive. In fact, their desire to lock in the payment was also supported by their dream of perhaps adding to their home as the boys get older. The neighborhood is an ideal location for a growing family and their oversized lot and house design are well suited for a future makeover.

**Table 3.3** Comparison of Mortgage Options for the Cabells

| | Current Loan | Option 1 | Option 2 | Option 3 |
|---|---|---|---|---|
| Interest rate | 6.750% | 5.625% | 5.500% | 5.875% |
| Mortgage term | 273 months | 360 months | 240 months | 240 months |
| Discount points | NA | 2.000 | 2.125 | 0.000 |
| Discount points cost | NA | $3,000 | $3,188 | $0.00 |
| Other closing costs | NA | $2,258 | $2,258 | $2,258 |
| Monthly principal and interest payment | $1,076.55 | $863.48 | $1,031.83 | $1,063.86 |
| Difference from current payment | NA | ($213.07) | ($44.72) | ($12.70) |
| Method 1: Basic break even | Formula (solving for the number of periods): Total refinancing cost/Difference in monthly payment | | | |
| Break even period | NA | 25 months | 122 months | 178 months |
| Method 2: Present value difference in payment and balance. | Formula (solving for the number of periods): Total financing cost = Present value of the annuity of the difference in the monthly loan payments + Present value of the difference in the loan balances at breakeven | | | |
| Break-even period using 9% required rate | NA | 44 months | 45 months | 24 months |
| Method 3: Present value difference in interest paid | Formula (solving for the number of periods): Total financing cost = Sum of the present value of the difference in interest expense between the original mortgage and the chosen alternative. | | | |
| Break-even period using 9% required rate | NA | 51 months | 40 months | 22 months |

The break-even analysis was completed using the three methods discussed earlier. The first method simply divides the total refinancing costs by the mortgage payment difference.

$$Breakeven\ months = \frac{Total\ Cost\ of\ refinance}{Original\ PMT - New\ Payment}$$

Again, this method completely ignores the time value of money. The other two methods are variations on the time value of money formula and more accurately reflect the benefits of refinance. For the second two methods, the Cabells set a required rate of return of 9%, which might be ambitious but is what they thought would be the rate they could receive on the money had they invested the entire amount in the § 529 plan.

The second method considers (1) the difference in monthly payment and assumes that the difference could have been invested in the 529 plan, and (2) the difference in outstanding balance on the mortgage at the break-even point. They did not really understand the algebra, but they were very surprised at the difference in outcome.

$$Costs\ of\ refinance = \frac{PMT_S}{i_S}\left(1 - \frac{1}{(1+i_S)^\Delta}\right) + \frac{\left[\frac{PMT_O}{i_O}\left(1 - \frac{1}{(1+i_O)^{t-\Delta}}\right) - \frac{PMT_A}{i_A}\left(1 - \frac{1}{(1+i_A)^{T-\Delta}}\right)\right]}{(1+i_S)^\Delta}$$

Where:

$PMT_S$ = difference in the loan payment between the original and the alternative

$PMT_O$ = monthly payment on original mortgage

$PMT_A$ = monthly payment on alternative mortgage

$I_S$ = monthly rate of return on the alternative investment account

$I_O$ = monthly rate on the original mortgage

$I_A$ = monthly rate on the alternative mortgage

t = remaining term, in months, on the original mortgage

T = Tterm, in months, on the alternative mortgage

Solving for:

$\Delta$ = time to break even in months

Again, this method provides a very different result. Using the more appropriate time value of money formulas shows the Cabells that the cost of refinancing their mortgage can be recouped in 45 months (mortgage Option 2) rather than 122 months, as the simple breakeven shows.

The third method considers the difference in interest paid over the term of the loan until the break-even point is reached. Again the Cabells were confused by the math, but they trusted the advisor's methods enough to agree with the outcome.

$$Costs\ of\ refinance = \sum_{t=1}^{\Delta}\left(PV\ IPMT_O - PV\ IPMT_A\right)$$

Where:

$$\text{PV IPMT}_O = \text{present value of the monthly interest payment on original mortgage}$$

$$\text{PV PMT}_A = \text{present value of the monthly interest payment on alternative mortgage}$$

$$I_S = \text{(embedded) monthly rate of return on the alternative investment account}$$

Solving for:

$$\Delta = \text{time to break even in months}$$

Method 3 also renders a very different result from the first option, but it is in closer agreement with the second option. Using this method shows the Cabells that the cost of refinancing their mortgage can be recouped in 40 months (again mortgage Option 2).

All three options offer the client potential savings, but there is an obvious trade-off between maximum payment reduction and maximum interest cost reduction.

Depending on clients' other goals and objectives, either option can offer benefits. One of those benefits is the ability to leverage their cash flow. If a client has numerous other good investment opportunities (good meaning that the expected rate of return exceeds the interest rate on the mortgage over the life of the mortgage), then choosing the option with the lowest monthly payment and leveraging the additional discretionary cash flow could have benefits. An interest-only mortgage can provide this benefit. However, if a client is more risk averse and would rather minimize the total cost of the mortgage, then choosing the option with the shortest Method 3 breakeven might be the optimal choice.

Once again, it is imperative to consider not only the pure numbers but also the attitudes, values, and goals of the client. Therefore, although Option 1 offered the greatest net increase in current cash flow and Option 3 has the lowest out-of-pocket cost, the Cabells decided that Option 2 was the best choice given short- and long-term considerations. They plan to be in the house for a number of years, so the expense associated with closing costs and discount points could be recouped in about 10 years. (A more accurate, but much more complex, calculation might discount all differences in the loans down to after-tax present value amounts to determine the break-even period.)

It seemed to Cheryl that this was a viable trade-off given the $45 in monthly savings and the 33-month reduction in the loan term. The strategy also had little impact on the Cabells' tax situation, indicating that the after-tax cost of the loan was not significantly different from the current loan. Cheryl and Tom had 7.25 years of payments behind them, and by refinancing with a 20-year mortgage they could immediately reduce the term of the loan by 2.75 years. Although the additional monthly cash flow of $213 was attractive under Option 1, they preferred to continue living frugally in exchange for avoiding 7.25 years of loan payments. They reasoned that the mortgage payments avoided with the shorter 20-year loan could be a nice addition to their retirement savings.

Cheryl and Tom expect their salary increases to continue, and with every passing year the boys' childcare costs will decrease. Both of these factors—more income and some reduced expenses—should allow them to meet their expenses and continue their savings.

Paying the discount points to secure the 5.5% rate for 20 years also seemed prudent given the Cabells' conservative investment philosophy. With a combined federal and state marginal tax bracket of 30%, they would need to earn a minimum of 8% before taxes to net a 5.6% return. Although they were comfortable projecting a 9% rate of return for their alternative investment, with their other projections of increased tax rates and a moderately slow economy for the next few years, the planner confirmed that the additional risk was not worth missing out on the 5.5% mortgage rate.

Finally, because the Cabells are financing only the mortgage loan balance, with no additional funding for home improvements or other "cash out" needs, the points are tax deductible over the life of the mortgage. Thus, of the $3,188 paid in points, $159 per year ($3,188 ÷ 20 years) can generally be claimed as an itemized deduction in addition to the interest paid on the mortgage.

Exhibit 3.9 illustrates how a refinance recommendation can be summarized for a client. Whereas the analysis to identify the optimal refinance recommendation can be extensive, a planner also has an obligation to help clients consider the other implications of this decision. For example, the appraisal required for the refinance might indicate a need for increased homeowner's insurance. Other spending implications should also be considered. The reduction in mortgage interest, although a savings, could also reduce the amount of itemized deductions and moderately increase the income taxes paid.

Plans for the increased cash flow associated with the lower mortgage payment should also be considered. Will the funds be used to reduce other outstanding consumer debt? Will the funds be redirected for other short- or long-term needs, such as an emergency fund, insurance protection, or retirement savings?

Although Cheryl and Tom Cabell are not engaged in a continuing planning relationship, the planner's initiative in exploring these issues could help the Cabells maximize their choices with the newly found $537 a year and encourage them to consider the planner for future needs.

**Exhibit 3.9** Cabells' Mortgage Recommendation Form

| Planning Recommendation Form | | | | |
|---|---|---|---|---|
| **Financial Planning Content Area** | Cash flow and net worth planning | | | |
| **Client Goal** | Refinance mortgage | | | |
| **Recommendation No.:** | 1 | **Priority (1–6)** lowest to highest: | | 6 |
| **Projected/Target Value ($)** | $150,000.00 | | | |

**Product Profile**

| | | | | |
|---|---|---|---|---|
| Type | 5.50% fixed-rate mortgage | | | |
| Duration | 20 years | | | |
| Provider | Hilton Mortgage Company | | | |
| Funding Cost per Period ($) | Monthly P&I of $1,031.94 | | | |
| Maintenance Cost per Period ($) | $0 | | | |
| Current Income Tax Status | Tax-qualified | X | Taxable | |
| Projected Rate of Return | N/A | | | |
| Major Policy Provisions | 1. Fixed-rate, 20-year term<br>2. 45-day lock<br>3. No prepayment penalty | | | |

**Procedural Factors**

| | | | | |
|---|---|---|---|---|
| Implementation by Whom | Planner | | Client | X |
| Implementation Date or Time Frame | Immediately | | | |
| Implementation Procedure | Contact Hilton Mortgage Company | | | |

**Ownership Factors**

| | | | | |
|---|---|---|---|---|
| Owner(s) | Thomas E. & Cheryl A. Cabell | | | |
| Form of Ownership | Tenancy in the entirety | | | |
| Insured(s) | Hilton Mortgage Company & Thomas E. & Cheryl A. Cabell | | | |
| Custodial Account | Yes | | No | X |
| Custodian | NA | | | |
| In Trust For (ITF) | Yes | | No | X |
| Transfer on Death (TOD) | Yes | | No | X |
| Beneficiary(ies) | NA | | | |
| Contingent Beneficiary(ies) | NA | | | |

| **Proposed Benefit** | Reduces monthly payment and increases discretionary cash flow; will reduce annual interest expense; reduces net worth because closing costs will be paid with monetary assets. |
|---|---|

# Learning Outcomes

1. Cash flow planning is the underpinning of the entire financial planning process, yet it may not get as much recognition as some other core content planning areas. For planners serving clients in the middle-income market, this may be a fundamental service that is necessary to identify income for meeting other goals. But too often, as income increases, the assumption may be made that cash flow planning is unnecessary, which may not be true unless the client clearly has excess cash flow and does not depend on debt. The determination and projection of net worth is an important planning tool, which enables a planner to review the use of short- and long-term debt and the allocation of assets to maximize earnings. Calculation of ratios enables a planner to more thoroughly interpret a client's financial situation. Cash flow planning, and all that it encompasses, is an important part of the financial planning process, because without it, making or tracking progress toward other goals would be impossible.

2. The cash flow planning process provides a window into a client's financial situation. Calculation of the income and expense statement (if appropriate) and the net worth statement provide insight into a client's efforts to manage income in support of short- and long-term goals. Financial ratios offer additional insights into strengths and weaknesses that may not be immediately evident from the financial situation documents. These efforts, in combination with an analysis of the client's assets and liabilities, serve as the foundation of the planning process and the identification of cash flow management strategies that can improve management, increase earnings, or reduce the cost of debt. Later the cash flow planning process offers a method for monitoring and tracking goal progress.

3. A client's temperament and personality, attitudes and beliefs, and financial knowledge and experience are likely quite evident in the income and expense and net worth statements. For example, a client's values and attitudes are often apparent from spending patterns, whereas risk tolerance and financial knowledge or experience may be inferred from the client's net worth statement. A client's emotional reaction to spending patterns or other financial decisions can offer additional useful insights during discovery. These examples of qualitative client situational information are perhaps more important than the actual quantitative data needed for the cash flow planning analysis. Care should be taken to explore qualitative situational factors fully in an effort to better explain a client's cash flow planning, and to provide necessary insights from which to approach the client about any recommended changes. Focusing too much on the numbers could weaken the foundation of the plan.

4. Care must be taken to thoroughly and accurately identify all dedicated and discretionary expenses to construct an income statement. Dedicated expenses are controlled (1) by contract or other similarly binding agreement or (2) by the client's commitment to protect (through insurance) and accumulate (through saving and investing) assets. On the other hand, within reason, the client has complete control over the amount of income attributed to individual discretionary expenses. If a client is over-committing income to savings, debt repayment, or uncontrolled spending, then the cash flow statement will reveal a negative cash flow or the commitment of future income to repay current expenses. Conversely, excess positive cash flow means income is available to support other goals or objectives.

5.  An income statement summarizes income and expenses for a predetermined period of time, typically one year. The resulting positive or negative cash flow indicates an opportunity or a challenge for the client and planner. A balance sheet summarizes assets and liabilities to reveal a client's net worth on the date of the assessment. Similarly, solvency or insolvency indicates an opportunity or a challenge for the client and the planner.

6.  The nine ratios discussed diagnose a client's liquidity (income adequate to cover expenses) and solvency (assets adequate to cover liabilities). Approximate benchmarks are used to interpret the ratios, although care must be used in interpreting the ratios across the life cycle. Care must also be taken to clearly delineate the determination of the income, expenses, assets and liabilities used in the ratio calculations because precise definitions must be matched to the client situation. Such standards ensure that accurate ratio calculations occur across time for the same client. However, variations in definitions can make it more difficult to compare ratios across clients.

7.  Whereas there is agreement that most clients should have some assets designated as an emergency fund, there is widespread disagreement on the number of months of expenses that should be protected and possible funding sources. Liquidity is the key to an emergency fund, but large sums committed to low-yielding savings alternatives are generally considered imprudent. Likewise, the unplanned selling of assets to cover an emergency situation could yield price and tax consequences. The amount and combination of assets designated for emergency situations will vary with a client's risk tolerance, the number of household earners, the use of credit, employment and income security, and other factors. A combination of "funded" and "unfunded" substitutes may be the best solution for many clients.

8.  Consumer debt, secured and unsecured, can enable a client to more quickly attain a desired lifestyle. The costs of borrowing, and the associated emotional stress, can be problematic for those who cannot manage excessive debt. Financial advisors—and in extreme situations, financial counselors—can help clients analyze the debt load and determine the best strategies for paying off, reducing, or consolidating debt. Central to this is the reduction and elimination of the costs of borrowing as well as an understanding of the factors that contributed to the excessive dependence on debt. Available assets, client attitudes, and client asset preferences must be balanced against the mathematical logic of interest earned and interest paid.

9.  The variety of mortgage alternatives available at any given time varies with the economic climate. But two basic considerations are important to standardize the process of matching the mortgage product, for a purchase or refinance, to the client situation. First, how long does the client anticipate remaining in the property, and what are the client's attitudes about and risk tolerance for the debt? Second, given the client's net worth and income, which mortgage product provides the best financial return, considering interest and tax implications? Mortgage debt is yet another situation where available assets, client attitudes, and client asset preferences must be balanced against the mathematical logic of interest earned and interest paid.

10. The strategies presented in this chapter represent examples of cash flow planning recommendations that are equally relevant for clients across the lifecycle. Although recommendations will differ based on each client's unique situation, the fundamentals of cash flow planning apply to all clients. As such, a thorough analysis of the qualitative and quantitative situational factors is necessary to ensure that appropriate and reasonable recommendations are identified and adopted by the client. As the foundation of the financial planning process, cash flow management allows client and planner to use the current financial situation to more fully understand the past and to establish cash flow management strategies that will foster future success in reaching the client's goals.

## Chapter Resources

Bradley, Susan. and Mary Martin. *Sudden Money: Managing a Financial Windfall*. New York: John Wiley & Sons, 2000.

Home Affordable Refinance Program (HARP) (http://www.makinghomeaffordable.gov).

Leimberg, Stephan R., Martin J. Satinsky, Robert J. Doyle, Jr., and Michael S. Jackson. *Tools & Techniques of Financial Planning*, 8th Ed. Cincinnati, OH: National Underwriter Company, 2007.

The *Financial Factilitator* and all fillable forms needed to complete text activities can be found on the student website at: http://pro.nuco.com/booksupplements/NUCollege-CaseBook2e.

## Quantitative/Analytical Mini-case Problems

1. Married clients have just been approved for a 20-year, $150,000 mortgage. They have been given a choice of two loans. One loan has an annual percentage rate (APR) of 8% and does not carry a fee, and the other has an APR of 7.5% but carries a discount fee of 2% of the initial loan amount. The fee for the second mortgage is payable in cash at loan inception and cannot be financed with the loan.

   From a present value cost perspective, which loan is the better deal, assuming they sell their home immediately after paying the 120th payment and require a 9% effective annual rate of return? In other words, which option has the lower cost?

   Assume all required payments are made at the end of each month and that interest is compounded monthly. Remember to consider the difference in loan payment, the difference in remaining balance at the time of sale, and the present value of the discount points on an after-tax basis assuming the points are fully deductible. The clients are in the 25% marginal tax bracket. (Hint: You can solve this problem at either $T_0$ or $T_{120}$.)

2. Suppose a client is in the market for a car. The client can afford to spend $500 per month, but she decides it is best to buy a cheap car now and use what is left of the $500 to save for a really nice one later. These savings will earn an effective annual rate of 9% interest. Suppose she decides to borrow $15,000 to buy a used car. The loan is for 48 months at a 7.8% APR. Three years later she sells this car for $4,500.

   How much money will the client have for her new car after paying off the old one assuming that all payments and compounding occurred on a monthly basis? (Do not consider sales or income taxes in the calculations.)

3. Married clients have just been approved for a 30-year, $150,000 mortgage, with an APR of 7%. However, they know that they do not want to make only the regular payment and that they do not want to take the entire 30 years to pay off the balance. So they have suggested two options they would like analyzed. Option 1 requires a fixed monthly payment of $1,200. Option 2 requires that they start with the regular payment but then increase that amount by an effective monthly rate of 0.35%.

   They want to know the answers to the following questions.

   a.  Which payment method will result in a faster payoff?

   b.  What is the difference in total interest payments between the two alternative payment methods? Hint: The total of payment for Option 2 involves using the formula for the partial sum of a geometric series.

   c.  Which repayment method results in higher home equity (the lower loan balance) after 14 years?

4. Puneet and Theresa are both 28 years old and have a two-year old child, Edward.  They have asked you to construct financial statements based on the information provided. In addition, you are to analyze their current financial situation by calculating and explaining the results of their financial ratios. How would you generally describe the financial situation of this family?

   Income and expense information:

   **Income**: Puneet and Theresa earned 95,000 in salary. Puneet earned $50,000 as a data analyst, and Theresa made $45,000 as a nursing supervisor. Puneet and Theresa also received $35 in interest from their money market account, which they reinvested.

   **Taxes:** Their W-2 tax statements indicate that they paid $7,267 in FICA taxes, $10,500 in federal income tax, and $2,900 in state income taxes. Real estate taxes on their home were $1,800. Personal property taxes on the two vehicles they own equal $360.

   **Insurance:** Medical insurance is provided by their respective employers; however, they have to pay a portion of the premium, which amounted to $1,400. Their personal automobile policy premiums totaled $1,600. Homeowners insurance premiums for the year were $1,200. Puneet and Theresa own term life insurance policies, and they paid $500 in premiums for both policies.

   **Loan payments:** Mortgage payments amounted to $20,253. Auto loan repayment for their two vehicles totaled $6,600. Student loan payments for Theresa's student loans when she was working toward her master's degree in nursing equal $4,500 for the year, and the boat payments for the year equal $3,112.

**Savings payments:** Puneet and Theresa contributed $4,000 to their retirement accounts, $1,200 to an education fund for their child, and $1,200 to their money market account, and the $35 in interest that they reinvested in the money market account.

**Daily living expenses:** Puneet and Theresa estimate, based on checking account records and credit card statements, that they spent approximately $4,000 on food at home. Clothing expenditures were estimated to be $1,800; laundry and dry cleaning expenses were $300; and personal care expenses were $1,000. Day care for Edward was $6,000. Expenses for gas and maintenance for their vehicles were $2,000. This year there were no auto repair costs.

**Variable expenses:** They estimate that they spent $1,600 on entertainment, which includes dining out and admission charges for plays, movies, and sporting events. Puneet and Theresa also spent $1,500 on recreation and travel, which is how they categorize vacation expenses. Charitable contributions for the year totaled $2,000. Hobby expenses were $360 for the year. Gifts for family and friends throughout the year were $2,000.

**Utilities:** Utilities for the year cost $4,000 , which included $1,840 for gas and electricity, $720 for water, and $1,440 for telephone, Internet access, and cable television.

**Home maintenance and improvements:** They spent $1,200 annually in this category.

**Miscellaneous expenses:** Unreimbursed medical expenses amounted to $300.

Asset and liability information:

**Assets:** They have $2,000 in their checking account, $11,000 in their money market account, $6,000 in a mutual fund investment account, $5,500 in the education savings account for Edward, and $20,000 in their retirement accounts. Their home has a fair market value of $185,000, and the blue book value of their vehicles is $7,000 for Vehicle 1 and $5,500 for Vehicle 2. Their furniture and household goods have an estimated value of $20,000; they have sporting equipment estimated at $2,500, and a boat valued at $12,500.

**Liabilities:** Theresa and Puneet's current unpaid bills equal $500 and they owe $700 on their Visa credit card but will pay the entire balance off before the due date. They routinely charge during the month, but *always* pay the balance in full each month. The balance on their home mortgage is $182,510; their auto loan balance for Vehicle 1 is $8,500, and $2,000 for Vehicle 2. The balance on the loan for the fishing boat is $11,855, and Theresa's student loan balance is $5,700.

5. Using the Butterfield case in Part VI of the text, calculate and interpret the ratios. All needed information is provided, except for the total credit available, which is $10,000 on the Visa and $11,500 on the Mastercard. Then, answer the following questions based on your findings.

   a. How would you rate the Butterfields' overall liquidity?

   b. How would you rate the Butterfields' overall solvency?

   c. Does their periodic savings rate meet the minimum suggested threshold?

   d. Are they spending too much on housing?

Be sure to frame your answers as if you are speaking to or presenting them to the client.

# Comprehensive Bedo Case—Analysis Questions

Several key pieces of information are needed to conduct an analysis of the cash flow and net worth situation for the Bedo household. Careful and accurate calculation of their gross income, expenses, and discretionary cash flow will establish the foundation of the financial plan. Earnings on the Bedos' monetary and investment assets must be calculated using the rates of return provided. Although insignificant in dollar terms, any § 79 benefit income should be included in the statement of cash flows. To calculate the Bedos' net worth, it will be necessary to determine the outstanding mortgage and automobile loans. Finally, it is advisable to review the planning assumptions and specific client goals.

1.  Develop a goal or goals for the Bedos' financial situation. When conceptualizing the goal or goals, consider the following.

    a.  Is the goal developed in agreement with any or all goals and objectives that the clients have identified as important to their financial planning?

    b.  What situational factors might influence their financial situation goals? Are these factors explicit, implied, or assumed? Is additional information required from the Bedos?

    c.  What is the desired outcome for the clients?

2.  Develop a list of globally accepted, client-specific, or planner-generated planning assumptions that will structure the financial situation analysis.

3.  As part of the analysis of the Bedos' current financial situation, develop an income and expense statement and a net worth statement. Be sure to calculate the following:

    a.  The amount of interest, capital gains, and other investment income earned by the Bedo household during the year.

    b.  Any additional income obtained by the Bedos, including § 79 plan employee benefit income.

    c.  Total income and expenses for the year.

    d.  The amount of discretionary cash flow available to the Bedos.

    e.  The amount of discretionary cash flow plus unallocated savings available to the household.

    f.  The net worth of the Bedo household.

4.  As part of the current financial situation analysis, calculate the following diagnostic financial ratios for the Bedo household:

    a.  The current ratio.

    b.  The emergency fund ratio.

    c.  The savings ratio.

    d.  The debt ratio.

    e.   The long-term debt coverage ratio.

    f.   The debt-to-income ratio.

    g.   The credit usage ratio.

    h.   The front-end mortgage qualification ratio.

    i.   The back-end mortgage qualification ratio.

5.    Calculate the following refinancing alternatives:

    a.   The monthly payment on a 15-, 20-, or 30-year refinance alternative, assuming closing costs are paid from available monetary assets.

    b.   The monthly payment on a 15-, 20-, or 30-year refinance alternative, assuming closing costs are included in the new mortgage balance.

6.    Summarize your observations about the Bedos' current financial situation, paying special attention to opportunities to reduce spending, optimize emergency fund balances, maximize earnings on monetary assets, and maximize tax and cash flow efficiency of debt.

7.    Based on the goals originally identified and the completed analysis, what product or procedural strategies might be most useful to improve the Bedos' cash flow and net worth situation? When reviewing the strategies, be careful to consider an approximate cost or savings, if applicable, as well as the most likely outcome(s) associated with each strategy.

8.    Write at least one primary and one alternative recommendation from selected strategies in response to each identified planning need. More than one recommendation may be needed to address all of the planning needs. Include specific, defensible answers to the who, what, when, where, why, how, and how much implementation questions for each recommendation.

    a.   It is suggested that each recommendation be summarized in a Recommendation Form.

    b.   Assign a priority to each recommendation based on the likelihood of meeting client goals and desired outcomes. This priority will be important when recommendations from other core planning content areas are considered relative to the available discretionary funds for subsidizing all recommendations.

    c.   Comment briefly on the outcomes associated with each recommendation.

9.    Complete the following for the Financial Situation Planning section of the Bedos' financial plan.

    a.   Outline the content to be included in this section of the plan. Given the preceding segments written, which segments are missing?

    b.   Write the introduction to this section of the plan (no more than one to two paragraphs). Be sure to include an explanation of the purpose of the financial situation analysis and define any terms used.

c. Given the emphasis on financial statements, ratios, and other numerical data in this section of the plan, how might this information be most effectively presented to the client? What interpretation or explanation of the data would be necessary? What data might be graphically summarized? Develop an example for the Bedos' plan, including the financial statement, the interpretation of the statement, and one graphic representation of the data. The latter should help the client interpret the data.

d. For one other issue discussed in this chapter (e.g., cash flow analysis and spending; debt restructuring or mortgage refinance; emergency fund or funding sources; or ratios), complete the analysis, write the interpretation, and graphically present the findings for inclusion in the Bedo plan.

10. Prepare a 10–15-minute presentation for the Bedos of your observations and/or recommendation(s) regarding their cash flow planning. Be sure to include visual aids or handouts.

## Notes

1. For additional information see:

   Griffith, R. "Personal Financial Statement Analysis: A Modest Beginning." In *Proceedings of the 3rd Annual Conference of the Association for Financial Counseling and Planning Education, 3*, 123–31.[AQ: Please provide name and location of publisher.] 1985.

   Prather, C. G. "The Ratio Analysis Technique Applied to Personal Financial Statements: Development of Household Norms." *Financial Counseling and Planning,* 1 (1990): 53–69.

   Lytton, R. H., E. T. Garman, and N. M. Porter. "How to Use Financial Ratios when Advising Clients." *Financial Counseling and Planning* 2 (1991): 3–23.

2. U.S. Census Bureau; Housing, "Table 14a. Seasonally Adjusted Homeownership Rates for the United States: 1980 to Present." Vacancies and Homeownership. Available at http://www.census.gov/hhes/www/housing/hvs/historic/index.html.

# Income Tax Planning

## Learning Objectives

1.  Understand the importance of income tax planning within the comprehensive financial planning process.

2.  Identify client situational factors that may uniquely affect a client's income tax planning goals.

3.  Discuss how planning for different sources of client income can affect a client's annual tax liability.

4.  Explain the 10-step tax planning procedure and demonstrate how income taxes are determined at the federal level.

5.  Explain the significance, and provide examples, of above-the-line and below-the-line deductions.

6.  Explain the alternative minimum tax (AMT) and possible triggers that could increase a client's tax liability.

7.  Explain the importance of proactive tax planning for retirement income.

8.  Identify prospective income tax planning strategies that can be used to help clients reach their income tax planning goals.

9.  Describe how a client's tax return can be used to recognize other planning opportunities.

# Key Terms

§ 529 plan

above-the-line deductions

Additional Child Tax Credit

adjusted gross income (AGI)

after-tax yield

Alternative Minimum Tax (AMT)

before-tax equivalent rate of return

below-the-line deductions

Certified Public Accountant (CPA)

child tax credit

cost basis

dispute

enrolled agent (EA)

equivalent taxable rate of return

home equity line of credit

home equity loan

Internal Revenue Service (IRS)

IRC § 79

IRS Form 1040

IRS Form W-4

IRS Schedule A

itemized deductions

marginal tax bracket

modified adjusted gross income (MAGI)

net *capital loss*

net unrealized appreciation

personal exemption

realized gain

standard deduction

statutory stock options

tax attorney

tax credits

taxable income

tax-exempt income

UGMA

UTMA

**Figure 4.1** The Systematic Financial Planning Process for Income Tax Planning

## TAX PLANNING: THE BASICS

Tax policy in the United States tends to be either progressive or regressive. With progressive taxes, the percentage of tax increases as taxable income increases. The tax rate burden in a progressive system falls disproportionately on higher-income earners. The federal income tax and the Alternative Minimum Tax (AMT) are progressive. With regressive taxes, the tax rate decreases proportionately as a person's taxable income decreases. The burden of tax, in a regressive system, falls on low-income earners. Self-employment and sales taxes are examples of regressive taxes. A 5% tax rate on food, for example, is proportionately more burdensome on someone earning $20,000 per year than on a person earning $100,000 annually, assuming that both eat the same amount and quality of food.

Several desirable outcomes are associated with income tax planning as part of comprehensive plan development. First, from a client's perspective, the assessment provides a roadmap for implementing strategies that can both reduce future tax liability and increase discretionary cash flow. Second, from a financial planner's point of view, a tax plan can serve as a valuable client-education tool. In addition to providing clients with background terms, definitions, and calculations, a tax plan can be used as a mechanism to facilitate client-planner discussions regarding retirement funding, insurance needs, college planning, and other client goals and expenses that can benefit from the use of tax-advantaged strategies.

The process of income tax planning hinges on a financial advisor's ability to understand, interpret, and apply basic individual income tax law to client situations. This requires a planner to gather data, compute results, and consider the integration of those results within other core content planning areas.

It makes sense for financial planners, who do not consider themselves tax experts, to establish working relationships with tax professionals such as **certified public accountants (CPAs), tax attorneys,** or **enrolled agents (EAs).** The **Internal Revenue Service (IRS)** recognizes these professionals as qualified to represent clients in tax disputes. A financial planner should also take the time to understand a client's knowledge of taxes and determine whether any previously undisclosed tax issues are present in the client situation. Referring a client to a CPA, attorney, or EA for complex tax help is often prudent, but such referrals do not remove the basic fact-finding obligations associated with comprehensive financial planning. For instance, a client might not initially disclose an outstanding tax debt with the IRS or state taxing agency. Calculating tax liabilities and making recommendations without such information could cause serious tax and legal problems for the client. In this situation, information about the client issue would be essential to making a referral decision.

However, simply relying on the help of a CPA, attorney, or EA is not enough. It is essential that a financial planner have a solid understanding of current tax laws and rules. This is true because almost every aspect of financial planning is either influenced by or directly affects a client's tax situation. Consider a recommendation to increase contributions to a 401(k) retirement plan. This recommendation may appear to have only retirement planning implications, but it also influences a client's cash flow and tax situation. Contributions to a qualified retirement plan help reduce the amount of income reportable for income tax purposes. This, in turn, helps reduce a client's annual withholding requirement, which can increase discretionary cash flow during the year. Conversely, by not reducing the withholding requirement, the client could avoid or reduce additional tax payments for investment earnings. The combined tax ramifications of this simple recommendation can be significant.

The purpose of this chapter is to review the basic steps necessary to analyze and evaluate a client's current tax planning situation as illustrated in Figure 4.1. This chapter also presents a variety of widely used tax planning strategies and an example of how some of these strategies can be evaluated to develop tax planning recommendations. However, unless a financial planner is also a CPA or an EA, it is prudent to include a tax planning disclaimer when presenting any tax calculations, estimates, or recommendations. A statement such as, "Before implementing the advice provided, please confirm these suggestions with your tax professional" provides some liability protection for advisors and helps promote collaboration with the client's other financial professionals.

## ANALYZE THE CLIENT'S CURRENT SITUATION

Review of a client's current tax situation starts by evaluating client situational factors related to the tax planning process. This is just another way of saying that a planner ought to know the client's tax planning goals as well as temperament and personality, attitudes, beliefs and values, financial knowledge and experience, and socioeconomic descriptors that could influence tax planning decisions. Understanding the emotional, personal, and nonfinancial aspects of a client's situation is as important as determining the client's tax liability.

Every client is unique, and qualitative values and attitudes in addition to quantitative client data make each planning situation distinctive. Some clients have a strongly held desire to shelter as much income from taxes as possible, whereas this may be less of a concern for others. Certain clients, for example, may wish to push the limits of the tax law, and others will be unwilling to risk a potential tax audit. This is one reason it is important to assess a client's risk tolerance as part of the data-gathering phase of the planning process. The following list illustrates some of the viewpoints a client might have regarding taxes:

- A strong desire to minimize taxes paid to the government;

- A willingness to pay "my fair share" of the tax burden;

- A wish to make charitable contributions for tax advantages and the benefit of society; or

- A desire to avoid being audited by the IRS.

The data-gathering phase of the financial planning process provides a very important context for tax planning. Recent or upcoming changes in a client's household situation can affect filing status, the number of **personal exemptions** claimed, or the availability of adjustments, itemized deductions, or credits. Common examples of important client situational issues include changes in marital status, reaching significant ages for taxpayers or dependents, an inheritance, a change in employment, a salary increase or decrease, the addition of a dependent (e.g., birth of a child, assuming expenses for a relative), the purchase of a second home, or the sale of a primary residence or second home. These examples of life cycle events and life transitions represent both important milestones in a client's life and potential tax planning issues.

The purchase, sale, or refinance of a personal residence provides an example of how client actions can trigger tax issues that call for advance planning. A married couple can exclude up to $500,000 ($250,000 for a single taxpayer) in gains on the sale of a primary residence. But to receive this exclusion, the client must have owned and used the home as a personal residence for two of the past five years—typically referred to as the *holding period requirement*. Any gains exceeding the excluded amount are generally taxed at the capital gains tax rate, currently a flat 15%. The itemized deduction for home mortgage interest is often cited as a tax benefit, but the deduction applies only to interest paid on the primary mortgage "initial acquisition" debt. And the deduction applies only to the interest paid on the first $1 million spent to acquire, build, or improve a residence. Home equity lines of credit or loans are often recommended as sources of funding emergency needs, college costs, or meeting other short-term cash flow needs.

Typically, lower interest costs and tax-deductible interest are recognized benefits of home equity debt, despite concerns about leveraging the home for other goals. But home equity debt interest is deductible only if the loan is the lesser of (1) $100,000 or (2) the fair market value of the home less the first mortgage debt. For AMT purposes, any refinanced indebtedness on which interest is deductible is limited to the amount of indebtedness prior to refinancing. Many clients know some mortgage-related tax issues, but few remember all of the details. A proactive financial planner anticipates a client's need for this type of information.

While maintaining a perspective on the client's tax planning situation, the planner must also consider these changes in light of any upcoming changes in the tax code. Tax planning involves taking actions that maximize each client's situation in anticipation of household and/or tax code changes. It is imperative that a client's wishes and concerns as well as potential changes in the tax situation be taken into account when developing planning strategies and recommendations. In some situations, the timing of an action can have a significant impact on taxes due.

## Determine and Quantify the Client's Income Tax Planning Needs

Determining and quantifying a client's income tax planning need is ultimately focused on the annual IRS Form 1040, and for most clients reducing tax liability. But simply calculating refunds or taxes due in no way reflects the full scope of income tax planning. For example, a planner may never prepare a client's tax forms, or tax form preparation might flow seamlessly with financial planning advice. Such advice could have little or no impact on the current year's Form 1040. Or a primary reason for a client seeking planning advice may be the resolution of an issue that results in a significant tax savings in the current year. Conversely, planning advice in the current year may not yield any tax implications for future years. The changing nature of the client's life and the fluidity of the tax code also call for financial advisors to plan while maintaining the flexibility to adapt, when necessary. In summary, determining and quantifying a client's income tax planning need as the first substep in analyzing the client's situation is unlike other core content planning areas. Although it may seem to be a discrete calculation, tax planning integrates with almost every other core content planning area.

A planner can start by obtaining a client's tax returns from at least the previous two years. An analysis of previous returns can provide a guide to trends in deductions, exemptions, and credits taken in preceding years. Reviewing past tax returns can also indicate discrepancies in cash flow and net worth figures. Previous tax returns can be used to provide planners with needed tax loss carry-forward information. Once a thorough review of prior years' returns has been completed, a client's current-year tax liability can be calculated or estimated. Projections for up to five years of returns may also be appropriate, depending on the nature of the client's planning and tax situation. Projections are an excellent way to inform a client of the interrelationships and tax implications of other core content planning recommendations.

Another part of the tax planning process is for the advisor to educate clients regarding the advisor's needs to review tax forms or collaborate with the client's tax professional to discuss a broad range of tax planning issues. This effort can help the client engage more actively in the tax planning process and more fully appreciate the relationships among client, planner, and the client's tax professional.

### Income: The Foundation of Income Tax Planning

When reviewing a client's cash flow and financial situation, it becomes apparent that many clients have income from any number of sources, which could have implications for several other core content planning areas. But from solely a tax planning perspective, one of the major objectives is typically to minimize a client's **average tax rate**—in other words, to reduce, on average, the amount of each dollar available for spending or saving that is lost to taxes. For tax planning purposes, income can be categorized in four ways: (1) income subject to the client's marginal tax rate; (2) income subject to a potentially lower-than-marginal tax rate; (3) income subject to a potentially higher-than-marginal tax rate; and (4) income not subject to tax. The latter category represents **tax-exempt income**. Examples include interest on municipal bonds, gifts, and inheritance, and several forms of government-provided payments like welfare and veterans' benefits.

To achieve the goal of reducing a client's total tax liability, a financial planner often starts with a focus on the client's **taxable income**, loosely defined as income that is usually subject to income tax. Examples of taxable income include salaries, pensions, royalties, rent, dividends, interest, capital gains, gambling winnings, hobby income, commissions, tips, § 79 income, and business income. But this categorization tells only part of the story. Within this list, salary, pensions, non-qualified dividends, interest income, gambling winnings (net of gambling losses), hobby income, commissions, tips, and § 79 income are subject to the client's marginal tax rate. Royalty payments and other business income are subject to a rate potentially higher than the client's marginal tax bracket because the client will most likely owe self-employment tax on the earnings. Under the current tax code, investment income, such as long-term capital gains and qualified dividends, are taxed at a rate that is likely to be lower than the client's marginal tax bracket. So the objective is simple: maximize income subject to a tax rate lower than the marginal tax rate and minimize income subject to a tax rate equal to or higher than the client's marginal tax bracket. To do so, however, it is important to understand more about the diverse sources of client income.

**Earned income.** As typically reported on a client's IRS W-2 Form, income earned from salaries, wages, tips, and commissions is easy to estimate but tough to reduce. The only realistic option a client has to reduce wage-based income is to increase elective deferrals or maximize employer-provided benefits, because most employer-provided benefits can be purchased with pretax dollars. In addition to the tax-deferral available through participation in an employer-sponsored qualified retirement plan, an employee might also be able to purchase life, medical, dental, disability, and long-term care insurance. Contributions to a § 125 cafeteria plan, if available, also serve to reduce reported income. Some benefit plans also allow for payment of unreimbursed medical expenses, child care expenses, or even select transportation costs. However it is important to carefully monitor and account for how employer-provided fringe benefits affect a client's tax situation. Internal Revenue Code (IRC) guidelines state that any fringe benefit provided to an employee by an employer is taxable unless specifically excluded in the IRC. Table 4.1 summarizes the tax status of many popular fringe benefits. More information about various employer-provided benefits is provided in applicable chapters throughout this book.

**Table 4.1** Special Rules for Determining the Tax Status of Select Fringe Benefits

| Type of Fringe Benefit | Treatment under Employment Taxes | | |
|---|---|---|---|
| | Income Tax Withholding | Social Security and Medicare | Federal Unemployment (FUTA) |
| Accident and health benefits | Exempt[1,2], except for long-term care benefits provided through a flexible spending or similar arrangement | Exempt, except for certain payments to S-corporation employees who are 2% shareholders | Exempt |
| Achievement awards | Exempt[1] up to $1,600 for qualified plan awards ($400 for nonqualified awards) | | |
| Adoption assistance | Exempt[1,3] | Taxable | Taxable |
| Athletic facilities | Exempt if substantially all use during the calendar year is by employees, their spouses, and their dependent children and the facility is operated by the employer on premises owned or leased by the employer | | |
| *De minimis* (without consequence) benefits | Exempt | Exempt | Exempt |
| Dependent care assistance | Exempt[3] up to a maximum exemption of $5,000 of dependent care assistance benefits each year ($2,500 for married employees filing separate returns) | | |

| | | | |
|---|---|---|---|
| Educational assistance | Exempt up to $5,250 of benefits each year | | |
| Employee discounts | Exempt[3] up to certain limits | | |
| Group-term life insurance coverage | Exempt | Exempt[1,4] up to cost of $50,000 of coverage. (Special rules apply to former employees) | Exempt |
| Health savings accounts (HSAs) | Exempt for qualified individuals up to HSA contribution limits | | |
| Lodging on your business premises | Exempt[1] if furnished for your convenience as a condition of employment | | |
| Meals | Exempt if furnished on your business premises for your convenience. Exempt if *de minimis*. | | |
| Moving expense reimbursements | Exempt[1] if expenses would be deductible if the employee had paid them | | |
| No-additional-cost services | Exempt[3] | Exempt[3] | Exempt[3] |
| Retirement planning services | Exempt[5] | Exempt[5] | Exempt[5] |
| Transportation (commuting) benefits | Exempt[1] up to certain limits if for rides in a commuter highway vehicle and/or transit passes ($230), qualified parking ($230), or qualified bicycle commuting reimbursement[6] ($20). Exempt if *de minimis*. | | |
| Tuition reduction | Exempt[3] if for undergraduate education (or graduate education if the employee performs teaching or research activities) | | |
| Volunteer firefighter and emergency responder benefits | Exempt | Exempt | Exempt |
| Working condition benefits | Exempt | Exempt | Exempt |

[1] Exemption does not apply to S-corporation employees who are 2% shareholders.

[2] Exemption does not apply to certain highly compensated employees under a self-insured plan that favors those employees.

[3] Exemption does not apply to certain highly compensated employees under a program that favors those employees.

[4] Exemption does not apply to certain key employees under a plan that favors those employees.

[5] Exemption does not apply to services for tax preparation, accounting, legal, or brokerage services.

[6] If the employee receives a qualified bicycle commuting reimbursement in a qualified bicycle commuting month, the employee cannot receive commuter highway vehicle, transit pass, or qualified parking benefits in that same month.

Source: IRS. *Employer's Tax Guide to Fringe Benefits* ( http://www.irs.gov/pub/irs-pdf/p15b.pdf ), p. 6 and also http://www.irs.gov/publications/p15b/ar02.html#en_US_2012_publink1000193623).

If the benefits received from an employer exceed the limits described in the table, or the benefits are deemed to be nonexempt, the client's taxable income will increase. So without adjustment the client could find that tax withholding is insufficient to cover the tax liability. It is important to account for fringe benefits whenever conducting a tax analysis

Finally, to reduce the amount of income reported, for example, a client who is self-employed can attempt to transfer personal expenses to deductible business expenses as reported on IRS Schedule C. This has the effect of reducing the amount of income reported, thereby reducing total income.

**Business income.** Two questions are typical when working with the tax implications of business income. First, was the client engaged in a business or simply a hobby? Second, if it is in fact a business, then is the client's engagement active or passive? The first helps determine the output of the activity—was there the intent to make a profit? The second question looks more at input—what is the level of involvement in the activity?

A planner might have a client who engages in activities where it is difficult to distinguish between a hobby and a business. Such situations should be monitored for tax planning opportunities. Modifying or racing cars, writing travel books, photography, and small-scale farming are examples of activities that some clients feel are more business than hobby. To address this issue, the IRS has developed several rules to help determine when an activity is a hobby and when it is a business. The IRS asks whether the activity is run like a business, how much time a person spends on the activity, and whether the activity is engaged in for profit. This last hurdle is crossed if the activity results in a profit in three of the last five years, including the most recent year.[1]

If income is generated as the result of a hobby then the income is reported on the IRS Form 1040, and expenses associated with that hobby are deductible on IRS Schedule A. However, if income is generated as the result of a solely owned business, then the income and business-related expenses are reported on IRS Schedule C.

IRS Publication 925 provides a definitional framework for passive and at-risk "active" activities. Both terms are used to describe a client's role in the decision and management process when making an investment. The key to determining whether an activity is passive is whether there is material participation in the operation. In other words, does the client work on a regular, continuous and substantial basis in operations, including most rental income (although there are a few exceptions)?

If a taxpayer does not materially participate, losses are passive. A passive activity loss is limited by the amount of passive income reported by the taxpayer. If a loss exceeds the income generated, the amount can be carried forward only to offset future passive income.[2]

On the other hand, at-risk loss is limited to the invested amount. If a loss exceeds the tax basis of the invested capital or property, then the remaining loss can be carried forward into subsequent years and used against nonpassive income.[3]

Unless fully qualified to deal with business income, a financial planner should seek advice from a tax professional or consult with the client's accountant. Care must be taken to match the appropriate income and expenses to ensure that all regulations are followed.

**Unearned (investment) income.** Because a financial planner has only a limited number of options to help clients reduce earned income, managing unearned or investment income such as dividends and capital gains becomes particularly important. For example, following the stock market meltdown of 2008, many investors sold securities at significant losses. Some justified the sale of stocks and other investments by assuming that they would be able to take large tax deductions. Unfortunately, some investors found that they were effectively limited to $3,000 in short-term **net capital losses**. Although excess losses can be carried forward, it is important for planners to help clients match losses against gains in particular years rather than having clients make investment and other financial decisions based on the client's assumptions about the tax code.

In 2008, Congress enacted a law that significantly affects how taxes are calculated for investors. The Emergency Economic Stabilization Act of 2008 made a significant change to the way investors report the cost basis of mutual fund holdings. The IRS defines **cost basis** as the cost of all shares held in an account or investment (e.g., mutual fund, exchange traded fund); *basis* refers to the original value of an asset, adjusted for dividends, stock splits, distributions, depreciation, and other tax allowances. A client's basis is the amount invested, which is used to determine the amount of gain or loss (realized and/or recognized) reported by a client when an asset is sold or exchanged.

Under most circumstances, the higher the basis the lower is the tax liability upon subsequent sale. Although cost basis is typically evaluated and determined by the dollar amount paid for an asset, basis can be transferred to others when a gift or exchange is made. When an asset is inherited, under current tax code, the cost basis is determined either as of the decedent's date of death, or the earlier of the alternative valuation date (see Chapter 13 for more information) or the date of transfer. New cost basis reporting rules require investors to elect one of the following seven cost basis methods for shares acquired after January 1, 2012:

1. Average cost

2. First in, first out (FIFO)

3. Last in, last out (LIFO)

4. Low cost

5. High cost

6. Loss/gain utilization

7. Specific lot identification

The IRS classifies mutual fund shares acquired before January 1, 2012, as noncovered shares. Mutual fund companies are not required to track or report cost basis for noncovered shares. The **average cost method** is the default choice if an investor does not elect a calculation based on one of the seven reporting methods. This method of reporting, as illustrated in Table 4.2, requires an investor to track the average cost of shares acquired over a period of time.

**Table 4.2** Average Cost Method Example

| Date of Purchase | Purchase Amount | Number of Shares Purchased | Calculation | Average Price per Share |
|---|---|---|---|---|
| 1/10/12 | $2,000 | 50 | $2,000/50 | $40.00 |
| 5/15/12 | $100 | 2 | $100/2 | $50.00 |
| 12/12/12 | $1,500 | 45 | $1,500/45 | $33.33 |
| Total Cost = $3,600 | | 97 | $3,600/97 | $37.11 |

The FIFO and LIFO methods of reporting assume that shares are depleted based on the date of acquisition, with either the first or last shares sold first. The low-cost approach exhausts the lowest price shares first. In the table, the shares purchased on 12/12/12 at $33.33 would be reported as first sold. The high-cost method assumes the highest price shares are sold first. This method of reporting subjects the investor to smaller taxable gains (maximum losses) initially while postponing larger taxable gains (smaller losses) into the future.

The IRS requires investors to use a somewhat complicated calculation when adopting the loss/gain utilization approach. Shares are assumed to be depleted in the following order:

1.  Shares with the greatest short-term loss

2.  Shares with a long-term loss

3.  Shares held less than one year (i.e., short-term) with no loss or gain

4.  Shares held longer than one year (i.e., long-term) with no loss or gain

5.  Shares with a long-term gain

6.  Shares with a short-term gain

This approach to cost basis accounting typically assumes that that shares with losses are depleted before shares with gains.

Finally, the specific lot identification method requires investors to indicate specifically which shares were sold. This approach allows for a secondary cost basis when shares cannot be identified. For many investors, this cost basis reporting method is the most time-intensive approach to share identification.

It is important to note that the cost basis reporting method can be changed, but only prospectively, not after a sale has occurred. This means that an investor should work closely with a financial planner and tax advisor before shares held in a mutual fund account are depleted to maximize tax-planning opportunities.

### Determine Income Tax Liability

Once all of the sources of income have been identified, a planner can determine a client's tax liability and begin to identify potential changes to reduce the client's average tax rate in either the current year or subsequent years. Two approaches can be used to determine a client's tax liability; both approaches occur as part of the current situation analysis. The first approach uses actual IRS tax forms, such as **IRS Form 1040** and IRS Schedules A, B, C, and D. The second approach, which may be slightly less accurate but more efficient, is to use some form of tax calculator or estimator. Either approach should lead to the same conclusion: the client will receive a refund, owe nothing, or owe additional tax.

Following is a basic 10-step income tax calculation that serves as a guide to calculating a client's tax liability, the overall tax planning process, and as an important client education tool.

1. Record potential gross income.

2. Exclude nontaxable income and pretax items.

3. Calculate gross income.

4. Subtract expenses for adjusted gross income (AGI) "above-the-line" deductions.

5. Reduce taxable income by either the standard deduction or by the itemized deduction amount "below-the-line" deductions.

6. Reduce taxable income by personal exemption amounts.

7. Calculate tax liability.

8. Reduce tax liability through the use of credits.

9. Add in other tax liabilities.

10. Determine the additional tax liability or the amount of the tax refund.

Following this simple 10-step approach to tax calculations ensures that all income is appropriately accounted for, expenses are recorded, and all tax-reduction tools and techniques are utilized. Of the 10 steps, steps 2, 4, 5, and 8 are areas where a financial planner can add the most value. In step 2, a planner can help the client plan to increase pretax expenses; in steps 4 and 5, a planner can help the client maximize "above-the-line" and "below-the-line" deductions, or adjustments to income that occur before the determination of adjusted gross income or itemized deductions that occur after the determination of adjusted gross income. Although the number of the "line" may change from year to year, the term refers to the line that identifies adjusted gross income. In step 8, the planner can help clients maximize available tax credits. Because of their importance, each of these steps is discussed further below.

In step 2, a planner can help clients maximize income from sources that are not subject to taxation. Municipal bonds and tax-free money market accounts can be used to reduce a client's reported income, because the interest earned from these accounts, although reflected in IRS Form 1040, is generally not included in the total income calculation.

In step 4, several different tax-planning strategies are available to help clients manage tax liabilities, but many of the benefits available in the tax code are subject to income limits. The limit most often imposed is based on **adjusted gross income (AGI)** or **modified adjusted gross income (MAGI)**. The actual definition or calculation of MAGI can vary with the tax issues in question. There are two methods for reducing AGI. One is to reduce the amount of income reported, as explained above, and the other is to increase negative adjustments to income.

A planner can help clients maximize their **above-the-line deductions**, which are also referred to as adjustments to gross income. Examples of expenses that can be used to reduce gross income include educator expenses, student loan interest, tuition fees, moving expenses, IRA early withdrawal penalties, and alimony paid. Other examples include making deductible contributions to a traditional IRA (but phase-out thresholds based on income for qualified plan participation could apply) or contributing to a healthcare savings account (HSA). For those who are self-employed, paying one-half of self-employment taxes, contributing to a self-employed retirement plan (e.g., a Keogh or SIMPLE plan), or purchasing health insurance are additional options that can be used to reduce gross income.

Adjustments to AGI often provide a marginal benefit for clients. For instance, if a client is in the 25% marginal tax bracket, a $1,000 deduction for AGI will generally result in approximately $250 in tax savings. All clients, subject to certain income phase-out restrictions, are eligible to deduct the preceding expenses. Clients who are close to triggering the AMT could consider deferring expenses that result in a lower AGI.

In step 5, a planner can help clients maximize below-the-line deductions. If above-the-line adjustments are either unavailable or exhausted, attention should turn to **below-the-line taxable-income reduction** by scrutinizing **itemized deductions**. Three areas where many clients can increase deductions and thereby reduce taxable income (assuming the client is not subject to the AMT) include converting non-tax-advantaged interest paid to deductible mortgage interest, increasing or accelerating taxes paid in a year, and increasing gifts to charitable organizations. A combination of any or all of these solutions can work to decrease taxable income. Charitable contributions are one expense that a client can influence directly compared to mortgage interest, real estate taxes, property taxes, or state and local income taxes. As a reminder, state and local income taxes and real property taxes are added back into taxable income to determine the AMT.

In step 8, the planner can help the client maximize available tax credits. A few of the most commonly used tax credits include the child and dependent care credit, the Lifetime Learning education credit, and the saver's tax credit. Maximizing available **tax credits** does not reduce a client's taxable income, but it does reduce tax liability. However, the availability of these credits may depend on a client's AGI or MAGI meeting various qualification thresholds, and on potential changes in the tax code.

---

### Tax Planning for Special Populations: Families with Children

Although the exact cost depends on the income level and size of a family or household, the U.S. Department of Agriculture estimated in 2010 that the cost of raising a child from birth to age 17 was more than $200,000.[4] That does not include the cost of prenatal care or the delivery or adoption of the child, which could increase the cost from $5,000 to $50,000 or more. In addition, many families have a goal to provide at least a minimum level of funding for post-secondary education. Although exact costs vary widely, the College Board estimated that a moderate, in-state, public college would cost more than $17,000 for tuition, fees, room, and board for the 2011–2012 academic year.[5] Therefore, between basic care and education, costs could exceed $300,000 per child. The IRS provides two very important tax credits to those who have qualifying expenses and meet the income limitations: the Child and Dependent Care Tax Credit and the Child Tax Credit.

The tax credit for child care and dependent care applies to the cost of care for qualified children under the age of 13 or to adult relatives who live with the taxpayer but are physically or mentally incapable of providing for themselves. The current Child and Dependent Care Tax Credit is the result of an expansion of the 2001 tax cuts that were extended through 2012 as part of the Tax Relief, Unemployment Insurance Reauthorization, and Job Creation Act of 2010; it currently allows for a maximum tax credit of 35% of qualifying expenses. Eligible families with one qualifying dependent can claim up to $1,050 (35% of $3,000) as a credit against their federal tax liability, and eligible families with two or more qualifying dependents can claim up to $2,100 (35% of $6,000) against their federal tax liability.[6] The federal credit can be used only to offset actual federal tax liability; any excess credit amount is lost. Unlike the Earned Income Tax Credit and the Child Tax Credit, the Child and Dependent Care Tax Credit is nonrefundable. This means that if a family does not earn enough money to owe federal income taxes, it cannot benefit from the credit. Finally, taxpayers who file "married filing separately" are ineligible to claim this credit.

The Child Tax Credit provides a maximum credit in 2012 of $1,000 for each qualifying child under age 17 (age 16 and under). Income limits apply, and for married taxpayers filing jointly the phase-out begins at $110,000. For married taxpayers filing separate returns, it begins at $55,000, and for all others the income phase-out begins at $75,000.[7]   There are seven tests to determine whether a child qualifies:

1. Relation test: the taxpayer's son, daughter, stepchild, foster child, brother, sister, stepbrother, stepsister, or descendant of any of them (for example, the taxpayer's grandchild, niece, or nephew)

2. Age test: was under the age of 17 at the end of the calendar year

3. Support test: did not provide more than half of his or her own support for the previous calendar year

4. Residence test: lived with the taxpayer for more than half of the year

5. Dependent test: is claimed as a dependent on the taxpayer's return

6. Joint return test: did not file a joint return for the year

7. Citizen test: was a U.S. citizen, a U.S. national, or a U.S. resident alien[8]

In addition to the basic tax credit, there is an Additional Child Tax Credit that can be claimed by taxpayers who do not receive the full benefit of the basic credit because they pay too little tax. In other words, this provision makes this credit refundable.

Figure 4.2 highlights some of the most common solutions available to reduce AGI either by maximizing above-the-line deductions or to reduce taxable income by maximizing below-the-line deductions and tax credits. The process of choosing a strategy or finding an area to concentrate on for a client starts by determining whether the client is losing some benefits available in the tax code because AGI is too high.[9] For example, if AGI is above certain thresholds, the client may lose the benefits of deducting a traditional IRA contribution, making a Roth IRA contribution, deducting qualified education expenses, or claiming several tax credits.

Whether a financial planner is directly involved in the preparation of a client's income tax forms or indirectly involved in the analysis of the client's tax situation as part of a comprehensive planning engagement, the planner may be responsible for implementing the changes necessary to increase the client's tax efficiency. The benefits for clients who use some or all of these tax liability reduction methods can be mitigated or enhanced by other planning considerations. Investment and planning strategies that minimize tax liability should always be considered as part of the process. However, tax planning strategies should not be considered in isolation; they should be considered in conjunction with each client's other overriding planning needs. For example, increasing a client's municipal bond allocation could be a viable strategy to reduce taxable income. However, if the tax-free rate on the bonds does not exceed the after-tax return on another form of fixed-income investment, the client could be better off paying the taxes. To make matters even more confusing, high levels of tax-exempt interest could trigger the AMT, thus effectively reducing the availability of several deductions, including home equity interest.

**Figure 4.2** Tax Planning Product and Solution Decision Tree

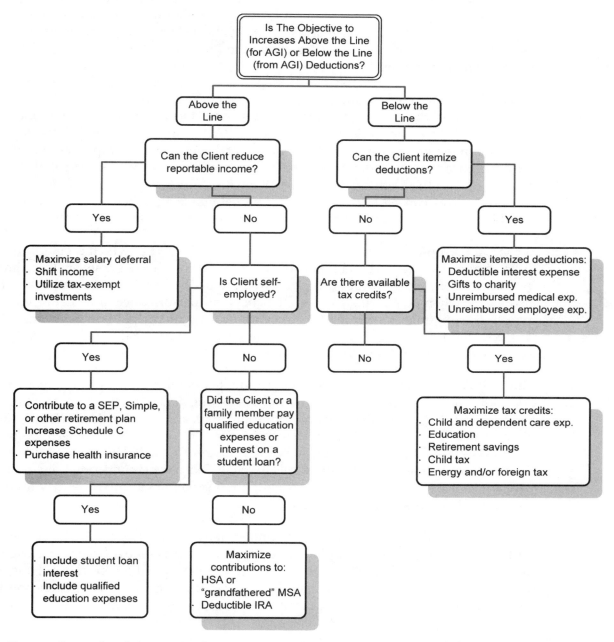

*Because of income-based phase-out or other reasons, not all of these options will be available to all clients.

The complexity of the AMT calculation is beyond the scope of the Federal, Social Security and State Tax Estimator Worksheet that is part of the Financial Facilitator. But the estimator, shown in Exhibit 4.1, helps expedite tax planning. It can easily be used to project different scenarios by applying the preceding strategies, such as reducing taxable income, increasing above-the-line and below-the-line deductions, and maximizing credits.

Several important considerations should be taken into account when using the tax estimator. First, the tax outputs can be integrated into other areas of the Financial Facilitator. This means that once data have been input into the tax worksheet, information generated can be used in other worksheets. For example, estimated tax liabilities based on the estimator or actual tax liabilities reported for the client should be entered into the Dedicated Expense Worksheet. Information about federal, state, and FICA taxes can be estimated in the tax estimator and then used to determine whether a client has over- or under-withheld taxes for the year.

Second, a **marginal tax bracket** is estimated; this is the rate at which each additional dollar earned is taxed. The tax bracket can be used in other worksheets to estimate insurance needs and education funding requirements. The marginal tax bracket is also useful when comparing the tax efficiency and performance of a client's current investment holdings. Given the tax rate and yield on municipal bonds, for instance, it is possible to compare the before- and after-tax returns of different securities, as explained in Chapter 2 and this chapter.

Third, the tax estimator estimates state income tax liability; however, the worksheet does not link to state-specific information. Users must input the exact state marginal tax rate and deduction, exemption, and adjustment information for a client's state of residence. The output calculations can be used, for example, to determine over- or under-withholding of state income taxes on the Dedicated Expense Worksheet. Researching state tax information is a useful skill because planners often have clients who are located in multiple states and, although professional software may account for these differences, some state-specific tax questions will surely arise.

Finally, users of the tax estimator are reminded that it does not accurately compensate for the taxation of long-term capital gains or qualified dividends, which are currently taxed at a lower rate (e.g., 0% or 15% contingent on marginal tax bracket.) Thus, the tax estimator over-estimates tax liability; the extent of the error will depend on the amount of the client's investment income relative to earned income.

**Exhibit 4.1** Federal, Social Security and State Tax Estimator

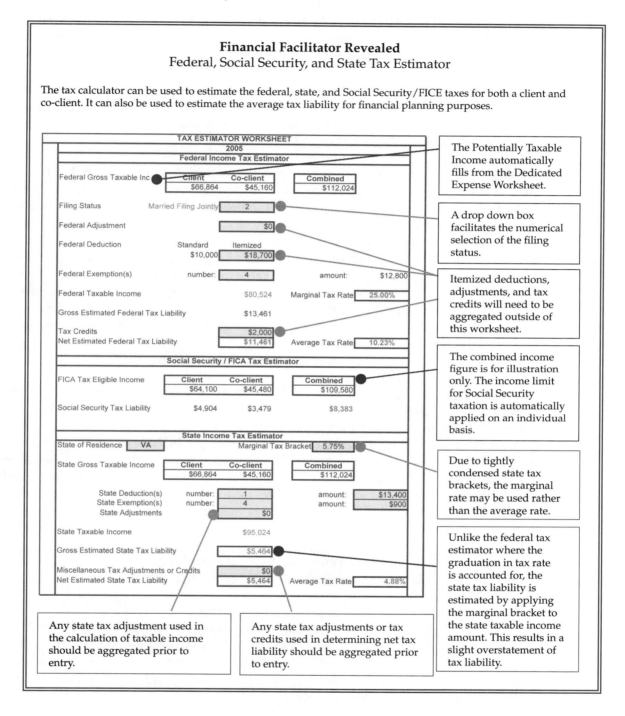

### Financial Facilitator Revealed
#### Federal, Social Security, and State Tax Estimator

The tax calculator can be used to estimate the federal, state, and Social Security/FICE taxes for both a client and co-client. It can also be used to estimate the average tax liability for financial planning purposes.

**TAX ESTIMATOR WORKSHEET**
**2005**

**Federal Income Tax Estimator**

| | Client | Co-client | | Combined |
|---|---|---|---|---|
| Federal Gross Taxable Inc | $66,864 | $45,160 | | $112,024 |

| Filing Status | Married Filing Jointly | 2 |
|---|---|---|

| Federal Adjustment | $0 |
|---|---|

| Federal Deduction | Standard | Itemized |
|---|---|---|
| | $10,000 | $18,700 |

| Federal Exemption(s) | number: | 4 | amount: | $12,800 |
|---|---|---|---|---|

| Federal Taxable Income | $80,524 | Marginal Tax Rate | 25.00% |
|---|---|---|---|

| Gross Estimated Federal Tax Liability | $13,461 |
|---|---|

| Tax Credits | $2,000 | | |
|---|---|---|---|
| Net Estimated Federal Tax Liability | $11,461 | Average Tax Rate | 10.23% |

**Social Security / FICA Tax Estimator**

| | Client | Co-client | | Combined |
|---|---|---|---|---|
| FICA Tax Eligible Income | $64,100 | $45,480 | | $109,580 |

| Social Security Tax Liability | $4,904 | $3,479 | $8,383 |
|---|---|---|---|

**State Income Tax Estimator**

| State of Residence | VA | Marginal Tax Bracket | 5.75% |
|---|---|---|---|

| State Gross Taxable Income | Client | Co-client | | Combined |
|---|---|---|---|---|
| | $66,864 | $45,160 | | $112,024 |

| State Deduction(s) | number: | 1 | amount: | $13,400 |
|---|---|---|---|---|
| State Exemption(s) | number: | 4 | amount: | $900 |
| State Adjustments | | $0 | | |

| State Taxable Income | $95,024 |
|---|---|

| Gross Estimated State Tax Liability | $5,464 |
|---|---|

| Miscellaneous Tax Adjustments or Credits | $0 | | |
|---|---|---|---|
| Net Estimated State Tax Liability | $5,464 | Average Tax Rate | 4.88% |

*Annotations:*

The Potentially Taxable Income automatically fills from the Dedicated Expense Worksheet.

A drop down box facilitates the numerical selection of the filing status.

Itemized deductions, adjustments, and tax credits will need to be aggregated outside of this worksheet.

The combined income figure is for illustration only. The income limit for Social Security taxation is automatically applied on an individual basis.

Due to tightly condensed state tax brackets, the marginal rate may be used rather than the average rate.

Unlike the federal tax estimator where the graduation in tax rate is accounted for, the state tax liability is estimated by applying the marginal bracket to the state taxable income amount. This results in a slight overstatement of tax liability.

Any state tax adjustment used in the calculation of taxable income should be aggregated prior to entry.

Any state tax adjustments or tax credits used in determining net tax liability should be aggregated prior to entry.

## Alternative Minimum Tax

Congress created the **Alternative Minimum Tax (AMT)** to prevent wealthy taxpayers from taking advantage of preferential deductions and paying little or no tax, whereas the regular tax law gives preferential treatment to some kinds of income and allows special deductions and credits for particular kinds of expenses. Therefore, clients who benefit from preferential provisions for regular tax purposes may have to pay the AMT. Although this law was originally written with only the wealthy in mind, in recent years more individuals have found themselves liable for these alternative taxes which, in all cases, are higher than regular taxes.

Common adjustments and tax preference items that can trigger the AMT include those related to personal exemptions, the standard deduction, miscellaneous itemized deductions, state and local tax, accelerated depreciation of certain property, incentive stock options, depletion allowances, intangible drilling costs, and certain tax-exempt interest. Taxpayers with substantial preference items in any given year might trigger the AMT. A taxpayer's taxable income is altered for AMT adjustments and preferences to calculate the alternative minimum taxable income (AMTI). The AMT has two tax rates: 26% on the taxable excess of tentative minimum taxable income over an exemption amount; and 28% on the taxable excess above that amount. AMT exemption amounts change periodically, but the 26% rate has historically been applied to the first $175,000 ($87,500 for married filing separate). The taxpayer's regular tax liability is subtracted from the tentative minimum tax to determine the AMT.

A few strategies can be used to reduce the impact of the AMT if it appears that a client might be subject to it. First, preference deductions should be reviewed and reduced, if possible. For example, it may be appropriate to exercise incentive stock options over time rather than all at once. Another strategy includes exercising incentive stock options in a year when other AMT preference items are minimal. Clients with significant depreciation expenses could consider shifting from accelerated to straight-line depreciation. Another strategy involves accelerating current-year income to help offset preference deductions. An increased bonus or salary advance could be used to increase income.

---

### Tax Planning for Special Populations:
### Executives with Incentive Stock Options (ISOs)

Incentive stock option (ISO) plans are a fairly common but very complex financial planning issue for planners who counsel corporate executives. If an employer grants a client an option to buy stock, there are three potential tax-triggering events. Clients may have to realize income for tax purposes when they (1) receive the option, (2) exercise the option, or (3) sell or transfer either the option prior to exercise or the stock after exercise.

There are two types of stock options: **statutory stock options** and nonstatutory stock options. A statutory plan includes a plan document outlining the conditions of the plan and the number of options to be granted to each employee. Typically, stock options granted under an ISO plan are statutory stock options. ISO plans have two potentially important advantages in comparison to nonstatutory stock options.

First, exercising the ISO option does not trigger any recognition of income or gain. Only the sale of the stock creates a taxable event, and tax is then due only on the difference between the market price at exercise and the sales price.[10] Conversely, with nonstatutory options, income tax must be paid on the difference in the exercise price and the market price in the year the option is exercised.

Second, if the stock is held until at least one year after the date of exercise, or two years from the option grant date, whichever is later, all of the gains on the sale of the stock will be at capital gains rates rather than ordinary income rates. However, if the stock is sold or transferred before the expiration of that holding period—called a *disqualifying disposition*—then all income or gains derived are considered ordinary income.[11]

Although the exercise of an ISO does not trigger a taxable event under the regular tax system, it could under the AMT system. For AMT purposes, the aforementioned tax treatment does not apply to the transfer of stock acquired as a result of the exercise of an incentive stock option.[12] Therefore, for AMT purposes, the difference in the fair market value of the stock and the exercise price of the ISO is treated as taxable income as soon as the executive vests in the right to exercise. In other words, once a client can exercise the option even the unrealized gain on the implied value, considered an AMT adjustment, is taxable in the current year at ordinary income tax rates.

This AMT adjustment has two effects: (1) the adjustment amount may become subject to the AMT and the tax may have to be paid if the filer is subject to AMT and (2) the tax basis in the stock becomes the fair market value on the date the AMT adjustment occurred. Unfortunately, the tax basis of the stock is different for AMT purposes and for regular income tax purposes; hence, the subsequent sale of the stock could generate a gain for regular income tax purposes, whereas it might not generate gain for AMT purposes.

## Document and Evaluate the Current Tax Planning Situation

The second step when analyzing a client's current tax situation involves documenting and evaluating the types of products and strategies a client is currently using to meet tax planning goals and objectives. In some cases, this part of the evaluation is simple. Whether a client is over- or under-withholding taxes may already be apparent. What may be more difficult to assess is the reason taxes are being over- or under-withheld. Over-withholding, for instance, may be because clients consider the process of changing withholding tedious and not worth the time. Financial planners know differently. In other cases, clients might over-withhold to receive a large refund every year. Sometimes clients see this as a boost to income rather than as a return of income. Again, financial planners know otherwise. At this stage of the process it is important for a planner not only to document a client's strategy, but to evaluate and communicate the benefits of the strategy to the client.

Although the term "document and evaluate" (in reference to the client's current tax planning situation) refers to a nebulous part of the systematic financial planning process, in a very real sense it refers to the interaction between the advisor and client to discuss the client's life and financial situation—including decisions that could affect taxes. In this context, the phrase can take on more meaningful nuances. As highlighted in this chapter, tax issues are interwoven throughout the financial planning process. This is particularly evident for money held in qualified retirement plans, where the IRS controls when clients can, cannot, or must access their money. Decisions can affect both the current-year tax situation and have broader implications for future tax scenarios. Consider these three examples.

A client's plan to take a distribution from a qualified retirement plan could result in a 10% early withdrawal penalty tax, in addition to regular income tax, on the taxable portion of the distribution received before age 59½. Under most circumstances, clients under the age of 59½ pay a 10% penalty on distributions (25% from a SIMPLE plan during the first two years of plan participation) in addition to income taxes due.[13] However, the 10% penalty may be waived under certain exceptions. There are exemptions for distributions caused by death or disability, to pay for higher education expenses, and sometimes distributions for a first-time home purchase. A similar 10% penalty also applies to distributions from annuities, IRAs, and other tax-deferred investments.

Required minimum distributions (RMDs) are another area of tax law that affects decisions about retirement planning and contextualizes the client's life. Clients who have assets in traditional, SIMPLE, or SEP IRAs, and those with assets in a qualified defined contribution plan (excluding Roth plans), must begin taking RMDs by April 1 of the year following age 70½. IRS Publication 590 provides a set of Uniform Lifetime Tables that are used to determine minimum distributions. The IRS penalty for failure to take the prescribed RMD is 50% of the amount that should have been withdrawn.

Although the core RMD rule is straightforward, there are several interesting twists to the statute that are important to understand. Some of these include options for "stretch" IRAs that reduce the RMD and extend tax-deferred growth over a longer time period; the alternative calculations of RMDs for inherited spousal and nonspousal IRAs and for surviving spouses who are more than 10 years younger than the decedent; and the option to do a tax-free RMD distribution to charity. The implications of these decisions are potentially far-reaching for the client's family and even society. But without advisor-client meetings to document and evaluate the client's current tax situation or the advisor informing the client of these tax planning options, the benefits might all be lost.

Some clients might have the option to accumulate company stock in their employer-sponsored retirement plans (e.g., 401k plan). Although other planning issues are related to the decision to include company stock in a retirement plan, distributions from such plans could be eligible for special tax treatment. First, it is important to remember that for taxation purposes the amount of a withdrawal from such a plan is considered in two parts: the cost basis and the accumulated value, or appreciation. The original cost basis of a withdrawal is taxed as ordinary income and therefore at the client's marginal tax rate. Any withdrawal above the cost basis amount is taxed at capital gains tax rates (capped at 15% in 2012). Second, it is important to consider that there are two options for withdrawing accumulated company stock—each resulting in different tax outcomes, the better of which may not be intuitively obvious. Clients who anticipate being in a higher marginal tax bracket in the future should consider taking company stock distributions directly rather than rolling assets into an IRA. The reason for this is that if the stock is rolled into a traditional IRA the entire withdrawal amount, basis and gain, is subject to taxation at ordinary rates upon final distribution from the IRA.

By taking an in-kind, lump-sum distribution from the qualified retirement plan and placing the assets in a *nonqualified* account, the client's stock assets become eligible for the **net unrealized appreciation** (NUA) tax treatment. In this case, the distribution is immediately taxable at ordinary income rates, but only the cost basis of the distributed amount of stock is subject to income tax, not the appreciation portion of the account. In addition, a 10% tax penalty may also be applicable if the client is under age 59½. This is almost the reverse of other plans, where the basis is not taxable but the gains are; the choice of a qualified account is typically a better option than a nonqualified account. With the NUA tax treatment a client recognizes the "income" rather than the "gain."

Because the stock was in a qualified retirement plan, the deferred income or employee-benefit dollars used to purchase the stock originally were never taxed, so income tax is owed at the time of distribution. When the client subsequently sells the stock, taxes will be due at the long-term capital gains rate on any NUA and the applicable capital gains rate (i.e., short- or long-term) on any additional appreciation. With careful planning, it may be a better option to pay income tax on the basis and capital gains tax on the appreciation later than to pay income taxes on the entire value later when using a qualified IRA account.

These examples illustrate that it is not enough simply to know how to calculate tax liabilities; rather, it is important to integrate tax calculation estimates with client situational factors. These examples, some of which are discussed in greater detail in Chapter 12, also demonstrate how understanding a client's current situation and the tax code can directly affect tax planning. Furthermore, tax planning can significantly influence a client's goals and decisions across the life cycle. They also illustrate a simple tax planning idiom: A client's current tax situation, or a planner's recommendations, should never be viewed in isolation. A financial planning strategy that might, at first glance, appear to benefit a client's financial situation could have underlying tax consequences that must be considered before making the recommendation.

---

### Tax Planning Tip: Challenging an IRS Decision

The IRS could impose penalties and enforce other deficiency actions when a client fails to pay the correct income, estate, or payroll tax. Although the IRS tends to be aggressive when enforcing deficiency notices, individual taxpayers can disagree and challenge the agency's findings. This is known as placing a ruling in IRS **dispute**. In most cases, the first step when disputing a deficiency involves filing an appeal with the administrative appeals office of the IRS. Once the appeal has been received, the appeals office will schedule a phone or in-person conference to discuss the case. Nearly all individual cases are settled at this level.

If not settled, the next step involves challenging the IRS decision by bypassing the appeals process and going directly to the courts. American citizens can take their claims to the United States Tax Court, the United States Court of Federal Claims, or the District Court where they reside. These courts are independent and not affiliated with the IRS; however, it is important to remember that a frivolous filing penalty of up to $25,000 can be imposed if a case is found to purposely cause a delay in collection. There are time limits and required paperwork for both courses of action, and as such, financial planners who are not attorneys, CPAs, or EAs should refer client deficiency cases to one of these professionals. However, planners should have a fundamental knowledge of the process of challenging an IRS decision. A number of IRS resources are available.[14]

## STRATEGIES

### Review Prospective Tax Planning Strategies

On December 16, 2010, Congress passed the Tax Relief, Unemployment Insurance Reauthorization, and Job Creation Act of 2010. This legislation provided for a short-term extension of tax cuts made in 2001 under the Bush administration, as well as making adjustments to the AMT and estate, gift, and generation-skipping transfer taxes. This act reinstated several important tax benefits that were set to expire. Although there is no certainty that all current tax benefits will remain in effect going forward, it is nonetheless important for financial planners to note that the following tax rates and benefits were extended for 2010–2012. Highlights of the bill follow.

*Two-year Tax Extension: Reductions in Individual Income Tax Rates through 2012*

- Continued income brackets at 10%, 25%, 28%, 33%, and 35%.

- Continued capital gains and dividend rates at 0% or 15%.

- Repealed the personal exemption phase-out (PEP).

- Repealed the itemized deduction limitation (Pease limitation) so there is no maximum for itemized deductions reported on IRS Schedule A.

- Extended the marriage penalty relief.

- Expanded the dependent care credit.

- Continued the Child Tax Credit of $1,000.

- Continued the earned income tax credit.

*Education Incentives Extended through 2012*

- Expanded Coverdell accounts and definition of education expenses

- Expanded exclusion for employer-provided educational assistance of up to $5,250

- Expanded student loan interest deduction

- Excluded from income amounts received under certain scholarship programs

- Continued American Opportunity Tax Credit of up to $2,500 for tuition expenses

*Temporary Extension of Investment Incentives*

- Extended the bonus depreciation for taxable years 2011 and 2012.

- Increased the maximum amount and phase-out threshold for small business expensing under IRC § 179. The maximum amount and phase-out threshold for tax year 2012 were increased to $125,000 and $500,000 respectively; future increase will be indexed for inflation.

*Temporary Employee Payroll Tax Cut*

- This legislation created a 2% payroll/self-employment tax holiday during 2011 that was later extended through 2012. The employer's share of the payroll tax remains unchanged, but employees pay only 4.2% on wages and self-employed individuals pay only 10.4% on self-employment income up to $110,100. Transfers from the general fund make up the difference in the Social Security trust fund.

*AMT Relief*

- This legislation increased the exemption amounts for 2010 to $47,450 (individuals) and $72,450 (married filing jointly) and for 2011 to $48,450 (individuals) and $74,450 (married filing jointly). It also allows nonrefundable personal credits against the AMT. Unfortunately, without congressional action to retroactively change the AMT exemption, it returned to $33,750 for a single filer and to $45,000 for joint filers for tax year 2012.

*Extensions of Certain Tax Provisions for Individuals through 2011 (These are expired as of the writing of this text; however, there were several Congressional initiatives that could reinstate one or more of the provisions.)*

- Above-the-line deduction of qualified tuition and related expenses was extended.

- Tax-free distributions of up to $100,000 from individual retirement plans for charitable purposes were extended.

- A 30% credit for energy-efficiency improvements to the home was extended (IRC § 25C).

- The deduction of state and local general sales taxes was extended.

- Parity for employer-provided mass transit benefits was extended.

- Provisions allowing for contributions of appreciated real property for conservation purposes were extended.

- The deductibility of mortgage insurance premiums for qualified residences was extended.

- Estate tax look-through of certain regulated investment company (RIC) stock held by nonresidents for decedents dying before January 1, 2012, was extended.

- Above-the-line deduction of certain expenses for elementary and secondary school teachers was extended.

Although the extension of the Bush era tax cuts provides some degree of planning flexibility, the fact that these extensions and adjustments are all temporary, typically lasting no more than two years means that considerable uncertainty continues to exist for clients. But perhaps this legislation demonstrates some important reminders for students and novice planners. Understanding the history of tax legislation and the tax code provides a valuable perspective when reviewing a client's financial situation or considering a possible tax planning strategy. This legislation highlights the significance of a planner's commitment to lifelong learning. Staying abreast of the changing tax code, even if the financial advisor does not prepare taxes, is a necessity. Finally, this legislation serves as a reminder that any strategy must be considered in light of its usefulness in the near term—and perhaps the need to take advantage of current opportunities before they expire—as well projected changes for the future. For example, the widespread concern that marginal tax rates might increase in the future makes Roth IRAs and Roth 401(k) plans more attractive for eligible clients, because they lock in the tax rate rather than gambling on the rate to be paid during retirement.

## Identify Prospective Income Tax Planning Strategies

The following strategies, some of which are shown in Figure 4.2, represent a cross-section of strategies used in the financial planning process. It is important to note that these strategies represent only a sampling of commonly used product and procedural strategies. Additionally, when reviewing their advantages and disadvantages, it is important to note that each client's situation will dictate which strategies are most appropriate. Finally, when in doubt about which strategy to recommend, consult with a CPA, EA, or other tax professional, or collaborate with the client's tax professional.

### Product Strategy 1: Convert Taxable Interest to Tax-exempt Interest

**Advantage:** This strategy helps reduce the amount of income reported on IRS Form 1040 by reducing the amount of interest income subject to tax. It is most appropriate for clients in the highest marginal tax bracket. This strategy can also be beneficial for clients in lower brackets whenever the return on a tax-exempt investment exceeds the after-tax return on taxable investments.

**Disadvantage:** Three potential drawbacks are associated with this strategy. First, municipal securities tend to trade less frequently and in smaller markets. Investors who use this strategy with individual securities could subject themselves to a higher degree of illiquidity and marketability than investors who purchase individual taxable securities. Second, the difference between a taxable and tax-free rate is not stable. In some instances, tax-free rates exceed after-tax rates of return. In other cases, a fully taxable security will provide a better return, even for high-marginal-tax-bracket clients. Third, certain tax-free interest can trigger the AMT. Clients with large amounts of tax-free interest should be aware that they may end up paying a higher tax rate if they trigger the AMT.

## Product Strategy 2: Replace Consumer Debt with Tax-advantaged Debt

**Advantage:** If a client has outstanding credit card bills or other short-term liabilities, one recommendation involves obtaining a **home equity loan** or **home equity line of credit** and using the proceeds to pay off short-term debt. This strategy should have two immediate results. First, it is likely that the client's monthly discretionary cash flow will increase. Home equity loans and lines of credit typically carry interest rates substantially below those paid for other open lines of credit. The reduction in interest paid should reduce monthly expenditures for debt payment.

Second, any interest paid on home equity loans and interest on expended lines of credit could be tax deductible if the client itemizes deductions. However, it is important to remember that there are several limitations to this strategy. First, home equity debt interest is deductible only if the loan is the lesser of (1) $100,000; or (2) the fair market value of the home, less first mortgage debt. Second, for AMT purposes, any refinanced indebtedness on which interest is deductible is limited to the amount of indebtedness prior to refinancing. Finally, initial acquisition debt interest is deductible for federal income taxes on only the first $1 million used to acquire, build, or improve a residence.

**Disadvantage:** This strategy places a client's home equity at risk by taking short-term consumption debt and extending payments into the future. This strategy should probably not be used if a client has a habitual spending problem or problems managing credit. Furthermore, this strategy may be limited or unavailable to clients subject to the AMT, because interest deductions for refinanced property can be denied under certain circumstances.

## Product Strategy 3: Consider Investing in a Roth rather than a Traditional IRA

**Advantage:** A traditional IRA, with deductible contributions and tax deferral, provides a good way to reduce taxable income while saving for retirement. Another strategy may be to make nondeductible contributions to a Roth IRA. Qualified distributions from a Roth IRA can be received tax free. This tax-free distribution of income from a Roth IRA in the future can, under certain circumstances, provide greater after-tax benefits than the immediate tax deduction and tax deferral of a traditional IRA.

**Disadvantage:** This strategy subjects a client to two risks. First, Congress may someday repeal the tax-free status of Roth IRAs. Second, if marginal tax rates are lower when a client retires, the traditional IRA with its tax deduction could be preferable. Also, income restrictions apply that prohibit Roth IRA contributions for some clients.

### Product Strategy 4: Compare 529 Plans, UGMAs, and UTMAs to Save Taxes and Plan for College

**Advantage:** § **529 plans** have gained popularity among financial planners and clients for two reasons. First, contributions are often given special state tax incentives. Second, withdrawals from such plans, if used in accordance with the rules, are tax free. **UGMA** or **UTMA** accounts can also be used to save for college. Effective tax planning is needed at the outset and throughout the planning process to make this recommendation work. The only way to obtain a long-term capital gain rate of 0% on custodial accounts is to make sure that asset sales do not push the child into a marginal income tax rate higher than 15%. Also, to obtain the low capital gains rate, asset sales in an account must generally occur after the child turns age 19 (age 24 if a full-time student). Asset sales prior to age 19 (age 24 if a full-time student) could result in distributions being taxed at the parents' marginal tax rate.

**Disadvantage:** Maybe the most important disadvantage planners and clients must understand is that funding educational expenses with custodial accounts does not guarantee that assets will be used for this purpose. With custodial accounts, parents lose control of the assets. Legally, assets are the property of the child, and at the age of majority, age 18 or 21 in most states, the child controls the use of those assets. Furthermore, in 2012, the annual gift exclusion of $13,000 applies to contributions per child; however, a special five-year provision can be elected that allows up to $65,000 to be contributed in one year to a § 529 plan without triggering a tax liability.

## Procedural Strategy 1: Match Withholdings to Tax Liability

**Advantage:** In the majority of cases, a client will be in the position of either over- or under-withholding taxes. In situations where a client is over-withholding taxes, it is the planner's responsibility to show how matching liabilities to withholding can enhance a client's financial situation. If the client can reduce withholding, the client can invest the increased cash flow immediately instead of waiting for a tax refund early the next year. For most clients, the amount earned on the accelerated cash flow is minimal.

In cases where a client owes more than was withheld, it is important to show both how the tax liability can be paid and how tax liabilities and withholding can be matched in future years. Failure to withhold enough or to make estimated payments, if required, can result in the taxpayer having to pay interest and penalties.

**Disadvantage:** Matching tax withholding to tax liabilities does not work well for clients who need a measure of forced savings. By reducing monthly withholding, discretionary cash flow will increase. Clients who tend to spend rather than save may find that this strategy reduces their net worth while actually decreasing their annual level of discretionary cash flow.

## Procedural Strategy 2: Maximize Deductions for Adjusted Gross Income

**Advantage:** This strategy provides clients who are not subject to a phase-out for deductions or personal exemptions based on the amount of the client's income one of the best ways to decrease taxable income. Examples of deductions for AGI include educator expenses, contributions to traditional IRAs, student loan interest, tuition fees, moving expenses, one-half of self-employment taxes, self-employed qualified plan contributions, IRA early withdrawal penalties, and alimony paid. It may be possible to prepay some of these expenses in high-income years, thus reducing income for tax purposes.

**Disadvantage:** The primary disadvantage associated with this strategy is that many of the deductions for AGI are applicable to only certain taxpayers (e.g., some deductions apply only to the self-employed). Also, many deductions from AGI can be subject to a phase-out based on income. In that case, a deduction for AGI, which reduces AGI, can have the effect of reducing a deduction from AGI. Similarly, personal exemptions also may be subject to phase-out based on AGI.

## Procedural Strategy 3: Increase Tax Credit Items

**Advantage:** A tax credit decreases tax liability dollar for dollar. Some of the most common tax credits are the: (a) foreign tax credit, (b) credit for child and dependent care expenses, (c) credit for the elderly or the disabled; (d) education credits; (e) retirement savings contributions credit; (f) child tax credit; and (g) adoption credit. Paying for the educational expenses of the taxpayer or other dependents is a way to take advantage of the education-based tax credits. For example, the use of the American Opportunity Tax Credit can reduce tax liability by up to $2,500 in any given year.

**Disadvantage:** One disadvantage of this strategy is that the approach may not work for high-income clients. Some of the preceding tax credits are subject to income phase-out restrictions, making them out of reach for high-income clients. Another potential disadvantage is that some of the credits are intended to help younger taxpayers and families and may not be available or of use to others.

## Procedural Strategy 4: Maximize Pretax Retirement Plan and Benefit Contributions

**Advantage:** One of the best ways to minimize taxes is to legally reduce the amount of income reported for tax purposes. Maximizing pretax retirement plan and benefit contributions is one method to reduce reportable taxable income. Contributing more to a qualified retirement plan, such as a 401(k) plan, is one strategy that reduces current taxes while increasing savings for retirement. Other contribution alternatives include taking full advantage of employer-provided health benefits, including medical, dental, eye, and disability insurance. Deductions for employer-sponsored insurance typically reduce taxable income. This tax-reduction strategy, in effect, reduces the overall cost of policy premiums, making group benefits more affordable in many cases.

**Disadvantage:** Like many of the procedural strategies presented in this chapter, this tactic is not available to all clients. For example, a client who currently maximizes qualified retirement plan contributions may not be able to implement this strategy. Furthermore, the types of group benefits provided by an employer may be limited. Additionally, when clients purchase group term life insurance it is likely they will incur a § 79 income tax liability (see Chapter 3 for more information on how to calculate § 79 income).

### Procedural Strategy 5: Maximize Qualified Dividends while Reducing Interest Received

**Advantage:** Dividend tax rates are currently capped at 15%, 0% for taxpayers in the 10% and 15% tax rate brackets, in 2012; however, these rates are subject to change. This means that income received in the form of qualified dividends will be taxed at a lower rate than ordinary interest income.

**Disadvantage:** Although dividends are currently taxed at a low rate compared to regular interest, implementing this strategy for any reason other than to increase the rate of return on long-term savings or to supplement a fixed-income portfolio can be risky. For example, using dividend-paying stocks to form an emergency fund could create a liquidity risk for a client. Further, tax laws are constantly in flux. It is possible that the tax-advantaged nature of dividends will be repealed in the future.

### Procedural Strategy 6: Maximize Long-term Capital Gains

**Advantage:** Investment property sold for a long-term gain is taxed at a maximum rate of 15% in 2012. Clients in the 10% and 15% marginal tax brackets pay 0% on capital gains in 2012. Holding capital assets for more than one year can reduce a client's tax liability.

**Disadvantage:** Employing this strategy imposes an opportunity cost on clients by creating an incentive to hold an asset longer than might otherwise be prudent. For instance, a gain can quickly turn to a loss over a relatively short period of time. It is sometimes better to capture a short-term gain than to risk a loss to ensure a lower capital gain rate. As with all tax law, it is possible that the tax advantage associated with long-term capital gains will be repealed in the future.

### Procedural Strategy 7: Donate Appreciated Investments to Charity

**Advantage:** This can be one of the best strategies to reduce current taxable income and eliminate assets from a client's gross estate. If an appreciated asset, such as a stock or mutual fund, is sold first and the proceeds donated to charity, the client will have to pay a capital gains tax on the sale. Even though the long-term capital gains tax rate is now low, selling first reduces the amount of the total donation to the charity by 0% or 15%. Instead, clients should generally donate property and securities rather than selling them. The charity can then sell the property on a tax-free basis. In this way, the total amount of capital gains can be excluded from income. This strategy also maximizes the total amount of the charitable donation.

**Disadvantage:** This strategy is beneficial only if the property donated provides a long-term gain. Short-term gain property donated to a qualified charity is deductible only up to the client's basis in the property. In such cases, the client loses the capital appreciation amount as a potential donation.

## *Procedural Strategy 8: Shift Medical Expenses to a Lower-income Year*

**Advantage:** It is very difficult for clients to treat unreimbursed medical expenses as an itemized deduction because of the 7.5% of AGI rule. One strategy that can work for clients who do have large medical bills is to shift these expenses into years when household income is lower. For example, if a client knows that he or she will terminate employment or retire, it may be helpful to postpone major medical expenses until that year, if possible. This tactic allows the medical expenses to be deducted if their total cost exceeds 7.5% of the client's new lower AGI.

**Disadvantage:** The primary disadvantage of this strategy is that it may be difficult, if not impossible, to postpone certain medical expenses. In many cases, medical bills and related expenses are the result of an emergency or unplanned event, and as such, a client may have little control over the timing of care and payment of expenses.

## *Procedural Strategy 9: Maximize the Number of Dependents, or Exemptions, Claimed*

**Advantage:** If a client is paying the majority of expenses for a child, parent, sibling, or other qualifying person, efforts should be made to determine whether the person can be claimed as a dependent. The benefit of this strategy is that additional exemptions can be claimed in any given year. This can result in a reduced level of income for tax purposes.

**Disadvantage:** Whenever a child becomes semi-independent, it creates a dilemma. It may be beneficial for a child who is in college, for instance, to claim that he or she is not a dependent. This could result in increased levels of financial aid and other benefits. However, doing so reduces the number of dependents claimed by a parent, which could result in increased tax liability.

## *Procedural Strategy 10: Consider Establishing a Business*

**Advantage:** All of the strategies provided up to this point have been general in nature and applicable to almost any client situation. This strategy, on the other hand, should be considered whenever a client's income exceeds phase-out limits for certain deductions and credits. Establishing a business could be a good way to convert non-tax-deductible expenses into income-tax-reducing deductions. For example, someone who opens a consulting practice could begin to deduct some expenses related to travel, entertainment, and marketing. Other potential deductions include home office expenses, cell phone charges, and computer equipment. Furthermore, a business owner can deduct contributions to certain types of retirement plans.

**Disadvantage:** Tax law requires that a business show an operating profit in at least three out of five years, or at least on honest attempt to generate a profit. Some clients who attempt to implement this recommendation run afoul of hobby loss rules, which define which expenses are deductible when an activity is not classified as a profit-making endeavor. The IRS looks very critically at a commercial enterprise that may really be a hobby rather than a legitimate business.

---

**Tax Planning Tip: The Primary Forms of Business Ownership**

Financial planners must be familiar with the six primary forms of business ownership: (1) sole proprietorship; (2) partnership; (3) limited liability partnership (LLP); (4) limited liability company (LLC), (5) S-corporation (S-corp), and (6) C-corporation (C-corp). A sole proprietorship is a single-person business that provides the owner with the least liability protection but the easiest form of income taxation. In effect, the company and individual are the same entity. A partnership, as the name implies, is a business owned by two or more individuals. Each partner is jointly responsible for the financial obligations of the company. An LLC provides greater liability protection than either a sole proprietorship or partnership while still allowing income to be taxed at the individual level. That is, earnings from the company are passed through to shareholders. Individuals, partnerships, trusts, and foreign investors can be shareholders. LLCs are inexpensive and easy to establish. An LLP combines elements of a corporation and a partnership. LLPs avoid double taxation by allocating profits among partners; however, unlike traditional partnerships, one LLP partner is not liable for another partner's misconduct or negligence. S-corps and C-corps have many similarities. Shareholders in each entity have limited liability. Both must have an elected board of directors and officers. The primary difference between the two revolves around the number of shareholders and the taxation of profits. S-corps limit the number of shareholders. More importantly, it is possible for C-corps to incur double taxation, meaning profits can be taxed at the corporate level first and then taxed again as dividends at the individual level. In the case of an S-corp, earnings pass directly through to shareholders, who are responsible for paying income tax directly, thus avoiding double taxation.

---

## Procedural Strategy 11: Use Like-kind Exchange Strategies Appropriately

**Advantage**: IRC §1031 features a provision for owners of investment property to exchange property without incurring immediate taxation. For this to be an effective tax-postponing strategy, a client must exchange his or her property for a similar kind or class of asset. For example, a business can be exchanged for another business, or an investment property (e.g., an apartment building) can be exchanged for another investment property (e.g., a rental house). Boot, defined as the receipt of non-like-kind property, can trigger taxation.

**Disadvantage**: Sometimes clients attempt to exchange investment securities or personal use property. The IRS will not allow such transfers. Furthermore, real estate can be exchanged only for real estate, which is defined as improved or unimproved land, buildings, warehouses, etc.

## Procedural Strategy 12: Understand the Implications of Realized and Unrealized Gains

**Advantage**: A **realized gain** (or loss) is calculated by subtracting the adjusted basis in property from the sale price of the property. Realized gains (or losses) are reported on a client's IRS Form 1040. Sometimes a gain (or loss) is not immediately recognized (i.e., reported on IRS Form 1040). In these situations the gain (or loss) is unrecognized. Examples of situations that might result in an unrealized gain (or loss) include completing a § 1031 like-kind exchange, the sale of personal use assets, and some gains on the sale of a personal residence (e.g., a $250,000 gain for a single taxpayer). Understanding when a gain or loss must be reported can be an effective tool to help clients maximize cash flow by managing and minimizing tax liabilities.

**Disadvantage**: Misinterpretation of gains rules can result in tax penalties. For example, selling personal property for a loss is not an eligible tax deduction strategy; however, selling personal property (e.g., sales at a garage sale) that results in a gain is technically taxable. Care must be taken whenever a like-kind exchange strategy is employed.

### Procedural Strategy 13: Calculate the Exclusion Ratio to Reduce the Tax on Annuity Distributions

**Advantage**: Careful attention should be paid in situations where a client is taking distributions from an annuity, IRA, or qualified plan. If any contribution was made using after-tax dollars, or if any of the contribution was taxed previously, a portion of the total distribution will be considered a tax-free distribution. Calculating the exclusion ratio can reduce the probability that a client will pay unnecessary taxes. The exclusion ratio formula is as follows:

$$\text{Exclusion Ratio} = \frac{\text{Total After-tax Contributions}}{\text{Total Expected Distributions}}$$

Where:

Total Expected Distributions is calculated by multiplying the monthly distribution by the number of expected distribution years times 12 (i.e., months per year).

For example, assume a client expects to receive $2,000 per month over a 20-year period. If the client originally invested $300,000 on an after-tax basis, the exclusion ratio would indicate that 62.5% of each distribution would be received tax free; that is, 37.5% of each distribution will be taxable.

**Disadvantage**: It is possible that distributions will last longer than the expected duration used in the formula. In these situations, all of the after-tax contributions are accounted for. This will result in all future distributions being fully taxable. Clients who fail to track cumulative distributions could incur tax penalties at some point in the future.

### Procedural Strategy 14: Compare Taxable and Tax-free Interest on a Taxable Equivalent Yield Basis

**Advantage**: Recall from Chapter 2 that financial planners should be adept at calculating taxable equivalent yields as a means of comparing taxable and tax-free fixed income investments. The following formula should be used as a means of determining the yield need for a taxable fixed-income investment to match that of a state and federally tax-free fixed income investment:

$$\text{Federal Tax - Exempt TEY} = \frac{\text{Taxable Bond Yield}}{[1 - FMTB]}$$

$$\text{State Tax - exempt TEY} = \frac{\text{Taxable Bond Yield}}{[1 - SMTB]}$$

$$\text{Fully Tax - exempt TEY} = \frac{\text{Taxable Bond Yield}}{[1 - (FMTB + (SMTB \times (1 - FMTB)))]}$$

Where:

TEY = Taxable equivalent yield

FMTB = federal marginal tax bracket

SMTB = state marginal tax bracket

For example, if a client lives in a state with a 5% marginal rate and is in the 25% federal marginal tax bracket, it is possible to compare to two bonds—a fully taxable 8.25% corporate bond and a 6.0% municipal bond. The TEY on the municipal bond would be is 8.42% if the bond was issued from a municipality in the same state as the client's state of residence. Therefore, the client would be better off purchasing the municipal bond. However, if the client purchased a municipal bond from another state, the interest would not be state tax exempt, so the TEY would be only 8.00%. In this case, the client should purchase the corporate bond and pay the tax.

It is not uncommon to find municipal bonds in a client's portfolio. An analysis may be required to determine whether municipal securities are in fact appropriate for a client. The following formula, which is simply a rearrangement of the preceding formulas to solve for the alternative variable, can be used to determine the **before-tax equivalent taxable rate of return** for an investment.

$$\text{Taxable Yield} = \frac{\text{Tax - Free Bond Yield}}{(1 - \text{Client's Marginal Tax Bracket})}$$

For example, a client in the 25% marginal tax bracket earning 4% interest on a municipal bond would need to earn at least 5.33% [4% ÷ (1 – 25%)] in a similar taxable bond to make the taxable alternative equivalent to the tax-free bond.

Another, similar formula is for **after-tax yield** (or equivalent tax-free rate of return), which can be calculated using the following formula:

After-tax yield = Taxable rate × (1 × client's marginal tax bracket)

Therefore, the same client who owned a taxable bond that yielded 4% interest ought to consider purchasing municipal securities whenever the yield on municipals is equal to or greater than 3% [4% × (1 – 25%)].

**Disadvantage**: Several assumptions are associated with the use of the preceding formulas. It is possible and likely that over time the marginal tax rates in a particular state will change. When this happens it is important to rerun the analysis. Also, bond rates change on a regular basis. What is an attractive tax-free rate today may be a less appealing rate tomorrow. Again, the use of this formula is not a one-time calculation; advisors are encouraged to conduct yield analyses on an ongoing basis. Finally, it is important to remember that the tax-exempt status of municipal bonds does not extend to all instances of the AMT calculation.

### Procedural Strategy 15: Understand when a Client Should Itemize Deductions

**Advantage**: According to the IRS, financial planning clients should itemize deductions if their allowable itemized deductions are more than the **standard deduction**. Some clients itemize deductions because they do not qualify for the standard deduction. **IRS Schedule A** is used to itemize the following deductions:

- Medical and dental expenses (subject to an AGI threshold)

- Deductible taxes, including state income and local property taxes

- Home mortgage points

- Interest expenses (e.g., interest on home mortgages)

- Contributions

- Casualty and theft losses (subject to an AGI threshold)

- Miscellaneous expenses (subject to an AGI threshold)

- Business use of home

- Business Use of Car

- Business Travel Expenses

- Business entertainment expenses

- Educational expenses

- Employee business expenses

- Casualty, disaster, and theft losses (subject to an AGI threshold)

**Disadvantage**: There are many rules and limitations applicable to itemizing deductions, but whenever clients have eligible expenses that exceed the standard deduction, they should claim the higher itemized amount. However, this in turn can create additional income reporting confusion for the subsequent year. For example, clients who claim the state income tax as an itemized deduction are required to report any refund of state tax overpayment as income on the federal income tax form the following year. Forgetting to claim the state tax refund as income can result in fines and penalties.

For clients who live in an income-tax-free state, IRS Schedule A should be completed using IRS guidelines for the sales tax deduction, in lieu of the income tax deduction, if continued by Congress. Assuming that a client should not complete IRS Schedule A because no state income taxes are paid could result in an increased federal tax liability.

### Procedural Strategy 16: Review Cost Basis Rules when Advising Clients about Gifts

**Advantage:** Sometimes clients are confused when calculating the tax gain or loss on an investment asset received as a gift. The rules relating to non-cash investment gifts can be found in IRS Publication 550 and are as follows:

- The holding period of the asset is transferred to the giftee.

- If the asset is sold for less than its fair market value on the date of the gift, the basis is the date-of-gift fair market value.

- If the asset is sold for more than the original basis of the asset (i.e., the amount paid when the asset was originally purchased), the original basis is used.

- If the asset is sold for less than the original basis but more than the date-of-gift fair market value, no gain or loss is recognized.

*Example*: Your client's father purchases bonds for $20,000. The father gifts the bonds to your client. At the time of the gift the bonds are worth $10,000. If the bonds are sold for $9,000, the client records a $1,000 loss. If the bonds are sold for $25,000, the client records a $5,000 gain. If the bonds are sold for $15,000, no gain or loss is recorded.

**Disadvantage:** Although not strictly a disadvantage, it is important to remind clients that whenever they give or receive a gift that could be deemed an investment they should record and retain information related to the date of the gift, its original basis, and the fair market value of the asset on the gift date. Without this information the IRS could limit claims of loss or maximize a sale gain if the client is audited. It is also worth noting that in cases where the current value of the asset is less than the original basis but more than the date-of-gift fair market value, the donee should be advised to sell the asset, capture the tax loss, and then transfer the assets to the giftee.

## CHAPTER-BASED CASE STUDY

## A Client-based Tax Recommendation Example

The quantitative analysis portion of the income tax planning process revolves around IRS Form 1040 and its accompanying schedules. To be a competent financial planner, it is necessary to have a thorough understanding of this tax form, which is the basis of all income tax strategies for individuals. Reviewing a client's IRS Form 1040 from previous years is useful in the planning process because this document shows not only the amount of income earned by a client, but also where large annual expenses are allocated. This information can then be used to develop tax strategies for future years so that tax liabilities are reduced and discretionary cash flow is increased.

In addition to providing insight into increasing discretionary cash flow, a client's IRS Form 1040 can be used to better understand retirement, insurance, and college planning issues. For example, based on retirement income replacement ratios, it is possible to determine whether a client is saving enough current income to meet future retirement income needs. Data from this form can be used to determine whether a client is maximizing employer-provided pretax benefits, such as a 401(k) plan. Clients who are employed but also have other income, which would also be shown on IRS Form 1040, may require special financial planning help. If, for instance, a client's tax return indicates that he or she generated consulting fees or gains from another business, there might be an opportunity to establish a retirement plan to shelter even more income from taxes. In other words, the first page of IRS Form 1040 can provide a quick glimpse into other investment and retirement opportunities for the planner and client to work on together.

IRS Form 1040 can also be useful in determining whether a client may need IRA rollover guidance and advice. If moving expenses are noted, this could suggest a separation from service from another employer. At the very least, noting these issues can lead to enhanced planner-client discussions. If a client is self-employed, a tax return can be a preplanning guide to financial service needs. Self-employed clients may need life, health, and disability benefits that, if managed correctly, can enhance the client's life while reducing future income tax via expenses, which also are shown on IRS Form 1041 and its schedules.

The number of dependents claimed on IRS Form 1040 can also present an interesting point of discussion for a planner and client. If a client has young dependents, in most cases this will result in reduced tax liability from a combination of personal exemptions and child tax credits. It could be appropriate to provide advice regarding education funding plans to clients in this situation.

As these examples show, tax planning differs from tax preparation in that planning involves more than simply crunching numbers to arrive at a client's projected tax liability. Tax planning, if done correctly, is holistic, taking into account both qualitative and quantitative issues and is integrative across core content planning areas. Tax planning strategies affect as they are affected by other recommendations in a comprehensive plan.

Tax planning is integrative to the extent that tax recommendations are incorporated into other parts of the planning process. Effective tax planning can provide insights into ways to increase monthly discretionary cash flow. Tax planning can also be used to prompt deeper planner-client discussions regarding retirement, investment, insurance, and education planning. Figure 4.3 illustrates one process that can potentially be used to narrow strategies down into one or more client recommendations. Note that this process is premised on the notion that, regardless of the approach chosen, the recommendation or recommendations match the client's tax planning goals and objectives.

**Figure 4.3** Decision Tree for Developing Tax Planning Recommendations

Finally, before making tax planning recommendations or recommendations in other core content planning areas, several issues should always be reviewed. This practice will help students and novice planners gain confidence that their recommendations reflect current and proposed tax code as well as the important and integrative role of taxes throughout the financial planning process. These issues include:

- possible AMT triggers;

- contribution levels to employer-provided tax-advantaged benefit plans;

- allocations among pretax, taxable, and tax-free investment assets;

- present and future business ownership interests;

- non-tax-advantaged debt compared to home equity debt; and

- where applicable, the ability to meet tax adjustment, deduction, and credit income limits.

## A Sample Recommendation: Matching Withholding to Liabilities While Increasing Charitable Contributions

A popular tax planning recommendation involves reducing the level of payroll withholding for clients who receives an annual refund. Clients who regularly receive refunds are, in effect, making an interest-free loan to the United States government. Over-withholding may be a valid strategy in cases where interest rates are low and a client has trouble saving money on a monthly basis, but for the majority of clients this approach does not make sense. Clients who over-withhold are paying a significant opportunity cost for this action. Over-withholding reduces the amount of monthly discretionary cash flow that can be used to meet other financial goals and objectives.

In this example, a client who is over-withholding taxes by $4,000 per year has come to her financial planner with the wish to increase monthly donations to her church. The client has committed to a building program at her church, but she has found that coming up with an extra $200 per month from discretionary cash flow is not as easy as she expected. Fortunately, her financial planner has developed a twofold recommendation that will help the client meet her objective. The planner's recommendation first requires the client to change **IRS Form W-4** withholdings so that approximately $333 less income is withheld on a monthly basis. This has the effect of increasing the client's monthly level of discretionary cash flow. (However, this has no effect on annual discretionary cash flow, because adjusting withholding, in effect, merely shifts the timing of when tax is paid for a year.) The client can then use this cash flow to fund her charitable giving objective.

Taxation and other planning benefits are associated with this recommendation. In this situation, the client's initial cash flow is increased by $333 per month and then decreased by $200 per month to fund the charitable contribution. This leaves the client with $133 per month that can be used to fund other financial planning goals, such as retirement. Assuming that the client itemizes tax deductions, the donations will result in a higher charitable deduction for the year. If the client is in the 25% marginal tax bracket, this will result in $600 of tax savings per year ($200 × 12 months × 25%). If the client's income remains stable, she can still expect a tax refund because the charitable donation will decrease her overall tax liability.

Moving from the review of tax strategies to the development of recommendations is straightforward. It is important to answer the seven implementation points—who, what, when, where, why, how, and how much—when developing recommendations. The planning recommendation form in Exhibit 4.2 illustrates how this recommendation can be summarized and presented.

**Exhibit 4.2** Income Tax Planning Recommendation Form

| Planning Recommendation Form | | | | |
|---|---|---|---|---|
| **Financial Planning Content Area** | Tax Planning | | | |
| **Client Goal** | Reduce Monthly Federal Tax Withholdings to Increase Monthly Discretionary Cash Flow | | | |
| **Recommendation No.** 5 | **Priority (1–6) lowest to highest:** | | | 5 |
| **Projected/Target Value ($)** | $4,000 annually | | | |

**Product Profile**

| | | | | |
|---|---|---|---|---|
| Type | NA | | | |
| Duration | NA | | | |
| Provider | NA | | | |
| Funding Cost per Period ($) | NA | | | |
| Maintenance Cost per Period ($) | NA | | | |
| Current Income Tax Status | Tax-qualified | X | Taxable | |
| Projected Rate of Return | NA | | | |
| Major Policy Provisions | NA | | | |

**Procedural Factors**

| | | | | |
|---|---|---|---|---|
| Implementation by Whom | Planner | | Client | X |
| Implementation Date or Time Frame | Beginning of next month | | | |
| Implementation Procedure | 1. Reduce W-4 withholdings at payroll department by $333 per month.<br>2. Increase monthly cash contributions to church by $200 per month. Be sure to obtain a written receipt for donations. | | | |

**Ownership Factors**

| | | | | |
|---|---|---|---|---|
| Owner(s) | NA | | | |
| Form of Ownership | NA | | | |
| Insured(s) | NA | | | |
| Custodial Account | | Yes | No | X |
| Custodian | NA | | | |
| In Trust for (ITF) | | Yes | No | X |
| Transfer on Death (TOD) | | Yes | No | X |
| Beneficiary(ies) | NA | | | |
| Contingent Beneficiary(ies) | NA | | | |

| **Proposed Benefit** | Monthly discretionary cash flow is increased by $133. Annual income tax charitable deduction increased by $600 ($200 ×12 months × 25% tax rate). |
|---|---|

As this example illustrates, almost all recommendations used in the income tax planning section of a comprehensive financial plan both affect and are affected by recommendations used in other parts of the plan. It is of critical importance that these interrelated and synergistic relationships be accounted for. In this example, the recommendation to decrease withholding while concurrently increasing charitable donations results in an increase in itemized deductions. Other effects include an increase in monthly discretionary cash flow, a decrease in potential estate tax liabilities, and a client who is able to meet her financial objectives.

# Learning Outcomes

1. Understand the importance of income tax planning within the comprehensive financial planning process. Nearly every tax planning decision and strategy can have an effect on a client's cash flow and net worth situation. This is the primary reason tax planning occurs early in the planning process. Specifically, it is important to know how much discretionary cash flow exists after taxes have been calculated before additional planning recommendations are made. Additionally, tax planning can serve either to increase or decrease a client's cash flow and net worth position.

2. A review of a client's current tax situation starts by evaluating client situational factors related to the tax planning process. A planner understands not only clients' tax planning goals, but their temperament, personality, attitudes, beliefs and values, financial knowledge and experience, and socioeconomic descriptors that influence tax planning decisions. Understanding the emotional, personal, and nonfinancial aspects of a client's situation is as important as calculating a client's tax liability. Additionally, a strong desire to minimize taxes paid to the government, or a willingness to pay "my fair share" of the tax burden, or even a simple desire to avoid being audited by the IRS can seriously shape a client's tax planning motivations.

3. Income is derived from any number of sources, including but not limited to earned income, business income, and investment income, and each of these sources is taxed differently. For example, earned income and business income are both taxed at a client's marginal tax rate, whereas investment income might be taxed at either the client's marginal tax rate or at the applicable capital gains rate. The other factor to consider when analyzing a client's income sources is the permanence of each source, in other words, how reliable and consistent the income stream is.

4. Generally, federal income tax liability is calculated using a 10-step process that first determines total income, then the amount of income subject to taxation after applying all deductions and exemptions. Next, total tax liability is calculated, and finally the net tax liability is determined after all tax credits for which the filer is eligible have been applied. Specifically, the 10-step tax determination process includes: (1) recording potential gross income; (2) excluding nontaxable income and pretax items; (3) calculating grossing income; (4) reducing AGI by using above the-line-deductions; (5) reducing taxable income by either the standard deduction or itemized deductions; (6) reducing taxable income through personal exemptions; (7) calculating the tax liability; (8) reducing tax liabilities by means of tax credits; (9) adding other tax liabilities; and (10) determining the amount owed or amount to be refunded.

5. *Above the line* versus *below the line* refers to the line where AGI is calculated on the personal income tax form. AGI is important to clients because it is used to determine a client's eligibility for certain retirement contributions, deduction limits, and tax credits, among other things. Examples of above-the-line deductions include health care savings account contributions, the deductible portion of self-employment taxes, small business qualified plan contributions, alimony, traditional IRA contributions, and student loan interest. Examples of below-the-line deductions include the standard deduction or mortgage interest, state income tax, real estate taxes, unreimbursed medical expenses (limits apply), qualifying job-related expenses, and tax preparation fees.

6. Congress created the AMT to prevent wealthy taxpayers from taking advantage of preferential deductions and paying little or no income tax. Whereas the regular tax law gives preferential treatment to certain income and allows special deductions and credits for certain expenses, the AMT removes much of these special allowances, thus resulting in a greater tax liability. Common adjustments and tax preference items that can trigger the AMT include personal exemptions, the standard deduction, miscellaneous itemized deductions, state and local taxes, accelerated depreciation of certain property, incentive stock options, and certain tax-exempt interest.

7. Tax planning is always important, but possibly never more so than for retirement income. All distributions from qualified retirement accounts are monitored by the IRS for potential tax implications. In fact, in several situations the IRS not only monitors but actually mandates action. For example, in most situations, if a client took a distribution *before* age 59½ the IRS would want the client to pay a penalty for accessing retirement money too early. And if the client failed to withdraw money *after* age 70½, again the IRS would collect a penalty.

   Additionally, there are many special situations that call for a tax-savvy solution, such as disposition of incentive stock options. In this case, depending on exactly how and when clients take the distribution from their employee-benefit company-stock account, clients might pay (1) income tax on the entire amount immediately, (2) income tax on the basis immediately and the capital gains later, or (3) income tax on the entire amount later. So being proactive with tax planning for retirement is paramount.

8. Many potential strategies are available to planners and clients; however, they all share the characteristic that they are used to reduce current or future income tax liability.

9. Although some financial planners outsource the calculation and filing of client tax returns to other professionals, it is nonetheless important for all financial planners to use a client's tax return to identify other planning opportunities. Clients seldom are in a position to determine, for example, whether owing municipal bonds compared to taxable corporate fixed-income securities makes sense from a tax perspective. Information from a client's tax return can help answer this question. Other areas of financial planning that can benefit from a tax planning review include cash flow planning, retirement accumulation planning, investment statement analysis, education funding planning, insurance needs analysis, and estate planning.

## Chapter Resources

Internal Revenue Service (www.irs.gov).

Leimberg, S. R., M. J. Satinsky, M. S. Jackson, and R. Gardner. *Tools & Techniques of Income Tax Planning*, 3rd Ed. Cincinnati, OH: National Underwriter Company, 2009.

Meyerowitz, Steven A. *Tax Facts on Insurance & Employee Benefits.* Erlanger, KY: National Underwriter Company, 2011.

Meyerowitz, Steven A. *Tax Facts on Investments 2012.* Erlanger, KY: National Underwriter Company, 2012.

The *Financial Factilitator* and all fillable forms needed to complete text activities can be found on the student website at: http://pro.nuco.com/booksupplements/NUCollege-CaseBook2e.

# Quantitative/Analytical Mini-case Problems

1. Liam is a 32-year-old single female. She has gross wages of $95,000 (before deferrals) and $18,000 withholding for federal income tax. Given the information below, will she likely have too much or too little withheld for the current tax year, assuming the following facts? How much? For simplicity, do not consider AMT.

    - She estimates total itemized deductions of $9,450.

    - The standard deduction for a single person is $5,450.

    - The personal exemption for a single person is $3,500.

    - She will not have any interest or dividend income or capital gains.

    - She will not contribute to an IRA.

    - She will defer 5% of her gross salary into the qualified retirement plan.

2. A client makes a tax-deductible contribution of $4,000 to a traditional IRA. The client is in the 25% marginal tax bracket. How much are the approximate tax savings?

3. A couple has owned and lived in their personal residence for 10 years. They purchased the home for $300,000. They sell the home for $900,000. How much of the gain is taxable?

4. A client has asked you to analyze the following investment alternatives for the highest after-tax rate of return under the assumption that the client is subject to a 28% marginal federal income tax and a 5% state income tax.

    - A corporate bond with a 7% pretax return

    - An out-of-state municipal bond with a 5.75% pretax return

    - An in-state municipal bond with a 5.5% pretax return

5. Your financial planner has just completed an analysis of your fixed-income holdings. She has determined each of your after-tax yields, but is cautioning you that the tax implications of your holdings could change if Congress changes marginal tax rates. Based on the following after-tax yields, which of these bonds would offer the greatest after-tax return if your federal marginal tax bracket increased from 25% to 30%, while your state marginal bracket remained 4.5%?

- A corporate bond with a 5.1% after-tax return

- An out-of-state municipal bond with a 5.0% after-tax return

- An in-state municipal bond with a 4.8% after-tax return

# Comprehensive Bedo Case—Analysis Questions

Before beginning the tax analysis for the Bedo family, it is important to review assumptions and data related to income, including wages and salaries, dividends, interest, capital gains, bonus income, and income attributable to employer-provided group benefits. When working with the data it will also be important to determine whether any phase-out limits based on income apply.

When reviewing their current situation, it will be helpful to formulate strategies that both increase discretionary cash flow and reduce tax liabilities. Recommendations should be as precise as possible.

For example, it is not enough to state that Tyler and Mia should match their tax withholdings to their tax liabilities. Exactly how should they do this? As their planner, it is acceptable to encourage both Tyler and Mia to complete a new IRS Form W-4 with their employer. It is also appropriate to indicate exactly how many exemptions they should claim on their W-4. Withholding tables can be found on the IRS Web site (www.irs.gov).

Use the following questions to guide you through the tax planning process.

1. Develop a tax planning goal for the Bedos. When conceptualizing this goal, consider the following.

   a. Is the goal developed in agreement with any or all goals and objectives that the clients have identified? What other goals have tax implications for the Bedos' financial plan?

   b. What situational factors might influence their tax planning goal? Are these factors explicit, implied, or assumed? Is additional information required from the Bedos, and if so, what?

   c. What is the desired tax planning outcome for the clients?

2. Are there globally accepted, client-specific, or planner-generated planning assumptions that will influence the income tax planning situation analysis? List these assumptions as they might affect income tax planning?

3. Make a list of specific federal income tax issues that should be evaluated as part of the documentation and evaluation of the Bedos' tax planning efforts.

4. Conduct a current income tax situation analysis for the Bedos. Be sure to calculate the following:

   a. the Bedos' gross income before adjustments and exclusions;

   b. their gross taxable income (Hint: this amount is arrived at after subtracting all pretax payroll contributions and deductions and other exclusion items.);

   c. the Bedos' adjusted gross income;

   d. the amount of interest paid on their principal residence for the tax year;

   e. the amount that should be claimed for their annual deduction (standard or itemized);

   f. their taxable income for the year; and

   g. the estimated amount of federal tax owed or the amount of refund they can expect, after applying tax credits.

5. Calculate the amount of FICA taxes withheld compared to the Bedos' actual FICA liability.

6. Considering the Bedos' marginal tax bracket, should they consider investing in municipal securities? Why or why not?

7. Summarize your observations about the Bedos' current tax situation as they might appear in a client letter or plan.

8. Based on the goals originally identified and the completed analysis, what product or procedural strategies might be most useful to satisfy the Bedos' tax planning needs? Where applicable, calculate an approximate annual tax savings, as well as the most likely outcome(s) associated with each strategy.

9. Write at least one primary and one alternative recommendation from the strategies selected in response to each planning need identified. More than one recommendation may be needed to address all of the planning needs. Include specific, defensible answers to the *who, what, when, where, why, how,* and *how much* implementation questions for each recommendation.

   a. It is suggested that each recommendation be summarized in a Recommendation Form.

   b. Assign a priority to each recommendation based on the likelihood of meeting client goals and desired outcomes. This priority will be important when recommendations from other core planning content areas are considered relative to the available discretionary funds for subsidizing all recommendations.

   c. Comment briefly on the outcomes associated with each recommendation.

10. Complete the following for the Income Tax Planning section of the Bedos' financial plan.

   a. Outline the information to be included in this section of the plan. Assume the financial advisor is not a CPA, attorney, or EA, does not provide income tax preparation services, and limits income tax work to a review of tax forms and a projection of changes in response to other planning recommendations. What content might be included in this section to inform the client? What disclaimers, if any, might be included?

b.  Draft an introduction to this section of the plan (no more than one paragraph).

c.  Define five key terms that would be included in the plan or glossary to assist the client with tax education or client interpretation of the plan.

11. Prepare a 10–15-minute presentation for the Bedos of your observations and/or recommendation(s) for meeting their life insurance needs. Be sure to include visual aids, Excel handouts, and other materials that will make the recommendations more meaningful to the clients.

## Notes

1.  *IRS Publication 535: Business Expenses*, p. 5. Available at http://www.irs.gov/pub/irs-pdf/p535.pdf.

2.  "Chapter 4—Material Participation," *IRS Passive Activity Loss ATG*. Available at http://www.irs.gov/businesses/small/article/0,,id=146335,00.html.

3.  "At-risk limits," *IRS Publication 925*. Available at http://www.irs.gov/publications/p925/ar02.html#en_US_2010_publink1000104672.

4.  USDA, *Expenditures on Children by Families, 2010*, p. 12. Available at http://www.cnpp.usda.gov/Publications/CRC/crc2010.pdf.

5.  The College Board, *Trends in College Pricing 2011*, p. 10, Table 1A. Available at http://trends.collegeboard.org/downloads/college_pricing/PDF/Trends_in_College_Pricing_2011_Tuition_and_Fee_Room_and_Board_Charges.pdf.

6.  *IRS Publication 503*: *Child and Dependent Care Expenses*, pp. 2–3. Available at http://www.irs.gov/pub/irs-pdf/p503.pdf.

7.  *IRS Publication 972: Child Tax Credit*, p. 3. Available at http://www.irs.gov/pub/irs-pdf/p972.pdf.

8.  *IRS Publication 972, Child Tax Credit*, p. 2.

9.  For the majority of taxpayers, adjusted gross income (AGI) and modified adjusted gross income (MAGI) are often the same for many purposes. Therefore, the terms are used interchangeably in this discussion. However, for some clients, or in certain situations, there will be a difference.

10. IRC § 421, *General Rules*, ¶ (a) Effect of Qualifying Transfer. Available at http://www.taxalmanac.org/index.php/Internal_Revenue_Code:Sec._421._General_rules.

11. IRC § 421, *General Rules*, ¶ (b) Effect of Disqualifying Disposition. Available at http://www.taxalmanac.org/index.php/Internal_Revenue_Code:Sec._421._General_rules.

12. IRC § 56, *Adjustments in Computing Alternative Minimum Taxable Income*, Subsection (b), ¶ 3. Available at http://www.law.cornell.edu/uscode/text/26/56.

13. *IRS Retirement Topics—Tax on Early Distributions*. Available at http://www.irs.gov/retirement/participant/article/0,,id=211440,00.html.

14. For additional information, see the following sources: *Appeals...Resolving Tax Disputes*. Available at http://www.irs.gov/individuals/content/0,,id=98196,00.html. *IRS Publication 5: Your Appeal Rights and How to Prepare a Protest if You Don't Agree*. Available at http://www.irs.gov/pub/irs-pdf/p5.pdf. *IRS Publication 1: Your Rights as a Taxpayer*. Available at http://www.irs.gov/pub/irs-pdf/p1.pdf. And *IRS Publication 556: Examination of Returns, Appeal Rights, and Claims for Refund*, "Appeal Rights." Available at http://www.irs.gov/publications/p556/ar02.html#d0e976.

# PART III: Analyzing and Evaluating a Client's Financial Status to Plan for Client Risk Protection

# Life Insurance Planning

## Key Terms

§ 1035 exchange

7-pay test

accelerated death benefit

annuities

annuity due

beneficiary

break points

buy term and invest the difference

buy/sell agreement

capital retention (CR)

cash surrender value

cash value insurance

chronic illness

contingent beneficiary(ies)

conversion provision

cost-of-living rider

cross-purchase plan

death benefit

declining balance term insurance

deferred annuity

disability waiver provision

discount rate

dividends

early distribution penalties

entity purchase plan

family member support ratio

fixed annuity

forced savings

fully paid term policy

growing annuity

guaranteed payout schedule

guaranteed renewable

guaranteed renewable provision

human life value (HLV) approach

immediate income annuities

immediate variable annuity

incidents of ownership

income multiplier approach

income retention approach

insurable interest

insured

interest-adjusted net cost method

internal rate of return yield method

joint and survivors annuity distribution

key person insurance

lapse

modified endowment contract

needs-based analysis

nonforfeiture provision

overfund

paid-up cash value policy

paid-up policy

perpetuity

policy owner

policy replacement analysis

primary beneficiary

replacement ratio

return of premium

return-of-premium term insurance

risk classification factors

substandard risk classification

substandard risks

surrender charge

term life insurance

terminal illness

traditional net cost method

triangulation

unholy trinity

universal life insurance

variable annuity

variable life insurance

variable universal life insurance (VUL)

viatical settlement

whole-life insurance

yearly-price-per-thousand method

yearly-price-per-thousand method formula

yearly rate of return method

**Figure 5.1** Systematic Financial Planning Process for Life Insurance Planning

214

# LIFE INSURANCE: THE BASICS

The origins of personal financial planning can be traced back to insurance professionals' attempts to streamline the process of integrating insurance into the overall financial life of clients. This began in the late 1960s. Before this time, financial planning as a profession, or even a codified process, did not exist. It is not surprising that the insurance industry had such a strong impact on the financial planning profession from the beginning. Life insurance is, after all, a major component of every comprehensive financial plan. Protecting a client's current assets and lifestyle should be a leading goal of every financial planner. Without first protecting a client's current financial situation, all other suggestions, goals, strategies, and recommendations could be undone by a simple twist of fate.

A client's life insurance need is typically assessed early in the financial planning process. The logic for the placement of analysis within the financial planning process is simple: clients must be adequately insured to cover the fiscal and psychological costs of premature death. This is especially true if a client is married and/or has dependents, a significant life partner, or other financial obligations that carry forward after the client's death, such as a substantial interest in a private firm.

Although nearly all clients have a strong desire to fund as many financial goals as possible, the need to purchase additional life insurance could, of necessity, take precedence over other goals. Insuring the life of a client to a reasonable extent should be one of the primary outcomes of the planning process. As such, life insurance protection should be highly ranked in a client's hierarchy of financial needs. However, many clients overlook the need for life insurance in their quest to realize other, more immediate and tangible goals. Think of it this way: without adequate life insurance, a college savings plan for children, a retirement plan, or other financial goals could be a lost cause for the surviving spouse or partner. Although no one likes to think about premature death, it is nonetheless an issue that must be discussed and planned for within the comprehensive financial planning process.

This chapter reviews the fundamental steps to be taken when analyzing and evaluating a client's current life insurance situation. The steps in the process reviewed in this chapter are illustrated in Figure 5.1, the Systematic Financial Planning Process for Life Insurance Planning. The chapter also includes a presentation of popular life insurance planning strategies and an example of how strategies can be compared and adapted to meet clients' needs.

# ANALYZE THE CLIENT'S CURRENT SITUATION

Central to the analysis of a client's current life insurance situation—and all aspects of the financial planning process—is a thorough knowledge of the client. To complete a comprehensive assessment, this knowledge must encompass an understanding of (a) the financial goals and objectives to be met by the insurance coverage in the event of premature death, (b) a broad range of personal characteristics that could affect the need for insurance, and (c) appropriate product recommendations, and documentation and review of any coverage currently available to the client. This part of the insurance planning process must be completed before any life insurance strategies can be considered.

## Understand a Client's Underwriting Factors

Life insurance strategies and recommendations must be evaluated against certain client **risk classification factors**, which determine the availability and cost of insurance. Although planners might not be expected to be familiar with specific company underwriting methods, a general knowledge of the factors considered is critical to effective planning. When reviewing a client's hazards and risk characteristics, planners should consider the following factors:

- Lifestyle

  Using tobacco, alcohol, or drugs

  Convictions for reckless driving, driving under the influence of alcohol or drugs, or receiving multiple speeding tickets

  Participating in sensation-seeking activities, including ultralight flying, scuba diving, or mountain climbing

  Personal character or household financial situation

- Occupation

  Working in a hazardous profession or occupation

  Piloting commercial, private, or military aircraft

- Medical condition or history

  Gender, age, height, and weight

  Family medical history

Individuals who, because of any of these factors, have a higher than standard risk of mortality are considered **substandard risks**. Depending on the company and the underwriting and reinsurance standards, client insurability factors could result in:

- a denial of the policy application;

- increased policy costs because of the risk factors; or

- the inclusion of riders that exclude certain causes of death or reduce the benefits to the premiums paid, policy reserve accumulations, or the greater of the two.

Life insurance planning, in particular, exemplifies the need for a broad-based exploration of a client's lifestyle, personal, and demographic profile. Additionally, a planner must collect the quantitative and qualitative data necessary to conduct a realistic needs assessment that will provide the coverage necessary to fulfill the client's goals. Throughout the life insurance planning process, the planner or planning team must demonstrate genuine client empathy, balanced with rigorous analytical skills.

## Determine and Quantify a Client's Need for Life Insurance

The need for life insurance is predicated on three basic notions:

1. People earn money during their working lives.

2. The money that they earn supports a desired standard of living.

3. A client's desired standard of living should not have to change because of the death of an earner.

The loss of a family member or a person who provides financial support to another is obviously a devastating emotional loss that cannot be overcome solely by insurance. However, such a loss could be compounded if the survivor(s) does not have adequate funds to (1) pay for the final expenses of the decedent or (2) maintain the same standard of living enjoyed prior to the death of the decedent.

The first step in the process of analyzing a client's current situation involves determining whether a client needs life insurance, and if so, the amount of coverage needed. Not all clients need life insurance. Figure 5.2 summarizes a series of questions related to financial responsibility, net worth, charitable giving, and insurability factors to consider when deciding whether a client has a current need for life insurance.

Of primary concern is whether the client is responsible for the financial welfare of another person (e.g., a spouse, child, or parent) or business entity. If the answer is no, the planner should determine whether the client's net worth is large enough to meet all final expenses (e.g., medical, burial, tax, and other needs). If net worth is sufficient, then no coverage may be needed unless there are reasons to justify putting a policy in place to ensure future access to coverage. Furthermore, if the client is projected to have a net worth in excess of final expenses, the issue of charitable donations should be considered. Similarly, if the client would like to be a benefactor to another person or organization, then life insurance coverage could be warranted. However, if the answer to all these questions is negative, a life insurance purchase could probably be delayed. If this is the case, the financial planner should continue to regularly monitor future circumstances to determine whether and when the need might arise.

The same issues must be considered if the client has financial dependents. In this situation, net worth must be sufficient to meet final expenses, the survivor's future income needs, and if relevant, any planned inheritance or charitable gifts. Otherwise, life insurance protection may be needed. Finally, in the event assets are sufficient to satisfy all of these expenses, the need for life insurance as an estate tax planning tool must be considered.

**Figure 5.2** Decision Tree for Determining a Client's Need for Life Insurance

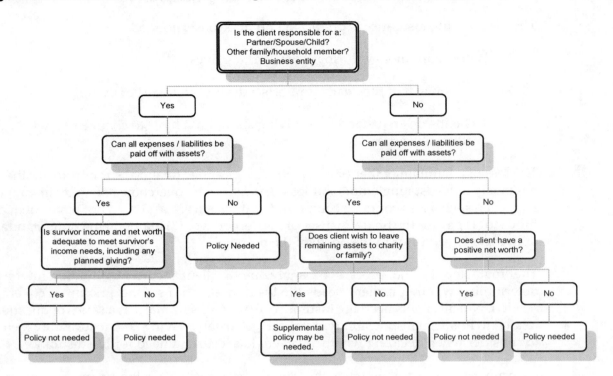

Assuming that a client needs life insurance, the analysis proceeds to answer the following question: "How much life insurance does this client need?" It is likely that the typical financial planning client already has one or more forms of life insurance. The majority of clients have some employer-provided group coverage, unless they are self-employed. When analyzing the current situation, the planner's role is to determine whether the amount of coverage is sufficient to meet the client's financial goals and objectives.

Five commonly used methods for determining a client's gross life insurance include the:

1. needs-based analysis approach;

2. human life value approach;

3. capital retention approach;

4. income retention approach; and the

5. simple income multiplier approach.

---

**Life Insurance Planning Tip: Social Security Death Benefit**

Anyone who is fully insured under Social Security is eligible to have his or her surviving spouse, and sometimes children, receive a lump sum death benefit of $255. Obviously, this lump sum payment is insufficient to pay for most final expenses; however, this is the maximum benefit available to those without a private insurance policy.

---

The human life value approach, the capital retention approach, and the income retention approach all employ time value of money formulas that were discussed in Chapter 2, whereas the other two methods do not. The easiest method, but also the most arbitrary, is the income multiplier approach. The most challenging, and arguably the most accurate of the methods for determining a client's insurance need, is the needs-based analysis approach.

## Needs-Based Analysis Approach

Although other commonly used methods (presented later in this chapter) provide a ballpark estimate of insurance need, planners are encouraged to conduct a comprehensive analysis to obtain a complete, life-cycle-based picture of a client's projected life insurance benefit need. The **needs-based analysis approach** provides the framework to complete a detailed analysis. Exhibits 5.1 and 5.2 illustrate the Needs-Based Analysis Life Insurance Calculator provided in the Financial Facilitator that accompanies this text. See the comment boxes in the exhibits for an explanation of the data inputs. Because of the life-cycle focus of this method, the financial needs, or costs, to be met by life insurance are projected and discounted for the effects of inflation, taxes, and potential investment returns. This approach includes the cost of specific goals or capital needs that the insurance proceeds should fund, as well as streams of income to supplement the survivors' income or replace income for the decedent, the surviving partner, or both.

**Exhibit 5.1** Life Insurance Calculator, Needs-Based Analysis Section One

**Financial Facilitator Revealed**
Life Insurance Calculator, Needs-Based Analysis Section One

The needs-based life insurance calculator can be used to calculate the life insurance needs for both a client and co-client. This portion covers the period of time from the death of the decedent until the children leave home.

| LIFE INSURANCE ESTIMATION WORKSHEET | | | | |
|---|---|---|---|---|
| Client's Age = | 55 | | Childrens' Ages | |
| Client's Total Income = | $64,200 | | 1 | 16 |
| Co-client's Age = | 47 | | 2 | 11 |
| Co-client's Total Income = | $46,500 | | 3 | 0 |
| Total Household Expenses = | $84,259 | | | |

| | Client's Death | | Co-client's Death | |
|---|---|---|---|---|
| **Needs-Based Analysis "Net" Total** = | $106,968 | = | $578,166 | |
| **Final Expenses** | | | | |
| Final Expenses (medical, funeral, burial, etc.) | $15,000 | | $15,000 | |
| Estate Administration (legal, executor, etc.) + | $2,000 | + | $2,000 | |
| Federal Estate Taxes (from Estate Tax Estimator) + | $0 | + | $0 | |
| State Estate Taxes (if any) + | $0 | + | $0 | |
| Other Immediate Needs (income taxes, etc.) + | $10,000 | + | $10,000 | |
| **Total Final Expenses** = | $27,000 | = | $27,000 | |
| | | | | |
| **Debt Elimination Expenses (not paid from estate)** | | | | |
| Credit Card and Consumer/Installment Debt | $9,525 | | $9,525 | |
| Automobile Debt + | $15,620 | + | $15,620 | |
| Desired Mortgage Reduction + | $118,876 | + | $118,876 | |
| Other Debt to be Paid Off at Death + | | + | | |
| **Total Debt Elimination Expenses** = | $144,021 | = | $144,021 | |
| | | | | |
| **Transitional Expenses (total estimated cost amounts)** | | | | |
| Education/Re-training Expenses for Survivor | | | | |
| Child Care and Homemaker Services + | | + | | |
| Other Transitional Needs + | | + | | |
| **Total Transitional Expenses** = | $0 | = | $0 | |
| | | | | |
| **Anticipated Household Expenses** | | | | |
| Which expenses should be used for calculations? | User-defined | | Historical | |
| | | | | |
| If "user defined" was choosen, enter new expenses => | $79,500 | | | |
| Selected expenses | $79,500 | | $84,259 | |
| **Determine Real Rate of Return on Investments Until Survivor's Retirement** | | | | |
| Assumed gross investment return | 9.00% | | 9.00% | |
| Combined (fed, state, & local) marginal tax bracket | 25.00% | | 25.00% | |
| Projected inflation rate | 3.00% | | 3.00% | |
| Projected real rate of return | 3.64% | | 3.64% | |
| | | | | |
| **Household Expenses during Dependency Period** (needs while children are at home) | | | | |
| Number of people remaining in household | 3 | | 3 | |
| Household Expense Ratio (assumed to | | | | |
| be 70% or greater of previous income) x | 78.00% | x | 78.00% | |
| Anticipated Annual Family Expenses = | $62,010 | = | $65,722 | |
| Eligible Soc. Sec. Dependent Survivor's Benefit - | $0 | - | $0 | |
| Anticipated Annual Survivor Earned Income | $46,500 | | $64,200 | |
| Pension Benefits and Income - | $0 | - | $0 | |
| Income to be Replaced Until Children/Dependents are | | | | |
| Self-Supporting = | $15,510 | = | $1,522 | |
| Years until youngest child reaches age 18 = | 7 | = | 7 | |
| **Total Dependency Period Expenses** = | $94,340 | = | $9,258 | |

Side notes:

This is the additional life insurance needed, after considering other policies and available assets.

Final expenses are typically considered as costs associated with a death and subsequent estate settlement.

Debt elimination and transitional expenses are not costs directly associated with the death. Rather they are lump sum amounts to be paid upon death to ease the survivor's transition.

User-defined vs. Historical:
To "back-out" savings or other expenses choose user-defined. To accept the same expenses as calculated on the income and expense statement choose historical.

The real rate of return is the asset appreciation rate after the affects of taxes and inflation are taken into account. This allows for present values to be used throughout the calculation. Note: This return will be separately calculated for the retirement period.

This section determines the expenses of the household before any children leave home. Note: This section will not apply to households without children.

This is the annual expense amount after adjusting for the reduction in household members.

Expenses typically change after a death based on how many people remain in the household. Enter the number of survivors here.

**Exhibit 5.2** Life Insurance Calculator, Needs-Based Analysis Section Two

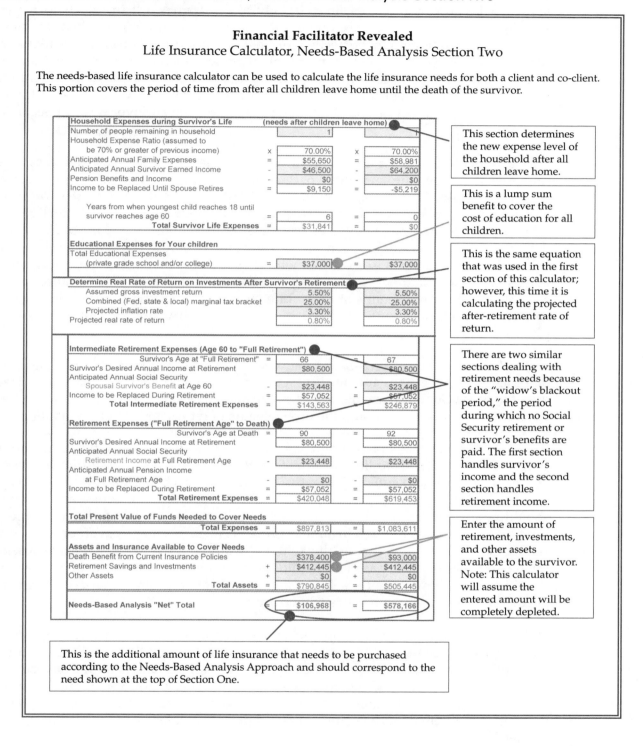

**Financial Facilitator Revealed**
Life Insurance Calculator, Needs-Based Analysis Section Two

The needs-based life insurance calculator can be used to calculate the life insurance needs for both a client and co-client. This portion covers the period of time from after all children leave home until the death of the survivor.

| Household Expenses during Survivor's Life | (needs after children leave home) | | | |
|---|---|---|---|---|
| Number of people remaining in household | | 1 | | 1 |
| Household Expense Ratio (assumed to be 70% or greater of previous income) | x | 70.00% | x | 70.00% |
| Anticipated Annual Family Expenses | = | $55,650 | = | $58,981 |
| Anticipated Annual Survivor Earned Income | - | $46,500 | - | $64,200 |
| Pension Benefits and Income | - | $0 | - | $0 |
| Income to be Replaced Until Spouse Retires | = | $9,150 | = | -$5,219 |
| Years from when youngest child reaches 18 until survivor reaches age 60 | = | 6 | = | 0 |
| Total Survivor Life Expenses | = | $31,841 | = | $0 |

This section determines the new expense level of the household after all children leave home.

| Educational Expenses for Your children | | | | |
|---|---|---|---|---|
| Total Educational Expenses (private grade school and/or college) | = | $37,000 | = | $37,000 |

This is a lump sum benefit to cover the cost of education for all children.

| Determine Real Rate of Return on Investments After Survivor's Retirement | | | |
|---|---|---|---|
| Assumed gross investment return | 5.50% | 5.50% |
| Combined (Fed, state & local) marginal tax bracket | 25.00% | 25.00% |
| Projected inflation rate | 3.30% | 3.30% |
| Projected real rate of return | 0.80% | 0.80% |

This is the same equation that was used in the first section of this calculator; however, this time it is calculating the projected after-retirement rate of return.

| Intermediate Retirement Expenses (Age 60 to "Full Retirement") | | | | |
|---|---|---|---|---|
| Survivor's Age at "Full Retirement" | = | 66 | = | 67 |
| Survivor's Desired Annual Income at Retirement | | $80,500 | | $80,500 |
| Anticipated Annual Social Security | | | | |
| Spousal Survivor's Benefit at Age 60 | - | $23,448 | - | $23,448 |
| Income to be Replaced During Retirement | = | $57,052 | = | $57,052 |
| Total Intermediate Retirement Expenses | = | $143,563 | = | $246,879 |

| Retirement Expenses ("Full Retirement Age" to Death) | | | | |
|---|---|---|---|---|
| Survivor's Age at Death | = | 90 | = | 92 |
| Survivor's Desired Annual Income at Retirement | | $80,500 | | $80,500 |
| Anticipated Annual Social Security | | | | |
| Retirement Income at Full Retirement Age | - | $23,448 | - | $23,448 |
| Anticipated Annual Pension Income at Full Retirement Age | - | $0 | - | $0 |
| Income to be Replaced During Retirement | = | $57,052 | = | $57,052 |
| Total Retirement Expenses | = | $420,048 | = | $619,453 |

There are two similar sections dealing with retirement needs because of the "widow's blackout period," the period during which no Social Security retirement or survivor's benefits are paid. The first section handles survivor's income and the second section handles retirement income.

| Total Present Value of Funds Needed to Cover Needs | | | | |
|---|---|---|---|---|
| Total Expenses | = | $897,813 | = | $1,083,611 |

| Assets and Insurance Available to Cover Needs | | | | |
|---|---|---|---|---|
| Death Benefit from Current Insurance Policies | | $378,400 | | $93,000 |
| Retirement Savings and Investments | + | $412,445 | + | $412,445 |
| Other Assets | + | $0 | + | $0 |
| Total Assets | = | $790,845 | = | $505,445 |
| Needs-Based Analysis "Net" Total | = | $106,968 | = | $578,166 |

Enter the amount of retirement, investments, and other assets available to the survivor. Note: This calculator will assume the entered amount will be completely depleted.

This is the additional amount of life insurance that needs to be purchased according to the Needs-Based Analysis Approach and should correspond to the need shown at the top of Section One.

The needs-based analysis approach is often considered the most accurate assessment approach because it provides financial advisors a framework in which to target specific costs at a specific point in time, using individual, customized discount rates. For example, funding might be needed for final expenses (including estate settlement costs), debt elimination, and transitional expenses. Income supplementation or replacement could be needed for household expenses both before and after children become financially independent, the costs of education (for survivor or children), and expenses for retirement periods both before and after the survivor's Social Security eligibility date.

This is particularly true for domestic partners. Because federal law does not recognize same-sex marriage, the surviving partner of a same-sex union does not receive survivor benefits from Social Security or ERISA-covered defined benefit or cash balance pension plans. Nor do survivors receive the unlimited marital deduction for estate tax purposes. The potential effects are a decrease in the standard of living for the surviving partner and a much higher estate tax liabilitiy. The same implications are applicable to opposite-sex couples who choose not to marry. For these and other reasons, financial planners are encouraged to conduct a thorough life insurance needs analysis matched to a client's lifestlye. Life insurance can provide a tax-advantaged solution for replacing lost Social Security and pension benefits and provide needed estate liquidity.

Use of the life insurance needs-based analysis is predicated on a thorough investigation of a client's life objectives and an earnest attempt to quantify client goals and desires over the life cycle. Furthermore, a reasonable attempt should be made to project the exact cost of all future goals and the probable rate of return and effects of inflation.

If care is not taken when projecting the future cost of a client's goals, the client could purchase too much or too little insurance. Either outcome could result in the client not realizing goals and suffering negative financial or psychological effects caused by reduced cash flow or unprotected needs. Although protection is important, caution should be used when projecting which goals to fund. It may be unwise to suggest funding certain goals through insurance proceeds (e.g., mortgage payoff or excessive college expense funding) that in all likelihood would not have been available absent the death of the spouse, partner, or child. Furthermore, a prudent financial planner should consider how a client's feelings of grief, guilt, or other emotional distress might affect how life insurance proceeds will be used.

In addition to the needs-based approach, financial planners commonly use four other methods to determine life insurance coverage needs. The first three of these use time value of money equations that can be adjusted for various factors to personalize the outcomes. The last method, again, is a simple multiplier that does not allow for as much personalization. Exhibit 5.3 illustrates how each method can be calculated using the Financial Facilitator. The comment boxes provide guidance and explanations for the data inputs.

**Exhibit 5.3** Life Insurance Calculator, Additional Estimation Methods

**Financial Facilitator Revealed**
Life Insurance Calculator, Additional Estimation Methods

The methods shown below are all variations of simple future value equations and are much easier and quicker to complete than a needs-based assessment. However, none of these methods place the projected survivor's expenses on a timeline. That is to say that they do not account for when the expenses are likely to occur. Therefore, calculation accuracy suffers.

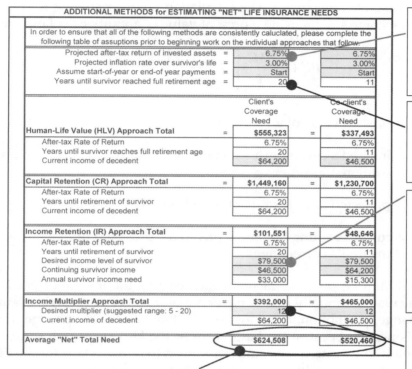

ADDITIONAL METHODS for ESTIMATING "NET" LIFE INSURANCE NEEDS

In order to ensure that all of the following methods are consistently caluclated, please complete the following table of assuptions prior to beginning work on the individual approaches that follow.

|  | | Client's | | Co-client's |
|---|---|---|---|---|
| Projected after-tax return of invested assets = | | 6.75% | | 6.75% |
| Projected inflation rate over survivor's life = | | 3.00% | | 3.00% |
| Assume start-of-year or end-of year payments = | | Start | | Start |
| Years until survivor reached full retirement age = | | 20 | | 11 |

|  | | Client's Coverage Need | | Co-client's Coverage Need |
|---|---|---|---|---|
| **Human-Life Value (HLV) Approach Total** = | | **$555,323** | = | **$337,493** |
| After-tax Rate of Return | | 6.75% | | 6.75% |
| Years until survivor reaches full retirement age | | 20 | | 11 |
| Current income of decedent | | $64,200 | | $46,500 |
| **Capital Retention (CR) Approach Total** = | | **$1,449,160** | = | **$1,230,700** |
| After-tax Rate of Return | | 6.75% | | 6.75% |
| Years until retirement of survivor | | 20 | | 11 |
| Current income of decedent | | $64,200 | | $46,500 |
| **Income Retention (IR) Approach Total** = | | **$101,551** | = | **$48,646** |
| After-tax Rate of Return | | 6.75% | | 6.75% |
| Years until retirement of survivor | | 20 | | 11 |
| Desired income level of survivor | | $79,500 | | $79,500 |
| Continuing survivor income | | $46,500 | | $64,200 |
| Annual survivor income need | | $33,000 | | $15,300 |
| **Income Multiplier Approach Total** = | | **$392,000** | = | **$465,000** |
| Desired multiplier (suggested range: 5 - 20) | | 12 | | 12 |
| Current income of decedent | | $64,200 | | $46,500 |
| **Average "Net" Total Need** | | **$624,508** | | **$520,460** |

Unlike the needs-based calculation, enter the after-tax rate of return. Note: This rate will automatically apply to the other calculators on this sheet.

The number of years until the survivor reaches the desired retirement age is automatically brought down from above.

Unlike the needs-based calculation that prescribes a similar ratio based on the number of people remaining in the household, a replacement ratio should be entered to determine the required income to be replaced.

While most professionals recommend that the multiplier fall in a range from 5 to 20, the most accurate number depends on two factors: (1) the number of years until retirement, and (2) the percentage of household income lost.

This is the average additional life insurance needed, the need after any existing policies and available assets are considered, for all of the calculators on this sheet and for the Needs-Based Approach calculator.

## Human Life Value Approach

The **human life value (HLV) approach** is used to determine the amount *currently* needed by a survivor or household to replace the insured's income that is lost upon the death of the insured. This approach bases the continuing stream of income from the life insurance benefits on the current income of the decedent had the decedent continued working until his or her normal retirement age. This projected income level can then be fine-tuned for self-maintenance costs, taxes, associated life insurance costs, or any other reasonable adjustment. The calculation involves solving for the present value of the lost income stream using a present value of annuity calculation, where:

$$PVA = \frac{PMT}{i}\left[1 - \frac{1}{(1+i)^n}\right]$$

PVA = present value of an annuity

PMT = insured's current gross income (see note at end of section about using net income)

I = projected after-tax rate of return on investment assets

n = future working lifetime = (insured's projected retirement age - insured's current age)

This equation should be used to calculate each client's life insurance needs, and it should be recalculated annually or whenever a major career or lifestyle event occurs (e.g., career change, promotion, raise, loss of job) that results in a change in income. Recalculation is needed because the basic form of the HLV approach suffers from a major flaw; namely, the insured's income is assumed to remain static for the life of the survivor. However, it is possible to automatically adjust for this weakness by using a growing annuity formula as discussed later in this chapter. If the goal is merely to replace income until retirement, recalculation or the purchase of a **declining balance term insurance** policy could be appropriate because, as time goes by, there are fewer years until retirement. As the name implies, a declining balance term insurance policy is one where the annual premium remains constant, but the face value of the policy declines yearly. These policies are typically associated with mortgage products.

## Capital Retention Approach

Similar to the HLV, the **capital retention (CR)** approach bases the continuing stream of income from the life insurance benefits on the current income of the decedent. But unlike the HLV approach, the CR approach uses a **perpetuity** (i.e., an annuity payable forever) to determine need. This method assumes that the survivor does not want to liquidate investment assets for current income. In other words, the capital is "retained." This income or payment level can be adjusted for self-maintenance costs, taxes, associated life insurance costs, or any other reasonable adjustment. Once the desired payment is determined, the resulting net income need is then divided by the projected rate of return of an investment portfolio, as shown in the following formula:

$$PVP = \frac{PMT}{i}$$

PMT = insured's current gross income
i = projected rate of return on investment assets

Because the CR approach assumes that a client's income needs continue forever, this calculation method normally results in the highest estimate of life insurance need. However, this approach also virtually guarantees that the survivor will not outlive the available capital. It is also the best approach for ensuring that future generations will receive an inheritance. Therefore, if providing for multiple generations is the goal, this life insurance estimation approach is worthy of consideration.

## Income Retention Approach

Unlike the previous two approaches, the **income retention approach** bases the continuing stream of income from the life insurance benefits on the expected income needs of the survivor. As such, this estimation procedure accounts for income earned or received by the survivor between the death of the decedent and the retirement of the survivor.

Beginning with the gross income of the decedent, reductions can be made for: (a) any continuous income earned by the survivor; (b) the income taxes associated with the decedent's income; (c) any preretirement benefits received from Social Security or pensions; and (d) other reasonable adjustments (e.g., annuity payments, interest, or dividend income). In other words, the amount of insurance purchased is assumed to cover only the net amount of income lost. As such, this life insurance estimation approach often yields the lowest approximation of required insurance coverage.

$$PVA = \frac{PMT}{i}\left[1 - \frac{1}{(1+i)^n}\right]$$

PVA = present value of an annuity
PMT = survivor's income need = (gross income need - all sources of continuing income)
i = projected after-tax rate of return on investment assets
n = future working lifetime = (survivor's projected retirement age - survivor's current age)

Although the formula for this approach is the same as for the HLV method, a planner who uses this methodology must first complete an assessment of current annual income need (i.e., total annual expenses and savings). Once the amount for a single year has been determined, the financial advisor must use the present value of an annuity formula to calculate the required amount of current coverage that would provide adequate supplementary income over the survivor's future working lifetime.

## Common Adjustments to Annuity Calculations

Although each of the life insurance calculation approaches discussed in this chapter uses one or more forms of present value equations, there are subtle differences among the methodologies, primarily in how payment is determined. With the human life value and capital retention approaches, the payment (PMT) in the time value of money formula is based simply on the insured's gross or net income. In the income retention approach, the PMT is based on current required replacement income (i.e., gross income reduced by any sources of continuing cash flow available to the survivor). Another major difference between the income retention approach and the human life value approach is that the number of years for the projection period (n) is based on the *survivor's* remaining working life, rather than the *insured's* remaining working life. The distinguishing characteristic of the methods discussed thus far is that each can be manipulated to consider additional client-specific information. All of the preceding calculations can be altered in several ways by changing how the variables are defined.

One of the most common adjustments is to change each formula to account for beginning-of-period payments rather than the typical end-of-year convention. Adding a $(1 + i)$ to the basic form of the appropriate formula adjusts for this change. Making this adjustment increases the present value outcome by exactly one year of interest to account for the funds being withdrawn *before* expenses, instead of at the end of the year *after* the expenses. When using the beginning-of-period convention, it is customary to refer to the equation as an **annuity due** rather than as an ordinary annuity.

Another common adjustment involves applying a growth rate to the formula, thus becoming a **growing annuity**. All of the other variables remain the same as in the previous equations, but there is an additional variable to take into account (i.e., that the decedent's income would have continued to increase). This affects the present value need by assuming that the income would have increased at a fixed rate over the projected time period. The growth variable "g" should be a reasonable estimate of the average annual increase. This adjustment will always result in a higher present value need and, therefore, is a more conservative approach to life insurance needs analysis planning. The following growth-adjusted formula can be used to estimate this conservative approach:

$$PVGAD = \frac{PMT_1}{(i-g)}\left[1 - \frac{(1+g)^n}{(1+i)^n}\right](1+i)$$

This growth-adjusted formula can provide a more realistic measure of a client's life insurance need by assuming that the client's income will increase over time. By assuming a salary growth rate, the insured's life insurance need increases. However, it is more likely that the assets provided from the life insurance settlement will be sufficient to provide the surviving household or partner an increasing stream of income over the survivor's life. For example, if a client (a) earns a current annual income of $75,000, (b) expects a 7% average after-tax return, (c) anticipates a salary growth rate of 4%, and (d) desires to work another 20 years, the amount of suggested life insurance coverage increases from about $850,000 to about $1,160,000 just by including a salary growth rate. Including a growth rate is prudent if salary is assumed to increase over the life cycle. However, because of this assumption, the total amount of insurance needed will initially be greater and may lessen the need to purchase additional life insurance in the future.

## Methodological Flaws

One reason multiple methods are used to estimate a client's life insurance need is that financial planners cannot agree on the inputs necessary to complete common needs analyses. Additionally, each client's circumstances can make one approach superior to another at any given time. In the fullness of time, each financial planner develops his or her favorite method(s) of evaluation. This is not necessarily a troublesome tendency, but it does point to an important observation; namely, it is very important to understand that each calculation method is, in some way, flawed. These flaws have to do with the overall approach and not the actual calculation. As previously discussed, nearly all of the problems inherent in the formulas used to estimate a client's insurance need can easily be overcome. However, the flaws in the approaches, or how the variables are defined and calculated, can be more difficult to surmount.

Two primary flaws are associated with the HLV approach. First, it does not consider other sources of income. Second, it does not consider to what extent a decedent's income supported the family. Although normally associated with the income-retention approach, using a **replacement ratio** (also known as **family member support ratio**) to determine annual income need for the survivor(s) is one method that can be used to adjust for any possible overstatement in required income. Financial planners often use replacement ratios ranging from a high of 100% to a low of 70%.[1] Commonly used standards of practice suggest that within a two-person household, the death of one adult reduces expenses by 30%. As household size increases, the percentage reduction in total living expenses declines. For example, for a surviving family of two, three, or four members, the expected reduction in expenses is 26%, 22%, and 20%, respectively. Expenses are generally reduced by only 2% with each additional surviving family member.

In addition to household size, other important factors in the choice of a replacement ratio include the survivor's earnings potential, the projected rate of return that can be earned on insurance proceeds, and other family issues, such as the need to eliminate debt or save for future goals. In effect, the more favorable the future looks for the survivor, the lower the replacement ratio that can be selected.

The flaw associated with the capital retention approach is that it considers the income stream to continue in perpetuity. This is obviously not the case, because people do not live forever. Income will obviously not continue in perpetuity. Therefore, this equation can overestimate the required amount of insurance coverage needed. This flaw is compounded if an unreasonable discount rate is used. If the **discount rate** (i.e., what the client is projected to earn on any investments) is overestimated, the formula will understate the coverage need. If the need is underestimated, the formula will overstate the required amount of insurance to be purchased.

Given the flaws inherent in any model, it is always wise to compare the results of multiple measures. For example, if the insured desires to leave an inheritance to children, the capital retention approach might be the most valid. Conversely, if there is a high probability that the survivor will remarry, and thus would not be overly dependent on insurance proceeds to maintain a standard of living, the income retention approach might be the most appropriate. In any case, understanding the flaws and adjustments for each method is crucial for preparing a thorough and defensible life insurance needs assessment.

## Income Multiplier Approach

The final life insurance estimation procedure is the **income multiplier approach**. This is one of the most widely used methods because of its speed in assessing life insurance need. Planners who use this technique multiply the insured's current income by a factor such as 8 or 10 to arrive at an insurance need; however, any number within a range can be used. For most situations, multiples between 5 and 15 are typical.[2] The exact number is usually determined by evaluating a number of issues, including age (or years until retirement) of the insured, number and ages of financial dependents, amount and types of debt, percentage of household income lost, and availability and continuity of a survivor's income. The more factors, the higher the multiplier.

For example, a client with several dependent children or other ongoing financial demands could require a multiplier of 12. A multiplier of 7 might be appropriate for an individual with few or no dependents and a low level of debt and final expenses. However, even a multiple of 15 could be inadequate for clients who are living well beyond their financial means or have a desire to leave a large legacy to children or charity. The choice of multiple is very subjective and almost always based on a financial planner's past experience in similar situations. The formula for this method is:

Current Need = Insured's Current Gross Income × Chosen Multiplier

Although gross income typically is used with this approach, net income can also be easily substituted. In either case, care must be taken when applying this formula as the only means of determining life insurance coverage needs. Because of the extremely general nature of this approach, even after years of experience, financial planners rarely use this as the sole measure. However, as mentioned earlier, this type of assessment can provide a quick, ballpark estimate before completing a more in-depth analysis.

## Tax Implications and Payment Options

Another potential adjustment that can be made to all of the life insurance estimation approaches presented in this chapter is to base the calculations on after-tax or "spendable" income. Because, in most cases, life insurance proceeds are income tax free, this methodology yields a more direct comparison to the income the survivor will actually be able to spend. To do this, simply substitute the after-tax income for the PMT previously shown. Although this adjustment has merit, care must be taken not to overestimate the tax advantages of life insurance proceeds. Generally, if the proceeds are received from a life insurance contract because of the death of the insured, the benefits are not considered taxable income and do not have to be reported. However, any earnings received on the death benefit would be considered taxable income. In other words, the periodic income derived from the invested settlement proceeds is taxable to the extent that it exceeds the original basis of the investment.

Another issue worthy of consideration is where the proceeds are invested. Generally, if the proceeds are taken as a lump sum and invested in taxable accounts, then the growth and/or income attributable to the account could be eligible for lower capital gains and qualified dividend tax rates. However, if the proceeds are left on deposit with the insurance company and paid as an installment or life annuity, then any interest received will be taxed at the beneficiary's marginal tax bracket.

Why does this matter when calculating life insurance need? The reason comes down to the following insight: the survivor can spend only after-tax income. Therefore, some discussion on how the proceeds would be received and taxed should be included in any comprehensive evaluation. IRS Publication 525, *Taxable and Nontaxaable Income*, should be consulted for additional information on the extent to which life insurance proceeds are taxed.

---

### Life Insurance Planning Tip: Using Income or Living Expenses

In some cases, planners substitute a household's current living expenses less the survivor's earnings for current income. The decision to make this choice will depend on a client's unique situation. The use of current living expenses will likely increase the amount of insurance needed. An alternative consideration involves whether current living expenses will be defined to include or exclude savings. A more complete discussion of this question was presented in Chapter 2.

---

## Determine the Additional Amount of Insurance a Client Should Purchase

Each of the estimation methods described above can be used to determine a client's gross life insurance need. To answer the question of how much life insurance a client needs, currently available life insurance coverage(s) and selected assets should be subtracted from the gross need figure. First, additional insurance need is calculated by subtracting the current face value of all in-force life insurance policies from the gross need, as shown below:

Additional insurance need =

Gross estimated insurance need – Face value of in-force policies

Second, in some cases, a client's retirement assets, other investments, or additional assets can also be used to reduce the gross amount of insurance required, as shown in Exhibit 5.2. For example, a client may wish, after consulting with a financial planner, to use the equity in a principal residence to reduce the gross life insurance need. Another client, on the other hand, could determine, after consulting with a financial planner, that a conservative estimate of gross need less current insurance is most appropriate. Whatever the case or client, it is the planner's responsibility to help clients consider the complexities involved in determining which assets to use in case of death. Furthermore, the true emotional and financial impact of tapping the equity established in a principal residence must be carefully considered. This could mean selling the family home, which is a very significant lifestyle change following the loss of a loved one.

Ideally, a client's financial situation will be modeled using each of the preceding life insurance estimation approaches to determine the amount of insurance needed. In practice, however, few planners use more than one or two of these methods. The insurance needs-based analysis method is the most comprehensive and accurate approach to calculating a client's life insurance needs, but it is common to find others who use the income multiplier approach.

Another device that can be used to determine a client's insurance need is to triangulate results from at least three of the calculation methods. Figure 5.3 shows the range of results from the different calculation methods that can be averaged into one dollar figure. **Triangulation** would take, for instance, the human life value ($555,323), the capital retention ($1,449,160), and the needs analysis approach results ($106,968), add them, and divide the sum by three. The average result, in this case, ($703,817) would flatten out the significant variances of each method alone. Triangulation can provide a more realistic indication of insurance needs. Note that the triangulation result of the three approaches mentioned is somewhere in the middle. In this regard, it is similar to the average need of $521,000 shown in Figure 5.3, which is the average of all five methods. However, taking an average can have its own drawbacks, because the different methods all measure different aspects of a client's financial situation.

**Figure 5.3** Client's Net Life Insurance Need Based on Different Analysis Methods

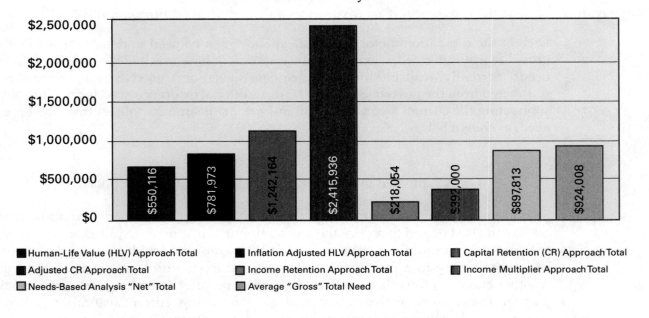

**Client's Net Life Insurance Need**

Based on Different Analysis Methods

■ Human-Life Value (HLV) Approach Total    ■ Inflation Adjusted HLV Approach Total    ■ Capital Retention (CR) Approach Total

■ Adjusted CR Approach Total    ■ Income Retention Approach Total    ■ Income Multiplier Approach Total

■ Needs-Based Analysis "Net" Total    ■ Average "Gross" Total Need

Once the amount of need is determined, that number must be converted into the most cost-effective purchase amount. Face value **break points** (e.g., more or less than $100,000 or more or less than $1 million), can significantly affect the cost of coverage. Companies refer to these price differentials as *insurance bands*, where more insurance could actually cost less than a lower amount in the previous band, or below the break point. To illustrate, assume that a company's pricing bands are $500,000 to $999,999, followed by $1 million to $1,999,999, etc. Based on a projected need of $895,000, buying $1 million of coverage could actually be less expensive than the $865,000 because the cost of $1,000 of coverage decreases with progressively higher bands. This is only one among many underwriting considerations that can affect policy pricing. However, whether comparison shopping with an insurance professional or online, asking about the break points or bands or experimenting with different amounts can provide significant cost savings and potentially more protection.

## Document and Evaluate Current Life Insurance Coverage

The second step in analyzing a client's current situation, and certainly a step that must be completed before a financial planner can recommend additional or alternative life insurance, entails documenting and evaluating all currently in-force coverage for household members. Coverage can be provided by an employer, purchased independently, or even provided as a benefit of having an account with a bank or credit union. Although there are numerous types and classifications of life insurance policies offered in the marketplace, most fall within one of the following six categories:

1. **Term life insurance**: The most basic and least expensive life insurance policy, term life insurance provides coverage for a specific number of years, usually at a fixed annual premium rate. Although term policies can be renewable (this is an optional rider), new policies usually cost more, because the premium on term policies is tied to the age of the client, and older clients pay higher premiums. To overcome the problem of clients having to renew at higher premium costs and for longer terms than desired, some companies offer term policies that continue until age 65 or expected retirement age, but that can be purchased at any age.

2. **Return-of-premium term insurance**: As the name implies, a return-of-premium term insurance policy refunds up to 100% of total premiums paid if the policy is held to the end of the term. In situations where a policy is terminated prematurely, only a portion of the premiums paid will be returned.

3. **Whole-life insurance**: As the most basic form of **cash value insurance**, a whole-life policy combines lifetime insurance protection with a continual buildup of cash value. Effectively, a portion of each premium payment is used to fund premiums associated with the purchase of life insurance, the costs associated with management of the policy, and cash value accumulation. A unique feature associated with whole-life insurance is the level lifetime premium. Loans can be taken against the accrued cash value.

4. **Universal life insurance**: As an alternative cash value policy, universal life insurance allows a policy owner to increase, defer, or decrease the annual premium, and to withdraw accrued cash values (although this would reduce

the policy's **death benefit**, which is defined as the policy's face value less outstanding loans and other expenses credited against the policy). Universal life insurance also allows a policy owner to change the face value periodically without proof of insurability. Like its cousin, whole-life insurance, universal life policies build cash value on a guaranteed return basis, which has traditionally been at least 4% annually.

5. **Variable life insurance**: Variable life insurance offers policy owners a fixed annual premium; however, unlike whole- or universal life policies, a variable contract provides an opportunity to earn higher returns on the cash value of the policy. Accrued cash can be invested in stock, bond, and money market investments through subaccount funds. As such, the cash value and death benefit associated with a variable life insurance policy fluctuates over time. It is important to note that insurance companies rarely guarantee cash values within variable products.

6. **Variable universal life insurance**: As the name implies, variable universal life insurance is a blended product that borrows features from universal and variable policies. A **VUL**, as the product is sometimes known, offers policy owners flexible premiums and a wide variety of investment options within the cash account. As with all cash value policies, outstanding loans accrue interest and reduce the death benefit when paid.

Once all currently in-force policies have been identified, it is important to document the ownership, or titling, of each. Whenever a life insurance contract is underwritten, three parties must be identified within the contract. The **policy owner** is the person or entity who has the right to name one or more beneficiaries. The owner is also entitled to all participating dividends and has the responsibility for paying the insurance premium. Policy owners can, at their discretion, surrender, transfer, or cancel a policy. A policy owner is any person or entity with an insurable interest in the insured, so it can be the insured, a family member, an employer, or a trust. The policy owner must provide evidence of an **insurable interest**, which is defined as possibly incurring a financial loss resulting from the death of the insured. The **insured** named in a policy is the person whose death prompts payment of the insurance policy's face value.

The **beneficiary** can be a person or entity (e.g., trust, business, or nonprofit organization) who receives the proceeds from a policy at the death of the insured. Generally, an owner can change a beneficiary unless the beneficiary choice was considered irrevocable at the time the policy was issued. Two types of beneficiaries exist. A **primary beneficiary** receives the proceeds of a life insurance policy when the insured dies. A beneficiary can be designated revocable (can be changed) or irrevocable. When a beneficiary is named irrevocable, the owner cannot change the beneficiary on the policy without the prior consent of the irrevocable beneficiary. Naming an irrevocable beneficiary also changes the owner's ownership rights. The owner cannot receive dividends, take a loan against the policy, pledge the policy as collateral for a debt, or surrender the policy without the written permission of the irrevocable beneficiary. These examples of the right to change, use, modify, or benefit from a policy are typically referred to as **incidents of ownership**.

A **contingent beneficiary** receives the proceeds in the event the primary beneficiary has predeceased the insured. Married clients with children often list their minor children as contingent beneficiaries to life insurance policies. Unfortunately, this can be a costly mistake, both financially and in relation to the speed at which policy proceeds can be distributed. Most states do not allow a child under the age of 18 to own monetary assets. Therefore, most insurance companies will not pay benefits directly to a minor. Because children cannot legally receive a death benefit, if a guardian or a trust (with the minor as the beneficiary) has not been named in a will, then the court will appoint a guardian or require that a trust be set up to manage the proceeds from the life insurance payout. The insurance company can hold the assets for the minor until a court-approved or court-appointed guardian is named to oversee the distribution and investment of insurance proceeds for the minor child. Without proper planning for the distribution of the proceeds to a minor child, the court can require that funds be held in an FDIC-insured account. This safe alternative could, however, preclude sufficient earnings to meet the child's future needs.

An individual can be the owner, insured, and beneficiary of the same policy; however, this is not generally recommended. The most common form of ownership is for the insured to own the policy. However, estate tax consequences must be considered. The face amount of the policy will be included in the gross estate of an insured owner who possesses any incidents of ownership. The policy proceeds will also be included in the gross estate if the insured or "my estate" or "for the benefit of my estate" is named as the beneficiary. This might not be an estate tax problem right away because of the unlimited marital deduction, because any assets the insured/owner left to the spouse are exempt from federal estate taxes. However, the additional value could increase the estate value for the surviving spouse, thus making it subject to estate taxes—often referred to as a "second to die" issue. On the other hand, if the proceeds are payable to children of the insured with the insured as owner, then the proceeds would be subject to estate tax if the value of the estate exceeds the estate tax exclusion.

Finally, two methods are available to change the ownership of a policy because of estate size or for other reasons: ownership can be transferred to another individual or to a trust. Transfer to another individual or entity with an insurable interest as a gift is irrevocable, and the value of the policy proceeds will be brought back into the estate if the transfer occurs within three years of the owner's death. If the current cash value plus any unearned premiums paid at the time of the gift exceed the annual gift tax exclusion ($13,000 in 2012), gift taxes are assessed and will be due upon the death of the original owner. Gift splitting with a spouse is allowed.

The second alternative is to establish an irrevocable life insurance trust, or ILIT, and transfer the policy ownership. To remove the policy from the estate, an owner must give up all incidents of ownership, and there are costs for establishing and managing the trust. With an ILIT an owner can ensure that premiums are paid, and with careful planning for the trust, the insured can gift money to the trust up to the annual exclusion amount to pay the premiums. For an example of ILIT use, see Chapter 14. The new owner should immediately update the beneficiary form. Furthermore, owning life insurance in an ILIT is a very effective way to mitigate tax and privacy issues for domestic partners.

It is also possible for each party of an insurance contract to be a separate person or entity. This is known as an **unholy trinity**. This also should be avoided. Consider a situation where a wife owns a policy in which the husband is the insured and the non-minor children are the beneficiaries. When the husband dies, the children will receive the insurance proceeds on a tax-free basis; however, the surviving spouse, as the owner, could owe a federal gift tax on the policy proceeds if the amount exceeds the annual gift exclusion ($13,000 per donee in 2012) and the total amount of the wife's gifts exceeds the lifetime gift tax exemption amount. The situation can become more troublesome if the wife, while the husband is still alive, transfers ownership of the policy or changes the beneficiaries—both of which are legal actions available to owners.

When reviewing a client's current life insurance situation, as well as when framing recommendations, the income and estate tax situation of the client as well as the age, maturity, and financial situation of any available beneficiaries must be considered. These ownership issues make the life insurance planning process more complex for some clients. Nevertheless, such considerations are important to every client review and equally important considerations when drafting recommendations for new insurance products, if necessary. Furthermore, an important role of the planner may be to work with the client, insurance professionals, and an estate attorney, as applicable, to correct or mitigate insurance contract issues.

If available, client-provided policies and policy illustrations are a valuable source of useful information for planners to document a client's current life insurance coverage. Life insurance policy information can be summarized as shown in Exhibit 5.4. This example illustrates the type of information needed to document the current situation and provides a format for communicating that information to clients in a financial plan. The summary also highlights the importance of identifying and keeping up-to-date the owner, beneficiary, and contingent beneficiary on each policy.

Once all currently in-force coverage is identified, some policies should be retained, and others should be replaced, canceled, or otherwise altered. Planners who make replacement recommendations without conducting a **policy replacement analysis** are overlooking an important portion of their professional responsibility to their clients. It is very important to review whether the forms and types of insurance held by a client are appropriate to meet the client's current and longer-term needs. If changes can be made to existing policies to better meet a client's needs, then every attempt should be made to do so.

**Exhibit 5.4** Sample Current Situation Analysis of Life Insurance for Vince and Anne Hurt

| Life Insurance Policy Information | | | | |
|---|---|---|---|---|
| | **Policy 1** | **Policy 2** | **Policy 3** | **Policy 4** |
| Type | Group Term | Whole-life | Group Term | Whole-life |
| Insurance Co. | New River Insurance | Blackwell Insurance | New River Insurance | Blackwell Insurance |
| Death benefit/ face amount of coverage | $144,000 (2 × salary) | $100,000 | $60,000 (1 × salary) | $100,000 |
| Person insured | Vince | Vince | Anne | Anne |
| Owner | Vince | Vince | Anne | Anne |
| Beneficiary | Anne | Anne | Vince | Vince |
| Contingent beneficiary | | | | Gary* and Lisa**, $50,000 each |
| Cash value | $0 | $4,000 | $0 | $4,000 |
| Premium amount | Employer-paid | $85 | Employer-paid | $70 |
| Payment Frequency | Monthly | Monthly | Monthly | Monthly |
| | Vince | | Anne | |
| Total coverage | $244,000 | | $160,000 | |

\* Vince and Anne's son, currently age 10
\*\* Vince and Anne's daughter, currently age 6

There may be times when existing policies must be replaced. Whether because of a change in the client's situation or a change in the tax laws, trying to force-fit older policies generally does not work well. Another issue that can arise is that the current policy could still be the right kind or face amount, but the insurer's financial strength could, over time, have come under pressure. Given the importance of a well-managed company to invest insurance product assets potentially over several decades, it is important that planners assess financial strength and default risk. Five third-party evaluators and their range of ratings are shown in Table 5.1. It is wise for planners to encourage the use of products from companies rated "A" or higher by any of the rating agencies. A planner may need to recommend replacing insurance products issued by companies with lower ratings.

Next, attention can turn to policy cost considerations. Term policies can be compared on the basis of premium dollars per $1,000 of coverage as long as comparisons are for similar face amounts. The complexity of cash value policies demands more rigorous review. Planners use a number of methodologies to evaluate the cost-effectiveness of cash value life policies. Commonly used methods include the **traditional net cost method,**[3] **the interest-adjusted net cost method,**[4] the **internal rate of return yield method,**[5] and the **yearly price per thousand method** (also known as the **yearly rate of return method**).[6] One approach that provides a quick insight into the "maintain or replace" question for a cash value policy is the yearly-price-per-thousand formula.

The yearly-price-per-thousand formula is effective in determining the cost per thousand a client pays for a policy. Using established benchmark costs, it is possible to compare cash value policies based on the age of the insured. This method is particularly well suited for analyzing whole-life and universal life insurance policies.

---

**Life Insurance Planning Tip: Use Caution When Terminating a Policy**

Underwriting issues can play a role in the decision to replace an insurance policy. In some cases, the cost of insurance, as shown in the yearly-price-per-thousand formula, can be high. This can lead to consideration of replacing the policy. However, a review of a client's insurability factors might suggest that it would be a mistake to cancel the policy because the client might either be unable to purchase or afford a new policy. A basic financial planning rule is as follows: policies should only be canceled or terminated *after* a new policy is in place.

---

The information needed to calculate the yearly-price-per-thousand formula is generally available from the insurance company underwriting the policy. The **yearly-price-per-thousand method formula** is:

$$YPT = \left[ \frac{(PMT + CV_0)(1 + i) - (CV_1 + Div)}{(DB - CV_1)(0.001)} \right]$$

YPT = yearly cost per thousand in coverage
PMT = annual premium payment
CV0 = cash value at beginning of the year
CV1 = cash value at end of the year
I    = projected after-tax rate of return
Div = current policy dividend
DB  = death benefit (most often face value)

The interest rate used in the formula should be the rate of interest that a planner and client estimate could be earned in another investment with similar safety and liquidity characteristics as those offered in a life insurance policy. The rate of return should be equivalent to a net after-tax yield. Once the cost per thousand of coverage is calculated, this amount is compared to benchmark price recommendations shown in Table 5.1

**Table 5.1** Benchmark Premium Prices Based on the Yearly-price-per-thousand Formula

| Age of Client | Yearly Price per $1,000 (Benchmark) |
|---|---|
| Less than 30 | $1.50 |
| 30–34 | $2.00 |
| 35–39 | $3.00 |
| 40–44 | $4.00 |
| 45–49 | $6.50 |
| 50–54 | $10.00 |
| 55–59 | $15.00 |
| 60–64 | $25.00 |
| 65–69 | $35.00 |
| 70–74 | $50.00 |
| 75–79 | $80.00 |
| 80–84 | $125.00 |

*Source:* Adapted from Belth, J. M. Life Insurance: A Consumer's Handbook, 2nd Ed. (Bloomington, IN: Indiana University Press, 1985).

If the yearly-price-per-thousand formula cost is less than the benchmark price, the client should maintain the policy. If the cost is greater than the benchmark price but less than two times the benchmark price, the client should still retain the policy. Only when the cost per thousand is greater than two times the benchmark price should a client consider replacing or exchanging a policy. The new policy should be priced favorably according to the yearly-price-per-thousand formula guidelines.

In this example, the yearly-price-per-thousand formula was calculated for whole-life policies owned by Adam and Katherine, two hypothetical clients. Note that the formula inputs are the same for both policies. However, the interpretation varies because of the couple's age difference. Adam is 36 years old and Katherine is 34.

$$YPT = \left[ \frac{(Cost + Beg\,of\,Year\,Cash\,Value) \times (1+i) - (End\,of\,Year\,Cash\,Value + Div)}{(Death\,Benefit - End\,of\,Year\,Cash\,Value) \times (0.001)} \right]$$

$$YPT = \left[ \frac{((600 + 475) \times 1.069) - (500 - 0)}{((500,000 - 500) \times 0.001)} \right] = \$13.11$$

$13.11 > $6.00 or two times the $3.00 benchmark

Adam is currently paying $13.11 per $1,000 of life insurance coverage, whereas the recommended benchmark for a male his age is $3.00 per $1,000 of life insurance coverage. Given that the premium cost per $1,000 of coverage is more than four times greater than the recommended yearly-price-per-thousand benchmark, a recommendation to replace the policy (assuming the coverage is needed) should be made. However, additional analysis might also be warranted to gain a better understanding about why

Adam's premium is so high. It could be that Adam is a very poor underwriting risk, in which case his advisor may not be able to obtain a policy quote with a lower premium.

This type of analysis offers the client several benefits. First, Adam might be able to stop paying for an overpriced policy. If so, the premium savings can then be used to purchase additional life insurance, if needed, or redirected to other financial goals. Second, if the client is a poor underwriting risk, this could uncover additional planning needs. There may be a need for a larger emergency fund, to increase life coverage on other financial dependents, or to alter lifestyle or other habits to mitigate the detrimental underwriting factors. Alternative sources of insurance through Adam's employer or other groups could offer additional coverage.

Replacing or consolidating policies, for any reason, must be done with care. The advisor must ensure that this recommendation is handled in the most advantageous manner possible, so that the client does not lose protection or incur undue additional expense. Furthermore, it is important that any existing policy not be terminated until a new policy is permanently in place.

### Options for Terminating or Accessing Benefits of a Life Insurance Policy

Both state and federal laws offer consumers options for terminating life insurance policies. State laws specify standard nonforfeiture options that companies must offer policyholders, and the Internal Revenue Code offers certain tax advantages for policy ownership. These consumer protections, as well as their implications for use in life insurance planning, are briefly considered here.

A **nonforfeiture provision** is available to owners of cash value life insurance policies. This provision gives a policy owner the ability to use the cash value of a policy to maintain some life insurance coverage without paying additional premiums or subjecting the cash value to current income taxation. Owners of cash value policies have three broad alternatives if they discontinue premium payments (i.e., cancel the policy), as shown in the Table 5.2.

The hypothetical policy in the sample nonforfeiture table is for a 35-year-old male smoker; the first premium is $241.60 for a policy with a face value amount of $10,000. The premium includes a disability waiver of premium ($4.30) and an accidental death rider ($7.80). Together, these add $12.10 to the base premium of $229.50.

**Table 5.2** Sample Whole-life Insurance Nonforfeiture Table

| End of Policy Year | Cash/Loan Value | Paid-up Insurance | Extended-term Insurance | |
|---|---|---|---|---|
| | | | Years | Days |
| 1 | $14 | $30 | 0 | 152 |
| 2 | $174 | $450 | 4 | 182 |
| 3 | $338 | $860 | 8 | 65 |
| 4 | $506 | $1,250 | 10 | 344 |
| 5 | $676 | $1,640 | 12 | 360 |
| 6 | $879 | $2,070 | 14 | 335 |
| 7 | $1,084 | $2,500 | 16 | 147 |
| 8 | $1,293 | $2,910 | 17 | 207 |
| 9 | $1,504 | $3,300 | 18 | 177 |
| 10 | $1,719 | $3,690 | 19 | 78 |
| 11 | $1,908 | $4,000 | 19 | 209 |
| 12 | $2,099 | $4,300 | 19 | 306 |
| 13 | $2,294 | $4,590 | 20 | 8 |
| 14 | $2,490 | $4,870 | 20 | 47 |
| 15 | $2,690 | $5,140 | 20 | 65 |
| 16 | $2,891 | $5,410 | 20 | 66 |
| 17 | $3,095 | $5,660 | 20 | 52 |
| 18 | $3,301 | $5,910 | 20 | 27 |
| 19 | $3,508 | $6,150 | 19 | 358 |
| 20 | $3,718 | $6,390 | 19 | 317 |
| Age 60 | $4,620 | $7,200 | 18 | 111 |
| Age 65 | $5,504 | $7,860 | 16 | 147 |

*Source:* Sample Life Insurance Policy (no date). Education and Community Services, American Council of Life Insurance, Washington, DC.

First, the client can request that the insurance company return the **cash surrender value** of the policy. The value of the cash received in excess of net paid premiums is subject to federal and state income taxation. Second, the cash value of the policy can be used to purchase a fully **paid-up cash value policy**. This will result in a significantly reduced face value policy. The benefit, however, is that no additional premiums will have to be paid. Third, the cash value can be used to purchase a **fully paid term policy**. The face value of the original cash value policy is retained in this case. The length of the term policy is then determined by the amount of the cash value available in the policy.

For example, as shown in the sample nonforfeiture table, at the end of 13 years of premium payments, with a substantial cash value of $2,294 buildup within a policy, the whole-life policy could be converted to a paid-up 20-year and 8-day term policy with a $10,000 face amount. Conversely, at the end of policy year 2, with a small cash value account of only $174, extended term coverage would be available for only 4 years and 182 days.

One of the nonforfeiture options could be appropriate for clients who have purchased an overpriced policy or for clients who find that a portion of the cash value distribution will be taxable. The nonforfeiture provision could also be useful to clients who made the mistake of buying a cash value policy when a more reasonably priced term policy would have provided the necessary protection. However, two caveats must be considered. First, life insurance that can be obtained using a nonforfeiture option could be costly compared to policies available in the marketplace. Nevertheless, the insurance protection might be a better alternative than the cash value. Second, the nonforfeiture option should not be used until a thorough analysis has been conducted and any new policy is in force.

An alternative to the nonforfeiture option is a § 1035 exchange. A tax advantage associated with life insurance policy ownership, the § 1035 exchange offers more options for replacing a policy. IRC Section 1035 allows for a policy owner to exchange a life insurance policy (i.e., contract) for another life insurance contract on a tax-free basis. In general, a **§ 1035 exchange** allows a policy owner to transfer the cash value from one policy to another without paying taxes on the distribution. This is substantially similar to a tax-free "rollover" of a policy's cash value.

Five specific types of § 1035 exchanges are allowed.

1.  A currently owned policy for a newly issued policy;

2.  An endowment contract policy for another endowment contract, with certain restrictions, or for an annuity contract;

3.  A currently owned policy for an annuity contract;

4.  An annuity contract for another annuity contract; or

5.  An annuity or life insurance contract for a long-term care contract.

In other words, it is possible to exchange a currently owned policy for another newly issued policy by the same or another insurance company. Simply stated, the process of transferring policies on a tax-free basis is analogous to conducting a custodian-to-custodian rollover of qualified retirement plan assets. Although IRC § 1035 can be used to exchange life insurance policies, the majority of § 1035 exchanges involve annuity contracts.

Why wouldn't a client simply withdraw the cash value instead of conducting a § 1035 exchange or taking the nonforfeiture option? The reason to consider a § 1035 exchange or the nonforfeiture option is to reduce the amount of taxable income reported by a client. If a client were to cash out a policy, the amount of cash received in excess of net premiums paid is fully taxable. For some clients, this taxable distribution can be substantial.

A few caveats are associated with the exchange strategy (e.g., keeping careful records of the exchange for tax purposes and obtaining a new policy prior to cancellation of the old policy). Nevertheless, on the whole, a § 1035 tax-free exchange strategy should be considered whenever a currently owned cash value policy is found to be disadvantaged in terms of performance or premium cost.

If the nonforfeiture option or a § 1035 exchange are not viable solutions for a client to terminate or access policy benefits, the options to surrender the policy to the insurance company or sell the policy to a third party remain. The latter are called **viatical settlements** or *life settlements*, depending on the reasons for and conditions of the sale. If a life insurance policy is surrendered or sold for a lump sum amount prior to the death of the insured, any amount received in excess of the net premiums paid is taxable as income. Losses are not recognized for tax purposes.

According to IRS Publication 525, proceeds resulting from the surrender of a policy or sale as the result of a viatical settlement that are paid as an **accelerated death benefit** before the insured's death are excluded from income if the insured is terminally or chronically ill. Someone has a **terminal illness** if life expectancy is 24 months or less from the date that a physician certifies that death is reasonably expected as a result of the insured's illness or physical condition. Neither are gains recognized when a policy is surrendered for the benefit of a chronically ill client. A person with a **chronic illness** is one who has been medically certified, within the previous 12 months, to require (1) substantial assistance because of the inability to perform at least two activities of daily living (i.e. eating, toileting, transferring, bathing, dressing, and continence) or (2) substantial supervision because of cognitive impairment. Accelerated death benefits paid to the chronically ill for costs incurred for qualified long-term care services are fully excludable, and benefits paid on a *per diem* or other periodic basis are excludable up to a limit.

In summary, both state and federal law offer consumers options for terminating life insurance policies and accessing the benefits. These decisions could be prompted by a variety of reasons to meet both short- and long-term client needs ranging from a policy loan for an immediate need to a §1035 exchange for an entirely different insurance product. In each case the client's need for life insurance protection, available cash flow to pay premiums, and the tax implications of the alternative must be considered. The complexity of these decisions could involve collaboration with the client's insurance professional or tax consultant.

---

**Life Insurance Planning Tip: Determining the Tax Status of Insurance Policy Dividends**

**Dividends** earned on life insurance and endowment policies are typically not taxable. The IRS considers dividends a **return of premium** to the client. However, dividends are taxable to the extent that total dividends received exceed total premiums paid. This is rarely the case. It is important to note that if dividends remain with the insurance company, and the dividends earn interest, the interest is fully taxable.

---

## Planning for Special Populations:
## Life Insurance Considerations for Divorcing Couples

Among the myriad of issues that must be considered as part of a divorce, life insurance must not be overlooked. In fact, before a divorce is final such decisions should be resolved, and if new coverage is needed, the purchase should be completed. A purchase promised for later may not occur, or the ex-spouse may not be eligible to purchase new insurance. Knowing this before the final decree means that an adjustment in the final settlement could be made.

Couples often have self-owned policies that name the spouse as beneficiary. When this is the case, the owner can simply change the beneficiary at the time of the divorce unless the ex-spouse is an irrevocable beneficiary, as described in this chapter, or other considerations apply.

Some couples cross-own their policies, where one spouse is the owner and beneficiary but the other spouse is the insured. This form of ownership may need to be altered or terminated upon divorce. But if gifting the policies to each other is a consideration, this should be done before the divorce to take advantage of marital gifting rules.

In some cases, one or both individuals might want to maintain the policy on the former spouse, assuming there is a continuing insurable interest. Insurable interest exists if there is financial reliance upon another person that would create hardship if the support ended. In instances where money or benefits are transferred directly from one party to another (e.g., spousal support or alimony, child support, continued insurance benefits as an agreement of decree) the insurable interest is clear. However, an insurable interest can remain after divorce for a number of reasons. By having life insurance in place, should the ex-spouse die, the proceeds of the policy could replace the stream of income support or be used to purchase health insurance or other benefits.

Minor children are possibly one of the most common reasons that an insurable interest would remain—and not just because of child support payments. In some cases, one parent might be granted primary custody of the child and the other parent provides health insurance for the child. Or a parent could be contributing to the future benefit of a child (e.g., a college fund). In these situations, the custodial parent could be granted the right to own a policy with the ex-spouse as the insured as long as the benefits are payable to the child or into a custodial account for the benefit of the child. This situation can also arise when the ex-spouse is unable or unwilling to self-own a policy because of the cost of ownership, an inability to purchase insurance for health or other reasons, or to avoid estate issues. In other cases, it may be done in lieu of alimony if the ex-spouse is in poor health or does not have much current income to distribute. Future policy proceeds can be given in lieu of current income.

> Another consideration could be which spouse is responsible for the premium payment. As owner, the custodial parent described in this situation would be responsible, but by divorce decree the ex-spouse could be responsible even if not the owner. Thus, by decree the ex-spouse would have to pay the premiums. Divorce does not necessitate changes to a policy unless estate or divorce settlement plans mandate them. Still, life insurance should be reviewed as part of a divorce.

## The Role of Annuities in the Insurance Planning Process

The equity and fixed-income market crises that began in 2008 have had important implications for investors and financial planners. Beginning in 2008, as access to credit markets tightened and in combination with worldwide economic contractions, investors' expectations must confront a new reality regarding returns. Rates of return, including interest on fixed-income securities, dropped to near-historic lows in 2011. The low rates of return on traditional investment products (e.g., stocks, bonds, money market accounts) have prompted investors to seek higher-yielding products that also afford greater levels of protection against volatility.

Annuities, once considered the product choice of retirees and excessively risk-averse investors, have increasingly gained popularity as a way to lock in higher rates of return while reducing volatility risk. For many investors, annuity products have replaced fixed-income holdings in asset allocation models. Given the importance and use of annuities, it is important for financial planners to understand the definitions and general operating characteristics of these products.

**Annuities** are products marketed and sold by insurance companies, and they come in two general forms: deferred and immediate income, although it is also possible to purchase hybrid annuity products. A **deferred annuity** is a tax-deferred investment that can be funded with a lump sum, a series of payments, or a combination of these two approaches. When a deferred annuity is purchased, the owner must choose either a fixed or variable annuity option. Investors who are interested primarily in security and complete minimization of variability in the investment account typically purchase a **fixed annuity**. Fixed deferred annuities are similar to certificates of deposit in that the insurance company provides a guaranteed interest rate on the account balance for a fixed number of years. However, unlike certificates of deposit, FDIC insurance does not apply. At the end of the period, the interest rate credited to the account can be changed.

Variable deferred annuities tend to be popular with younger and more aggressive investors. The term **variable annuity** refers to the type of investments held within the annuity account. Whereas a fixed deferred annuity provides a guaranteed interest rate on assets in the annuity, the rate of return on a variable product is based on the investments held in the account. Usually, variable products offer mutual funds and guaranteed investment contracts as investment options. It is very important to note that, unlike typical mutual funds that can often be purchased without a commission, fund and investment choices within annuity products tend to be more expensive. Insurance companies typically charge fees and expenses above and beyond what the funds levy. Furthermore, almost all deferred annuity products contain **early**

**distribution penalties** that can last up to 15 years, meaning any distribution will be reduced by the **surrender charge**. Together, fees, expenses, and surrender charges make annuity products an expensive investment alternative.

Financial planners can recommend either a fixed or variable deferred annuity product to clients who have maximized their use of qualified retirement plans and other tax-deferred investment alternatives. Because a 10% penalty could be imposed on distributions before age 59½ , these products are inappropriate for clients seeking short-term or emergency fund investment choices. It is also important to remember that annuities avoid probate by means of beneficiary designation. Account values can be paid as a lump sum over a period not to exceed five years, or as a lifetime stream of income at the death of the annuitant. A beneficiary spouse can elect to assume ownership of the annuity, thus maximizing the tax deferral of the product.

**Immediate income annuities** represent a fast-growing segment of the annuity marketplace. Income annuities are usually purchased by retirees or others who need a guaranteed (although not federally insured) source of income for life or a fixed period of time. The primary difference between a deferred annuity and an income annuity is that immediate income annuity holders receive income from the annuity on a regular basis rather than deferring income to a later period. (A deferred annuity can be converted to an income annuity at a future point in time.) When a fixed-income annuity is purchased, the insurance company guarantees an income stream for a given period of time. Some annuity products can even include a **cost-of-living rider** (i.e., inflation protection). It is important to note, however, that this guarantee is based on the insurer's claims-paying ability and financial strength. As is the case when purchasing any insurance product, financial planners should always assess the strength of an insurance company before basing a purchase recommendation on either the rate of return offered or the commission provided to the planner.

Although not as popular as fixed-income annuities, **immediate variable annuity** products are also available. To maintain certain tax advantages, insurance companies are required to guarantee income for life from a variable annuity; however, they are not required to guarantee the amount of each payment. In effect, the level of payout from a variable annuity depends on the investment choices made in the account. This product is most appropriate for younger clients who have a relatively high level of risk tolerance.

Distributions and rules associated with immediate annuities can get quite complex. Income payments from annuity products vary by company, but generally the client's gender, age, and purchase value are used to estimate either guaranteed or projected income from an annuity product. Those who choose a variable annuity can receive more or less than the projected annual income amount based on the underlying performance of the investments in the account. When a client is married, a **joint and survivors annuity distribution** choice can be selected. A 100% and 50% survivor benefit is traditional.

To illustrate the distribution of annuity income, consider a male client born in 1950 who purchases a $500,000 immediate fixed-income annuity in 2011.[7] A typical annuity product would guarantee him a monthly payment of $2,204. At death, his spouse, also born in 1950, would receive no survivor benefit. A 100% guaranteed lifetime survivor benefit option would reduce the monthly income stream to $2,181, with all payments ending at the death of the wife. A 50% survivor option would generate $2,519 per month in current income and leave $1,259 per month to the surviving spouse, with all payments ending at her death.

Many financial planners and clients worry about the irrevocable nature of immediate income annuity products. Although it is true that if a traditional product is purchased (thus maximizing current monthly income) all asset values held in the annuity will revert to the insurance company at the death of the owner or last beneficiary, certain income distribution alternatives reduce the possibility of purchasing an annuity, receiving a few payments, passing away, and forfeiting the present value of the asset. Today most insurance companies provide a 10- or 20-year **guaranteed payout schedule**. Using the preceding example, if the client purchased a 100% survivor product with a 20-year payout guarantee, the initial monthly payment would be $2,181 per month. If both the husband and wife were to pass away in less than 20 years, the insurance company would guarantee distributions to additional beneficiaries until the 20-year period was fulfilled.

As this discussion highlights, the use of annuity products in a client's financial plan has grown beyond the retiree market. Today, many financial planners incorporate fixed-income annuity products into portfolios as a substitute for traditional fixed-income holdings. The risk-return tradeoff (the risk being the financial stability of the insurance company) must always be considered, but in cases where a guaranteed long-term fixed rate is needed, an annuity could be an important tool in the insurance and financial planning process. For clients who have maximized other forms of deferred savings, variable annuity products that allow financial planners to actively manage portfolio assets can also be powerful investment tools.

## STRATEGIES

### Review Prospective Life Insurance Planning Strategies

At this juncture of the life insurance planning process, the planner should be armed with the necessary qualitative and quantitative data to consider various life insurance strategies. It is assumed at this point in the analysis that the financial planner has a thorough knowledge of the client's need for life insurance as well as an assessment of gross and additional coverage needs and the client's current coverage. The next step in the life insurance planning process focuses on the identification of realistic strategies to protect the client's dependents, assets, or charitable wishes. General product considerations as well as specific strategies for meeting the client's needs must be reviewed. Although the adage "buy the most insurance you can afford" sounds simple, developing sound advice can be much more complex.

### Choosing between Cash Value and Term Policies: General Considerations

Before reviewing specific life insurance strategies, a planner should consider whether a client's current and projected needs are best met through a term or cash value policy. Table 5.3 compares term and cash value polices.

**Table 5.3** Comparison of Term and Cash Value Insurance Policy Characteristics

| Characteristic | Term | Cash Value | | | |
| --- | --- | --- | --- | --- | --- |
| | Renewable | Whole-life | Variable | Universal | VUL |
| Length of policy | 1–30 years | Life of insured* | Life of insured* | Life of insured* | Life of insured* |
| Premium from year to year | Fixed or increasing | Fixed | Fixed | Flexible | Flexible |
| Cash value | No | Yes | Yes | Yes | Yes |
| Guaranteed cash value | NA | Yes | No | No | No |
| Interest earned on cash value | NA | Fixed | Based on investments chosen | Based on annually adjusted fixed rate | Based on investments chosen |
| Death benefits | Guaranteed | Guaranteed | Guaranteed minimum (may be less than face value) | Option A: guaranteed; Option B: guaranteed minimum (may be less than face value) | No guarantee (may be greater than or less than face value) |
| Ability to skip premiums | No | No | No | Yes | Yes |

*Some policies terminate at age 95 or 100.

The decision process involved when choosing between a term policy and a cash value policy must include several important factors. Figure 5.4 illustrates the general decision process to broadly consider both kinds of product. The first and foremost factor is the goal of the policy: Will the policy be purchased to cover a temporary or permanent need? If the need is permanent or very long term, perhaps greater than 20 years, a client might want to consider a low-cost, cash value policy. Furthermore, if a planner ascertains that a client's current health status is poor or has the potential to deteriorate significantly, a cash value policy could be an appropriate recommendation. Cash value policies generally last for the life of a client. Therefore, no additional medical tests would be required to maintain the policy, even if the client's subsequent risk class would make insurance prohibitively expensive. Some term policies are **guaranteed renewable** and do not require new medical tests. But the review cannot stop at the client's current health condition. Determining a client's family health history, lifestyle, and occupational risk factors offers insights into the choice of a permanent or temporary type of insurance. For a client who reports numerous issues that could affect the underwriting decision, a permanent type of insurance could be more appropriate than a term policy.

**Figure 5.4** Decision Tree for Choosing between a Cash Value Policy (CVP) and a Term Policy

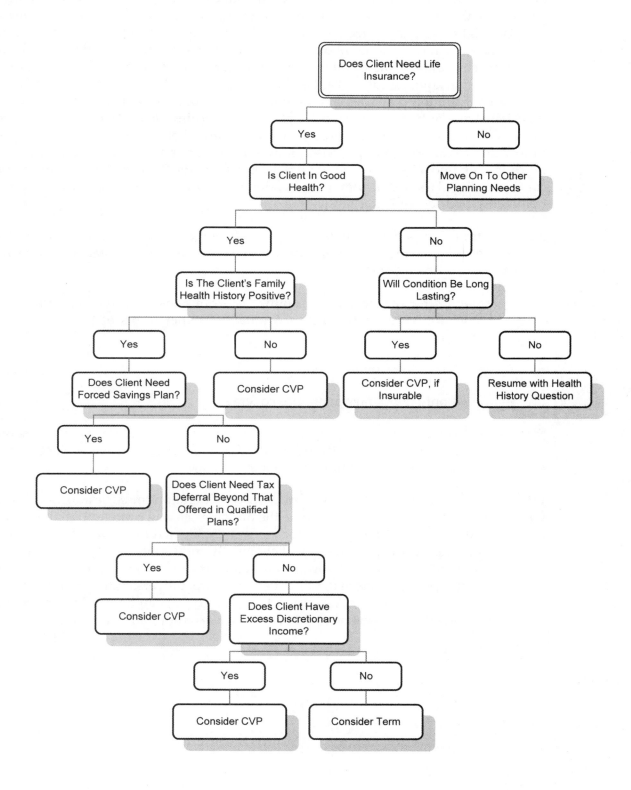

Medical history and coverage period are not the only important factors when determining which kind of policy to recommend. Cash value policies offer a savings component that is not generally available in a term policy. Under certain circumstances, a client might want the **forced savings** or investment availability of a cash value policy. Access to and the amount of tax-advantaged investments a client has available should be considered. Clients who earn significant yearly income will find that they are able to quickly take full advantage of 401(k), 403(b), 457(b), and other qualified defined contribution plans, leaving high levels of income subject to taxation. This is especially true for business owners. High-income-earning clients may need a way to invest a significant amount of money each year into other tax-deferred investments. Life insurance can serve this purpose. However, it is important to note that putting too much money into a life insurance contract can violate the 7-pay test and result in the contract being classified as a modified endowment contract (with less favorable tax treatment), as discussed later in this chapter.

Finally, a term life policy provides adequate coverage at a fraction of the cost of a cash value policy if the client's lifestyle, occupation, and health status suggest no underwriting concerns, and the client:

- qualifies for but does not maximize contributions to defined contributions plans, individual retirement accounts, and other forms of tax-advantaged investments;

- is not a business owner; and

- needs only temporary insurance coverage.

Some new term policies, generally with a longer term, provide a return of some premiums, with payment of a death benefit after the policy term ends. Also, some term policies can be converted into permanent coverage.

When a cash value policy is chosen, a few more considerations must be addressed. The following questions can be used to guide the decision-making process: Will the policy be wholly funded at the time of purchase, or over the life of the contract? Will the cash value policy offer an array of investment choices through subaccounts or simply be a "savings account" with rate of return controlled by the insurance company? If a cash value insurance policy is selected, will it be whole-life, universal life, variable life, or variable universal life (VUL)? A decision tree (Figure 5.5) can be used to determine initially which cash value policy might be the most appropriate for a client.

**Figure 5.5** Decision Tree to Choose the Type of Cash Value Policy

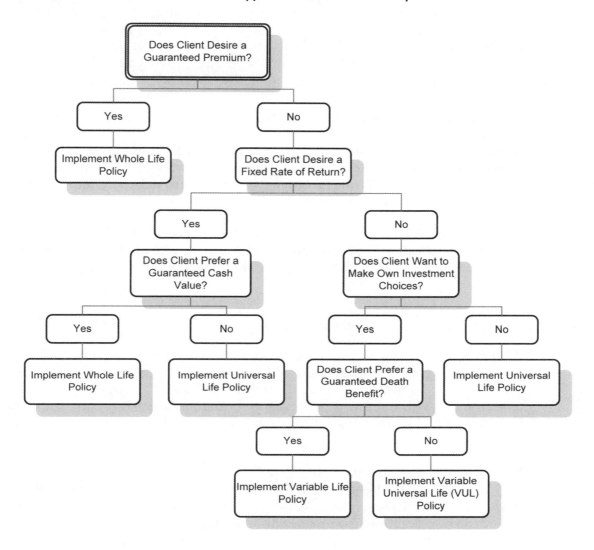

## Identify Prospective Life Insurance Strategies

Regardless of the specific strategies and/or recommendations a planner proposes, some essential analyses must be conducted. Just as the planner has due diligence responsibilities when evaluating existing client coverage, the same process must be repeated for prospective life insurance products. Cost evaluation methodologies using policy illustrations should be used to determine the most cost-effective coverage to meet the client's needs. Ideally, the product search should be restricted to highly rated insurance companies with a reputation for quality customer service.

Financial planners have a multitude of generic life insurance planning alternatives available to meet client objectives. It is the professional duty of the planner to constantly improve product knowledge and keep abreast of new strategies and products for meeting client needs, even beyond the requirements for professional licensure and certification. Following is a brief review of common product and procedural strategies for financial advisors to consider, including their basic advantages and disadvantages.

## Product Strategy 1: Purchase a Whole-life Policy

**Advantage:** For a client who demands greater product certainty, this strategy provides a fixed annual premium, guaranteed cash value, known rate of return, and guaranteed death benefit. Clients who are considered a substandard risk could find that whole-life is the only type of cash value policy available.

**Disadvantage:** Whole-life insurance does not allow clients to control the rate of return earned on cash value. Typically, the rate of return is quite modest—not more than 5% annually. Furthermore, both face value and premium are fixed, which reduces policy flexibility.

## Product Strategy 2: Purchase a Universal Policy

**Advantage:** Universal life provides clients with the opportunity to earn a conservative rate of return greater than that offered in a whole-life policy. This strategy should be considered for clients who want a guaranteed fixed rate of return with the opportunity to earn more with improved performance of the insurance company's investments. Universal life also provides clients with some flexibility in terms of changing the annual premium.

**Disadvantage:** Unlike a variable life policy, universal life does not allow a client to fully manage the assets—and consequently the rates of return—in the cash account. Also, it is unlikely that a client will earn more than a 1% to 2% real return over an extended period of time. The greatest disadvantage, however, is that unless the policy is properly funded and possibly prefunded, it is possible for it to **lapse** (i.e., that coverage be terminated) because of nonpayment of premium and/or a reduction in cash value due to low rates of return earned on the cash account. Although lapsing is possible with any form of universal life policy, the flexibility associated with the frequency and amount of premium payments could make this a greater risk than for a variable universal life policy because of the availability of higher-risk, higher-return assets in which to invest with a VUL policy. (See Product Strategy 4.)

## Product Strategy 3: Purchase a Variable Policy

**Advantage:** This strategy offers clients the opportunity to manage their investments in the cash account, which makes it possible to earn a higher tax-advantaged rate of return. More diversification is possible than that provided by a whole- or universal life policy. This product is appropriate for clients who demand some guarantee in terms of annual premium, but who are also willing to assume greater investment risk over time.

**Disadvantage:** Variable life insurance is relatively inflexible. Premiums are fixed on a yearly basis, regardless of how well the cash value is invested, and the death benefit is typically fixed.

## Product Strategy 4: Purchase a Variable Universal Life (VUL) Policy

**Advantage:** Variable universal life insurance is the most flexible cash value policy. Premiums can be changed annually. The client can direct the investments in the cash account, and the death benefit can grow to exceed the face value. It is also possible to skip premium payments if the account earns a sufficiently high rate of return. This strategy also provides high-income clients with the opportunity to maximize diversified tax-advantaged savings more than in qualified defined contribution plans. Clients with an above-average financial risk tolerance could find this strategy appealing because it allows them to invest the cash value aggressively.

**Disadvantage:** Whenever a VUL policy is sold, the insurance company provides a cash value growth illustration to the client; some illustrations can be quite optimistic. The premium, based partially on the assumed rate of return, could be too low to fully fund the policy. A policy that assumes high returns in the subaccounts could be underfunded as a result of lower realized market returns achieved over the period. If a policy becomes underfunded, the insurance company will require the client to increase the premium. This strategy can also subject a client to relatively high administrative, insurance, and subaccount fees. Consequently, a client may need above-average returns on investments simply to cover administrative, premium, and interest costs.

## Product Strategy 5: Purchase a Single-premium Variable Universal Life Policy

**Advantage:** This strategy allows a client to pay a one-time premium that will result in a higher guaranteed face value in the future. Some planners recommend this strategy as part of an estate reduction plan that allows clients to reposition assets to reduce estate taxes or to leverage assets for gifts to beneficiaries or charities. For example, an average 50-year-old client can use a $10,000 one-time premium to purchase between $25,000 and $30,000 of life insurance.

**Disadvantage:** As with any variable life insurance strategy, this approach can fail if the realized rate of return earned in the cash account falls below projections. Also, a single-premium policy is generally classified as a modified endowment contract (subject to less favorable tax treatment).

## Product Strategy 6: Purchase a One-year Term Policy

**Advantage:** This strategy provides the maximum amount of pure coverage at the lowest annual cost and is most appropriate for a client who needs to avert possible income loss or asset replacement for one year or less. This strategy satisfies a temporary need caused by a change in employment or other life-cycle event that dramatically increases the need for insurance protection.

**Disadvantage:** Without a **guaranteed renewable provision** (i.e., the right to renew the policy on the policy's anniversary date at a higher premium without fear of denial), this strategy exposes the client to the possibility of becoming uninsurable when the policy terminates. This strategy also eliminates multiple-year cost savings and guarantees that the client will pay a higher premium when the new policy is issued.

## Product Strategy 7: Purchase a Multiyear Term Policy

**Advantage:** This strategy allows a client with a limited insurance budget to purchase the maximum amount of pure life insurance over an extended period of time. The annual premium is fixed for the term of the policy. Policies can be purchased with terms ranging from 2 to 40 years.

**Disadvantage:** Usually, this strategy is presented as a **buy term and invest the difference** tactic based on the term policy premium and premium for a comparable cash value policy. Essentially, a client who buys term and invests the difference takes what would have been paid for a cash value policy and invests the difference between that premium and the cost of the term policy in a basket of stocks and bonds. Over time, the value of the investments should grow large enough to replace the face value of the term policy when the insurance coverage expires. This strategy can fail when a client fails to actually save the difference in premiums or when the investment rate of return achieved on the savings is below expectations. Regardless, however, because of the term nature of the insurance, coverage ceases at the end of the term, and the annual premium increases upon policy renewal.

## Product Strategy 8: Purchase a Return-of-premium Term Policy

**Advantage:** A return-of-premium term insurance policy is a hybrid between pure term and whole-life insurance. These polices guarantee to repay all premiums to the policy owner if the insured outlives the term of the policy. If the insured dies during the term of the policy, the full face value is paid.

This type of policy appeals to young, healthy clients who want some kind of return on their premium investment but do not want to spend the extra premium to purchase a cash value life insurance policy. Return-of-premium polices offer two significant advantages. First, the cost can be as much as 60% to 70% less than the premium for a cash value policy. Second, the returned premium can be received on a tax-free basis.

**Disadvantage:** The primary disadvantage associated with this strategy deals with a client's self-discipline. If the client allows a policy to lapse, the return-of-premium option is of little value. Returned premiums seldom exceed 35% of actual premiums paid if a policy lapses. Another disadvantage is that the premiums repaid do not earn interest during the term of the policy. Therefore, the inflation-adjusted "time value of money" could be greatly reduced depending on the term of the policy. Obviously, the longer the term, the greater the loss of purchasing power. However, some money received could be better than no money returned.

### Procedural Strategy 1: Purchase Insurance through a Group Term Policy

**Advantage:** This strategy is designed for clients who are able to purchase life insurance on a pretax, group-rate basis, which makes the insurance very affordable. Coverage is typically available to any employee (or in some cases, members of fraternal, professional, or other groups), regardless of insurability factors. This provides at least a minimum level of insurance to pay for final debts and expenses.

**Disadvantage:** Aside from the benefits of guaranteed insurability and relatively low cost, lack of coverage diversification can be a major disadvantage of this strategy. If most or all of a client's life insurance is purchased through an employer, conversion to individual coverage is typically unavailable should the client cease working. Even a change in position with a reduction in salary could affect insurance coverage and cost. Payment of income taxes on employer-provided premiums (generally for coverage in excess of $50,000) is another disadvantage.[8]

### Procedural Strategy 2: Combine a Group Term Policy with a Low-cost Private or Individual Policy

**Advantage:** This combination insurance strategy is most appropriate for clients who have access to low-priced group insurance, but who want the assurance of supplemental, continuous coverage of a private policy. This strategy is also appropriate for clients who anticipate leaving employment before retirement, or those who fear a **substandard risk classification** in the future due to health habits, medical history, or work history. As a precaution, insurance diversification and lifetime coverage can be assured by purchasing a cash value policy or guaranteed renewable term rather than depending solely on employer-provided coverage.

**Disadvantage:** The primary disadvantage associated with this strategy is that the additional insurance will probably be more expensive than the group coverage and will not offer the ability to purchase coverage with pretax dollars. Furthermore, to be most cost effective, the purchase must be made at a relatively young age.

### Procedural Strategy 3: Combine a "Base" Cash Value Policy with Group or Private Term Policies

**Advantage:** This strategy offers the guarantee of permanent insurance protection coupled with the lower-cost options of group or private term insurance. It offers clients increased flexibility to add lower-cost term coverage during periods of high insurance coverage need (e.g., when children are young or in college), while maintaining a smaller "base" amount of permanent protection.

**Disadvantage:** During the early years of strategy implementation, when client earnings are lower, the higher-cost, cash value policy could limit the amount of coverage a client can afford relative to the amount of term insurance that could have been purchased.

### Procedural Strategy 4: Include Conversion and Renewability Features in Term Policies

**Advantage:** An attractive feature of some term polices is a **conversion provision**, which allows the policy owner to exchange a term policy for a cash value policy without proof of insurability. This rider could be valuable for those who think that they could become uninsurable in the future or face a significantly higher risk classification. When purchasing a term policy, it is also possible to obtain a guaranteed renewable provision, which guarantees that the policy owner can renew the policy for an extended period of time without proof of insurability.

**Disadvantage:** A conversion provision usually has time limits. The guaranteed renewable provision does not guarantee a fixed premium rate, only the ability to lengthen the term of the policy regardless of underwriting considerations. Clients interested in locking in a steady annual premium should consider purchasing a cash value policy.

### Procedural Strategy 5: Include a Disability Waiver Provision when Purchasing a Policy

**Advantage:** Almost all policies provide a **disability waiver provision**. This optional provision enables an insurance policy to remain in effect during a period of a disability without the additional cost of continuing premium payments. In effect, this provision supplies a waiver of premiums if the policy owner becomes disabled. The probability of becoming disabled far exceeds the probability of premature death during most of a client's working years. Consequently, from a cost/benefit analysis perspective, this provision is generally worth the expense.

A variation of the idea of continuing coverage for the client is a waiver of premium for unemployment if an individual is unemployed and eligible for unemployment benefits. Restrictions apply regarding how long premiums will be paid or how often the waiver can be used.

**Disadvantage:** The inclusion of a disability waiver provision increases the annual cost of a policy, sometimes substantially. The unemployment waiver provision can be offered as a no-cost rider or added for a fee. A client's situational factors and risk tolerance must be considered in the cost-benefit analysis provision in consultation with an insurance professional when recommending any rider.

### Procedural Strategy 6: Beware of Modified Endowment Contracts

**Advantage: Modified endowment contract** (MEC) status applies to any contract purchased after June 1988 that fails the **7-pay test**. As defined by IRC Section 7702A, the 7-pay test refers to any contract "if the accumulated amount paid under the contract at any time during the first seven contract years exceeds the sum of the net level premiums which would have been paid on or before such time if the contract provided for paid-up future benefits after the payment of seven level annual premiums." This basically means that if a contract could have been self-supporting after seven years based on the premiums of the first seven years and additional amounts were deposited, some of the tax benefits of the life insurance contract will be lost. The purpose of the law is to discourage policyholders from making very large premium payments during the first seven years of the contract to create a **paid-up policy** that leverages the tax advantaged status of the deposits.

**Disadvantage:** Few disadvantages are associated with this strategy. If a policy is an MEC, any death benefit provided under the contract will qualify for income tax-free treatment. However, any distribution—whether a loan, withdrawal, surrender, or settlement from an MEC—will be taxed on an income-first basis. Furthermore, if the insured is less than age 59½, a 10% penalty also applies to the taxable portion of most distributions.

### Procedural Strategy 7: Use Viatical Settlements or Accelerated Death Benefits when Appropriate

**Advantage:** A **viatical settlement** occurs when a terminally ill insured client sells a life insurance policy to a third party for perhaps as much as 80% of the death benefit. Alternatively, an insurance company could pay **accelerated death benefits** to the insured when the insured is terminally ill, either through a policy feature, a rider that is added to the policy, or policy surrender as described earlier in this chapter. In the case of a policy feature or rider, a portion of the face value of the policy (e.g., stated amount or percentage) is paid to the client once certain medical situations are documented, and the balance is paid at the death of the insured. Service or interest charges may apply. In the case of a viatical settlement when the policy is sold to a third party, the face value of the policy is paid to the viatical holder at the death of the insured.

For federal income tax purposes, the amount received by a terminally ill insured client in a viatical settlement or as an accelerated death benefit is treated as an amount paid under the life insurance contract by reason of the insured's death and thus is generally tax-free.

Viatical settlements are increasingly used by individuals who have exhausted lifetime limits on their medical policies or who want the funds to make the end of life more comfortable for themselves or others. The viatical settlement provides the dying person with immediate funds to pay for caregivers, medical or pharmaceutical treatment, or living expenses. The policy option for accelerated death benefits offers clients the same advantages, but it may not be available in the client's insurance products.

**Disadvantage:** When considering a viatical settlement, it is important to consider immediate benefits to the insured, the household, and caregivers compared to the longer-term effect of no insurance proceeds for the beneficiary. If chosen, the cost of the viatical settlement should be compared among different companies to get the maximum benefit for the client.

In some policies, the accelerated death benefit may be a policy feature, but for other products the rider must be added to a new policy when purchased, or in some cases it can be added to an existing policy. If added, the cost of the rider must be considered relative to the client's perceived need or medical history, and cost comparisons among companies should be considered.

## Procedural Strategy 8: Use a Life Settlement when Appropriate

**Advantage:** For elderly clients who no longer need insurance or estate tax protection, selling a policy to a life settlement company offers several benefits. First, to be worthwhile, the settlement must be for more than the cash surrender value. Second, the client benefits from the immediate availability of the funds for reinvesting, supplementing income, or meeting medical needs. Third, the client avoids the premiums required to maintain the policy, which is a form of future savings. At the death of the insured, the face value of the policy is paid to the settlement company.

**Disadvantage:** When considering a life settlement, it is important to recognize that life settlement companies prefer that the insured be at least 65 years old with a policy providing a minimum face value of $100,000. Other guidelines apply that could affect the availability of a settlement offer. Policy owners with a life expectancy of less than 12 years are preferred, but those in declining health could receive a higher offer. The policy should have been in force for two years, and the client should be expected to live for at least two more years.

Contingent on the cost basis of the policy, the cash surrender value, and the settlement offer, the life settlement payment could be taxable. Fees or commissions also apply, so it is important to consider offers from other settlement firms.

---

### Planning for Special Populations:
### Life Insurance for the Small Business Owner

Life insurance plays an extremely important role for the owner of a small or closely held business, because the business may be the primary source of income and perhaps the bulk of the client's net worth. When an owner dies, revenue can decline or cease and there may not be an easy way to extract value from the business to support the survivors. Many typical estate planning needs are amplified in the case of business ownership. Without an effective estate plan, including a business succession plan, the business may have to close or be liquidated to pay estate taxes. With the proper use of life insurance, a business owner can plan to provide the liquidity needed to pay any estate tax liability.

But beyond immediate liquidity needs, there are two additional reasons that life insurance is so critically important to small business owners: (1) key person insurance to protect the company, and (2) buy-sell funding agreement to protect the partners.

**Key person insurance** is life insurance on the vital person or persons who are crucial to a business. The purpose of key person insurance is to help a company survive the financial loss associated with the death of the person who makes the business work. The business might not be viable without the services of the owner or another key person. Therefore, to ensure the continuation of the business, the company purchases a life insurance policy on the key employee(s), pays the premium(s), and is the beneficiary of the policy(ies). If the insured dies, the company receives the face value of the insurance. The company can then use insurance proceeds for expenses until it can find a replacement person, or if necessary, pay off debts, distribute money to investors, pay severance to employees, and close the business in an orderly fashion. In a tragic situation, key person insurance provides companies with options other than immediate bankruptcy.

A **buy/sell agreement** reduces the number of difficulties a business faces when an owner dies by allowing the business to continue. The agreement is typically between the owners, an owner and a family member, the owners and the business entity, or an owner and employees.

Buy-sell agreements are typically defined as either a cross-purchase plan or an entity purchase plan. In either case, in a partnership the agreement facilitates the surviving partner(s)' purchase of the deceased partner's business interest from the heirs or the estate at an agreed-upon price. Buy-sell agreements work similarly for limited liability companies and their members, and for corporations and their shareholders.

In a **cross-purchase plan,** each partner, not the partnership, buys a life insurance policy on each of the other partners. Each partner owns, pays the premiums, and is the beneficiary of the insurance policies on the other partners in an amount equal to each partner's investment or business equity as set forth in the buy/sell agreement. At a partner's death, the other partners purchase the deceased partner's interest in the partnership.

In an **entity purchase plan the individual** partners enter into an agreement with the partnership (the legal entity representing the business), which owns, pays the premiums, and is the beneficiary of the policies. At a partner's death, the partnership purchases the deceased partner's interest in the partnership. This plan only works when more than two partners are involved.

However, any plan should include a funding method. There are several options for the future business owner to fund a buy-sell agreement, including borrowing funds, establishing a savings account within the company, or establishing an employee stock ownership plan.  However, the death of an owner typically creates a significant financial burden on the business and its remaining partners. To mitigate this risk, many buy-sell agreements are established to be funded with the proceeds of life insurance, although life insurance used in this manner can be very expensive because of the size of the policy.

In either of these situations, a buy/sell agreement is executed as follows:

- An agreement is prepared that sets forth the entity or the prospective business owner's obligation to buy, the price of the business, and the method of payment. (The price should be periodically reviewed based on a current valuation of the business.)

- The entity or the prospective business owner purchases, funds, and is named the beneficiary of a life insurance policy on the current owner, as the insured.

> • Upon the death of the owner, the death benefit of the insurance policy is used to buy the business, shares, or interest from the decedent's estate.
>
> Because two-party partnerships are automatically dissolved with the death of one partner, a buy-sell agreement is especially important, but this business continuation method can be used with partnerships, limited liability companies, or closely held private corporations.

## CHAPTER-BASED CASE STUDY

### A Client-based Life Insurance Recommendation Example

Determining the face amount of coverage and the specific policy or policies to purchase—in other words, the strategy—is insufficient for making a sound client recommendation. More specifically, the recommendation should go beyond the strategy to clearly state how the life insurance policy contract should be structured. Considerations unique to life insurance recommendations include:

- who owns the policy;

- who receives the benefit from the policy, and

- how policy proceeds will be disbursed.

This attention to the structure of the policy contract promotes smooth and timely asset transfer by maximizing tax benefits and minimizing legal issues upon the death of the insured. When purchasing a policy, care must be taken to consider the income, gifting, and estate tax implications of potential scenarios. Periodically, during advisor-client review meetings, it is important to reconsider the beneficiaries and ensure that they still match the client's wishes. Finally, after significant life or family events it is important to again review insurance policy contract features. The following reminders could be useful:

- Avoid having the insured as owner of the policy if the client's estate is likely to be greater than the federal estate tax exclusion amount.

- Avoid naming the policy owner or the owner's estate as beneficiary because of: (1) possible estate tax or state inheritance tax implications; (2) lack of protection of the funds from creditors; and (3) delays with the probate court that will make the funds inaccessible.

- Avoid establishing a trust to manage life insurance proceeds and naming an individual as the beneficiary of the policy. The proceeds will go to the beneficiary instead of the trust.

- Avoid delays in updating the policy beneficiary after major life events. In a few states, divorce automatically revokes a beneficiary designation naming the ex-spouse. Otherwise, an ex-spouse could receive policy proceeds years after the divorce.

- Avoid naming only a single, primary beneficiary and opt instead for naming a primary beneficiary with one or two contingent beneficiaries. Should a sole beneficiary predecease the insured, the insurance proceeds would then be payable to the estate unless a second in-line contingent beneficiary (or two) is named.

- Avoid naming minor children as beneficiaries unless the will names a guardian or trust to manage the funds on behalf of the children. If the court has to appoint someone, there will be additional expense—paid from the insurance proceeds.

- Avoid stating a specific amount of policy proceeds to be paid to multiple beneficiaries, opting instead for a stated percentage of the policy proceeds. Because of dividends, outstanding loans, or other variations, the face value of the policy might not, at the time of death, be exactly the face amount initially stated in the distribution.

## A Sample Recommendation: Purchase a Variable Universal Life (VUL) Policy

In essence, a VUL policy bundles pure life insurance with a cash account that can be invested in a mix of asset classes via subaccounts within the policy. As the name implies, a VUL policy is a hybrid product that is similar to a variable policy in the types of investments allowed in the cash account and comparable to a universal policy because the policy owner has the option of flexible premiums. Depending on the return from cash account investment choices, the policy death benefit could be substantially higher than the policy face value. Conversely, if invested imprudently or during periods when rates of return on equity investments are low or negative, the policy could lapse with no cash value.

The use of a VUL strategy is most appropriate for investment-savvy clients who want to maximize tax-advantaged savings while providing beneficiaries with a base amount of life insurance proceeds. A target client might want an investment vehicle that allows tax-deferral of savings beyond what is typically available in a defined contribution retirement plan or other tax-advantaged investments. A high-net-worth/high-income client could, theoretically, **overfund** a VUL policy by annually contributing five- and six-figure amounts to the policy. However, the face value of the policy would have to be quite large to accept this type of funding.

The success of the VUL strategy is contingent on two factors. First, the client must be willing to overfund the policy for many years. Second, the client must invest the cash account in fairly aggressive investments to achieve a high annualized rate of return. In a bull market, the VUL policy strategy can work extremely well to build nontaxable wealth. Following this strategy, clients can take loans against their policy, spend the loan proceeds, and simply repay the loan interest.[9] In effect, the client creates a tax-free retirement portfolio, and upon death the beneficiaries reap a substantial tax-free windfall.

A VUL recommendation could be presented using an Insurance Recommendation Form, such as that shown in Exhibit 5.5.

**Exhibit 5.5** The Jones' Life Insurance Recommendation Form

**Planning Recommendation Form**

| Financial Planning Content Area | Life insurance and investments | | | |
|---|---|---|---|---|
| **Client Goal** | Maximize tax-qualified investment opportunities | | | |
| **Recommendation No.:** | 1 | **Priority (1–6) lowest to highest:** | | 5 |
| **Projected/Target Value ($)** | $500,000 (face value) | | | |

**Product Profile**

| Type | Variable universal life policy | | | |
|---|---|---|---|---|
| Duration | Lifetime | | | |
| Provider | Northern Nevada Insurance Company | | | |
| Funding Cost per Period ($) | $6,000 annually | | | |
| Maintenance Cost per Period ($) | $0 | | | |
| Current Income Tax Status | Tax-qualified | X | Taxable | |
| Projected Rate of Return | 7% (with a guaranteed minimum of 1.5% on fixed-asset account.) | | | |
| Major Policy Provisions | 1. Loan provision<br>2. Automatic premium loans<br>3. Waiver of premium for periods of disability (restrictions apply) | | | |

**Procedural Factors**

| Implement by Whom | Planner | | Client | X |
|---|---|---|---|---|
| Implementation Date or Time Frame | Immediate | | | |
| Implementation Procedure | Contact Northern Nevada Life Company | | | |

**Ownership Factors**

| Owner(s) | Mary E. Jones | | | |
|---|---|---|---|---|
| Form of Ownership | Sole | | | |
| Insured(s) | John D. Jones | | | |
| Custodial Account | Yes | | No | X |
| Custodian | NA | | | |
| In Trust For (ITF) | Yes | | No | X |
| Transfer on Death (TOD) | Yes | X | No | |
| Beneficiary(ies) | Mary E. Jones, spouse (100%) | | | |
| Contingent Beneficiary(ies) | William I. and Sarah B. Jones, children (50% each) | | | |

| **Proposed Benefit** | Immediate life insurance protection with the added benefit of accumulating tax-advantaged assets for use during retirement. |
|---|---|

The Joneses are high-net-worth clients who are experienced, risk-tolerant investors seeking additional tax-advantaged investments. John does not have sufficient life insurance and they are comfortable with the advantages and potential disadvantages of a VUL policy. To avoid future estate tax issues for John, it is recommended that Mary own the policy. She is identified as the primary beneficiary, with their college-age children identified as the contingent beneficiaries. Note that the contract would be structured with loan and automatic premium loan provisions, both of which are central to the effective use of this product recommendation. Because of concerns over John's family medical history and his extensive career-related travel, he, Mary, and their planner agree that a disability waiver is important to include, although it would add to the cost of the policy. Finally, the form summarizes other specific information needed to implement the recommendation, as well as the projected immediate and long-term benefit to the Jones household.

A recommendation to purchase a VUL policy provides select clients with the opportunity to build substantial cash value through a combination of contributions and aggressive investing in the investment subaccounts. When the client has to fund a major expenditure, assuming expected levels of performance, a loan can be taken against the policy. An important assumption is that the account has sufficient earnings to pay both the loan interest and the ongoing pure insurance costs. Otherwise, continued annual loan interest or premium payments will be needed and the cost of insurance will continue to increase as the insured ages. When matched to the appropriate client situation, the recommendation to purchase a VUL policy can satisfy an insurance need and potentially serve as a funding source for education, retirement, or other special needs considered in the planning process.

## Learning Outcomes

1. As discussed throughout this chapter, life insurance planning plays an important role in a comprehensive financial planning framework. A client's life insurance need is normally evaluated early in the planning process to determine the fiscal and emotional costs associated with the client's premature death. Without proper levels of insurance in place—and funded—a client's entire financial plan could potentially collapse in the event of premature death, resulting in liquidity constraints and unfunded tax liabilities.

2. An essential first step in the life insurance planning process involves identifying common risk classification factors used in the life insurance underwriting process. Client lifestyle characteristics, such as using tobacco, alcohol, or drugs; a history of reckless driving; participating in sensation-seeking activities; and exhibiting low financial risk tolerance are all indicators of potential underwriting problems. These factors also suggest high premiums and the possibility of limited coverage. Other factors that might indicate that a client is a substandard risk include working in a hazardous profession, piloting aircraft, being overweight, or having a family history of medical problems.

3.  Five quantitative approaches are commonly used to identify a client's need for life insurance. Financial planners must be familiar with the use and application of each of the following methods: (1) needs-based analysis; (2) human life value; (3) capital retention; (4) income retention; and (5) simple income multiplier approach. Rather than relying on one or two of these measures, it is often a good idea to triangulate results into an average need. This triangulated dollar estimate can be recommended to a client.

4.  Although each insurance company in the marketplace has distinct names for its life insurance products, most policy types can be classified into one of the following six groups: (1) term; (2) return of premium term; (3) whole; (4) universal; (5) variable; and (6) variable universal life. Competent financial planners, even those who do not deal daily with life insurance planning issues, should be able to identify each type of policy and match the appropriate policy to a client's needs.

5.  Many financial planners regularly conduct a policy replacement analysis. It is common for financial planners to use the yearly price per thousand method formula to estimate the approximate cost of a cash value life insurance policy. Benchmarks developed by Joseph Belth can be used to determine whether a client should hold or replace a currently in-force policy.

6.  Clients who own cash value policies normally have several choices available through nonforfeiture provisions included in their contract when considering the termination of an in-force policy. Options include surrendering the policy for the cash value, using the cash value to purchase a paid-up cash value policy, or using the cash value to buy a fully paid term policy. Sometimes, however, it makes better financial sense to exchange a policy for another type of insurance product. Five alternatives exist under what is known as a § 1035 exchange: (1) exchange the current policy for a newly issued policy; (2) exchange an endowment contract for another endowment contract; (3) exchange a current policy for an annuity contract; (4) exchange an annuity contract for a new annuity contract; or (5) exchange an annuity contract for a long-term care contract.

7.  Annuities, as used in the life insurance planning process, can be categorized in one of two ways: deferred and immediate income. Deferred annuities provide a tax-advantaged means for accumulating assets for future goals. Immediate annuities represent a way for clients to convert current financial assets into income-generating sources of income. Within any annuity product, clients can choose to invest in either a fixed-income or variable-income contract. Annuity products are gaining in usage among aging clients. Thus, it is essential that financial planners have a strong working knowledge of the types and uses of annuity products. Furthermore, a working familiarity with key annuity terms and features, such as joint-and-survivor payout alternatives, payout schedules, and early distribution penalties, is a characteristic that distinguishes the most competent financial planners.

8.  The decision to recommend either a term or cash value policy is more complicated than simply implementing a "buy term and invest the difference" strategy. Foremost, every insurance recommendation should be based on a client's need for a policy. Permanent cash value policies might be more appropriate when a client has a long-term enduring financial need. In situations where the financial need is short and temporary, term insurance may be

more appropriate. Other factors to consider when drafting life insurance recommendations include understanding the medical history of the client and his or her family. Clients who could face underwriting challenges in the future should consider purchasing permanent life insurance today. Additionally, the aspect of forced savings can be important for some clients, resulting in a recommendation to purchase a cash value policy. Regardless of the final recommendation, financial planners must consider issues related to triggering the 7-pay test, which could limit the attractiveness of a policy recommendation.

9. As the examples provided in this chapter illustrate, there are a multitude of life insurance planning recommendations, both product and procedural, that can be used to help a client reach his or her financial goals. An important aspect of the financial planning process involves identifying and recommending prospective life insurance planning strategies that can be used to meet a client's unique financial situation and life goals. Financial planners who become experts at identifying the needs of current and prospective clients in relation to life insurance planning topics will find that the client-planner relationship greatly improves over time. Recommending life insurance strategies focused on helping clients reach their financial goals provides an excellent pathway for developing and strengthening relationships.

## Chapter Resources

Baldwin, B., *The New Life Insurance Investment Advisor* (New York: McGraw Hill, 2002).

Belth, J. M., *Life Insurance: A Consumer's Handbook*, 2nd ed. (Bloomington, IN: Indiana University Press, 1985).

General life insurance and tax source: *Tax Facts on Life Insurance & Employee Benefits* (Cincinnati, OH: National Underwriter Company, published annually).

Leimberg, S. R. and R. J. Doyle, *Tools & Techniques of Life Insurance Planning*, 4th ed. (Cincinnati, OH: National Underwriter Company, 2007).

Life and Health Insurance Foundation for Education, general life insurance information (http://www.naifa.org/consumer/life.cfm)

The *Financial Factilitator* and all fillable forms needed to complete text activities can be found on the student website at: http://pro.nuco.com/booksupplements/NUCollege-CaseBook2e.

# Quantitative/Analytical Mini-case Problems

1. Theresa Cortez is the primary breadwinner for a family of four. Her husband has been unable to work since the onset of severe vertigo 2½ years ago. Their two children are both in high school and, presumably, college bound. After attending your seminar about life insurance planning, she has come to you to determine whether she has enough life insurance. Besides the small disability check that her husband receives, she is the only source of income—albeit a good income of $84,000 per year. At your request, she has brought her most recent annual income and expense statement that shows the family's annual expenses of $55,000, annual taxes of $17,000, and savings of $12,000.

   Calculate Theresa's current insurance need using the Human Life Value approach for each of the following four scenarios, assuming her remaining working life is 26 years and the projected discount rate is 8.0% before taxes, compounded daily.

   a. Using her gross income.

   b. Using her gross income and a growth rate of 3.5%.

   c. Using her net income.

   d. Using her net income and a growth rate of 3.5%.

   Which of these four methods would result in the most reasonable estimation of insurance need?

2. John Wilson is a 42-year-old computer programmer, husband, and father of four. He wants to use the capital retention approach to determine how much life insurance he should purchase. Because of his $105,000 salary and their four children, his wife does not work outside the home. The family's current annual living expenses are approximately $75,000, including $8,000 in annual IRA contributions. He prefers to use the capital retention approach (CRA) so that he can be reasonably assured that his family will not exhaust the proceeds of his policy. However, he also wants to consider the possible reduction in expenses and apply a 70% replacement ratio to the calculation.

   a. Calculate John's insurance need using the capital retention approach, an after-tax discount rate of 5.5%, and assume end-of period payment of benefits.

   b. Calculate John's insurance need using the human life value approach (HLV), an after-tax discount rate of 5.5%, a remaining working life of 25 years, and assume end-of period payment of benefits.

   After your presentation, John was bewildered about why the HLV and CRA calculations resulted in significantly different insurance needs. Using the two formulas as a guide, explain to John why this result occurred.

3.  Morgan is a 32-year-old nurse. She is in good health and has applied for a new cash value life insurance policy. She is interested in knowing whether she should surrender her current policy and purchase the new policy offered through a AAA-rated firm. If all of the contract and company characteristics are similar, and the current face value of her policy is sufficient, should she maintain or replace her current policy? Assume the following factors:

    •   Yearly premium: $1,900

    •   Cash value at the beginning of the period: $13,456

    •   Cash value at the end of the period: $13,927

    •   Projected after-tax rate of return: 3.50%

    •   Current policy dividend: $350

    •   Death benefit: $200,000

# Comprehensive Bedo Case—Analysis Questions

Before beginning the Bedo household life insurance analysis, it will be important to review assumptions related to salaries, assets, and client goals (e.g., funding education and retirement). When reviewing their current life insurance situation, note the proportion of insurance held by the Bedos from private policies and employer-provided group term policies. Evaluating the cost of these policies will also be beneficial. Use the following questions to guide the life insurance planning process.

1.  Develop a life insurance planning goal for the Bedos. When conceptualizing this goal, consider the following:

    a.  Is the goal developed in agreement with any or all goals and objectives that the clients have identified regarding life insurance planning?

    b.  What situational factors might influence their life insurance goals? Are these factors explicit, implied, or assumed? Is additional information required from the Bedos?

    c.  What is the desired outcome for the clients?

2.  Make a list of the lifestyle, occupational, and health underwriting factors that should be evaluated for the Bedos. How might this information be obtained? How might it be useful in the current life insurance situation analysis? Also, make a list of life events that could impact the life insurance planning analysis for Tyler and Mia and that should be reviewed at future client meetings.

3.  Develop a list of globally accepted, client-specific, or planner-generated planning assumptions that will structure the life insurance situation analysis.

4.  Using the formulas or the Financial Facilitator, calculate both Tyler's and Mia's gross and additional life insurance need using each of the following approaches:

    a.  Needs analysis approach

    b.  Human life value approach

    c.  Capital retention approach

    d.  Income retention approach

    e.  Income multiplier approach

5.  How might these results change if a growth rate is applied to the desired benefit amount? What if the Bedos wanted to replace after-tax rather than gross income?

6.  Using the life insurance calculation approach that best fits their situation or triangulation, state how much additional life insurance, if any, Tyler and Mia might need. Provide a brief, client-friendly explanation of how this number was determined. What graphic presentations might be used to convey this information to the clients?

7.  Calculate the yearly price per thousand in coverage for Tyler's current whole-life policy. Based on your findings, should Tyler consider replacing this policy? Provide a brief, client-friendly explanation of this analysis and the interpretation to include in the Bedos' plan. What graphic presentations might be used to convey this information to the clients?

8.  Calculate the yearly price per thousand in coverage for Mia's current whole-life policy. Based on your findings, should Mia consider canceling this policy or exchanging it for a term policy? Are there tax implications to consider? Provide a brief, client-friendly explanation of this analysis and the interpretation to include in the Bedos' plan.

9.  Does Becky need life insurance, and if so, what type of policy would be most appropriate for her? Provide a brief explanation of this analysis and the interpretation to include in the Bedos' plan.

10. Based on the information collected, financial advisors have a responsibility to fully document and inform clients of the analysis and results. This information can be communicated by letter or in a comprehensive or a modular plan. Using bullet points summarize your observations about Tyler's, Mia's, and Becky's current life insurance situation and the planning need(s) identified.

11. Based on the goals originally identified and the complete analysis, what product or procedural strategies might be most useful to satisfy the Bedos' life insurance protection needs? Be sure to consider strategies matched to the planning needs identified for each member of the household. When reviewing these strategies, be careful to consider the approximate cost of implementation, as well as the most likely outcome(s) associated with each strategy.

12. Write at least one primary and one alternative recommendation from select strategies in response to each planning need identified. More than one recommendation may be needed to address all of the planning needs. Include specific, defensible answers to the who, what, when, where, why, how, and how much implementation questions for each recommendation.

   a.  It is suggested that each recommendation be summarized in a Recommendation Form.

   b.  Assign a priority to each recommendation based on the likelihood of meeting client goals and desired outcomes. This prioritization will be important when recommendations from other core planning content areas are considered relative to the available discretionary funds for subsidizing all recommendations.

   c.  What considerations should be taken into account when naming beneficiaries to any new life insurance policies for the Bedos?

   d.  Comment briefly on the outcomes associated with each recommendation.

13. Prepare a 10–15 minute presentation for the Bedos of your observations and/or recommendation(s) for meeting their life insurance needs. Be sure to include visual aids, Excel handouts, and other materials that will make the recommendations more meaningful for the clients.

## Notes

1.  A *Kiplinger's* article provides an example of how replacement ratio calculations are commonly discussed, calculated, and used in practice. Available at http://www.kiplinger.com/magazine/archives/how-much-life-insurance-do-you-need.htm.

2.  Prudential Financial, "Consumer Insights Research," January 13, 2011, as reported in The Life Insurance Coverage Gap. Available at http://research.prudential.com/media/managed/documents/research_perspective/RP_The_Life_Insurance_Coverage_Gap.pdf.

3.  The traditional net cost method subtracts total premiums paid from a policy's projected dividends plus cash surrender value. What remains is divided by the projected holding period. This equates to an annual cost of ownership. One criticism of this methodology is that the calculation does not account for the time value of money associated with premium payments. This evaluation procedure is not widely used because the calculation often results in a negative cost of ownership.

4.  This method of evaluation adjusts the traditional net cost estimate for the time value of money associated with premium payments.

5.  Sometimes called the net payment cost index, this approach assumes that premiums and policy dividends are accrued over a set period of time, typically 20 years, with a fixed rate of return (e.g., 4%) paid on the policy cash value. Total dividends are then subtracted from the total of all premium payments. This figure is then averaged, using a time value of money adjustment, to estimate an average annual net premium cost.

6.  Joseph Belth originally developed the yearly price per thousand method. A complete description of the method can be found in Belth, J. M., *Life Insurance: A Consumer's Handbook*, 2nd Ed. (Bloomington, IN: Indiana University Press, 1985).

7.  Calculations based on estimates from Fidelity Investments online income calculator. Available at http://gie.fidelity.com/estimator/gie/gielanding?refpr=annufixincom011.

8.  Issues related to Section 79 imputed income are addressed in the Tax Planning chapter.

9.  This is known as *pension maximization*, a technique discussed in Chapter 12, Retirement Planning.

Chapter 6

# Health Insurance Planning

## Learning Objectives

1. Understand the importance of health insurance within the comprehensive financial planning process.

2. Identify the proposed changes to be enacted between 2010 and 2014 for households, Medicare recipients, employers, and insurance companies as a result of the Patient Protection and Affordable Care Act (PPACA) of 2010.

3. Identify client situational factors that could uniquely affect a client's need for and selection of health care coverage.

4. Demonstrate how to determine and quantify a client's need for and selection of health care coverage.

5. Summarize the most important health insurance plans and provisions, including the role of health savings accounts (HSAs) and high-deductible plans in health insurance planning.

6. Understand how Medicare and Medigap coverage affects insurance planning.

7. Evaluate a client's available health insurance coverage and options.

8. Explain how to incorporate Consolidated Omnibus Budget Reconciliation Act (COBRA) and Health Insurance Portability and Accountability Act (HIPAA) protections into a health insurance plan.

9. Assess the role of IRC Section 125 Plans and flexible spending arrangements in the health insurance planning process.

10. Identify and recommend appropriate and reasonable health insurance strategies matched to a client's situation.

# Key Terms

§ 125 Plan

annual limit

Archer medical savings account

cafeteria plan

Consolidated Omnibus Budget Reconciliation Act of 1985 (the COBRA law)

coinsurance

copayment

cost-sharing

deductible

dependent care flexible spending arrangement/account (FSA)

end-stage renal disease

exclusive provider organization (EPO)

flexible benefit plan

flexible spending arrangement/account (FSA)

formulary

grandfathered plans

health care flexible spending arrangement/ account (FSA)

Health Insurance Portability and Accountability Act of 1996 (HIPAA)

Health maintenance organization (HMO)

health savings account (HSA)

high-deductible health plan (HDHP)

lifetime maximum

managed care plan

medical loss ratio

Medicare

Medicare Advantage Program

Medicare Part A

Medicare Part B

Medicare Part C (Medicare + Choice Plan)

Medicare Part D

Medicare SELECT

medigap

opting out

out-of-pocket expenses

point-of-service (POS) plan

pre-existing condition

preferred provider organization (PPO)

premium-conversion plan

premium-only plan

private fee-for-service plan

qualifying event

special needs plan

stop-loss limit

traditional indemnity health insurance plan

uniform coverage

**Figure 6.1** Systematic Financial Planning Process for Health Insurance Planning

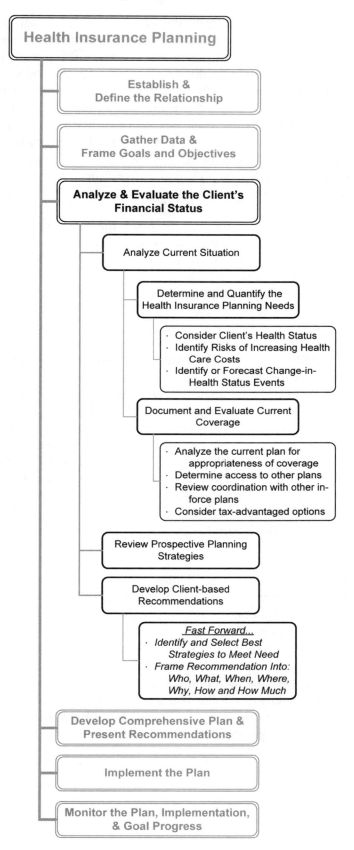

## HEALTH INSURANCE: THE BASICS

Health insurance is the most popular and widely used form of nonproperty insurance in the United States today. Health insurance or the lack thereof, is a topic that goes beyond traditional financial planning. When working with clients, planners should anticipate the fear of financial loss associated with the costs of health care and related **out-of-pocket expenses**, which are defined as the maximum amount of unreimbursed expenses, or the **deductible** a client must pay before insurance benefits begin. Health coverage is one of the most complex types of insurance offered in the marketplace–whether through an employer or a private health insurance contract. Although financial planners may or may not sell the actual insurance that they recommend, it is nevertheless important that planners understand the basic issues involved in medical insurance planning and policy selection.

This chapter provides a review of the fundamental steps that can be used to analyze a client's current health insurance situation by focusing on available insurance products and services. The process is outlined in Figure 6.1, The Systematic Financial Planning Process for Health Insurance Planning. This chapter retains a more traditional approach to health insurance needs planning, because the health insurance marketplace is still in transition after passage of The Patient Protection and Affordable Care Act (PPACA) in 2010.

Exorbitant health care costs, in addition to the need to provide more universal access to health insurance, prompted Congress to draft PPACA, which was signed by President Barack Obama on March 23, 2010, and subsequently amended by the Health Care and Education Reconciliation Act of 2010 on March 30 of that year. PPACA changed the U.S. health care landscape almost immediately, and many other dramatic changes are proposed. PPACA was intended to improve the performance, transparency, and accountability of health insurers and health insurance products; however, it is important to note that many of its reforms will not become effective until 2014 or later. One of the most controversial reforms is the *individual mandate*, or the requirement that most U.S. citizens and legal residents (exclusions apply) have qualifying health coverage or pay a maximum tax penalty of $695 per year, phased in between 2014 and 2016.[1]

A number of reforms address health insurance costs and transparency. Effective in 2011, insurance companies had to publicly justify proposed increases averaging 10% or more for individual or small group policies. Referred to as *rate review*, this practice entails states, in conjunction with the U.S. Department of Health & Human Services (HHS), to begin reviewing unreasonable premium increases before they take effect. To learn about proposed increases in individual states, visit http://companyprofiles. healthcare.gov/. Also effective in 2011, health insurers are required to spend between 80% and 85% of premium dollars on medical care and health care quality improvement rather than administrative costs. Companies whose administrative costs exceed this limit, referred to as the *medical loss ratio*, are required to provide customer rebates starting in 2012.

Several other reforms are discussed in this chapter, but a detailed discussion of the many PPACA reforms is beyond its scope. Appendix 6A highlights select aspects of PPACA that are of particular importance to planners.

Because PPACA reforms will not be fully enacted until 2014 or later, and in the interim they could be the focus of other Congressional actions, planners are cautioned to monitor this legislation carefully. The impact on American households, Medicare recipients, employers, and insurance companies is significant, and ultimately the changes in coverage and cost will influence the systematic financial planning process.

An additional caution is warranted. Health insurance policies, both individual and employer-provided, issued prior to March 23, 2010, and that have covered at least one person continuously since that day, are considered **grandfathered plans**. Some of the reforms listed in Appendix 6A may not apply to grandfathered plans, and if the plans maintain their grandfathered status in the future, they will remain exempt from some reforms. To maintain this status, a plan cannot reduce or eliminate benefits for particular conditions, increase employee cost sharing above specific thresholds, reduce the employer share of the premium cost, or change insurers. Once a plan loses its grandfathered status, it must comply with PPACA rules. Plan documents must clearly state whether a plan has grandfathered status. This will be an important feature for planners to monitor as they review current client coverage or the availability of other employer-provided plans.

## ANALYZE THE CLIENT'S CURRENT SITUATION

Analyzing a client's current health insurance situation is relatively straightforward, but nuances must be considered. Insurance information is typically collected during the data-gathering phase of the planning process. By exploring current and future needs for coverage, as well as the coverage currently available, the planner and client become informed of issues that could affect the need for or selection of health insurance coverage. Issues to consider during this step include:

- family health status and related health history;

- family demographics that could trigger insurance needs;

- assets available for use in case of a catastrophic health claim;

- lifestyle choices that could influence the availability of insurance benefits;

- working in a hazardous profession or occupation; and

- concerns about future unemployment, career changes, or retirement.

The next step in analyzing the current situation focuses on reviewing the client's current coverage or tax-advantaged accounts. Gathering a variety of information about a client's health insurance situation is critical to a thorough analysis.

## Determine and Quantify the Client's Need for Health Insurance

Unlike the analysis of life insurance needs, where the answer to the question of "how much" yields a dollar need for life insurance, determining how much health insurance coverage is necessary is less straightforward. Yet the logic underlying the questions is similar. Recall that the formulas for determining an optimal level of life insurance typically consider financial risks or potential financial needs to be funded through life insurance proceeds. Similarly, determining the amount of health insurance needed must focus first and foremost on the potential financial risks or needs to be met. Family health history can be an important indicator. Anticipating significant medical expenses based on family history, for example, will help determine whether the lifetime coverage limit for a plan is sufficient.

Unfortunately, quantifying need and the associated costs is challenging. Given the vagaries of life, there is no way to predict a major accident or disease. The impact of premium payments on cash flow can be significantly less than the impact of possible uninsured losses on net worth or the potential restrictions on care for the uninsured. Fear of the unknown must also be tempered by client realities and the logic of balancing insurance premium costs with competing financial objectives.

Considering the different group coverage options available to two-income households, clients may wonder if "he, she, or we" should purchase/provide health insurance coverage. The planner can be instrumental in helping clients analyze the optimal balance between "how much coverage," "whose coverage," and premiums paid. But resolving such questions hinges on a thorough analysis of the current situation so that both planner and client are alerted to potential needs for health insurance coverage.

Some may question how **opting out** can affect health insurance coverage decisions. Two-income households should consider questions of coordinating benefits between plans, the cash flow advantage of opting out of coverage, and the ease of recordkeeping through one plan. Clearly, opting out should not be a consideration unless comprehensive coverage is available through another household member. The situation becomes even more difficult with children. If both parents provide family coverage, then the parent whose birthday comes first in the year is considered the primary provider according to the coordination-of-benefit rules developed by the National Association of Insurance Commissioners.

PPACA provides two important new benefits for children: Young adult children, up to age 26, are now eligible to receive coverage through a parent's health insurance plan if the plan covers children. The new requirement applies to new plan years beginning after September 23, 2010. However, until 2014, grandfathered group plans do not have to offer dependent coverage up to age 26 if a young adult is eligible for group coverage outside of their parent's plan. Otherwise, children may join or remain on a parent's plan even if they are married, not living in the same household, attending school, not financially dependent on the parent, or are eligible to enroll in their own employer's plan.

This change in law alters a major health insurance planning challenge but creates another one. Previously a child's 19th birthday, or if a full-time college student, then graduation or the 23rd birthday, typically precipitated the loss of health insurance coverage under a parentally provided policy. Although in many cases young adults could continue coverage under their parent's health insurance policy because of the **Consolidated Omnibus Budget Reconciliation Act of 1985** (the **COBRA** law, discussed in more detail later in the chapter, this was often a costly and short-term solution. Unrestricted coverage until age 26 is a widespread solution for young adults who are continuing their education, unemployed, ineligible for benefits, or eligible only for high-cost benefits. The new planning challenge will be to compare the following alternatives, for both quality of coverage and cost-effectiveness, considering premium costs and **cost-sharing** (e.g., copayments, coinsurance and deductibles):

- For couples, opt out of one plan for the coverage provided by the other spouse.

- For couples, each spouse have a plan so long as one plan allows for the coverage of a child.

- For couples and children, continue the child's coverage until age 26 on the parental policy or have the child choose an employer-provided plan.

- If a child chooses an employer-provided plan, then consider whether the parents/partners continue the current plan or consider each having a plan, if both are employed.

Health care plan decisions are not irrevocable. The plan must provide written notification of the 30-day period when adult children can be enrolled for the upcoming plan or policy year. Once enrolled, the child is eligible for coverage for the entire policy year.

The second important PPACA advantage for children and their families is the requirement that benefits or coverage cannot be limited, excluded, or denied to children under the age of 19 who have a pre-existing condition. This reform protects children with a physical or mental condition that has been diagnosed or would normally require treatment (i.e., a **pre-existing condition**). However, the rule applies whether or not the disability or condition was discovered or treated before applying for coverage. This rule applies to all employer-provided health plan years and individual policy years beginning after September 23, 2010. The only exclusion to this rule is grandfathered individual policies purchased before March 23, 2010.

PPACA also provides additional coverage to adults with pre-existing conditions. Effective July 1, 2010, uninsured adults with pre-existing conditions who have been uninsured for at least six months are eligible for coverage through the new, temporary Pre-existing Condition Insurance Plan (PCIP). PCIP can be run by the state or by HHS. To learn more about the availability of these plans in each state, see http://www. healthcare.gov/law/features/choices/pre-existing-condition-insurance-plan/index.

html. This program serves as a bridge until 2014, when insurance companies are prohibited from denying or limiting coverage or charging higher premiums because of a pre-existing condition.

---

**Health Insurance Planning Tip: Continuation of Coverage for Young Adults**

Clients with children who are approaching age 26 and who do not have access to an employer-provided plan should consider purchasing a short-term individual health insurance policy. Although families with COBRA-eligible coverage have a window of 63 days for a child to find replacement coverage without being subject to pre-existing condition rules, families with a non-COBRA-eligible policy do not have a grace period for pre-existing conditions. In either situation, the child will have no health insurance coverage during the lapse, thus necessitating a short-term policy. If an individual policy is not purchased, after six months without insurance, the child can purchase coverage through the PCIP program. Assuming no Congressional changes, in 2014 health insurance will be required (some exceptions do apply) or the uninsured will be subject to a tax of $695 or 2.5% of income, whichever is greater, but coverage will also be available regardless of a pre-existing condition.

---

Finally, the health plans of retired or self-employed clients need special evaluation. Some retired clients may be covered under a former employer's health plan, although the availability of this benefit has declined. Typically, this type of coverage is secondary to Medicare, as it is for military retirees' TRICARE for Life coverage and federal retirees' Federal Employee Health Benefits Program benefits, but not always. Knowing exactly how a client's available plans are structured is important. If a client qualifies only for Medicare, the use of Medicare supplemental plans should be reviewed, including the six-month window for purchasing a Medigap policy after the client turns age 65 or enrolls in Medicare Part B.

Self-employed clients could be restricted in the type of coverage available, as may clients who work for small employers. Both self-employed clients and those who work for small employers (50 or fewer employees) may own an **Archer medical savings account (MSA)**. The Archer MSA, precursor of the HSA, is obsolete, except for those who were eligible prior to December 31, 2007. However, MSA funding can continue, assuming the owner is still eligible, or the Archer MSA can be rolled over into an HSA.

These accounts provide a method for making tax-deductible contributions to a tax-deferred account to save for future medical expenses. They are discussed more later in this chapter. Additional information is available in IRS Publication 969, *Health Savings Accounts and Other Tax-Favored Health Plans*.

As a result of the PPACA tax credit incentive, more small employers (those with 25 or fewer full-time employees whose average annual wages are $50,000 or less) can purchase health insurance for employees. For tax years 2010 through 2013, employers are given a tax credit of up to 35% of the employer's contribution (25% of a nonprofit employer's contribution) with the tax amount increasing in 2014, assuming all rules are satisfied. Unfortunately, the restrictions on this program limit its widespread effectiveness. Some self-employed individuals might be able to access group coverage through a spouse or partner until more widespread, cost-effective provisions of PPACA become available. Otherwise, planners and clients must continue to thoroughly analyze underwriting issues, product providers, and the needs of the small business owner and employees, as well as their tax implications.

Although planners may have little flexibility when recommending specific health insurance plans to clients, they can be instrumental in the choice of plan and introducing the plan options available. The majority of Americans purchase health insurance through employer-sponsored plans. The cost of employer-sponsored plans can be significantly less than the premium for purchasing insurance in the private market, as illustrated by the following examples. In comparing employer-sponsored and private market costs, one source reported that the average employee paid $58 a month for health insurance in 2007, with the employer paying the remaining annual premium of $3,785. In contrast, the average private individual annual premium from 2006 to 2007 cost $2,613, or $218 a month. But depending on state regulations and the age and health status of the individual, private health insurance premiums could be $10,000 to $12,000 annually.[2] Another study reported that in 2006, the average American paid $4,118 for a single-person private policy; however, for those in a group plan the actual cost was less than $800, or approximately 20% of the total premium.[3] But this significant difference in cost between employer-provided and private insurance is not always the case due to the size, type, or claims history of the covered group, despite the fact the employer and employee share the premium. The majority of plans offered through an employer are generic, although multiple managed care plans and options for coverage may be available, as well as a high-deductible health plan option. Compounding the complexity of this analysis is the availability of multiple plans in two-earner households and households with employed young adults, as noted above.

Analysis of a client's situation should include a comprehensive evaluation of other types of medical coverage or benefits, potential or actual, from one or both spouses or partners, assuming coverage is available for domestic partners. Premiums are typically cheapest for a **high-deductible health plan (HDHP),** insurance that requires that a high deductible be met before the insurance pays any claims. Used in conjunction with an HSA—a form of tax-advantaged medical savings—the client can accumulate funds for future health expenses; if these are not spent, they can grow tax deferred until retirement. This is true even if the client chooses at some point—perhaps when children are present in the home—to replace the high-deductible plan with a managed care plan, such as a health maintenance organization. Or perhaps the benefits available in a § 125 plan, such as a **flexible spending account (FSA)**—another example of a tax-advantaged plan—also should be considered. § 125 plans, commonly known as *cafeteria plans* because of the range of choices provided, enable employers to offer their employees a choice between cash and a variety of pretax benefits. These plans are addressed in more depth later in this chapter.

### Choosing the Health Insurance Plan: General Considerations

Before considering specific health insurance planning strategies, a planner should ascertain whether a client's current and short-term needs are best met through a traditional indemnity health insurance plan, one of the managed care plan options, or an HDHP, which can be structured after either model. **Managed care plan** options attempt to manage access to and coordination of services while promoting efficient, high-quality care, all with the objective of controlling health care costs. The standard in- or out-of-network methods common to managed care plans compare to a **traditional indemnity plan** where the insured can obtain services from any provider, but typically at a higher premium and service fee. Table 6.1 provides a comparison of the five primary health insurance plans available in the marketplace.

The **preferred provider organization (PPO)** plan, **point-of-service (POS) plan**, and **health maintainence organizaion** (HMO) are three of the most common managed care plans. The PPO offers the most flexibility in seeking health care, whereas the HMO is typically the most restrictive. The hybrid POS plan shares features of the PPO and HMO, and the **exclusive provider organization (EPO)** plan is similar to but more restrictive in its provider network than the HMO. To be reimbursed, the insured must obtain services from an EPO network provider

**Table 6.1** Comparison of Health Insurance Plans

| Plan Type | Traditional Indemnity Plan | Preferred Provider Organization (PPO) | Point-of-service (POS) Plan | Health Maintenance Organization (HMO) | High-Deductible Health Plan (HDHP) |
|---|---|---|---|---|---|
| *Cost* | Highest | Middle-high | Middle-low | Lowest of managed cost plans | Lowest of all plans available |
| *Physician Choice* | Least restrictive, but restrictions are increasing to control costs | Restricted to network; may go outside network with higher deductible and copayment | Restricted, but insured may see out-of-network provider for additional cost | Restricted | Depends on whether the HDHP is an indemnity, PPO, POS, or HMO plan, but certain requirements must be met to qualify as an HDHP. Offers copays for office visits only after the deductible has been met. For 2012, the minimum deductible for one insured is $1,200; $2,400 for families. Out-of-network providers can cost more than in-network providers. |
| *Hospital Choice* | Least restrictive, but restrictions are increasing to control costs | Restricted to network; may go outside network with higher deductible and copayment | Restricted to network | Restricted | Depends on whether the HDHP is an indemnity, PPO, POS, or HMO plan, but certain requirements must be met to qualify as an HDHP. Offers copays for office visits only after deductible has been met. For 2012, the minimum deductible for one insured is $1,200; $2,400for families. Out-of-network providers can cost more than in-network providers. |

| Plan Type | Traditional Indemnity Plan | Preferred Provider Organization (PPO) | Point-of-service (POS) Plan | Health Maintenance Organization (HMO) | High-Deductible Health Plan (HDHP) |
|---|---|---|---|---|---|
| *Appropriate for Whom?* | Households that demand maximum choice | Households that would like some choice but with lower expenses than a traditional plan | Households that use medical services frequently, but occasionally visit out-of-network providers | Households that use medical services frequently | Households that are<br>• generally healthy and medical expenses are limited to preventive care OR not healthy and typically hit the lower limits on catastrophic coverage in other plans and incur out-of-pocket expenses for exclusions (e.g., drug or other costs);<br>• financially that are disciplined savers and who can fund the annual maximum of the HSA ($3,100 for individuals; $6,250 for families in 2012) to cover expenses; and<br>• comfortable with in-network providers to maximize savings. |
| *Among Firms Offering Health Benefits, Availability of this Plan, 2011[1]* | 3% | 50% | 24% | 16% | 23% |
| *Estimated Annual Group Plan Cost for a Family, 2011* | No cost estimate provided due to limited availability | $15,404 | $15,260 | $15,288 | $13,704[2] |

1. Kaiser/HRET Survey of Employer-Sponsored Health Benefits, 2011. Among Firms Offering Health Benefits, Percentage of Firms That Offer the Following Plan Types, by Firm Size, 2011, Publication Date: 9/27/2011. Available at http://ehbs.kff.org/?page=charts&id=2&sn=19&ch=2130.

2. Kaiser/HRET Survey of Employer-Sponsored Health Benefits, 2011. Average Monthly and Annual Premiums for Covered Workers, Single and Family Coverage, by Plan Type, 201. Publication Date: 9/27/2011. Available at http://ehbs.kff.org/?page=charts&id=2&sn=16&ch=2069.

Keep in mind that choices typically are limited to plans offered by a client's employer and that annual plan changes are allowed. But it is important to explore client preferences that reflect both quantitative aspects of the analysis as well as qualitative or more intangible preferences. The latter may supersede cash flow issues, when something as personal as family health care is at stake.

Figure 6.2 identifies decision criteria to help address which type of health plan—traditional indemnity, PPO, POS, or HMO—may be the most appropriate. It is important to note that the same options can also be offered as an HDHP, so the decision criteria and research on the plan would be similar once the HDHP alternative has been chosen. Helping clients choose the type of health insurance that best matches lifestyle, health situation, medical usage, and anticipated wellness is an important consideration when making health insurance recommendations.

**Figure 6.2** Health Insurance Plan Decision Tree

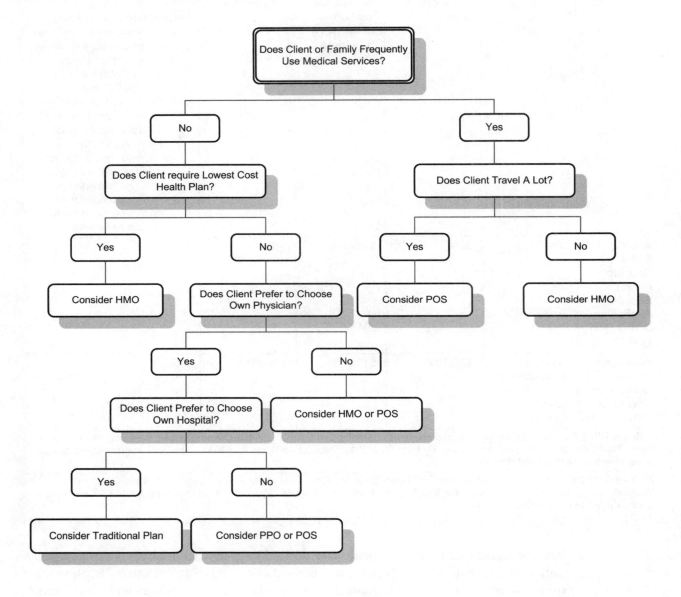

Another choice that aligns with the choice of health insurance is the use of a tax-advantaged account. Because these decisions must be coordinated, it is important that planners be aware of the features of each to help clients effectively manage their costs or save for the future. The availability of these accounts also varies with the individual's employment. Table 6.2 summarizes the features of the **health care flexible spending arrangement,** the health reimbursement account (HRA), the **health savings account (HSA),** and the Archer MSA. Some of these accounts are also discussed later in this chapter.

**Table 6.2** Comparison of Tax-advantaged Accounts for Health Care Expenses

| Plan Type | Traditional Indemnity Plan | Preferred Provider Organization (PPO) | Point-of-service (POS) Plan | Health Maintenance Organization (HMO) | High-Deductible Health Plan (HDHP) |
|---|---|---|---|---|---|
| *Cost* | Highest | Middle-high | Middle-low | Lowest of managed cost plans | Lowest of all plans available |
| *Physician Choice* | Least restrictive, but restrictions are increasing to control costs | Restricted to network; may go outside network with higher deductible and copayment | Restricted, but insured may see out-of-network provider for additional cost | Restricted | Depends on whether the HDHP is an indemnity, PPO, POS, or HMO plan, but certain requirements must be met to qualify as an HDHP. Offers copays for office visits only after the deductible has been met. For 2012, the minimum deductible for one insured is $1,200; $2,400 for families. Out-of-network providers can cost more than in-network providers. |
| *Hospital Choice* | Least restrictive, but restrictions are increasing to control costs | Restricted to network; may go outside network with higher deductible and copayment | Restricted to network | Restricted | Depends on whether the HDHP is an indemnity, PPO, POS, or HMO plan, but certain requirements must be met to qualify as an HDHP. Offers copays for office visits only after deductible has been met. For 2012, the minimum deductible for one insured is $1,200; $2,400 for families. Out-of-network providers can cost more than in-network providers. |
| *Appropriate for Whom?* | Households that demand maximum choice | Households that would like some choice but with lower expenses than a traditional plan | Households that use medical services frequently, but occasionally visit out-of-network providers | Households that use medical services frequently | Households that are <br> • generally healthy and medical expenses are limited to preventive care OR not healthy and typically hit the lower limits on catastrophic coverage in other plans and incur out-of-pocket expenses for exclusions (e.g., drug or other costs); <br> • financially that are disciplined savers and who can fund the annual maximum of the HSA ($3,100 for individuals; $6,250 for families in 2012) to cover expenses; and <br> • comfortable with in-network providers to maximize savings. |

| Plan Type | Traditional Indemnity Plan | Preferred Provider Organization (PPO) | Point-of-service (POS) Plan | Health Maintenance Organization (HMO) | High-Deductible Health Plan (HDHP) |
|---|---|---|---|---|---|
| *Among Firms Offering Health Benefits, Availability of this Plan, 2011*[1] | 3% | 50% | 24% | 16% | 23% |
| *Estimated Annual Group Plan Cost for a Family, 2011* | No cost estimate provided due to limited availability | $15,404 | $15,260 | $15,288 | $13,704[2] |

[1] Kaiser/HRET Survey of Employer-Sponsored Health Benefits, 2011. Among Firms Offering Health Benefits, Percentage of Firms That Offer the Following Plan Types, by Firm Size, 2011, Publication Date: 9/27/2011. Available at http://ehbs.kff.org/?page=charts&id=2&sn=19&ch=2130.

[2] Kaiser/HRET Survey of Employer-Sponsored Health Benefits, 2011. Average Monthly and Annual Premiums for Covered Workers, Single and Family Coverage, by Plan Type, 201. Publication Date: 9/27/2011 Available at http://ehbs.kff.org/?page=charts&id=2&sn=16&ch=2069.

*Sources*: C. Rapoport, Congressional Research Service. *Tax-Advantaged Accounts for Health Care Expenses: Side-by-Side Comparison.* Available at http://assets.opencrs.com/rpts/RS21573_20100618.pdf.

J. Mulvey, Congressional Research Service. *Health Savings Accounts: Overview of Rules for 2011.* Available at http://op.bna.com/mdw.nsf/id/plon-8csks5/$File/CRShsareport.pdf.

IRS Publication 969, *Health Savings Accounts and Other Tax-Favored Health Plans.* Available at http://www.irs.gov/publications/p969/index.html.

---

## Health Insurance Planning Tip:
## Important Health and Flexible Spending Account Changes

Effective 2011, qualified distributions from an HSA, an Archer MSA, an FSA, or an HRA exclude over-the-counter (nonprescription) drugs. The IRS defined a medicine or drug as a qualified expense only if the medicine or drug (a) requires a prescription, (b) is available without prescription, and a prescription is written for it, or (c) is insulin. PPACA also increased the tax on nonqualified distributions from an HSA or an Archer MSA from 10% and 15%, respectively, to 20% in 2011.

---

### Planning for Special Populations:
### Health Insurance for Same-sex Couples

Rising costs and access to health care are recognized problems in the United States, but for same-sex couples, taxes are an additional hurdle. Current federal law and the laws of many states do not recognize same-sex partnerships, causing people enrolled in domestic partner benefits to incur extra taxes—if employers allow access. (The same is also true for nonmarried, opposite-sex couples who choose to enroll in domestic partner benefits, although some employers bar access because the couple could marry and receive benefits.) The IRS considers the benefits received by the nonmarried, nondependent spouse imputed income, and the cost of the benefit provided is added to the employee's ordinary income.

The imputed income can cost in two ways. First, taxes are due on the imputed cost of the benefit—taxes not paid for benefits when received by married couples. Second, the additional inputed income could push the employee into a higher tax bracket, thus incurring additional taxes on other income. The company offering the benefits is also responsible for any additional income or payroll taxes due on the phantom income reported to the employee.

The same practice is applied if a partner's children are added to the health coverage. In situations where one partner is the legal guardian of a child, it might be possible to co-adopt the child, thereby obtaining coverage. If the child is a dependent of the employee, coverage would be available.

To compensate, some companies choose to "gross up" the employee's income in the amount of the additional tax payment due. In January 2012, Ernst & Young LLP and its affiliates became the first Big Four accounting firm to offer this perk by reimbursing lesbian, gay, bisexual, and transgender (LGBT) employees for the additional federal and state taxes paid on same-sex domestic partners' medical benefits in the United States. According to the Human Rights Campaign (HRC), more than 30 for-profit employers and municipalities offer the tax equalization benefit.[4]  According to the HRC, calculating the gross-up amount is a two-step process. First, the taxes due on the fair market value of the benefit are calculated. Then, because that amount will be added to the employee's income and additional taxes will be due, that tax amount is also calculated. The sum of the two tax payments equals the gross-up amount for tax equalization.

The situation is worse if a client is covering a domestic partner through an HDHP, despite the benefit of being eligible to contribute up to the annual maximum for a family account. If reimbursement is made from the HSA for a nondependent domestic partner's health care expenses, the distribution is taxable and subject to an additional 20% penalty tax if the account owner is younger than age 65. All HSA distributions for nonqualifying expenses are added to the annual gross income and subject to the 20% penalty tax.

However, a domestic partner covered by the HDHP may also be eligible to establish his or her own HSA, if eligible. To be eligible for an HSA, the partner cannot have other medical coverage or be claimed as the dependent of another taxpayer. Opening two HSAs allows each domestic partner to receive tax-free distributions from his or her individual account. This strategy also allows both partners to contribute up to the family coverage limit to each HSA; they are not constrained by the limit set for spouses.

Finally, if the domestic partner is the beneficiary of an HSA, all tax advantages end at the death of the account owner. The balance, or fair market value of the account, is taxable to the surviving domestic partner in the year of death. This is true for any HSA when the designated beneficiary is not a spouse.

## Medicare Planning and Eligibility

Generally, **Medicare** is available for people age 65 or older, younger people with disabilities, and people with **end-stage renal disease**, i.e., permanent kidney failure requiring dialysis or a transplant. Medicare has three primary parts. Part A is a hospital insurance plan. Part B is a voluntary medical insurance plan with a monthly premium. Part D is a prescription drug benefit. Those who did not pay Medicare taxes for at least 10 years or were never married may not be eligible for Part A, but they may be able to purchase coverage if they are age 65 or older and a citizen or permanent resident of the United States. A brief description of Parts A, B, and D follows. To learn more about the changes in Medicare plans and benefits, see www.medicare.gov.

**Medicare Part A**, hospital insurance, helps cover costs for inpatient care in hospitals, critical access hospitals, and skilled nursing facilities. Benefits for the latter are available only following a related three-day hospital stay. Part A also covers hospice care for the terminally ill and some home health services prescribed by a doctor, including durable medical equipment and supplies. In addition to services and supplies covered as part of hospital or skilled nursing home care, Part A·includes coverage for pints of blood received at a hospital or skilled nursing facility. Although the costs of some benefits are fully covered, coinsurance and deductibles also may apply.

**Medicare Part B**, medical insurance, provides benefits for doctors' services, outpatient hospital care, some home health services, and some other medical services excluded from Part A, such as the services of physical and occupational therapists or speech pathologists. Part B helps pay for these covered services and diagnostic testing and supplies when they are judged to be medically necessary. The listing of covered services is extensive, ranging from ambulance services when medically necessary to transplants, yet restrictions and limitations on services apply.

The base monthly Part B premium in 2012 is $99.90 for those with 2011 income less than $85,000 ($170,000 for those filing a joint tax return). The premium is higher for those with incomes that exceed this threshold. This monthly premium is generally deducted from the client's Social Security, Railroad Retirement, or Civil Service Retirement check. In addition to the monthly premium for Part B, annual deductible and coinsurance provisions also apply. Effective in 2007, premium charges for Part B are "means tested." In 2012, consumers with incomes in excess of $85,000, or $170,000 for couples, are required to pay a higher premium for Medicare Parts B and D, Medicare prescription drug coverage, with the premium prorated on the basis of income. Singles earning more than $214,000 a year, or couples earning more than $428,000, will pay $319.70 a month in 2012. Some programs are available to reduce Part B premiums for those with limited income.

**Medicare Part D,** Medicare prescription drug coverage, provides coverage for both brand-name and generic prescription drugs at participating pharmacies. Medicare prescription drug coverage provides protection for people who have very high prescription drug costs. Everyone with Medicare is eligible for this coverage, regardless of income and resources, health status, or current prescription expenses. In 2011 and subsequent years, the annual election period is from October 15 through December 7, during which time anyone with Medicare can enroll in Part D or change Part D plans. A client's decision to enroll in Part D depends on the kind of health care coverage available at retirement. Clients can join either a Medicare prescription drug plan or a Medicare Advantage

Plan or other Medicare Health Plan that offers drug coverage. According to the Social Security Administration, when clients join Part D they will pay a monthly premium, which varies by plan, and a yearly deductible. In 2012, the maximum deductible is $320. Clients also pay a part of their prescription costs, including a copayment or coinsurance.

PPACA attempts to close the Medicare doughnut hole, or the coverage gap that many with Medicare Part D coverage and high prescription drug costs encounter annually. In 2012, the donut hole starts when the drug plan pays a total of $2,930 in medication costs (typically referred to as the *initial coverage period*) and continues until the individual has spent $4,700 out of pocket. While in the donut hole, an individual must pay all prescription drug costs. From 2011 to 2020, a combination of PPACA-mandated government subsidies and manufacturer discounts will progressively reduce out-of-pocket costs for covered drugs purchased during the doughnut hole period. By 2020, the coverage gap will be closed, in that individuals will pay only 25% of the cost of prescription drugs until the annual out-of-pocket spending limit is met. In 2012, individuals will pay 86% of the cost of covered generic drugs and 50% of the cost of covered brand-name drugs purchased in the doughnut hole.

Individuals in the doughnut hole enter catastrophic coverage after their out-of-pocket expenses for drugs on the plan's **formulary**, or list of covered drugs, reaches the stated annual limit, and Part D payment for prescriptions resumes until the end of the year. The money spent on drugs that are not covered on the plan's formulary does not count toward the catastrophic coverage threshold. Medicare Part D coverage resets each year on January 1st.

The Medicare + Choice program, which is sometimes referred to as **Medicare Part C**, is an alternative to traditional Medicare programs. Part C coverage was ushered in as part of the Medicare Prescription Drug, Improvement, and Modernization Act of 2003. Medicare Part A and Part B coverage is required to be eligible. **Medicare + Choice Plans** allow consumers to seek benefits through a private health maintenance organization (HMO), a special needs plan for targeted audiences, a private fee-for-service plan (PFFS) through a private insurance company, or a preferred provider organization (PPO). (The latter two will probably cost more). Part C plans may include extra benefits such as prescription drugs, dental care, and routine physical and vision services.

Originally enacted in 1997, this program has been renamed the **Medicare Advantage Program** and was expanded in 2006 to offer more choices for both urban and rural consumers. For example, Congress created **special needs plans** to allow insurance companies to target enrollment to special needs individuals, including those who are (a) institutionalized, (b) dually eligible, and/or (c) suffering from severe or disabling chronic conditions. To identify Medicare Advantage Programs available in a geographic area and any extra benefits offered by these plans, visit the Medicare Personal Plan Finder at www.medicare.gov.

The Medicare Advantage MSA is an Archer MSA for those who are enrolled in Medicare Part A and Part B and have an HDHP that meets Medicare guidelines. The tax-exempt trust or custodial account is funded by the Medicare program—no personal contributions are allowed—to pay for qualified medical expenses of the account holder. Funds in the account can earn interest or dividends, grow tax-deferred, and are not taxed if used for qualified medical expenses. Medicare Advantage MSAs are administered through the Medicare program; for more information see www.medicare.gov or IRS Publication 969, available at www.irs.gov.

A variety of expenses are not covered under either Medicare Part A or Part B. Some exclusions affect only select groups of Medicare beneficiaries (e.g., exclusions for acupuncture, cosmetic surgery, or health care received outside the United States). Other exclusions for routine physicals, eye care, foot care, dental care, hearing aids, or custodial care at home or in a nursing home affect far more consumers. In 2011, PPACA eliminated cost sharing (e.g., copayments, coinsurance, and deductibles) for select Medicare-covered preventive services. It is important that financial planners and their clients be fully informed of both exclusions and covered services to more accurately project medical costs. Clients who assume that they are covered may find themselves exposed to unreimbursed costs if they use these services. Such knowledge can help planners develop strategies to cover these expenses with private sources of insurance, such as Medigap coverage, or through self-insurance techniques. Clients who overestimate the cost of care may unnecessarily limit their lifestyle, gifting, or spending for other goals to save more for future medical costs.

As these examples illustrate, the question of the amount of health care protection a client needs is relevant, but potentially complex. The answer to this question, beyond insights available from the client's situational factors, is further complicated by changes over the life cycle as well as the changing array of health care plans or tax-advantaged accounts available. The second step when analyzing a client situation, to document and evaluate current coverage, expands the analysis and informs the decision regarding the best options to choose.

---

### Planning for Special Populations:
### Health Insurance Options for Early Retirees

Until all PPACA reforms are in place to provide broader access to cost-effective health insurance, one of the biggest challenges for those who wish to retire early is health care. Clients may want to retire early for many reasons—to leave a job they dislike or find stressful, to pursue more leisure or volunteer activities, to take on more family responsibilities, or to pursue education or training for a second career. With fewer companies offering retiree health coverage, regardless of age, those who wish to retire prior to Medicare eligibility at age 65 may have to be creative. The following list of alternatives could match the needs of some clients:

- If available, continue coverage through the employer, but be sure to inquire about the coverage (same or more limited), the cost, the potential increase in premiums, and whether coverage is available until age 65.

- If available, continue coverage with the employer through the Early Retiree Reinsurance Program (ERRP), which reimburses employers for health care costs paid by or on behalf of early retirees (age 55 years or older) who are ineligible for Medicare. This PPACA reinsurance program was to be funded from 2010 through 2013, until 2014 when the exchanges are available to provide other, more affordable health care coverage.

- For a couple or partners, consider having one continue working to provide health insurance benefits while the other retires or cuts back to part-time work, assuming the domestic partner can be covered. However, this change must be planned to coordinate the addition of the spouse/partner to the coverage as a qualifying event (rules apply) or during open enrollment.

- Seek part-time employment that includes access to health insurance.

- If the employer and the client are COBRA eligible, use the COBRA benefit to continue health insurance for the 18 months before the client reaches age 65. This could be an expensive alternative, because the client will be responsible for the full premium cost (employer and employee portions) and the 2% up-charge, but it would provide coverage for the employee, the spouse, and any dependents. Because of the continuous coverage, HIPAA protection would guarantee access to an independent policy, regardless of pre-existing conditions, although the cost could be prohibitive. Note that restrictions on access to coverage for pre-existing conditions are prohibited by PPACA, regardless of age, starting in 2014.

- Buy an independent policy, although this, too, could be a very expensive alternative, and health conditions could prohibit underwriting approval to secure an independent policy. When seeking coverage for a couple or family, inquire about pricing for individual and family coverage with an insurance broker with access to multiple companies, or shop different companies individually. Age is a consideration for pricing, so purchasing individual policies could be cheaper than a family policy. If a family policy is purchased, be sure to do so in the name of the younger spouse so he/she will not lose coverage when the older spouse/partner transitions to Medicare.

- Consider any membership organizations, either professional, trade, or community/public service, that might offer group health insurance access. Coverage may be limited, but group rates could make this a more cost-effective option, especially for someone with few health issues. The cost and requirements to maintain group membership must also be considered.

- Consider state-provided high-risk pools for those who are otherwise uninsurable. However, because of the new PPACA PCIP plans, to be eligible there must be a pre-existing condition and a six-month period without insurance. An accident or health incident during those six uninsured months could be financially devastating.

Regardless of how badly a client may want to retire, an important caveat is not to act until health coverage and a budget with ample cash flow have been confirmed. Early retirement may be the goal, but not at the cost of jeopardizing the future.

## Document and Evaluate Current Health Insurance Coverage

The second step in the analysis of a client's current situation focuses on documenting and analyzing all health insurance coverage currently in force and the use of tax-advantaged accounts for all household members. At this point, planners should have a solid foundation for considering the match between current and projected needs, as outlined above, and available health care plans and tax-advantaged accounts in place.

Essentially, a planner can assist a client who has an employer-sponsored plan(s) in two ways. First, the planner can offer advice regarding the attractiveness of the plan(s) by conducting a thorough evaluation of plan features. Until all aspects of PPACA are implemented, the following factors should be evaluated to ensure that the coverage meets current and anticipated needs:

- current **deductible**—amount the insured pays before the insurance company contributes;

- current **copayment**—fixed fee the insured pays for services in addition to what the insurance company will pay;

- current **coinsurance**—percentage of service expense paid by the insured above the deductible amount (e.g., if a plan has a 20% coinsurance clause, the insured is responsible for paying the deductible and 20% of each bill up to the maximum annual stop-loss limit);

- current **stop-loss limit**—the maximum amount of out-of-pocket expenses paid by an insured, which includes deductibles, copayments, and coinsurance, or what PPACA refers to as *cost sharing*;

- **lifetime maximum** on covered benefits—eliminated by PPACA for most health benefits in employer-provided group plans or individual policies issued or renewed after September 23, 2010. Plans may set a lifetime limit on health care services not defined as essential by PPACA.

- **annual limit** on covered benefits—restricted by PPACA for most health benefits in employer-provided group plans or individual policies issued or renewed after March 23, 2010. For a plan year or policy year effective on or after September 23, 2011, but before September 23, 2012, the limit cannot be less than $1.25 million. For a plan year or policy year effective on or after September 23, 2012, but before January 1, 2014, the limit cannot be less than $2 million. No annual limits are allowed on most covered benefits after January 1, 2014. Plans can set annual limits on health care services not defined as essential by PPACA.

- excluded coverage;

- out-of-network restrictions, freedom of choice, network of providers, and cost differentials if an HMO, PPO, POS, or EPO;

- current annual premium; and

- access to COBRA and HIPAA benefits.

If a particular insurance plan is the only one available to a client, then the analysis stops here, aside from perhaps establishing a flexible spending account if deemed to be a prudent method for meeting out-of-pocket expenses.

The second and maybe more important way a planner can offer advice is in cases where more than one health plan is available, either by one employer, or for couples or partners, across both employers. If multiple plans are available, then a similar cost-benefit analysis should be conducted. For instance, some organizations provide employees with the choice of a traditional indemnity plan, a managed care plan (e.g., HMO, PPO, POS, or EPO), or a high-deductible health plan. To maximize benefits and control costs, thorough analysis is needed, perhaps with the assistance of personnel from human resources or employee benefits or an independent health care insurance specialist.

On the basis of this information, a planner and client can begin to take action to adequately protect the health of the client's household while minimizing or eliminating duplicative coverage. It is also important to recognize that the choice of plan may change over the life cycle. Decisions about the coordination of benefits between two plans must also be considered, as well as the option for each spouse/partner to carry an individual plan, if no coverage is required for children. However, care must be taken when a high-deductible health plan is used because coverage by any other health plan is not permitted. Exceptions to this rule include accident, disability, dental, vision, long-term care, or specified disease insurance (e.g., cancer).

Coordination between types of tax-advantaged accounts must also be considered. For example, if a client is funding both an FSA and an HSA, funds from the FSA should be exhausted first so that funds can remain in the HSA for the future. (It is important to note that there are specific rules governing the allowable use of FSA funds in conjunction with an HSA. In this case, the FSA is limited or restricted, generally to preventive care costs.) Similarly, to the extent that qualified expenses could be reimbursed from either a FSA and a HRA (recall that the employer can also define allowable reimbursements from the IRS-approved list), expenses from the FSA would be used first, typically to maintain the HRA balance. In other words, when a client has access to two different tax-advantaged accounts, the "use it or lose it" rule should take priority, consistent with all other plan rules. Planners can be instrumental in educating clients on the account selection as well as funding, coordination, and withdrawal of funds from these accounts to effectively manage health care expenses.

Special consideration must be given to couples with children. In cases where both parents are providing family coverage, the child's primary coverage will be determined by which parent's birthday comes first in the calendar year. In such cases, any coverage provided by the other parent, spouse, or guardian will be considered excess coverage for benefit purposes. In the case of unwed or divorced parents, the primary provider of coverage is generally the parent granted custody, unless determined otherwise by a court decree. Therefore, matching a client's lifestyle, as well as budget or health needs, with an appropriate plan is one way for a comprehensive financial planner to add value to the client/planner relationship.

Although analysis of the client's current situation based on client-provided information is the advisor's responsibility, another important task is communicating findings to the client. Summarizing and presenting a review of current policy coverage and recommendations can be done in a number of ways. Increasingly, planners are choosing a brief format that presents only essential information. Exhibit 6.1 provides a simple but thorough approach.

**Exhibit 6.1** Health Insurance Planning Summary for the Garwood Family

### Health Care Cost Planning

*Current Situation Analysis and Observations:*

- George, you are currently providing coverage for your family of five under a health maintenance organization (HMO) plan, an employer-provided benefit, paid on a pre-tax basis with monthly premiums of $700. Dental and vision insurance are not included.

- Based on the data you provided, your household is annually paying:

- $150, average expenses, for dental care;

- $750, average expenses, for eye care;

- $8,400 in health insurance premiums;

- $380 annually in medical copayments; and

- $300 annually for prescriptions.

*Assumptions:*

- The entire family is in good health, with no diagnosed chronic health conditions.

- Out-of-pocket expenses will remain constant, except for inflationary increases.

- All family members visit health care providers annually for preventive care, and the family adheres to a healthy lifestyle.

- Open enrollment for both George's employer and Donna's employer occurs in May and June, respectively, so that new plan information will be available for a comparison prior to the close of the open-enrollment period.

*Recommendations:*

1. Despite your past assumption that George's employee benefits were better, we recommend that we, in conjunction with you and your Human Resource representatives, conduct a thorough review of the health care plan options available. This comparison should consider the cost of copays, deductibles, and coinsurance, as well as the network of providers available. This will help us identify the most cost-effective, comprehensive plan for your family.

2. Consider opening a Flexible Spending Account (FSA) matched to your projected annual out-of-pocket expenses not covered by health insurance. Funded with pre-tax salary withdrawals, FSA contributions are not subject to state (5.75%), federal (25%), and FICA taxes (7.65%), which means a tax savings of 38.4% would have been realized on your out-of-pocket expenses last year as shown below:

   [$150 dental + $750 eye + $380 copay + $300 drugs] × 38.4% = $607

A $600 savings is significant! Most FSA accounts offer a debit card for convenient payment. You may be charged a small monthly fee to establish the account, but we can consider that, with other costs, as a part of the review of available plans in the spring. Also, generally no annual carryover of balance is allowed, typically called the "use it or lose it" rule, so it is important that we accurately estimate the annual eligible out-of-pocket expenses. You should receive employer information on eligible expenses; many plans offer an Internet site to assist with estimating the optimal amount.

*Implementation:*

*To Do List:* George and Donna, in April/May please review all health plan information in conjunction with Human Resources personnel and/or our staff. Monitor the dates for open enrollment so that you can (1) implement any changes in plan selection, and/or (2) enroll for the Flexible Savings Account. We are very willing to assist you with these important decisions. Not only does the choice of health care alternatives affect your access to and payment for care, but any cost savings yield additional cash flow for funding other goals.

## STRATEGIES

### Review Prospective Health Insurance Planning Strategies

After completing an analysis of the client's current and projected health plan needs, the second step in the analysis and evaluation of a client's financial status focuses on the array of strategies for choosing the most appropriate product(s), structuring the insurance contracts, coordinating benefits between contracts, coordinating benefits with social insurance, if applicable, and establishing or optimizing other tax-advantaged accounts to meet the client's needs. Increasing a client's confidence to handle the financial loss associated with serious or chronic illness and to minimize the lingering financial and emotional effects of that loss solidifies a strong client-planner working relationship.

### Identify Prospective Health Insurance Planning Strategies

The following broad strategies represent a cross-section of product and procedural approaches often used by financial planners to meet a client's health insurance needs over the life cycle. Understanding a client's needs as well as preferences on health care coverage can further inform the review of specific product and procedural strategies. Fundamental advantages and disadvantages of each are noted, as well as unique caveats that must be considered.

#### *Product Strategy 1: Establish a Health Savings Account in Conjunction with a Qualified High-deductible Health Plan (HDHP) (For clients aged 64 or younger and not a dependent of another individual)*

**Advantage:** This strategy works well for self-employed clients, for those without access to cost-efficient group plans, or for those with access to qualifying high-deductible group health plans, an option increasingly available from more employers. The combination of a health savings account (HSA) and an HDHP offers a number of benefits to those who have minimal health care needs and want greater control over the cost of medical care and insurance. Because of the high-deductible plan, premiums are significantly lower than typical health care plans.

To qualify as a high-deductible health insurance plan in 2012, an individual insurance plan must have at least a $1,200 deductible and an annual stop-loss limit of no more than $6,050. For a family plan to qualify, the deductible must be at least $2,400, with a maximum stop-loss limit of $12,100.

The HSA is similar to an individual retirement account (IRA) for health care-related expenses. The client has access to a catastrophic health plan, and the benefit of an above-the-line tax deduction for post-tax contributions or a tax-exemption for pretax contributions to the account. If available to an employee, an HSA can be funded up to the 2012 contribution limit of $3,100 for an individual and $6,250 for a family, with pretax salary reductions or with employer contributions that may be available through a Section 125 Plan. Contributions are not subject to state or federal income tax or FICA withholding. A catch-up contribution of $1,000 is also available for persons aged 55 to 64.

Assets in the account grow tax deferred as they accumulate. Distributions for qualifying medical expenses are excluded from income. Any funds remaining in the account not used for medical expenses can be used after age 65 for any purpose without penalty.

To be eligible for an HSA, a person must be covered by a qualifying high-deductible health insurance plan and not be covered by other health insurance, such as a spouse's plan or spouse's FSA. Other allowable coverage includes dental and vision insurance as well as coverage for a specific disease or illness as long as it pays a specific dollar amount when the policy is triggered. Also, the person must be younger than age 65, the age of eligibility for Medicare. In addition, the person must not be a dependent of another person.

**Disadvantage:** Only clients covered by a qualifying high-deductible health insurance plan are eligible for an HSA. Annual contribution limits as well as the allowable above-the-line tax deduction are limited, but they increase annually. Distributions made for any reason other than to pay for qualified medical expenses are subject to income taxes. In addition, such distributions are subject to a 20% penalty unless made after death, disability, or age 65. Premiums paid for a high-deductible health plan are not eligible as an itemized tax deduction.

**Caveat:** HSA accounts are portable and require contributions to be managed, typically through mutual funds or bank accounts. As is the case whenever an investment is made, the custodian of the account should be evaluated in terms of investment alternatives, costs, and fee structure. Many smaller banks—and even some specialty banks—act as HSA trustees. They offer fixed-interest funds and other account types for qualified deposits.

### Product Strategy 2: Maximize the Benefits of a § 125 Plan (for Employed Clients)

**Advantage:** IRC § 125 provides employees with several advantages for choosing, using, and paying for health insurance premiums, health care expenses, and other benefits. **§ 125 plans**, commonly known as **cafeteria plans** or **flexible benefit plans**, make it possible for employers to offer employees a choice between cash and a variety of nontaxable benefits. Such plans must allow employees to choose between two or more qualified benefits (i.e., life insurance, health insurance, accidental death and dismemberment, long-term disability insurance, child and dependent care costs or adoption assistance, group legal services, or medical expense reimbursement) and cash, or another taxable benefit that is treated as cash. Nontaxable benefits, such as disability insurance purchased with after-tax dollars, can also be included in a cafeteria plan.

The benefits chosen are typically paid for with pretax dollars through employee salary reduction agreements or "credits" provided by the employer. Employee contributions are made by contributing a portion of salary, on a pretax basis, to pay for qualified benefits. Salary reduction contributions are not considered to be actually or "constructively" received by the participant. Therefore, contributions are generally not considered wages for federal or state income tax purposes (some exclusions apply). Also, plan contributions generally are not subject to FICA. In addition, employer-provided credits, often stated in dollar amounts, are used to purchase qualified, or nontaxable, benefits. Although the credits may vary with employee age, service, or salary, the plan cannot offer an undue advantage to highly compensated employees.

Because of their complexity, cafeteria plans are generally available in midsize to large firms. Self-employed clients are ineligible to establish these plans, although other tax advantages for health and retirement plan contributions are available to them.

Once an employee has elected benefits for a plan year, the choice can be changed only in limited circumstances. Under change-in-status rules, a plan may permit participants to revoke an election or make a new election with respect to accident and health coverage, dependent care expenses, group-term life insurance, or adoption assistance if a qualifying event occurs and the participant makes the change in a plan within 31 days of the qualifying event.

Qualifying change-in-status events include:

- a change in legal marital status;

- a change in number of dependents or eligible family members;

- a change in employment status of the employee or changes affecting the employment of a covered family member;

- cases where the dependent satisfies or ceases to satisfy the requirements for eligibility;

- a change in residence for the employee, spouse, or dependent; and

- the commencement or termination of an adoption proceeding, for purposes of adoption assistance.

Many cafeteria plans offer a salary reduction agreement, or **premium-conversion plan,** or **premium-only plan** for the purchase of health or life insurance coverage. Pretax salary reduction agreements can also be used to fund an HSA and high-deductible health plan. A flexible spending arrangement, also referred to a **flexible spending account (FSA)** is another tax-favored tool that allows employees to accumulate pretax dollars (exempt from state, federal, and Social Security taxes) through salary reductions for the reimbursement of select expenses. Both health care FSAs and dependent care FSAs are established and maintained in a similar manner. For both, allowable reimbursements are limited to those eligible for the medical deduction or the dependent care tax credit, respectively.

The **health care FSA** can be used to pay for cost sharing (e.g., copayments, coinsurance, and deductibles) as well as other medical, dental, or eye care costs not covered by health insurance. Over-the-counter drugs, vitamins, dietary supplements, and cosmetic procedures are excluded, but expenses for an herbal remedy or a weight loss program, if prescribed by a physician as medically necessary, could be covered. In 2012 there are no standard limits, though most employers cap the maximum allowable contribution. Beginning in 2013, FSA contributions will be limited to $2,500 each year with annual inflation increases, as mandated by PPACA.

The **dependent care FSA** is used to pay for qualified dependent care expenses, such as child care and elder care costs incurred, when both spouses are employed, unless one is disabled or a full-time student. The maximum tax-free reimbursement for a dependent care FSA is $5,000 ($2,500 for a married employee filing separate tax returns), although income restrictions apply to determine the maximum allowable contribution.

It is important to recognize that the health care FSA and dependent care FSA differ on the uniform coverage, or risk-of-loss rule. **Uniform coverage** means that the maximum amount of reimbursement (i.e., the annual election) must be available to the health FSA participant at all times. For example, if an employee elects a monthly salary reduction of $100 for an FSA, then the annual election of $1,200 (less any prior year reimbursements) must be available for employee reimbursement at any time during the plan year without regard to the employee's actual accumulated balance. The plan may not accelerate the payment schedule based on the employee's prior claims. Conversely, the dependent care FSA account can reimburse *only* with funds deposited into the account, based on the monthly salary deductions available in the participant's account to date.

For both health and dependent care FSAs, reimbursements can be made only for claims incurred during the plan year and cannot be paid in advance. FSA expenses are treated as having been incurred when the participant is provided with the medical care or dependent care resulting in an expense, not when the participant is billed or pays for the care. Reimbursement requests can be submitted, with restrictions, after the plan year ends for expenses incurred during the plan year. IRS changes in 2005 permit a 2½-month grace period for the health FSA "use it or lose it" provision, but few employers have adopted the change because of the easier-to-manage "use it or lose it" plan year provision. The plan year is typically 12 months, as specified by the employer plan.

**Disadvantage:** § 125 plan options usually must be chosen before the beginning of the plan year during the open enrollment period. Once established, adjustments to the amount of salary reduction during the year are not allowed, unless there is a qualifying change of family or work status. Careful estimates of out-of-pocket medical and dependent care expenses are necessary to avoid the loss of contributions if flexible spending accounts are used. Because of the "use it or lose it" rule, any balance remaining in the account at year-end will most likely be forfeited. Preplanning medical expenses to occur within one year is a way to coordinate the "bunching" of medical services as a way to avert the loss of account funds. In addition to non-qualifying health expenses, premiums for other health care coverage or for long-term care insurance are also excluded. Dependent care reimbursements from an FSA reduce the total dependent care expenses eligible for calculation of the dependent care credit.

## Product Strategy 3: Purchase a Medigap Policy to Supplement Medicare Coverage (for Clients Age 65 or Older)

**Advantage:** Traditional **Medigap** insurance is available to residents of most states. Medigap policies are sold by private insurance providers to pay for health care costs not provided by Medicare Parts A and B, such as out-of-pocket expenses for copays, co-insurance, or deductibles. Some Medigap plans also fill in for "gaps" in coverage not provided by Medicare Parts A and B. A few states—Massachusetts, Minnesota, and Wisconsin—have their own specific Medicare supplemental policies and are not considered here. Acceptance by an insurance company into a Medigap plan is guaranteed once a client reaches age 65 and enrolls in Medicare. Clients have six months to apply for a Medigap policy. Clients cannot be turned down, regardless of health status, if they apply within the six-month window. However, anyone covered by Medicaid or by a Medicare Advantage Plan is typically ineligible to purchase Medigap insurance.

Nearly all Medigap insurance is sold as a standardized plan that must meet federal and state laws. As shown in Table 6.3, 10 standard plans are available, ranging from the most basic coverage in Plan A to other plans, with different features, having different alphabetical titles up to Plan N. Every insurance company offering Medigap insurance is required to provide the same standard coverage for each plan, although premiums may differ significantly. Each company offering Medigap insurance must offer Plan A, but companies may have some, all, or none of the other plans available in a state or geographic region within a state.

Basic benefits include

- in-patient hospital care: covers the cost of Part A coinsurance and the cost of 365 extra days of hospital care during the client's lifetime after Medicare coverage ends;

- medical costs: covers the Part B coinsurance (generally 20% of Medicare-approved payment amount) or copayment amount, which may vary according to service; and

- blood: covers the first 3 pints of blood each year.

**Table 6.3** Standard Medicare Supplement, or Medigap, Plans and the Percentage of Costs Covered for Benefits

| Benefits | A | B | C | D | F* | G | K | L** | M | N |
|---|---|---|---|---|---|---|---|---|---|---|
| Part A coinsurance and hospital costs up to an additional 365 days after Medicare benefits are used | 100% | 100% | 100% | 100% | 100% | 100% | 100% | 100% | 100% | 100% |
| Part B coinsurance or copayment | 100% | 100% | 100% | 100% | 100% | 100% | 50% | 75% | 100% | 100%*** |
| Blood (first 3 pints) | 100% | 100% | 100% | 100% | 100% | 100% | 50% | 75% | 100% | 100% |
| Part A hospice care coinsurance or copayment | 100% | 100% | 100% | 100% | 100% | 100% | 50% | 75% | 100% | 100% |
| Skilled nursing facility care coinsurance | | | 100% | 100% | 100% | 100% | 50% | 75% | 100% | 100% |
| Part A deductible | | 100% | 100% | 100% | 100% | 100% | 50% | 75% | 50% | 100% |
| Part B deductible | | | 100% | | 100% | | | | | |
| Part B excess charges | | | | | 100% | 100% | | | | |
| Foreign travel emergency care (up to plan limits) | | | 100% | 100% | 100% | 100% | | | 100% | 100% |

*Note:* The Medicare supplement policy covers coinsurance only after the insured has paid the deductible (unless the supplement policy also covers the deductible).

*Plan F also offers a high-deductible plan. If this option is chosen, the insured must pay for Medicare covered costs up to the deductible amount of $2,070 in 2012 before the Medicare supplement plan pays anything.

**After meeting the annual out-of-pocket limit (i.e., $4,660 for Plan K and $2, 330 for Plan L) and the annual Part B deductible (i.e., $140 in 2012), the Medicare supplement plan pays 100% of covered services for the rest of the calendar year.

***Plan N pays 100% of the Part B coinsurance, except for a copayment of up to $20 for some office visits and up to a $50 copayment for emergency room visits that do not result in an inpatient admission.

*Source:* Centers for Medicare and Medicaid Services. *Choosing a Medigap Policy: A Guide to Health Insurance for People with Medicare,* p 11. Available at http://www.medicare.gov/Publications/Pubs/pdf/02110.pdf.

Beginning in 2006, two new standard Medigap plans became available. These two plans do not include the entire core benefit package. Instead they offer catastrophic coverage at a lower premium.

- Plan K includes (a) coverage of 50% of the cost sharing otherwise applicable under Parts A and B, except for the Part B deductible; (b) coverage of 100% of hospital inpatient coinsurance and 365 extra lifetime days of coverage of inpatient hospital services; (c) coverage of 100% of any cost sharing otherwise applicable for preventive benefits; and (d) a limit on annual out-of-pocket spending under Part A and Part B to $4,660 in 2012.

- Plan L includes (a) coverage of 75% of the cost sharing otherwise applicable under Parts A and B, except for the Part B deductible; (b) coverage of 100% of hospital inpatient coinsurance and 365 extra lifetime days of coverage of inpatient hospital services; (c) coverage of 100% of any cost sharing otherwise applicable for preventive benefits; and (d) a limit on annual out-of-pocket spending under Part A and Part B to $2,330 in 2012.

Another alternative is a **Medicare SELECT plan**. These plans are similar to traditional Medigap plans; however, SELECT coverage utilizes a managed care approach, similar to an HMO or PPO, where clients must use either an in-network or preferred provider, which can make the premiums less expensive than comparable plans.

Medigap insurance offers the advantages of a standardized insurance policy, with a range of supplemental coverage, for those on Medicare. With careful selection and attention to company ratings and consumer satisfaction rankings, a Medigap policy can be a cost-effective solution to the limitations of Medicare coverage. To make a cost-effective selection, advisors and their clients should compare the projected Medigap premium with potential out-of-pocket costs for deductibles, coinsurance, and other health care needs not covered by Medicare. Medigap policies are particularly useful for clients who are not offered or cannot afford to continue any company-provided health benefits after retirement.

**Disadvantage:** Premium costs for the 10 standard plans can vary, so comparison shopping among providers is advisable. Clients who do not enroll within six months of turning age 65 can be denied coverage or shifted to higher-risk groups at higher premiums.

**Caveat:** It is illegal for an insurance company to sell clients a Medigap policy that substantially duplicates any existing coverage, including Medicare coverage. A client can postpone purchasing a Medigap policy if working past age 65 and covered by employer-sponsored health insurance, or if not working but still covered by a spouse's employer-sponsored plan. Clients can still enroll in Medicare, but the employer-sponsored insurance will be the primary payer, and Medicare will be the secondary payer. Medicare will pay any costs covered by Medicare that are not covered by the employer's plan. If clients find themselves in this situation, they may want to enroll in Medicare Part A, because it is free. Remember, however, that if clients enroll in Medicare Part B, the open enrollment period for Medigap begins.

### Product Strategy 4: Establish a Health Savings Account (HSA) in Conjunction with a Qualified High-deductible Health Plan (HDHP) (for Young Adults)

**Advantage:** This strategy works well for young, healthy adults because it could provide another avenue to save for retirement. While a person is healthy, single, and without dependents is a great time to maximize contributions to an HSA. Additionally, an HSA can be invested in a wide variety of risk- and age-appropriate investment vehicles so a reasonable return can be generated on unused deposits. It could be argued that under the right set of circumstances a person should invest in an HSA even before maximizing Roth or Traditional IRA contributions.

Money deposited into a Roth IRA can be withdrawn only after five years, and then only the contributions can be withdrawn without taxes or penalties. To withdraw earnings, in addition to the five-year rule, one of a number of qualifying events or exceptions must be met. One exception deals with unreimbursed health care expenses; however, to meet the rule of the exception, the unreimbursed health care expenses must exceed 7.5% (increasing to 10% under PPACA in 2013) of the account owner's AGI. No such limitation exists for HSA withdrawals, plus any money remaining in the account when the account owner reaches age 65 may be withdrawn for any reason without a tax penalty, although ordinary income tax is owed. Money deposited into a Traditional IRA also can be withdrawn only for a qualifying event, such as paying medical expenses that exceed the AGI limit, but there is no predetermined time limit.

And although the income-based phase-out limits on a Roth IRA are quite high, the phase-out on a deductible, Traditional IRA, if the account owner is eligible for a qualified retirement plan, is only $58,000. Therefore single people with income exceeding the phase-out threshold could make a deductible contribution to an HSA even if they had maximized their Roth IRA contribution because HSA deposits are not included in the combined maximum funding levels.

**Disadvantage:** Overfunding an HSA in preference to a Roth IRA can create additional tax consequences at retirement given that qualified Roth IRA distributions are tax free, whereas distributions at age 65 or after will be taxed at ordinary income tax rates. Also, the HSA acts more like a Traditional IRA than a Roth IRA in that contributions to an HSA are made on a pretax basis, but again are taxed upon withdrawal.

An additional issue is that if the account owner must take a withdrawal from an HSA prior to age 65 and for a reason other than a qualified medical expense, the penalty on the withdrawal is 20%—twice the penalty rate on IRA accounts.

### Procedural Strategy 1: Monitor Health Insurance Coverage and Encourage Clients to Do the Same

**Advantage:** Comprehensive planners should routinely conduct ongoing reviews of clients' health insurance plan coverage as part of the planning process. For this reason, it may seem redundant and unnecessary to clients. Including this strategy as a specific recommendation or in a structured client-planner to-do list reminds clients that they too have a responsibility for staying abreast of plan changes and insurance triggers. Both planners and clients need to monitor the ongoing PPACA changes scheduled to occur over the next few years.

**Disadvantage:** In many cases, the flexibility to change a health plan within a given year will be minimal and likely limited to the plan's open enrollment period. Nevertheless, it is prudent to recommend that clients continue to monitor both potential employer-provided and PPACA-mandated alternatives or modifications available to them or their spouse/partner, as well as any other household changes that could affect health care planning options.

## Procedural Strategy 2: Use COBRA to Bridge Employment Termination or Continue Group Health Coverage for Dependents

**Advantage:** The COBRA law requires employers with 20 or more employees offering group health plans to provide employees and certain family members the opportunity to continue group health coverage in a number of instances when coverage would otherwise have lapsed. The lapse must occur as the result of an employee **qualifying event**, defined as:

- voluntary or involuntary termination of employment, except in the case of gross misconduct;

- coverage termination due to a reduction in hours worked;

- eligibility for Medicare;

- divorce or legal separation; or

- death.

Two other nonemployee qualifying events also are included in COBRA: (a) dependents who cease to meet the dependency definition; and (b) the filing of Chapter 11 bankruptcy by the employer.

The employee must pay for the entire cost of continuing coverage through COBRA. The employee or qualified beneficiary may be charged 102% of the applicable premium for this benefit. Although expensive, coverage is available, whereas a privately provided individual policy might not be available, might offer more limited coverage, or be equally expensive.

Employers must send COBRA notifications to employees and their spouses when the employee is first covered under the group health plan. They must also send notices to both the employee and qualified beneficiaries whenever a qualifying event occurs. The latter notice must be sent within 14 days of learning of the qualifying event.

Qualified beneficiaries have 60 days to elect continuation of coverage. The maximum period that this continued coverage must be provided is generally 18 months, but in some cases it is 36 months. Depending on the state, there may be a *small group COBRA* benefit available.

**Disadvantage:** A timely response is required. Election of coverage continuation must occur within 60 days of employer-provided COBRA notification. The cost of insurance continuance can be 102% of total premiums, calculated as the employer and employee contributions and a 2% surcharge. Thus, it is possible that a policy that cost a client $2,500 annually as an employee may actually cost, for example, as much as $6,500 when COBRA benefits are used. The effect on cash flow must be weighed relative to the potential financial loss of an uninsured accident or illness for one or more household members.

## Procedural Strategy 3: Maximize the Benefits of HIPAA to Extend COBRA Coverage

**Advantage:** The original COBRA law was amended by the **Health Insurance Portability and Accountability Act of 1996 (HIPAA)**. The first change dealt with the extension of COBRA coverage to disabled beneficiaries. COBRA required that the 18-month maximum coverage continuation period be extended to 29 months if the qualified beneficiary was determined under the Social Security Act to have been disabled at the time of the qualifying event. HIPAA provided that if the disability existed at any time during the first 60 days of COBRA coverage, then the 29-month period applies. The 29-month period also applies to a nondisabled qualified beneficiary of the covered employee.

HIPAA also provide that a newborn infant or child placed for adoption with the covered employee during the period of COBRA coverage is entitled to receive COBRA continuation coverage as a qualified beneficiary. COBRA coverage can be terminated early for individuals who are covered under another group health plan. HIPAA provides that COBRA coverage can be cut short even if the new plan has a pre-existing condition exclusion unless the exclusion applies to a condition for which the insured is receiving treatment.

The most universally applicable modification dealt with the length of time pre-existing conditions can be excluded from a group policy. For instance, an employer may require that a new hire wait 60 days or more before participating in a group plan. Once the elimination period has been met, all medical expenses for the employee will be covered, after deductibles and copayments have been paid. HIPAA states that pre-existing conditions cannot be secondarily excluded once the waiting period has been satisfied, as long as there has not been a break in health care coverage. HIPAA allows individuals to switch jobs and obtain employer-sponsored health insurance coverage without satisfying any waiting period for pre-existing conditions as long as the employee had at least a full year's coverage through a previous position and the person enrolls in the new group plan without a break of 63 days or more. Beginning in 2014, PPACA will eliminate all pre-existing condition exclusions currently in place.

To take advantage of HIPAA, a person must prove that he or she was insured during the previous 12 months and has not been uninsured for more than 63 days. Workers who could be unemployed for more than 63 days should consider purchasing the (1) COBRA "bridge" or (2) an individual short-term policy to maintain continuous coverage, and thus avoid loss of coverage for pre-existing conditions. (Some insurers do not consider short-term medical or individual coverage to be creditable toward the continuous coverage requirement.) If no insurance is purchased, coverage from the Pre-existing Condition Insurance Plan (PCIP) is available after six months.

The maximum allowable pre-existing condition exclusion period is 12 months for regular enrollment and 18 months for late enrollment. (Someone who does not enroll in a plan on the earliest date on which coverage can become effective or does not enroll during a special/open enrollment period is defined as a *late enrollee*.) Group coverage time of less than one year with a previous employer applies to these limits (i.e., prior coverage of three months would reduce the waiting period with the new employer to nine months). The exclusion can be applied only to expenses associated with the pre-existing condition. HIPAA defines these as any condition for which treatment was received during the six months prior to enrolling with the new employer.

These term and coverage limits are very important and should be discussed with any client who is anticipating a job or career change, change in employment or marital status, or other qualifying event. Recommending the COBRA bridge or the purchase of a private individual policy is especially important whenever a client has a pre-existing condition and anticipates being between positions, or ineligible for coverage, for more than 63 days.

**Disadvantage:** Although the HIPAA changes in the extension of disability coverage, coverage for an adopted child, and continuation of COBRA coverage for the treatment of a pre-existing condition are beneficial, their applicability is fairly limited. Eliminating the exclusion on pre-existing conditions is more widely applicable, but utilizing the benefit requires careful planning to ensure that continuous coverage requirements are met and consistent with individual insurers' requirements. Election of the COBRA bridge benefit requires a timely response and can be expensive—as can a privately provided individual policy. But the fiscal and emotional benefits of continuous insurance protection, including pre-existing condition coverage, should not be overlooked.

## CHAPTER-BASED CASE STUDY

### A Client-based Health Insurance Recommendation

As with each financial planning issue, once an analysis of the current situation is complete, the next step is to cull or combine possible strategies and develop an actionable recommendation. Implementation is also an important part of any financial plan, but attention to timing is especially important when health insurance issues are considered. For example, the client and planner may meet during one month, and the open enrollment for employer-provided plans can occur during another month (often different months for two-income households). The need to change coverage because of demographic or lifestyle changes can occur at yet another time. It is necessary that planners and clients coordinate the necessary actions.

Health care plans must provide ample, yet cost-effective coverage for all household members while meeting the client's desires for flexibility regarding care providers. For these reasons health care planning recommendations can offer unique challenges— many of which focus on issues of *coordination*, as outlined below.

- *Coordination of plans.* A combination of product and procedural strategies may be necessary to best meet the need to coordinate benefits and primary and secondary payments across multiple employer group plans or between plans. Plan choices must also be coordinated with the use of tax-advantaged options to pay for unreimbursed medical expenses or policy premiums. Options to consider, if applicable, include premium conversion, flexible spending accounts, health reimbursement accounts, health savings accounts, or the inclusion of premium costs or medical expenses as an itemized income tax deduction. For the self-employed, the effect of premium costs as an adjustment to income or an above-the-line deduction must also be considered. Finally, a recommendation to change a health care provider can also affect the decision of long-term care provider, as well as the decision to participate in an HSA-qualified health plan or a flexible spending account. All these aspects of plan coordination must be taken into account.

- *Coordination of plan changes.* Most clients will be eligible to make changes only during the annual open-enrollment period or in response to a qualifying midyear event. Of course, these limitations do not apply if the client purchases an individual policy, but this is the exception and not the rule. As with any sound recommendation, health care recommendations must be developed in anticipation of events that could create coverage gaps or restrictions.

  Life events to consider in scheduled client meetings or that necessitate a health care policy review include:

  - childbirth;

  - marriage/divorce/widowhood;

  - employment change (especially retirement);

  - a child reaching the age of 26, if ineligible for an employer-provided plan; or

  - a change in the overall health of the client or other household member.

  Coordinating needed health care plan changes and these life events to the extent possible can help clients avoid hasty decisions. In the worst case, coordination could help avoid a negative impact on cash flow resulting from a lapse in coverage or coverage replacement with a more expensive policy. Furthermore, if there is a break in continuous coverage, then the client could be subject to pre-existing condition exclusions for 12 to 18 months in accordance with HIPAA. It is important to note that PPACA will eliminate this restriction in 2014.

- *Coordination of timing.* With most other forms of insurance, a planner can directly execute or at least facilitate the implementation of plan recommendations. However, health insurance changes are often left solely to the client. While waiting for open enrollment periods for household members covered by different plans, clients could forget or fail to make the necessary changes. It is very important that the planner and client have a system in place to ensure that new plan information is shared with the planner for review (if this is part of the client services offered) and that the client make the changes.

In addition to coordinating the timing of plan changes, the client may also need to coordinate the timing of health care expenditures to maximize benefits. For example, the "bunching" of medical expenses in one year may allow a client to periodically satisfy the 7.5% floor for claiming an itemized tax deduction. (Beginning in 2013, the AGI floor for medical expense deductions will increase from 7.5% to 10% for those under age 65. For those 65 and older, PPACA waives the increase for tax years 2013–2016.) Conversely, the same strategy of bunching expenses can allow for more effective management of a health FSA or the coordination of periodic elective expenses (e.g., new eyeglass frames) with health FSA funding.

## A Sample Recommendation: Maintain Existing Group Coverage but Add a Flexible Spending Account

Comprehensive health insurance plans often offer additional coverage for vision and dental needs for an additional premium cost. Depending on the age and health status of household members, expanded coverage of this kind may be most cost effective when children are younger or during the later years of employment when a client's health care costs might be increasing. Although this example may be a gross generalization, it is important to attempt to match anticipated medical costs with the coverage purchased.

Routinely selecting the least expensive or most expensive health insurance coverage without regard to the suitability of the plan can have a negative effect on cash flow. Fear of the unknown questions of health status and future benefit needs could encourage a risk-averse client to select the most expensive coverage, "just in case." Conversely, those who are more comfortable with risk or who have not seriously considered the ramifications of limited or no coverage might select the least expensive coverage. The benefits of coverage relative to anticipated household costs as well as the alternatives of meeting these expenses with post-tax dollars and a possible tax deduction or pretax dollars in an FSA must be weighed.

Sujana, a health-conscious divorced professional with no children, decided that turning age 50 warranted a comprehensive financial checkup. She had recently completed a comprehensive physical exam and knew that health care costs might start to rise with increasing age and more frequent diagnostic testing. Her doctor had declared her in excellent physical health, but her conservative nature and her concern over personal and financial independence prompted her to pursue an equally extensive financial checkup.

The planner asked about the types of health plans she had available at work, including the option of a high-deductible plan, and her typical annual out-of-pocket spending on health care. The planner also asked if she had considered an FSA—the same question her accountant had asked. Questions about the number of employees where she worked baffled Sujana until the planner explained that company size controlled the availability of federally authorized protection against a lapse in insurance benefits should she leave the company or experience other qualifying events.

Based on her research from the company's Internet site, Sujana learned that both a preferred provider organization (PPO) and health maintenance organization (HMO) were offered, but the latter was not available at her company location. The monthly premium for comprehensive coverage for a single person was $32 per month, with five options for different combinations of out-of-network provider, vision, hearing, and expanded dental benefits. Applicable premiums ranged from $40 to $57 per month, depending on the combination of benefits.

Because of her good health, Sujana's medical expenses last year totaled only $1,225, over half of which was spent on her annual ophthalmologist exam and new eyeglass frames and lenses. No expense for dental care was incurred due to the basic services included in the comprehensive plan. Expanded dental would pay up to $1,500 annually for restorative and orthodontic services, neither of which she anticipated needing. Sujana's current health care providers were all in-network. Based on this information, Sujana and her planner agreed that only two options were viable: add vision care to her coverage or consider an FSA.

The plan packaged vision, hearing, and expanded dental together at a monthly premium of $49, or an additional cost of $17 per month. Because Sujana did not reasonably anticipate a need for the hearing or expanded dental coverage, analysis focused on the vision care. Over a 24-month period, she would pay a maximum of $35 for a routine examination and the plan would pay up to $75 for frames and up to $75 for bifocal lenses. A review of her expenses revealed that for an additional $404 in premiums, Sujana would receive approximately $220 in benefits (maximum of $70 to the ophthalmologist and $150 for frames and lenses). Given her anticipated need for services, adding the package of vision, hearing, and expanded dental was not deemed cost effective.

Because of the combination of salary, good health, and top-quality health care coverage, Sujana was unlikely to ever incur out-of-pocket expenses in excess of 7.5% of her adjusted gross income, and this would be even more difficult with the increase in 2013 to 10% of AGI. Her plan year deductible was $200 and the out-of-pocket expense limit was $1,500. However, an FSA offered the benefit of tax-advantaged dollars (30% federal and state marginal tax bracket plus 7.65% FICA). Given Sujana's most recent annual expenses of $1,225, an FSA offered an estimated tax savings of $461 [$1,225 × (30% + 7.65%)].

Sujana learned that no fees were incurred to establish an FSA account. The allowable annual deposit ranged from $200 to $5,000 per plan year. On the basis of her anticipated expenses and the "use or lose it" rule, Sujana and her planner agreed that funding the account for $1,080 was a good compromise. This would result in a tax savings of approximately $407 [$1,080 × (30% + 7.65%)], which could offset any post-tax dollars that might be necessary to meet expenses in excess of $1,000.

With the analysis complete and the recommendation resolved, Sujana made notations to sequence the necessary steps for action. She learned that the FSA plan year ran from July 1 through June 30, with all account forms due to the employer by May 15. To maximize the benefits, she would need to postpone her routinely scheduled spring eye care exam until after July 1. The health care plan year follows the calendar year of January through December, with an open enrollment period during the preceding October. No changes to her basic coverage would be necessary.

Exhibit 6.2 illustrates how a recommendation to maintain current coverage and add a flexible spending account can be explained and presented to a client. All of the recommendation forms developed for a client's plan can be a useful guide for writing the plan or tracking implementation.

**Exhibit 6.2** Insurance Planning Recommendation Form

### Planning Recommendation Form

| | | | | |
|---|---|---|---|---|
| **Financial Planning Content Area** | Health Insurance | | | |
| **Client Goal** | To maximize cost-effective health care options. | | | |
| **Recommendation No.:** | | **Priority (1–6) lowest to highest:** | | 5 |
| **Projected/Target Value ($)** | $1,080 tax-exempt salary withdrawal | | | |

**Product Profile**

| | | | | |
|---|---|---|---|---|
| Type | Flexible spending account for health care | | | |
| Duration | July 20XX–June 20XX | | | |
| Provider | NECO Insurance | | | |
| Funding Cost per Period ($) | $1,080 tax-exempt contribution | | | |
| Maintenance Cost per Period ($) | $0 | | | |
| Current Income Tax Status | Tax-qualified | X | Taxable | |
| Projected Rate of Return | NA | | | |
| Major Policy Provisions | NA | | | |

**Procedural Factors**

| | | | | |
|---|---|---|---|---|
| Implement by Whom | Planner | | Client | X |
| Implementation Date or Timeframe | Before May 15, 20XX | | | |
| Implementation Procedure | Contact employer benefits office and submit forms to NECO Insurance | | | |

**Ownership Factors**

| | | | | |
|---|---|---|---|---|
| Owner(s) | Sujana A. Manawyth | | | |
| Form of Ownership | NA | | | |
| Insured(s) | Sujana A. Manawyth | | | |
| Custodial Account | Yes | | No | X |
| Custodian | NA | | | |
| In Trust For (ITF) | Yes | | No | X |
| Transfer On Death (TOD) | Yes | | No | X |
| Beneficiary(ies) | NA | | | |
| Contingent Beneficiary(ies) | NA | | | |

| | |
|---|---|
| **Proposed Benefit** | Given the current employer-provided health insurance plan options, no change is recommended. However, funding an FSA for health care expenses will result in a net tax savings of approximately $407 on projected annual eligible reimbursements. |

# Learning Outcomes

1.  Although health insurance planning typically is not considered the most glamorous aspect of financial planning, the process of helping clients evaluate their health insurance need is vitally important. Helping clients make choices that maximize benefits, reduce costs, increase tax-advantaged purchases, and facilitate peace of mind are good reasons to incorporate health insurance planning into every comprehensive review of a client's financial situation. Furthermore, as this chapter highlights, sound health insurance planning can lead to increases in a client's level of discretionary cash flow by helping manage out-of-pocket expenses related to health care costs.

2.  Arguably the most sweeping social legislation since the Great Depression, the Patient Protection and Affordable Care Act (PPACA) of 2010 has created dramatic shifts in the way consumers, financial planners, and policy makers view health care in the United States. Provisions of PPACA impact nearly every aspect of health care as it is currently provided. Although many provisions will not go into effect until 2014, many aspects of PPACA are already in force. Over the next five to ten years, the health care environment will change significantly. It is imperative that financial planners stay abreast of legislative changes to help their clients maximize benefits, minimize costs, and reduce surprises resulting from PPACA both today and in the future.

3.  Each client's financial, physical, and emotional situation is unique. Client situational factors need to be evaluated carefully when assessing and selecting appropriate health care plans, products, and services. Although the number of situational factors is almost limitless, this chapter has highlighted the need for financial planners to consider, at a minimum, the following client characteristics: (a) family health status and related health history; (b) family demographics, which can trigger insurance needs; (c) assets available for use in case of a catastrophic health claim; (d) lifestyle choices that can affect the availability of insurance benefits; (e) working in a hazardous profession or occupation; and (f) concerns over future unemployment, career changes, or retirement.

4.  As discussed in the chapter, determining and quantifying a client's need for and selection of health care coverage is not an easy financial calculation. In some respects, this aspect of planning can best be described as a combination of art and science. Rather than producing strictly a dollar need, as with a life insurance analysis, planning for health insurance focuses both on potential financial risks or needs to be met as well as the client's psychological needs (e.g., decreasing the financial fears associated with disease and discomfort). Helping clients deal with not only the financial realities associated with health care but also the worries associated with the unknown is one way to strengthen the client-planner relationship.

5.  Financial planners often get into the habit of speaking in acronyms. This is particularly true in relation to health care planning. It is important for financial planners to have a working knowledge of terms such as traditional indemnity; managed care plans such as HMO, PPO, POS, and EPO; and high-deductible health plans. Although each of these terms represents a type of health insurance coverage, each plan is distinct, offering advantages and disadvantages for clients. Of particular importance when helping clients manage health care costs while providing an opportunity for financial planners to provide guidance associated with accumulated savings is the increasing role of high-deductible plans and HSAs in health care planning. Well-qualified financial planners should not only know the basic provisions of

these products but also be able to summarize their associated strengths and weaknesses to clients.

6. As clients transition from working life toward retirement, they face many new challenges and opportunities. One common source of anxiety among those considering retirement deals with health care costs and health insurance alternatives. Even clients who continue to work past age 65 must grapple with health insurance issues. Because of this, financial planners need a firm understanding of the key rules, guidelines, products, and services targeted toward seniors. Specifically, understanding how Medicare and Medigap policy coverage affects health insurance planning is essential. The monetary and psychic costs associated with hastily made Medicare and Medigap choices can easily come back to haunt clients and their financial advisors.

7. In some respects, evaluating a client's available health insurance coverage and options is the easiest aspect of health insurance planning. Although the landscape for health insurance in the United States will change dramatically in 2014, financial planners still need to consider a number of factors when assessing how well a client's coverage is meeting current and anticipated needs. These factors include evaluating current: (a) deductibles, (b) copayment levels, (c) coinsurance requirements, (d) policy stop-loss limits, (e) policy lifetime maximum benefit, (f) excluded coverages, (g) out-of-network restrictions, (h) premiums, and (i) access to COBRA and HIPAA benefits.

8. The economic environment of the 21st century has been marked by uncertainty and financial instability, both at the national and household level. One result has been a relative increase in job insecurity among financial planning clients. It is not uncommon for clients to change jobs five to seven times in a career. Each move requires the analysis of health care packages, as well as an investigation of health insurance needs while transitioning to a new position. Further, as children age and enter the workforce, they too are experiencing job instability. The days when a parent's plan might drop a child from coverage has extended from the teen years to the age of 26. Still, some children find that they cannot afford insurance, even if living somewhat independently of their parents. It is because of these and other factors that financial planners need to have a working familiarity with PPACA, COBRA, and HIPAA rules and regulations.

9. Assessing the role of Section 125 Plans and flexible spending arrangements—also known as premium-conversion or premium-only plans—is an essential skill for financial planners interested in developing strong client-planner relationships that include health insurance analysis. FSAs are a useful tool not only from the perspective of paying out-of-pocket health care costs, but also from a cash flow and tax planning perspective. Clients who contribute to an FSA do so with pretax dollars. Contributions are exempt from state, federal, and Social Security taxes. Although there is a "use it or lose it" provision associated with FSAs, the ability to pay for health and dependent care costs with pretax dollars almost always outweighs the potential risks of losing unused savings.

10. Although the number of product and procedural strategies available to financial planners dealing with client health care issues is somewhat limited, there are ample opportunities to recommend strategies that increase client cash flow, improve lifetime health coverage, and maximize client satisfaction. Exploring concepts related to the use of health savings accounts, flexible spending arrangements, high-deductible insurance plans, Medigap policies, and, of course, understanding provisions related to PPACA, provides an outstanding way to identify and recommend appropriate and reasonable health insurance strategies matched to a client's situation.

# Chapter Resources

§ 125 Plan information (http://www.irs.gov/govt/fslg/article/0,,id=112720,00.html).

*Choosing a Medigap Policy: A Guide to Health Insurance for People with Medicare* (http://www.medicare.gov/Publications/Pubs/pdf/02110.pdf).

General insurance information and quotes ( www.insurance.com).

Health insurance cost information (www.nchc.org).

Health savings account information (www.hsabank.com or www.hsafinder.com or *www.treasury.gov/resource-center/faqs/Taxes/Pages/Health-Savings-Accounts.aspx.*

Insurance Information Institute (http://www.iii.org/individuals/healthinsurance/).

*Medicare and You* (http://www.medicare.gov/Publications/Pubs/pdf/10050.pdf).

Medicare information (www.medicare.gov).

Patient Protection and Affordable Care Act (PPACA) of 2010 (http://www.dol.gov/ebsa/healthreform/).

Publication 969, *Health Savings Accounts and Other Tax-Favored Health Plans* (http://www.irs.gov/publications/p969/index.html).

*Your Guide to Medicare Medical Savings Account (MSA) Plans* (http://www.medicare.gov/Publications/Pubs/pdf/11206.pdf).

The *Financial Factilitator* and all fillable forms needed to complete text activities can be found on the student website at: http://pro.nuco.com/booksupplements/NUCollege-CaseBook2e.

# Quantitative/Analytical Mini-case Problems

1.  A 40-year-old, unmarried client has been contributing to an HSA for the last three years using a salary reduction agreement through his employer. The stated effective annual rate on the account is 3% and the interest is compounded on a monthly basis. The client is in the 25% marginal

federal tax bracket and the 5% marginal state tax bracket. Use this information to answer the following questions.

   a.  How much money does the client currently have in the HSA if the client has deposited $200 per month and did not make any withdrawals?

   b.  Because the client is in exceptionally good health, the client is also using this account as an additional retirement savings vehicle. How much money will the client have in the account at age 65 if the client maintains his current level of contribution?

   c.  How much will the client have at age 65 if the client contributes $2,850 every year?

   d.  How much will the client have at age 65 if the client contributes $2,850 every year if it is assumed that the contribution and catch-up provision limits increases to 2.5% each year? (Ignore any minimum or maximum dollar change limitations.)

2.  A 52-year-old client has come to you for assistance with funding her HSA. Her doctor has told her that she will be facing knee replacement surgery within the next five years. She was also told that her out-of-pocket expenses (deductibles, copays, and various other uncovered expenses including rehabilitation) for the operation would total $4,000 if the operation happened today. Her open enrollment period is currently open. She plans to wait exactly five years for the surgery.

How much money should she contribute on a monthly basis if the account pays a stated rate (APR) of 4% compounded quarterly. To determine her out-of-pocket expenses at the time of her surgery, inflate the current cost by an effective annual rate of 7%.

3.  Ludwig has just accepted a position at a midsize firm that provides three health insurance plan choices for employees. Basic information about each plan is provided below (note: Plan C is a high-deductible health plan with a savings option). Ludwig must make a plan choice immediately. He can afford the annual premium for any of the plans and/or the HSA contribution. Although no one can predict a future health emergency, Ludwig estimates that he will likely incur $500 in medical expenses during the next year. Given this forecast, what policy should he purchase to minimize his net health insurance cost for the year?

| Plan provisions | Plan A | Plan B | Plan C |
|---|---|---|---|
| Annual deductible | $300 | $150 | $1,500 |
| Coinsurance | 20% | 35% | 20% |
| Annual stop-loss limit | $1,400 | $2,000 | $3,000 |
| HSA eligible | No | No | Yes |
| HSA yearly employer contribution | NA | NA | $400 |
| HSA minimum employee contribution | NA | NA | $100 |
| Yearly premium | $190 | $175 | $94 |

4.  David Cohen, a 24-year-old, single, healthy male has just opened an HSA in conjunction with his qualified HDHP. He wants to determine how much the account might be worth if he funds it primarily for retirement purposes.

   a.  How much would the account be worth at age 65 if David makes the maximum deposit of $3,100 per year for the next seven years before changing to his employer's standard health plan because of family health concerns and discontinuing contributions to the HSA? Assume that David earns only 3% per year for the next seven years while he might need the money, but after he changes plans he increases his risk and expects an annual return of 6%.

b.  How much would the account be worth at age 70 if David makes the maximum deposit of $3,100 per year for the next eight years, but he also has to take a $5,500 qualified distribution at age 28? Assume that David earns only 2% per year for the next seven years while he might need the money, but after he changes plans he increases his risk and expects an annual return of 7%.

c.  If David took a $10,000 nonqualified distribution from his HSA prior to age 65, how much in federal income tax and penalties would he owe? Assume that he is in the 25% marginal tax bracket.

# Comprehensive Bedo Case – Analysis Questions

Often, health insurance is overlooked in the planning process because it is generally employer provided. As such, the planner has little control over selection of the product or coverage. Health insurance assessment, however, should not be overlooked in the planning process. Adequate lifetime limits should be examined, as should other aspects of the coverage and the potential for future changes.

Strategies using § 125 Plan and FSA alternatives should also be developed based on the Bedos' annual health care spending patterns, deductibles, and copayments. Although it is unlikely that a planner would recommend that either Mia or Tyler purchase a private insurance policy, a cost analysis of other available policies offered during the open enrollment periods would be appropriate. The family's goal of living a financially satisfying life must be weighed against the relative costs of health care options.

1.  Develop a health insurance planning goal for the Bedos. When conceptualizing this goal, consider the following.

    a.  Is the goal developed in agreement with any or all goals and objectives that the clients have identified regarding health insurance planning?

    b.  What situational factors might influence their health insurance goal? Are these factors explicit, implied, or assumed? Is additional information required from the Bedos? If so, what?

    c.  What is the desired health insurance planning outcome for the clients?

2.  Make a list of the lifestyle, occupational, and health factors that should be documented and evaluated for the Bedos. How might this information be obtained? How might it be useful in the current health insurance situation analysis? Also, make a list of life events that could affect the health insurance planning analysis for Tyler and Mia and that should be reviewed at subsequent client meetings.

3.  Are there globally accepted, client-specific, or planner-generated planning assumptions that will influence the health insurance situation analysis? List the assumptions as they might appear in a plan.

4.  Make a list of specific policy features that should be evaluated as part of the documentation and evaluation of the Bedos' health insurance planning efforts.

5.  Conduct a current health insurance situation analysis for the Bedos. Be sure to assess the following:

    a.  The after-tax costs of their current plans compared to purchasing an individual policy.

    b.  The use of a tax-advantaged account as a health insurance planning tool.

    c.  How COBRA impacts health insurance planning for the Bedos.

    d.  Should one of the Bedos' employers offer the option, would another managed care plan or high-deductible health plan and HSA be a viable option for this household? What criteria would be considered in this decision?

6.  Summarize your observations about the Bedos' health insurance planning situation as they might appear in a client letter or plan.

7.  Based on the goals originally identified and the completed analysis, what product or procedural strategies might be most useful to satisfy the Bedos' health insurance protection needs? When reviewing the strategies, be careful to consider an approximate cost of implementation, as well as the most likely outcome(s) associated with each strategy.

8.  Write at least one primary and one alternative recommendation from selected strategies in response to each identified planning need. More than one recommendation may be needed to address all of the planning needs. Include specific, defensible answers to the who, what, when, where, why, how, and how much implementation questions for each recommendation.

    a.  It is suggested that each strategy be summarized in a Recommendation Form.

    b.  Assign a priority to each recommendation based on the likelihood of meeting client goals and desired outcomes. This priority will be important when recommendations from other core planning content areas are considered relative to the available discretionary funds for subsidizing all recommendations.

    c.  Comment briefly on the outcomes associated with each recommendation.

9.  Complete the following for the Health Insurance section of the Bedos' financial plan.

    a.  Draft an introduction to this section of the plan (no more than one paragraph).

    b.  Explain the purpose of an FSA and its potential benefit for the Bedos.

10. Prepare a 10–15-minute presentation for the Bedos of your observations and/or recommendation(s) for meeting their health insurance planning needs. Be sure to include visual aids or handouts.

# Notes

1.  As this book goes to press, legal issues surrounding the constitutionality of the healthcare reform law and other issues related to it are scheduled to be heard by the U.S. Supreme Court. Matters pertaining to the ability of the government to mandate that individuals buy health insurance (generally referred to as "the individual mandate") and whether the Court must wait for the tax to be imposed on those who do not wish to pay it (known as "anti-injunction") and the expansion of the Medicaid program required under PPACA are to be heard beginning in March 2012. However, because of the anti-injunction component, a decision on the health reform law may be delayed until 2015. And opponents have argued that the individual mandate is critical to the proposed requirement to offer health insurance coverage to everyone regardless of pre-existing conditions. If the individual mandate is unconstitutional, as argued, it is likely that the health insurance requirement will also fail. Planners and clients must continue to monitor the future of PPACA.

2.  S. L. Bradford, "Buying Private Health Insurance," *Smart Money*, January 7, 2008. Available at http://www.smartmoney.com/spend/family-money/buying-private-health-insurance-14819/.

3.  Branscome, J. M. *State Differences in the Cost of Job-Related Health Insurance, 2006.* July 2008. Data compiled from Medical Expenditure Panel Survey data. Available at http://meps.ahrq.gov/mepsweb/data_files/publications/st208/stat208.pdf#xml=http://meps.ahrq.gov/cgi-bin/texis/webinator/search/pdfhi.txt?query=cost+of+insurance&pr=MEPSFULLSITE&prox=page&rorder=500&rprox=500&rdfreq=500&rwfreq=500&rlead=500&sufs=0&order=r&cq=&id=4eaaac951ca, p. 1.

4.  Human Rights Campaign. Domestic Partner Benefits: Grossing Up to Offset Imputed Income Tax. Available at http://www.hrc.org/resources/entry/domestic-partner-benefits-grossing-up-to-offset-imputed-income-tax.

# Select Provisions of the Patient Protection and Affordable Care Act (PPACA) of 2010

| Year in Effect | Provisions Impacting Households |
| --- | --- |
| 2010 | Young adult children, up to age 26, may receive coverage through a parent's individual or group health insurance policy. Until 2014, grandfathered group health plans are not required to offer coverage to dependents eligible for employer coverage. |
| 2010 | Health insurance companies are prohibited from denying claims for covered children under the age of 19 because of a pre-existing condition. |
| 2010 | A temporary program to provide health insurance coverage to individuals with a qualifying pre-existing medical condition who have been uninsured for at least six months is established. The Pre-existing Condition Insurance Plan (PCIP) is operated by the states or HHS. For enrollment data for the PCIPs in all 50 states, go to Statehealthfacts.org.<br>Maximum cost-sharing is limited to the current legal HSA limit. |
| 2010 | Insurers are prohibited from rescinding coverage except in cases of fraud or material misrepresentation on the application; the law prohibits rescission of coverage due to errors or other technical mistakes on the application. |
| 2010 | Plans providing coverage for emergency services must do so without prior authorization, regardless of whether they are participating or nonparticipating providers. Emergency service charges for cost-sharing (e.g., copayments, coinsurance, and deductibles) cannot be greater for out-of-network providers than for in-network providers. But out-of-network providers are permitted to bill for any balance between the insurer's allowed amount and the provider's billed charges.<br>Note: This does not currently, and will not in the future, apply to grandfathered group health plans as long as grandfathered group health plan status is maintained. |
| 2010 | Women can receive treatment from a network obstetrician or gynecologist without first obtaining preauthorization or a referral from their primary care provider.<br>Note: This does not currently, and will not in the future, apply to grandfathered group health plans as long as grandfathered group health plan status is maintained. |
| 2010–2014 | Lifetime and annual benefit limits are prohibited on most benefits in employer-provided plans and individual policies, as explained below:<br>• Annual benefit limit restricted (2010–2013. From 9/23/12–12/31/13, the limit is $2 million.)<br>• Annual benefit limit prohibited (2014 and beyond, including grandfathered plans)<br>• Lifetime limits on most benefits prohibited |
| 2011 | The tax penalty on distributions from an HSA or an Archer Medical Savings Account (MSA) that are not used for qualified medical expenses increase from 10% and 15%, respectively, to 20%. |
| 2013 | The threshold for the itemized deduction for unreimbursed medical expenses increases from 7.5% to 10% of adjusted gross income; the increase for taxpayers age 65 and older is waived for tax years 2013–2016. |
| 2013 | The amount of contributions to a flexible spending account (FSA) for medical expenses is limited to $2,500 per year, increasing annually by a cost-of-living adjustment. |

| Year in Effect | Provisions Impacting Households |
| --- | --- |
| 2013 | The Medicare Part A (hospital insurance) tax rate on wages increases by 0.9% (from 1.45% to 2.35%) on earnings over $200,000 for individual taxpayers and $250,000 for married couples filing jointly, and a 3.8% tax is imposed on unearned income for higher-income taxpayers. |
| 2014 | All coverage exclusions are prohibited (including grandfathered plans) for pre-existing conditions, regardless of age. |
| 2014 | Waiting periods of longer than 90 days for employer-sponsored group coverage (including grandfathered plans) are prohibited. |
| 2014 | Cost-sharing subsidies and premium tax credits must be provided to eligible lower-income individuals and families to reduce out-of-pocket spending at the point of service. |
| 2014 | Most U.S. citizens and legal residents (exclusions apply) are required to have qualifying health coverage. Those without coverage pay a maximum tax penalty of $695 per year, phased in between 2014 and 2016. |

| Year in Effect | Additional Provisions Impacting Medicare Recipients |
| --- | --- |
| 2011–2013 | The beneficiary coinsurance rate in the Medicare Part D coverage gap will decrease gradually from 100% to 25% by 2020. In 2011, Medicare recipients became eligible for a 50% discount from pharmaceutical manufacturers on brand-name prescription drugs purchased in the Medicare Part D "doughnut hole"; beginning in 2013, federal subsidies are phased in to reduce coinsurance to 25% by 2020.<br>In 2011, federal subsidies for generic prescriptions filled in the Medicare Part D coverage gap begin, with the goal of providing federal subsidies of 75% of the generic drug cost by 2020. |
| 2011 | Select free, preventive services, such as annual wellness visits, screenings, vaccinations, and personalized prevention plans (i.e., smoking cessation) are provided for Medicare enrollees. Check with the provider to ensure that the services are free when covered by a Medicare Advantage Plan. |
| 2011 | The threshold for income-related Medicare Part B premiums for 2011 through 2019 are frozen at 2010 levels, causing more people to pay income-related premiums. The Medicare Part D premium subsidy is reduced for those with incomes above $85,000/individual and $170,000/couple. |

| Year in Effect | Provisions Impacting Businesses |
| --- | --- |
| 2010 | Small employers (those with 25 or fewer full-time employees and average annual wages of $50,000 or less) that purchase health insurance for employees are given a tax credit: 35% to 50% of employer cost or, for nonprofits, 25% to 35% of employer cost. All credits are phased in from 2010 to 2014, and they will continue, if all rules met.<br>• For tax years 2010 through 2013, a tax credit of up to 35% of the employer's contribution is provided.<br>• For tax years 2014 and later, for eligible small businesses that purchase coverage through the state Exchange, a tax credit of up to 50% of the employer's contribution is provided. |
| 2011 | Small employers that establish wellness programs receive grants for up to five years. |
| 2014 | Employers with 50 or more full-time employees that do not offer coverage are assessed a fee of $2,000 per full-time employee; the first 30 employees are excluded from the assessment. Applies to employers who do not offer health coverage and have at least one employee who receives a premium tax credit. Employers with more than 50 employees that offer coverage but have at least one full-time employee receiving a premium tax credit will pay the lesser of $3,000 for each employee receiving a premium credit or $2,000 for each full-time employee, excluding the first 30 employees |
| 2014 | Employers may offer employees rewards (premium discounts, waivers of cost-sharing requirements, or additional benefits) of up to 30% of the cost of coverage for participating in a wellness program and meeting certain health-related standards. |

| Year in Effect | Additional Administrative and Insurance Companies Impacts |
|---|---|
| 2010 | All health insurance plans are required to provide first-dollar coverage for a defined set of preventive health benefits; insurers are required to include wellness and prevention benefits such as immunizations and screenings with no cost to the insured. |
| 2010 | Plans are to provide an independent, external review of denied health insurance claims. |
| 2010–2013 | Employers are allowed to reduce health care costs through a temporary "reinsurance" program for early retirees (age 55 years or older) who are ineligible for Medicare. Under the law, participating employers, including state and local governments, are reimbursed for 80% of medical claims between $15,000 and $90,000 incurred by retired employees. |
| 2011 | Health insurance companies are required to publish detailed information about the percentage of each premium dollar the company spends on health care (called a medical loss ratio). |
| 2014 | Health insurance companies in the individual and small group markets are prohibited from charging higher premiums based on gender or health status. Premiums may vary only according to age, geography, tobacco use, and family coverage status. |
| 2014 | Create state-based American Health Benefit Exchanges and Small Business Health Options Program (SHOP) Exchanges to provide qualified coverage to individuals and small businesses with fewer than 100 employees. Exchanges are administered by a government agency or nonprofit organization and facilitate individuals' application to Exchange and other health care programs. State actions may be tracked using the Exchange Monitor on Statehealthfacts.org. |
| 2014 | Coverage for the individual and small group market, offered inside or outside of the Exchange, must include an "essential health benefits package" that provides:<br>• physician services; emergency services; hospitalization; maternity and newborn care; mental health, substance abuse, and behavioral health treatment; prescription drugs; rehabilitation services; laboratory services; and pediatric services.<br>• limited annual cost-sharing to the high-deductible health plans of the current law that qualify for HSAs. Deductibles for health plans in the small group market are limited to $2,000 for individuals and $4,000 for families, but exceptions apply.<br>• the creation of four categories of plans (bronze, silver, gold, platinum) based on the proportion of plan benefits covered. |
| 2018 | A 40% excise tax is assessed on "Cadillac health plans," or high-cost health benefit packages provided by employers. The first $10,200 of plan costs for an individual and the first $27,500 of plan costs for a family are excluded from the tax. |

**Note:** Some of the reforms listed here do not apply to grandfathered plans.

*Sources:*

H. Chaikind, C. W. Copeland, C. S. Redhead, and J. Staman. PPACA: A Brief Overview of the Law, Implementation, and Legal Challenges. Congressional Research Service. Available at http://www.nationalaglawcenter.org/assets/crs/R41664.pdf

Illinois Department of Insurance. Illinois Law v. The Patient Protection and Affordable Care Act

Positive Change From National Reform (Summary), June 2010. Available at: http://www.insurance.illinois.gov/hiric/comparisonsum.asp

The Henry J. Kaiser Family Foundation. Health Reform Source, Implementation Timeline. Available at: http://healthreform.kff.org/timeline.aspx

The Henry J. Kaiser Family Foundation. Focus on Health Reform. Summary of New Health Reform Law. April 15, 2011. Available at: http://www.kff.org/healthreform/upload/8061.pdf

U.S. Dept. of Health and Human Services. Provisions of the Affordable Care Act, By Year. Available at: http://www.healthcare.gov/law/timeline/full.html

# Disability Insurance Planning

## Learning Objectives

1. Understand the importance of disability insurance within financial planning.

2. Identify client situational factors that could uniquely affect a client's need for and selection of disability income coverage.

3. Demonstrate how to determine and quantify a client's need for and selection of short- and long-term disability income protection.

4. Summarize the definitions of disability and the basic forms of disability insurance, including different provisions available in the marketplace.

5. Identify the different sources of income replacement benefits that could be available to a disabled client.

6. Evaluate a client's current disability insurance coverage and options.

7. Identify and recommend appropriate and reasonable disability income protection strategies matched to a client's situation.

# Key Terms

any-occupation definition

automatic-increase option

average income tax rate

benefit integration

cost-of-living adjustment benefit

disability

elimination period

Family and Medical Leave Act (FMLA)

future-increase option

group disability replacement rider

guaranteed-renewable provision

income replacement ratio

long-term disability policy

loss-of-income test

modified own-occupation policy

noncancelable provision

own-occupation definition

recurrent disability provision

residual disability provision

short-term disability policy

social security rider

split-definition policy

waiver-of-premium clause

Workers' Compensation

**Figure 7.1** Systematic Financial Planning Process for Disability Insurance Planning

## DISABILITY INSURANCE: THE BASICS

A stark reality is facing the U.S. workforce. Among those of working age, more are likely to become disabled than to die in any given year. The Americans with Disabilities Act defines a **disability** as broadly meaning a physical or mental impairment that substantially limits a person's major life activities.[1] The incidence of disability varies based on many factors, including but not limited to gender, age, lifestyle, and occupation. Generally speaking, a 42-year-old worker is more than three times as likely to become disabled than to die during his or her working lifetime.[2] The purpose of this chapter is to review the steps for conducting a disability insurance planning analysis. The Systematic Financial Planning Process for Disability Insurance Planning is summarized in Figure 7.1.

As illustrated in Table 7.1, the probability of becoming disabled for 90 days or longer is significantly greater than the probability of death until a client reaches age 60 or older, although on a continually decreasing basis. This information is important for a planner to understand because it illustrates the fact that the need for disability insurance actually decreases over time. This is more similar to life insurance than health insurance, where the need generally increases as a client ages.

**Table 7.1** Probability of Death or Disability by Age

| Current Client Age | Probability of Death prior to Age 67[1] | Probability of Disability (Lasting 90 Days or Longer ) prior to Age 65[2] |
|:---:|:---:|:---:|
| 25 | 24% | 54% |
| 30 | 23% | 52% |
| 35 | 22% | 50% |
| 40 | 21% | 48% |
| 45 | 20% | 45% |
| 50 | 18% | 39% |
| 55 | 15% | 32% |
| 60 | 9% | 9% |

1.  Calculation is a simple summation of the probability of death at every age from the current age to age 67. Social Security Administration, Actuarial Publications, Period Life Table. Available at http://www.ssa.gov/oact/STATS/table4c6.html.

2.  National Association of Insurance Commissioners , 1985 Individual Disability Table A and B as reported by Kenneth Black, Jr., and Harold D. Skipper, Jr., in Life & Health Insurance, 13th Ed. (Upper Saddle River, NJ: Prentice Hall, 2000), 149. Often referenced as 85CIDA or 85CIDB.

The reported incidence of disability can vary greatly from the raw data presented in the original 1985 Insurance Commissioners' study that still serves as the primary source for projecting the probability of disability.[3] For instance, some data are segmented not only by age, but also by cause of disability claim as shown in Table 7.2, or by gender and occupation category of the claimant as shown in Table 7.3.

**Table 7.2** Probability of Disability from Accident or Illness by Age

| Current Client Age | Probability of Disability (Lasting 90 Days or Longer) prior to Age 65 |
|:---:|:---:|
| 25 | 40.3% |
| 30 | 38.5% |
| 35 | 36.5% |
| 40 | 34.0% |
| 45 | 30.5% |
| 50 | 26.2% |
| 55 | 20.5% |

*Source:* New York Life,  Disability Income Worksheet.  Based on data from the 1985 National Association of Insurance Commissioners' Individual Disability Table A.  Available at http://www.newyorklife.com/nyl/v/index.jsp?vgnextoid=9a7ba2b3019d2210a2b3019d221024301 cacRCRD.
Often referenced as 85CIDA.

It is obvious that different occupations have differing incidences of disability; therefore, when determining whether to issue a policy and the applicable premium, underwriters take into account the likelihood of disability based on the applicant's profession. There are four basic classifications for disability insurance underwriting: Class 1—Professional; Class 2—Skilled; Class 3—Nonhazardous or light manual labor; and Class 4—Hazardous or heavy manual labor.

**Table 7.3** Probability of Disability by Occupational Class and Gender

| Occupational Class | Probability of Disability (Lasting 90 Days or Longer) prior to Age 65, Male | Probability of Disability (Lasting 90 Days or Longer) prior to Age 65, Female |
|:---:|:---:|:---:|
| 1 | 18.0% | 26.2% |
| 2 | 33.3% | 38.2% |
| 3 | 46.1% | 48.9% |
| 4 | 49.2% | 52.3% |

*Source:*  Adapted from Robert W. Beal, FSA, The Real Risk of Disability in the U.S. May 17, 2007, p. 7. Milliman, Inc. Available at http://www.lifehappens.org/media1/LIFEDIResearch.pdf.  Based on 1985 National Association of Insurance Commissioners' Individual Disability Table A, often referenced as 85CIDA.

More detailed information is also available, such as the probability of disability occurring by age and gender within a specific occupational category.  For example, in Class 1—Professional, females are generally more likely to experience a disability lasting 90 days or longer, prior to age 65, than a male. At age 20 the probabilities are 29.9% and 20.2%, respectively for female and male Class 1 workers, and by age 40 the probabilities have declined to 24.8% for females and 18.2% for males.[4] Only by age 55 are probabilities more similar, at 13.5% for women and 12.6% for men working in professional, technical, and managerial occupations that are generally limited to office duties.[5]

Developing a basic understanding of disability statistics like those shown in these tables can be useful to financial planners. The more planners understand about the incidence of disability, the more effective they can be in exploring client situational factors to assess the need for disability insurance and the likelihood of insurance availability. Disability statistics can also be used to help a client objectively evaluate the need for insurance protection or alternative strategies to prepare for possible financial implications. In fact, the Council for Disability Awareness provides a Personal Disability Quotient calculator to help consumers estimate their chances of disability (see http://www.disabilitycanhappen.org/chances_disability/pdq.asp). Disability is not only more likely to occur between the ages of 25 and 65 than death, but it can often be more expensive. For a disabled individual, normal costs of living continue and often increase because of health care and rehabilitation expenses. Those very costs, compounded by the potential loss of most or all income earned, compel financial planners and clients to consider disability insurance needs.

When clients become disabled, they lose their most important financial asset: the ability to earn income. Without adequate disability coverage, clients might lose not only their income stream, but they could be forced to liquidate assets to meet the cost of living. The reduction or elimination of an income stream coupled with the untimely liquidation of assets can have disastrous effects on net worth and on the ability to fund long-term goals or reduce debt.

Whereas health insurance policies cover direct costs incurred as the result of sickness or disability, disability insurance policies cover the loss of earned income. Unearned income, such as passive, investment, or unearned business income, is not insurable with a disability policy. As with most insurance coverage, disability policies come in a variety of forms and coverage amounts, which vary by individual or group coverage. The amount of coverage available is related to the insured's earnings, and the amount of coverage purchased is typically a percentage of income and is normally purchased as monthly or annual income replacement. Just as deductibles and copayments make the insured partially responsible for the cost of health care, disability policies have elimination periods, benefit periods, and income replacement percentages.

Following an **elimination period**, or a waiting time during which no benefits are paid and the client can recover, benefits begin. **Short-term disability policies** cover short periods of lost income and typically begin coverage after the claimant has exhausted medical and personal leave days from work. They typically offer from six months up to a maximum of two years of benefits and are coordinated to work with a long-term disability policy so that the benefit period on the short-term policy matches the elimination period on the long-term policy. **Long-term disability policies** then provide benefit coverage for as little as three years or as long as a lifetime. Although some policies provide lifetime benefits, this is rare. Policies typically offer coverage until a specific age, such as 65 or 67. **Income replacement ratios** vary, but most policies offer a replacement of around 60% of predisability earned income. Additional information about standard long-term disability policy options is outlined in Table 7.4.

**Table 7.4** Long-term Disability Policy Definitions and Options Available

| Option | Description | Options Available | Typical Selection |
|---|---|---|---|
| Elimination period | Period of time the insured must be totally disabled before benefits can begin | 30, 60, 90, 180, or 365 days | Minimum: 180 days<br><br>Preferred: Matched to short-term policy benefit period or paid leave available |
| Benefit period | Period of time the insurance company is obligated to pay the monthly disability benefits | 3, 5, 10, or 20 years, until age 65, or lifetime | Minimum: 5 years<br><br>Preferred: Age of eligibility for Social Security/Medicare |
| Qualification period | Period of time the insured must be totally disabled before residual benefits can begin | Same as elimination period | Minimum: 180 days<br><br>Preferred: 30 days |
| Definition of occupation | Determines the conditions under which disability income benefits are paid | Own occupation or any occupation | Own occupation is preferred but should be coordinated with residual benefit rider |
| Residual benefit rider | Pays a partial benefit when the insured is not totally disabled | | Recommended, but coordinated with definition of occupation |
| Cost-of-living adjustment (COLA) rider | Total disability and residual benefits each year are increased by a specified percentage | | Recommended for maximum coverage, but expensive |

For example, Sasha has an employer-provided, group, long-term disability policy; the stated replacement ratio is 70% of gross income, and Sasha pays the entire premium with after-tax dollars. At first glance this may seem like adequate coverage; however, after analyzing the actual benefit that Sasha would receive, a financial planner might realize that there is actually a shortfall in covering his monthly expenses. Based on Sasha's gross monthly income of $4,200, he would receive a benefit of only $2,940 ($4,200 × 0.70).

The income replacement ratio can be linked to either gross (pretax) or net (post-tax) income, but either way the calculation is the same (covered income × replacement ratio), although the ratio is typically higher if after-tax income is used to calculate the monthly benefit. Although income-replacement ratios vary, disability policies also typically have a minimum and maximum income (or benefit) level that would override the replacement ratio in cases of very high or very low monthly income.

Disability insurance policies can also have a provision that coordinates income replacement benefits with Social Security Disability Insurance (SSDI) benefits; this is known as **benefit integration**. Benefit integration is necessary because in some cases the total amount of benefits paid under both private and social insurance can exceed the original income of the claimant; this is known as *over-insurance*. This creates a moral hazard wherein the claimant has no incentive to resume working. There are several methods for calculating the net benefit to be paid after integration with Social Security benefits; however, the most common is a straight dollar offset. In this situation the gross benefit of the private insurance is reduced by the amount of the Social Security benefit on a dollar-for-dollar basis.

Returning to Sasha, if his disability qualified him to receive SSDI benefits and his policy had an integration clause, his gross benefit would be reduced. In the original example he was to receive a monthly benefit of $2,940; however, if he received a monthly benefit of $800 from Social Security then the payment from his private insurance would decrease to $2,140. Although this may not seem like a problem, because Sasha is still receiving the aforementioned amount, he now has to deal with satisfying the definition of disability and the paperwork of two different sources.

In addition to short- and long-term disability insurance, another form of insurance could offer some protection if a client is injured while at work or becomes ill as a result of work. Workers' Compensation insurance provides income replacement benefits as well as payments for medical claims and vocational training benefits. Although exact insurance coverage amounts vary from state to state (e.g., Virginia covers 66.6% of after-tax earned income, Michigan covers 80% of after-tax earned income), these benefits are not subject to income tax.[6]

Most states require business owners to provide Workers' Compensation insurance or proof of self-insurability if they have any employees. (One notable exception is that in California any roofing contractor must carry Workers' Compensation insurance even if the contractor does not have any employees).[7] This insurance requirement was established so that employees injured on the job would not have to sue for lost wages or medical expenses incurred from a workplace accident.

## ANALYZE THE CLIENT'S CURRENT SITUATION

Almost all earners need insurance to provide income replacement in the event of disability. Only those with substantial wealth can continue their lifestyle without some annual inflow of income. Even then, long-term asset depletion can seriously erode all but the largest of fortunes when no earned income is available to meet current expenses.

These considerations are relevant for those of average means and of particular concern for single persons. If, as the result of a disability, an individual's earning capacity is significantly reduced or eliminated, what revenues are available to maintain current lifestyle? Without disability income replacement insurance or considerable net worth, options are limited. Minimally, two-earner households have the advantage of a second income source, but much depends on whether one spouse's disability will affect the earnings of the other spouse because of possible caregiving responsibilities.

Unlike scenarios when a spouse in a heterosexual marriage becomes disabled, the issue of paying for hospital and day-to-day living expenses can be much more burdensome for those in domestic partner relationships. In a domestic partner relationship—particularly in states that do not recognize same-sex marriage—any support above the maximum gift amount ($13,000 per year) to help pay for rent, mortgage, utility, or other daily expenses is considered a taxable gift from one partner to the other. Although a partner could pay a hospital directly for health care costs to avoid the gift tax, this is not always a practical solution to offset other expenses associated with disability. For this reason, disability coverage is highly recommended for those involved in a domestic partner relationship.

An alternative that provides some protection for a disabled person's job if not income, or to care for a disabled family member is the **Family and Medical Leave Act** (FMLA). Although the FMLA guarantees a job upon return to work, leave is without pay and the protected leave period is limited to 12 workweeks per 12-month period.[8] Although these 12 weeks are in addition to any accrued vacation or other form of personal leave, the employee could still fall far short of the time necessary to fully recover and return to work.  FMLA also allows a qualified employee to use the leave to care for a son or daughter, spouse or parent with a serious health condition. However, unless the state specifically recognizes the partner as a spouse, either by means of same-sex or common law marriage, the FMLA does not provide leave for domestic partners.

Self-employed clients, in particular, can be hit hard economically and personally as they assume domestic duties, especially when children and possible caregiving duties are involved. These issues, and many others, are central to the analysis of a client's current situation when planning for disability insurance needs.

Analyzing a client's current disability insurance coverage is relatively simple, but projecting the need for disability insurance protection clearly is not. Insurance information and client situational factors are collected during the discovery and data-gathering phase of the systematic planning process. Issues to evaluate, some of which have been mentioned already as background for analyzing the client's situation, include:

- assets available for use in case of a catastrophic health claim;

- family health status and related health history;

- marital status, household situation, number of wage earners or other family demographics that can trigger insurance needs;

- self-employment or employment in a hazardous profession or occupation;

- lifestyle or recreational choices; and

- attitudes, such as risk tolerance.

By exploring the possible future need for disability income protection and currently available coverage, the planner and client become informed of issues that could affect the selection of disability income protection strategies. The next step in the analysis is the review of the client's currently in-force coverage or the availability of other resources. Gathering a variety of information about a client's disability insurance situation is critical to a thorough analysis of the current situation and is the foundation for identifying appropriate strategies and recommendations.

## Determine and Quantify the Client's Need for Disability Insurance

Not every income earner has access to or the ability to pay for disability insurance. Far too many people ignore the risk of disability or assume that alternate employment would be available to provide some income. For those who acknowledge the need, the amount of coverage must be considered for both short- and long-term income replacement needs. Answering this question is particularly important to self-employed clients, especially those who are single. The first step when analyzing a client's disability insurance situation focuses on addressing the issues of the need for and the amount of disability insurance coverage necessary.

Unlike life insurance planning, where needs calculators are widely available to planners and the public, few disability calculators exist. Most calculators offer a simplistic estimate based on an income replacement ratio, or at most they reduce the estimated need by projecting benefits from existing group coverage and Social Security. Independent financial planners who do not rely on integrated planning software will have to develop their own disability needs assessment methods and calculations, because no standard methodology exists.

Exhibits 7.1 through 7.4 provide examples of the disability analysis worksheets included in the Financial Facilitator. These worksheets incorporate factors to consider when assessing the short- and long-term disability income replacement needs of a household when one or two earners become disabled. In general, the amount of coverage needed is contingent on several issues:

- the amount of leave available;

- the amount of savings available;

- the income from a partner or spouse;

- the projected length of the disability period;

- the projected severity of the disability; and

- the desired lifestyle of the earner.

Although projecting the length and severity of a disability may seem pointless because of the endless possibilities, this estimation must be done. For example, if a client works in a high-risk industry where the probability of severe disability is great, then the client might be more likely to receive Social Security benefits. In addition to government-provided coverage, a number of alternatives are available to meet income replacement needs. For short-term disabilities, employer-provided sick leave or vacation time could yield 100% of after-tax earnings for a limited time, or an emergency savings fund or other financial assets could be liquidated to provide money until a short-term policy provides some level of income replacement.

Exhibit 7.1 illustrates how different elimination and benefit periods can be entered or altered in the Financial Facilitator. The output from this analysis can help the planner and client choose the optimal disability insurance needs outcome. This method allows planners to approach the short-term coverage need in two ways: by (1) advising the client to liquidate financial assets to cover 100% of expenses for as long as needed; or (2) suggesting that the client share the financial responsibility with the insurance company as soon as possible. In either case, longer elimination periods and lower monthly benefit amounts result in reduced premiums.

Under the first method, a planner might recommend a policy with a longer elimination period, for example 180 days instead of 90 days, but with a higher earned-income replacement-percentage benefit, such as 70% instead of 50%. The longer a client can comfortably support a chosen lifestyle from savings, other sources of income, or employer leave, the less dependent the client is on insurance coverage.

In the second scenario, a planner might recommend the shortest elimination period available but with a lower monthly benefit. For example, if the client is currently saving a significant portion of earnings but has not built up a considerable amount, the monthly income replacement benefit could be reduced to match the client's expenses excluding the amount currently contributed to savings.

**Exhibit 7.1** The Disability Calculator, Information Section

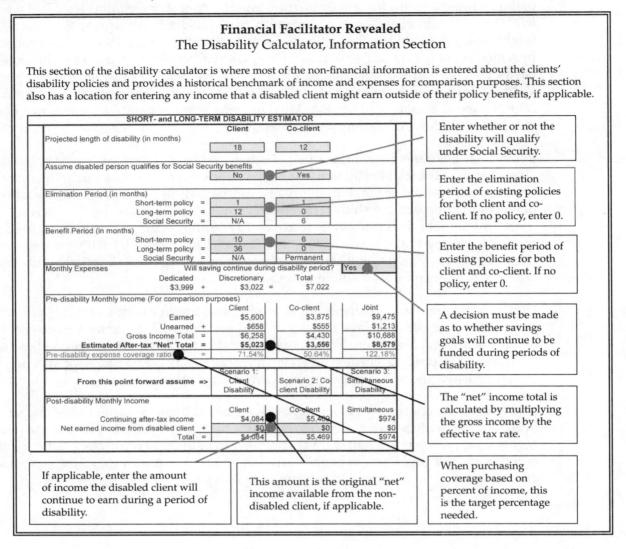

For long-term disabilities, the establishment of an emergency savings fund is even more important. Although 180-day elimination periods are the most common for long-term disability policies, a longer elimination period extending to one year will further reduce the premium cost of the policy. In addition to the emergency fund, some of the same aspects of a client's financial capacity to fund short-term expenses are also relevant to the assessment of income replacement needs for long-term disability. The amount of investment assets available, income from a partner or spouse, the severity and length of the disability, and the lifestyle of the earner are considered. Complexity is further heightened by other planning factors, such as access to available local, state, or federal insurance benefits or Veteran's Administration benefits (if the disability occurs during active or reserve service). Additionally, federal taxation of benefits must also be considered; state taxes could also apply but they vary by state and are ignored for simplicity in the Financial Facilitator. Exhibits 7.2 and 7.3 show how various sources of income are included in the calculation and illustrate how taxes reduce the net benefit the client receives.

**Exhibit 7.2** The Disability Calculator, Short-term Benefits Section

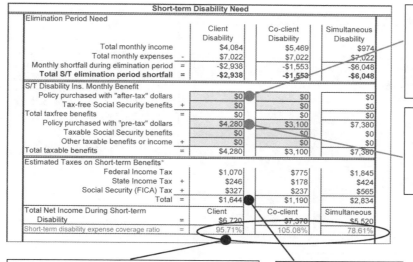

**Financial Facilitator Revealed**
The Disability Calculator, Short-term Benefits Section

This section of the disability calculator determines the difference between short-term disability income available and current monthly expenses. The difference in this section is displayed as a ratio. If the ratio is less than 100%, then the client is adequately covered. If the ratio is more than 100% then the client will not have enough benefit income to cover expenses.

| Short-term Disability Need | | Client Disability | Co-client Disability | Simultaneous Disability |
|---|---|---|---|---|
| **Elimination Period Need** | | | | |
| Total monthly income | | $4,084 | $5,469 | $974 |
| Total monthly expenses | - | $7,022 | $7,022 | $7,022 |
| Monthly shortfall during elimination period | = | -$2,938 | -$1,553 | -$6,048 |
| **Total S/T elimination period shortfall** | = | **-$2,938** | **-$1,553** | **-$6,048** |
| **S/T Disability Ins. Monthly Benefit** | | | | |
| Policy purchased with "after-tax" dollars | | $0 | $0 | $0 |
| Tax-free Social Security benefits | + | $0 | $0 | $0 |
| Total taxfree benefits | = | $0 | $0 | $0 |
| Policy purchased with "pre-tax" dollars | | $4,280 | $3,100 | $7,380 |
| Taxable Social Security benefits | | $0 | $0 | $0 |
| Other taxable benefits or income | + | $0 | $0 | $0 |
| Total taxable benefits | = | $4,280 | $3,100 | $7,380 |
| **Estimated Taxes on Short-term Benefits** | | | | |
| Federal Income Tax | | $1,070 | $775 | $1,845 |
| State Income Tax | + | $246 | $178 | $424 |
| Social Security (FICA) Tax | + | $327 | $237 | $565 |
| Total | = | $1,644 | $1,190 | $2,834 |
| Total Net Income During Short-term Disability | = | Client $6,720 | Co-client $7,379 | Simultaneous $5,520 |
| Short-term disability expense coverage ratio | = | 95.71% | 105.08% | 78.61% |

Enter the monthly benefit from any policies the client purchased using after-tax dollars, through an employer-provided cafeteria plan or other private provider.

Enter the monthly benefit from any policies the client purchased using pre-tax dollars, through an employer-provided cafeteria plan.

Ratios show the percentage of expenses the client's disability benefits can cover during a period of disability. Ratios should ideally be more than 100% to avoid any possible income shortfalls. However, due to purchase limitations, this may not be possible.

This is the total tax liability on disability earnings and taxable benefits.

**Exhibit 7.3** The Disability Calculator, Long-term Benefits Section

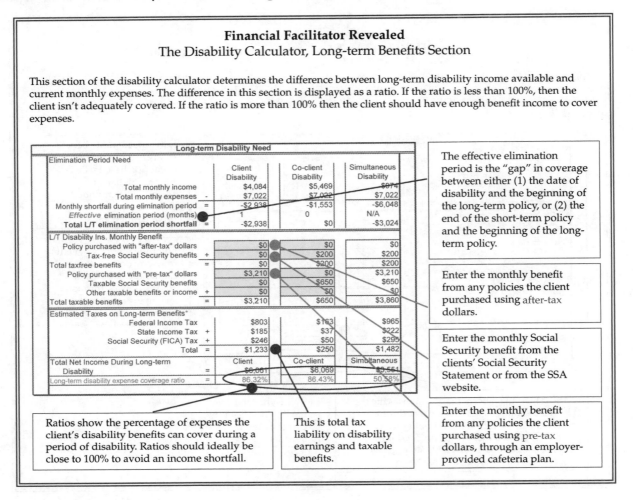

### Financial Facilitator Revealed
### The Disability Calculator, Long-term Benefits Section

This section of the disability calculator determines the difference between long-term disability income available and current monthly expenses. The difference in this section is displayed as a ratio. If the ratio is less than 100%, then the client isn't adequately covered. If the ratio is more than 100% then the client should have enough benefit income to cover expenses.

The effective elimination period is the "gap" in coverage between either (1) the date of disability and the beginning of the long-term policy, or (2) the end of the short-term policy and the beginning of the long-term policy.

Enter the monthly benefit from any policies the client purchased using after-tax dollars.

Enter the monthly Social Security benefit from the clients' Social Security Statement or from the SSA website.

Enter the monthly benefit from any policies the client purchased using pre-tax dollars, through an employer-provided cafeteria plan.

Ratios show the percentage of expenses the client's disability benefits can cover during a period of disability. Ratios should ideally be close to 100% to avoid an income shortfall.

This is total tax liability on disability earnings and taxable benefits.

The key figure for determining an insurance need is generally based on an income replacement ratio of 60% to 70% of earned income. However, some planners prefer to estimate income needs more conservatively by using a 100% income replacement ratio. For example, assume that a client currently earns $90,000 per year before taxes. Using a 70% income replacement ratio, the client's total annual disability need is $63,000 of available, or after-tax, income. This amount is equivalent to the client's after-tax income before the disability, assuming a 30% combined federal and state marginal tax bracket. However, this seemingly straightforward estimation is complicated by three factors that must always be considered:

1. Disability insurance pays a fixed amount of monthly indemnity, but the amount that can be purchased is limited to prevent over-insurance, or the disincentive to return to work.

2. Disability policies often have an integration clause, also to protect against the moral hazard of over-insurance by instituting an offset for other benefits.

3. Disability benefits can be subject to income tax depending on whether the recipient paid the premiums and whether the premiums were paid with pretax or post-tax dollars.

Projected sources of disability replacement income, such as existing disability group or private policy benefits; local, state, or federal disability benefits; investment income; and veterans' benefits should be subtracted from the total income replacement need. This amount should also be reduced by the amount of projected earnings by the disabled client as well as income from other household earners. The net result, as shown in Exhibit 7.4, is the amount of income that (1) must be replaced by additional disability insurance, if additional insurance can be purchased, or (2) foregone.

To estimate Social Security disability income benefits, consult the client's annual benefit statement, or use the online calculators on the Social Security Web site (http://www.socialsecurity.gov/planners/benefitcalculators.htm). Disability benefits are based on average lifetime earnings and calculated similarly to the calculation of retirement benefits.

**Exhibit 7.4** The Disability Calculator, Results Section

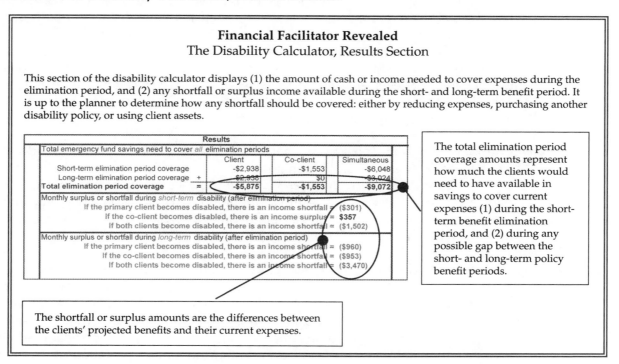

As shown in Exhibits 7.1 through 7.4, disability insurance analyses consider a client's actual expenses as well as financial assets and other income sources to meet elimination period and insurance shortfall financial needs. The accuracy of this analysis method is also enhanced by incorporating the effects of taxation on benefits received. Finally, this approach allows the planner and client to consider different scenarios, such as reducing expenses, increasing income, purchasing additional disability coverage, or liquidating assets, to arrive at the best combination of insurance and self-insurance approaches.

### Planning for Special Populations:
### Disability Insurance for High-Income Earners

Disability planning for the high earner may seem like a Wall Street executive complaining that her bonus was cut by 80% to a mere $350,000. But high-income earners, like moderate earners, are accustomed to a certain lifestyle. A disability could create serious financial repercussions. Multiple mortgages, private school tuition for children, and domestic help could all be considered fixed expenses not easily continued in the event of a disability.

Many disability insurance policies limit the maximum monthly benefit regardless of the stated percent of coverage. This is especially prevalent in group policies. For example, a group disability policy could impose an absolute limit of $6,000 of monthly benefits or limit the amount of earned income includable in the benefits calculation to $120,000 of annual income. In either case, a high-income earner could face a situation where the group disability policy covers far less than the stated 60% of income.

Although many high-income earners might also have sizable net worth that could provide adequate unearned or investment income to fill the earnings gap, others might not have nearly enough to support their current lifestyle, which could create undue hardship on the earner's family. In these cases, the executive, doctor, or entertainer might want to purchase a supplemental disability income policy. These policies, although expensive, offer a much higher income limit—in some cases, $1 million or more—and are normally underwritten by specialty insurers, such as Lloyd's of London.

In addition to filling an income gap, a supplemental policy can provide an extra layer of financial protection that replaces a larger percentage of total compensation because it includes incentive pay, bonuses, or commissions as part of the earnings covered. Although moral hazard prohibits any policy from providing benefits greater than earned income, a supplemental policy can offer additional guarantees and enhanced portability.

The issue of disability insurance covering only earned income creates an additional issue for self-employed business owners—not all of whom are high-income earners, but they might be. Business owners often overlook the fact that their business generates income attributable to the owner's work that is not covered under the disability income insurance definition of *personal, earned income*. An example of this is a business that generates $250,000 of revenue per year based on the activities of the owner, but the owner draws a salary of only one-half that amount, choosing to reinvest the remainder in the company. That reinvestment would decrease or even cease as a result of a lost-time injury or illness and would not be replaced by a standard disability insurance policy. Strategies to prepare for this uncertainty are available, but the important point is not to overlook these issues when advising self-employed business owners.

## Document and Evaluate Current Disability Insurance Coverage

The second step to analyze and evaluate a client's situation involves reviewing in-force disability coverage. Of those covered by disability insurance, most have group insurance instead of private coverage. It is important for planners to determine the type of coverage a client has (e.g., short- or long-term) and what provisions the coverage includes or excludes. Examining a policy for the definitions of disability and occupation, elimination period requirements, and any pre-existing condition exclusions is extremely important.

Of paramount importance is defining the type of disability coverage to purchase. Policies fall into two categories, **any-occupation** and **own-occupation,** based on the policy owner's ability to maintain gainful employment in a specific or nonspecific occupation. An any-occupation policy pays reduced or no benefits as long as the insured can maintain any employment, regardless of the level of skill or compensation relative to pre-disability employment. With an own-occupation policy, at least partial benefits are paid if the claimant cannot continue to hold gainful employment on a similar skill and compensation level as before the disabling event. Much more information on this topic, as well as modified own-occupation policies, are discussed in the Strategies section of this chapter.

Although a client can be covered through an employer-sponsored plan and therefore changing the policy could be difficult or impossible, if plan provisions are unattractive (e.g., do not provide sufficient coverage, or the policy is from a company with a poor claims record, a history of customer complaints, or low financial ratings) the client may have to opt out of the group coverage. In this case, the planner could recommend that the client purchase an individual private policy or, at a minimum, retain any free group coverage and purchase a supplemental individual policy. Although, again, it is important to consider the potential for apparent over-insurance that could reduce a client's ability to purchase a supplementary policy.

A planner can also provide an important service by helping clients understand the relationship between taxation of any future disability benefits received and the taxation of current disability premiums paid. Clearly, this question could be affected by a number of qualitative and quantitative considerations. For risk-averse clients with a family history of chronic or debilitating health conditions, paying taxes on the imputed income derived from employer contributions could result in significant tax savings on disability benefits.

---

### Disability Insurance Planning Tip: Tax Credit for Benefits

When disability benefits are included in gross income, a federal tax credit might be available to clients who are totally and permanently disabled. However, income guidelines and other restrictions apply in the calculation of the credit. For more information, see Publication 524: *Credit for the Elderly or the Disabled*, at http://www.irs.gov/pub/irs-pdf/p524.pdf.

---

For private or employer-provided policies, the taxability of benefits is based on who paid the annual premium during the plan year in which the disability occurs. For purposes of determining the extent of taxability, there are six basic premium payment scenarios, as shown in Table 7.5.

**Table 7.5** Taxability of Disability Insurance Benefits Matrix

| Scenario | Type of Policy | Premiums Paid by | Premiums Included in Income | Taxability of Benefits |
|----------|----------------|------------------|------------------------------|------------------------|
| 1 | Group | Employer | No | Yes |
| 2 | Group | Both | No | Yes |
| 3 | Group | Employer | Yes | No* |
| 4 | Group | Both | Yes | No* |
| 5 | Group | Employee | Yes | No* |
| 6 | Individual | Owner | N/A | No |

*Taxes will be due on the portion of benefits attributable to any employer-paid premiums over the preceding three policy years.

If the client is insured through a group plan paid for completely by the employer and elects to exclude employer contributions from taxable income, any future benefit received is fully taxable to the employee. For employees who irrevocably elect to include the employer contributions as income (and therefore they are taxable in the current year), any benefits resulting from a disability occurring during the plan year would avoid taxation, prorated to the portion of employer-provided premium contributions made over the preceding three policy years. If the premium cost is shared between the employer and the employee (i.e., a contributory plan), then taxes will be due on the portion of benefits attributable to the employer-paid premiums over the preceding three policy years. If the premium is paid completely by the insured with after-tax dollars, all benefits will be received tax free. When conducting a disability insurance analysis, it is very important that financial planners consider whether a client is better served to pay the taxes on the premiums received today or the benefits received in the future. Helping clients financially prepare for the unknown is a basic tenet of financial planning, and in this case client situational factors such as marital/partner situation, type of employment, self-employment, or recreational pursuits must be considered.

Again returning to the Sasha example, assume that this time the premiums for his policy are fully covered by his employer, he does not elect to pay income taxes on the premiums, and the stated replacement ratio is still 70% of gross income. Based on Sasha's gross monthly income of $4,200, he would now receive a net benefit of only $2,352 [($4,200 × 0.70) × 0.80], assuming an **average income tax rate** of 20%. The average tax rate is simply the ratio of local, state, federal, and FICA income tax paid to the amount of taxable income. However, if Sasha had chosen to pay income tax on the premiums paid on his behalf, then the benefits of the policy would be excludable from income tax.

For government-sponsored plans, it is easier to determine potential tax liability. Workers' Compensation benefits are fully taxable. A portion of benefits received from Social Security is tax free. The taxability of Social Security disability benefits follows the same guidelines as other Social Security benefits (i.e., retirement and survivor benefits). As shown in Table 7.6, the amount of Social Security disability benefits subject to federal income tax is determined by the client's annual income, including tax exempt income. It is important to note that for married-filing-separately clients, the income threshold, referred to as the *base amount*, is zero, which means all Social Security benefits would be taxed from the first dollar if the client *lived with the spouse at any time during the tax year.*

**Table 7.6** Limits for Social Security Disability Benefits Taxation

| Benefit Taxation Level | Filing Status and Base Amount | |
|---|---|---|
| | One-half of Social Security Disability Benefits Plus Annual Income* for Other Filers** | One-half of Social Security Disability Benefits Plus Annual Income* for Joint Filer |
| 0% | $0 to $25,000 | $0 to $32,000 |
| Up to 50% | $25,000 to $34,000 | $32,000 to $44,000 |
| Up to 85% | Above $34,000 | Above $44,000 |

*Annual income is defined as all income, including tax-exempt income, and is not reduced by exclusions for the following:

- interest from qualified U.S. savings bonds;

- employer-provided adoption benefits;

- foreign earned income or foreign housing; or

- income earned by bona fide residents of American Samoa or Puerto Rico.

For more information, see IRS Publication 915. Available at http://www.irs.gov/publications/p915/ar02.html#en_US_2011_publink100097874.

**Other filers include those filing as single, head of household, qualifying widow/widower with a dependent child, or married individuals filing separately who did not live with their spouses at any time during the year. The base amount is $0 for married persons filing separately who lived together during the year.

*Source:* IRS, *Social Security and Equivalent Railroad Retirement Benefits,* 2011. Available at http://www.irs.gov/publications/p915/ar02.html#en_US_2011_publink100097874. See "Are Any of Your Benefits Taxable" and "How Much is Taxable?"

**Planning for Special Populations: Families with Disabled Children**

Wage earners' disabilities have obvious emotional and financial repercussions. But families with a disabled child, whether disabled from birth or as the result of an accident or illness, face very different financial planning hurdles. Although this situation does not fit the standard disability insurance planning need, because there is no loss of income, a disability to a child, whether psychological or physical, can be equally financially devastating and in extreme cases can mean a loss of income for life.

Social Security provides a financial safety net for such situations as long as the child's disability results in "marked and severe functional limitations" for at least 12 continuous months; this program is known as *Supplemental Security Income* (SSI).[9] In general a child must meet the same eligibility requirements pertaining to disability status and income as an adult, but additionally the parents or caregiver's income must also be within eligibility limits if the child is under the age of 18. In addition to SSI, a minor child would also be eligible for state-provided medical services such as reduced-cost or free clinics.

Having a disabled child creates issues in addition to the obvious financial and emotional strain.  Education planning can be much more complex. Instead of planning for college funding, a family or caregiver may be faced with determining the need, availability, and cost of a special education environment for grade school. Estate planning is another area that becomes more difficult when a child is receiving public aid. Bequeathing assets to a child with a physical disability may not be prudent, but bequeathing assets to a developmentally disabled child may be impossible or even illegal. In either case, a special-needs trust may be the most prudent way for parents to leave assets to a child without potentially disrupting or terminating the child's eligibility for Social Security or Medicaid benefits. The lesser-known support trust could be another vehicle for leaving assets to children; however, beneficiaries of such trusts are normally ineligible for financial assistance.

Once a child reaches the age of 18 and is still eligible for Social Security benefits, then SSI can stop and Social Security Disability Insurance begin provided the parent is insured under Social Security *and* is receiving retirement or disability benefits or is deceased.[10]  The biggest difference between the two programs is that benefits paid under the SSDI benefit program are not need-based, meaning that the child could work for additional income, if able. Furthermore, if the child is ineligible for SSDI benefits because of the parent's status, the child can continue on SSI under certain circumstances.

Planning for a family with a disabled or special-needs child  obviously takes a great deal of expertise given (1) the sensitivity of the planning and the advisor-client trust required and (2) the complexity of navigating the numerous legal, tax, and policy guidelines that must be followed.

# STRATEGIES

## Review Prospective Disability Insurance Planning Strategies

Analysis of a client's current situation provides a foundation for the review of potential strategies to best meet the client's short- and long-term disability income replacement needs. This is the third step in the disability insurance planning process. Although the analysis of a client's current situation is the advisor's responsibility, an equally important task is communicating findings to the client as a foundation for understanding any changes needed.

The review of current policy coverage within a comprehensive plan can be summarized and presented in a number of ways. Exhibit 7.5 provides a simple but thorough approach, using a table and summary bullet points to present recommendations for a client's disability coverage.

**Exhibit 7.5** Disability Insurance Summary for Gerald and Jessie Kinder

### Disability Insurance Summary for Gerald and Jessie Kinder

|  | **Policy 1** | **Policy 2** | **Policy 3** | **Policy 4** |
|---|---|---|---|---|
| Insured | Gerald | Gerald | Jessie | Jessie |
| Type of policy | Group, short-term | Group, long-term | Group, short-term | Group, long-term |
| Provider | Select Insurance Co. | Surety Insurance Co. | Select Insurance Co. | Surety Insurance Co. |
| Benefit | 80% of gross salary | 60% of gross salary | 100% of gross salary | 60% of gross salary |
| Waiting period | 0 days | 90 days | 0 days | 90 days |
| Benefit period | 90 days | 5 years | 90 days | To age 65 |
| Frequency | Monthly | Monthly | Biweekly | Biweekly |
| Premium | Employer-paid | Employer-paid | Employer-paid | $15 |
| Frequency | Monthly | Monthly | Biweekly | Biweekly |
| Taxation of premiums | Premiums included in income | Premiums included in income | Premiums excluded from income | Premiums paid with after-tax income |

## Observations:

- Client insurance is provided through three employer-sponsored plans and one private plan.

- Disability is defined as own occupation in all policies.

- Each policy has a cost-of-living adjustment (COLA).

- Short-term coverage is sufficient, because the entire elimination period of the long-term policy is covered.  Gerald's long-term policy is adequate but not ideal, because it does not provide coverage until the age of retirement.  Should a disability extend beyond the average length of disability for a 40-year-old, he would be dependent on Social Security Disability benefits, assuming he qualified.

- Jessie's short-term disability benefits would be subject to income taxes; however, all other disability benefits for both Jessie and Gerald would be received tax free.

- Current emergency savings funds are adequate to meet household needs, assuming Gerald or Jessie remains employed. Employed spouses who use the Family and Medical Leave Act are not paid, but they are guaranteed employment.

# Identify Prospective Disability Insurance Planning Strategies

The following product and procedural strategies represent just a sampling of alternatives used by financial planners in practice. When planning for a client's disability protection, it is important to consider strategies for choosing the most appropriate product(s), structuring the insurance contracts, coordinating benefits between group and individual contracts, and coordinating benefits with social insurance, if applicable. Strategies to meet both short- and long-term needs must be considered, as well as coordination between the two.

## Product Strategy 1: Purchase an Own-occupation Policy

**Advantage:** The most generous disability insurance definition is known as *own-occupation disability coverage*. Under this definition, an insured receives benefits if, as the result of sickness or injury, the client is unable to perform the specific duties of his or her own occupation. The difference between the "own" and "any" occupation definitions is significant. It is quite possible that a client becomes disabled and unable to work in the chosen occupation but is able to perform the duties of another, unrelated occupation. In this case, if the client's coverage is any-occupation, no benefit is received. Most clients prefer an own-occupation policy.

**Disadvantage:** The insurance industry is moving away from offering the more narrowly defined own-occupation policy; thus, own-occupation coverage could be more difficult to find. Policies that are available can be quite expensive. Insurance professionals report that a premium equivalent to 5% of a client's gross income is not unrealistic.

## Product Strategy 2: Purchase a Modified Own-occupation Policy

**Advantage:** Trends within the privately provided or nongroup disability insurance market are ominous. Although own-occupation policies are appropriate for the majority of clients, finding such a policy is becoming increasingly difficult. Several insurance companies have either stopped offering own-occupation policies or significantly reduced the number of policies issued on a yearly basis. When and if an own-occupation policy can be obtained, the annual premium can be quite expensive.

The reason for this is the increasing number of claims being filed and the high costs associated with providing benefits to those who become disabled. Increasing costs are due, in part, to the types of disabilities that precipitate these claims. For instance, in the past nearly all disabilities were physical in nature. More recently, the number of mental and emotional disability claims has skyrocketed. This has had the most significant negative impact on coverage availability and premiums.

To meet the needs of the market while protecting the underwriting profitability of insurance companies, some firms have begun to offer modified own-occupation and split-definition disability policies (see below). A **modified own-occupation** policy is one that pays only if an insured is unable to engage in his or her chosen occupation and is also unable to work in a reasonable alternative occupation—or one for which the client is qualified by education, training, or experience. This strategy is appropriate in cases where a client does not qualify for an own-occupation policy or is unable to afford the premium for an own-occupation policy. The premium for a modified own-occupation policy can be significantly less than for an own-occupation policy.

**Disadvantage:** Although the premium is less than for own-occupation coverage, some clients find that the premium still exceeds their insurance budget. A projection of 1% to 3% of gross client income provides a rough estimate of the premium cost for a disability policy, but elimination period, benefit period, age, optional riders, premium structure, occupational class, gender, state, health, amount and type of coverage, and benefit amount all influence cost.[11]

### Product Strategy 3: Purchase a *Split-definition* Policy

**Advantage:** A **split-definition policy** incorporates the preceding modified own-occupation definition with a short- and long-term disability definition. Specifically, to obtain benefits, the insured must be unable to engage in his or her own occupation for a certain period of time, usually two years. After the specified period, benefits are continued if the insured is unable to engage in a suitable and reasonable occupation.

It is apparent from these definitions that insurance companies want to encourage clients to re-enter the workforce as soon as possible. To this end, a **loss-of-income test** can also be used to determine benefit eligibility. This method considers earnings before the disability, earnings in the new position, and the maximum benefit coverage originally provided by the policy. If eligible, the insured receives a percentage of the maximum monthly benefits relative to the percentage of earned income lost between the two jobs.

This strategy is cost effective and a more readily available alternative than an own-occupation policy. The initial benefit period is contingent on the inability to perform all or the principal duties of the insured's occupation. This time offers the insured the opportunity for rehabilitation or other training, which could be necessary to pursue employment that is a reasonable match, or fit, according to prior training, education, or experience. The "split" in the definition and the coverage periods allows benefits to continue if the insured is unable to pursue related employment.

**Disadvantage:** The initial period is typically two years, which may be insufficient for retraining, counseling, and therapy to adequately prepare the insured for re-entry into a related occupation. But benefits do not continue unless the insured is unable to function in any related occupation as defined by prior training, education, or experience.

### Product Strategy 4: Purchase an *Employer-* or *Group-provided* Policy

**Advantage:** This strategy allows a client to purchase group plan coverage, which typically costs less than a private policy. This strategy may use pretax dollars or, in some cases, taxable dollars. Medical examinations are usually not required. An initial waiting period might apply to new employees. Existing employees may be eligible to enroll only during an annual open-enrollment period.

**Disadvantage:** Because of the pretax premiums, any benefits received are taxed at the recipient's current federal marginal tax bracket. This can be offset by the credit for the disabled, if the individual is eligible, including retirement for permanent and total disability. If the option to pay premiums with after-tax dollars is available, any benefits received avoid taxation.

Coverage is typically standardized for an entire employment group. In a fluctuating job environment, primary coverage through an employer can be problematic. Disability coverage ends at termination of employment, leaving clients vulnerable to disability losses at the most inopportune time.

### Product Strategy 5: Consider a Mortgage Disability Insurance Policy

**Advantage:** This strategy offers a client another insurance alternative if the earned income replacement ratio is lower than needed to meet the majority of expenses, or if the individual is the sole source of income.

**Disadvantage:** Disability insurance offered through a mortgage company has additional drawbacks that are not generally mentioned at the time of sale. The insurance policy itself could be a fully restrictive policy, meaning that a client must be completely unable to engage in gainful employment to collect. Additionally, there may be a waiting period before it starts to pay, a time during which premiums must still be paid. This is not always the case, so research is necessary. Finally, the cost of such insurance is often based on the amount of the loan—so much per thousand dollars of coverage needed. Private disability insurance is based on the income needed and is usually a percentage of latest salary; thus, a client is probably able to draw more using this method than if the benefit payment was based on the mortgage alone.

### Procedural Strategy 1: Do Not Purchase Group or Individual Disability Coverage and Rely on Social Security Benefits

**Advantage:** The disability insurance definition used by the Social Security Administration is by far the most stringent. The qualification for coverage is based strictly on an any-occupation definition. To collect benefits, the insured must be currently eligible to receive Social Security benefits and be permanently and totally disabled. According to the Social Security Administration, *permanently disabled* means that the disability is expected to last at least 12 months, and *totally disabled* means that the insured is unable to work at any occupation. Furthermore, there is a five-month elimination period, and benefits do not include reimbursement for related medical expenses. Finally, the recipient can have no more than an average of $1,010 in earned income per month in 2012.[12] This is the limit for substantial gainful activity (employment), and it is established annually by the Social Security Administration.

The one advantage to Social Security coverage is that the cause of a disability does not have to be work related to qualify. So even if someone slipped in the shower, as long as the disability meets the other permanent and total criteria, benefits can be received after the elimination period.

**Disadvantage:** Given the restrictions on the definitions of permanent and total disability, the mandatory elimination period, and the lack of reimbursement for related medical expenses, the general recommendation for clients is not to rely solely on Social Security disability benefits. Consider these benefits only as a supplement to an existing long-term policy. As of 2011, the Social Security Administration reported an average monthly disabled worker's benefit of $1,111, and benefits for spouses and children being $299 and $331, respectively.[13]

### Procedural Strategy 2: Increase the Waiting Period and Increase Emergency Savings Fund

**Advantage:** Extending the waiting period in a policy significantly reduces the cost of coverage for a short- or long-term disability policy. If a large enough emergency fund or other assets earmarked for liquidation are available, it may be possible to eliminate the need for short-term coverage. Compared to a 90-day wait period policy, a 180-day wait period can reduce the cost of long-term coverage by approximately 1% of a client's gross income.

**Disadvantage:** Increasing the elimination period and increasing an emergency savings fund could subject a client to potentially significant opportunity costs. A client can sacrifice higher rates of return on assets held as emergency savings to implement this strategy. The untimely forced sale of assets earmarked for this purpose could result in significant losses.

### Procedural Strategy 3: Reduce the Wage Replacement Ratio

**Advantage:** This strategy reduces the premium cost relative to a policy with a higher wage replacement ratio. Reducing the amount of cash flow needed to fund a disability policy can provide a more cost-effective solution that ensures some income protection. It could allow for accumulating assets to meet this need as well as other household needs or goals.

**Disadvantage:** Purchasing a policy with, for example, a 60% wage replacement ratio could leave a client underinsured. This could negatively impact other short- and long-term financial objectives, unless the client has the financial wherewithal to cover any possible difference between the benefit amount and actual living expenses.

**Caveat:** In most situations, this strategy should be reserved for two-income households. Reducing the replacement ratio can be a better alternative than no protection. But for many households, especially those already living at or beyond their means, further reducing available income could have an immediate disastrous effect on a client's disability cash flow situation.

### Procedural Strategy 4: Purchase a Policy with a Recurrent Disability Provision

**Advantage:** A common client question is, "What happens if I become disabled a second time as the result of a previous injury or illness?" It is not uncommon for an insured to become disabled, recover from the disability, return to the workforce, and then become disabled a second time.

It is important for those employed in high-risk professions to obtain a **recurrent disability provision** as part of the original disability contract. Recurrent disability provisions state that if a policyholder becomes disabled again within six months or up to one year, the disability will be considered a continuation of the previous claim. Without a recurrent disability provision, an insurance company can impose another elimination period before beginning benefits a second time.

**Disadvantage:** The primary disadvantage associated with this strategy is that the addition of this provision adds to the cost of the policy. As with other provisions, this could negatively impact other short- and long-term financial objectives by diverting cash flow that could be used for other objectives.

## Procedural Strategy 5: Purchase a Policy with Partial or Residual Benefit Provisions

**Advantage:** The **residual disability provision** could be the most important rider available. A large percentage of all disability insurance claims either start or end in a residual disability claim. The basis of a residual claim is that those insured are either still or once again actively engaged in their occupation, but because of a sickness or injury they are suffering from either a loss of time and/or productivity or a loss of income.

The preferred residual provisions provide coverage based on lost income rather than on the loss of job responsibilities caused by a disability. The amount of the benefit is prorated according to the disability. For example, someone who is 50% disabled would receive a 50% benefit. Someone who was determined to be 30% disabled would receive a 30% benefit. It is assumed that the person will then work part time to increase monthly income.

**Disadvantage:** The primary disadvantage of this strategy is that it adds to the cost of the policy. However, this provision tends to add to the value of the policy because it pays benefits when policies without it would not. Most residual benefit provisions also institute a benefit floor of $250 to $500 to minimize the administrative cost of very small benefit payments.

## Procedural Strategy 6: Ensure Adequate Benefits by Including Appropriate Provisions in Individual Policies

**Advantage:** The availability and cost of several provisions that allow benefits to increase as inflation (or earnings potential) increases should be considered before an individual policy is purchased. The obvious advantage to these provisions is that, as a client's cost of living increases, the available benefit will also increase, thereby protecting the client against "outgrowing" the policy.

The first provision to consider is a **cost-of-living adjustment (COLA) benefit**. This provision takes effect only after a client makes a disability insurance claim, and then only if the disability lasts for more than one year. This provision is based on the inflation rate or an amount specified in the policy, depending on the percentage option chosen when the policy is purchased. It will increase the monthly benefit each year, up to the maximum elected, as long as the client is filing a continual claim.

The second provision to consider is the **future-increase option** that allows for client-requested incremental increases in policy benefits. This provision helps protect future earnings and is effective before a claim is made. Without this provision, or the similar **automatic-increase option**, a disability insurance policy protects only the amount of income earned at the time the policy is purchased. In other words, most policies do not automatically "grow" the potential benefit amount. This future-increase option provision guarantees insurability for a certain period of time so that, as the insured ages and earned income increases, the monthly benefit can also increase regardless of health changes.

**Disadvantage:** Adding provisions will add to the cost of a policy. The COLA provision can be quite expensive, but the future-increase option typically is inexpensive. However, given the importance of these provisions, each should be included in a private policy unless the cost makes the underlying policy prohibitively expensive. But the trade-off in not protecting future earning potential should not be ignored.

### Procedural Strategy 7: Ensure Continuation of Coverage by Including Appropriate Provisions

**Advantage:** The availability of several provisions that help ensure continuity or continuation of coverage should be a key decision point when selecting a policy. A **group disability replacement rider** guarantees a client the ability to convert a certain percentage of the group disability benefit into an individual plan, thus making the group long-term disability policy portable. A **waiver-of-premium clause,** which pays all future premiums in the event of disability, is also an important provision to consider. Obviously it would not be beneficial for a disabled client to lose coverage because of nonpayment just when coverage is needed most.

A **guaranteed-renewable provision** protects the insured from policy cancellation by allowing the insured to renew a policy without proof of insurability. However, if available, a noncancelable policy is even better than a guaranteed-renewable policy. A **noncancelable provision** allows for the guaranteed renewal of the policy at a predetermined premium—an essential provision for controlling costs. The policy cannot be canceled, and if desired, the insured can renew for a specific number of years or until age 65 or 67 (depending on the policy).

**Disadvantage:** Each of these provisions adds to the cost of the policy. However, given their importance, each provision should be included unless the cost makes the underlying policy prohibitively expensive. The only other disadvantage to any of these provisions concerns the guaranteed-renewable provision. Although the policy cannot be cancelled for any reason other than nonpayment, this provision allows the insurance company to increase the annual premium for all individuals covered by the policy.

### Procedural Strategy 8: Purchase a Policy with a Social Security Rider

**Advantage:** Monthly benefits for private or group coverage can be affected by policy provisions that coordinate the benefit amount with Social Security or worker's compensation benefits. Known as a **Social Security rider**, this provision decreases the amount of policy benefits paid if the insured meets both the policy definition of disability and qualifies for Social Security benefits. This rider should substantially reduce the policy premium. Group policies specifically offset Social Security in their contracts.

There are different types of Social Security offset riders in the individual market. In some instances, individual policy Social Security offset riders assure the client of a certain level of benefits if Social Security does not pay benefits. This is often the case because of the broadly defined any-occupation definition.

**Disadvantage:** To encourage rehabilitation, the total combined benefit is less than the income received before the disability. For example, group benefits, which are typically limited to 60% to 70% of salary, are likely to be reduced if the insured is also eligible for Social Security or Workers' Compensation benefits.

## Procedural Strategy 9: Coordinate Noninsurance Strategies with Short-term Disability Coverage

**Advantage:** For the average worker, the likelihood of short-term disability far exceeds that of long-term disability. Nonfinancial strategies such as maintaining a moderate reserve of employer-provided sick leave or vacation time could provide full salary and benefits for a short time. Emergency funds or other financial assets could be liquidated, if necessary, to extend the elimination period on a short-term policy and reduce premium cost. If group or individual short-term coverage is unavailable or judged to be too expensive, noninsurance strategies can be a cost-effective alternative; but client management is necessary.

**Disadvantage:** Contingent on individual client and employer-provided benefits, noninsurance strategies might not be available, or there may be employer restrictions on sick leave or vacation reserves. Increasing the elimination period by increasing an emergency savings fund subjects a client to potentially significant opportunity costs. Higher rates of return could be sacrificed, or the untimely forced sale of assets could result in significant losses.

## Procedural Strategy 10: Pursue Other Sources of Disability Benefits, when Applicable

**Advantage: Workers' Compensation** is administered through state compensation boards and funded by participating employers. These programs grant benefits to employees who are injured at work or suffer a work-related illness. Although specific program provisions vary from state-to-state, benefits include medical treatment, partial wage replacement, and survivor benefits. In some states, clients might also be eligible for compulsory temporary benefits. These are basically state-sponsored disability insurance pools.

Generally the Workers' Compensation program can be thought of as a combination health and disability policy. But unlike Social Security benefits, Workers' Compensation covers only disabilities that occur during the normal course of employment. The other basic difference from Social Security is that employees are eligible for Workers' Compensation benefits for short-term, long-term, partial, and total disabilities.

Because of this broad coverage, some disabled workers can file claims with both Social Security and the state office of Worker's Compensation, but the combined benefit amount cannot exceed 80% of the worker's average current earnings.

Clients who find themselves unemployed after a disability could be eligible for state-sponsored unemployment insurance, although some restrictions may apply and benefits generally end after 39 weeks. Private unemployment insurance could also be available on a limited basis. However, the costs associated with this type of insurance are prohibitive and generally not worth the premiums. Benefits from private policies are related to previous earnings and typically equal no more than 50% of a person's earnings. This is further limited by a total dollar maximum monthly benefit. It is important to note that neither state-sponsored nor private unemployment benefits are designed for long-term disability situations.

Finally, settlements from a liability or negligence claim resulting from a disabling accident could provide assets or income. But this is a worst-case scenario and receipt of any financial benefits could potentially be delayed for years.

**Disadvantage:** Restrictions on applicability, availability, benefit amounts, and benefit periods limit the usefulness of these sources of disability benefits in the planning process. But for eligible clients, these benefits are a useful supplement that should not be overlooked.

## CHAPTER-BASED CASE STUDY

## A Client-based Disability Insurance Recommendation

In today's economic environment, insurance companies with an A.M. Best rating of A or higher, or similar ratings from another rating service, should be used for a client's primary disability policy. Although this is true in general, other policy considerations are unique to disability coverage selection. For example, disability policies from firms with a lower rating may be the only option for clients with pre-existing conditions or health problems. The policy chosen should cover physical as well as mental or emotional health disabilities and should not exclude coverage for Alzheimer's or Parkinson's disease. A hospital stay should not be a prerequisite to obtain benefits. In addition to these basic disability policy components, the following general guidelines (i.e., tenets) are recommended to guide planners when making recommendations.

*Tenet 1*

Long-term policies are more important than short-term policies. A basic outcome of the financial planning process is an emergency savings fund or the identification of emergency sources of income. Self-insurance could be the best option for managing a short-term disability. By planning to use emergency funds, including cash assets, short-term liquid securities, or available lines of credit, clients can avoid the additional cost of short-term coverage. This could provide additional incentive to build and maintain an emergency fund and credit.

The greatest financial risk for most clients is a long period of disability. As such, the general rule is to purchase a long-term policy that provides benefits until age 65 or 67, when Social Security and other retirement benefits can be used to fund income needs. Short-term coverage, although important and perhaps the cheaper of the two options, should be a secondary consideration.

## Tenet 2

Choose the longest elimination period that is financially feasible, but at least a 90-day elimination period, because increasing the elimination period significantly lowers the annual premium. Again, the financial planning process answers the question of how a client will fund living expenses during the elimination period. Expenses during this short period of disability can be covered from employer-compensated sick leave or other vacation time, emergency savings and other emergency income sources, or if necessary, supplemented with available lines of credit.

## Tenet 3

Purchase the maximum benefit that a client can reasonably afford. As a general rule, most clients require a benefit equal to at least 70% of gross monthly income. This benefit target should be reduced only if the policy costs exceed a client's insurance budget.

## Tenet 4

Purchase a policy with an inflation protection provision that provides an annual inflation adjustment to the benefit. Regardless of the percentage of income initially replaced, the long-term benefits will soon become too low because of the effects of inflation.

## Tenet 5

Purchase a noncancelable and guaranteed-renewable policy, if available and affordable; otherwise, purchase a guaranteed-renewable policy. Including both riders is ideal, but these policies are typically offered only to low-risk occupational groups at a high premium. A guaranteed-renewable policy offers continual coverage subject to premium increases. But any premium increase applies to all policyholders in the same insurance classification and cannot be modified for individuals. Any premium increase must be approved by the state insurance department contingent on a company's adverse claims history.

*Tenet 6*

Always attempt to locate an own-occupation policy for a client. If unavailable, or if the premium exceeds the client's budget or willingness to pay, recommend a modified own-occupation policy. If this policy is still too expensive, recommend a split-definition policy. Only after these policies have been explored should an any-occupation policy be considered.

*Tenet 7*

Protect yourself as a competent professional with a liability release form. If a client declines a recommendation to purchase disability insurance, a liability release should be signed. Thus, should the client, the client's spouse, or other family members question the lack of contingency planning to protect the household from a temporary or long-term loss of income, the planner is protected. The client's signature on the liability release acknowledges that the planner made a recommendation that was declined. But it is important that the advisor remain sensitive to and respectful of the client's choice when requesting a liability waiver.

---

**Disability Insurance Planning Tip: Average Premiums for Individual Disability Insurance**

The average cost of a high-quality policy generally approximates 1% to 3% of a client's annual gross earned income.[14] The definition of disability or type of policy chosen is the primary determinant of cost. It is up to the planner to adjust the premium to fit the needs of each client based on the elimination period, benefit period, and monthly benefit chosen. Extending the elimination period lowers the premium. As with most planning issues and estimates, it is best to over-estimate the premium than to be too conservative with disability cost estimates.

---

## A Sample Recommendation: Purchase a Long-term Modified Own-occupation Policy

Although it is almost always a good idea to recommend an own-occupation policy, coverage may be unavailable, the client might not qualify for this type of coverage, or the cost might be prohibitive. The disability insurance policy recommendation can be summarized using the Planning Recommendation Form in Exhibit 7.6.

**Exhibit 7.6** Disability Planning Recommendation Form

### Planning Recommendation Form

| | |
|---|---|
| **Financial Planning Content Area** | Disability planning |
| **Client Goal** | To provide financial stability in case of disability. |

| **Recommendation No.:** | 7 | **Priority (1–6) lowest to highest:** | 6 |
|---|---|---|---|

| | |
|---|---|
| **Projected/Target Value ($)** | Approximately $45,000 per year |

**Product Profile**

| | | | | | |
|---|---|---|---|---|---|
| Type | Modified own-occupation, Long-term disability policy | | | | |
| Duration | Guaranteed renewable until Age 65 | | | | |
| Provider | Sunflower Insurance | | | | |
| Funding Cost per Period ($) | $1,250 annual premium | | | | |
| Maintenance Cost per Period ($) | $0 | | | | |
| Current Income Tax Status | Tax-qualified | | Taxable | X | |
| Projected Rate of Return | N/A | | | | |
| Major Policy Provisions | 1. 180-day elimination period<br>2. Inflation protection rider<br>3. 70% of gross income replacement | | | | |

**Procedural Factors**

| | | | | |
|---|---|---|---|---|
| Implement by Whom | Planner | X | Client | |
| Implementation Date or Time Frame | Within 30 days | | | |
| Implementation Procedure | Insurance application will be prepared for your signature; the first month's premium is due with the application. | | | |

**Ownership Factors**

| | | | | |
|---|---|---|---|---|
| Owner(s) | Robert F. Nusalsang | | | |
| Form of Ownership | N/A | | | |
| Insured(s) | Robert F. Nusalsang | | | |
| Custodial Account | Yes | | No | X |
| Custodian | | | | |
| In Trust For (ITF) | Yes | | No | X |
| Transfer On Death (TOD) | Yes | | No | X |
| Beneficiary(ies) | NA | | | |
| Contingent Beneficiary(ies) | NA | | | |

| | |
|---|---|
| **Proposed Benefit** | Provides replacement of 70% of client's income, if disability eligible, until age 65. |

In this example, Bob Nusalsang is a divorced 35-year-old with a 6 year-old son. Bob is employed by a small information technology consulting firm that offers great life, health, and retirement programs, but no disability insurance. Bob is particularly concerned about this.

As a single-income household, Bob recognizes that his financial future is in his hands and his strong values of independence and self-reliance make disability protection a priority. Although he has significant investments and plans to continue investing, he is not comfortable risking his future, and that of his son's education, to chance or self-insurance.

The logic supporting this recommendation highlights several potential positive client outcomes. First, premium costs tend to be lower than for an own-occupation policy. Second, the definition of disability is more favorable than that used for an any-occupation policy.

Other outcomes are associated with this recommendation, however. If Bob should become disabled and unable to work in a reasonably suitable occupation, income would be available until age 65, at which time he could transition into other forms of income and health care assistance. This recommendation, although funded by a somewhat costly annual premium, decreases the possibility of Bob making significant compromises in his standard of living or of depleting other assets in case of disability. This means that other goals, such as education or retirement funding, could stay on track even in the event of a disability. Finally, this recommendation satisfies the client's personal and emotional needs with the reasonably priced compromise of a modified own-occupation policy instead of the more costly own-occupation policy.

# Learning Outcomes

1.  Disability insurance planning may be the most important and frequently overlooked aspect of financial planning because of the simple fact that disability insurance is often part of a client's employee benefits package. However, a middle-aged worker is three times more likely to become disabled than to die during his or her working lifetime. Additionally, the incidence of personal bankruptcy has been closely linked to both medical expenses and job loss; so in the event of a disability the client could be facing both of these factors. Disability insurance is not excessively expensive and could provide the necessary funding to help a client or family avoid, or at least mitigate, a potentially devastating financial loss.

2.  Any number of situational factors can affect a client's need for and selection of disability income coverage; however, some of the most critical factors include: (1) the number of wage earners in the household; (2) whether the client is providing support for minor children or disabled adults; (3) the availability of assets or credit; (4) whether the client has qualified for Social Security Disability Insurance; (5) the hazard level of the client's job and whether he or she is self-employed; (6) the client's lifestyle choices; and (7) the client's risk tolerance.

3.  Calculating the appropriate amount of disability insurance is quite complex because it requires consideration of income and expenses, assets available to support lifestyle (i.e.,

bank accounts, undrawn lines of credit), and employee benefits (i.e., vacation and sick leave, FMLA availability, group disability policies). For example, a client might not have a short-term disability policy, but one may not be needed because of a generous leave policy from work (mitigation) or the availability of liquid assets (self-insurance). Again, several factors determine the amount of long-term disability coverage needed. A client could opt for a larger monthly replacement percentage and a longer elimination period or a lower replacement ratio and a shorter elimination period for roughly the same cost. In either case it would be assumed that the client had assets that could be used to cover a gap or shortfall in benefits. Additionally, if a there is another earner in the household and the household could meet monthly expenses on the income of the remaining earner, there might be less need for coverage, or a smaller amount of coverage could be purchased.

4.  For purposes of disability insurance, disability can be classified broadly as either own-occupation or any-occupation; any-occupation is the stricter classification. With an own-occupation policy claimants are considered disabled and therefore eligible for benefits if they are unable to perform the duties required by their original or "own" job. Under an any-occupation policy, claimants are considered eligible to collect benefits only if their disability is severe enough to keep them from preforming the duties required for any meaningful work. In addition to these classifications of disability, a policy provision called a *residual benefits rider* is typically available for purchase. This rider offers added protection for partial disability or for claimants who can return to work on a part-time basis. Finally, some policies offer a cost-of-living adjustment rider that continues to increase benefits as inflation increases.

5.  In addition to traditional disability income replacement policies, a client might have access to or be eligible for Social Security Disability Income and/or Workers' Compensation insurance. To be eligible for SSDI a worker must be totally disabled and expect that disability to last for at least 12 continuous months. To be eligible for Workers' Compensation, the event that precipitated the disability must have occurred at work or when functioning in a working capacity. In addition, a disabled employee might have unused sick or personal leave that could be used for a short-term disability.

6.  Five basic questions must be answered when evaluating a disability policy: (1) How restrictive is the definition of disability? (2) How long does the insured have to wait before benefits are paid? (3) How much of a client's expenses (measured as a percentage of gross or net income) will be replaced during the benefit period? (4) Will the benefits remain fixed or will they increase with the rate of inflation? and (5) How long will the benefits continue?

7.  Many possible strategies can be recommended based on a client's situational factors and the quality of any in-place disability policies. However, most recommendations should center on a client's willingness and capacity to sustain the loss of income. Clients must be made aware that most disabilities not only reduce income but also increase expenses; therefore, recommendations should consider the likelihood and severity of any possible disability. Finally, strategies should also consider the policy provisions (e.g., inflation riders, classifications of disability, residual benefit clauses) that make the most sense for a client, because clients in a dual-earner household or one with adequate access to assets might not need the same amount of coverage or a policy with many added provisions.

# Chapter Resources

Council for Disability Awareness (http://www.disabilitycanhappen.org/).

Disability Insurance Education—Glossary of Disability Insurance Terms. Available at http://www.instantdisabilityinsurancequote.com/html/disability-insurance-education-glossary.html.

Elias, Stephen, and Kevin Urbatsch. *Special Needs Trusts: Protect Your Child's Financial Future.* Berkeley, CA: Nolo Press, 2011.

General disability insurance information Web sites: http://www.iii.org/individuals/DisabilityInsurance/www.ssa.gov/disability/.

Information about Medicare (www.medicare.gov).

Nadworny, John W., and Cynthia R. Haddad. *The Special Needs Planning Guide: How to Prepare for Every Stage of Your Child's Life.* Baltimore: Brookes Publishing, 2007.

Rajput, Minoti. "Planning for Families of Children with Disabilities." *Journal of Financial Planning* August, 2001: 74–84.

Russell, L. Mark, and Arnold E. Grant. *Planning for the Future: Providing a Meaningful Life for a Child with a Disability after Your Death.* Planning for the Future, Inc., 2005.

Social Security Benefit Calculator (disability, retirement, survivor): http://www.socialsecurity.gov/planners/benefitcalculators.htm.

Stenken, Joseph F., *2011 Social Security & Medicare Facts.* Erlanger, KY: National Underwriter Company, 2011.

The *Financial Factilitator* and all fillable forms needed to complete text activities can be found on the student website at: http://pro.nuco.com/booksupplements/NUCollege-CaseBook2e.

# Quantitative/Analytical Mini-case Problems

1. Tarek Framborgia is considering the purchase of a disability policy. He is currently 35 years old and earns $50,000 per year as a quality control engineer for a major industrial company. His greatest concern is that with his moderately strenuous job responsibilities and his potential for increasing earnings he be adequately covered should an off-the-job accident keep him from continuing his career. He has come to you with the following list of problems and questions.

   a. If I purchase a policy that pays a fixed benefit of 90% of my current salary, how long will it be before this amount covers only 70% of my future salary if I assume salary increases of 4% per year?

   b. Assuming the same policy as above, if I purchase a policy with a provision for future increases of $1,000 per year, how long will it cover at least 70% of my income?

   c. If I assume that both my salary and the inflation rate increase at 4% per year, and that there is no floor or ceiling to my potential benefit increases because I purchase both the COLA and future increase option provisions on the above policy, how much should my annual benefit be in 25 years?

2. Samantha O'Reilly has come to your office for a second opinion about her individual long-term disability policy. She was told that her best option for reducing the cost of her policy was to choose a long elimination period. But she has become worried that she will not be able to pay her monthly expenses for the year-long elimination period. She has some savings, but she is afraid that is not enough.

   a. If her current annual salary is $43,000, her taxes are $8,000, and she just barely manages to fund her Roth IRA each year with $5,000, how much of an emergency fund would she need to meet only her living expenses?

   b. How long would it take her to achieve the emergency fund goal above if she currently has $18,500 saved, invests $300 per month, and earns an annual percentage yield or APY of 4.25% after taxes in her money market mutual fund?

   c. If she could reduce her elimination period to nine months for an additional premium of $10 per month, how much would she need to save on a monthly basis in the same money market account to reach her emergency fund goal within 12 months? Could she afford this savings payment if she suspended her IRA contribution for one year?

3. Deshawn Carter has just received his open-enrollment notification and has asked you to assess his disability insurance coverage. He currently has a long-term, any-occupation disability policy available through his employer that pays a benefit of 80% of his $85,000 gross annual income. Deshawn has previously chosen to have his premiums deducted from his salary on a before-tax basis, and the premium dollars are not being added back into his taxable income. He has asked you to determine the net after-tax benefit he would receive should he become disabled under each of the following situations:

   a. No changes are made to his policy.

b.  He elects to have the pretax dollars used to pay his policy premiums added back into his taxable income. (Remember to remind Deshawn that this is an irrevocable election.)

c.  His employer has offered to pay 50% of the premium on his behalf, and Deshawn would elect to pay the other half of the premium with after-tax dollars. (Remember to address with Deshawn how the income tax impact of this election will change his net benefit over the next several years, assuming his salary remains static.)

4.  One of your clients has just realized that her own-occupation disability policy has a Social Security benefits integration clause, meaning that her policy will have a dollar-for-dollar reduction in benefits paid if she qualifies for Social Security disability. According to her most recent Social Security benefits statement, she would be eligible for $1,325 per month for a permanent and total disability. How much would her disability policy pay as a monthly benefit under the following circumstances if her current annual salary is $62,000, her policy pays 70% of gross, and she pays for the policy with after-tax dollars?

a.  Her disability meets the definition for her policy, but it doesn't meet the Social Security definition.

b.  Her disability meets the definition for her policy and also meets the Social Security definition.

c.  How much would her total combined monthly disability benefits equal if she meets both definitions of disability and her policy does not have a benefits integration clause? Why could this be problematic? In other words, why might this create a moral hazard?

# Comprehensive Bedo Case—Analysis Questions

Certain key data are needed before a disability needs analysis can be conducted for the Bedos. It is important to summarize the type of disability coverage currently in force for Tyler and Mia. Data such as the type of coverage available—short- or long-term—and the provider of the coverage—employer or private company—should be reviewed. Insurance company ratings and policy costs should also be considered. Other information needed to advise the Bedos includes the availability of Social Security benefits; the client's assumptions regarding the availability of these or other benefits; and the specific assets, expenses, or goals that the clients are willing to adjust in the event of a disability.

1.  Develop a disability insurance planning goal for the Bedos. When conceptualizing this goal, consider the following:

a.  Is the goal developed in agreement with any or all goals and objectives that the clients have identified regarding disability insurance planning?

b.  What situational factors might influence their disability insurance goal? Are these factors explicit, implied, or assumed? Is additional information required from the Bedos, and if so, what?

c.  What is the disability insurance planning outcome desired for the clients?

2.  Make a list of the lifestyle, occupational, and health factors that should be documented and evaluated for the Bedos. How might this information be obtained? How might it be useful in the current disability insurance situation analysis? Also, make a list of life events that could affect the disability insurance planning analysis for Tyler and Mia and should be reviewed at future client meetings.

3.  Are there globally accepted, client-specific, or planner-generated planning assumptions that will influence the disability insurance situation analysis? List the assumptions as they might appear in a plan.

4.  Make a list of specific policy features that should be evaluated as part of the documentation and evaluation of the Bedos' disability insurance planning efforts. For each feature, write a definition or explanation that could appear in this section of the plan or in the plan glossary.

5.  Use the Financial Facilitator to calculate the income replacement need to be met by short- and long-term disability insurance for both Tyler and Mia, given their employer-provided policies.

    a.  What is the resulting need if individually disabled?

    b.  What is the resulting need should they both be simultaneously disabled?

    c.  How does the assumption on qualification of Social Security benefits affect the calculation? Explain the advantages and disadvantages of planning for disability with or without Social Security benefits.

    d.  What are the tax implications of these benefits?

    e.  What are the implications for their emergency fund given the applicable waiting periods?

6.  Based on the information collected, financial advisors have a responsibility to fully document and inform clients of the analyses and results. This information can be communicated through a letter or via a comprehensive or modular plan. Summarize your observations about Tyler's and Mia's current disability insurance situation and the planning need(s) identified. Incorporate text, bullets, and graphics in your explanation.

7.  Based on the goals originally identified and the completed analysis, what product or procedural strategies might be most useful to satisfy the Bedos' disability insurance protection needs? Be sure to consider strategies matched to the planning needs identified for Tyler and Mia, individually. When reviewing the strategies, be careful to consider an approximate cost of implementation, as well as the most likely outcome(s) associated with each strategy.

8.  Write at least one primary and one alternative recommendation from the strategies selected in response to each identified planning need. More than one recommendation might be needed to address all of the planning needs. Include specific, defensible answers to the who, what, when, where, why, how, and how much implementation questions for each recommendation.

    a.  It is suggested that each recommendation be summarized in a Recommendation Form.

    b.  Assign a priority to each recommendation based on the likelihood of meeting client goals and desired outcomes. This priority will be important when recommendations from other core planning content areas are considered relative to the discretionary funds available to subsidize all recommendations.

    c.  Comment briefly on the outcomes associated with each recommendation.

9.  Complete the following for the Disability Insurance section of the Bedos' financial plan.

    a.  Outline the content to be included in this section of the plan. Given the segments written previously, which segments are missing?

    b.  Write the introduction to this section of the plan (no more than one to two paragraphs).

10. Prepare a 10–15-minute presentation for the Bedos of your observations and/or recommendation(s) for meeting their disability protection needs. Be sure to include visual aids, Excel handouts, and other materials that will make the recommendations more meaningful for the clients.

## Notes

1.  U.S. Equal Employment Opportunity Commission, *Facts About the Americans With Disabilities Act*. Available at http://www.eeoc.gov/eeoc/publications/fs-ada.cfm.

2.  John R. Ingrisano, *The Disability Income Insurance Decision*. Available at http://www.aafpins.com/Old%20Web%20Site/aafpins/mono2.html.

3.  "Report of the Committee to Recommend New Disability Tables for Valuation," *Transactions of the Society of Actuaries*, 37 (1985): 449–601. Available at http://www.soa.org/library/research/transactions-of-society-of-actuaries/1985/january/tsa85v3713.pdf.

4.  Guardian Disability Insurance Brokerage, *Chances of a Long Term Disability*. Available at http://www.disabilityquotes.com/disability-insurance/chances.cfm.

5.  Guardian Disability Insurance Brokerage, *Chances of a Long Term Disability*. Available at http://www.disabilityquotes.com/disability-insurance/chances.cfm.

6.  *Virginia Workers' Compensation Commission Chronological Compensation Benefits Chart*. Available at http://www.vwc.state.va.us/portal/vwc-website/HelpfulResources/CustomerAssistance/CustomerAssistanceBeneAmt. Also Michigan Department of Labor and Economic Growth, *An Overview of Workers Compensation*, p. 22. Available at http://www.michigan.gov/documents/wca_PUB-004_135317_7.pdf.

7.  Contractors with a C39 Roofing Classification Are Ineligible to File an Exemption for Workers' Compensation Insurance Coverage even with No Employees. Information available at http://www.cslb.ca.gov/Resources/FormsAndApplications/ExemptionFromWorkersCompensation.pdf.

8.  *The Family and Medical Leave Act (FMLA)*. Available at http://fmlaonline.com/.

9.  Social Security Administration, *Benefits for Children with Disabilities*. Publication No. 05-10026, January 2012, ICN 455360. Available at http://www.ssa.gov/pubs/10026.html#a-0=0.

10. Social Security Administration, *Frequently Asked Questions: Benefits for Disabled Children*. Available at http://ssa-custhelp.ssa.gov/app/answers/detail/a_id/156/~/benefits-for-disabled-children.

11. Guardian Disability Insurance Brokerage, *Common Questions: How Much Does Disability Insurance Cost?* Available at http://www.disabilityquotes.com/disability-insurance/disability-insurance-cost.cfm.

12. Social Security Administration, *OASDI and SSI Program Rates and Limits, 2012*. Available at https://www.socialsecurity.gov/policy/docs/quickfacts/prog_highlights/.

13. Social Security Administration, *Monthly Statistical Snapshot, January 2012*. Available at http://www.socialsecurity.gov/policy/docs/quickfacts/stat_snapshot/.

14. AffordableInsuranceProtection.com, *How Much Does Disability Insurance Cost?* Available at http://www.affordableinsuranceprotection.com/disability_premiums.

# Long-term Care Insurance Planning

## Learning Objectives

1. Understand the importance of long-term care insurance within the comprehensive financial planning process.

2. Identify client situational factors necessary for analyzing a client's need to purchase long-term care insurace or to self-insure.

3. Demonstrate how to determine and quantify a client's need for long-term care insurance.

4. Evaluate a client's long-term care insurance coverage and options.

5. Explain the primary advantages and disadvantages of linked-benefit life and annuity products for providing long-term care protection.

6. Explain how Medicaid qualification and the transfer and recovery of assets can influence the determination of need for long-term care protection.

7. Summarize the most important long-term care insurance policy types and provisions.

8. Identify and recommend appropriate long-term care insurance strategies matched to a client's situation.

# Key Terms

accelerated payment options

activities of daily living (ADLs)

acute care

adverse selection

bed hold provision

benefit bank

chronic care

continuing care retirement community

expense-reimbursement contract

extension of benefits option

fee-for-service contract

guaranteed purchase option

guaranteed renewable

indemnity plan or policy

integrated policies

life care contract

linked-benefit products

long-term care insurance

medicaid planning

modified contract

noncancellable

nonexempt transfer

nonforfeiture clause

partnership plan long-term care insurance

pool-of-money policy

reimbursement plan

reduced paid-up coverage nonforfeiture option

return of premium nonforfeiture option

residual death benefit

restoration of benefits provision

risk triggers

shortened benefit period nonforfeiture option

spousal survivorship

waiver of premium clause

**Figure 8.1** Systematic Financial Planning Process for Long Term Care Insurance

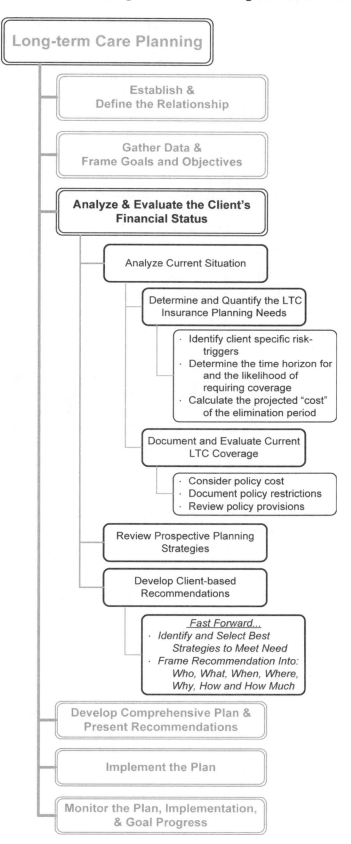

## LONG-TERM CARE INSURANCE: THE BASICS

Once known as *nursing home insurance*, long-term care insurance continues to be redefined. Policies can cover a range of services from home health care, care at an adult day care center, in-home care, assisted living care, skilled nursing care, hospice care, or some combination of these needs. Some policies cover home modifications. Some policies also include benefits for respite care, which pays for substitute care given when a primary caregiver takes a vacation or break. A typical respite care clause will cover up to 21 days per calendar year of substitute care.

Because **long-term care insurance** coverage is designed for care that is not purely "medical care" and is not provided in a hospital, health insurance offers no coverage, and Medicare offers only limited coverage under certain conditions. Hospitals provide **acute care**, or care that is immediate or short-term. Long-term care facilities provide for the progression of **chronic care**, or care that may be continuous or long-term.

Long-term care facilities run the gamut from basic assisted living facilities that provide only domestic help to facilities with 24-hour medical staff capable of dispensing medication and handling minor medical emergencies. With increased care comes increased cost. Facilities also offer a variety of living conditions, including group arrangements, semiprivate living quarters, and private rooms or even suites. With increased amenities and privacy come higher costs.

These costs are staggering and vary widely by geographic area. States such as Alaska, Massachusetts, and New York have, on average, higher costs of living, so facilities in those states are correspondingly more expensive. Median 2011 costs for semiprivate nursing home rooms ranged from a low of $46,355 in Texas to $114,975, $116,800 and $222,285 in New York, Massachusetts, and Alaska, respectively.[1]

In 2011, the U.S. median annual cost for a semiprivate room in a nursing home or skilled care facility was $70,445, a 5.7% increase over 2010. The median cost of a private room was $77,745 in 2011, reflecting a 4.35% compound annual inflation rate since 2005.[2] The *Genworth Financial 2011 Cost of Care Survey* also reported that adult day health care, which provides community-based protective care during the day, was also expensive. The national median rate was $60 per day, or a median annual cost of $15,600 per year for support services, but less than 24-hour care. The daily rate ranged from $15 to $160. For those still capable of more independent living, the median cost of a one-bedroom unit in an assisted living facility was $39,135, reflecting a six-year annual growth rate of 6.0% during a period when real estate prices were sharply declining across the United States.[3]

According to the *2011 MetLife Market Survey of Nursing Home, Assisted Living, Adult Day Services, and Home Care Costs*, there is no relief in sight. Assisted living base rates rose 5.6% from 2010 to 2011, and the average cost of a private room in a nursing home increased by 4.4%.[4] To put these numbers in perspective, with an annual increase of 5.5%, a 40-year-old client who lives to age 86 and spends the last 2.5 years in a skilled-care facility would spend a minimum of $1.4 million on long-term care.

With steady increases in life expectancy, improved medical care, and the aging of the Baby Boomers, it is increasingly likely that some clients, regardless of age, will require some kind of long-term care. Based on data from 2004 and 2005, The Kaiser Commission on Medicaid Facts estimated that more than 10 million Americans need long-term services and support to meet daily activity needs. Additionally, the Commission noted that $178 billion was spent on long-term care services in 2006. Of that, 40% was paid by Medicaid, 23% was paid by Medicare for post-acute care, and 22% was paid out-of-pocket, but only 9% was paid by private insurance.[5] Consequently, purchasing long-term care coverage as part of either an insurance or estate plan is an important consideration for clients and advisors. The purpose of this chapter is to examine the underlying process used to analyze and evaluate a client's long-term care insurance situation. The steps involved in the process are shown in Figure 8.1. An example of a client-based long-term-care policy selection process is also provided.

## ANALYZE THE CLIENT'S CURRENT SITUATION

Analysis of a client's long-term care situation is built on information similar to that required for the analysis of health insurance needs. Issues to consider include:

- family health status and related health history;

- family demographics and preferences that can affect the need for care;

- assets available for care expenses, as well as the goals competing for those assets; and

- lifestyle and profession or occupational choices that could affect the future need for long-term care.

For example, the likelihood of developing Alzheimer's disease, the most common type of dementia, is greater for someone with a first-degree relative (i.e., a parent or sibling) who has the disease. For an individual with more than one first-degree relative diagnosed, the risks of the disease are even greater. Further complicating the analysis is consideration of the continuum of care that may begin at home, transition to an assisted living facility, and finally progress to a skilled nursing facility or what is typically called a *nursing home*.

Eligibility for long-term care insurance benefits is based on functional ability, cognitive ability, or medical necessity. Functional ability is determined by the insured's ability to perform a certain number of **activities of daily living (ADLs)**, which measure the ability to perform routine personal care functions. Benefits begin when the insured is unable to perform two of the six activities (some policies may require three of five ADLs) listed below:

1. Eating

2. Toileting (e.g., getting to, from, on, and off the toilet)

3. Transferring from a bed to a chair

4. Bathing

5. Dressing

6. Maintaining continence (e.g., ability to control bladder and bowel movements)

Cognitive disability, such as Alzheimer's disease or other dementias or organic cognitive disorders, is another eligibility trigger and one of the primary reasons for admission to a care facility today. The Alzheimer's Association reports, based on various studies, that at least half of elderly adult day care clients, almost half of nursing home residents, and 45% to 67% of the residents of assisted living facilities have Alzheimer's disease or another form of dementia.[6] Such mental incapacities are isolated triggers and should not be linked to any ADLs.

Medical necessity is the final qualification for long-term care insurance eligibility. A client is eligible for long-term care benefits if, as the result of an illness, injury, or chronic condition, the insured requires medically necessary care and assistance. Some policies require that a company representative perform the screening, but others allow the client's physician to do the assessment, which is typically considered the better option.

Beyond the issue of eligibility for policy benefits is the related issue of policy eligibility for favorable tax treatment. The Health Insurance Portability and Accountability Act (HIPAA) of 1996, along with Internal Revenue Code (IRC) § 7702B, set forth the requirements for long-term care policies to be considered "qualified" and therefore eligible for the premiums to be tax deductible and the benefits in excess of premiums paid to be excluded from income. To be considered a qualified policy, the benefit payment must be contingent on (1) a chronic illness that lasts for at least 90 days; (2) the loss of at least two ADLs; and (3) severe cognitive impairment or impairment that requires supervision. Tax qualification under HIPAA also precludes medical necessity as a stand-alone trigger for benefit payment. In addition to these benefit-related requirements, to claim the cost of premiums as a tax deduction the insured must also itemize tax deductions and claim medical expenses that exceed the adjusted gross income (AGI) limitation of 7.5%.

The primary benefit of purchasing a tax-qualified policy is that the premiums may be tax-deductible, whereas no portion of the premium cost is a tax-deductible expense if the policy is not tax qualified. But the advantages of not purchasing a tax-qualified policy include unlimited benefits, less restrictive qualification for benefits, and a shorter qualification period. Given the AGI limitation and the age-based maximum deductibility of premium limits, as shown in Table 8.1, this cost-reduction strategy will work only for clients who have substantial additional out-of-pocket medical expenses.

**Table 8.1** Maximum Deductibility for Eligible Long Term Care Premiums, 2012

| Attained Age in Year | Maximum Deduction per Person |
|---|---|
| 40 or under | $350 |
| 41–50 | $660 |
| 51–60 | $1,310 |
| 61–70 | $3,500 |
| 71 or over | $4,370 |

*Source*: Data from American Association for Long-term Care Insurance (http://www.aaltci.org).

For example, a 50-year-old single client with an AGI of $50,000 per year would need to have more than $3,090 of other IRS Schedule A unreimbursed medical expenses to receive any tax benefit from the long-term care premium (($50,000 × 7.5%) – $660). But married clients between 61 and 70 years old—with the same AGI and each paying annual premiums of $2,500—would not require any additional out-of-pocket medical costs to qualify for the tax deduction. In this case, their deduction would be $1,250 (($2,500 × 2) – ($50,000 × 7.5%)). This would result in approximate tax savings of $187.50 ($1,250 ×15%) given that they are in the 15% marginal tax bracket. However, it is important to note that under the 2010 Patient Protection and Affordable Care Act (PPACA), effective January 1, 2013, the 7.5% floor increases to 10% unless the taxpayer or spouse is age 65 or older. But in either case, the cost associated with the more restrictive benefit qualification must also be considered. It would be a disservice to the client, given the negligible tax savings, if the client was never eligible for benefits under the qualified plan but would have been eligible for benefits under a nonqualified plan.

Understanding eligibility for long-term care insurance benefits provides an important foundation for determining and quantifying a client's need for insurance coverage. This assessment is perhaps one of the most complex and subjective of any of the core financial planning content areas, and perhaps one of the most difficult to discuss.

---

### Long-term Care Planning Tip: Continuing Care Retirement Communities

According the to the AARP, **continuing care retirement communities** (CCRCs) combine independent living, assisted living, memory or special care, and skilled nursing home care in a tiered approach for those who want to prepare for health care need transitions. Rather than moving from one facility to another as health care needs change, a retiree enters a CCRC as an independent person living in a single-family home or apartment. When the need arises, the person can transfer to assisted living or nursing care facilities within the community. And for couples who need different types of care, the community can accommodate both needs while promoting independence and togetherness. Many CCRC residents prefer the notion of living in one location with an available continuum of care. Family members also like the idea of consistent friendships within the community as well as familiarity with the caregiving services. But CCRCs can be expensive. Clients who wish to consider this type of living arrangement in retirement should consider the costs and plan accordingly. According to the AARP, Some CCRCs require nonrefundable entrance fees (e.g., $100,000 to $1 million) and monthly maintenance charges (e.g., $2,000 to $5,000).[7] It is also common for the monthly fee to increase over time and as the health care needs of the resident change.

Three CCRC contracts are common. The first is a **life care contract,** also called an *extensive contract*. This provides unlimited assisted living, medical treatment, and skilled nursing care over a resident's lifetime with no additional charges. A **modified contract** offers residents a choice of services for a predetermined period of time. At the end of that time period, additional services may be purchased. Finally, a **fee-for-service contract** provides access to a CCRC, but once assisted living and/or skilled nursing care is needed, the resident will be required to pay market rate for additional services and care.

When working with clients to select the appropriate CCRC facility, it is important to consider factors associated with the financial viability of the CCRC as well as other licensing and inspection reports. Qualitative issues to consider include facilities and grounds, staff, food, transportation, and interests shared with other residents. Third-party accreditation and review standards are available, such as from the Commission on Accreditation of Rehabilitation Facilities/Continuing Care Accreditation Commission (CARF/CCAC) or LeadingAge.

## Determine and Quantify a Client's Need for Long-term Care Insurance

Planners should base long-term care recommendations on a thorough review of a client's situation and projected needs. Determining need is not easy—although most companies will sell to clients between the ages of 18 and 84 who are in reasonably good health and able to care for themselves. Unlike life insurance or health insurance that everyone eventually uses, long-term care insurance is truly a gamble. The analysis of a client's current situation begins by answering two important questions:

1. Does the client's current health, family medical history, or personal situation suggest that long-term care may be needed in the future?

2. Does the client have sufficient monetary resources or a family support network to "self-insure" in the event that long-term care may be needed in the future?

Notice that the first question does not address finances. This ordering is purposeful and based on the subjective factors that help characterize a client's situation and affect the pending decision. The emotion surrounding a client's decision to purchase long-term care insurance is second only to the decision to purchase life insurance. There is little reason to consider an objective assessment of the financial ramifications of long-term care without first addressing a client's fears, preferences, and even cultural biases about care.

Some of the concerns clients might face center not only on who will care for them, but also who will care for those for whom they have traditionally provided care and support. Guilt about the possibility of being unable to care for family can be a very powerful emotion. Other concerns surrounding a diagnosis or the need for custodial care might be more egocentric, such as feelings of shame, inadequacy, or failure. Women, who tend live longer than men, may be in greater need of paid care services.

Single individuals, because of the lack of a family network, might require paid care services. The loss of privacy and the potential reversal of family roles are additional concerns, especially between parents and children. Besides these intrinsic barriers, home design, space limitations, or the geographic location of family members can pose even greater barriers for long-term care alternatives.

Although such fears may seem rational to clients or their children (if they are involved in the decision making), they can create barriers to open communication in the planning process. For example, a 2010 survey of adults ages 18 to 90 revealed that more than 90% of respondents had not talked to their spouses, adult children, or parents about any of the following: their preferred long-term care option, the role of family members in managing care, and how to pay for long-term care.[8] Eighty-six percent of respondents in the same survey felt it was important for their financial professional to discuss long-term care with them, but only 9% of respondents had actually done so.[9]

A financial professional must be able to adequately empathize with these issues while encouraging clients to fully explore the biases that may shape decisions about long-term care needs. This could start by helping clients confront their understanding, or lack of knowledge, of the protection and limitations of Medicare, Medicaid, private insurance, and personal assets. Clients might also be ignorant of the range of care available or the associated costs. Allowing time for the discussion to evolve and approaching the conversation with sensitivity to the emotional and cognitive needs of the client are good strategies to encourage client action.

By promoting the discussion of health, medical history, and caregiving preferences, a planner might be able to soothe a client's fears, enabling a more productive outcome. Certain personal, family, and lifestyle **risk triggers** should be closely reviewed when evaluating the potential need for long-term care expenses. In some cases, for example, family health history may be the most important evaluative factor for a planner to understand when helping a client analyze potential need. Anticipating the probability of incurring assisted living or skilled nursing facility expenses, based in part on family history, will help determine whether and how much long-term care coverage is needed. Furthermore, awareness of a genetic health issue can also help determine when a policy should be purchased.

Specifically, the following risk triggers should be considered:

- personal health status (e.g., diabetes, alcoholism, high blood pressure);

- related family health history (e.g., coronary artery disease, cancer, Alzheimer's disease, or Parkinson's disease);

- lifestyle choices (e.g., high-risk activities, tobacco or other drug usage); or

- working in a hazardous profession or occupation (e.g., steel worker, emergency medical technician).

These triggers could compromise a client's future health status and increase the likelihood of needing chronic care or custodial care. Considered in conjunction with the client's care preferences and biases, both client and advisor will have a better idea of what challenges or financial demands the future may hold.

In addition to risk triggers, a client's age is another important factor when considering the need for and future cost of long-term care insurance. According to the American Association for Long-Term Care Insurance (AALTCI), in 2007 only 3% of coverage claimants were under age 60, compared to 55.2% of claimants who were 80 or older. Almost a third of claimants were between the ages of 70 and 79.[10] As a client ages, the likelihood of needing services may become more apparent. This phenomenon, known as **adverse selection**, is the tendency for persons with a greater chance of loss to seek coverage.

Adverse selection is controlled by the insurance company underwriting process, which results in higher premiums for those with greater need or more likelihood of making a policy claim. Therefore, the older the purchaser, the higher the periodic premiums, but the fewer premiums paid. The younger the purchaser, the lower the periodic premium, but the greater the number of premiums paid—unless a fixed-pay policy is chosen.

Clients under the age of 40 typically are not advised to purchase a long-term care policy because the cost/benefit tradeoff makes long-term care coverage unfavorable for young clients. A young person who owns a policy is unlikely to make use of services for an extended period of time. As such, the opportunity cost associated with premium payments usually outweighs the benefits of being insured. Beyond the financial savings of delaying the purchase, clients under the age of 40 are also more likely to have living parents or other family members who could help care for them in the event of a disability or illness that would otherwise have required a stay in a care facility.

Conversely, clients over the age of 55 typically should consider purchasing some sort of long-term care coverage. The reduced availability of an extended family network or of family members to care for an older adult, the increased immediacy of need, and the sheer cost of a long-term stay in a care facility make long-term care insurance at this stage of life very important for some clients. These same factors can be relevant regardless of a client's age. For example, a younger client with no extended family network, spouse, or partner to provide care may need and want a policy simply for peace of mind, so that if care is needed, coverage would be available.

By age 65, clients should have a reasonable idea about their individual likelihood of need. After age 70, policy cost and physical condition may eliminate the option. As reported in 2004 by *Consumer Reports*, a plan that costs a 50-year-old $1,625 annually will cost a 60-year-old $3,100 and a 70-year-old $7,575. Furthermore, one out of four 65-year-olds fails the physical and is rejected for long-term-care insurance. At age 75, one in three is rejected.[11]

Owning long-term care insurance typically does not make financial sense for those under age 40, but many planners with clients in the 40 to 55 age range take a wait-and-see approach. With college or wedding costs for children, as well as the need to accelerate retirement savings, discretionary cash flow may be insufficient to meet all financial goals. Although there may be many reasons to delay the purchase of long-term care insurance, an early purchase could be in a client's best interest. By purchasing a policy while younger and still working, a client has more income to meet financial obligations. For example, if a 45-year-old client purchased a 20-pay policy, then the client's long-term care needs would be funded before or near the time of retirement. This would free up cash flow during retirement and protect the client from future premium increases.

Whereas client risk profile and age can offer insight into the need for long-term care insurance, a more definitive answer may come from the client's available monetary resources for funding care services. Assuming a client is at least age 40 and that there is evidence to suggest that long term-care may be needed in the future, a client's situation analysis hinges on the retain-the-risk versus the insure-the-risk approach. This issue is addressed in the second question above, which asked, "Does the client have sufficient monetary resources or a family support network to 'self-insure'?"

The following rules could help an advisor, in consultation with a client; answer the financial part of that question:

**Rule 1:** If a client has a net worth between $250,000 and $1.5 million, exclusive of the value of the home, a long-term care policy may be worth considering. This type of client may not have sufficient resources to fully self-insure. If an extended stay in a care facility was needed, the cost would significantly reduce the client's net worth. Lifetime premiums, as a percentage of net worth, often indicate the need for long-term care coverage.

**Rule 2:** Clients with a net worth in excess of $1.5 million, exclusive of home value, should consider self-insuring. Clients with this level of net worth can often afford to self-insure the risk of entering a care facility or fund needed services while remaining at home. Assuming an average stay in a care facility, usually quoted as 30 months, it is unlikely that this cost would deplete assets below $1 million for most clients, thus preserving wealth for other goals.

**Rule 3:** Clients with a net worth less than $250,000, exclusive of home value, should consider self-insuring. Although this rule seems harsh, a client at this level of net worth would be expected to spend down assets and use Medicaid benefits to pay for an extended period of care, if necessary. The cost of premiums, in comparison to such a low level of net worth, makes purchasing a policy inefficient. But clients living in a Partnership Plan state, discussed later in the chapter, could purchase a lower-cost, state-certified policy and protect a certain level of assets while remaining Medicaid eligible. In addition to Medicaid qualification restrictions, clients could lose control over care decisions, and in-home care typically is not an option.

As with all "rules," exceptions apply. For example, consider a client with a net worth of $2 million who wants to preserve the money for a charitable or family legacy. To protect this wish, the client could purchase a long-term care policy, even though the cost of care is otherwise affordable. Another exception would be a married couple with $750,000 in assets who decides that the much younger spouse would care for the older spouse should chronic care be required. As long as the couple jointly reaches an informed decision, the choice to self-insure should be honored. Figure 8.2 summarizes how a client's age, family health history, or current financial situation can generally be incorporated into determining the need for long-term care insurance.

**Figure 8.2** Long-term Care Insurance Planning Decision Tree

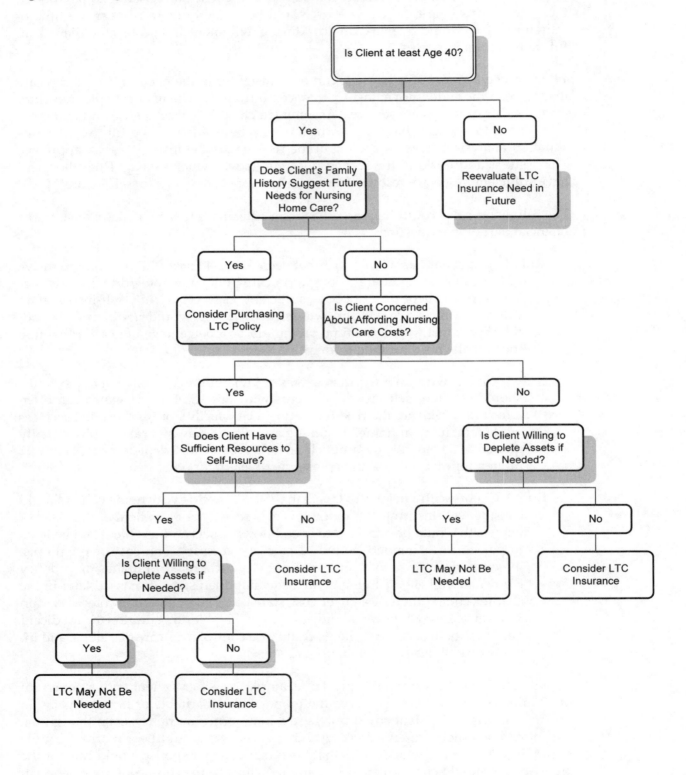

Once the need for long-term care insurance has been established, attention must turn to the quantification of that need. Just as the determination of need is not always straightforward, neither is the decision regarding the amount of coverage to purchase. The continuum of services covered; differences in the respective costs of those services; and uncertainty regarding when, where, and how long services may be needed confound discussions on the amount of coverage. Additional factors, such as the ages of the client, spouse, or partner and the corresponding cost of coverage purchased now or later must be considered. A number of policy provisions are available to tailor a policy to a client's needs, but they may also add to premium cost. Conversely, experts caution that restricting coverage too much in an effort to reduce premiums may render the policy virtually useless.

When purchasing a long-term care policy, client and planner should consider several factors. The first factor is the range of services covered and the corresponding actual benefit amount. Most comprehensive long-term care insurance policies, or **integrated policies**, cover a range of services, although the amount of coverage may vary by service. The client may use home care, adult day care, assisted living care, nursing home care, or hospice care until the maximum benefit or the stated period expires.

The choice of maximum benefit is typically based on nursing home costs. But coverage amounts for other services vary and may be the same as the nursing home amount, a percentage of that amount contingent on the type of care used, or a smaller stated per-day coverage amount contingent on the service. Some policies cover only the insured, but others offer coverage for couples—a difference that can significantly affect the amount of coverage needed when matched to the needs of the client(s). Finally, it is important to note that policy benefits can be limited to specific coverage, such as facility-only or home-care only.

The majority of long-term care policies provide a specified "per-day" benefit. This amount can range from less than $100 to more than $300 per day. The appropriate amount should be based on a thorough review of facility costs in the area where the care is most likely to be received. For example, based on the *Genworth Financial 2011 Cost of Care Survey*, the median annual cost of a private room in a nursing home ranged from a low of $52,925 in Oklahoma to $227,760 in Alaska.[12] Furthermore, this report revealed stark differences in the costs of assisted living and nursing care facilities within the same state, as well as differences among states.

The second factor when quantifying coverage need is the length of the coverage period. Most policies offer coverage periods between two (or, in some states, a minimum of three) and five to seven years, although some may offer coverage for a lifetime. (The latter can be prohibitively expensive.)  The length of coverage must be matched to the individual client's projected need for coverage, available resources, and ability to pay for the premiums.

The third factor considered when quantifying coverage need is how a policy pays the benefit. Some policies pay a full daily limit regardless of actual charges for long-term care services. In other words, the full cost of a day of service is "exhausted" regardless of actual cost, and with some older policies any excess benefit is lost. Most policies pay the actual amount of charges incurred up to the daily limit chosen. Still other policies provide a set dollar benefit that is not measured by calendar usage, but rather by a lifetime maximum dollar amount. For example, a four-year, $100-per-day policy would list a total benefit of $146,000 (4 × 100 × 365). But the insured's actual benefit received could vary depending on the type and length of care.

If the policy is a **pool-of-money policy**, also known as an **expense-reimbursement contract**, then regardless of the benefit per day received, the policy would pay $146,000 prior to expiration. If the policy is a *stated period*, or *indemnity policy*, however, then it will pay only for the specified period of years, whether or not the client receives the maximum $100-per-day benefit. In other words, the only way to receive the full $146,000 is to be eligible for the maximum per-day benefit for the full four years. A pool-of-money policy refers to the maximum lifetime benefit amount. A stated-period policy refers to benefits indemnified or paid over a period of time. Benefits from an individually owned long-term care policy are typically received tax free, except for benefits from an indemnity policy. Benefits are subject to federal tax only if the amount paid exceeds the higher of the cost of qualified long-term care or $300 per day (the 2011 limit).[13]

Clearly a pool-of-money, or expense-reimbursed, contract is superior to an indemnity contract. A pool of money might allow a client to extend a four-year benefit to longer-term coverage if the reimbursement did not require the maximum daily amount. In addition to direct reimbursement for services, other plans feature a per-diem cash payment based on the daily benefit amount and the number of eligible days in a payment cycle, regardless of the type of services used once eligibility is established. The cash payment option offers more flexibility because the recipient of the benefits determines how the money is spent.

The fourth factor to consider when quantifying the need for long-term care insurance is the elimination period of a policy. This factor affects the amount of proposed coverage, the cost of coverage (the longer the waiting period, the lower the premium), and the client resources available to pay for care during the waiting period. Almost all policies have waiting periods before benefits are payable, ranging from 0 days (known as "first-dollar coverage") to, more commonly, 15 to 90 days, although it can be as long as 365 days.

Policies define the days that count toward the elimination period or deductible differently, the primary consideration being "days of service," meaning how long the insured received paid care, or simply "calendar days." Some policies count actual qualifying service days or weeks (based on a defined number of qualifying days within a week), and they may count only consecutive days or random qualifying days over a period of time. Some policies also change the elimination period based on other factors, including previous stays in a care facility within the last 12 months, a hospital stay immediately preceding a move to a care facility, or a change in the insured's health.

The fifth factor to consider when quantifiying coverage need is an inflationary increase in the cost of long-term care services. Although this can be important for any client, it is especially important for younger clients, because the difference between increasing service costs and policy benefits must be drawn from personal assets. An inflation rider provides an annual automatic increase in coverage limits in one of three ways. The annual inflation factor can be a simple fixed percentage, a compound fixed percentage, or it can be based on the Consumer Price Index or other measure of inflation. Policies typically offer a 2% to 5% inflationary increase, but other options may be available. Both the amount of increase and the kind of factor influence the cost of the rider, with choices that yield a greater increase in benefits, level of protection, or greater cost. Some sources refer to the inflation rider as a cost-of-living adjustment, or COLA.

A compound fixed percentage increase is recommended, unless clients are in their 60s or older, when a simple fixed percentage may offer suffcient protection. But clients should be cautioned that waiting until this age to purchase a policy will increase the cost and, depending on health status, could render them uninsurable. A second caution is also warranted. The inflationary increase should be automatic, not contingent on the insurability of the client, as some policies require.

Two more options for increasing coverage are available and can affect the amount of coverage purchased initially. A different inflation protection approach is a guaranteed purchase option that allows the insured to increase daily coverage automatically at periodic intervals (e.g., every three to five years) with no evidence of insurability. This provision offers additional flexibility, but it does increase the premium based on the insured's age at the time of exercise. If the option is not exercised, it is typically lost. Another option is to choose a significantly higher daily benefit than currently needed, with the idea that the cost of care will increase to or exceed the benefit amount. This can be more cost effective than adding an inflation rider. But higher-than-expected out-of-pocket costs may be necessary if the cost of care increases more than anticipated and no other inflation protection has been included.

Incidental to the consideration of inflationary increases in the cost of care is the issue of future premium costs relative to retirement income available. For those on a fixed income, premiums that were once affordable can, over time, become prohibitively expensive. Without a well-diversified retirement plan and ample savings, purchasing long-term care insurance that will subsequently lapse may not be the most productive use of premium dollars.

Although there may not be as many different policy types as other forms of insurance, the complexity and cost of long-term care policies can truly confound decision making for planners and clients. Emotional issues involved in the purchase decision add to this complexity. It is imperative that financial planners be familiar with the various aspects of the policy but, more importantly, with the process to help clients assess their situations. So for planners the question becomes who might need it and who might not? Answering that question requires both planner and client to recognize that a long-term care policy may be a cornerstone in protecting a client's financial well-being and provide confidence to face the future.

### Planning for Special Populations: Long-term Care Insurance Issues for Women

Women are particularly affected by the issue of long-term care. On one hand, they are more likely to be caregivers, by choice or because financial support for paid care is unavailable. On the other hand, women are more vulnerable to the need for paid care services because they live longer and spend more years of their lives alone, on average. Almost 70% of women age 75 or older, compared to about 30% of men, are widowed, divorced, or never married.[14] Older women also tend to have lower incomes and access to fewer resources. Consider the following statistics:

- Almost two-thirds of family caregivers, defined as those providing care and assistance for an older adult or someone with a chronic or disabling situation, are female (65%).  The "average" U.S. caregiver is a 49-year-old woman who works outside the home but spends about 20 hours each week providing unpaid care to her mother for nearly five years.[15]

- The Alzhiemer's Association reports that 60% of family caregivers and other unpaid caregivers of people with Alzheimer's disease and other dementias are women. The caregivers are white (70%), married (66%), and aged 55 or older (56%). Nearly half of the caregivers (44%) work full or part time. Little relief for unpaid caregivers is available, because 50% of them live in the same household as the person with Alzheimer's or other dementias for whom they provide care.[16]

- The AALTCI reports that longevity, an average of five years more than men, explains why women use more long-term care services than men. More than 70% of nursing home residents are women, and 75.7% of assisted living community residents are women. Of those who remain independent aged 75 or older, women are 60% more likely than men to need help with one or more ADLs.[17]

- Almost two-thirds of all Americans living with Alzheimer's disease are women. A larger proportion of women than men have Alzheimer's or other dementia primarily because women live longer than men, on average, not because women are more likely to develop dementia. According to the research, age-specific onset does not vary by gender.[18]

- When asked about what would be or has been a barrier to discussing long-term care, women were more worried than men (72% to 57%, respectively) about upsetting their families by talking about long-term care needs or options.[19]

- A 2011 study reported that, based on a representative sample of U.S. adults age 25 and older with an income of $50,000 and higher, men were twice as likely as women (69% and 31%, respectively) to have purchased long-term care insurance in the last six to 10 years.[20]

- According to the AALTCI, women represented just over 60% of the 2010 purchasers of life insurance policies with long-term care coverage. One-third (34%) of the women who purchased new life insurance policies with long-term care riders in 2010 were between the ages of 55 and 64, and nearly 40% were between the ages of 65 and 74. Male purchasers tended to be slightly older.[21]

Financial advisors have an opportunity to empower women to change the course of their lives by discussing long-term care planning. For many individuals, the question focuses on whether there is a need. But for many women, whether thinking about themselves or others in their lives, the question may not be *if*, but *when*. Helping women understand their options and make informed choices by planning for that uncertainty is a value-added service that only a well-informed financial professional can provide.

## Document and Evaluate Current Long-term Care Insurance

The Center for Retirement Research projected that, of those turning 65 in 2010, about two-thirds would need long-term care at some point in their lives, and 33% would need to enter a nursing home for three months or longer. Nine percent were projected to need care for nine years or longer.[22] Based on a 2007 study, the AALTCI, the industry's professional organization, reported that approximately 8 million Americans own long-term care insurance, , with 400,000 new policies issued in 2007.[23] Employer group plans are increasingly available, but they still are not widespread. But some group plans do offer coverage for parents of employees, a benefit that should not be overlooked if available to clients.

Consequently, many clients are unlikely to have coverage available to document or evaluate. But if a policy is in force, coverage, cost, and company ratings are important considerations. Coverage can vary widely, depending on the age of the policy, and it should be evaluated in light of a client's current situation. Policy premiums should be evaluated for affordability today as well as for possibly decades into the future, when dramatically increased premiums may consume more of a retirement income. Insurance company ratings provided by A. M. Best, Moody's, Standard & Poor's, or Weiss should be reviewed to assess the ability of a company to meet future claims.

One of the most beneficial options that can be purchased with a long-term care policy is the **nonforfeiture clause**, especially if a client is younger or still in exceptional health. In some policies this is known as a **benefit bank**. This clause allows the insured to receive some residual benefit in the event of policy lapse or death before making a claim. Many states require nonforfeiture on policies, or the company may voluntarily offer it as an option. The nonforfeiture option adds to the cost of a basic policy premium—in some cases, as much as 40%, and by some estimates as much as 100%.[24] Different types of nonforfeiture options are available, and costs vary by company.

Nonforfeiture options are similar to those for cash value life insurance. These options include a reduced lifetime (or paid-up) benefit, a reduced benefit period, or a return of premium. The **reduced paid-up coverage option** provides that a specified amount of coverage is available until the death of the client, but the daily benefit is permanently reduced, and with some companies the coverage is limited to nursing home care. The **shortened benefit period option** provides the insured the benefit originally offered, but the duration of coverage is limited based on the dollar amount of the premiums paid. With the **return of premium option**, a percentage of the premiums paid is returned after policy lapse or death.

For insureds who did not purchase a nonforfeiture option, some policies offer contingent nonforfeiture benefits upon lapse (CBL). Based on a standardized table recommended by the National Association of Insurance Commissioners (NAIC) 2000 Model Act and Regulation, this benefit is available when a policy lapses because of increased premium cost. Availability of the option is based on a comparison of the insured's age and the percentage increase in premium cost, either for a single increase or for cumulative increases, compared to the initial premium amount. Like other nonforfeiture options, CBL is available only when required by state law or when voluntarily offered by the company. The options are reduced paid-up benefits (available indefinitely, but with a reduced daily benefit) or a shortened period of benefits (with the original coverage benefit available, but for a limited time).

For clients who are considering long-term care policy lapse or replacement, planners must carefully study the nonforfeiture and CBL options available. In some cases, continuing a policy for even a short period of time can affect the nonforfeiture benefits available. As is true with other types of insurance, clients should be cautioned not to cancel a policy until another is in force. Furthermore, a pre-existing condition clause in the new policy could limit coverage initially. Also, premium costs will reflect the increased age of the client at the date of purchase. These are two distinct disadvantages that should not be overlooked.

Finally, a § 1035 exchange of one long-term care tax-qualified policy for another policy could be another option for a client with an in-force policy. The suitability of the new product must be documeneted. Further discussion of this option follows.

# STRATEGIES

## Review Prospective Long-term Care Insurance Planning Strategies

The long-term care planning landscape continues to change rapidly. Several important trends will have an impact on the way long-term care product recommendations are made in the future. Increasing premium costs, commonly described as double-digit and in some cases projected to be as high as 40%, have caught people with policies—and those seeking to purchase—by surprise, and they have significantly reduced sales.[25] High claims, a low-interest-rate environment, a low policy lapse rate, and a tendency toward adverse selection, among other factors, have forced several companies such as MetLife out of the long-term care market; they stopped offering the product in 2010.

Other companies are offering innovative products by packaging life insurance and long-term care products together, or by packaging annuity and long-term care products together. As a result of the Pension Protection Act of 2006 (the Act), effective in 2010, insurance companies can offer life insurance and annuity products with a long-term care insurance rider, and the benefit payments would not be treated as taxable distributions of policy gains. This contributed to the availability of innovative linked-benefit products. Investments in the contract may fund the long-term care insurance rider, but neither that cost nor the benefits are taxed as a policy distribution. However, these expenses do reduce the investment in the contract, which may have implications if the contract is surrendered, or upon the death of the owner. This combining of products, often referred to as **linked-benefit products** or *asset-based products*, will provide additional choices—and complications—for consumers and financial planners.

The Act also modified  the provisions of IRC § 1035 to allow for the tax-free exchange of a life insurance or annuity product to purchase a qualified long-term care policy, or the exchange of one long-term care policy for another. This change protects from taxation a client's gains from existing life insurance or annuity contracts by allowing their tax-free exchange for another product. These changes, which stemmed from the Pension Protection Act of 2006, made it possible for clients to protect their futures more easily by means of a deferred annuity with a long-term care benefit; to exchange an annuity or life insurance product to purchase a long-term care insurance policy; or to exchange an annuity or life insurance contract for a similar product with a qualified long-term care rider.

It is important to note that neither an annuity contract nor a traditional long-term care contract can be exchanged, tax-free, for a life insurance policy with or without a qualified long-term care rider. A nonqualified single-premium immediate annuity is also eligible for a tax-free exchange to purchase long-term care insurance. Care must be taken to handle the exchange appropriately through the insurance companies, with the advice of a tax professional, and to be certain that any death benefit surrendered (in the case of life insurance) is no longer needed.

Finally, **Partnership Plan**s that started in the 1980s but became available to all states in the Deficit Reduction Act of 2005 are helping families meet long-term care insurance needs by providing tax and asset protection benefits. These plans encourage long-term care planning by linking insurance coverage and Medicaid eligibility, and they support the goal of reducing Medicaid spending for a rapidly increasing elderly population. According to the Center for Retirement Research at Boston College, Medicaid paid nearly 40% of the national long-term care tab in 2008.[26]

Financial planners must help clients develop a long-term care strategy regardless of a client's age, health status, or financial situation. As with other aspects of the planning process, the uncertainty of the future provides the context for the choices considered. For many, long-term care insurance offers the advantages of greater choice among care alternatives, including the option for the often-preferred in-home or in-community care, as opposed to residential or custodial care. For some, it eliminates or reduces the need for extended family to pay for care. For others, any private insurance delays dependence on Medicare or Medicaid, with their complicated federal and state regulations regarding eligibility for care, assets, and asset transfers. Those who cannot medically qualify for long-term insurance face these and other issues surrounding asset accumulation and preservation. Two product trends, linked-benefit products and partnership plans, offer planners and their clients' additional options. Discussions of both follow.

## Long-term Care and Life Insurance Combination Products

The question "what if I never need long-term care?" coupled with the expense of the insurance are primary reasons the average American fails to purchase long-term care coverage. Realizing that people feel constrained when faced with what they consider to be a lose-lose scenario, a number of firms within the insurance industry have created a product that combines the advantages of cash value life insurance with long-term care coverage. Financial planners and consumers have enthusiastically embraced these combination or hybrid products because clients perceive dual value—they obtain long-term care coverage while building cash value that can be used if the long-term care benefit is never needed.

Although products vary by company, most hybrid products add a long-term care rider to a cash-value (whole or universal) life insurance policy. Policies are available as a single premium or, in some cases, with a recurring premium. Regardless of the product, an accelerated benefits rider makes the policy death benefit available to pay for long-term care expenses. An **extension of benefits option** adds a multiple to the face value of a policy for additional long-term care expenses. For example, with this option, a $100,000 face value policy might provide an additional $200,000 in long-term care coverage. Both the death benefit of the policy and the extension of benefits would be available to pay long-term care costs. Unlike traditional long-term care policies that offer greater choice in the length of time qualifying care must be provided before policy benefits begin, a 90- or 100-day elimination period is common.

According to the AALTCI, insurance companies use different formulas when qualifying claims. **Reimbursement plans** repay actual expenses up to the policy maximum monthly benefit amount. Another approach is known as an **indemnity plan**, which pays a monthly maximum as long as the policyholder provides evidence of an ongoing need within covered expenditures. An indemnity plan tends to be more expensive. Policyholders determine the total long-term care amount and maximum monthly payment when purchasing a policy. Typical payment periods range from 24 to 60 months, although a few lifetime plans are also available. Policies may pay for a range of care options (in-home, assisted living, or adult day care) or be limited to nursing home care. Regardless of policy type, the benefit amount must fall within IRS-defined guidelines and conform to federal regulations for both life insurance and long-term care insurance coverage to maintain qualified tax status.

As with all life insurance products, several policy provisions are available for an additional premium. A **return of premium** option is very popular with consumers. This optional feature provides a full refund of all premiums paid (exclusive of loans, withdrawals, or policy benefits paid). If a client requests a return of premium, the policy is then cancelled. A **residual death benefit** makes the full life insurance benefit available if the long-term care coverage feature is not used. Some policies provide a minimal residual death benefit to cover final expenses if all policy benefits are exhausted. Inflation protection can also be purchased. This additional feature provides some protection against increasing long term-care costs.

It is important to remember that clients must meet underwriting standards for a hybrid policy, but requirements vary by product. However, applying for a hybrid policy before it is needed is imperative. Some companies offer joint policies for couples, which may ease underwriting concerns if one spouse is reasonably healthy.

The following example, described by the AALTCI, illustrates how a linkded-benefit life and long-term care plan works. A client with $400,000 in retirement assets is 60 years old and in good health. He plans to leave his nest egg to his adult children. The client could purchase a $200,000-face-value hybrid policy, naming his children as beneficiaries. By adding an extension of benefits rider, he could have up to $400,000 in long-term care coverage, or $6,000 per month for five years. Using a return of premium option, the client can cancel at any time and receive his premium payments back, but if necessary, the policy could protect the retirement assets intended for the heirs. Typically, the long-term care benefit rider is paid with a one-time premium of available assets. In 2011, the average premium was $65,000. A § 1035 exchange of an existing life insurance policy could be used.

## Long-term Care and Annuity Combination Products

Hybrid products combining annuity and long-term care features also appeal to clients who want protection for long-term care costs but fear that they will not ultimately need the coverage. Although features vary by company and individual product, several general product characteristics add to the appeal—and the complexity—of these hybrid annuity products. It is important to note that product availability also varies by state. Thus, working with a knowledgeable professional is important. Many planners, in the best interests of their clients and to remain within their competence limits, collaborate with someone who specializes in long-term care products once a client need has been established.

Both fixed and variable annuities may offer a long-term care rider, although fixed products are more common. Some linked-benefit annuity and long-term care products require health underwriting, and others do not. The latter feature is particularly attractive to those who may be uninsurable. However, the available term of long-term care benefits varies for these products. Annuities that do not require underwriting typically limit coverage to no more than 36 months, and longer benefit periods are available for products that require health underwritng. Of the products that do not require underwriting, some may be purchased before care is needed, and others can be purchased afterwards.

Funding options also vary by product. Lump-sum,or single, payments are required, but if funds are not available, a traditional annuity contract or a life insurance contract can be exchanged, through § 1035, for an annuity with a long-term care rider. For annuities that require health underwriting, up to 60% of the value in a qualified account such as a 401(k) or IRA can be used through a § 1035 exchange to purchase the product. This option can benefit couples, in that qualified funds of one spouse may be used to purchase a shared-benefit product that could offer protection for both. Linked-benefit annuity and long-term care products have certain disadvantages, including high surrender charges, low fixed returns on premiums, and the opportunity costs associated with funding long-term care insurance with a lump-sum payment rather than over time.

An example reported by Phipps may illustrate how this product can be used.[27] Consider a 60-year-old female who purchases a 20-year long-term-care fixed annuity with a 5% inflation-adjustment rider for long-term care coverage and a lump-sum premium of $50,000. This coverage provides the client with an initial $100,000 (two times the premium) in long-term care coverage for a maximum of the six-year benefit period. If no distributions are taken from the policy, the account will increase to $265,330 of long-term care coverage, or a maximum of $3,685 per month at the end of 20 years, assuming a 3.5% compound interest rate less administrative fees. If the long-term care coverage is not needed, the client may continue to defer the account value or begin taking distributions when the annuity matures. Upon her death, her heirs would receive the premium of $50,000 less any long-term care benefits paid *or* the accumulated anuity value, whichever is larger.

Despite the complexity of hybrid annuity products, the long-term care protection available, if needed, is typically based on four factors:

- the amount of the single premium paid;

- the term of benefits selected (generally four or six years);

- the addition of an inflation factor and its amount (e.g., 3% or 5%); and

- the multiplier (sometimes called the *leverage factor*) applied to the initial premium paid to determine the maximum long-term care benefit, typically 1.5 or two times if inflation protection is chosen *or* two or three times if inflation protection is not chosen.

Clients should be cautioned to fully understand and compare products prior to purchase. Also recall that, as a result of the Pension Protection Act of 2006 provision that took effect in 2010, distributions for long term-care coverage are made on a tax-free basis. This tax savings could benefit a client who previously purchased a traditional annuity, but who could now purchase a hybrid product with a § 1035 exchange and avoid the taxes that would have been paid on the gains in the original product.

### Partnership Plans and Medicaid: Changing the Future of Cost-benefit Analysis

Medicaid is a federally funded program to provide health and long-term care services to those with few resources and very limited income. States administer the Medicaid program individually to provide nursing home care and, to a limited extent, in-home and community care services to those who meet financial and functional eligibility requirements. Medicaid will not pay for long-term custodial care for individuals until most of their assets have been spent and income is limited. **Medicaid planning** involves efforts to distribute or "spend down" assets to meet the means tests (i.e., a maximum of $2,000 in "countable" assets are owned in the individual's name, although this amount may vary by state) and other eligibility requirements for Medicaid long-term care benefits.

Planners are not allowed to recommend that clients forgo the purchase of a long-term care policy with the intent of spending down assets to become Medicaid eligible. When someone applies for Medicaid, the Medicaid agency reviews all transfers of assets that the applicant or his or her spouse have made in the prior 60 months; this is typically called the *look-back period*. Nonexempt transfers or transfers disallowed by Medicaid during this period cause the loss of Medicaid eligibility (what is called a *penalty period*) that begins when the individual is eligible for Medicaid benefits. The length of the penalty period is determined by dividing the value of the transferred asset by the average monthly private-pay rate for nursing facility care in the state. This penalty means that more of an individual's assets must be liquidated or, if unavailable, that the extended family may have to offer assistance.

According to the Omnibus Budget Reconciliation Act of 1993, the state has the right to reclaim the amount paid for the care of a Medicaid applicant. And because of the means testing to qualify for Medicaid, the home is usually the only property of substantial value that a Medicaid recipient is likely to own. But federal law also allows a married Medicaid recipient to transfer the home to his or her spouse without penalty. Then, should the spouse choose to protect the home, some states allow the spousal owner to gift the home to others. This creates a number of issues, beyond the obvious questions of whether the donor will be able to remain in the home. A second issue focuses on the donor's potential need for long-term care. If Medicaid was to be needed, all transfers within the prior 60 months would be reviewed, and any **nonexempt transfer** or a disallowed transfer of assets, during that prior five-year period would trigger a penalty period and ineligbibility for aid. A third issue is the potential gift tax that could result.

When analyzing a client's capacity to fund a long-term stay in a care facility, planners must consider a client's desires regarding the location, the type of care anticipated, and family or charitable legacy relative to the assets available. Public/private partnership plans encourage long-term care planning by linking insurance coverage and Medicaid eligibility. Partnership programs, which are now available in more than 35 states, split the cost of custodial care between personal assets and state payments while allowing the recipient to maintain assets based on a predetermined formula established by the state.

According to state insurance commissioners, such as the Kansas Insurance Department, partnership plans encourage consumers to partner with a state-based program as they purchase qualified private long-term care insurance policies. Partnership-qualified policies are available from licensed insurance professionals and financial planners. To qualify, policies must meet state and federal partnership requirements. People who purchase a qualifying long-term care policy may still qualify for Medicaid after depleting their insurance benefits, provided they meet all other Medicaid eligibility criteria. In effect, a long-term care partnership program provides dollar-for-dollar asset protection. Each dollar paid by a partnership policy entitles a consumer to keep a dollar of assets sheltered from Medicaid recovery.

It is important to note that, although these plans help protect assets from liquidation, they do not waive the income limit or functional eligibility required for Medicaid— functional eligibility requirements that may exceed the eligibility requirements for the private policy that had been providing care services. Another downside of these partnerships is that benefits may or may not be portable from state to state, depending on individual state agreements that allow for reciprocity among states. Finally, Medicaid plans typically restrict coverage to services provided in a nursing home.

The increased availability of partnership plans further complicates long-term care planning for some clients. Advisors must be knowledgeable about the coordination of services and eligibility guidelines between private insurance and Medicaid coverage or be able to offer referrals to knowledgeable professionals who specialize in long-term care planning. Out-of-pocket expenses to supplement the cost of care provided by the private policy also must be considered.

> ### Planning for Special Populations: Long-term Care Insurance Issues for Same-sex Couples
>
> Clients who are involved in a same-sex relationship must take steps to adequately insure against the costs associated with long-term care expenses. Unlike heterosexual married couples who can provide financial support for each other without triggering the federal gift tax, same-sex couples cannot. Helping a partner pay for long-term care expenses may trigger gift taxes if the transfer exceeds the yearly maximum gift amount.
>
> Married couples can transfer assets without penalty to each other in such a way as to qualify for Medicaid and to shelter assets for the benefit of the community spouse. However, partners in a same-sex relationship may not be afforded the same protection. Thus, a home, which would be a protected asset for the benefit of the community spouse, may not receive the same treatment for the community partner in a same-sex relationship. At the death of the homeowner, a lien on the property could force its sale for recovery of Medicaid expenses paid, leaving the surviving partner homeless. Federal law prohibits imposing this lien if beneficiaries are married to someone of the opposite sex who still lives in the home. Long-term care insurance can alleviate or minimize these costs and the potentially devastating outcomes, personally and financially, associated with illness and health care needs.
>
> Under Department of Health and Human Services guidance issued in June 2011, states have the option to allow community partners in a same-sex relationship to keep their homes while their partners are receiving Medicaid support for long-term care, such as care in a nursing home. States may—but are not required to—include same-sex couples in the same Medicaid protections, equivalent to those of heterosexual married couples. This guidance did not state what level of legal protection the same-sex couples must obtain, i.e., marriage or civil union, to qualify for such protection.

## Identify Prospective Long-term Care Insurance Strategies

When purchasing long-term care insurance, it may be prudent to discuss with clients methods that optimize the cost/benefit ratio of the policy. One of the easiest ways to accomplish this, aside from adjusting the amount of the benefits, is to weigh the benefit period and the elimination period against the premium. A long benefit period and a short waiting period will result in a relatively expensive policy. Conversely, a policy with a short benefit period and a long waiting period may leave the client uninsured when insurance is most needed. A client's gender must also be considered. Because women tend to live longer than men, their benefit period may need to be longer. But if a client can afford the premium, a lifetime benefit, regardless of gender, may be best.

The average stay in a long-term care facility is 30 months; but the median length of stay, according to the AALTCI 2008 LTCi Resource publication is between 12 and 36 months. Clients have a 50% chance of incurring a stay of longer than three years.[28] To err on the side of caution, all of the following strategies assume that a client will spend at least three years in a long-term care facility and insure the projected total cost. These strategies are listed in descending order of total projected policy cost.

## Product Strategy 1: Purchase a Policy with a Lifetime Benefit Period and a 180-day Elimination Period

**Advantage:** This strategy is appropriate in cases where the probability of needing skilled care for an extended period of time is high, based on defined risk triggers. Assuming a three-year or longer care period and having a 180-day elimination period results in the client self-funding for six months up front, but it ensures that the client will never exhaust coverage. This strategy is most suitable for clients who are predisposed to chronic diseases that could incapacitate them for years, such as Alzheimer's disease, severe osteoarthritis, Type 2 diabetes, or Parkinson's disease.

**Disadvantage:** Two disadvantages are associated with this strategy. First, the cost of insurance for this level of coverage can be very high. Second, this strategy requires a client to maintain assets equivalent to the cost of care during the elimination period, which in light of current average monthly costs could equal $20,000 to $50,000, not including the projected 7% increase in annual costs. An alternative to reduce the cost of coverage would be to extend the elimination period to a full year, if that option is available from the insurer and the client has enough assets to cover the cost. Another option would be to limit the lifetime benefit period, a feature that significantly increases the premium.

## Product Strategy 2: Purchase a Long-term Care Policy with a Four-year Benefit Period and a 90-day Elimination Period

**Advantage:** This strategy is appropriate in cases where the probability of needing skilled care for an extended period of time is moderate to average, based on defined risk triggers. Assuming a three-year care period and having a 90-day elimination period result in the client self-funding for only 90 days up front. Even that could be offset by Medicare, if the client qualifies for coverage. This strategy is most suitable for a client who is predisposed to terminal coronary artery disease or stroke, where the length of stay is not as long and has a higher probability of meeting the requirements for Medicare coverage. Should the length of stay exceed the benefits, the family has some time to consider alternatives for meeting the cost of care. According to the AALTCI, only 12% of patients stay for an average of five years or more in a nursing home; the largest single group of patients, 30.3%, stays an average of one to three years.[29]

**Disadvantage:** Three possible disadvantages are associated with this strategy. First, insurance for this level of coverage can be fairly expensive. Second, this strategy requires a client to maintain assets equivalent to the elimination period, in this case, $10,000 to $25,000, not including the projected 7% increase in annual costs. Third, the client could exhaust coverage should the long-term care extend beyond the four-year coverage period. A longer elimination period would reduce the cost of insurance, but it would increase the client's savings requirement.

## Product Strategy 3: Purchase a Fixed-premium, Restricted-coverage Long-term Care Policy with a Four-year Combined Benefit Period and a 90-day Elimination Period

**Advantage:** This strategy is appropriate in cases where the probability of needing custodial care is average to low. The fixed premium results in a higher initial premium. Restricting the types of coverage reduces the overall cost of the insurance. One method of restricting the coverage would be to have two years of coverage for assisted living care and two years for nursing care. Assuming a three-year combined care period and having a 90-day elimination period result in a client self-funding for three months up front. But as long as one type of care does not exceed two years, the client's coverage should not be exhausted.

**Disadvantage:** The primary disadvantage associated with this strategy is that the total four-year benefit period would not be available for either assisted living or nursing care. Experts advise against limiting policy coverage to the point that the policy offers a false sense of security for the premiums paid but actually offers little protection. Eliminating benefits or key provisions from a comprehensive policy to make the premium affordable may be less effective than having no coverage at all.

## Product Strategy 4: Purchase a Fixed-premium Long-term Care Policy with a Two-year Benefit Period and a 180-day Elimination Period

**Advantage:** This strategy is appropriate in cases where the probability of needing custodial care is average to low. Although fixing the premium results in a higher initial premium, it makes planning for expenses easier for the client. Assuming a three-year care period and having a 180-day elimination period result in the client self-funding for six months up front and six months at the end. If funding allows and the option is available, a one-year elimination period may be preferable because this option substantially reduces the cost of insurance and still requires the client to self-fund only one year of coverage.

**Disadvantage:** The three primary disadvantages associated with this strategy are: (1) the cost of insurance may still be significant for some clients; (2) this strategy requires a client to maintain an emergency level of savings equivalent to the elimination period; and (3) the shorter coverage period could leave a client unprotected in the event of an abnormally long care period.

## Product Strategy 5: Self-insure the Long-term Care Need

**Advantage:** This strategy is appropriate in cases where the probability of needing custodial care is moderate to low. If a client's asset base is sufficient to support up to four years of expenses in today's dollars, long-term care insurance may not be needed. This strategy is particularly appropriate for clients with a net worth in excess of $1.5 million and whose insurance coverage and other assets are adequate to care for surviving family members.

**Disadvantage:** If a client is strongly committed to leaving an inheritance to individuals or assets to charity, this strategy could significantly diminish the assets available. With nursing home care costs ranging from approximately $40,000 to $200,000 annually, contingent on location and care provided, the cost of even four years of nursing care can be a significant sum. Assisted living facility care is almost as expensive and often precedes a move to a nursing facility. Clients who want to leave a legacy should consider the benefits of a long-term care insurance policy.

### Product Strategy 6: Self-insure with a Life Insurance Backup

**Advantage:** This strategy is best suited for a client whose asset base is sufficient to support at least partial funding of a long-term care stay. If a life insurance policy is available that allows for a living benefit to be paid for the costs associated with long-term care, even if the client is not terminally ill, then long-term care insurance may not be needed. This could be a good strategy for a client who has a life insurance need but wants added protection should nursing care, such as skilled care or hospice, be needed.

**Disadvantage:** If a client is strongly committed to leaving an inheritance in the form of life insurance benefits, using the living benefit would reduce the amount of the legacy and/or leave the survivors underinsured at the time of death. This insurance should be purchased well in advance of possible need. Policies vary regarding the qualifications that must be met to receive the living benefit, so a complete understanding of the requirements as well as an evaluation of the cost of the rider should be considered.

### Product Strategy 7: Self-insure with a Medicaid Backup

**Advantage:** This strategy is appropriate for clients with less than $250,000 in net worth, exclusive of the home. Clients with this asset profile may find that the premiums associated with long-term care insurance outweigh the benefits provided.

**Disadvantage:** It is possible that a client's asset base could be depleted if nursing home care is required, which would result in the client becoming dependent on Medicaid to pay for care.

### Product Strategy 8: Take Advantage of Available Policy Discounts

**Advantage:** In some states, a 10% to 30% discount is available for married couples who insure jointly with the same insurer. Another way of decreasing the cost of coverage for a married couple is by sharing a common benefit pool. Some individual plans allow couples to transfer benefits to each other from the same policy or sometimes between policies. A **spousal survivorship** option, available on some plans, requires both spouses to buy separate coverage. If one spouse dies after coverage has been in effect for a certain number of years, usually 10 years, then the surviving spouse's policy becomes paid up. Finally, as with health insurance, long-term care insurance offers "good-health" discounts for people who do not take unnecessary health risks or have a history of debilitating diseases.

**Disadvantage:** Because policies vary so much by company, shopping for discounts in addition to other needed provisions can be time consuming. Working with a knowledgeable professional can reduce the time spent comparing policies.

### Product Strategy 9: Use a Long-term Care Partnership Program to Protect Client Assets

**Advantage:** Long-term care Partnership Programs allows policy owners to protect a portion or all of their assets if they ever need to apply for and use Medicaid services. Typically, clients should be encouraged to purchase a three- to five-year long-term care policy with a specific dollar amount of coverage. Should a client need long-term care coverage, the policy will pay benefits up to the maximum dollar amount of the policy, for example $250,000, over the policy term. After depleting the coverage, the client may qualify for Medicaid. These policies provide dollar-for-dollar protection of assets equal to the policy coverage limit (e.g., $250,000). That is, each dollar that a policy pays out entitles the client to shelter a dollar of assets from Medicaid.

**Disadvantage:** Under provisions of the federal Deficit Reduction Act of 2005, each state is authorized to enact Partnership Programs, but not all states have such programs. To qualify for asset protection, Partnership Program plans must be tax qualified, include certain consumer protection provisions, and provide inflation protection.

## Product Strategy 10: Purchase a Hybrid Life Insurance Policy with Long-term Care Benefits

**Advantage:** These cash value products, both whole-life and universal, are ideal for clients who want to be protected against long-term care costs but desire to transfer any remaining assets to heirs. The policy protects assets and offers benefits even if the long-term care benefit is never needed. Underwriting may be more or less stringent than traditional long-term care policies, so purchasing early is prudent.

**Disadvantage:** Care should be taken that the policy provides benefits for a variety of care situations, not only nursing home care. Most policies do not provide for payment of benefits beyond five years, so clients anticipating the possibility of a longer stay because of medical or family history should consider a traditional long-term care policy. Despite potential future availability of assets for heirs, the initial purchase requires a sizeable lump sum for the single-premium payment, and returns on the life insurance policy are low.

## Product Strategy 11: Purchase a Hybrid Deferred Annuity with Long-term Care Benefits

**Advantage:** Insurance companies are issuing both fixed- and variable-annuity products offering a guaranteed lifetime withdrawal option that includes the benefits of an annuity with a long-term care multiplier. Not all products require health underwriting, and for those that do, underwriting can be less strict than for a traditional long-term care policy. Once the qualifications for benefits are met (based on ADLs), there are few policy restrictions on how the funds are used to pay for care. Funds are received tax free, but the federal tax savings must be considered relative to the potentially lower return on the annuity when compared with other taxable investment options. The lump-sum payment is convenient for some purchasers who have chosen to self-insure but want the added security of the linked product and the tax benefits. The residual value also offers security, assuming no long-term care benefits are needed or the benefits do not exhaust the entire value.

**Disadvantage:** Clients must be medically underwritten to quality for some products. A client in poor health will not have access to these hybrid annuity products but could have access to those that do not require underwriting. Clients must have significant assets available to (1) make the single premim payment, and (2) insure sufficient long term-care benefits, depending on projected need. Furthermore, because of surrender fees, clients must be certain that no part of the funds will be needed for the first five to 10 years. And, once the policy matures, any withdrawals from the annuity will reduce the long-term care benefit. Returns on hybrid fixed annuities tend to be less than on traditional annuities, so projected need for long-term care coverage must be weighed against product returns on a hybrid product or the purchase of two traditional products (an anuity and long-term care insurance). Also, earnings on the current asset should be compared to earnings on the hybrid product before making the purchase. Finally, the hybrid must be purchased early enough to allow for the 20-year maturity to fully access benefits.

---

### Long-term Care Insurance Planning Tip:  Definition of a Couple

Although definitions may vary by company, most apply a broad definition of couple when applied to long-term care products and riders. Typically a couple is defined as

- married;

- partners (same- or opposite-sex) who live together for a specified period, often at least three years; or,

- two people of the same generation (i.e., sibling, cousin, etc.) living together and sharing expenses for a specified period, often at least three years.

---

## Procedural Strategy 1: Purchase Policy No Earlier than Age 50 to 55

**Advantage:** Clients younger than age 50 generally should not purchase long-term care insurance unless they know that they have a high likelihood of needing care at an early age and for an extended time. One possible scenario would be if a client knows of a genetic predisposition for early-onset Alzheimer's disease or Parkinson's disease and could be uninsurable in the future.

**Disadvantage:** Clients who wait until at least age 50 to purchase long-term care coverage implicitly self-insure the risk of needing long-term care coverage earlier than age 50.

## Procedural Strategy 2: Purchase a Joint Policy

**Advantage:** It can be significantly less expensive for a married couple (or an unmarried couple that meets the policy definitional requirements) to purchase a joint policy than to purchase two individual policies with the same benefit amount and period. With this type of policy, the couple shares the pool of benefits, either individually or simultaneously. This can be a very useful strategy when both partners want long-term care coverage but only one has a high propensity for using the policy. Generally, this strategy should be recommended in situations where both spouses are close in age. Wide dispersions in age between spouses can trigger excessive policy premiums. However a joint policy allows the couple to maximize eligible tax deductibility for the premium when there is a difference in ages between the spouses.

**Disadvantage:** Although the annual premium for this type of coverage is lower, the total benefit available for each spouse is also lower should both become benefit eligible. To compensate, a large inflation factor is recommended to increase the daily or monthly benefit should both members of the couple require benefits simultaneously. This strategy may be unsuitable for spouses who are of significantly different ages because of the higher premiums.

## Procedural Strategy 2: Purchase Linked, or Shared-care, Policies

**Advantage:** For a married couple (or an unmarried couple that meets the policy definitional requirements), benefits can be increased by linking individual policies with a shared-care rider, which essentially provides sequential access to the benefits available to each individual, thus doubling the benefit, if necessary. Benefits can be drawn on simultaneously by each spouse, but combining the benefits is only available after one spouse has exhausted individual coverage. Thus, assets will be needed to supplement the cost of care if benefit coverage is insufficient for all costs. Discounts can be available when spouses apply for coverage at the same time.

**Disadvantage:** The shared-care rider adds to the cost of the policies, but it is cheaper than buying additional benefits. Linking policies with reduced individual benefits can be a workable strategy unless the cost of care for one partner exceeds the benefit available, thus requiring other assets to supplement that cost. The second spouse to need benefits will have access only to the remainder of his/her unused benefits, which could be insufficient.

## Procedural Strategy 4: Increase the Coverage Period but Decrease the Daily Benefit

**Advantage:** If a client has adequate funds to self-insure but does not want to risk the chance of depleting savings, then sharing the cost of care might be an excellent alternative strategy. By choosing a lower daily benefit, such as $75 or $100, and increasing the benefit period to five years or more, the client should have adequate protection in the event of an abnormally long care period.

**Disadvantage:** Without incorporating an inflation guard rider in the policy, choosing a low initial benefit amount could put undue strain on a client's finances, regardless of the coverage period. To offset this possibility, a planner could recommend a pool-of-money policy, rather than a stated period, or indemnity, policy so that a client can draw a higher amount, up to actual costs incurred, until the policy is exhausted.

## Procedural Strategy 5: Educate Clients that Long-term Care Costs Are Generally Not Covered by Medicare

**Advantage:** Clients are often misinformed about Medicare coverage and may need guidance to prepare for unexpected long-term care costs. Medicare coverage for home care is limited to skilled-nursing care when homebound under a doctor's care. Skilled nursing home care, limited to 100 days, is covered only within 30 days of a three-day or longer hospital stay. And hospice care in a Medicare-approved hospice is available only if a doctor certifies that the individual has six or fewer months to live.

Furthermore, restrictions on the services covered, benefit periods, benefit payments, and client copayments apply in each situation. Without long-term care insurance and with only limited Medicare benefits, clients are effectively self-insuring against the costs associated with skilled nursing care. Unfortunately, these clients are often unaware of the actual costs involved, or how dramatically different the cost could be in one area or one type of facility versus another.

**Disadvantage:** Advisors have a responsibility to help clients become better informed about the myriad of options for planning for long-term care and the implications for asset accumulation and asset preservation. Implications for adult children who may provide care or share in the cost of insurance premiums or the cost of care services must also be considered. Although clients should not rely on Medicare as a long-term care provider, some clients may not be able to afford the cost of long-term care coverage.

### Procedural Strategy 6: Tailor the Policy to the Client with Appropriate Provisions

**Advantage:** Provisions customize the policy to better meet the needs of the client. Guaranteed renewability or better yet, noncancelability are recommended provisions that add to the cost of a policy. **Guaranteed renewable** means that as long as premiums are paid on time, the insurance company cannot cancel the policy, unless it does so for an entire risk category. But premiums can continue to increase. **Noncancelable** also means that the policy is in force as long as premiums are paid, but unlike the guaranteed renewable policy, premiums are fixed for the duration of the policy. Not all companies offer noncancelable policies; guaranteed renewable policies are more commonly available.

Some plans offer ways for clients to shorten the length of time that premiums are due. **Accelerated payment options** include 10-pay, 20-pay, or pay-until-age-65 options. Each of these payment options allows for a fixed payment period beyond which no further premiums are due. This can be a very beneficial feature for clients who can afford to "pre-pay" the higher premium, thus avoiding payment later when income may be reduced or medical expenses may have accelerated. The amount of the premiums no longer required could also become available for funding other goals.

Another feature available on some long-term care policies is the **restoration of benefits provision**. This feature is conditional and restores benefits that have been used under a policy, as long as the benefit pool has not been exhausted. For example, if a client has a six-year benefit policy and uses up five years of benefits, all of the policy benefits can be restored if they are not needed for a certain length of time, most likely 12 months. To trigger the restoration, a physician must certify that the insured no longer needs long-term care, and the insured must resume paying premiums if a waiver of premium had been granted.

The **return of premium** provision adds approximately 70% to 80% to the base premium, but it will repay the difference between premiums paid and benefits collected upon the insured's death. To collect on this feature, most insurers require the policy to have been in force for a certain period of time, such as 10 years. Although this feature is moderately expensive, it may be a useful planning tool if a client is uncertain about the probability of using the policy but wants the assurance of coverage for care, if needed.

The **bed hold** or **reservation feature** preserves the bed or room in a long-term care facility should the client need to leave for a period of time, typically two weeks to two months, or for a certain cause, such as a stay in a hospital. In other words, the facility cannot "rent out" the room simply because it is temporarily unoccupied. This can be a very valuable feature if care facility vacancies in the geographic area are at a premium.

**Disadvantage:** As with all types of insurance products, adding provisions and riders to a policy tends to increase the cost of insurance. Premium costs can increase significantly by adding all of the preceding provisions to a basic policy; it isimportant to compare policy costs from different companies.

## Procedural Strategy 7: Use Tax-advantaged Methods to Purchase Long-term Care Coverage

**Advantage:** A portion of the long-term care premiums paid for a tax-qualifed policy may be eligible for a medical expense deduction for clients who own their own businesses (including S-corporation owners, LLC members, and partnership owners) and individual taxpayers who file Schedule A as part of IRS Form 1040. For individuals, tax-qualified long-term care insurance premiums paid for themselves, their spouse s,or any tax dependents (e.g., parents) can be claimed a as a personal medical expense. The following deductible amounts are available regardless of a client's adjusted gross income (AGI):

Additionally, clients who purchase health insurance through a high-deductible plan and a health savings account (HSA) can use distributions from the HSA to pay long-term care insurance premiums up to the maximum eligible premium amount shown in Table 8.1 This results in a pretax purchase method for long-term care insurance. Some states also offer tax incentives (i.e., deductions or credits) for long-term care premiums.

**Disadvantage:** The deductibility of long-term care premiums exclusive of the 7.5% AGI threshold is available only to business owners. Individuals can deduct premiums only if all unreimbursed medical expenses, including long-term care premiums up to the eligible amount shown in Table 8.21, exceed 7.5% of AGI, and effective January 1, 2013, the 7.5% floor increases to 10% unless the taxpayer or spouse is age 65 or older. If an HSA is used to purchase long-term care coverage, clients will lose the IRS Schedule A deduction. Bear in mind that distributions from § 125 plans and flexible spending accounts may not be used to pay long-term care insurance premiums.

## Procedural Strategy 8: Consider Group Long-term Care Coverage

**Advantage:** For those who need long-term care insurance, group coverage may be an acceptable option, especially for people who might not meet the underwriting standards to qualify for an individual policy. However, for those who can qualify individually, adverse selection may force healthy clients to pay increasing premiums to subsidize the costs of others in the group.

**Disadvantage:** Because of the group policy guaranteed or modified-guaranteed offering (i.e., little or no medical history or health underwriting required), adverse selection can result in large premium increases. Additionally, most group policies do not offer automatic inflation protection, but increases in coverage through a guaranteed purchase option, which is based on the age of the insured. Excercising this benefit can be expensive, so the benefits available may be quite limited as the client ages. Group long-term care premiums often appear to be inexpensive, but the policy limitations may actually make group insurance more expensive than an individual policy or self-insuring the costs via other assets.

## CHAPTER-BASED CASE STUDY

### A Client-based Long-term Care Recommendation

Long-term care insurance recommendations flow directly from a review of possible coverage strategies. In some cases, it may be best to purchase a policy immediately, while for other clients, waiting until a later date might be more appropriate. The impact on other planning areas such as the federal income tax deduction must also be considered, if applicable. Also, some states offer a state income tax deduction or credit based on annual long-term care insurance premiums. Implications for other life insurance protection needs or estate planning issues also should be considered. Finally, some clients may be well served by a self-insurance strategy. For these situations, the decision to self-insure must be considered relative to plans for retirement income needs, asset management, and estate transfer.

Regardless of the client situation, planning for long-term care can be a complex decision that must take into consideration a variety of qualitative and quantitative factors. This chapter has attempted to identify some of those factors, but most important may be the recognition that such factors are uniquely characteristic of each individual client situation.

### A Product Recommendation: Purchase Long-term Care Coverage

Calvino, 58, is a recently widowed father of two adult daughters. He is now concerned with his own mortality. Hereditary cognitive disorders are common in his family, but symptoms have not typically appeared until later in life. His mother, now 87, has lived for more than a decade with Alzheimer's disease. Ever since his wife's death two years ago, Calvino has maintained that if he ever shows signs of mental decline, "Put me in my BMW and point me toward a cliff." This is, obviously, a very radical attitude, but understandable given his experiences during the past several years.

His two daughters have both reassured him that if something was to happen and he could no longer take care of himself, he could move in with one of them. But Calvino has two reservations about this. First, they live on opposite coasts and he does not want to make either daughter feel isolated, nor does he want to relocate. Second, he does not want to be a financial burden on his children or inhibit their social or professional growth. He says that "unless she really convinces me that she wants me to move in, I would rather seek other alternatives." He continues, "I know how much of a burden taking care of mom was on dad before he died and she moved to the assisted living facility. I don't want to ask my girls to change their lives for me."

Given his opinions about family-provided care, Calvino is in a position to look at more formal alternatives. A self-professed insurance skeptic, he wants to maintain as much independence and flexibility in coverage as possible. But he also realizes that if something happens and he does not have insurance, he will not be able to leave as much of a legacy for his daughters.

Given Calvino's predisposition for cognitive impairment, it is essential that the eligibility guidelines of the long-term care policy not be based solely on physical impairments. Additional policy provisions should be included in this type of client-specific recommendation. For Calvino, it is appropriate to recommend a policy that has a noncancelable clause, a waiver of premium clause, and inflation protection. The inflation protection is especially important because it may be a number of years before he needs the coverage. The policy should also clearly state that the policy becomes effective after the client's physician certifies a need for care, because requiring an insurance company physician to certify the need for care could result in delayed eligibility or receipt of benefits.

The purchase of a long-term care policy could change Calvino's need for life insurance. Respecting Calvino's desire to maintain flexibility in his insurance plan, as an alternative to a long-term care policy, the planner also suggested a universal life policy with a living benefit rider that could be used to pay for long-term care. In addition to increased flexibility, the benefit of this option is that, in the event that long-term care is never needed, Calvino saves the cost of a separate long-term care premium, and his heirs benefit from his life insurance purchase.

After speaking with his financial planner, Calvino received the information shown in Exhibit 8.1. Given his preference for formalized care, his financial planner determined that each of the following policies would be viable alternatives.

A long-term care insurance recommendation cannot be made in isolation, because it will have an impact on other sections of a comprehensive financial plan. First, the additional cost of funding long-term care coverage will decrease Calvino's discretionary cash flow. Second, the recommendation may affect the need to create or increase an emergency savings fund.

Fortunately, neither of these has a significant negative impact on Calvino's financial situation. He has adequate income to cover any of the options and more than $1 million in financial assets. However, the planner did consider Calvino's sizable net worth an important factor in not recommending a lifetime benefit. In the worst-case scenario, Calvino would have adequate funding to continue long-term care without interruption and without state assistance should the need extend beyond two or five years, respectively.

Once Calvino made a final policy selection, the Long-Term Care Insurance Recommendation Form illustrates how his financial planner presented the recommendation.

**Exhibit 8.1** Comparison of Long-term Care Coverage Options

| | "Ideal" Coverage | Option 1: 5-yr LTC | Option 2: 4-yr LTC | Option 3: Universal Life |
|---|---|---|---|---|
| *Value of Coverage* | | | | |
| Benefit per day | $125 | $125 | $125 | -- |
| Maximum total benefit | Unlimited | $230,000 | $160,000 | $200,000 |
| Reimbursement plan | No | No | No | |
| *Types of Coverage* | | | | |
| Nursing home | | | | |
| Skilled care | Yes | Yes | Yes | -- |
| Intermediate care | Yes | Yes | Yes | -- |
| Assisted living (% of daily maximum) | Yes (100%) | Yes (100%) | Yes (75%) | -- |
| Home-based | | | | |
| Skilled care (% of daily maximum) | Yes (75%) | Yes (100%) | No | -- |
| Custodial care (% of daily maximum) | Yes (75%) | No | No | -- |
| Coverage period (yrs) | | | | |
| Nursing home | Lifetime | 5 | 2 | -- |
| Assisted living | Lifetime | 5 | 2 | -- |
| Home-based | Lifetime | 5 | 0 | -- |
| Eligibility triggers | | | | |
| Physical (No. of ADLs) | Yes (1) | Yes (2) | Yes (2) | -- |
| Cognitive | Yes | Yes | Yes | -- |
| Medical necessity | Yes | Yes | Yes | -- |
| Stated period/pool of money | Pool | Pool | Pool | |
| Provisions | | | | -- |
| Inflation rider | Yes | Yes | Yes | -- |
| Waiver of premium | Yes | Yes | Yes | -- |
| Restoration of benefit | Yes | No | No | |
| Bed hold/reservation | Yes | No | Yes | |
| Nonforfeiture | Yes | No | No | -- |
| Return of premium | Yes | No | No | |
| Restrictions | | | | |
| Prior hospitalization | No | No | No | -- |
| Elimination period (days) | -- | 180 | 90 | -- |
| State partnership plan | -- | No | No | |
| Payment options | -- | 10-pay | -- | Pay to age 85 |
| Fixed payment | -- | Yes | No | -- |
| Guaranteed renewable | Yes | Yes | -- | Yes |
| Noncancelable | Yes | No | Yes | -- |
| *Annual premium** | -- | $3,200.00 | $2,550.00 | $5,850.00 |

*Policy premiums are for illustration purposes only. They are extrapolated based on available data and do not represent any actual company policy.

**Exhibit 8.2** Long-term Care Insurance Recommendation Form

## Planning Recommendation Form

| | |
|---|---|
| **Financial Planning Content Area** | Long term Care Insurance Planning |
| **Client Goal** | Purchase Long term Care Coverage |

| **Recommendation No.:** | 1 | **Priority (1–6) lowest to highest:** | 4 |
|---|---|---|---|

| | |
|---|---|
| **Projected/Target Value ($)** | $160,000 total benefit pool |

**Product Profile**

| | | | | |
|---|---|---|---|---|
| Type | Long -term care (4-year split benefit) | | | |
| Duration | Noncancelable | | | |
| Provider | Midwest Health Corporation | | | |
| Funding Cost per Period ($) | $2,550 per year (paid monthly) | | | |
| Maintenance Cost per Period ($) | $0 | | | |
| Current Income Tax Status | Tax-qualified | | Taxable | X |
| Projected Rate of Return | NA | | | |
| Major Policy Provisions | 1. 90-day elimination period<br>2. Waiver of premium<br>3. Cognitive disease eligible<br>4. Inflation rider<br>5. Bedhold | | | |

**Procedural Factors**

| | | | | |
|---|---|---|---|---|
| Implementation by Whom | Planner | | Client | X |
| Implementation Date or Time Frame | Within in one (1) year | | | |
| Implementation Procedure | Contact Jennifer Black of Midwest Health Corporation to complete application process. | | | |

**Ownership Factors**

| | | | | |
|---|---|---|---|---|
| Owner(s) | Calvino Mercadante | | | |
| Form of Ownership | Sole | | | |
| Insured(s) | Calvino Mercadante | | | |
| Custodial Account | Yes | | No | X |
| Custodian | NA | | | |
| In Trust For (ITF) | Yes | | No | X |
| Transfer On Death (TOD) | Yes | | No | X |
| Beneficiary(ies) | NA | | | |
| Contingent Beneficiary(ies) | NA | | | |

| | |
|---|---|
| **Proposed Benefit** | Provides a 4-year, $125-per-day benefit. The policy is an expense reimbursement, or pool-of-money benefit rather than an indemnity plan. Covers assisted living at a maximum rate of 75% of the nursing care benefit. It does not cover home-based care, nor does it provide a return-of-premium death benefit. |

# Learning Outcomes

1.  The aging of the Baby Boomers coupled with a steady increase in life expectancy is fueling a rapid increase in the cost of and need for care for the elderly. This continuum of care includes home health care services, care at an adult day care center, in-home care, assisted living care, skilled nursing care, hospice care, and in some instances, a combination of these needs. As the cost of long-term care in the United States approaches $200 billion, providing care is either a direct client expense that financial planners must help fund or an indirect expense paid for by the tax-funded Medicare and Medicaid programs. Thus, it is imporant for planners to help clients prepare to fund future long-term care expenses, for themselves or extended family members, as part of a comprehensive financial planning process. Central to long-term care planning is client education on the possible contribution of Medicare, Medicaid, insurance products, and self-insurance to meet future needs.

2.  Identify the client situational factors necessary to analyze a client's need to purchase long-term care insurace or self-insure. Although planning for the uncertainlty of long-term care needs is not an en exact science, advisors typically focus on two issues: the client and the client's resources. Specifically a client's age, health, family health history, lifestyle choices, and occupational choices (i.e., risk triggers) can directly influence the likelihood of needing long-term care services. A client's financial and personal resources (network of family or friends) directly influence decisions regarding how to provide or pay for any necessary long-term care services. As part of this situational analysis, advisors often apply the rules of thumb linked to clients' net worth of less than $250,000, between $250,000 and $1.5 million, and over $1.5 million. These measures, clients' preferences, and projected care needs all influence the decision to purchase long-term care insurance or self-insure.

3.  The need for long-term care insurance is based on client preferences; net worth; and the projected need for care based on age, personal health, family health history, lifestyle choices, and occupational choice. The first two may be more easily identified, while the latter are more random. All three also significantly influence the projected cost of care and the amount of insurance to be purchased. Specifically, five factors are considered when quantifying the amount of insurace coverage to purchase, including the (1) range of services covered and benefit amount; (2) coverage period; (3) method by which benefits are paid (i.e., pool of money or indemnity); (4) elimination period; and (5) inflation rider to increase coverage limits.

4.  Planners asked to evaluate an existing long-term care policy should first determine whether the client really needs coverage or self-insurance is a better option. Then, factors that determine the amount of insurance needed as well as other riders that affect coverage should be reviewed. If the decision to discontinue a policy is made, a client has the option to (1) let the policy lapse; (2) exercise the nonforfeiture clause, if available; (3) exercise the CBL, if available; or (4) exercise a § 1035 exchange for another, more suitable long-term care insurance contract. With the latter option, care must be taken because the new policy premium will reflect the client's current age.

5.  Linked-benefit (or hybrid) life and annuity products offer clients the certainity of the base policy—death or annuity benefits, respectively—coupled with the availability of long-term care coverage, if needed. These products help clients manage the risk of paying for but not requiring long-term care protection, at the same time offering the certainty of

estate protection or policy benefit for heirs. Heatlh underwriting may be less stringent or unnecessary—a benefit for some clients. But the single-sum payment may be a deterrent. Individual policy features can make the hybrid policies less favorable than purchasing two separate policies if both are needed.

6. Without the benefit of a long-term care partnership plan to protect assets, qualification for Medicaid eligibility requires clients to "spend down" assets to meet the means tests (i.e., a maximum of $2,000 in countable assets owned in the individual's name, although this amount may vary by state), and a lien could be placed on any remaining assets for recovery by Medicaid for benefits paid. Conversely, assets transferred by an individual within 60 months of needing Medicaid benefits could trigger a penalty period and ineligbibility for aid. Clients who wish to retain assets and avoid these rules could find a partnership plan, if available in their state, a good option to protect some level of assets for heirs or a legacy.

7. Long-term care insurance contracts typically are reimbursement plans that provide for a specific amount of coverage, or indemnity plans that pay for a specific period of time. Other provisions that customize a policy include the elimination period, the inflation rider, the nonforfeiture clause, an accelerated payment option, a restoration of benefits provision, a return of premium provision, the bed hold or reservation feature, and the spousal survivorship option. Additionally, policies can be guaranteed renewable or noncancelable and special provisions such as a joint policy or shared-care policy may be available only to couples. Policy discounts also may apply.

8. Numerous product and procedural strategies are available to advisors to customize long-term care planning recommendations to individual client needs. Strategies reflect differences in products available, product coverage and features, and the tax or other advantages of different products. Other strategies focus on client education to help clients choose between long-term care product options and self-insurance options. For many clientes, a combination of strategies may be needed.

# Chapter Resources

AARP (http://www.aarp.org/).

Administration on Aging (www.aoa.gov).

American Association for Long-Term Care Insurance (http://www.aaltci.org/).

Commission on Accreditation of Rehabilitation Facilities/Continuing Care Accreditation Commission (CARF/CCAC) (http://www.carf.org/Providers.aspx?content=content/Accreditation/Opportunities/AS/CCAC.htm).

Comparison of Nursing Homes (www.medicare.gov/NHcompare).

Comprehensive long-term care insurance information (www.longtermcarelink.net).

LeadingAge (http://www.leadingage.org/).

Long-term Care Partnership Only (http://ltcpartnershiponly.com/index.html).

Medicare (www.medicare.gov).

National Clearinghouse for Long-Tterm Care Information (www.longtermcare.gov).

Weiss Ratings (www.weissratings.com).

The *Financial Factilitator* and all fillable forms needed to complete text activities can be found on the student website at: http://pro.nuco.com/booksupplements/NUCollege-CaseBook2e.

# Quantitative/Analytical Mini-case Problems

1. Ambra is age 50 and single. She is concerned about funding long-term care insurance costs in the future. Based on family history, she has determined the following:

   - She will likely need long-term care coverage beginning at age 78;

   - She will need coverage for six years;

   - Long-term care costs in her area are currently $72,000 per year;

   - Long-term care costs are increasing by 5% annually;

   - She can earn 7% on her savings and assets;

   - She currently earns $98,000 per year; and

   - She has saved $75,000 that she is willing to earmark for long-term care costs.

   Use this information to answer the following questions:

   a. What is the future value cost of long-term care coverage when Ambra enters a nursing facility?

   b. What is the total cost of coverage for six years when Ambra enters a nursing facility (present value of cost determined at age 78)?

c. How long will Ambra's long-term care savings last when she enters a nursing facility?

d. Assume that Ambra has other property valued at $250,000. If she is willing to use this asset to help pay for long-term care costs, does she need long-term care insurance at this time?

2. Recently, a married couple requested that you assist them by writing a modular, or targeted, long-term care financial plan. The clients both turned 54 this month and are fairly wealthy but not rich. Specifically, they wanted to consider self-insuring for any long-term care costs. However, they do not know whether they have adequate assets to self-insure. Use the following client assumptions to answer their questions.

- The current cost of an assisted living facility is $95 per day and the nursing care facility is $135 per day.

- Cost of care will increase at an annual effective rate of 6% throughout the time period. Assume cost increases occur annually.

- Both clients will simultaneously enter care facilities at age 77, spend three years in assisted living and one year in nursing care, and die at age 81.

- For simplicity, assume that all expenses, whether premium payments or direct costs, are to be paid at the end of each year.

- The policy includes a **waiver of premium provision**. In other words, once the clients begin to receive benefits for a long-term care stay, premium payments cease.

- Premiums are not paid during the elimination period.

- The clients currently have $40,000 that could be set aside for long-term care expenses. But if long-term care insurance is purchased, this same account would be used to pay for the insurance premiums.

- The effective annual required rate of return on invested funds is 6.5%.

- For simplicity, assume that all months have 30 days.

Use this information to answer the following questions:

a. How much will assisted living care cost per year when the clients reach age 77?

b. How much will nursing care cost per year when the clients reach age 80?

c. What is the total present value need for one person at age 77?

d. Given the future value of assets saved for long-term care needs compared to future costs, should the couple plan to self-insure the need?

# Comprehensive Bedo Case—Analysis Questions

Long-term care insurance is sometimes overlooked because younger clients typically do not require this kind of coverage. Also, from a cost perspective, long-term care insurance is most appropriately purchased during a relatively short window of opportunity, between the ages of 50 and 65. Although many clients may not need long-term care insurance, because of their age, health, or assets, it is still important to conduct a thorough long-term care analysis as part of a client's comprehensive insurance analysis.

The Bedo family's health status is an important consideration when considering long-term care coverage strategies. A review of Tyler's and Mia's health history and their access to long-term care coverage through their employers must be considered. The family's goal of living a financially satisfying life must be weighed against the potentially high costs of insuring both Tyler and Mia for long-term care expenses.

1.  Develop a long-term care planning goal for the Bedos. When conceptualizing this goal, consider the following:

    a.  Is the goal developed in agreement with any or all goals and objectives that the clients have identified regarding long-term care planning?

    b.  What situational factors might influence their long-term care goal? Are these factors explicit, implied, or assumed? Is additional information required from the Bedos? If so, what?

    c.  What is the desired long-term care planning outcome for the clients?

2.  Make a list of the lifestyle, occupational, and health factors that should be documented and evaluated for the Bedos. How might this client information be obtained, or collected, from the Bedos? How might it be useful in the Bedos' long-term care situation analysis? Also, make a list of life events that could affect long-term care planning analysis for Tyler and Mia and that should be reviewed at future client meetings.

3.  Are there globally accepted, client-specific, or planner-generated planning assumptions that will influence the long-term care situation analysis? List the assumptions as they might appear in a plan.

4.  Make a list of specific policy features that should be evaluated as part of the documentation and evaluation of the Bedos' long-term care insurance planning efforts. For each feature, write a definition or explanation that could appear in this section of the plan or in the plan glossary.

5.  Conduct a current long-term care situation analysis for the Bedos. Be sure to assess the following:

    a.  Tyler's and Mia's need for long-term care insurance today.

    b.  The Bedos' need for long-term care insurance in the future.

    c.  How will Medicare or Medicaid benefits influence the Bedos' need for long-term care insurance?

    d. What, if any, are the tax implications of a policy purchase?

    e. What are the implications for their emergency fund, given different elimination periods?

6. Summarize your observations about the Bedos' long-term care planning situation as they might appear in a client letter or plan. Incorporate text, bullets, or graphics in your explanation.

7. Based on the goals originally identified and the completed analysis, what product or procedural strategies might be most useful to satisfy the Bedos' long-term care planning needs? When reviewing the strategies, be careful to consider the approximate cost of implementation as well as the most likely outcome(s) associated with each strategy.

8. Write at least one primary and one alternative recommendation from selected strategies in response to each identified planning need. More than one recommendation may be needed to address all of the planning needs. For each recommendation, include specific, defensible answers to the who, what, when, where, why, how, and how much implementation questions.

    a. It is suggested that each recommendation be summarized in a Recommendation Form.

    b. Assign a priority to each recommendation based on the likelihood of meeting client goals and desired outcomes. This priority will be important when recommendations from other core planning content areas are considered relative to the available discretionary funds for subsidizing all recommendations.

    c. Comment briefly on the outcomes associated with each recommendation.

9. Complete the following for the long-term care section of the Bedos' financial plan.

    a. Outline the content to be included in this section of the plan. Given the segments written above, which segments are missing?

    b. Write the introduction to this section of the plan (no more than one to two paragraphs).

10. Prepare a 10–15-minute presentation for the Bedos of your observations and/or recommendation(s) for meeting their long-term care planning needs. Be sure to include visual aids or handouts.

## Notes

1. *Genworth 2011 Cost of Care Survey.* Available at http://www.genworth.com/content/etc/medialib/genworth_v2/pdf/ltc_cost_of_care.Par.14625.File.dat/2010_Cost_of_Care_Survey_Full_Report.pdf, p. 20.

2. *Genworth 2011 Cost of Care Survey, Executive Summary.* Available at http://www.genworth.com/content/etc/medialib/genworth_v2/pdf/ltc_cost_of_care.Par.85518.File.dat/Executive%20Summary_gnw.pdf, p. 2.

3. *Genworth 2011 Cost of Care Survey,* p. 22.

4. *2011 MetLife Market Survey of Nursing Home, Assisted Living, Adult Day Services, and Home Care Costs.* Available at http://www.metlife.com/mmi/research/2011-market-survey-long-term-care-costs.html#findings.

5. Kaiser Commission on Medicaid Facts, *Medicaid and Long-Term Care Services and Supports,* March 2011. Available at http://www.kff.org/medicaid/upload/2186-08.pdf, p. 1.

6. Alzheimer's Association, "2011 Alzheimer's Disease Facts and Figures," *Alzheimer's & Dementia* 7, no. 2 (2011): 40. Available at http://www.alz.org/downloads/Facts_Figures_2011.pdf.

7. AARP, *Continuing Care Retirement Communities: What They Are and How They Work.* Available at http://www.aarp.org/relationships/caregiving-resource-center/info-09-2010/ho_continuing_care_retirement_communities.html.

8. AgeWave/Harris Interactive, *America Talks: Protecting Our Families' Financial Futures*. Available at https://pro.genworth.com/content/etc/medialib/genworth_v2/pdf/industry_expertise/retirement.Par.89331.File.pdf/America_Talks.pdf, pp. 34–35.

9. AgeWave/Harris Interactive, *America Talks: Protecting Our Families' Financial Futures.*

10. American Association for Long-Term Care Insurance, *2008 LTCi Sourcebook*. Available at http://www.aaltci.org/long-term-care-insurance/learning-center/fast-facts.php.

11. "Do You Need Long-term-care Insurance? (CR Investigates)," *Consumer Reports* (2003). Available at http://www.accessmylibrary.com/coms2/summary_0286-19498415_ITM.

12. *Genworth 2011 Cost of Care Survey*, p. 21.

13. American Association for Long-Term Care Insurance, *Long-term Care Insurance Tax-deductibility Rules*. Available at https://www.aaltci.org/long-term-care-insurance/learning-center/tax-for-business.php.

14. American Association for Long Term Care Insurance, *Long-term Care—Important Information for Women*. Available at http://www.aaltci.org/long-term-care-insurance/learning-center/for-women.php.

15. Lynn Feinberg, Susan C. Reinhard, Ari Houser, and Rita Choula, *Valuing the Invaluable: 2011 Update The Growing Contributions and Costs of Family Caregiving* (Washington, DC: AARP Public Policy Institute), 1. Available at http://assets.aarp.org/rgcenter/ppi/ltc/i51-caregiving.pdf.

16. Alzheimer's Association, *Facts and Figures*, 25.

17. American Association for Long Term Care Insurance, *Important Information for Women*.

18. Alzheimer's Association, *Facts and Figures*, 14.

19. AgeWave/Harris Interactive, *America Talks*, 30.

20. AgeWave/Harris Interactive, *America Talks*, 30.

21. American Association for Long Term Care Insurance, *Women Buy Majority Life—Long-term Care Insurance*. Available at http://www.aaltci.org/news/long-term-care-insurance-association-news/women-buy-majority-life-long-term-care-insurance.

22. Alicia H. Munnell and Josh Hurwitz, "What Is 'CLASS' and Will It Work?" Center for Retirement Research *Issue in Brief*, 11, no. 3: 1. Available at http://crr.bc.edu/images/stories/Briefs/IB_11-3.pdf.

23. American Association for Long-Term Care Insurance, *2008 LTCi Sourcebook*.

24. *What if You Cannot Afford to Continue Paying the Long Term Care Premium? Nonforfeiture Benefits in Long Term Care Insurance Policies*. Available at http://law.freeadvice.com/insurance_law/long_term_care/can-not-afford-to-continue-paying-long-term-care.htm.

25. Ingrid Case, "Long-Term Care: Crisis Brewing," *Financial Planning*. Available at http://www.financial-planning.com/fp_issues/2011_4/crisis-brewing-2672143-1.html?zkPrintable=1&nopagination=1; also *Study Examines Long-term Care Insurance Rate Increases*, American Association for Long-Term Care Insurance. Available at http://www.aaltci.org/news/long-term-care-insurance-association-news/study-examines-long-term-care-insurance-rate-increases.

26. Munnell and Hurwitz, "What Is 'CLASS'?"

27. J. L. Phipps *New: A Hybrid Annuity with LTC Coverage*. Available at http://www.bankrate.com/finance/insurance/new-a-hybrid-annuity-with-ltc-coverage-1.aspx.

28. American Association for Long-Term Care Insurance. *2008 LTCi Sourcebook*. Available at http://www.aaltci.org/long-term-care-insurance/learning-center/fast-facts.php.

29. American Association for Long-term Care Insurance, *What Is the Probability You'll Need Long-term Care? Is Long-Term Care Insurance A Smart Financial Move?* Based on the 2008 LTCi Sourcebook. Available at http://www.aaltci.org/long-term-care-insurance/learning-center/probability-long-term-care.php.

# Property and Liability Insurance Planning

## Learning Objectives

1. Understand the importance of property and liability insurance within the comprehensive financial planning framework.

2. Describe the risk management process and how financial planners can use risk reduction techniques within the financial planning process.

3. Explain what is meant by the term *risk control* and how insurance companies price policies using insurance scores.

4. Identify client information necessary to complete a comprehensive property and liability insurance needs analysis.

5. Demonstrate how to determine and quantify a client's need for and selection of homeowners and personal automobile insurance policies and provisions designed to manage potential property loss and liability exposures.

6. Understand the purpose of excess liability, or umbrella, policy coverage as a tool for managing a client's exposure to risk resulting from members of a household or property.

7. Understand and apply the 80% rule as an aspect of homeowners insurance planning.

8. Identify and recommend appropriate and reasonable property and casualty insurance strategies matched to a client's situation.

## Key Terms

80% rule

actual cash value

all-risk policy

attractive nuisance

auto loan/lease coverage endorsement

basic form

broad form

building code upgrade endorsement

coinsurance penalty

collision damage waiver (CDW)

collision coverage

combined single-limit coverage

comprehensive coverage

contents form

earthquake insurance

endorsement

excess liability insurance coverage

extended replacement cost endorsement

Federal Emergency Management Agency (FEMA)

floater

flood insurance

guaranteed auto protection (GAP)

hold-harmless agreement

homestead exemption

indemnify

inflation endorsement

insurance score

loss damage waiver (LDW)

loss prevention

maximum possible loss

maximum probable loss

medical expense coverage

modified coverage form

multipolicy discount

named perils

National Flood Insurance Program (NFIP)

Open peril

pair and set clause

personal article or property endorsement

personal article policy

personal automobile policy (PAP)

personal injury coverage

personal property endorsement

renter's policy

replacement cost

replacement cost coverage endorsement

rider

risk avoidance

risk control

risk management

risk reduction

risk retention

risk sharing

risk transferring

special form

typical loss

umbrella liability policy

underinsured motorists coverage

uninsured motorists coverage

upside-down

write your own company (WYO)

**Figure 9.1** Systematic Financial Planning Process for Property and Liability Insurance

## PROPERTY AND LIABILITY INSURANCE: THE BASICS

Prior insurance chapters in this text provided a review of client-specific and environmental factors that influence the analysis of general life and health insurance needs. This chapter extends this review by showing how analyses related to a client's need for adequate property and liability coverage are also essential within the financial planning process. Without adequate liability coverage, for instance, a single accident or event could place a family's financial future in jeopardy and negatively impact the client's ability to fund other financial goals. In today's increasingly litigious society, it is imperative that clients be protected from financial losses associated with personal property and casualty claims. This protection begins with a review of each client's unique property and liability coverage situation.

Driving a car, for example, is as much a means for getting from point A to point B as it is a tool that can inflict damage on another person or someone else's property. Owning a house may also present perilous opportunities for loss that require adequate insurance coverage. For instance, a client's swimming pool can be both a haven for relaxation as well as an **attractive nuisance**—a dangerous condition that is likely to attract children and others to a homeowner's property. Most homeowners invest heavily in their homes. For many, a large portion of net worth is associated with home equity. Uninsured damage or claims against the property can adversely affect this important investment. Financial planners need to assess and discuss possible insurance exposures with their clients or risk their clients having to invade financial assets to pay for losses that could have been transferred to a third party, such as an insurance company. Because property and liability insurance typically can be purchased for reasonable amounts, an oversight related to this area may be deemed a serious financial planning omission when viewed within a comprehensive financial plan.

This chapter considers ways to maximize a client's protection planning for property and liability exposures. The fundamental steps involved with the analysis and evaluation of a client's property and liability situation are outlined in Figure 9.1, the Systematic Financial Planning Process for Property and Liability Insurance Planning.

## ANALYZE THE CLIENT'S CURRENT SITUATION

Managing risks involves identifying, analyzing, and ranking a client's personal, household, and family lifestyle for potential threats that could lead to financial loss and identifying methods to reduce or eliminate the impact of that loss. In its simplest form, this is the premise underlying **risk management** methodologies. The success of any risk management method is contingent on timing. Recognizing a client's risk exposure after a loss has occurred is pointless. Thus, it is essential to take the time before a loss occurs to carefully evaluate risk exposures.

Five primary risk reduction techniques should be considered when analyzing a client's property and casualty insurance situation. Two of these techniques deal with reducing the likelihood of loss (i.e., **loss prevention**) and two deal with reducing the cost of loss. There is one additional possibility: **Risk retention** involves having the client accept the loss or gain resulting from a risk. Risk retention is an appropriate risk management strategy when the costs associated with insurance are significantly greater than the potential losses involved. By definition, any risk that is not prevented, avoided, or transferred is retained by the client. Sometimes retention is the only way to handle risk. There may be no economically viable option to prevent a risk or to indemnify a client for it (e.g., acts of war). Retention may also be the best way to deal with risks that are predictable and not costly.

Clients who do not want or cannot afford to retain the risk of loss may reduce or eliminate it. Clients can prevent a loss from occurring by reducing or, in the extreme, avoiding the behavior that could lead to a loss. Alternatively, a client can indemnify the loss by sharing or, in the extreme, transferring the cost of replacing missing, damaged, or stolen items.

The two primary methods of reducing, or controlling, the likelihood of a loss include **risk avoidance** and **risk reduction**. However, both avoiding and reducing risk require a client to alter behavior, possessions, or their personal, household, or working environment. For instance, to avoid an auto theft loss, the client could choose not to own a car. This approach to risk management may not be feasible or even possible. Instead, the client may seek to reduce the likelihood of loss by safeguarding the car with a vehicle alarm or tracking system. This is an example of risk reduction.

If controlling the likelihood of loss is impractical, a client can **indemnify** the loss by sharing the cost associated with the risk with another person or organization, typically an insurance company. The two primary indemnification methods include **risk transferring** and **risk sharing**. Both of these methods establish an agreement or contract (e.g., an indemnity or **hold-harmless agreement** or insurance contract) prior to a loss. The agreement outlines the moral and financial responsibilities of both parties. When contractually transferring risk, clients (ideally with the help of their financial advisor) must identify potential risks, determine the likelihood of loss, and calculate the estimated financial exposure associated with that risk. Conversely, the insurance company determines the risks, probabilities, and costs associated with insuring the risks. Insurance is often the preferred risk management mechanism when risks pose the possibility of moderate or high financial loss but the anticipated frequency of loss is low or unpredictable.

---

### Homeowners Insurance Tip: Deductible Requirements

Nearly all homeowners policies require that the insured pay a deductible before being reimbursed for damages. There is an inverse relationship between the deductible and the premium. Increasing the deductible can reduce the annual premium, thereby increasing a client's level of discretionary cash flow. This cash flow can be used to build an emergency fund to help offset future insurance costs and losses. This will ensure availability of the "first dollars" for the deductible payment and allow the insured to more comfortably accept the risk of a higher deductible. It is not uncommon to recommend that a homeowners policy deductible be the lesser of $1,000 or 1% of the value of the dwelling.

---

A financial planner should strive to educate his or her clientele about the advantages associated with evaluating risk and engaging in **risk control** as an ongoing process that involves identifying and analyzing the severity and likelihood of potential loss exposures. To understand risk control is to recognize issues related to maximum possible loss, maximum probable loss, and typical losses, as well as the likelihood of each. The **maximum possible loss** is the largest loss that can occur. Theoretically, for liability purposes, there is no limit on the maximum possible loss because there generally is no way to be certain what a jury might award. The **maximum probable loss** is the greatest loss that has the highest probability of occurring. The **typical loss** is the one that occurs most frequently.

Safeguarding against the maximum possible loss requires insurance to cover catastrophic losses, regardless of how likely or unlikely it is that a catastrophic event might occur. When analyzing a client's homeowners coverage, a planner should make certain that the limits of liability and property coverage shield the client from potentially bankrupting financial responsibility.

Recommending strategies that deal with the maximum probable loss is a bit more ambiguous. For example, if a client has a house fire, will the fire in all probability consume the entire home or just a portion, such as the kitchen? This is a question without a fixed answer. The likelihood of a serious loss to a home depends on various factors, such as whether the house is frame or masonry, where it is located, and the type of fire protection available in the community. These same factors influence the cost of insurance to protect a home and property.

Whereas issues of maximum possible or probable loss may set the upper boundaries of coverage sought, protection must also be available for the most likely, or typical, loss. It is unreasonable to suggest, for example, that all of a client's possessions should be sold simply to avoid the possibility of theft. Whole-house theft is not typical. But a planner could suggest that a client purchase an in-home safe to store valuables or an insurance policy **endorsement** (i.e., a separate policy that covers the value of goods above standard policy limits) to provide additional coverage for such valuables. The first suggestion advises the client to retain the risk and to reduce the probability of loss. The second suggestion advises loss sharing. A planner could combine both suggestions and recommend purchasing the safe and the insurance. This would most likely decrease the insurance premium and offer the best financial protection.

A thorough knowledge of a client's personal and financial situation is central to all aspects of financial planning, but nowhere is this more evident than when planning for property and casualty insurance. Seemingly mundane—and in some cases intrusive—questions about a client's home, personal property, pets, hobbies, autos, and driving habits must be considered. To complete a comprehensive assessment, the planner and client must explore issues concerning the client's lifestyle, the client's aversion to risk, property owned, and the ways in which property is used by members of the insured's household. This information provides the basis for determining property and liability insurance needs as well as appropriate product recommendations.

## Determine and Quantify a Client's Need for Property and Liability Insurance

Beyond a lender's requirement for homeowners insurance or the state-mandated requirement of auto insurance to license a vehicle, most Americans think of property insurance in the context of replacing damaged, lost, or stolen property. Although the financial impact of property loss may be significant, by far the greater risk comes from liability claims resulting from the actions of the insured or members of the insured's household.

Factors that can affect the need for property and liability insurance parallel the issues that influence underwriting and the rating used to determine insurance costs. Although the factors that insurance companies use vary for homeowners and auto insurance, two consistent and very important issues must be considered when determining the level of insurance coverage to recommend.

First is the territory or location of the property. Aside from moving, this factor is beyond the insured's control when purchasing auto or homeowners insurance. Location influences the need for flood insurance or earthquake coverage. Retrofitting or modernizing a home to improve its disaster resistance may reduce policy costs and the potential for loss.

Second is the client's **insurance score**, which is calculated from data collected by the major national credit bureaus. The Federal Trade Commission defines an insurance score as a numerical summary of a person's past credit delinquencies, bankruptcies, debt ratios, credit-seeking behavior, credit history, and use of credit.[1] Insurance companies typically use insurance scores to estimate whether a person is likely to make premium payments and the number of claims someone is, in all likelihood, going to file over any period of time. A client's insurance score tends to be inversely correlated with claims costs. In other words, the lower the client's insurance score, the higher the likely cost of future claims and the higher the insurance premium. For clients with credit problems, efforts to reduce the reliance on credit and to make timely payments can, over time, improve their credit and insurance scores, both of which can impact other aspects of the client's financial life, primarily by reducing the cost of credit and insurance premiums.

Answering the question of the need for and optimal amount of property and liability coverage is not a straightforward process. Most agree on the need to transfer risk through insurance. But how much of that risk to transfer or the amount of protection to purchase is often a matter of interpretation. One approach that can be used to answer this important question involves considering the following queries:

- What is the maximum loss possible?

- What is the maximum loss probable?

- What is the typical loss?

Considering these questions in light of a client's net worth and risk tolerance can help frame the choice of how much coverage to purchase. Other factors unique to the individual client household must also be considered. The following overview provides a broad summary of some of these issues; it also describes the basic insurance concepts commonly associated with property and casualty insurance coverage.

### Homeowners Insurance

Homeowners policies (often referred to by the acronym *HO*) are generally packaged as standard policy forms. Table 9.1 compares seven of the most widely available homeowners policy forms. An important feature that differentiates HO policies is the protection from perils. A **named perils policy** protects against financial loss resulting from perils, either 11 or 17, that are specifically named within a policy. *Open peril* is a term used to describe an **all-risk policy** that covers losses from all causes unless specifically excluded in an insurance contract. These exclusions typically include flood, earthquake, war, nuclear accident, and mold. Corresponding to these two types of policies is the related issue of burden of proof. With a named perils policy, the homeowner (or renter) must provide evidence that the loss was caused by a named peril listed in the policy. In contrast, with the open peril policy, a loss is covered unless the insurance company can provide evidence that the loss was excluded from the policy.

Type of construction and local construction costs, access to and quality of community fire protection, occupancy and use of the home, and home safety features all affect policy needs and costs for clients seeking HO insurance coverage. When providing insurance recommendations within a financial plan, it is important to include references to home safety features, which typically reduce the cost of insurance. Clients who enhance existing safety features may qualify for additional discounts. Policy type and the limits of coverage affect the cost of all policies. As such, issues surrounding the cost to replace the home and its contents should be carefully reviewed when conducting an insurance analysis.

Beyond the basic limits of Part C coverage for personal property, additional coverage is available for select items that are either inadequately covered or excluded from coverage under a homeowners policy. These provisions, called *endorsements* (or *riders*) and *floaters*, and their terminology and use are often confusing.

For the most part, the terms *endorsement* and *rider* are synonymous and refer to a provision that materially changes coverage in the underlying contract. Technically, an endorsement is the actual change in coverage, and a **rider** is the document that changes the coverage. Normally the term *endorsement* is used when referring to general changes in policy coverage, including guaranteed replacement cost coverage, inflation protection, identity theft, or modified coverage of assets, that are included or "scheduled" under the special limits of the liability section. Examples of scheduled assets include jewelry, furs, firearms, collectibles, art, precious and semiprecious metals, securities held in physical form, and business assets. Although a basic homeowners policy provides some coverage, the value of such items can quickly exceed the limits of coverage—typically $200 to $2,500—depending on the asset and the insurance company. A scheduled **personal property endorsement** would increase coverage on a specific asset basis, a class of asset basis, or a blanket basis. Professional appraisals are often required to establish the value of an item. Annual reviews should include any new property (i.e., not covered at the time of purchase) to ensure that adequate ongoing coverage is in place.

**Table 9.1** Typical Homeowners Policy Forms and Coverage

### Seven Forms of Homeowners Policies*

| Form | Part A Dwelling | Part B Other Structures | Part C Personal Property | Part D Loss of Use | Part E Typical Personal Liability Limit | Part F Typical Medical Payments to Others Limit |
|---|---|---|---|---|---|---|
| Basic Form (HO-1)# <br><br> Named 11 perils policy¶ | Replacement value | 10% of dwelling coverage | 50% of dwelling coverage | 10% of dwelling coverage | $100,000 | $1,000 per person per incident |
| Broad Form (HO-2) <br><br> Named 16 perils policy | Replacement value | 10% of dwelling coverage | 50% of dwelling coverage | 30% of dwelling coverage | $100,000 | $1,000 per person per incident |
| Special Form (HO-3) <br><br> Named 16 perils policy for personal property | Replacement value | 10% of dwelling coverage | 50% of dwelling coverage | 30% of dwelling coverage | $100,000 | $1,000 per person per incident |
| Contents Form (HO-4) <br><br> Named 16 perils policy for personal property | Does not apply | Does not apply | Usually stated in dollar amount | 30% of personal property coverage | $100,000 | $1,000 per person per incident |
| Comprehensive Form (HO-5) <br><br> All perils, except specific exclusions | Replacement value | 10% of dwelling coverage | 50% of dwelling coverage | 30% of dwelling coverage | $100,000 | $1,000 per person per incident |
| Joint Owner's Form (HO-6) <br><br> Named 16 perils policy | $1,000 - $5,000 minimum limited to semi-permanent features in the unit | Does not apply, or included in Part A | Usually stated in dollar amount | 50% of personal property coverage | $100,000 | $1,000 per person per incident |
| Modified Coverage Form (HO-8) <br><br> Named 11 perils policy | Market value of structure | 10% of dwelling coverage | 50% of dwelling coverage | 10% of dwelling coverage | $100,000 | $1,000 per person per incident |

*Discussion here and throughout this chapter is based on the standard Insurance Service Office (ISO) policy forms used throughout the U.S. Policy variations may apply as some insurers use the American Association of Insurance Services (AAIS) forms, some insurers design their own forms, and in some instances, state mandated modifications may apply. For more information see www.iso.com.

#HO-1 policies are generally no longer available.

¶ Named 11 perils typically include: (1) Fire or lightning; (2) windstorm or hail; (3) explosion; (4) riot or civil commotion; (5) damage caused by aircraft; (6) damage caused by vehicles; (7) smoke; (8) vandalism or malicious mischief; (9) theft; (10) volcanic eruption; and (11) falling objects. The additional 5 perils to total 16 include: (12) weight of ice, snow or sleet; (13) accidental discharge or overflow of water or steam from within plumbing, heating, air conditioning, automatic fire-protective sprinkler system, or from a household appliance; (14) sudden and accidental tearing apart, cracking, burning, or bulging of a steam or hot water heating system, an air conditioning or automatic fire-protective system; (15) freezing of a plumbing, heating, air conditioning, automatic, fire-protective sprinkler system, or of a household appliance; and (16) sudden and accidental damage from artificially generated electrical current (does not include loss to a tube, transistor or similar electronic component). For more information see the Insurance Information Institute at http://www.iii.org/policymakers/home/

The second type of coverage available for personal property is called a *floater policy*. Originally called an *inland marine policy*, a **floater** is typically a separate minipolicy that "floats" coverage of an asset that frequently changes location—most often jewelry, firearms, art, or musical instruments. A personal article, personal effects, or personal property policy (different companies use different terms) works in much the same way as the personal property endorsement. Whereas an endorsement is an extension of a homeowners policy written by the same insurer, a floater is a separate policy that may or may not be written by the same company and often has different features. This type of policy can benefit a client because having a separate policy for such coverage allows for more flexibility in coverage limits and deductibles.

Finally, the planner and client should consider other property exclusions that may be relevant. For example, theft of property typically is excluded from coverage for college-age students who vacate their dorm rooms or apartments for more than 45 days during the summer or for alternative educational opportunities. Although an obscure circumstance, this question, as well as others, relating to coverage for property moved by a college student away from the insured residence should be considered, because policies vary. Clients who operate a home business will find that insurance restrictions may require the addition of a home business insurance endorsement. HO policies typically include up to $2,500 of coverage for business property kept at home, but standard coverage characteristically excludes many business exposures from liability claims and losses of high-value business property.

Clients often worry about issues related to medical claims resulting from property ownership. The medical payments (Part F) and liability coverage (Part E) of a homeowners policy extend beyond situations on the insured's property to liability losses caused by the activities of the insured, the activities of a residence employee in the course of employment, and the activities of an animal owned or cared for by the insured. It may be wise to increase the medical payments or liability coverage as a result of the athletic participation or hobbies of household members, as well as pet ownership. For example, some states have passed legislation making the owner of a dog that bites someone strictly liable for the injuries. Information about dog ownership often is considered when underwriters are rating and offering insurance coverage. Homeowners with swimming pools also may pay higher insurance premiums. A knowledgeable planner or insurance professional should be consulted to explore these issues and to ensure sufficient protection, either through the HO policy or in conjunction with an excess liability or umbrella policy, which is described in more detail later in the chapter.

### Auto Insurance

Driver characteristics, such as age, gender, marital status, and driving record, use of the auto, and number and types of cars covered are considerations in **personal automobile policy (PAP)** insurance price and coverage analyses. How vehicles are used (e.g., for pleasure, commuting to work, or business or farm activities) significantly affects PAP prices and the liability limits needed. Driver education and good student discounts may be used to reduce premiums for households with young drivers, as may the discount for a college student away from home without a car.

Auto insurance is often viewed simply as a requirement to operate a motor vehicle. And, as shown in Table 9.2, New Hampshire is the only state that does not have compulsory liability insurance. Aside from the fact that state minimum liability requirements are generally inadequate, attention to the liability limits in a PAP is important for another reason. Typically the split-limit liability coverage chosen is the same amount of **uninsured** or **underinsured motorists insurance** offered by the policy. Bodily injury and property damage coverage protect the insured from the losses sustained as a result of an accident with an uninsured, or underinsured, driver. Studies by the Insurance Research Council, as reported by the Insurance Information Institute, suggest that from 2003 to 2009, approximately 14% of U.S. drivers were uninsured.[2] State variations range from a high of 28% in Mississippi to a low of 4.5% in Massachusetts, with a few states (e.g., Alabama, Texas, West Virginia) implementing online verification systems to track those in violation.[3] Individuals who reside in areas where there is a concentration of uninsured drivers may want to consider higher limits of uninsured or underinsured motorists insurance. Currently, only Illinois, Kansas, Maine, Maryland, Massachusetts, Minnesota, Missouri, Nebraska, New Hampshire, New Jersey, New York, North Carolina, North Dakota, Oregon, South Carolina, South Dakota, Vermont, Virginia, Washington DC, West Virginia, and Wisconsin require drivers to carry uninsured motorist coverage. Of these, only 12 also require underinsured motorist coverage.[4]

Beyond the direct protection of insured motorist, a secondary—and perhaps less obvious—protection is also available. Consider the example of a client who chooses split-limit coverage of $1 million /$1 million/$1 million liability coverage *and* uninsured or underinsured motorists insurance. The liability coverage protects the client's assets and future income from losses caused by an accident for which the client or the client's family members were determined to be at fault. Conversely, if the client is involved in an accident for which an uninsured or underinsured driver (for example, PAP with only $100,000 of liability insurance) is at fault, the client's PAP provides additional protection. Assuming the client was disabled as a result of the accident, the $100,000 would leave little, if any, coverage for lost income. The client's protection of $1 million might not replace a lifetime of income, but it would provide significantly more than that of an uninsured or underinsured driver and a PAP with lower coverage limits. Although this is no substitute for adequate disability insurance, for a client who spends significant time commuting or traveling for work, the additional PAP coverage could be relatively inexpensive protection for this isolated loss.

In addition to understanding the basic components of a traditional PAP, financial planners are sometimes required to help clients deal with insurance issues related to leased cars and those where the insured is considered to be **upside-down**, meaning that they owe more on the car than the car is worth in the marketplace. An **auto loan/ lease coverage endorsement** provides coverage for the potential gap between the actual cash value of an auto and the amount the insured owes on the auto loan or lease. If a vehicle is deemed a total loss after an accident, the owner may owe more on the vehicle than the insurance will pay as its actual cash value. **Guaranteed auto protection (GAP)** pays the difference between the actual cash value settlement and the remaining balance on the loan or lease.

**Table 9.2** State Minimum PAP Split-Limit Liability Requirements

| State/District | Split-limit Liability Minimums | State/District | Split-limit Liability Minimums |
|---|---|---|---|
| Alabama | 25/50/25 | Montana | 25/50/10 |
| Alaska | 50/100/25 | Nebraska | 25/50/25 |
| Arizona | 15/30/10 | Nevada | 15/30/10 |
| Arkansas | 25/50/25 | New Hampshire | 25/50/25* |
| California | 15/30/5 | New Jersey | 15/30/5 |
| Colorado | 25/50/15 | New Mexico | 25/50/10 |
| Connecticut | 20/40/10 | New York | 25/50/10 |
| Delaware | 15/30/10 | North Carolina | 30/60/25 |
| Florida | 10/20/10 | North Dakota | 25/50/25 |
| Georgia | 25/50/25 | Ohio | 12.5/25/7.5 |
| Hawaii | 20/40/10 | Oklahoma | 25/50/25 |
| Idaho | 25/50/15 | Oregon | 25/50/20 |
| Illinois | 20/40/15 | Pennsylvania | 15/30/5 |
| Indiana | 25/50/10 | Rhode Island | 25/50/25 |
| Iowa | 20/40/15 | South Carolina | 25/50/25 |
| Kansas | 25/50/10 | South Dakota | 25/50/25 |
| Kentucky | 25/50/10 | Tennessee | 25/50/15 |
| Louisiana | 15/30/25 | Texas | 30/60/25 |
| Maine | 50/100/25 + minimum of $1,000 for medical payments | Utah | 25/65/15 |
| Maryland | 30/60/15 | Vermont | 25/50/10 |
| Massachusetts | 20/40/5 | Virginia | 25/50/20 |
| Michigan | 20/40/10 | Washington | 25/50/10 |
| Minnesota | 30/60/10 | Washington D.C. | 25/50/10 |
| Mississippi | 25/50/25 | West Virginia | 20/40/10 |
| Missouri | 25/50/10 | Wisconsin | 50/100/15 |
| | | Wyoming | 25/50/20 |

**Note:** Some states allow the minimum requirement to be met with a combined single-limit policy. Coverage amounts vary by state.

*New Hampshire does not require the purchase of auto insurance, but drivers must be able to prove they can meet the New Hampshire Motor Vehicle Financial Responsibility Requirements in the event of an "at-fault" accident. The 25/50/25 minimum is recommended coverage.

*Source:* The Insurance Information Institute. Available at http://www.iii.org/issues_updates/compulsory-auto-uninsured-motorists.html and/or other Internet sources to confirm any discrepancies found among Web sites, such as the following: Wisconsin Dept. of Transportation, DMV, http://www.dot.wisconsin.gov/drivers/vehicles/ins-req.htm; Wyoming Automobile Insurance Guide, http://insurance.state.wy.us/consumfm/word60/Auto.doc, p. 4.

Renting a car while on business or for personal reasons causes many clients anxiety. Whether to purchase the insurance offered by rental car companies can be a confusing issue. Normally, clients who carry **collision coverage**—a policy provision which covers damage to a policy holder's auto resulting from physical contact with another object—on their personal car will find that the coverage extends to rental cars as well. Usually **comprehensive coverage** also carries over to a rental car. This coverage provides reimbursement for noncollision damage or theft of the automobile; however, it is important to note when advising clients that they are responsible for paying the policy deductible and that the insurance company will consider the policy to be excess coverage, meaning the insurance company will look first to see whether the insured purchased coverage from the rental car company before paying a claim.

Drivers who have many claims on file with their insurance company, and those who are highly risk averse, should consider purchasing insurance as part of the rental agreement. Rental car insurance is known as a **loss damage waiver (LDW)** or a **collision damage waiver (CDW)**. Purchasing an LDW/CDW allows the insured to walk away from an accident, or if the car is stolen or vandalized, without having to pay a deductible, unless the rental company can show that the driver was reckless or driving while under the influence of drugs or alcohol. Costs for LDW/CDWs average between $7 and $20 per day. Sometimes clients will ask financial planners whether accidental death and/or personal property insurance coverage should be purchased when renting a car. Normally, the answer is no. The cost of accidental death insurance can be very high, and most often, reimbursement for lost personal property falls under a client's HO policy.

### Excess Liability Coverage

Although clients often think of insurance as a tool to reimburse property losses, financial planners are quick to point out that liability coverage may be a more important need for clients. Typical homeowners and personal automobile policies provide basic levels of liability protection. Often, however, these limits are very low. In some states, for example, someone may drive legally with as little as $5,000 in liability coverage. Although it is possible and prudent for clients to purchase additional liability coverage of $300,000 to $500,000 on individual homeowners, auto, or watercraft policies, additional—and perhaps more cost-effective—coverage should be purchased through an **excess liability** or **umbrella liability policy**. These policies provide coverage for losses above liability limits within HO and PAP policies, and stated HO and PAP policy liability coverage is typically required before an excess liability policy can be purchased. Umbrella contracts are not standardized, so coverage can vary. These insurance contracts also typically provide **personal injury coverage** (e.g., claims alleging libel, slander, or invasion of privacy) that may not be included in other policies.

Although $1 million is the minimum policy available, financial planners often recommend $2 million to $5 million in coverage. A rule of thumb is to roughly match the umbrella protection, at a minimum, to the client's net worth. But other factors, such as earnings potential, risk tolerance, personal risk and lifestyle profile, and the availability of assets to be attached to pay for a claim beyond the coverage of the policy, also must be considered.

## *Other Considerations for Securing Property and Liability Protection*

Standard HO policies typically provide reimbursement for losses associated with fire (including wildfires), windstorms, hail, and freezing pipes. Standard policies, however, exclude damage caused by disasters, such as flooding and earthquakes, and for those who live in hurricane coastal areas, windstorms. Clients who live in areas prone to flooding must consider flood coverage. A lender may, in fact, require flood insurance before a mortgage can be acquired. Floods are the most common and widespread of all natural disasters, except for fire. The federal flood insurance requirement applies to any structures located in an eligible community or one that is designated a Special Flood Hazard Area in the emergency program.

The flood insurance program is administered by the Federal Insurance and Mitigation Administration (changed from the Federal Insurance Administration), which is part of **FEMA (Federal Emergency Management Agency)**. An insurance agent or broker may issue a policy directly from the **National Flood Insurance Program (NFIP),** or a client can secure coverage from a **write your own (WYO) company**. WYO companies are private insurance companies that provide flood insurance under a special arrangement with the NFIP. WYO companies provide and service policies, while the NFIP retains the risk, thus expanding the availability of flood protection to more homeowners and communities. Policies are also available for renters and condominium unit owners.

**Flood insurance** provides reimbursement for the overflow of inland or tidal waters and surface waters. Mudslides caused by a flood are also covered. Flood insurance will not cover damage from rain, snow, hail, sewer back-ups, or water damage that results from something a homeowner can control. As with all types of property insurance, premiums reflect the risk of loss, and a deductible does apply. Premiums for coverage start at approximately $130 per year for those living in low- to moderate-risk areas.[5] The minimum deductible is $500, but a homeowner can choose to increase the deductible, which will result in a reduced annual premium.

At least 39 states are subject to moderate or major earthquakes.[6] **Earthquake insurance** provides catastrophic coverage for those who live in areas prone to earthquakes and also provides coverage for landslide, mudslide, mudflow, mine subsidence, or other earth movement. Earthquake policies typically have deductibles equal to 10% to 25% of the policy limit. Some policies apply the deductible separately to the contents, the structure, and any unattached buildings, so care must be taken to carefully evaluate the policy.

As with all types of property insurance, premiums reflect the risk of loss, including location and the probability of an earthquake, as well as building materials and other structural considerations. Premiums for a $500,000 home in a high-risk earthquake community can run as high as $2,000 a year, with a deductible equal to 10% of the limit of coverage. In other parts of the country, an earthquake endorsement can be purchased much less expensively.

Some planners advise clients to self-insure against earthquake losses. Other planners argue that the cost of insurance plus the deductible is reasonable considering the unpredictability and potential magnitude of earthquake damage. The value of the home and potential replacement costs relative to the client's total net worth should be a major consideration. Earthquake damage to autos would be covered under comprehensive insurance, included in the automobile policy.

Many states provide homeowners with the opportunity to protect a portion of home equity in a personal residence from creditors, which can include liability claims. This protection is provided through a **homestead exemption** or **declaration**. Protection may or may not be automatic, depending on the state. To qualify, a client must live in the residence, and it may be necessary to file a form with the local municipality. Equity protection amounts and guidelines vary by state.

---

### Planning for Special Populations: Random Thoughts on Property and Liability Insurance

Whereas some core content planning areas present unique planning challenges for select segments of the population, property and liability risk management issues can be a challenge simply because of the property owned or lifestyle activities. Consider the following:

**For jewelry owners**. How many people typically walk around with thousands of dollars in their pocket? Yet, a diamond ring, wedding band, watch, or other jewelry could easily amount to $10,000 or more. Jewelry owners make three common mistakes. First, clients often assume that jewelry is covered by their homeowners policy, not realizing that relatively low limits apply (typically $2,500) and that policies do not cover loss, damage, or the loss of a diamond from the setting. A deductible will also apply, further reducing the stated, limited protection. **Personal article policies**, which are relatively inexpensive, provide comprehensive jewelry coverage, typically without a required deductible.

The second common mistake is the failure to periodically update jewelry appraisals, because value fluctuates with changes in the price of gold, silver, diamonds, or other precious stones and metals. Recommendations on how often new appraisals should be done vary, but waiting more than a few years is inadvisable. Without a current assessment, a gap in coverage could result in a loss—of not only the item of jewelry, but also in the amount of insurance proceeds to replace it. A personal articles policy policy is an all-perils policy and protects from loss, theft, or damage to the item, as well as loss of gemstones and diamonds. A **pair and set clause** offers additional protection for items sold as a pair or a set, as in a matching diamond ring and wedding band or a pair of earrings. A broad form pays for full replacement of both items, but a standard form pays only to replace, or duplicate, the missing component. Personal articles policies typically include inflation protection, based on the purchase price or appraised value when insurance is initially puchased, and require no deductible.

The third common mistake is failure to maintain an up-to-date inventory. Appraisals required to purchase personal article policies (or to add a personal article endorsement) provide needed documentation, but it is still important to maintain a complete inventory of all jewelry. Care should be taken to continually update the inventory and buy coverage for new purchases. In fact, specialized insurance is available to protect items purchased during a specific time period, such as while traveling, so that insurance is immediately available until a personal articles policy or endorsement can be obtained.

**For those serving on corporate or nonprofit organization boards.** Individuals are often honored, and quite motivated, to serve on the board of directors of a nonprofit organization. Most corporations and nonprofit organizations purchase directors' and officers' (D&O) liability insurance to protect those serving in this capacity. But if the coverage is inadequate or is *not* purchased, then a liability suit that names the officers and directors could expose their personal assets to any claims or jury awards. An excess, or umbrella, liability policy provides limited protection in this situation, specifically for bodily injury or property damage, and it may also pay for the costs of defending the individual. Another option is for the client to purchase a directors and officers liability policy to protect against non-bodily injury claims (e.g., discrimination or termination of employment) arising from misstatement, misleading statement, breach of duty, or errors and omissions. The policy may or may not provide for legal and court fees, and deductibles often apply.

The data collection and discovery process could reveal a couple's love for animals and service on a struggling, local animal shelter board. But the clients might never have considered how a dog bite at a shelter-sponsored event could threaten their personal wealth. A qualified insurance specialist is best equipped to address that possibility and to recommend the necessary insurance protection. A financial advisor plays a valuable role in asking the questions to uncover the issue and to recommend that the necessary actions be taken.

**For anyone, protecting against identity theft.** Clients may not have considered insurance coverage in the event of a stolen identity. In fact, according to the Federal Trade Commission (FTC), the No. 1 consumer complaint in 2011, for the 11th straight year, was identity theft.[7] Placing fraud alerts with credit reporting bureaus, shredding documents with personal or financial information, and using "strong" passwords are all recommended methods of prevention, but what if those measures fail? In 2008, almost 10 million Americans were reportedly victims of identity theft, a 22% increase over the previous year.[8] The FTC estimates that consumer costs associated with identity theft are about $50 billion annually.[9] Identity theft can continue undetected until the victims check their credit reports, notice an incorrect charge on their credit card statement, or are contacted by a debt collector.

One method to mitigate such loss at the household level is to insure for it. Some homeowners policies provide at least a modest form of coverage. This may be limited to a particular type of transaction (e.g., forgery, electronic fund transfer, or credit card fraud) or a nominal amount of coverage (e.g., $500–$1,000) depending on the company. The first layer of additional protection is available with an endorsement on the homeowners policy to enhance both the scope and coverage amount for a potential loss. Additional coverage may be available with an excess liability, or umbrella, policy.

> Discussing methods of identity protection and loss mitigation during the conversation about the financial planning firm's own commitment to the security of records, transactions, and communication is another value-added service for clients. Planning firms also use Web sites, client newsletters, or other client outreach methods to educate busy clients, who think identity theft, could not happen to them.

## Document and Evaluate Current Property and Liability Insurance

The second step in the assessment of a client's current situation focuses on gathering, summarizing, and analyzing all currently in-force property and liability policies. This entails conducting a comprehensive review of a client's homeowners, personal automobile, excess liability, and other miscellaneous policies. A basic checklist is shown in Exhibit 9.1.

**Exhibit 9.1** Questions to Use When Assessing Property and Liability Insurance Coverage

| Assessing Homeowners Insurance Coverage | Yes | No |
|---|---|---|
| Is client's home insured for 100% replacement value rather than market value? | | |
| Is coverage on the home at least 80% of the estimated replacement value? | | |
| Has the home recently been appraised for its estimated replacement value? | | |
| Does the policy have an inflation endorsement? | | |
| Does the policy have a building code, sewer back-up, identity theft, or other endorsement? | | |
| Has client made a household possessions inventory? | | |
| Does client have a video or pictures to supplement the inventory? | | |
| Is the household possessions inventory/documentation held in a safe place outside of the home? | | |
| Does client's homeowners policy have adequate contents insurance protection? | | |
| Does client need special coverage for collectibles and other hard-to-replace items? | | |
| Does client have written appraisal for expensive items (silver, jewelry, furs, etc.)? | | |
| Does client have endorsements or individual policies for these items? | | |
| Does client carry comprehensive (open perils) coverage on household contents? | | |
| Does client carry replacement cost coverage on household contents? | | |
| Does client need/have coverage for any watercraft? | | |
| Does client need extended theft coverage? | | |
| Is coverage for medical payments to others sufficient? | | |
| Is liability coverage sufficient? Is it coordinated with an umbrella policy? | | |
| Does the deductible match client's ability to pay out of pocket for losses? | | |
| Have all available discounts been taken? | | |
| Does client own any seasonal residences that might need special insurance treatment? | | |
| Does client own an historic home that might need special insurance treatment? | | |

| Assessing Automobile Insurance Coverage | Yes | No |
|---|---|---|
| Are liability limits sufficient? Are they coordinated with an umbrella policy? | | |
| Is coverage for medical payments to others sufficient? | | |
| Is uninsured and under-insured motorist's coverage sufficient to protect the client, if needed? | | |
| Does client still need comprehensive or collision coverage, given the age of the vehicle(s)? | | |
| Does client have coverage for any off-road or recreational vehicles? | | |
| Do deductibles match client's ability to pay for losses from cash flow or assets? | | |
| Have all available discounts been taken? | | |
| **Assessing Liability Insurance Coverage** | **Yes** | **No** |
| Does client have an umbrella liability policy? | | |
| Does client have potential liability exposure from serving as an officer or director of a for-profit or not-for-profit organization? | | |
| Does client have potential liability exposure resulting from volunteer activities? | | |
| Does client have a nanny, housekeeper, or lawn/garden help? | | |
| Are liability homeowners and auto policies coordinated with client's umbrella policy? | | |
| **Assessing Need for Flood and Earthquake Insurance** | **Yes** | **No** |
| Does client need, or qualify for, flood insurance? | | |
| If maximum losses were incurred, could client afford to pay damages from cash flow and/or assets? | | |
| Does client need/have earthquake insurance? | | |
| Can client afford the premium for flood or earthquake insurance? | | |

Two issues should guide the review. First, is the current level of coverage sufficient to insure property losses fully? Second, is the client adequately protected against liability claims? Each issue should be considered in greater depth; however, the questions presented in Exhibit 9.1 serve as the basis of this analysis.

Once these questions have been answered, it becomes easier to assess a client's need for additional property and liability insurance. Any "no" answer should be addressed when developing strategies and developing client recommendations. The client current situation summary illustrated in Exhibit 9.2 shows how a client's property and liability insurance situation can be summarized and presented within a comprehensive financial plan. This illustration combines a summary table with bulleted observations.

**Exhibit 9.2** Sample Client Current Homeowners Insurance Situation Summary

### Homeowners Insurance Policy

| Type | HO-3 | Auto | Auto | Excess Liability |
|---|---|---|---|---|
| Insurance company | Northern Lights | Northern Lights | Northern Lights | Northern Lights |
| Premium amount | $450 | $850 | $400 | $180 |
| Premium frequency | Annual | Semiannual | Semiannual | Annual |
| Liability coverage | $300,000 | $100/$300/$100 | $100/$300/$100 | $1,000,000 |

Observations:

- You have an H0-3 Special Form policy. This policy covers losses to the dwelling and other structures for open perils protection (all perils, except flood, earthquake, war, and nuclear attack are included in the policy). Personal property is limited to named peril protection, which means only losses occurring as a result of the specific named perils (e.g., fire, lightening, theft) are covered.

- You have actual cash value coverage on your home and contents.

- The deductible on your homeowners policy is $500.

- You have limited coverage for your rare books, artwork, and jewelry under your homeowners policy.

- You do not have additional endorsements or personal articles policies to cover your rare books, artwork, or jewelry beyond the applicable policy limits.

- Both auto insurance policies provide full protection (liability, medical expense, uninsured/underinsured motorists, and damage to your auto) and have a $500 deductible.

## The 80% Rule and Other Homeowners Insurance Considerations

As reported by Nationwide Mutual Insurance Company, two out of every three homes in the United States are underinsured. The average amount of under-insurance is 22%, with some homes underinsured by 60% or more.[10] As these data suggest, it is imperative that financial planners assess each client's home insurance coverage to ensure adequate reimbursement for potential losses. Some homeowners policies include an 80% rule to determine the level of reimbursement when a loss is incurred. The 80% rule provides one way to verify whether a HO policy limit is sufficient to provide full replacement for a major loss. Based on the value of the residence at the time of loss, if the amount of coverage is equal to 80% of the replacement cost, then full replacement of the damaged portion will be paid, up to the limits of the policy less the deductible, with no reduction for depreciation. If the insured does not carry insurance equal to at least 80% of the replacement cost, the insured is penalized through a coinsurance clause when the loss is paid.

Financial planners should remind clients that insurance is based on **replacement cost**, which is defined as the actual amount needed to rebuild or repair property, rather than the market value of that property. Market value may be higher or lower than replacement cost, depending on the geographic area in which the home is located. Although it is always a good idea to recommend a 90% to 100% replacement cost policy with an inflation endorsement, it is essential that the 80% rule be met. Otherwise, a client may not be completely reimbursed for future losses or damage.

If the amount of insurance on a structure, divided by 80% of the applicable replacement cost, is equal to or greater than 1, then the homeowner will be reimbursed for the lesser of the replacement cost or the amount of the policy. However, if the amount of insurance on the structure, divided by 80% of the applicable replacement cost, is less than 1, then the insured will not qualify for full repair or replacement. In this situation, the insured will be paid the actual cash value of the part of the structure damaged or destroyed less the deductible *or* the reimbursement amount calculated using the following formula:

$$\frac{\text{Amt of Insurance Coverage}}{80\% \times \text{Replacement Cost}} \times \text{Value of Loss} = \text{Value of the Claim}$$

The deductible amount will be subtracted from all settlements, regardless of whether the insured has met the 80% rule. **Actual cash value** settlements typically depreciate a property to account for its age. Replacement cost settlements typically do not include depreciation.

Assume, for example, that a client owns a home with a replacement value of $190,000. Unfortunately, over the years the policy has not kept pace with the rising values of real estate costs and the home is currently insured for only $130,000 with a $500 deductible. If the insured incurs a loss of $20,000, the insurance company will reimburse the client only $17,105, as shown below:

$$\left( \frac{\$130,000}{80\% \times \$190,000} \times \$20,000 \right) - \$500 = \$17,105 - \$500 = \$16,605$$

The $2,895 not reimbursed on the $20,000 claim is considered to be the client's **coinsurance penalty**. However, this is the reimbursement before applying the $500 deductible. Therefore, the actual amount received by the client will be $16,605. To maintain full reimbursement to the limit of the policy, the house should have been insured for a minimum of $152,000 ($190,000 multiplied by 80%).

In general, it is important to remember three rules when evaluating the current coverage limits on a client's home: (a) the 80% rule applies primarily to partial losses; (b) if the actual cash value exceeds the 80% rule limit, the insured receives the larger amount; and (c) the total reimbursement will never exceed the face amount of the policy less the deductible. Table 9.3 provides guidance on how the 80% rule can impact client outcomes in the event of a loss. Most other coverage levels are determined as a percentage of the coverage on the structure, so the ripple effect of under-insurance can have a significant effect on large losses.

**Table 9.3** Coverage and Coinsurance Illustration

**Possible Coverage and Coinsurance Outcomes**

| Amount of Insurance Coverage | Coverage Ratio to Property Value | Payment for Total Loss (Less $2,500) | Insured Coinsurance Percentage | Payment for Partial* Loss (Less $2,500) | Insured Coinsurance Penalty |
|---|---|---|---|---|---|
| $250,000 | 100% | $250,000 | 0% | $50,000 | 0% |
| $200,000 | 80% | $200,000 | 20% | $50,000 | 0%** |
| $150,000 | 60% | $150,000 | (1– (60/80)) or 25% | $37,500 | 25% |
| $100,000 | 40% | $100,000 | (1– (40/80)) or 50% | $25,000 | 50% |

Based on a home value of $250,000 and an HO policy with a $2,500 deductible.
\* $50,000 loss
\*\* 80% rule

Coverage in excess of the 80% rule is available and often recommended. With insurance equal to the full replacement cost of the structure, an endorsement that provides specified additional amounts of insurance can be added. This coverage is often referred to as an **extended replacement cost endorsement.** This policy provision provides reimbursement of 20% or more above policy limits. This may be necessary when the costs of labor and building supplies are at a premium because of extensive losses in a region (e.g., in the aftermath of a hurricane or tornado).

Bringing an older home up to date to meet current building code requirements, as whenever major repairs or reconstruction must occur, can also significantly add to replacement costs. A **building code upgrade endorsement** may save the client large out-of-pocket expenses. Some policies provide coverage that helps offset expenses associated with bringing a dwelling up to residential code standards after a loss; however, the amount of coverage is typically limited to 10% of the amount of insurance on the dwelling. Other policies provide no coverage for this necessary expense. These choices must be considered in light of a client's risk tolerance and emergency funds available for unreimbursed losses. A common financial and insurance planning refrain applies: All coverage should be reviewed periodically.

For clients who rent or own a condominium or cooperative, the 80% rule is not an effective measure of coverage. Other factors must be considered. Foremost is the named perils coverage on the contents, which some clients may wish to extend to protect against all risks except specific exclusions. Clients protected by an HO-4 or HO-6 policy (see Table 9.1 for a comparison of common policies) should include replacement cost and inflation guard endorsements for maximum protection. A careful inventory of contents to determine their estimated replacement cost is necessary to provide full protection in the event of a major loss. Condominium or cooperative owners must consider the level of coverage on unit property for which they are responsible, such as built-in cabinetry, appliances, or other surface treatments (e.g., carpet, tile, wallpaper) relative to their actual cash value or replacement cost. Upgrading to replacement cost and inflation guard protection offers broader protection, but it will increase premium costs as well.

**Planning for Special Populations: Property and Liability Protection for Cohabiting Couples, Housemates, or Partners**

Insurance companies can deny claims from an auto accident caused by a driver who *routinely* has access to a car but is not included on the policy as a driver *or* for a fire caused by a live-in partner or roommate who is not included on the homeowners policy. The property owners, of the car and the home, respectively, never suspected that they, and the actions of their partners, were not protected in these situations. So what is required to provide protection for the property and potential liability claims against the owner's assets or future income? Well, it all depends! But it is essential that financial planners review the titling—and insurance coverage—of jointly used assets as part of the insurance planning analysis.

In the auto situation, most companies will allow a multicar policy for unrelated individuals who share the same "garage address" for their vehicles. If this is unavailable or is not the method preferred by a nontraditional couple or housemates, then the other option is to add the partner or roommate to the auto policy of each of the insureds. With either method, the premium cost will be based on the driving records of both individuals. This is required for regular access to, and use of, the other partner's car. If access to the other's car is limited to a random, occasional occurrence, then it is not necessary to add the partner as a driver. If there is only one car, but both partners routinely drive it, then both must be named as insured drivers on the policy.

Similarly, if the home is owned by one partner, then coverage must be extended to the housemate. Typically, homeowners policies are written to match the deed and protect only the insured and his or her immediate family. To extend coverage, several options are available. The nonowner's name may be added to the policy as an additional insured, although not all companies will allow this. Some companies add a rider, or cohabitant form, for an additional occupant. If this is not available or is not the method preferred by the clients, then the nonowner should purchase a renters policy, even if no rent is actually being paid. The renters policy will provide protection for the personal property in the home, and more importantly, provide liability and other HO-4 coverage (for more information see Table 9.1), if needed. If the home is rented, a joint renters policy may be available; otherwise, each partner should purchase an individual policy.

Contingent on the insurance options chosen from these alternatives, a similar strategy may be available to purchase excess liability, or umbrella, insurance. State laws and company policies vary, so be sure to consult with an insurance professional. However, individuals who are not married or do not own property jointly typically cannot purchase an excess liability policy together; individual umbrella policies will be necessary. Either way, the protection should be matched, at a minimum, to the net worth of the individuals, and potentially to an even higher amount to protect assets adequately.

# STRATEGIES

## Review Prospective Property and Liability Insurance Strategies

Answering the key property and liability questions presented in Exhibit 9.1 and reviewing a client's current coverage and liability limits can help financial planners and their clients discover gaps in current insurance coverage and opportunities to enhance in-force policies. Generally, these needs can require an increase in current coverage or the purchase of a new policy. The way an insurance contract is structured will affect the cost and amount of insurance obtained. The following discussion describes commonly used property and liability insurance strategies to meet a typical client's needs. When reviewing these strategies, it is important to consider that, in practice, financial planners often go beyond these basic tactics to help their clients navigate the complex property and casualty insurance environment.

## Identify Prospective Property and Liability Insurance Planning Strategies

The following product and procedural strategies represent only a sampling of alternatives used by financial planners. When planning for a client's property and liability protection, it is important to consider strategies for choosing the most appropriate product(s) and effectively structuring the insurance contracts.

### Product Strategy 1: Purchase an HO-3 Policy with at Least $300,000 in Liability Coverage

**Advantage:** An HO-3 policy provides the broadest open perils coverage available for a given structure. This type of policy covers personal property losses for named perils only. An endorsement to provide open perils coverage on the contents is available for those who prefer the most comprehensive coverage, assuming an HO-5 is unavailable. If the HO-3 provides only $100,000 in liability coverage, it should be increased to $300,000, which is what many financial planners consider a minimum level of protection. Increasingly, a minimum of $500,000 of liability protection is recommended. An umbrella policy can be added for additional liability protection.

**Disadvantage:** The primary disadvantage associated with this strategy is the higher premium cost associated with the contents endorsement and the higher liability limit, especially if an open perils endorsement for contents is chosen. This higher cost can be partially offset by a high deductible.

### Product Strategy 2: Maximize Homeowners Coverage with Endorsements

**Advantage:** To personalize and maximize coverage, a wide variety of endorsements, such as a personal articles endorsement, a personal injury endorsement, an identity theft endorsement, or home office coverage, can be written as an addendum to a homeowners contract. The choice of appropriate endorsements must be matched to a client's individual needs, but two endorsements are broadly applicable.

A **replacement cost coverage endorsement** provides for lost, stolen, or destroyed property to be replaced with equivalent property with no reductions for depreciation.

Some policies use **actual cash value** as the basis for replacing property. Actual cash value provides reimbursement on the basis of the replacement value of the property *less* depreciation. Older property, whose age exceeds the specified useful life of "x" years, has no reimbursement value. Consequently, reimbursement could be pennies on the dollar relative to the value of the loss or the amount needed for even minimal replacement. Although slightly more expensive, replacement cost coverage is recommended in most situations.

An **inflation endorsement** ensures that property coverage automatically adjusts annually in response to rising prices. An extended replacement cost endorsement and a building code upgrade endorsement, discussed previously in this chapter, provide additional protection from losses occurring to a structure.

**Disadvantage:** Endorsements add to the cost of an annual premium. Professional appraisals may be necessary to secure coverage. These costs, as well as the time and effort to complete a well-documented possessions inventory, may discourage some clients. But a quick tally of the potential financial losses, without the additional coverage of the endorsements, may persuade clients to add endorsements to their current coverage.

### Product Strategy 3: Purchase Lowest-Cost Personal Automobile Policy

**Advantage:** Refer to Table 9.2 for a state-by-state listing of split-limit liability requirements. It is possible to purchase policies with these limits at a relatively low cost.

**Disadvantage:** The least effective way to shop for automobile insurance involves comparing policies on premium alone. Although a policy with low liability limits may be purchased for a modest annual premium, buying automobile insurance on premium alone can be dangerous. First, a client is more likely to be underinsured for liability exposure. Second, low-cost insurance providers should be reviewed for financial stability, claims history, and customer satisfaction. Further, some low-cost policies require that claims be made via telephone or the Internet. Although this often sounds reasonable before an accident, the inherent limitations of such claims adjustment procedures can be severe in a serious accident. Having a competent and well-trained agent is often worth the extra premium.

### Product Strategy 4: Purchase at Least a $1 Million Umbrella Liability Policy

**Advantage:** Rapidly increasing jury awards for liability claims have escalated the need for additional liability insurance to protect current assets and future income. High-net-worth clients are especially at risk for liability exposure. Often the greater the perceived ability of an individual to pay, the greater the likelihood of a liability lawsuit. The annual cost of an umbrella policy is quite reasonable. A $1 million policy can be purchased for $300 or less annually in most cases. In addition to the additional financial protection it provides, an umbrella policy provides peace of mind. For a very modest annual cost, clients can sleep easier knowing that they are protected in case of a liability claim.

**Disadvantage:** Liability limits on homeowners and personal automobile policies generally must be increased to obtain an umbrella policy. A minimum of $300,000 in liability coverage for a homeowners policy typically is required. Higher split-limit coverage, such as 250/500/100, or a $500,000 single limit, is normally required for automobile policies. These policies provide the first level of coverage in case of litigation. Once these policy limits are reached, the umbrella policy provides additional protection up to the limits of the policy.

If the umbrella policy is used for a claim that is excluded from a HO or PAP, a deductible ranging from a low of perhaps $250 to as much as several thousand dollars may be imposed. For example, payment of a deductible would be required for a lawsuit that is excluded from homeowners coverage. This must be considered when establishing emergency fund limits.

### Procedural Strategy 1: Drop Collision Coverage on Autos Six to Eight Years of Age or Older

**Advantage:** The costs associated with repairing significant damage on most late-model standard automobiles almost always exceeds the book value of the automobile. In such cases, an insurance company may elect not to repair the car. Rather, they may pay the insured the book value (minus the deductible) and declare the car a total loss. Paying premiums for collision coverage on a car in this situation may not be cost effective.

This strategy will reduce the premium and increase annual discretionary cash flow. However, the insured must recognize that, without physical damage protection, any loss other than an at-fault accident caused by another driver with insurance will mean that the insured must pay for all repair costs or replace the auto with another auto.

**Disadvantage:** This strategy is least effective when the insured drives a high-value or collectible car. Also, the out-of-pocket expenses associated with a loss can still be quite high. This may require a client to hold more in liquid assets than might be desired.

### Procedural Strategy 2: Choose the Highest Deductible a Client Can Afford

**Advantage:** A higher deductible is preferred, unless the client has no emergency savings. Raising a HO policy deductible from $500 to $1,000 could save a client up to 25% on annual premium costs.[11] Similarly, raising a PAP deductible from $200 to $500 could reduce collision and comprehensive coverage costs by 15% to 300%, and increasing a deductible to $1,000 could save 40% percent or more in annual premium costs.[12]

**Disadvantage:** Client out-of-pocket expenses will increase in case of a loss. This strategy requires clients to increase their emergency funds, which may temporarily divert savings and assets from funding other goals. Planners should conduct a cost-benefit analysis to determine how long it will take to recoup costs if a claim occurs earlier or later in the savings process.

### Procedural Strategy 3: Increase Liability Limits

**Advantage:** In general, liability limits on a HO policy should be increased to a minimum of $300,000. Financial advisors often recommend that clients have a minimum of $100,000/$300,000/$100,000 in split-limit coverage on a PAP policy. A minimum of $500,000 **combined single-limit coverage** is recommended, with the insurance company paying covered liabilities up to this amount regardless of the distribution between bodily injury and property damage liability. Increasing liability coverage decreases the likelihood of being underinsured for losses caused to others. Furthermore, these amounts are generally the minimum required to purchase excess liability insurance.

**Disadvantage:** Increasing liability limits will result in an annual premium increase. But the premium cost must be considered relative to the protection of assets and future income, in the event of a large award from an at-fault accident. The increased premium cost can be partially offset by increasing the deductible and taking advantage of all discounts.

### Procedural Strategy 4: Reduce Premiums with Discounts

**Advantage:** Clients may be eligible for insurance premium discounts. For example, an older client who drives infrequently may be eligible for a low-mileage discount, and clients with teenagers or college-age children should inquire about good student discounts. In many states, it is also possible to receive a discount for taking a driver's education course. Clients who insure a home and automobile with a single insurer may receive a **multipolicy discount**. Homeowners policy discounts may be available for smoke detectors or security systems, including dead-bolt locks.

**Disadvantage:** The only real disadvantage associated with this strategy is the amount of time involved in researching, requesting, or validating eligibility for certain discounts. There may be a significant opportunity cost between the amount of time spent obtaining a discount and the amount of premium saved. Clients should instruct their insurance agents to recommend applicable discounts.

### Procedural Strategy 5: Review Insurance Rates before Purchasing a New Car

**Advantage:** Insurance rates are, in part, based on the type and value of the car being insured. Cars with lower repair rates will be less expensive to insure than those with higher repair rates. Likewise, a lower-priced car will be less expensive to insure than a more valuable one. Cars with outstanding safety records, passive restraint systems, and antitheft devices also generate lower premiums.

**Disadvantage:** This strategy can significantly limit a client's choice in cars. Additionally, adding features that will reduce premium costs may increase the overall cost of the vehicle. The best advice: when auto shopping, check the cost of coverage on all models considered. Insurance premiums can vary significantly for autos that appear similar in style, features, and cost.

## Procedural Strategy 6: Bundle Homeowners and Personal Auto Policies to Reduce Annual Premiums

**Advantage**: Clients, particularly those with a high insurance score, should shop aggressively for HO and PAP bundled coverage. The marketplace is competitive and discounts are widely available for those with a strong history of premium payment and low-incident levels of filing claims. An easy way to reduce annual premiums involves bundling a HO and PAP policy together, using a replacement value endorsement. When determining the level of HO insurance to purchase, insurance agents and brokers often recommend using the cost per square foot associated with building in a local area as a guide. Average insurance rates, for bundled and unbundled policies, can be obtained at www.homeownersinsurance.com.

**Disadvantage**: A clear disadvantage associated with bundling coverage relates to sometimes being held captive by one insurance company. Although a single provider may offer competitive rates on, for example, HO policies, there is no guarantee that the company will also be competitive with PAP policy rates. It is important for financial planners to work with their clientele to shop competitively for bundled policies that provide the lowest net premium cost.

## Procedural Strategy 7: Use Appropriate Business Structure to Help Clients Limit Liability

**Advantage**: Although not solely a property and casualty insurance issue, clients who own a business as a sole proprietorship who also use personal property as a function of their business need to understand that they are exposed to potential unlimited personal liability for claims against either the business or the individual. Normally, this liability cannot be controlled with a HO policy or an excess liability insurance contract. Although a sole proprietorship can be easy to manage, there are better alternatives to protect clients from liability. Five alternatives should be considered when working with small business owners. These alternatives, with a brief description, are listed below:

1. **C-corporation**: Limited liability for owners; relatively complex to manage. The corporate structure can provide an effective way to provide tax-advantaged fringe benefits for employees and owner-shareholders.

2. **S-corporation**: Limited liability for owners; income flows through from corporation to owners; may not have more than 100 shareholders.

3. **LLC**: Liability limited to member's contribution to firm; members rather than shareholders; less cumbersome than a corporation.

4. **LLP**: Liable for actions of all partners, but not liable for errors and omissions of partners.

5. **Partnership**: Liable for action of all partners.

**Disadvantage**: The costs, both financially and administratively, are higher for these arrangements than for sole proprietorships. Also, changing from a corporate structure back to a sole proprietorship can be expensive. Sometimes clients feel these costs outweigh the potential liability associated with owning a business; nonetheless, financial planners should always address liability exposure and recommend alternative forms of business ownership, when appropriate, within a comprehensive financial plan.

## CHAPTER-BASED CASE STUDY

## A Client-based Property and Liability Insurance Recommendation Example

Adequate levels of property and liability insurance are essential components of a well-designed financial plan. Liability coverage is especially important. Clients who under-insure themselves for liability protection may place their entire financial future in jeopardy because there is virtually no cap on the amount that a jury can award an injured party.

Clients who are in the process of accumulating assets, and those who are in the asset preservation stage of the financial planning life cycle, should be encouraged to manage their liability exposures with insurance. Recommendations associated with property and liability coverage require planners to answer the "who, what, when, where, why, how, and how much" implementation questions as specifically as possible. Although not all recommendations are the same for every client, a few guidelines can be used to simplify the answers to these questions. Some of the most common financial planning property and liability insurance recommendation rules are discussed here.

Four parameters can be used whenever a HO policy is recommended to a client. In general, clients should purchase maximum liability protection, but never less than a $300,000 limit. This should be coordinated with an umbrella policy of at least $1 million. Second, the coverage should be as comprehensive as possible. Third, first-party losses should be paid on a replacement cost basis, with an annual inflation adjustment. Finally, any and all discounts should be explored, including higher deductibles. Premium discounts also may be earned by implementing property protection devices and by buying all policies from the same insurance company.

Four rules apply to recommendations regarding personal automobile policies. First, clients should obtain the maximum affordable level of liability coverage, which should be coordinated with coverage for uninsured and underinsured motorists and an umbrella policy. Second, **medical expense coverage** should be evaluated. Policy payments to others within the policy should be maximized if the insured frequently has passengers who are not family members. Third, clients need to take advantage of premium reductions for discounts and higher deductibles. Finally, collision insurance, which covers damage to a policy holder's auto resulting from physical contact with another object, should be monitored yearly and eliminated once the automobile's value drops substantially. It is also important to monitor comprehensive insurance coverage as well. In situations where a client owns an older car, comprehensive coverage can be reduced or eliminated as a way to decrease the annual premium.

The general rule when recommending an umbrella policy is that the amount of insurance should be at least $1 million, coordinated with the homeowners and personal automobile policy. Higher coverage is preferable. Deductible rules follow a similar logic. Higher annual deductibles reduce the cost of insurance. High-net-worth clients may be able to afford very high deductibles. The reduction in premium associated with a high deductible can then be used to purchase additional liability coverage. Moderate-net-worth clients will need to find a trade-off point where the cost of insurance matches their insurance budget. A deductible that matches that point should be recommended.

These general rules can be used as property and liability insurance coverage guidelines. The following example illustrates how a property and liability insurance recommendation can be developed using this methodology.

## A Sample Recommendation: Increase Liability Limits and Purchase a Watercraft Endorsement

After Barry Corsaw, the youngest of four sons, talked his dad, George, into purchasing a new $9,000 110-horsepower Jet Ski®, the whole family found a new summertime activity to enjoy while living at their lakefront home. Everyone in the family would invite friends over for rides and jet skiing. Insurance was the last thing on their minds. George even mentioned, "What can I hit on a lake 20 miles long and 7 miles wide?" Little did he consider that property damage is not the only loss covered by insurance. He continued, "Well, if someone gets hurt, their medical insurance will pay. If something happens to the Jet Ski, my homeowners insurance will cover the cost of the damages, and under the worst case scenario my umbrella policy will cover any difference."

Upon hearing his father's response, the eldest son, Walker, a graduate student in financial planning, did some research to determine whether his dad faced potential loss. Walker confirmed that, even if the watercraft were covered for damage, most policies exclude many common causes of property loss and impose a low, typically $1,500 coverage limit. Also, if the watercraft was stolen while away from the primary "garaging" location, it would not be covered. He informed his father that, although all homeowners policies were not written so restrictively, it was safe to say that typical homeowners coverage of watercraft is inadequate. Walker went on to tell his father that homeowners policies do not usually cover liability claims arising from the operation of inboard motor boats owned by the insured if the craft has more than 50 horsepower, a restriction that includes personal watercraft such as Jet Skis and WaveRunners®.

Upon hearing this, George, anxious to avoid any losses, decided to contact a local financial planning firm that offered comprehensive planning services as well as "targeted" financial planning. In this case, George was very concerned about this potentially enormous liability exposure, not to mention the cost of the property loss if the Jet Ski was damaged or stolen. The planner promptly told George that none of his original coverage assumptions were correct, and if someone driving or riding on the Jet Ski got hurt, any lawsuit brought would be his responsibility. To ensure adequate coverage, the planner suggested a full review of George's property and casualty insurance policies. The information that was presented to George is shown in Exhibit 9.3.

**Exhibit 9.3** Property and Casualty Insurance Information for George Corsaw

### Comparison of Homeowners Coverage Options

| Type of Coverage | Homeowners Policy | | Automobile Policy | | Umbrella | |
|---|---|---|---|---|---|---|
| | Existing | Suggested | Existing | Suggested | Existing | Suggested |
| Total liability coverage limit | $100,000 | $300,000 | $300,000 | $500,000 | $1,000,000 | $1,000,000 |
| Property damage coverage | Replacement cost | Replacement cost | Actual cash value | Actual cash value | NA | NA |
| Property damage deductible(s) | $500 | $1,500 | $1,000/ $500 | $1,000/ $500 | $250 | $500 |
| Jet Ski endorsement | NA | Yes | NA | NA | NA | NA |
| Jet Ski damage coverage limit | $1,500 | Actual cash value | NA | NA | NA | NA |
| Medical payments | $1,000 | $3,000 | $1,000 | $3,000 | NA | NA |
| Annual premium | $635.00 | $712.00 | $2,291.00 | $2,406.00 | $320.00 | $245.00 |

The first recommendation the planner made was to increase the liability coverage limit on George's homeowners policy from $100,000 to $300,000. Raising the deductible would offset some of the resulting premium increase. The second recommendation was to increase the liability coverage on the automobile policy from a single-limit $300,000 to a single-limit $500,000 policy. Since George already had fairly high deductibles, $1,000 on collision and $500 on comprehensive, the planner suggested no changes. The planner also informed him that the increased liability limits on auto and homeowners policies would reduce the premium on his umbrella policy.

Although George was in agreement with these recommendations, he did not understand what this had to do with his Jet Ski. The planner explained that changing the deductibles was only a precursor to adding a watercraft endorsement on the existing homeowners policy. Without the changes, the endorsement would be significantly more expensive. The effect of the endorsement was to increase the damage coverage, to expand the coverage for bodily injury and property damage liability, and to include a medical-payments-to-others benefit.

Although not the case here, the planner also explained that some insurance companies offer a separate watercraft policy if the watercraft does not meet the homeowners policy requirements. Whereas a separate policy provides similar coverage, it can be more expensive. The planner further explained that because an umbrella policy offers only liability protection, no property damage claims for his Jet Ski could be made.

By more closely coordinating George's coverage, the planner closed some of the gaps in coverage, provided higher liability limits, and kept the premium costs reasonable and affordable. Exhibit 9.4 illustrates how these recommendations could be summarized and presented to a client.

**Exhibit 9.4** George Corsaw Insurance Recommendation Form

### Planning Recommendation Form

| | |
|---|---|
| **Financial Planning Content Area** | Property and liability insurance coverage |
| **Client Goal** | Obtain maximum property damage and liability coverage related to recent purchase of Jet Ski |

| Recommendation No. | 1 | Priority (1–6) lowest to highest: | 6 |
|---|---|---|---|
| **Projected/Target Value ($)** | Net annual premium increase of $117 | | |

**Product Profile**

| | | | | |
|---|---|---|---|---|
| Type | Homeowners, auto, and umbrella policies | | | |
| Duration | Annual | | | |
| Provider | Pearis Mountain Insurance Company | | | |
| Funding Cost per Period ($) | HO-3, $712 annually<br>Auto, $2,406 annually<br>Umbrella, $245 annually | | | |
| Maintenance Cost per Period ($) | $0 | | | |
| Current Income Tax Status | Tax-qualified | | Taxable | X |
| Projected Rate of Return | NA | | | |
| Major Policy Provisions | 1. Add watercraft endorsement to the HO-3 policy.<br>2. Increase the HO-3 liability coverage from $100,000 to $300,000 and the auto liability from $300,000 to $500,000.<br>3. Increase the HO-3 and auto medical payments coverage from $1,000 to $3,000.<br>4. Increase the property damage deductible on the HO-3 from $500 to $1,500.<br>5. Increase the umbrella policy deductible from $250 to $500. | | | |

**Procedural Factors**

| | | | | |
|---|---|---|---|---|
| Implementation by Whom | Planner | | Client | X |
| Implementation Date or Time Frame | Immediately | | | |
| Implementation Procedure | Contact Pearis Mountain Insurance Company | | | |

**Ownership Factors**

| | | | | |
|---|---|---|---|---|
| Owner(s) | George E. and Christine A. Corsaw | | | |
| Form of Ownership | JTWROS | | | |
| Insured(s) | George E. and Christine A. Corsaw and Hilton Mortgage Company | | | |
| Custodial Account | | Yes | No | X |
| Custodian | NA | | | |
| In Trust For (ITF) | | Yes | No | X |
| Transfer on Death (TOD) | | Yes | No | X |
| Beneficiary(ies) | NA | | | |
| Contingent Beneficiary(ies) | NA | | | |

| | |
|---|---|
| **Proposed Benefit** | Provides property damage loss and liability protection on the Jet Ski. Increases liability limits on the HO-3 and auto policies, which, with the increase in umbrella policy deductible, reduces the umbrella premium. Increases medical payments protection on both the HO-3 and the auto policies. |

In addition to reviewing George's property and casualty situation and answering any questions about the Insurance Recommendation Form, the planner also advised George to complete a periodic review of his actual insurance policy documents when meeting with his insurance professional. He explained to George that it was very important that the following items be checked for accuracy:

- Names and addresses

- Social Security Numbers

- Dwelling construction type

- Dwelling or outbuilding additions

- Deductibles

- Schedules and endorsements

If any item on a policy document is incorrect or inaccurate, immediate steps should be taken to correct it. Accurate documentation will lead to more efficient claims settlement should a loss occur.

Finally, the planner talked with George to confirm that he was pleased with the benefits associated with the proposed premium expenditures. George agreed that in many cases the purchase of insurance, especially liability coverage, provided psychological benefits as well as potential future financial reimbursement. In fact, he had declared the Jet Ski off-limits for anyone until this issue was resolved. Conducting an annual review or a spot evaluation can help a client see the value, both psychologically and fiscally, of proper insurance planning.

# Learning Outcomes

1.  The role of a property and liability insurance planning analysis within the comprehensive financial planning process sometimes gets relegated to a quick review, especially when compared to analyses related to life and long-term care planning issues. This is unfortunate. Although often overshadowed, issues related to property loss and liability exposure can influence almost every other aspect of a client's financial situation. It is imperative, as such, that financial planners adequately review and evaluate a client's personal, household, and family lifestyle issues as a way to identify threats that could lead to financial loss.

2.  The risk management process can be defined as identifying, analyzing, and ranking a client's personal, household, and family lifestyle for potential threats that could lead to financial loss and identifying methods to reduce or eliminate the impact of that loss. Five risk reduction techniques can be used to manage client property and casualty risks: (1) risk retention, (2) risk avoidance, (3) risk reduction, (4) risk transference, and (5) risk sharing. Insurance contracts represent an example of transferring and/or sharing risk with a third party.

3. Risk control refers to the ongoing process of identifying and analyzing the severity and likelihood of potential loss exposures. Issues related to maximum possible losses, maximum probable losses, and typical losses dominate the risk control process. Insurance companies regularly engage in risk control evaluations. This is one factor that determines the price of insurance. Additionally, insurance underwriters rely on insurance scores as a method for pricing policies. An insurance score is similar to a credit score. Both scores are calculated by considering a client's credit history, debt level, and previous financial behavior. Insurance firms use scores to predict premium payment history and the number of claims someone is likely to file. Low scores are generally associated with high insurance premiums.

4. Information and situational factors to assess the need for property and liability insurance focus on the assets and lifestyle of a client's household. Initially, attention is on identifying all of the property to protect and the possible risk exposures associated with a client's activities and those of other family members. But the risk management and control process is an ongoing activity. Financial planners can strengthen the client-planner relationship by periodically updating client information to maintain and improve a client's property and liability insurance protection. Minimally, financial planners should, at regular intervals, review client data related to (a) the names and addresses of all household members; (b) dwelling construction type; (c) dwelling or outbuilding improvements or additions; (d) changes in car ownership; (e) liability policy limits; (f) policy deductibles; and (g) HO and PAP schedules and endorsements. By including property and liability reviews in meetings with clients, issues related to property loss and/or liability exposure can be minimized both currently and in the future.

5. Although planners and clients collaborate with licensed insurance agents to manage the client's risk exposure, planners can play a significant role. It is important for financial planners to have a fundamental knowledge of typical liability exposures resulting from property ownership and the activities of a client's household. Planners also need to be competent in comparing different HO and PAP insurance types and provisions designed to manage client risk exposures. Through the data collection and discovery process, planners develop a profile of a client's situation that enables them to advise clients on: (a) forms of HO coverage, (b) PAP provisions, (c) excess liability planning, (d) flood/earthquake coverage, and (e) factors associated with premium rate determinations.

6. Excess liability, or umbrella, policy coverage is an essential tool that can be used to help clients manage exposure to insurance risk. Typically, financial planners recommend that clients purchase at least $1 million in excess liability coverage, although higher limits are sometimes more appropriate. To qualify for an umbrella policy, clients will be required to increase liability limits in both HO and PAP coverage. Although implementation of this planning strategy will result in increased annual premium charges, the benefits associated with enhanced liability protection are well worth the cost.

7. A key calculation within the property and liability planning section of a financial plan involves determining whether clients are currently in conformity with the 80% rule. Although not universally used by all insurance companies, the 80% rule provides an indication of the level of reimbursement that will occur if a client incurs a loss and makes a claim against the HO policy. If the amount of insurance on a structure, divided by 80% of the applicable replacement cost, is equal to or greater than 1, then the homeowner will be reimbursed for the lesser of the replacement cost or the amount of the policy. If the result of the calculation is less than 1, the client will not qualify for full repair or replacement.

8. Ensuring that a client has adequate levels of property and liability insurance is an important aspect of financial planning, especially for those who are engaged in comprehensive financial planning. The strategies presented in this chapter represent examples of insurance recommendations that can be incorporated into plans for clients who are either in the asset accumulation or asset preservation stage of the life cycle. Although recommendations will differ based on each client's unique situation, the fundamentals of property and liability insurance planning apply to all clients. Thus, identifying and recommending appropriate and reasonable insurance strategies is a measure of a financial planner's abilities and an important way to potentially help clients protect property, assets, and future income.

## Chapter Resources

Insurance Institute for Business and Home Safety (www.disastersafety.org).

Insurance Information Institute (www.iii.org).

National Flood Insurance Program (floodsmart.com or www.fema.gov/nfip/ or 1-800-638-6620).

Policy Forms Used by the Top 10 Homeowners' Insurance Groups in Nevada (http://doi.nv.gov/scs/Homeowners.aspx). Nevada is the only state offering this service to consumers, but other states are expected to follow this initiative.

Property Casualty Insurers Association of America (http://www.pciaa.net/web/sitehome.nsf/main).

United Policyholders™ Empowering the Insured (www.uphelp.org).

The *Financial Factilitator* and all fillable forms needed to complete text activities can be found on the student website at: http://pro.nuco.com/booksupplements/NUCollege-CaseBook2e.

## Quantitative/Analytical Mini-case Problems

1. Ricardo Juarez is purchasing a homeowners insurance policy. He is very concerned about inflation and wants to make a determination about purchasing the optional inflation protection rider. He has identified several scenarios and wants to know how often he needs to revisit his coverage to maintain at least 80% of replacement cost. Base all calculations on an initial home value of $250,000 and initial coverage of 100% on the dwelling and contents.

a. He believes that current housing prices will increase at 4% per year. How long will his coverage meet the 80% rule if he does not buy inflation protection? How long would he be covered if he purchases an inflation protection rider that offers annual compound increases of 3%?

b. Given the recent declines in housing values, he believes a recovery is coming and that housing prices will increase at 7% per year for the next five years before slowing to a permanent 4% annual appreciation rate. How long will his coverage meet the 80% rule? First assume that Ricardo does not purchase an inflation protection rider, and then assume that he purchases an inflation protection rider that offers annually compounded increases of 3%.

c. Ricardo believes that housing prices still have a ways to fall before any meaningful recovery. He believes that future housing prices will decrease at an annual rate of 4% for the next three years before the long-term trend of 5% annual increases resumes. Assuming that he does not purchase an inflation protection rider, how long will his coverage meet the 80% rule?

d. He believes that future price increases will be very unstable. With this uncertainty, he wants to have the inflation rider protection of 3% compounded annually. Assume actual housing price changes for the next five years are 3%, -7%, -2%, 8%, and 12%. Will his coverage meet the 80% rule at the end of this five-year period? What if he does not purchase the optional rider?

e. Based on the results from above, what can be said about how frequently insurance coverage needs to be reevaluated?

2. Your client has coverage of $90,000 on a dwelling. The replacement value of the dwelling is $125,000. The policy coinsurance requirement is 80%. The client has chosen a $500 deductible. Calculate the amount of loss reimbursement a client should receive for each of the following losses.

a. The amount of the loss is $60,000.

b. The amount of the loss is $90,000.

c. The amount of the loss is $120,000.

Now assume that the client increases the amount of coverage to $105,000. To offset some of the premium increase, the client chose to increase the deductible to $1,050. The policy coinsurance requirement is 80%. The replacement value of the dwelling is $125,000. Calculate the amount of loss reimbursement for each of the following losses.

a. The amount of the loss is $90,000.

b. The amount of the loss is $105,000.

c. The amount of the loss is $120,000.

# Comprehensive Bedo Case – Analysis Questions

Specific client data are needed to conduct a thorough property and liability analysis. A copy of the client's homeowners and personal automobile policies should be obtained. The 80% rule should be reviewed in relation to the Bedos' homeowners coverage and the value of their property. Any personal property that might be excluded or have limited coverage should be identified for coverage with policy endorsements. Special attention should also be placed on examining liability limits in the homeowners, auto, or umbrella policies.

1. Develop one or more property and liability insurance planning goals for the Bedos. When conceptualizing this goal, consider the following:

   a. Is the goal(s) developed in agreement with any or all goals and objectives that the clients have identified regarding property and liability insurance planning?

   b. What situational factors might influence their property and liability insurance goal? Are these factors explicit, implied, or assumed? Is additional information required from the Bedos, and if so, what?

   c. What is the desired property and liability insurance planning outcome for the clients?

2. Make a list of the lifestyle factors or property ownership issues that should be documented and evaluated for the Bedos. How might this information be obtained? How might it be useful in the current property and liability insurance situation analysis? Also, make a list of life events that could affect the property and liability insurance planning analysis for Tyler and Mia and that should be reviewed at future client meetings.

3. Are there globally accepted, client-specific, or planner-generated planning assumptions that will influence the property and casualty insurance situation analysis? List the assumptions as they might appear in a plan.

4. To determine and quantify the Bedos' current property and liability insurance planning needs thoroughly, assess the following:

   a. Possible liability exposures faced by the Bedos.

   b. Their current level of homeowners insurance coverage compared to industry benchmarks.

   c. The amount of liability coverage in the Bedos' homeowners policy compared to their possible liability exposure.

   d. The need for specific policy endorsements.

   e. The split-limit coverage limits on their personal automobile insurance policies.

   f. The need for Part D Coverage for Damage to Your Car automobile insurance coverage.

   g. The need for an umbrella, or excess liability, policy.

5. List and comment on other policy features that should be evaluated as part of the documentation and evaluation of the Bedos' property and liability insurance planning needs and efforts, including, but not limited to, the following.

   a. Do the Bedos have sufficient documentation to verify property or values in the event of a loss?

   b. Assume that the Bedos were shopping for a new car. What attributes of the car would result in a lower annual insurance premium?

6. Based on the information collected, financial advisors have a responsibility to fully document and inform clients of the analyses and results. This information may be communicated through a letter or a comprehensive or modular plan. Summarize your observations about Tyler and Mia's current property and liability insurance situation and the identified planning need(s). Be sure to discuss their homeowners, auto, and, if needed, excess liability insurance. Incorporate text, bullets, and graphics into your explanation.

7. Based on the goals originally identified and the completed analysis, what product or procedural strategies might be most useful to satisfy the Bedos' property and liability insurance protection needs? Be sure to consider strategies matched to the planning needs identified. When reviewing the strategies, be careful to consider the approximate cost of implementation, as well as the most likely outcome(s) associated with each strategy.

8. Write at least one primary and one alternative recommendation from the selected strategies in response to each identified planning need. More than one recommendation may be needed to address all of the planning needs. Include specific, defensible answers to the who, what, when, where, why, how, and how much implementation questions for each recommendation.

   a. It is suggested that each recommendation be summarized in a Recommendation Form.

   b. Assign a priority to each recommendation based on the likelihood of meeting client goals and desired outcomes. This priority will be important when recommendations from other core planning content areas are considered relative to the available discretionary funds for subsidizing all recommendations.

   c. Comment briefly on the outcomes associated with each recommendation.

9. Complete the following for the Property and Liability Insurance section of the Bedos' financial plan.

   a. Outline the content to be included in this section of the plan. Given the segments written above, which segments are missing?

   b. Write the introduction to this section of the plan (no more than one to two paragraphs).

   c. Define, explain, or interpret at least five policy features or concepts (e.g., the 80% rule) that would be included in this section of the plan. For each, write a definition or explanation that could appear in this section of the plan or in the plan glossary.

10. Prepare a 10–15-minute presentation for the Bedos of your observations and/or recommendation(s) for meeting their property and casualty insurance needs. Be sure to include visual aids, Excel handouts, and other materials that will make the recommendations more meaningful for the clients.

## Notes

1. Federal Trade Commission, *Credit-based Insurance Scores: Impacts on Consumers of Automobile Insurance.* Available at http://www.ftc.gov/os/2007/07/P044804FACTA_Report_Credit-Based_Insurance_Scores.pdf, p. 1.

2. Insurance Information Institute. *Compulsory Auto/Uninsured Motorists.* Available at http://www.iii.org/issues_updates/compulsory-auto-uninsured-motorists.html.

3. Insurance Information Institute, *Compulsory Auto/Uninsured Motorists.*

4. Insurance Information Institute, *Compulsory Auto/Uninsured Motorists.*

5. National Flood Insurance Program, *Residential Coverage: Homeowner.* Available at http://www.floodsmart.gov/floodsmart/pages/residential_coverage/homeowner.jsp.

6. National Earthquake Hazards Reduction Program, *Earthquake Hazards Reduction Act of 1977, As Amended.* Available at http://www.nehrp.gov/about/PL108-360.htm.

7. Federal Trade Commission, *FTC Releases List of Top Consumer Complaints in 2010; Identity Theft Tops the List Again.* Available at http://www.ftc.gov/opa/2011/03/topcomplaints.shtm.

8. Finklea, K. M. (January 2010). *Identity Theft: Trends & Issues.* Available at http://www.fas.org/sgp/crs/misc/R40599.pdf, p. 1.

9. Finklea, *Identity Theft*, p. 1.

10. Nationwide. *Underinsurance: A Common Problem.* Available at http://www.nationwide.com/underinsurance.jsp.

11. Insurance Information Institute. *Trying to Save Money? Avoid the Five Biggest Insurance Mistakes!* Available at http://www.iii.org/press_releases/trying-to-save-money-avoid-the-five-biggest-insurance-mistakes.html.

12. Insurance Information Institute. *How Can I Save Money on Auto Insurance?* Available at http://www.iii.org/articles/how-can-i-save-money.html.

# PART IV: Analyzing and Evaluating a Client's Financial Status to Plan for the Growth and Distribution of Assets

# Investment Planning

## Learning Objectives

1. Understand the importance of investment planning within the comprehensive financial planning process.

2. Understand and practice the steps involved in conducting an investment planning needs analysis.

3. Identify and distinguish between interior and exterior factors as they pertain to asset selection.

4. Explain the roles of strategic and tactical asset allocation as they pertain to the realization of a client's investment portfolio.

5. Evaluate a client's investment profile and develop an investment policy statement that matches the client's goals and risk tolerance.

6. Demonstrate the appropriate use of benchmarks and performance statistics as methods for comparing investment performance.

7. Develop investment strategies matched to a client's primary objective of capital appreciation, capital preservation, or current income.

8. Identify and recommend appropriate and reasonable investment planning strategies matched to a client's situation.

# Key Terms

benchmark

call option

capital appreciation

capital preservation

client situational factors

Coefficient of determination ($R^2$)

current income

downside risk

exterior asset allocation factors

information ratio

interior asset allocation factors

investment policy statement (IPS)

Jensen's alpha

Modern Portfolio Theory

Modigliani measure

put option

risk capacity

risk perception

risk tolerance

Sharpe ratio

strategic asset allocation

systematic risk

tactical asset allocation

time horizon

total risk

Treynor index

unsystematic (or idiosyncratic) risk

**Figure 10.1** Systematic Financial Planning Process for Investment Planning

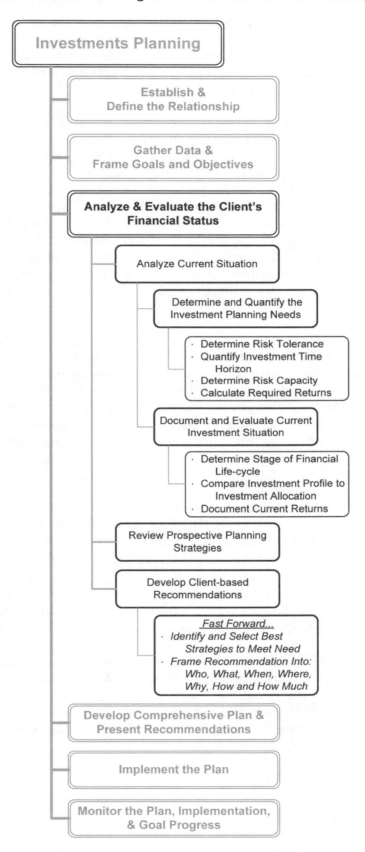

## INVESTMENT PLANNING: THE BASICS

Few investors or investment managers outperform the broad financial markets over extended periods of time. Some investment pundits use this observation to encourage people to go it alone for financial and investment planning. Other financial planners use this observation to argue that individuals should work closely with professional advisors for several reasons.

First, financial planning—and investment planning in particular—is a game of probabilities. A financial planner should be familiar with the odds of success and failure associated with different financial planning strategies. The planner can use that knowledge to help clients make informed decisions even in difficult times.

Second, the financial planner should understand that much of what constitutes success or failure in the realm of personal finance is related to persistence. People are, by nature, prone to procrastination and indecision. A financial planner can help a client take action through implementation and ongoing management. Simple and sometimes boring investment routines and pragmatism often lead to great success. In other words, financial planners can be effective coaches to prompt clients' continued action.

Third, financial planners can be very helpful in one of the most important aspects of investment planning, namely, asset allocation. Economic and market changes often mean that investment plans must change. Unfortunately many investors, especially those who manage their own portfolios, lose touch with their investments. They forget why they purchased an asset or why a particular investment strategy was being used. Worse, some investors fall in love with a stock or investment strategy and are unable to sell even when the stock, markets, or world events have changed unfavorably. Financial planners must assimilate tax, legal, and market changes important to the management of portfolios and the education of clients.

An investment plan should be developed on the basis of a combination of factors, but foremost are the client's goals. The framing of goals and objectives takes place early in the client/planner relationship, during Step 2 of the financial planning process. By the time investment recommendations are made, specific goals and objectives should already have been defined, ordered, and assigned priority in the financial plan. For instance, some clients might rank retirement as their principal goal, whereas others might state that funding a child's education is their number one priority. The type of investment plan developed must match the goals and time frame of the client.

The purpose of this chapter is to review some of the important issues surrounding the analysis of a client's investment situation. The steps in the investment planning process are illustrated in Figure 10.1. The chapter also includes a presentation of popular investment planning strategies and an example of how strategies can be compared and adapted to meet the needs of clients through client-specific recommendations.

# ANALYZE THE CLIENT'S CURRENT SITUATION

Analyzing a client's current investment management situation involves a combination of qualitative and quantitative assessments. To this end, investment planning is as much an art as it is a logical system based on fixed rules. A planner must understand a client's perspectives on wants and needs, idealism and reality, as well as a broad range of personal characteristics that can affect investment decisions. A client's stage in the life cycle as well as goals, time frame, risk tolerance, knowledge and experience, expectations, and financial capacity to engage in risk-taking behaviors all play an interrelated role in determining the best investment approach for a given client.

Regardless of what financial planning model is used for investment planning, the first factors that should be reviewed before developing a specific investment plan are a client's goals and objectives. If goals have not been determined, it is essential to do so before proceeding with any investment planning. Without a clear understanding of the goal (e.g., new home, retirement, university endowment), when it must be funded, its time horizon (e.g., next year, 10 years, at age 65), and the amount of funding needed, it is unrealistic to assume that an investment plan can be drafted that will remain valid over time.

## Determine and Quantify the Client's Investment Planning Needs

The first step to analyze the client's current investment planning situation focuses on determining and quantifying the client's planning needs. Temperament, personality, attitudes, and beliefs are particularly salient factors in the development of efficient, effective, client-specific recommendations. Too often, investment planning decisions are based initially on assets available, with insufficient consideration of other **client situational factors** that should be instrumental in the products and strategies chosen. Although the assessment of a client's investment planning need is multifaceted, most professionals agree that an investment plan should be based on five key interrelated factors.

The five factors introduced include a client's risk tolerance, expectations about future market conditions, knowledge and experience, time horizon, and the financial capacity to withstand risk. The first three represent client situational factors that are inferred, meaning that they are more reasoned than measured. A more complete understanding of these and other situational factors should emerge from the evolving planner-client relationship during the discovery and data-gathering involved in Step 2. Insights into the client's temperament and personality as well as attitudes, beliefs, and behaviors should also guide the advisor when formulating an investment plan. The last two factors, time horizon and financial capacity to withstand risk (or loss), are more quantitative in nature because they can more easily be measured.

It is essential to consider both qualitative and quantitative situational factors before and during the development of investment strategies. An increased focus on the codification of investment policy statements is an example of focusing on the "whole" client. For example, the investment plan, client communication, and client education might, of necessity, be quite different for a highly emotional and reactive client who is unduly influenced by short-term market trends than for a client who has a more tolerant, long-term outlook.

Arguably, the most important situational factor in the investment planning process is a client's **risk tolerance**, Factor 1, which is defined as the maximum level of uncertainty a client is willing to accept when making an investment decision. Developing an understanding of, and an appreciation for, both the time and psychological dimensions of risk is essential.

It is possible for a client to have both a long time horizon and a low tolerance for risk. However, in almost all cases a person's risk tolerance supersedes other influential factors in asset allocation choices. To help mitigate the effects of risk-averse behavior, a planner must be willing to explain to clients that goal achievement may be impossible in s given time horizon if the client is unwilling to accept higher risk. But even with additional coaching, if a client's tolerance for risk is low, it is likely that an aggressive strategy will be abandoned if the client is faced with prolonged losses.

Occasionally, a client's risk tolerance is so low that the financial advisor has almost no choice but to recommend very liquid insured accounts (e.g., savings account, CDs, and money market deposit accounts). In the most severe cases, a client might require the sole use of FDIC-insured bank accounts. Then it is up to the planner to optimize the client's earning power while maintaining complete FDIC coverage of the client's accounts. Although the use of insured accounts is limiting, these investments could be in the best interest of the client and the only way a planner can persuade the client to stay the course. In cases such as this, annuities are one way to convince a client to invest in the market with a small safety net, because many insurance products have a guaranteed death benefit.

The second factor influencing investment planning decisions is managing a client's expectations, or Factor 2. These expectations include what the planner can do, the general economy, and most notably, achievable rates of return. The most successful planners rarely compete based on their ability to generate the highest possible rates of return. Instead, the best planners work daily to manage client expectations about performance.

Consider a planner who suggests an allocation designed to achieve a 10% annualized return but only manages to generate an 8% return. The 8% return might be poor, average, or excellent in relation to the market environment. In fact, the return may be superior to almost all other strategies available; however, clients working with this planner might very well be disappointed. Some clients leave a planner because they expected a higher return and were not appropriately coached to understand the relative nature of investing.

Now consider a planner who consistently informs clients that a 6% return is reasonable, but over the course of three to five years generates 8% returns for clients. The return is the same as for the aggressive planner, but the outcome is significantly different. Clients working with the second planner are likely to feel that they have received a bonus. This demonstrates the importance of managing client expectations when it comes to investment returns. A planner should always attempt to achieve the appropriate amount of risk-adjusted return, but in some cases it is wiser to "under-promise and over-deliver" than the other way around.

An investment plan should be tempered by a client's expectations and satisfaction with the current financial situation. Managing expectations requires a planner not only to measure but understand the client's view of market trends, both past and future. Viewing the investment marketplace and economy without a planner's knowledge to rationalize the client's viewpoint is akin to trying to see underwater without goggles on. While wearing the goggles of experience, the planner can see more clearly what is happening and can adjust more quickly to changing conditions. It is, therefore, necessary to account for investment and economic expectations when developing investment plans. A person's outlook, be it negative or positive, should be used as a moderating factor when developing an investment plan.

Exhibit 10.1 provides a sample of questions that help ascertain a client's expectations about the future economy and satisfaction with the client's current situation. Answers to the first question are particularly important when developing investment planning strategies. If a client truly believes that the economy will perform worse in the future, and if the planner concurs, the level of risk taken to meet a financial goal should be reduced accordingly. Similar adjustments, either positive or negative, can be made based on responses to other questions. For instance, if a client is dissatisfied with a chosen career, this could be an indicator that a career change is possible or that the potential for significant promotions or salary increases may be limited. It would be imprudent to invest the client's assets aggressively—thereby reducing marketability and liquidity—if there is a possibility that those assets will be needed to fund job search expenses and other costs. Furthermore, the capacity to withstand financial risk and the availability of assets to invest must be realistically assessed.

**Exhibit 10.1** Examples of Expectation and Satisfaction Questions

1. Over the next five years, do you expect the U.S. economy, as a whole, to perform better, worse, or about the same as it has over the past five years?
   a. Perform better
   b. Perform worse
   c. Perform about the same

2. How satisfied are you with your current level of income?

   1  2  3  4  5  6  7  8  9  10

   Lowest level             Highest level

3. How satisfied are you with your present overall financial situation?

   1  2  3  4  5  6  7  8  9  10

   Lowest level             Highest level

4. Overall, how satisfied are you with your current job or position within your chosen career?

   1  2  3  4  5  6  7  8  9  10

   Lowest level             Highest level

5. Rate yourself on your level of knowledge about personal finance issues and investing.

   1  2  3  4  5  6  7  8  9  10

   Lowest level             Highest level

As should be apparent, expectation and attitude assessments can provide only a starting point in client/planner discussions. However, questionnaires and scale items are not necessarily prescriptive in and of themselves; it takes a planner's insights and experience to decipher the impact that temperament, personality, attitudes, and beliefs have on the investment planning process.

Additionally, a planner is expected to know the investment terrain and a client's level of investment knowledge and experience (Factor 3). Beyond the regulatory requirements of understanding a client's knowledge level, financial planners will have fewer objections to overcome if they present investment alternatives that the client already understands or has experience with. The fifth sample question can be helpful to determine how much to reduce the variance of returns or overall volatility of a portfolio.

Much research in the past decade has concluded that, holding other factors constant, clients with low levels of financial knowledge tend to view risk differently than clients with a high degree of financial knowledge,. This view of risk is commonly referred to as *risk perception*, and it is different from risk tolerance. It has been determined that risk tolerance does not dramatically change with knowledge, whereas risk perception does.[1]

Again, risk tolerance is loosely defined as an investor's ability to accept or handle risk on a psychological level, whereas **risk perception** is a client's belief or judgment about risk, and it has much to do with the familiarity, quantifiability, or controllability of the risk. In fact, a recent study found that only financial literacy proved relevant when analyzing changes in risk perception.[2] This is fairly intuitive because the more educated a client is regarding financial markets the better the client's understanding of the negative outcomes associated with risk will be. Because financially educated clients are more familiar with the risks, they have a greater awareness of potential losses implying some control over and relative acceptability of loss. Therefore, it could be hypothesized that investing too aggressively for someone unfamiliar with investment markets is a recipe for panic selling if and when a prolonged bear market hits.

Conversely, by increasing a client's level of knowledge about investment and establishing shared expectations about the probable performance of an investment, the plan has a greater likelihood of success. To return to the goggle example, planners should help clients see by sharing the goggles. This accomplishes two things at once. First, the client's level of knowledge increases. Second, the planner gains greater insight into the client's perspective by occasionally removing the goggles.

Although the qualitative factors of investment planning are critical to the long-term viability of a plan, the quantitative factors of time horizon and risk capacity may be more important in the short term. Suggesting that a client invest heavily and aggressively in a retirement account is certainly sound advice if the client is 50 years old and risk tolerant and retirement funding is the client's primary goal. But making the same suggestion to an equally risk-tolerant 25-year-old who does not have an emergency fund might ignore the time available to realize the goal or the financial capacity to take on the risk associated with this plan.

Time can be either a client's greatest asset or greatest liability. **Time horizon,** Factor 4, can be defined as the time period between goal formation and goal achievement. For instance, someone who starts planning for retirement at age 25 will find that time is a great ally. Someone else who waits until age 50 to plan for retirement will most likely discover that time is an enemy. Time allows a client to invest more conservatively and maintain the same likelihood of goal achievement. Some would argue that a long-term conservative investment strategy results in the highest probability of a positive outcome. Another way of viewing a longer time horizon is that a client can invest less money on a periodic basis at a higher expected rate of return because greater volatility can be withstood.

For example, assume that two clients have the same goal of saving $1 million by age 65. Both have $250 per month available for saving. One client is 25 years old, and the other is 35 years old. In this situation, the older client would need an average rate of return of about 12.6% to reach the goal. This is possible, but at what level of risk? Comparatively, the younger client needs only to average about 8.5% to achieve the same goal. This is also possible, even probable—and at a much lower level of risk. As the example illustrates, the greater amount of time a client can devote to saving and investing for a goal, the higher the likelihood that the client will accomplish the goal. Because risk and return in the securities market are highly positively correlated, those with longer time horizons are generally more likely to reach their financial objectives.

Finally, a client's capacity to accept risk is an important factor to consider when making investment plans. **Risk capacity**, Factor 5, measures the amount of financial cushion or safety net available to a client both before and after an investment decision has been implemented. Some clients are not prepared to take risks with their assets because they simply do not have enough assets compared to their other financial obligations. Documenting and assessing a client's risk capacity is especially important when tempering initial portfolio risk profiles based on time horizon and risk attitude. Often, the maximum amount of risk that a client should be willing to take, given the client's time frame, risk tolerance, expectations, and attitudes, is higher than what the client can fiscally afford to lose.

The best way to assess a client's capacity for accepting risk in an investment portfolio is to review the financial situation with financial ratio analysis. Because ratios focus on the relationships between financial assets and liabilities or income and expenses, the planner can assess a client's need for financial liquidity and stability. This is done by determining how many ratios meet prescribed benchmarks (see Chapter 3) and the availability of an emergency fund. A client who has several ratios that meet or exceed the benchmarks could have significant risk capacity. Excess capacity gives a client additional flexibility with long-term investments because the client has the capital to cover an unexpected expense without liquidating long-term assets. Another client who meets or exceeds only one or two ratios could be considered to have a lower capacity to absorb risk. The need for additional liquidity and stability would indicate that the planner should not recommend long-term volatile investments, even if the client has the tolerance.

### Determine a Client's Required Rate of Return

The discussion up to this point has dealt with a client's investment in relation to the client's preferences or current financial situation. However, there are times when investment decisions must be based on projected investment outcomes rather than current attitudes and financial circumstances. In such cases, rather than making allocations that happen to result in a certain rate of return, a planner and client can allocate a portfolio to achieve the necessary rate of return. This reverse engineering has its advantages if all goes as planned; however, if the results are not achieved, then maintaining client satisfaction will be harder because the client might be less comfortable with the level of risk exposure or the amount of volatility.

An example of reverse engineering can be seen in the 35-year-old client who wants to retire at age 65 with $1 million; if he has $250 to invest on a monthly basis, the portfolio must be allocated to achieve an annual rate of return of more than 12.6% (ignoring the impact of income taxes). This rate of return is simply the required rate that achieves the objective and it does not consider the client's risk tolerance or risk capacity.

In principal, calculating the required rate is a simple time value of money equation where the future value is $1 million, the present value is $0, the periodic payment is $250, and the number of periods is 360 [(65 − 35) × 12]. In practice, having a required rate of return dictate an asset allocation rather than having the client's risk profile dictate the targeted return is a dubious proposition and should be recommended only for a knowledgeable client with the capacity to accept the risk.

Unfortunately, if the client's risk profile does not match the required portfolio, then the client has a difficult choice to make. The client must learn to be comfortable with the additional risk required, increase the amount of money available for savings, reduce the desired goal amount, or delay goal achievement. Any of these compromises could derail an investment plan and undermine the client-planner relationship.

### Determine a Client's Asset Allocation

Asset allocation is the way a client's investment dollars are spread among different financial asset classes. Financial assets can be broken into many categories for asset allocation purposes, based on either the client's preferences or current and projected market conditions. Exhibit 10.2 briefly outlines the primary asset classes and a suggested use for each.

When allocating a client's assets, planners must consider not only the asset classes available, but also interior and exterior asset allocation factors. **Interior asset allocation factors** are client-centric and involve answering two primary questions. First, what is the client's goal—**current income, capital appreciation, or capital preservation**? Second, how aggressively allocated does the portfolio need to be to achieve the goal? *Aggressiveness* can be loosely defined as the amount of additional risk a portfolio is subject to for a corresponding incremental increase in potential returns. In other words, the more aggressive the portfolio, the greater the expected return of the portfolio, but the higher the anticipated volatility—or risk.

**Exhibit 10.2** Summary of Investments by Asset Classification

**Equity (stocks).** The primary purpose of equity investing is capital appreciation. Stocks have historically had the highest asset returns after adjusting for inflation. A secondary purpose of current income is possible if investing in stocks that pay a high dividend.

Subclassifications:

- Large-cap—stocks with a market capitalization over $10 billion. These stocks are typically mature, dividend-paying companies.

- Mid-cap—stocks with a market capitalization between $2 billion and $10 billion. These stocks may not pay dividends, but they have higher growth rate prospects than large-cap companies.

- Small-cap—stocks with a market capitalization under $2 billion. These stocks typically do not pay dividends because they are less mature but fast-growing companies that retain earnings to fuel growth.

**Debt (bonds).** The primary purpose of debt investing is current income. Bonds typically pay interest on a regular and recurring basis without the possibility of interest reinvestment. A secondary purpose of capital appreciation is possible if investing in a declining interest rate environment.

Subclassifications:

- Treasury/government agency—bonds issued by the Treasury Department or a federal government agency.

- Municipal—bonds issued by state and local governments. Can be further classified as general obligation bonds or revenue bonds.

- Corporate—bonds issued by public corporations. Can be further classified as investment-grade or high-yield issues.

- Zero coupon—bonds sold at a discount to par value that do not pay a periodic payment. Typically, these bonds are issued by the federal government in the form of Treasury Strips; however, other zero-coupon issues are available.

**International.** The primary purpose of international investing is capital appreciation, especially during times of superior international growth. Subclassifications include the equity and debt of both developed markets and emerging markets.

**Commodities.** The primary purpose of investing in commodity assets, for the average investor, is capital appreciation, especially in times of rapid hard asset price growth. Commodities can serve as an inflation hedge. Subclassifications include precious metals, natural resources, energy products, livestock, and agricultural products.

**Real estate.** The primary purpose of real estate investing is current income. Real estate investment trusts (REITs) typically pay dividends on a regular and recurring basis. Capital appreciation, as a secondary focus, is possible with some forms of direct real estate investment. Subclassifications include raw land, agricultural, commercial, residential, and mortgage-backed obligations.

Table 10.1 summarizes the risk and return characteristics of commonly used investments. The level of aggressiveness required within an asset allocation structure depends heavily on the difference between the current value of invested assets and the desired level of invested assets. From a purely time value of money perspective, there are only two factors that control the difference between the amount of money initially (or periodically) invested and the desired future value of the portfolio: rate of return and time horizon. Therefore, unless a client wants to delay the realization of a goal or is willing and able to invest more money, the planner's only choice is to increase the aggressiveness of the portfolio in an attempt to achieve a greater rate of return.

**Table 10.1** Summary of Investment Characteristics by Investment Type

| Asset | Risk (Aggressiveness) | | | Potential Return | |
| --- | --- | --- | --- | --- | --- |
| | Liquidity | Marketability | Risk | Current Income | Capital Appreciation |
| **Direct Investment** | | | | | |
| Cash | High | High | Low | Low | None |
| Savings accounts | High | High | Low | Low | None |
| Certificates of deposit | Moderate | High | Low | None | Low to average |
| Treasury bills | High | High | Low | None | Low to average |
| Treasury bonds | High | High | Low | Low to average | Low to average |
| EE and I savings bonds | High | High | Low | None | Low to average |
| HH savings bonds | High | High | Low | Low to average | None |
| Federal agency bonds | High | High | Low | Average | Average |
| Municipal bonds | Moderate | Moderate | Moderate | Average | Average |
| Investment-grade corporate bonds | Moderate | High | Moderate | Average | Low |
| Speculative-grade corporate bonds | Moderate | Moderate | Moderate | High | Low to high |
| Zero-coupon bonds | Moderate | Moderate | Moderate | None | Average to high |
| Preferred stock | Moderate | Moderate to High | Moderate | Average to high | None to low |
| Common stock | Moderate to High | High | Moderate to High | Low to average | Low to high |
| Collectibles (coins, stamps, art, etc.) | Low | Low to moderate | High | None | Dependent on supply and demand |
| Precious metals | Low to moderate | Moderate | Moderate to High | None | Dependent on supply and demand |
| Real estate | Low | Low | High | Low to high | Dependent on supply and demand |
| **Indirect Investment** | | | | | |
| Money market funds | High | High | Low | Low to average | None |
| Bond funds/ETFs | High | High | Low | Average to high | Low to average |
| Stock funds/ETFs | High | High | | Low to average | Average to high |
| Commodity funds | Moderate to High | Moderate to High | High | Low to average | Low to high |
| Real estate investment trusts (REITs) | Moderate to High | Moderate to High | High | Average to high | Low to average |
| **Derivative Investment** | | | | | |
| Options and Warrants | Low | Low to Moderate | High | None to average | Dependent on underlying security |
| Futures | Low | High | High | None | Dependent on underlying contracts |

Investments are bought and sold not only because of changing investor goals, risk attitudes, and time horizons, but also because of changing exterior factors. **Exterior asset allocation factors** such as the current and prospective economic environment are not client-centric, and a planner should consider them when changing an asset allocation model. This process of economically based asset allocation can be outlined by asking the following questions.

- What have been the recent and long-term returns of the various asset classes?

- Are domestic interest rates rising or falling?

- What is the difference in stock yields and bond yields?

- Are the projected monetary and fiscal policies of the United States conducive to strong long-term growth?

- Will the U.S. dollar rise or fall in value relative to foreign currency?

- What are projected domestic and international growth rates?

- Will inflation or rising commodity prices stunt growth domestically or internationally?

- Will foreign investments offer superior risk-adjusted returns?

It is important that the client understand why certain asset allocations are recommended. A planner must be careful not to overwhelm the client with too much financial or economic information. To begin the economic allocation process, most financial planners mentally segregate assets into a two-by-two investment selection matrix (Figure 10.2).

**Figure 10.2** Investment Selection Matrix

| | | Goal | |
|---|---|---|---|
| | | **Appreciation** | **Income** |
| Inflation | **High** | Commodities | Real estate |
| | **Low** | Stocks | Bonds |

The matrix consists of stocks, bonds, commodities, and real estate (hard assets such as collectibles are typically not considered investment assets because their value is determined more by supply and demand). Each one of these categories has pros and cons, but the strategic allocation of all types of assets yields the greatest benefit. The basic premise behind this mental accounting is that real assets, such as commodities and real estate, often perform better than financial assets, like stocks and bonds, in times of high or increasing inflation; and the opposite often holds true in times of low or decreasing inflation.

By considering the impact of economic conditions, a planner can optimize portfolio allocation by changing the weight of a particular class of assets. An example of an allocation that might perform equally well in times of high or low inflation is a portfolio split 25% among each asset class. However, this might not work if the client wanted to maximize current income. So the planner must change the portfolio based on both the economy and the client's goal.

The current income versus capital appreciation question helps the planner develop basic guidelines for the allocation that best suits the client. Typically, planners recommend real estate and bond holdings to maximize the income potential of a portfolio, and stock and commodity holdings to maximize the appreciation potential. However, a 25% equal allocation might not work because, for example, high inflation is anticipated. So the planner must focus on both the economy and the client's goal.

The next question might be whether the investment focus should be foreign or domestic. The primary objective of foreign investment is reduction of the systematic risk associated with investing in only one country or region. However, superior returns could also be achieved with international investing by capitalizing on changes in currency exchange rates or higher international growth rates associated with emerging or recovering markets. In either case, adding international diversification to an asset allocation model can increase the overall risk-adjusted return of a client's portfolio.

The final question pertains to the current and projected interest rate environment. The rule for fixed-income securities (bonds) is that as rates rise values fall. Therefore, a planner should allocate a portfolio that is not overly sensitive to rising or falling interest rates. Returning to the original 25% balanced allocation example, it is easy to see that in a time of rising interest rates a planner might want to reduce the bond allocation to mitigate possible negative consequences.

## Asset Allocation Strategies

Once the classes of appropriate assets have been selected, a planner must determine how to combine them into a cohesive portfolio. Portfolio construction begins with the client and is based on the client's risk tolerance, risk capacity, time horizon, and investment objectives. All too often the return tail wags the risk dog rather than the other way around. The construction of a portfolio should target a specific risk level; it is then up to the financial planner to optimize the return. Risk can be qualified either by standard deviation or beta, but it is important to remember that a client may not be satisfied with a huge loss even if the loss was less than that of the overall market. So targeting a specific beta may not be the best place to start.

Two additional issues arise from attempting a beta-weighted portfolio. First, beta is a risk measure relative to a benchmark, so it is representative only if the asset allocation model is very similar to the benchmark from which it was calculated. Second, an issue arises from the fact that the capital asset pricing model (CAPM) derives beta using a linear regression model. Thus, because all of the asset-class betas are linear, the beta of a targeted portfolio is the simple weighted-average beta of the underlying asset classes.

Much more information about specific investment statistics is available in Appendix 10A, but following is an example of the difference that results from attempting to target a portfolio beta versus a portfolio standard deviation.

For example, using the data in Table 10.2 and an asset allocation of 50% domestic equities; 25% international equities; 10% commodities; and 5% each to real estate, bonds, and cash, it is possible to achieve a portfolio beta of 0.88 to the S&P 500 Index with a standard deviation of 23.6. The S&P 500 had a standard deviation across the same period of only 21.1, so although the portfolio exhibits only 88% of the systematic risk of the market, it exhibited nearly 112% of the total variability of return. However, it is also possible to construct a portfolio with a beta of 0.92 with a standard deviation of only 20.8, exhibiting 92% of the systematic risk and 98% of the total risk.

**Table 10.2** Sample Risk and Return Statistics

| Asset | 10-year Arithmetic Average Return | 5-year Standard Deviation | Asset Beta vs. Best Index |
|---|---|---|---|
| Equity 1 | 7.00 | 20.21 | 0.757 |
| Equity 2 | 8.41 | 19.08 | 0.887 |
| International equity | 9.29 | 28.51 | 1.046 |
| Real estate | 17.10 | 35.19 | 1.131 |
| Commodity | 14.59 | 39.42 | 0.682 |
| Real estate bond | 5.93 | 3.18 | 1.058 |
| Treasury bond | 6.32 | 3.77 | 1.066 |
| Corporate bond 1 | 10.33 | 13.09 | 1.372 |
| Corporate bond 1 | 3.57 | 11.33 | 0.850 |
| Money market | 3.50 | 1.78 | 0.211 |

Based on the previous example, it becomes very clear that portfolios with similar betas can have very different total risk profiles. Developing an asset allocation based on standard deviation that gives the client a strong understanding of how much the value of the portfolio can change over time in absolute terms rather than one based on beta, which explains the changes only in relative terms, could go a long way toward helping a planner manage clients' expectations for their portfolios.

### Portfolio Management—Strategic vs. Tactical Asset Allocation

**Strategic asset allocation** is the process of setting target (percentage) allocations for each class of asset based on the long-term objective of the portfolio. The portfolio is then periodically rebalanced back to the original asset allocation percentages. This is necessary because different asset classes appreciate and depreciate at different rates and times in the market cycle. This is the basis of the buy-and-hold investing strategy, where strategic asset allocations change only as the client's goals and needs change.

Historically the standard three-asset-class model has predominated, where the portfolio is divided among domestic equities, debt, and cash. However, based on continued research and in light of recent economic events, a more diversified approach has become more prevalent. Currently, a five-asset-class model is more common, where in addition to the original three, real estate and commodities are being included to a greater extent. Greater emphasis is also placed on international equity and debt holdings.

For example, if a client wants a portfolio designed for maximum capital appreciation with tax minimization and has a secondary goal of maintaining purchasing power over an extended period of time, a planner might recommend a portfolio that comprises 50% domestic equities; 25% international equities; 10% commodities; and 5% each to real estate, zero-coupon bonds, and cash—similar to the allocation used in the previous example. This allocation would then be rebalanced annually to maintain these targets until a client-centric factor dictated a change. For instance, if a client were to lose her job, it might be prudent to alter the composition of the portfolio to reduce volatility.

In the long run, strategic allocations are the most important determinant of total return for a broadly diversified portfolio. **Tactical asset allocation**, on the other hand, allows for a more active management style by setting a range of percentages in each asset class (e.g., a domestic equity range of 45% to 60%) rather than a fixed target of 50%. This range gives a planner the ability to be more opportunistic about changing allocations to match current market conditions. Based on economic forecasts, tactical allocations attempt to add value (alpha) by overweighting asset classes that are expected to outperform on a relative basis and "underweighting" those expected to underperform. This is not always an attempt to time short-term swings in the market; rather, this approach opens the door for changes to allocation when longer-term economic conditions might favor one asset class over another. For instance, having 5% of a portfolio invested in real estate might make very good sense over the long-term, but not having as much or any exposure to real estate in 2008 would turn out to have been a very wise move.

To some extent tactical asset allocation is a dynamic strategy that actively adjusts the allocation of a portfolio based on short-term market forecasts, with the objective of increasing appreciation potential. Sector rotation is a fairly basic form of tactical asset allocation in which a portfolio manager attempts to outperform a market index such as the S&P 500 by tracking the economic cycle. Sector rotation, as in investment approach, was first introduced as a way to incorporate National Bureau of Economic Research (NBER) data on the business cycle into investment decisions. Proponents of the strategy use their analysis on the current phase of the business cycle and relative currency valuations to anticipate industrial and household demand for goods and services. For example, during an economic contraction demand for commodities typically decreases, which then relaxes the general price pressure on downstream goods. So although this environment might be bad for commodity-driven business sectors, it could be positive for financial sectors where falling interest rates can boost corporate income.

Another form of tactical allocation is the construction of core-and-satellite portfolios. The core-and-satellite investing style is designed to maximize returns while minimizing trading expenses and tax liabilities. The approach comprises two types of investments: core holdings and satellite (i.e., speculative or rotational) investments. Financial advisors who use this strategy first decide how much to allocate to core portfolio investments, those that an investor intends to hold through a number of business and market cycles—the central idea of strategic allocation. Often, core investments are held as index positions. Core investments are rarely managed tactically, resulting in high tax efficiency. The remainder of the assets is dedicated to the satellite portion of the portfolio. Satellite holdings are actively managed. These investments tend to be short-term holdings that allow a financial advisor to position assets tactically for maximum capital gain potential.

As previously mentioned this portfolio management style is attempting to add alpha by enhancing the return of an asset class upswing by adding exposure. When a money manager increases a position in or exposure to a market movement she is adding leverage. For example if a portfolio has a "normal" strategic allocation that results in a portfolio Beta of 0.8, the market increases 12%, and the risk-free rate was 2% then, according to CAPM the portfolio should rise only 10% [2% + (0.8x(12% – 2%))]. However, if the portfolio was changed in advance of this market move to have a beta of 1.1, then CAPM predicts that the portfolio would rise by 13% [2% + (1.1x(12% – 2%))].

It is important to note that attempting to "add alpha" in this manner is different than trying to do so through superior asset selection, as this type of market timing doesn't truly "add alpha," rather it adds beta. Returning to the previous example, if the manager mistimed the market and increased the beta just before a market downturn of 12%, then the portfolio would have lost 13.4% [2% + (1.1x(-12% – 2%))]. Whereas, if a manager is truly "adding alpha" then not only is the appreciation potential enhanced but the downside risk is mitigated.

## The Use of Single or Multiple Asset Allocation Models

Another issue that should be considered when building an asset allocation model is whether the client and the planner choose to treat assets as if they were in a single bucket that supplies all goals or in multiple buckets, each with a single goal. For instance, instead of choosing a single moderate allocation for all assets, the planner and client might opt to select an aggressive allocation for retirement assets and separately build a more conservative model for a shorter-term goal, such as a down payment on a home or a child's wedding. The financial planning profession does not have a preference between these two methods.

There is a debate among academics regarding portfolio management strategies, investment planning, and asset allocation approaches. Some financial planning practitioners and academics believe that a client's total asset allocation structure should be evaluated all at once. Advocates of this approach argue that a client's financial situation is integrated and, as such, it is impossible to solve one financial situation without affecting other client issues. Furthermore, these advocates maintain that it is simply foolish, for instance, to consider a person's portfolio for retirement separately from assets saved for an emergency, because few clients would maintain their retirement savings in the face of an emergency.

Other academics and planners argue that, in fact, clients and planners alike tend to use mental accounts to separate assets for different purposes. Clients often keep assets in low-yielding savings accounts even though they could invest the funds for high rates elsewhere. Why? Behavioral finance theory could provide an answer. According to the theory, nearly all people separate assets into mental accounts. People sometimes feel that they need immediate access to cash. They are willing to sacrifice return for this security. The use of mental accounts may not always be prudent in financial planning, but it makes perfect sense when helping people to manage their daily lives. Because of the psychological ramifications associated with money and investing, a large number of planners argue that asset allocation models should be developed for each client goal and objective.

Using a separate allocation methodology, a client would be shown a current and recommended asset allocation for various planning case issues, including an emergency savings allocation, a life insurance allocation (assuming a variable or variable universal life policy is used), a retirement planning allocation, an education funding allocation, and other situational funding allocations. Each separate allocation would show the portfolio's asset categories, rates of return, and relevant modern portfolio statistics.

Regardless of which method is used, it is important to be as specific as possible when describing a portfolio and asset allocation approach. This is particularly true when detailing changes in a portfolio. Clients need to know whether their current asset allocation approach matches their risk profile. If not, specific recommendations should be made to adjust the portfolio to match this parameter. Implementation strategies should be both concise and precise, telling a client when, where, and how a change should be made. The results of changes should also be documented. Apart from how a planner and client think about the mental accounting of assets, the most basic idea behind asset allocation is not to put all investment assets in one basket.

---

### Planning for Special Populations: Investment Planning for the Suddenly Wealthy

From technology company founders to professional athletes to lottery winners, most people can think of someone who instantly became super-wealthy and famous. But, with the exception of entrepreneurs who built wealth from a business enterprise, many lottery winners and athletes end up in financial ruin as a result of their investment and lifestyle choices.

However, for each one of these individuals, there are hundreds if not thousands of others who instantly became much wealthier as the result of an insurance settlement, inheritance, trust, or retirement. It does not take a tremendous sum of money to completely change the financial situation of an entire family; a sum as small as $50,000 or $100,000 dollars can make an enormous difference. The impact of this money could be 10- or 15-fold in 35 or 40 years if invested correctly. For example, a young family saving $5,000 per year for retirement would have about $550,000 saved in 30 years; however, with an additional $100,000 today, that sum would instead be more than $1 million more—a threefold increase. So instead of a $44,000 per year retirement annuity, they would have a $121,000 annual retirement annuity (assuming a 25-year time horizon and a 6% annual rate of return). But all too often the money is spent on comparatively frivolous items or on a general improvement in the immediate standard of living.

Sometimes people with sudden money go out and buy multiple houses, cars, and vacations beyond even what their new wealth would support. But perhaps even more meaningful is the emotional toll that a financial windfall can exact. Some recipients use the occasion to make excessive gifts to charity.  Although seemingly a well-intended, such acts might spring from a feeling of unworthiness or from guilt about receiving the money.

Susan Bradley, a financial advisor who has done groundbreaking work in the area of sudden wealth, describes the inner experience of sudden money as resembling a chute of emotions.[3] This chute leads the recipient into a general state of emotion that includes fear, isolation, grief, and insecurity, but that could lead to resentment or even paranoia depending on the events that led to the windfall. The Money, Meaning, and Choices Institute (MMCI) even coined a phrase: "Sudden Wealth Syndrome." Both Ms. Bradley and MMCI have determined that sudden wealth basically makes people stop listening to those whom they should and start listening to those whom they should not. MMCI attributes this to "identity confusion."[4] Susan Bradley suggests not making any financial or emotionally charged decisions for an extended period of time after a windfall event.  The National Endowment for Financial Education goes so far as to suggest that cash for six to twelve months of living expenses should be kept separate from the remainder of the windfall so recipients can mentally and emotionally adjust to their new status.[5]

In summary, investment planning for the suddenly wealthy takes a lot of time and patience from both planner and client to ensure the long-term success of a plan. And it might not focus on investing activities as much as it does on general financial well-being.

## Document and Evaluate the Current Investment Management Situation

The second step in analyzing a client's current situation, and certainly a step that must be completed before a planner can recommend additional or alternative investments, entails documenting and evaluating all investment plans currently in place, whether assets are allocated or unallocated for a specific goal. An initial assessment might focus on the client's stage in the financial life cycle and whether current investment plans match life cycle objectives and other client characteristics. It must be noted that changing family dynamics (e.g., delayed marriage, remarried or repartnered families) can limit the usefulness of the life cycle approach, but even broad generalizations can be very important when educating clients.

The financial life cycle is typically conceptualized in three stages: protection, accumulation, and distribution. This approach can provide direction and meaning by helping clients understand and anticipate how each financial decision affects subsequent decisions. Following is a short discussion of how the investment focus, or overall objective, changes as a client progresses through life cycle stages.

During the protection stage, a client should develop a budget and emergency fund to meet unexpected expenses. Regrettably, some young clients can focus on the later stages too early and be unprepared for the unexpected. As a result, they can find themselves raiding investment assets in the event of an emergency. Having a financial planner focus on protection ensures that clients' future risk capacity matches or exceeds their risk tolerance. Also, having the tolerance to invest aggressively but lacking the capacity to do so can result in unnecessary frustration for both client and planner.

Next is the accumulation stage, during which a client begins to build wealth. This stage can last from 20 to 40 years or longer. Generally, clients want to save for retirement, purchase a bigger home, fund a child's education, or buy a new car. The list can go on and on. The financial planner's responsibility is to recommend actions that will enable the client to meet these savings objectives as efficiently as possible. By closely monitoring the client's investment profile for changes and reallocating the portfolio as necessary, a planner can safely and effectively guide the client through the most challenging stage of the client's financial life.

Although the last stage, distribution, may seem to be neatly separated from the accumulation stage by retirement, many clients continue to accumulate wealth well into retirement. At this point in the life cycle, the planner begins to suggest titling and gifting strategies that minimize potential asset transfer difficulties. Portfolio allocation and reallocation also become much more intense, because failure in this stage could be disastrous.

All of these distinctions make it counterintuitive to state that a client might never actually "complete" each stage before moving to the next. But in reality, changing stages is more a change in focus than a discrete point in time. A client could be accomplishing tasks in all three phases at once. In summary, life cycle investment planning is not only about the concerns of today or next week, it is about anticipating the needs of the client as the client ages. By viewing each financial decision as part of a whole, planners and clients alike can consider both the short- and long-term effects that current decisions have on a client's future life goals.

## Determine a Client's Investment Profile

Once the five initial factors of investment planning have been established (i.e., risk tolerance, expectations about future market conditions, knowledge and experience, time horizon, and capacity to withstand risk), the planner can begin to combine them to build a client's investment profile. Initially this can be estimated by looking at the person's time frame and risk tolerance for goal achievement. Table 10.3 illustrates how the combination of time frame and risk tolerance can be used to estimate a baseline for investment risk (i.e., volatility) that would be appropriate for a given client goal.

**Table 10.3** Portfolio Risk Guidelines Based on Client Time Horizon and Risk Tolerance

| Time Frame | High Risk Tolerance | Moderate Risk Tolerance | Low Risk Tolerance |
|---|---|---|---|
| 10+ years | Aggressive | Moderately Aggressive | Moderate |
| 7 to 10 years | Moderately Aggressive | Moderate | Moderate |
| 3 to 7 years | Moderate | Moderate | Moderately Conservative |
| 1 to 3 years | Moderately Conservative | Moderately Conservative | Conservative |
| Less than 1 year | Conservative | Conservative | Conservative |

The fact that clients typically have more than one goal, each with a different time horizon, implies that multiple investment strategies need to be designed. To use this table, it is essential that planners use a reliable and valid risk assessment instrument. It is also important to remember that the guidelines shown in the table must be tempered by an assessment of a client's attitudes, expectations, and risk capacity. Given this caveat, however, the guidelines provide general guidance on the level of risk that could be appropriate for a client.

> *Example.* A client is saving for retirement in 20 years. After taking a risk assessment quiz, it is apparent that the client is neither a real risk taker nor a risk avoider. Given the length of time as the primary factor, an aggressive portfolio could be prescribed as a starting point in client discussions.

Knowing only a client's time frame and risk tolerance is not enough to formulate an effective investment plan. These factors alone tell less than half the story. To get a full picture of a client's investment profile, it is also important to assess a client's investment attitudes and expectations. For instance, some clients might be open to any kind of investment within their portfolio, and others may prefer to employ screens to eliminate certain types of investments. Screens related to socially responsible investing, religious beliefs, or political affiliations are examples of how attitudes can affect the structure of an investment plan. Other types of attitudes need to be evaluated as well. It would be helpful, for example, to know whether a client is content with regard to the current level of investment income, taxes paid on investment earnings, and level of volatility.

Answers to these kinds of questions can help an advisor either moderate or enhance the risk profile of a portfolio beyond what might be appropriate if only time and risk were accounted for. Exhibit 10.3 presents some attitudinal questions a planner can ask. A planner can use a client's strong preferences to better understand what might be driving a client to seek help with investments.

**Exhibit 10. 3** Client Investments Attitude Questionnaire

Name _____     **Investment Attitudes Questionnaire**

| Put an X in the box to the right that reflects your first reaction to the statement. | Strongly Disagree | Disagree | Neutral | Agree | Strongly Agree |
|---|---|---|---|---|---|
| 1. Keeping pace with inflation is important to me. | | | | | |
| 2. I am comfortable borrowing money to make a non-home purchase investment. | | | | | |
| 3. Diversification is important to investment success. | | | | | |
| 4. The current return I am making on my investments is acceptable. | | | | | |
| 5. I need to earn more spendable income from my investments. | | | | | |
| 6. I am comfortable with the volatility I experience with my current portfolio. | | | | | |
| 7. Reducing the amount of taxes paid on my investments is a top priority. | | | | | |
| 8. I am willing to risk being audited by the IRS in exchange for higher returns. | | | | | |
| 9. I am willing to risk being audited by the IRS in exchange for paying less tax. | | | | | |
| 10. My friends would tell you that I am a real risk taker. | | | | | |

The process of documenting a client's investment preferences and evaluating alternatives is the basis of constructing an investment policy statement. An **investment policy statement (IPS)** is a document to acknowledge agreement with and willingness to follow the parameters guiding the investment or management of a client's funds. The IPS, normally written by the planner and signed by both planner and client, integrates the client's risk tolerance, risk capacity, and investment philosophy with the planner's proposed investment methods to establish parameters for the investment strategies.

Because of the communication between planner and client required to develop a comprehensive IPS, it is possible this communication occurred during the discovery process prior to the development of the plan. However, in some firms the plan precedes the IPS because the plan is developed as a foundation for establishing the kind of portfolio needed to maximize the likelihood of achieving a client's goals. For example, if the advisor's planning approach typically begins with the transfer of assets to the firm for management, then the IPS is provided with the other initial documents. But if the advisor's planning approach is to develop a plan, after which the client can choose to contract for investment management services, then another contract would be initiated and the IPS would be developed to govern the related services.

Some advisors even develop multiple IPSs individually matched to the investment management plan aligned with different client goals. For example, two investment policy statements might be necessary for managing retirement assets if risk tolerance factors and acceptable investment management strategies are very different for spouses or partners. Regardless of the number of statements or where the IPS is situated in the written document, its inclusion is not only a necessity to lessen financial planner liability through appropriate planning disclosure, but also because of its vital link to the planning process, and as a reminder to the client and planner of the importance of adhering to the established guidelines.

Today's litigious environment suggests that financial planners—even those whose investment advice is secondary to their planning activities—should use an IPS to disclose and document the professional expectations for the management and investment of client assets. Practicing full disclosure with a client-signed IPS is a prudent procedure because it establishes a mutually agreed-upon standard of conduct while reducing the possibility of a future lawsuit brought by a client who claims misrepresentation or poor performance.

---

### Planning for Special Populations: Minority Investing

Based on the premise that investors should not put all their eggs in one basket, Lazetta Rainey Braxton, founder of Financial Fountains LLC in Chicago, posed the following question:

What would happen if financial advisers applied the basic intent of [Modern Portfolio Theory] MPT to matters of racial diversity in the financial profession? Diversification theory would suggest that a firm's business relationships (portfolio) with intentionally diverse asset classes (racial and ethnic groups) can maximize a firm's return (profits and social equity) and minimize its risk (inability to attract and retain minorities as employees or clients and a loss of economic sustainability).[6]

Some background might be helpful for firms that wish to pursue Ms. Braxton's proposal:

- Before the real estate bubble burst in the late 2000s, real estate had historically been the favored investment among African-Americans. According to *The Ariel Investments 2010 Black Investors Survey*, for the first time in the 12-year history of the survey, more African-Americans chose stocks and stock mutual funds as the "best investment overall" relative to real estate.[7] Less than a third of Blacks and Whites (30% and 27%, respectively) said real estate was the "best investment overall" as compared to 41% of Blacks and 55% of Whites who picked equities.[8]

- Business ownership is a primary source of building wealth among Hispanics. But African-Americans are nearly twice as likely as those in the general population (35% and 19%, respectively) to have a dream of starting a small business.[9]

- After controlling for demographic and behavioral variables, African-Americans were 35% less likely than Whites to invest, as found in the Ariel Investments *2001 Black Investors Survey*.[10] Study results revealed a positive relationship between income and investing for African-Americans—a relationship not found among Whites, for whom income was not a determinant of investing. The subsequent 2007 study revealed that after controlling for demographic factors, Whites were nearly twice as likely to be investors as African-Americans.[11]

- The failure to invest is also reflected in retirement savings. Based on a 2009 study that analyzed data from 57 companies and almost 3 million participants, 66% of Black employees and 65% of Hispanic employees participated in 401(k) plans, compared with 77% of White workers and 76% of Asian workers.[12] According to the results, regardless of age and income, Black and Hispanic workers were less likely to participate and saved less in comparison to Asian workers, who had the highest savings rate. African-Americans also had the lowest rate of equity investments, and equity ownership differences for Asians and Hispanics as compared to Whites were minimal.

- Although less familiarity with investments has been identified as a possible contributing factor, research has shown that Blacks and Hispancis have lower investment risk tolerance than Whites, even after controlling for income and other household characteristics.[13]

Given these observations, what steps might be necessary to apply MPT principles to the financial planning profession? Several suggestions include:

- Increase education on investment principles to encourage a broader understanding of the market and increase familiarity with equities and other investments. Given that familiarity affects risk perception, this change in addition to education on different investments might increase tolerance for risk within the investment market.

- Increase the diversity of the financial services workforce to provide greater language and cultural diversity to serve a broader clientele. Care must be taken that translations of documents are not only accurate, but also consistent with the culture. *InvestmentNews* reported a translation of accelerated death benefits that in some translations read "die faster benefits"—a difference in literal and cultural accuracy.[14]

- Focus on the importance of building strong advisor-client relationships that are based on trust. Anecdotal reports from advisors suggest that working with minority clients can take more time, but the dividend on that investment is referrals to an underserved market.

### Comparing a Client's Investment Profile to the Current Portfolio

Taken together, a client's time frame, risk tolerance, knowledge, expectations, and risk capacity can be used as the basis for better understanding the client's current situation. Once this part of the current situation analysis is concluded, it is appropriate to look at portfolio characteristics in more detail. Specifically, it is important to document whether the client's current portfolio matches the client's investment profile and goals.

> *Example.* A client has a long-term time horizon, a moderate level of risk tolerance and financial knowledge, generally positive attitudes and expectations regarding investing, and an intermediate level of risk capacity, but a portfolio that is invested fairly conservatively. The planner concludes that more portfolio risk could—and probably should—be taken by the client, thus increasing the expected return of the portfolio.

One of the key questions associated with an investment planning current situation analysis is whether a client needs to make a portfolio change to better meet financial goals. There is no definite, quantitative way to answer this question. But distinct approaches can be employed to make the process easier.

One approach to quantifying how a portfolio corresponds to a client's investment profile is to document relevant portfolio characteristics using a standardized form, and then compare these characteristics to market benchmarks. Exhibit 10.4 is one example of a form that can be used in this process.

This form begins by documenting the situational factors that affect a client's investment profile. An investor profile, based on these factors, is then determined. Although no universal scale is available, this table uses a five-step investment risk profile scale—5: High; 4: Above average; 3: Moderate; 2: Below average; 1: Low. A planner then matches these risk classes with recommended portfolio allocations. (A completed form with a model allocation is shown in the comprehensive example later in this chapter.)

The client portfolio allocation profile is the basis for choosing a benchmark portfolio. Benchmark statistics should then be entered into the table. For example, if a planner determines that a client's investment profile falls in the moderate range, then statistics for a balanced growth portfolio could be entered in the benchmark column. Next, relevant portfolio statistics should be summarized and actual portfolio statistics compared to the benchmark.

**Exhibit 10.4** Investment Profile and Portfolio Summary Form

| Investment Profile and Portfolio Summary Form | | | |
|---|---|---|---|
| **Client Investment Profile** | | | |
| Qualitative | Circle the appropriate response. | | |
| Risk tolerance | High | Moderate | Low |
| Knowledge/experience | High | Moderate | Low |
| Market expectations | Positive | Neutral | Negative |
| Quantitative | | | |
| Time horizon | Long | Intermediate | Short |
| Risk capacity | High | Moderate | Low |
| Client risk profile* | | Client allocation profile** | |
| **Portfolio Measures** | **Current Statistics** | **Benchmark Statistics** | **Comparison to Benchmark** |
| **Targeted portfolio allocation profile**** | | | |
| **Observed portfolio allocation profile**** | | | |
| **Portfolio statistics** | | | |
| Beta | | | |
| Alpha | | | |
| $R^2$ | | | |
| Sharpe ratio | | | |
| Treynor ratio | | | |
| **Fixed income measures** | | | |
| Bond duration | | | |
| Average bond quality | | | |
| **Asset allocation (%)** | | | |
| Cash | | | |
| U.S. stock | | | |
| Foreign stock | | | |
| Bond | | | |
| Other | | | |
| **Sensitivity analysis** | | | |
| 3-year average return | | | |
| Worst 1-year loss | | | |
| Best 1-year gain | | | |
| Does portfolio match investment profile? | Yes / No | Yes / No | |

\* Scale: 5: High; 4: Above average; 3: Moderate; 2: Below average; 1: Low

\*\* Scale: 6: Aggressive growth; 5: Growth; 4: Moderate growth; 3: Balanced growth; 2: Conservative growth; 1: Income

## *Use of Financial Market Benchmarks*

Indices track the performance of a select group of equities, bonds, or in some specialized cases, equities and bonds. The news media typically report indices as indicators of general market conditions or movements, but indices are also useful as benchmarks or standards of measurement for individual securities or portfolios. For a meaningful comparison, it is important to select a **benchmark** that most closely matches both the type of security and the corresponding level of risk. In other words, a planner is attempting to find a "system" to which to compare the asset.

The simplest method for determining the best benchmark is to first find one or more benchmarks that seem to have a general fit, for example the S&P 500 index as a benchmark for a large-cap stock fund. Next, it is best to perform a simple linear regression of historical returns of the asset versus the historical returns of the benchmark. A planner can then review the **coefficient of determination ($R^2$)** for each regression and select the benchmark that resulted in the largest $R^2$. The $R^2$ runs a continuum from zero to one; the larger the $R^2$ the more that the variability in returns of the asset is explained by variability in returns of the benchmark; therefore, the more closely the asset matches the benchmark or "system."

In addition to benchmarking individual assets, many advisors benchmark entire portfolios. To gauge overall portfolio performance, the returns for several indices reported over the same time period are matched proportionately to the assets in the portfolio. In other words, weighted average returns are compared based on the actual portfolio and the matching benchmarks for corresponding market sectors. Information to track the performance of most securities over time should be readily available, either free from the Internet or from the advisor's custodian, broker dealer, or other third-party source. Although numerous indices track different market segments (nationally, regionally, and internationally), some of the most commonly used indices are listed in Tables 10.4 and 10.5. However, it is important to note that a decision to purchase or sell a security should not be based solely on performance relative to the benchmark index; it should consider other aspects of the client's situation as well.

In some cases, this analysis can lead to quick and apparent conclusions. For example, a portfolio that carries a higher beta (risk), a lower annualized rate of return, and hence a more negative alpha than the benchmark could lead to the conclusion that the client is taking too much risk for the return received. Therefore, the planner could recommend reallocating the portfolio.

**Table 10.4** Select Widely Used Equity Market Indices

| Market Sector | Corresponding Index by Provider | | | |
|---|---|---|---|---|
| | **S&P/Barra** | **Russell** | **Morgan Stanley** | **1Wilshire/DJ** |
| All U.S. stocks | S&P Total Mkt | 3000 | Market 2500 | Wilshire 5000 |
| *U.S. Equity (Size segmented)* | | | | |
| Mega-cap | — | — | — | DJIA 30 |
| Large-cap | S&P 500 | 1000 | Large-cap 300 | Wilshire 750 |
| Mid-cap | S&P 400 | Mid-cap | Mid-cap 450 | Wilshire 500 |
| Small-cap | S&P 600 | 2000 | Small-cap 1750 | Wilshire 1750 |
| *U.S. Equity (Style segmented)* | | | | |
| Large growth | Barra Growth | 1000 Growth | — | Target large Growth |
| Mid-growth | — | Mid-cap Growth | — | Target large value |
| Large value | Barra Value | 1000 Value | — | Target mid-growth |
| Mid-value | — | Mid-cap Value | — | Target mid-value |
| *U.S. Equity (Sector segmented)* | | | | |
| Consumer | S&P Consumer | — | — | — |
| Health care | S&P Health Care | — | — | DJ Health Care |
| Utilities | S&P Utilities | — | — | — |
| Financials | S&P Financials | — | — | DJ Insurance |
| Technology | S&P Technology | — | — | DJ Telecom |
| *International Equity (Region segmented)* | | | | |
| Global | S&P Global 1200 | — | AC World Index | — |
| International (non-emerging) | S&P 700 | — | AC World Index (Ex. U.S.) | DJ Developed Mkts |
| Emerging market | IFCI | — | Emerging Markets | DJ Emerging Mkts & DJ Latin America |

However, not all analyses are that simple. During the early 2000s, for instance, portfolios that were overweighted in bonds and cash tended to outperform portfolios that were more balanced. These fixed-income-heavy portfolios almost always showed betas that were lower, alphas that were higher, and returns that were superior to balanced portfolio indices. So on paper these portfolios looked better than what might actually be the case going forward. Over the long run, remember that risk and return are positively related. In the short term, this relationship might not hold. To believe that risk and return would continue to be uncorrelated could lead to the serious underachievement of client goals if and when the relationship reverted back to normal.

**Table 10.5** Select Widely Used Fixed-income Market Indices

| Market Sector | Corresponding Index by Provider | | |
|---|---|---|---|
| | **S&P** | **Wilshire/DJ** | **Barclay's** |
| *All U.S. bonds* | — | — | U.S. Universal |
| *U.S. Treasury (Term segmented)* | | | |
| Long-term | BG Cantor U.S. T-bond | — | |
| Intermediate | — | | U.S. Treasury |
| Short-term | BG Cantor U.S. T-bill | | --- |
| TIPS | BG Cantor U.S. TIPS | | U.S. Treasury TIPS |
| *Corporate Debt (Quality segmented)* | | | |
| U.S. Investment Grade | — | — | U.S. Long Credit |
| U.S. High-Yield | — | — | U.S. Corp High-Yield |
| *International (Region segmented)* | | | |
| Global | — | — | Multiverse |
| International | Int'l Corp Bond | — | Global Aggregate |
| Emerging market | — | — | Global Emerging Markets |
| *Specialty* | | | |
| Real Estate (REITS) | U.S. REIT | 2Wilshire RESI* | — |
| Global Real Estate | — | Global RESI* | — |
| U.S. municipal | Municipal Bond | — | U.S. Municipal |
| U.S. mortgage-backed | — | — | U.S. MBS |

*Real Estate Securities Index

This is an example of a situation where a financial planner needs to evaluate a portfolio's characteristics using experience and skill. A client who should be taking a balanced growth investment approach should not allow the percentage of assets held in any one asset class to dramatically exceed the benchmark level. If this occurs, the planner should again consider reallocating assets. If the current allocation is not changed, this implies that either the client's goal(s) had changed or that the desired level of risk had changed. This might be the result of a change in economic expectations, risk capacity, or another factor.

## Performance Measures—Applications of Comparative Statistics

Performance measures of excess performance break into two categories: absolute measures and ratio measures. As summarized in Table 10.6, different measures categorize risk differently and have a more specific view of what risk is: **total risk** versus **downside risk**, or **systematic risk** versus **unsystematic risk**. Total risk is the most basic measure and quantifies the general likelihood of an unexpected outcome, whereas downside risk limits the quantification of risk to both unexpected and negative outcomes. Systematic risk measures quantify the risk inherent in the entire market, whereas unsystematic risk quantifies the risk associated with a single asset or asset class within a market.

Precision of measurement is important to the planner when trying to make decisions about the effectiveness of portfolio management or asset selection. The more active the planner is in attempting to mitigate a specific type of risk or maximize a return based on a particular investment philosophy, the more precise the planner must be in isolating those variables to make accurate comparisons.

**Table 10.6** Summary of Commonly Used Portfolio Risk Measures

| Name (Symbol) | Definition/Formula |
|---|---|
| Variance ($\sigma^2$) and Std deviation ($\sigma$) | Absolute measures of the average variability or spread of periodic returns. This measures the total risk of unanticipated outcomes. $$\sigma_i^2 = \frac{1}{T-1} \sum_{t=1}^{T} \left( r_{i,t} - \bar{r}_i \right)^2 \qquad \sigma = \sqrt{\sigma^2}$$ |
| Semi-variance ($\sigma^2$) and Semi-deviation ($\sigma$) | Absolute measures of the average variability or spread of periodic returns that do not meet the targeted return: downside risk. $$\sigma_i^2 = \frac{0.5}{T-1} \sum_{t=1}^{T} \left( r_{i,t} - \bar{r}_i \right)^2 \qquad \sigma = \sqrt{\sigma^2}$$ Formulas assume "normal" distribution. (For more information, see Appendix 10.A.) |
| Coefficient of variation (CV) | A measure of dispersion of a probability distribution. It is defined as the ratio of the standard deviation ($\sigma$) to the mean ($\mu$). Formula = $CV = \dfrac{\sigma}{\bar{r}}$ |
| Coefficient of determination ($R^2$) | A measure of systematic, or market-related, variability. $R^2$ ranges from 0 to 100 and reflects the percentage of an asset's movements that are explained by movements in the benchmark. The remainders (residuals) are a rough measure of the unsystematic component of risk. Formula = Linear regression-based |
| Beta (ß) | The beta coefficient is a measure of the security's volatility relative to the market. This is a "relative" measure of volatility. Because beta reflects only the market-related or systematic portion of a security's risk, it is a narrower measure than standard deviation. Formula = $\beta = \dfrac{\sigma_{i,M}}{\sigma_M^2}$ |

Five performance statistics are commonly used for risk-adjusted, return-based portfolio evaluation. The first two statistics discussed the Sharpe ratio and the Modigliani measure, use a measure of total risk for the risk-based adjustment; the next two, the Treynor index and Jensen's alpha, use a systematic risk measure for the adjustment. The final performance measure, the information ratio, is not actually a risk-based adjustment; rather, it tries to capture whether a planner or asset manager is enhancing portfolio performance through active management.

### Sharpe Ratio

The **Sharpe ratio** standardizes portfolio performance in excess of the risk-free rate by the standard deviation of the portfolio. Higher Sharpe ratio scores are better. However, the ratio is not useful unless an investor has a comparable portfolio to judge the score against. Additionally, because the Sharpe ratio uses a measure of total risk for risk adjustment, a planner should use this method primarily for comparing undiversified portfolios or concentrated positions. The Sharpe ratio can be calculated using the following formula:

$$S_i = \frac{R_i - R_f}{\sigma_i}$$

Where:

$S_i$ = Sharpe ratio

$R_i$ = Actual return of the asset (or portfolio)

$R_f$ = Risk-free rate

$\sigma_i$ = Standard deviation of asset (or portfolio)

*Example:* First assume that Laini's portfolio achieved an average annual return of 12% with an annualized standard deviation of 16%, and the market portfolio achieved an annual return of 13% with a standard deviation of 18%. Secondly, it is known that the risk-free opportunity returned 5% per year. Applying the formula, Laini's Sharpe ratio would be $(12-5)/16 = 0.437$. But what does this mean? Without a point of comparison, it means almost nothing. So by calculating the Sharpe ratio of the market for a comparison $(13-5)/18 = 0.444$, it can be determined that Laini's portfolio is inferior to the market portfolio.

The Sharpe ratio is still not easy to interpret. As with all ratio values, it is fairly difficult to interpret the results in absolute terms, and only slightly less so in relative terms when there is a benchmark for comparison. Negative ratios also lack intuitive meaning. The following Modigliani method removes both of these limitations because it returns a percentage rather than an abstract ratio value.

## Modigliani Measure

The **Modigliani measure**, which calculates the absolute amount of risk-adjusted return, is based on the Sharpe ratio and helps put the results into a more intuitive form: return. It starts with the Sharpe ratio and then applies a risk adjustment to convert the Sharpe back into percentage return form, adds the risk-free rate, then subtracts the return of the market.

$$M_i^2 = \left[ R_f + \sigma_m \left( \frac{(R_i - R_f)}{\sigma_i} \right) \right] - R_m$$

Where:

$M^2$ = Modigliani measure

$R_f$ = Risk-free rate

$R_i$ = Return of the asset or portfolio

$\sigma_m$ = Standard deviation of the market or benchmark

$\sigma_i$ = Standard deviation of the asset or portfolio

$R_m$ = Return on the market

*Example.* Returning to the previous example and based on the formula above, Laini's $M^2$ measure would have been −0.125%. So, although she returned 1% less than the market with a standard deviation of two less than the market, her risk-adjusted return remained negative. This coincides with the fact that her Sharpe ratio was lower than the market. This measure nicely quantifies the exact amount of risk-adjusted underperformance she achieved.

## Treynor Index

The **Treynor index** is also a measure of standardized risk-adjusted performance. Instead of using standard deviation as a measure of absolute volatility, the formula uses beta as a measure of systematic risk. Just like the Sharpe ratio, the Treynor index number is useful only in terms of comparing one portfolio to another. However, because the Treynor uses a systemic measure of risk, this index should be used only with well-diversified portfolios. A Treynor index score can be calculated using the following formula:

$$T_i = \frac{R_i - R_f}{\beta_i}$$

Where:

$T_i$ = Treynor index

$R_p$ = Actual return of the portfolio

$R_f$ = Risk-free rate

$\beta$ = Beta

*Example.* Assume Chris' portfolio return was 12%, the risk-free rate was 3%, and beta of Chris' portfolio was 0.85. The Treynor index for the portfolio would be 0.106 [(0.12 – 0.03)/0.85].

## Jensen's Alpha

Another useful statistic is **Jensen's alpha** or the **Jensen Performance Index**. Alpha measures the relative under- or over-performance of a portfolio compared to a benchmark—typically a representative, diversified market portfolio. Alpha measures the difference between the actual returns of a portfolio and its expected risk-adjusted performance. The following formula is used to determine the Jensen alpha of a portfolio:

$$\alpha = R_p - \left[ R_f + \beta \left( R_m - R_f \right) \right]$$

Where:

$\alpha$ = Alpha (derived from the assumption of investment risk)

$R_p$ = Actual return of the portfolio

$R_f$ = Risk-free rate

$\beta$ = Beta

$R_m$ = Return on the market

A positive alpha indicates that a portfolio exceeded expectations on a risk-adjusted basis. A negative alpha suggests that a portfolio underperformed the market on a risk-adjusted basis. A reallocation of assets might be warranted if a portfolio shows a long history of significant underperformance.

*Example.* Returning to Chris's portfolio from the previous example, if Chris actually earned a rate of return of 12% over the three-year period, she would conclude that on a risk-adjusted basis she did better than expected. Her portfolio would have generated a positive alpha of 1.35% (12% – 10.65%). If the portfolio were managed by a professional money manager, one could conclude that the manager added value above what would have been expected given the risk taken.

## Information Ratio

The **information ratio** is the excess return of the portfolio (alpha) generated by active management compared to the standard deviation (tracking error of alpha) generated by the active management. This is most useful when a financial planner is attempting to "beat" a benchmark through superior asset selection or market timing. This differs from other ratios in that the benchmark is no longer the risk-free asset, as both the Sharpe ratio and Treynor index assume. This ratio can be calculated using the following formula.

$$IR = \frac{(r_p - r_B)}{\sqrt{Var(r_p - r_B)}} = \frac{\alpha}{\varepsilon_T}$$

Where:

$IR$ = Information ratio

$\alpha$ = Alpha (derived from active management, not solely investment risk)

where alpha is the difference between the portfolio return and the benchmark return

$\varepsilon_T$ = Tracking error of alpha where the error is the standard deviation of the alpha return

*Example.* If a portfolio manager achieved an annual alpha of 2.5% with an annualized tracking error of 6.25%, then the information ratio would be 0.4.

But once again a problem exists with the interpretation of the ratio: what does 0.4 mean? Is it good or bad? Generally it is good, because the ratio is positive; therefore, it is known that the manager added value—positive alpha. But how good is good enough? Much research has been done, but still there is no easy answer. One could easily say that negative is bad, but that could be ascertained simply by calculating the alpha.

An additional note of caution regarding the use of the information ratio is that it is traditionally calculated using arithmetic averages, which do not allow for differences in the leverage applied by different managers.

**Table 10.7** Summary of Portfolio Relative Performance Measures

| Name (Symbol | Definition/Formula |
| --- | --- |
| Sharpe ratio | A measure of risk-adjusted performance calculated by dividing the excess return of a portfolio by a measure of total risk. Higher values are desirable. This measure is most appropriate when analyzing portfolios where unsystematic risk is still prevalent.<br><br>Formula = $S = \dfrac{E(r_i) - r_f}{\sigma_i}$ |
| Modigliani measure ($M^2$) | A measure of risk-adjusted performance that results in a percentage measure for under- (negative values) or over- (positive values) performance, based on total risk within the asset or portfolio.<br><br>Formula = $M_i^2 = \left[ R_f + \sigma_m \left( \dfrac{(R_i - R_f)}{\sigma_i} \right) \right] - R_m$ |
| Treynor index | A measure of risk-adjusted performance calculated by dividing the excess return of a portfolio, return beyond the risk-free rate, by its beta. Higher values are desirable and indicate greater return per unit of systematic risk. This measure is most appropriate when analyzing portfolios where only systematic risk remains.<br><br>Formula = $S = \dfrac{E(r_i) - r_f}{\beta_i}$ |
| Jensen's alpha ($\alpha$) | Return in excess of capital asset pricing model (CAPM) return. In other words, alpha is the difference between the security's actual performance and the performance anticipated in light of the security's systematic risk (beta) and the market's behavior.<br><br>Formula = $\alpha = \overline{r_i} - E(r_i)$ |
| Information ratio | A measure of risk-adjusted performance calculated by dividing the excess risk-adjusted return (alpha) of a portfolio by the tracking error (standard deviation of alpha). Higher values are desirable. This measure is most appropriate when analyzing actively managed portfolios where either market timing or asset selection is being used in an attempt to exceed a benchmark.<br><br>Formula = $IR = \dfrac{\alpha}{\varepsilon_T}$ |

Although the comparison of statistics can be documented in terms of higher, lower, or the same, there are few rules to determine whether the current portfolio is superior or inferior to the benchmark. **Modern portfolio theory**, the process of mean-variance optimization, its related statistics, and various other investment rules can be used to determine whether a client's portfolio is efficient and effective. However, in many cases the choice to recommend portfolio changes comes down to a planner's professional judgment. Experience, knowledge, and skill help a planner determine whether a portfolio is appropriate for a client's needs considering the current economic situation, client attitudes and expectations, and an analysis of risk tolerance and capacity. The integrated nature of these, and other situational factors, makes investment planning challenging.

Throughout the comprehensive financial planning process, including insurance, retirement, and special situation planning, it is essential that a planner know how a client's assets are invested. A client's asset allocation strategy for each goal can tell a planner much about how well a client is progressing toward meeting certain objectives. Analytical tools can easily generate modern portfolio statistics that provide an insight into the relative position of a portfolio. Planners need to understand and be able to interpret these statistics for clients.

# STRATEGIES

## Review Prospective Investment Strategies

Clients tend to seek the help of a financial planner for investment planning guidance for one of three reasons: (1) they want to increase the capital appreciation potential of their investments; (2) they want to increase the amount of current income earned from their investments; or (3) they want to reduce the amount of taxes paid on their investments. However, clients are often unaware of what may be necessary to increase their real return, their risk-adjusted return, or their after-tax return. It is up to the planner to help the client understand methods to measure returns and to determine a realistic return. In other words, it is the planner's job to manage the client's expectations. An experienced financial planner can also look for strategies that act as an inflation hedge or reduce risk. The best planning strategies accomplish more than one objective, such as ones that hedge inflation and provide current income.

## Identify Prospective Investment Management Strategies

Because of the wide variety of investment products available, an equally diverse number of strategies can be used to meet client goals and objectives. Although the tendency when dealing with investments is to focus on specific products, the procedure involved in investment planning can be just as important.

Take, for example, recommending the purchase of municipal bonds. This might be a great strategy for a client, unless it is poorly executed by purchasing the bonds within a tax-advantaged account. Because the rules for the IRA or other tax-deferred account determine whether a distribution is taxable or not, there is no benefit for earnings that originate from a tax-exempt interest. Although no rules forbid this investment strategy, the planner may be doing a client a great disservice by executing the strategy in this manner. Advising a client to double-check the beneficiary on a retirement account, or retitle a mutual fund so that both spouses are on the account are examples of procedural strategies.

### *Product Strategy 1: Use Zero-coupon Bonds if Anticipating Changes in Interest Rates*

**Advantage:** Zero-coupon bonds are purchased at a discount on their face value. These types of bonds pay no interest; instead, bond owners accrue interest over time. Zero-coupon bonds are unique in that maturity and duration of the bond are basically the same.

This means that a bond with a maturity and modified duration of five years will typically move up or down by approximately 5% with a 1% change in interest rates over a one-year period. Someone who believes that interest rates are going to fall can speculate on rising bond prices by purchasing long-maturity zero-coupon bonds to obtain the maximum price appreciation. On the other hand, someone who believes that rates will increase could sell long-term zero-coupon bonds and replace them with short-maturity bonds.

**Disadvantage:** Investors who use zero-coupon bonds in their taxable portfolios should be aware that, although they receive no income from the bonds, all accrued interest is taxable in the year of accrual. Any capital gains captured from this strategy will also result in a tax liability. The price of zero-coupon bonds is sensitive to changes in interest rates.

### *Product Strategy 2: Adjust the Duration of the Bond Portfolio if Anticipating Changes in Interest Rates*

**Advantage:** The modified duration of a bond or bond portfolio tells an investor approximately how much a bond or portfolio will change in value in relation to a change in interest rates. A modified duration equal to 5 means that if interest rates increase by 1% over a one-year period the bond will decline in value by approximately 5%. If interest rates decline by 1% over a one-year period, the bond should increase by approximately 5%.

Knowing this, an investor can adjust a bond portfolio's exposure to interest rate changes by adjusting duration. For instance, if a planner believes that interest rates will fall, the planner could increase the duration of the bond portfolio to capture the increase in principal that should accompany the interest rate change. If, on the other hand, interest rates are expected to increase, the duration of the bond portfolio could be reduced.

**Disadvantage:** In general, this strategy is an effective way to reduce interest rate risk within a bond portfolio. However, duration can be misleading in certain situations.

For instance, the duration of a mortgage-backed security is often misleading. If rates rise, mortgage-backed bond prices fall. If interest rates decline, these same bonds might not go up in value as much as their duration indicates because of the negative convexity induced. The reason for this is that as interest rates decline, home owners tend to refinance their mortgages, leading to prepayment of mortgage loan obligations. This effectively reduces the duration and potential capital gain advantage of mortgage-backed securities.

### Product Strategy 3: Increase Client Income by Investing in Real Estate Investment Trusts (REITs)

**Advantage:** REITs are structured in a way that allows investors to pool their investments in a publicly traded company that then purchases a portfolio of real estate. REITs can invest in land, buildings, shopping centers, apartment buildings, offices, and mortgages. REIT investments are attractive for income-oriented investors because REITs are required to distribute 90% of the income received from rents, dividends, interest, and other gains, such as income from the sale of securities and property.

**Disadvantage:** Although REITs tend to be high-income-producing investments, several factors can make these securities problematic for clients. First, real estate tends to be cyclical, and given that REITs can invest in local markets, rates of return earned on real estate assets are usually tied to local market conditions. There is no guarantee that currently high yields will persist into the future. Furthermore, lack of liquidity in the commercial real estate markets means that REITs carry more risk than other dividend-paying stocks.

### Product Strategy 4: Write (Sell) Covered Calls to Increase Portfolio Income

**Advantage:** Suppose a client owns a stock that has appreciated in value. The client would like to sell the stock to capture the profit, but at the same time would not mind holding the stock if income could be generated from the asset. Writing a covered call could be a good strategy to achieve the client's objective.

Writing a call provides immediate premium income for the client, which effectively reduces the cost basis of the original stock. If the price of the stock goes up, the stock may be called away, but this results in generally the same outcome as selling the stock now. If the price of the stock should fall, the call option serves as a hedge, reducing or eliminating the loss on the stock price decline.

**Disadvantage:** Opportunity costs are linked with this strategy. If the price of the stock goes up dramatically, the client will lose both the stock and the price appreciation. If the client purchases back the option, the client will pay much more than the premium earned originally, which will result in a reduced gain.

Further, the commission associated with writing covered calls can be quite high, a percentage of assets, for those selling one or a few options. The strategy is only cost effective if large blocks of options are traded.

### Product Strategy 5: Increase Portfolio Income by Reducing Bond Quality Mix in a Portfolio

**Advantage:** Because of the inverse relationship between bond quality and interest rate—the lower the grade, the higher the interest rate paid—clients who need additional income may want to include lower-grade speculative bonds in their portfolios. One way to do this is through junk bond mutual funds, which provide diversification and professional management as a way to reduce the increased risk associated with this strategy.

**Disadvantage:** This strategy has many potential pitfalls. First, clients who purchase lower-grade bonds, especially junk bonds, run the risk that the bonds will not be redeemed because of default. Also, lower-grade bonds are more volatile whenever interest rates change. So an increase in interest rates results in a greater loss in value than would a similar higher-rated bond. Finally, junk bonds tend to trade more like stocks than bonds. This means that lower-grade bonds are impacted by both a company's financial situation and interest rates, which subjects the bond holder to greater overall risk.

## Product Strategy 6: Reduce Tax Costs by Investing in Dividend-paying Stocks

**Advantage:** Taxes on qualified stock dividends are capped at 15% for taxpayers in the 25% marginal tax rate and above, and 0% for taxpayers who are in lower marginal tax brackets. This means that clients who need income from their investments should consider shifting assets toward dividend-paying stocks. The net after-tax yield, given the lower tax on dividends, means a higher return for clients.

**Disadvantage:** It is important to remember that some dividends from stock and bond mutual funds are not considered to be qualified for the lower tax rate. To take advantage of this strategy, a client might need to build a diversified portfolio of individual stocks. This means potentially higher transaction costs, which for smaller portfolios could negate the tax advantage of receiving dividends. Furthermore, the costs—particularly in time—to manage a stock portfolio may not be worth the marginal tax benefit.

## Product Strategy 7: Decrease Tax Liability by Investing in Municipal Securities

**Advantage:** One of the basic tenets of investing is that an analysis of tax-free yields compared to fully taxable yields should be conducted on a regular basis for those investing in fixed-income securities. Clients in the highest marginal tax brackets often find that municipal securities provide a higher after-tax return than similar fully taxable bonds, even if the initial yield is higher on the taxable bonds. The following formula can be used to determine whether owning a tax-free bond investment is better than owning a taxable security.

$$\text{Tax-free Rate} = \text{Taxable Rate} \times (1 - \text{Marginal Tax Bracket})$$

For example, assume that a client can earn 4% in a fully taxable bond fund and is in the 25% marginal federal tax bracket. The equivalent tax free rate is 3% (4% × [1 – 25%]). The client would be just as well served by investing in a municipal bond fund with a yield of at least 3%.

This strategy is even more effective if a client purchases municipal securities from the state in which the client lives. In such cases, interest earned is usually both federal and state tax free.

**Disadvantage:** The primary disadvantage associated with this strategy is that sometimes a client will conduct a tax-equivalency calculation and determine that the relationship between taxable and tax-free rates is fixed. In fact, the relationship between rates can change frequently, meaning that this analysis should occur more frequently than it often does.

Also, clients must be aware that municipal securities generally have a lower degree of liquidity and marketability than some corporate and nearly all federal government debt. The importance of assessing each credit agency's debt rating cannot be overemphasized.

## Product Strategy 8: Invest in a Variable Annuity to Reduce Current Taxes

**Advantage:** Variable annuities provide clients with multiple advantages. Notably, annuities can be tax efficient. Dividends, interest, and capital gains earned in any given year are deferred until a later date. This can be quite beneficial for clients who will be in a lower marginal tax bracket in retirement than today, and for clients who employ tactical asset allocation strategies resulting in many trades.

**Disadvantage:** Variable annuity products should be used only in situations where a client has a long-term investment horizon. This strategy is inappropriate for clients who need assets to fund expenses, such as the purchase of a home, car, or business. Some variable annuity products can be quite expensive. Additionally, income distributions are taxed at the client's full marginal income tax bracket.

## Product Strategy 9: Hedge Inflation in a Fixed-income Portfolio with Treasury Inflation-indexed Securities

**Advantage:** Treasury inflation-protection securities (TIPS) are 10-year bonds issued by the federal government. Purchasing TIPS is a strategy designed to reduce inflation risk. The principal value of a TIP security is adjusted on a semiannual basis to account for inflation, as measured by the consumer price index. At maturity, the redemption price is equal to the greater of the inflation-adjusted principal amount or par value. The coupon rate for TIPS is fixed, but payments to bond holders can increase over time as the inflation-adjusted principal amount increases.

**Disadvantage:** Several potential disadvantages are associated with TIPS. First, the initial coupon rate for new issues is significantly less than yields on comparable non-inflation-adjusted debt. This means that, if inflation stays quiescent or there is deflation, the bond holder receives less annual income than other investors. Second, bond holders must pay taxes on the increase in the inflation-adjusted principal amount on a yearly basis, not at maturity. This is why TIPS make the most sense in tax-deferred portfolios.

## Product Strategy 10: Hedge a Portfolio against Inflation with Hard Assets and Precious Metals

**Advantage:** During times of high inflation, hard assets and precious metals tend to outperform other assets, especially fixed-income and equity assets. There are many reasons for this, but in general, the limited supply of these assets makes them an attractive alternative to other securities during inflationary times.

**Disadvantage:** The disadvantages associated with this strategy can offset the advantages of holding hard assets. First, hard assets and precious metals entail holding costs that can be substantial. A place needs to be devoted to holding the physical assets, and insurance may have to be purchased to guard their value in case of loss or theft. All of these costs work to erode the potential for gain that this strategy offers.

Also, the value of hard assets and precious metals is determined primarily by supply and demand factors. If a new supply enters the market, the value of the assets is almost certain to fall. When inflation becomes less of a factor, the value of hard assets tends to stagnate or fall.

### Product Strategy 11: Protect a Client against Interest Rate Risks by Creating a Laddered Fixed-income Portfolio

**Advantage:** Clients often want to limit the maturity and duration of a fixed-income portfolio to reduce interest rate risk. Unfortunately, doing so usually reduces the level of income generated from the portfolio. One strategy to increase the average yield from a portfolio of fixed-income securities while limiting average portfolio maturity involves creating a ladder.

For instance, a client could purchase equal dollar amounts of 3-, 6-, 9-, and 12-month certificates of deposit (CDs). Whenever one CD matures, another 12-month CD could be purchased. This plan provides a weighted average maturity of less than 12 months but a yield greater than that offered on a 3-month CD. Furthermore, this strategy enhances a client's liquidity situation, because there is always a CD near maturity. Obviously, the strategy could be extended beyond 12 months by adding CDs with longer maturities. The same strategy can be used to develop bond portfolios.

**Disadvantage:** Although this strategy is relatively simple to implement, it requires constant monitoring to remain effective. New securities must be purchased on a regular basis. This makes analysis of the fixed-income market extremely important. Replacing securities that mature with assets of similar credit quality and yields requires more work than simply buying and holding one or a few securities.

### Product Strategy 12: Purchase Rental Real Estate to Reduce Taxes and Generate Cash Flow

**Advantage:** A client's comfort level, knowledge, and experience with certain types of investments often dictates which strategy will dominate an investment plan. Some clients prefer to invest directly in real estate rather than through stocks, bonds, and other investment assets. Rental real estate can provide clients with deferred capital gains, tax shelter, an inflation hedge, and cash flow.

**Disadvantage:** Lack of liquidity and potentially limited marketability are two significant disadvantages associated with this strategy. Clients who are considering rental real estate must also remember that costs for ongoing operating expenses can sometimes escalate more quickly than rents in certain locations. This is especially true in cases where the client hires a management firm to handle all aspects of rental ownership.

Another disadvantage associated with real estate investing is that it requires the temperament and skill of a trained property manager to consistently make money. For example, client owners of rental properties must sometimes be plumbers, electricians, painters, sales agents, and evictors. Not everyone is capable of performing these activities. It may be possible to hire a management firm to oversee properties, but the costs associated with management can erode the return on investment generated from a property.

### Product Strategy 13: Understand the Purpose of Call and Put Options

**Advantage**: Investors increasingly are looking for ways to hedge the inherent risks associated with investment in the markets. Options provide one mechanism to reduce the risk related to owning a basket of securities. A **call option** allows an investor to purchase an asset at a predetermined price in the future. For example, an investor might believe that the price of a stock will increase in the future. Rather than purchase the shares directly, the investor can purchase a call option. If the stock should increase in value, the investor can "call" his or her broker, pay the predetermined price (which will be lower than the current stock price), and then sell the stock in the market for a higher price. The net result is a profit with very little initial investment.

A **put option** is a way for an investor to sell an asset at a predetermined price in the future. Put options are often used to hedge a portfolio of stocks. Say an investor owns a diversified portfolio. The investor is worried that the markets might fall. He or she could purchase a put option. If prices do indeed decline, the value of the portfolio will fall, but the value of the option will increase, thus hedging the portfolio. Put and call options can be purchased for individual securities or for larger baskets of investments; these are called *index options*.

**Disadvantage**: The primary disadvantage associated with option trading is that each option purchased adds a cost to the investment process. It is important to note that options have a limited duration—usually from a few days to a few months. If an option is unexercised by the owner, the value eventually declines to zero. Additionally, if the option is exercised, the investor must also pay a commission on the shares acquired. Options are usually a good investment only in a volatile marketplace. This is the reason that some investors not only buy options, but they sell them as well.

For example, assume that a shareholder owns 100 shares of stock X. The investor believes that the stock price will remain about where it is for the next year. That shareholder could sell a call option into the marketplace. Basically, the investor is betting against the person who buys the option. The buyer believes the price will go higher, whereas the seller thinks the price will decline or stay the same. Some speculators sell call and put options *naked*. This is a very risky approach to investing. A naked option writer sells calls and puts without actually owning the underlying security. If the price moves against the seller he or she will be forced to enter the market and pay market prices. This strategy exposes the seller to unlimited market risk. In summary, although options trading can be an effective way to hedge a portfolio against market risk, the costs associated with the strategy must be incorporated into the return expectations associated with investing.

### *Procedural Strategy 1: Balance Long- and Short-term Tax Gain and Loss Selling to Maximum Tax Savings*

**Advantage:** This strategy is premised on the fact that only $3,000 in short-term losses can be used to offset regular income in any given year. If a client has more short-term losses than short- and long-term gains, those losses must be carried forward into future years. By matching investment losses with asset gains, it may be possible to minimize the negative impact of taxes on portfolio performance.

**Disadvantage:** It may not always be possible to match losses and gains. It might be better to take a short-term loss than to wait and potentially have the investment liquidated with no value at all.

### *Procedural Strategy 2: Reallocate the Current Portfolio to Match the Client's Changing Investment Profile*

**Advantage:** Reallocating portfolio assets can be counted as one of the most basic investment planning strategies available. Because risk and return are positively related, it is reasonable to assume that, over time, a portfolio invested more aggressively should outperform other less risky portfolios. However, as a client's time horizon, risk tolerance, or risk capacity changes, investment allocations should also change.

**Disadvantage:** Although this is an easy recommendation to make, actual implementation entails many pitfalls. For example, reallocating assets through the sale of existing assets and the purchase of new assets has tax implications as well as certain up-front costs. And it is unreasonable to assume that asset returns will improve in the short term simply by taking more risk. This relationship holds true only over extended periods of time.

### *Procedural Strategy 3: Invest in Low-cost Mutual Funds to Maximize Performance*

**Advantage:** Mutual funds represent the most widely used investment company product. Mutual funds are professionally managed, pooled-asset investment companies formed to meet a specific investment objective. In effect, mutual funds pool assets from a number of investors, and the mutual fund hires a portfolio manager who uses the assets to purchase stocks, bonds, or other assets.

Mutual funds are an attractive investment choice for clients, because funds tend to provide diversification at a relatively low cost. Additionally, mutual funds provide investors of modest means access to professional management at very reasonable entry levels. Shares in some funds can be purchased for as little as $100.

The most useful predictor of a fund's future performance is the expense ratio. Funds with lower expense ratios historically and empirically tend to outperform others.

**Disadvantage:** Choosing low-cost mutual funds is an easy prescription, but sometimes a difficult process. There could be situations where a low-cost mutual fund is unavailable. In such cases, other determinants of mutual fund performance should be used to screen potential fund investments.

## Procedural Strategy 4: Consider Adding Exchange-traded Funds to Client Portfolios

**Advantage:** Exchange-traded funds (ETFs) are emerging as a popular investment company product. Unlike traditional mutual funds, ETFs can be traded throughout the day, similarly to a stock, bond, or option. This gives ETFs a unique advantage over funds while retaining most of the attributes offered by mutual funds.

Exchange-traded funds are distinguishable from mutual funds in two respects. First, very few ETFs are actively managed. Until recently, nearly all ETFs mimicked a market index, such as the S&P 500, Dow Jones Industrial Average, or other market indices. Second, investment companies develop ETFs by using *creation units*, which are then pooled into baskets of securities. These baskets of securities mirror the underlying index, and these securities are bought and sold by investors. This allows an investor to purchase one or more units of an ETF, and when ETF investors wishes to sell their investments they can either sell units to other investors on the secondary market or they can sell them back to the investment company, though this is rarely done.

An ETF investment strategy provides investors with multiple advantages, as summarized in Table 10.8. In general, ETFs allow clients to develop well-diversified portfolios with low annual expenses. ETFs also offer liquidity and marketability to a greater extent than index mutual funds. Moreover, ETFs are completely transparent, which means that the exact components and weightings of securities held in the portfolios are always known. Mutual funds, on the other hand, are only partially transparent, because they have to make only their holdings known on a periodic basis, and even then they are allowed to delay the publication of the data for a certain period of time to protect their marketability.

Other ETF advantages include tax efficiency and investment style stability. ETFs are tax efficient because portfolio turnover is low or even zero, which results in few taxable distributions. ETFs also allow financial planners to develop portfolios with fixed allocations to certain market benchmarks. Unlike mutual funds that tend to exhibit style drift, investing via an ETF almost guarantees exposure to a chosen asset class and market.

**Table 10.8** Indirect Investment Ownership Options Comparison

| Investment Attribute | ETF | Index Fund | Managed Fund |
|---|---|---|---|
| Tradability | Can trade during market hours | Can trade once per day | Can trade once per day |
| Ability to sell short | Yes | No | No |
| Transparency | High | Moderate to high | Low to moderate |
| Diversification | Low to high | Moderate to high | Low to high |
| Tax efficiency | Very high | High | Low to high |
| Subject to style drift | Low | Low | Low to high |

**Disadvantage:** The primary disadvantage associated with ETFs is the lack of active management. Once an ETF is created, the underlying assets do not change. This means that the opportunity to outperform the market, on a risk-adjusted basis, is very low. Also, because ETFs are traded like stocks, clients incur trading commissions whenever shares are bought and sold.

## Procedural Strategy 5: Use the Discounted Dividend Valuation Model to Value Shares of Stock

**Advantage**: The discounted dividend valuation model, sometimes referred to as the *dividend growth model*, can be used to value a share of stock using the present value of all future dividends. This method of valuation provides a starting point in valuing a stock. The formula is:

$$Value = \frac{D_0(1+g)}{(i-g)}$$

Where,

$D_0$ = Current dividend

$i$ = Required rate of return

$g$ = Dividend growth rate

**Disadvantage**: The model relies on two unknown assumptions: the dollar amount of future dividends and the growth rate of those dividends. As such, estimated values vary dramatically based on the assumptions used to measure value. Also, if the dividend growth rate exceeds the required rate of return a null value is obtained.

## Procedural Strategy 6: Calculate Key Financial Statement Ratios as a Stock Valuation Technique

**Advantage**: The use of the following types of financial statement ratios can provide an important insight into the relative value of individual equities.

- **Profit margin:** net income/total sales

- **Return on equity**: net income/shareholder's equity

- **Debt-to-equity ratio**: long-term debt/shareholder's equity

- **Price-to-earnings ratio**: market capitalization/net income*

- **Price-to-sales ratio**: market capitalization/total sales or total revenue*

- **Price-to-book ratio**: market capitalization/shareholder's equity*

\* Each of these ratios can also be determined on a per-share basis by dividing the answer by the number of shares outstanding.

**Disadvantage**: Financial ratios provide a picture only of past performance. Should a firm's sales, net income, debt, or other calculation inputs change, estimated values also change.

## CHAPTER-BASED CASE STUDY

### A Client-based Investments Recommendation Example

Many investment planning strategies are available to help clients achieve their financial goals. The ones identified above are only a sampling of the alternatives available. For clients with more specialized needs (e.g., high net worth, business owners, extended families), the number, type, and complexity of strategies becomes even larger. It is important to remember when molding strategies into specific client recommendations that the client's goals should dominate the process.

Planners and clients often find that the simplest strategy is best. It is tempting to develop very complex and intricate recommendations; this is not always appropriate or necessary.

The average client simply needs guidance answering one of three core investment questions: How can I increase my rate of return? How can I maintain my current level of wealth? How can I generate more income from my assets? Although answers to these questions can be complex, depending on the client situation many solutions are quite easy to understand and implement.

In many ways, the development and presentation of investment planning recommendations is the most important part of financial planning. Lack of implementation by the client is the leading cause of plan failure. Therefore, it is imperative that recommendations be easy to understand, conceptually valid, and cost effective.

For the majority of investment planning recommendations, any prudent person should be able to quickly understand the reasoning behind the recommendation and the potential outcomes associated with its implementation. All of this means that answers to the core issues of who, what, when, where, why, how, and how much ought to be clear, concise, and understandable. However, planners should always solicit client collaboration in decision making and implementation, depending on the extent of the planner-client engagement. No client wants to be pushed into accepting a recommendation that is not fully explained, no matter how concise, well-intentioned, or suitable it may be.

The issue of fiduciary responsibility is significant for planners who offer investment planning services. Documenting that certain records have been obtained from a client and showing that important information has been shared with clients are important first steps in the recommendation, development, and implementation process.

## A Sample Recommendation: Reallocate a Portfolio for Changing Economic Conditions

The primary purpose of investment planning is to determine whether a client's current portfolio situation is suitable, reasonable, and appropriate for a given financial goal or objective. This scenario considers Tobias Fleischer, a middle-aged, married father of one son. Tobias recently realized that his retirement account, which performed so admirably several years ago, is no longer keeping up with the market.

During their first meeting, the planner had Tobias complete a risk tolerance questionnaire and provide some basic information about his finances. Based on the information provided, the planner developed Exhibit 10.5 as a summary of Tobias' financial ratios and completed Exhibit 10.6, Tobias' Investment Profile and Portfolio Summary Form, to document and evaluate Tobias' current investment planning situation for his retirement account.

**Exhibit 10.5** Tobias' Financial Ratio Summary

| Ratio | Client Outcome | Benchmark |
|---|---|---|
| Current ratio | 1.10 | > 1.00 |
| Emergency fund ratio | 9 months | 3–6 months |
| Debt ratio | 38% | < 40% |
| Savings ratio | 5% | > 10% |
| Long-term debt coverage ratio | 2.35 | > 2.50 |

The planner drew a number of conclusions. Tobias's quantitative and qualitative investment profile is squarely in the moderate risk area and his stated investment objective is capital appreciation for retirement. Taxes are not a concern, because the portfolio in question is in a 401(k) account. For the qualitative measures, both Tobias's risk tolerance and knowledge level are moderate, which suggests that he should be able to withstand, as well as understand, a reasonable level of portfolio volatility. Furthermore, he has positive expectations about future market prospects. This positive outlook is also indicative of an investor who would be willing to experience some short-term volatility for the potential benefit of achieving superior long-term gains.

In terms of socioeconomic descriptors, Tobias' time horizon for goal achievement is long-term, over 10 years, and his-risk capacity is moderate. His planner reasonably assigned this risk capacity ranking because the financial ratios indicate that Tobias is solvent, has a funded emergency savings account, and has positive savings ratios. The only point of concern is his debt level.

**Exhibit 10.6** Tobias' Investment Profile and Portfolio Summary Form

| Client Investment Profile | | | |
|---|---|---|---|
| Qualitative | Circle the appropriate response. | | |
| Risk tolerance | High | (Moderate) | Low |
| Knowledge/experience | High | (Moderate) | Low |
| Market expectations | (Positive) | Neutral | Negative |
| Quantitative | | | |
| Time horizon | (Long) | Intermediate | Short |
| Risk capacity | High | (Moderate) | Low |
| Client risk profile* | Moderate | Client allocation profile** | Moderate growth |

| Portfolio Measures | Current Statistics | Benchmark Statistics | Comparison to Benchmark |
|---|---|---|---|
| Targeted portfolio Allocation profile** | Moderate growth | Moderate growth | |
| Observed portfolio Allocation profile** | Conservative growth | N/A | Lower |
| Portfolio statistics*** | | | |
| Beta | 0.11 | 0.85 | Lower |
| Alpha | 1.59 | 1.32 | Higher |
| $R^2$ | 30.00 | 84.00 | Lower |
| Sharpe ratio | 0.83 | 0.34 | Higher |
| Treynor ratio | 36.81 | 5.87 | Higher |
| Fixed-income measures | | | |
| Bond duration | 2.90 | 4.20 | Lower |
| Average bond quality | AA | AA | Same |
| Asset allocation (%) | | | |
| Cash | 70.00% | 7.00% | Higher |
| U.S. stock | 18.00% | 52.00% | Lower |
| Foreign stock | 5.00% | 10.00% | Lower |
| Bond | 7.00% | 27.00% | Lower |
| Other | 0.00% | 4.00% | Lower |
| Sensitivity analysis | | | |
| 3-year average return | 5.15% | 4.33% | Higher |
| Worst 1-year loss | -2.58% | -10.60% | Higher |
| Best 1-year gain | 13.82% | 25.33% | Lower |

| Does portfolio match investment profile? | Yes | No | Yes | No | |
|---|---|---|---|---|---|
| | | X | | X | |

* Scale: 5: High; 4: Above average; 3: Moderate; 2: Below Average; 1: Low

** Scale: 6: Aggressive growth; 5: Growth; 4: Moderate growth; 3: Balanced growth; 2: Conservative growth; 1: Income

*** Portfolio statistics compared to a broad-based market index

Both the debt ratio and the long-term debt coverage ratio only marginally meet industry benchmarks. This could mean that his planner should review some additional debt reduction strategies before reallocating the portfolio. However, because Tobias is solvent, meaning that he has enough assets to pay off all debt, Tobias' planner simply confirmed his comfort with the existing level of debt and continued with the reallocation recommendation.

Therefore, both quantitative measures support the notion that Tobias is willing and able to be more aggressive with his investment allocation approach. In other words, Tobias is psychologically and fiscally capable of taking on additional risk to achieve a higher rate of return to meet his financial goal. Given this information, it is likely that his planner will assign Tobias somewhere between a moderate and an above-average risk profile.

Situational factors reflecting both qualitative and quantitative information obtained by Tobias' planner provide a framework for analyzing the current portfolio. Current portfolio statistics are shown in the column titled "Current Statistics." Because Tobias's risk profile is moderate, the selected benchmark is a moderate-growth portfolio. Statistics for the benchmark portfolio are shown in the column titled "Benchmark Statistics."

After entering the data, a planner would first notice that the beta, alpha, mean returns, and Sharpe and Treynor indices of Tobias' original portfolio exceed the benchmark. This is reasonable, because the risk, as measured by beta, is lower, resulting in higher risk-adjusted returns. On the surface, it appears that the current portfolio is working quite well for Tobias. This is a case, however, where modern portfolio statistics can lead to a biased conclusion regarding the match between Tobias's investment profile and the appropriateness of the portfolio.

**Figure 10.3** Tobias' Current Allocation

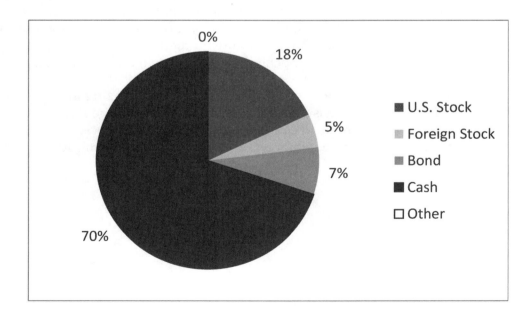

Looking further, Tobias' financial planner would quickly notice that Tobias' current asset allocation (shown in Figure 10.3) does not match the selected benchmark allocation shown in Figure 10.4, meaning that the client has not maximized his investment allocation. In this case, Tobias would probably miss out on future market returns and have almost no chance of beating inflation with a 70% cash position. Neither does the current portfolio match the stated objective of capital appreciation. The current allocation would be more appropriate for a client with a current income or capital preservation goal.

**Figure 10.4** Tobias' Benchmark Allocation

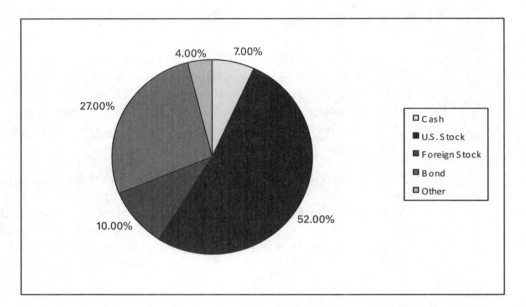

Armed with the knowledge of Tobias' risk profile and his current portfolio allocation, the planner's recommendation should be that the portfolio needs to be reallocated as shown in Figure 10.5. However, one objection the planner might have to overcome is that the current portfolio has recently outperformed the market. Tobias may not fully understand why this happened or why it is unlikely to continue.

The question that needs to be addressed when analyzing this portfolio is whether the conditions will persist into the future. According to the information provided by the client to generate the investment risk profile, the answer is no. Both Tobias and his planner expect the equity market situation to continue improving.

It is this belief, which is a very qualitative yet important situational factor, that experienced financial planners would most often use as the basis of their portfolio recommendation. An improving economic situation, given the client's time horizon, risk tolerance, positive attitudes, and risk capacity, suggests that holding 70% of the portfolio in cash will lead to future underperformance. Tobias' investment risk profile exceeds the portfolio's actual risk level, so unless the client and planner change their economic outlook, this portfolio should be assessed as inappropriate for the goal and reallocated. Stated another way, the client's investment profile indicates that he should take more risk to earn higher potential future returns.

**Figure 10.5** Tobias' Recommended Allocation

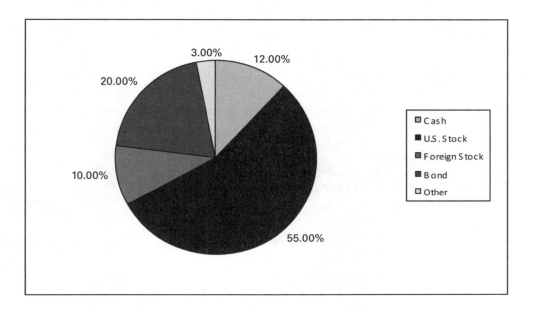

It is important that the key questions of implementation be addressed in relation to reallocating portfolio assets. Making a reallocation recommendation easy to understand and implement is important. If a client's questions and objections are not addressed, there is the possibility that action will not be taken. The Recommendation Form can be used to summarize the investment planning recommendation. It summarizes and codifies the reallocation recommendation and provides a cost estimate associated with implementation, a benefit statement, and specific implementation procedures relating to who should reallocate the assets, when the action should be taken, and how implementation should take place.

**Exhibit 10.7** Tobias' Planning Recommendation Form

## Planning Recommendation Form

| | |
|---|---|
| **Financial Planning Content Area** | Investment planning |
| **Client Goal** | Reallocate portfolio to obtain higher long-term returns. |

| **Recommendation No.** | 1 | **Priority (1–6) lowest to highest:** | | 6 |
|---|---|---|---|---|
| **Projected/Target Value ($)** | | 8.50% to 10.25% RoR | | |

### Product Profile

| | | | | |
|---|---|---|---|---|
| Type | Qualified retirement account | | | |
| Duration | 15+ years | | | |
| Provider | Lindsey, Graham & Associates Planning, LLC, using various investment companies as itemized below. | | | |
| Funding Cost per Period ($) | Estimated transaction costs $1,200 (includes transfer fees, account maintenance fees, and contingent deferred sales charges) | | | |
| Maintenance Cost per Period ($) | $0 | | | |
| Current Income Tax Status | Tax-qualified | X | Taxable | |
| Projected Rate of Return | 8.50% to 10.25% | | | |
| Major Policy Provisions | See Implementation Procedure | | | |

### Procedural Factors

| | | | | |
|---|---|---|---|---|
| Implementation by Whom | Planner | X | Client | |
| Implementation Date or Time Frame | Immediately | | | |
| Implementation Procedure | Reallocation of funds can be implemented either by client or planner; if planner implements, client will need to provide written acceptance of strategy. The specific reallocation procedure is as follows:<br>1. Reduce cash position by 58%.<br>2. Allocate 37% of cash into the following equity funds:<br>   a. (12%) Germain and Lukajic Stock Fund<br>   b. (12%) DuPaul, Batteman, and Bull Growth Fund<br>   c. (13%) Coombs, Flaman, and Hanchuck Small-cap Fund<br>3. Sell current bond fund and reallocate an additional 6% of cash into the Jobin and Dora Bond Fund.<br>4. Use 5% of cash to increase holdings in the foreign stock fund from 5% to 10% of assets.<br>Reallocate 5% of assets from cash to the Arbinger REIT Fund, a specialized real estate trust. | | | |

### Ownership Factors

| | | | | |
|---|---|---|---|---|
| Owner(s) | Tobias Fleischer | | | |
| Form of Ownership | Sole owner | | | |
| Insured(s) | NA | | | |
| Custodial Account | Yes | | No | X |
| Custodian | | | | |
| In Trust For (ITF) | Yes | | No | X |
| Transfer On Death (TOD) | Yes | | No | X |
| Beneficiary(ies) | Agathe Fleischer (Wife) | | | |
| Contingent Beneficiary(ies) | Adam Fleischer (Son) via testamentary trust w/trustee named in will | | | |

### Proposed Benefit

1. Should result in an increase total risk-adjusted rate of return over the next 10 years.
2. Should reduce income earned within the account by an estimated $300 per year.
3. Although the income earned is not taxable, the change in allocation is more in keeping with capital appreciation objective.

The outcomes briefly noted in Exhibit 10.7 indicate that implementation of this recommendation could have effects on other parts of the financial plan—in this case, estate planning for Tobias's minor child. Documenting these effects when the actual plan is being written for later reference is an important step in the recommendation and implementation phase of the investment planning process.

Investment planning recommendations, more than nearly any other recommendations a planner can make, have the potential to significantly impact other parts of the financial plan. This is particularly true because the achievement of financial goals is also closely tied to the performance of a client's portfolio. So, depending on the situation, whether it is retirement planning, education funding, or special needs planning, the impact of a recommendation to reallocate assets can be significant.

Finally, because the account that is being reallocated is a tax-qualified retirement account, proper ownership and beneficiary titling is paramount for successful implementation.

# Learning Outcomes

1.  The development of an investment plan is based on a combination of interior and exterior factors, but foremost is the client's goal. The type of investment plan developed must match the goal and time frame identified with the client, along with the client's risk tolerance and risk capacity. The investment plan might be the most revisited portion of the financial plan because it is subject to so many client-centric events and economic events and the soundness of investment choices is one of the primary determinants of success or failure in realizing future goals.

2.  The steps involved in conducting an investment planning analysis start with a complete understanding of the client and end with the construction of the portfolio. First a planner must understand the five situational factors that affect a client's investment planning. These include risk tolerance, expectations about future market conditions, knowledge and experience, time horizon, and the capacity to handle risk. The first three factors are inferred, meaning that they are more reasoned than measured; whereas the other two factors are more quantitative in nature because they can be more objectively measured. Next the planner must determine the rate of return desired or required to meet the client's objectives. Unfortunately, sometimes the client's risk profile does not match the required portfolio. Once the desired rate is determined, appropriate asset classes are selected and the planner can finally determine how to combine these asset classes into a single cohesive portfolio or, in some cases, multiple portfolios.

3.  When allocating a client's assets, planners must consider not only the asset classes available, but also interior and exterior asset allocation factors. Interior asset allocation factors, which involve the goal of the client's portfolio and how aggressively the assets in the portfolio can be allocated within the risk comfort level of the client, are client-centric in nature. Assets should not be allocated in the same way for a risk-averse client seeking some appreciation while attempting to preserve capital as for a client seeking maximum appreciation while minimizing potential tax liability. Investments are also allocated or reallocated based on exterior factors pertaining to the current and prospective economic landscape. Although

exterior factors can be more easily quantified, interpreting them and their effects on a portfolio can be more difficult, because they encompass asset classes' returns, domestic interest rates, stock and bond yields, monetary and fiscal policies, and inflation.

4.   Strategic asset allocation is the process of setting target allocations for each class of assets based on the long-term objective of the portfolio. The portfolio is then periodically rebalanced back to original asset allocation percentages. The strategic allocation of a portfolio is the most important determinant of total return. Tactical asset allocation, on the other hand, allows for more active management by setting a range of percentages in each asset class rather than a fixed target. This range gives the planner the ability to be more opportunistic about changing the allocations when longer-term economic conditions might favor one asset class over another. Two examples of tactical allocation strategies are sector rotation and core and satellite.

5.   Once the five client factors of investment planning are established, the planner can start combining them with the client's investment attitudes (e.g., social or religious preferences) and expectations about the future to build the client's investment profile. The process of documenting a client's investment preferences and evaluating the alternatives is the basis of constructing an investment policy statement. This IPS guides the investment and management of a client's investments and is included in a client's investment plan as a way (1) to reduce financial planner liability through appropriate planning disclosure and (2) as a reminder to the client and planner of the importance of adhering to established guidelines.

6.   Indices track the performance of a select group of financial assets, but they are also useful as standards of measurement for a client's portfolio. For a meaningful comparison, it is important to select a benchmark that closely matches both the type of security and the corresponding level of risk. The simplest method for determining the best benchmark is to find one that seems to  generally fit the asset or asset class being evaluated, e.g.,  large-cap fund versus large-cap benchmark. It is also recommended that a linear regression of returns be done to validate the similarity of the benchmark. With some additional work this analysis can also be performed for entire portfolios. Once an appropriate benchmark is identified, the next step in evaluating a portfolio is to calculate one or more performance statistics. There are two primary classes of performance measures: absolute and ratio. Although different measures categorize risk differently, the precision of measurement is important to planners when trying to make decisions about the effectiveness of portfolio management or asset selection.

7.   Clients tend to seek the help of a financial planner for investment planning guidance to increase the capital appreciation potential of their investments, to increase the amount of current income earned from their investments, or to reduce the amount of taxes paid on their investments. However, clients are often unaware of what might be necessary to increase their real, risk-adjusted, or after-tax returns. Therefore, nothing is more important than a planner's ability to match one or more investment alternatives to a client's objective. However, selecting only a few from the vast array of choices takes a great deal of time and skill. And although the tendency when dealing with investments is to focus on specific products, the procedure involved in investment planning can be equally important. Planners and clients often find that the simplest strategy makes for the best recommendation.

8.   In many ways, the development and presentation of investment planning recommendations is the most important part of financial planning. Although there may be a temptation to develop complex and intricate recommendations, this is not always appropriate or even

necessary. In fact, lack of implementation by the client is the leading cause of plan failure. However, some of the best planning strategies accomplish more than one objective, such as hedging inflation while providing current income, or maximizing long-term appreciation while minimizing tax consequence. As such, it is imperative that recommendations be easily understood, conceptually valid, and cost effective. Of paramount importance when developing or choosing strategies is to remember that the client's goals should dominate the process. Planners should always solicit the client's collaboration in decision making and implementation. For the majority of investment planning recommendations, a client should be able to quickly understand the reasoning behind them and the potential outcomes associated with their implementation. This means that answers to the core issues of who, what, when, where, why, how, and how much should be clear, concise, and understandable.

## Chapter Resources

Benninga, S. *Financial Modeling*, 3rd Ed. Boston: MIT Press, 2008.

Boone, N., and L. Lubitz. *Creating an Investment Policy Statement.* Denver, CO: FPA Press, 2004.

Investment Risk Tolerance Quiz (http://njaes.rutgers.edu/money/riskquiz/).

FinaMetrica Risk Profiling System (http://www.riskprofiling.com/home).

FINRA Mutual Fund Expense Analyzer (http://apps.finra.org/fundanalyzer/1/fa.aspx).

Leimberg, S., et al. *The Tools and Techniques of Investment Planning,* 2nd Ed. Cincinnati, OH: National Underwriter Company, 2006.

Murray, Nick. *Behavioral Investment Counseling*. Mattituck, NY: The Nick Murray Company, Inc., 2008.

Shefrin, H., & Mario Belotti. "Behavioral Finance: Biases, Mean-Variance Returns, and Risk Premiums." *CFA Institute Conference Proceedings Quarterly*. June (2007): 4–11. Available at http://www.ifa.com/pdf/behavioralfinancecp.v24.n2.pdf.

Siegel, L.B. *Benchmarks and Investment Management*. Charlottesville, VA: CFA Institute, 2003.

Susan Bradley's Sudden Money Institute (www.suddenmoney.com).

The *Financial Factilitator* and all fillable forms needed to complete text activities can be found on the student website at: http://pro.nuco.com/booksupplements/NUCollege-CaseBook2e.

# Quantitative/Analytical Mini-Case Problems

1. Use the information provided in the table below to calculate the weighted-average before-and-after tax rate of return of this portfolio.

| Asset | Allocation | Amount | Rate of Return Before Tax | Rate of Return After Tax |
|---|---|---|---|---|
| Fund A | Large growth | $ 75,000.00 | 9.00% | 6.75% |
| Fund B | Mid-value | $100,000.00 | 8.00% | 6.00% |
| Fund C | Money market | $ 94,000.00 | 2.00% | 1.50% |
| Fund D | Small growth | $ 14,000.00 | 12.00% | 9.00% |
| Fund E | Small value | $ 35,000.00 | 4.00% | 3.00% |
| Fund F | High-quality bond | $ 45,000.00 | 3.00% | 2.25% |
| Fund G | Low-quality bond | $112,000.00 | 5.00% | 3.75% |

2. Use the information shown in the following table to calculate the statistics below. (Refer to Appendix 10A, if necessary, for a refresher on the formulas and purpose of each.)

| Year | Portfolio Return | Market Return |
|---|---|---|
| 1 | 12.00% | 9.00% |
| 2 | 9.00% | 8.00% |
| 3 | 22.00% | 19.00% |
| 4 | -4.00% | -1.00% |
| 5 | 2.00% | 5.00% |
| 6 | 25.00% | 19.00% |
| 7 | 15.00% | 15.00% |
| 8 | -6.00% | -4.00% |
| 9 | 11.00% | 9.00% |

   a. Geometric average of portfolio and market

   b. Arithmetic average of portfolio and market

   c. Standard deviation of portfolio and market

3. Use the Single Asset Statistic sheet within the Portfolio Analysis Excel file found on the Web site to calculate the following statistics using the data provided.

   a. Beta of each asset using the appropriate index provided

   b. CAPM expected return of each asset using the appropriate index provided and a risk-free rate of 0.25%

    c.   Jensen's alpha of each asset

    d.   Sharpe ratio of each asset

    e.   Modigliani measure of each asset using the appropriate index provided

    f.   Treynor index of each asset

4.   Use the Portfolio Statistics sheet within the Portfolio Analysis Excel file found on the Web site to calculate the following statistics for both the rebalanced and non-rebalanced portfolios and answer the questions. (To complete this question you will need to enter the following weights into the Excel spreadsheet in the highlighted cells: U.S. Large Cap = 20%, U.S. Mid-cap = 10%, U.S. Small Cap = 10%, U.S. Corporate Bond = 15%, U.S. Gov't Bond = 15%, U.S. Balanced = 5%, Global Equity = 5%, Non-U.S. Equity 15%, Emerging Mkt. Equity = 5%.)

    a.   Beta, expected return of each asset, using CAPM, and Jensen's alpha using the appropriate custom benchmark portfolio

    b.   What do you notice about the difference in expected return and alpha between the two portfolios?

    c.   Sharpe ratio and Treynor index

    d.   Modigliani measure using the appropriate custom benchmark portfolio

    e.   What do you notice about the difference in the two ratios and the Modigliani measure between the two portfolios?

# Comprehensive Bedo Case—Analysis Questions

Almost all of the Bedos' goals have an investment component. For example, saving for retirement, college, and a home addition all require the analysis of investment planning factors. Each investment-funded goal will require documentation of the Bedos' time horizon, risk tolerance, and investment attitudes for the goal—which could include investment restrictions imposed by the clients, expectations about the future, and risk capacity.

Furthermore, these facts could differ for each goal. For instance, the maximum amount of risk that the Bedos are comfortable taking for retirement might be different from the level of risk they are prepared to take with Becky's education funding. Thus, it is important to review the client information as well as relevant assumptions, tax rates, and the Bedos' global asset allocation structure.

*Note*: Sufficient information is not yet available to quantify the education planning need or the retirement planning needs for the Bedos; thus, all references to these goal as they relate to investment planning must be addressed in generalities, with the integration of the investment strategies for the education planning and retirement planning more fully resolved in Chapters 11 and 12, respectively.

1.  Develop a list of investment-funded planning goals (e.g., emergency fund situation, retirement investment plan, education funding goal, and the art gallery and home improvement goals) for the Bedos. When conceptualizing these goals, consider the following:

    a.  Is each goal developed in agreement with any or all goals and objectives that the clients have identified regarding investment planning?

    b.  What situational factors might influence their investment-funded goals (e.g., emergency fund situation, retirement investment plan, education funding goal, and the art gallery and home improvement goals)? Are these factors explicit, implied, or assumed? Is additional information required from the Bedos?

    c.  What is the desired outcome for the clients for each of these goals?

2.  Make a list of life events that could impact these goals for Tyler and Mia and that should be reviewed at future client meetings. Some events could affect all of the goals, and others only certain goals.

3.  Develop a list of globally accepted, client-specific, or planner-generated planning assumptions that will structure the situational analysis and planning for each goal.

4.  Summarize the Bedos' time horizon, risk tolerance, investment attitudes, economic expectations, and risk capacity for each of their investment-funded goals (e.g., emergency fund situation, retirement investment plan, education funding goal, and the art gallery and home improvement goals).

5.  Summarize your observations about Tyler's and Mia's current planning efforts and the identified planning need(s) for each of the investment-funded goals (e.g., emergency fund situation, retirement investment plan, education funding goal, and the art gallery and home improvement goals). Complete an Investment Profile and Portfolio Summary Form for each goal to determine whether changes are needed. Incorporate text, bullets, and graphics in your explanation. For example, what information might be shown graphically, and specifically what kind of graphs might most effectively convey this analysis to the Bedos?

6.  Based on the goals originally identified and the completed analysis, what product or procedural strategies might be most useful to satisfy the Bedos' planning need(s) for each of the investment-funded goals (e.g., emergency fund situation, retirement investment plan, education funding goal, and the art gallery and home improvement goals)? Be sure to consider strategies matched to the planning needs identified. When reviewing strategies, be careful to consider the approximate cost of implementation as well as the most likely outcome(s) associated with each strategy.

7.  In response to each identified planning need for the investment-funded goals (e.g., emergency fund situation, retirement investment plan, education funding goal, and the art gallery and home improvement goals), write at least one primary and, if applicable, one alternative recommendation from the strategies selected. Include specific, defensible answers to the who, what, when, where, why, how, and how much implementation questions for each recommendation.

    a.  It is suggested that each recommendation be summarized in a Recommendation Form.

b.  Assign a priority to each recommendation based on the likelihood of meeting client goals and desired outcomes. This priority will be important when recommendations from other core planning content areas are considered relative to the available discretionary funds for subsidizing all recommendations.

c.  Comment briefly on the outcomes associated with each recommendation.

8.  Depending on the organization of the plan, a comprehensive plan might or might not include a discrete section on investment planning. It could be included in the plan to address all investment-funded goals, or investment planning information could be incorporated in the section corresponding to individual goals (e.g., education planning or retirement planning). Given these options, choose one approach and complete the following for the Bedos' financial plan:

a.  Outline the content to be included in this section of the plan. Given the segments written above and/or elsewhere in other chapters related specifically to investment-funded goals, which segments are missing?

b.  If applicable, write the introduction to this section of the plan (no more than one to two paragraphs).

c.  Define, explain, or interpret at least five terms related to investment planning. For each, write a definition or explanation that could appear in a section of the plan or in the plan glossary.

9.  Prepare a 10–15-minute presentation for the Bedos of your observations and/or recommendation(s) for meeting their investment planning goals. Be sure to include visual aids, Excel handouts, and other materials that will make the recommendations more meaningful for the clients.

## Notes

1.  C. Sahm, *How Much Does Risk Tolerance Change?* Finance and Economics Discussion Series. Divisions of Research & Statistics and Monetary Affairs, Federal Reserve Board, Washington, D.C. 2007.

2.  K. Sachsea, H. Jungermanna, and Belting, "Investment Risk – The Perspective of Individual Investors," *Journal of Economic Psychology* 33 (2012): 437–447.

3.  Susan Bradley. *Sudden Money: Managing a Financial Windfall.* (New York: Wiley, 2000).

4.  Money, Meaning and Choices Institute. *Sudden Wealth.* Available at http://www.mmcinstitute.com/about-2/sudden-wealth-syndrome/.

5.  National Endowment for Financial Education (NEFE). *Financial Psychology and Life-changing Events: Financial Windfall.* (Denver, CO: NEFE Press, 2004).

6.  Lazetta Rainey Braxton, "Minorities Can Enrich Financial Services Industry," *Investment News*, August 15, 2010. Available at http://www.investmentnews.com/apps/pbcs.dll/article?AID=/20100815/REG/308159998&cslet=Un hOY2lLVDlKL09aK2pjMXNkbTdUZmhxbytmcXVHMD0=.

7.  Ariel Investments, *The Ariel Investments 2010 Black Investors Survey: Saving and Investing Among Higher Income African-American and White Americans.* Available at http://www.arielinvestments.com/images/stories/landing_pages/Black_Investor/2010bisreportslides.pdf.

8.  Ariel Investments, *2010 Black Investors Survey*, 7.

9.  Prudential Financial Inc., "The African American Financial Experience," *2011 Prudential Research Study.* Available at http://www.prudential.com/media/managed/aa/AAStudy.pdf.

10. Ariel Investments, *The Ariel Mutual Funds/Charles Schwab & Co., Inc. Black Investor Survey: Saving and Investing Among Higher Income African-American and White Americans*, June 2001. Available at http://www.arielinvestments.com/landmark-surveys/.

11. Ariel Investments *Ariel-Schwab Black Investor Survey 2007*, 11. Available at ttps://www.arielinvestments.com/landmark-surveys/.

12. Ariel Investments, *The Ariel/Hewitt Study: 401(k) Plans in Living Color: A Study of 401(k) Savings Racial Disparities Across Racial Groups*, 2009, 7. Available at https://www.arielinvestments.com/images/stories/PDF/arielhewittstudy_finalweb_7.3.pdf.

13. Sherman D. Hanna, Cong Wang, and Yoonkyung Yuh, "Racial/Ethnic Differences in High Return Investment Ownership: A Decomposition Analysis," *Journal of Financial Counseling & Planning* 21, no. 2 (2010): 45–59. Available at http://6aa7f5c4a9901a3e1a1682793cd11f5a6b732d29.gripelements.com/pdf/vol_21_issue_2_hanna_wang_yuh.pdf.

14. *Lisa Shidler, "Blacks, Hispanics Lag In Retirement Savings,"* Investment News, July 19, 2009. Available at http://www.investmentnews.com/apps/pbcs.dll/article?AID=/20090719/REG/307199981&cslet=UnhOY2lhMzlLUE9WK2pjMXNkbTdUZmRxcitmcXVXUT0=.

# Modern Portfolio (Mean-variance) Review

## WHAT CREATES "RETURN"

For an investment market to exist there must be people or institutions with more money than they need, and others who need more money than they have. The interests of these two groups are at odds. Those who need money want access to it at the lowest possible cost. Those who have money want the greatest possible compensation— in fact; they demand two types of compensation for the use of their money. First, they want to be compensated for delaying the opportunity to spend the money. This minimum compensation that clients require for delaying consumption when they are unwilling to accept any other risk is called the **risk-free rate** of return.

The second compensation is for accepting risk, or the **risk premium**. Multiple risk premiums can be assigned to an investment. Equity investments typically are assigned risk premiums associated with business risk and market risk. Bonds, on the other hand, receive a risk premium for default risk and interest rate risk. International investments might have premiums for exchange rate risk, liquidity risk, or political risk. This is not to say that these risks and risk premiums are exclusive to any single investment class; these examples represent typical assignments. A general understanding of why investment returns are not static over time is crucial for financial planners because it affects portfolio construction and management.

## WHAT CAUSES "VARIANCE" OF RETURNS

**Default risk**, or credit risk, is the risk that investors might not be paid what they are owed contractually. Because U.S. Treasury issues are backed by the full faith and credit of the U.S. government, these issues are said to be default-risk free. However other investments, such as money market mutual funds or bank accounts, are also virtually default-risk free and therefore offer similar rates of return.

The T-bill rate is often quoted as the risk-free rate, except even the risk-free rate of return is not totally free of risk. The T-bill rate is quoted as a nominal rate of return, and thus its return is affected by inflation. However, because inflation affects all nominally priced investments, freedom from default risk earns the T-bill the "risk-free" designation as a shortcut term. A premium on the risk-free rate is needed for clients to be willing to accept any additional risk. The risk premium depends on the type, severity, and probability of the risk, as well as the time horizon of the investment.

When a client is considering investment in other corporate or municipal issues, either equity or debt, it is always prudent to consider the default or credit risk of the entity, but this is difficult to quantify. Therefore, it is simpler to review credit rating agencies' opinion of default risk using Table 10A.1.

**Table 10A.1** Bond Rating Agencies and Descriptions

### Investment-grade Bonds

| Moody's | S&P | Fitch | Rating Description |
|---------|-----|-------|--------------------|
| Aaa | AAA | AAA | Highest investment bond rating |
| Aa | AA | AA | Very high investment grade rating |
| A | A | A | Medium investment grade rating |
| Baa | BBB | BBB | Lower investment grade rating |

### Speculative-grade Bonds—High Yield

| Moody's | S&P | Fitch | Rating Description |
|---------|-----|-------|--------------------|
| Ba | BB | BB | Highest grade junk bond |
| B | B | B | Speculative grade junk bond |
| Caa | CCC | CCC | Low grade junk bond |
| Ca | CC | CC | Default grade junk bond |
| C | C | C | Issue that pays no interest |
| --- | D | D | Issue in default |

A lesser-known risk that became extremely important in the 2008 financial crisis is **liquidity risk**. This is the risk that an investor will not be able to convert an asset into cash in a timely manner or without a loss of value. For example, in the fall of 2008 many investors could not redeem their money from money market mutual funds in a timely manner because the investments underlying the portfolio had become illiquid, meaning that the mutual fund could not sell the asset for cash to process the shareholder's request. Although it is now known that the liquidity crisis was temporary, it created enough panic that investors are still nervous about money market mutual funds four years later.

Possibly the most costly risk faced by investors and noninvestors alike is **inflation risk**. Consumers can spend either now or later. But to spend later in an inflationary environment means that a consumer will have to spend more money, in nominal terms, to purchase the same amount of goods and services. Therefore, the purchasing power of the money declines over time. It is worth noting that the majority of individuals who keep their money in savings accounts generally do not receive adequate compensation for the inflation risk they take on. If, for instance, inflation averages 4% and an account earns only 1% in interest, the real purchasing power of the savings declines by approximately 3% annually— before taxes are incorporated into the calculation. Table 10A.2 reports inflation as measured by the Consumer Price Index (CPI).

**Table 10A.2** U.S. Annual Inflation Rates (1992–2011)

| Year | Inflation Rate | Year | Inflation Rate |
|------|----------------|------|----------------|
| 1992 | 2.9% | 2002 | 2.4% |
| 1993 | 2.7% | 2003 | 1.9% |
| 1994 | 2.7% | 2004 | 3.3% |
| 1995 | 2.5% | 2005 | 3.4% |
| 1996 | 3.3% | 2006 | 2.5% |
| 1997 | 1.7% | 2007 | 4.1% |
| 1998 | 1.6% | 2008 | 0.1% |
| 1999 | 2.7% | 2009 | 2.7% |
| 2000 | 3.4% | 2010 | 1.5% |
| 2001 | 1.6% | 2011 | 3.0% |

*Source*: U.S. Bureau of Labor Statistics, *Consumer Price Index History Table*. Available at http://www.bls.gov/cpi/#tables.

Notice that inflation, averaging approximately 2.5%, has remained relatively benign. Yet, even at recent inflation rates, it would take about $165 in 2012 to purchase what could have been bought for $100 in 1992. For example, if inflation edged up to 5% on average, clients would lose half of their purchasing power about every 14 years. To counteract this erosion of purchasing power, minimally clients expect compensation that offsets this reduction. Therefore, a financial planner should generally attempt to develop portfolios that can at least match the rate of inflation.

Risk is at the root of most clients' concerns when they make investments. Beyond individual sources of risk, investors face two primary forms of risk: systematic and unsystematic.

**Systematic risk,** also called *market risk,* is embedded in the system of financial markets. This type of risk generally cannot be eliminated through diversification. Assume, for example, that the markets experience a significant one-day drop in value, such as occurred in 1929 and 1987. Regardless of the amount of diversification within a portfolio, anyone invested in the stock market lost money on unhedged investments on those days.

Examples of systematic risks that investors face include **political risk** (regulatory or tax code) and **exchange rate risk**. Political changes can have a widespread impact on the markets. For U.S. investors, these can range from changes in the tax code to increased regulation of business. Political risks can be even more exaggerated if the portfolio contains overseas investments, particularly in emerging markets. Generally, the political systems in such countries are less developed and new leadership can signal dramatic change. U.S. investors who invest overseas must also account for changes in exchange rates. In general, a declining dollar makes U.S. exports and foreign investments more attractive. When the dollar strengthens against foreign currencies,

U.S. investors can actually lose money on foreign investments, even if the investments make money nominally.

Another important systematic risk is the overall level of compensation investors require for taking risk. During the Internet bubble of the late 1990s, investors were willing to accept little compensation for additional levels of risk. At any time, investors as a whole might demand more compensation for the risks they take, which causes the value of securities either to stop increasing (stagnate) or to start decreasing (deflate). This was the case immediately following September 11, 2001.

Unsystematic risk or *firm risk*, on the other hand, is a type of risk that can be managed and reduced through diversification. **Diversification** involves blending assets that are not highly correlated within a portfolio to reduce risk exposure. Business failure is perhaps the greatest unsystematic risk. Businesses can fail because of poor management (**business risk)** or for taking on too much debt (**financial risk)**.

# MODERN PORTFOLIO STATISTICS—MEAN-VARIANCE ANALYSIS

## Asset Mean "Average"

As discussed in Chapter 2, the most basic investment statistic is the average return, known as the arithmetic average, or *mean*. It is sometimes designated by the Greek letter $\mu$. Typically this is the most easily understood investment statistic, the one most sought after by investors, and the most quoted by investment providers. This statistic is also the basis of all other modern-portfolio-theory-related statistics such as variance, standard deviation, the coefficient of variation, and the Sharpe ratio.

$$\text{Average Return (AR)} = \frac{r_1 + r_2 + r_3 + ... + r_n}{n}$$

Where:

r = return for period

n = number of periods

However, unless a client is investing in a fixed-return asset, such as a bank CD, then most periodic returns vary over time; so an average return tells only half of the story. Basically, this means that although the returns should average out in the end, returns during any given period likely will be either above or below the expected long-term average. When returns vary around an average, most predictions of future returns assume that the average will prevail.

## Asset Variance

One of the primary measures of risk deals with the fluctuation of individual returns around an average return. The greater the dispersion of returns is, the higher the return volatility; hence, the higher the risk. The difference between the average return and the range of possible outcomes is known as **variance**, denoted by $\sigma^2$. Variance is calculated by subtracting each individual outcome from the average outcome and then squaring the difference.

$$\sigma^2 = X_t - \mu$$

Where:

$\sigma^2$ = variance

$X_t$ = outcome

$\mu$ = average (mean)

Although the individual security variance statistic is informative, average variance is the more important statistic. This calculation simply involves adding variances together and then dividing the sum by one less than the number of outcomes in the sample.

$$\sigma_t^2 = \frac{(x_1 - \mu)^2 + (x_2 - \mu)^2 + (x_3 - \mu)^2 + ... + )x_4 - \mu)^2}{n - 1}$$

Where:

n  = number of observations or units

*Example.* Assets A and B have the following returns.

| Nominal Rates of Return | Asset A | Asset B |
|---|---|---|
| 2003 | -12.0% | -2.9% |
| 2004 | 4.2% | 6.5% |
| 2005 | 11.8% | 9.0% |
| 2006 | 6.1% | -3.7% |
| 2007 | 9.3% | 7.5% |
| Arithmetic mean | 3.88% | 3.28% |

By applying the preceding formula, a planner can determine that Asset A has a variance of 0.00873 and Asset B has a variance of 0.00370.

## Asset Standard Deviation

**Standard deviation,** denoted as a lower-case sigma ($\sigma$), is a risk measure related to and predicated on variance. Standard deviation is the square root of variance and is more often quoted and used in investment statistics than variance. Standard deviation can be very useful in determining the dispersion of possible—or past—outcomes in relation to an expected outcome. Total risk, which comprises systematic and unsystematic risk, is typically measured by standard deviation.

$$\sigma_i = \sqrt{\frac{(x_1 - \mu)^2 + (x_2 - \mu)^2 + (x_3 - \mu)^2 + \dots + )x_4 - \mu)^2}{n - 1}}$$

Where:

$\sigma$ = standard deviation

$n$ = number of observations or units

$r_i$ = actual return

$\mu$ = average return

Using the table of data from the variance example, it is easy to see that, because the annual outcomes are different, the standard deviation will be greater than zero. (In fact, the only time that standard deviation and variance are zero is when all outcomes over the analysis period are identical.) Using the preceding formula or applying the square root formula to the variance derived above, the standard deviations are calculated as 9.34% and 6.08% respectively for Assets A and B.

## Asset Coefficient of Variation

The **coefficient of variation** (CV) is another measure of dispersion (range), but in this case it is a relative measure based on average returns. CV is a ratio of unit of risk per unit of return. Therefore, it is easy to see that, for this ratio, smaller numbers are superior to larger ones. CV is useful to compare the risks of various investments with different expected returns. Therefore, calculating the CV for a single asset provides little insight. The equation for CV is:

$$CV = \frac{\sigma}{\mu}$$

Where:

$\sigma$ = standard deviation

$\mu$ = mean

Again, consider the same two possible investments, Asset A and Asset B. To determine which asset offers the greatest return for a given level of risk, the risk of each asset (standard deviation) must be divided by the average return of each asset (arithmetic mean).

| Nominal Rates of Return | Asset A | Asset B |
|---|---|---|
| 2003 | −12.0% | −2.9% |
| 2004 | 4.2% | 6.5% |
| 2005 | 11.8% | 9.0% |
| 2006 | 6.1% | −3.7% |
| 2007 | 9.3% | 7.5% |
| | | |
| Arithmetic mean | 3.88% | 3.28% |
| Variance | 0.87% | 0.37% |
| Standard deviation | 9.34% | 6.08% |

CV Asset A = 9.34/3.88 = 2.41

CV Asset B = 6.08/3.28 = 1.85

By comparing the two assets without an adjustment for risk, a financial planner might choose Asset A, the riskier asset, because of its higher average return. However, after calculating the CV for both assets, the planner could conclude that Asset A does not offer enough additional return for the increased level of risk.

Another use of CV involves determining the appropriate level of return for an increased level of risk. Returning to the preceding example, a financial professional sees that Asset B experiences 1.85 points of risk for each point of return. Therefore, for the planner to choose Asset A, a similar or lower ratio is needed. To determine the level of return necessary for the level of risk associated with Asset A, use the following CV formula:

$$\text{Required return of Asset A to equalize the CV} = \frac{\sigma A}{\text{CV of Asset B}}$$

$$\text{Required return to select Asset A} = \frac{9.34\%}{1.85} = 5.05\%$$

## Correlation and Covariance of Two Assets

Diversification is a method used to reduce unsystematic risk in a portfolio. However, to maximize the benefit derived from diversification, it is important for a financial planner or portfolio manager to select assets that do not react the same way to a given economic environment. Covariance and correlation are measures of the degree to which multiple assets move in tandem.

Covariance measures the linear relationship between two random variables. The formula for covariance is:

$$\sigma_{ij} = \sigma_i \, \sigma_j \, \rho_{ij}$$

Where:

$\sigma_{ij}$ = covariance of assets i,j

$\sigma$ = standard deviation

$\rho_{ij}$ = correlation of assets i,j

Notice that the preceding formula for solving covariance and the formula for solving correlation are identical. The variables have simply been rearranged to isolate the unknown. Unfortunately, if both correlation and covariance are unknown, then the equation is rendered useless. Therefore, an alternative equation must be used, one that is not predicated on the other, but on the periodic returns of each asset. The formula to solve for covariance if the correlation is unknown is:

$$\sigma_{ij} = \frac{1}{n-1} \sum_{t-1}^{n} (r_{i,t} - \mu_i)(r_{j,t} - \mu_j)$$

Where:

$\sigma_{ij}$ = covariance of assets i,j

$n$ = number of observations or units

$r_i$ = actual return at each period "t"

$\mu$ = average return

The easier to interpret of these two statistics is the **correlation coefficient,** which scales covariance based on the product of the standard deviation of two measured assets. The correlation coefficient is often denoted by the Greek letter *rho* ($\rho$).

Correlation is measured on a scale of –1 to +1, with a value of zero indicating that there is no relationship between two variables. If assets are positively correlated, it means that as one asset rises (or falls) the other asset usually does the same. If the assets are negatively correlated, then as one asset rises the other asset falls, and as one asset falls the other asset rises. If assets are positively correlated to a degree of +1, meaning that they are perfectly correlated, then not only will both assets rise at the same time, they will rise at the same rate. The inverse of this is also true if the assets are perfectly inversely correlated (-1). The formula for correlation is:

$$\rho_{ij} = \frac{\sigma_{ij}}{\sigma_i \, \sigma_j}$$

## Standard Deviation of a Two-asset Portfolio

Now that all of the statistics about Assets A and B are known, the power of investment statistics can be applied to a combination of these two assets—a portfolio. Unfortunately a financial planner cannot simply weight asset standard deviations to calculate the standard deviation of a portfolio as can be done with returns, because this ignores the covariance of the assets when used in tandem. Therefore, the following equation must be used to determine the standard deviation of a two-asset portfolio.

$$\sigma_p = \sqrt{w_i^2\sigma_i^2 + w_j^2\sigma_j^2 + 2w_iw_j\sigma_{i,j}}$$

Where:

$\sigma$ = standard deviation

$w$ = weight "allocation" of each asset

$\sigma_{ij}$ = covariance

# MODERN PORTFOLIO STATISTICS—USING PROBABILITIES

## Expected Return

So far statistics have been calculated based on historical—or known—data. But as the investment disclaimer states, "past performance does not guarantee future results." For a financial planner to plan, some assumptions about the future must be made. These assumptions become the basis of expectations.

Clients expect a certain level of return to compensate for a variety of risks. This "expected" return, denoted $E(r)$, can be mathematically calculated by adding the appropriate risk premiums to the risk-free rate of return, as follows.

$$E(r) = r_f + IP + DP + BP + \ldots$$

Where:

$E(r)$ = expected return

$r_f$ = risk-free rate

$IP$ = inflation risk premium

$DP$ = default risk premium

$BP$ = business risk premium

For simplicity, these risk premia are typically grouped together as one aggregated risk premium that accounts for both systematic and unsystematic risks. Once an expected rate of return is calculated, it is important for a financial planner to determine whether rates of return available in the marketplace are adequate for the level of risk that the client is willing to accept. Also, a financial planner must perform a sensitivity analysis to determine how likely the projected returns are.

## Expected Return (Using Probabilities)

One of a financial planner's most common tasks is to conduct a scenario analysis that considers possible outcomes under various market conditions. However, to facilitate client communication, these scenarios can be aggregated into the most likely outcome—or at least an average representation of the various scenarios.

Assigning and using probabilities is the easiest way to aggregate these outcomes. If a planner looks at three possible market conditions—boom, normal, and bust—and assigns each outcome a probability, then the planner can determine an "average" or most likely outcome.

*Example*: A planner determines that in any given year there is a 20% likelihood of above-normal returns (boom), a 65% chance of average returns (normal), and a 15% possibility of below-normal returns (bust). The planner also determines that the corresponding returns would be 21%, 9%, and –12%, respectively. With this information and using the following formula, the planner can calculate the most likely—or average—outcome to be 8.25%.

$$E(r) = (p_1 \times r_1) + (p_2 \times r_2) + (p_{n-1} \times r_{n-1}) + ... + (p_n \times r_n)$$

Where:

$E(r)$ = expected return

$p$ = probability of outcome

$r$ = return (outcome)

$n$ = number of outcomes

$$E(r) = (20\% \times 21\%) + (65\% \times 9\%) + (15\% \times -12\%) = 8.25\%$$

## Standard Deviation and Confidence Levels

If returns are normally distributed, nearly 100% of all possible outcomes fall within three standard deviations above or below the mean. Therefore, a planner can reasonably predict the minimum and maximum periodic return value for any period of time.

Risk can be quantified using measures of volatility. Standard deviation is a measure of historical returns as they are dispersed around an average. Although the standard deviation of a portfolio can change, planners usually assume that historical standard deviation is somewhat predictive of the future volatility of a portfolio. To use this measure of risk effectively, a financial planner has to understand the following confidence levels.

1.  Approximately 68% of all observations fall within one standard deviation of the mean.

2.  Approximately 95% of all observations fall within two standard deviations of the mean.

3.  Approximately 99% of all observations fall within three standard deviations of the mean.

*Example.* A portfolio returned an average of 12% and the standard deviation was 15%. Applying the three confidence levels, a planner could be 68% confident that a client's actual returns fell within a range of –3% and 27% (12% +/– 15%). A 95% confidence level would suggest that returns ranged from –18% to 42% (12% +/–30% (2 × 15%)) in any given year. A 99% confidence level suggests that returns ranged from –33% to 57% (12% +/– 45% (3 × 15%)) in any given year.

Standard deviation plays a central role in helping financial planners understand the dynamics of portfolio management. The measure of standard deviation, along with covariance and variance, makes up the core basis of modern portfolio theory.

## POSTMODERN PORTFOLIO STATISTICS

The two primary flaws of modern portfolio theory are that statistical analysis assumes that returns are normally (symmetrically) distributed around the mean, and that standard deviation is the appropriate measure of risk.  Both of these assumptions fail. First, investment returns are not normally distributed; they are closer to log-normal with slightly negative (left) skewness. This is important because the normal distribution erroneously assumes that one-half of the outcomes are below the average outcome and one-half are above. Second, investors dislike a negative surprise more than they like positive surprises.  Put another way, the risk of the undesirable outweighs the risk of the unknown, and standard deviation simply measures the likelihood of the unanticipated happening—whether the outcome is positive or negative. To overcome these shortcomings, Markowitz himself suggested that models based on semivariance (focusing on downside risk) are preferable.

### Log-normal Distributions

The log-normal probability distribution arises from a continuous distribution of returns where the logarithm of those returns is normal, rather than the returns themselves being normal. This results is a distribution curve of returns that is skewed slightly to the left or right; it has been determined that, in developed markets, skewness is to the left.  To a planner and client, this skewness means that the geometric mean (average) and the geometric median (50% level) are unequal. In other words, if a distribution is skewed to the left, then more than 50% of the outcomes are below the mean outcome.

### Asset Semivariance

Semivariance generally can be defined as one-half of the orginial variance, and if a planner is working with a normal distribution, that is correct. However, in the case of log-normal distributions, semivariance is either greater than or less than one-half, depending on the direction of skewness and which side of the distribution is being measured.

## Downside Risk (DR)

Because it was previously asserted that planners and clients dislike losses even more than they like gains, it makes sense to target the side of the distribution that fails to meet the standard rather than the side that exceeds it. In this case, the standard is the expected or mean outcome, and the side that fails is the left side where relative returns are negative (even if absolute returns can be either positive or negative). As an interesting note, the target could be defined as any minimum return deemed acceptable, for example, the internal rate of return that satisfies an investment objective. First the semivariance would be calculated by squaring only the negative deviations from the mean (all outcomes above the target would be entered as the target, thereby resulting in a squared difference of zero). Taking the square root of the sum of these squared deviations results in semideviation, also known as *downside deviation*, a measure of downside risk.

## The Sortino Ratio

The most popular method for ranking investment opportunities is by ratio. Typically the ratio is of excess return (return greater than a target) over a measure of risk (e.g., total [$\sigma$], systemic [$\beta$], negative outcome [DR]). Whereas the Sharpe ratio measures excess return over total risk, and the Treynor ratio measures excess return over systemic risk, the Sortino ratio measures excess return over only the risk of negative outcomes, or downside risk. This ratio is very useful when attempting to determine the likelihood of a particular investment or strategy not meeting the minimum acceptable return when the distribution of outcomes is non-normal, which has been previously determined. This utility arises from the fact that the minimum acceptable return target can be any number; it is not limited to a simple arithmetic or geometric mean.

# SENSITIVITY ANALYSIS: CAPITAL ASSET PRICING MODEL (CAPM)

## CAPM Expected Return

Once a financial planner knows the return on the market, the risk-free rate of return, and the beta of a portfolio, the planner can calculate an expected risk-adjusted rate of return for the portfolio. The formula used to calculate an expected rate of return is known as the **capital asset pricing model (CAPM)**. The CAPM formula is shown here:

$$R_{Exp} = R_f + \beta(R_m - R_f)$$

Where:

$R_{Exp}$ =   expected risk-adjusted rate of return

$R_f$   =   risk-free rate

$\beta$    =   beta

$R_m$   =   return on the market

The risk-free rate of return is most often indexed to Treasury bill rates, or other risk-free, short-term rates. Some financial planners use the 10-year rate to approximate the long-term horizon assumed of a stock holding or the one-year rate as a proxy for a one-year forecast horizon. The return on the market used most often for domestic portfolios is the S&P 500. However, other benchmarks can be used. For example, if a portfolio is composed of technology and Internet stocks, the NASDAQ index could be an appropriate benchmark. A portfolio comprising primarily non-U.S. stocks might be benchmarked against the Europe, Australia, and Far East (EAFE) index.

> *Example.* Assume that Chris has a well-diversified retirement portfolio. Over the past three years, the beta of the portfolio was calculated to be 0.85. The risk-free rate at the time of the analysis was 3%, and the market returned 12%. What risk-adjusted return should Chris have received during the three-year period?

> CAPM Return = $0.03 + [0.85 \times (0.12 - 0.03)] = 10.65\%$

This means that Chris should have received 10.65% on a risk-adjusted basis over the three-year period. Anything below this expected rate of return would suggest that Chris took unsystematic market risk that he was not compensated for.

## Beta

The main weakness associated with measuring volatility using standard deviation is that it is security/portfolio specific. It is difficult to compare one portfolio against another using standard deviation. Many planners instead use **beta** as a measure of volatility to solve this problem. Beta is a relative measure of risk and is most often used as a measure of systematic risk in the stock market, but it can also measure the volatility of a portfolio compared to a market index.

Beta is generally estimated by using a linear regression for each asset, based on historical asset returns and the corresponding market returns. Beta is sometimes estimated as:

$$\beta = (\sigma_p / \sigma_m) \times \rho_{p,m}$$

Where:

$\sigma_p$    =   standard deviation of the portfolio

$\sigma_m$   =   standard deviation of the market

$\rho_{p,m}$ =   correlation between portfolio and market

*Example.* Assume that the standard deviation of a portfolio of stocks is 14%, and the standard deviation of a market index, such as the S&P 500, is 12%. If the correlation between the portfolio and market is 0.90, the beta of the stock portfolio must be 1.05 [$(0.14 \div 0.12) \times 0.90$].

The beta of the market is, by definition, 1.00. Most typically, the S&P 500 is used as the market index. A portfolio with a beta of less than 1.00 is considered less volatile than the market. On the other hand, a beta of greater than 1.00 implies volatility in excess of the market. Beta is useful because the number can be used to tell a client approximately how much less or more volatile a portfolio is in comparison to the market. A beta of 1.10 indicates, for example, that a portfolio is approximately 10% more volatile than the index. Beta coefficients are theoretically continuous, meaning that scores can range from less than zero to a positive number. In practice, however, beta coefficients for diversified portfolios rarely exceed 4.0 on the high or –2.0 on the low side.

One note of caution in relation to beta is in order. Planners who use beta should do so only with well-diversified portfolios. Beta becomes very unstable and unreliable when used with single securities or non-diversified portfolios. In such cases, it is often best to use standard deviation as the measure of portfolio risk.

# Education Planning

## Learning Objectives

1. Understand the importance of education planning within the comprehensive financial planning framework.

2. Identify the client situational factors necessary to complete a comprehensive education funding analysis.

3. Demonstrate how to calculate and interpret education funding need.

4. Identify alternative sources of funding (i.e., scholarships, loans, or grants) that can mitigate the client funding required for education.

5. Evaluate a client's current education funding.

6. Identify alternative accounts used to fund education costs and demonstrate how to analyze each relative to the client situation.

7. Identify and recommend appropriate and reasonable education funding strategies matched to a client's situation.

# Key Terms

§ 529 prepaid tuition plan

§ 529 savings plan

§ 2503(c) minor's trust

Coverdell Education Savings Account (CESA)

Crummey trust

dependent student

expected family contribution (EFC)

Federal Supplemental Educational Opportunity Grant (SEOG)

Free Application for Student Aid (FASFA)

independent student

Parent Loans for Undergraduate Students (PLUS)

Pell grant

Perkins loan

Stafford loan

**Figure 11.1** Systematic Financial Planning Process for Education Planning

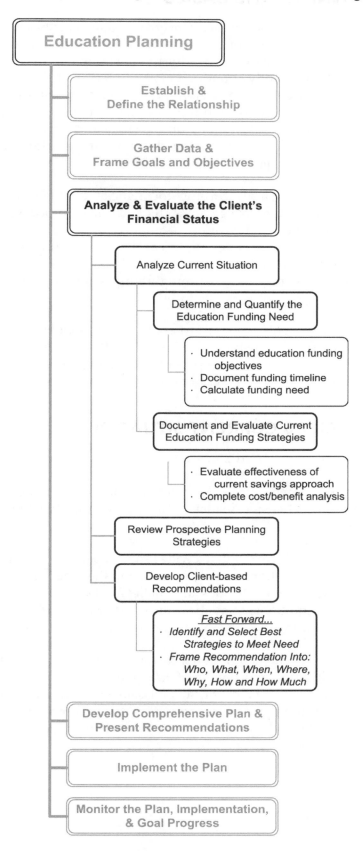

# EDUCATION PLANNING: THE BASICS

Education funding is a primary concern for many clients and planners. Often it is this issue that prompts a client to seek professional planning services. Although parents tend to be the most interested in education planning, this is not the only group that can be involved. Frequently, grandparents and relatives have a stake in helping a family plan for a child's education. A grandparent's objective may be strictly to help fund the grandchildren's education. On the other hand, the objective might include reducing the taxable estate. So, depending on the client and situation, education planning can be important to clients with young children, clients with children who are about to enter college, and clients with grandchildren.

Families are increasingly turning to financial planners to help answer questions about funding future college costs. As such, it is important for advisors to have a working knowledge of the variety of tax-advantaged and non-tax-advantaged options available for individuals and families as they plan to fund education expenses. Taxes, timing, assets, income, competing financial goals, and a host of other considerations serve to further complicate a seemingly simple question, "How do we pay for college expenses?"

This chapter presents the steps to analyze and evaluate a client's current education funding situation as illustrated in Figure 11.1. Education funding strategies commonly used by financial planners are provided as examples. The chapter concludes with an illustration of how strategies can be turned into client-specific recommendations.

# ANALYZE THE CLIENT'S CURRENT SITUATION

A number of interrelated steps are involved in the analysis of a client's education planning situation. Knowing one's client is the basis of all education funding and planning recommendations. To complete not only an education funding assessment but also a comprehensive financial plan, it is essential that a client's goals and objectives guide the process.

It is possible—and likely—that a wide range of personal client beliefs and expectations will affect the education funding analysis and the type of recommendations ultimately made. In fact, client attitudes and beliefs, especially as they are interpreted into planning assumptions, may be more important and potentially problematic in education planning than in any other core content planning area.

Getting to know client situational factors must precede actual quantitative analyses or the identification and review of strategies. Just as strategies in any planning area must be matched to the client, this customization must be considered in education planning. The timing of planning efforts, the assumptions needed (which can vary dramatically depending on the timing), and client situational factors can preclude the use of some otherwise beneficial strategies.

## Determine and Quantify the Education Planning Need

Education funding and planning strategies and recommendations must be consistent with a client's personal beliefs and values. Parents, guardians, or other family members may have different attitudes about how to pay for education either for themselves or their children; and planning for their children's education must often be balanced with planning for other goals—most often, retirement. A thorough assessment to determine and quantify education planning needs can help clients make decisions that are in closest alignment with their goals.

Two fundamental questions in education planning require answers: (1) how much will the education cost, and (2) how will these costs be paid? However, many underlying factors need to be considered. Foremost is not using the term *college* at first, but instead initiating these discussions as being about *education, higher education,* or *post-secondary education.* These terms allow clients to acknowledge without bias that their children might or might not be interested in college, but that other options such as trade, technical, or arts programs may be the more likely choice. For some clients the topic of paying for education can focus on the cost of private elementary or secondary school rather than public education. The following general questions offer one way to explore some of the situational factors surrounding education planning:

- Do you plan to save enough to pay for higher education before the child enters the educational program?

- Do you plan to pay for the educational program after or while the child is enrolled in the educational program?

- Do you expect others to pay for the child's education?

- Do you plan to use some combination of the foregoing to pay for the child's education?

Once a client has defined the direction of the education planning effort, then focused planning with the client can begin. Although discussion in this chapter is limited to planning for college education expenses, the principles are applicable to planning for other types of education expenses as well.

Thoroughly and openly discussing these questions can help the advisor and client explore the range of client situational factors that impact education planning decisions. For example, some clients may firmly refuse to fully pay for college costs, although they are financially capable of doing so. Based on their values and attitudes, they may want the child to contribute through earnings or loans. Another client might insist on funding college costs to the exclusion of other planning needs. To such clients, it is important that their child not have to struggle for an education as they perhaps did. Although these scenarios are extreme, they illustrate how personality, values, attitudes, experience, and socioeconomic descriptors converge to influence education planning.

For example, clients who plan to accumulate funding before a child enters college will likely initiate disciplined savings early and focus on the desired amount. Those who plan to pay during or after the student attends college may be doing so by necessity or choice—because of a failure to start early, competing financial goals, life events that prevented or interrupted savings, or any number of other reasons. Such clients have no reservations about incurring debt through public or private sources, or postponing other goals to contribute to educational expenses. They, as well as the clients who plan on someone else paying, may expect the child to contribute through borrowing or working (summers, vacations, during the academic year, or through cooperative working/learning programs). Other parents may view student loan debt or employment during the academic year as an unnecessary burden on their child.

In addition to the child, others who will pay could include providers of scholarships and grants awarded on the basis of aptitude (e.g., scholastic, athletic, artistic), interest (e.g., leadership, community service), or need. Other family members might be expected to contribute insignificant or significant amounts before, during, or after college through direct or indirect gifts, trusts, or estate distributions. Finally, some parents are amenable to any combination of these funding approaches that will allow their children to attend the college of their choice.

The real significance of these personal beliefs in determining a client's planning need hinges on the application of these beliefs as assumptions in the planning process. As illustrated below, conducting an education funding assessment relies on several key assumptions, which frame the funding need and recommendations. However, these assumptions can be invalidated at any time and will likely change as a child ages.

The guidance given to a client who believes strongly that a child will receive financial assistance or not attend college will differ significantly from that given to a client committed to saving. Clients who trust that their child will receive financial aid for merit or need might consider funding retirement as an alternative goal or as a contingent source of education funding.

On the other hand, a client who is uncertain about financial aid could be directed toward tax-efficient strategies that will maximize account growth without jeopardizing available aid. However, should this client's child unexpectedly receive support, placing savings into qualified education savings plans could result in a significant opportunity cost and higher taxes. For example, if the assets held in a Coverdell Education Savings Account (CESA) are not used for educational purposes, any distributions become fully taxable and subject to a 10% penalty.

In summary, the choice of which or how much of each goal to fund is complicated by the uncertainty of the assumptions used when determining education funding needs. Prior to quantifying this need, planners should first understand what priority a client places on education planning and which assumptions to include in the planning. For some clients, education funding will be the highest priority. For others, education funding will rank below other financial planning goals. Many of these issues can be revealed during the discovery process of gathering data and framing goals and objectives, but if they are not, then a discussion focused on education planning should occur.  Specific issues to address with a client include:

- Determining how much value a client or household places on receiving higher education;

- Prioritizing education planning within the comprehensive planning framework;

- Establishing the primary reason education funding is desired, including feelings of obligation or benevolence, as well as other tax considerations (e.g., preferences for tax-advantaged savings opportunities to defer or avoid income taxes, availability of income tax adjustments or credits reductions in estate taxes);

- Establishing guidelines regarding what the client or household believes is a reasonable amount to pay for a college education for one or more dependents;

- Identifying the level of control a client wants to retain in the management of assets devoted to education funding needs;

- Assessing a child's probability of receiving a scholarship or grant based on unique skills, abilities, or interests; and

- Determining a client's expectation of receiving financial aid.

Of these factors, some are wholly determined by the client, and the planner must respect them without judgment. Other fact-based considerations, such as preferences regarding taxes and control over the account, can be used by planners to directly influence the strategy recommendations.  Once a planner has a solid understanding of a client's perceived roles, attitudes, and goals surrounding education planning, the next step is to determine the cost of this goal.

Education planning involves documenting a client's specific education funding objective(s), determining gross need, and then determining whether or not the client is on track to meet the objective(s) given all other assumptions about the funding situation. The conversation can be guided by the following questions.

1.  When will the child(ren) begin college?

2.  What type of college might the child(ren) want or be encouraged to attend?

3.  How much are college costs increasing annually for this type of college?

4.  What are projected costs for the targeted college when the child(ren) begins college?

5.  How much of the projected college cost does the client intend to provide?

6.  How much of the projected cost does the client expect to be funded by scholarships, grants, and loans?

7.  Does the client currently have assets earmarked for this goal?

8.  How much is the client, or other family members, currently saving for this goal?

9.  Does education planning include funding for graduate education? (If so, the preceding questions must be reconsidered for this scenario.)

Assessing a client's educational funding needs is a relatively straightforward procedure. Table 11.1 illustrates the information needed to complete a basic education funding needs analysis, the likely source of data, and the calculations required.

**Table 11.1** Summary of Data and Calculations for a College Savings Need Analysis

| Data Needed for Analysis | Source of Data |
|---|---|
| Rate of return | Client/planner assumption |
| Years to complete college | Client/planner assumption |
| Initial additional periodic savings amount | Client/planner assumption |
| Initial periodic increase in savings amount | Client/planner assumption |
| Annual cost of college today | Planner research |
| College expense inflation rate | Planner research |
| Current age of child | Client data |
| College age of child | Client data |
| Present value of assets currently saved | Client data |
| **Calculations Required for Analysis** | **Completed by** |
| College real interest rate | Planner |
| Future value cost of college | Planner |
| Future value of assets currently saved | Planner |
| Future value of additional periodic savings | Planner |

To complete the analysis, a planner must determine the rate of return most likely to be generated in the accounts in accordance with the risk tolerance of the account owner. The choice of a single rate-of-return figure may be overly simplistic because it is possible for clients to (1) have a combination of before- and after-tax investments earmarked for education, and/or (2) have an age-based portfolio where the rate of return will decrease over time as risk is removed from the portfolio and goal realization nears. It is also likely that some investments (e.g., U.S. Savings Bonds, 529 Plans, and CESAs) will generate tax-free returns. Planners who would like to generate more precise figures should estimate returns for each possible before- and after-tax investment as well as for taxable and tax-free investments. Once individual account returns have been determined, the planner can then calculate the weighted-average return on which to base future-value calculations.

Other information needed to complete an analysis includes the assumed rate of inflation for college expenses, the child's current age, expected age when entering college, and the number of years of college to be funded. The current cost of the college of choice is needed. Finally, the amount of assets already saved and a projected annual savings amount must be determined.

The process for determining the present-value cost of education is similar to most other time value of money calculations. Although Table 1 outlines the required inputs and considerations, the following is a more detailed, step-by-step process[1] that uses the basic time value of money equations presented in Chapter 2.

1. Determine the future-value (FV) cost of education for a single year at the time the child begins college using the future-value equation below, where the present value (PV) is the current annual cost of college, the interest rate (i) is the projected annual increase (inflation rate) in college cost, and $n$ is the number of years until college begins.

$$FV = PV(1+i)^n$$

2. Find the total cost of education (all years) at the time the child begins college using the present value of a growing annuity equation below, where the payment (PMT) is the first-year cost of college as calculated in Step 1. Because college is normally paid as an annuity, the annual increase in college cost is the growth rate, the estimated rate of return becomes the interest rate, and $N$ is the number of years in college. This is also an annuity due because college tuition is typically paid at the beginning of each semester.

$$PV = \frac{PMT}{i - g}\left( 1 - \frac{(1+g)^n}{(1+i)^n} \right)(1+i)$$

3. To determine the cost of college today (as if the client were going to set aside the requisite amount immediately), calculate the present value of the total cost of education as discounted from the first year of college back to today using the present value of a lump sum equation below, where future value is the total cost in Step 2. The interest rate is the estimated rate of return, and $n$ is the number of years until college begins.

$$PV = \frac{FV}{(1+i)^n}$$

4. If money is already dedicated to this goal, subtract that amount from the total present cost of education in Step 3. The result is the lump sum amount needed immediately to meet the education goal.

*Funding Shortfall = Total Need - Amount Already Dedicated*

5. If the client is going to fund the shortfall on a periodic basis, the planner needs to determine the monthly savings required until college begins by using the present value of an annuity payment formula, where the present value is the lump sum amount in Step 4. The inputs for the formula include the expected rate of return and the anticipated growth rate of the periodic payment, if applicable. Again, $n$ is the number of years until college begins.

$$PV = \frac{PMT}{i-g}\left(1 - \frac{(1+g)^n}{(1+i)^n}\right)$$

Rearranging the formula to isolate PMT yields:

$$PMT = \frac{PV(i-g)}{\left(1 - \frac{(1+g)^n}{(1+i)^n}\right)}$$

This payment is the required periodic payment, assuming that the client wants to save enough to achieve the goal without regard to other funding sources.

To illustrate this process, consider this example to determine a one-time lump sum payment (as well as monthly savings) to fully fund a child's education. The current annual cost of the preferred college is $12,000, and to ensure adequate funding the planner and client assume annual cost increases of 5% per year both before and during college. If the child is to begin college in exactly four years, will attend for four years, no money has been saved for this goal, and the planner projects an effective annual rate of return of 8.30%,[2] what is the required savings amount if the client is going to set aside the entire amount today? What is the required monthly savings amount?

1. Determine the future-value cost of education for the first year of school.

$$FV@T_4 = \$12,000(1.05)^4 = \$14,586.08$$

| Input | Keystroke | Result |
|---|---|---|
| 0 | [PMT] | PMT = 0.00 |
| 12000 [+/-] | [PV] | PV = -12,000.00 |
| 5 | [I/Y] | I/Y = 5.00 |
| 4 | [N] | N = 4.00 |
| [CPT] | [FV] | FV = 14,586.08 |

*Note:* The PV is input as a negative because an investment is an assumed outflow, and for this step the inflation rate is treated as an interest rate to determine the "inflated" cost of the goal.

2. Find the total cost of education (for all years) needed at the time the child begins college.

$$PV@T_4 = \frac{14{,}586.08}{0.083{-}0.05}\left(1-\frac{(1.05)^4}{(1.083)^4}\right)(1.083)=\$55{,}731.37$$

| Input | Keystroke | Result |
|---|---|---|
| 14586.08 | [PMT] | PMT = 14,586.08 |
| 0 | [FV] | FV = 0.00 |
| 3.1429* | [I/Y] | I/Y = 3.1429 |
| 4 | [N] | N = 4.00 |
| [CPT] | [PV] | PV = -55,731.37 |

*The calculator needs a serial rate to handle growing annuities. See Chapter 2 for details.

3. Determine the present value of the savings required as a lump sum.

$$PV@T_0 = \frac{\$55{,}731.37}{(1.083)^4} = 40{,}512.20$$

| Input | Keystroke | Result |
|---|---|---|
| 0 | [PMT] | PMT = 0.00 |
| 55731.37 | [FV] | FV = 55,731.37 |
| 8.30 | [I/Y] | I/Y = 8.30 |
| 4 | [N] | N = 4.00 |
| [CPT] | [PV] | PV = -40,512.20 |

4. There are no current savings, so the lump sum amount needed immediately to meet the education goal equals $40,512.20 ($40,512.20 – $0).

5. Determine the monthly savings needed to meet the education goals. (Note: To solve for a monthly payment, the planner must use the equivalent monthly rate for both the rate of return and the rate of payment growth, if applicable).

$$PMT = \frac{\$40,512.20(0.00667)}{\left(1 - \dfrac{1}{1.00667^{48}}\right)} = \$989.02$$

| Input | Keystroke | Result |
|---|---|---|
| 40512.20 | [PV] | PV = 40,512.20 |
| 0.667* | [I/Y] | I/Y = 0.667 |
| 48 | [N] | N = 4.00 |
| 0 | [FV] | FV = 0 |
| [CPT] | [PMT] | PMT = -989.02 |

*°To calculate the monthly payment, either the interest rate must be in a monthly EPR format or the number of payments per year must be reset to 12.

6. Because the client did not indicate that any money was currently being contributed to the goal, monthly savings needed to meet the education goal equals $989.02.

Education funding needs can also be easily calculated using a standardized spreadsheet. Exhibit 11.1 shows the Education Cost Estimator Worksheet included in the Financial Facilitator. The process for calculating an education funding need used in the worksheet is similar to the method described above. However, rather than calculating needs for one person at a time, the spreadsheet can accommodate analyses for up to three people.

## Mitigating the Need—Financial Aid

In some situations, a client's situational factors or beliefs could require a planner to determine alternatives to cover the projected cost of education, but in other cases the estimated cost of education may be so exorbitant that additional, cost mitigation methods are necessary. An important service a planner can provide is to help a client better understand the financial aid system and how planning choices can affect the likelihood of receiving aid. It is likely that nearly all clients (or their children) will apply for financial aid at some point in the educational planning process. In fact, this should be encouraged, regardless of family income.

**Exhibit 11.1** Education Cost Estimator

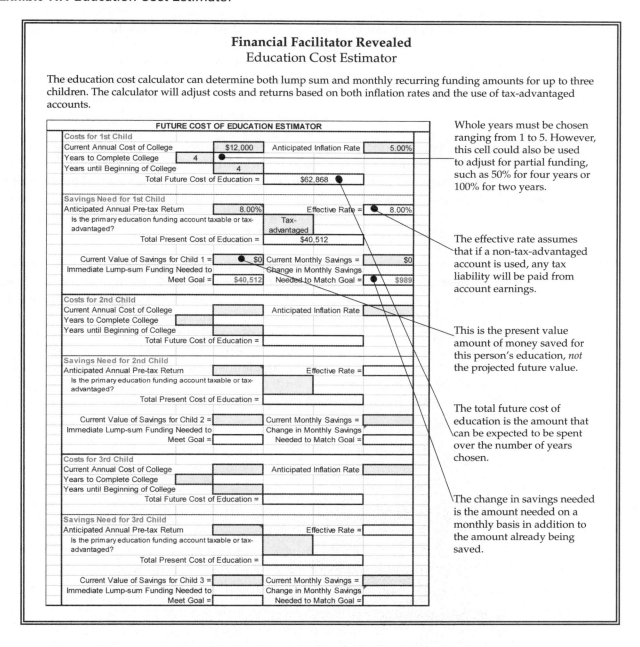

It is important that parents and children start to discuss acceptable college costs early, and financial aid planning should begin in earnest no later than the child's junior year in high school. The longer planning is postponed, the more likely the chance to exercise certain strategies to increase financial aid offers will be lost. The following discussion highlights some of the most popular forms of financial aid available today and how a client, working with a financial planner, can assess the current situation to determine financial aid availability.

The first step involves understanding the basic financial aid application process. Information related to parent and student income and assets is input into a form called the **Free Application for Federal Student Aid (FAFSA)**, which can be opened, completed, and saved at the Department of Education Web site (www.fafsa.ed.gov). Once the application has been completed online or via paper submission, a Student Aid Report is sent to the client. This report provides the client with an **expected family contribution (EFC),** an indicator of a family's ability to pay for college. Schools use it to determine a student's eligibility for various financial assistance programs.

Eligibility may vary among schools. If the cost of college is higher than the EFC, the student could be eligible for need-based student financial aid. Four financial factors influence the expected family contribution for a dependent student: (1) the parents' income; (2) the parents' assets; (3) the child's income; and (4) the child's assets. Parental income includes all sources of income, taxable and nontaxable, received by the parents in the previous year. Certain adjustments are made.

Because student status is significant in determining financial aid, it is important to understandthe difference between a dependent and an independent student. Except for some exceptional circumstances, a student is considered a **dependent student** for financial aid purposes unless one of the criteria for independent student status is met. For financial aid purposes, students are not automatically independent if parents stop claiming them as a tax exemption or refuse to provide support for college education. A common misconception is that not being claimed on a parent's income tax for two years establishes the child as an independent student. *Tax status and federal financial aid status are not the same.* To qualify as an **independent student** for financial aid purposes, children must:

- be 24 years of age or older during the year they apply for financial aid;

- be married;

- have legal dependents of their own (i.e., provide more than half of their support);

- be enrolled in graduate school;

- since turning age 13, be a ward of the court, be in foster care, or have both parents deceased;

- be a veteran of the U.S armed forces or serving on active duty;

- be (or have been) an emancipated minor or in legal guardianship;

- be homeless or at risk of being homeless as defined (criteria apply); or

- be judged "independent" by a university administrator, even though the preceding criteria do not apply but documentation for the extenuating circumstance is provided.

A questionnaire to determine dependency is available at http://www.finaid.org/calculators/dependency.phtml.

Financial aid comes in three basic forms: (1) scholarships, (2) loans, and (3) grants. Nearly all scholarships offered in the United States are university or program specific. However, a number of national scholarships are available. Scholarships can be either need or merit based. Students interested in scholarships should generally apply through their university, college, and academic unit.

Federal student loans are available through two primary programs: Stafford and Perkins. **Stafford loans** are federally sponsored loans for educational expenses. Prior to July 2010, Stafford loans were offered under the Federal Family Education Loan Program, and funds were provided by private banks and credit unions. But after passage of the Health Care and Education Reconciliation Act of 2010, the Federal Direct Loan Program handles both Stafford and Perkins loans, and the federal government provides funding directly by through participating schools.

There are two types of Stafford loans, subsidized and unsubsidized. The subsidized Stafford is a need-based loan where the federal government pays the interest for the student on the loan as long as the student is enrolled at least half-time. Unsubsidized Stafford loans are available to all students (who are eligible for federal aid) regardless of need. The unsubsidized Stafford loan accrues interest from the date of disbursement. Both loans offer payment deferral, meaning the student is not required to make interest payments while attending college at least half-time, and both offer a six-month grace period after the deferment period ends before repayment is required.

Annual loan limits for undergraduate students are determined by their grade level and dependency status. Interest rates on Stafford Loans are quite reasonable—the rates are set periodically by Congressional Act—and currently fixed at 6.8% for both subsidized and unsubsidized student loans disbursed in 2012. Loans disbursed prior to July 2006 carried a variable interest rate capped at 8.25%.[3] Some students may be eligible to receive a **Perkins loan**, a need-based loan that charges a flat 5% interest rate, allows repayment to be deferred until nine months following graduation, and features a 10-year repayment period.[4]

Parents rather than students apply for the **Parent Loan for Undergraduate Students** (PLUS). A PLUS loan can be taken out for an amount equal to the difference between the college-defined cost of attendance and all other financial aid received. For loans disbursed prior to July 2006, the interest was variable based on market conditions and capped at 9%; however, loans disbursed since that time have a 7.9% annual interest rate.[5] A primary difference between Stafford and PLUS loans is that PLUS loans require repayment beginning approximately 60 days after the loan is fully disbursed rather than being deferred until graduation.

All Direct Loan Program loans offer a variety of repayment plans, as listed below:

- Standard—up to 10 years, with a minimum monthly payment of $50.[6]

- Extended—up to 25 years, with the option of fixed or graduated payments (increasing every two years); must have more than $30,000 in qualifying debt to be eligible).[7]

- Graduated—up to 10 years (or 20 years if also qualified under the extended plan) with payment increasing every two years. Later payments are prohibited from being more than three times any other payment on the loan.[8]

- Income contingent—an applicant income-based formula capped at 20% of discretionary income with a repayment period of 25 years, after which any outstanding balance is forgiven but taxed as current income.[9] The annual payment calculation is based on adjusted gross income (AGI), plus spouse's income (if applicable), family size, and the total amount of Federal Direct Loans.

- Income based—maximum repayment period can exceed 10 years, but it is only available to those experiencing partial financial hardship; under certain circumstances, loan cancellation may be available.[10] Payment may adjust annually matched to income. Partial financial hardship is determined by a calculation where, under a standard 10-year repayment plan for all eligible loans, the total annual payment due exceeds 15% of discretionary income.[11] The Health Care and Education Reconciliation Act, passed in 2010, reduces the maximum payment percentage from 15% to 10% and also reduces the forgiveness of any remaining loan balance from 25 years to 20 years. These changes are effective for new borrowers of new loans made on or after July 1, 2014.[12]

The income-contingent and income-based repayment plans are not available to PLUS borrowers. It is important that clients be reminded that the longer the loan period, the more interest will be paid.

Finally, supplemental loans can be obtained to fund unpaid educational costs. These private education loans, also known as *alternative education loans*, are available through private lenders. Private education loans tend to cost more than education loans offered by the federal government, but they are less expensive than credit card debt. Loans are not subsidized and origination, guarantee, or repayment fees may apply. Repayment is typically deferred while a student is in school (interest payments may be paid or deferred), and the repayment periods can be as long as those of direct loans, although such features vary by lender.

Pell grants are the most widely recognized form of federal education funding support. A federal **Pell grant** is a tax-free gift to a student to offset college expenses; it is awarded based on family need as determined by the EFC. Universities and colleges can award **Federal Supplemental Educational Opportunity Grants** directly to needy students. Priority for these need-based federal grants is given to federal Pell grant recipients. Some states and universities also provide grants, but almost always such grants are based on need rather than merit.

For most of the aforementioned forms of financial aid, some component of need or expected contribution is used to determine eligibility or availability. Therefore, a common planning need for clients who are not averse to "working the system" is working with the four factors that influence perceived need on the FASFA form. Planners and clients must determine not only the amount of money that will be available for college expenses, but who will own that money. Ownership is important because the percentage of assets required to fund college costs depends on whether the assets are held in the child's, parent's, or guardian's name. Dependent students are expected to contribute 20% of assets and 50% of income to education expenses, and parents are expected to contribute only 22% – 47% of assets and 2.6% – 5.6% of income.[13] These amounts differ for independent students.

Armed with some knowledge of the financial aid system, a planner can advise parents regarding how to work more proactively with high school staff and targeted college financial aid programs to determine more accurately the likelihood of merit- or need-based financial assistance. The same strategy can be applied to identifying institutions, both public and private, that could offer the most assistance given the student's profile. Finally, this information, plus projected payment scenarios, can help parents feel more comfortable about taking on education loan debt for themselves or their children.

---

**Planning for Special Populations:**
**Random Thoughts on Planning for College Education Challenges**

Rapidly increasing college costs coupled with a weak stock market and poor employment conditions have parents and students anxious about college costs and college debt. It is important that students and planners be familiar with a variety of education planning strategies. Consider the following ideas for targeted client groups:

**Divorced Parents.** According to an article in the *Journal of Family Issues*, parental contributions to education funding decline after divorce.[14] Married parents meet 77% of tuition costs and contribute about 8% of their income to a child's college expenses, whereas divorced parents meet only 42% of their children's financial needs and contribute only about 6% of their income.[15] This is attributable to all of the usual factors, but the resultant impact on education planning can be mitigated by careful divorce planning.

State laws differ in their treatment of parental support for education; some may require payments for college expenses, although most do not. Without an agreement in the divorce decree, there may be no legal requirement for educationl expense assistance. Financial aid officers may require documentation of the noncustodial parent's legal obligation to assist with college expenses, because financial aid depends on only the custodial parent's (and, if applicable, the new spouse's) income and assets unless there is legal documentation of required support.

**Parents with Credit Issues**: Whereas unsubsidized Stafford loans do not require a credit check, collateral, or cosigner for the student, this is not true for PLUS loans, which are offered to parents. (It should be noted, however, that students who are currently in default on any federal student loans may not be eligible to receive any form of federal financial aid.) Parents who have a weak credit history because of late payments, foreclosure, or other issues related to the market downturn or loss of employment will likely be ineligible. In this case, once the parent is denied, the child will be eligible to borrow a maximum of $57,500 total debt via Stafford loans, the same amount as an independent undergraduate, instead of the maximum $31,000 available to a dependent undergraduate. Regardless of a student's status, the subsidized Stafford loan amount, if eligible, is limited to $23,000. Annual limits apply and the maximum loan amount is not guaranteed. Private student loans are another alternative, but they lack the consumer protections of federal loans, so shopping to compare terms and conditions is important.

Parents with credit issues may be well served to write or visit the financial aid office to explain how recent events such as unemployment, reduction of income, or other circumstances have negatively impacted their capacity to pay for college expenses and to request reconsideration for financial aid. It is also important to remind clients that EFC and award packages are unique to each institution, and in some cases, flexibility regarding awards rests with the financial aid adminstrator.

**Parents with High-school-age Students**: The recommendation to "start early" typically refers to saving for college, but it also applies to setting parameters for which colleges or universities are or are not affordable. In fact, this conversation should occur two to three years *before* high school graduation for several reasons. First, it avoids the emotional dilemma when a parent and child must agree that an institution, perhaps the child's top choice, is simply too expensive to consider. Second, it can motivate the child to more proactively develop a competitive application for the schools identified or to be more responsible in seeking employment or saving for college expenses. Finally, narrowing the list saves on the cost of visits to schools and application fees, although these are marginal expenses.

Deborah Fox of Fox College Funding LLC suggests that a "college match" can yield significant savings, perhaps as much as the cost of a year or more. This idea means perhaps not applying to the parents' alma mater or the big-name state university, but to select colleges where academic record, talents, extracurricular activities, or field of study place the student in the top 20% to 25% of applicants.[16] This strategy yields merit aid—another form of financial aid that is not need-based—and could be available at private or public institutions.

**Parents with Children in College.** Results of the Fidelity Investments® fifth annual national College Savings Indicator study revealed that more parents and children are making sacrifices to pay for college in 2011 compared to 2007, as shown below:[17]

- 59% report having a child work part-time, compared to 49% in 2007;

- 48% report having a child live at home and commute, compared to 38% in 2007;

- 46% report asking the child to help pay for college, compared to 36% in 2007;

- 44% report asking the child to graduate in fewer semesters, compared to 13% in 2007;

- 44% report encouraging the child to attend a public college or university, compared to 34% in 2007;

- 18% report having the nonworking spouse go back to work, as opposed to 11% in 2007; and

- 17% report a parent getting a second job, compared to 11% in 2007.

Planning for education typically focuses on principles related to timing (start early), taxes (take advantage of tax-deferred accounts), and priorities (there are more options to fund education than retirement). But the true value of the planner-client relationship may be more evident in the creativity to suggest additional funding alternatives, such a those listed above, and to help clients recognize that they or their childern are not alone in making lifestyle changes to fund education.

## Document and Evaluate Current Education Planning Strategies

The second step in analyzing a client's current situation involves documenting and evaluating all current education funding strategies and determining whether the client is on track to meet the goal. The client may already have accounts or other efforts in place that should be reviewed for consistency with goal parameters. Rather than merely determining the dollar amount of assets accumulated to meet a need, this step focuses attention on assessing the effectiveness of savings strategies and determining whether other strategies might be more appropriate. The following questions help a financial planner review education funding strategies already in place, whether they were chosen by the client or a financial professional.

- Is the client using tax-advantaged savings alternatives?

- Are the fees and expenses associated with the savings programs appropriate?

- Who owns the assets? Who controls the assets? Who is the beneficiary of the assets?

- How are assets allocated and what is the expected rate of return?

- Is the client able to contribute additional assets or income to the need?

- What alternatives, if any, could increase the likelihood of achieving the client's education objectives?

For example, a client may already have a § 529 plan in place. Although § 529 plans are a popular tax-advantaged savings vehicle for funding future education expenses, there is a wide variety of plans available. Therefore, a planner must review the details of each plan. Some § 529 plans are broker provided, whereas others can be established by an individual. Performance, fees, investment choices, flexibility of program usage, disclosure of plan information, and reputation for shareholder service vary markedly by individual states' § 529 plans and company sponsors. Fee structure in particular, which can include annual fees, administrative fees, program fees, distribution fees, and other fees associated with the mutual fund share class (e.g., institutional or A shares are commonly used) can affect performance.

---

**Education Planning Tip:**
**Changes to Expected Family Contribution for § 529 Plans and CESAs**

Beginning July 2009, § 529 plan assets and Coverdell Education Savings Account (CESA) assets owned by a dependent student, or by a student's custodian, are not included in the student asset section of the FASFA as other nonqualified assets or UGMA/UTMA accounts would be. Instead, they are now reported under parental assets. This could have a tremendous impact on the "need" calculation.

For example, if a student held $20,000 of assets in a § 529 plan account, $4,000 (20% of $20,000) would have been considered available for funding prior to the change; but after the change only $1,120 (5.6% of $20,000) of those same assets is considered available. This change increases apparent "need" by $2,880.

---

As part of a current situation analysis, advisors must review any plan choices relative to other § 529 plans available, notwithstanding state tax or monetary incentives that might affect the choice. Account balances can be moved into new plans once a year, but fees may apply. Also, some states assess taxes on rollovers into out-of-state plans to recapture previous tax breaks. This kind of analysis is needed for any products in use as well as for prospective product strategies under consideration.

Once these questions have been answered and analysis begins, it becomes easier to assess a client's need for additional education planning. The sample client education planning summary provided in Exhibit 11.2 shows how this planning need can be summarized and presented within a comprehensive financial plan.

As the financial planner explains in the sample education summary, another important consideration is the impact of various savings alternatives on financial aid eligibility or eligibility to claim a Hope Credit (temporarily altered and enhanced by the passage of the American Opportunity Tax Credit, but set to expire at the end of 2012) or a Lifetime Learning Credit, assuming the client meets income and other guidelines. Although Azalea's parents did not want to consider the possibility of scholarships in this example, they were encouraged to contemplate the potential of various funding strategies even with a funding goal still 10 years away. Planning well in advance of the beginning of college is crucial to maintain the flexibility to balance funding alternatives, ownership options, and tax implications.

**Exhibit 11.2** Sample Client Education Planning Summary

## Education Planning Summary

Your primary goal is to accumulate at least $40,000 to assist Azalea to fund her college education at a 4-year public in-state school. Azalea is 8 years old and should attend college from 2022 until 2025. You have accumulated $1,550 in a mutual fund account, and wish to fully fund this goal by August 2022. You have further stated that you are willing to take a little additional risk, initially, but are very concerned about the long-term effect of market volatility. If necessary, you are willing to take money from your Roth IRA accounts to assist her, but want a dedicated account for her education savings. This goal is very important to you.

### Assumptions

Given our assumptions of the current in-state public school cost of $16,000 per year for tuition, fees, room and board and an average annual increase of 5%, we projected that Azalea will need approximately $120,000 to fund 4 years of college. Because it is too early to consider scholarships, financial aid would be a consideration. Based on this assumption, we recommend that you maintain ownership of the assets you provide. Financial aid formulas treat assets in the parents' name more favorably than money saved in the child's name. Azalea will be expected to contribute inherited funds and savings toward her education or to seek employment. You initially planned to start saving $2,200 per year in the mutual fund account but have agreed to increase that to $3,000.

### Analysis

The graph below compares a 529 plan tax-free account, *assuming* all rules are followed for distributions, and your current taxable account. The tax-free account would yield approximately $15,000 more by 2022 due to the proposed difference in funding, $2,200 and $3,000, respectively, and taxation. The graph assumes the same rate of return and beginning balance for each account; state taxes are ignored. Complete analysis and explaination can be found in Appendix D.

### Recommendation & Implementation

Open an AnyState 529 College Savings Plan (we will discuss titling and the state tax implications when completing the paperwork) with the Real Life Mutual Fund Company. We will assist you to select an appropriate age-based portfolio that will automatically shift the asset allocation in coordination with Azalea's time horizon for entering college, and recommend automatic checking account withdrawals to fund the account.

---

**Education Planning Tip: Understand the American Opportunity Tax Credit**

The American Opportunity Tax Credit alters the Hope Credit for 2010, 2011, and 2012, and further reduces federal income tax liability in several ways. First, the American Opportunity Tax Credit increases the maximum credit to 100% of qualified tuition and related expenses for each eligible student up to a maximum of $2,500 and makes 40% of the credit refundable. Second, it expands eligibility to four years of an eligible student's postsecondary education. Generally, the credit can be claimed if a client pays qualified tuition and related higher education expenses for an eligible student (including the client). Third, it increases the availability of the credit by increasing the modified adjusted gross income (MAGI) limit to $90,000 for a single filer and $180,000 for joint filers. Those who file "married filing separately" may not claim the tax credit.[18] See IRS Publication 970 for more detail.[19]

---

Tax planning and education planning may be the most difficult financial objectives to jointly optimize, because many of the most attractive options from an ongoing income tax liability perspective (e.g., § 529 plans, CESAs) could interfere with the ability to also claim the Hope or Lifetime Learning Tax Credits. Table 11.2 summarizes this information for some of the more widely used funding alternatives.

# STRATEGIES

## Review Prospective Education Planning Strategies

Clients who want to fund a child's education often face a tough dilemma, namely, deciding whether to save for potential college costs or fund retirement plans. The time horizons for saving for these goals are generally different, but they often overlap. Furthermore, a child may decide not to go to college or to go to a more or less expensive college, or the child could qualify for a scholarship or other financial aid.

One method to hedge the possibility that college expenses will be lower than expected, funded through other means, or simply unneeded is to fund both goals in one account. This means that future college costs, coupled with retirement funding needs, can be combined into one or more tax-deferred contribution plans. An employer-sponsored retirement plan, a Roth IRA, or a traditional IRA can be used to fund a portion of or all projected college costs.

For example, if a Roth IRA is opened at least five years before education funding is needed, all contributions (but not earnings) can be taken out on a tax-free basis. If a client dips into account earnings to pay qualified higher education expenses before age 59½, the distributed earnings are generally taxable but free of the penalty tax on early distributions.

Any withdrawals from a traditional IRA would be taxable (except to the extent the distribution is attributable to nondeductible contributions, determined on a pro rata basis). To the extent the withdrawal is used to pay qualified higher education expenses, the penalty tax on early distributions would not apply.

**Table 11.2** Potential Impact of Asset Ownership on Financial Aid and Tax Credits

### Assets Owned by the Dependent Student

| Education Savings Plan | Change in Expected Family Contribution | Hope[1] and Lifetime Learning Tax Credit Impact |
|---|---|---|
| UGMA/UTMA | Increased (20% of balance)* | No impact |
| 529 Savings Plan (UGMA/ UTMA) | Increased (2.6% – 5.6% of balance) * | Expenses paid with distribution cannot be claimed for tax credit** |
| Coverdell Education Savings Account (CESA) | Increased (2.6 %– 5.6% of balance) * | Expenses paid with distribution cannot be claimed for tax credit** |
| Crummey Trust[2] | Increased (20% of balance) * | No impact |

### Assets Owned by the Parent

| | | |
|---|---|---|
| 529 Savings Plan | Increased (2.6% – 5.6% of balance) * | Expenses paid with distribution cannot be claimed for tax credit** |
| Series EE Savings Bonds (Tax-free Education Withdrawals) | Increased (2.6% – 5.6% of balance) * | Expenses paid with distribution cannot be claimed for tax credit** |
| Retirement Plans | None | No impact |
| Variable Universal Life Insurance | None | No impact |

### Assets Owned by Others (e.g., Grandparent) but with Student as Beneficiary

| | | |
|---|---|---|
| 529 Savings Plan | None*** | Expenses paid with distributions cannot be claimed for tax credit** |

* Hurley, Joseph F. (2011). Family guide to college savings 2011–2012, JFH Innovative, LLC, Pittsford, NY.
** Clients may take distributions from these plans. However, distributions must be spent on expenses not already claimed with the Hope or Lifetime Learning Credits.
*** Distributions from plans owned by a third party will be added back as income on the FAFSA.

1. Altered for 2009–2012, but not permanently renamed as the American Opportunity Tax Credit, at the time of publication.

2. A Crummey trust allows the beneficiary a window of opportunity to access the gift made, thereby completing the gift and removing the donated amount from the estate of the donor, although the intent is for the money to remain in the trust for a specified purpose or time period.

---

### Education Planning Tip: Traditional IRA Accounts

There is no hard-and-fast rule about the best time to convert a traditional IRA to a Roth IRA; however, there is a worst possible time—while your children are in college. Qualified retirement accounts are excluded from assets when calculating the EFC for financial aid; however, income derived from those sources is not. So, although a distribution from IRAs to pay qualified educational expenses is allowable and therefore will not trigger a tax penalty, it will count as income and could affect the income component of the EFC the following year.

A lesser-known consideration is the impact of conversion. Converting a traditional IRA to a Roth IRA is a taxable event. In other words, the amount of the conversion is typically taxable as ordinary income in the year of conversion, although there have been numerous temporary changes to this rule. So a planner must consider long-term tax implications of IRA distributions and conversions to the account owner, as well as the near-term financial aid implications to the dependent student of the account owner.

---

In general, for purposes of the education exception to the penalty tax on early distributions, distributions are covered only to the extent that they do not exceed the qualified higher education expenses of the taxpayer, the taxpayer's wife, or the child or grandchild of either, and if the expenses are paid during the same year as the distribution. Eligible expenses include tuition, fees, books, supplies, and room and board for a student attending undergraduate or graduate school at least half-time.

Figure 11.2 illustrates some of the decisions that could influence the choice of college funding alternatives. These and other product and procedural strategies, as well as the associated advantages and disadvantages of each, are discussed below. It is likely that one or more strategies will be needed to achieve a client's education funding goals. Different strategies should be fully evaluated relative to a client's situation before combining them in a recommendation.

**Figure 11.2** Decision Tree for Select Education Funding Strategies

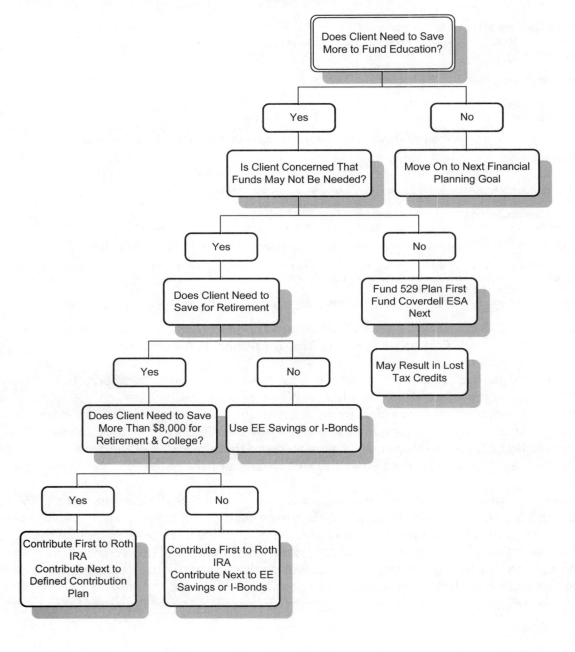

# Identify Prospective Education Planning Strategies

Planners and their clients have numerous alternatives available as they plan for funding education expenses. In addition to the accounts shown in Table 11.2, less common and less advantageous funding alternatives include insurance and home equity loans. Regular investment accounts (e.g., savings, mutual funds, or brokerage accounts) are another possibility, but generally they do not offer income tax benefits.

A variety of grants, loans, scholarships, and other financial aid sources are available. Others seek funding from private education loans or even family or personal loans. Students sometimes fund a part of the cost through summer jobs or on- or off-campus employment during the school term. Finally, some students pursue careers associated with loan forgiveness programs as a means to defray after-college repayment.

Few other core financial planning content areas offer such an extensive range of strategies with the opportunity to align availability, advantages, and disadvantages with a client's unique situation. Some of the most common education planning strategies are listed below, but they do not represent all of the creative approaches that can be considered.

## Product Strategy 1: Save for College Using a § 529 Plan

**Advantage: § 529 savings plans,** named after § 529 of the Internal Revenue Code (IRC) that created them in 1996, offer a number of advantages for clients who want a tax-advantaged education funding tool.

First, a significant dollar amount can be contributed on an annual basis. This makes a § 529 plan advantageous compared to a CESA.

Second, investments in the account grow tax free, and withdrawals used for qualified college expenses are free from federal income tax.

Third, some states offer state income tax advantages in addition to those offered by the federal government. States with an income tax often provide a state income tax exclusion for qualified withdrawals. Furthermore, most—but not all—states allow a deduction or credit for contributions to a § 529 plan, and some offer direct grants or monetary incentives. Some states have "tax-parity" legislation that extends state tax deductions to residents investing in out-of-state § 529 plans.

The fourth benefit involves control over the account. The account owner maintains control over how funds are invested and distributed. A parent, grandparent, relative, or friend can establish an account for a designated beneficiary. The owner can even decide when withdrawals should be taken and for what purpose.

Another unique advantage of § 529 plans involves their usefulness in estate planning. A client can contribute up to $65,000 to a § 529 plan in 2012 without triggering the federal gift tax. In effect, by implementing this strategy a client can use up to five years of gift tax annual exclusions in one year. Joint tax filers can contribute twice as much, and there are no limits to the number of beneficiaries for gift tax purposes. In addition, amounts in a § 529 plan account are generally not included in the account owner's gross estate for federal tax purposes.

A beneficiary can use § 529 plan college savings program funds at any accredited college, university, technical, vocational, or graduate school anywhere in the United States. This means that withdrawals can be used to pay for expenses in Kansas, for instance, even though the § 529 plan was sponsored by Nebraska.

Furthermore, no income limitations or age restrictions are associated with § 529 plans. Lifetime contribution limits for § 529 plans are considerably higher than any other tax-advantaged college saving plan. The lifetime maximum contribution is based on each state's projected cost of college. In many states, the maximum lifetime contribution limit can exceed $250,000.

**Disadvantage:** Advisors need to be aware of some potential drawbacks associated with § 529 plans. A beneficiary could decide not to attend college or to attend a less expensive school. Earnings withdrawn for nonqualified expenses are generally subject to federal and state income tax as well as a 10% federal penalty tax. Instead of taking a nonqualified distribution, an account owner could transfer an account to another family member, including siblings, first cousins, spouses, and even back to the client.

Another potential problem involves investment choices within § 529 plans. Nearly all states have pre-established asset allocation models that are used to direct investments within a plan. Accounts for young beneficiaries typically are invested aggressively, and in some cases annual management and maintenance fees can be high. Asset allocation typically becomes more conservative as the beneficiary ages. The choice of mutual funds within an account is almost always restricted, and historically the number of times an account owner can make changes within a plan has been limited to once a year.

Finally, investments held in the account are considered assets of the parent, and as such they increase the EFC for financial aid, but not as much as if the child held them.

A **§ 529 prepaid tuition plan** is a form of § 529 plan that provides an opportunity to prefund college expenses. Three important issues must be acknowledged before using a § 529 prepaid tuition plan. First, the amount of contribution is based on the age of the beneficiary and anticipated college costs in the state offering the plan. Second, the account owner has no control over how the account is invested. The sponsoring state manages the account and guarantees that tuition will be paid, regardless of account value. Third, and maybe most important, § 529 prepaid tuition plans typically guarantee benefits only for public institutions within the state sponsoring the plan, although some plans offer more flexibility.

## Product Strategy 2: Save for College Using a CESA

**Advantage: Coverdell Education Savings Accounts** (CESAs) help parents and grandparents save for a qualified beneficiary's education expenses. A CESA is a trust or custodial account set up for the purpose of paying qualified education expenses for a designated beneficiary. Principal and earnings from the account can be used to pay qualified higher education expenses, including tuition, fees, books, supplies, and equipment required for enrollment or attendance. Other expenses include amounts contributed to a qualified tuition program and room and board expenses. Distributions can be used to pay expenses at public, private, and religious elementary and secondary schools, as well as for postsecondary education expenses. This means that, unlike any other tax-advantaged program, a CESA can be used to pay for private day school expenses.

The designated beneficiary of a CESA must be under the age of 18 when an account is established, unless the beneficiary has special needs. Any balance in a CESA must be distributed within 30 days after the date the beneficiary reaches age 30, unless the beneficiary has special needs. There is no limit to the number of CESAs that can be established for one beneficiary. However, contributions can be made only in cash, and the total contributions made to all CESAs for any beneficiary in one tax year cannot be greater than $2,000. This means that a client cannot contribute $2,000 to an account while a grandparent contributes another $2,000. Also, contributions to CESAs are restricted by income phase-out rules.

The primary financial planning advantage associated with a CESA is that distributions are tax free to the extent the distribution does not exceed the beneficiary's qualified education expenses. If a distribution does exceed the beneficiary's qualified education expenses, a portion of the distribution is taxable. A CESA can be rolled over into a § 529 plan. Also, the Hope Credit or the Lifetime Learning Credit can be claimed for certain qualified higher education expenses in the same year in which the student receives a tax-free withdrawal from a CESA. However, the distribution cannot be used for the same educational expenses for which the credit was taken.

**Disadvantage:** Two limitations are associated with this college savings approach. First, many financial planning clients could find that their income exceeds threshold limits, making contributions out of the question. Second, and more importantly, the annual $2,000 contribution limit severely restricts the usefulness of this tool in accumulating assets for education.

To maximize this type of account, a client must start saving early in a child's life and save the maximum allowable each year. If, for instance, a client saved $2,000 each year for 15 years earning 9% on average, the account would be worth only $58,722 at the end of the period.

Also, if assets are not used by the child's 30th birthday and are not assigned to a close family member, the client will incur income tax and a 10% penalty on earnings that accumulated on a tax-free basis within the account.

### Product Strategy 3: Save for College Using a Roth IRA

**Advantage:** For those eligible to do so, contributing to a Roth IRA is an excellent strategy for clients who want to save for a contingent educational funding need, but who have a primary goal of saving for retirement. If funds are needed for college or other education needs, distributions of contributions can be received tax free as long as the Roth IRA has been open for at least five years. If earnings are withdrawn prior to age 59½ and used to pay qualified educational expenses, taxes may be due on such distributions, but the early distribution penalty will not apply.

**Disadvantage:** The primary disadvantage associated with this strategy is that it is unlikely that enough funding can be generated to cover 100% of college costs at a moderate- to high-expense college. Reducing this retirement asset may benefit the child, who may have other education funding alternatives, but it could jeopardize the owner's retirement plan. Thus, this strategy may be more appropriate for a grandparent than a parent, depending on other situational factors. Additionally, distributions from Roth IRAs can adversely affect a subsequent financial aid application because of the increased income.

### Product Strategy 4: Save for College Using Variable Universal Life (VUL) Insurance

**Advantage:** This strategy, which is somewhat unorthodox outside the insurance industry, can be quite effective in meeting education funding goals. The principal advantages associated with this strategy include being able to maximize funding and investing in assets that can grow substantially over time. Ultimately, this strategy is beneficial if growth within the variable account is high enough to allow the client to take loans to pay for college expenses and have remaining assets generate returns to pay the interest and repayment charges. Also, if the insured dies, insurance proceeds could be used to pay for education.

**Disadvantage:** The chief disadvantage associated with this strategy is that, to fully fund a VUL at the level necessary to accumulate a significant account value, a large face value policy is needed. The premium cost of such a policy can be prohibitive. Furthermore, ongoing administrative and subaccount fees can reduce overall rates of return on assets. Unless managed and invested well, a VUL can terminate with a zero cash balance. Also, rates credited by the insurer are reduced when a loan is made.

### Product Strategy 5: Save for College Using Series EE and Series I Bonds

**Advantage:** A parent's savings bonds can be cashed in tax free to pay for a child's college tuition. The amount that can be contributed on a yearly basis is higher ($30,000 for married clients) than what can be contributed to a CESA or traditional or Roth IRAs.

Individuals must meet certain requirements for distributions from savings bonds to be tax free. First, a client must be at least 24 years old on the first day of the month in which the bond was purchased. Second, when using bonds for a child's education, the bonds must be registered in the *client's and/or spouse's name*. A child can be listed as a beneficiary on the bond, but not as a co-owner. Third, if a client uses bonds for the client's own education, the bonds must be registered in the client's name. Finally, if a client is married and uses the bonds for educational purposes, the client must file a joint return to qualify for the exclusion.

Unlike distributions from CESAs, only payments made to postsecondary institutions, including colleges, universities, and vocational schools that meet the standards for federal assistance (such as guaranteed student loan programs) qualify for the program. Qualified educational expenses include tuition and fees such as lab fees and other required course expenses. Expenses paid for any course or other education involving sports, games, or hobbies qualify only if required as part of a degree- or certificate-granting program. The costs of books, room, and board are not considered qualified expenses. Savings bonds can be used to fund qualified state tuition plans, such as a

529 Plan. When determining the amount of qualified expenses, a client must reduce the amount of total expenses by the amount of scholarships, fellowships, employer-provided educational assistance, and other forms of tuition reduction received. Finally, expenses must be incurred during the same tax year in which the bonds are redeemed.

Up to $30,000 in Series EE and Series I savings bonds can be purchased by married clients ($15,000 for single clients) in any given year. To exclude the interest from gross income, a client must use both the principal and interest from bonds sold to pay qualified expenses. If the amount of eligible bonds cashed during the year exceeds the amount of qualified educational expenses paid during the year, the amount of excludable interest is reduced using a pro rata formula. For example, assume that bond proceeds equal $20,000 ($16,000 principal and $4,000 interest) and the qualified educational expenses are $16,000. The amount of interest that can be excluded is $3,200 ([$16,000 expenses ÷ $20,000 proceeds] × $4,000 interest).

**Disadvantage:** Like most tax benefits, certain household income limitations apply. The full interest exclusion is available only to clients with modified adjusted gross income (which includes the interest earned) under certain limits. Also, savings bonds are included as a parent asset, which can increase the EFC used in financial aid formulas. Furthermore, rates of return are relatively low, which limits a client's ability to fund expenses from interest earned. The early withdrawal penalty during the first five years and the relatively low rate of return require that this strategy be implemented well in advance of when the funds are needed.

## Product Strategy 6: Use a Home Equity Loan to Pay for Additional College Expenses

**Advantage:** This strategy is appropriate for clients who wish to borrow against their home equity to contribute to their child's education. In general, clients receive a tax deduction for the interest paid on a home equity loan (for up to $100,000 of debt) if they itemize deductions and are not subject to the Alternative Minimum Tax. Loan repayment typically ranges from 5 to 15 years, and prepayment penalties may apply.

**Disadvantage:** Closing costs and other associated fees to establish and service the loan apply, and repayment begins immediately. Clients who use this strategy place a lien against their home equity that must be repaid over a number of years. If a child chose not to finish school or to use the proceeds of the loan for expenses other than college, the parents could have mortgaged their own financial future to fund something unintended.

## Product Strategy 7: Structure Student Loans Appropriately

**Advantage:** This strategy is premised on the fact that certain education loans are better than others. Of course, need-based loans may not be available to some clients. Generally, a Perkins loan should be taken first. These loans carry a low fixed rate of interest and provide payment deferral. Stafford loans should be used once Perkins loans have been maximized. Subsidized Stafford loans are preferable, but unsubsidized Stafford loans are available to anyone. Finally, PLUS loans can be taken by parents, assuming an acceptable credit history. These loans allow parents to make payments over an extended period of time.

Private or alternative education loans should be the last loan consideration, because interest rates and fees are typically higher for these loans. The applicant's FICO score is a major determinant of the rate offered for a private loan. Rates vary by lender, so comparison shopping is recommended.

**Disadvantage:** No matter what type of loan is taken, or when the loan is received, if the debt is not managed well either the client or the client's child can run into financial difficulties. Debt should be taken on only if absolutely necessary, or when the cost of debt is less than the return earned on investment assets.

### Product Strategy 8: Use Retirement Accounts Rather than Education Savings Products to Save for College Expenses

**Advantage:** Student financial aid formulas do not take into account assets held in defined contribution plans or self-employed retirement plans, such as Keoghs. By maximizing contributions to these plans, and then taking loans against account values if needed, it may be possible to reduce the expected family contribution when applying for financial aid.

**Disadvantage:** The primary disadvantage associated with this strategy is that if early withdrawals are needed, a 10% penalty may apply. Also, some private universities may require that retirement assets be listed for calculating the EFC for financial aid purposes.

### Product Strategy 9: Use 401(k) and 403(b) Account Loans to Fund Education Expenses

**Advantage:** Although not universal, many 401(k) and some 403(b) plans allow an account owner to borrow the greater of $50,000 or 50% of account value at any given time. Typically, loans can be taken for up to five years with a minimal rate of interest. This strategy allows a client to minimize the financial aid EFC by sheltering assets in a 401(k) or 403(b) plan, and then later use loan proceeds to pay for excess college expenses.

**Disadvantage:** Using retirement assets to fund a dependent child's college expenses could cause the parent's retirement plan to become underfunded. Once a loan is taken, loan proceeds stop earning market rates of return. An opportunity cost exists where the amount of interest repaid will almost always be less than the amount of interest and capital gains that could have been earned. Loan repayment starts immediately. If employment ends, the loan must be repaid in 30 days or less or taxes and penalties may apply.

### Procedural Strategy 1: Consider the Advantages and Disadvantage of a Child Filing Taxes as an Independent Taxpayer

**Advantage:** Often, clients assume that the best tax filing strategy is to claim a child as dependent for the maximum length of time possible. Other clients assume that the best way to maximize financial aid is to have the child file taxes as an independent taxpayer. Doing so could result in a client forfeiting a tax exemption or credit.

However, not being claimed as a dependent on the parent's taxes does not confer independent student status on the child for financial aid purposes. The rules relating to independent student status for the purposes of filing for financial aid are different from those for tax purposes.

Several factors must be considered, including parental income, support for the child, the child's eligibility for financial aid, the parents' eligibility for the adjustment for education expenses or the education credit, and the marginal tax bracket of the parents. If the issue is isolated to taxes, generally the greater savings results from a parent continuing to claim the exemption.

**Disadvantage:** The benefit from savings on the client's income taxes may be negligible if the dependent could actually qualify as an independent student and receive maximum financial aid. However, it is important that both issues, the potential impact on income taxes and the impact on financial aid eligibility, be considered separately or in combination depending on the individual client situation.

### *Procedural Strategy 2: Shift Income Two Years Prior to Applying for Financial Aid*

**Advantage:** Current financial aid formulas are based on a family's prior year level of income. By shifting income so that it is recognized earlier than the year prior to application, it may be possible to reduce the EFC.

**Disadvantage:** Although it may be possible to capture certain capital gains two years early, it may not be feasible to shift enough income to make this strategy work. Other disadvantages include the potential for creating a higher tax burden before the financial aid application than is gained in financial aid.

### *Procedural Strategy 3: Fund a 2503(c) Minor's Trust Before the Child Turns Age 21*

**Advantage:** Funding a **2503(c) minor's trust** completes a gift to a minor under IRC § 2503(c), thereby removing the assets from the estate of the grantor while maintaining some level of control over the distribution and use of the assets.

**Disadvantage:** Gifts made to the trust are irrevocable and must be made before the child turns 21. Additionally, all of the proceeds from the trust must be used for the benefit of the beneficiary prior to the age of 21, unless a "window" is provided to the beneficiary immediately following the 21st birthday, which grants the beneficiary access before it converts into a Crummey trust. As with all trusts, set-up and administration fees can be quite high in comparison to the corpus of the trust. Finally, trust assets are considered assets of the child, and income derived from the trust is income to the child; therefore, it will have a significant impact on financial aid contribution calculations.

### *Procedural Strategy 4: Fund a Crummey Trust*

**Advantage:** Funding a **Crummey trust** completes a gift to a minor by allowing temporary access to the gift, thereby removing the assets from the estate of the grantor while maintaining some level of control over the distribution and use of the assets. Another benefit is that Crummey trusts, unlike § 2503(c) trusts, can name multiple beneficiaries.

**Disadvantage:** Gifts made to the trust are irrevocable. As with all trusts, set-up and administration fees can be quite high in comparison to the corpus of the trust. Finally, trust assets are considered assets of the child, and income derived from the trust is income to the child; therefore, it will have a significant impact on financial aid contribution calculations.

### Procedural Strategy 5: Shift UGMA/UTMA Assets Two Years Before the Child Turns Age 18

**Advantage:** Current financial aid formulas penalize families when a child holds sizable assets in UGMA/UTMA accounts. Although a parent cannot take back money held in a UGMA/UTMA account, it may be possible to use account assets to purchase goods and services for a child above and beyond items generally thought of as basic living expenses. For example, assets can be used to pay tuition to a precollege camp. Doing so increases the likelihood of receiving a larger financial aid award.

**Disadvantage:** This strategy should be recommended with caution. Gifts made to an UGMA/UTMA account are irrevocable. They should not be used for the benefit of a parent or guardian or for costs that are deemed to be basic expenses the parent or guardian may be obligated to pay. Also, the effectiveness of this strategy disappears if account transfers are not made at least two years before filing for financial aid.

### Procedural Strategy 6: Use EE Savings Bonds to Fund a § 529 Plan

**Advantage:** Proceeds from the sale of Series EE and Series I savings bonds can be received tax free when used either to pay for a family member's educational expenses or when funding a § 529 plan or a CESA. Several requirements must be met. The account beneficiary must be the client, the client's spouse, or a dependent of the client. To qualify for the interest exclusion, the bonds must be issued in the parent's name and purchased after 1989, must be used to pay for qualified higher education expenses or funding a § 529 plan or CESA, and the parent must meet the modified AGI guidelines for the interest exclusion (income phase-outs apply). Those filing "married filing separately" are ineligible for the exclusion. This allows savings bonds to be used on a tax-free basis to earn a potentially higher rate of return in a § 529 plan. Furthermore, because many states provide an incentive to contribute to an in-state (and in some instances an out-of-state) § 529 plan, doing so can yield a higher overall tax benefit.

**Disadvantage:** By transferring savings bond assets to a § 529 plan, a client limits the availability and use of these assets for other goals, especially if the client's child does not need to use account assets for education.

### Procedural Strategy 7: Increase Annual Savings Dedicated to Goal

**Advantage:** One final and obvious strategy involves increasing the amount of savings dedicated to the education funding goal. The more that can be saved on a monthly or yearly basis, the more likely that the goal will be met. It may be possible to involve grandparents or other family or friends in this effort.

**Disadvantage:** This strategy is based on the premise that the client or others have additional discretionary cash flow and unallocated savings to contribute to the educational goal. If this assumption is incorrect, this strategy will not work.

## *Procedural Strategy 8: Decrease the Level-of-support Assumption*

**Advantage:** Clients who attempt to achieve an education funding objective but still find themselves coming short of their goal may want to consider decreasing the cost-of-college assumption used in the analysis. Although it is nice to want to fund a child's full educational costs at an expensive university, it may be fiscally impossible. Therefore, reducing the cost to be covered and focusing on obtaining scholarships, grants, and loans may be a way to meet at least a portion of future educational costs.

**Disadvantage:** Reducing the support assumption and instead relying on a child to receive grants and scholarships can be a problematic approach to planning. The uncertainty associated with grants and scholarships makes these sources of funding difficult to predict. An unrealistic reliance on these forms of funding can leave a client significantly short of actual future assets to fund these expenses. This alone would be detrimental, but it can also limit alternative funding planning.

## *Procedural Strategy 9: Increase the Risk/Return Trade-off Assumptions*

**Advantage:** Clients may underestimate their risk tolerance when accumulating assets for education funding needs. This especially applies when funding efforts are postponed (not initiated when the children are young) and therefore the time horizon for goal attainment is shortened. If this is the case, this strategy calls for the client to reallocate assets to increase the rate of return on savings. Increasing the rate of return on investment assets will amplify the compounding of returns, which helps make an education goal more achievable.

**Disadvantage:** Not all educational funding products allow a client to systematically change the asset allocation of savings to increase returns. For instance, many § 529 savings plans use a fixed asset allocation based on the beneficiary's age. In other words, the risk exposure in the portfolio decreases as the beneficiary gets closer to college age. Also, if a Roth IRA or retirement plan is used to partially offset college costs, increasing the return may not match well with the return assumptions used in the retirement plan.

## *Procedural Strategy 10: Decrease Assumed College Inflation Rate*

**Advantage:** One factor that drives the future high cost of funding educational goals is the constant increase in the price of tuition and fees. One way to manipulate an educational funding analysis is to decrease the assumed rate of tuition inflation. Doing so will make the future cost of education appear more affordable; that is, the amount of savings necessary will be less. The inflation rate for college costs varies over time and by type of institution, but valid data on which to base assumptions are available. However, once a reasonable inflation rate has been chosen, it is unwise to "cook" the numbers simply to assuage a client's concerns. A better alternative is to explain the discrepancy in funding the education goal and to consider other alternatives.

**Disadvantage:** This is a perilous strategy that should be used only in extreme cases where the cost of college is significantly more than the projected future value of client educational assets. In effect, decreasing the tuition inflation rate assumption goes against 20 years of historical data, which suggest that tuition costs will continue to rise, with some projections indicating double-digit increases. But it may give the client some solace that their efforts will pay off as long as the actual rate of inflation is less than originally projected.

### Procedural Strategy 11: Assign the Correct Priority to Paying off Student Loan Debt

**Advantage:** Because the interest rate on student loans is in many cases substantially lower than other forms of borrowing, the cost of servicing this debt is relatively inexpensive. The debtor may be better served by maximizing cash flows to other goals, such as building an emergency fund, rather than paying off the student loan debt more quickly. This will enhances liquidity and reduces the likelihood that other, more expensive types of borrowing are incurred because of unforeseen circumstances.

**Disadvantage:** By diverting money from student loan debt service, the borrower will incur greater interest expense over the life of the loan. However, the interest might be tax deductible.

# CHAPTER-BASED CASE STUDY

## Sample Client-based Education Planning Recommendation

Developing education planning recommendations follows the same general process used in other areas of financial planning. Specifically, education planning recommendations flow directly from a client's primary education funding objective. Recommendations should evolve from both a quantitative analysis of a client's current situation and a review of situational factors, such as the expectations of the child receiving financial aid, the client's willingness to fund certain expenses while not funding others, and the level of control a client wishes to maintain over assets and savings. These personal expectations and attitudes strongly influence the type of recommendations that are most suitable for a client.

The process of combining education funding strategies into one or more client-specific recommendations depends on a number of factors. At least initially, the choice of appropriate strategies may be driven by the education planning need. Figure 11.3 illustrates a hierarchical approach that can be used to select appropriate strategies for a client recommendation.

**Figure 11.3** Ranking and Using Education Funding Strategies

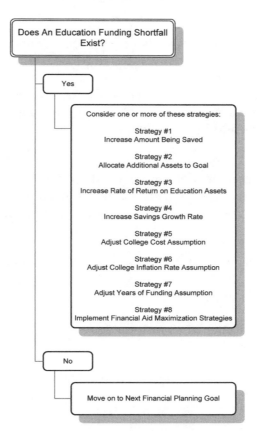

Before a recommendation is presented to a client, steps should be taken to confirm that the recommendation meets both the education funding need and the client's stated expectations. For instance, recommending that a client reduce the college cost assumption to make funding feasible could run contrary to a client's strong desire to have the child attend an expensive university. It may be better, in a situation similar to this, to determine whether the client would be willing to maintain the high cost assumption but realize that only a portion of the child's education costs can be funded. Such a candid approach helps the planner more effectively manage client expectations. It also enables the client to consider other options to maximize goal funding relative to any trade-offs in lifestyle that may be called for or the attainment of other goals. An overriding objective of comprehensive financial planning is to empower clients to make these decisions more effectively.

# A Sample Recommendation: Using Series EE Savings Bonds to Fund a § 529 College Savings Plan

Numerous strategies are available to help clients reach their education funding objectives, and there are many ways to present these alternatives. Examples of tax-advantaged funding mechanisms include § 529 college savings plans, UGMA/UTMA accounts, savings bonds, and C ESAs. The following sample recommendation examines one financial planner's process for choosing among these education planning solutions when working on a client case.

Early this year, Timur asked his financial planner Jackie to conduct an education funding assessment to determine whether he was in a position to help fund his daughter's future college expenses. Before running the numbers, Jackie talked with Timur about his wishes, desires, and education funding objectives. This is what she learned:

- Timur's objective, as an unmarried father, was to establish an education fund to help offset most, but not all, of his 9-year-old daughter's future college expenses at age 18.

- He was in the 25% marginal federal tax bracket and the 5% state tax bracket at the time.

- He had already accumulated $9,000 in Series EE savings bonds for this objective.

- Although he was happy to help fund educational costs, he was reluctant to give up too much control over the assets.

- He very much wanted to explore earning a higher rate of return on assets held for education funding, if he could do so without taking undue risk.

Jackie also realized that because Timur's objective was to use EE savings bonds to fund education, she needed to assess whether Timur would be eligible for the income tax exclusion. She was certain that (1) the account beneficiary was a dependent of the client; (2) the bonds were issued in Timur's name after 1989 and he was older than 24 at the time; and (3) the funds were intended to pay for qualified education expenses. However, she wanted to confer with Timur's accountant to verify his MAGI and filing status before making any recommendations.

After speaking with the accountant and determining that Timur's filing status and income level were within the guidelines to file for the exclusion, Jackie conducted an education funding needs assessment and determined that he was not making a high enough return on his Series EE savings bonds to meet his objective. She concluded that, to meet his objective, he would either need to reallocate his bonds to earn a higher rate of return or continue to hold the bonds and significantly increase savings. Given Timur's cash flow situation and his desire to fully fund other goals, this second alterative was unrealistic.

Jackie determined that she needed to evaluate four education funding strategies before making a recommendation to Timur. Exhibit 11.3 illustrates the logic that Jackie used to compare holding the Series EE savings bonds with using the proceeds from the sale of the bonds to establish a UGMA/UTMA account, a CESA, or a § 529 savings plan.

Timur's EE bonds have a market value of $9,000 and a cost basis of $6,000. The bonds will earn 3.5% annually and can be redeemed at any time. Jackie made a planning assumption that any tax paid on redemption reduces the savings available for education purposes (e.g., in Strategy 2) and that any tax savings increases the amount invested in the education account (e.g., in Strategy 4). Assume alternative strategies are implemented either immediately (e.g., in Strategies 2 and 4) or at the beginning of each year (e.g., in Strategy 3).

Jackie is leaning toward the § 529 plan because of (1) the ownership flexibility, (2) the tax-advantaged growth, (3) the strong investment choices available, and most importantly (4) the tax deduction for contributions into a § 529 plan in Timur's state. Jackie prepared Exhibit 11.3 to guide the discussion with Timur and to summarize the information for each of the strategies considered.

Given these financial advantages, and the fact that opening a § 529 plan matches closely with Timur's stated objectives and personal preferences, it was relatively easy for Jackie to move forward with the formation of a recommendation. Exhibit 11.4 shows how the recommendation to use the proceeds from the sale of Series EE savings bonds to fund a § 529 plan could be presented using an Education Planning Recommendation Form.

A recommendation to use Series EE savings bonds to fund a § 529 plan offers clients who have the objective of subsidizing all or part of a child's college education the opportunity to build significant account value over time. If this strategy is also supplemented with annual contributions to the § 529 plan, it may be possible to accomplish three financial planning outcomes: (1) reduce current income taxes through a contribution tax deduction (or credit in some states); (2) reduce future estate taxes by transferring assets to the plan; and (3) maximize education savings. When matched to the appropriate client (i.e., those who own savings bonds and want to save for a child's education), this recommendation can offer a winning combination for tax efficiency and goal maximization.

**Exhibit 11.3** A Comparison of Education Funding Strategies for Timur Smith

| Comparison of Education Funding Strategies | | | |
|---|---|---|---|
| **Hold EE Savings Bonds** | **Establish UGMA/ UTMA Account** | **Establish a Coverdell Education Savings Account** | **Open a 529 Savings Plan** |
| **Advantages** | | | |
| • Tax-deferred growth<br>• Tax-free if used for college expenses<br>• Assets do not need to be used for college expenses | • Unlimited dollar contributions allowed<br>• Kiddie Tax would apply | • Tax-deferred growth<br>• Tax-free if used for college expenses<br>• Can be used to fund a wide variety of educational expenses | • Tax-deferred growth<br>• Tax-free if used for college expenses<br>• $250,000 lifetime limit<br>• Allows Timur to maintain the flexibility of ownership |
| **Disadvantages** | | | |
| • Low rate of return | • Gifts are irrevocable<br>• Child gains ownership at age of majority<br>• Fully taxable | • Limited to $2,000 annual contribution<br>• Loss of asset control<br>• Subject to taxation and penalties if not used for educational purposes | • Subject to taxation and penalties if not used for educational purposes |
| **Immediate Tax Cost/Benefit of Funding Plan with EE Savings Bond Assets (Reduces or Increases Education Account)** | | | |
| NA | -$750, which is the federal tax on the sale of the bonds (no state tax on Series EE Savings Bond proceeds) | $0, contributions to a CESA can be made tax free using proceeds from Series EE Savings Bonds | $450, contributions to a 529 Plan may be made tax free using proceeds from Series EE Savings Bonds, plus Anystate offers a tax deduction. |
| **Rate of Return if Used for College** | | | |
| 3.50% | 4.90% (after-tax) | 7.00% (pre-tax) | 7.00% (pre-tax) |
| **Tax-Adjusted Future Value When Child Enters College** | | | |
| $12,266.08 | $12,689.17 | Due to contribution limits, Timur will make the following contributions:<br>Year 1: $2,000<br>Year 2: $2,000<br>Year 3: $2,000<br>Year 4: $2,000<br>Year 5: $1,603<br><br>$15,574.29 | $17,373.44 |

**Exhibit 11.4** Timur's Education Planning Recommendation Form

## Planning Recommendation Form

| | |
|---|---|
| **Financial Planning Content Area** | Education planning |
| **Client Goal** | Fund child's education |
| **Recommendation No.** 1 | **Priority (1–6)** lowest to highest: 6 |
| **Projected/Target Value ($)** | |

**Product Profile**

| | | | | |
|---|---|---|---|---|
| Type | 529 Plan | | | |
| Duration | 9 Years | | | |
| Provider | Anystate | | | |
| Funding Cost per Period ($) | $9,000 one-time cost | | | |
| Maintenance Cost per Period ($) | Minimal Anystate and mutual fund fees | | | |
| Current Income Tax Status | Tax-qualified | X | Taxable | |
| Projected Rate of Return | 7.00% | | | |
| Major Policy Provisions | NA | | | |

**Procedural Factors**

| | | | | |
|---|---|---|---|---|
| Implementation by Whom | Planner | | Client | X |
| Implementation Date or Time Frame | January 2 | | | |
| Implementation Procedure | Redeem $9,000 in Series EE Savings Bonds. Place proceeds in checking account. Our office has prepared the Anystate 529 Plan application for you. Name Annie, your only child, as the plan beneficiary. The application requires your signature. Send check for $9,450 (includes $450 tax savings) with application to plan provider. | | | |

**Ownership Factors**

| | | | | |
|---|---|---|---|---|
| Owner(s) | Timur Smith | | | |
| Form of Ownership | 529 custodian | | | |
| Insured(s) | NA | | | |
| Custodial Account | Yes | X | No | |
| Custodian | Annie Smith | | | |
| In Trust For (ITF) | Yes | | No | X |
| Transfer on Death (TOD) | Yes | | No | X |
| Beneficiary(ies) | Annie Smith | | | |
| Contingent Beneficiary(ies) | NA | | | |

| | |
|---|---|
| **Proposed Benefit** | The projected future value of the account, when Annie turns age 18, is approximately $17,370. Opening the account today will result in a $450 state tax deduction (the $450 savings is also contributed to the account). If distributions are used for qualified educational expenses, no state or federal tax liability will be incurred. |

# Learning Outcomes

1. As the cost of a college education and college loan debt reach unprecedented heights, planning for education funding has become an important financial planning topic for parents, grandparents, and other family members. Planners have responded by assuming a more proactive role that goes beyond the projection of costs and needed investments to helping clients plan to maximize need- and merit-based aid, to choose tax-advantaged accounts, and to creatively combine strategies that help clients balance the cost of education against potentially negative consequences. These deleterious outcomes include a significantly reduced lifestyle during the college years, a significant reduction in retirement savings, or launching children with a heavy future commitment to repay college loans.

2. A wide range of personal client situational factors, both qualitative and quantitative, affect planning for education funding and the type of recommendations ultimately made. Unknown situational information and the short time frame for planning with full information further complicate the planning process. Additionally, education funding is a highly emotional topic for parents and children, and a goal that many clients are willing to compromise other goals for, including retirement. Client attitudes, values, and expectations, which influence planning assumptions, may be more important and potentially problematic in education planning than in any other core content planning area. Thus, it is important that planners take the time to fully explore client situational factors as a foundation for the planning of education funding.

3. Planners rely on professional software to quickly calculate and project education funding costs under different scenarios. Both financial planning students and planners need to fully understand the time value of money principles used to calculate future costs and the income streams to accumulate and disperse the funds. Because the costs of education can be met through numerous sources (i.e., family savings, child savings or income, merit-based or need-based aid, etc.), scenario planning with different assumptions is an important value-added service that relies on a thorough knowledge of the calculations and related cash flows.

4. Merit-based and need-based funding (i.e., scholarships, loans, or grants) can significantly reduce or defer the cost of education for parents and students. A first step for everyone is to file the FAFSA annually. Despite the fact that financial planning clients may not be eligible for most need-based aid, family situational factors (i.e., size of family, multiple children in college, medical debt/issues, etc.) and the student's profile (i.e., talents, aptitude, extracurricular activities, discipline of study, etc.) could increase eligibility for financial assistance. Being proactive in selecting schools where the student is competitive, identifying college- and community-based sources of aid, and broadly applying for aid are important strategies. Finally, planners can add value by helping clients understand the federal and private educational loan programs as well as other possible sources for borrowing funds (i.e., home equity, retirement accounts, life insurance) to mitigate the funding need.

5. The complexity of planning for college education funding and the variety of alternative approaches advocated can make it difficult for clients to choose and implement the most effective strategies. Planners can help clients explore the emotional issues and understand

the advantages and disadvantages of different accounts. Access to and control of the funds, the timeline for accumulating and disbursing the funds, the effect on financial aid, and tax implications are primary considerations that must be evaluated. Tax consequences include (1) tax-deferred vs. taxable growth; (2) tax-free vs. taxable withdrawals; (3) annual income tax reductions from state incentives, the federal adjustment for interest paid, or the credit for costs incurred; and (4) shifting assets to potentially reduce or avoid estate taxes.

6.  The availability of tax-deferred savings and tax-free withdrawals is limited to funding retirement, health care, and education. CESAs, § 529 savings and prepaid plans, and Series EE bonds all offer these advantages, assuming all guidelines regarding income, purchase, and disbursement are met, as applicable. State tax incentives for the § 529 accounts are another advantage, but they must be considered relative to account earnings, fees, and other features when choosing an in- or out-of-state account. Although these accounts are popular education savings alternatives, numerous other dedicated or dual-purpose accounts are available and offer unique benefits. Access to and control of funds, the timeline for accumulating and disbursing the funds, the effect on financial aid, and tax implications are important considerations to evaluate, relative to the individual client situation.

7.  Individual client qualitative and quantitative situational factors should guide choices for every client recommendation, but this is particularly true when planning for education funding. The situational factors, range of assumptions, and variety of available strategies increase the complexity of identifying appropriate and reasonable education funding recommendations. For most clients, a combination of accounts or strategies offers the best alternatives for dealing with multiple scenarios based on different sets of assumptions. It is important to remember that planning for education is also planning for retirement and the next generation.

# Chapter Resources

Bassonette, Zac. *Debt-Free U: How I Paid for an Outstanding College Education Without Loans, Scholarships, or Mooching off My Parents.* New York, Penguin Group, 2010.

Darvis, Rick. *College Solution: A Roadmap to Selecting Your Best Strategy to Fund College And Retirement...without Going Broke.* Mason City, IA, Stone People Publishing Co., 2005.

Department of Education, 2012–2013 *Expected Family Contribution Formula Guide* (January 2012 Update) can be found at http://www.ifap.ed.gov/efcformulaguide/attachments/010512EFCFo rmulaGuide1213.pdf.

Federal student financial aid information can be found at www.studentaid.ed.gov.

For information regarding tax benefits for education, visit the IRS Web site at http://www.irs. gov/publications/p970/index.html.

Information about student loans and the Free Application for Federal Student Aid (FAFSA) can be found at www.fafsa.ed.gov.

Information about loans available for higher education can be found at www.finaid.org.

National Institute of Certified College Planners (NICCP) can be found at http://university.niccp.com/default.aspx.

The Princeton Review and Kalman Chany. *Paying for College Without Going Broke, 2012 Edition (College Admissions Guides)*. Framingham, MA: The Princeton Review, 2011.

The *Financial Factilitator* and all fillable forms needed to complete text activities can be found on the student website at: http://pro.nuco.com/booksupplements/NUCollege-CaseBook2e.

## Quantitative/Analytical Mini-case Problems

1. Johanna and Ryan just put their two boys (grades 6 and 2) on their respective school buses for the first day of school and realized that they are growing up fast. So they called you and stated that they wanted to save, starting today, at the beginning of every month for the next six years (until the older child goes to college) to pay for one-half of school expenses for both children. You know that tuition, room, and board this year cost $18,000 at their selected school, and you expect 5% effective annual inflation for education expenses. They also said that they know the children's grandparents are going to make a gift of $48,000 toward this cause in exactly three years.

   Assume that both children attend the same college for four years each. Also assume that the annual tuition bill is due at the beginning of each academic year, and the first payment is exactly 72 months away. How much money will they need to invest on a monthly basis to meet their education goal assuming a required effective annual rate of 10.471% (10% APR with monthly compounding)?

2. A client wants to begin a savings program for her eight-year-old son. She has been reading about the various accounts available for college savings programs, but she is confused about which type of account would be best. Her primary concerns are taxes, account ownership, and flexibility. She has developed a list of questions that she would like answered at the next meeting.

   a. Which account would allow for the greatest flexibility given that she is a single mother, is not expecting to have any additional children, and is not absolutely certain that her son will attend college?

   b. Given the following account assumptions, which account would require the lowest monthly contribution to attain her goal of saving $50,000 in 10 years? (The savings goal ends at the beginning of her son's first year of college.) Assume that she makes a fixed payment at the end of each month for the next 120 months. Also assume that any account set-up fees or annual fees are paid on a monthly basis in addition to the required savings deposit.

| | Account Type | | |
| --- | --- | --- | --- |
| | **Nonqualified** | **Roth IRA** | **§ 529 Plan** |
| Projected market gross annual return | 9.5% | 9.5% | 9.5% |
| | | | |
| Annual expense ratio (target date fund) | 0.0% | 1.1% | 1.1% |
| Program fees* | 0.0% | 0.0% | 0.6% |
| | | | |
| Annual account fee | $0 | $12.00 | $24.00 |
| Annual applicable tax rate** | 20.0% | 0.0% | 0.0% |
| | | | |

*Program fees include management and state administration fees.

**Assume that all withdrawals from qualified accounts are used for a qualified purpose and therefore are not subject to income tax or early withdrawal penalties.

c. Depending on the account type chosen in part b, who should "own" the account, assuming her son has earned income? Consider both financial aid eligibility and flexibility of use.

3. Broderick, an independent student, graduated from college in May 2011 with $37,000 (not including accrued interest charges) in unsubsidized Stafford Loan debt and realized that he is in over his head. He has come to you for answers. Answer the questions based on the following disbursement schedule:

| Disbursement Date | Total Disbursement Amount | Interest Rate |
| --- | --- | --- |
| Aug 2007 | $8,000 | 6.8% |
| Aug 2008 | $9,000 | 6.8% |
| Aug 2009 | $10,000 | 6.8% |
| Aug 2010 | $10,000 | 6.8% |

a. What was the actual aggregated balance on his loans the August after he graduated?

b. What is the monthly payment if he chooses the standard 10-year repayment plan?

c. How much will he pay in total to pay off the aggregate loan? How much interest will he pay, assuming all payments are made as agreed?

d. What is the monthly payment if he chooses the extended 20-year repayment plan?

e. How much will he pay in total to pay off the aggregate loan? How much interest will he pay, assuming all payments are made as agreed?

f. How much additional interest would Broderick pay if he chose the extended payment option?

4. Rahel, a dependent student, graduated from college in May 2011 with the maximum ($31,000) allowable amount in Stafford Loan debt; however, this was far less than the total cost of her schooling. Additionally, her parents had planned far enough in advance that Rahel demonstrated each year sufficient financial need to qualify for the maximum amount under the subsidized loan program. Her parents are wondering how much their planning paid off, so they have posed the following questions to you. Base your analysis on the disbursement schedule.

| Disbursement Date | Total Disbursement Amount | Subsidized Amount | Unsubsidized Interest Rate | Subsidized Interest Rate |
|---|---|---|---|---|
| Aug 2007 | $5,500 | $3,500 | 6.8% (APR) | 6.8% (APR) |
| Aug 2008 | $6,500 | $4,500 | 6.8% | 6.0% |
| Aug 2009 | $7,500 | $5,500 | 6.8% | 5.6% |
| Aug 2010 | $7,500 | $5,500 | 6.8% | 4.5% |

a. What was the actual total balance on her loans the August after she graduated?

b. How much total interest did Rahel avoid on her subsidized loans during college and since her graduation (the subsidy continues during the six-month grace period) as a result of the subsidy?

c. What is the combined monthly payment, based on the standard 10-year repayment plan, for her subsidized loans?

d. What would her combined monthly payment have been if her loans had not been subsidized? (Although not completely accurate, assume that the balance in August was still the same.)

e. How much additional interest would Rahel have paid if she had not qualified for any subsidized loans?

f. How much was the subsidy worth? (Hint: Add the answer in part b to the answer in part e.)

# Comprehensive Bedo Case Analysis Questions

Determining the Bedos' education funding need is fundamentally a comparison of total assets needed and the total value of assets saved to date. The Bedos want to fund 100% of four years of college for Becky, who is age 5 and is assumed to start college at age 18. The current cost of college is $10,000 per semester. It will be important to review the following: assets currently used for education funding, the rate of return on assets used for education funding, the growth rate of savings, and the assumed rate of inflation for college costs.

Once the cost of their education goal has been established, planning strategies must be incorporated into a recommendation to empower the Bedos to achieve it. It is essential to review the case for assumptions regarding which assets they are willing to allocate to their education funding goal and to ascertain the maximum amount of risk they are willing to take with their education fund assets.

Use the following questions to guide the education planning process.

1. Develop one or more education planning goals for the Bedo household. When conceptualizing this goal(s), consider the following:

    a. Is the goal(s) developed in agreement with any or all goals and objectives that the clients have identified regarding education planning?

    b. What situational factors might influence their education planning goal? Are these factors explicit, implied, or assumed? Is additional information required from the Bedos, and if so, what?

    c. What is the desired education planning outcome for the clients?

2. Are there globally accepted, client-specific, or planner-generated planning assumptions that will influence the education planning situation analysis? List the assumptions as they might appear in a plan.

3. To determine and quantify the Bedos' current education planning need, thoroughly consider the following:

    a. The future value of one year of college when Becky turns age 18

    b. The total amount of assets needed when Becky turns 18 to fully fund four years of college

    c. The amount the Bedos need to save annually to meet their education goal(s)

4. List and discuss some of the advantages and disadvantages associated with an in-state § 529 plan. Should the Bedos consider plans offered by other states, and if so, which state?

5. Summarize your observations about Tyler's and Mia's current education planning efforts and the planning need(s) identified. Incorporate text, bullets, and graphics in your explanation. For example, what information might be shown graphically, and specifically what kind of graphs might convey the analysis to the Bedos most effectively?

6. Based on the goals originally identified and the completed analysis, which product or procedural strategies might be most useful to satisfy the Bedos' education planning needs? Be sure to consider strategies matched to the planning needs identified. When reviewing strategies, be careful to consider the approximate cost of implementation as well as the most likely outcome(s) associated with each strategy.

7. Write at least one primary and one alternative recommendation from the selected strategies in response to each identified planning need. Include specific, defensible answers to the who, what, when, where, why, how, and how much implementation questions for each recommendation.

   a. It is suggested that each recommendation be summarized in a recommendation form.

   b. Assign a priority to each recommendation based on the likelihood of meeting client goals and desired outcomes. This priority will be important when recommendations from other core planning content areas are considered in relation to the discretionary funds available for subsidizing all recommendations.

   c. Comment briefly on the outcomes associated with each recommendation.

8. Complete the following for the Education Planning section of the Bedos' financial plan.

   a. Outline the content to be included in this section of the plan. Given the segments written above, which segments are missing?

   b. Write the introduction to this section of the plan (no more than one or two paragraphs).

   c. Define, explain, or interpret at least five terms or concepts related to education planning. For each, write a definition or explanation that could appear in this section of the plan or in the plan glossary.

9. Prepare a 10–15-minute presentation for the Bedos of your observations and/or recommendation(s) regarding their education planning. Be sure to include visual aids or handouts.

## Notes

1. This process assumes that periodic savings payments occur at the end of each period; that periodic saving payments for college will cease when the child begins college; and that the annual college expense payment occurs at the beginning of each school year. All of these assumptions can be changed to fit the individual situation, but corresponding changes in the calculations will be necessary.

2. An effective annual rate (EAR) of 8.30% is equivalent to an 8% rate compounded monthly.

3. Department of Education, Student Loans Overview, *Fiscal Year 2012 Budget Request*. Available at http://www2.ed.gov/about/overview/budget/budget12/justifications/s-loansoverview.pdf, p. S-12.

4. FinAid, The Smart Student™ Guide to Financial Aid. *Student Loans*. Available at http://www.finaid.org/loans/studentloan.phtml.

5. FinAid, The Smart Student™ Guide to Financial Aid. *Parent Loans*. Available at http://www.finaid.org/loans/parentloan.phtml.

6. Department of Education. Federal Student Aid. Direct Loans. *Repayment Plans*. Available at http://www.direct.ed.gov/RepayCalc/dlindex2.html.

7. Department of Education, *Repayment Plans*.

8. Department of Education, *Repayment Plans*.

9. Department of Education, *Repayment Plans*.

10. Department of Education, *Repayment Plans*.

11. Equal Justice Works. *Partial Financial Hardship*. Available at http://www.equaljusticeworks.org/resources/student-debt-relief/income-based-repayment/partial-financial-hardship.

12. FinAid, The Smart Student™ Guide to Financial Aid. *Health Care and Education Reconciliation Act of 2010*. Available at http://www.finaid.org/educators/20100330hcera.phtml.

13. Joseph F. Hurley, *Family Guide to College Savings 2011–2012* (Pittsford, NY: JFH Innovative, 2011), 66.

14. R. Turley and M. Desmond, "Contributions to College Costs by Married, Divorced, and Remarried Parents," *Journal of Family Issues* 32, no. 6 (2011): 767–790.

15. R. Turley and M. Desmond, "Contributions to College Costs."

16. Donald Jay Korn, Financial Planning, *College Panic*. Available at http://www.financial-planning.com/fp_issues/2009_8/college-panic-2663445-1.html. For additional information, see Deborah Fox, Financial Planning, *Coming up Short*. Available at http://www.financial-planning.com/fp_issues/2009_1/coming-up-short2638481-1.html.

17. Fidelity.com, *Fidelity® Study Finds Significant Shifts Over Five-Year Period in How Families Tackle Rising College Costs*. Available at http://www.fidelity.com/inside-fidelity/individual-investing/csi-2011.

18. IRS, *American Opportunity Credit*. Available at http://www.irs.gov/publications/p970/ch02.html.

19. Additional information is available online at IRS, *American Opportunity Credit*, http://www.irs.gov/publications/p970/ch02.html#d0e1386.

# Retirement Planning

## Learning Objectives

1. Understand the importance of retirement planning, for both accumulation and distribution, within the comprehensive financial planning process.

2. Identify client situational factors that could uniquely affect a client's retirement planning goals.

3. Understand and practice the steps involved in conducting a retirement needs analysis.

4. Explain the role of Social Security in the retirement planning process.

5. Compare the characteristics and underlying use of qualified and non-qualified retirement plans.

6. Describe the appropriate use and limitations of contributory, rollover, inherited, and spousal traditional and Roth IRAs as retirement savings vehicles.

7. Develop retirement plan withdrawal strategies that match a client's income needs and life expectancy.

8. Describe and correctly utilize qualified plan and IRA distribution rules matched to a client's situation and need for retirement income.

9. Identify and recommend appropriate and reasonable retirement planning strategies matched to a client's situation.

# Key Terms

401(k) plan

403(b) tax-sheltered annuity

457 plan

average indexed monthly earnings (AIME)

capital depletion approach

capital needs analysis

capital preservation approach

combined income

defined benefit plan

defined contribution plan

deterministic modeling

employee stock ownership plan (ESOP)

exclusion ratio

fixed annuity

fixed payment annuity

fully insured

glide path portfolio

guaranteed annuity

guaranteed lifetime annuity

highly compensated employee

inclusion ratio

individual retirement arrangement or agreement (IRA)

inflation-adjusted capital preservation approach

Internal Revenue Code (IRC)

IRA rollover

joint and survivor annuity

Keogh plan

key employee

legacy

legacy pool

life annuity

life with period certain annuity

money purchase plan

Monte Carlo modeling

non-qualified deferred compensation plan (NQDC)

non-qualified plan

normal retirement age (NRA)

Pension Benefit Guaranty Corporation (PBGC)

pension plan

pool of assets

primary insurance amount (PIA)

profit-sharing plan

qualified domestic relations order (QDRO)

qualified retirement plan

rabbi trust

recharacterization

replacement ratio

required minimum distribution (RMD)

retirement annuity

retirement capital needs analysis

retirement planning

reverse mortgage

rollover

Roth IRA

Roth IRA conversion

Roth 401(k)

safe harbor 401(k)

secular trust

sequence risk

shortfall risk

simplified employee pension

SIMPLE IRA

SIMPLE 401(k)

snowbirds

Social Security

step transaction doctrine

stochastic modeling

stock bonus plan

target benefit plan

transfer

transfer incident to divorce

trustee-to-trustee transfer

variable annuity

variable universal life insurance

younger spouse exception

**Figure 12.1** Systematic Financial Planning Process for Retirement Planning

## RETIREMENT PLANNING: THE BASICS

When viewed historically, **retirement planning**—the process of helping a client to define and prepare for retirement by developing strategies for asset accumulation, asset distribution, and monitoring of plan progress—can be seen as a relatively new phenomenon. Prior to the industrial revolution, people rarely planned to retire in the way retirement is defined today, nor did they live as long to spend as many years in retirement. Nearly everyone worked until they could work no longer. Those who did outlive their working careers relied on the charity of family, friends, religious groups, or community resources for assistance with elder needs. Today, beyond leaving one's primary source of employment, which most agree on, retirement can mean pursuing part-time or full-time employment in the same or a different occupation. Or it can mean pursuing leisure or volunteer activities. Although retirement activities can vary widely, for most people retirement represents a longer life segment—offering both opportunities and challenges.

Not until the latter half of the 19th century was retirement planning considered necessary. Germany was the first nation to implement a social retirement system. By the mid-1930s, almost all western countries had some form of government-sponsored social security structure. In the relatively short time span from the 1930s to the 2010s, Americans' expectations regarding retirement needs and obligations changed dramatically. Today, nearly all Americans are covered by Social Security or another retirement plan, and the thought of entering old age without some level of asset accumulation to help pay living expenses is nearly unheard of among those contemplating retirement.

Depending on the individual financial planner's business model and scope of services provided, retirement planning services can focus on one or two perspectives: the employer's or the employee's. In some situations, a client can be both. However, especially when a planner is working with a business owner to build an employer-sponsored retirement plan, it is important that financial planners who are not attorneys avoid the appearance of practicing law. Planners are allowed to promote, market, and sell a plan; explain retirement plan alternatives; discuss issues related to the **Internal Revenue Code (IRC)**; and gather data; but they must not provide legal advice. Not only is it appropriate, at times, to discuss aspects of the IRC with clients; it is essential that financial planners have a strong working knowledge of the code because at its core the IRC serves as the basis of all qualified retirement planning. It organizes all federal tax law, as enacted by Congress in Title 26 of the U.S. Code (26 U.S.C.). In this capacity, a planner can help employers decide which plans might work best for their business and most effectively meet the retirement needs of the employer and/or the employees.

Financial planners can also advise employees who might be constrained by plan offerings through their employers. In some cases, planners must seek better alternatives because of plan limitations. Under no circumstances, however, may a financial planner who is not an attorney draft a plan document, draft a contract, or provide legal advice to clients. In every instance, the retirement planner should avoid conflicts of interest, and if a conflict arises, disclose this information to those affected.

It is also possible—especially for financial planners who work primarily with those who are already retired—for clientele to include the unemployed. This chapter focuses primarily on the planner's role when working directly with individual clients, not employers. Although some types of plans or strategies may be considered from an employer's perspective, assessing employers' needs and developing a business retirement plan are not the focus of this chapter.

This chapter provides an overview of the analysis and evaluation process undertaken by financial planners when reviewing a client's current retirement planning situation. This process, which is described and illustrated, follows the steps shown in Figure 12.1. This chapter reviews common retirement planning strategies that can be used to meet retirement objectives and presents an example of how strategies can be incorporated into a recommendation. Because the average working client is the main focus, little attention is given to planning for clients who are self-employed, owners/partners in a closely held business, or highly compensated executives who might have privileged "golden handcuffs" or other non-qualified plan arrangements that can affect the timing of and resources available for retirement.

## ANALYZE THE CLIENT'S CURRENT SITUATION

The primary difference between a retirement planning analysis and other analyses discussed in this text involve the number of variables and assumptions that can be changed to alter plan recommendations. Although this aspect of financial planning is similar to education or investment planning, the amount of funding required for the goal and the time frame, both for accumulation and distribution, make retirement planning much more complex in many respects. Furthermore, the longer time frames associated with the cycle of saving and spending can act as a two-edged sword. On the one hand, early planning offers the benefits associated with the time value of money and extended market performance; however, on the other hand, the long lag between savings behaviors and retirement expenditures increases opportunities for life and market events to derail planning efforts.

It is the financial planner's responsibility to review financial planning assumptions, question anticipated outcomes, and help clients establish targets for a realistic retirement date, rate of return, and lifestyle benchmarks. In no section of the comprehensive plan is it more important to provide clients with as many reasonable alternatives as possible. As in many aspects of financial planning, there are multiple paths to retirement success.

Even so, the financial planner, using a combination of educational background and professional judgment, is ultimately charged with the responsibility for choosing and recommending the optimal path to meet a client's retirement goal(s). A well-designed retirement plan integrates a client's situational factors with the assumptions and strategies most likely to achieve the client's desired lifestyle. A plan that can meet these standards and remain adaptable to other life-cycle changes, such as the need for long-term care or competing financial needs for children or parents, separates a superior retirement planning analysis from a mediocre one.

## Determine and Quantify a Client's Retirement Planning Needs

Ideally, retirement planning is a lifelong process that starts with funding an IRA or employer-provided plan from high school or college earnings. From that point, and for the first few decades of employment, saving for retirement focuses primarily on the most productive strategies for accumulating assets. However, in reality, life events (e.g., divorce or changes in employment) can derail anyone's accumulation plans. Competing goals, such as the need to fund a child's education or support parents or in-laws, can delay or reduce cash flow directed toward retirement accumulation goals. But at some point, perhaps 10 or more years before retirement—or unfortunately for some individuals not until after retirement—the following key question must be considered: "What does retirement mean to you?"

Financial planners should proactively help clients—particularly pre-retirees—visualize life during retirement. This is important to ascertain the client's fiscal, personal, and emotional readiness to transition away from the primary workplace into a new lifestyle. Furthermore, conceptualizing retirement helps both advisor and client determine whether expectations are realistic or whether interim strategies or research is needed to accomplish the client's retirement goals.

For example, does a client want to work during retirement? Or would the client prefer to fill the days volunteering for a variety of community, national, or international pursuits? Many retirees can comfortably walk away from the demands of a busy professional career without ever looking back. Others derive a strong sense of self and self-esteem from their profession. When they leave the workplace, the loss of that identity can be overwhelming. The need to combat depression or to fill endless empty days can create unanticipated challenges.

Issues such as the individual's purpose and meaning during retirement should be explored to delve deeper into client needs. Finding an answer to questions surrounding these themes can shed light on the level of freedom and flexibility a client desires in retirement. For someone who wants to travel, explore new hobbies or interests, or start a second career, strategies to meet retirement needs may be very different than for someone who wants to live a quiet life with more time for family and friends.

It is also important to document issues related to legacy. **Legacy** refers to a person's need or desire to leave a remembrance or lasting memorial after death. Some people have a strong desire to leave a legacy to their children or grandchildren. Others see their legacy in grander terms. They may want to endow a fund through a university, hospital, church, or other charitable or social cause. Helping clients establish realistic nonfinancial goals and expectations before retirement is one way a financial planner can enhance the perceived value of services offered.

An important lifestyle question centers on where a client will live during retirement. Some clients plan to stay in the home and town where they currently live. Others wish to move elsewhere either because of their interests, job opportunities, a lower cost of living, or to be closer to family. Still others plan to divide the year between more than one location.

The choice of housing in retirement will significantly affect a client's need for income. For example, **snowbirds**—those living in warm climates in the winter and cool climates in the summer—may have greater income needs than those who remain in their current homes. A related consideration is the choice to move to a state with lower income, real estate, or property tax rates. This decision can save clients a considerable amount of money, which can be used to fund other expenses or activities.

Another important factor that must be assessed is the client's health coverage in retirement. A 2006 Employee Benefit Research Institute study reported that a couple retiring at age 65 would need $295,000 to cover health insurance premiums and other out-of-pocket expenses in retirement assuming an average life expectancy.[1] The study assumed that health insurance was available from a former employer, with the retiree paying the entire premium. Living to age 95 would increase the cost to $550,000 for the couple. Certainly these estimates, which do not include long-term care costs, are alarming to anyone planning for retirement, but particularly so for clients faced with a decision to retire prior to the normal retirement age.

Early retirement poses unique challenges and opportunities when conducting a retirement planning analysis. The choice of early retirement may be voluntary, based on a client receiving an inheritance or reaping the gains from a well-made investment. At other times, however, the choice may be involuntary. Company-sponsored early retirement alternatives might be offered on a mandatory basis or as a voluntary workforce reduction strategy. When an employer sponsors an early retirement package, the client is usually given an incentive, such as an enhanced retirement benefit or an extension of medical benefits, but sometimes the employee is forced to deal with decreased cash flow and minimal benefits.

The need for adequate medical coverage, especially among those who retire early, is of paramount importance for clients with a history of medical problems and for those who plan to retire before age 65 when coverage under Medicare becomes available for most Americans. Medicare coverage is generally unavailable to those who retire early unless they are disabled. This causes an insurance gap that should be evaluated prior to retirement. Two commonly used strategies can be used to meet medical needs until age 65.

First, a client could negotiate with an employer for continued medical coverage. Some employers provide health coverage to all retirees, but this is rare. If available, early retirees might be able to continue coverage with the employer through the Early Retiree Reinsurance Program, which reimburses employers for health care costs paid by or on behalf of early retirees (age 55 years or older) ineligible for Medicare. This Patient Protection and Affordable Care Act reinsurance program is to be funded from 2010 through 2013; in 2014 the state-based American Health Benefit Exchanges will be available to provide other more affordable health care coverage. Second, clients who work at firms with 20 or more employees might be able to extend medical insurance coverage via COBRA. Some states mandate medical extensions similar to COBRA for even smaller employers. In either case, the out-of-pocket premium will be significantly higher than what the client paid as an employee. This strategy is premised on the assumption that an outside policy or one provided through a COBRA-like extension will be needed until age 65. Utilizing this strategy requires the client to begin saving 5 to 10 years prior to retirement into an account to be used exclusively to pay insurance premiums. For additional ideas on securing coverage, see *Planning for Special Populations: Health Insurance Options for Early Retirees* in Chapter 6 on health insurance planning needs.

Although the issues are likely more complex for early retirees, the same lifestyle and client situational factors must be considered whether a client is considering early or normal-age retirement. Regardless of a client's age, it is important for planners to assess the client's financial and nonfinancial willingness and ability to retire successfully. Client situational factors to consider from the perspective of the client and spouse, partner, or significant other include the following:

- attitude about retiring, or specifically about retiring early;

- motivation for retiring or retiring early;

- willingness to continue working in another firm or industry;

- willingness to establish a consulting practice or other business venture;

- types of personal, leisure, or volunteer activities that the individual(s) would engage in while retired;

- health status;

- willingness to relocate, either to a specific designation or to a lower-cost area; and

- willingness or need to provide support for other family members (e.g., children, grandchildren, parents, in-laws).

Although all pre-retirees should analyze the following quantitative financial factors to assess fiscal readiness, those considering early retirement must carefully consider the:

- ability of their accumulated asset base, plus other forms of income, to provide adequate retirement income;

- impact of early retirement on Social Security benefits;

- impact of early retirement on defined benefit plan distributions;

- effect of retirement on health benefits;

- impact of early retirement on the working status of a spouse or partner;

- tax implications of lump-sum benefits (e.g., unused sick and vacation days) received from an employer; and

- relocation and retirement transition expenses.

A complete retirement needs analysis should be completed before the anticipated retirement date to determine a client's potential standard of living while in retirement as well as projected quality of life, regardless of whether an early, on-time, or late retirement option is chosen. For many clients, this analysis will confirm that their early planning has been effective. For others, however, the analysis could indicate the need for additional savings or a change in lifestyle choices.

Once a client and planner have envisioned the ideal—or perhaps most likely—lifestyle and income picture for retirement, considering both the active and inactive years associated with aging, attention must turn to quantifying the cost of the projected retirement need. Fundamentally, retirement planning involves (a) documenting a client's specific retirement income funding goal, (b) determining gross need over a client's life expectancy, and (c) determining whether the client is on track to meet the asset accumulation objective given all other assumptions about the funding situation. Although the analytical approach may appear straightforward, these three essential components of the projection must be accurately matched to a client's situation. Each is now briefly considered.

Income or living expense **replacement ratios** are widely used by planners to estimate a client's retirement income funding goal. An accepted generalization is that a client will need 70% to 80% of currently available income in retirement. That is, the target should be to replace at least 70% of current income on the client's first day of retirement. In general, low- and high-income-earning households need the highest replacement ratios.

The argument for using less than 100% as a replacement ratio is that a retiree's expenses will be reduced by the expenditures associated with employment. Evidence suggests, however, that this assumption may be incorrect. More retirees are engaging in activities and hobbies that require as much or more income in retirement as was earned prior to retirement. Some expenses, such as those for health care, could increase significantly during retirement. Choices about other major expense categories during retirement, like housing or taxes, significantly affect the income replacement ratio choice.

In many cases, contingent on a client's plans, the first needs analysis calculations can be estimated with a 100% income replacement assumption, which can be relaxed if it is determined that the client will be unable to meet asset accumulation requirements.

## Select Retirement Needs Calculations

Determining the gross pool of assets needed over a client's life expectancy involves conducting a traditional **retirement capital needs analysis.** As the name implies, this projection determines the capital needed from all sources to support the estimated retirement income requirement, while allowing for the effects of inflation over a client's life expectancy. Financial planners use this type of analysis to help pre-retirees understand how allocating assets and saving money can influence taxes due and the amount of income and assets available during retirement.

The steps necessary to calculate capital depletion, capital preservation, and inflation-adjusted approaches to retirement needs are based on the time value of money equations presented in Chapter 2. All of the steps used in the following examples, plus additional ones that were omitted from these earlier examples for simplicity, are illustrated in the exhibits from the Financial Facilitator that appear later in this chapter.

The financial planner must make several assumptions, in consultation with the client, before calculating retirement estimates. The first key assumption involves determining whether contributions toward the retirement goal will grow or remain fixed. That is to say, will each subsequent payment increase by a predetermined amount, such as the inflation rate? In effect, this assumption comes down to using a fixed annuity or a geometric varying annuity assumption. A second assumption involves the length of the retirement period or the number of years that the client will engage in saving for the goal. The third assumption involves determining the rate of return expected during retirement. The last key assumption is the timing of income received by the client during the retirement period. This determines whether the adviser needs to use an annuity due adjustment. (Typically a retirement annuity is calculated based on a beginning-of-period payment—an annuity due assumption.)

Once these calculation inputs have been determined, the financial planner—again working closely with the client—must calculate the amount of the first retirement payment. The amount of this payment should be based on the client's current (or projected) income. The projection could simply be an estimated target value, such as a dollar figure (e.g., $100,000) or a percentage of current living expenses. Once all variables are known, the planner can calculate the amount required to fully fund the level of savings needed on an annual basis to meet the accumulated asset objective as of the retirement date.

To facilitate the presentation of these calculations, two loosely defined terms are used. First is the **retirement annuity,** the amount of money required to fund a client's retirement period. Second is the **legacy pool**. This is the amount of money that a client wants to have left at the end of the retirement period (i.e., the amount that the client wants to own on the date of death).

The **capital depletion approach**, when used to estimate the capital required to fund income needs on the first day of retirement, assumes that at the end of the retirement planning period no additional client assets will remain available to the client or heirs. In other words, all client assets available for retirement will be depleted by the time of the client's death. Therefore, the legacy pool value will be zero and can be ignored for this approach.

Basic time value of money formulas are used to determine the present value of the retirement annuity need assuming a future value (legacy value) of zero. Then, based on the present value required, the client can determine the periodic savings amount needed to achieve the savings goal. In each of the following examples, only the present value of the need is calculated. The periodic savings amount calls for an additional calculation based on the client's funding requirement.

> *Example:* A client desires to fund a retirement account with enough money to last for 30 years. The planner knows that the client wants the first payment to be $100,000 and occur at the beginning of the first year of retirement. Further, the planner knows that subsequent payments are to increase 4% annually to keep pace with anticipated inflation. Assuming an effective annual rate of 10%, how much

money will the client need at retirement? Using the present value of a growing annuity, it can be determined that the client requires $1,492,564.

$$PVGA_n = \frac{PMT_1}{(i-g)}\left[1 - \frac{(1+g)^n}{(1+i)^n}\right](1+i)$$

Where:

$i$ = 10%

$g$ = 4%

$PMT_1$ = $100,000

$n$ = 30

$$PVGA_n = \frac{\$100,000}{(0.10 - 0.04)}\left[1 - \frac{(1.04)^{30}}{(1.10)^{30}}\right](1.10) = \$1,492,564$$

The capital depletion method results in the lowest savings need, because it is assumed that the client will deplete the account over the course of retirement. Therefore, reaching this threshold is the minimum level of retirement planning funding that must be met.

Many clients could be uncomfortable with the fundamental assumption of depleting all assets over their life expectancy. First, there is the possibility of outliving the available assets. Second, the capital depletion approach leaves nothing as a legacy to heirs or charities. In cases where the minimum capital depletion scenario can be satisfied with asset projections, the planner should also calculate the retirement need using the **capital preservation approach**.

To determine the pool of assets (i.e., legacy pool) needed to preserve a client's capital (i.e., so that the client's asset base does not decline during retirement), the planner must conduct one additional time value of money calculation. As with the previous approach, the present value of the pool of assets (retirement annuity) figure must be estimated. However, this legacy pool figure should also be included as a future value. Therefore, the resulting present value of the legacy pool should be added to the present value of the retirement annuity to determine a new amount needed on the first day of retirement. In effect, the present value of the legacy pool grows while the present value of the retirement annuity is depleted. At the end of the planning period, the client has exactly the same nominal amount available as on the first day of retirement. The following example should bring additional clarity to this process.

*Example:* Return to the previous example where a client requires a growing annuity with a beginning payment of $100,000. However, in addition, the client desires to leave a legacy equal to the beginning value of the retirement annuity. The adjustment to the previous example may seem unexpectedly simple. The client needs to accumulate only an additional $85,537 on the first day of retirement, because this is the amount that would result in a future value equal to $1,492,564 at the time of the client's death. Using this approach, the client needs a total of $1,578,101 saved at retirement ($1,492,564 + $85,537). The present value of a lump sum is used to solve for the additional amount needed.

$$PV_n = \frac{FV}{(1+i)^n}$$

Where:

i  = 10%

FV = $1,492,564 (the amount needed to fund the retirement annuity)

n  = 30

$$PV_n = \frac{\$1,492,564}{(1.1)^{30}} = \$85,537$$

This approach maintains the client's assets such that the balance of assets is nominally the same at the beginning of retirement and at the end of life expectancy.

Determining how best to preserve a client's asset base is often a difficult task given the complexity of assumptions and the need to generate sufficient income to support the client during retirement. However, in cases where capital preservation can be achieved, a third projection can be undertaken. This is known as the **inflation-adjusted capital preservation approach**. It may be possible not only to preserve a client's assets, but also to account for inflation such that at life expectancy the real value of the retirement assets is equal to the nominal value at retirement.

*Example:* Return to the previous example where a client requires a growing annuity with a beginning payment of $100,000. However, in addition, the client wishes to leave a legacy with an ending purchasing power equal to the beginning purchasing power of the retirement annuity. Again, the adjustment to the original example is quite simple. To maintain equivalent purchasing power, the client needs to a have an additional $277,429 saved at the time of retirement. Using this approach, the client needs a total of $1,769,993 saved at retirement ($1,492,564 + $277,429).

$$Serial\ Rate = \frac{(1+i)}{(1+g)} - 1$$

$$Serial\ Rate = \frac{(1.10)}{(1.04)} - 1 = 5.77\%$$

Using the serial rate, the following present value equation is used to calculate the required additional amount needed to preserve the purchasing power of the client's legacy.

$$PV_n = \frac{FV}{(1+i)^n}$$

Where:

i  =  5.77%

FV =  $1,492,564 (The inflation-adjusted amount desired at the end of retirement.)

n  =  30

$$PV_n = \frac{\$1,492,564}{(1.0577)^{30}} = \$277,429$$

This approach greatly increases the targeted nominal value of the client's account while maintaining the real value of the client's assets from the beginning of retirement until the end of the client's life expectancy.

Almost all of the numerical inputs used in a **capital needs analysis** come from a client's cash flow statement and balance sheet. Other sources of data include Social Security benefit statements, estimates of Social Security income, and employer-provided estimates of defined benefit payouts, if any.

Assumptions, on the other hand, tend to be based on a combination of a planner's knowledge and experience and a client's goals. Assumptions are particularly sensitive to the economic environment, and care should be taken to choose realistic standards and periodically review and update them in planning projections. Usually, clients expect a planner to provide initial planning assumptions, anticipating that certain changes will be made as client-planner discussions progress.

One of the first requirements to assess retirement planning need involves helping the client determine the amount of income needed during retirement. In the majority of cases, an income replacement ratio is chosen based on a percentage of total client income. It is generally a good idea to discuss income needs with clients in today's dollars. Using inflated (nominal value) dollars at an early stage in the process serves only to confuse and panic clients. When clients see or hear that their income need will be in the hundreds of thousands—and possibly millions—of dollars, they sometimes become apprehensive about the effectiveness of planning in the context of their current level of income, which is, by definition, less than future-value projections.

It is not uncommon for some planners to base the replacement ratio on living expenses rather than income. This approach has the advantage of helping clients determine how much they will need to earn to maintain a comfortable retirement lifestyle. It can also be a more meaningful approach if the client is currently saving a significant percentage of income.

Once income issues have been addressed, other sources of guaranteed retirement income must be documented. For clients with a defined benefit plan, obtaining an estimate of future income is relatively straightforward. Benefits administrators working for a client's employer can usually produce an estimate of defined benefit plan payments. This figure, in present value dollars, should be subtracted from the client's projected retirement income need. The present value of the estimated Social Security benefit should also be subtracted from the projected retirement income or living expenses needed.

Earnings rates for periods prior to and after retirement also should be estimated. It is important to remember that these rates of return should be based on the client's current asset allocation and retirement savings approach. Rate of return assumptions might need alteration after the initial analysis, but during the first projection it is necessary to show the client the *current situation*, given the facts at the moment, rather than use projections that assume that other planning recommendations have been implemented. The planner should also determine a client's current marginal tax bracket and then estimate the marginal tax bracket expected in retirement. These estimates will be used to determine the after-tax value of accumulated savings.

The final assumption—and one of the most important to be made—is how long a client will remain in retirement. Obviously, the longer the period, the greater the need for asset values large enough to meet future income or expense needs. If the assumed length of retirement is too short, it is likely that a client will outlive available assets. It is also increasingly important to consider the possibility of long-term care funding. Finding the right balance among these assumptions is very important.

Exhibits 12.1, 12.2, and 12.3 illustrate how retirement income needs can be estimated using the Financial Facilitator. Call-out boxes explain the data input. Note that some cells in the sheet self-populate from other worksheets.

In summary, the capital depletion approach to projecting a client's retirement planning need should be determined first. Often more than one planning assumption needs adjusting to help a client reach the retirement planning goal. For example, increasing rate of return assumptions based on a revised (e.g., riskier) asset allocation model, in tandem with directing more assets and savings toward retirement, could meet the need.

**Exhibit 12.1** Retirement Needs Estimator, Section One

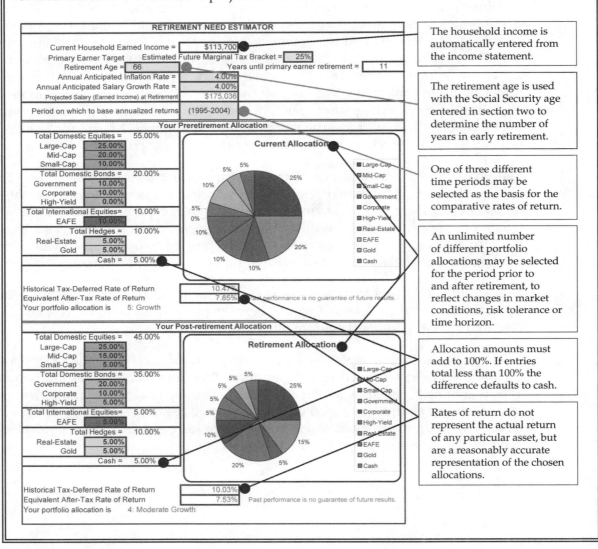

**Financial Facilitator Revealed**
Retirement Need Estimator, Section One

The retirement needs estimator is used to determine the amount of savings needed for retirement based on various user-defined inputs. This portion of the estimator projects future salary and calculates portfolio growth rates. Portfolio allocations can be entered based on current allocations or ideal allocations to maximize projected returns.

### RETIREMENT NEED ESTIMATOR

| | |
|---|---|
| Current Household Earned Income = | $113,700 |
| Primary Earner Target     Estimated Future Marginal Tax Bracket = | 25% |
| Retirement Age = 66     Years until primary earner retirement = | 11 |
| Annual Anticipated Inflation Rate = | 4.00% |
| Annual Anticipated Salary Growth Rate = | 4.00% |
| Projected Salary (Earned Income) at Retirement | $175,036 |
| Period on which to base annualized returns | (1995-2004) |

The household income is automatically entered from the income statement.

The retirement age is used with the Social Security age entered in section two to determine the number of years in early retirement.

#### Your Preretirement Allocation

| | |
|---|---|
| Total Domestic Equities = | 55.00% |
| Large-Cap | 25.00% |
| Mid-Cap | 20.00% |
| Small-Cap | 10.00% |
| Total Domestic Bonds = | 20.00% |
| Government | 10.00% |
| Corporate | 10.00% |
| High-Yield | 0.00% |
| Total International Equities= | 10.00% |
| EAFE | 10.00% |
| Total Hedges = | 10.00% |
| Real-Estate | 5.00% |
| Gold | 5.00% |
| Cash = | 5.00% |

**Current Allocation**

Legend: Large-Cap, Mid-Cap, Small-Cap, Government, Corporate, High-Yield, Real-Estate, EAFE, Gold, Cash

One of three different time periods may be selected as the basis for the comparative rates of return.

| | |
|---|---|
| Historical Tax-Deferred Rate of Return | 10.47% |
| Equivalent After-Tax Rate of Return | 7.85% |
| Your portfolio allocation is | 5: Growth |

Past performance is no guarantee of future results.

An unlimited number of different portfolio allocations may be selected for the period prior to and after retirement, to reflect changes in market conditions, risk tolerance or time horizon.

#### Your Post-retirement Allocation

| | |
|---|---|
| Total Domestic Equities = | 45.00% |
| Large-Cap | 25.00% |
| Mid-Cap | 15.00% |
| Small-Cap | 5.00% |
| Total Domestic Bonds = | 35.00% |
| Government | 20.00% |
| Corporate | 10.00% |
| High-Yield | 5.00% |
| Total International Equities= | 5.00% |
| EAFE | 5.00% |
| Total Hedges = | 10.00% |
| Real-Estate | 5.00% |
| Gold | 5.00% |
| Cash = | 5.00% |

**Retirement Allocation**

Legend: Large-Cap, Mid-Cap, Small-Cap, Government, Corporate, High-Yield, Real-Estate, EAFE, Gold, Cash

Allocation amounts must add to 100%. If entries total less than 100% the difference defaults to cash.

| | |
|---|---|
| Historical Tax-Deferred Rate of Return | 10.03% |
| Equivalent After-Tax Rate of Return | 7.53% |
| Your portfolio allocation is | 4: Moderate Growth |

Past performance is no guarantee of future results.

Rates of return do not represent the actual return of any particular asset, but are a reasonably accurate representation of the chosen allocations.

**Exhibit 12.2** Retirement Needs Estimator, Section Two

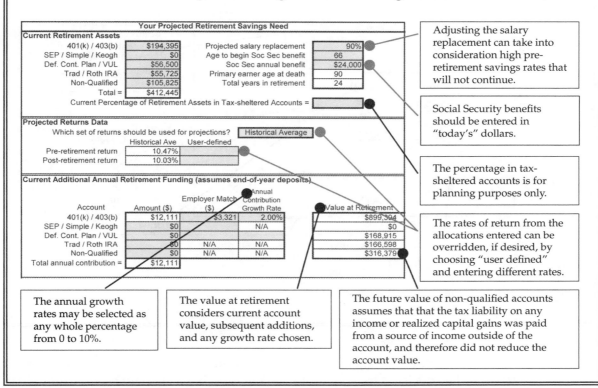

**Exhibit 12.3** Retirement Needs Estimator, Results Section

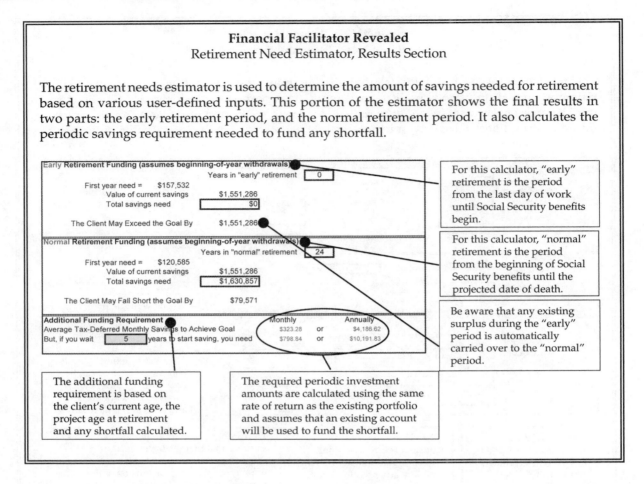

Figure 12.2 outlines the hierarchical steps to follow when evaluating a client's current situation. The decision tree begins by asking whether a client needs additional savings to meet a capital depletion objective. If the answer is yes, a series of assumption changes and strategies is presented, beginning with allocating additional resources to the goal. If these adjustments do not allow a client to meet the retirement savings goal, the planner is prompted to determine the client's willingness to reduce the income needed in retirement. The process continues until the capital depletion projection is achieved for the client's life expectancy. However, caution must be exercised when changing planning assumptions to ensure that the assumptions are valid and defensible. Overly conservative estimates could compromise a client's current standard of living, and assumptions that are too generous could seriously threaten retirement funding by generating savings recommendations that would be insufficient if rate of return or inflation estimates deviate significantly from reality.

Once the capital depletion model is fully funded, the focus of potential funding strategies proceeds to Step Two at any point on the decision tree shown in Figure 12.2. Here, attention turns to projecting the funding needed for the capital preservation and inflation-adjusted models, depending on the client's preference.

**Figure 12.2** Decision Tree for Determining Retirement Planning Strategy

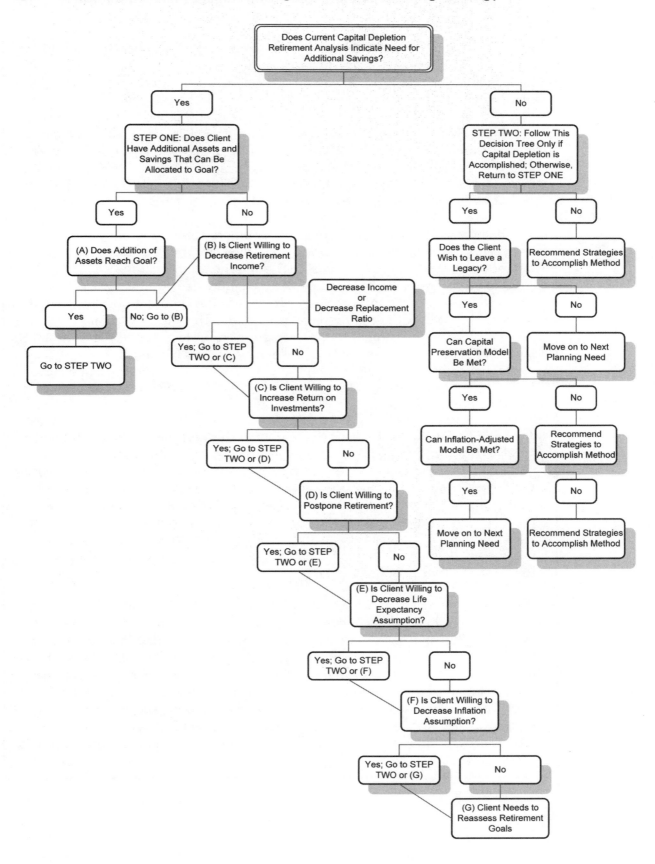

## Planning for Special Populations: Retirement Planning for Young Adults

For the first time in nearly 70 years, an entire generation of Americans has grown up watching their parents lose their savings, their homes, their cars, and their jobs. In addition, Ponzi schemes have instilled distrust and heightened the fear of many potential investors. These factors have resulted in a younger generation that is investing as conservatively as their parents and grandparents.[2] Not since the Great Depression has there been such a financially devastating course of events as the decade of the 2000s. Just as the Depression shaped the saving and spending habits of what is commonly known as the Traditional generation, the Internet bubble and housing crisis have shaped and will continue to shape the financial habits and paradigms of the Millennial generation.

The names Millennials, Gen Y, or Echo Boomers typically identify those born between 1980 and 1995; they comprise nearly 80 million Americans. Other date ranges often cited for the Millennial or Gen Y generation include 1977 to 1998 or 1980 to 2000. People born in this period were between ages 1 and 16 when the dot-com bubble burst and between ages 8 and 23 when the housing collapse nearly brought down the entire financial system. This group is clearly cautious when evaluating investment and retirement risks. In fact, according to an MFS Investing Sentiment Survey, 40% of Millennials agreed with the statement "I will never feel comfortable investing in the stock market."[3] But in the same survey, 62% agreed that they enjoy investing.[4] This is a difficult dichotomy to overcome in the planning process.

Two additional issues to consider are that (1) Millennials will be the most indebted group of college graduates in the history of the United States, and (2) they will be the best-connected, most well-informed group in the history of the United States. But they are also new to the world of personal finance—a personal financial world that has become more complex—and a world where it is becoming apparent that learning how to manage money has evolved into a life skill. These are major issues for young people and for those who strive to provide financial advice to young people. On the bright side, this group seems to be more serious about savings, but in what?

Data points to younger generation investors who prefer to invest in tangible assets rather than purely financial ones; assets such as land, gold, energy, mineral rights, and bank deposits seem to be more in vogue than at any time since the 1930s. Coincidentally, energy and tangible assets such as gold have enjoyed sustained rallies for much of the Millennials' lives. But those who have watched their parents lose their retirement account values to accounting fraud (e.g., Enron), Ponzi schemes (e.g., Bernie Madoff), greed (e.g., Global Crossing, Inc), arrogance (e.g., AIG), or ignorance (e.g., Lehman Brothers) are looking for more stable returns, guarantees, and income generation in their own retirement accounts.

One final issue is that this generation will have to plan for a retirement that is practically devoid of private, corporate-sponsored pension plans. Although this avenue of retirement savings has been in decline since the 1970s, at least some members of all of the previous generations had access to a defined-benefit plan; now, that is almost solely reserved for government employees. In 1977 nearly two-thirds of active participants in employer-sponsored retirement plans were covered by a defined benefit; however, by 2007 that ratio had fallen to 22.5%.[5]

In summary, the Millennials enjoy investing, but they do not trust the stock market. They are willing to save, but not willing to risk; and they have an appetite for investing in asset classes that, in the long-term, perform no better than inflation.[6]

## Document and Evaluate Current Retirement Planning Efforts

The second step when analyzing a client's current retirement planning situation involves documenting and evaluating all current retirement planning strategies. This analysis considers four questions:

1. Is the amount of money the client is saving enough to meet the goal (discussed in the previous section)?

2. Is the client optimizing the asset class mix to ensure the best risk-adjusted return (discussed in Chapter 10 on investment planning)?

3. Is the client utilizing the optimal types of accounts (i.e., qualified or pretax versus non-qualified or post-tax) to ensure the best tax-adjusted return?

4. Is the client maintaining adequate financial flexibility to meet changing goals or emergencies?

Although question 1 may be the most important aspect to review early in the accumulation phase of retirement planning, question 4 becomes more important to evaluate as a client nears or enters retirement. Questions 2 and 3 represent important planning issues across the life cycle, as well as issues that might need to be reconsidered because of changes in the economy or market or tax policy changes.

Whereas the first step in the analysis of the client's current situation focused on determining the dollar amount of assets needed to meet the retirement need, the second step of documenting and evaluating current retirement planning efforts focuses attention on the effectiveness of savings strategies and whether other tactics are more appropriate. For example, the client (and spouse or partner) may have one or more employer-provided plan(s), IRA account(s), or other personal tax-advantaged or non-tax-advantaged assets designated for retirement funding. All of these account types must work in unison toward this common goal, not only during the accumulation phase (preretirement), but also during the distribution phase (postretirement). Both of these phases of retirement planning require planners to continuously document and evaluate a client's current retirement planning efforts. Clients might seek planning advice during the accumulation phase, when a long-term plan can be developed, but more likely the client will wait until approaching retirement to seek advice. In this situation, the time frame may be limited to only a few years of accumulation planning. At this point, the primary focus should be on helping the client envision and define the retirement years and then plan the distribution phase, perhaps in conjunction with some form of employment. Following is a discussion of how to document and evaluate current retirement planning efforts across the life cycle among pre-retirees, near-retirees, and retirees.

### Pre-retirees: Analysis of Current Retirement Planning Efforts

Financial professionals often use the analogy of the three-legged stool as a framework for considering a client's retirement planning situation. The three commonly identified legs of the stool supporting retirement are

1. resources from the government through **Social Security** benefits—a government-backed retirement system that provides monthly inflation-adjusted benefits;

2. resources from employer-provided retirement plans; and

3. resources from personal savings.

In light of the Baby Boom generation's recent and expanding efforts to redefine retirement, some professionals have suggested adding a leg to the stool: employment during retirement and the use of home equity. A Fidelity Research Institute 2007 Retirement Index report noted that, although 60% of pre-retirees plan on working to supplement their retirement income, 22% of retirees in that same survey were forced into early retirement because of poor health.[7] So although employment, either in the same or a different professional pursuit, may be an alternative, like other retirement funding sources, the option of postretirement employment is characterized by unique benefits and risks. The same also can be said of home equity, which prior to 2007, most assumed was stable or appreciating. The significant loss of value resulting from home losses post-2008 eroded the retirement portfolios of many pre-retirees, forcing them to postpone retirement because of concerns over the value and liquidity of real estate. Each of the primary funding sources of retirement (i.e., Social Security, retirement plans, savings, and employment) is briefly reviewed to establish the framework of the three- or four-legged stool.

**Social Security within the funding mix.** Virtually all working Americans are covered by Social Security, which is funded through employee and employer payroll deductions. A few categories of workers are not covered through the Social Security system. For instance, certain municipal or state employees whose employers have opted out of the system are exempt from Social Security taxes. Federal workers hired before 1984 are generally not covered by Social Security. Some religious ministers and Christian Science practitioners can also opt out of Social Security. The largest category of privately employed exempt workers includes railroad workers covered under the Railroad Retirement Act. Although most Social Security benefit calculations can be estimated online, customized to the client's earnings record online, or estimated by a Social Security representative, it is important that students and novice planners have a working knowledge of Social Security terms and benefit calculation methods.

The Social Security Administration uses the **average indexed monthly earnings** (**AIME**) calculation to determine a worker's Social Security benefit upon early, regular, or postponed retirement. According to the Social Security Administration, two primary calculations need to be made, consecutively, to arrive at AIME.[8]

The first calculation is the adjustment for inflation of the retiree's top 35 years of earnings, not to exceed the Social Security maximum taxable income in that specific year. (Fewer years may sometimes be used.) The calculation begins by dividing the current national average wage index by the national average wage index in the year the individual incurred wages. This calculation is made for each year. This indexing adjustment is completed for all years with the exception of the most recent two years. The total indexed earnings amount is then divided by the total number of months in those years.

The second calculation involves multiplying each year's earnings by the index calculated for that specific year. This effectively adjusts each year's earnings to the current year's wages, as indexed for inflation. Calculation outcomes are added together and then divided by the number of months to arrive at AIME. AIME is then used to calculate the Social Security **primary insurance amount** (**PIA**), which is just a fancy term for the monthly benefit.[9]

Social Security benefits are generally based on an average of the 35 years of highest earnings, although the PIA is specifically used to determine retirement, disability, and survivor benefits that are paid *monthly* to a single individual. According to the Social Security Administration, PIA is calculated by first determining the worker's AIME, a factor the Social Security Administration provides. The PIA calculation is as follows:

PIA  = 90% of the first $X of AIME

+ 32% of the AIME in excess of $X and less than $Y

<u>+ 15% of the AIME in excess of $Y</u>

In the preceding equation, $X and $Y are called *bend points*, which are adjusted annually according to the national average wage index. In 2012 the value for $X was $767 and the value for $Y was $4,624. PIA is the amount the worker will receive for retirement at full retirement age.

> *Example*: Irina Dalakis, a 40-year-old account executive for a major pharmaceutical company, has begun to wonder how much she can expect to receive as a monthly benefit from Social Security to supplement her other retirement savings. Based on her AIME of 6,875, she would receive $2,262.00 per month in retirement benefit.[10]

$$PIA = (0.90 \times 767) + (0.32 \times (4{,}624 - 767)) + (0.15 \times (6{,}875 - 4{,}624))$$

$$PIA = 691.30 + 1{,}234.24 + 337.65$$

$$PIA = 2{,}262.19$$

It is important to note that PIA is reduced or increased for early or delayed retirement. When designing a retirement plan, it is important to remember that those who are eligible for Social Security may receive retirement, disability, survivorship, and Medicare benefits concurrently. A small lump sum death benefit of $255 is also available to survivors of a fully insured person.

To be **fully insured** in the Social Security system, a client must generally have 40 quarters of employment coverage. In 2012, a person receives one quarter of coverage for each $1,130 of earnings (wages or self-employment income), up to a maximum of four quarters per year. It is possible to be *currently* rather than *fully* insured. Individuals with at least six quarters of coverage credits in the last 13 quarters are considered currently insured.

A client who is fully insured is entitled to Social Security benefits at retirement. **Normal retirement age (NRA)** is 65 for clients born before 1938. The NRA increases in two month increments for every year an individual is born between 1938 and 1943. Anyone born from 1943 to 1954 has a normal retirement age of 66 years. For anyone born from 1955 to 1960, the NRA increases in two month intervals until age 67. Age 67 is currently the maximum Social Security normal retirement age.

It is possible to retire prior to the NRA. Age 62 is the earliest age at which Social Security retirement benefits can be received. A retiree's monthly benefit is reduced by 5/9 of 1% for every month of early retirement for the first 36 months, and by 5/12 of 1% for every month in excess of 36. Someone whose NRA is 66 and who claims benefits at age 64, for example, will receive a 13.33% reduction in benefits (5/9 × 0.01 × 24). Someone who's NRA is 67, who claims benefits at age 62, will receive a 30% reduction in benefits, as shown below:

$$\left[\left(\tfrac{5}{9} \times 0.01 \times 36\right) + \left(\tfrac{5}{12} \times 0.01 \times 24\right)\right]$$

Clients also can delay the receipt of Social Security benefits. Doing so results in a permanent increase in benefits. The actual increase depends on the age of the client, but generally a worker can expect between a 6.5% and 8% increase in benefits for every year of deferment between the normal retirement age and age 70.

For retirement planning purposes, survivor benefits are available to the spouse of an insured individual. A spouse who has no work history or a limited work history can draw Social Security benefits based on their spouse's work history. The payment is typically 50% of the insured's benefit, but this can be reduced if the surviving spouse is younger than the insured. Although several states currently recognize same-sex marriage, federal laws do not.[11] This means that rules associated with Social Security benefits and qualified retirement plans do not provide the same ownership or beneficiary clauses as those provided to same-sex couples. This effectively means that there are no survivorship benefits available through Social Security for same-sex couples, nor are joint-and-survivor benefits provided automatically under ERISA-covered defined benefit or cash-balance plans, discussed later in this chapter.

The Social Security Administration regularly sends statements to persons covered by Social Security that provide an estimate of future Social Security benefits in today's dollars, based on actual Social Security wages. Another easy way to estimate a client's approximate annual benefit in today's dollars is to use the Social Security Benefit Estimator on the Internet at www.socialsecurity.gov/OACT/quickcalc/index.html. This tool provides a rough estimate of how much a client and spouse can expect to receive at retirement.

A question commonly asked of financial planners is whether a client should take early Social Security retirement benefits. Before answering this question, the planner should perform a present value break-even calculation to determine the best time to begin drawing the benefit. Issues to consider when addressing this question include the client's life expectancy, current earnings projections, prospects for salary increases, and other employment opportunities. A general early benefit rule was published in 2012. Under the rule, a single person should take early Social Security benefits only if the rate of return earned on the benefits exceeds the inflation rate by 5%.[12]

In effect, the client who postpones retirement benefits is wagering that he or she will live long enough to recoup the opportunity cost associated with delaying the benefit, and as such, the client must earn a sufficient real return to break even on the reduced benefit received. As long as the recipient's age and health profile matches statistical averages, the 5% rule is usually appropriate. Someone who takes an early benefit may think that having additional cash flow now rather than later is worthwhile both financially and psychologically. As suggested by the 5% rule, this may be true if the early paid benefits can be saved and reinvested at a rate higher than inflation.

It is important to take into account possible tax issues when helping clients make decisions regarding the timing of benefits. Social Security payments can increase a client's income tax liability. The amount of benefits subject to tax depends on each client's combined income (not solely adjusted gross income [AGI]) and filing status. **Combined income** is the sum of AGI, tax-exempt interest, and one-half the Social Security benefit. For example, if the combined income of a single filer in 2012 is between $25,000 and $34,000, up to 50% of Social Security benefits could be taxed. If the combined income of a single filer is more than $34,000, up to 85% of the benefits can be taxed. For those filing joint returns, break points are $32,000 and $44,000, respectively. For married individuals filing separate returns, the break point is $0.

A person who retires before their NRA and receives Social Security retirement benefits can lose some or all of the benefits by working. Retirees who have not yet reached their NRA for all of 2012 can earn up to $14,640 without losing benefits. If earnings exceed this amount, part of the Social Security benefit is lost; the penalty in lost benefits is severe. For every $2 a client earns above this amount, $1 in benefits is lost. For those who will reach their NRA in 2012, the Social Security Administration will deduct $1 from benefits for each $3 earned above $38,880 until the month a client reaches full retirement age. After NRA has been reached, a retiree can earn an unlimited dollar amount without penalty.

In summary, Social Security benefits can be an important supplement to other retirement funding sources. But questions surrounding access to the funds, the amount of the projected funds, and the potential impact on income taxes due on all retirement income cannot be overlooked in the planning process. For couples, the issues can be even more complex. These complexities must be analyzed as clients approach retirement.

**Qualified and non-qualified employee benefits within the funding mix.** Employer-provided retirement plans can be broadly categorized as either qualified or non-qualified. **Qualified retirement plans** are recognized and described in the IRC. Qualified plans provide employees and employers certain tax advantages because they meet qualifications established by tax law. Contributions to an employee's qualified retirement plan are generally excluded from current taxable income. Employers enjoy an immediate tax deduction for contributions made to a qualified retirement plan for their employees. Although certain rules place limits on contributions, it is possible for some employers to offer more than one kind of plan.

Qualified retirement plans can be further differentiated into two categories: defined benefit plans and defined contribution plans. A **defined benefit plan**, or **pension plan,** provides a specific guaranteed benefit at retirement that is usually calculated using a formula typically based on a percentage of salary and years of service. For example, a benefit of 1.5% of final pay for each year of service up to 25 years is common. Using this formula, someone who has worked at a firm for 20 years would be eligible to receive 30% of final pay as a yearly benefit in retirement for the remainder of the retiree's life. Again, no joint and survivor benefits are provided automatically under ERISA-covered defined benefit or cash-balance plans.

A **defined contribution** plan provides an individual account for each participant and offers benefits to employees based on the value of that account upon retirement. The most common form of employer-provided retirement plan in the United States is the defined contribution plan.

Although defined benefit plans were very common throughout the 1970s, the most common type of qualified plan offered today is the defined contribution plan, such as a 401(k) plan. A **401(k) plan** offers employees the opportunity to contribute pretax dollars to their accounts. Many plans provide some form of matching contribution by the employer. A 401(k) plan can also include a **Roth 401(k)** feature, which allows the contribution of after-tax dollars. Two specialized types of 401(k) plan designs are available: the **SIMPLE 401(k) plan** and the **safe harbor 401(k) plan.**

Defined contribution plans include all **profit-sharing plans**, as well as **stock bonus plans,** and **employee stock ownership plans (ESOP). Money purchase plans** and **target benefit plans** are also included. Certain types of retirement plans are not technically qualified plans, yet they operate in a similar manner and provide tax-deferred earnings growth. Examples include **simplified employee pension** accounts (SEP accounts) and **Keogh plan** accounts for small businesses, **403(b) tax-sheltered annuities** for nonprofit employers, and **457 plans** for state, local, and municipal government employers. Table 12.1 provides summary data for each of these defined contribution plans.

**Table 12.1** A Comparison of the Funding Characteristics of Defined Contribution Plans for 2012

| Plan Type | Maximum Contribution per Participant (Elective Deferral) | Maximum Annual Addition[1] per Participant (based on Max. Compensation of $250,000)[2] | Mandatory Yearly Employer Contributions? | CODA/ 401(k) Permitted? | Forfeitures Generally Required To Be Redistributed? | In-Service Withdrawals Allowed? | Immediate, Mandatory Vesting for Employer Contributions? |
|---|---|---|---|---|---|---|---|
| *Large-employer-sponsored Plans* | | | | | | | |
| Money purchase | After-tax allowed | The lesser of 100% of income or $50,000 | Yes | No | Yes | No, but loans are allowed | No |
| Target benefit | Not allowed | The lesser of 100% of income or $50,000 | Yes | No | Yes | No | No |
| Profit-sharing | Not allowed | The lesser of 100% of income or $50,000 | No[3] | Yes | Yes | Yes | No |
| Stock bonus | $50,000 | The lesser of 100% of income or $50,000 | No[3] | Yes | Yes | Yes | No |
| ESOP | $50,000 | The lesser of 100% of income or $50,000 | No[3] | Yes | Yes | Yes | No |
| 401(k)[4] | $17,000 + $5,500 age 50+ catch-up | The lesser of 100% of income or $50,000 | No | NA | No | Yes | No |
| Roth 401(k) | $17,000 + $5,500 age 50+ catch-up (after-tax) | The lesser of 100% of income or $50,000 | No | NA | No | Yes; after 5 years of participation, or age 59½ | No |
| Thrift and savings | Varies | The lesser of 100% of income or $50,000 | Generally, yes | No | Yes | Yes | No |
| 403(b)[4] | $17,000 + $5,500 age 50+ catch-up | The lesser of 100% of income or $50,000 | No | No | No | Yes | Yes |
| 457[4] | $17,000 + $5,500 age 50+ catch-up or 100% of compensation | $17,000 or 100% of compensation | Not allowed | No | NA | Yes; unforeseen emergency only | NA |
| *Small-business-sponsored Plans* | | | | | | | |
| SEP[5] | Not allowed | The lesser of 25% of net earnings or $50,000 | No | No | NA | Yes; same as IRA | Yes |
| SARSEP/ 408(k)[6] | The lesser of 25% of compensation or $17,000 | The lesser of 25% of net earnings or $50,000 | No | No | NA | Yes; same as IRA | Yes |
| Keogh[5] money purchase | Employees may not contribute | Up to 25% of earned income | Yes | No | Yes | No | No |

| Plan Type | Maximum Contribution per Participant (Elective Deferral) | Maximum Annual Addition[1] per Participant (based on Max. Compensation of $250,000)[2] | Mandatory Yearly Employer Contributions? | CODA/ 401(k) Permitted? | Forfeitures Generally Required To Be Redistributed? | In-Service Withdrawals Allowed? | Immediate, Mandatory Vesting for Employer Contributions? |
|---|---|---|---|---|---|---|---|
| Keogh[5] profit-sharing | Employees may not contribute | Up to 25% of earned income | No[3] | No | Yes | Yes; after 5 years of participation, or age 59½ | No |
| SIMPLE IRA | $11,500 + $2,500 age 50+ catch-up | See[7] below | Yes | No | NA | Yes; same as IRA | Yes |
| SIMPLE 401(k)[4, 8] | $11,500 + $2,500 age 50+ catch-up | $18,850 or $21,350 age 50+ | Yes | Yes | NA | Yes; same as IRA | Yes |

1. Annual additions are equal to the sum of employer contributions, employee contributions, both deductible and nondeductible, and unvested forfeitures.
2. There is an additional limitation on the maximum amount of employer contribution that is tax-deductible to the employer.
3. No mandatory annual employer contributions required, but employers must make substantial and regular contributions.
4. A targeted, non-refundable tax credit for low- to moderate-income savers is available for 401(k), 403(b), 457(b), and IRA contributions.
5. SEP and KEOGH: the effective maximum contribution percentage takes into account net earnings instead of total compensation.
6. Salary Reduction (SAR) SEPs have not been eligible for new establishment since 1997.
7. For a SIMPLE IRA, employers must make either a dollar-for-dollar matching contribution up to 3% of an employee's compensation (can elect to lower the percentage to no less than 1% for no more than 2 out of 5 years ending in the current year), or 2% of compensation for all eligible employees earning at least $5,000 regardless of elected salary reductions.
8. The maximum total contribution to a SIMPLE 401(k) plan for 2012 is $18,850 (salary deferral of $11,500 + 3% contribution of maximum salary of $250,000 + catch-up contributions). The maximum permitted contribution for a SIMPLE 401(k) plan is the maximum elective deferral plus the 3% matching contribution.

Employers may find that nondiscrimination rules and dollar limits placed on qualified plans restrict the usefulness of these retirement planning tools, especially as a means for providing benefits to executives and highly compensated employees. **Non-qualified plans** give employers more flexibility in offering benefits to these select groups, but they generally offer fewer tax advantages. An example of a non-qualified plan is a **non-qualified deferred compensation plan** (NQDC), which is defined as an agreement between an employer and employee where the employee agrees to accept payments at some specified time in the future. Employees are sometimes allowed to contribute to an NQDC, in which case contributions are considered fully vested. However, employer contributions are not as secure compared to contributions to a similar qualified plan. In exchange for less security, an employee can be compensated with contributions far exceeding current limits on qualified plans.

Two non-qualified deferred compensation arrangements are commonly used by employers when benefit plans are negotiated with highly compensated employees: rabbi and secular trusts. A **rabbi trust** is an irrevocable arrangement between an employer and employee. (The name stems from the first trust assessed by the IRS in which a congregation established this type of arrangement for its rabbi.) Under this agreement, the trust is considered to be unfunded, meaning that the employee cannot access assets until all contractual obligations have been met (typically at retirement). Because the plan is unfunded, the employer cannot deduct contributions to the trust until distributions are made. The employee is not taxed until he or she receives a trust distribution (e.g., upon retirement, death, disability, or employment termination). Because of the non-qualified status of the plan, assets held in the trust are subject to claims of the employer's creditors in case of bankruptcy. A **secular trust** provides employees additional security. Assets held in the trust are not subject to creditor claims against the employer. However, because the assets are more secure, all employer contributions to the plan are immediately taxable to the employee.

---

### Retirement Planning Tip:
### The Role of the PBGC in the Retirement Planning Marketplace

The  (**Pension Benefit Guaranty Corporation (PBGC)**) was created when President Ford signed the Employee Retirement Income Security Act (ERISA) into law in 1974. The primary role of the PBGC is to protect participants in qualified defined benefit plans from losing benefits when a plan is terminated because of underfunding. PBGC is a government corporation that serves the role of insuring pension plan account balances; however, PBGC insurance covers only a fraction of the benefit level of a terminated pension plan. PBGC benefits are based on an employee's age, the previous promised defined benefit plan payout, and the amount of plan benefits that remain after plan termination. PBGC insurance is funded by premiums collected from pension plan sponsors (based on a premium per participant), earnings from assets held by PBGC, and recoveries from the sponsors of terminated defined benefit plans.

---

**Personal savings within the funding mix.** Every client who begins planning for retirement faces the same critical retirement question: "Are current asset allocation and saving strategies sufficient to create a **pool of assets** large enough to meet retirement goals?" Fifty years ago, this question was not as crucial as it is today. In earlier decades, a higher percentage of Americans could retire comfortably on a combination of defined benefit pension distributions, Social Security benefits, and small personal savings.

Today, the financial landscape is quite different. The majority of workers in the United States no longer have access to a defined benefit plan, and those who do may find that the amount of income replaced is insufficient to meet retirement income needs. Furthermore, few Americans can live entirely on Social Security benefits. Consequently, nearly all Americans who hope to retire comfortably must rely on their own willingness and ability to save money. Thus, it is important to generate a pool of assets, combined with those from qualified and non-qualified sources, which will be large enough to generate income during a client's retirement years.

The traditional or Roth **individual retirement arrangement or agreement (IRA)** is typically the first personal retirement savings vehicle recommended, assuming an individual has earned income. IRAs were introduced in 1974 with a maximum contribution of $1,500. The Roth IRA was introduced in 1997. The popularity of these accounts coupled with the opportunities for rollovers, transfers, and conversions between IRAs and other retirement arrangements have resulted in large account balances. IRAs provide an option to grow assets on a tax-deferred (traditional) or tax-free (Roth) distribution basis, which offers financial planning clients unique tax benefits not available with other personal savings alternatives. Characteristics of traditional and Roth IRAs are summarized in Table 12.2.

**Table 12.2** A Comparison of Traditional and Roth IRAs

| Feature | Traditional IRA | Roth IRA |
|---|---|---|
| Eligibility | Must receive earned income in the year of contribution<br><br>Up to the calendar year when age 70½ is reached<br><br>Spousal IRA—Up to the calendar year when the spouse is age 70½ | Must receive earned income in the year of contribution<br><br>2012 modified adjusted gross income( MAGI) phase-out<br>Single filers:<br>$110,000–$125,000<br>Joint filers:<br>$173,000–$183,000<br><br>Spousal IRA—Any age |
| Maximum annual contribution | Lesser of $5,000 or 100% of earned income in 2012 plus $1,000 catch-up for those age 50 or older<br><br>Spousal:  See specific rules regarding nonworking or low-earning spouses<br><br>Rollover:  No limit or income guidelines for rollover contributions | |
| Federal income tax treatment of contributions | Fully deductible for those ineligible for an employer plan (an exception applies for a non-employer eligible spouse who files a joint return if MAGI exceeds $173,000 for 2012) or if eligible below a certain AGI (in 2012: $92,000 joint or $58,000 single)<br><br>Partially deductible for employees eligible for an employer plan with MAGI within a certain range (in 2012: $92,000–$112,000 joint or $58,000–$68,000 single)<br><br>Nondeductible for employees eligible for an employer plan with MAGI above a certain amount (in 2012: $112,000 joint or $68,000 single) | Not deductible<br><br>Taxable portion of traditional IRA conversion taxed at ordinary income rates |
| Earnings | Earnings grow tax deferred. Distributions of earnings *and tax-deductible contributions* are taxable. | Earnings grow tax deferred. Qualified distributions of earnings and contributions are exempt from federal taxation. |
| Tax on qualified distribution | Money from a qualified distribution of earnings and/or tax-deductible contributions *is* included in gross income for federal income tax purposes. | Money from a qualified distribution is *not* included in gross income for federal income tax purposes. |
| Tax on Withdrawals of Contributions? | Yes, unless the contributions were not tax-deductible | No, because no tax deduction was received for the contributions. |

| Tax on Distribution of Earnings? | Yes | Yes, unless the distribution is "qualified" meaning that:<br>• The account is open for 5 years AND,<br>• Distribution made on or after age 59½; or<br>• Distribution made to the estate or a beneficiary of the owner upon death of the owner; or<br>• Distribution made to the owner after meeting the definition of disabled according to the IRS code; or<br>• Distribution used to pay for qualified first-time homebuyer expenses. |
|---|---|---|
| Is There a 10% Penalty on Withdrawals? | Yes <u>on both tax-deductible contributions and earnings</u>, unless:<br>• Penalty-free withdrawals available for any reason after age 59½, or for the following prior to age 59½. However, income tax may apply.<br>• Withdrawal occurs because of the IRA owner's disability or death<br>• Withdrawal meets 72½ standards.<br>• Withdrawal used to pay for unreimbursed medical expenses that exceed 7½% of adjusted gross income (AGI).<br>• Withdrawal used to pay medical insurance premiums after the IRA owner has received unemployment compensation for more than 12 weeks.<br>• Withdrawal used to pay the costs of a first-time home purchase ($10,000 lifetime maximum).<br>• Withdrawal used to pay for the qualified expenses of higher education for the IRA owner and/or eligible family members. | Yes <u>on earnings only</u>, unless:<br>• Penalty-free withdrawals available for any reason after age 59½, or for the following prior to age 59½. However, income tax may apply.<br>• Withdrawal occurs because of the IRA owner's disability or death<br>• Withdrawal meets 72½ standards.<br>• Withdrawal used to pay for unreimbursed medical expenses that exceed 7½% of adjusted gross income (AGI).<br>• Withdrawal used to pay medical insurance premiums after the IRA owner has received unemployment compensation for more than 12 weeks.<br>• Withdrawal used to pay the costs of a first-time home purchase ($10,000 lifetime maximum).<br>• Withdrawal used to pay for the qualified expenses of higher education for the IRA owner and/or eligible family members. |
| Required Minimum Distributions | Must begin by April 1 of the next year after attaining age 70½. | No required minimum distributions. |
| Penalty Tax for Insufficient Distributions | Penalty of 50% of the amount that should have been distributed | No penalties apply. |
| Penalty for Excess Contributions | 6% | 6% |

| Compensation for IRA Purposes | 1. Wages and Salaries |
| --- | --- |
| | 2. Commissions |
| | 3. Self-Employment Income |
| | 4. Alimony and Separate Maintenance |
| | 5. Military Differential Pay |
| | 6. Non-taxable Combat Pay |

As illustrated in Table 12.2, some features are common to both types of IRAs. First, almost any type of investment can be purchased, excluding life insurance and collectibles. Second, IRAs cannot be used as collateral for a loan. Third, under federal bankruptcy law, IRAs enjoy limited (up to $1 million) protection from creditors.

Beyond the taxation differences of traditional and Roth IRAs, there are four distinct types of IRAs, determined by funding source: contributory, rollover, inherited, and spousal. This can be easily remembered by the acronym *CRIS*. The contributory IRA is what most people are familiar with as the IRA with the funding limitation (e.g., $5,000 per year for worker's under the age of 50 in 2012) and earned income requirement (e.g., 100% of earned income up to the funding limit). However, the other three types do not have an earned income requirement and only the spousal IRA has an annual funding limit. The option to fund a spousal IRA for a non-working married partner (also limited to $5,000 per year for people under the age of 50) is another benefit for couples seeking additional alternatives for retirement savings.

Rollover and inherited IRA accounts are distinctive for two reasons. The owner cannot contribute to these accounts after establishment, and these IRAs may not be commingled. This means that the owner cannot combine assets from one IRA with those of another, with one exception: the rollover IRA is funded with assets that were originally contributed to another qualified retirement account (e.g. 401(k), 403(b), etc.) and distributed, typically as the result of a separation of service. The inherited IRA is an account originally funded by another person, with the original owner bequeathing the account to an heir. Multiple inherited IRAs from the same owner and of the same type (e.g., traditional or Roth), can be combined, or commingled, if all rules are followed.

At the end of 2010, IRA assets totaled $4.7 trillion, representing 27% of U.S. retirement assets.[13] At midyear 2010, 40% of—or 49 million—U.S. households owned some form of IRA.[14] Given the prevalence of these accounts, it is important for financial planners to understand rules related to the inheritance of IRAs as a way to help clients avoid paying unnecessary taxes and penalties. The following points highlight important inherited IRA rules for non-spousal beneficiaries:[15]

1. When a non-spouse beneficiary inherits an IRA, he or she must either begin lifetime distributions by December 31 of the year after the year of the decedent's death or choose a five-year distribution alternative. The five-year distribution is available only if the owner died before the required distribution beginning date for a traditional IRA. If the five-year distribution plan is chosen, the beneficiary can elect to revert to a lifetime distribution plan as long as the first distribution was made by December 31 of the year following the decedent's death.

2. The 10% penalty for distributions prior to age 59½ does not apply to inherited IRAs; only taxes would be due upon distribution. The 60-day rollover rule does not apply to inherited IRAs; any distribution is subject to tax.

3. Non-spouse beneficiaries cannot roll over inherited IRAs into an existing or new IRA, but they can transfer the funds to a new custodian or combine multiple inherited IRA accounts of the same type and from the same owner into one account. Care must be taken in titling the account according to IRS requirements, as follows: "IRA FBO Jane Smith as beneficiary of Dan Brown" or "IRA FBO Dan Brown (dec'd); Jane Smith (beneficiary)."

4. Non-spouse beneficiaries may not convert an inherited IRA into a Roth IRA or an inherited Roth IRA.

5. When calculating required minimum distributions (RMDs), inherited IRAs must remain separate from other IRAs owned by the beneficiary. RMDs are discussed later in this chapter; for more information, see IRS Publication 590, *Individual Retirement Arrangements (IRAs)*.

Most rules are similar for a spouse who inherits an IRA, although a spouse can roll over an inherited IRA into an existing or new IRA of the same type, which allows for more discretion on the RMDs from a traditional account. Figure 12.3 illustrates these general rules. However, extreme caution is warranted when working with a client inheriting spousal retirement assets or IRAs because the options are contingent on several different factors (e.g., age of spouse at death, age of surviving spouse, financial situation and the need for and timing of need for assets, potential estate tax situation of the surviving spouse), including the following:

- Transfer the inherited assets into an inherited IRA with rules similar to that for a non-spousal inherited IRA; or

- Roll over the assets into an existing or new IRA with the RMD based on the age of the surviving spouse; or

- Roll over or convert the assets into a new or existing Roth IRA; or

- Disclaim, within nine months of the spouse's death, all or part of the inherited assets.

Finally, an important caveat is the reminder that clients complete the necessary documentation to establish a beneficiary(ies) for an inherited IRA or a new spousal IRA funded with inherited assets. This is important to ensure that the client's wishes for bequeathing the assets are satisfied and to protect the client's estate from potential additional estate taxation.

**Figure 12.3** Decision Tree for Planning for an Inherited IRA

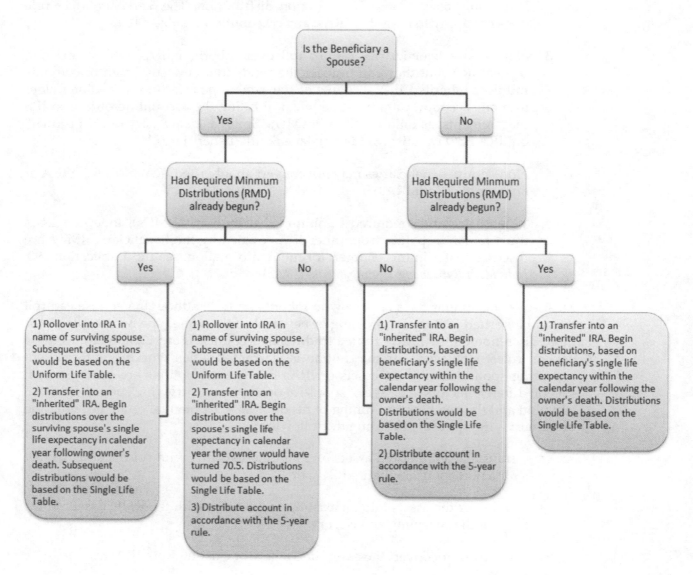

There are the two primary ways to move assets between qualified accounts without incurring an income tax liability: transfer and rollover. Typically, a **transfer** refers to moving assets directly from one custodian to another without the owner of the account ever taking possession of the funds. This is the most typical method for moving funds from one IRA account to another. The other method for moving funds from an employer-sponsored plan into an IRA is called a **rollover,** and there are two forms: indirect and direct. In the case of an indirect rollover the owner takes temporary (60 days or fewer) ownership—called *constructive receipt*—of the funds. The original custodian sends the assets to the owner, who then sends them to the new custodian, thereby completing the rollover. The direct method works the same as the transfer, where the owner never has constructive receipt of the funds.

A third method for moving funds—conversion—creates an income tax liability. Converting a traditional IRA to a Roth IRA is a strategy frequently used to gain the benefits of the Roth IRA. In its most basic form, a **Roth IRA conversion** occurs when a client converts assets held in a traditional IRA into a Roth IRA. Conversion triggers income tax in the year of the conversion on the value of the account (excluding any non-tax-deductible contributions that were previously taxed) on the day of the conversion. This allows the assets to continue to grow tax deferred with the option of making withdrawals on a tax-free basis. Because of the tax implications, and the potential to push some clients into a higher tax bracket, care must be taken when using this strategy. Some or all of a conversion can be undone (called a **recharacterization)** should the tax situation, the cash flow to pay the taxes, or the value of the accounts decline significantly. Undoing a Roth conversion involves moving the money from the Roth IRA back to a traditional IRA using the custodian's forms for a Roth recharacterization. It is also possible to execute a partial recharacterization and move part of a Roth IRA back to a traditional IRA. However, care must be taken to follow the rules carefully for a conversion and recharacterization, regarding both the process and the time line.

Beginning in 2010, income limits associated with Roth conversions were removed. This was the result of the Tax Increase Prevention and Reconciliation Act of 2005. The Act, however, did not eliminate the income restrictions associated with Roth contributions, thereby creating a significant tax loophole. High-income clients, clients who believe that their marginal tax rate will be higher in retirement than it is currently, and those who wish to postpone RMDs are the most anxious to hold wealth in Roth IRAs. These clients are also the most likely to convert traditional IRA assets into Roth IRAs. This is where the loophole comes into play. High-earning households typically are excluded from contributing to a Roth IRA, but not to non-deductible traditional IRAs. Some planners have recommended, therefore, that high-income clients contribute the maximum allowed to a traditional IRA. They are then encouraged to convert the IRA to a Roth. Because both transactions include only after-tax contributions, the strategy has no immediate tax consequences.

Although this strategy is being used, financial planners should be forewarned that the IRS requires IRA aggregating for calculating taxes due on conversions. If a client holds any pre-tax IRA assets, it is likely that this conversion strategy will trigger income taxation.[16] Further, some have argued that the IRS could assert the **step transaction doctrine**, which states that a series of actions taken to complete a single comprehensive transaction will be taxed on the overall economic outcome of the transaction. That is, the IRS may conclude that clients who use this type of conversion strategy constructively made an improper Roth IRA contribution. As such, this loophole should be used with great caution.

Other personal retirement saving strategies that offer tax advantages include **variable universal life insurance** policies (VULs), annuities, and home equity. A **VUL** allows a client to purchase a term insurance policy while also investing in tax-deferred mutual funds through available subaccounts in the policy. With appropriately planned investment strategies, it is possible for the cash account to gain significant value over time. Unlike qualified plans that restrict annual contributions, a VUL can accept very large annual premiums, assuming sufficient face value of the policy and careful attention to modified endowment contract restrictions. In fact, a VUL could be funded with an amount several times the annual funding limit applicable to qualified defined contribution plans. Furthermore, the cash value in such accounts is generally sheltered from taxes and creditors. Accessing savings for retirement is relatively straightforward. The most common distribution strategy involves taking tax-free loans against the policy value. If sufficient assets remain within the VUL subaccounts, earnings can be used to pay back the loan without reducing the client's level of cash flow. Of course, this strategy assumes that a relatively high rate of return can be earned over an extended period of time on assets held in the subaccounts.

Investing in an annuity, either with a lump sum payment or a series of contributions, offers another tax-deferred retirement savings option. Investment earnings, whether fixed or variable, generally grow tax deferred until withdrawn. Distributions are taxed as ordinary income. No annual contribution limits apply, and distributions are not required at age 70½ as is generally required by traditional IRAs or employer-sponsored plans. A variety of fees (e.g., surrender, annual, investment management, and insurance) could apply. A 10% federal penalty does apply, in addition to ordinary income tax, if withdrawals are made prior to age 59½, unless certain exceptions are met. Similar to qualified retirement plan assets, annuities are generally protected from creditors in most states.

As indicated earlier in the chapter, a Fidelity Research Institute report noted that some financial planning experts now refer to home equity as the fourth leg of the retirement funding stool—although this source of funding has come under pressure since the real estate collapse of the late 2000s.[17] The emotional tie to the asset, a desire to retire in the home, or the desire to convey the asset to heirs are influential factors that should be considered when adding home equity as a retirement asset. Nevertheless, the home can represent, either by necessity or choice, one of the largest retirement assets for many clients. A significant advantage associated with home equity is the tax-advantaged nature of the asset. A couple can exempt from taxes gains of up to $500,000 (or $250,000 for a single filer) generated from the sale of a principal residence. A common planning recommendation involves having clients who are entering retirement consider using the proceeds from the sale of their home to buy a smaller house and using the balance of the proceeds to supplement retirement income.

Finally, there is a seemingly endless variety of non-tax-sheltered personal investment assets, ranging from financial to personal to real, which can be earmarked to fund retirement. Although these assets offer no special retirement tax benefits, accumulation and distribution restrictions typically do not apply, thereby increasing financial flexibility.

**Determining the funding mix.** Traditionally, the three-legged retirement stool consisted of income from Social Security, employer-provided accounts, and personal savings. Increasingly, a fourth leg, either post-retirement employment or home equity, is being used to supplement retirement income. Yet the reality of retirement planning suggests that all of these sources offer distinct advantages and disadvantages when considering an individual's perspective and the respective characteristics of each client's unique situation. Determining which sources of income to include in the funding mix begins as a mathematical exercise, given the parameters of accumulation, distribution, and taxation; but it must also include subjective factors such as the emotional investment, values, and preferences of the client. Given the number of interrelated steps involved in the analysis of a client's current retirement planning situation, it is essential that financial advisors have a thorough understanding of the client's financial and emotional needs. Assessing a client's situation encompasses an understanding of how both contribute to a client's lifestyle aspirations as well as their financial needs and resources.

During the client data-gathering phase of the financial planning process, a planner should take steps to obtain information from clients not only about current savings and assets, but also about where the client might wish to live, the anticipated retirement lifestyle and activities, and any fears a client might have about retirement. When viewed from a purely financial perspective, each step in the retirement planning process should be devoted to helping clients balance the need to maximize income in retirement (i.e., create a large pool of assets) with the desire to minimize current savings allocations focused toward retirement. Managing a balance among planning assumptions, including date of retirement, length of time in retirement, and rates of return earned prior to and during retirement, is essential if clients are to fully enjoy and satisfy their income and lifestyle aspirations both today and while in retirement.

---

### Planning for Special Populations: Retirement Planning for Divorcing Couples

Divorce is hard enough without the IRS getting involved, but that is exactly what will happen without careful planning and advice to protect a couple's retirement accounts. In the past, a couple's largest asset was their home; however, in the wake of the housing collapse, it is often their retirement accounts. Liquidating a 401(k) or IRA to be able to give half to the former spouse can leave both with about 25% of its pretax value. In this division, the only partner to get half is Uncle Sam. In the event of a divorce, liquidating a qualified retirement account will result in a taxable event, where 25% to 40% will be owed in income taxes and another 10% tax penalty will apply for early distribution: divorce does not qualify as a hardship withdrawal.

Fortunately, a divorce court can approve a tax-exempt transfer of assets from the qualified account of one spouse into the qualified account of the other. This is known as a **transfer incident to divorce**. A **qualified domestic relations order (QDRO)** can be used to divide pension rights, or other accounts covered under ERISA, between spouses. This way any potential tax liability can be shared or avoided. A QDRO may be issued as part of the divorce decree, as part of the property settlement, or as a separate order. A QDRO establishes rights and protections pertaining to the division of assets that the divorce decree may not. In some marriages, only one spouse contributes to a retirement plan because the other spouse may not work or earn enough to contribute. Upon separation or divorce, a QDRO provides the mechanism to divide the retirement account without incurring current taxes or penalties.

It may appear to be easier to split an IRA account than to divide employer-provided retirement plans. A common mistake is to plan to use the unlimited spousal gifting rules, but these rules do not apply to qualified accounts. Although a divorcing couple will not necessarily need a QDRO to divide IRA accounts, they will need the court to mandate the tax-free division of property under Section 408(d)(6) of the IRC.[18]

### Near-retirees: Analysis of Current Retirement Planning Efforts

Much of the preceding discussion assumes that a client has several years remaining before retirement. Near-retirees are often defined as those who are age 50 to 55 or older; other authors use the term to refer to someone within five or so years of retirement. Regardless of the exact age or number of years until retirement, these clients have a different set of planning needs than someone 25 or more years away from retirement who is concerned only with wealth accumulation. For one thing, the near-retiree should already have a fairly sizable retirement nest egg, so the primary planning issue might be wealth preservation instead of wealth accumulation, although this is not always the case. The concern could be how to significantly increase savings and take advantage of account catch-up provisions to more quickly save for retirement, if the retirement nest egg has not been sufficiently funded.

The client's questions could also be focused on distribution, such as, "How much income can be safely distributed annually from accumulated assets?" In other words, what will be the client's standard of living in retirement? How might a few more working years, full- or part-time, impact retirement income? Or conversely, if the client retires sooner, are retirement assets sufficient to provide for income and legacy goals? Documenting and evaluating a client's current situation in relation to post-retirement planning issues is just as— if not more—important than dealing with pre-retirement accumulation planning concerns. Although the future is still uncertain, time horizon and other assumptions might be based more on fact than conjecture, as can be the case in the early years of retirement planning.

### Retirees: Analysis of Current Retirement Planning Efforts

The retirement planning process to transition clients from near-retiree to retiree status is significantly different than the process of planning for retirement, and certainly more emotional. First, there is rarely any time remaining for a client to accumulate assets through qualified plans, IRAs, or other employer-sponsored plans. Although it may be possible for a retired client to establish a business or seek other employment, which would allow for additional asset accumulation, this may not be an option for people who intend to give up work in their senior years rather than continue working. Second, there is less room for error when establishing retirement asset earnings, inflation, and life expectancy assumptions. A planner will know approximately the assets available to generate income. If any of the key planning assumptions are violated, a client could deplete these assets too soon or make unnecessary sacrifices that compromise the client's desired quality of life.

**The capital withdrawal process—A deterministic model.** How much a client can withdraw annually from a pool of retirement assets can be determined using the following process. However, as discussed later, **deterministic models** using only a static, or constant, mean return throughout the modeling period provide a very elementary projection.

1. Determine the value of the pool of available assets at the beginning of retirement. Although not all client assets will be used to fund retirement (e.g., home equity), assets that can be used should be valued at the market value as of the projected date of retirement.

2.  Choose a reasonable after-tax rate of return for retirement. It is sufficient to stress that a planner should always take into account a client's risk tolerance, expectations, time horizon, and preferences (e.g., asset class limitations) when estimating the rate of return. The return should not subject a client's assets to risks beyond those necessary to achieve the desired standard of living.

3.  Choose a realistic average rate of inflation during retirement, or determine the client's desired rate of increase for the retirement annuity. Although not always the case, it does not hurt to be conservative in this choice (i.e., to slightly overstate projected inflation). Just as investment losses are more detrimental early in the withdrawal period, high inflation early in the withdrawal period can create lasting problems for meeting a client's desired standard of living.

4.  Calculate the inflation-adjusted rate of return applicable to the client using the serial interest rate formula:

$$Serial\ Rate = \frac{(1+i)}{(1+g)} - 1$$

5.  Determine the client's life expectancy. A client's individual life expectancy can be estimated using the Single Life Expectancy Table shown in Table 12.2. (This is the same table referenced elsewhere in this chapter, used for calculating RMDs by beneficiaries of inherited IRA accounts). If a client is married, the client and spouse's joint and survivor life expectancy (i.e., how long at least one of them will live, or until both will be deceased) can be determined using a joint and survivor life expectancy table. These tables should be used as a starting point in the analysis. Other important information, including a person's ancestral life expectancy patterns, current health, occupation, and hobbies, can be used to increase or decrease assumptions regarding a client's life expectancy. For planners who want a conservative estimate, using a table factor life expectancy and adding at least five years is worth considering.

**Table 12.3** Single Life Expectancy Table

**Single-life Expectancy Table[1]**

| Age | Divisor | | Age | Divisor |
|-----|---------|---|-----|---------|
| 56 | 28.7 | | 84 | 8.1 |
| 57 | 27.9 | | 85 | 7.6 |
| 58 | 27.0 | | 86 | 7.1 |
| 59 | 26.1 | | 87 | 6.7 |
| 60 | 25.2 | | 88 | 6.3 |
| 61 | 24.4 | | 89 | 5.9 |
| 62 | 23.5 | | 90 | 5.5 |
| 63 | 22.7 | | 91 | 5.2 |
| 64 | 21.8 | | 92 | 4.9 |
| 65 | 21.0 | | 93 | 4.6 |
| 66 | 20.2 | | 94 | 4.3 |
| 67 | 19.4 | | 95 | 4.1 |
| 68 | 18.6 | | 96 | 3.8 |
| 69 | 17.8 | | 97 | 3.6 |
| 70 | 17.0 | | 98 | 3.4 |
| 71 | 16.3 | | 99 | 3.1 |
| 72 | 15.5 | | 100 | 2.9 |
| 73 | 14.8 | | 101 | 2.7 |
| 74 | 14.1 | | 102 | 2.5 |
| 75 | 13.4 | | 103 | 2.3 |
| 76 | 12.7 | | 104 | 2.1 |
| 77 | 12.1 | | 105 | 1.9 |
| 78 | 11.4 | | 106 | 1.7 |
| 79 | 10.8 | | 107 | 1.5 |
| 80 | 10.2 | | 108 | 1.4 |
| 81 | 9.7 | | 109 | 1.2 |
| 82 | 9.1 | | 110 | 1.1 |
| 83 | 8.6 | | 111+ | 1.0 |

[1.] For ages 0 to 55, see IRS Publication 590, *Individual Retirement Arrangements (IRAs)*.

*Source:* IRS. *Individual Retirement Arrangements (IRAs)*, Publication 590, p. 87. Available at http://www.irs.gov/pub/irs-pdf/p590.pdf#page=104.

6. Calculate the withdrawal. There are two basic methods that can be used for this step. Both methods can be adjusted to account for inflation to preserve purchasing power. If so, withdrawals will increase each year to reflect inflation.

The first method assumes a depletion of all assets at the end of the client's life expectancy (i.e., at the end of retirement), which is referred to as **the capital depletion withdrawal method or approach.** This method is based on a growth-adjusted present value of an annuity due calculation.

*Example:* Assume retirement assets equal $500,000 at the time of retirement, yearly distributions increase by 4%, assets earn 8% annually, and retirement is planned to last for 20 years at which time assets are depleted. The amount that can be withdrawn at the beginning of the first year equals $34,947; the amount would then be increased by 4% in each succeeding year.

$$Serial\ Rate = \frac{(1+i)}{(1+g)} - 1 = \frac{1.08}{1.04} - 1 = 3.846\%$$

$$\$500,000 = \frac{PMT}{0.03846}\left(1 - \frac{1}{1.03846^{20}}\right)(1.03846)$$

$$PMT = \frac{\$500,000 \times 0.03846}{\left(1 - 1.03846^{-20}\right) \times 1.03846} = \$34,947$$

Where:

i   = 3.846%

FV  = 0

PV  = $500,000

n   = 20

Solving for PMT also returns approximately $34,947.

*Note:* Remember to set the calculator to beginning-of-period payments.

The second distribution approach is called the **capital preservation method or approach**, which assumes that the client's assets at retirement will be preserved throughout the client's lifetime. The capital preservation method can also increase the capital each year to reflect inflation. Payments can be determined using a present value of a growing perpetuity due calculation.

*Example:* Assume retirement assets equal $500,000 at the time of retirement, yearly distributions increase by 4%, assets earn 8% annually, and retirement is planned to last for 20 years, at which time assets would still be equal to the inflation-adjusted future value of $500,000. The amount that can be withdrawn at the beginning of the first year equals $18,519; this amount would then increase by 4% in each succeeding year. Using the same serial rate as before:

$$\$500,000 = \frac{PMT}{0.03846}\left(1 - \frac{1}{1.03846^{20}}\right)(1.03846) + \frac{500,000(1.04^{20})}{1.08^{20}}$$

$$\$500,000 = \frac{PMT}{0.03846}\left(1 - \frac{1}{1.03846^{20}}\right)(1.03846) + 235,050.77$$

$$\$500,000 - \$235,050.77 = \frac{PMT}{0.03846}\left(1 - \frac{1}{1.03846^{20}}\right)(1.03846)$$

Therefore, what is actually available to support retirement is the difference in the $500,000 saved and the $235,050.77 needed to ensure the inflation-adjusted future value of the account.

$$PMT = \frac{\$264,949.23 \times 0.03846}{\left(1 - 1.03846^{-20}\right) \times 1.03846} = \$18,519$$

Note: In this case the calculator cannot handle this problem directly with the TVM keys because there is a future value involved and serial rates cannot be used to directly solve for future values. Therefore, the present value of the remaining balance must be subtracted before beginning. Again, the calculator is set to beginning-of-period payments.

Where:

    I    = 3.846%

    FV = 0

    PV = $264,949.23

    n    = 20

Solving for PMT also returns approximately $18,519.

Thought about another way, the present value of the account is increasing in perpetuity by the rate of inflation. So if the account is always increasing in value at a rate equal to increases in the annual withdrawal, then it is a simple present value of a growing perpetuity.

$$\$500,000 = \frac{PMT}{0.08 - 0.04}(1.08)$$

$$PMT = \frac{\$500.000 \times (0.08 - 0.04)}{1.08} = \$18,519$$

A non-random deterministic withdrawal model can be easily developed to help clients gain an idea of how long their retirement account balances will remain funded.

Consider how to project estimated withdrawal amounts for a client who enters retirement at age 65 with $100,000 in assets. Table 12.3 was created in Excel based on the following assumptions:

- A 5% annualized before-tax rate of return;

- A 3% annualized inflation rate;

- A 4% annual distribution rate;

- A distribution rate that increases by the rate of inflation; and

- An RMD based on the Uniform Life Table (described later in the chapter).

**Table 12.4** Deterministic Withdrawal Illustration

| Age of Client | Beginning Balance | Yearly Distribution | Distribution Rate |
|---|---|---|---|
| 65 | $500,000 | $20,000 | 4.00% |
| 66 | 504,000 | 20,600 | 4.09 |
| 67 | 507,570 | 21,218 | 4.18 |
| 68 | 510,670 | 21,855 | 4.28 |
| 69 | 513,256 | 22,510 | 4.39 |
| 70 | 515,283 | 23,185 | 4.50 |
| 71 | 516,702 | 23,881 | 4.62 |
| 72 | 517,462 | 24,597 | 4.75 |
| 73 | 517,508 | 25,335 | 4.90 |
| 74 | 516,781 | 26,095 | 5.05 |
| 75 | 515,220 | 26,878 | 5.22 |
| 76 | 512,759 | 27,685 | 5.40 |
| 77 | 509,328 | 28,515 | 5.60 |
| 78 | 504,853 | 29,371 | 5.82 |
| 79 | 499,257 | 30,252 | 6.06 |
| 80 | 492,455 | 31,159 | 6.33 |
| 81 | 484,361 | 32,094 | 6.63 |
| 82 | 474,880 | 33,057 | 6.96 |
| 83 | 463,914 | 34,049 | 7.34 |
| 84 | 451,359 | 35,070 | 7.77 |
| 85 | 437,103 | 36,122 | 8.26 |
| 86 | 421,030 | 37,206 | 8.84 |
| 87 | 403,015 | 38,322 | 9.51 |
| 88 | 382,928 | 39,472 | 10.31 |
| 89 | 360,629 | 40,656 | 11.27 |
| 90 | 335,972 | 41,876 | 12.46 |
| 91 | 308,801 | 43,132 | 13.97 |
| 92 | 278,952 | 44,426 | 15.93 |
| 93 | 246,253 | 45,759 | 18.58 |
| 94 | 210,519 | 47,131 | 22.39 |
| 95 | 171,557 | 48,545 | 28.30 |
| 96 | 129,163 | 50,002 | 38.71 |
| 97 | 83,119 | 51,502 | 61.96 |
| 98 | 33,198 | 33,198 | 100.00 |
| 99 | 0 | 0 | 0.00 |
| 100 | 0 | 0 | 0.00 |

The first column reports the client's age from 65 to an assumed death at age 100. The second column shows the client's account balance adjusted for annual withdrawal and account earnings. The third column shows the annual 4% distribution, adjusted for inflation. The effective distribution rate shown in the last column is estimated by dividing the yearly distribution amount by the beginning balance. Over time, the effective distribution rate will rise in response to inflation. These calculations provide an alternative method of estimating capital withdrawal amounts described in the previous section.

Similar to what has been reported in the literature, using these conservative assumptions it is possible for a client to fully fund withdrawals for 33 years. If the client lives beyond age 97, a shortfall will occur. Data can also be graphically represented by charting the yearly income and ending balance columns, as shown in Figure 12.4. It is interesting to note that a client's situation can be improved by increasing the rate of return assumption from 5% to 6%, as shown in Figure 12.5. A 1%- increase in the return assumption fully funds the client's projected life span to age 100, with a remaining balance of $400,005. However, this illustrates an important criticism associated with this type of deterministic modeling. Specifically, the assumptions in the model remain static throughout the modeling period. Some have argued that this is not a reasonable way to model the reality of market returns.

**Figure 12.4** Graph of Deterministic Withdrawal Illustration: 5% Annualized Before-tax Rate of Return

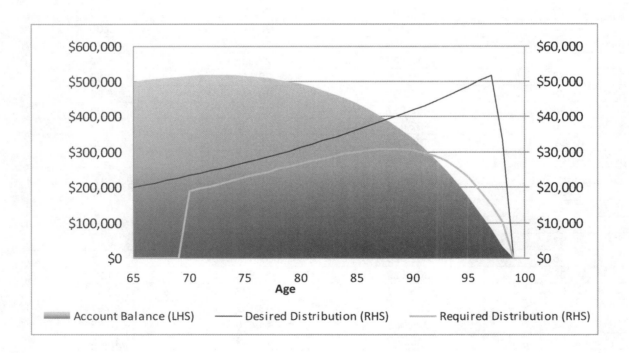

**Figure 12.5** Graph of Deterministic Withdrawal Illustration: 6% Annualized Before-tax Rate of Return

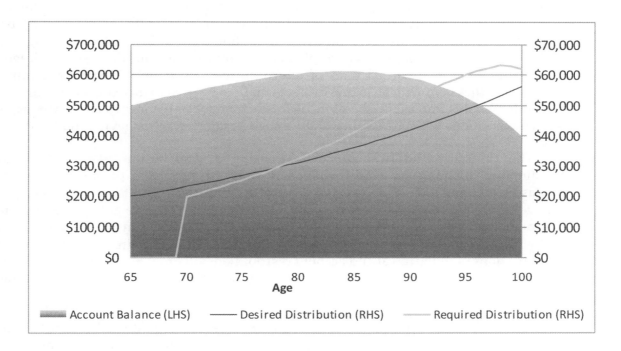

For example, investment returns for most investors during the period 2000 through 2012 were quite low. Had a planner based rate-of-return assumptions on prior period estimates of 9% or higher, which has been a traditional benchmark, a deterministic model would be in jeopardy of failing. Additionally, deterministic models sometimes fail as a result of **sequence risk**. This is the risk associated with receiving a below-average return during the first few years of distributions compared to earning higher returns later. Clients who begin distributions just before a market decline must earn higher rates in the future to reach their average return need. This means that the likelihood of having an asset shortfall is greater for such clients. Furthermore, these potential errors in retirement projections demonstrate the need for an ongoing client-planner relationship, where planners can continually update projections and advise a client on needed changes.

**The capital withdrawal process—A stochastic model.** As discussed in Chapter 11 on investment planning, **stochastic modeling**, or what is known as **Monte Carlo modeling**, has gained favor as a projection tool for withdrawal analyses. A stochastic approach basically randomizes rate-of-return, inflation, and life expectancy assumptions using thousands of data point observations to estimate features of plan success or failure. This approach to modeling, however, suffers from a weakness associated with the use of historical data. That is, stochastic models assume that future market returns will, to some extent, mirror past data. To summarize, neither deterministic nor stochastic modeling procedures work perfectly. Both rely on past data and the professional judgment of the model designer. For simplicity, deterministic models can be effective if the assumptions used are quite conservative. For example, assuming a real 6% to 6.5% return going forward is reasonable. This assumes a risk premium of approximately 3%, with a similar 3% inflation rate.[19]

Of primary interest to the financial planner tasked with helping a client choose an appropriate withdrawal strategy is the issue of what *safety* means. Some clients will be satisfied only by knowing with 100% certainty that they cannot outlive their retirement savings. An annuity approach may be the best alternative for this kind of client. On the other hand, a more risk-seeking client might find a 5% to 10% risk of running out of money over a 30-year period acceptable. They may see the upside to such a situation. It is possible that earned rates of return on their portfolio will surpass estimates, leaving the client with an excess of assets that can be used to increase income or legacy gifts. What is important, therefore, is for each financial planner to actively engage in conversations with clients about topics such as safety, risk, longevity, and legacy.

**The capital withdrawal process—choosing a distribution plan.** Traditionally, financial planners have been trained to think of retirement planning in terms of asset accumulation and investment growth, with the ultimate objective being the development of a retirement nest egg. Little thought went into an equally important planning issue—how clients should structure withdrawals from accumulated savings when they retire. As the surge of Baby Boomers entering retirement continues, the questions of withdrawal and account distribution will grow in importance. For many advisors, this is already a key issue as they help their clientele consider retirement income alternatives.

Upon retirement, retirees face an important question regarding the distribution of income from accumulated savings. Financial advisors typically recommend that clients withdraw funds from taxable accounts before taking distributions from qualified retirement plans (e.g., a 401(k), 403(b), 457 plan) to maximize the tax deferral of the other accounts.[20] Assets held in tax-free accounts (e.g., a Roth IRA) would be distributed last. Two exceptions to this general rule exist. First, clients who will not take meaningful distributions prior to death may want to withdraw from tax-deferred accounts first to obtain the maximum step-up in basis on other assets at the time of death. Second, whenever the after-tax return on taxable accounts exceeds the return on qualified tax-deferred account assets, distributions from the tax-deferred accounts should occur first.[21] The one caveat to the second point is obviously the risk aspect, because higher returns normally mean higher risk.

Taking distributions from taxable accounts can offer some tax advantages. Lower rates have recently been available for long-term capital gains, and a client may be able to time the taxation of any capital gains, further reducing the average tax rate by looking for offsetting capital losses. In certain circumstances, taking distributions from these investments first could actually reduce income taxes. Postponing the redemption of tax-deferred accounts, taxed as ordinary income when withdrawn, allows these accounts to continue growing on a tax-deferred basis. Assuming the rules for tax-free distributions from Roth accounts are met, leaving those accounts until last allows for a longer period of tax-deferred growth and tax-free distributions.

Planners and their clients have the most flexibility in choosing the distribution method that best meets the client's needs when working with non-qualified accounts or with IRAs, because employer-sponsored qualified retirement accounts may have additional limitations on withdrawal options. Employers often require employees who separate from service to take a distribution. Distributions from qualified plans (401 (k), 403(b), 457 plan, etc.) can generally be made in a couple of ways. Accumulated assets can, depending on plan policy, be left in the plan itself, which may allow the client to take distributions as needed—on a regular periodic or irregular basis. Or the employer may require the former employee to take a lump sum distribution of all plan assets.

A client who takes a lump sum distribution from a qualified defined contribution plan must be given the opportunity to roll over the proceeds of the distribution into an IRA or other eligible qualified plan. Once the plan assets have been rolled over to an IRA, the client has the same distribution options as for any other IRA account. For clients who are no longer employed, rolling defined contribution plan assets into a Roth IRA allows them to maintain the account balance even longer by avoiding the RMD. But this rollover to a traditional IRA followed by conversion to a Roth IRA is a taxable event; so while the account would once again grow tax deferred, income taxes would be owed on the converted amount in the year of the conversion. As with all retirement strategies, tax implications should be considered during both accumulation and distribution.

The following discussion examines the forms of distribution and the associated income tax considerations. For taxation purposes, there are two categories of distribution payments:

1.  Non-annuitized payments (e.g., lump sum "one-time" distributions, discretionary installment payments, irregular distributions)

2.  Annuitized payments

It is important to note throughout this discussion that an annuitized payout is not synonymous with an insurance company annuity. Although the insurance product derives its name from the process, they are not the same.

Most plans offer lump sum distributions. Clients who take a lump sum distribution will trigger a 20% federal income tax withholding requirement. The IRS requires plan sponsors who issue lump sum payments to withhold taxes as a way to ensure that the recipient can pay any tax liability. The benefit of a lump sum payment is that the total account value (minus taxes) is available to make an investment or purchase. The drawback is that a client will lose tax-deferred compounding of the earnings. This disadvantage is another reason why financial planners often suggest that a client roll over the account balance into an IRA or other eligible plan. Rollovers allow retirement assets to be managed in a way that preserves the tax-deferral of the retirement account proceeds.

Additionally, a plan participant could opt, if available, for discretionary periodic withdrawals, which could be done on a planned or an ad hoc basis. This is in fact the most common method for handling distributions, because it maintains the greatest flexibility and can be matched most closely to the deterministic withdrawal streams discussed earlier in the chapter.

**The capital withdrawal process—The role of the insurance company.** Almost universally, everyone's fear after retirement is outliving their money. In the academic community this is known as **shortfall risk**, or the percentage of time a portfolio will run short of the money needed to pay distributions. Spitzer summarized the trade-offs involved when making distribution choices in retirement in relation to shortfall risk.

His primary conclusions were as follows.[22] First, the use of annuities reduces shortfall risk significantly. The difference in risk falls from 0% with 100% annuitization to 6% without the use of annuities. Second, the use of annuities reduces a client's gross estate dramatically. Whereas, without annuitization someone can expect their final estate to be 150% of their starting portfolio value, the use of annuities reduces this amount to about 20%. In other words, retirees must choose between legacy and security. Retirees who are more interested in retirement income security, versus leaving heirs a legacy, should consider the use of annuitization as a retirement planning distribution tool.

A great deal of academic analysis has gone into the question of how much can be safely withdrawn from accumulated savings to minimize account shortfalls. Given the amount of research on the topic, one might assume that a general consensus or quantifiable approach has emerged in the field. Unfortunately, this is not the case. Instead, financial planners have few set rules for use when it comes to distribution preferences, alternatives, and strategies. Consider the following portfolio withdrawal guidelines used in the profession currently:

- Upon retirement, annuitize all account assets into a fixed-income annuity product with a 5% initial payout.[23]

- At retirement, allocate retirement assets 50% to 60% in stocks with the remaining balance in bonds, and withdraw 4% adjusted for inflation.[24]

These two withdrawal rules could not be further apart in concept and practice. The first approach transfers the income distribution question from the financial planner/client to an insurance company. Certainly, the annuitization strategy provides a level of certainty that cannot be achieved through active portfolio management, but the tactic subjects the client to premature forfeitures due to early death as well as inflation risk. The second distribution approach is also somewhat problematic. Almost all of the studies used to generate the "4% withdrawal rule" have been based on historical equity returns from the early 1900s through the first few years of the 21st century. Regrettably, many retirees who implemented this withdrawal rule beginning anytime after the year 2000 have been hard pressed to maintain a reasonable rate of return to match increases in consumer prices.

Additional research has been conducted to examine how well commonly used withdrawal strategies fare in practice. Consider one of the most widely used withdrawal approaches. An advisor positions a client's retirement portfolio in a balanced mix of stocks and bonds. The client is then advised to withdraw 4% of the account balance on an annual basis. It has been shown historically that if the distributions are adjusted for inflation, there can be as much as a 19% probability that the client will run out of money within 30 years. Increasing the stock allocation to 75% reduces the shortfall possibility to approximately 16%.[25] Others have argued that the possibility of running into a shortfall, even with a 50%/50% mix of stocks and bonds, is only 6%.[26] This means that clients using a 4% distribution approach have between a 6% and 19% probability of outliving their retirement nest eggs.

Annuitized distributions are the final way to manage retirement income. Annuitization is basically an underwriting process where the issuer of an annuity—in the United States this must be an insurance company—determines the likely remaining life span of the annuitant, thereby calculating the cost of guaranteeing the stream of periodic payments to the annuitant. The annuity product is actually an insurance wrapper of sorts that guarantees the payment stream, but the client's assets are used to make the payments.

Annuitization provides greater certainty of income for longer periods of time while also reducing the asset base subject to RMD, because the IRS assumes that the periodic payments from an annuity will suffice for the RMD. This last point effectively increases the after-tax rate of return for assets held in annuity accounts.

Annuitization is basically an irrevocable choice of planned distribution, and it comes in one of three basic forms: fixed period, single lifetime, or joint lifetime. Annuitization shifts the shortfall risk to the underwriter, because the annuitant could still outlive the principal but cannot outlive the payment stream, assuming a life annuity. Because of the underwriting and the guarantees provided, canceling or surrendering an annuity contract can be quite expensive, so the choice of an annuitized distribution should be made carefully.

Annuity payments are based on two factors: (1) the desired length of time the contractually obligated payments last, and (2) the assets underlying the contract. The second item is discussed first. Two basic categories of annuities are available: fixed and variable. In return for a lump sum payment or series of payments, a **fixed annuity** provides an income stream based on a fixed, guaranteed interest rate, similar to a fixed income security or bank account. This option carries very little to no market risk. **Variable annuity** products, on the other hand, can offer clients a higher degree of inflation protection in exchange for an element of risk. Instead of providing a client with a fixed rate of return, variable annuities make payments based on the returns generated from the value of the securities in the portfolio. This option can offer a higher payout as long as market conditions are favorable, but in exchange the annuitant has chosen to accept a certain degree of market risk and payout variability.

A case can be made against retirees' use of annuities; the case is strongest against life annuities. A **life annuity** pays out either a fixed or inflation-adjusted stream of income for as long as the annuitant lives. If all goes as planned, in other words if a client dies when he or she is forecast to based on the mortality tables, then "nobody wins." However, if the client outlives the forecast, then the insurance company must continue to pay; whereas without the insurance guarantee the client would theoretically have run out of money. If the client dies prematurely, any remaining principal balance in the annuity is forfeited at death. As a result, life annuities generally appeal only to individuals who have an above-average life expectancy and very high risk aversion.

A strong case can be made for the use of a **guaranteed annuity.** Although less commonly available in the marketplace, a **fixed payment (or period-certain) annuity** provides either a fixed or inflation-adjusted payout for a specific number of years, usually 5, 10, 20, or 30 years, regardless of how long the annuitant lives. In this case, the annuitant could outlive the payment stream, but if the annuitant were to die prematurely a secondary beneficiary would continue to receive payment until the end of the guaranteed period. The use of guaranteed annuities is warranted as a retiree's income increases, risk aversion increases, and overall equity and bond market volatility intensify.[27]

Some annuities combine certain aspects of both life and guaranteed annuities. **Guaranteed lifetime annuities**, as the name implies, provide lifetime income to a client. Most lifetime annuities cease payments upon the client's death (also as the name implies). However, it is possible to obtain annuities with a guaranteed minimum number of distribution years; these are sometimes referred to as a **life with period certain annuities**. If an annuitant were to die during the "period certain," then payments would continue to a secondary beneficiary until the end of that period.

The foregoing discussion assumes that a client is unmarried or has elected a single life payout. However, an additional annuitization choice must be made available for married individuals investing money from an IRA or qualified account. In such plans, it is illegal for a married person to exclude a spouse from receiving a survivor annuity unless the spouse signs a notarized affidavit waiving rights to the annuity payment. **Joint and survivor annuities** provide annuity payments for the lives of the client and a surviving beneficiary, typically a spouse. Choosing a joint and survivor annuity will initially result in a reduced benefit. Typical examples of joint and survivor annuities include 50%, 66 2/3%, and 100% annuity payouts. For example, a 100% annuity would continue the annuity payout at 100% of what was received before the first annuitant's death. A 50% joint and survivor annuity will pay one-half of the payout to the survivor for the survivor's life.

If an annuity or other periodic taxable distribution option is taken, all or a portion of the payments received will most likely be taxable. If the annuity is inside an IRA, then the entire payment is taxable as ordinary income, but if the annuity is not within an IRA then any return of principal is not taxed. In other words, the extent to which the distributions are taxed is based on the adjusted taxable basis of plan assets. In a case where all contributions to a plan are made with "pretax" dollars, meaning that the IRS has not collected tax revenue on the money invested, as is the case with most employer-sponsored retirement plans, then all distributions from the plan will be fully taxable. At the other extreme are Roth accounts, either IRA or 401(k)/403(b). Assets held in these accounts are based on money contributed to the plan that was taxed prior to deposit. Thus, distributions from the plan will be exempt from federal taxation in most cases.

Distribution planning becomes more difficult when some of the assets have been contributed on a pretax basis and some on an after-tax basis, or when there is some other reason why the adjusted tax basis is not zero. In these situations, annuity distributions from a traditional IRA (or any tax-qualified annuity) are taxed using an **inclusion ratio** (or the inverse **exclusion ratio**). The taxable portion of a periodic distribution can generally be estimated using the following formula.

$$Inclusion\ Ratio = \frac{(Annual\ Distribution \times Expected\ Distribution\ Time) - Aftertax\ Contributions}{(Annual\ Distribution \times Expected\ Distribution\ Time)}$$

*Example:* Assume a client retires and receives a $2,000 monthly annuity payout, and that the client's life expectancy is 20 years. If the client contributed $150,000 to the annuity, 68.75% of each distribution would be subject to income taxes, based on the formula.

$$Inclusion\ Ratio = \frac{((\$2,000 \times 240) - \$150,000)}{(\$2,000 \times 240)} = 68.75\%$$

**The capital withdrawal process—required minimum distributions (RMDs).** Also referred to by some sources as *minimum required distributions*, or MRDs, RMDs from qualified plans, traditional IRAs, and 403(b) plans generally must begin by April 1of the year following the year in which the retiree turns age 70½. (Different rules may apply to pre-1987 contributions to 403(b) plans.) Certain plans might permit employees (other than 5% owners) to wait until April 1 of the year following retirement, if not later. This delayed option is not available for IRAs. A penalty of 50% applies to the extent that RMDs are not made. Generally, RMDs are computed by dividing the account balance at the end of the preceding year by the client's life expectancy factor, based on one of three tables: (a) the Uniform Lifetime Table, (b) the Single Life Expectancy Table (for use by beneficiaries), or (c) the Joint and Last Survivor Life Expectancy Table (for the use of owners whose spouses are more than 10 years younger and are the sole beneficiaries of their IRAs). The appropriate table to use depends on the type of account, beneficiaries, and ages of the account owner and beneficiary. Lifetime distributions are generally based on the Uniform Lifetime Table factors shown in Table 12.5.

**Table 12.5** Uniform Lifetime Table

| Uniform Lifetime Table | | | | |
|---|---|---|---|---|
| **Age** | **Divisor** | | **Age** | **Divisor** |
| 70 | 27.4 | | 94 | 9.1 |
| 71 | 26.5 | | 95 | 8.6 |
| 72 | 25.6 | | 96 | 8.1 |
| 73 | 24.7 | | 97 | 7.6 |
| 74 | 23.8 | | 98 | 7.1 |
| 75 | 22.9 | | 99 | 6.7 |
| 76 | 22.0 | | 100 | 6.3 |
| 77 | 21.2 | | 101 | 5.9 |
| 78 | 20.3 | | 102 | 5.5 |
| 79 | 19.5 | | 103 | 5.2 |
| 80 | 18.7 | | 104 | 4.9 |
| 81 | 17.9 | | 105 | 4.5 |
| 82 | 17.1 | | 106 | 4.2 |
| 83 | 16.3 | | 107 | 3.9 |
| 84 | 15.5 | | 108 | 3.7 |
| 85 | 14.8 | | 109 | 3.4 |
| 86 | 14.1 | | 110 | 3.1 |
| 87 | 13.4 | | 111 | 2.9 |
| 88 | 12.7 | | 112 | 2.6 |
| 89 | 12.0 | | 113 | 2.4 |
| 90 | 11.4 | | 114 | 2.1 |
| 91 | 10.8 | | 115 + | 1.9 |
| 92 | 10.2 | | | |
| 93 | 9.6 | | | |

*Source:* IRS. *Individual Retirement Arrangements (IRAs)*, Publication 590, p. 102. Available http://www.irs.gov/pub/irs-pdf/p590.pdf.

The Uniform Lifetime Table can be used by all IRA owners (i.e., unmarried owners; owners whose spouses are fewer than 10 years younger ; owners for whom the spouse is not the sole beneficiary) except under the following circumstances:

- IRA owners for whom the sole beneficiary of the account is a spouse who is more than 10 years younger than the owner. In that situation, the Joint Life Expectancy Table is used, thereby reducing the RMD to preserve tax-deferred earnings.

- Inherited IRA owners (non-spousal or spousal if titled as an inherited IRA). In this situation, the Single Life Expectancy Table is used.

*Example:* Assume that an individual turned age 82 this year and has a traditional IRA valued at $100,000 at the end of the previous year. The planner would simply divide $100,000 by 17.1 to determine the current year MRD of $5,848.

The **younger spouse exception** provides a longer payout for IRA owners whose sole beneficiary is a spouse who is younger by more than 10 years and the only beneficiary of the account. These owners can calculate their lifetime RMD based on the ages of both owner and spouse, using a Joint and Last Survivor Life Expectancy Table. This effectively reduces the amount of the required distribution, thereby preserving the tax-deferred status of the account balance.[28]

Most distributions from qualified plans before age 59½ are subject to federal and state income taxation and could be subject to a 10% early distribution penalty. The following exceptions from the early distribution penalty are available for certain distributions:

- Distributions made at the death of the owner/participant.

- Distributions attributable to the disability of the owner/participant.

- Certain distributions made in the form of substantially equal periodic payments over the life of the person (or lives of the person and a beneficiary).

- Distributions to the extent of medical expenses that exceed 7.5% of a person's adjusted gross income.

- Distributions made to someone age 55 or older who has separated from service (this exception does not apply to IRAs).

- Certain distributions ordered by a court, such as a qualified domestic relations order (QDRO) (not applicable to IRAs).

- Distributions to the extent of health insurance premiums paid during unemployment (IRAs only, not applicable to qualified plans).

- Distributions to the extent of certain college costs (not applicable to qualified plans).

- Certain distributions for the first-time purchase of a home, up to $10,000 (not applicable to qualified plans).

## STRATEGIES

### Review Prospective Retirement Planning Strategies

Developing retirement planning strategies and recommendations involves integrating qualitative and quantitative client situational factors. It is important to determine at the outset a client's goals, dreams, and aspirations for retirement. Where clients want to live, what they want to do, and how they will spend or donate money are all critically important factors to know before making recommendations. Examples of quantitative factors include asset values and savings amounts, and assumptions related to rates of return, inflation, and life expectancies. Once these factors have been reviewed, it is time to consider outputs from the estimates to quantify the client's retirement planning situation.

At the end of the retirement situation analysis, an advisor will know whether a client is on track to meet retirement goals, based on all planning assumptions. If so, few changes in the plan may be needed. If, on the other hand, the client's current retirement assets and savings approaches are insufficient to meet stated goals, it will be necessary to help the client implement changes to meet the retirement objectives.

For those who enjoy solving puzzles, the retirement planning process can be both fun and challenging because designing a plan to help a client reach a retirement goal involves a great deal of creativity. The next step in the planning process involves the development of strategies and recommendations that move a client from planning to action.

### Identify Prospective Retirement Planning Strategies

Planning for retirement can encompass decades of planning to identify and implement the most effective accumulation and distribution strategies responsive to changing financial, economic, and tax environments. Some of the most commonly used retirement planning strategies, both product and procedural, are illustrated below. The tools and techniques listed are only a sampling of the techniques used in practice.

#### Product Strategy 1: Balance Contributions to Tax-deferred Plans and IRAs

**Advantage:** This strategy is premised on the notion that saving money on a tax-deferred basis is one of the best ways to accumulate wealth for retirement. The choice of which type of plan to use—an employer-sponsored plan or an IRA—is complicated. Figure 12.6 provides a rudimentary decision tree to help determine funding priorities based on plan type.

**Figure 12.6** Choosing between a Defined Contribution Plan and IRA Contributions

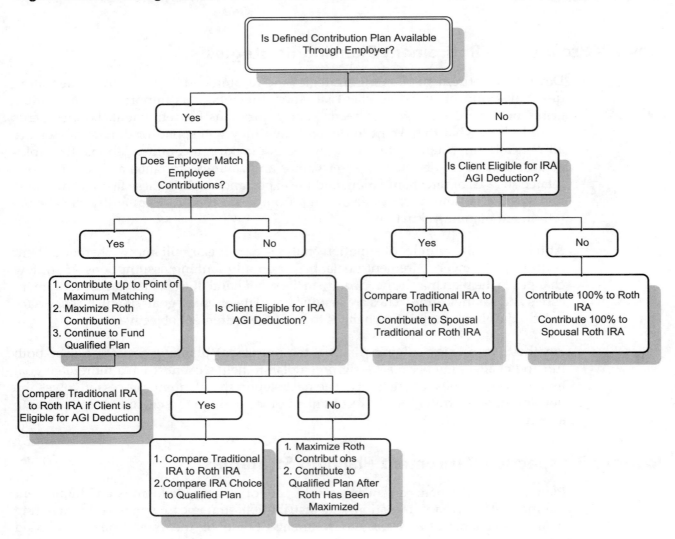

As shown in the decision tree, clients should be encouraged to contribute to a defined contribution plan when employer matching is available. Maximizing the match is important. If, for example, an employer matches dollar-for-dollar on the first 4% of contributions, a client would be foolish to pass up this offer. In effect, the employer is guaranteeing the client an immediate 100% return on contributions up to 4%, and that is before any earnings are generated from the contribution.

Next, benefits associated with employer-sponsored plans must be compared to advantages offered by IRAs. In many cases, contributing either to a tax-deductible or Roth IRA may be more beneficial than contributing to a defined contribution plan. If eligible, the tax-deductible plan offers an immediate income tax savings and tax-deferred growth, whereas the Roth offers the advantages of tax-deferred growth and tax-exempt earnings if the distribution rules are followed. Furthermore, IRAs offer more freedom of account choice than employer-provided plan offerings.

Once deductible or Roth IRA contributions have been maximized, clients who can afford additional contributions up to the maximum allowable limits should contribute to qualified and other employer retirement plans (e.g., 403(b) and 457 plans). These plans provide immediate income tax reduction and tax deferral on account growth.

**Disadvantage:** The greatest limitation of this strategy is that not all clients will be able to fully benefit from it. For 2012, a **highly compensated employee (HCE)** is anyone who was a "5% owner" at any time during 2012 or anyone who receives in excess of $115,000 in compensation during 2012 and, if elected by the employer, is in the top 20% of employees based upon compensation. A **key employee** is someone who is (a) an officer with income in excess of $165,000 in 2012, (b) a 5% owner, or (c) a 1% owner with compensation in excess of $150,000. Highly compensated employee contributions to a 401(k) plan can be limited by the contributions made by non-highly-compensated employees. Also, higher-income clients typically cannot deduct traditional IRA contributions, and they may be unable to contribute to a Roth IRA. Other disadvantages include potential penalties associated with early withdrawals and the possibility of paying higher taxes if the client's marginal rate is higher once distributions begin. Other clients may not have available discretionary cash flow to benefit from multiple accounts.

## Product Strategy 2: Increase Contributions to Retirement Plans and IRAs

**Advantage:** Assuming that a client's retirement goals and assumptions are realistic, one of the simplest strategies for meeting the retirement accumulation goal is to allocate additional assets and savings to the retirement plan. Certain defined contribution plans and some IRA-based plans allow employees 50 years of age or older to make catch-up contributions beyond the maximum annual allowable contribution. The contribution catch-up information shown in Table 12.6 summarizes catch-up provisions as they apply to 401(k), 403(b), 457, and IRA plans. This strategy has the advantage of taking already accumulated assets or unaccounted-for sources of cash flow to build retirement wealth.

**Table 12.6** Retirement Plan Catch-up Provisions

| Plan | 2010 and beyond | |
|---|---|---|
| 401(k) | $5,500 Indexed to inflation in $500 increments | |
| Roth 401(k) | $5,500 | |
| 403(b) | $5,500 Indexed to inflation in $500 increments | |
| 457 | $5,500 Indexed to inflation in $500 increments | |
| SIMPLE IRAs and SIMPLE 401(k) plans | $2,500 Indexed to inflation in $500 increments | |
| IRA | $1,000 | $1,000 |

*Sources:* IRS. 401(k) *Resource Guide—Plan Participants—Limitation on Elective Deferrals.* Available at http://www.irs.gov/retirement/participant/article/0,,id=151786,00.html.

IRS. *Retirement Topics—Catch-Up Contributions.* Available at http://www.irs.gov/retirement/participant/article/0,,id=211396,00.html.

IRS. *Determinations —Summary of EGTRRA Changes for Retirement Plans.* Available at http://www.irs.gov/retirement/article/0,,id=218383,00.html.

**Disadvantage:** Reallocating assets and savings toward retirement plan goals could jeopardize other important financial planning goals, including building an emergency fund, funding insurance needs, and paying for education expenses. However, depending on the type of account used, some retirement savings can still offer options for certain expenses, such as education.

## Product Strategy 3: Fully Fund an Individual Retirement Account

**Advantage:** Assuming that a client has contributed to a defined contribution plan to the point of receiving the maximum employer match, investing in an IRA should be the next consideration. The choice of traditional or Roth IRA generally depends on two factors: (1) the ability to deduct contributions to a traditional IRA, and (2) the marginal tax rates at the time of contribution and withdrawal. Clients who are eligible to make tax-deductible contributions generally find a traditional IRA attractive whenever the marginal tax rate will be lower when the client retires and distributions are made. Clients who are eligible to make contributions to Roth IRAs will generally find a Roth IRA attractive if marginal tax rates will be higher after retirement (assuming Roth IRA distributions are qualified). The Roth IRA is generally a better choice when a contribution to a traditional IRA is not deductible, unless contributions cannot be made to a Roth IRA. Table 12.7 illustrates how tax rates impact IRA funding decisions. Furthermore, in some cases it may be worth fully funding a client and spouse Roth IRA before also contributing to a qualified plan, especially in cases where employer matching is unavailable.

**Table 12.7** Impact of Tax Rates on Traditional and Roth IRA Distributions

| Type | Contribution | Contribution Tax Rate | Distribution Tax Rate | After-tax Distribution |
|------|-------------|----------------------|----------------------|------------------------|
| Traditional IRA | $5,000 | 25% | 25% | $13,659 |
| Roth IRA | $3,750 | 25% | 25% | $13,659 |
| Traditional IRA | $5,000 | 25% | 15% | $15,481 |
| Roth IRA | $3,750 | 25% | 15% | $13,659 |
| Traditional IRA | $5,000 | 15% | 25% | $13,659 |
| Roth IRA | $4,250 | 15% | 25% | $15,481 |

This table is based on the following assumptions:
- Number of years until distribution = 15
- Rate of return = 9%
- Roth IRA contribution = traditional IRA contribution × (1 – pre-retirement tax rate)
- Roth distribution is qualified

**Disadvantage:** Choosing to contribute to either a traditional or Roth IRA before funding a qualified plan means that a client will lose an important tax reduction tool (i.e., the ability to fund qualified retirement savings with pretax dollars). Another disadvantage is that contributions to and accumulations in IRAs are not always protected from creditors. IRA asset protection differs from state to state. Furthermore, deductible contributions to a traditional IRA or contributions to a Roth IRA may be unavailable because of phase-outs based on modified AGI.

## Product Strategy 4: Elect Pension Maximization

**Advantage:** Pension maximization generally starts with taking a 100% single life payout from a defined benefit plan or annuity. As a result of the single life payout, the monthly benefit will be significantly larger than a comparable joint and survivor payout. Under a pension maximization arrangement, the extra amount is used to purchase life insurance, which is used to fund a survivor's income need if the participant predeceases the spouse. If a permanent form of insurance is used, a portion of the cash value can be used in later years to supplement retirement income.

**Disadvantage:** Pension maximization will not work when a client is uninsurable. The strategy also might not work when a client's life expectancy is significantly longer than an affordable term of insurance, or when the amount of insurance that can be purchased is insufficient to fund the difference between the single life payout and the joint and survivor payout.

## Product Strategy 5: Use a Reverse Mortgage to Increase Retirement Income

**Advantage:** A **reverse mortgage** is a type of loan that is generally provided to a client on either a monthly payout or a line of credit basis. No interest or principal is due until the end of the mortgage term. Payments received by a client are not taxable. Payments received do not impact Social Security or Medicare benefits.

**Disadvantage:** Although a reverse mortgage allows a client to convert a portion of home equity to current income while living in the home, it is possible that all equity will be used by the end of the loan term, leaving nothing for the client or heirs. Furthermore, if a client saves a portion of the payments received, this could negatively affect Medicaid and Supplemental Security Income eligibility. Additionally, interest paid is not deductible until the end of the loan term. Finally, reverse mortgages have come under intense federal and state scrutiny because of generally high lender fees and expenses. The costs associated with these products could, in some cases, exceed the benefits.

## Product Strategy 6: Use Variable Universal Life as a Retirement Planning Tool

**Advantage:** In some cases, a highly compensated client needs to shelter income and assets to such an extent that qualified plans are of modest help. For example, a highly paid executive might quickly exhaust his or her ability to shelter assets in an employer plan due to maximum annual contribution limits. It is also likely, given the executive's income level, that the client cannot make a contribution to a Roth IRA because of phase-outs based on income. What is an executive to do? One solution might be for the firm to implement a non-qualified retirement plan. This can be an expensive option. It could also be a risky alternative for the executive, because assets held in a non-qualified plan could be subject to firm creditors. One realistic solution for solving this issue involves the use of a variable universal life insurance policy.

VULs provide an opportunity for a client (or the client's employer) to change the face value of a policy and yearly premiums paid. In effect, a VUL allows a client to purchase a term insurance policy while also investing in tax-deferred mutual funds. If invested appropriately, the cash account can grow in value over time. Unlike qualified plans that restrict annual contributions, a VUL can accept very large annual premiums. In fact, a VUL can easily be funded with multiples of the yearly limit applied to qualified defined contribution plans. Furthermore, the cash value in such accounts is sheltered from taxes and creditors. In most cases, the client owns the account outright.

Once the cash value of an account generates enough annual income to cover policy expenses (called *the tax-free funding level*), all additional earnings and premiums work to increase cash values. Assume that the executive is ready to retire. Also assume that over the course of 20 or 30 years, the executive funded the VUL to the fullest extent. If the account has gone up in value, the executive can start to take policy loans out against the value of the account. The insurance company will charge interest on these loans, but the executive generally owes no tax on the borrowed amounts unless he or she failed to make a loan payment. With a large enough account cash balance, the interest plus insurance expenses can continue to be covered by account earnings. Year after year, the executive can borrow money from the account.

**Disadvantage:** Obviously, multiple factors come into play using this type of planning technique. First, the level of funding necessary to make the scenario realistic over time is quite large. Second, and most importantly, the client must invest aggressively over the VUL holding period. It is important to note that the account value must be of such size at the time of retirement to meet ongoing retirement income needs and also pay interest and insurance expenses. Another disadvantage is that this strategy is appropriate in only a limited number of cases, which limits the usefulness of the product in meeting the needs of many clients. If the policy is a modified endowment contract, loan payments are treated as taxable distributions to the extent that cash value exceeds investment in the contract.

### Product Strategy 7: Use Glide Path Portfolios That Match a Client's Investment Time Horizon

**Advantage:** A retirement **glide path portfolio** refers to the allocation of investments within a retirement account, most often mutual funds, which automatically adjust from risky to conservative as the client/investor ages. The glide path refers to the notion that the portfolio slowly adjusts to an increasingly conservative asset allocation the closer to retirement or the target-date maturity of the fund. At that time, the portfolio will be almost entirely in Treasury securities or other low risk/return assets and the client will have the choice of continuing to own the fund, purchasing an annuity or reallocating the assets into the retirement income portfolio. These products provide two main advantages. First, the need to reallocate holdings is eliminated. Second, portfolio risk falls as the client's risk capacity declines.

**Disadvantage:** The term *glide path portfolio* is a marketing term used to describe what are generally known as *target-date maturity funds*. Although each company that provides a target-date product defines the glide path differently, all funds using this strategy reduce equity exposure over time. Depending on the reallocation from equity to low risk/return assets, this can run counter to academic studies showing that nearly everyone, regardless of age, should have some exposure to equities as an inflation and longevity hedge. By following a traditional glide path strategy, clients could find that their overall portfolio is too conservative dependent on the ratio of these retirement assets within the client's broader portfolio. For example, fixed-income assets tend to make up a high percentage of income sources for the majority of U.S. retirees (e.g., Social Security, annuities). Care must be taken that when glide path portfolios are included in the broader portfolio the allocation to fixed-income securities is not too great.

### Procedural Strategy 1: Allocate Additional Resources to Retirement Goals

**Advantage:** In many cases, a current situation analysis will indicate that a client's current level of assets and ongoing savings is insufficient to fully fund retirement. In such situations, other existing nonallocated assets can be used for retirement (i.e., other assets that have not been allocated to a particular client goal). Use of other assets and savings could be key to reaching a retirement goal; another approach would be to increase annual account contributions to the annual maximum. Table 12.1 provides a summary comparison of the most commonly used retirement plans available to clients when implementing the savings component of this recommendation.

**Disadvantage:** The primary disadvantage associated with this strategy is that using unallocated assets and savings for retirement means that these resources will be unavailable to meet other client goals, including education funding and estate planning needs.

### Procedural Strategy 2: Decrease Projected Income or Living Expense Requirements

**Advantage:** A shortfall in retirement savings could exist even after committing unallocated assets and savings toward the retirement goal. It is possible that the amount of income or living expenses being replaced is too high. This strategy calls for the client to reevaluate the retirement income need. By reducing the need, it might be possible to use existing resources to fully fund retirement.

**Disadvantage:** Emotionally, asking a client to reassess his or her income need can be quite difficult. Some clients could interpret this suggestion as indicating that they are extravagant. Also, it is possible that the client's income need is realistic and that income cannot be cut without seriously decreasing a client's quality of life in retirement.

### Procedural Strategy 3: Adjust the Life Expectancy Assumption

**Advantage:** Changing the years in retirement assumption (i.e., life expectancy) is one way to decrease a client's total asset need without decreasing the projected amount of annual income received.

**Disadvantage:** The obvious disadvantage associated with this strategy is that a client could outlive the accumulated asset base. The fiscal and emotional strain on the client and other family members could be devastating. Elderly individuals who have planned well for retirement often worry about outliving their resources. Adjusting the life expectancy assumption, unless there is valid information on which to base this decision, could mislead a client and further limit alternative retirement saving options or available spending reductions.

## Procedural Strategy 4: Increase Rate-of-return Assumptions

**Advantage:** Increasing the rate-of-return assumption within retirement planning models is the easiest way to obtain the theoretical feasibility of retirement goals. Hypothetically, it is possible to meet retirement objectives, holding all other inputs static, by increasing portfolio returns.

**Disadvantage:** Rate-of-return assumptions must be based on a combination of a client's time horizon, risk tolerance, capacity for risk taking, asset class preference, and expectations about the future. Assuming a rate of return that is higher than is commensurate with a client's risk profile almost inevitably leads to plan failure. So, even though it is theoretically possible to make a retirement plan work by increasing portfolio return assumptions, in practical terms it may not be possible to actually manage assets in a way that generates such returns without exposing the client to greater levels of risk. Further, overestimating expected returns in a portfolio might subject a financial planner to suitability challenges if returns are not realized.

## Procedural Strategy 5: Postpone Retirement

**Advantage:** It may be reasonable to recommend that a client postpone retirement one or more years. The advantage of this strategy is that it generally results in a higher Social Security benefit. The strategy also allows existing assets to grow for additional years.

**Disadvantage:** This strategy may not be feasible for clients who face forced retirement because of medical problems or loss of employment. Also, this strategy forces clients to work longer than hoped and expected, which can result in a reduced level of morale and willingness to maintain proactive financial planning strategies. As an alternative, in situations where one spouse will earn more by claiming a spousal benefit rather than their own Social Security benefit, a good strategy involves having the high-earning spouse file for benefits at NRA. This allows the low-earning partner to file for spousal benefits. The higher-earning partner can then, if desired, halt his or her request, thus allowing the benefit value to increase. Even though the high-earning spouse will not receive a benefit, the spousal benefit will be paid immediately.

## Procedural Strategy 6: Decrease the Inflation Rate Retirement Assumption

**Advantage:** In cases where adjusting other assumptions leaves a client short of the capital accumulation goal, another strategy is to reduce the assumed inflation rate for the retirement time period. This will result in a lower assumed gross asset need at retirement, which will make the value of assets and savings appear more likely to meet client needs.

**Disadvantage:** Implementing this strategy is fraught with risk. Inflation is often the greatest financial risk facing retirees on a fixed income. If actual inflation exceeds the assumed level, then it is likely that a client's assets will quickly be depleted over the course of his or her life.

### Procedural Strategy 7: Decrease the Income Replacement Ratio

**Advantage:** This strategy is similar to Procedural Strategy 2, which called for decreasing a client's income need while in retirement. The advantage of this strategy is that decreasing the percentage of income projected to be replaced will result in a lower total funding need at the date of retirement.

**Disadvantage:** Implementing this strategy could reduce a client's standard of living to a level that is less than preferable, and in an extreme situation, unrealistic. The ultimate consequence is less money to fund leisure activities, gifting strategies, travel, entertainment, or other expenses.

### Procedural Strategy 8: Continue to Work (Part-time) while in Retirement

**Advantage:** This recommendation has the dual advantage of providing additional cash flow in retirement while providing meaningful activity for the client while retired. For some executives and former business owners, this could mean periodic consulting. For others, it might mean working a permanent part-time job. The additional cash flow reduces the amount of retirement income to be replaced from assets, savings, and retirement plans. Working while retired is also an excellent way to keep both mind and body active. Some retirees find that their dreams of retirement are larger than the reality, and employment provides some with the opportunity to contribute to society in a meaningful way.

**Disadvantage:** Working while retired can have a significantly negative impact on Social Security benefits. Clients who receive Social Security benefits before reaching NRA are limited in the amount that can be earned without losing benefits. Another disadvantage associated with this strategy is that for many clients the thought of working defeats the goal of retiring. This, like many of the procedural strategies presented, can have a negative impact on attitudes and willingness to continue planning.

### Procedural Strategy 9: Understand Qualified Plan Coverage Rules

**Advantage**: When designing or evaluating a qualified retirement plan for an organization (e.g., a small business owner) it is important to understand the following coverage eligibility rules:

- Defined benefit plans must benefit the lesser of 40% of eligible employees or 50 eligible employees.

- Defined contribution plans must provide a benefit to 70% or more of

    - non-highly compensated employees, or

    - the ratio of non-highly compensated employees to highly compensated employees, or

    - the average benefit ratio for non-highly compensated employees to highly compensated employees must be at least 70%, and

    - the plan must not be nondiscriminatory.

**Disadvantage**: Any plan that fails these coverage rules is considered non-qualified for tax purposes, resulting in lost tax deductions for the organization and potential loss of tax deferral for employees.

## Procedural Strategy 10: Understand Who Could Be Excluded from a Qualified Retirement Plan

**Advantage**: Providing a qualified retirement plan can often be an expensive benefit for businesses. By understanding who could be excluded from plan participation, it is possible to save plan expenses for a business owner client. In general, anyone under the age of 21 or those who work less than 1,000 hours per year can be excluded. Any employee who has worked for 1,000 hours in a 12-month period and is at least 21 years of age is eligible for plan participation.

**Disadvantage**: Excluding certain employees from a qualified plan can result in reduced productivity, resulting in higher employee turnover. Furthermore, business owners must weigh the potentially negative effects of excluding employees (e.g., low morale) against the actual dollar amount saved in benefit costs.

## Procedural Strategy 11: Understand Social Security Eligibility for Divorced Clients

**Advantage**: Increasingly, financial planners are called on to help clients prepare for retirement prior to, after, or during a divorce. It is important to understand how divorce can impact a client's eligibility for Social Security benefits. According to the Social Security Administration, if a client is divorced (even if the other person has since remarried), the client can qualify for benefits on the record of the ex-spouse. This is an important consideration for many women who were primary homemakers without an earnings record. To receive benefits, a client must:

- have been married to the ex-spouse for at least 10 years;

- have been divorced at least two years;

- be at least 62 years old;

- be unmarried; and

- be ineligible for an equal or higher benefit on his or her own work or someone else's work.

**Disadvantage**: These eligibility rules can place some clients in a financially awkward position. For example, if a client was married for less than 10 years, he or she might not be eligible for benefits under the ex-spouse's record. The rules also prohibit a client from remarrying; however, clients sometimes marry first only to discover that their benefits have been lost. The primary disadvantage for younger divorced clients under current rules is that to receive benefits and/or to be considered insured for Medicare, the client may have to reenter the workplace to establish an income record.

## Procedural Strategy 12: Consider IRA Transfer Rules when Advising Clients about Rollover Alternatives

**Advantage**: The IRS currently allows assets to be transferred tax free from a qualified retirement plan or another IRA to an IRA. Three transfers are allowed. A **trustee-to-trustee transfer** occurs when one trustee directly moves a client's assets to another trustee. Because there is no distribution to the client, the transfer is tax free. According to the IRS, because this type of transfer is not a rollover, it is not affected by the one-year waiting period required between rollovers. The second transfer is called a *rollover*. An **IRA rollover** is a tax-free distribution of cash or other assets from a retirement plan made directly to a client. It is the client's responsibility to contribute assets to the IRA. Clients must generally roll over the entire contribution by the 60th day after receiving the distribution. The third transfer method is known as *transfers incident to divorce*. If assets in a traditional IRA are transferred from an ex-spouse to your client via a divorce or separate maintenance decree, the assets held in the IRA, starting from the date of the transfer, are treated as belonging to the client. The transfer is tax free.

**Disadvantage**: Knowing the transfer rules is important as a tool for reducing tax liabilities and penalties. If a client fails to roll over a distribution within 60 days, in the absence of a waiver, the client must treat the amount as a taxable distribution. These amounts are taxable in the year distributed, even if the 60-day period expires the next year. For clients under age 59½, it is likely that they will have to pay a 10% additional tax on early distributions. It is also important to note another disadvantage associated with a rollover. Generally, if a client makes a tax-free rollover of any part of a distribution from a traditional IRA, he or she cannot, within a one-year period, make a tax-free rollover of any later distribution from that same IRA. Clients are also prohibited from making a tax-free rollover of any amount distributed within the same one-year period from the IRA into which they made the tax-free rollover. The one-year period begins on the date that clients receives an IRA distribution, not the date they roll it into an IRA. There is third disadvantage. If an eligible rollover distribution is paid directly to a client, the payer must withhold 20% for federal tax purposes. This rule applies even if the client plans to roll over the distribution to a traditional IRA.

## Procedural Strategy 13: Include Post-retirement Income Tax Considerations when Conducting a Retirement Needs Analysis

**Advantage**: A key factor determining the feasibility of a retirement needs analysis involves the client's place of residence. Each state taxes pension benefits—and in some cases even Social Security benefits—differently. Various sources, such as Kiplinger, AARP, and the National Conference of State Legislatures, provide a state-by-state comparison of taxes—income, sales, and real estate, for example—levied on retirees. By understanding the income tax status of Social Security and private, state, and federal pensions at the state level, a financial planner can provide a more accurate income projection. For example, some states lik Nebraska, Rhode Island, North Dakota, Utah, and Vermont offer no income tax exemptions for Social Security or pension benefits.[29] Other states, such as Georgia, exempt Social Security benefits and up to $35,000 of any kind of retirement income from state taxation; Kentucky also exempts Social Security benefits from state income taxes plus up to $41,110 per person of retirement income, including public and private pensions and annuities.[30] Other taxes, such as state sales taxes, real estate taxes, and estate and inheritance taxes, are reviewed by some sources to rank states as "best or worst" states for retirees.

**Disadvantage:** For some clients, it may be impossible to relocate to a state that provides a more competitive tax environment. There might also be situations when a client would rather pay higher taxes than move. Under such circumstances, this tax information should be used to help clients plan for avoiding or paying taxes rather than as a comparison of tax havens.

# CHAPTER-BASED CASE STUDY

## A Client-based Retirement Recommendation Example

Client-based retirement recommendations should be designed to use available resources to the highest and best use to meet client goals. This means incorporating quantitative and qualitative factors into one or more recommendations that answer the who, what, when, where, why, how, and how much questions related to implementation issues. On the quantitative side, a recommendation ought to be developed by narrowing possible strategies into ones that maximize client outcomes while minimizing costs related to savings and asset usage.

For example, in some cases, it will be difficult for a client to increase savings toward retirement objectives without sacrificing savings for another goal. In such situations, it is prudent to attempt to design recommendations that can be used to meet more than one financial planning goal. The use of a Roth IRA is an example of how one product can be strategically positioned to meet either of two objectives. Principal invested in a Roth IRA can generally be withdrawn on a tax-free basis to help pay for future expenses, such as a child's education. If funds are not needed for education in the future, the assets can then be used to help fund retirement objectives.

Other quantitative factors need to be considered when developing recommendations. Issues related to health insurance coverage and the taxation of Social Security and other benefits in retirement are fundamental examples of factors that influence the choice of appropriate recommendations.

Qualitative factors must also be evaluated in the context of moving from strategy prioritization to recommendation presentation. Planners should evaluate how a recommendation, if implemented by a client, will affect the client's lifestyle while in retirement. Maximizing tax-deferred savings vehicles while eschewing after-tax investments before retirement, for instance, could lead to alterations in a client's lifestyle while retired.

Assume that a client plans to live in a state with a high income tax rate when retired. Maximizing tax-deferred investments almost guarantees that income generated from these assets will be taxed at a high state tax rate. If, on the other hand, the client invests in dividend-paying stocks using after-tax dollars, the client's tax burden will probably be lower.

As this example shows, it is important to account for lifestyle and other qualitative issues before making a recommendation. Issues such as where a client's family plans to live in retirement, what activities they would like to engage in while retired, and what type of legacy they would like to leave all influence the type of recommendation(s) that should be made.

## A Sample Recommendation: Increase Contributions to a 401(k) Plan

After gathering information from her client and analyzing relevant data, Jamie is ready to make a retirement planning recommendation. Jamie has determined that her client, Bob Smith, has to save approximately $4,000 more per year, on a pretax basis, to fully fund his retirement goal.

Before choosing a retirement planning product as the funding mechanism, Jamie went over the notes that she took when talking with Bob about his retirement dreams. Jamie noted that Bob plans to move to Las Vegas in retirement. Bob's number-one leisure activity is golf, and he thinks that with the warm weather, city amenities, and relaxed lifestyle options, he will very much enjoy retirement.

Jamie was pleased to learn that Bob is interested in moving to Nevada for another reason. She knows that Nevada is an income- and estate tax-free state. Using a tax-deferred retirement plan such as a 401(k) to fund Bob's need makes sense because his total marginal tax bracket should be less in retirement than it is today. The tax benefits he will receive today make this an attractive recommendation.

The Retirement Planning Recommendation Form shown in Exhibit 12.4 illustrates how Jamie might summarize the 401(k) recommendation.

**Exhibit 12.4** Smith Retirement Planning Recommendation Form

### Planning Recommendation Form

| | | | | | |
|---|---|---|---|---|---|
| **Financial Planning Content Area** | Retirement planning | | | | |
| **Client Goal** | Increase contributions to 401(k) Plan | | | | |
| **Recommendation No.** | 1 | **Priority (1–6) lowest to highest:** | | 6 | |
| **Projected/Target Value ($)** | $4,000 annual increase in 401(k) contributions | | | | |

**Product Profile**

| | | | | |
|---|---|---|---|---|
| Type | Company-sponsored retirement plan | | | |
| Duration | 5+ years; monthly | | | |
| Provider | Employer | | | |
| Funding Cost per Period ($) | $333 increase per month | | | |
| Maintenance Cost per Period ($) | $0 | | | |
| Current Income Tax Status | Tax-qualified | X | Taxable | |
| Projected Rate of Return | 8.4% | | | |
| Major Policy Provisions | NA | | | |

**Procedural Factors**

| | | | | |
|---|---|---|---|---|
| Implementation by Whom | Planner | | Client | X |
| Implementation Date or Time Frame | Immediately | | | |
| Implementation Procedure | Employer allows one annual change to your salary reduction agreement; obtain necessary forms from payroll office and increase annual contribution by $4,000. | | | |

**Ownership Factors**

| | | | | |
|---|---|---|---|---|
| Owner(s) | Bob Smith | | | |
| Form of Ownership | Jenny Smith | | | |
| Insured(s) | NA | | | |
| Custodial Account | Yes | | No | X |
| Custodian | NA | | | |
| In Trust for (ITF) | Yes | | No | X |
| Transfer on Death (TOD) | Yes | | No | X |
| Beneficiary(ies) | Jenny Smith | | | |
| Contingent Beneficiary(ies) | NA | | | |

| | |
|---|---|
| **Proposed Benefit** | Although cash flow is initially decreased by $4,000, implementation will result in tax savings (25% of contribution) of approximately $1,000, for a net decrease in discretionary cash flow of $3,000. |

In this case, Jamie assigns the recommendation a very high priority, because without adequate funding Bob will be unable to meet his retirement goal. Using the 401(k) vehicle also means that Bob's reportable income will decrease by $4,000 as a result of using the pretax contribution feature. Assuming that Bob is in the 25% marginal tax bracket, this will result in a tax savings of $1,000. Rather than costing Bob $4,000 in cash flow to fund the recommendation, Bob's current net after-tax cost is only $3,000.

Each retirement recommendation is client specific and unique. This example illustrates how one recommendation can affect other areas of a client's financial situation. As shown, increasing pretax contributions to a retirement plan results in a lower tax liability for Bob. Note that this example shows an assumed rate of return of 8.4%. If this rate of return is not achieved, Bob's goal could be jeopardized.

# Learning Outcomes

1.  This chapter highlights the importance of retirement planning in the comprehensive financial planning process. For nearly all clients, planning and saving for retirement require a significant commitment to resource allocation. In addition to issues related to the use of cash flow to build a retirement nest egg, clients, working with their financial planner, must also grapple with questions related to housing preferences, recreational choices, and overall lifestyle factors as they plan for retirement. Clients who postpone tasks associated with retirement planning will find that the strategies, tools, and techniques available to reach retirement goals are limited. Financial planners can serve their clientele well by promoting early and ongoing retirement planning activities.

2.  Although retirement planning entails a high degree of quantitative analysis, it is essential that financial planners account for client situational factors that could uniquely affect a client's retirement planning goals. As illustrated in this chapter, the following lifestyle issues can impact the process associated with retirement planning: retirement attitudes, early retirement aspirations, postretirement work attitudes, leisure activity hopes and dreams, health status, and relocation preferences.

3.  Conducting a retirement capital needs analysis is a key aspect of the retirement planning process. The steps involved in calculating capital depletion, capital preservation, and inflation-adjusted approaches require a firm grasp and application of time value of money concepts. It is each financial planner's responsibility to develop assumptions related to rates of return, inflation, life expectancy, and timing of payments, and to balance these assumptions against each client's retirement aspirations and financial goals. When used appropriately, using time value of money concepts it is possible to estimate a client's retirement need.

4.  Competent financial planners must have a sufficient working knowledge of the Social Security system to help their clients plan for retirement. Even for clients with other sources of retirement income, Social Security benefits tend to be a significant source of fixed income during retirement. Because of this, issues related to retiring either before or after NRA create complexities that require planners to incorporate both qualitative and quantitative client data into distribution analyses. It is not enough to rely on general planning rules when helping clients make decisions related to the timing of retirement or the receipt of Social

Security benefits. Rather, when making Social Security recommendations, financial planners must account for a client's life expectancy, the need for Social Security benefits as a source of income, the probability a client will work while retired, and other factors.

5. Although qualified retirement plans such as 401(k) arrangements often dominate how clients think about saving for retirement, it is important for financial planners to understand that retirement savings can occur using both qualified and non-qualified products. Qualified plans provide an immediate tax reduction and tax deferral for plan participants; further, employers receive a current tax deduction for qualified plan contributions. These features make qualified plans attractive options for most clients as they begin to save for retirement. Unfortunately, qualified plans come with many restrictions; caps on employee and employer contributions are significant constraints. As such, financial planners may find that non-qualified products can be used to help clients more effectively reach their retirement goals. Annuity products and non-qualified plans (e.g., rabbi and secular trusts) can be added to the product mix to help ensure that clients are best able to reach their retirement goals, and once in retirement, maintain an adequate standard of living.

6. Rather than relying on one or a few retirement planning savings vehicles, it is often most prudent for financial planners to incorporate a mix of qualified defined contribution, pension, and traditional and Roth IRAs (in their various forms as contributory, rollover, inherited, and spousal accounts) into each client's retirement savings program. The use of Roth IRAs and 401(k)/403(b) plans is an area of planning that will continue to grow in the future. These tools allow clients to use after-tax dollars to fund investments that grow tax deferred, and if all rules associated with the plans are met, distributions can be taken in the future on a tax-free basis. Assuming that marginal tax rates could be higher in the future should drive more pre-retirees to use these tax-deferred savings plans today.

7. Although the tendency of many financial planners—and their clients—is to focus on capital accumulation issues in the retirement planning process, it is equally important to develop retirement plan withdrawal strategies that match a client's income needs and life expectancy. Deterministic modeling techniques can be used to generate simplified income distribution projections. These projections can be presented to clients mathematically and graphically. Planners should also be familiar with stochastic modeling theory as an alternative to deterministic approaches to distribution planning.

8. Rules related to qualified plan and IRA distributions are complex. Factors related to early retirement, job transfers, and the use of plan assets for nonretirement purposes each have an impact on a client's retirement plan, as well as tax and cash flow implications. Understanding what might trigger a taxable distribution and federal tax penalty is considered a minimal standard of competency for financial planners. In addition, the ability to identify and calculate RMDs, exceptions to distribution rules, and QDRO exemptions is an essential skill for financial planners. Finally, understanding issues related to IRA rollovers and annuity distribution alternatives represent a characteristic of competency among financial planners.

9. Few aspects of the financial planning process provide as much leeway for financial planners to develop client-specific recommendations as retirement planning. The ability to identify and recommend appropriate and reasonable retirement planning strategies matched to a client's situation is a necessary skill for all financial planners.

# Chapter Resources

Academic papers on sustainable withdrawal rates (research category) (http://www.planipedia. org/index.php/Sustainable_Withdrawal_Rates_).

Complete information about qualified plans from IRS Publication 560 (http://www.irs.gov/ pub/irs-pdf/p560.pdf). Complete summary of ERISA legislation (http://aging.senate.gov/crs/ pension7.pdf).

Department of Labor site for Qualified Retirement Plan information (http://www.dol.gov/ebsa/ publications/wyskapr.html).

Leimberg, Stephan R., et al. *Tools & Techniques of Retirement Income Planning.* Cincinnati, OH: National Underwriter Company, 2007.

Mortality tables (http://www.cdc.gov/nchs/nvss/mortality_tables.htm).

Social Security Benefit Estimator (www.socialsecurity.gov/OACT/quickcalc/index.html).

Stenken, Joseph F. *2012 Social Security & Medicare Facts.* Erlanger, KY: National Underwriter Company, 2012.

Wagner, William J. *Ultimate IRA Resource* (including IRA Calculator), 3rd Ed. Cincinnati, OH: National Underwriter Company, 2006.

The *Financial Factilitator* and all fillable forms needed to complete text activities can be found on the student website at: http://pro.nuco.com/booksupplements/NUCollege-CaseBook2e.

# Quantitative/Analytical Mini-Case Problems

1.  Marybeth and Anneal are beginning to contemplate retirement. They have saved a total of $500,000 for retirement and they are each just 45 years old. They realize that they have not saved sufficiently to be able to retire early, fully retire without some part-time employment, or replace 100% of their preretirement income. But they are willing to explore different avenues.

    Marybeth and Anneal have a combined annual income of $125,000 and believe that their salaries will keep pace with inflation at 4% per year. They are also comfortable assuming that the effective annual rate of return for their retirement assets will be 9% before retirement and 6.5%

after retirement. For now, Marybeth wants to keep the planning simple, projecting that they will both die in exactly 40 years and that their retirement assets will be depleted with the exception of $100,000 to cover funeral and burial costs. Lastly, they do not want to continue saving after they retire (either partly or fully).

As their financial planner, provide some assistance with these calculations. The two primary options are listed below. Considering all previous information, which outcome requires the lowest monthly (end-of-month) contribution if they also require that their retirement annuity grow by 4% per year to keep pace with inflation? (Ignore the effects of income taxes and social security on the answer.)

a. To retire at age 55 with an income replacement ratio of 60%.

b. To retire at age 65 with an income replacement ratio of 100%.

2. Tara, age 44, plans to retire at age 67. Her life expectancy, accounting for family medical history, is age 97. Tara is single and currently earns $56,000 per year as a university librarian. At her normal retirement age she expects to receive $28,700 in Social Security benefits (today's dollars). She will also receive a small defined benefit pension in the amount of $13,500 from a local municipality. She has come to you to determine whether she is on track to meet her retirement goals. Use the following assumptions and information to answer the questions that follow:

- She would like to use a 90% income replacement ratio, based on current earnings.

- She is currently contributing $2,400 per year into a 403(b) plan [no employer match].

- Inflation is assumed to be 3.50%.

- She can earn a 6.50% after-tax rate of return on assets before retirement.

- She can earn a 4.50% after-tax rate of return on assets after retirement.

a. How much does Tara need, on her first day of retirement, to fund a capital depletion model of retirement?

b. Given her current level of savings, is Tara on target to reach her retirement goal?

c. If she has a shortfall, how much more must she save per year to reach her goal?

d. If she would like to obtain a capital preservation goal for retirement, how much will she need to have saved on her first day of retirement?

e. Given a capital preservation goal, is she saving enough on a yearly basis currently?

f. How much, in total, must she save yearly to reach a capital preservation model of retirement?

3. Annette Robinson is a 63-year-old recent widow and is attempting to do some tax and investment planning pertaining to her late husband's traditional IRA account. She has sought your advice as to the best course of action. She has informed you that her husband was 69 at the time of his death and had not begun taking his RMD.

a. What are the three distribution methods available to Annette?

b. Which method should she choose to maximize tax deferral? Based on the appropriate life table, how much would her first required distribution be? When would this distribution happen?

c. Which method should she choose to maximize the distribution? Based on the appropriate life table, how much would her first required distribution be? When would this distribution happen?

d. Which alternative would not have been available had her husband begun his required distributions?

e. If Annette had been younger than 59, which alternative would allow her to take distributions without incurring the tax penalty?

# Comprehensive Bedo Case – Analysis Questions

Tyler and Mia have clearly stated that they would like to retire at age 62, and they would like their plan to include reduced Social Security benefits. The first step in the analysis involves working with relevant assumptions, such as before- and after-retirement inflation rate and marginal tax rate assumptions, savings rates, and portfolio values to determine whether they are on track to meet their retirement goal. If the answer is negative, it will be necessary to determine which assets and savings sources are available for the retirement goal. As a reminder, it is important to work through the retirement planning needs assessment in a logical, step-by-step order.

Every attempt should be made to achieve the Bedos' retirement goal using the capital depletion method. Only after attempting to meet this goal should changes in assumptions be made. Once the funding need is met using the capital depletion method, the next step is to attempt to fund retirement using the capital preservation method. If this goal can be met, the third step is to attempt to implement an inflation-adjusted approach. In other words, it is important to show the Bedos that different alternatives exist and that each alternative has both advantages and disadvantages.

Use the following questions to guide the retirement planning process.

1. Develop a retirement planning goal for the Bedos. When conceptualizing this goal, consider the following.

   a. Is the goal developed in agreement with any or all goals and objectives that the clients have identified regarding retirement planning?

   b. What situational factors might influence their retirement planning goal? Are these factors explicit, implied, or assumed? Is additional information required from the Bedos, and if, so what?

   c. What is the desired retirement planning outcome for the clients?

2.  Make a list of life events that could affect the retirement plans for Tyler and Mia and that should be reviewed at future client meetings.

3.  Are there globally accepted, client-specific, or planner-generated planning assumptions that will influence the retirement planning situation analysis? List the assumptions as they might appear in a plan.

4.  Calculate the following for the Bedos.

    a.  The total value, in current dollars, of assets that have been accumulated by the Bedos for retirement.

    b.  The value at retirement of the retirement assets (including planned future contributions) using the current weighted average rate of return for the retirement assets.

    c.  The net amount of income needed in today's dollars that must be replaced to meet the Bedos' retirement goal.

    d.  The amount of assets needed to completely fund the Bedos' retirement, starting at age 62, using a capital depletion assumption.

    e.  The additional savings the Bedos need at age 62 to meet a capital preservation retirement goal using the assumed after-tax rate of return.

    f.  The amount needed to be saved annually to fund an inflation-adjusted retirement scenario using the assumed after-tax rate of return.

    g.  The amount the Bedos need to save monthly to fully fund their future home expansion using the assumed after-tax rate of return.

    h.  The amount the Bedos need to save monthly to fully fund Mia's art gallery in retirement using the assumed after-tax rate of return.

5.  Clients often request a modular plan for retirement goals. Using text, bullets, and graphics, summarize your observations about Tyler and Mia's retirement planning situation and the identified planning need(s). Based on the information collected, fully document and inform the Bedos of the analyses and results.

6.  Based on the goals originally identified and the completed analysis, what product or procedural strategies might be most useful to satisfy the Bedos' retirement planning needs? Be sure to consider strategies matched to Tyler and Mia's identified planning needs, individually and as a couple. When reviewing the strategies, be careful to consider the approximate cost of implementation as well as the most likely outcome(s) associated with each strategy.

7.  Write at least one primary and one alternative recommendation from the selected strategies in response to each identified retirement planning need. More than one recommendation may be needed to address all planning needs. Include specific, defensible answers to the who, what, when, where, why, how, and how much implementation questions for each recommendation.

    a.  It is suggested that each recommendation be summarized in a Recommendation Form.

b. Assign a priority to each recommendation based on the likelihood of meeting client goals and desired outcomes. This priority will be important when recommendations from other core planning content areas are considered relative to the available discretionary funds for subsidizing all recommendations.

c. Comment briefly on the outcomes associated with each recommendation.

8. Complete the following for the Retirement Planning section of the Bedos' financial plan.

a. Outline the content to be included in this section of the plan. Given the segments written above, what segments are missing?

b. Write the introduction to this section of the plan (no more than one or two paragraphs).

c. Write an explanation of the capital depletion approach, the capital preservation approach, and the inflation-adjusted approach to retirement planning.

9. Prepare a 10–15-minute presentation for the Bedos of your observations and/or recommendation(s) for meeting their retirement planning goals. Be sure to include visual aids, Excel handouts, and other materials that will make the recommendations more meaningful for the clients.

## Notes

1. Employee Benefit Research Institute. "Savings Needed to Fund Health Insurance and Health Care Expenses in Retirement." *EBRI Issue Brief*, no. 295 (2006). Available at www.ebri.org/publications/ib/index.cfm?fa=ibDisp&content_id=3650.

2. Marksjarvis, G. "Gen Y: Time Is on Your Side with the Stock Market." *The Bulletin*. September 22, 2011. Available at http://www.bendbulletin.com/apps/pbcs.dll/article?AID=/20110922/NEWS0107/109220343/1163/1163&nav_category=1163&template=print.

3. MFS Investment Management. *MFS Investing Sentiment Survey Offers Insight into Generation Y Investing Behaviors*. Available at https://www.mfs.com/wps/portal/mfs/us-investor/market-outlooks/news-room/press-releases/!ut/p/c5/04_SB8K8xLLM9MSSzPy8xBz9CP0os3j_QKNAf3MPIwN342BnAyMXE39j01BjQ5cAI6B8JLK8j4UjUN7fLczbLMDA3dKQgG4_j_zcVP2C3IhyAEF8gjE!/dl3/d3/L2dBISEvZ0FBIS9nQSEh/?contentId=templatedata%2finternet%2farticle%2fdata%2fnews%2fpr_sentiment2011_geny_part5.

4. MFS Investment Management, *Investing Sentiment Survey*.

5. Department of Treasury. *Statistical Trends in Retirement Plans*. August 9, 2010. Figure 3, p. 7. Text available at http://www.treasury.gov/tigta/auditreports/2010reports/201010097fr.pdf.

6. Information about the inflation-adjusted performance of popular asset classes is available at http://www.investorsfriend.com/asset_performance.htm.

7. Fidelity Research Institute. (2007, March). "The Fidelity Research Institute Index." *Research Insights Brief*. Summary report available at http://nsresearch.com/media/Mar.12.07_Retirement.pdf .

8. Social Security Administration. *Social Security Benefit Amounts*. Available at http://www.ssa.gov/OACT/COLA/Benefits.html.

9. A complete calculation example can be found at http://www.ssa.gov/oact/ProgData/retirebenefit1.html.

10. Social Security benefits are always rounded down to the next lower dollar. For more information, see http://www.ssa.gov/oact/ProgData/retirebenefit2.html.

11. See Marriage/Relationship Recognition Law by state to identify states that recognize same-sex marriage. Available from the Human Rights Campaign at http://www.hrc.org/laws_and_elections/state.asp.

12. Lemons, D., "When to start collecting Social Security Benefits: A Break-even Analysis," *Journal of Financial Planning 25*, no. 1 (2012): 52–60.

13. Investment Company Institute, *2011 Investment Company Factbook*, 51st Ed. Available at http://www.ici.org/pdf/2011_factbook.pdf, p. 112.

14. Investment Company Institute, *2011 Investment Company Factbook*, p. 113.

15. Caudill, A., "Inherited IRA myths." *Journal of Financial Services Professionals*, 65 no. 5 (2011): 38–41.

16. For more information on the tax loophole, see http://www.kitces.com/blog/archives/242-Dodging-The-Income-Limits-on-Roth-Contributions-Strategy-Or-Abuse.html.

17. Fidelity Research Institute, "The Equity You Live In: The Home as a Retirement Savings and Income Option," *Research Insights Report* (2007). Summary report available at http://www.capitalfundingroup.com/EquityYouLiveIn1__1_.pdf.

18. I.R.C. Section 408 is available online at http://www.law.cornell.edu/uscode/text/26/408.

19. J. Y. Campbell, P. A. Diamond, and J. B. Shoven, *Estimating the Real Rate of Return on Stocks over the Long Term*. Papers presented to the Social Security Advisory Board. Report (2001). Available at http://www.ssab.gov/publications/financing/estimated%20rate%20of%20return.pdf.

20. W. Reichenstein, "Tax-efficient sequencing of account to tap in retirement." *Trends and Issues*, TIAA-CREF Institute, (2006, October). Available at http://www.tiaa-crefinstitute.org/ucm/groups/content/@ap_ucm_p_tcp_docs/documents/document/tiaa02029501.pdf.

21. J. J. Spitzer and S. Singh, "Extending Retirement Payouts by Optimizing the Sequence of Withdrawals," *Journal of Financial Planning, 19 no.* 4 (2006): 52–61.

22. J. J. Spitzer, "Managing a Retirement Portfolio: Do Annuities Provide More Safety?" *Journal of Financial Counseling and Planning, 20 no.* 1 (2009): 58–69.

23. W. P. Bengen, "Baking a Withdrawal Plan 'Layer Cake' for Your Retirement Clients," *Journal of Financial Planning, 19* no. 8 (2006): 44–51.

24. W. P. Bengen, "Conserving Client Portfolios during Retirement, Part III." *Journal of Financial Planning, 10* no.6 (1997): 84–97.

25. P. L. Cooley, C. M. Hubbard, and D. T. Walz, "A Comparative Analysis of Retirement Portfolio Success Rates: Simulation versus Overlapping Periods." *Financial Services Review, 12* (2003): 115–129.

26. J. J. Spitzer, J. C. Strieter, and S. Singh, "Guidelines for Withdrawal Rates and Portfolio Safety during Retirement," *Journal of Financial Planning, 20* no. 10 (2007): 52–59.

27. M. A. Milevsky and V. R. Young, "Annuitization and Asset Allocation," *Journal of Economic Dynamics & Control, 31* (2007): 3138 –3177.

28. See IRS Publication 590 at http://www.irs.gov/publications/p590/ar02.html for this table.

29. National Conference of State Legislatures, *State Personal Income Taxes on Pensions & Retirement Income: Tax Year 2010*. Available at http://www.ncsl.org/documents/fiscal/TaxonPensions2011.pdf , pp. 9, 10, and 11.

30. Kiplinger, *Retiree Tax Heavens (and Hells)*. Available at http://www.kiplinger.com/tools/retiree_map/.

# Estate Planning

## Learning Objectives

1. Understand the importance of estate planning within the comprehensive financial planning framework.

2. Identify and explain the three purposes of estate planning.

3. Identify influential situational factors and questions that can be asked to help determine a client's estate planning needs.

4. Determine and evaluate the factors associated with a client's estate tax liability.

5. Describe the steps associated with calculating the estate tax.

6. Explain how the Tax Relief Act of 2010 affected estate planning calculations for some clients.

7. Identify prospective estate planning strategies that can be used to help clients reach their estate planning goals.

# Key Terms

§ 2503(b)

§ 2503(c)

A-B trust arrangement

adjusted taxable gift

advance medical directive

agent

annual exclusion

attorney-in-fact

bypass trust

charitable remainder annuity trust (CRAT)

charitable deduction

charitable giving

charitable lead trust

charitable remainder unitrust (CRUT)

codicil

community property

credit

credit shelter bypass trust

direct skip

directive to physicians

disclaimer

donor-advised charitable fund

durable power of attorney for health care

estate planning

estate tax

estate tax exclusion

family limited partnership

generation-skipping transfer

gift

gift splitting

grantor retained annuity trust (GRAT)

grantor trusts

gross estate

health care proxy

incapacity

income beneficiary

income in respect of a decedent

irrevocable trust

irrevocable life insurance trust (ILIT)

IRS Form 1041

joint tenancy with the right of survivorship (JTWROS)

letter of last instructions

living trust

living will

marital deduction

marital trust

medical directive

medical power of attorney

payable on death (POD)

pooled income fund

portable estate exemption

power of attorney

private foundation

probate

proxy

public foundation

QTIP trust

qualified disclaimer

qualified personal residence trust (QPRT)

qualified terminable interest property (QTIP)

remainder beneficiary

revocable trust

skip person

springing power of attorney

standard family trust

taxable estate

tenancy by the entirety

tenancy in common

transfer on death (TOD)

trust

unified credit

Uniform Gifts to Minors Act (UGMA)

Uniform Transfers to Minors Act (UTMA)

will

**Figure 13.1** Systematic Financial Planning Process for Estate Planning

642

## ESTATE PLANNING: THE BASICS

Estate planning is usually considered the end-of-life distribution of assets; however, a more complete understanding is that estate planning is as much about ownership as it is distribution.  From a financial planning perspective, **estate planning** involves helping clients make decisions about the accumulation, preservation, and ultimate distribution of assets, as well as planning for other end-of-life decisions, including custodial and guardianship situations for incapacitation or minor children. Through proper estate planning, clients can dispose of property upon death in a tax-efficient and cost-effective manner while providing for dependents or other interests—all in a manner consistent with individual beliefs and values. Recommendations related to probate, asset transfers, gifts, estate taxes, settlement costs, and other personal end-of-life decisions are components of a comprehensive estate plan.

Estate planning is an essential part of any well-conceived financial plan. An estate planning analysis can identify potential weaknesses in a client's financial situation that can reduce assets available for beneficiaries, charities, or other legacy goals. Steps taken to analyze a client's situation and to develop estate planning recommendations can serve multiple outcomes. First, estate planning recommendations can maximize a client's financial assets via potential savings on taxes and estate settlement costs. Second, a well-crafted estate plan can protect a client's privacy. Third, estate planning can help ensure that legacy goals are achieved. Fourth, estate planning can give clients peace of mind by confirming that their final financial and life wishes will be enacted.

The purpose of this chapter is to present the essential steps involved in an estate planning analysis, as illustrated in Figure 13.1. The chapter provides a broad overview of estate and gift taxes, including how to estimate a client's gross and taxable estate. Common planning strategies are presented, including the need for a range of estate planning documents, the use and application of trusts, and the implementation of charitable and other gift strategies. The chapter concludes with a discussion of how estate planning strategies can be shaped into client-specific recommendations.

## ANALYZE THE CLIENT'S CURRENT SITUATION

A number of steps are involved in the analysis of a client's current estate planning situation. It is essential that planners engage in discussions and fact-finding exercises that lead to fully knowing their clients. This means understanding the client situational factors, both qualitative and quantitative, associated with the client's personal and financial situation. A client's overarching financial goals as well as specific estate planning objectives need to be reviewed. There must be a thorough exploration of the client's estate distribution desires and wishes. Only after the full range of personal, emotional, and financial factors have been considered should a planner, either individually or in conjunction with an estate attorney, make recommendations directly associated with estate planning objectives.

Sometimes novice financial planners fail to fully appreciate the role of estate planning in the comprehensive financial planning process. Often, it is assumed that estate planning is an activity designed only for the wealthy, and as such, it is further assumed that less wealthy clients may need only a cursory estate plan review. These assumptions are incorrect. Although complex and sophisticated strategies are typically reserved for high-net-worth clients, this does not negate the need for fundamental estate planning preparation for all clients. Planning efforts in the domain of estate planning can serve to preserve a client's assets, but more importantly, they make the process of dealing with end-of-life scenarios easier for surviving family members or heirs. It is a good idea to remember that, although these holistic goals may be the objective of the financial planner, considerable client education may be needed before these goals can be addressed.

It is also important to acknowledge the tension that surrounds estate planning for both clients and planners. It is common for clients and even financial planners to be anxious when thinking about their own or a loved one's death. This is further complicated by the need to be sensitive and respectful of the diverse religious and cultural beliefs, traditions, and ideologies that provide a context for death and the transfer of property. Being cognizant of these issues is a prudent approach whenever estate planning issues are first broached with new or existing clients.

Advisors agree that many clients are resistant to implementing estate planning recommendations, often postponing the preparation of documents from a few months to even years. Sometimes this myopic response to the need for estate planning is based on a host of client fears—which the advisor may need to help the client address. Planners must also use care in balancing their role as educator, trusted advisor, or intermediary between the client and other estate planning professionals, such as an attorney, CPA, insurance professional, custodian, or trust officer. The emotionalism and sensitivity of the client's information and professional and legal boundaries must be carefully balanced to limit any conflicts of interest and to promote collaboration among professionals to help each client reach estate and legacy financial goals.

## Determine and Quantify Estate Planning Needs

Although a client's values, social position, or culture are influential situational factors in determining and quantifying planning needs for all core planning content areas, these factors are particularly ubiquitous in estate planning. Sensitivity to a client's family, cultural, and religious beliefs and attitudes is an important financial planner consideration. Estate planning needs can run the gamut from bequests to immediate or extended family members or friends to providing care or a trust for a cherished pet. The prevalence of remarriages and other nontraditional family relationships, as well as the need for multigenerational planning, further complicate and, in some situations, challenge traditional property law.

These same issues can create unique planning needs to provide for "my, your, and our" heirs, or conversely, to selectively choose or exclude potential heirs or recipients of gifts in post-death asset transfer planning. A client's need for control over assets, either before or after death, can shape estate planning needs, including predetermined conditions (e.g., age or the emotional or financial ability to manage assets) for gifts or distributions from one or more trusts. When working in the estate planning domain, it is wise to remember that what may seem like an odd request to a financial planner may be quite reasonable from the client's perspective. Being sensitive to each client's goals and respectful of different individual, religious, and cultural perspectives is an important trait of successful financial planners.

Consider some common estate planning objectives among financial planning clients. For some, privacy could be a primary concern. For others, the goal might be reducing or avoiding the taxes associated with property transfer. Keeping family secrets confidential might be a primary concern of yet another client. For some clients, charitable giving may take precedence over family bequests. Others might refuse to consider charitable or family gift strategies, regardless of the logical benefit of reducing the taxable estate. The principal concern of other clients could be the reduction or avoidance of settlement costs, including probate and income taxes. As these examples illustrate, few simple rules can be universally applied when working with clients on estate planning issues. Developing an objective perspective focused on helping each client reach the desired objective exemplifies sensitivity, objectivity, and competence. Fundamentally, the determination of estate planning needs focuses on three issues: (a) planning for the transfer of assets in a way that is consistent with the client's wishes and preserves the estate by reducing taxes, probate fees, and other settlement costs; (b) providing for survivors or other financial or charitable needs; and (c) complying with the client's final wishes regarding incapacitation and other end-of-life decisions.

The quantification of a client's estate planning need could involve a number of issues related to estate liquidity (e.g., probate or other state death taxes, debt, income taxes), which are considered later in this chapter and could affect many more clients. But the primary question centers on the payment of federal estate taxes. The answer hinges on the value of the client's **taxable estate** (i.e., the taxable value of assets owned by a decedent at his or her death) relative to the federal estate tax threshold—a number that has ranged from $1 million to $5 million over the past few years. Reaching this threshold can trigger planning needs and strategies that otherwise might not have been necessary. For instance, if it is determined that a married client's **gross estate** (i.e., the value of everything owned on the date of death) currently exceeds or probably will exceed the estate tax unified credit exclusion amount in the near future, then proactive planning strategies are needed to reduce the gross estate —possibly through gifting or the use of trusts. But both of these strategies are also subject to distinct tax considerations, despite the primary intent to reduce or eliminate the estate tax.

### The Estate Tax Calculation

The **estate tax** is a levy on a client's right to transfer property at death and is based on the value of the client's taxable estate at the time of death. A client's taxable estate is the gross estate less allowable deductions. The gross estate includes the fair market value of all property that the client owned or had an interest in at the time of death, or in some cases within three years of death. IRS Form 706 is used to account for these assets. The fair market value of assets at a client's death or as of an alternative valuation date is used, whichever will result in the most advantageous cost basis for the distributed assets. The assets included in the gross estate consist of cash and securities, real estate, revocable trusts, business interests, and other assets, as listed below:

- Life insurance proceeds payable to the estate or, if the client held incidents of ownership in the policy, to the client's heirs;

- The value of certain annuities payable to the estate or heirs;

- The value of certain property transferred within three years before death; and

- Trusts or other interests established by the client or others in which the client had certain interests or powers.

A client's taxable estate is determined by subtracting certain deductions from the gross estate. Allowable deductions include outstanding mortgages and other debts as well as the following deductions used to determine the taxable estate:

- Expenses of estate administration: funeral expenses paid out of the estate, debts owed at the time of death, taxes, and certain estate losses;

- Marital deductions, including all property passing to a surviving spouse;

- Charitable deductions; and

- The state death tax deduction.

It is important to deduct only the portion of a liability attributable to the client. Only the part of a client's debt attributable to a listed asset is deductible. For example, married couples holding a principal residence as joint tenants with right of survivorship (JTWROS) can list only half of the fair market value of the property as an asset. As such, the deceased client can deduct only one-half of the outstanding mortgage balance.

A **marital deduction** is available for the value of all property that passes from one spouse to another. Under current law, the marital deduction is unlimited, meaning that one spouse can leave all of his or her assets to a spouse free of estate and gift taxes. A **charitable deduction** is available for the value of the property that passes to a charity.

After the net amount is computed, the **adjusted taxable gifts** or the value of lifetime taxable gifts made after 1976 are added to this figure, resulting in the taxable estate. The tax is then computed on the new balance or taxable estate. Tax is also calculated on the adjusted taxable gifts and subtracted from the tax on the taxable estate. The tax is also reduced by the available unified credit and other available credits, such as the credit for prior taxes paid or a foreign death tax credit. A **credit** is the dollar amount that reduces or eliminates a tax.

Exhibits 13.1 and 13.2 illustrate the data needed to complete an estimation of estate taxes due for two clients. Exhibit 13.1 from the Financial Facilitator illustrates an estimate for the estate taxes due at the death of one or two clients in 2011 or 2012. Exhibit 13.2 illustrates the estimation of taxes due based on a second-to-die scenario. See the call-out boxes for additional explanation of data input details.

**Exhibit 13.1** Estate Tax Estimator, Section One

### Financial Facilitator Revealed
#### Estate and Gift Tax Estimator, Section One

The estate tax estimator can simultaneously determine the amount of federal estate tax liability for both the client and co-client, including any gifts or marital transfers. This portion of the calculator determines the tax liability upon the first death.

| FEDERAL ESTATE TAX ESTIMATOR | | |
|---|---|---|
| **First Death Tax Liability** | | |
| | **2005** | |
| | Client Death | Co-client Death |
| **Balance Sheet** | | |
| Assets | | |
| Financial (Non-retirement) | $72,150 | $58,675 |
| Retirement | $246,275 | $60,345 |
| Education | $0 | $0 |
| Real | $275,000 | $275,000 |
| Personal/Collectible | $27,615 | $21,329 |
| Use | $42,000 | $42,000 |
| Life Insurance | | |
| The decedent is NOT the insured. | | |
| (Cash-value only) | $0 | $0 |
| The decedent was the insured. | | |
| (Death benefit amount) | $378,400 | $93,000 |
| Trust Assets (includable in estate) | | |
| QTIP property | $0 | $0 |
| Revocable trust property | $0 | $0 |
| **Gross Estate** | $1,041,440 | $550,349 |
| Gift taxes paid during most recent three years prior to 1st death. | $0 | $0 |
| **"Grossed-up" Estate** | $1,041,440 | $550,349 |
| **Expenses (paid from estate)** | | |
| Funeral / burial expenses | $15,000 | $15,000 |
| Estate admin / legal expenses | $10,000 | $5,500 |
| Outstanding liabilities | $140,771 | $124,326 |
| Income taxes | $15,000 | $10,000 |
| Executor fee (approx 2%) | $0 | $0 |
| Charitable contributions | $10,000 | $10,000 |
| **Total expenses** | $190,771 | $164,826 |
| **Reductions (prior to or at first death)** | | |
| Qualified marital transfer | $500,669 | $35,523 |
| Planned tax-free gifts | $0 | $0 |
| Assets to be irrevocably removed prior to date of first death | $0 | $0 |
| **Total reductions** | $500,669 | $35,523 |
| **Taxable Estate** | $350,000 | $350,000 |
| Taxable lifetime gifts | $0 | $0 |
| **Gift-adjusted Taxable Estate** | $350,000 | $350,000 |
| **First Death Estate Tax Liability** | | |
| Gross tax liability | $104,800 | $104,800 |
| Estate tax credit | $555,800 | $555,800 |
| Credit for total gift taxes paid | $0 | $0 |
| First death estate tax liability | $0 | $0 |

Neither Unifed Transfer Tax Credit is being fully used.

Only individually held assets should be entered.

Asset values should be reasonably inflated from the present values entered on the balance sheet to reflect any anticipated growth between now and the forecasted year of death.

Enter the cash value of any policies owned or controlled by the decedent at the time of death.

Policies payable to or for the benefit of decedent's estate, or if the decedent held incidents of ownership at death (or within 3 years of death) should be included.

Only near-term gifts and transfers should be included, due to the incalculable future value and subsequent impact on estate value.

The value of any gifts that did not qualify for gift tax exclusions at the time the gift was completed should be aggregated and entered.

Any gift taxes paid at the time the gift was completed should be aggregated and entered, including the amount entered earlier for the previous three years.

A warning shows up if the Unified Credit is not fully used; however, in some cases, maximizing this credit is not the best estate planning strategy.

**Exhibit 13.2** Estate Tax Estimator, Section Two

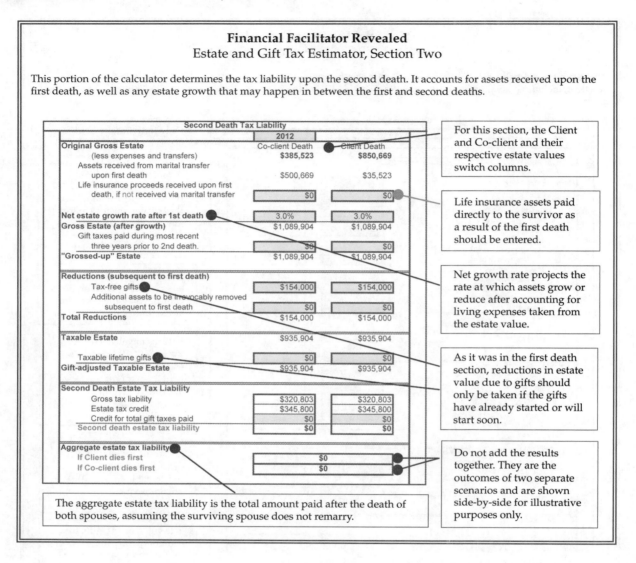

An additional tax, beyond the standard estate tax calculation, may be necessary for **income in respect of a decedent** (IRD). This generally is a tax based on any income that the deceased person was entitled to receive prior to death but that was not actually received until after death. Examples of IRD include salary earned but not paid until after the taxpayer's death, retirement account distributions, royalties, rents, dividends, interest, and other similar forms of income. IRD items must be included in the decedent's gross estate and the beneficiary of the income is then taxed at the beneficiary's marginal tax rate. However, the beneficiary might be able to deduct his or her portion of any estate taxes generated by the inclusion of the IRD.

---

**Estate Planning Tip: Guidelines for Valuing Art and Collectibles**

The valuation of art, collectibles, and other keepsakes owned by a deceased relative often causes heirs confusion. Two values exist: the catalog value, available for most items; and the market value. Catalog values are used primarily for insurance purposes; however, heirs sometimes assume that an inventory based on catalog values is equivalent to market value. This is rarely true. In the case of collectibles such as stamps and books, market value may be as little as 20% of the unadjusted (for condition of the item[s]) catalog value.[1] That is, a collection will almost always generate less in cash value than the cost it would take to replace the collection. In some situations, catalog and market values tend to be close. The valuation of precious metals, for example, usually falls much closer to catalog valuation. When reporting the worth of a valuable collection for estate planning purposes, it is important to work with an experienced appraiser who can translate catalog values into market values.

---

## The Tax Relief Act of 2010

On December 16, 2010, Congress passed the Tax Relief, Unemployment Insurance Reauthorization, and Job Creation Act of 2010 (the Act). This legislation extended the estate, gift, and generation-skipping transfer (GST) taxes but increased the exemption threshold and lowered the marginal tax rates. This legislation set the exemption at $5 million per person and $10 million per couple (for 2011) and established a top tax rate of 35% for estate, gift, and GST taxes for two years, through 2012. The Act also indexed the exemption amount for 2012 to inflation. Finally, the legislation reunifies the estate and gift tax rate, so that a single lifetime exemption can be used for both lifetime gifts and/or upon-death bequests.

The **unified credit** applies to both the gift tax and the estate tax and is subtracted from any gift or estate tax that a client may owe. The credit amount was increased from $1,730,800 to $1,772,800[2] in 2012, which effectively exempts $5,120,000 from estate and gift taxes, although this credit is reduced based on the decedent's lifetime taxable gifts, and an estate tax return for a U.S. citizen or resident needs to be filed only if the gross estate exceeds the applicable exclusion amount. Once an estate exceeds the exemption amount, the maximum tax rate applied is 35%.

The Act also allows for the portability of any unused exemption; in other words, it allows the executor of a deceased spouse's estate to transfer any unused exemption to the surviving spouse. The **portable estate exemption**, which is in effect until 2013, allows the unused portion of a spouse's **estate tax exclusion** (i.e., the amount of assets that can be transferred tax free at the death of a client) to be shifted to the surviving spouse. This means that even if the first-to-die spouse fails to use his or her entire exemption ($5 million in 2012), the unused estate exemption can be utilized by the second-to-die spouse. In effect, the portable estate exemption allows up to $10 million for a married couple in 2012 to be sheltered from taxes. Therefore, the Act makes it a good idea for all clients to file IRS Form 706 to maintain the portable estate exemption, even if the first-to-die's estate is not taxable.

If Congress fails to extend the estate tax law, the portable estate exemption will disappear in 2013. Without an extension of the Act, the estate tax exemption will drop to $1 million, and the maximum estate tax rate will rise from 35% to 55%.

## Gift Tax

Because the federal government taxes estates upon transfer, it stands to reason that a person should not be able to avoid this tax simply by giving all of the estate away just before death. Therefore, the federal gift tax is linked, in 2012, to the estate tax. However, the gift tax is backwards from most other taxes in that the gift is taxable to the giver (donor) rather than the receiver (donee). The gift tax applies to transfers of property by **gift** and occurs whenever property (including money) or the use of or income from property is given without expectation of receiving something of at least equal value in return. Additionally, if a client sells something at less than its full value, or if an interest-free or reduced-interest loan is made, the IRS will most likely consider a portion of the sale a gift.

The general rule is that any gift is a taxable gift. However, there are certain exceptions to this rule. Generally, the following gifts are not taxable:

- Annual gifts that do not exceed the exclusion for the calendar year;

- Gifts to a client's U.S. citizen spouse (limits apply for a non-U.S. citizen spouse);

- Tuition expenses a client pays directly to the educational institution for the benefit of someone else;

- Medical expenses a client pays directly to the institution or person providing care for the benefit of someone else;

- Gifts to a political organization for its use; and

- Gifts to qualified charities (a deduction is available for these contributions).

A separate **annual exclusion** applies to each person to whom a client makes a gift. In 2012, the annual exclusion is $13,000, but this amount is indexed to inflation. In general, a client can give up to $13,000 to any number of people in 2012. As long as the gift value is equal to or less than $13,000, none of the gift amount is taxable. If a client is married, the client and spouse can effectively give up to $26,000 to the same person without making a taxable gift; this is known as **gift splitting**.

Generally, clients need not file a **gift tax** return, IRS Form 709, unless they give someone other than a spouse money or property worth more than the annual exclusion. Although a return may be required, no actual gift tax will become payable until cumulative lifetime taxable giving exceeds the applicable exclusion amount. Clients who give money or assets to others are primarily responsible for the payment of the gift tax. When discussing gift tax issues with clients, it is important to remind them that the person who receives the gift generally will not have to pay any federal gift tax.

*Example.* Assume that a client gifts $25,000 to her son, $25,000 to her daughter, $8,000 to her niece, and $2,500 each to the seven other members of her bridge group; all gifts are made within the same calendar year—in this example, 2012. Although the client made gifts totaling $75,500, each gift is treated separately. After applying the $13,000 annual exclusion, all of the individual gifts under $13,000 are not taxable, only the individual gift amounts in excess of $13,000 to each child is taxable. The gift tax on the $24,000 [($25,000 – $13,000) × 2] in nonexcludable gift is $4,680 using the applicable 2012 tax rate. Because the gift to each child is taxable, the client must file IRS Form 709 to claim the gifts, although the client could opt to subtract the tax from her unified credit rather than pay the tax. Based on the 2012 unified tax exclusion of $1,772,800, this would leave her with a remaining exclusion of $1,768,120 to be used in later years should she opt to not pay the gift tax.

Tax basis must also be considered when gifting property in that the donee's basis will be different depending on whether the property was received as a "gift" or an inheritance. When property is inherited, the donee's tax basis becomes the value of the property as of the donor's date of death (or alternate valuation date if chosen by the custodian of the estate); however, if the property is transferred as a gift, then the donee does not receive a step-up in basis, meaning the donee's original tax basis still applies.

*Example.* Your parent left you the family farm, which has an original tax basis of $145,000, but the market value is $500,000. If the farm was received as a gift and then sold for the market value, you would owe capital gains tax on the $355,000 difference between the basis and sales price. Additionally, your parent might be responsible for gift tax on the $487,000 difference between the annual exclusion and the market value. However, if you inherited the property upon death, then you would not owe any capital gains tax on the sale, and so long as the total value of lifetime taxable gifts did not exceed the exclusion, your parent's estate would not owe any estate tax on the transfer.

Some financial transactions are a little tricky when it comes to determining whether or not a gift has actually been given. Adding a joint tenant to a bank account is not considered a gift; that is, until the new owner withdraws the funds. But adding a joint tenant to real estate *is* a gift if the new owner has the right to sell the interest in the property, even if the owner does not exercise this right. (It is important to note that adding joint owners to assets will override the distributions directed by the will because property law supersedes the instructions of the will or probate rulings. More information about joint ownership is provided later in the chapter.)

Finally, it is important to realize that although many other taxes can be filed jointly, gift tax returns are filed on an individual basis. So if a married couple gave a single person a gift in excess of twice the annual exclusion, then the gift would be evenly split and each spouse would need to file individual IRS Forms 709 for one-half of the amount in excess of twice the exclusion amount. For example, in 2012, a gift of $150,000 would require separate filings of IRS Form 709 for the amount of $112,000, assuming no other gifts in excess of the annual exclusion amount.

### Generation-skipping Transfer Tax

The GST is a levy on the portion of an estate that skips over one generation. Any gift or property assignment to someone two or more generations below the person making the transfer (or 37½ years younger that the donee, known as a **skip person**) is generally considered a **generation-skipping transfer**. Typically, a generation skip occurs when a distribution is made from a grandparent to a grandchild, thereby skipping a generation. This is known as a **direct skip**. Direct skips can occur whether the donor/decedent is living or deceased, but in cases where the death of the middle generation occurs before the gift is made, the GST tax is avoided. The tax can also be avoided whenever a donor/decedent and beneficiary are not related and the beneficiary is at least 37½ years younger than the donor.[3]

Transfers to a trust—as well as certain transfers within or from a trust—are subject to the GST tax; such transfers are taxed at the highest estate tax rate in effect at the time of transfer.

### Use of Trusts

Given the number of potential tax liabilities, it may be advisable to explore the use of trusts in addition to gifting strategies. A **trust** is an arrangement that grants a trustee legal title to assets. A trustee is required to act as a fiduciary when managing assets for the benefit of trust beneficiaries. In most cases, a beneficiary is the person who holds the beneficial title to trust assets. In general, trust income is passed directly from the trust to the **income beneficiary**, as opposed to the **remainder beneficiary**—the person or entity entitled to receive the assets upon termination of the trust. Often the income and remainder beneficiary are the same person or entity. It is also possible for a trust to have only income beneficiaries.

Because a trust transfers the rights of ownership to a third-party trustee, a trust is a useful strategy to financially provide for a person or persons unable to care for themselves because of legal or medical incapacity. **Incapacity** can be defined in several ways, including lack of ability, lack of legal standing, lack of legal power, or the inability to plan, delegate, provide for, or manage one's legal and financial affairs. Medical incapacity is usually the result of illness or accident, whereas legal incapacity is most common in situations where minor children or developmentally disabled adults are involved. Less acknowledged are situations where an adult has maladaptive behaviors such as a drug or gambling addiction, legal issues, behavioral problems, or a history of poor financial decision making. Trusts are often established in response to the need to provide care for incapacity. However, in some situations, clients should be proactive in planning for their own incapacity. Individuals who fail to plan for the possibility of incapacity face potential risks and costs, including:

- placing the management of their assets and health decisions under the control of a third party;

- the loss of standing to direct the distribution of assets to heirs and charities before and after death;

- the inability to legally execute or delegate their own financial affairs; or

- the possibility of depleting family assets because of legal battles associated with conservatorship issues.

There are two main types of trusts: testamentary trusts, funded upon death; and living trusts, funded prior to death. The most common type of testamentary trust is a **standard family trust** (also known as an **A-B trust arrangement**), a legal tool established to hold assets and transfer income to a surviving spouse without the surviving spouse actually taking ownership of the assets. Upon the death of the surviving spouse, a trustee then distributes the remaining assets to beneficiaries, often referred to as *remaindermen*.

In addition to the distinction between living and testamentary trusts, living trusts can also be subclassified as either irrevocable or revocable. **Revocable trusts** are also known as **grantor trusts,** because the trust or trust assets can be revoked or modified by the grantor. **Irrevocable trusts**, as the name implies, cannot be modified, amended, or revoked by the grantor; only the trustee has this authority according to trust document guidelines.

All income and deductions associated with a revocable trust are treated as part of the grantor's individual tax return, although grantors are required to complete the entity part of **IRS Form 1041**. At the death of the grantor, the executor of a grantor's estate is also required to file IRS Form 1041 for the revocable trust.

An irrevocable trust, on the other hand, is considered a separate entity from the grantor, and as such, IRS Form 1041 must be completed each year that the trust has remaining income. With an irrevocable trust, income that is distributed is taxed first to beneficiaries. If income remains in the trust, the trust itself is subject to trust tax rates and must file IRS Form 1041 and pay applicable income taxes. If the trust has more than $600 in gross income, or if one of the beneficiaries is a nonresident alien, the filing can become more complicated.

One of the disadvantages of using trusts can be the higher trust tax rate assessed to income that remains within the trust. However, this may not be a disadvantage depending on the sources of income within the trust and the marginal tax rate of trust beneficiaries. The IRS classifies all trusts as simple or complex for the purposes of annual income taxes; complex trusts, whether living or testamentary, are subject to their own tax rates as reported on IRS Form 1041.  The Internal Revenue Code (IRC) defines a simple trust as one that:

- distributes its income, instead of  allowing discretionary distributions;

- makes no mandatory or discretionary distributions of  principal; and

- makes no distributions to or has any principal set aside for charity.

Should the trust not meet the preceding criteria, it is classified as a complex trust and is subject to trust income tax rates for that tax year.

## Quantifying Estate Planning Issues beyond Federal Estate Taxation

Assertions regarding the determination and quantification of estate planning needs are premised on clients having or putting into place, regardless of situational factors or estate size, certain basic estate planning documents (e.g., wills, letters of last instruction, and advance medical directives—all of which are discussed later in this chapter). Reviewing life goals with a client can be an important foundation for establishing estate planning preferences. A number of key questions can be used to determine a client's estate planning preferences and better assess client estate planning and estate liquidity needs. Answers to these questions directly impact the size or distribution of an estate. In situations where the estate is not large enough to trigger estate tax issues, other financial issues threaten to reduce the estate, or if not planned for properly they can create other problems for heirs.

Before considering these questions, it is important to clarify whether the client, and if applicable the spouse or partner, is a U.S. citizen. Specifically, planning needs differ for noncitizens or resident aliens and can affect asset titling, gifts, estate transfers, and estate taxes. Property owned in the United States must be probated in a U.S. court, so similar considerations apply. It is generally important for noncitizens to have U.S. estate planning documents, even if documents were prepared in another country. Because citizenship adds another layer of difficulty to the estate planning process, it is a critical consideration. Another critical consideration is a client's marital status, because estate planning for domestic partners is more complicated, as described later in this chapter. Additional questions to determine a client's estate planning needs are listed below:

- Does the client wish to avoid **probate** (i.e., the legal and public procedure that validates a will and the distribution of assets as described in a will) or reduce probate assets?

- Is reduction of state death taxes a primary client need?

- Is protection of assets from creditors a concern?

- Is reduction of income taxes a primary client need?

- Does the client want to leave some or most of the estate to a spouse or partner?

- Are there special needs (e.g., mental or emotional health issues, retardation, physical handicaps) or other financial management issues that must be considered?

- Does the client have a desire to leave some or most of the estate to children? If yes, are they minor children or children with special needs, regardless of age?

- If an estate is to be left to children, will each child share equally, and if a child should predecease the parent, how will that child's share be distributed?

- Does the client want to leave some or most of the estate to other dependents besides spouse, partner, or children? If yes, are there special needs (e.g., mental or emotional health issues, mental or physical handicaps) or other financial management issues that must be considered?

- Does the client wish to leave a charitable bequest? If charitable giving is a priority, which organizations are most important?

- Does the client have financial or managerial ties to a small business or a closely or privately held business that must be planned for within or outside of the estate plan?

- Which assets will be used to pay for final expenses and debt reduction?

- Is preplanning for a medical situation or emergency or long-term care an important client objective?

- Does the client have any special wishes that should be accounted for in the estate plan?

Each of these questions can lead to an in-depth discussion between a financial planner and client—and in some cases spouses, partners, or other family members—about life goals, legacies, estate planning objectives, and end-of-life issues. Answers to these and similar questions can then be used as background for initiating an assessment of a client's estate plan.

---

**Estate Planning for Special Populations:
Domestic Partners without Civil Unions**

Nearly 14 million U.S. households were classified as unmarried by the Census in 2010. Of these, 10% represent same-sex couples.[4] Without proper planning, many of the health care and end-of-life rights that exist for married couples may be nonexistent for non-married couples regardless of the sexual orientation of the partners. As with many issues dealing with end-of-life and estate planning, the regulations and governing laws vary from state to state and, in some cases, are in nearly constant flux. So the best advice a planner can give to domestic partners is that if there is any question regarding rights or privileges, do not rely on general state procedures; rather, create a legal document that is allowable under the law. It is important for unmarried couples to execute detailed and legally enforceable instructions; the primary documents used for this are the general power of attorney (POA), the medical POA or advance medical directive (AMD), the appropriate trust documentation, and custodial documentation, if applicable.

Designating a **proxy** (also known in some states as an attorney-in-fact or agent) to make decisions regarding financial affairs (via a general, durable, or springing POA) or medical affairs (via a medical POA) is important protection. By executing a POA, a client can decide who will be the agent should the client become unable to act or make decisions. Without a POA, someone else—most likely an immediate family member—will have to petition a court to be appointed guardian and/or conservator to handle financial matters. This process can be expensive and the family member may not be the client's choice to have this decision-making authority. In addition to financial affairs, assisting a client with a plan for health care decision making during a period of disability or incapacitation is crucial. Virginia law, for example, provides an order of priority for making medical decisions; it includes guardian, spouse, child over age 18, parents, adult siblings, and other blood relatives, but makes no mention of a partner. Issues as seemingly simple as visitation rights and the ability to make financial and health care decisions for a partner may not exist unless a couple has updated health care proxies, living wills, AMDs or medical POAs (depending on the state of residence) and durable POAs in place. Without these documents, decisions regarding finances and health matters can revert to family or government-appointed guardians. Only through the execution of state-specific documents can a client guarantee that a domestic partner has rights and the ability to assist with financial and medical issues.

Another concern—potentially greater for same-sex couples—is avoiding courts, because all aspects of a last will and testament become public record during probate. The probate process means notifying potential heirs, thus giving them a chance to contest the will. Therefore, trust documentation should be in place for the disposition of any estate. Although a will may be important for other reasons, a revocable living trust can serve as a substitute for a will, thereby avoiding the probate process and keeping the transfer of assets confidential—and in most cases, uncontestable.

Finally, should the clients have children, it is advisable to draft a shared custody agreement if allowable under state law. Some states allow the legal parent to draft a contract for shared custody with a domestic partner. This could be very helpful in keeping the family together if the biological or legal parent dies; however the reverse is also true in that if the family breaks up, custody would still be shared.

Although having comprehensive estate and financial planning documents in place is important for everyone, it is especially important for unmarried couples. If the proper estate planning documents are not in place, then a domestic partner will likely have no rights in making financial or medical decisions on the client's behalf and might not inherit from the estate if the client passes away intestate or without a living trust. Whereas most clients do not like discussing such matters, the issues raised by this process can save time and money, avoid unnecessary litigation and disputes, and ensure that their wishes are followed and their partners respected.[5]

## Document and Evaluate Current Estate Planning Efforts

The next step in analyzing a client's estate planning situation entails documenting and evaluating the client's current estate planning approach. A client's estate plan may have been thoroughly conceptualized and executed or developed haphazardly. There might be no plan, which indicates an avoidance of the subject on the part of the client. According to a 2011 ABC News poll, only 50% of all U.S. adults have a

**will**—a document written to direct the distribution of one's property at death, and even fewer—only 42%—have a living will, **health care proxy,** or AMD for directing end-of-life or health care decisions (i.e., someone a client appoints, such as a family member or friend, to make health care decisions for the client if the client is unable to make his or her own decision).[6]

A planner must evaluate the strategies, products, or legal techniques a client is currently using to accumulate, preserve, and distribute assets over time. Although no one but an attorney should ever draft a legal document, every planner who performs comprehensive financial planning should help clients think through the complex issues associated with planning an estate. As part of this review, it is imperative that financial planners determine whether a client (and spouse or partner) possesses any of the following documents, when they were drafted, and whether they are still applicable.

- Client will(s): A legal document outlining how property will be transferred at death

- **Letter(s) of last instruction**: A document written to a significant other (usually a spouse) to provides directions regarding the execution of a client's will

- **Codicil**: An attachment or amendment to an existing will

- **Power of attorney** (medical or financial): A legal document appointing another person to act for the client if the client becomes incapacitated

- **Living will** or **advance medical directive** (AMD): A directive written for the use of a physician or hospital that outlines a client's wishes regarding medical and end-of-life treatment in the event of the client's incapacitation

The costs of drafting a will, power of attorney, trust, or other legal document can vary greatly. A client's net worth can affect the number and complexity of documents, which can result in higher costs. Although the initial expense might dissuade some clients from implementing recommendations, the decision to forgo these documents can significantly increase the costs, time, and frustration of survivors, who must now handle the estate in accordance with state or federal mandates.

In addition to these legal documents, any prepaid, contracted, or even informal final arrangements should also be discussed and the location of any contracts determined, if applicable. Finally, it is important to verify and review the following documents to develop a comprehensive profile of the client situation and confirm locations for future use.

- Birth certificate(s) for all household members

- Marriage certificate(s) and/or divorce decree(s)

- All in-force insurance policies with beneficiary designations

- Life, health, long-term care, and annuity policies and beneficiary designation form(s) for individual and group policies

- Title(s) to personal property and deed(s) to real property in the state of residence or other states

- Inventory of any special property such as jewelry, fine art, or a collection (e.g., stamps, coins, wine, firearms) including a schedule of beneficiaries

- Brokerage account statements or other evidence of security ownership (e.g., stock certificates)

- Business agreements and documentation for any outstanding unpaid debts or unsettled legal claims

- Income tax returns for the previous three years

- The location of a safety deposit box, an inventory of contents, the location of key(s), and a determination of whether state law requires that the box be sealed until inventoried by a representative of the court

When reviewing a client's current will, planners should look for signs that a change or codicil might be needed. The following list includes a number of indicators that a client's will or estate plan should be reviewed by an attorney.

- The will was drafted more than five years ago.

- The client has additional beneficiaries who are not listed in the will.

- The client now has fewer beneficiaries than are listed in the will.

- There has been a major change in the beneficiaries' family or financial circumstances.

- The client has indicated verbally that the client wishes to distribute assets differently from what is listed.

- The client's health has diminished since drafting the will.

- The client's marital status has changed since drafting the will (marriage, remarriage, divorce, or death of a spouse).

- The birth or adoption of one or more grandchildren has occurred.

- A significant estate planning law was passed since the date of the will or the date of the last review, if any.

- There has been a significant increase or decrease in the client's wealth or income since the will was drafted.

- The client has purchased additional life insurance.

- The client has started a business.

- A change in the named guardian is needed.

- A change in the executor or contingent executor is needed.

- Property has been purchased in a different state.

- The client has moved, thereby changing the state of residence.

In addition to obtaining copies of a client's estate planning documents and studying them, the planner and client should also discuss other professional relationships with attorneys, accountants, stockbrokers, tax preparers, or insurance providers. Obtaining this comprehensive information helps ensure that all relevant estate planning issues will be addressed in an orderly, systematic manner. For instance, the focus of an estate plan can be significantly different for a client who does not have a will compared to a client who has estate-appropriate legal documents.

After reviewing a client's current estate plan, a variety of issues may need to be addressed. These will help the planner focus on strategies to form recommendations for the client. A client's last will and testament often needs immediate remedial attention. The checklist shown in Exhibit 13.3 will help novice planners and students assess a client's current will and end-of-life documentation to determine whether legal documents should be retained or rewritten.

### Additional Consideration: Ownership

Possession versus property is a distinction that few people consider outside of estate planning. Possessions are generally personal items such as clothing, jewelry, electronics, and other household items that typically do not have a formal document of ownership or formal means of transfer. By contrast, property such as houses, land, and cars are formally deeded or titled, and the state of ownership or residency tracks the ownership of these items primarily for tax purposes. The two primary subclassifications of property are personal property, which can be moved, and real property, which is permanently attached to land and therefore cannot be moved.

Titling assets properly is one tool to help manage a client's estate plan. Generally, whenever someone is added to the title of a property the IRS considers it a taxable gift to the new owner equal to the fair market value of the new ownership position. Understanding when a taxable gift might be incurred can save a client significant gift and estate taxes. If the original owner can make a withdrawal from the asset account without the permission of the new owner, no gift tax will be due until the new owner takes a distribution. For example, no gift tax is due when a joint owner is added to a bank account until the new owner makes a withdrawal. As an interesting note, if a security is held in street name, no gift tax is incurred upon joint titling; however, if a security is held JTWROS, a gift tax may be incurred.

**Exhibit 13.3** Estate Planning Documentation Checklist

### Estate Planning Documentation Checklist

| Question | Yes | No |
|---|---|---|
| 1. Is the client's name correct on all documents? | | |
| 2. Is the spouse's or partner's name correct on all documents? | | |
| 3. Are the children's names and ages (if applicable) correct on all documents? | | |
| 4. Is the executor properly named? | | |
| 5. Is a guardian for dependent children named? | | |
| 6. If named, is the guardian still the appropriate choice? | | |
| 7. Are special bequests adequately identified? | | |
| 8. Are charitable bequests up to date and adequately identified? | | |
| 9. Is the simultaneous death clause appropriate for the state of residence? | | |
| 10. Are trust documents referred to in the will? | | |
| 11. Does the will refer to a particular trust if a trust exists? | | |
| 12. Have trusts, other than testamentary trusts, been funded? | | |
| 13. Have special considerations been made for parents? | | |
| 14. Have special considerations been made for siblings? | | |
| 15. Have special considerations been made for grandchildren? | | |
| 16. Are codicils up to date and accurate? | | |
| 17. Does the client have a power of attorney in place? If so, what kind and what powers are included? | | |
| 18. Has the client written a letter of last instructions? | | |
| 19. Depending on the state of residence and need, has the client drafted: | | |
|    • a living will? | | |
|    • an advance medical directive? | | |
|    • a medical power of attorney? | | |
|    • a HIPAA authorization? | | |
| 20. Does the client share time in different states? If so, are all documents appropriate and in place? | | |
| 21. Is there a current list of all financial professionals, including the estate attorney, available for the survivors or the executor? | | |

Financial planners are advised to thoroughly understand the ramification of federal and state laws in relation to joint ownership titling. As exemplified by security titling, adding a new owner may or may not trigger the gift tax. Clients would be quite disappointed to find that the titling process, which they thought would be beneficial, triggers a gift tax liability.

The following titling methods can be used for property owned by more than one person:

- *Tenancy in common*: Used by two or more individuals; ownership interests need not be equal; each owner can sell, exchange, or otherwise dispose of his or her interest without the consent of the other owners; there are no survivorship rights.

- *Joint tenancy with right of survivorship (JTWROS)*: Used by two or more individuals; ownership is equal among owners; ownership passes automatically to survivors upon the death of an owner; ownership can be terminated by death, mutual agreement, and divorce.

- *Tenancy by the entirety*: Used only by married couples; survivorship interest passes automatically to the surviving spouse.

- *Community property*: Used only by married couples living and acquiring property in community property states; survivorship interest does not automatically pass to the surviving spouse.

In the case of JTWROS and **tenancy in common**, creditors can access the value of the co-owner's interest. Only tenancy by the entirety protects a couple's home from creditor or liability claims against one member of the couple. Some states, such as Virginia, also allow married couples to title investment assets as tenants by the entirety. Potential gift taxes can arise with a change in titling.

Ten states provide married couples with an alternative to **tenancy by the entirety**, which is a common form of titling for property owned by a married couple. Alaska, Arizona, California, Idaho, Louisiana, Nevada, New Mexico, Texas, Washington, and Wisconsin each have a form of community property law. **Community property** refers to all assets obtained while a couple is married. Each spouse legally owns one-half of each asset purchased as community property.

Community property is unique, however, in that any property owned by a spouse prior to marriage remains the sole property of that spouse unless it is commingled with community property assets. Furthermore, if a spouse receives a gift or inheritance while married, those assets remain the separate property of the spouse.

One advantage associated with community property titling is that, upon the death of one spouse, all assets receive a 100% step-up in basis. This compares favorably to the 50% step-up in basis for assets held by spouses as **joint tenancy with right of survivorship (JTWROS)** (i.e., titling procedure in which ownership of an asset transfers automatically at death to the surviving owners) or as tenancy by the entirety. Few banks, title companies, or other financial service firms automatically title marital assets as community property. A financial planner who fails to guide his or her community property clientele in the appropriate use of this titling option could cause clients to pay higher taxes in the future because of the lost step-up in basis associated with JTWROS titling.

Another possibility for transferring ownership as part of an estate plan is the use of a **qualified disclaimer**. According to IRC § 2518, a "qualified disclaimer" refers to "an irrevocable and unqualified refusal by a person to accept an interest in property."[7] For the disclaimer to be qualified, it must meet the following guidelines:

- It must be in writing.

- It must be received no later than nine months after the bequest is made, or if the beneficiary is a minor at the time of the bequest, no later than nine months after the child reaches the age of 21.

- The beneficiary must not accept any interest or benefit from the bequest.

- The beneficiary must not maintain any control or interest concerning who is to receive (inherit) the asset after filing the disclaimer.

Disclaimed assets are treated as though they were never transferred, which allows them to be transferred to another person or entity. This strategy can be useful in situations where the beneficiary already has a sizable estate and additional assets are not needed or desired. For a disclaimer to be qualified for federal and state tax purposes, the written disclaimer must be in compliance with IRC § 2518, as well as any state disclaimer statues that might apply. This can be an effective tool in the estate planning process.

---

### Estate Planning for Special Populations: Newly Separated or Divorced

Although state laws differ greatly regarding spousal rights, they all agree on one thing: your spouse is your spouse until a divorce is final. This can cause a great deal of difficulty, especially when the divorce is contested by one party or children are involved. In some states, uncontested divorce between spouses with no common children can be completed after six months of legal separation; however, this is the best-case scenario. On the other end of the spectrum, divorces can take years to resolve. This lag creates the need to carefully consider all aspects of an estate plan, including but not limited to wills, trust beneficiaries, qualified account beneficiaries, the custody of minor children, medical and durable powers of attorney, and life insurance contacts.

Divorce is really a two-phase process. Phase one is the legal separation—when two people are still married but realize that the marriage no longer works and will not continue, and it is not simply physical separation. Phase two is divorce—when the request for the dissolution of the marriage is granted by the court system. The period of legal separation is messier in that the soon-to-be ex-spouse still retains marital rights.

If a client has estate planning documents in place with the current spouse, the client should consider revoking and restating all of the estate planning documents before filing for divorce. In California, for example, the spouse who is contemplating divorce is not mandated to notify his or her spouse of any changes in estate planning documents, life insurance beneficiary designations, or retirement account beneficiary designations. However, the client may not be able to change these documents after filing a petition for divorce because California, ironically enough, and some other states issue Family Law Restraining Orders, sometimes called ATROs (automatic temporary restraining orders), which prevent certain activities from occurring during the divorce proceedings.[8]

These restraining orders do not allow the revocation of a trust, the changing of life insurance beneficiaries, or the changing of retirement plan or IRA account beneficiaries, among other constraints and limitations. The intent is to maintain the status quo of assets and ownership interests until the division of assets is final. So what was changeable before filing is no longer. However, if a client has already filed for divorce, the client should be able to update the will, financial POA, and AMDs.

Although other states, notably Arizona, automatically change spousal rights upon the granting of divorce,  Arizona law dictates that (1) a divorced person's will remain valid, but the ex-spouse is disqualified as a potential beneficiary of the estate; (2) if one or both spouses should die before any joint marital property trust is dissolved as part of the divorce settlement, each spouse's share of the trust is distributed as if there were no surviving spouse; (3) an ex-spouse is automatically removed as an agent named in a financial or health care power of attorney, as a beneficiary on life insurance contracts, as a beneficiary for accounts with pay-on-death, transfer-on-death and in-trust-for designations; and (4) any property held as JTWROS automatically converts to tenancy in common so that the property will no longer automatically pass to the survivor.[9]

Qualified retirement accounts are notoriously difficult because of ERISA, the federal law governing such accounts. The U.S. Supreme Court has ruled that plan administrators can rely solely on beneficiary designations. Thus, an ex-spouse remains a beneficiary of one of these plans until the plan participant submits a new beneficiary designation.[10] In fact this ruling upholds an ex-spouse's claim on residual assets even after the death of the account owner. Although this ruling does not extend to IRA accounts, the IRA custodian will likely treat the ex-spouse as beneficiary if the custodian has no knowledge of the divorce, so funds could be legally but inadvertently distributed to a former spouse. The best advice that planners can offer a recently divorced client is to systematically update all documentation that mentions the former spouse to ensure that the client's wishes for property ownership and division are met.

# STRATEGIES

## Review Prospective Estate Planning Strategies

Two important considerations should be reviewed before identifying estate planning strategies. First, it is important to consider what might be considered basic estate planning strategies before introducing more complex tactics. Never assume that a client, regardless of wealth or income, has necessary, basic documents in place, such as a will, POA, living will, or AMD. This means that although there are opportunities for a financial planner to develop multifaceted estate planning strategies, these should generally wait until the fundamental aspects of estate planning have been addressed.

Second, it is important to remember that financial planners who are not attorneys should proceed carefully when developing and presenting estate planning recommendations. It is illegal for nonattorneys to draft legal documents for clients. The best approach is to work collaboratively with the client and the attorney on estate planning issues. This method of planning preserves the planner's fiduciary responsibility to act in the best interest of the client but limits the possibility of being sued by a client who later feels that a strategy was inappropriate; it also limits exposure to penalties for the unauthorized practice of law. Most importantly, a collaborative approach between planner and attorney will likely provide a better outcome for the client because of the insights available from the planner's more comprehensive knowledge of the client situation. Finally, planner recommendations should include a **disclaimer**, such as "Prior to implementing these recommendations, please confirm these suggestions with an attorney."

## Identify Prospective Estate Planning Strategies

The strategies related to an estate planning analysis can range from basic to extremely complex. The intent of this section is to provide examples of common (i.e., fundamental) estate planning strategies. Readers interested in developing more complex strategies and recommendations should consider *Principles of Estate Planning* 1st edition, published by the National Underwriter Company.

### Product Strategy 1: Prepare a Will

**Advantage:** This estate planning strategy should be the first advice given to a client who does not currently have a will and those whose wills are out of date. A will ensures that a client's wishes are followed appropriately rather than relying on the intestate laws of the client's state of residence.

**Disadvantage:** It is important for clients to recognize that having a valid will does not avoid probate and the associated disadvantages. It is important to remind them that, upon the death of a decedent, a will becomes a public document through the probate system. The value of the assets conveyed in the will is subject to probate fees, and in some states the probate process can be lengthy and expensive. The cost of a will might also be a deterrent; clients can expect to pay between $200 and $750 for a basic attorney-drafted will, and the cost increases with the complexity of the situation. Finally, this is often the most resisted recommendation of any in a financial plan. Planners must patiently encourage clients to act rather than postpone preparation of this important estate planning document.

### Product Strategy 2: Write a Letter of Last Instructions

**Advantage:** All clients should write a letter of last instructions. This letter can include special wishes that might not otherwise be included in a will or trust document. For example, a client can specify where the client would like to be buried, the name of the caterer that the client would like to use at the funeral, and other requests.

**Disadvantage:** Clients who write a letter of last instructions should take care to update the letter whenever they redraft their will or other legal documents. Great confusion can result if more than one letter is found at the date of death.

### Product Strategy 3: Prepare a Living Will, Power of Attorney, or Advance Medical Directive

**Advantage:** Several important documents are fundamental to the estate planning process. Because the commonly used terms and legal requirements vary by state, care must be taken when recommending this strategy.

A living will is a legal document that establishes the medical situations in which a client no longer desires life-sustaining or life-prolonging treatment. A living will is essentially a document that involves the client and the client's physician, and it often includes wishes regarding the use of cardiopulmonary resuscitation, intravenous therapy for nutrition or medication, feeding tubes, and ventilators for artificial breathing. However, it is very important that the family be informed of an individual's wishes. A living will might also be known as a *declaration* or **directive to physicians** or in some states as an *advance medical directive*. Typically, a living will is relevant only in situations of terminal illness or injury when an individual is incapable of making care decisions.

An alternative to a living will is a **durable power of attorney for health care**, also called a **medical power of attorney**. This legal document appoints another person, called an **agent, attorney-in-fact**, or **proxy**, to make health care decisions for the client when the client is unable to do so as a result of physical or mental incapacitation. The addition of the term *durable* makes this or another power of attorney remain in effect or take effect in the event of mental incompetence. The agent can make decisions for nonterminal situations or, if a living will is available, help ensure compliance with the individual's wishes.

Generally, a **medical directive** or **advance medical directive** combines the protection of a living will in terminal situations with the broader powers of a durable power of attorney for health care into one document. A proxy or attorney-in-fact is appointed, as well as a contingent individual, or successor agent, should the primary person be unavailable to serve. Neither the medical power of attorney nor the medical directive obligates the agent or proxy with financial responsibility for the costs of medical care.

A power of attorney appoints a person or organization to handle a client's affairs. A durable power of attorney remains in effect or takes effect in the event of subsequent disability or incapacity. A power of attorney can be general, giving broad powers for most—if not all—financial affairs, or be limited to a specific list of responsibilities. With an extremely broad general power of attorney, a client might, in effect, give a third party "all legal powers that I have myself." A powerholder with an unlimited power of attorney may or may not be able to make gifts to him- or herself or family members; this will depend on state law and the prior history of the client. Powers of attorney are relatively inexpensive to establish, simple, private, and flexible. Courts also universally recognize powers of attorney.

When planning for incapacitation and overall health care issues, clients should be encouraged to have a living will and a medical power of attorney, as well as a power of attorney for financial affairs. In this way, the client's care and death decisions can be made confidentially using state-specific documents, and the client's financial affairs can be managed with a power of attorney.

**Disadvantage:** The greatest disadvantage associated with this strategy is psychological, not fiscal. Planners may face resistance among clients when this strategy is presented. Some clients find the thought of planning for their own incapacity and the sharing of decision-making authority difficult and uncomfortable. As a result, some clients might resist implementing this strategy, but planners must patiently encourage client consideration.

The use of a **springing power of attorney** (i.e., powers available only after a specific event, such as an illness or disability, and perhaps after validation by a physician) is one alternative. Clients should also be assured that the power of attorney can be revoked at any time.

Depending on individual state law, an attorney or witnesses may or may not be required, so minimal costs might be involved. Clients who own property or live for periods of time in different states each year should exercise particular caution with these documents, because state reciprocity may not apply.

## Product Strategy 4: Avoid Probate by Using a Living Trust

**Advantage:** Two reasons to consider establishing a **living trust** (i.e., a trust created during a client's life) are minimization of probate involvement and the publicity surrounding public documentation of a family's financial situation at a client's death. Other advantages include continuation of income and distributions to heirs from assets held in the trust after the death of the client, the ability of a trustee to manage assets, and the likely appropriate distribution of assets to heirs at the client's death. Other advantages include reducing the possibility of someone claiming that asset transfers were against the decedent's wishes and a reduction in legal costs for those with property in more than one state.

**Disadvantage:** A significant disadvantage associated with this strategy is that clients sometimes confuse avoiding probate with avoiding estate taxation. Assets held in a revocable living trust are included in the client's gross estate for estate tax purposes. Also, income that is taxable to the trust, rather than to the grantor or the beneficiaries, is generally taxed at a higher rate (e.g., tax rates on trusts are based on compressed income tax brackets). Furthermore, although living trusts are effective in helping a client avoid probate, unless all titled assets are retitled or originally titled in the name of the trust, this goal may not be achieved.

### Product Strategy 5: Establish an A-B Trust Arrangement for Clients with a High Net Worth

**Advantage:** An A-B trust arrangement is another name for a strategy using a **credit shelter bypass trust** with a marital deduction trust (also known as a standard family trust). This technique can save a high-net-worth family substantial amounts of estate tax if properly implemented. In effect, this strategy guarantees that both spouses will maximize the use of their estate tax unified credit applicable exclusion amount. This strategy can also be an effective way to guarantee that a surviving spouse receives annual income but avoids some of the pitfalls of asset ownership, with the remaining assets going to ultimate beneficiaries upon the death of the surviving spouse.

In this arrangement, the **marital trust**—the A Trust—is established at the same time as the **bypass trust**—the B Trust—is created. The marital trust is typically funded with all of the assets in excess of the estate tax unified credit applicable exclusion amount using the unlimited marital deduction. The marital trust is usually either a POA or a QTIP trust. In either of these types of trust arrangements, the surviving spouse must be given an income interest in the trust. In the POA trust, the spouse must also be given a general power of appointment over trust assets. As a result, marital trust assets are generally included in the surviving spouse's gross estate. For this reason, a bypass trust is also established, which is funded with assets protected by the unified credit of the first spouse to die. The bypass trust ensures that the first spouse does not lose use of his or her estate tax unified credit; but the trust bypasses the surviving spouse's estate.

When the Tax Relief Act of 2010 created the portable estate exemption, it effectively eliminated the need for most A-B trust arrangements. This law allows a surviving spouse to utilize any unused exclusion amount from the first-to-die spouse. As long as the couple was married at the date of the first death and the surviving spouse elects the exemption on IRS Form 706, the full value of a joint estate, at least $10 million, can be sheltered from federal estate taxes in 2012. Unless Congress acts to make the law permanent, the portable estate exemption will disappear in 2013. This level of uncertainty makes the complete disuse of A-B trusts unlikely. Some financial planners argue that even if the law becomes permanent, A-B trust arrangements will continue. These trusts allow for asset protection, particularly for those with estates exceeding $10 million. Assets in a B trust are generally inaccessible to creditors. A-B trusts also provide asset protection in cases where the surviving spouse remarries. If the portable estate exemption is elected and the surviving spouse remarries, the exemption amount could be reduced.

**Disadvantage:** This strategy has some disadvantages. First, establishing the trust agreements requires that all other estate planning documents be revised, including the "evening out" of assets through retitling. (Remember: jointly held assets pass via property laws.) Retitling could result in a sizable upfront cost in both time and money for clients. This makes the strategy less attractive for clients whose combined assets are not, or will not be, greater than the estate tax unified credit applicable exclusion amount in the future. Second, the irrevocable nature of the bypass trust means that the surviving spouse generally can access only income generated from assets, which could limit the spouse's standard of living if the assets fail to generate adequate income in the future.

### Product Strategy 6: Decrease Estate Tax Liability and Generate Income by Using a CRAT, CRUT, or Pooled Income Fund

**Advantage:** This estate planning process is designed to benefit a charity while enhancing a client's financial situation. If proper gift planning is conducted and ultimately implemented, it may be possible to accomplish several distinct goals simultaneously. First, income tax liability can be reduced. The amount of the income tax charitable deduction is affected by the type and use of the asset given. Second, gift and estate taxes can be lessened. Third, benefits can be provided to charitable organizations. Fourth, giving can provide the donor a feeling of goodwill.

**Charitable giving** involves providing gifts of money, income, and assets to charitable organizations. To qualify for a charitable donation, a client must give assets to a recognized charity in the United States, a U.S. territory, or a political subdivision. Nonprofit organizations include most religious, scientific, and charitable organizations, some fraternal societies and associations, and certain veterans associations and organizations. To receive a tax deduction and exclude assets from an estate, a client should consider outright gifts, as well as using one or more of the following trust arrangements: a charitable remainder annuity trust, a charitable remainder unitrust, a pooled income fund, or a charitable lead trust (discussed in Product Strategy 13).

When a client contributes to a **charitable remainder annuity trust (CRAT)**, the noncharitable beneficiary generally receives, on an annual basis, a fixed annuity payment equal to or greater than 5%, but not more than 50% of the initial net fair market value of the trust. The benefit may be structured as an annuity for life or a term certain. Once established, no additional contributions can be made to the CRAT. At the end of the term, the remainder goes to charity.

A **charitable remainder unitrust trust (CRUT)** is similar to a CRAT, but fundamentally different in the way in which payments are made to the beneficiary. The noncharitable beneficiary generally receives, annually, a payment equal to a fixed percentage between 5% and 50% of the assets held in the trust as revalued on an annual basis. The benefit can be structured as a unitrust for life or a term certain. In some instances, payments are set at the lower of the unitrust amount or trust income, with or without a make-up provision. This means that distributions can be limited to earnings, and there is no requirement to use principal to pay beneficiaries. Further, additional donations to a CRUT are allowed. At the end of the term, the remainder goes to charity.

A **pooled income fund** is a charitable device created and maintained by a charity. The donor makes an irrevocable gift that is pooled with similar gifts from other donors. The charity manages the commingled assets, and payments based on the income earned by the account are made to beneficiaries on a pro-rata basis for life. At the end of the term, the remainder goes to charity.

**Disadvantage:** Gifts made to charitable organizations are irrevocable. It is also possibile that payments from these trusts will not keep pace with inflation over time. Because a unitrust is a variable annuity, a CRUT can provide a hedge against this. In general, clients must be committed to the charity and acknowledge that the use of their donated assets might not represent their values or choices in the future. The irrevocable nature of charitable gifts is something each client must weigh against the qualitative and quantitative benefits received.

## *Product Strategy 7: Establish a Donor-advised Charitable Fund*

**Advantage:** A **donor-advised charitable fund** is an irrevocable account established by a custodian to accept, manage, and distribute donations to a client's chosen charities. The donor, while losing access to the assets for personal use, controls which charity receives a donation, when the donation will be made, how often the donation will be granted, and how much will be distributed. Although distributions cannot be used for pledges, private benefit, or political contributions, any legitimate charitable activity can receive benefits from a donor-advised fund.

The primary advantage associated with establishing a donor-advised charitable fund is that, although contributions are irrevocable, the client retains control over the timing and amount of annual distributions to a charity. Furthermore, the client can generally determine which charity will receive distributions. This choice can change yearly, so if a charitable organization veers from the client's objectives for giving, a different charity can be chosen in subsequent years.

There are tax advantages as well. Just like a regular charitable contribution, assets transferred to a donor-advised fund reduce a client's gross estate. Gifts of appreciated stock offer the added benefit to the donor of avoiding the capital gains on the appreciation. A portion of contributions can also be used to reduce federal income tax liability through an itemized deduction.

**Disadvantage:** Several disadvantages are associated with this strategy. First, the number of donor-advised charitable fund providers is relatively limited, although financial services providers like Charles Schwab, Fidelity, and Vanguard offer these services. Second, the costs associated with such funds can be quite high. Annual fees of 2% to 5% are common, but they are still more reasonable than establishing a private foundation. Third, unlike CRATs and CRUTs, the donor cannot retain the right to receive payments.

---

### Estate Planning Tip: Private vs. Public Foundations

Private and public foundations are tax-advantaged entities that allow individuals to donate goods, services, and assets while receiving an income tax deduction (assuming the donor itemizes deductions). **Private foundations** generally receive their asset contributions from one or a few sources. Assets are then used to fund the ongoing operations of a charity or nonprofit organization. **Public foundations** typically receive funding from a wider public audience. Assets are then used to support a variety of community charities. Caps on the deductibility of contributions exist. The maximum deductibility for cash donations to private foundations is capped at 30% of adjusted gross income. Cash donations to public foundations are capped at 50% of adjusted gross income. Private foundations have very strict reporting requirements that require disclosure of asset values and donation sources. Private foundations must, by law, also distribute the equivalent of 5% of the fair market value of all investable assets per year.

### Product Strategy 8: Decrease the Gross Estate by Contributing to a § 529 Plan

**Advantage:** This strategy works well when a client's objective is to help save for a child or grandchild's education while reducing his or her own estate tax liability. A single client can contribute up to five years of annual exclusion gifts to a § 529 plan for a beneficiary in any given year (once every five years) gift tax free. By making five years of contributions in one year, a married couple can contribute $130,000 on a tax-free basis (2 × 5 × $13,000 gift tax annual exclusion) per child in 2012.

**Disadvantage:** Clients who use this strategy must remember that if they elect to contribute the maximum amount allowable in a given year, they generally cannot make another tax-free contribution for five years. Furthermore, the client will be required to file a gift tax return at the time of the contribution to account for the gift.

### Product Strategy 9: Establish a Qualified Personal Residence Trust (QPRT) or Grantor Retained Annuity Trust (GRAT) to Reduce Estate Liability

**Advantage:** A **qualified personal residence trust (QPRT)** is designed to hold a client's home for later transfer to an heir(s). QPRTs are used by clients who would like to reduce the value of their gross estate in the future but still retain the right to live in their house, which may be their single greatest asset. If a client outlives the term of the trust, the property is transferred to the beneficiary. At that point, the client can generally continue to live in the property by agreeing to pay rent (based on an independent appraiser's fair market value rental) to the new property owner. If the client should die before the trust terminates, the full value of the home is included in the client's gross estate.

A **grantor retained annuity trust (GRAT)** is similar to a QPRT, but instead of holding a personal residence the trust holds other assets, such as stocks, bonds, mutual funds, and income-producing real estate. The trust makes annuity payments to the grantor for a certain number of years. At the trust's termination, the assets are transferred to the trust's beneficiaries.

QPRTs and GRATs can be effective tools for reducing a client's gross estate while providing the client with immediate access to housing or an annuity stream. Implementing this strategy allows a client to remove a potentially rapidly appreciating personal residence or other assets from the client's estate if the client can outlive the term of the trust.

**Disadvantage:** Several disadvantages are associated with this strategy. The trust is generally includable in the grantor's gross estate if the grantor dies during the trust term. Although the value of the property can be excluded from the gross estate if the grantor survives the trust term, the client could owe a gift tax on the present value of the remainder in the QPRT or GRAT. The shorter the term of the trust, the higher the potential gift tax will be. However, the longer the term, the more likely that the client will not outlive the trust term, which would defeat the purpose of the strategy.

Even though the QPRT owns the client's personal residence, it is the client's responsibility to pay all expenses related to upkeep, insurance, and taxes on the property. Also, if a client should outlive the duration of a QPRT, the client would need to negotiate with the owners of the property to continue living in the house.

### Product Strategy 10: Establish a Family Limited Partnership

**Advantage:** A **family limited partnership (FLP)** is a tool that can be used by high-net-worth business-owner clients to reduce estate tax liability, decrease income tax liability, and transfer ownership of a business to relatives over time. In the simplest form of an FLP, a client establishes a limited partnership, keeping a general partnership interest in it as well as some limited partnership interests. This enables the client to retain control over the day-to-day activities of the business. Initially, some limited partnership interests can be given or sold to family members. Over time, the client gives interests in the limited partnership to children, grandchildren, and other family members.

As income is generated in the business, the limited partners report their share of earnings. This can help a client reduce current tax liabilities. However, unearned income of a child under age 19 (24 if a full-time student) is generally taxable to the child at the parent's marginal tax rate.

Over time, however, the real advantage of this technique is that it is possible to transfer ownership of a privately held firm from one generation to another on a tax-free basis, using a combination of the gift tax annual exclusion and the unified credit. Furthermore, valuation discounts are often available for transfers of minority interests and lack of marketability.

**Disadvantage:** Some key disadvantages are associated with this strategy. First, even though a partnership can be established with relatively few upfront costs, the actual partnership document must be thorough and the parties need to continually observe partnership formalities to obtain tax benefits. Second, ongoing costs can become high because of accounting issues. Third, by establishing a partnership, the client may be taking on general liability for family members that the client might not otherwise want. Fourth, a gift tax might apply if future partnership gifts exceed the annual exclusion. Finally, implementing this strategy can result in a higher probability of being audited.

### Product Strategy 11: Use an Irrevocable Life Insurance Trust to Reduce Gross Estate

**Advantage:** In many respects, an **irrevocable life insurance trust (ILIT)** strategy can be one of the best ways to remove a high-value asset from a client's gross estate. Using this strategy, a client transfers an existing life insurance policy to a trust. Premiums are then funded using the gift tax annual exclusion (i.e., the client gifts the premium amount to the trust, which then pays the insurance premium). Assuming the grantor-insured lives for more than three years after the gift, this has the advantage of removing the life insurance policy from the gross estate and allows for further estate reduction by using annual gifts to fund premium payments. Of course, if the trustee purchases the policy on the client's life using trust assets, the insured never has an incident of ownership and there is much greater assurance that policy proceeds will be estate tax excludable.

**Disadvantage:** A significant disadvantage associated with this strategy is that the transfer of ownership in a life insurance policy is considered a gift. If the value of the gift exceeds or for some reason does not qualify for the gift tax annual exclusion, a client may have to use up some or all of his or her unified credit and perhaps owe gift tax. Another disadvantage is that the cost of establishing and maintaining an ILIT to some extent offsets the tax benefits gained.

## Product Strategy 12: Establish a QTIP Trust When Applicable

**Advantage:** A **QTIP trust** is often used to obtain a marital deduction for **qualified terminable interest property (QTIP)**. These trusts are useful for divorced individuals entering a remarriage with children, or when a wealthy spouse wishes to ensure adequate income for the surviving spouse but has a strong desire to be sure that at the spouse's death assets remaining in the trust will pass to the wealthy spouse's children. Two important rules apply to the use of QTIP trusts:

1. The surviving spouse must be given the right to all income from the trust (paid at least annually).

2. No one can be given the right to direct that the property will go to anyone else as long as the surviving spouse is alive.

If these rules are met, assets passing to the trust become eligible for the marital deduction. Property that remains in the trust after the surviving spouse's death then goes to the beneficiary originally named by the donor or decedent.

**Disadvantage:** Like any marital deduction trust, a QTIP trust is subject to estate tax at the surviving spouse's death. That is, QTIP trusts are ineffective tools for those wishing to reduce or eliminate estate tax liabilities.

## Product Strategy 13: Reduce Taxes by Using a Charitable Lead Trust

**Advantage**: A **charitable lead trust (CLT)** allows a client to gift assets to a charity, receive a tax deduction for the gift, and potentially reduce estate taxes. Unlike other charitable gifting strategies, a CLT provides a charity with an annuity income rather than assets. At the end of the annuity period, e.g., 20 years, any assets remaining in the trust are distributed to the client's remainder beneficiaries (e.g., children, grandchildren, trusts). The longer the term of the annuity payment, the larger the tax deduction and reduction in estate value will be.

**Disadvantage**: For estate tax purposes, the return of the asset to the remainder beneficiary is considered a gift; however, the gift value is based on current market interest rates and the present value of the assets when donated, not the appreciated value. IRS rules make the use of a CLT strategy complicated. Gifts to CLTs do not qualify for the annual gift exclusion. Also, the IRS will impose a tax on the sale or exchange of property in a CLT within the first two years. Finally, a CLT could be disallowed if the IRS suspects self-dealing.

### Procedural Strategy 1: Use Annual Gifts to Reduce a Client's Gross Estate

**Advantage:** One of the most effective ways to decrease a client's gross estate involves taking full advantage of the $13,000 (in 2012) gift tax annual exclusion per donee. Using this strategy, a client can give up to $13,000 per year gift tax free to as many individuals (related or not) as the client desires. Married couples can double gifts through gift-splitting techniques and provide up to $26,000 per year to each donee gift tax free. It is possible to reduce an estate substantially over time simply by systematically making gifts to one or more persons.

**Disadvantage:** The primary disadvantage associated with this strategy is that, once a gift has been made, the transfer is irrevocable. Further, gifts to others cannot be used to generate income for the donor. Gifts of more than $13,000 (in 2012) effectively decrease a client's unified credit and subject the donor to gift taxation.

### Procedural Strategy 2: Increase Charitable Giving to Reduce Estate Tax

**Advantage:** Lifetime charitable giving provides clients with three primary advantages. First, gifts typically can be deducted, at least in part, as an itemized deduction for federal income tax purposes. Second, the full value of gifts made to qualified charities reduces a client's gross estate, which can reduce tax liability. Third, if established through a CRAT, CRUT, or pooled income fund, charitable gifts can also provide lifetime payments to, for example, the donor and the donor's spouse.

**Disadvantage:** Like all giving strategies, donating assets to charity results in loss of use of the property. Gifts are irrevocable, regardless of whether a client has a change of heart at a later date or needs the assets back to fund other goals. Issues related to family disagreements over charitable donations should also be considered.

### Procedural Strategy 3: Make Gifts to Custodial Accounts (UGMA/UTMA)

**Advantage:** State laws for custodian accounts are titled either **Uniform Gifts to Minors Act (UGMA)** or **Uniform Transfers to Minors Act (UTMA)**. If UGMA/UTMA is used, an adult must be named custodian of the account. When a child reaches the age of majority, which is typically age 18 or 21 depending on the state of the child's residence, the assets become the full property of the young person.

Certain tax advantages are associated with using UGMA/UTMA. First, the donor's gross estate can generally be reduced through the use of annual gifts. Second, income-producing assets can be shifted to children and grandchildren in a way that possibly reduces the total amount of income tax paid. Gifts to custodial accounts qualify for the annual exclusion for both gift tax and GST tax purposes.

**Disadvantage:** Several disadvantages are associated with this strategy. To begin with, all gifts to custodial accounts are irrevocable, and upon the child's age of majority—typically18 or 21—the assets become the sole property of the child. Unearned income of a child under age 19 (24 if a full-time student) is generally taxable to the child at the parent's marginal tax rate. The loss of property use and the inability to guarantee that assets will be used for a specific purpose make this strategy problematic for some clients.

## Procedural Strategy 4: Make Gifts to § 2503(b) or 2503(c) Trusts for Minor Child

**Advantage:** Certain trusts can be used to transfer assets to minor children and grandchildren using the gift tax annual exclusion.

A **§ 2503(b) trust** generally requires the income from assets held in the trust to be distributed for the child's benefit at least annually. However, the principal need not be distributed at the age of majority.

A **§ 2503(c) trust** allows all income to grow within the trust, but distribution of trust assets must generally occur at the child's age of majority. A § 2503(c) trust is similar to UGMA/UTMA in this respect, but different in that a clause can be inserted into the trust document that gives the child a right to demand distribution from the trust for a limited period of time upon reaching the age of majority. If the distribution is not requested within this time period, the trust can continue into later years. Unlike a gift under UGMA/UTMA, the property can remain within the trust beyond the child's age of majority.

**Disadvantage:** The asset and the income from the asset are no longer available to the donor. If a § 2503(b) trust is used, income generated within the trust must be distributed at least annually to the child.

## Procedural Strategy 5: Adding Co-owners to Accounts

**Advantage:** Many times clients feel an emotional obligation to add family members to accounts. If they want the account to pass automatically at death, clients should consider using a **payable on death (POD)** or **transfer on death (TOD)** account. A POD is used for bank accounts, and a TOD is used for security titling. Clients are sometimes tempted to use forms of co-ownership as a way to avoid probate.

**Disadvantage:** Although adding a spouse, child, or other person as a co-owner to property may sound like an attractive strategy initially, the long-term ramifications of this strategy can be quite negative. For example, co-owning all assets with a spouse almost guarantees that assets will transfer directly to the spouse through the unlimited marital deduction. This could result in over-qualifying the spouse's estate for the marital deduction, resulting in more federal estate tax due at the surviving spouse's death than might otherwise have been the case. Adding a co-owner other than a spouse to property can result in gift tax. Additionally, co-owners can lose the ability to receive a full step-up in basis on co-owned property. Finally, care is needed to avoid a conflict with POD or TOD arrangements that take precedence over intentions stated in the will.

## Procedural Strategy 6: Make Complete and Appropriate Use of Property Transfer Law by Using Beneficiary Designations

**Advantage:** One of the simplest ways to reduce probate fees and retain client privacy is to ensure that all financial assets have designated beneficiaries and contingent beneficiaries, and that these designations are kept up to date. Changes precipitated by a death, divorce, or other personal situation should not be overlooked.

**Disadvantage:** Like many other estate planning issues, beneficiary designations require clients to face their mortality and make choices. Too often, no designation is made or "payable to the estate" is chosen by default.

## Procedural Strategy 7: Make Sure Everyone Is Informed when Appointing Others in an Estate Plan

**Advantage:** Clients are well served by financial planners who help them carefully consider potential family conflicts, conflicts of interest, or the qualifications required for those appointed to serve a function within an estate plan (e.g., a guardian for children or the executor of a will). Individuals chosen must fully understand and accept the responsibilities inherent in their appointed role. This also extends to medical providers and other family or household members who should be fully informed of a client's end-of-life preferences and decisions. For example, copies of the living will, AMD, or medical power of attorney should be distributed among appropriate medical, financial, and legal professionals, as well as the spouse, partner, or family.

**Disadvantage:** Emotional distress and perhaps a loss of privacy are the primary disadvantages of this strategy. Although family discussions may be uncomfortable, it is critical that guardians and executors be informed of the choice and are willing to serve. Furthermore, it is important for these appointees to understand their financial obligations. Certainly, any preliminary distress will be less traumatic than disclosing this information after the death of the client, or failing to appoint anyone so that court involvement is necessary.

## Procedural Strategy 8: Take Care to Accurately Account for Life Insurance in the Gross Estate

**Advantage**: It is important to know when and how much life insurance is included in a client's gross estate. The face value of a policy is always included if a decedent owns the insurance and is the insured. The face value amount is reduced by any outstanding policy loans and accrued dividends. If the decedent owns the policy but is not the insured, the interpolated terminal reserve value of the policy plus any unearned premium will likely be included in the gross estate. Often, this value is close to the cash value of a nonterm policy.

**Disadvantage**: Failing to account for the appropriate value of life insurance in the gross estate can produce significant estate miscalculations.

# CHAPTER-BASED CASE STUDY

## A Client-based Estate Planning Recommendation Example

The estate planning analysis is integrative with other plan components. Some might argue that estate planning is the most integrative section in a comprehensive financial plan. For example, to calculate a client's potential estate tax liability, it is necessary to review a client's cash flow and net worth statements. This can suggest another need, namely the availability of liquid assets for meeting immediate expenses for the decedent or survivors until insurance proceeds or other assets are available. Income tax issues also play a part in estate planning analysis. The tax basis of certain assets and the potential capital gains associated with the sale or purchase of other assets must be taken into account when making recommendations for lifetime gifts and transfers at death.

The integration of life insurance planning and estate planning is typically recognized, but some of the details of that relationship may be less obvious. Life insurance certainly plays a role in the estate planning process, especially as it pertains to who should own the policy and who should be the beneficiary. If a client owns a significantly large life insurance policy, the use of an ILIT could be appropriate, especially if the client's estate is estimated to exceed the estate tax unified credit applicable exclusion amount. If the client's spouse owns the policy, the proceeds are generally includable in the spouse's gross estate.

An overriding concern associated with owning life insurance, beyond the obvious monetary benefit, is to ensure that life insurance proceeds do not create undue distribution hardships and unexpected estate or income tax consequences. The most efficient and effective method used to control these issues involves ensuring that appropriate beneficiaries are named and that the policy is owned by the most appropriate person or entity (e.g., a trust). Any incident of ownership by the decedent-insured could cause the proceeds of the policy to be included in the gross estate. If the life insurance proceeds become an asset of the estate, the same life insurance purchased to increase estate liquidity or pay for estate taxes could instead increase the very estate taxes they were meant to pay.

If having spouses or the insured as owner or beneficiary, respectively, sometimes creates estate planning problems, placing children in these roles can complicate matters even more. Children create a new set of potential problems. To be named a primary beneficiary, a child generally must be more than 18 years of age and mentally and emotionally competent to handle large financial decisions. In addition, naming as beneficiary a third-party who is not a party to the contract (e.g., insured or owner) and not the owner's/insured's spouse could trigger unintended gift tax consequences. For example, a husband who purchases a life insurance policy on his wife but names his two children as beneficiaries is, in essence, making a gift to the children for the face amount of the policy upon the death of his wife. An additional complication is that if the husband transfers ownership of the policy to his children within three years of his death, then the life insurance proceeds could be included in his estate.

Although there are many possibilities regarding who should own or be the beneficiary of life insurance policies when estate taxes are of no consequence, there are fewer good choices if taxes are an important issue. Therefore, establishing a trust to serve as either the owner or the beneficiary of a life insurance policy could make the estate transfer a much smoother process. A well-developed estate plan must reflect the integration of multiple planning areas and keep pace with the changing legislative environment. This requires periodic review and update, but the long-term effects can benefit multiple generations of a client's family or other social causes.

## A Sample Recommendation: A Multifaceted Gifting Technique

The following example shows how Sarah, a comprehensive financial planner, moved from strategy development to recommendation formation when working with a client named Kevin Gray. At the time, Kevin was a 56-year-old single man living in Virginia. Kevin was referred to Sarah by a longtime client. When they began working together, Sarah told Kevin that she worked with clients only on a comprehensive basis. She also indicated that, although she was not an attorney and could not draft legal documents, she would review his estate situation and make recommendations when she felt it was appropriate.

Several months ago, Sarah had Kevin complete a client data-gathering questionnaire. She used data from the questionnaire in combination with information obtained through personal interviews with Kevin to calculate his level of discretionary cash flow, net worth, and tax situation. She also used information provided by Kevin to formalize his short- and long-term financial goals. Only after all of this work had been completed did Sarah turn her attention to her favorite topic: estate planning.

Sarah reviewed the notes she had taken during previous meetings with Kevin. She knew that Kevin had a strong desire to help his alma mater, church, and family members financially, both during his lifetime and after his death. She knew that Kevin had a current net worth of $7.2 million and that his assets should continue to grow over the next 20 to 30 years. Kevin was in the 25% marginal tax bracket, had a positive monthly cash flow, and was confident that he could afford to contribute up to $15,000 per year to charities and family members. Each contribution would consist primarily of cash generated from asset sales. Sarah knew that, based on Kevin's asset base and current occupation, he did not need additional income, either today or during retirement.

Kevin had conflicting goals and concerns regarding estate planning issues. He wanted to reduce his current taxable income while keeping an eye on estate tax reduction. He also valued education and wanted to provide a scholarship fund to his alma mater. Several years ago, he had approached the university about making a donation, but he was not pleased with how the foundation office had treated him. Since that time, Kevin's skepticism had grown and he was hesitant to make an irrevocable gift to an institution that might mismanage the assets.

Sarah knew that Kevin needed guidance on several estate planning issues. Intuitively, she began to work through a process of strategy identification and recommendation development. She determined that Kevin needed to update his will and letter of last instructions. He also needed a living will, power of attorney, and AMD. She also believed that, given his marital status and net worth, he needed a living trust. She noted the approximate costs associated with each recommendation and concluded that, if he used one attorney to draft all of the documents, the cost would be less than $4,000.

To Sarah, these recommendations were basic and prudent. Her main concern was that Kevin's gross estate was significantly higher than the estate tax unified credit applicable exclusion amount. If the tax law did not change by 2013, Sarah knew that Kevin's estate would be subject to a sizable tax bite that would limit his ability to maximize his estate planning goals. Her training, experience, and knowledge suggested that a gift plan recommendation would be the ideal way to reduce taxes on his estate, increase cash flow by means of charitable tax deductions, and maximize transfers to charities and family members.

Sarah initially considered several gift strategies. She knew that at a very basic level, Kevin could begin to give assets away to noncharitable beneficiaries such as family members. If the gifts were less than the gift tax annual exclusion, no gift tax would be due. If Kevin needed an immediate income tax charitable deduction for a gift and also to receive lifetime payments, charitable giving alternatives such as CRATs and CRUTs would make more sense. If, on the other hand, Kevin had a desire to play an active role in determining which charities received funding on an annual basis, and if he was willing to forgo payments from a trust, establishing a donor-advised fund might be an appropriate recommendation. Based on her experience, she also realized that it was possible and likely that more than one gift strategy could be used in her final recommendation.

Sarah now faced a decision, namely, which of the gifting strategies should she recommend to Kevin? She began the procedure of narrowing down the strategies by reviewing Kevin's goals and temperament. She knew that although Kevin would like to receive an income tax deduction for any gifts made, he did not really need income from the gift. Unless there was no alternative, Sarah felt that using an income-producing gift strategy would be inappropriate. This helped her eliminate the use of a CRAT, CRUT, and pooled income fund from the list of potential strategies. It occurred to her that Kevin could combine gifts to a donor-advised fund with annual gifts to family members.

Before making this recommendation, Sarah decided to compare the combined strategy of using a donor-advised fund with separate annual gifts to the other three strategies. She knew that Kevin would face set-up and administrative costs with any strategy, but she wanted to document these before making a final decision. Sarah's calculations are summarized in Table 13.1.

**Table 13.1** Sarah's Notes for Estimating Strategy Costs

| Calculation | Strategies Considered | | | |
| --- | --- | --- | --- | --- |
| | Annual Gift | Donor-advised Fund | Charitable Gift | Donor-advised Fund and Annual Gift |
| Cost of contribution | $0 | $300 Sarah estimated that management fees would average 2% of total contributions per year | $0 | $200 Based on a $10,000 gift to a donor-advised fund, charging 2% of contributions per year, plus $5,000 gift to family members |
| Percentage of contribution used for gift purposes | 100% | 98% | 100% | 99% |
| Estimated income tax benefit (at a 25% marginal tax rate) | $0 | $3,750 ($15,000 x 25%) | $3,750 ($15,000 x 25%) | $2,500 ($10,000 x 25%) |
| Total value of the strategy | $15,000 | $18,450 | $18,750 | $17,300 |

Sarah's calculations showed that the costs associated with each strategy were reasonable. In fact, making a contribution to a charity or a donor-advised fund provided a tax benefit that offset any costs associated with managing assets. Sarah ruled out recommending that Kevin give his family $15,000 per year because Kevin would not receive an income tax charitable deduction. She also decided against making direct charitable contributions even though the total value of the gift was the highest of the four solutions. She believed Kevin would be unlikely to implement this recommendation because of his growing mistrust regarding the management of assets held by some charitable organizations.

Her final recommendation came down to a choice between a 100% contribution to a donor-advised fund and a split contribution to a donor-advised fund and family members. The donor-advised fund strategy offered a reduction in Kevin's gross estate, an immediate tax deduction for contributions made to the fund, and the ability to manage distributions from the fund. Kevin could use contributions and earnings held inside the fund as gifts to one or more charities in a given year. If, at some point in the future, a charity lost Kevin's favor, he could change the amount donated to the charity. The ability to control the assets while maximizing tax benefits made this strategy very attractive. Sarah also liked the fact that she could manage the assets held in the account for Kevin.

However, Sarah opted to recommend a combination strategy. The fact that Kevin wanted to help his family by giving them financial gifts on a yearly basis made the combination strategy the most appropriate for Kevin, in her opinion. At this point in the recommendation process, her only question involved the percentage of Kevin's annual $15,000 gift that should go to the donor-advised fund versus his family. Sarah had originally thought that a $10,000/$5,000 split between the fund and the nephew would be optimal, but she was not sure how Kevin would feel about this allocation. So she decided to recommend this split to Kevin and allow him to alter the recommendation if necessary. Sarah felt that the best way to help Kevin understand the basic components of the recommendation was to review questions related to implementation. She used a planning recommendation form to summarize her recommendation. An example of how Sarah completed the form is shown in Exhibit 13.4.

**Exhibit 13.4** Kevin Gray's Estate/Trust Recommendation Form

### Planning Recommendation Form

| | | | | |
|---|---|---|---|---|
| **Financial Planning Content Area** | Estate and gift planning | | | |
| **Client Goal** | Provide annual gifts to charities and family | | | |
| **Recommendation No.** | 1 | **Priority (1–6) lowest to highest:** | | 5 |
| **Projected/Target Value ($)** | $15,000 per year | | | |

**Product Profile**

| | | | | |
|---|---|---|---|---|
| Type | Donor-advised fund and annual gift | | | |
| Duration | Yearly | | | |
| Provider | Donor-advised fund: National Heritage Foundation | | | |
| Funding Cost per Period ($) | $15,000 | | | |
| Maintenance Cost per Period ($) | 2% of each contribution made to the fund, or approximately $200 per year | | | |
| Current Income Tax Status | Tax-qualified | X | Taxable | |
| Projected Rate of Return | Conservative | | | |
| Major Policy Provisions | Once fund size reaches $10,000, assets can be actively managed. At that point, an annual management fee may apply. | | | |

**Procedural Factors**

| | | | | |
|---|---|---|---|---|
| Implementation by Whom | Planner | | Client | X |
| Implementation Date or Time Frame | Begin monthly contributions October 1 | | | |
| Implementation Procedure | Our firm will prepare foundation documents for approval by the National Heritage Foundation; once the account is established, client may begin contributing to the fund; distributions from the fund may be made only to charitable entities approved by the IRS.<br>Gifts to the client's nephew can begin whenever the client is comfortable doing so; the annual gift should not exceed $5,000. | | | |

**Ownership Factors**

| | | | | |
|---|---|---|---|---|
| Owner(s) | At account set-up, the donor-advised fund becomes its own legal entity; sample name could be the Kevin Gray Foundation. | | | |
| Form of Ownership | Trust | | | |
| Insured(s) | NA | | | |
| Custodial Account | Yes | | No | X |
| Custodian | NA | | | |
| In Trust for (ITF) | Yes | | No | X |
| Transfer on Death (TOD) | Yes | | No | X |
| Beneficiary(ies) | Any charity approved by the IRS; family members through direct gifts | | | |
| Contingent Beneficiary(ies) | NA | | | |
| **Proposed Benefit** | Contribution to the donor-advised fund will result in an income tax deduction at the client's marginal tax rate(s); all gifts, including those to the nephew, will result in a reduced gross estate. | | | |

# Learning Outcomes

1.  In some respects, estate planning is the most integrative of the core financial planning topics. Whenever a financial planner engages in an estate planning review, by default the planner must deal with a multitude of factors, including cash flow and net worth documentation, tax analyses, insurance frameworks, and investment management issues. As this chapter highlights, almost every aspect of a client's financial life affects, to some extent, estate planning issues. Additionally, each client's unique situation helps shape the type of recommendations that a financial planner makes. Some clients have a strong desire to minimize taxes. Others desire privacy. Still other clients wish to share their wealth with family and community organizations. These examples suggest that no single strategy or tool is always appropriate when framing estate recommendations. It is imperative that each financial planner, working with his or her clientele and collaborative professionals, develop recommendations that can be implemented in a way that maximizes each client's unique financial and lifestyle goals.

2.  The estate plan should accomplish three objectives including: (a) planning for the cost-effective transfer of assets in a way that is consistent with the client's wishes and preserves the estate: (b) providing for survivors or other financial or charitable needs; and (c) planning for the client's final wishes regarding incapacitation and other end-of-life decisions. Regardless of the size of the estate, these three objectives should guide an estate plan.

3.  Before embarking upon a quantitative review of a client's estate planning situation, it is important for financial planners to identify influential situational factors and questions that can be asked to help determine a client's estate planning needs. Obtaining a clear idea of a client's values, social position, and culture can help shape an estate plan. In addition, asking questions related to privacy desires, feelings about taxation and charitable giving, and special needs are equally important factors shaping the way in which estate planning recommendations are formulated.

4.  When determining and evaluating the factors associated with a client's estate tax liability, financial planners must have a keen understanding of both the definitions and applications of several key terms. For example, differentiating between a client's gross and taxable estate and the process used to arrive at the taxable estate is important. Additionally, understanding how the unified credit applies to both taxable gifts and asset transfers is important when estimating a client's estate tax liability. The ability to describe and determine the annual gift exclusion and how gift splitting affects the value of a client's estate plays an equally important role in shaping tax calculations.

5.  Four critical steps are associated with describing and calculating a client's estate tax liability. First, the value of the client's gross estate must be estimated. Second, the taxable estate must be calculated by subtracting from the gross estate funeral and administrative expenses, debts, taxes, charitable donations, and any marital transfers. Third, the value of taxable lifetime gifts must be added back into the taxable estate figure—unless the gift taxes were paid at the time the gift was made. This results in what is known as the adjusted taxable estate. The fourth and final step involves determining the tax payable. To arrive at this figure, the remaining exclusion amount is subtracted from the adjusted taxable estate. What remains is subject to taxation. Alternatively, the tax can be calculated first and the applicable credit amount can be subtracted to determine remaining liability.

6.  The Tax Relief Act of 2010 has had a significant impact on the type of estate planning calculations and recommendations being made in the financial services marketplace. The Act created the portable estate exemption, which effectively shields as much as $10 million from federal estate taxation for married couples. The Act changed the way many financial planners counsel clients. For example, A-B trust arrangements were once commonly recommended as a strategy to maximize the unified credit available to married couples. A-B trusts, although still recommended, are no longer as widely used because the portable estate exemption accomplishes the same objective with less cost. Other changes resulting from the Act include linking the estate and gift tax and eliminating previous restrictions on stepped-up basis. The Act has also left many estate planning rules and strategies in limbo. Unless Congress takes steps to make the Act permanent, the estate planning landscape will change in 2013.

7.  Few aspects of financial planning provide as many opportunities to recommend strategies to meet multiple client goals as the estate planning process. Recommendations can be divided into product and procedural strategies. Product strategies encompass basic recommendations such as drafting a will, putting in place a living will, and using appropriate asset titling, to more complicated strategies including the use of trust arrangements, charitable giving techniques, and FLPs. Procedural strategies involve aspects of planning that enhance client outcomes while reducing taxes and/or administrative nuisances. Examples include the use and monitoring of custodial accounts, beneficiary designations, and life insurance. Viewed holistically, the estate planning process can be seen as a unifying procedure that helps clients better understand the lifetime accumulation, preservation, and ultimate distribution of assets.

# Chapter Resources

Garrett, S., and D. A. Neiman. *Money without Matrimony: The Unmarried Couple's Guide to Financial Security.* Chicago: Dearborn, 2005.

Hertz, F. C., and E. Doskow. *Making It Legal: A Guide to Same-sex Marriage, Domestic Partnerships, and Civil Unions.* Berkeley, CA: Nolo Press, 2009.

Information on the unified credit (http://www.irs.gov/publications/p950/ar02.html).

IRS Form 706 filing instructions for 2011 (http://www.irs.gov/pub/irs-pdf/i706.pdf).

Leimberg, S. R., J. H. Ellis, S. N. Kandell, R. G. Miller, T. C. Polacek, and M. S. Rosenbloom. *Tools & Techniques of Estate Planning*, 15th Edition. Erlanger, KY: National Underwriter Company, 2011.

Pride Planners (professional association dedicated to same-sex and non-married financial and estate planning) (www.prideplanners.org).

The *Financial Factilitator* and all fillable forms needed to complete text activities can be found on the student website at: http://pro.nuco.com/booksupplements/NUCollege-CaseBook2e.

# Quantitative/Analytical Mini-case Problems

1. Sandomir and Rasia Kolbe, ages 58 and 57 respectively, and their three grown children recently attended Sandomier's father's funeral in Poland. They realized that they did not know the effect of federal estate tax on their own estate, nor did they have any legal documentation supporting end-of-life medical or financial decisions. So upon returning home, Rasia called her mother for a recommendation regarding financial professionals to interview. Her mother suggested an attorney for the legal documents and her own financial planner for other estate planning needs. Assume all family members are U.S. citizens. Financial information for the Kolbe family follows:

### Current Division of Assets

| Assets | Total | Sandomir | Rasia | Joint |
|---|---|---|---|---|
| Cash and savings | $83,500 | $4,500 | $7,000 | $72,000 |
| Securities and annuities (nonqualified) | 625,000 | 0 | 0 | 625,000 |
| Securities and annuities (qualified) | 55,000 | 0 | 55,000 | 0 |
| Retirement plans | 605,000 | 425,000 | 180,000 | 0 |
| Automobiles | 105,000 | 0 | 0 | 105,000 |
| Personal property | 150,000 | 0 | 0 | 150,000 |
| Residence | 500,000 | 0 | 0 | 500,000 |
| Other real estate | 350,000 | 0 | 0 | 350,000 |
| Business interests | 225,000 | 0 | 225,000 | 0 |
| Life insurance (see table below) | 164,000 | 84,000 | 80,000 | 0 |
| | | | | |
| Total assets | 2,862,500 | 513,500 | 547,000 | 1,802,000 |

### Current Life Insurance Information

| | Face Value | Cash Value | Owner | Insured | Beneficiary |
|---|---|---|---|---|---|
| Life Policy # 1 (Term) | $220,000 | $0 | Employer | Sandomir | Sandomir |
| Life Policy # 2 (Whole) | 250,000 | 45,000 | Sandomir | Sandomir | Rasia |
| Life Policy # 3 (Whole) | 150,000 | 30,000 | Rasia | Sandomir | Children |
| Life Policy # 4 (Term) | 20,000 | 0 | Rasia | Rasia | Sandomir |
| Life Policy # 5 (VUL) | 300,000 | 50,000 | Rasia | Rasia | Sandomir |
| Life Policy # 6 (Whole) | 50,000 | 9,000 | Sandomir | Rasia | Sandomir |
| Life Policy # 7 (Whole) | 150,000 | 30,000 | Sandomir | Rasia | Children |
| | | | | | |
| Total life insurance | 1,140,000 | 164,000 | | | |

Based on the Kolbes' financial information, the lawyer and the financial planner jointly made these recommendations.

Recommendation 1: Establish testamentary trusts for both Sandomir and Rasia.

Recommendation 2: Retitle assets in preparation of funding trusts.

Recommendation 3: Transfer life insurance ownership to the three children.

To assist the Kolbes in their estate planning, answer the following questions.

a. What type of trust(s) might be recommended in keeping with the clients' desires of minimizing estate taxes, maximizing privacy, and easing ownership transfer?

b. How might the assets be retitled to ensure that all trusts can be adequately funded?

c. What are some of the challenges associated with transferring ownership of the insurance policies to the children? Describe some of the problems with the current life insurance designations. What other strategies could also be considered for alleviating any potential estate, gift, or income tax issues?

d. Besides completing wills and trust documents, what other legal documents should the Kolbes consider?

2. Assume the following estate planning information for a client and spouse.

| | Client (Jane) | Spouse (John) | Joint* |
|---|---|---|---|
| Assets | $6,300,000 | $1,200,000 | $500,000 |
| Debts | | | 100,000 |
| Funeral | 20,000 | 20,000 | |
| Estate administration | 20,000 | 20,000 | |
| Charitable contribution | 20,000 | 20,000 | |
| Marital plan | A/B | A/B | |

*Jointly owned with right of survivorship between client and spouse

a. If Jane were to pass away first, in 2012, what is her tax liability before the marital deduction?

b. If John were to pass away first, in 2012, what is his tax liability before the marital deduction?

c. Using the portable estate exemption, how much of their combined estate is taxable in 2012?

d. If Jane and John fail to take advantage of the portable estate exemption by forgetting to file IRS Form 706 at the death of the first spouse, will there be a tax liability in 2012, assuming the second spouse also passes shortly thereafter? Describe an estate planning strategy that can be used to minimize any estate tax liability in this situation.

3.  Brenda is wealthy, single, and generous. During the previous year she made the following gifts:

    • Gift of stock to the local art museum (a 501(c)(3) nonprofit organization): $245,000

    • College tuition payment for niece: $29,000 made directly to the institution

    • Medical bills for elderly neighbor: $18,000 paid directly to the hospital

    • Home down payment gift to daughter: $30,000 paid directly to the mortgage lender

    • Cash gift to son: $15,000

    • Use the gift tax rates shown below as a guide to answer the following questions:

### Federal Gift Tax Rates for Clients Dying After 2010

| Taxable Amount | Rate | | |
|---|---|---|---|
| $0 to $10,000 | 18% | minus | $0 |
| $10,001 to $20,000 | 20% | minus | $200 |
| $20,001 to $40,000 | 22% | minus | $600 |
| $40,001 to $60,000 | 24% | minus | $1,400 |
| $60,001 to $80,000 | 26% | minus | $2,600 |
| $80,001 to $100,000 | 28% | minus | $4,200 |
| $100,001 to $150,000 | 30% | minus | $6,200 |
| $150,001 to $250,000 | 32% | minus | $9,200 |
| $250,001 to $500,000 | 34% | minus | $14,200 |
| $500,000 or more | 35% | minus | $19,200 |

Source: IRS. *2011 Instructions for Form 709: U.S. Gift (and Generation-Skipping Transfer) Tax Return.* Available at http://www.irs.gov/pub/irs-pdf/i709.pdf, p. 15.

a.  What is the total amount of taxable gifts in 2012?

b.  What is Brenda's gift tax liability in 2012?

c.  Assuming a unified credit of $1,772,800, what alternatives does Brenda have in terms of paying the gift tax liability?

# Comprehensive Bedo Case—Analysis Questions

Before beginning the estate planning analysis for the Bedos, it is important to review case details related to asset ownership, liabilities, and other assumptions, including estate tax growth rates. A review of the household net worth statement will help with the gross estate calculation for both Tyler and Mia. *The effect of state taxes paid should be ignored for purposes of the case narrative.*

An assumption must be made as to who will predecease whom. It is typical to assume that the primary breadwinner of the household dies first. In this case, this means that Tyler predeceases Mia.

Tyler's gross estate would, therefore, include one-half of all jointly held property plus the fair market value of any other personally owned assets, including life insurance. Funeral and administrative expenses and debts should be deducted to arrive at Tyler's adjusted gross estate. For this purpose, debt is limited to a lien, mortgage, or other form of debt that is attached to assets included in the estate. Tyler's taxable estate should then be calculated. The use of the unlimited marital deduction ought to be considered in the initial analysis.

A similar analysis should be conducted for Mia. It is possible that upon Mia's death federal estate tax may be due.

Use the following questions to guide you through the estate planning process:

1.  Develop an estate planning goal for the Bedos. When conceptualizing this goal, consider the following.

    a.  Is the goal developed in agreement with any or all goals and objectives that the clients have identified regarding estate planning?

    b.  What situational factors might influence their estate planning goals? Are these factors explicit, implied, or assumed? Is additional information required from the Bedos?

    c.  Identify life events that could affect the estate planning analysis for Tyler and Mia and that should be reviewed at future client meetings.

    d.  What is the desired outcome for the clients?

2.  Develop a list of globally accepted, client-specific, or planner-generated planning assumptions that will structure the estate planning situation analysis.

3.  Using the Financial Facilitator, calculate the following scenarios for the Bedo household as part of the analysis of their current estate planning situation. For each scenario, ignore any applicable state estate taxes.

    a.  Scenario 1. The amount of federal estate tax due if Tyler were to predecease Mia and they both died in 2012.

    b.  Scenario 2. The amount of federal estate tax due if Mia were to predecease Tyler and they both died in 2012.

4.  Evaluate and comment upon the following:

    a.  The appropriateness of Tyler's current will.

    b.  The appropriateness of Mia's current will.

    c.  Given their current situation, what other estate planning documents should the Bedos have in place?

5.  A planner's observations and results from analyses can be communicated through a letter or a comprehensive or modular plan. Using some combination of text, bullets, or graphics, summarize your observations about the estate planning situation and the identified planning need(s) of the Bedo household.

6.  Based on the goals originally identified and the completed analysis, what product or procedural strategies might be most useful to improve the Bedos' estate planning situation? Be sure to consider strategies matched to the planning needs identified for each member of the household. When reviewing strategies, be careful to consider the approximate cost of implementation as well as the most likely outcome(s) associated with each strategy.

7.  Write at least one primary and one alternative recommendation from selected strategies in response to each identified planning need. More than one recommendation may be needed to address all of the planning needs. Include specific, defensible answers to the *who, what, when, where, why, how,* and *how much* implementation questions for each recommendation.

    a.  It is suggested that each recommendation be summarized in a Recommendation Form.

    b.  Assign a priority to each recommendation based on the likelihood of meeting client goals and desired outcomes. This priority will be important when recommendations from other core planning content areas are considered relative to the available discretionary funds for subsidizing all recommendations.

    c.  What considerations should be taken into account when naming beneficiaries to any new life insurance policies for the Bedos?

    d.  Comment briefly on the outcomes associated with each recommendation.

8.  Complete the following for the estate planning section of the Bedos' financial plan.

    a.  Outline the content to be included in this section of the plan. Given the preceding segments written, which segments are missing? What disclaimers, if any, could be important to include in this section of the plan?

    b.  Draft an introduction to this section of the plan (no more than one paragraph).

    b.  Identify at least five terms, concepts, or planning strategies that could be included in this section of the plan. For each, write a definition or explanation that would be helpful to the typical client with limited knowledge of estate planning.

9.  Prepare a 10–15-minute presentation for the Bedos of your observations and/or recommendation(s) for meeting their estate planning needs. Be sure to include visual aids, Excel handouts, and other materials that will make the recommendations more meaningful for the clients.

## Notes

1.  Napoleon, Philatelic Estate Disposition for the Novice, *American Philatelist*. Available at http://stamps.org/userfiles/file/Estate/PhilatelicEstateDispositionfortheNovice.pdf, p. 159.

2.  *IRS Instructions Booklet for Form 950: Introduction to Estate and Gift Taxes.* Available at http://www.irs.gov/publications/p950/ar02.html.

3.  *IRS Form 706 Instructions: Generation Assignment.* Available at http://www.irs.gov/instructions/i706gst/ch01.html.

4.  R. F. Stolz, "Estate Planning for Unmarried Couples: What Financial Planners Need to Know," *Journal of Financial Planning* 25, no. 2 (2012): 20–24.

5.  Additional information and planning techniques for same-sex couples can be found at http://www.fpanet.org/journal/BetweentheIssues/LastMonth/Articles/PlanningIdeasandConsiderationsforUnmarriedCouples/.

6.  Gary Langer, *Poll: Americans Not Planning for the Future.* Available at http://abcnews.go.com/Business/story?id=86992&page=1#.TvpMeZg5tFI.

7.  Legal Information Institute, Cornell University Law School, 26 USC § 2518 – Disclaimers. Available at http://www.law.cornell.edu/uscode/text/26/2518.

8.  California Family Law Form 110 (FL110) Summons Pertaining to Divorce. Available at http://www.courts.ca.gov/documents/fl110.pdf.

9.  Arizona State Legislature, Title 25-318, *Disposition of Property; Retroactivity; Notice to Creditors; Assignment of Debts; Contempt of Court.* Available at http://www.azleg.state.az.us/FormatDocument.asp?inDoc=/ars/25/00318.htm&Title=25&DocType=ARS.

10. Legal Information Institute, Cornell University Law School, *Kennedy* v. *Plan Administrator for DuPont*, Case No. 07-636. Opinion available online at http://www.law.cornell.edu/supct/html/07-636.ZS.html.

# PART V: Review of the Systematic Process

Chapter 14—The Financial Planning Process: Steps 4 to 6

# The Financial Planning Process: Steps 4 to 6

---

## Learning Objectives

1. Describe the benefits of utilizing a systematic financial planning process.

2. Explain how client-based recommendations are developed and guide the financial planning process.

3. Describe the three issues that guide the development of a plan within Step 4: Develop the Comprehensive Plan and Present Recommendations.

4. Discuss the pivotal role that the presentation of the plan plays in the success of the advisor-client relationship.

5. Identify and discuss the questions that guide Step 5: Implement the Plan.

6. Explain the process of monitoring a financial plan and why it is important to a successful advisor-client relationship.

7. Explain the dichotomy between the importance of monitoring a financial plan and the responsibility for monitoring it.

# Key Terms

cash flow orientation to planning

goal orientation to planning

impact analysis

implementation

to-do list

**Figure 14.1** The Systematic Process of Financial Planning

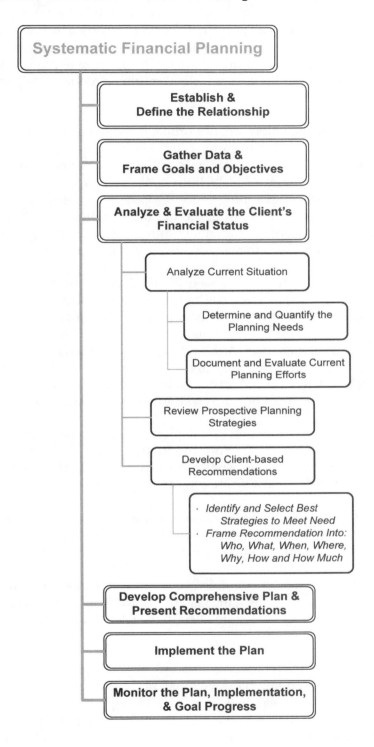

"I have all of this information and data about the client, now what do I do?" This is a common question among students faced with their first comprehensive client profile, whether approaching a "paper case" or conducting discovery and data collection with a real client. Either situation contributes to students' anxiety. The paper case affords no option for additional questions or clarification —there is no real client to get to know. On the other hand, a real client might engender a palpable fear of failure: what if the advice is wrong?

These students' reactions are not unlike those of novice planners faced with their first clients. As explained in Chapter 1, this book, written as a companion to *The Process of Financial Planning, Second Edition*, applies the systematic six-step financial planning process shown in Figure 14.1. Both books were written in the hope of developing a systematic financial planning process based on the general financial planning process promoted by the CFP Board and other organizations.[1] Both books were written with the intent of equipping students with a systematic, nearly step-by-step process that would empower them to answer the question, "Now what do I do?"

Chapters 3 through 13 addressed the analysis encompassed in Step 3, Analyze and Evaluate the Client's Financial Status, for each of the core content planning areas. An explanation of how client-specific analyses can be conducted and how planning strategies and recommendations can evolve from these analytical techniques was the focus of each chapter. Although developing financial planning strategies to meet specific client goals and objectives is an important part of the financial planning process, this activity is not an end in itself. Three more equally important steps crucial for client success must be addressed in the systematic financial planning process:

1. Financial planning strategies, once chosen, must be integrated into a comprehensive (or modular) plan, and then presented as client recommendations. The case studies presented throughout this book provide examples of how strategies can be transformed into recommendations.

2. The plan and recommendations must be implemented. In some respects, this step in the process is the most important. Without implementation, the plan and recommendations are nothing more than a "hoped for" outcome.

3. Implemented recommendations must be monitored to ensure that a client is progressing toward the goals and that the plan and recommendations continue to be appropriately matched to the client's life and the economic, tax, and legal environments.

The purpose of this chapter is twofold. First, it presents a method by which client-specific recommendations developed in Step 3, as illustrated for each of the core content planning areas in Chapters 3 through 13, are prioritized, integrated, and funded for formulation into a comprehensive financial plan to present to the client. Second, a summary of Step 5, Implement the Plan; and Step 6, Monitor the Plan, Implementation, and Goal Progress; are presented.

## DEVELOPING CLIENT-BASED RECOMMENDATIONS: A QUICK REVIEW

Which financial planning strategies should a planner recommend to a client? In a perfect world, the answer is simple: Choose strategies that best meet the client's goals and objectives and implement each one. In practice, however, this approach is difficult to follow and seldom used. This is an impractical approach when a client's financial resources do not allow full and complete implementation. The procedure also fails when a client's goals conflict, or when the client does not accept some of the advisor's recommendations.

It is essential that client and planner be able to prioritize recommendations relative to the goals and objectives. Ranking goals and the associated recommendations may require a client to make difficult choices among planning needs that reflect personal wants, desires, and needs and advisor-recommended needs that the client may not have identified. This is particularly true for clients with insufficient assets, savings, and discretionary cash flow to fund all recommendations. Clients may need to grapple with questions such as, "Is retirement more important than funding my child's education?" and "Is funding a future goal more important than maintaining current lifestyle choices?" It is such dilemmas that suggest three important practices in the planning process:

1.  The advisor must have broad insight into the client's perspective to guide the formulation of the recommendations into a plan; this comes from knowing the client.

2.  That same knowledge of the client and the need to resolve planning dilemmas supports the practice of offering the client alternatives or options for goal achievement.

3.  When resources are limited and a client has multiple goals that are ranked similarly (e.g., retirement and education funding), it may be necessary for a financial planner to look for strategies that can be used to meet multiple goals.

For example, funding a Roth IRA is a strategy that can be used to meet a portion of an education funding need as well as a retirement objective. This strategy can be a powerful recommendation for a client with limited financial resources, assuming that the client has maximized any applicable employer match in a qualified retirement plan.

Central to the theme of recommendation development is the concept that a client's temperament, personality, preferences, attitudes, family history, financial knowledge, and experience must also be used to shape the recommendations. This information, which is typically gathered during the client data collection and discovery step of the financial planning process, plays a key role in helping determine which strategies might make the most effective recommendations. For example, assume that a client has a strong aversion to investing in gambling, alcohol, and tobacco stocks, and a decision must be made to recommend investing in either an index fund or a diversified socially screened mutual fund. In this situation, it is likely that the client's preference for a socially screened portfolio will outweigh other factors in the recommendation decision. (Formalizing these preferences in an investment policy statement would be an important approach to guide the financial planning process.)

It is also important for financial planners to take into account their own temperament, risk tolerance, personality, knowledge, experience, and biases when selecting strategies and making recommendations. It is very difficult for any planner to be totally objective and consider the client's goals and preferences exclusively. This is not to imply that planners are biased; each financial planner—like most other professionals—has preferred strategies. For example, some planners use variable universal life insurance as the primary tool in recommendations designed to help clients save for multiple financial goals. Other planners find the use of variable universal life insurance products inappropriate for the majority of their clientele. Rather than debate who is right or wrong, the best practice is for planners to know their clients and themselves. By acknowledging preferences and other factors, planners can be forthright in their communication with clients as well as their own assessment of the objectivity of their planning approach.

The idea that a client might not actually implement all recommendations sometimes comes as a surprise to those who have been trained using case study methodologies. In nearly all case studies, a client's situation lends itself to multiple "solutions" to satisfy a client's goals. The planner's recommendations might even include issues not identified by the client. The case study methodology gives students practice in the art (creativity) and science (analysis) of generating client-centered recommendations. It is common to find that case study clients have sufficient assets, savings, and discretionary cash flow to fund all goals and objectives—a characterization often not true of the "typical" client (depending on the business model of the planner). What students find difficult in such situations is prioritizing client needs and conceptualizing comprehensive and integrated plans—that the client can afford—to meet the needs. This can even be true of a modular plan, where implementation must be integrated into the client's current financial situation. In practice, however, few clients have sufficient financial resources to implement all recommendations.

In these situations, there are no definitive standards of practice to help a financial planner determine which strategies should be recommended to a client or in what priority recommendations should be ranked. An overriding question might be, "Which recommendation will potentially cause the most harm to the client if it is *not* implemented?" In many respects, these decisions result from professional judgment gained through study, experience, and personal knowledge applied to a client's unique character and situational factors.

The Recommendation Form, as part of the systematic planning process, helps planners focus on essential issues to include in an actionable recommendation. This useful planning tool summarizes the answers to the seven critical recommendation questions of *who, what, when, where, why, how,* and *how much* into one simple format. When initially identifying possible recommendations, the form is useful for summarizing and projecting the costs and benefits of the recommendations in meeting client goals. As the plan develops, it may be necessary to combine, sort, and rank recommendations from other core content planning areas, and the forms can quickly be revised for the costs and benefits of each recommendation. Once final, the forms can be used to document information for planning staff or to communicate with the client. Possibly one of the most beneficial uses of the form is documenting the titling of assets and beneficiary designations. Examples of completed Planning Recommendation Forms appear in Chapters 3 through 13 as a model for encapsulating the information necessary for each core content planning area.

# STEP 4: DEVELOP THE COMPREHENSIVE PLAN AND PRESENT THE RECOMMENDATIONS[2]

Just as the stroke of midnight separates yesterday from today, client-based recommendations are the outcome of Step 3 and the input for Step 4. Resolving the multiple issues inherent in even a simple comprehensive case involves the development and integration of recommendations from multiple strategies that originate from the core content planning areas. Strategies lead to recommendations, which lead to plans. But just as midnight balances yesterday and today, plans must balance on the axis between the **goal orientation** and **cash flow orientation** to planning, both of which ground the financial planning process in a client situation. In other words, the plan must balance equally the commitment to achieving the client's goals and the reality of the assets, or cash flow, available to fund those goals.

Attention to cash flow (which can include discretionary income as well as other available assets) ensures that the plan is realistic and affordable, both in the current planning period and projecting into the future. The goal orientation ensures that the plan represents the client's values, needs, and desires interpreted into their most important goals both now and in the future. As one goal is accomplished, a new goal can be identified and new recommendations initiated. Careful tracking of cash flow ensures that funding one goal does not expose the client to unwarranted risk or leave the client unprepared for unexpected negative financial consequences. Although it is important that the financial plan maximize and stabilize cash flow across the client's planning period, the significance of the goals motivates sustained client commitment. In summary, both a goal orientation and a cash flow orientation are necessary for a successful plan, yet neither can fully protect the client from the unknowns of life, which can derail even the best plan.

## Developing the Financial Plan

The constantly evolving relationship between planner and client grounds the financial planning process and plan development. Mutually agreed-on goals and client situational factors serve as the foundation of the analysis of each core content area and the identification of possible strategies. Using knowledge of the applicable strategies, the available funding sources (i.e., all sources of income, assets, employee benefits, inheritance), and the client situation, the planner proposes actionable client-based recommendations. These recommendations, the output of Step 3, are the input for Step 4, where they are manipulated and molded into a comprehensive plan or, when applicable and if multiple recommendations are made, into a targeted plan.

The development of the comprehensive plan occurs in response to the following three questions:

1. Given the client's planning needs, have all recommendations been identified and a preliminary priority assigned?

2. Given the client's planning needs, what are the impacts or consequences, beneficial and detrimental that could result from implementing all of the proposed recommendations?

3. Given the client's planning needs, are all proposed recommendations affordable from available discretionary cash flow, short-term or liquid savings, or other assets?

Answering these questions with confidence is a complex and intellectually challenging exercise that truly represents the professional judgment gained from experience. Repeated use of the forms and checklists in the systematic financial planning process provides a method to build the expertise to manage this dynamic part of the planning process. Some might assert that the forms are excessive, tedious, and perhaps even a waste of time. With experience, this could become increasingly true —until faced with an unusual or more complex client situation. For students and novice planners, the objective of the repeated use of the forms is to build the capacity —in both knowledge and skill—to offer financial planning advice confidently. This framework of professional proficiency, practiced consistently, will foster the almost reflexive ability to formulate well-crafted comprehensive financial plans for clients. Following is a discussion of the significance of each question and the related forms that guide the process.

## Have All Recommendations Been Identified and Prioritized?

The Recommendation Form, completed for each of the recommendations developed in Step 3 of the process, summarizes the answers to the seven critical questions (i.e., who, what, when, where, why, how, and how much) required for an actionable recommendation. The forms help planners quickly identify the cost and priority of each recommendation. It is helpful to have this valuable information easily accessible when comparing competing recommendations across the core content planning areas. Up to this point, these recommendations may have been considered only relative to other recommendations developed for a particular core content planning area. But to develop the plan, recommendations from one core content area (e.g., life insurance) must compete against recommendations from another core content area (e.g., education savings), assuming there is insufficient funding for all recommendations, as is often the case. Also, cost and priority can easily be revised as all of the recommendations are considered in relationship to each other.

Another form used in the systematic planning process, the Comprehensive Planning Checklist, challenges students and novice planners to carefully consider key questions related to each of the core content planning areas. In essence, this form, shown in Appendix 14A, helps answer the broader question, "Has anything been overlooked?"

Although these questions do not address comprehensive or sophisticated analysis of every client situation, they do challenge the planner to carefully consider key questions related to each of the core content planning areas. In essence, the form helps the user quickly complete a self-assessment of the planning process to ensure that oversights have not occurred. The form provides a framework for reviewing and summarizing a client's individual circumstances in each of the core planning areas, as well as fundamental interactions across planning areas, as represented by the "↔" symbol. It is impossible to encapsulate a process as broad and dynamic as financial planning in a simple form. This limitation cannot be overlooked. However, this form offers the advantage of focusing attention on the most common planning needs and patterns of interaction, whether developing a targeted or a comprehensive plan.

### What Are the Consequences of Implementing the Proposed Recommendations?

Just as financial planning recommendations are not made in a vacuum; neither do the projected consequences of implementing recommendations occur independently. Implementing one recommendation tends to have a ripple effect throughout a client's financial plan, as shown in Table 14.1, which summarizes some of the most common results, or financial interactions, that might be generated by frequently used recommendations. Because of the far-ranging effects of seemingly simple recommendations, it is important for financial planners to incorporate an **impact analysis** as part of the systematic planning process.

A review of these effects may suggest that additional strategies should be considered to meet the client's financial goals and objectives. Consider, for example, the relatively simple recommendation to purchase additional life insurance. If the insurance is owned by the insured who is also the client, or if the beneficiary is the estate of the insured, the insurance will be included in the client's gross estate. If the amount of the insurance is substantial, this inclusion could trigger an estate tax liability. In practice, a cross-impact analysis would indicate that the client ought to reconsider the ownership and titling of the insurance and/or take steps to resposition assets to reduce potential estate tax liabilities. Although there are strategies for changing ownership in the future, impact analysis encourages planners to be proactive and thorough in planning rather than reactive in the future.

**Table 14.1** Select Recommendations That Have Multiple Impacts on a Client's Financial Situation

| Recommendation | Potential Result |
|---|---|
| Refinance mortgage (results will vary depending on whether closing costs are/are not included or if cash is/is not taken) | 1. Change cash flow<br>2. Change net worth[a]<br>3. Change tax liability |
| Restructure debt | 1. Change cash flow<br>2. Change net worth<br>3. Change tax liability |
| Change federal tax withholding | 1. Change cash flow |
| Change state tax withholding | 1. Change cash flow |
| Reallocate non-qualified portfolio assets | 1. Change cash flow (only if earnings are not reinvested)<br>2. Change net worth[b]<br>3. Change tax liability |
| Liquidate non-qualified portfolio assets | 1. Change cash flow (only if earnings are not reinvested)<br>2. Possible change in net worth depending on how the assets are used [b]<br>3. Change tax liability |
| Increase retirement savings | 1. Change cash flow<br>2. Change net worth<br>3. Change tax liability<br>4. Change estate tax situation |
| Purchase additional life insurance | 1. Change cash flow<br>2. Possible change in net worth depending on type of insurance<br>3. Change estate tax situation |
| Retitle assets | 1. Change cash flow<br>2. Change net worth<br>3. Change tax liability<br>4. Change estate tax situation |
| Begin gift strategies | 1. Change cash flow<br>2. Change net worth<br>3. Change tax liability<br>4. Change estate tax situation |

[a] Assuming closing costs are paid from assets rather than current income.
[b] Transaction costs or sales charges may apply.

The Recommendation Impact Form offers a systematic method to verify that any potential interactions among the recommendations have not been overlooked. This form should be completed for each recommendation and then revised, if necessary, as final recommendations are determined. Should cash flow or other assets be insufficient for funding all recommendations, completing the Recommendation Impact Form shown in Exhibit 14.1 might help planners identify mutually exclusive recommendations that could be integrated and achieved by another multipurpose planning product or procedure. Use of the forms can also help students and novice planners *complicate* the planning process—not in the sense of making it more difficult, but in the sense of more broadly informing the planning process.

**Exhibit 14.1** Recommendation Impact Form

**Recommendation Impact Form**

**Recommendation:**

| Recommendation No. | | | | | |
|---|---|---|---|---|---|
| **Planner Decision** | Accept | | Reject | | Modify | |
| **Client Decision** | Accept | | Reject | | Modify | |

**Financial Impact**

| | |
|---|---|
| Annual impact on cash-flow ($) | |
| Immediate impact on net worth ($) | |

| Planning Issue | Degree of Significance | | | | Notes |
|---|---|---|---|---|---|
| | Major | Modest | Minor | None | |
| Financial situation—cash management | | | | | |
| Tax planning | | | | | |
| Life insurance planning | | | | | |
| Health insurance planning | | | | | |
| Disability insurance planning | | | | | |
| LTC insurance planning | | | | | |
| Property and liability insurance planning | | | | | |
| Investment planning | | | | | |
| Education or other special needs planning | | | | | |
| Retirement planning | | | | | |
| Estate planning | | | | | |
| Other planning need | | | | | |
| Other planning need | | | | | |

By seriously considering the impact of each recommendation on the other core content planning areas, as shown later in Exhibit 14.6 for Terry Meredith, planners can gain new insights into the client situation that otherwise might never have been considered. Likewise, if an advisor cannot reasonably and knowledgeably assess the impact of the recommendations, more research or consultation with other professionals may be warranted. As such, the systematic approach, which may justifiably be criticized for stifling creativity, could actually encourage a greater depth and range of thinking. Ultimately, it is important that a consistent approach be used to rank and order recommendations in a way that is comfortable for the advisor. To be effective, whatever approach is chosen must encourage the financial planning professional the freedom and responsibility to shift paradigms when analyzing and reviewing a client's situation.

Although integrating core financial planning content areas is beyond the scope of engagement of an advisor focused on single-issue analysis, whether offering advice or promoting product sales, the importance of the impact analysis should not be overlooked. Projecting the integration of all recommendations using impact analysis ensures financial planners that a client has enough discretionary cash flow and assets to fully fund—and continue funding—all recommendations. Furthermore, the impact analysis gives advisors another perspective on the logic and assumptions upon which a plan is based. The Planning Recommendation Form, the Comprehensive Planning Checklist, and the Impact Analysis Form can help planners fully integrate plan recommendations. The systematic approach depends on the repeated use of planning forms and protocols to guide and document the planning process. With repeated use, this process should become so routine that basic norms of practice will be established and applied with every client.

## Are All Proposed Recommendations Affordable?

In addition to the impact of the recommendations, funding them is another critical question that must be resolved before a plan can be finalized. Developing a plan is the culmination and integration of available cash flow and the goals most critical to a client. Although creative options may be available, generally planners and clients are limited to considering one or more of the following alternatives, which are summarized in Figure 14.2.

- Fully fund the most important recommendation in support of the goal determined by the planner and the client; prioritize other recommendations and corresponding goals or planning needs and apply the remaining funds.

- Agree to fund all recommendations, but stagger their implementation over a reasonable period of time that will not adversely affect the client's financial situation. This approach assumes that additional assets will become available to facilitate future funding as the result of an influx of income, assets, or the completion of goal funding, thus freeing up money to be redirected to another goal(s).

- Reconsider the recommendations and "downsize" or reduce one or more of the suggested funding alternatives so that all recommendations receive some funding.

- Review mutually exclusive recommendations that might be integrated and achieved through a different multipurpose planning product or procedure (e.g., a Roth IRA or life insurance).

- Prioritize the recommendations and goals, fund those that are most important, and eliminate or postpone other recommendations.

- Increase available funding for all or some of the recommendations. This might be done by reducing spending (for goods, services, or debt) or by increasing personal income, liquidating assets, or reallocating other assets for higher earnings.

**Figure 14.2** Alternative Options for Funding Recommendations

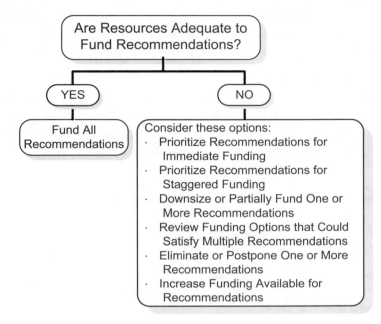

The priority for funding usually centers on the recommendations that most closely match a client's goals or that provide protection from the greatest perceived risk of loss. Complementary recommendations that can be used to meet more than one goal might also emerge as a priority. For instance, recommending that a client fund a Roth IRA can serve the dual goals of saving for retirement and a child's college expenses.

Although comprehensive plans are more complex, the synthesis of goals and funding strategies applies to both comprehensive and targeted (or modular) plans. The same is true of analysis in support of product sales, because a client must be convinced that the product fulfills a recognized need or goal *and* is worthy of funding. Planner and client could face an either/or situation that hinges on the availability of discretionary cash flow or other assets to fund recommendations. If funding is insufficient, the planner, working from knowledge of the client situation or directly with the client, must conduct a cost-benefit analysis to determine the best use of available funds relative to the proposed "ideal" recommendations.

**Cash flow and net worth tracking.** Concurrent with considering the impact of recommendations and funding alternatives is a planner's responsibility to diligently track the financial effects of proposed recommendations. A financial plan is contingent on the availability of discretionary cash flow, savings, or other available assets to actually fund the recommendations. As such, there is one absolute rule that successful financial planners must incorporate into their professional practices. In addition to thoroughly and objectively justifying the choice of recommendations in a client's plan, planners must also clearly explain to the client how costs associated with the plan can be funded. One way to ensure that all recommendations can be implemented is to track cash flow and asset changes concurrently as recommendations are determined.

An effective way to monitor funding is to use a cash flow and savings tracker, which can be easily developed using Excel™. A completed form, shown in Exhibit 14.2, illustrates how this planning tool can be used to document the effects of each recommendation on cash flow and net worth. The tracker's principal purpose is to help advisors document that sufficient cash flow, savings, and assets are available to implement recommendations.

**Exhibit 14.2** Available Cash Flow and Other Assets Tracker Form

| | | | Annual Cash Flow Tracker | | | | |
|---|---|---|---|---|---|---|---|
| | | | | | Running Balances | | |
| Recommendation | (Cost)/ Benefit | Frequency (single/annual) | Discretionary Cash Flow ($1,300) | Monetary Assets $9,500 | Other Assets $42,000 | Liabilities $12,000 | Net Worth $39,500 |
| Payment savings from mortgage refinance | $2,800 | A | $2,800 | $0 | $0 | $0 | $0 |
| | | | $1,500 | $9,500 | $42,000 | $12,000 | $39,500 |
| Pay mortgage closing costs | ($1,300) | S | $0 | $0 | ($1,300) | $0 | ($1,300) |
| | | | $1,500 | $9,500 | $40,700 | $12,000 | $38,200 |
| Pay-off credit card debt | ($12,000) | S | $0 | $0 | ($12,000) | ($12,000) | $0 |
| | | | $1,500 | $9,500 | $28,700 | $0 | $38,200 |
| Payment savings from paying off credit card debt | $5,900 | A | $5,900 | $0 | $0 | $0 | $0 |
| | | | $7,400 | $9,500 | $28,700 | $0 | $38,200 |
| Purchase life insurance | ($1,000) | A | ($1,000) | $0 | $0 | $0 | $0 |
| | | | $6,400 | $9,500 | $28,700 | $0 | $38,200 |
| Increase education funding | ($4,400) | A | ($4,400) | $0 | $4,400 | $0 | $4,400 |
| | | | $2,000 | $9,500 | $33,100 | $0 | $42,600 |
| Take $2,000 out of savings and contribute to an IRA | ($2,000) | S | $0 | ($2,000) | $2,000 | $0 | $0 |
| | | | $2,000 | $7,500 | $35,100 | $0 | $42,600 |
| **Final Balance** | | | **$2,000** | **$7,500** | **$35,100** | **$0** | **$42,600** |
| **Aggregate Change** | | | **$3,300** | **($2,000)** | **($6,900)** | **($12,000)** | **$3,100** |

In this example, the client begins the financial planning process with a discretionary cash flow equal to –$1,300. In other words, the client was "short" more than $100 per month, which probably contributed to the credit card debt of $12,000. The client has "unallocated" savings equal to $3,000 and another $42,000 in unallocated assets in a money market account and miscellaneous investments. Unallocated funds are those not specifically designated for goal accomplishment, other than for an emergency fund or other savings.

Initially, the planner recommends that the client refinance the mortgage. This results in a $2,800 per year decrease in expenses (ignoring any income tax changes, and assuming that the refinancing will not subject the client to the Alternative Minimum Tax). The decrease in annual expense flows directly to the client's discretionary cash flow, which is now a positive $1,500 (–$1,300 + $2,800). However, refinancing the mortgage also results in $1,300 in closing costs, which is paid from unallocated assets. This reduces the assets available for other purposes to $40,700. Implementing an immediate payoff of the credit cards further reduces unallocated assets by $12,000 to $28,700. Implementation of the recommendation also results in a $5,900 increase in discretionary cash flow because the client will no longer be making monthly credit card payments. This brings the available discretionary cash flow balance to a total of $7,400.

Purchasing life insurance at an annual cost of $1,000 and savings of $4,000 annually for a college fund further reduces available cash flow to $2,000. The planner and client agreed that maintaining such flexibility is important for the household. Implementing a recommendation to reallocate the $2,000 of unallocated savings toward retirement reduces that account from $3,000 to $1,000. The client now has enough cash flow, savings, and assets to implement all recommendations but will utilize $2,000 of the unallocated savings and more than $13,000 in unallocated assets. Projected final balances equal $2,000 for available annual cash flow, $1,000 of unallocated savings, and a remaining balance of $28,700 ignoring any applicable taxes or transaction costs.

As noted, the cash flow tracker is a useful tool to confirm that sufficient cash flow, savings, and assets are available to implement recommendations. And, if several recommendations are competing for funding, both the Recommendation Form and the Available Cash Flow and Other Assets Tracker Form can be modified easily to reflect final recommendation features. Once finalized, the forms can be used to document this information for planning staff or to communicate information to the client. The Recommendation Forms are useful to summarize and project the costs and benefits of individual recommendations to meet client goals. The Tracker Form is an effective tool for communicating the costs of individual recommendations—and the entire plan—to the client.

In the simplest sense, a plan must provide a realistic and workable road map for the actions required, immediately and in the future, to give the client the greatest likelihood of protecting and growing assets. One of the most effective ways to motivate client action involves systematically summarizing recommendations so that implementation does not seem overwhelming. An Implementation Checklist bridges the gap between tracking the financial implications of the plan and summarizing the information needed to describe and implement each recommendation. As such, the Implementation Checklist provides an abridged plan that can be a useful reference for planning staff and client.

An Implementation Checklist that summarizes all recommendations is a useful tool in both modular and comprehensive plans. However, checklists can also be completed for each core content planning area or for specific segments of time. For example, a client with staggered goals or goals with staggered or changing funding schedules might best be served by having one checklist for each of several six-month periods. And in some instances one comprehensive checklist may suffice, contingent on the complexity of the plan or the client's role in implementing it. An Implementation Checklist for Doug and Emily is shown in Exhibit 14.3. It summarizes five recommendations for Doug and Emily by using the framework of the seven key questions to guide recommendations and their subsequent implementation. Changes to Doug and Emily's cash flow and net worth situation are also explained. A realistic and defensible summary of projected results can motivate and sustain client action—and provide a valuable foundation for writing a plan.

**Exhibit 14.3** Implementation Checklist for Doug & Emily Miscatt

**Implementation Checklist for Doug & Emily Miscatt**

| Recommendation (What) | Who | When | Where | Why | How | Cash Flow Impact | Net Worth Impact (How Much) |
|---|---|---|---|---|---|---|---|
| Refinance your home mortgage at 5.875% for 25 years. | Doug and Emily | Start the process this week; interest rates are volatile. | First National Bank offers this loan with no points and $1,300 in closing costs. | Refinancing your mortgage will increase your monthly/yearly cash flow. | Meet with Tommy Links to complete the mortgage application or use the online application portal. Sell $1,300 of XYX Mutual Fund. No taxes will be paid because of carry-over losses. | + $2,800 | -$1,300 |
| Pay off all credit card balances. | Doug and Emily | Within the month | Discover and Best Buy | This will eliminate high-interest debt by using liquid, low-earning assets to increase your cash flow. | Sell $12,000 of XYX Mutual Fund to pay the balances on your Discover and Best Buy cards. No taxes will be paid because of carry-over losses. Pay any outstanding balances each month. | + $5,900 | None |
| Purchase a $75,000 whole-life policy for Doug. | Doug and Emily | Within the next 6 weeks | With the Cia and Associates Insurance Brokerage | This will provide permanent life insurance in response to Doug's concerns over family health history and financial risk. | Meet with an insurance professional at Cia & Associates Insurance Brokerage to complete the application. | ($1,000) | None |
| Increase your quarterly contribution by an additional $1,100. | Doug and Emily | Time of the next quarterly payment | With the existing Anystate 529 Savings Plan | This will allow you to meet your goal of having $50,000 saved for Freddy's education. | Increase the amount of your quarterly check or electronic payment to $2,500. | ($4,400) | +$4,400 |
| Total Impact of Recommendations on Cash Flow and Net Worth | | | | | | +$3,300 | +$3,100 |
| Discretionary Cash Flow after Implementing Recommendations | | | | | | $2,000 | |
| Net Worth after Implementing Recommendations | | | | | | $42,600 | |

## The Plan—Modular, Targeted, or Comprehensive

Conceptualization of a plan may require planners to analyze competing recommendations, strategies, goals, or other client-specific information to formulate the most cost-effective, risk-adjusted plan for meeting a client's needs. What appeared initially, or in isolation, to be the best recommendation may subsequently have to be modified or abandoned when considered in relation to all other planning recommendations, needs, restrictions, or choices. Ultimately, every financial plan evolves from this linear yet more realistic recursive process.

One of the challenges facing planners who write comprehensive financial plans is how to account for the integrative nature of recommendations, implementation, and monitoring in the plan. The analysis, recommendations, and projected outcomes must be completely integrated into each individual section of the plan as well as across all core content planning areas. A sample outline of a comprehensive plan is shown in Exhibit 14.4; for an explanation and examples of the entries in the outline, see Chapter 9 in *The Process of Financial Planning: Developing a Financial Plan, Second Edition.*

Targeted financial plans, focused on only one or two goals, are less challenging, but they still must clearly communicate analysis, recommendations, and projected outcomes. Regardless of the type of plan prepared, it must clearly reflect a client's situational factors and goals. In other words, the plan must resonate with the individuality of the client and be adaptable to the client's financial lifestyle. That is not to say that changes in the client's financial situation will not be warranted or recommended, but that the changes must be in alignment with the client's ability to cope with and implement the changes.

When writing a plan, the following suggestions may be helpful:

1. Describe the current situation for each of the core content areas as if no other recommendations have been made or implemented.

3. Present all recommendations within a core content section (e.g., the retirement planning section) on the basis of the current situation analysis.

2. Describe alternatives or alternative outcomes in client circumstances where a recommendation in one core content area is based on the implementation of a recommendation in another core content area. For example, show alternative recommendations and alternative outcomes when education funding is done with or without gifting from grandparents.

4. Conclude a plan by illustrating a client's projected situation assuming all recommendations are implemented.

**Exhibit 14.4** Sample Outline for a Comprehensive Financial Plan

I. Cover Page

II. Letter to Client

III. Copy of the Original Client Engagement Letter

IV. Table of Contents

V. Other Introductory Materials (optional)
   a. Mission/vision statement
   b. Statement of principles or core values
   c. Ethics statement, privacy statement
   d. Review of assumptions
   e. Investment policy statement

VI. Client Profile, Summary of Goals and Assumptions

VII. Executive Summary or Observations and Recommendations

VIII. Individual Core Content Planning Sections
   a. Cash flow analysis
   b. Net worth analysis
   c. Tax analysis
   d. Insurance/risk management analysis
      i. Life insurance
      ii. Health and disability insurance
      iii. Long-term care insurance
      iv. Property and liability insurance
      v. Umbrella insurance
      vi. Other insurance needs
   e. Investment analysis
   f. Retirement analysis
   g. Estate planning analysis
   h. Specialized analyses
      i. Education funding
      ii. Planning for special needs
      iii. Refinancing scenarios
      iv. Saving for special objectives

IX. Implementation and Monitoring Section

X. Client Acceptance Letter or Client Engagement Letter

XI. Appendices
   a. Calculations and projections
   b. Educational materials

The fourth rule implies that a reanalysis and recalculation of certain client data should occur. Minimally, the following information should be recalculated to project the client's financial situation in one year (or some other time frame), assuming that recommendations are implemented:

- Available discretionary cash flow;

- Net worth balance;

- Income tax situation; and

- Estate tax situation (when applicable).

Recalculating these measures to reflect projected outcomes is another way to motivate clients. For instance, if a client can be shown that refinancing debt, reallocating portfolio assets, purchasing additional forms of insurance, and implementing other recommendations will result in positive outcomes, it is more likely that the client will take action. Revised cash flow, net worth, income tax, and estate tax projections can be included as a separate section in the plan or in an appendix, perhaps titled *Key Financial Measures in 20XX* to reflect projected status one year in the future. Some financial planners incorporate future projections (tabular or graphic) for each core content planning area of the plan. Different time frames coordinated to the individual goal or planning need can be used to project the short-, intermediate-, or long-term impact of the successfully implemented recommendation(s) on the client's future.

Either approach helps clients grasp how recommendations are integrative within a plan, and to see the potential impact of financial planning. However, it is extremely important that any projections include appropriate disclaimers (e.g., "past performance is no guarantee of future returns," "all projections are based on historical data, which may not be reflected in future returns," "projections are hypothetical") so as not to mislead clients or give the impression of guaranteed returns or outcomes. Other disclaimers include reminders to the client that "This plan is based on data provided by the client as of [specified date]" or "Please consult your tax or legal professional for assistance in reviewing and implementing these recommendations."

## Presenting the Plan

Although advocates for the profession of financial planning have worked hard to dissociate financial *planning* from *selling*, in reality sales and marketing skills are integral to an advisor's success. The planner actually is selling something, explicitly or implicitly, from the obvious (i.e., financial advice, products, or services) to something more subtle (i.e., client education or a suggested change in a client's attitudes, money scripts, or behaviors). Regardless of a planner's business model, the presentation to a client is the opportunity to "close the deal" for both advisor and client. Without revenue, a planner cannot remain in business, but without plannning advice, products, or services, the client's life could also be very different.

A well-designed plan is the foundation of an effective presentation to clients. Such plans and presentations are easier for clients to understand and more likely to motivate client action. Good presentations are the result of effective communication (involving both verbal and nonverbal communication skills as well as the written and graphic messages in the plan, handouts, or PowerPoint), thorough preparation, and genuine concern for the client. The planner, in the roles of advisor, educator, and mediator, must offer explanations to engage the client and empower the client to make decisions about plan alternatives. As these decisions are resolved, a final plan will emerge for the client's acceptance. Training and experience are critical to successful client presentations that motivate action by *projecting* but not *promising* results.

Ultimately, the decision rests with the client. If a client decides on a course of action contrary to the plan, or if rejected recommendations could potentially jeopardize the client's financial situation in the future or raise questions about the professional judgment of the planner, a liability release signed by the client should be considered. Ultimately, this stage of the planning process should end with a realistic plan for achieving the client's financial and life goals and lay the foundation for what could potentially be a long-term planner-client relationship.

To build such a relationship, clients and planners are best served by unbiased presentations that acknowledge that tax, legislative, economic, or personal life-changing events positively or negatively affect planning projections. Periodic reviews and adjustments (i.e., monitoring) offers clients the greatest likelihood of reaching financial goals. How to maintain and foster that relationship by implementing and monitoring the plan is the focus of Steps 5 and 6.

## STEP 5: IMPLEMENT THE PLAN

**Implementation** refers to putting a recommendation into action. Sometimes the financial planner performs the action or coordinates implementation, and at other times the client or other professionals direct implementation. Without a thorough, defensible, and easily understood description of how each recommendation can be implemented, it is likely that some clients will fail to do so, or fail to be convinced by the recommendations. Some advisors argue that providing clients with a reasonable implementation plan could, in fact, be the most important part of a financial plan.

Implementation hinges on three key interrelated factors. First, recommendations need to be put in place—that is, action must be taken. A financial plan that is not implemented is of little value to anyone. Second, it is essential that a client have the financial capacity to implement recommendations. Where monies to fund a recommendation should come from, or where cash assets should be deposited, has to be clearly identified. Finally, the effects of implementation on a client's discretionary cash flow and net worth situation ought to be shown. Students and novice planners can avoid oversights by using the seven questions in the systematic financial planning process to guide recommendations and implementation.

### Who Should Implement the Recommendation? What Should Be Done? Where Should It Be Done?

Once a planner and client agree on a plan, implementation begins. A recommendation is only as good as the planner's, client's, or other professionals' ability—working together or independently—to effectively implement it. In the simplest terms, *who* will do *what*, and *where* should it be done? Depending on the planner's business model and the products or services offered, plan implementation approaches differ among planners, and perhaps even across clients served by the same planner. Some advisors will take most, if not all, of the responsibility for carrying out various aspects of the plan and ask little of the client (assuming such authority is granted). Other planners will inform or assist the client, who has primary responsibility for executing some or all of the recommendations.

Some recommendations might require clients to work with professionals with whom they have an existing relationship (e.g., an insurance agent, broker, or banker), and other recommendations will require the forging of new relationships. Providing clients with a professional referral is one method to help a client move from recognition that action needs to be taken to actually implementing recommendations. If referrals are made, clients should be notified if fees are shared between the planner and consulting professionals. Planners often consider themselves the hub of a wheel as they facilitate plan implementation in collaboration with the client and multiple other parties (e.g., the client's accountant, attorney, trust administrator, or personal assistant).

In conjunction with the question of *who* are the issues of *what* and *where*. The latter may refer, literally, to the place a client must go to access the provider of a recommended product or service (e.g., a URL or mailing address). *What* represents the variety of traditional insurance, investment, retirement, and other ancillary financial planning products and services that emanate from the strategies identified in Step 5 to a wide range of concierge services. For example, some planners provide high-net-worth clients a variety of time- and money-saving services (e.g., shopping and negotiating transportation or mortgages, or handling routine bill payment for themselves or extended family members).

*What*, in this instance, can also refer to the client information that may be shared with other professionals, contingent on client disclosure agreements or the scope of the agreement giving the advisor the authority to act on the client's behalf. In some instances, the client will be the go-between among all of the financial service providers. In other cases, the client will sign a disclosure document that allows the financial planner to contact other providers (e.g., tax preparer, lawyer, trust administrator) directly. Such situations require the utmost care and trust in the planner-client relationship, and the boundaries of authority must be clearly documented.

## Why Should It Be Done? When Should the Recommendation Take Place?

Regardless of the range of the advisor's products or services or whether the client is solely or partly responsible for implementing recommendations, ultimately the actual implementation rests with the client. Although it is often assumed that clients acting in their own best interest will put plans into action, this is not always the case. The implementation issues of *why* and *when* can become inextricably intertwined. Regardless of the reason for inaction, lack of implementation is the single greatest deterrent to meeting financial goals. Therefore, it is imperative that planners take steps to examine—and in some cases supervise or facilitate—the timeliness and effectiveness of client implementation if such responsibilities are part of their business plan and the engagement agreed to with the client.

One of an advisor's primary goals is to use the plan and its presentation effectively to educate and motivate the client regarding (1) *why* the recommendations are viable solutions to the client's concerns and (2) *when* implementation should occur to best meet the client's objective in a timely manner. Because a client pays for a plan does not mean that the client is motivated to act. It may be necessary to remind the client that, without proper implementation, the ability to reach long-term financial goals is jeopardized. Other clients may know logically *why* they should implement, but emotional or other barriers (e.g., fear, lack of time or knowledge, or avoidance of difficult decisions) could be significant deterrents to *when* they implement. Recall that temperament, personality, beliefs, attitudes, and money scripts are significant influences in a client's financial life.

Keeping clients motivated to take action in the short term and over the longer term is a trait that separates the best planners from the rest. Furthermore, it takes careful attention to detail to keep the implementation and outcome of a plan on track. For example, it is important that clients realize and commit—both intellectually and personally—to the complexities of implementation. It is equally important to acknowledge that the implementation of the recommendation and the fulfillment of the goal may occur in different time frames, as outlined in the following examples:

- Immediate implementation and immediate completion (e.g., filing a change-of-beneficiary form for a retirement account).

- Immediate implementation and delayed completion (e.g., opening a § 529 plan and contributing $500 per month for the next five years to fund the client's education goal).

- Delayed implementation and immediate completion (e.g., opening a flexible spending account and changing the health insurance plan during the next open enrollment six months in the future).

- Delayed implementation and delayed completion (e.g., increasing retirement savings by $500 per month in five years once § 529 funding is completed).

The meaning of "immediate or delayed implementation" is fairly obvious, but the meaning of "immediate or delayed completion" is not as transparent. A goal that is completed immediately, such as paying off credit card debt, suggests that there is very little or no continuous action needed to achieve the desired result. However, if the results require periodic or continuous action and/or monitoring, then the goal should be categorized as a delayed-completion goal. Typically this type of goal requires more commitment and effort by both client and planner to see through to fruition.

## How Should Implementation Take Place? How Much Should Be Purchased, Saved, and Invested to Implement the Recommendation?

The final two implementation issues are *how* and *how much*. Often the best answers to these practical and perhaps technical issues are convenience and cost. These queries may appear simplistic given the range of business models, recommendations, and products and services available, but cost and convenience are important regardless of how implementation is handled. One of the most effective ways to motivate client action involves systematically summarizing recommendations so that implementation can be easily understood and accomplished. The use of an implementation checklist, as explained earlier, can guide implementation within each core content area, across different periods of time, or as a comprehensive summary of the entire plan. Another way to motivate action is to create specific to-do lists for clients. Altfest[3] suggests that after a **to-do list** is delivered to a client it be followed soon thereafter with a follow-up phone call from someone on the planner's staff to ask whether the client had any difficulty in taking action. In this way, a client can be motivated to take action to report back that a recommendation was successfully implemented.

Financial planners are often adept at answering *how much*, but frequently they are much less comfortable with helping clients address the fears and concerns associated with *how*. The results of the client goal analysis, built on defensible assumptions and sound analytical approaches, will yield an answer to the question of *how much should be purchased, saved or invested*. The planner's technical knowledge and the implementation checklist can provide the client with concise implementation instructions for *how* to put the recommendations into action. Note, however, that fears and concerns about *how* may have a more significant impact on the client than even an experienced advisor recognizes at first.

Explicitly, a client may be apprehensive about having insufficient financial knowledge, experience, or perseverance to implement the plans. Implicitly, the client's fears or attitudes about money could be a source of anxiety. What an advisor might interpret as reluctance to implement could actually be the client's lack of confidence to implement—regardless of the amount of income available or the logical benefit to the client. At this juncture of the financial planning process, advisor sensitivity to the impact of these client situational factors is an important first step toward gaining the skill and confidence needed to explore these issues with clients. Such efforts to fully understand and respect the client's issues contribute to a more trusting planner-client relationship.

Managing client expectations is another area of concern to planners. Too often a client assumes that if the plan is executed perfectly, the planner's recommendations will result in the projected outcome—with no deviations. But the client may not fully understand that the planner (1) built the recommendation on the best (but imperfect) information available at the time; (2) used professional judgment to determine the best (but not foolproof) course of action; and (3) framed both the action and the expected outcome on the basis of mutually agreed-upon assumptions (some of which could ultimately prove invalid). Managing client expectations when implementing and monitoring a plan hinges on three important concepts:

1. The client must acknowledge that the plan is based on the information provided to the planner; consequently, withholding relevant information, giving "socially acceptable" answers, or otherwise knowingly or unknowingly misleading the advisor will result in an unsound plan.

2. The client must be fully informed of the function and formulation of hypothetical projections in the financial planning process.

3. The client must be educated about financial trends and economic issues to provide a valid and reliable context for gauging plan results.

The latter can be accomplished through planner-client interactions, such as periodic monitoring meetings, newsletters, or Web site postings. These also provide opportunitis for an advisor to continue to assist and motivate the client to *act in the client's best interest*.

# STEP 6: MONITOR THE PLAN, IMPLEMENTATION, AND GOAL PROGRESS

Sometimes it is easy to lose track of *why* a financial plan was written. The real reason that clients need a comprehensive financial plan is to ensure that their short-, intermediate-, and long-term financial goals are met. Only by looking at how all components of a client's financial life fit together can a full picture of financial threats, opportunities, and successes be drawn. Likewise, whether or not a client is on target to meet goals can be determined only by tracking and monitoring client outcomes. Monitoring a client's situation enables a planner to determine the client's progress toward goals as well as the client's response to other economic or personal/life event changes. Continued monitoring also affords an opportunity for financial planners to add value to the planner-client relationship by helping clients respond to situations, reduce anxiety, and feel in control of and confident about their financial situation. The sixth and final step involves ongoing monitoring of:

- the *plan* as a malleable element in a client's life responsive to the client's changing situation and goals;

- the *effectiveness of the plan* as a comprehensive approach to meeting a client's needs in the current regulatory, economic, tax, and market environments;

- the *implementation* of the recommendations to date;

- the viability of the *products and services* incorporated into the implementation and their continued usefulness to meet the client's needs; and

- the *outcomes* associated with the recommendations and the progress toward goal achievement.

It is important to recognize that monitoring can incorporate periodic evaluation or ongoing review of products and services. The extent of these monitoring activities—whether periodic or ongoing—varies with the advisor's business model and agreed-on engagement with the client. However monitoring is conducted, this last step in the financial planning process is important for several reasons:

1. Monitoring compels a planner to stay in touch with a client to assess how well the plan is meeting the client's life and financial goals and objectives. Proactive planners will try to anticipate their clients' changing needs and facilitate dialogue to identify potential responses. It is equally important to encourage clients to proactively initiate questions in response to changing wants, needs, life cycle events, or life transitions (e.g., planning in anticipation of a divorce; a marriage, with or without a prenuptial agreement; or the birth of a child). Periodic contact from a planner can motivate a client to continue to take action or initiate changes, which can benefit the client's financial situation as well as the advisor from a continuous revenue stream.

2. Periodic monitoring of a client's situation ensures that previously made recommendations, products, and services are still appropriate and useful for the client's situation. A client's needs, attitudes, or capacity to fund goals can change dramatically. It is essential, therefore, that a planner who is engaged

by a client on a long-term basis periodically monitor both quantitative data and qualitative, or situational, life issues.. Examples of quantitative product criteria for review include product and provider performance, product and provider ratings, fees and expenses, and other features unique to the product in question, such as the need for portfolio rebalancing.

3.  Monitoring keeps planner and client on track to (1) make time-sensitive changes in response to the client's need or changes in the economy, the stock market, or taxes; (2) determine how implemented recommendations, and the underlying products, have affected (or are affecting) other areas of the client's financial plan; or (3) implement recommendations that were delayed until a future date (e.g., redirecting funds from a § 529 plan to retirement savings because a college savings goal has been met). In this respect, monitoring involves assessing the cross-impact of one recommendation on other areas of a client's financial situation after implementation, just as they were projected before implementation.

4.  Monitoring provides an opportunity for planner and client to celebrate what has been accomplished.  Despite the professionalism required of planner-client relationships, often there is a genuine personal relationship and mutual concern for the well-being of planner and client. Monitoring activities foster that relationship and provide an opportunity to express appreciation.

Monitoring is multifaceted and integrative. Few aspects of a financial plan can be evaluated in isolation, even when considering a core content planning area. Significant changes to a plan may entail reevaluation of a client's planning needs or priorities, including analysis of the client's situation, identification of prospective strategies, and development and presentation of recommendations. Depending on the extent of the changes, new recommendations may be needed for an isolated goal or core content planning area, or for several goals integrated across multiple areas of the plan. Without consistent monitoring, a client's plan can inadvertently become obsolete, and an obsolete plan defeats the purpose of proactive planning.

With an understanding of *what* this step of the systematic financial planning process entails and *when* monitoring should occur, it is important to consider *who* does monitoring. Monitoring can be the responsibility of

- the client;

- the planner, or the planner in coordination with other product or service providers (recall the idea of the planner as the hub of  the wheel that coordinates implementation and monitoring);

- a variety of product or service providers with no coordination; or

- no one.

The advisor's business model and scope of the established planner-client relationship generally set the parameters for monitoring, which can vary widely.  Some aspects of monitoring pertain only to planners who are soliciting an ongoing relationship (i.e., for services, products, or servicing products) with their clients. Some advisors are consistently involved with their clients, offering counsel on how to achieve financial and life goals. For planners who conduct their practices on a medical model (i.e., with a treat-as-needed approach), or for these creating modular plans (e.g., on a single problem, issue, or core content planning area), monitoring is beyond the scope of the planner-client engagement. The planner may not have the opportunity to follow up with a client because implementation and monitoring are the client's responsibility and the client may or may not re-engage the advisor for to review and evaluate progress. In a more sales-based or product-delivery type model, service may not include monitoring of the situation once a product is sold to meet a specific need. Monitoring may be limited to periodic review of the client's progress on a multiple-year schedule.

For the greatest likelihood of client success, a financial plan must be responsive to change. The plan must mature in concert with the client and the life cycle progression just as it must be responsive to unforeseen events or the need for different products or services. Failure to monitor the implementation and results of the recommendations is inconsistent with the intent of the financial planning process. Unfortunately, though, that is sometimes the case and likely detrimental to client and advisor, both of whom are missing opportunities. During the monitoring stage a good planner can demonstrate the value-added benefit of the planner-client relationship. But this requires that both the personal relationship and business relationships between planner and client support such a trust-based exchange.

## CHAPTER-BASED CASE STUDY

There are multiple ways to move from strategy development to client recommendations. Over time, every financial planner develops a unique approach to solving the planning puzzle. The following example illustrates how one financial planner worked through the complex process of recommendation development using a combination of experience, knowledge, and professional judgment.

Terry Meredith was watching television when an advertisement caught his attention. The message encouraged viewers to think about recent changes in their lives. Examples included buying or selling a home, getting married or divorced, having a child, or changing jobs. The message was clear: viewers who had experienced a life-changing event were encouraged to reconsider their life insurance needs. The advertisement went on to state that "buying term and investing the difference" was an ideal solution for many consumers.

Terry took the advertisement to heart as he thought about how his life had changed over the past few months, and even more over the past few years. He had recently purchased a new home with a 30-year mortgage of $300,000. He knew he needed more insurance protection and was intrigued by the idea of buying a term policy while making investments in another account. He knew it was time to call his financial advisor to pursue the idea—and tell him about the new house.

Mario Belmonte, Terry's comprehensive financial planner, was pleased to receive a call from Terry. They set up an appointment for later in the week. In preparation for the meeting, Mario reviewed Terry's client information file and identified some key pieces of information that Mario needed to update.

After a short time of chatting about the new house and how much Terry and his son Brady were enjoying their weekends and holidays there, Terry got right to the point to explain why he had called. First, he was worried that if he were to die, Brady would lose his father and a home that he had come to love. Terry realized that a teenager did not need his own house, but in a few years, Brady would be a young adult. Second, Terry wanted to make sure that if something happened to him, all of his debts would be paid so that Brady would receive as much inheritance as possible. When Terry saw the life insurance advertisement touting the advantages of buying term and investing the difference, he thought that this strategy might be the way to expand his investments while protecting assets for his son.

As Terry and Mario talked, Mario made the following observations:

- Terry, a nonsmoker, is age 37 and in excellent health. He is divorced with no plans for remarriage.

- Annual gross salary is approximately $220,000 per year in total income, with $15,000 to $20,000 fluctuations possible from year to year.

- Terry has one child, Brady, age 10.

- Terry has been saving steadily for retirement in his 401(k). In addition, he has an ample emergency fund and appoximately $10,000 in unallocated savings.

- Terry reports a moderate level of risk tolerance.

- Terry's life insurance coverage consists of $200,000 in 20-year term coverage with 15 years remaining. The insurance premium is $400 per year. Terry's employer offers only $100,000 of life insurance coverage.

Terry and Mario have been working together for a number of years. Mario initially prepared Terry's financial plan following Terry's divorce. Over time, Mario has helped Terry increase his discretionary cash flow, decrease his tax liabilities, save for retirement, and protect assets and future income through insurance. For example, about three years ago, Mario recommended a modified own-occupation disability plan that Terry subsequently purchased. When they first started working together, Mario conducted a life insurance needs analysis and determined that Terry required approximately $200,000 in additional coverage. The majority of Terry's need was based on his mortgage at the time, student loan debt, and the desire to leave an inheritance for Brady. Overall, Mario has enjoyed working with Terry because Terry seems to value his advice and he has assets and income that make implementation of recommendations possible.

Mario agreed that buying a term life insurance policy might be the best solution for Terry, but Mario also explained that he wanted to explore some other strategies as well. Mario knew that a solid analytical approach had appealed to Terry in the past. In many ways, Terry was seeking confirmation of the strategy and wanted an answer that fit with the remainder of his financial planning situation. Terry trusted Mario to be sure that nothing was overlooked. Mario was certain that he could help Terry. They agreed to meet the following week.

Mario began his analysis by updating Terry's life insurance needs calculation. This included updating the mortgage and other debt information, as well as some other projections regarding Brady's education costs. Mario determined that Terry needed an additional $250,000 in life insurance that would cover Terry's life for at least 10 years or longer.

Mario quickly generated a preliminary list of life insurance alternatives and mulled over the advantages and disadvantages associated with term, whole-life, universal life, variable life, and variable universal life policies. Mario used his knowledge of Terry's situation to begin eliminating potential solutions. For example, he knew that Terry was relatively young with a moderate level of risk tolerance. Based on this, he eliminated whole-life insurance as a solution. Whole-life, while very stable, would not meet Terry's need for obtaining a rate of return higher than the conservative return that would be generated on this type of investment. Variable life insurance was ruled out because of Terry's fluctuating income. A variable policy could be a drag on his cash flow and offer no premium flexibility.

After this process of strategy elimination, Mario arrived at three possible solutions:

1.  A 20-year term life policy, using a "buy term and invest the difference" strategy;

2.  A universal life (UL) policy; or

3.  A variable universal life (VUL) policy.

Mario knew that any life insurance recommendation for Terry would have to be both reasonable and affordable. The term insurance strategy provided Terry with the lowest absolute costs, as Mario obtained a quote of $640 per year for a 20-year, $250,000 term policy. Mario knew that a "buy term and invest the difference" solution worked best when the client was disciplined and committed to saving the difference between the cost of the term insurance and the cost of cash value insurance. Mario was confident that Terry would do this, given how carefully he had followed Mario's initial advice to reduce debt following the divorce while at the same time increasing savings. Terry had persistently followed the plan, while calmly coping with a very stressful and emotional time following the divorce.

Mario also knew that even though Terry was not anxious about financial decisions, he was cautious and wanted to be well prepared. As an added precaution, Mario recommended that the term policy include a waiver of premium for disability and a guaranteed renewability rider so that Terry could continue protection with either eventuality. Mario suspected that Terry would judge the additional cost to be worth the protection, but he would provide quotes with and without the riders for Terry's consideration.

The UL insurance strategy offered the benefit of flexibility in the insurance face value and annual premium, which would be useful for Terry during times when his income declined. Mario concluded that, although not the optimal solution for Terry, a UL policy would give Terry a tax-advantaged way to save money. The solution would also allow a cash account to grow that could be used for any need Terry might have. Mario was quoted a premium of $2,700 per year for a $250,000 UL policy.

A VUL policy was priced similarly to the UL policy. The VUL offered a mix of asset classes via mutual funds or unit trusts, typically called subaccounts, similar to that in the variable policy (which Mario had originally dismissed). The VUL had the added benefit of flexible premiums. The VUL solution would allow Terry the greatest amount of flexibility in terms of premiums, cash value, investments, and face value changes. Mario knew that under the best of circumstances, the death benefit generated with the cash account investments could be substantially higher than the original face value. In the worst case, the policy could lapse with no cash value.

Mario was very confident that Terry would stay committed to the 20-year term strategy. Terry had already proven willing to pay premiums in the past. Mario was less certain that Terry would stay committed to the UL or VUL solutions. Mario's primary concern centered on Terry's fluctuating annual income. If rates of return achieved in the subaccounts of the VUL, for instance, did not meet expectations, Terry might be required to increase his annual premium. Doing so in any given year might be difficult. As such, Mario discounted the UL and VUL solutions relative to the 20-year term policy.

Knowing Terry's interest in using factual analyses to guide his decisions, and given that all three products offered distinct advantages and disadvantages, Mario decided to do a mathematical comparison. He assumed that although the cash value policies were higher in upfront cost, each strategy was similar in total cost. If the 20-year term policy was chosen, Terry would incur a $640 reduction in cash flow for the premium, and a $2,060 reduction in cash flow as the difference between the term cost and the UL policy cost. The latter funds would be available for "investing the difference."

For the initial comparison, Mario developed a spreadsheet based on the following factors:

1. A $250,000 face value policy;

2. A $2,700 UL policy cost;

3. A $140 per year UL policy premium expense;

4. Pure insurance costs, using yearly price-per-thousand estimates;[4]

5. A $640 initial term policy premium;

6. A $3,750 projected premium to renew the term policy in 20 years, assuming that Terry is insurable;

7. A projected rate of return in the UL policy and in other investments of 8%; and

8. An income tax rate of 20%.

Mario's calculations, shown in Table 14.2, indicate that the UL policy would be canceled when Terry turns age 77. Even using a generous 8% rate of return, there would be insufficient premium plus available cash to cover the cost of one year of insurance at that time. In other words, Terry would lose all his cash value plus the face value of the policy. Note that for this UL policy to be sustainable, the initial premium amount would need to be significantly higher. However, an increased premium would be unaffordable for Terry.

Mario then considered the term solution. He assumed that Terry would be disciplined and invest the difference between the UL premium and the term policy premium into an account earning 8%. Mario also assumed that in year 21 Terry would purchase another 20-year policy. Mario made this assumption to make the comparison equal, although he knew that Terry might not need that much coverage by that future date. However, at that time the premium would increase dramatically to $3,750 per year, which would be over $1,000 more than the projected UL policy.

**Table 14.2** Comparison of Universal Life Insurance and 20-year Term Life Insurance Policies

| Policy: Universal Life | $ 250,000 | | | | Policy: 20-Year Term | $ 250,000 |
|---|---|---|---|---|---|---|
| Initial Premium | $ 2,700 | | | | Initial Premium | $ 640 |
| | | | | | Renewal Premium @ age 57 | $ 3,750 |
| Rate of Return | 8.00% | | | | Tax Rate | 20% |
| | | | | | Rate of Return | 8.00% |

| Age | Cost/ $1000[1] | Annual Premium | Net Annual Premium | Cost | Value @ End of Period | Term Difference in Value | After-tax Value |
|---|---|---|---|---|---|---|---|
| 37 | $3.00 | $ 2,700 | $ 2,560 | $ 750 | $ 1,810 | $ 2,060 | $ 1,648 |
| 38 | $3.00 | $ 2,700 | $ 2,560 | $ 750 | $ 3,765 | $ 4,285 | $ 3,428 |
| 39 | $3.00 | $ 2,700 | $ 2,560 | $ 750 | $ 5,876 | $ 6,688 | $ 5,350 |
| 40 | $4.00 | $ 2,700 | $ 2,560 | $ 1,000 | $ 7,906 | $ 9,283 | $ 7,426 |
| 41 | $4.00 | $ 2,700 | $ 2,560 | $ 1,000 | $10,099 | $ 12,085 | $ 9,668 |
| 42 | $4.00 | $ 2,700 | $ 2,560 | $ 1,000 | $12,466 | $ 15,112 | $ 12,090 |
| 43 | $4.00 | $ 2,700 | $ 2,560 | $ 1,000 | $15,024 | $ 18,381 | $ 14,705 |
| 44 | $4.00 | $ 2,700 | $ 2,560 | $ 1,000 | $17,786 | $ 21,911 | $ 17,529 |
| 45 | $4.00 | $ 2,700 | $ 2,560 | $ 1,625 | $20,143 | $ 25,724 | $ 20,579 |
| 46 | $6.50 | $ 2,700 | $ 2,560 | $ 1,625 | $22,690 | $ 29,842 | $ 23,874 |
| 47 | $6.50 | $ 2,700 | $ 2,560 | $ 1,625 | $25,440 | $ 34,290 | $ 27,432 |
| 48 | $6.50 | $ 2,700 | $ 2,560 | $ 1,625 | $28,410 | $ 39,093 | $ 31,274 |
| 49 | $6.50 | $ 2,700 | $ 2,560 | $ 1,625 | $31,618 | $ 44,280 | $ 35,424 |
| 50 to 54 | $10.00 | $ 2,700 | $ 2,560 | $ 12,500 | $46,810 | $ 77,148 | $ 61,718 |
| 55 to 59 | $15.00 | $ 2,700 | $ 2,560 | $ 18,750 | $61,797 | $115,344 | $ 92,275 |
| 60 to 64 | $25.00 | $ 2,700 | $ 2,560 | $ 31,250 | $69,153 | $163,318 | $130,654 |
| 65 to 69 | $35.00 | $ 2,700 | $ 2,560 | $ 43,750 | $65,294 | $233,808 | $187,046 |
| 70 to 74 | $50.00 | $ 2,700 | $ 2,560 | $ 62,500 | $37,624 | $337,381 | $269,904 |
| 75 | $80.00 | $ 2,700 | $ 2,560 | $ 20,000 | $23,194 | $363,321 | $290,657 |
| 76 | $80.00 | $ 2,700 | $ 2,560 | $ 20,000 | $ 7,609 | $391,337 | $313,069 |
| 77 | $80.00 | $ 2,700 | $ 2,560 | $ 20,000 | $(9,222) | $421,594 | $337,275 |

1. The premium cost for insurance within the universal life policy is based on the price-per-thousand method as originally developed by Joseph Belth, Ph.D. The cost figures for Dr. Belth's benchmarks can be found in Baldwin, B. G. (2002), *The New Life insurance Investment Advisor*, 2nd Ed. New York, NY: McGraw-Hill, p. 207.

If Terry purchased the term policy and invested the difference in premiums, Mario estimated that Terry would accumulate more than $85,000 in his account, or about $68,000 on an after-tax basis at age 55. Mario noted that either before- or after-tax amounts would be more than the projected cash value of $49,364 for the universal policy at that time. By age 77, when the universal policy was projected to be cancelled, Terry would have accumulated more than $300,000 in after-tax account value. This amount would significantly exceed the face value of the policy should he die after age 77. If Terry were to use a tax-advantaged account (e.g., Roth IRA) for his investment, the tax-free account value would exceed $400,000.

Mario decided that he did not need to do the same analysis comparing a term policy to a VUL policy; the only way the outcome would change is if Terry could earn significantly more than 8% per year in the cash account. Given Terry's risk tolerance profile, Mario concluded that making this assumption would be imprudent because he would have to invest the cash account in aggressive investments to achieve such a high annualized rate of return after expenses. Mario knew that a VUL policy was most appropriate in situations where a client needs an investment vehicle for tax-deferral of savings beyond what is typically available in a defined contribution retirement plan and other tax-advantaged investments (e.g., IRA). This profile did not describe Terry. Given these factors, Mario determined that the VUL solution would subject Terry to too many risks. Furthermore, purchasing a UL or VUL policy could lead to a high level of regret, especially if the policy were to lapse without cash value. This risk is minimized using the 20-year term policy solution and the greater flexibilty of the investment available. Mario concluded that the 20-year term policy strategy best matched Terry's situation and projected needs at this time. The pure life insurance covered his need, and the extra savings outside of the insurance could grow to leave an inheritance for Brady.

Because Mario had focused his analysis solely on the life insurance question, he thought it wise to complete a Recommendation Impact Form to project the effect on other areas of Terry's financial situation. In general, Mario concluded that implementation of the recommendation would not significantly affect other financial planning areas, other than a reduction in annual discretionary cash flow and a change in the way Terry's assets were managed. An example of the completed Recommendation Impact Form is shown in Exhibit 14.5. But when Mario considered the estate tax impact, he decided one final analysis was warranted.

**Exhibit 14.5** Terry Meredith Life Insurance Recommendation Impact Form

## Recommendation Impact Form

**Recommendation: Purchase a $250,000 20-year term life insurance policy with disability waiver provision and guaranteed renewability rider**

| Recommendation No. | 1 | | | | | |
|---|---|---|---|---|---|---|
| **Planner Decision** | Accept | X | Reject | | Modify | |
| **Client Decision** | Accept | X | Reject | | Modify | |

**Financial Impact**

| | |
|---|---|
| Annual Impact on Cash flow ($) | $640 reduction |
| Immediate Impact on Net Worth ($) | $0 |

| Planning Issue | Degree of Significance | | | | Notes |
|---|---|---|---|---|---|
| | Major | Modest | Minor | None | |
| Financial situation – cash management | X | | | | Implementing recommendation will decrease annual cash flow. |
| Tax planning | | X | | | Term policies provide no cash value and no option to defer taxes on savings. Depending on the investments, tax liability could increase. |
| Life insurance planning | X | | | | This strategy will maximize your life insurance coverage at a minimal cost. |
| Health insurance planning | | | X | | Unlike a cash value policy, it will be difficult to obtain a viatical settlement. |
| Disability and LTC insurance planning | | | X | | An accelerated death benefit rider or the option to initiate this benefit for a fee will allow access to a portion of the death benefit if the insured is diagnosed with a terminal illness or in some cases, if nursing home care is needed. |
| Property and liability insurance planning | | | | X | |
| Investment planning | X | | | | Higher premiums for a cash value policy can be invested. |
| Education or other special needs planning | | | X | | Higher premiums for a cash value policy can be invested. |
| Retirement planning | | X | | | The policy will terminate unless renewed at the beginning of retirement; if terminated, client would be uninsured during retirement. |
| Estate planning | | X | | | Self-ownership of a life insurance policy will increase the estate. |

By all indications, the 20-year term policy using a "buy term and invest the difference" strategy was determined to be the most effective recommendation for Terry. But Mario decided to triangulate, or reconsider, the recommendation from two other perspectives: Brady's and his own. A quick call to Terry confirmed that his other term policy was still payable to Terry's estate, because at the time of the initial purchase too many things were changing in Terry's life to make a definitive choice. Now, with increased life insurance, the value of the new home, and steadily growing retirement and other personal assets, it was time to seriously consider what this decision could mean for Brady and Terry's potential estate tax liability.

Whereas Terry's intent was to provide for Brady, without proper estate plans in place the assets could be subject to greater settlement costs. And there was also the question of direct ownership and titling until Brady reached age 18. Mario knew that a funded irrevocable life insurance trust (commonly referred to as an ILIT) could be established to purchase the policy and pay the future premiums for the benefit of Brady until some predetermined age when the corpus would be fully available to Brady. This was an issue that Mario and Terry needed to more fully investigate with an attorney. The trust would offer no income tax protection on the earnings of the deposited funds, but the income tax consequences would probably be minimal. In addition, Mario made a note to talk with Terry about changing the beneficiary designation on the in-place life insurance policy.

In preparation for their meeting, Mario prepared a Planning Recommendation Form, shown in Exhibit 14.6, to summarize the recommendation and provide documentation to share with Terry.

Now, thinking from his own perspective, Mario reflected on the planner-client relationship. He noted that other planners, working on the same case, might have arrived at a different conclusion based on their own particular knowledge, background, and interpretation of the facts. He knew that advisor compensation varied with the life insurance products he had considered, and that although he could help Terry consider some of the estate planning issues, an attorney would be needed to fully implement the plan. Yet Mario was convinced that his consultation with Terry had been both efficient and effective. By continuing to build on their relationship, he could more easily analyze the situation and offer recommendations that meet Terry's immediate needs and lay a foundation for future work. Another question they still needed to explore related to the options for "investing the difference" and whether Terry wanted Mario's assistance. Bottom line: Mario was convinced that his approach was prudent, defensible, client-specific, and offered opportunities for a long-term planner-client relationship.

**Exhibit 14.6** Terry Meredith Insurance Recommendation Form

**Planning Recommendation Form**

| | |
|---|---|
| **Financial Planning Content Area** | Life Insurance |
| **Client Goal** | Maximize Life Insurance Protection |

| **Recommendation No.** | 1 | **Priority (1–6) lowest to highest:** | 6 |
|---|---|---|---|
| **Projected/Target Value ($)** | $250,000 (Face Value) | | |

**Product Profile**

| | |
|---|---|
| Type | 20-year term life policy |
| Duration | 20-year term, renewable |
| Provider | Zellers Insurance Company |
| Funding Cost per Period ($) | $640 annually |
| Maintenance Cost per Period ($) | $0 |
| Current Income Tax Status | Tax-qualified ☐ Taxable ☐ |
| Projected Rate of Return | 0% on the life insurance; 8% before-tax assumed on the investment account for the "premium difference" |
| Major Policy Provisions | 1. Guaranteed renewable<br>2. Waiver of premium for periods of disability (restrictions apply) |

**Procedural Factors**

| | | | | |
|---|---|---|---|---|
| Implement by Whom | Planner | | Client | X |
| Implementation Date or Time Frame | Upon establishment of the trust | | | |
| Implementation Procedure | Contact Zellers Insurance Company | | | |

**Ownership Factors**

| | | | | |
|---|---|---|---|---|
| Owner(s) | Trust for Brady C. Meredith | | | |
| Form of Ownership | Trust | | | |
| Insured(s) | Terry Meredith | | | |
| Custodial Account | Yes | | No | X |
| Custodian | NA | | | |
| In Trust For (ITF) | Yes | | No | X |
| Transfer On Death (TOD) | Yes | | No | X |
| Beneficiary(ies) | Trust for Brady C. Meredith, (100%) | | | |
| Contingent Beneficiary(ies) | NA | | | |

| | |
|---|---|
| **Proposed Benefit** | Immediate life insurance protection, with the added benefit of "investing the difference" in the cheaper term premium for other goals. |

# Learning Outcomes

1. The systematic financial planning process based on the general financial planning process promoted by the CFP Board and other organizations provides a consistent method, characterized by several forms, for practicing the financial planning process. For students and novice planners, the objective of the repeated use of the forms is to build a reflexive capacity of both knowledge and skill to confidently craft financial plans and offer planning advice. By practicing this framework, users will develop the reflexive professional proficiency to conduct analyses, interpret the results in the many dimensions of a client's financial situation, develop recommendations, and synthesize them into a viable, affordable plan matched to client' needs. The forms include the Recommendation Form, the Comprehensive Planning Checklist, the Recommendation Impact Form, and the Available Cash Flow and Other Assets Tracker Form, and the Implementation Checklist. In addition to providing a systematic structure for conducting the financial planning process, the forms are useful for communicating information to planning staff and clients.

2. Client-based recommendations evolve from the data collection and discovery that occur as part of the advisor-client relationship. Recommendations are matched to the client's planning needs but reflect the situational factors that characterize the client and to a lesser extent, the advisor and the advisor's business model. Alternative recommendations should be offered to give the client choices, but available resources (i.e., discretionary cash flow, savings, and investments) are the major determinant of recommendations that are included in the plan and implemented. Several methods were presented for dealing with resource constraints (e.g., stagger the funding of recommendations; downsize the goal and required funding), but a favored strategy is one that can be used to satisfy or save for multiple goals.

3. Several issues guide the development of a plan within Step 4: Develop the Comprehensive Plan and Present Recommendations. Fundamentally the issues relate to the tenuous balance between the goal orientation to planning—planning for what is important to the client—and the cash flow orientation to planning—planning for what the client can afford. The two are not mutually exclusive, nor are they always compatible. Three questions that guide Step 4 focus on the client's planning need and clarify (1) whether all necessary recommendations have been identified; (2) whether the consequences of the recommendations have been identified; and (3) whether the recommendations are affordable. The first two questions align with the goal orientation to planning; the third question, as well as identification of alternative funding options, corresponds to the cash flow orientation.

4. The presentation of a plan is pivotal in the financial planning process. Its outcome affects the advisor's business development and the client's access to financial planning advice, products, and services. The presentation should educate the client, motivate client action, and objectively project potential outcomes for the client. Clients may be asked to make decisions about alternatives in the plan and their willingness to implement it.

5. The seven questions of *who, what, when, where, why, how,* and *how much* guide the development of action-oriented recommendations as well as Step 5: Implement the Plan. The same questions are reflected directly or indirectly in several of the forms included in the systematic planning process. In particular, the Implementation Checklist integrates these questions by tracking the financial impact of the recommendations on the client's cash flow

and net worth. Although seemingly simplistic, these questions challenge planners to plan in detail for the implementation of multiple recommendations as well as the associated cash flows.

6. Contingent on the advisor-client engagement agreement, Step 6: Monitor the Plan, Implementation, and Goal Progress, can include all or some of these activities: (1) following the plan and its match to the client's life situation as well as the changing regulatory, economic, tax, and market environments; (2) following the implementation of the plan and the need for continued implementation of delayed recommendations or other necessary actions; (3) following the viability and success of the products and services implemented; and (4) following the outcomes to date and progress toward the client's goals. Few aspects of the plan can be evaluated in isolation because the monitoring actions should continue to integrate the plan with the client's life. Monitoring encourages interaction between advisor and client and provides opportunities to enrich the advisor-client relationship.

7. Monitoring all of the products and services in a financial plan to keep the plan current, effective, and responsive to a client's life is a very important part of the financial planning process. Without continued monitoring, the plan could become obsolete. But responsibility for monitoring can rest with the client, the planner, other professionals, product or service providers, or no one. Ideally, the planner serves as the hub of the wheel and coordinates and monitors all aspects of implementation and monitoring because both steps are likely intertwined. Not all clients want to delegate, and not all business models or planner-client engagements support anything more than periodic or isolated monitoring. The tension between what needs to be done and who does it, if anyone, is important to resolve because monitoring adds value for the both client and advisor.

## Chapter Resources

Certified Financial Planner Board of Standards, Inc. (www.cfp.net)
Insurance company ratings can be monitored at:

A.M. Best Company (www.ambest.com).

Fitch Ratings (http://www.fitchratings.com/).

Moody's Investor Service (http://www.moodys.com/cust/default.asp).

Lytton, R., J. Grable, and D. Klock. *The Process of Financial Planning: Developing a Financial Plan*, 2nd Ed. Erlanger, KY: National Underwriter, 2012.

The *Financial Factilitator* and all fillable forms needed to complete text activities can be found on the student website at: http://pro.nuco.com/booksupplements/NUCollege-CaseBook2e.

# Quantitative/Analytical Mini-case Problems

1. You are preparing to meet with Adam, Kate, and their 3-week-old baby girl Cooper. They have lived life to the fullest but have recently realized that all of this excess is going to seriously jeopardize their long-term finances. They have done a fair job of saving but have also habitually overspent their annual income by financing the difference on credit cards, which has resulted in $17,000 in credit card balances. In the last year Kate and Adam have attempted to make significant changes in their spending and have excellent financial records. They have enlisted your help.

   You have numerous recommendations for them pertaining to almost every aspect of their financial lives, particularly for insurance and retirement planning, and you have compiled a list of these recommendations along with the associated cost and frequency of payment. One of your first recommendations is to build a $10,000 emergency fund, because you never know what might happen with a newborn. Currently the only monetary asset is a five-year, $15,000 bank CD that Adam inherited from his great-aunt. Luckily it is coming due in a few months, so they will be able to access the money.  They also have $85,000 in other financial assets and $26,170 in nonmortgage liabilities.

   When you started your analysis, you realized that Adam and Kate had only $2,250 in annual discretionary cash flow, so you knew that you had to recommend that they reallocate some assets and organize some of their debt. Given the low interest rate environment, they had inquired with a local lender and wanted your advice on a mortgage refinance.  You determined that they could take out $32,500 of their home equity and still be approved for a 5.75% 20-year mortgage, which would give them enough to pay the $6,330 in closing costs and pay off their credit card debt, with the remainder going toward their home equity line of credit (HELOC). The payment on the new mortgage is only $40 less than their old mortgage, but they did not want to extend the term beyond 20 years. Besides, the reduction in the HELOC balance also reduces that monthly payment by $125.

   Now that they have a child, you think that they should each have life insurance (Adam was actually overinsured, given his company benefits); they should reevaluate their property and casualty insurance coverage and see an attorney to get their affairs in order. Finally, Kate has informed you that their parents are going to provide generously for Cooper's education, so you are comfortable recommending that they reduce funding there to accomplish some additional goals, namely saving for retirement. You have sketched out your recommendations in the following table.

| Recommendation Summary | Annual Value (Cost) / Benefit | Frequency of (Cost) / Benefit |
|---|---|---|
| Refinance the mortgage (5.75%, $158,300, 15 yrs.) with cash out | $480 | Annual |
| Use the cash out proceeds to pay closing costs, HELOC ,and high-interest credit cards | $32,500 | Single |
| Closing costs and points for the refinance | ($6,330) | Single |
| Pay off high-rate (16.5%) credit card balances | ($17,000) | Single |
| Pay down variable-rate (6.5%) HELOC | ($9,170) | Single |
| Reduce HELOC payment ($125/mo) | $1,500 | Annual |
| Eliminate credit card payments ($510/mo) | $6,120 | Annual |
| Liquidate mutual fund (fund emergency fund account) | $10,000 | Single |
| Liquidate CD upon maturity (fund emergency fund account) | $4,000 | Single |
| Allocate money from CD and mutual fund to emergency savings account | ($14,000) | Single |
| Federal tax refund | $1,956 | Single |
| Reduce education funding , Cooper | $1,800 | Annual |
| Drop $1 million term life insurance, Adam | $600 | Annual |
| Purchase $1 million term life insurance, Kate | ($770) | Annual |
| Enhance property and casualty insurance (homeowners, auto, umbrella) | ($850) | Annual |
| Increase 401(k) contribution, Adam | ($1,500) | Annual |
| Increase 403(b) contribution, Kate | ($1,500) | Annual |
| Contribute to Roth IRA, Adam | ($3,000) | Annual |
| Contribute to Roth IRA, Kate | ($3,000) | Annual |
| Plan estate (wills, general power of attorney, letter of last instruction, and advance medical directive) | ($1,000) | Single |
| Financial planning fee | ($2,500) | Single |

To prepare for the meeting, you need to:

a. Complete a Recommendation Form and an Impact Form for at least one of the recommendations to explain your planning process to Adam and Kate.

b. Complete a Comprehensive Planning Form to ensure that no planning needs have been overlooked.

c. Complete a Cash Flow and Other Assets Tracker to determine the aggregate impact of your recommendations on their discretionary cash flow and net worth.

# Comprehensive Bedo Case Analysis Questions

Before finalizing the recommendations and integrating them into a comprehensive plan to help the Bedos meet their financial goals, it is important to review all of the assumptions related to Tyler's and Mia's temperament, personality, attitudes, family history, financial knowledge, experience, and other factors. Finally, the Planning Recommendation Forms resulting from the independent situation analysis conducted for each of the core planning areas must be reviewed. Do recommendations serve to meet the Bedos' primary goals and objectives and at the same time reflect their situational factors? Use the following questions to guide the plan development, implementation, and monitoring steps of the financial planning process.

1.  For each of the core content planning areas, one or more planning goals were identified for the Bedo household. When conceptualizing the comprehensive plan, consider the following:

    a.  Are the goal(s) in agreement with any or all goals and objectives that the clients have identified?

    b.  What is the desired outcome for the clients? Are there planner-identified needs or outcomes that must be presented to the Bedos?

    c.  What situational factors might influence their ranking of these goals? Are these factors explicit, implied, or assumed? Is additional information required from the Bedos, and if so, what?

    d.  Have all globally accepted, client-specific, or planner-generated planning assumptions been identified and considered? List the assumptions as they might appear in a plan.

2.  Review all of the Planning Recommendation Forms prepared for the primary and alternative recommendations for each core content planning area. Then, considering the forms and the Bedos' goals, complete the Comprehensive Planning Checklist.

3.  For each recommendation (primary and alternative, where applicable), complete a Recommendation Impact Form to review the cross-impacts of each recommendation.

4.  Based on the priority originally assigned to each recommendation, review the priorities relative to the knowledge of the entire client situation. Be sure to consider the likelihood of meeting the clients' goals and desired outcomes, as well as the approach that will most effectively protect and grow assets. Sequence all of the recommendations to reflect these priorities.

5.  Given these priorities and their corresponding goals and recommendations, and the Bedos' discretionary cash flow and other available assets, choose the most important recommendation(s) to fund first. Which recommendations, if any might be (1) downsized or (2) postponed to increase funding opportunities for more immediate recommendations? Be sure to review the preceding for ideas regarding how to meet the Bedos' goals most effectively and efficiently. Do current recommendations utilize the Bedos' resources to the highest and best use?

6. Advisors are encouraged to provide clients with alternative approaches to reach the same goal, when applicable. Does this situation apply to the Bedos? What alternatives might realistically be offered to them? Are there any recommendations that, in consultation with the Bedos, might be eliminated given their goals, temperaments, personalities, attitudes, and financial knowledge and experience? Are there recommendations that the Bedos might choose to ignore?

7. Once the recommendations with the greatest likelihood of effectively and efficiently meeting the Bedos' goals and objectives are finally identified, summarize the financial impacts of each recommendation made using a Cash Flow and Other Assets Tracking Form. Make adjustments as needed to match the recommendations to the cash flow and assets available.

8. Develop an Implementation Checklist to clarify all of the details to be stated in response to the seven key questions.

9. Conduct a cross-impact analysis for the Bedos one year in the future by recalculating and projecting the following, assuming all recommendations will be implemented as planned:

   a. The cash flow situation;

   b. The household net worth;

   c. The income tax situation; and

   d. The estate and estate tax situation.

10. Develop a summary of the goals and recommendations that comprise the Bedos' plan. Based on the initial drafts written in Chapters 3 through 13 and the revisions made during plan development, clearly state each recommendation. Be sure to state specific, defensible answers to the *who, what, when, where, why, how*, and *how much* implementation questions for each recommendation. (Refer to the Implementation Checklist.) As assigned, prepare this as a Summary of Goals and Assumptions, as an Executive Summary, or as a Summary of Goals, Observations, and Recommendations for inclusion in the plan.

11. What barriers might a planner face when working with the Bedos that could lessen their motivation or timely action to implement recommendations? What approaches might be incorporated in the plan, included in the presentation, or both to help motivate the Bedos to take action?

12. Using the short presentations prepared in Chapters 3 through 13 of your observations and/or recommendation(s) and the final integrated plan develop a presentation for the Bedos. As assigned, the presentation could be a summary, highlighting only the goals, recommendations, and implementation *or* a longer presentation could provide a more detailed explanation of the entire planning process. Be sure to include visual aids, Excel handouts, and other materials that will make the plan more meaningful to Tyler and Mia.

13. Monitoring, in its most multifaceted and integrative form, involves a review of the client's life situation and its relationship to the plan, the implementation of the plan, the viabilty of the products and services chosen, and outcomes to date. Develop a list of three to five questions or issues representing each of these components to review with the Bedos at their first annual review meeting. How might those questions change by the time of the fifth annual review? Be specific.

14. For one of the following situations, list the most important situational factors and conceptual planning issues for the affected core content planning areas if the Bedos reported that:

   a. Tyler or Mia wanted to stop work and go to law school, with a substantial projected salary increase in five years

   b. Mia was pregnant and for health or personal reasons needed to stop working for a few years

   c. Tyler or Mia got a promotion resulting in a $10,000 annual salary increase

## Notes

1. Certified Financial Planner Board of Standards, Inc., CFP Board's Standards of Professional Conduct. Available at http://www.cfp.net/Downloads/2010Standards.pdf, pp. 13–27.

2. This section of the chapter was excerpted from the companion text, R. Lytton, J. Grable, and D. Klock, *The Process of Financial Planning: Developing a Financial Plan* (Cincinnati, OH: National Underwriter, 2006).

3. K. C. Altfest, *Keeping Clients for Life: How to Build a Successful Financial Practice* (New York: John Wiley and Sons, 2001).

4. For more information on this approach, see Chapter 5.

# Comprehensive Planning Checklist

Comprehensive Planning Checklist for _____

| Cash Flow Analysis to Maximize Client's Discretionary Cash Flow | | | Recommendation Needed? | |
|---|---|---|---|---|
| 1. Has planner reviewed financial ratios and compared them to benchmarks? | Yes | No | Yes | No |
| 2. Have steps been taken to designate savings or other assets for use as an emergency fund or source of emergency income? | Yes | No | Yes | No |
| 3. Has planner reviewed client budget or income and expense statement for possible expense reductions? | Yes | No | Yes | No |
| 4. Has planner verified that the client is able and willing to proactively save money on a regular basis? | Yes | No | Yes | No |
| 5. Have debt reduction or debt restructuring alternatives been reviewed? | Yes | No | Yes | No |
| 6. Have mortgage refinancing alternatives been reviewed? | Yes | No | Yes | No |
| 7. Are there other client-specific cash management issues to consider? | Yes | No | Yes | No |

| Tax Analysis to Minimize Taxes and Maximize Client's Discretionary Cash Flow | | | Recommendation Needed? | |
|---|---|---|---|---|
| 8. Have tax projections for 1, 3, or 5 years been done to guide the planning process? | Yes | No | Yes | No |
| 9. Has client income tax withholding been matched to tax liability? | Yes | No | Yes | No |
| 10. Has client FICA withholding been matched to FICA liabilities? | Yes | No | Yes | No |
| 11. Has planner reviewed client's tax situation to ensure that other tax-reduction opportunities have not been overlooked? | Yes | No | Yes | No |
| 12. Is the client currently subject to the AMT? Have projections been made for the next 1, 3, or 5 years? | Yes | No | Yes | No |
| 13. Has planner checked to determine whether client is maximizing tax-reducing insurance alternatives? | | | | |
|    a. Health flexible spending account? | Yes | No | Yes | No |
|    b. Dependent care flexible spending account? | Yes | No | Yes | No |
|    c. Employer provided life, health, disability, or LTC benefits? | Yes | No | Yes | No |
|    d. Any other § 125 cafeteria plan benefits? | Yes | No | Yes | No |
| 14. Are there other client-specific tax management issues to consider? | Yes | No | Yes | No |

| Insurance Analysis to Limit Client's Household Risk Exposures | | | Recommendation Needed? | |
|---|---|---|---|---|
| 15. Has a life insurance analysis been conducted? | Yes | No | Yes | No |
| 16. Has a disability insurance analysis been conducted? | Yes | No | Yes | No |
| 17. Has a long-term care (LTC) insurance analysis been conducted? | Yes | No | Yes | No |
| 18. Has a health insurance analysis been conducted? | Yes | No | Yes | No |
| 19. Has a property, casualty, and liability insurance analysis been conducted? | Yes | No | Yes | No |
| 20. Are there other client-specific risk management issues to consider? | Yes | No | Yes | No |

| Investment Planning Analysis to Maximize Client's Return | | | Recommendation Needed? | |
|---|---|---|---|---|
| 21. Has an investment funding goal been identified? | Yes | No | Yes | No |
| 22. Is the client on track to meet the targeted amount and date? | Yes | No | Yes | No |
| 23. Are asset allocation and investments suitable given the client's time horizon, risk tolerance, and other assumptions? | Yes | No | Yes | No |
| 24. Is the client fully benefiting from tax-advantaged investments? | Yes | No | Yes | No |
| 25. Are there other client-specific investment planning issues to consider? | Yes | No | Yes | No |

| Education or Special Needs Planning Analysis to Maximize Client's Return | | | Recommendation Needed? | |
|---|---|---|---|---|
| 26. Has an education funding goal been identified? | Yes | No | Yes | No |
| 27. Is the client on track to meet the targeted amount and date? | Yes | No | Yes | No |
| 28. Are asset allocation and investments suitable given the client's time horizon, risk tolerance, and other assumptions? | Yes | No | Yes | No |
| 29. Is the client fully benefiting from tax-advantaged accounts? | Yes | No | Yes | No |
| 30. Are there other client-specific education planning issues to consider? | Yes | No | Yes | No |
| 31. Has a special needs funding goal(s) been identified? Is the client on track to meet the targeted amount(s) and date(s)? | Yes | No | Yes | No |
| 32. Are asset allocation and investments suitable given the client's time horizon, risk tolerance, and other assumptions? | Yes | No | Yes | No |
| 33. Are there other client-specific special needs planning issues to consider? | Yes | No | Yes | No |

| Retirement Planning Analysis to Maximize Client's Return | | | Recommendation Needed? | |
|---|---|---|---|---|
| 34. Has a retirement funding goal been identified? | Yes | No | Yes | No |
| 35. Is the client on track to meet the targeted amount and date? | Yes | No | Yes | No |
| 36. Are asset allocation and investments suitable given the client's time horizon, risk tolerance, and other assumptions? | Yes | No | Yes | No |
| 37. Is the client fully benefiting from any available match? | Yes | No | Yes | No |
| 38. Is the client fully benefiting from tax-advantaged accounts? | | | | |
| 39. Are other retirement funds available? | Yes | No | Yes | No |
| 40. Are there other client-specific retirement planning issues to consider? | Yes | No | Yes | No |

| Estate Planning Analysis to Minimize Estate Taxes and Ensure Client's Final Wishes | | | Recommendation Needed? | |
|---|---|---|---|---|
| 41. Has the client begun giving assets to dependents, other family members, or charity? | Yes | No | Yes | No |
| 42. Are documents in place to distribute property and provide for dependents, heirs, or charities? | Yes | No | Yes | No |
| 43. Have steps been taken to minimize probate, estate, or inheritance taxes? | Yes | No | Yes | No |
| 44. Have steps been taken to minimize settlement costs, including legal and accounting fees? | Yes | No | Yes | No |
| 45. Are funds available, or plans in place, for the payment of estate taxes and settlement expenses? | Yes | No | Yes | No |
| 46. Are documents in place to guide incapacitation or other end-of-life decisions? | Yes | No | Yes | No |
| 47. Are documents in place to care for, or name guardians for, children or other financial dependents? | Yes | No | Yes | No |
| 48. Are documents in place to care for a pet, if applicable? | Yes | No | Yes | No |
| 49. Has a letter of last instructions been prepared to provide for the distribution of personal and digital assets (i.e. accounts, music, pictures, etc.) as well as other final wishes? | Yes | No | Yes | No |
| 50. Are there other client-specific estate planning issues to consider? | Yes | No | Yes | No |

| Cross-planning Analysis: Have the Following Interactions Been Considered? | | | Recommendation Needed? | |
|---|---|---|---|---|
| 51.  Net worth ↔ insurance? | Yes | No | Yes | No |
| 52.  Income taxes ↔ insurance? | | | | |
|     a.  Health flexible spending accounts? | Yes | No | Yes | No |
|     b.  Dependent care flexible spending accounts? | Yes | No | Yes | No |
|     c.  Employer-provided life, health, disability, and LTC benefits? | Yes | No | Yes | No |
| 53.  Income taxes ↔ mortgage refinance? | Yes | No | Yes | No |
| 54.  Life insurance ↔ estate planning? | Yes | No | Yes | No |
| 55.  Life/LTC hybrid ↔ life insurance? | Yes | No | Yes | No |
| 56.  LTC ↔ estate planning? | Yes | No | Yes | No |
| 57.  Education funding ↔ estate planning? | Yes | No | Yes | No |
| 58.  Education funding ↔ income tax planning? | Yes | No | Yes | No |
| 59.  Investment planning ↔ income tax planning? | Yes | No | Yes | No |
| 60.  Retirement planning ↔ income tax planning? | Yes | No | Yes | No |

# PART VI: Financial Planning Case Studies

The Zimmer Case: A Financial Situation Mini-case

The Ande Case: A Tax Planning Mini-case

The Roth Case: A Tax Planning Mini-case

The Shim Case: An Insurance Planning Mini-case

The Butterfield Case: An Insurance Planning Mini-case

The Little Case: An Investment Situation Mini-case

The Cantrell Case: An Investment Planning Mini-case

The Alpha Case: A Retirement Planning Mini-case

The Edwards Case: A Retirement and Employee Benefits Mini-case

The Mayfield Case: A Retirement Planning Mini-case

The Dion Case: An Estate Planning Mini-case

The Graham Case: A General Planning Mini-case

The Case of the Good Gone Bad—A Play in Three Scenes: An Ethics Case

# Introduction to Case Studies

This appendix includes 13 mini-cases: (a) eight 10-question mini-cases; (b) four 20-question cases; and (c) an ethics case. In general, the mini-cases are designed to test both definitional and basic applied financial planning concepts. The longer 20-question cases provide more detail in terms of background, assumptions, and complications. Additionally, each of the longer cases, although comprehensive in context, focuses on one central theme, as follows:

1. Graham case: general financial planning

2. Cantrell case: investment planning

3. Mayfield case: retirement planning

4. Butterfield Case: insurance planning

Instructors and students interested in additional writing applications will find these cases appropriate for use as either modular/targeted or comprehensive financial planning narratives. That is, each case contains more information than needed to answer the core multiple-choice questions. (Instructors are provided with answers in the Instructor's Manual.) These longer cases also include open-ended discussion questions.

The ethics case is intended to be used as an interactive in-class exercise. It is designed to be lighthearted and obvious in the planner's violation of multiple professional standards. The case is designed to assess key Certified Financial Planner ™ Board of Standards, Inc., (CFP Board) *Code of Ethics and Professional Responsibility* terms, rules, and standards.

Before beginning work on these cases, it is important to remember the following case assumptions:

1. Case information and assumptions are closely linked to the Financial Facilitator spreadsheet package provided with the book. Using the assumptions provided, financial planning students should generally be able to use the spreadsheets to arrive at mathematical solutions to all core financial planning problems (e.g., cash flow, net worth, retirement). This does not mean, however, that the cases can be solved only by using the spreadsheet package. To the contrary; it is possible to solve each case using traditional calculators, formulas, and commercially available software.

2. Assumptions within a particular case are divided into sections. For example, each case has unique assumptions related to insurance planning, retirement planning, estate planning, etc. Students should use only the assumptions provided in each section to solve math and strategic planning questions related to that section. In other words, it is possible—and likely—that rate-of-return assumptions, for instance, will be different for insurance and retirement planning purposes. When solving any question, students should use the assumptions related to the specific section. Furthermore, it is important to remember that case assumptions, particularly those related to rate-of-return data, will be different from data in the current market environment. It is essential, however, to use only the information provided in each case when answering the questions. Bringing in additional assumptions, return data, or other information from the "real world" will result in wrong answers and frustration.

3. Readers (e.g., instructors and students) who would like to add realism to each case may want to consider changing the Anystate and Anycity location assumption to a specific state. Income tax information was originally developed for each case based on a model state, as shown below:

   - Graham case: Arizona

   - Cantrell case: South Dakota

   - Mayfield case: Ohio

   - Butterfield case: Virginia

# The Zimmer Case

## A FINANCIAL SITUATION MINI-CASE

Today's date is December 31, 20XX, and Bonita Zimmer has stopped by your office for her year-end annual financial planning review. The following narrative provides important details about Bonita.

Bonita just turned 30 years of age. She lives in a house that she purchased three years ago for $110,000, right before housing prices began to skyrocket. She was fortunate to purchase the home with $18,000 in down payment money received from her father (who is married) and a loan for the remainder. She was able to obtain a 6.5% 30-year mortgage.

Bonita is a hard worker and good saver. Over the past eight years—since graduating from college—she has accumulated a nice-sized nest egg. Table VI.1 summarizes her asset and liability situation.

**Table VI.1** Bonita Zimmer's Assets and Liabilities

| Assets | Value | | Liabilities | Value |
|---|---|---|---|---|
| Savings account | $9,000 | | Mortgage balance | $88,704 |
| Checking account | $2,000 | | Credit card balances | $3,200 |
| 6-month CD | $2,500 | | Car loan | $9,500 |
| Principal residence | $367,000 | | | |
| Car | $12,000 | | **Total assets** | $403,500 |
| Personal property | $11,000 | | **Total liabilities** | $101,404 |
| | | | **Net worth** | $302,096 |

Bonita has been saving for an emergency fund. Her goal is to maintain a liquid account balance equal to six months of total expenses. Table VI.2 summarizes Bonita's income and expense situation. Note that Bonita lives in an income tax-free state.

**Table VI.2** Bonita Zimmer's Income and Expenses

| Income or Expense | Amount (Yearly) |
|---|---|
| *Income* | |
| Annual income | $55,000 |
| Reinvested interest income | $400 |
| *Expenses* | |
| Mortgage payment | $6,978 |
| Real estate taxes and insurance | $2,200 |
| Utilities | $2,400 |
| Groceries | $3,000 |
| Dining out | $2,400 |
| Credit card payments | $960 |
| Car payments | $4,400 |
| Gas | $900 |
| Auto insurance | $1,200 |
| Auto and household maintenance | $1,800 |
| Entertainment | $3,200 |
| Federal taxes | $6,540 |
| FICA | $4,320 |
| Personal care | $1,500 |
| Clothing | $3,000 |
| Charitable donations | $2,200 |
| Gifts to others | $3,000 |
| Miscellaneous expenses | $2,400 |
| Reinvested interest | $400 |

Please use this information to answer the following case questions.[1]

---

# Case Questions

1.  If Bonita sells her current residence for full fair market value (excluding commissions and closing costs), and she purchases a new residence for $180,000 in the same calendar year, the amount of proceeds subject to capital gains tax is

    a.  $7,000

    b.  $28,296

    c.  $187,000

    d.  $257,000

2.  Which of the following statements is true assuming that the money Bonita received for the down payment on her house from her father was a gift rather than a loan?

    I.   Bonita must pay a gift tax on the amount that exceeds the gift tax annual exclusion.

    II.  Her father should have filed a gift-splitting election with the IRS to avoid incurring a gift tax liability.

    III. Bonita should have filed a gift-splitting declaration with the IRS to avoid incurring a gift tax liability.

    IV.  The basis in the house is increased by the amount of any taxes paid on the down payment gift.

    a.  II only

    b.  I and III only

    c.  II and IV only

    d.  III and IV only

    e.  I, III, and IV only

3.  Bonita is concerned that she could be overextended on her monthly mortgage payment. Do you agree with her?

    a.  Yes, because her total debt-to-income ratio exceeds the accepted benchmark of 36% of gross income.

    b.  No, because her monthly housing cost-to-income ratio is less than the accepted benchmark of 28% of gross income.

    c.  Yes, because her monthly housing cost-to-income ratio is greater than the accepted benchmark of 28% of gross income.

    d.  No, because her monetary assets are greater than six months of total expenses, which allows her to overextend her monthly mortgage obligation.

4.  Which of the following statements is correct regarding Bonita's cash flow situation?

    a.  Her level of discretionary cash flow, if used for savings, is below the recommended benchmark average of 10% of gross income.

    b.  Her level of expenditures for principal, interest, tax, insurance (PITI), and other debt payments exceeds the recommended maximum of 36% of gross income.

    c.  She needs to save additional money in liquid assets to achieve her six-month emergency fund goal.

    d.  Both (a) and (c) are correct.

    e.  Answers (a), (b), and (c) are correct.

5.  Bonita has been dating Jason for nine months. He has proposed marriage. If Bonita accepts the proposal and they purchase a home together after they get married, which method can they use to title the property that will provide automatic survivorship rights, assuming they live in a non-community property state?

    I.   Joint tenants with right of survivorship (JTWROS).

    II.  Tenants by the entirety.

    III. Tenants in common.

    a.  I only

    b.  II only

    c.  I and II only

    d.  I and III only

    e.  II and III only

6. Bonita is considering changing jobs and plans to roll over the vested portion of her qualified retirement plan into either an IRA or the qualified retirement plan of her new employer. Reasons why a direct rollover into the new plan, rather than an IRA, would be more appropriate include which of the following?

    I. The new employer's plan is the only way Bonita can get a distribution at retirement in the form of a life annuity.

    II. The new employer's plan contains a provision for loans.

    III. There will be no tax penalty if a lump sum benefit is withdrawn from the new plan at early retirement after attaining age 50.

    IV. Lump sum withdrawals from the new employer's plan after age 59½ will be eligible for 5- or 10-year forward-averaging.

    a. II only

    b. I and III only

    c. II and III only

    d. II and IV only

7. Bonita received a bequest of 100 shares of XYZ stock from a relative who died on March 1 of this year. The relative bought the stock at a total cost of $5,500. The value of the 100 shares of XYZ stock was $5,750 on March 1. On July 1, Bonita sells the stock for $6,250, incurring expenses for the sale of $250. The taxable gain on the sale will be a

    a. $250 long-term capital gain.

    b. $250 short-term capital gain.

    c. $500 long-term capital gain.

    d. $500 short-term capital gain.

8. Bonita is considering establishing a trust for her mother that will pay out $1,000 each month. The trust department will act as trustee. Bonita will retain the right to revoke the trust and be the remainder beneficiary of the trust. If the trust earns $15,000 for the year, who must pay the income tax on earnings?

    a. Bonita pays on $15,000.

    b. Bonita's mother pays on $12,000, the trust on $3,000.

    c. Bonita's mother pays on $12,000, Bonita on $3,000.

    d. The trust pays on $15,000.

9.  If Bonita and Jason do get married and buy a house, they have identified two mortgage alternatives when taking out a loan. The first alternative is a 30-year 7% mortgage with 5 discount points to be paid at closing. The second alternative is an 8% mortgage with 2 discount points to be paid at closing. Assuming they can qualify for either loan, which of the following aspects should Bonita and Jason consider when choosing between these two alternatives?

    I.   Monthly PMI expenses. —

    *regardless of what loan is chosen, these expenses will be the same.*

    II.  Estimated length of ownership.

    III. Monthly utility expenses. —

    IV.  Cash currently available.

    a.  I and II only

    b.  II only

    c.  II and IV only

    d.  IV only

    e.  I, III, and IV

10. Bonita is considering purchasing an expensive piece of jewelry next month. The local jeweler is offering a three-year financing plan to help her pay for the jewels. For the purposes of preparing Bonita's financial statements for next year, you should

    I.   list the jewels as an investment asset.

    II.  list the loan amount as a current or short-term liability. *no ... 3yrs long-term*

    III. list the jewels as a use asset. —

    IV.  list the loan payment as a fixed expense on the income and expense statement. —

    a.  I and II only

    b.  II and III only

    c.  III and IV only

    d.  I and IV only

    e.  II and IV only

# The Ande Case

## A TAX PLANNING MINI-CASE

Today's date is July 1. Larry and Lolita Ande, both age 44, are reviewing their tax situation for the current year. They have been married for a number of years and have one adult child. They file their own tax returns, and this is the first time they have had questions about their tax situation. Table VI.3 summarizes their financial position for tax purposes. Use this information to answer their tax questions.

**Table VI.3** The Andes' Annual Tax Position

| Tax Item | Amount |
|---|---|
| Larry's earnings | $50,000 |
| Lolita's earnings | $43,000 |
| Federal tax withholdings | $12,300 |
| State income tax withholdings | $4,100 |
| State and local sales taxes paid | $2,300 |
| FICA withholdings | $6,273 |
| Bank account interest* | $1,600 |
| State tax refund from previous year | $900 |
| Home mortgage interest paid | $5,300 |
| Real estate taxes paid | $1,800 |
| Charitable contributions | $4,000 |
| Unreimbursed medical expenses | $800 |
| Stock ownership: United Motor Company** | Current value: $4,000<br>Basis: $8,000 |
| Whole-life insurance policy | Face value: $100,000<br>Cash value: $7,800<br>Owner: Larry<br>Beneficiary: Lolita<br>Insured: Larry<br>Policy dividend: $300 |

*They earn 4% on their account balance. Short-duration municipal bond funds are currently yielding 3.4%.
**They purchased the stock three months ago and still own the stock today.

The Andes itemized deductions for their federal return last year. Currently, neither Larry nor Lolita has access to a qualified retirement plan through their work, and they have not funded IRAs up to this point. They have access to a § 125 flexible spending account through Lolita's employer. To date, they have not funded the account. Open enrollment for the § 125 account lasts for the next 30 days. For the purposes of solving this case, use the tax information shown in Table VI.4.

**Table VI.4** Marginal Tax Rate, Deduction, and Exemption Amounts

| Taxable Income | Tax Rate |
|---|---|
| $16,050 or less | 10% |
| $16,050 to $65,100 | 15% |
| $65,100 to $131,450 | 25% |
| $131,450 to $200,300 | 28% |
| $200,300 to $357,700 | 33% |
| Over $357,700 | 35% |
|  |  |
| Standard deduction | $10,900 |
| Personal exemption | $3,500 |

Please use this information to answer the following case questions.

# Case Questions

1.  Which of the following statements is true?

    I.   If Larry were to pass away this year, Lolita would be required to claim the face value of the life insurance received for federal income tax purposes.  *False*

    II.  If Larry uses a transit pass valued at $100 per month given to him by his employer to commute to and from work, he will be required to add the value of the pass to his income for tax purposes.  *False*

    III. If the Andes want to reduce gross income for tax purposes, they could contribute to a flexible spending plan to cover the cost of unreimbursed medical expenses.

    IV.  Although the face value of the life insurance policy would be tax free to Lolita if Larry were to pass away, the cash value would be fully taxable as income at the federal level.  *False*

    a.   II only

    b.   III only

    c.   I and III only

    d.   II and IV only

    e.   II, III, and IV only

2.   Larry and Lolita are considering moving their bank account balance to a safe municipal bond mutual fund. Before making the switch, they should be aware of which of the following?

    I.   Given their federal marginal tax bracket, the bank account provides a higher after-tax yield.

    II.   Interest and capital appreciation from the municipal bond fund is federally income tax exempt.

    III.   Interest from the bonds will be state income tax free if the bonds held in the fund are from the state where the Andes live.

    IV.   Municipal bond interest that is used to reinvest in the fund will grow on a tax-free basis.

    a.   I only

    b.   III only

    c.   II and III only

    d.   II, III, and IV only

    e.   I, II, III, and IV

3.   Which of the following tax items will be included when calculating the Andes' gross income this year?

    I.   Lolita's salary.

    II.   The state tax refund from the previous year.

    III.   The capital loss in United Motor Company.

    IV.   Dividends earned, but not received, on the insurance policy.

    a.   I and II only

    b.   I and IV only

    c.   II and III only

    d.   I, II, and IV only

    e.   I, III, and IV only

4. The Andes do not know whether they should take the standard deduction or itemize deductions this year. Which of the following statements is true in relation to this issue?

   a. It does not matter which deduction amount they choose because they are equal.

   b. They should claim itemized deductions because this amount is greater than the standard deduction.

   c. They should claim the standard deduction because this amount is greater than itemizing deductions.

   d. If they sell the United Motor Company stock, the loss will reduce their itemized deductions, making the standard deduction more attractive.

   e. Both c and d are correct.

5. Lolita and Larry are thinking about adding to their family next year. If they do have a child, Lolita plans to be a stay-at-home mom. Larry is concerned about what will happen to their tax situation when Lolita stops working. One issue, in particular, that they would like to discuss with their financial planner is whether they should sell the United Motor Company stock this year or wait until next year. What is the best recommendation in their situation?

   a. They should sell the stock this year while they are in the 25% marginal tax bracket because this will result in a larger deduction than waiting and selling when they are in a lower bracket.

   b. They should sell the stock next year, making the deduction more valuable as an offset to Lolita's lost income.

   c. They should sell the stock this year because the full value of the loss can be used this year to reduce their gross income level.

   d. They should sell the stock next year because they currently do not need a tax loss to reduce their reportable income.

6. The Andes have considered moving to another state across the country so that Larry can work with his brother. Larry and his brother work in a similar business. If they do move, which of the following expenses will be an allowable moving expense deduction?

   I. Payment of real estate expenses on the sale of their current home.

   II. Any loss that they incur when selling their personal residence.

   ˣ III. Cost of travel expenses, such as lodging, while in transit from one town to another.

   IV. Cost of meals while in transit from one town to another.
   NO

   a.   III only

   b.   I and III only

   c.   II and III only

   d.   III and IV only

   e.   II and IV only

7.   Which of the following tax planning strategies provides the greatest immediate tax benefit for the Andes?

   a.   Contributing the maximum allowable to a Roth IRA.

   b.   Making the maximum allowable deductible contribution to a traditional IRA. *immediate tax deduction*

   c.   Establishing and contributing to an immediate fixed annuity.

   d.   Purchasing additional whole-life insurance.

8.   Larry is considering changing jobs. A potential employer has offered him several employee benefits that make the job offer very attractive. Which of the following employee benefit alternatives will help reduce the Andes' reportable gross income for federal income tax purposes?

   I.   The immediate right to contribute to a 401(k) plan. —

   II.   Employer-provided parking.

   III.   Group term life insurance equal to three times salary.

   IV.   The right to contribute to a § 125 plan. —

   a.   I only

   b.   I and II only

   c.   I and IV only —

   d.   II, III, and IV only

   e.   I, II, III, and IV

9. One month ago Lolita's uncle gave Larry and Lolita a check for $25,000. He said that he had won some money while gambling in Reno. He wanted to share his good fortune with family. Larry is concerned about the tax ramifications of this transaction. Which statement(s) below is (are) true in this situation?

    I.   Larry and Lolita must pay state and federal income tax on the full $25,000.

    II.   Larry and Lolita must split the tax liability with Lolita's uncle.

    III.  Lolita's uncle must pay state and federal income taxes on the winnings. —

    IV.  Lolita and Larry need not pay any tax because the $25,000 is a gift. —

  a. I only

  b. II only

  c. III only

  d. II and III only

  e. III and IV only

10. If Larry and Lolita finalize a divorce this year and the court orders Larry to pay alimony in the amount of $700 per month for six months (through December), and then $700 per month for 15 years or until Lolita dies, which of the following statements will be true?

  a. Larry and Lolita may not file married filing jointly when completing this year's tax return.

  b. Lolita must file as head of household when completing this year's tax return.

  c. Larry may take a $4,200 deduction from gross income related to the alimony payments.

  d. Lolita need not report the alimony paid, or any child support payments, when she files taxes in future years.

  e. Both a and c are correct.

# The Roth Case

## A TAX PLANNING MINI-CASE

Your clients, Ira and Flora Roth, have come to you for some basic tax-planning advice and guidance. Here are the facts you need to help them.

- Ira's earned income: $65,000

- Flora's earned income: $52,000

- They live in Kansas and own a municipal bond issued by the city of Wichita (not a private activity bond). The bond's face value is $100,000 and it has a 3.5% coupon.

- Ira paid $12,000 in alimony for the year to a former spouse.

- During the year they had the following transactions:

    - Sold XXP stock for $11,000; originally purchased many years ago for $5,000.

    - Purchased 100 shares of HHP stock for $3,000 in April of the year.

    - Sold a KSU corporate bond originally purchased on February 6 of the year for $15,000 (basis); they received $11,000 for the bond on November 12.

    - Redeemed $4,300 worth of EE savings bonds in July that they had held for 12 years; the bonds earned 6% interest and had doubled in value.

    - Sold 1,000 shares of UNR stock at $7 per share that they had purchased earlier in the year for $13 per share.

- Flora (age 61) received annuity distributions of $22,000 from a nonqualified annuity. At the beginning of the year, the annuity had a value of $300,000 and an after-tax basis of $100,000. Her remaining life expectancy is 13.64 years.

- Ira (age 57) terminated employment and took a distribution of $100,000 from his 401(k) plan with the intent of rolling the money over to a Fidelity IRA in 30 to 45 days. His remaining life expectancy is 14.80 years.

- Ira and Flora paid $3,000 in housing expenses for their grandchild Chuck as a way to help offset some of his college expenses. They paid the $3,000 directly to Chuck.

- During the year, they paid the following items:

  - $12,600 in unreimbursed medical expenses

  - $7,000 in mortgage interest

  - $3,500 in property taxes

  - $3,000 in state income taxes

  - $2,800 in state and local sales taxes

  - $1,000 to the Salvation Army

  - $2,400 to their church

  - $750 to Kansas State University

  - $500 in legal fees

  - $100 in safe deposit box fees

- They contributed $3,200 to a § 529 plan to help pay for Chuck's college expenses.

## Case Questions

1. How much in long-term capital gains did the Roths have for the year?

    a. −$3,000

    b. $0

    c. $1,000

    d. $6,000

2. Which of the following statements is true?

   a. The Roths had $1,000 in short-term losses for the year.

   b. The Roths had $4,000 in short-term losses for the year.

   c. The Roths had $10,000 in short-term losses for the year.

   d. The Roths had $15,000 in short-term losses for the year.

3. How much (rounded) of Flora's annuity distribution is taxable this year?

   a. 33%

   b. 67%

   c. 75%

   d. 100%

4. Which of the following statements is true?

   a. Ira's employer will withhold $20,000 in federal taxes from the 401(k) distribution.

   b. Ira will owe an immediate 10% penalty on the 401(k) distribution.

   c. Ira will need to contribute only $80,000 to the IRA rollover to avoid penalties.

   d. Ira needed to roll over the money to the IRA within 30 days to avoid taxes and penalties.

5. Had the Roths decided to give the XXP stock to a charity, they should have

   I. sold the stock first and then made the donation for a deduction.

   II. donated the stock first and then taken the deduction.

   III. donated cash to the charity then sold the stock.

   a. I only

   b. II only

   c. III only

   d. I, II, or III, because they result in the same tax outcome

6. Assuming they had decided to donate the KSU bond to a charity, they should have

    I.   sold the bond first and then made the donation for a deduction.

    II.  donated the bond first and then taken the deduction.

    III. donated the bond first and then deducted the loss.

  a.  I only

  b.  II only

  c.  III only

  d.  I, II, or III, because they result in the same tax outcome

7. How much can the Roths deduct from their federal taxes for the § 529 plan contribution?

  a.  $0

  b.  $1,000

  c.  $2,000

  d.  $1,600

  e.  $3,200

8. In addition to the information already known about the Roths, you learn that Flora owns a vacant lot in Topeka that she purchased as an investment. She would like to exchange the lot so that she does not incur a tax liability. Which of the following properties can she take in trade to receive like-kind tax treatment?

  a.  A duplex in Wichita.

  b.  Collector coins owned by a coin dealer.

  c.  A mortgage on a rental house in Topeka.

  d.  A or c only.

9.  Instead of doing a straight exchange with someone, assume that Flora finds a person who is willing to provide her a combination of property and cash for her vacant lot. Flora will receive $5,000 cash and a vacant lot in town valued at $10,000 (basis of $8,000). If her original lot has a fair market value of $20,000 and a basis of $5,000, how much will Flora realize on this transaction?

    a.  $0

    b.  $5,000

    c.  $8,000

    d.  $10,000

    e.  $15,000

10. Using the information in the previous question, how much gain must Flora recognize on the exchange for income tax purposes?

    a.  $0

    b.  $5,000

    c.  $10,000

    d.  $15,000

    e.  $20,000

# The Shim Case

## AN INSURANCE PLANNING MINI-CASE

Kevin and Sonya Shim are conducting an insurance review with their financial planner. Kevin and Sonya consider themselves middle-Americans—with a small but positive cash flow and a modest net worth. Kevin (age 63) is just a few years away from retirement, whereas Sonya (age 61) plans to work a few more years once Kevin officially retires. The following discussion provides a summary of the Shims' insurance planning situation.

## Life Insurance

Kevin owns a $250,000 universal life insurance policy. Sonya is the insured and their son Wilbur (age 37) is the beneficiary. The policy has a cash value of $23,450 and a living benefits provision; all account earnings are used to offset premium expenses. Sonya owns a 20-year $100,000 level-term life policy that she purchased five years ago. She pays approximately $450 per year in premium costs.

## Property and Casualty Insurance

Kevin and Sonya own a home as JTWROS that has a market and replacement value of $245,000. The house is insured with a Standard HO-3 policy for $210,700. The policy requires that the Shims pay a $500 deductible per claim occurrence. Other provisions include the following:

- 10% coverage on detached structures

- Coverage up to $250 for cash

- Coverage up to $1,500 for collectibles, artwork, and similar assets

- Personal property contents coverage equal to 20% of the insured dwelling

- Living expense coverage for six months

- Coverage up to $100,000 for personal liability

- A replacement cost coverage endorsement is in place.

The Shims' two cars are insured under a personal automobile policy with split-limit coverage of $250,000/$500,000/$50,000. They also have a $1-million-dollar excess liability policy.

## Health Insurance

The Shims are covered under Sonya's group health insurance plan. The traditional plan has a lifetime maximum benefit equal to $1 million for the family, a $500-per-person deductible, and an 80% coinsurance clause, with a family stop-loss limit of $2,500.

Use the preceding case information to answer the questions that follow.

# Case Questions

1.  In preparation for retirement, Kevin is exploring his Social Security and Medicare insurance coverage. Which of the following is a benefit provided by Medicare?

    a.  Hospice benefits for terminally ill persons.

    b.  A stop-loss limit for annual medical expenses in excess of $2,500.

    c.  Coverage for custodial care.

    d.  Coverage for nonprescription drugs.

2.  Kevin is considering purchasing a 12-year-old pickup truck for use when he goes hunting. The truck that he has his eye on has 90,000 miles but is in generally good condition. Which of the following insurance coverage(s) should Kevin probably exclude when purchasing an insurance policy for this truck?

    I.   Part A—liability coverage.

    II.  Part B—medical payments coverage.

    III. Part C—uninsured motorist coverage.

    IV.  Part D—damage to insured's auto coverage.

    a.  IV only

    b.  II and IV only

    c.   I, II, and III

    d.   I, III, and IV

    e.   II, III, and IV

3.    If Sonya were to die today, which of the following is true in relation to the $250,000 universal life insurance policy owned by Kevin?

    a.   Kevin will continue to own the policy for the benefit of Wilbur.

    b.   Kevin will make a taxable gift of life insurance proceeds to Wilbur.

    c.   Kevin will receive an amount equal to the cash value, and Wilbur will receive the remainder of the life insurance value as a tax-free gift.

    d.   Kevin will receive the proceeds of the policy.

    e.   Kevin must include the $250,000 face value of the policy as an asset when he calculates Sonya's taxable estate.

4.    What will be the result if Sonya decides to cancel her term life insurance policy?

    a.   She will incur a $2,250 tax liability based on the level of premium paid over the past five years.

    b.   She will receive $450 in premium paid for last year's coverage as a refund from the insurance company, and this amount will be fully taxable at the Federal level.

    c.   She will not have a tax liability associated with the cancellation.

    d.   She would incur a tax liability on the face amount received if she were to die after canceling the policy but before receiving refunded premiums.

5.    If the Shims sustain an $80,000 loss to their dwelling from a fire, how much will the insurance company pay (after the deductible) toward the dwelling loss claim?

    a.   $64,000

    b.   $68,000

    c.   $79,500

    d.   $80,000

6.  If a shed valued at $13,000 in the backyard is also destroyed in the fire, what is the maximum amount that the insurance company will pay, prior to the deductible, to replace the shed and any other detached dwellings?

    a.  $225,000

    b.  $25,000

    c.  $21,070

    d.  $13,000

    e.  $1,300

7.  Sonya believes that her husband is a reckless driver, and she worries about what will happen if he is ever in a serious car accident. If Kevin is involved in a car accident and causes physical harm to another motorist in the amount of $300,000, how much will be paid from the personal automobile policy (PAP) and how much from the excess liability policy?

    a.  $300,000 PAP and $0 excess liability.

    b.  $0 PAP and $300,000 excess liability.

    c.  $150,000 PAP and $150,000 excess liability.

    d.  $50,000 PAP and $250,000 excess liability.

    e.  $250,000 PAP and $50,000 excess liability.

8.  How much will the Shims' health insurance company pay if Sonya files a claim for a broken foot that cost $2,000 for emergency room treatment, $700 for bone setting, and $300 in rehabilitation services?

    a.  $0

    b.  $500

    c.  $2,000

    d.  $2,500

    e.  $3,000

9. The Shims are curious about the alternatives available when planning for possible nursing home care costs in the future. Which of the following long-term care insurance strategies listed below is an appropriate financial planning alternative for the Shims?

    I.   Use the living benefits provision within an accelerated death benefit rider available in the universal life insurance policy.

    II.   Purchase a life insurance policy that has a long-term care insurance endorsement.

    III.   Systematically save for future health care costs and use Medicare as the primary insurance coverage for long-term care expenses.

    IV.   Use Medicaid coverage for long-term care expenses after age 65.

  a.  II only

  b.  I and II only

  c.  II and III only

  d.  III and IV only

  e.  I, II, and III only

10. Currently, neither Kevin nor Sonya has disability insurance coverage. Kevin and Sonya would like more information about disability insurance. Which of the following statements is (are) true in relation to disability insurance?

    I.   Shorter elimination periods result in lower premium costs.

    II.   Benefits paid from employer-provided group disability plans are received income tax free.

    III.   If a guaranteed renewable contract is used, the insurance company cannot increase premiums on individual policies but can raise premiums for all individuals covered by the policy.

    IV.   Disability policies are nearly always designed to provide lifetime benefits.

  a.  I only

  b.  I and II only

  c.  II and III only

  d.  III only

  e.  II, III, and IV only

# The Butterfield Case

## AN INSURANCE PLANNING MINI-CASE

John Butterfield, 49, and his wife Haley Butterfield, 44, live in a relatively new home on the outskirts of Anycity, Anystate. They have been married for 23 years and have three children. Both John and Haley are in excellent health. Their son Troy, age 20, is a baseball player on scholarship at the University of Anystate. Daughter Holly, age 17, hopes to attend State University next fall as a cadet to begin pursuing a career in the Marine Corps.

The choices of their first two children have allowed the Butterfields to concentrate their college saving goals on Naomi, the youngest, at age 13. John and Haley have come to you for help in addressing several insurance planning questions and concerns. Use the following information to conduct a review of their financial situation and use your analyses to answer the questions that follow the case narrative.

## Global Assumptions (Valid unless otherwise Specified in Certain Instances)

- Inflation: 3.5%

- All income and expense figures are given in today's dollars.

- Federal marginal tax bracket: 25%

- State marginal tax bracket: 5.75%

- Any qualified plan or IRA contribution growth rates are assumed to stop at the federally mandated limit unless otherwise restricted.

- All nominal rates of return are pretax returns.

## Income Issues

John has worked for the last 14 years as an engineer for CNS Design. He has an $81,000 salary. He would like to retire at age 67.

Haley has worked as a CPA for 17 years, the last 14 of which have been out of their home. Though her earnings vary from month to month, she estimates that she will earn $65,000 this year. She wants to retire at the same time as John.

They also assume that their salaries will increase, on average, by 3.5% per year over their working lives. This year they anticipate earning $600 in interest and non-qualified mutual fund dividend distributions, which will be reinvested.

## Expense Issues

Table VI.5 provides a summary of the Butterfields' fixed (non-discretionary) and variable (discretionary) expenses.

**Table VI.5** Summary of Expenses

| Expense | Amount | Frequency |
|---|---|---|
| Pretax health care premiums | $200 | Monthly |
| 401(k) contributions ✗ add 50% matching | $540 ✗12 | Monthly | 9,720 |
| Keogh contributions ✗ | $7,800 | Annually |
| Mortgage | $1,600 | Monthly |
| Home equity loan | $625 | Monthly |
| Auto loan #1 | $310 | Monthly |
| Auto loan #2 | $500 | Monthly |
| Credit cards and installment debt | $2,100 | Annual |
| Auto insurance | $1,100 | Semiannual |
| Homeowner's insurance | $825 | Annual |
| Disability insurance (pretax) | $200 | Monthly |
| Life insurance | $400 | Annual |
| IRA contributions (Haley) ✗ | $750 ✗4 | Quarterly | 3000 |
| IRA contributions (John) ✗ | $750 ✗4 | Quarterly | 3000 |
| Subscriptions | $650 | Annual |
| Telephone | $1,560 | Annual |
| Digital cable television | $125 | Monthly |
| Hobbies | $750 | Annual |
| Entertainment | $1,500 | Annual |
| Education payments (spending money Troy) | $5,000 | Annual |
| Travel costs for first child while in college | $1,200 | Annual |
| Groceries | $75 | Weekly |
| Food away from home | $3,400 | Annual |

| Real estate taxes | $1,300 | Annual |
|---|---|---|
| Household maintenance | $2,700 | Annual |
| Utilities | $175 | Month |
| Clothing | $1,500 | Annual |
| Dry cleaning | $50 | Month |
| Personal care | $500 | Annual |
| Furnishing | $1,000 | Annual |
| Allowances | $2,000 | Annual |
| Medical copayments | $700 | Annual |
| Prescriptions | $250 | Annual |
| Gas | $2,500 | Annual |
| Personal property tax | $400 | Semiannual |
| Banking fees | $75 | Annual |
| IRA fees | $80 | Annual |
| Travel | $100 | Monthly |
| Contributions to church | $125 | Monthly |
| Vacations | $3,000 | Annual |
| Christmas gifts | $2,400 | Annual |

**Home mortgage.** They are eight years into a 30-year 7.5% mortgage that had an original balance of $228,850, with a current outstanding balance of $206,602.

**Home equity loan.** The loan balance was used to pay off credit cards and purchase a vehicle for Troy to use at college. Since the loan was first taken, they have accumulated additional credit card debt. The monthly payment is approximately 2% of the outstanding balance. The credit line expires and will be due and payable in seven years. They have paid $3,000 in interest over the past year.

**Auto Payments.**

Auto 1: Balance is $8,500 with 2.5 years remaining.

Auto 2: Balance is $25,000 with 57 months remaining.

## Tax Issues

After reviewing their pay stubs, John and Haley calculated that their total annual federal withholdings and/or estimated tax payments totaled $20,250. Their state withholdings amounted to $8,000. Social Security withheld was $10,985. The Butterfields file taxes as "married filing jointly" and have $30,241 in itemized deductions for the year.

The Butterfields are eligible for a $5,000 state income tax deduction, and five $1,000-personal exemptions for John, Haley, and the children. The marginal tax bracket for their state is 5.75%.

## Specific Client Goals

- Under any circumstance, they want to provide 50% of the cost of Holly's and Naomi's college education costs, and all of Troy's education costs that are not covered by scholarships.

- They want to maintain their current standard of living in retirement or in the event of either spouse's premature death.

- They want to protect their income and assets in the event of a catastrophic accident or illness, so that they can pass on their assets to their children.

- They both want to continue funding their IRAs to the current maximum limit.

See Table VI.6 for information on the Butterfields' assets and liabilities.

**Table VI.6** The Butterfields' Assets and Liablities

| Asset | Amount | Ownership |
|---|---|---|
| Checking account | $950 | Client |
| Large-cap mutual fund | $9,000 | Client |
| Checking account | $1,200 | Co-client |
| Small-cap mutual fund | $17,250 | Co-client |
| Life insurance cash value | $3,800 | Co-client |
| Checking account | $2,800 | Joint |
| Savings account | $7,500 | Joint |
| Money market account | $10,050 | Joint |
| Mid-cap mutual fund | $40,000 | Joint |
| Artwork | $25,000 | Joint |
| 401(k) | $62,000 | Client |
| Keogh retirement plan | $125,000 | Co-client |
| Individual retirement account (IRA) | $38,000 | Client |
| Individual retirement account (IRA) | $41,500 | Co-client |
| Home | $315,000 | Joint |
| Honda | $17,500 | Joint |
| Toyota | $38,000 | Joint |
| Collectibles | $13,000 | Co-client |
| Furniture | $17,500 | Client |
| Other assets | $69,000 | Joint |
| Misc. assets | $39,000 | Joint |
| **Liabilities** | **Amount** | **Ownership** |
| Visa credit card | $2,500 | Co-client |
| MasterCard | $4,900 | Joint |
| Mortgage | $206,602 | Joint |
| Home equity loan | $32,000 | Joint |
| Honda | $8,500 | Joint |
| Toyota | $25,000 | Joint |
| Short-term installment debt | $21,000 | Client |

# Current Insurance Data

## Property and Casualty

**Auto**. All vehicles

Liability: $300,000 single limit (including uninsured motorist)

Medical payments coverage: $1,000 limit per person

Deductible: $250 collision; $100 comprehensive

Premium: $1,100 every six months

*Auto 1*: 20XX Honda Accord LX Sedan

Mileage: 30,000

Color: light blue

Engine: 6-cylinder

Transmission: manual

Payment: $310/month

Balance: $8,500 with 2.5 years remaining

Worth: $17,500

*Auto 2*: 20XX Toyota Sequoia Limited (4×4)

Mileage: 5,500

Color: silver

Engine: 8-cylinder

Transmission: automatic

Payment: $500/month

Balance: $25,000 with 57 months remaining

Worth: $38,000

**Home**. Single-family dwelling

Insured value: $245,000

Replacement value: $315,000

Deductible: $500

Personal property: 50% of dwelling

Bodily injury: $100,000

Personal injury: $0

Other endorsements: None

**Umbrella**: None

**Professional liability**: None

**Business**: None

## Life and Health

**Life.** Haley has a $50,000 universal life policy with XYZ Insurance Co. She pays the annual premium of $400. The policy has a current cash value of $3,800 (the cash value at the beginning of the period was $3,600). John is the primary beneficiary and Haley is the owner. At the time of purchase, policy projections were based on after-tax U.S. Treasury rates of 6%.

John has an employer-provided term policy that pays one times his annual salary. The face amount of the policy is reduced by 50%, regardless of his salary, at age 65 and terminates at age 70.

Other life assumptions:

- For planning purposes, the Butterfields would like to use 80% of their combined incomes, before taxes, to represent their total household expenses in the event of a death.

- Final illness and burial expenses are estimated to be $15,000 each.

- Estate administration expenses are expected to be approximately $5,200 each.

- Child care expenses will be $10,000.

- Full retirement age, for insurance purposes, is assumed to be age 67.

- The Butterfields need $100,000 in annual income per year, before taxes, while retired. They would like to use this assumption for both insurance and retirement planning purposes.

- Social Security benefit while children are still at home is $32,000 if John dies, and $29,000 if Haley dies, in today's dollars.

- At age 60, Haley is eligible for a $13,000 annual Social Security survivor benefit, while John is entitled to a $10,000 annual survivor benefit (in today's dollars).

- In the event of either spouse's death, the other spouse plans to stop working at age 60 and begin taking early retirement survivor benefits (if available).

- For conservative planning purposes, the Butterfields do not plan on using interest and/or dividends as an income source when planning insurance needs.

- At full retirement (i.e., at age 67) John will receive $18,000 per year in Social Security benefits; Haley will receive $16,500 in benefits (in today's dollars).

- Assumed ages at death for John and Haley are 90 and 92, respectively.

- The assumed gross rate of return on insurance assets, in the event of death, is 9%.

**Health.** The Butterfields' health insurance is provided by Blue Cross/Blue Shield. The monthly premium of $600 is paid 66% by John's employer, with the remainder paid out of pocket. The plan has a deductible of $250 per person and a family copayment of 20%. The out-of-pocket per-family cap on copayments is $1,000 per year. The lifetime maximum on major medical is $500,000 per person.

**Long-term care.** None.

**Disability.** John's disability coverage is a group disability contract provided by his employer. It pays a $5,000 monthly benefit until age 65. The contract has a liberal "own occupation" definition. The elimination period is 120 days. Haley does not have a disability policy. In the event of a disability, the Butterfields would like to continue saving for other goals; however, they do not want to rely on Social Security disability benefits when estimating disability income needs.

**Vacation/medical leave.** John has accumulated 30 sick days, which is the maximum he is allowed to carry. He could accrue one week per year if he fell below the maximum. He also is eligible for three weeks of vacation per year. He can carry over one week, but this has not previously been done.

## Education Funding Goals

The Butterfields would like to assume that education expenses will increase 6.50% per year. They are comfortable assuming a growth rate of 9.00% per year for educational assets and savings in a tax-advantaged account before and after college begins (6.75% if assets are held in a taxable account). Each of the children is talented academically (GPA > 3.0) and in terms of extracurricular activities.

Troy is currently enrolled at University of Anystate. Current cost: $14,700/year (waiver).

- He is on a ¾ baseball scholarship. His parents budget $5,000 per year in extra support; they pay tuition not covered in the scholarship and give Troy what is left from their $5,000 budget as a spending allowance.

- The Butterfields have also allocated $1,200 per year to help pay for Troy's travel expenses.

- He has completed one year of college.

- His health insurance is provided under his father's group health plan.

Holly wants to attend State University; current cost: $10,500/year (possible tuition waiver).

- Wants to go to school on an ROTC scholarship and fund any additional expenses out of pocket from money earned during summers.

Naomi's college funding goals are unknown, but her parents want to plan for college costs of $16,500 per year (in today's dollars).

- They prefer to use tax-advantaged savings plans to fund any expenses.

## Retirement Information

The Butterfields would like to retire when John turns age 67. Based on today's dollars, they are willing to reduce their income by 80% of current income while retired. At full retirement (i.e., age 67) John will receive $18,000 per year in Social Security benefits; Haley will receive $16,500 in benefits (in today's dollars) at age 67. When planning, they are comfortable assuming a 9.00% rate of return before retirement, and a 5.75% return after retirement. Contributions to their defined contribution plans are anticipated to increase 3% annually. They anticipate being in a combined 25% marginal tax bracket in retirement. Inflation before and after retirement will be 3.50%; their incomes should keep pace with inflation. John's employer matches 401(k) contributions $0.50 cents on the dollar. IRA assets are held in Roth accounts. Assumed age at death for John is age 90 and age 92 for Haley.

## Estate Information

They both have simple wills. John leaves his estate to Haley and Haley leaves her estate to John. They believe that, on average, their estate will grow by 4% after the first spouse's death. Other assumptions include:

- Funeral expenses are expected to be approximately $12,000 each.

- Estate administrative expenses will be $5,200 each.

- The Butterfield do not expect to pay any executor fees.

# Case Questions

1.  Which of the following strategies can the Butterfields use to improve their cash flow situation?

    a.  Pay off credit card balances with monetary assets.

    b.  Decrease insurance deductibles.

    c.  Reduce IRA contributions and use the proceeds to purchase a variable universal life insurance policy.

    d.  All of the above.

2.  The Butterfields' current ratio is (rounded): ~ *balance sheet*

    a.  0.62

    b.  0.79

    c.  1.68

    d.  3.00

3.  The Butterfields' savings ratio, using gross earned income and including employer 401(k) matching but excluding reinvested interest and dividends, is (rounded):
    X
    *expense statement*

    a.  4%

    b.  10%

    c.  16%

    d.  22%

4.  John and Haley both have retirement account balances. They would like to know what their options will be when they reach retirement. Which of the following statements describes their IRA retirement situation?

    I.   John can roll over his 401(k) account balance into an IRA. *yes.*

    II.  Haley cannot roll over her account balance because her assets are held in a Keogh.

    III. Both John and Haley can roll over their account balances into an IRA and take a special five-year averaging tax technique on amounts withdrawn at that time.

    IV.  Haley can roll over her Keogh account balance into an IRA.

    a.  III only

    b.  I and II only

    c.  I and III only

    d.  I and IV only

5.  Which of the following is true if Haley closes her accounting firm to join a large consulting company this year?

    a.  Health Insurance Portability and Accountability Act (HIPAA) rules guarantee that her new employer will immediately pay for any pre-existing conditions she might have.

    b.  She will need to continue her current insurance coverage under COBRA provisions.

    c.  She will be required to drop her current coverage through John's employer if she accepts insurance through her new employer.

    d.  She can remain on John's health insurance policy until she is fully covered under her new employer's insurance plan.

6.  If John, Haley, and Naomi were involved in an accident that required medical care, how much would their health insurance pay, including deductions and copayments, given the following expenses? John $1,800; Haley $3,700; Naomi $4,200.

    a.  $1,750

    b.  $7,160

    c.  $7,950

    d.  $8,950

7.  An HO-3 policy (Special Form) with no endorsements excludes which of the following perils?

    a.  Flood

    b.  Fire

    c.  Collapse caused by a covered peril

    d.  Weight of ice

    e.  Volcanic eruption

8. If the Butterfields suffer a $47,000 homeowner's loss due to fire, how much will the insurance company pay on the claim, accounting for any deductible and co-pay provisions?

   a. $45,193

   b. $45,693

   c. $46,500

   d. $47,000

9. The Butterfields recently lived through a major wind storm. The experts said it was not a tornado, but John and Haley would argue otherwise. Their home was terribly damaged. It has been estimated that it will cost $250,000 to fix the house. Excluding listed deductibles and copayments, how much must the Butterfields pay out of pocket toward the repairs?

   a. $0

   b. $500

   c. $5,000

   d. $7,500

10. The Butterfields might be able to reduce their automobile insurance premiums by taking which of the following discounts?

   a. A good student discount.

   b. A multicar discount.

   c. A farm use discount.

   d. Both a and b

11. Which of the following statements is (are) true about the Butterfields' PAP?

   I. They are covered if injured while driving someone else's car.

   II. They are covered while driving either the Honda or Toyota.

   III. They are covered if they rent off-road motorcycles to tour the desert while on vacation.

   a. I only

   b. II only

   c. I and II only

   d. I, II, and III

12. During a recent thunderstorm, the Butterfields' Honda Accord received $2,300 in damage from hail. How much will their PAP pay for this claim?

    a. $0

    b. $2,050

    c. $2,200

    d. $2,300

13. Haley is worried that her oldest son Troy will be without health insurance after he graduates from college in a few years. Which of the following are examples of appropriate insurance coverage recommendations for Troy once he graduates?

    I.   Extend his current coverage through a COBRA extension.

    II.  Purchase insurance through an offshore Asian state-sponsored high-risk pool.

    II.  Purchase insurance through a private company.

    a. I only

    b. I and II only

    c. I and III only

    d. II and III only

    e. I, II, and III

14. Which of the following risk management recommendations is (are) most appropriate to help the Butterfields manage their risk exposures?

    I.   Purchase an excess liability insurance policy.

    II.  Decrease their homeowner's coverage to 80% of the home's value.

    III. Eliminate collision coverage on the Toyota.

    IV.  Purchase an endorsement to cover their art collection.

    a. I and III only

    b. II and IV only

    c. II and III only

    d. I and IV only

15. Which of the following strategies can the Butterfields use to increase their current discretionary cash flow situation?

    a.  Increase the deductible in their PAP policy.

    b.  Purchase an umbrella liability insurance policy.

    c.  Decrease the deductible in their HO policy.

    d.  All of the above.

16. The Butterfields are not sure whether they are paying an appropriate premium for their universal life insurance policy. Which statement below is true in relation to this concern?

    a.  The universal life policy is fairly priced according to the yearly-price-per -thousand formula.

    b.  Even though the yearly-price-per-thousand formula states that the policy is overpriced, given Haley's health status, she should hold the policy because she probably will not qualify for another policy.

    c.  Even though the universal policy is expensive, they should not replace it because the cost is less than two times the yearly-price-per-thousand formula benchmark price.

    d.  Haley should replace the universal policy because, according to the yearly-price-per-thousand formula, the cost is more than two times the benchmark price.

17. Haley would like to know the difference between variable life insurance and universal life insurance. Which of the following statements most accurately describes the difference?

    a.  Variable life insurance uses subcontracts that are invested to generate a guaranteed rate of return.

    b.  Universal life insurance uses a fixed mortality charge, and variable life insurance does not.

    c.  Variable life insurance has a death benefit that varies, and universal life insurance provides only a fixed death benefit.

    d.  Universal life insurance provides a crediting rate based on the insurance company's general account subject to a minimum guarantee, and variable life insurance uses subaccounts that can fluctuate based on market returns.

18. Which of the following is an advantage for John and Haley if they decide to fund their children's college expenses using a § 529 plan?

    a.  The contribution will allow them to take a federal and state income-tax deduction, which will reduce their overall tax liability.

    b.  If a beneficiary of the § 529 plan does not use the assets, John and Haley can name a new beneficiary of the account.

c. Because of the special tax structure of § 529 plans, the assets held in the plan will not increase the expected family contribution for financial aid.

d. All of these answers are advantages.

19. Which of the following is an advantage associated with the Butterfields' current health insurance coverage?

    I. John's employer pays two-thirds of the total premium, which makes the cost of the policy reasonably low.

    II. The deductible and co-payment associated with the policy is better than or equal to traditional health insurance policies found in the marketplace.

    III. The lifetime maximum benefits are sufficiently high.

a. II only

b. I and II only

c. II and III only

d. I, II and III

20. Which of the following is true for John if he purchases additional life insurance through his employer?

a. Few exclusions are associated with these types of policies.

b. Because most group term policies have a conversion feature, he can be assured that upon termination of employment he can continue his coverage.

c. He can tailor the coverage to his own needs.

d. All of the above are true.

# Discussion Points and Questions

1.  Briefly summarize the relevant facts of the case relating to insurance planning.

2.  If the Butterfields were going to purchase additional life insurance, what type of policy, what face value, and what riders would be most appropriate given their ages and needs?

3.  Explain the advantages and disadvantages of having John purchase additional life insurance through his employer.

4.  Describe the 80% co-insurance rule and report to the Butterfields how this rule affects their homeowners coverage.

5.  What actions can the Butterfields take to reduce their insurance premiums while maintaining adequate coverage in terms of liability and property coverage?

6.  Explain why the Butterfields should consider purchasing an excess liability insurance policy.

7.  Describe the purpose of long-term care insurance and indicate whether and when the Butterfields should consider purchasing this type of insurance.

8.  Report on the advantages and disadvantages associated with the Butterfields' current health insurance policy.

# The Little Case

## AN INVESTMENT SITUATION MINI-CASE

Lucas Little has been asked by his client to review the financial statements of Stuff Stores Company. Mr. Little's client is considering making a substantial purchase of Stuff Stores stock. Before doing so, the client would like to know a bit more about the financial stability of the company. The information in Table VI.6 should be used to conduct a basic analysis of Stuff Stores' financial situation.

**Table VI.6** Annual Financial Data for Stuff Stores Company ($ millions)

| Financial Attribute | Year 1 | Year 2 | Current |
|---|---|---|---|
| Market capitalization | 200,000.5 | 212,234.0 | 249,926.5 |
| Total sales | 139,208.0 | 166,809.0 | 193,295.0 |
| Net income (earnings) | 4,430.0 | 5,377.0 | 6,295.0 |
| Dividends per share | .16 | .20 | .24 |
| Shares outstanding | 4,474.8 | 4,443.8 | 4,464.5 |
| Total assets | 64,654.0 | 70,349.0 | 78,130.0 |
| Debt | 16,891.0 | 18,712.0 | 18,824.0 |
| Shareholder's equity | 19,136.0 | 24,216.0 | 31,343.0 |
| Cash flow | 7,580.0 | 8,194.0 | 9,604.0 |

Other relevant data include:

- Beta for Stuff Stores stock: .85

- Standard deviation for Stuff Stores stock: 14.5%

- Average return for Stuff Stores stock: 10.5%

- Risk-free rate of return: 4.0%

- Return on the market: 9.0%

Information on similar stocks is shown in Table VI.7.

**Table VI.7** Data for Similar Stocks

| Company | Stock Beta | Stock Standard Deviation | Average Stock Return |
|---|---|---|---|
| Wigwam Stores, Inc. | .90 | 15.5% | 8.0% |
| Maryland Markets | .80 | 12.0% | 9.0% |
| Pacific Mercantile, Inc. | .89 | 15.0% | 11.0% |

Please use this information to answer the following questions:

# Case Questions

1. Based on current information, what is the net profit margin for Stuff Stores?

   a. 1.98%

   b. 2.97%

   c. 3.26%

   d. 3.56%

   e. 3.88%

2. Based on current information, the price to earnings ratio (P/E) for one share of Stuff Stores stock is:

   a. 1.29

   b. 7.97

   c. 20.08

   d. 26.02

   e. 39.70

3. When comparing Stuff Stores stock to similar stocks in the market, which has the highest required rate of return?

   a. Stuff Stores Company.

   b. Wigwam Stores, Inc.

    c.   Marryland Markets.

    d.   Pacific Mercantile, Inc.

    e.   Stuff Stores Company and Pacific Mercantile, Inc. are the same.

4.   Based solely on past performance compared to the required rate of return, which stock should Mr. Little's client avoid?

    a.   Stuff Stores Company.

    b.   Wigwam Stores, Inc.

    c.   Marryland Markets.

    d.   Pacific Mercantile, Inc.

    e.   Both Marryland Markets and Pacific Mercantile, Inc.

5.   Mr. Little would like to rank the four stocks in a standardized way before making a recommendation to his client. Using the average stock return data provided, rank the four stocks from highest to lowest using the Sharpe ratio.

    I.   Stuff Stores Company.

    II.  Wigwam Stores, Inc.

    III. Maryland Markets.

    IV. Pacific Mercantile, Inc.

    a.   II, III, I, and IV

    b.   IV, III , II, and  I

    c.   III, I, IV, and II

    d.   IV, I, III, and II

    e.   I, IV, III, and II

6.   Mr. Little's client has noticed that the price of Stuff Stores Company stock has remained steady during the past six months. He is convinced that the stock will continue to trade in a narrow range. He would like to make money on the stock, however. Which of the following strategies will cause Mr. Little's client to experience the greatest potential loss if Stuff Stores' stock price begins to fluctuate more widely?

    a.   Selling a naked put option.

    b.   Selling a naked call option.

    c.   Selling a covered call option.

    d.   Buying a call option.

    e.   Buying shares in Stuff Stores Company directly.

7.   Assume that Mr. Little's client decides to purchase shares in Stuff Stores stock to add to his sizable portfolio. The client tells Mr. Little that he does not want to incur the cost of selling the stock or the entire portfolio. The client also does not want to risk mistiming the market should stock prices start to fall. One strategy for the client to protect against a possible decline in both Stuff Stores stock price and the value of the portfolio would be to

    a.   buy an index call option.

    b.   sell an index call option.

    c.   buy an index put option.

    d.   sell an index put option.

    e.   avoid all options strategies because the client cannot protect against the decline with these options.

8.   If the market risk premium were to increase, the value of common stock, including Stuff Stores Company stock, (holding all other factors constant) would[1]

    a.   not change because this does not affect stock values.

    b.   increase to compensate the investor for increased risk.

    c.   increase because of higher risk-free rates.

    d.   decrease to compensate the investor for increased risk.

    e.   decrease because of lower risk-free rates.

9.   Mr. Little thinks that he has found an interesting bond investment for his client's portfolio. Mr. Little, when searching for investment ideas, focused on his client's goal of return maximization. The bond has a face value of $1,000 with a maturity date in seven years. The bond's coupon rate is 6.25% compounded annually. Today, the bond sells for $1,185.00. The indenture agreement states that the bond can be called for $1,100 after five years. Which of the following statements is (are) true?

    a.   The current yield is greater than both the yield to maturity and yield to call.

    b.   Given the client's investment objective, this bond should do particulary well if interest rates start to increase.

c. Mr. Little can lock in a yield to maturity that is higher than the current yield by purchasing the bond today.

d. The value of the bond today in comparison to the spread in the yield to maturity and the current yield indicates tht this bond will not be called early.

10. According to the dividend growth model method of stock valuation, which of the following statements is true, assuming that Mr. Little's client has a required rate of return of 16% and that the dividend has grown from .16 to .24 in three years?

    I. The current Stuff Stores stock price exceeds the calculated value.

    II. The current Stuff Stores stock price is less than the calculated value.

    III. Using the dividend growth model as the only measure, the Stuff Stores stock is undervalued.

    IV. The market price and the calculated value for Stuff Stores match closely, as expected given the high degree of efficiency in the markets.

a. I only

b. III only

c. II and III only

d. III and IV only

# The Cantrell Case

## AN INVESTMENT PLANNING MINI-CASE

Gabriel and Sarah Cantrell, both age 26, were married four years ago. They have one daughter, Joyce, who is now age 3. They also have a new son, Lee, who is age 1. They live at 1315 Devonshire Drive in Anytown, Anystate, 78901.

Gabe works for TG Ag Services as a sales representative. He has been working since he turned age 16, and has spent the last five years with TG Ag Services. Gabe earns $45,000 per year.

Sarah started working when she was 15 years old. Four years ago she took a clerk position at Dave's Discount Store in downtown Anytown. She makes $27,500 per year.

Use the following information to conduct a review of the Cantrells' financial situation.

## Global Assumptions (Valid unless otherwise Specified in Certain Instances)

- Inflation: 3.5%

- Anystate has no state-imposed income tax.

- All income and expense figures are given in today's dollars.

- Planned retirement age: 67 for both

- Federal marginal tax bracket: 15%

- State marginal tax bracket: No state income tax

- All nominal rates of return are pretax returns.

## Income Issues

Currently Gabe earns $45,000 per year, and Sarah earns $27,500. Both Gabe and Sarah assume that their salaries will increase at the rate of inflation. They make approximately $60 (all of which is reinvested) in interest annually. They have no other sources of income.

## Expense Summary

Before meeting with you, they summarized their expenses. These are shown in Table VI.8. Their assets and liabilities are summarized in Tables VI.9 and VI.10, respectively.

**Table VI.8** The Cantrells' Dedicated and Discretionary Expenses

| Expenses | Amount | Frequency |
|---|---|---|
| Health care expenses (Gabe)* | $300.00 | Monthly |
| Health care expenses (Sarah)* | $50.00 | Monthly |
| 401(k) contribution (Gabe)* | $1,800.00 | Annually |
| 401(k) contribution (Sarah)* | $1,375.00 | Annually |
| SS/Medicare (FICA) withholdings | $5,225.00 | Annually |
| Federal tax withholdings | $4,500.00 | Annually |
| Mortgage payments | $714.25 | Monthly |
| Credit card payments | $20.00 | Monthly |
| Auto insurance | $800.00 | Semiannually |
| Homeowner's insurance | $600.00 | Annually |
| Subscriptions | $480.00 | Annually |
| Telephone expense | $1,800.00 | Annually |
| Home Internet | $90.00 | Monthly |
| Hobbies (Sarah) | $1,450.00 | Annually |
| Recreation/entertainment | $200.00 | Monthly |
| Groceries | $400.00 | Monthly |
| Food away from home | $3,000.00 | Annually |
| Real estate taxes | $1,482.00 | Annually |
| Private mortgage insurance | $50.00 | Monthly |
| Household maintenance | $750.00 | Annually |
| Utilities | $3,300.00 | Annually |
| Clothing | $2,200.00 | Annually |
| Laundry services | $300.00 | Annually |
| Personal care | $50.00 | Monthly |
| Furnishing | $750.00 | Annually |
| Child care*** | $600.00 | Monthly |
| Eye glasses | $300.00 | Annually |
| Medical deductibles | $50.00 | Monthly |
| Unreimbursed medical expenses | $100.00 | Annually |
| Gasoline | $1,100.00 | Annually |
| Car registrations | $575.00 | Annually |
| Personal property tax | $450.00 | Annually |
| Safe deposit box fee | $1.00 | Monthly |
| Accounting fees | $150.00 | Annually |
| Charitable contributions | $100.00 | Monthly |
| Vacations | $2,800.00 | Annually |
| Gifts to family members | $1,000.00 | Annually |

*Pretax § 125 plan expenses
**Pretax expenses
***The child care provider is licensed in Anystate.
*Note:* Last year the Cantrells paid $711 in Anystate sales taxes.

## Asset Summary

**Table VI.10** A Summary of the Cantrells' Assets

| Asset | Amount | Ownership |
|---|---|---|
| *Financial Assets* | | |
| Checking account | $350.00 | Joint |
| Savings account | $500.00 | Joint |
| EE savings bonds | $1,000.00 | Joint |
| *Retirement 401(k) Assets* | | |
| Large-cap funds | $5,000.00 | Gabe |
| Mid-cap funds | $2,500.00 | Gabe |
| Small-cap funds | $2,500.00 | Gabe |
| Government bond funds | $1,000.00 | Sarah |
| Mid-cap funds | $2,500.00 | Sarah |
| Small-cap funds | $1,000.00 | Sarah |
| *Other Assets* | | |
| Primary residence | $124,000.00 | Joint |
| Buick Regal | $12,000.00 | Joint |
| GMC pickup | $9,800.00 | Joint |
| Collectibles | $1,200.00 | Joint |
| Golf clubs and equipment | $3,800.00 | Joint |
| 16-foot sailboat w/2-HP motor | $9,600.00 | Joint |
| Furniture | $13,000.00 | Joint |
| Other assets | $4,700.00 | Joint |

## Liability Summary

**Table VI.11** A Summary of the Cantrells' Liabilities

| Liability | Amount | Ownership |
|---|---|---|
| Visa credit card* | $2,400.00 | Joint |
| MasterCard** | $500.00 | Joint |
| Mortgage | Unknown | Joint |

*17.95% APR
** 14.25% APR

Gabe and Sarah purchased a new home in town exactly two years ago today. The original mortgage was in the amount of $116,000 for 30 years at a 6.25% rate. They have made precisely 24 payments on the mortgage.

## Life Insurance and Planning Issues

Gabe and Sarah would like you to analyze their life insurance situation using the following assumptions and facts:

- Upon the first death, household expenses will decrease to $55,000 per year.

- Final expenses are expected to be $9,500 each.

- Estate administration costs are anticipated to be $3,500 each.

- All outstanding liabilities will be paid at the first death.

- They would like to prefund $10,000 in child care expenses at the death of the first spouse.

- They would like to prefund college costs in the event of a spouse's death. They plan to invest any insurance proceeds for this goal in a tax-advantaged educational savings plan.

- They can earn 7% before taxes on any life insurance proceeds both pre- and postretirement.

- They anticipate that their marginal federal tax rate will increase to 25% in retirement.

- They would like to replace $58,000 in retirement income for the surviving spouse.

- They are willing to use all of their retirement savings to offset life insurance needs.

- In the event of either spouse's death, the other spouse plans to stop working at age 60 and begin taking early retirement survivor benefits (if available).

- For conservative planning purposes, the Cantrells do not plan to use interest and/or dividends as an income source when determining insurance needs.

- Gabe's employer provides a term policy for two times his salary at no cost, which continues during periods of disability but terminates at retirement. Sarah is the beneficiary of the life insurance policy.

- Sarah's employer also provides two times her salary in term coverage at no cost, which continues during periods of disability but terminates at retirement. Gabe is the beneficiary of the life insurance policy.

- The surviving spouse's income is not expected to change after the death of the first spouse.

See Table VI.12 for information on the Cantrells' Social Security and life insurance.

**Table VI.12** Social Security Survivor Benefit Information

| Beneficiary | Amount (Monthly)* |
|---|---|
| Sarah and children (until last child turns age 18) | $2,582.50 |
| Gabe and children (until last child turns age 18) | $1,843.10 |
| Sarah (ages 60–67) | $1,048.00 |
| Gabe (ages 60-67) | $1,118.00 |
| Sarah (at age 67) | $1,466.00 |
| Gabe (at age 67) | $1,563.00 |

\* Income test limits could apply. See www.ssa.gov for more information.

## Additional Insurance Information and Planning Issues

Both TG Ag Services and Dave's Discount Store are large employers in the area; each employs more than 20 people at any given time. The Cantrells do not currently have disability or long-term care insurance policies. Both are healthy, with both sets of parents still alive and well. Their home is currently covered by an HO-3 policy with an inflation rider and a $1,000 deductible. Both automobiles are insured with split-limit coverage of $25/$50/$10 and a $500 deductible.

## Retirement Information and Planning Issues

The following information should be used when evaluating the Cantrells' current retirement planning situation:

- They anticipate being in the 25% federal marginal tax bracket after retirement.

- They are comfortable assuming that working with you, their financial planner, they can generate a 10.00% rate of return before retirement.

- When retired, they would prefer to maintain a conservative growth asset allocation that will generate an 8.25% rate of return.

- If retired today, they would like to replace 80% of their combined income.

- At retirement Gabe will be eligible to receive $1,563.00 in monthly Social Security benefits.

- At retirement Sarah will be eligible to receive $1,096.00 in monthly Social Security benefits.

- They are comfortable assuming a life expectancy of 100 years.

- Gabe currently contributes 4% of his salary to his company's 401(k) plan; his employer matches 50% on the first 6% contributed; his plan has a maximum deferral limit of 12% of salary.

- Sarah currently contributes 5% of her salary to her company's 401(k) plan; her employer matches 50% on the first 5% contributed, up to the maximum annual limit.

- Inflation before and after retirement is assumed to be 3.50%.

- Contributions to their 401(k) plans will increase by 3% even though their salaries are expected to increase by the rate of inflation.

## Estate Information and Planning Issues

Both Gabe and Sarah have professionally prepared wills; Gabe's will leaves all of his assets to Sarah, and Sarah's will leaves all of her assets to Gabe. Their wills name their attorney as the estate executor, and in the event of a simultaneous death it is assumed that Gabe will predecease Sarah. Other estate planning facts include:

- Funeral and burial expenses will be $7,500 each.

- Estate and legal costs will be $2,000 each.

- Executor fees will be approximately 2% of the gross estate *before* the marital transfer.

- The net growth rate of the survivor's estate is estimated to be 4% annually.

- Both wills name Sarah's sister Lindsey as the guardian of their children.

- All individually owned assets that pass via property law or contract (e.g., IRAs, qualified plans, bank accounts, life insurance) name the surviving spouse as the primary beneficiary; no contingent beneficiaries have been named.

- No other estate planning documents are known to exist.

Table VI.13 provides a summary of the current yield and rate information applicable to this case.

**Table VI.13** Yield and Rate Information for Use in the Cantrell Analysis

| Investment Class | Yield |
|---|---|
| Checking account | 0.00% |
| Savings account | 3.00% |
| Taxable money market fund | 3.50% |
| EE and I bonds | 3.50% |
| Loan Rates | |
| 30-year mortgage* | 6.50% |
| 15-year mortgage* | 6.00% |
| Home equity line of credit* | 7.25% |
| Home equity loan* | 7.35% |
| 5-year auto loan | 7.90% |
| Personal loan | 8.50% |

*APR includes closing costs over life of loan.

# Goals and Objectives

The Cantrells' primary objective at this point is to fully fund four years of college for their two children. They have already been in contact with the universities that they hope their children will attend. Gabe and Sarah learned that the annual cost of college (including tuition, room, and board) in today's dollars is $18,000 at each school. College costs are estimated to increase by about 6% annually.

They would like to have the total amount needed to pay for a child's college costs available on the first day of college. Given their moderate level of risk tolerance, they are comfortable planning for these expenses using a 7% rate of return. They would also like to use a tax-advantaged investment to save for college.

Their second goal is to retire at age 67, using the assumptions already listed.

In preparation for a meeting with the Cantrells, you have been given a monitored list of mutual funds used by your firm. Your firm's investment committee will allow you to use any of the funds listed below when developing investment recommendations for the Cantrells (see Table 1VI.14).

**Table VI.14** Mutual Funds Approved for Cantrell Recommendations

### Market Indexes

| | RoR* | SD | Corr ( r ) with Index | Yield |
|---|---|---|---|---|
| T-bills | 4.00% | 2.00% | 1.00 | 4.00% |
| Equity market | 12.00% | 17.00% | 1.00 | 2.00% |
| Bond market | 8.00% | 9.00% | 1.00 | 4.70% |

| Fund | Stated Equity Fund Objective | RoR* | SD | Corr ( r ) with Stock Market | Yield |
|---|---|---|---|---|---|
| | Approved Mutual Funds | | | | |
| Super Big Fund | Large-cap fund | 13.00% | 18.00% | 0.95 | 2.00% |
| Maxi Fund | Large-cap fund | 12.20% | 17.40% | 0.92 | 2.00% |
| Multivariate Fund | Mid-cap fund | 14.00% | 18.30% | 0.90 | 1.00% |
| Germain Fund | Mid-cap fund | 13.30% | 16.90% | 0.89 | 1.25% |
| Efficacy Fund | Small-cap fund | 11.00% | 19.00% | 0.85 | 0.25% |
| Software Fund | Small-cap fund | 12.00% | 21.00% | 0.70 | 0.00% |
| Clinical Fund | International fund | 10.00% | 13.00% | 0.68 | 2.00% |
| Image Fund | International fund | 9.80% | 11.00% | 0.63 | 1.00% |
| Measures Fund | Precious metals fund | 6.00% | 13.00% | 0.40 | 0.50% |
| Thumb Fund | Real estate fund | 11.00% | 11.00% | 0.99 | 4.00% |
| Factors Fund | Real estate fund | 9.90% | 12.00% | 0.89 | 5.30% |
| **Column Averages** | | **11.11%** | **15.51%** | **0.80** | **1.75%** |

| Fund | Stated Bond Fund Objective | RoR* | SD | Corr ( r ) with Bond Market | Yield |
|---|---|---|---|---|---|
| Alumni Fund | Gov't bond fund | 7.80% | 8.00% | 0.95 | 4.50% |
| Bush Fund | Gov't bond fund | 8.20% | 8.50% | 0.90 | 5.00% |
| National Fund | Corporate bond fund | 8.40% | 9.00% | 0.98 | 5.10% |
| CDR Fund | Corporate bond fund | 7.56% | 9.20% | 0.85 | 5.40% |
| Fast Fund | High-yield bond fund | 9.90% | 13.00% | 0.75 | 7.00% |
| Mobile Fund | High-yield bond fund | 10.30% | 12.80% | 0.60 | 8.20% |
| **Column Averages** | | **8.69%** | **10.08%** | **0.84** | **5.87%** |

*Rates of return include yields.

Use the information provided in the case narrative to answer the questions that follow.

# Case Questions

1. How much total § 79 income (rounded) for the year must the Cantrells report for tax purposes?

    a. $0

    b. $6

    c. $29

    d. $32

    e. $35

2. Which of the following is true?

    a. Interest earned by the Cantrells adds to their level of discretionary cash flow.

    b. § 79 income earned by the Cantrells adds to their level of discretionary cash flow.

    c. Contributions to Gabe's 401(k) plan reduce discretionary cash flow.

    d. All of the above are true.

    e. A and b only are true.

3. The Cantrells are eligible for which of the following tax credits?

    I.   income tax credit.

    II.  Child and dependent care tax credit.

    III. Earned Child tax credit.

    IV.  Low-income housing tax credit.

    a. I and II only

    b. II and III only

    c. III and IV only

    d. II, III, and IV only

4. The Cantrells' current net worth situation can best be described as

    a. A positive $78,356

    b. A negative $2,900

    c. A positive $116,094

    d.   A negative $113,194

    e.   A positive $194,950

5.    When completing their tax return, the Cantrells should

    a.   file married filing separately.

    b.   claim a deduction from AGI for retirement plan contributions.

    c.   use the sales tax deduction when calculating the amount they can claim for itemized deductions.

    d.   claim Anystate income taxes as a tax credit.

6.    Which of the following strategies can the Cantrells use to improve their discretionary cash flow situation?

    I.   Refinance their first mortgage using a 15-year loan.

    II.   Pay off some or all credit card debt with financial assets.

    III.   Reduce the amount being withheld for federal taxes.

    IV.   Increase the amount of reinvested interest earned on investments.

    a.   I and III only

    b.   II and III only

    c.   II and IV only

    d.   II, III, and IV only

7.    The Cantrells' current level of discretionary cash flow is enough to

    a.   fund this year's savings need for one child's college education.

    b.   fund both children's savings need for college education this year.

    c.   pay off credit card debts within one year.

    d.   fund both a and c.

8.    Which of the following statements is true?

    a.   The Cantrells need to save an additional $3,700 per year to meet their retirement goal.

    b.   The Cantrells will fall short of their retirement goal by more than $1.5 million using their current retirement planning strategy.

    c.   The Cantrells must reduce their life expectancy in retirement to retire at age 67.

    d.   Both a and c.

    e.   None of the above.

9.   Which of the following is true regarding the Cantrells' estate situation?

    I.   The value of Gabe's group life insurance policy will be excluded from his gross estate.

    II.   The full value of jointly held liabilities can be deducted as an expense from the gross estate at the passing of the first spouse.

    III.   If Gabe and Sarah establish § 529 plans for their children by contributing $5,000, the assets held in the accounts will be excluded from Gabe and Sarah's gross estate.

    IV.   The Cantrells should begin a gifting strategy to reduce their taxable estate.

    a.   I only

    b.   III only

    c.   I and II only

    d.   II and III only

    e.   I, III, and IV only

10.   All of the following are examples of tax-advantaged education savings alternatives appropriate for use by the Cantrells except:

    a.   A § 529 plan.

    b.   A Coverdell savings plan.

    c.   EE savings bonds.

    d.   An immediate annuity.

11.   Sarah's grandmother has decided to gift Gabe and Sarah $150,000. Which of the following strategies can the Cantrells fund with this gift?

    I.   Fully prefund their children's college education costs.

    II.   Earmark the gift as a source of emergency funds.

    III.   Use the gift to fully offset Gabe's need for additional life insurance.

    a.   I only

    b.   III only

c. I and II only

d. II and III only

12. Rank the following funds in terms of their total portfolio risk (volatility), highest to lowest:

   I. Maxi Fund

   II. Software Fund

   III. Image Fund

   IV. Clinical Fund

   a. I, II, IV, and III

   b. I, II, III, and IV

   c. II, I, IV, and III

   d. II, I, III, and IV

13. Which fund's expected rate of return, as measured by CAPM, is the lowest?

   a. Super Big Fund

   b. Efficacy Fund

   c. Image Fund

   d. Measures Fund

14. Rank the following funds based on the Sharpe ratio (highest to lowest):

   I. Thumb Fund

   II. Germain Fund

   III. Multivariate Fund

   IV. Super Big Fund

   a. I, II, IV, and III

   b. I, II, III, and IV

   c. II, I, IV, and III

   d. II, I, III, and IV

15. Rank the following funds based on the Treynor index (highest to lowest):

    I.    Clinical Fund

    II.   Image Fund

    III.  Measures Fund

    IV.  Thumb Fund

  a.  I, II, IV, and III

  b.  I, II, III, and IV

  c.  II, I, IV, and III

  d.  II, I, III, and IV

16. Rank the following funds based on the Sharpe ratio (highest to lowest):

    I.    Germain Fund

    II.   Image Fund

    III.  Multivariate Fund

    IV.  Thumb Fund

  a.  I, II, IV, and III

  b.  I, II, III, and IV

  c.  II, I, IV, and III

  d.  IV, I, III, and II

17. Rank the following funds based on the Treynor index (highest to lowest):

    I.    Germain Fund

    II.   Image Fund

    III.  Multivariate Fund

    IV.  Thumb Fund

  a.  I, II, IV, and III

  b.  I, II, III, and IV

  c.  II, IV, I, and III

  d.  IV, I, III, and II

18. Which of the following funds has the highest alpha?

    a.  Super Big Fund

    b.  Thumb Fund

    c.  Germain Fund

    d.  Factors Fund

19. Assume that the correlation and standard deviation data for the bond funds are linked to the bond market index. Which bond fund has the highest alpha?

    a.  Mobile Fund

    b.  Fast Fund

    c.  National Fund

    d.  CDR Fund

20. Which of the following statements is correct?

    I.  High-yield bond funds are affected by both interest rate changes and changes in the economic performance of the company issuing the bonds.

    II.  Risk-adjusted performance can best be measured by beta.

    III.  An investor who wanted to rank a list of diversified mutual funds could feel comfortable using the Treynor index.

    IV.  If an investor wanted to rank a list of sector funds, the Treynor index would be more appropriate than the Sharpe ratio.

    a.  II only

    b.  I and IV only

    c.  I and III only

    d.  II and IV only

# The Alpha Case

## A RETIREMENT PLANNING MINI-CASE

Alpha Corporation is considering its alternatives in relation to establishing a retirement plan for its employees. Please help the CFO of Alpha Corporation answer the following questions:

## Case Questions

1. Alpha Corporation has 100 full-time nonunion employees. What is the minimum number of employees that must be allowed to participate in the company's defined benefit plan?

   a. 40

   b. 50

   c. 75

   d. 100

2. The CFO would like to implement a 401(k)/profit sharing plan. If 75% of the firm's employees stay with the company for only two years (i.e., the firm has high turnover), and the remainder stay for an average of at least 10 years, which vesting schedule should the CFO choose if she wants to minimize plan administration costs?

   a. 2–6 year graduated

   b. 3-year cliff

   c. 3–7 year graduated

   d. 5-year cliff

3.  Jana, age 25, has worked for Alpha Corporation on a part-time basis (i.e., 900 hours per year) for four years. Is she eligible to participate in the firm's 401(k) plan?

    a.  Yes, because she is older than age 21.

    b.  No, because she has not accumulated enough hours for the year.

    c.  Yes, because she has worked for more than two years.

    d.  No, because she has not worked for at least five years.

4.  The CFO's husband, Bud (age 43), also works at Alpha Corporation. He earns $28,000. He just contributed $3,000 to a Roth IRA. When must he begin taking distributions from the Roth IRA?

    a.  Never

    b.  At age 59½

    c.  At age 70½

    d.  At age 75

5.  The CFO would like to establish a deferred compensation plan for herself. She wants any money contributed to the plan to be protected from the firm's creditors. Which nonqualified deferred compensation plan should she choose?

    a.  A rabbi trust

    b.  A secular trust

    c.  A 457 plan

    d.  An unfunded promise-to-pay plan

6.  The CFO feels bad about having a plan for the exclusive benefit of key employees, including herself. She would like you to recommend a qualified plan that would allow her to restrict employee contributions but would permit the firm to make contributions as a tool to increase employee productivity. Which of the following three plans should she use?

    I.   A defined benefit plan

    II.  A stock bonus plan

    III. An ESOP

    a.  I only

    b.  II only

    c.  II or III only

    d.  I, II, or III

7. Which type of plan should the CFO choose if she wants Alpha Corporation to absolutely guarantee benefits to eligible employees (i.e., employees will know exactly how much they will receive when they retire)?

    a. A 401(k) plan

    b. A profit-sharing plan

    c. A target benefit plan

    d. A defined benefit plan

8. Micala, an employee of Alpha Corporation, is 53 years old. She is considering divorcing her husband Jack. They have been married for nine years. If Micala gets a divorce, is she eligible to receive a spousal benefit from Jack's Social Security benefit?

    a. No, because they have not been married for 10 years.

    b. Yes, because they have been married for at least five years.

    c. No, because as someone with a job she can claim only her own Social Security benefit.

    d. Yes, because she is younger than age 60 at the time of divorce.

9. Christina (age 41) terminates employment with Alpha Corporation, and she rolls over her 401(k) account balance to an IRA. Which of the following statements is true, assuming that she takes the money directly before rolling it over?

    I. She must roll over the full amount of the distribution within 60 days to avoid taxation and penalties.

    II. If she distributes $200,000 from the 401(k) plan, she must roll over $160,000 to avoid a penalty.

    III. If she fails to roll over the full distribution, she will incur a 10% penalty.

    a. I only

    b. III only

    c. I and II only

    d. I and III only

10. Which of the following health insurance options does Christina have as a result of quitting her job with Alpha Corporation?

    a. She is ineligible for COBRA coverage because Alpha Corporation employs fewer than 100 employees.

    b. She is eligible for COBRA coverage because Alpha Corporation employs more than 20 employees.

c. COBRA coverage will cover expenses associated only with pre-existing conditions.

d. Both b and c are correct.

# The Edwards Case

## A RETIREMENT AND EMPLOYEE BENEFITS MINI-CASE

Nick Edwards owns a used car dealership. He is age 60, has worked in the business for 30 years, and earns $110,000 per year. He has several employees with varying years of experience and tenure at the dealership. As the owner of the company, Nick has come to you for advice regarding the establishment of a retirement plan. He is also interested in learning more about employee benefits as a tool to help him recruit and retain good salespersons.

Over the course of several weeks of meetings with Nick you have compiled a list of attributes he would like to see in a retirement plan:

- He wants his employees to contribute to the plan.

- He is willing to match employee contributions if necessary.

- He wants the plan to be an incentive to increase productivity.

- He is willing to pay all of the plan's administrative costs.

- He would prefer not to assume any investment risk on the part of employees.

- He would be happy with a payroll deduction for his firm of 10% to 15% per year.

- Although he is willing to match contributions, he would prefer to maintain flexibility so that in low-profit years he could skip matching if needed.

- He does not want 100% immediate vesting for employees.

- He has no opinion regarding the ability of employees to make in-service withdrawals.

- He would like to maximize his own benefits, but not at the expense of running afoul of IRS highly compensated employee rules.

You have learned that, in addition to retirement benefits, Nick offers a mix of employee benefits, including life, health, and disability insurance for his employees. Information about these plans is summarized below:

- Group term life insurance equal to two times annual earnings.

  - Table VI.15 shows the cost per $1,000 of life insurance protection offered through an employer on a monthly basis for tax purposes

- Group health insurance benefits

  - Traditional plan with a $500 annual deductible and 80/20 coinsurance provision

  - Out-of-pocket maximum equal to $5,000 annually

  - Lifetime limit of $750,000

  - Benefit coverage includes employee and spouse only

  - Financed 100% through the dealership

- Group short-term disability insurance

  - Benefit equal to 50% of salary for six months

  - 30-day waiting period

**Table VI.15** Cost per $1,000 of Employer-provided Life Insurance Protection

| Attained Age on Last Day of Employee's Tax Year | Cost Per $1,000 of Protection for One-month Period |
|---|---|
| Under 25 | $.05 |
| 25–29 | .06 |
| 30–34 | .08 |
| 35–39 | .09 |
| 40–44 | .10 |
| 45–49 | .15 |
| 50–54 | .23 |
| 55 – 59 | .43 |
| 6 –64 | .66 |
| 65–69 | 1.27 |
| 70 and above | 2.06 |

Nick's best employee is Emily James. Emily has worked at the dealership full-time for seven years. She is 56 years old and makes $74,000 per year. Other employees' relevant data are shown in Table VI.16.

**Table VI.16** Relevant Employee Data

| Name | Salary | Years w/Firm | Age | Status |
|------|--------|--------------|-----|--------|
| Kate | $36,000 | 6 | 28 | Full-time employee |
| Mark | $32,000 | 4 | 47 | Full-time employee |
| Joyce | $32,000 | 4 | 34 | Full-time employee |
| Bill | $30,000 | 2 | 36 | Full-time employee |
| Jack | $15,000 | 3 | 20 | Part-time employee (< 1,000 hours/year) |
| Andy | $12,000 | 2 | 17 | Part-time employee (< 1,000 hours/year) |
| Mary | $6,000 | 1 | 19 | Part-time employee (< 1,000 hours/year) |

Use this information to answer the following questions.

# Case Questions

1.  How much must Emily James report in yearly § 79 income (rounded) for tax purposes, assuming she stays employed for the year?

    a.  $42

    b.  $98

    c.  $506

    d.  $6,000

2.  Nick purchased a $100,000 participating whole-life insurance policy on his life. To date, he has paid $50,000 in total premiums and received $10,000 in dividends. The policy currently has a net cash value of $15,000 and is subject to a $30,000 outstanding loan. If Nick decides to surrender the policy, he would realize a gain of

    a.  $0

    b.  $5,000

    c.  $10,000

    d.  $15,000

3.  Currently, Nick's brother Tommy owns an auto repair shop across town. Tommy owns the shop as a sole proprietorship. Nick has suggested that Tommy think about converting the shop to a corporation. Advantages for incorporating the repair shop into a C corporation include which of the following?

    I.   Allowing the flow-through of corporate profits to shareholders that could be taxed at each owner's marginal tax bracket.

    II.  Withdrawing accumulated profits at capital gain rates.

    III. Providing tax-favored fringe benefits to employee shareholders.

    IV.  Changing the form of business with ease once a corporation has been formed.

    a.  II only

    b.  III only

    c.  I and III only

    d.  I and IV only

4.  Assuming that Nick is most interested in implementing a retirement plan that offers flexibility, low costs, and limited paperwork and regulation, he should consider establishing a:

    a.  Cash balance plan

    b.  401(k) plan

    c.  Roth 401(k) plan

    d.  SIMPLE plan

    e.  Stock bonus plan

5.  Based on Nick's desires, as outlined in the list you developed, which of the following plans would meet his needs?

    I.   A 403(b) plan

    II.  A profit sharing plan

    III. A stock bonus plan

    IV.  A defined benefit plan

    a.  I and IV only

    b.  II and IV only

    c.  II and III only

    d.  I, II, and III only

    e.  II, III, and IV only

6.    Using the most restrictive vesting schedule and participation rules available, Nick can exclude which of the following employees from participating in a qualified defined contribution plan?

        I.    Bill

        II.   Jack

        III.  Andy

        IV.  Mary

    a.  I and II only

    b.  II and III only

    c.  I and IV only

    d.  I, II, and III only

    e.  II, III, and IV only

7.    Nick is concerned about how he will fund contributions to a defined contribution plan. You recommend that he use a unit formula based on employee compensation and years of service. The formula is calculated using one unit of credit for each year of service and one unit of credit for each $10,000 in earnings. If Nick is willing to allocate $30,000 in total contributions in any given year, using a total allocation of 80 units (and disregarding any key employee or top-heavy restrictions), what is the maximum amount that will be contributed to Nick's account?

    a.  $9,675

    b.  $13,225

    c.  $15,375

    d.  $22,750

8.    Nick's daughter, who is hoping one day to take over ownership of the dealership, is interested in your discussion with her father. She would like her father to receive the maximum plan benefit available before and after retirement. She would also like to establish a plan that guarantees her father a steady source of income during retirement. If you follow the daughter's desires, which of the following plans would be most appropriate?

    a.  A SIMPLE plan

    b.  A money purchase plan

    c.  A stock bonus plan

    d.  A defined benefit plan

    e.  A target benefit plan

9.  Nick is intrigued by his daughter's idea. However, he is still adamant about providing the best possible benefits to his employees, in addition to himself. The thought of maximizing tax deductions for contributions is something he would like to consider. Assuming that the dealership has steady to increasing levels of cash flow, which of the following plan(s) would be most appropriate?

       I.  A defined benefit plan.

      II.  A target benefit plan.

     III.  A 401(k) plan.

     IV.  A stock bonus plan.

      V.  A Roth 401(k) plan.

    a.  I and V only

    b.  I and II only

    c.  IV and V only

    d.  II, III, and IV only

    e.  I, II, III, and V only

10.  Joyce, one of Nick's employees, has come to you for advice. She would like guidance on choosing between contributing to a defined contribution plan and a Roth IRA. Assuming that Nick establishes a 401(k) plan, which of the following statements is true for Joyce?

    a.  If Nick's firm matches contributions to the 401(k) plan, she should contribute to the plan at least to the point of obtaining the match.

    b.  Under no circumstances will the 401(k) plan provide a better after-tax return than the Roth IRA.

    c.  If Joyce believes that tax rates in retirement will be higher than rates today, she should contribute to the 401(k) plan rather than the Roth IRA.

    d.  Regardless of employer matching, Joyce should maximize her contribution to the Roth IRA before contributing to the defined contribution plan.

# The Mayfield Case

## A RETIREMENT PLANNING MINI-CASE

Peter and Ann Mayfield, both age 52, recently sought your help in planning their financial future. Peter is the Anytown, Anystate, city manager. His wife is active in many civic organizations but not employed outside of the home. They live at 123 Maple Street, in Anytown. They have been married for slightly more than 25 years.

Their two children, Nick and Nedra, have both moved away from home and started their own families. In fact, Nick and his wife have two children, Lisa and Timmy, ages 3 and 2, respectively. Table VI.17 presents additional information about the Mayfields.

## Additional Personal Information

**Table VI.17** The Mayfields' Personal Information

| Occupation—Peter | City Manager<br>123 Elm Street<br>Anytown, Anystate 01010<br>26 years of employment |
|---|---|
| Occupation—Ann | Homemaker<br>26 years of employment |

## Global Assumptions (Valid unless otherwise Specified in Certain Instances)

- Inflation: 3%

- All income and expense figures are given in today's dollars.

- Federal marginal tax bracket: 25%

- State marginal tax bracket: 4.5%

- Any qualified plan or IRA contribution growth rates are assumed to stop at the federally mandated limit unless otherwise restricted.

- All nominal rates of return are pretax returns.

- They are currently qualified for Social Security benefits.

## Income Issues

Peter currently earns $90,000 per year and expects his salary to increase at 3% per year until retirement. As shown in Table VI.18, Peter contributes 10% of his salary to his employer-sponsored 403(b) plan. He receives a 33% match from the city. Ann and Peter are covered by an employer-sponsored health care plan, which has a premium of only $50 per month and is paid for directly out of Peter's paycheck on a pretax basis. The Mayfields currently use interest earned from their municipal bond holdings to supplement their income.

## Dedicated and Discretionary Expenses

**Table VI.18** The Mayfields' Dedicated and Discretionary Expenses

| Source of Expense | Amount | Frequency |
|---|---|---|
| Pretax medical premiums | $600 | Annually |
| 403(b) contributions | $750 | Monthly |
| Social Security withholdings | $6,839 | Annually |
| Federal tax withholdings | $10,000 | Annually |
| State tax withholdings | $3,400 | Annually |
| Mortgage payment (P&I) | $511.63 | Monthly |
| Credit card payments | $450 | Annually |
| Auto insurance | $550 | Semi-Annually |
| Homeowner's insurance | $50 | Monthly |
| Life insurance (private policy) | $780 | Annually |
| **Other insurance** | **Not calculated by client** | |
| Umbrella policy | $150 | Annually |
| Peter's traditional IRA contribution | $2,000 | Annually |
| Ann's traditional IRA contribution | $2,000 | Annually |
| Unallocated savings | $1,000 | Quarterly |
| Subscriptions | $50 | Monthly |
| Telephone charges | $1,560 | Annually |
| Alarm system | $40 | Monthly |
| Internet and cable | $90 | Monthly |
| Hobbies | $100 | Monthly |

| Recreation | $400 | Monthly |
|---|---|---|
| Health club dues | $90 | Monthly |
| Groceries | $3,900 | Annually |
| Eating-out expenses | $4,900 | Annually |
| Real estate taxes | $1,600 | Annually |
| Household maintenance | $90 | Monthly |
| Utilities | $2,160 | Annually |
| Clothing | $1,700 | Annually |
| Dry cleaning | $60 | Monthly |
| Personal care | $100 | Monthly |
| Stereo equipment | $800 | Annually |
| Yard maintenance service | $900 | Annually |
| Eye glasses | $725 | Annually |
| Health insurance co-pays | $500 | Annually |
| Prescriptions | $400 | Annually |
| Other medical expenses | $350 | Annually |
| Gas and car maintenance | $800 | Semiannually |
| Car licenses (not tax deductible) | $250 | Annually |
| Parking in city | $100 | Annually |
| Trains and taxis in city | $300 | Annually |
| Personal property tax | $750 | Annually |
| Safe deposit fees | $40 | Monthly |
| Bank fees | $4 | Monthly |
| IRA fees | $45 | Annually |
| Tax preparation fees | $450 | Annually |
| Charitable contributions | $300 | Monthly |
| Business travel* | $1,500 | Annually |
| Vacations | $1,000 | Quarterly |
| Business expenses* | $250 | Annually |
| Alcohol expenses | $250 | Semiannually |
| Postage stamps | $125 | Annually |
| Gifts to children/grandchildren | $1,300 | Semiannually |
| Other misc. expenses | $500 | Annually |

*Peter's employer does not reimburse these expenses.

## Asset and Liability Information

Table VI.19 presents the Mayfields' asset and liability information.

**Table VI.19** The Mayfields' Assets and Liabilities

| Asset/Liability | Value | Notes |
|---|---|---|
| Checking account | $13,000 | No interest earned on asset |
| Municipal money market fund (general obligations) | $240,000 | 2.50% federal annual tax-free yield |
| I-bonds* | $42,000 | Market value |
| Peter's 401(k) | $975,000 | Invested in equities |
| Peter's traditional IRA | $52,000 | Invested in equities |
| Ann's traditional IRA | $35,000 | Invested in equities |
| Primary residence | $375,000 | |
| Mazda | $6,700 | 5 years old |
| Honda | $5,200 | 6 years old |
| Household furnishings | $30,000 | |
| Yard equipment | $7,500 | |
| Other misc. assets | $14,000 | |
| Visa credit card | $2,500 | 14.90% interest rate |
| MasterCard | $4,000 | 9.90% interest rate |
| Discover card | $1,000 | 18.90% interest rate |
| Macy's credit card | $500 | 21.00% interest rate |
| First mortgage | $25,685 | Home purchased 25 years ago; $75,000 financed at 7.25% for 30 years; 300 payments made to date |

Note: All nonretirement assets are jointly owned.
*The I bonds have been owned for 4 years.

## Tax Information

The Mayfields' marginal state tax rate is 4.5%. The state income tax is tied to the federal AGI figure. The Mayfields are eligible for two state exemptions in the amount of $1,300 each and a state standard deduction of $10,000. The Mayfields are also eligible for $6,000 in state income tax adjustments. The municipal money market mutual fund is made up of general Anystate state obligations.

# Insurance Information and Planning Issues

## Life Insurance

Peter purchased a $250,000 10-year term policy when he turned age 50. Peter is the owner and insured. Ann is the beneficiary. In addition, Peter's employer provides him with a group term policy in the amount of one times his salary. When estimating life insurance needs, the Mayfields would like to make the following assumptions:

- Life expectancy: age 95 each

- Final expense needs: $12,000 each

- Estate administration needs: Peter: $36,500; Ann: $9,500

- Other immediate needs: $12,000 each

- They would like to pay off all debts at the first death.

- Anticipated expense needs at first death: $85,000 per year before and after retirement (in today's dollars).

- They believe they can earn 6% on any proceeds from insurance prior to retirement.

- They believe they can earn 5% on insurance proceeds after retirement.

- They anticipate being in a combined 25% federal and state marginal tax bracket after retirement.

- Projected inflation rate: 3%

- In the event of a spouse's death, Peter and Ann plan to stop working and collect early Social Security benefits at age 60. They will receive $16,500 at that time.

- For conservative planning purposes, the Mayfields do not plan to use interest and/or dividends as an income source when planning insurance needs.

- Full retirement benefits, at age 66, are $23,580.

- In addition to Peter's life insurance, they are willing to use all of their retirement, investments, and monetary assets to meet insurance needs.

## Disability Insurance

Peter's employer provides both short- and long-term disability coverage. His short-term coverage pays 100% of his earned income for the first six months of disability. There is no wait period for this coverage. Peter's long-term coverage has a six-month wait period and pays a benefit equal to 60% of earned income until age 65. All premiums, for both policies, are employer paid. If Peter were to become disabled, they would not continue to save for other goals. In case of disability:

- Total household expenses in the event of death or disability are $85,000.

- When calculating life insurance needs, the Mayfields are willing to use all their combined retirement savings to offset insurance needs.

- The Mayfields assume that in the event of a possible disability neither will be eligible for Social Security disability benefits.

- For life insurance planning purposes only, they would like to replace $85,000 per year, in today's dollars, for retirement.

### Long-term Care Insurance

The Mayfields do not currently have long-term care insurance.

## Retirement Information and Planning Issues

The following information should be used when evaluating the Mayfields' current retirement planning situation:

- Peter does not have a defined benefit plan at this time.

- Retirement age for reduced Social Security benefits is age 62; they plan to retire and take benefits at the earliest possible date.

- Retirement age for full Social Security benefits is age 66.

- Their individual life expectancies are 95 years of age.

- In the event of the death of one spouse, the surviving spouse is eligible to receive $16,500 per year starting at age 60 from Social Security.

- At age 62, Peter's annual Social Security benefit will be $17,950 in today's dollars; Ann is eligible to receive a survivor benefit equal to $8,367.

- At age 66, Peter's annual Social Security benefit will be $24,420 in today's dollars; Ann is eligible to receive one-half of this amount.

- At age 70, Peter's annual Social Security benefit will be $32,900 in today's dollars; Ann is eligible to receive a survivor benefit.

- They would like to replace $90,000 in yearly income, in today's pretax dollars, on their first day of retirement. (Note that this figure is different from the assumption they want to use for insurance planning purposes.)

- Ann is the beneficiary of Peter's qualified retirement plan assets.

- For retirement planning purposes only, they believe that they can earn a 7.6% rate of return prior to retirement and a 5% rate of return after retirement.

- Inflation before and after retirement is expected to be 3%.

- Peter's salary will increase at the rate of inflation.

- All annual retirement savings will increase by the rate of inflation (3%) prior to retirement.

- The Mayfields are willing to assume that they will remain in the same marginal tax bracket after they retire.

- All nonretirement assets are owned as JTWROS at this time.

### Estate Information and Planning Issues

- Final funeral, burial, and medical expenses for life insurance and estate planning purposes will be $12,000 each.

- Estate administration costs are anticipated to be $1,500, and executor fees will be approximately $35,000 for Peter and $8,000 for Ann.

- In the event of death, the Mayfields will need approximately $12,000 to cover immediate needs.

- They would like to leave a legacy for their grandchildren by fully funding both children's college education costs should Peter or Ann die.

- Assumed investment return on assets in the event that one spouse dies is 6.00% annually.

- The value of the surviving spouse's net estate is expected to grow by 4.00% annually.

## Additional Planning Assumptions

The Mayfields would like to maintain their monetary assets as an emergency fund if possible, and use interest earned as a "slush fund" while in retirement.

# Goals and Objectives

The Mayfields are very much looking forward to retirement. They hope to spend more time with their growing grandchildren. Given this goal, they plan to retire when Peter turns age 62. They would like to know if they are currently on track to meet this goal.

Their second goal involves establishing an education funding plan to help their grandchildren pay for college expenses. They would like to fund one year of college tuition and room and board for each grandchild. Tuition plus expenses for colleges they have looked at average $18,000 per year. They believe that college costs will continue to rise at a 6% rate, but to offset some of this increase they are comfortable assuming an 8% rate of return in a tax-advantaged education savings account, which is roughly equivalent to a 5.5% after-tax rate of return.

Use the information provided in this narrative to answer the following case questions.

# Case Questions

1.  How much money market fund income did the Mayfields earn during the year?

    a.  $0

    b.  $6,000

    c.  $6,325

    d.  $7,200

2.  Which of the following statements is true?

    I.  Peter must report $110 in § 79 income for tax purposes.

    II.  Because Peter is over age 50, he does not need to report § 79 income.

    III.  § 79 income helps reduce a client's taxable income.

    IV.  § 79 income should be accounted for as a taxable expense on the income and expense statement.

    a.  II only

    b.  I and II only

    c.  I and IV only

    d.  II and III only

    e.  II, III, and IV only

3.  How much of the Mayfields' gross income is considered total income for tax purposes on IRS Form 1040?

    a.  $96,110

    b.  $90,000

    c.  $86,510

    d.  $80,510

4.  All of the following statements about the Mayfields' level of discretionary cash flow are incorrect except:[1]

    a.  After paying all dedicated and discretionary expenses, the Mayfields have a negative cash flow.

    b.  Total dedicated expenses are greater than discretionary expenses.

    c.  Savings expenses make up the largest dedicated/fixed expense item for the Mayfields.

    d.  The Mayfields' savings ratio, including employer matching contributions, exceeds 10%.

5.  Which of the following are strengths related to the Mayfields' financial situation?

    a.  Their savings rate, as measured by the savings ratio, is acceptable at this time.

    b.  Their debt as a percentage of net worth is low as measured by industry ratios.

    c.  They could easily pay off all of their debt using monetary assets.

    d.  All of the above.

6.  Which of the following is true?

    a.  The Mayfields should choose to itemize deductions on IRS Form Schedule A.

    b.  Given their age, they will receive enhanced personal exemptions for this year's taxes.

    c.  They can claim a tax credit for gifts made to their grandchild this year.

    d.  The Mayfields' standard deduction is greater than their itemized deduction.

    e.  Both a and b are correct.

7.  During a benefits presentation for all city employees, the presenter talked about the need for those in attendance to think about long-term care needs. Peter was shocked to learn how much one year of nursing home care would cost. He is worried about depleting assets if he or his wife should need this type of care. He wants to know whether he and his wife should purchase long-term care insurance. Which of the following statements best represents the strategy that the Mayfields should consider?

    a.  Purchase long-term care insurance because their net worth, exclusive of home value, is less than $1.5 million.

    b.  They do not need long-term care insurance because they can afford to self-insure the costs of care.

    c.  They should expect to spend down assets to a point where they will become eligible for Medicaid, and as such, they do not need long-term care insurance.

---

1.  It is recommended that the Financial Facilitator be used to answer this question.

    d.  They do not need long-term care insurance because they can use a combination of assets, Medicare funding, and Medicaid reimbursement to fund care needs.

8.  Peter was recently approached by a financial adviser who wanted Peter to consider investing in a variable annuity for retirement. A few days later the adviser called Peter again and said that a variable universal life (VUL) insurance policy could also be used to fund retirement needs. Which of the following statement(s) is (are) true in relation to annuities and VULs?

    I.  Given their favorable tax treatment, variable annuities and VUL policies allow earnings to grow tax deferred until withdrawn.

    II.  Distributions from the annuity, after age 59½, will be taxed at the long-term capital gain rate if the annuity has been in existence for at least one year.

    III.  Distributions from the VUL policy, if made in the form of a loan, will be taxed at the Mayfields' marginal tax rate.

    IV.  Distributions in the form of a VUL loan need not be reported on IRS Form 1040 for tax purposes.

    a.  I and II only

    b.  III and IV only

    c.  I and IV only

    d.  II, III, and IV only

9.  Reducing a client's life expectancy assumption will have which of the following effects?

    a.  Increase the amount of life insurance needed.

    b.  Decrease the amount of retirement assets needed.

    c.  Increase the amount of retirement assets needed.

    d.  Both a and c are correct.

10.  Which of the following disability insurance statements is true?

    a.  All of the benefits received by Peter from his disability coverage will be taxable because his employer paid the premium.

    b.  None of the benefits received by Peter from his disability coverage will be taxable because his employer paid the premium.

    c.  If Ann becomes disabled, she is eligible for coverage under her state's workers' compensation program.

    d.  Both a and c are correct.

    e.  Both b and c are correct.

11. Peter and Ann have been discussing the possibility of retiring as early as age 60. What do the Mayfields need to consider as factors that will impact the costs, risks, and benefits of this objective when conducting their planning?

    a. Distributions from their qualified retirement plans at that time will be subject to a 10% early withdrawal penalty.

    b. They can deal with the loss of health insurance by extending their current health insurance coverage using both COBRA and HIPAA benefits until age 65, at which time they will be eligible to enroll in Medicare.

    c. The cost of Medicare will increase dramatically for each year that they postpone enrolling after age 60.

    d. None of the above.

12. Which of the following strategies should the Mayfields consider to increase their level of discretionary cash flow?

    a. Pay off credit card debt with monetary assets.

    b. Open a home equity line of credit.

    c. Increase contributions to Peter's 403(b).

    d. Increase IRS W-4 withholdings on an annual basis.

    e. A and b only.

13. If Peter and Ann want to pay off their credit card debt, which of the following assets should they use first?

    a. Money market fund

    b. Proceeds from a 403(b) loan

    c. I-bonds

    d. Home equity

14. Suppose that the Mayfields decide to retire at age 60. How much do they need in assets at that time to fund income needs from ages 60–62, assuming that they still want $90,000 (in today's dollars) in annual income starting on their first day of retirement?

    a. $114,009

    b. $225,847

    c. $228,018

    d. $231,438

15. Peter and Ann are concerned about estate planning details. They have heard about income in respect of a decedent (IRD).  They realize that their retirement plans could be subject to IRD taxation. Which of the following statements is true in relation to IRD property?

     I.    IRD property will be included in the Mayfields' estates at fair market value.

     II.   IRD property does not receive a step-up in basis.

     III.  IRD property is subject to income taxation when the heir or estate collects income from the property.

     IV.  IRD property will be included in the Mayfields' estates at a step-up in basis value.

     a.   I and III only

     b.   II and IV only

     c.   I, II, and III only

     d.   II, III, and IV only

16. Which of the following factors should help drive the Mayfields' decision to fund a capital preservation approach of retirement planning compared to a capital depletion method?

     a.   Their desire to leave a legacy at the death of the second spouse.

     b.   Their willingness to dedicate additional cash flow today to fund the higher retirement asset need in the future.

     c.   Their willingness to decrease their income replacement ratio assumption.

     d.   All of the above.

17. Calculating the future value of regular savings using a geometrically varying annuity assumption will tend to

     a.   reduce the future value of the asset.

     b.   reduce the tax liability of the asset.

     c.   increase the future value of the asset.

     d.   increase the interest rate used to calculate future value.

18. Peter and Ann would like to establish a gifting program for their grandchildren. They have two desires. First, they want to implement a strategy that does not allow the grandchildren to access principal prior to age 21, except to pay expenses for the welfare of the child. Second, they want to maintain the maximum flexibility in terms of the types of assets that they can gift. Which of the following alternatives meet(s) their desires?

   a.   A Uniform Gifts to Minors Act account

   b.   A § 2503(b) trust

   c.   A § 2503(c) trust

   d.   All of the above

   e.   B or c only

19. What is (are) the advantage(s) associated with suggesting prepaying the Mayfields' mortgage at this time?

   a.   The loss of the interest deduction will require them to claim the standard deduction.

   b.   Their annual level of discretionary cash flow will increase, which can be used to fund other financial goals and objectives.

   c.   They will have the satisfaction of knowing that they own their home outright.

   d.   All of the above.

   e.   B and c only.

20. The Mayfields should consider which of the following estate planning strategies to reduce the likelihood of owing federal estate taxes in the future?

   a.   Maximizing use of the marital deduction.

   b.   Gifting strategies to reduce the value of Peter's gross estate.

   c.   Using a credit equivalency or bypass trust arrangement.

   d.   A and b only.

   e.   B and c only.

## Discussion Question

Describe how the Mayfields' asset allocation approach may need to change as they get closer to their retirement goal.

# The Dion Case

## AN ESTATE PLANNING MINI-CASE

Marcel and Clio Dion are taking steps to begin evaluating their estate planning situation. Marcel is 60 years old. Clio is 53 years old. They have two children, ages 13 and 18. Marcel is a successful executive with a Fortune 500 company, and Clio has achieved success as a cosmetics home sales trainer.

Currently, their wills state that if either Marcel or Clio were to pass away, the surviving spouse would inherit everything. Both Marcel and Clio value their privacy, but they have not established a trust at this time. They have an interest in providing charitable support to their church, but they have not made any sizable contributions. Table VI.20 summarizes their asset, liability, and estate expense situation.

**Table VI.20** Asset, Liability, and Expense Situation for the Dion Family

| Assets | Value | Ownership |
|---|---|---|
| Checking account | $26,000 | JTWROS |
| Savings account | $20,000 | JTWROS |
| Money market account | $90,000 | JTWROS |
| Other monetary assets | $0 | JTWROS |
| EE/I bonds | $100,000 | JTWROS |
| Mutual funds (basis less than fair market value) | $1,720,000 | JTWROS |
| Other investment assets | $250,000 | JTWROS |
| Primary residence | $700,000 | JTWROS |
| Other housing assets (vacation home) | $240,000 | JTWROS |
| Vehicles | $86,000 | JTWROS |
| Personal property | $134,000 | JTWROS |
| Retirement assets (e.g., 401(k) and IRA) | $768,000 | Marcel |
| Retirement assets (e.g., 401(k) and IRA) | $345,000 | Clio |
| Other assets | $48,000 | Jointly held but not titled |
| Life insurance (variable universal life)* | $1,500,000 | Marcel |
| Life insurance (universal life) | $250,000 | Clio |
| **Liabilities** | **Value** | **Ownership** |
| Mortgage on vacation home | $112,000 | Joint |
| Debts | $86,000 | Joint |
| **Expenses** | **Costs** | |
| Funeral and final expenses assumed the same for both | $25,000 | |

*Clio is the beneficiary of Marcel's policy, and Marcel is the beneficiary of Clio's policy.

Use this information to answer the questions that follow:[1]

---

1.  Questions 1, 2, and 3 are from "Released CFP® Certification Examination Questions," "1994 & 1996 Certification Exam Questions," and "1999 Case Scenario and Questions." Copyright © 2008, Certified Financial Planner Board of Standards, Inc. All rights reserved. Used with permission.

## Case Questions

1. Identify the statement(s) below that correctly characterize(s) property interests held by Marcel that, at death, pass by operation of law.

    I.   If the property passes according to the operation of law, the property avoids probate.

    II.  If the property passes according to the operation of law, it will not be included in the decedent's gross estate.

    III. Property that passes by operation of law cannot qualify for the marital deduction.

    IV.  The titling on the instrument determines who shall receive the property.

    a.  I only

    b.  I, II, and III only

    c.  I and IV only

    d.  I, II, and IV only

    e.  II and III only

2. As Marcel and Clio think about the value of their adjusted gross estate, they are unsure which assets and expenses might be deductible. Which of the following is a deduction from the gross estate used to calculate the adjusted gross estate?

    a.  Costs associated with maintaining estate assets.

    b.  Nontaxable gifts made within three years.

    c.  Federal estate tax marital deduction.

    d.  Property inherited from others.

3. Currently, the Dions own their personal residence as JTWROS. If instead they owned the property as a tenancy by the entirety, how could this form of ownership be terminated?

    I.   Death, whereby the survivor takes the property.

    II.  Mutual agreement.

    III. Divorce, which converts the estate into a tenancy in common or a joint tenancy.

    IV.  Severance, whereby one spouse transfers his or her interest to a third party without the consent of the other spouse.

    a.   IV only

    b.   I and III only

    c.   II and IV only

    d.   I, II, and III only

    e.   I, II, III, and IV

4.    One of Marcel's primary financial planning goals includes making lifetime gifts to his children. He would like to do this to help his children and to reduce his potential estate tax liability. If he moves forward with his plan to maximize the value of the strategy, he should make gifts of property that

        I.   are expected to depreciate in the future.

        II.   are expected to appreciate in the future.

        III.  have already depreciated significantly.

    a.   I only

    b.   II only

    c.   III only

    d.   I and III only

    e.   I, II, and III

5.    What is the value of Marcel's adjusted gross estate if he were to pass away today and before Clio?

    a.   $2,475,000

    b.   $3,225,000

    c.   $3,851,000

    d.   $3,975,000

6.    There are several weaknesses associated with the Dions' current estate plan. Which of the following are the significant weaknesses within their plan?

        I.   Failure to utilize the marital deduction.

        II.   Failure to maximize the unified credit.

        III.  Failure to utilize charitable gift strategies to reduce the taxable estate.

        IV.  Failure to avoid probate.

    a.   I and III only

    b.   II and IV only

    c.   I, II, and III only

    d.   II, III, and IV only

    e.   I, II, III, and IV

7.   In view of combined estate values for Marcel and Clio, and knowing that one of their planning objectives is the reduction of estate taxes, which of the following estate planning techniques might be appropriate?

      I.   Placing the life insurance policies in an irrevocable trust.

      II.   Establishing a revocable living trust and funding it by using the unlimited marital deduction and the full unified credit.

      III.  Making use of the gift tax annual exclusion.

      IV.  Establishing a qualified terminable interest property (QTIP) trust to pass property to their children.

    a.   II and III only

    b.   I and III only

    c.   II and IV only

    d.   II, III, and IV only

    e.   I, II, III, and IV

8.   Calculate Clio's taxable estate assuming that Marcel passes away first, followed closely by Clio's death.

    a.   $6,029,000

    b.   $6,484,000

    c.   $7,860,000

    d.   $7,736,000

    e.   $7,984,000

9. The Dions are considering making a sizable charitable gift to their local university using assets held in their mutual fund accounts. The primary purpose of their gift strategy is to reduce their taxable estate while providing a benefit for the university. Which of the following strategies will maximize the effectiveness of this estate planning strategy?

   a. Give the mutual funds first to their oldest child, who can then sell them with a stepped-up basis and use the proceeds as a donation to the university.

   b. Donate the mutual funds directly to the university and allow the university to sell the funds.

   c. Sell the mutual funds first and then donate the cash proceeds to the university.

   d. Transfer the mutual funds to a noncharitable irrevocable trust and then donate the trust income to the university.

10. The local university has approached the Dions about making a charitable contribution. After discussing the possibility of making a donation, Marcel and Clio have decided that they would be willing to make the donation if they could receive an immediate tax deduction and income based on a fixed percentage of the amount donated (valued annually). They would also like to have the ability to increase their donation amount in future years. Which of the following charitable giving alternatives best serves the Dions' desires?

   a. A charitable remainder unitrust.

   b. A charitable remainder annuity trust.

   c. A pooled income fund.

   d. A grantor retained annuity trust,

# The Graham Case

## A GENERAL PLANNING MINI-CASE

Onslo Graham is 59 years of age. His wife, Daisy, is age 58. They have been married for nearly 30 years. The Grahams currently live at 3456 Speedway, Anycity, Anystate 01010. They have an adult child, Rose, who recently turned age 28. Rose also lives in Anycity.

Because of their strong relationship, they have tended to own all of their assets jointly even though Daisy has been a homemaker all of their married lives. Onslo does have one real estate asset that is not jointly owned.

Onslo is the general manager of Tarantula Industries, a closely held corporation, which owns a hockey team in an expanding southwestern minor league. The team is headquartered at 555 West Verity Road, Anycity, Anystate 01010. Onslo has been involved in professional sports management for nearly 25 years, and he currently earns $137,500 per year in income. Rose is also actively involved with the team. She works in the front office and manages day-to-day operations. Onslo and Daisy hope that Rose will eventually take over management of the team once Onslo retires.

Use the following information to conduct a review of the Grahams' financial situation.

## Global Assumptions (Valid unless otherwise Specified in Certain Instances)

- Inflation: 4%

- All income and expense numbers are given in today's dollars.

- Planned retirement age: 66 for both

- Federal marginal tax bracket: 25%

- State marginal tax bracket: 4.72%

- Any qualified plan or IRA contribution growth rates are assumed to stop at the federally mandated limit unless otherwise restricted.

- All nominal rates of return are pretax returns.

- As of the date of the case, the Grahams are not subject to the alternative minimum tax (AMT).

- They are currently qualified for Social Security benefits.

## Income Issues

Onslo currently earns $137,500 per year and expects his salary to increase at 5% per year until retirement. They also receive $15,403 in nonqualified dividends and interest from miscellaneous other investments, all of which are reinvested. Onslo and Daisy are covered by employer-sponsored health care. The premium, which is paid by Onslo directly, is $2,400 per year. Onslo also contributes $9,600 into a 401(k) plan. The plan provides matching at 33 cents on the dollar with no maximum beyond IRC statutory limitations. These expenses are paid for with pretax dollars.

## Expense Summary

Based on his salary, Onslo had $27,000 withheld for federal, Social Security, and Medicare taxes. He also had $6,565 withheld for state taxes. Table VI.21 summarizes other expenditures.

**Table VI.21** Other Dedicated and Discretionary Expenses for the Grahams

| Expense | Amount | Frequency |
|---|---|---|
| Mortgage payments | $1,829.50 | Monthly |
| Home equity loan payments | $286.67 | Monthly |
| Auto payments | $483.33 | Monthly |
| Credit card payments | $3,500.00 | Annually |
| Auto insurance | $1,300.00 | Semiannually |
| Homeowners insurance | $450.00 | Semiannually |
| Life insurance | $3,200.00 | Annually |
| Umbrella liability insurance | $125.00 | Annually |
| Disability insurance | $2,250.00 | Annually |
| IRA contributions (Daisy) | $2,000.00 | Annually |
| IRA contributions (Onslo) | $2,000.00 | Annually |
| Subscriptions | $500.00 | Annually |
| Telephone expense | $91.67 | Monthly |
| Home Internet | $50.00 | Monthly |
| Hobbies (Daisy) | $500.00 | Yearly |

| Hobbies (Onslo) | $100.00 | Yearly |
|---|---|---|
| Recreation/entertainment | $100.00 | Monthly |
| Club dues | $500.00 | Yearly |
| Groceries | $500.00 | Monthly |
| Food away from home | $400.00 | Monthly |
| Real estate taxes | $600.00 | Semiannually |
| Household maintenance | $200.00 | Monthly |
| Utilities | $300.00 | Monthly |
| Clothing (Daisy) | $300.00 | Monthly |
| Clothing (Onslo) | $600.00 | Semiannually |
| Laundry services | $100.00 | Monthly |
| Personal care | $100.00 | Monthly |
| Furnishing | $1,000.00 | Yearly |
| Yard maintenance | $100.00 | Monthly |
| Medical copayments (Daisy) | $10.00 | Monthly |
| Medical copayments (Onslo) | $10.00 | Monthly |
| Prescriptions (Daisy) | $300.00 | Yearly |
| Unreimbursed medical expenses | $10.00 | Monthly |
| Gasoline | $100.00 | Monthly |
| Car registrations | $320.00 | Yearly |
| Parking and tolls | $400.00 | Yearly |
| Personal property tax* | $450.00 | Yearly |
| Safe deposit box fee | $100.00 | Yearly |
| Monthly bank fees | $2.00 | Monthly |
| IRA fees | $40.00 | Yearly |
| Accounting fees | $400.00 | Yearly |
| Charitable contributions | $400.00 | Monthly |
| Travel expenses | $2,500.00 | Yearly |
| Vacations | $2,500.00 | Semiannually |
| Alcohol expenses | $350.00 | Annually |
| Gifts to family members (Daisy) | $500.00 | Quarterly |
| Gifts to family members (Onslo) | $500.00 | Annually |
| Other miscellaneous expenses | $500.00 | Semiannually |

*Amount includes applicable car registration property tax.

## Tax Issues

The Grahams complete their own tax returns using a nationally known tax preparation software package. Onslo pays his company's accountant to double-check his calculations. Onslo and Daisy file married filing jointly and they claim themselves as exemptions. They are currently in the Anystate 4.72% marginal tax bracket, where taxes are linked with the federal AGI figure. They are eligible for a $1,250 state standard deduction and a $275 exemption per person. Onslo is considered an employee of his firm and does not pay self-employment income taxes. The Grahams' assets are summarized in Table VI.22. Their liabilities are summarized in Table VI.23.

## Asset Summary

**Table VI.22** Summary of the Grahams' Assets

| Asset | Amount | Ownership |
|---|---|---|
| **Financial Assets** | | |
| Checking account | $6,500 | Joint |
| Savings account | $10,000 | Joint |
| Taxable money market mutual fund | $230,000 | Joint |
| I-bonds | $15,000 | Joint |
| Government bond funds | $41,000 | Joint |
| Corporate bond funds | $45,000 | Joint |
| High-yield bond funds | $15,000 | Joint |
| Large-cap funds | $151,600 | Joint |
| Mid-cap funds | $70,600 | Joint |
| Small-cap funds | $37,000 | Joint |
| Rental real estate portfolio* | $2,100,000 | Onslo |
| **Retirement Assets** | | |
| Large-cap funds (401k) | $40,000 | Onslo |
| Mid-cap funds (401k) | $35,000 | Onslo |
| Small-cap funds (401k) | $15,000 | Onslo |
| Corporate bond funds (401k) | $27,000 | Onslo |
| International funds (IRA) | $19,000 | Onslo |
| High-yield bond funds (IRA) | $17,500 | Daisy |
| **Other Assets** | | |
| Primary residence | $375,000 | Joint |
| Mazda MPV | $25,000 | Joint |
| Ford Taurus | $7,800 | Joint |
| Artwork | $2,500 | Joint |
| Hockey collectibles | $1,500 | Joint |
| Sporting/hobbies supplies | $3,500 | Joint |
| 14-foot aluminum boat | $7,000 | Joint |
| Furniture | $28,000 | Joint |
| Other assets | $6,500 | Joint |

*The rental real estate is income and tax neutral; the property does not generate income or losses for cash flow or tax purposes.

## Liability Summary

**Table VI.22** Summary of the Grahams' Liabilities

| Liability | Amount | Ownership |
|---|---|---|
| Visa credit card | $12,000 | Joint |
| MasterCard | $8,000 | Joint |
| Discover card | $7,500 | Joint |
| Garts sporting goods card | $5,000 | Joint |
| Loan due in 45 days | $2,500 | Onslo |
| Mortgage | $235,984 | Joint |
| Home equity loan | $29,471 | Joint |
| Mazda loan | $9,177 | Joint |

| Loan Factors | Home Mortgage | Home Equity Loan | Mazda Loan |
|---|---|---|---|
| Original loan amount | $275,000 | $30,000 | $25,000 |
| Interest rate | 7.00% | 8.00% | 6.00% |
| Length of loan | 30 Years | 15 Years | 5 Years |
| Number of payments made | 120 | 6 | 40 |

## Life Insurance Information and Planning Issues

Onslo and Daisy would like you to analyze their life insurance situation using the following assumptions and facts:

- In the event of a death, household expenses would drop to $105,000 per year.

- Final expenses (funeral and burial costs) will be $25,000 for each person.

- Estate and legal costs will be $69,930 for Onslo and $16,135 for Daisy.

- All outstanding liabilities will be paid at the first death.

- Other immediate needs should be funded with $10,000 each.

- They would like to plan conservatively in the event of a death by assuming a 6% before-tax rate of return on any insurance proceeds both pre- and post-retirement.

- They will be in a combined state and federal tax bracket of 30% before retirement.

- Full retirement age is 66 for both Onslo and Daisy.

- They would like to replace $90,000, before taxes, while in retirement for the surviving spouse.

- Daisy is eligible to receive $1,958 per month (in today's dollars) as a Social Security survivor benefit at age 66 (assumes that Onslo dies today).

- Onslo will receive $2,024 Social Security benefits per month (in today's dollars) in retirement at age 66.

- They are eligible to receive survivor benefits equal to a 71.5% reduction in full benefits from age 60 to 66.

- In the event of either spouse's death, the other spouse plans to stop working at age 60 and begin taking early retirement survivor benefits.

- For conservative planning purposes, the Grahams do not plan on using interest and/or dividends as an income source when determining insurance needs.

- They are willing to use all their retirement savings and $350,000 in other assets to offset life insurance needs.

- Onslo expects his salary to remain the same following Daisy's death.

- Daisy does not expect to work after Onslo's death.

Table VI.23 summarizes life insurance policy information for Onslo and Daisy.

**Table VI.23** Life Insurance Policies

| Policy Type | Face Value | Cash Value | Owner | Insured | Beneficiary | Premium |
|---|---|---|---|---|---|---|
| 20-year term (12 years remaining)* | $250,000 | NA | Onslo | Onslo | Daisy | Paid by Onslo and Daisy; $1,000 yearly |
| 20-year term (20 years remaining)* | $150,000 | NA | Onslo | Onslo | Daisy | Paid by Onslo and Daisy; $1,200 yearly |
| Group term | $50,000 | NA | Onslo | Onslo | Daisy | Employer paid |
| Whole-life** | $100,000 | $21,250 | Onslo | Daisy | Rose | Paid by Onslo and Daisy; $1,000 yearly |

*Both insurance companies are rated A by A.M. Best.
**Cash value at beginning of year was $21,250; current dividend is $100; an equivalent after-tax yield is 6%.

## Disability Insurance Information and Planning Issues

The Grahams have not focused too heavily on disability planning issues. They do know that they do not want to account for Social Security benefits in the event of a disability. A few years ago Onslo purchased a long-term policy in the private market (not through a cafeteria plan at work). Information about the policy is summarized below:

- The policy is defined as own-occupation and is issued by an A.M. Best A-rated company.

- The policy has a six-month elimination period.

- The policy pays 50% of Onslo's current salary until age 65.

- All premiums are paid with after-tax dollars.

- If disabled, they would like to continue to save for objectives.

## Other Insurance Information and Planning Issues

The Grahams do not currently have a long-term care insurance policy. Both are healthy with both sets of parents still alive and well. In fact, Onslo and Daisy skate twice a week at the team's local indoor practice arena.

They have worked with the same property and casualty insurance agent for 25 years. Their agent encouraged them to purchase a $1-million umbrella policy four years ago. This required that the Grahams increase the split-limit coverage on their personal automobile policies to $100/$300/$100. Their current HO-3 homeowners policy provides 100% inflation protection coverage.

Current yield information for use when solving case questions is provided in Table VI.24.

## Current Yield Information

**Table VI.24**

| Investment Class | Yield |
|---|---|
| Checking account | 0.00% |
| Savings account | 2.00% |
| Taxable money market fund | 3.00% |
| Anystate municipal money market fund | 2.40% |
| EE savings bonds | 3.50% |
| I bonds | 4.50% |
| Government bonds | 4.50% |
| Corporate bonds | 5.00% |
| High-yield bonds | 6.50% |
| Real estate | 3.75% |
| Gold | 0.00% |
| Large-cap stocks | 2.00% |
| Mid-cap stocks | 1.00% |
| Small-cap stocks | 0.00% |
| **Loan Rates** | |
| 30-year mortgage* | 5.95% |
| 15-year mortgage* | 5.75% |
| Home equity line of credit* | 5.85% |
| Home equity loan* | 7.35% |
| 5-year auto loan | 6.10% |
| Personal loan | 8.25% |
| *APR includes closing costs | |

## Retirement Information and Planning Issues

The following information should be used when evaluating the Grahams' current retirement planning situation:

- They would like to retire when Onslo reaches age 66.

- They anticipate being in the 25% marginal tax bracket while in retirement.

- Prior to retirement, they are comfortable assuming that future rates of return will be 10.72% before taxes on their retirement assets and savings.

- If retired today, they would like to replace 90% of Onslo's salary.

- At retirement, Onslo will be eligible to receive $2,024 (in today's dollars) in Social Security benefits per month.

- Daisy has not yet earned 40 quarters for Social Security benefits, but she does qualify for spousal benefits.

- They are comfortable assuming a life expectancy of 95 years.

- Contributions to Onslo's 401(k) will increase by 3% each year.

- Daisy is the primary beneficiary of Onslo's retirement assets.

- All qualified assets held outside of the 401(k) are in traditional IRAs.

- After retirement they plan to allocate retirement assets to generate a before-tax return of 8.7%.

## Estate Information and Planning Issues

Onslo and Daisy have separate wills. Onslo's will leaves all his assets to Daisy. Daisy's will leaves all of her assets to Onslo. Their wills name their attorney as estate executors, and in the event of a simultaneous death it is assumed that Onslo predeceases Daisy. Other estate planning facts include:

- Funeral and burial expenses will be $25,000 each.

- Estate and legal costs will be $5,000 each.

- Executor fees will be approximately 2% of the gross estate before the marital transfer.

- The net growth rate of the survivor's estate is estimated to be, on average, 4% annually.

- Daisy is the sole beneficiary of Onslo's IRA and retirement plan assets.

- Onlso is the sole beneficiary of Daisy's IRA assets.

- Daisy has a strong allegiance to the University of Anystate. She would like to leave a legacy gift to the university, if possible.

- No other estate planning documents are known to exist.

# Goals and Objectives

The Grahams have two primary goals. First, they would like to know whether they are on or off track to meet an age 66 retirement date. Second, they feel that a thorough review of their current estate situation is in order. Specifically, they would like to minimize any estate taxes paid in the event of death. Other planning objectives include reviewing their discretionary cash flow, net worth, and life insurance situation. They are looking for guidance on how to improve their general financial well-being.

# Case Questions

1. Which of the following statements most accurately reflects the Grahams' current discretionary cash flow position?

    a. Their discretionary cash flow is greater than $0 but less than $1,000.

    b. Their discretionary cash flow is less than $0 but greater than –$1,000.

    c. Their discretionary cash flow is greater than $1,000 but less than $8,000.

    d. Their discretionary cash flow is less than $–1,000 but greater than $8,000.

2. Which of the following statements is (are) true?

    I. Retirement plan assets make up approximately 5% of the Grahams' total assets.

    II. Given their age and income profile, one would expect the Grahams to have a substantially higher level of net worth.

    III. The Grahams' savings ratio, including reinvested dividends and interest, is below industry benchmark levels.

    IV. The Grahams' emergency fund ratio is adequate at this time.

    a. I and II only

    b. II and III only

    c. I and IV only

    d. I, III, and IV only

3. Which of the following strategies can the Grahams use to increase their discretionary cash flow situation?

    I. Refinance their first mortgage using a 15-year fixed-rate loan.

    II. Pay off outstanding credit card debt using money market mutual fund assets.

    III. Use a two-year home equity loan to refinance the Mazda car debt.

    a. II only

    b. I and II only

    c. II and III only

    d. I and III

4.  According to your tax calculations, which of the following statements is (are) true?

    a.  The Grahams should use the standard deduction rather than itemize expenses.

    b.  Given their AGI, the Grahams can deduct Daisy's IRA contribution because she is not an active participant in a qualified plan.

    c.  Even though Onslo is an active participant in a qualified plan, the Grahams can deduct his IRA contribution because he is over age 50 this year.

    d.  Both a and b are correct.

5.  Which of the following tax planning statements is true?

    I.   The Grahams should, based on tax-equivalent investment calculations, transfer their money market mutual fund assets to an Anystate municipal money market fund.

    II.  By paying off their home equity loan early, they will increase discretionary cash flow but lose a tax deduction.

    III. Using municipal bond investments will increase both the Grahams' level of discretionary cash flow and their taxable income.

    IV.  Increasing 401(k) contributions will decrease the amount of taxes the Grahams will pay at the federal level.

    a.  I and II only

    b.  II and IV only

    c.  I, II, and IV only

    d.  II, III, and IV only

6.  All of the following life insurance observations are true except?

    a.  Based solely on the relative cost of the policy, Onslo should consider using a §1035 exchange procedure to replace the $100,000 whole-life insurance policy.

    b.  The death benefit from Onslo's current life insurance policies is less than his calculated life insurance need.

    c.  Term life insurance will provide the Grahams with the maximum amount of coverage for the lowest premium but leave them uninsured at some point in the future.

    d.  Using the nonforfeiture provision in the whole-life insurance policy will result in a decrease in discretionary cash flow.

7. Which of the following statements is true?

    a. The Grahams can afford to self-insure short-term disability needs by using a combination of cash flow and nonretirement assets.

    b. Because Onslo purchased his disability policy in the private market, if he receives benefits, then 100% of this income will be subject to federal income taxation.

    c. If the Grahams used all of their financial assets, excluding insurance cash values and Onslo's rental real estate interests, they would be able to self-insure Onslo's net long-term disability need.

    d. Both a and c are correct.

8. Assume that long-term care costs in Anycity are currently $45,000 per year, and that these costs are increasing by 5% annually. If the Grahams anticipate that Daisy will enter a nursing home when she turns age 71 and stay for five years, and they can earn a 7% rate of return on investments, which of the following statements is true?

    a. The Grahams currently have enough financial assets to self-insure nursing home costs for Daisy.

    b. The Grahams do not need to worry because Daisy will qualify for Medicare benefits at that time.

    c. The cost of coverage for five years will exceed the Grahams' ability to self-insure the loss.

    d. Even if they wanted to purchase long-term care insurance, the cost to purchase this insurance today is prohibitively high.

9. To retire at age 66—based on the value of their current retirement assets—the Grahams need to consider which of the following?

    a. Be willing to reduce their income need in retirement.

    b. Increase the rate of return earned on retirement savings and assets.

    c. Increase the age-of-death assumption.

    d. All of the above.

    e. A and b only.

10. Given what they currently have saved, which of the following statements is (are) true in relation to their current retirement planning situation?

    a. The Grahams currently have adequate cash flow to fund their age 66 retirement goal.

    b. If Onslo can convert his rental real estate holdings to cash prior to age 66, the Grahams can meet their retirement goal.

   c.   Postponing retirement by one year will allow them to reach their retirement goal without using any additional assets.

   d.   None of the above.

   e.   B and c only.

11.   Which of the following assets would pass directly to Daisy if Onslo were to die today?

   a.   His 401(k) assets.

   b.   Proceeds from his group term life insurance policy.

   c.   His ownership interest in their house.

   d.   All of the above.

12.   What is the approximate value of Onslo's gross estate today?

   a.   $1,000,000

   b.   $2,000,000

   c.   $3,000,000

   d.   $4,000,000

13.   At Onslo's death, assuming Daisy is still alive,

   a.   if Anystate is a community property state, Daisy will receive a step-up in basis equal to 50% on all jointly owned taxable property.

   b.   if Anystate is a community property state, Daisy will receive a step-up in basis equal to 100% of all community property.

   c.   Daisy will retain the original basis in all property held jointly.

   d.   Daisy will be required to pay estate and gift taxes on all property received from Onslo.

14.   What action(s) can Onslo take today to ensure a smooth transfer of his rental real estate holdings to either Daisy or Rose at his death?

   I.   Change the title from individual to trust ownership.

   II.   Consider a buy-sell agreement provision by funding the agreement with a life insurance provision so that the daughter can then buy the rental company from the mother (assume Daisy would be the owner because she is the beneficiary of the property).

   III.   Use a grantor retained annuity or unitrust to pass these assets to Rose.

a. I only

b. III only

c. I and II only

d. I, II, and III

15. Which of the following estate planning tools generally allow Onslo Graham to maintain full control of his assets today while minimizing estate taxes at his death in the future?

    I.   An A-B trust arrangement funded at his death.

    II.  A QTIP trust arrangement.

    III. An irrevocable living trust arrangement.

    IV. A funded revocable living trust arrangement.

a. I only

b. I and II only

c. I and III only

d. III and IV only

16. Onslo and Daisy have indicated to you that they are considering adding Rose as a co-owner on their checking and savings accounts. They have heard that gift and/or income taxes could apply if they decide to move forward with the idea. Which of the following statements best describes the tax consequences of adding Rose to the account?

a. Rose will owe a gift tax on one-third of the account balance when she is added to the account.

b. Onslo and Daisy might owe a gift tax when Rose makes a withdrawal from the account.

c. Rose will owe only federal income tax on her share of the account when either Onslo or Daisy dies.

d. Onslo and Daisy will owe a gift tax when Rose is added to the account.

e. Both a and d.

17. Daisy has been talking with a planned giving officer from the University of Anystate about funding a charitable trust that will also provide income during retirement. She and Onslo would like to begin funding the trust immediately and retain the right to add to the fund in future years. Which of the following gift alternatives will meet the Grahams' objective?

a. A charitable remainder unitrust.

b. A charitable reminder annuity trust.

   c.   A pooled-income fund.

   d.   All of the above.

   e.   Both a and c.

18.  Recently, Onslo indicated being concerned about the general strength of the stock market. As he and Daisy get closer to retirement, he is worried that the market will drop at just the moment they need to be drawing money from their equity fund holdings. Even so, he is reluctant to sell his stock funds at this time. Which of the following investing strategies could provide Onslo with a solution to his dilemma?

   a.   Periodically sell an index option put.

   b.   Periodically buy an index option put.

   c.   Periodically write a covered put.

   d.   Periodically buy an index option call.

19.  Onslo has occasionally thought about buying municipal bond securities, but he never has because he does not have great faith that his local elected officials will make good on the bonds. Which of the following municipal bond alternatives would be most appropriate for Onslo, assuming that he wants to know that bond interest and principal will be paid from earnings on a project rather than tax revenues?

   a.   Debenture bonds.

   b.   General obligation bonds.

   c.   Revenue bonds.

   d.   Income bonds.

20.  Before selling their taxable bond securities and purchasing municipal bond securities to reduce tax liabilities, Onslo and Daisy ought to consider which of the following factors as true in their situation?

   a.   Given their level and sources of income and deductions, there is the possibility that owning certain municipal bond securities that generate preference item interest will subject them to the AMT.

   b.   Anystate will tax all interest earned on bonds issued by another city in their state but not by Anycity, where Onslo and Daisy file taxes.

   c.   Although state income tax free, any municipal bond interest that they earn will still be taxable at the federal level.

   d.   Both a and c.

## Discussion Points and Questions

1. Briefly summarize the relevant facts of the case.

2. Are there any areas in the Grahams' expense summary that can be reduced to improve their cash flow situation?

3. If the Grahams were going to purchase additional life insurance, what type of policy would be most appropriate given their age and needs?

4. What factors do the Grahams need to take into account regarding health insurance as they begin to think about retirement?

5. The Grahams' current retirement plan assumes the depletion of assets at the death of the surviving spouse. How much more do the Grahams need in assets on their first day of retirement to fully fund a capital preservation model of retirement if the following assumptions are used?

    a. They want to replace 90% of Onslo's salary in retirement.

    b. Onslo's salary is increasing by 5% annually.

    c. Social Security benefits are increasing by 4% annually.

    d. Inflation will remain at 4% throughout retirement.

    e. They can earn an 8.7% rate of return on investments in retirement.

    f. At retirement, they have a 29-year life expectancy.

6. Discuss property ownership and titling characteristics for the Grahams, assuming that they live in a community property state.

7. What can the Grahams do to avoid probate?

8. What action(s) can Onslo take today to ensure a smooth transfer of his rental real estate holdings to either Daisy or Rose at his death?

9. What type of gift strategies can be used by the Grahams to reduce their estate tax situation?

10. What other creative estate planning techniques can be used in this case?

# The Case of the Good Gone Bad

## A PLAY IN THREE SCENES[1]

To solve this case you must have access to Certified Financial Planner Board of Standards, Inc. (CFP Board) *Standards of Professional Conduct*, including the *Code of Ethics and Professional Responsibility*, *Rules of Conduct*, *Financial Planning Practice Standards*, *Disciplinary Rules and Procedures*, and *Candidate Fitness Standards*, which can be found at http://www.cfp.net/Downloads/2010Standards.pdf. Information from the *Process of Financial Planning: Developing a Financial Plan*, Second Edition, the companion text to this book, can also be used to help answer questions.

### Characters:

Ashley: A CFP® professional

Bill Jackson: Ashley's client and friend

Jane Jackson: Bill's wife and Ashley's friend

Phil Rheem: A prominent attorney in the area

Ben Pyles: Ashley's broker/dealer representative

## Background

Ashley has been a Certified Financial Planner (CFP®) professional and registered representative for more than 10 years. She prides herself on her excellent work and ethical standards. Ashley was recently ranked by her local newspaper as one of the top 50 planners in her region, and she was recently recognized at an awards banquet.

---

1. This fictional (and lighthearted) play is intended to be acted out in class. The case takes approximately 15 minutes to complete. A minimum of 30 minutes should be allocated to answer case questions.

At 9:30 on a bright Thursday morning, Ashley received a phone call from a long-time client, Bill Jackson. Although Bill is married, Ashley manages only Bill's sizable investment portfolio. Bill is one of the wealthiest men in the area. He and Ashley have had a long client/planner relationship, and he considers her to be worthy of his full trust. Ashley and Bill have long been good friends, and dealing with Bill has always been a pleasure for her. When Ashley answers the phone, she is aware of Bill's altered mood and she immediately becomes concerned.

**Bill:** *(In a hushed tone.)* Ashley, I need to talk with you about asset protection.

> **Narrator:** Ashley could sense that Bill was quite disturbed, and she wondered why this type of question might cause such panic in a person.

**Ashley:** Bill, your assets are fully protected. Your trust is fully secure, and your brokerage account has comprehensive SIPC coverage. Why the concern about asset protection all of a sudden?

**Bill:** *(More persistent.)* Listen Ashley, I just need to know how not to let anyone touch my investments or my property without my permission.

> **Narrator:** Ashley was now getting annoyed; she could not figure out for the life of her what brought on this sudden panic about asset protection.

**Ashley:** Bill, are you in some sort of trouble? What is going on?

> **Narrator:** There was silence on the other end of the line, and Ashley could sense the tension as she held the receiver. Finally, a long sigh came from Bill, and Ashley was temporarily relieved.

**Bill:** *(Pauses.)* Ashley, you and I have been friends for a long time. Our kids played with each other. For heaven's sake, I couldn't even count the number of barbecues our two families have had in my backyard .... Those were the easy times, Ashley—everything was so simple back then. Ashley, I don't know how to tell you this, *(long pause)* but I am leaving Jane. Another thing, she doesn't know yet.

> **Narrator:** Ashley was shocked. She and Jane had been good friends for years—better friends than she was with Bill.

**Ashley:** Bill, what are you talking about? Why would you and Jane split up?

> **Narrator:** Again, there was a long sigh on the other end of the line; then Ashley heard a voice—a female voice—but it wasn't Jane's. Ashley now knew why Bill wanted a divorce. He had met someone new. It wasn't a unique scenario for Ashley; she had seen it happen to a few of her other "50-something" friends. "After Jane has supported Bill for so long, he is going to trade her in for a newer model. What a creep!" Jane thought to herself. Well, there was no way she was going to let Bill leave Jane with

nothing. In fact, Ashley thought to herself, "I'll fix it so that Jane is better off than she has ever been, and I'll make that slimeball pay!"

**Ashley:** Bill, you know I will do anything to help you out. I mean, after all, you have been so good to me over the years. Let me look into the situation, and I will call you back on Monday morning. Can you wait that long?

> **Narrator:** Ashley smiled on the other end of the line as she waited for Bill's response. She leaned back in her chair and began planning out her strategy. Bill's voice came back over the line a lot calmer than it had been at the beginning of their conversation.

**Bill:** Thanks Ashley, Monday will be fine.... I really didn't think you would understand, I mean … you know … since you and Jane have been such good friends.

**Ashley:** Well, Bill, you are my client, and what you do with your personal life is not a professional concern of mine. I'll call you on Monday. Have a good weekend.

**Ashley:** (*Talking to herself.*) Yeah, have a *great* weekend, you weasel—because it is the last good one you'll have after I get through with you.

> **Narrator:** As soon as she hung up the phone, Ashley immediately called Jane at the club. Ashley knew Jane always played tennis on Thursday mornings with a group of other "housies," as they liked to refer to themselves. When Jane finally got to the phone she sounded winded from the run up to the clubhouse.

**Jane:** (*In a cheerful voice.*) Hello Ashley, what in the world has given me the pleasure of hearing from you this morning?

**Ashley:** Jane, listen, I think there are some things we need to discuss; is there any way you can meet me for lunch this afternoon?

**Jane:** (*Suddenly serious.*) Well, normally I have lunch with my tennis group, but I'm sure they won't mind if I cancel. What is this about?

**Ashley:** Jane, I'll talk to you about it at lunch. Does *Le Marie* sound good to you … say 1:00?

**Jane:** Yes, that will be fine. I'll see you there at 1:00.

> **Narrator:** Later that afternoon when Ashley and Jane were at Le Marie for lunch, Ashley finally looked Jane in the eye and began to tell her the whole story.

**Ashley:** Listen, Jane, this is really hard for me to say. I don't even know where to begin. But, this morning I got a phone call from your husband. Can I just ask you one question?

**Jane:** *(Concerned.)* Ashley you know you can talk to me about anything. What is it?

**Ashley:** Jane, how is your marriage?

**Jane:** Ashley, what is this about? What do you mean how is my marriage?

**Ashley:** Bill is having an affair.

**Jane:** *(Suddenly angry.)* What are you talking about? Bill has always been faithful and for your information our marriage is fine. Now, if you have nothing else to say I will be leaving.

> **Narrator:** As Jane is getting up to leave, Ashley's voice softens and she touches Jane's arm.

**Ashley:** *(More softly.)* Jane, I know Bill is having an affair. Today when he called me I heard "her" voice in the background. And Bill was calling to figure out how he could protect his assets from someone—*(long pause)*—and that someone is you.

> **Narrator:** Jane sat down quietly and leaned her head in her hands. She was clearly shaken but didn't seem to be too surprised.

**Jane:** Oh, Ashley ... if you only knew how hard it's been these last few years. Bill has been so distant. But, I never expected him to be unfaithful. I mean after all of this time. After everything I have given him. I mean I gave up my life and my career to be his perfect "trophy wife."

> **Narrator:** Jane was suddenly struck with anger. She didn't know what she could do, but there was no way she was going to let Bill leave her with nothing. After all she had sacrificed; she was not going to let him make her a poor little old lady without a penny to her name!

**Jane:** So, what can you do to help me? Would you act as my financial advisor?

**Ashley:** I thought you would never ask. First, I need some information. Who is your lawyer? You know you are going to need to hire a good divorce attorney—do you have someone in mind?

**Jane:** I have always worked with Phil Rheem. He was a dear friend of my father, and he was the one who handled my father's estate when he passed away; normally all he handles are divorce cases. I will stop by his office after I leave here.

**Ashley:** Also, I will be setting up a trust for your assets.

**Jane:** Are you qualified to do that sort of thing?

**Ashley:** Oh don't worry, I can take care of it—I've got a lot of experience with trusts and it will save us some time instead of having to worry about jumping through all the legal hoops.

> **Narrator:** On the way back from lunch, Ashley was thinking about where to begin. She knew she wanted to leave Bill with nothing, but she also needed to make sure Jane was able to continue living the life she had become accustomed to.

## Scene II

> **Narrator:** Later that afternoon Ashley returned to her office. She knew that the day ahead was going to be a long one.
>
> The afternoon before, after she had left the office she stopped by Phil Rheem's law practice. Even though Ashley did not know Phil on a casual basis, she had worked with him on a number of different occasions when she had clients with complicated estate matters. Ashley had told Phil's secretary that the matter was urgent and she needed to see him immediately. When she entered Phil's office he was reviewing a case file that he placed to the side as he stood up to greet her.

**Phil:** Well ... Good afternoon, Ashley. What is it that gives me the good fortune to see your pretty face in my office today?

> **Narrator:** Ashley had never really cared for Phil's charming style—she found it to be condescending and irritating. Nevertheless, he was the perfect type of attorney who had the power and connections to do what she needed him to do for her.

**Ashley:** (*Sounding charming herself.*) Good afternoon to you too, Phil. You know it is always *my* pleasure when I have a chance to work with you.

> **Narrator:** Phil motioned for Ashley to sit down in one of the overstuffed leather chairs in front of his giant mahogany desk. As Ashley took a seat, she noticed the open file on Phil's desk. She glanced at it only briefly, but she noticed the name typed at the top of the papers. Ashley then realized that the file contained all of the legal documents for Bill Jackson's trusts. Of course, she also had a copy of them, but these were the originals, and the man who had signed and prepared them was sitting right in front of her. She silently crossed her fingers that Mr. Rheem would be as helpful as she was hoping.

**Ashley:** Phil, (*Pausing, then speaking in a direct tone.*) I am going to get right down to business here. (*Pausing again.*) I am here about Jane Jackson. Her husband has been a client of mine for more than 10 years. I am sure you are acquainted with Bill?

**Phil:** Yes, I have worked with Bill on a few previous business matters.

**Ashley:** Well, this morning Bill contacted me. He was interested in protecting his assets. When I talked to him he seemed so frantic that I was concerned, of course. I could not understand where this sudden panic had come from, and it wasn't until I found out that he was going to leave his wife that it all made sense to me. Bill wants to make sure that his wife, Jane, will not be able to lay a finger on any of his wealth, which—if I may say say—Jane helped him to build. So, as you can see, this little situation has put me in quite a bind.

**Phil:** Yes, I can see where it would. Well, (pause) as Jane may have told you, I have been acquainted with her family for a long time. Her father and I used to play golf together out at the club. He was a great man. He helped me get my start in this profession. It saddened me greatly to see him pass away. (*Leaning back in his chair and sighing.*) I must tell you that I would have done anything for that man—I would be willing to do whatever it takes to protect Mrs. Jackson; she deserves at least that much.

**Ashley:** (*Leaning back in her chair.*) Thank you, Phil. I knew you would understand. Jane and I have talked, and she is willing to do whatever it takes also. I know she will be getting in touch with you soon about filing for divorce, but I felt like I needed to see you myself—I am sure you understand.

**Phil:** Of course I understand. (*Pause.*) Now don't you worry your pretty little head about a thing; I will make sure Jane is completely taken care of. Now, if you'll excuse me I'll make a few calls and see what I can do for you.

**Ashley:** Thank you, Phil. And you know that if you ever need anything, just give me a call. I will always be glad to return the favor.

## Scene III

**Narrator:** Later that night, Ashley sat down in her still, dark office and pulled a file out of her briefcase. She switched on the desk lamp and opened the file containing Bill Jackson's original trust documents. Yesterday, when she was in Phil's office, she had secretly slipped them into her briefcase when he momentarily stepped out to talk with his secretary. She knew that she was treading in deep waters here, but it seemed so simple to her. Slowly, Ashley stood up and walked over to the shredding machine in the corner of the room, and one by one, she fed each sheet into the metal teeth that ground up the original documentation that Bill Jackson had ever established a trust.

The following morning she returned to her office. She picked up the phone and hit the speed dial. She was directly connected with Ben Pyles, her broker/dealer representative.

**Ashley:** Ben, yes, hello? And how are you this morning? Yes, it is early. Well, you know I wanted to get a jump on a few things before heading off for the weekend. Listen, I need to make a few trades for a client—his name is Bill Jackson. His account number is 9008765. (*Pausing, waiting for him to answer.*) Yes, that's right. I want to go ahead and liquidate the account. (*Pause.*) No, I do not want to reinvest the proceeds into a money market account. Just make a check out to Bill and Jane Jackson and send it to their home address. Secondly, I would like for you to liquidate Bill's second account and invest the proceeds in the following penny stocks.

**Narrator:** Ashley listed several penny stocks, directing Ben to split the assets evenly among the stocks she had given him. Ashley was fully aware that by moving the assets from the second account into penny stocks that Bill would almost certainly incur a loss. She also knew that this could hurt Jane by reducing the amount of assets available in the divorce, but she suspected that the account was nothing more than a place where Bill stashed money to pay for his own personal expenses. She felt justified in taking the action.

**Ashley:** *(Pausing and softly giggling.)* Now, Ben, you know I wouldn't do anything that wasn't in the best interest of my client. I tried to talk him out of these trades, but he was insistent. I guess he read some article in a personal investing magazine. It is all a bunch of bologna if you ask me, but I work for him so I have to do what he wants. You know…that's just the way the business goes. *(Pausing again.)* Well, I guess that will be all for me. You have a nice weekend. Tell your wife hello for me. Take care now. Goodbye to you, too.

**Narrator:** When the receiver finally clicked down, Ashley leaned back in her chair. She sighed to herself. She hated to see Bill and Jane's marriage end; it seemed like they were always so happy. But she wasn't going to allow Bill to make a mockery of all of Jane's sacrifice and devotion. No, Bill Jackson was going to be the sorry one in the end. By Monday morning , he wouldn't know what had hit him.

## Case Questions

1.  When asked later about her actions, Ashley affirmed that she did what she thought was right at the time because it served the interest of her friend. She argued that even though her actions might be wrong, the consequences for Jane were positive. Her view of the ethical situation was driven by which ethical outlook?

    a.   Normative ethics.

    b.   Teleological ethics.

    c.   Deontological ethics.

    d.   Disclosure ethics.

2.  Which of the following statements is true?

    I.    Ashley is in violation of CFP Board *Practice Standards and Code of Ethics.*

    II.   Ashley is in violation of SEC financial adviser rules.

    III.  Although some of Ashley's actions are questionable, nothing she did would fall under the rule making of the FINRA (NASD).

    a.   I only

    b.   III only

    c.   I and II only

    d.   I, II, and  III

3.   Which of the following will provide liability protection for Ashley in this case?

   a.   E&O insurance.

   b.   The arbitration clause in investment management contracts.

   c.   Disclaiming fiduciary status as a registered representative.

   d.   None of the above.

4.   According to the definition of what constitutes a client, found in the terminology of financial planning practice standards section of CFP Board *Practice Standards and Code of Ethics*, who among the following is not considered Ashley's client?

   a.   Bill

   b.   Jane

   c.   Phil

   d.   Both a and b

   e.   Both b and c

5.   Did Ashley break CFP Board *Practice Standards and Code of Ethics* confidentiality rules when she contacted Phil Rheem without the consent of Jane—even though Jane was most likely not going to be upset with Ashley?

   a.   Yes, because personal information was given without Jane's consent, a violation occurred.

   b.   No, because Jane could not be harmed by the use of her personal information.

   c.   No, because Ashley is allowed to share client information with other professional advisors.

   d.   Because Jane is only a friend of Ashley's, the CFP Board *Practice Standards and Code of Ethics* do not apply.

6.   Would Jane's attorney, Phil Rheem, need to follow the CFP Board *Practice Standards and Code of Ethics*?

   a.   Yes, because any professional who deals with a CFP® professional must also follow the standards.

   b.   No, because Phil is not a CFP® professional.

   c.   Yes, because as an attorney, he must abide by all applicable and published ethical standards.

   d.   Attorneys have no ethical standards, so he does not have to follow CFP Board rules—or any other rules, for that matter.

7. The Principle of Integrity states that "A CFP® professional shall offer and provide professional services with integrity." Which of the following statements is true in relation to this principle?

    I.   This principle allows for honest mistakes and innocent errors.

    II.   This principle allows a client who is dissatisfied with his or her planner to sue for lack of disclosure.

    III.  This principle requires CFP® professionals to provide fee-only services whenever a client requests an initial planning review.

   a. I only

   b. II only

   c. III only

   d. I and II only

   e. II and III only

8. Prior to her trouble with the Jacksons, Ashley prospected for clients using seminars. She advertised herself as Ashley Smith, CFP®, RIA. Is this permissible?

   a. Yes, so long as she describes what the certifications mean during her seminar.

   b. No, because the SEC does not allow the use of RIA in marketing materials.

   c. Yes, as long as she tells the audience that she is not also a registered representative.

   d. It depends on the size of the seminar and whether or not she is promoting the sale of securities.

9. CFP Board *Practice Standards and Code of Ethics* indicate that a CFP® professional may not solicit clients using false or misleading advertisements. Which of the following statements is *not* an example of a misleading statement/advertisement?

   a. "Our mutual fund portfolios have averaged over 18% returns during the last three years."

   b. "We guarantee a 100% improvement on your portfolio's annual return."

   c. "Our firm offers fee-based services, but also receives commissions from the investment products sold."

   d. "I practice as a fee-only planner, but I receive a commission on the insurance products I sell."

10. About a year ago Ashley was dealing with a client, Bob Hernandez, who was trying to minimize estate taxes. Ashley was not clear on all of the estate laws, so she called an attorney friend who deals primarily with criminal cases to help resolve a few of Bob's questions. Did Ashley violate rules related to planning competence within CFP Board *Practice Standards and Code of Ethics*?

    a. No; she called a qualified person for help.

    b. Yes; she should not be dealing with estate planning issues at all as a CFP® professional.

    c. Yes; she should have contacted a qualified estate attorney.

    d. No; she acted in the best interest of her client.

11. Which of the following statements is true?

    I.   If a CFP® professional must earn continuing education credits from a licensing board other than CFP® Board, he/she does not have to meet CFP continuing education credits.

    II.  A CFP® professional shall not engage in any conduct that reflects adversely on his or her integrity or fitness as a CFP® professional.

    III. All CFP® professionals are prohibited from actively practicing other professions and offering services in related fields, regardless of license and practice standards.

    a. I only

    b. II only

    c. III only

    d. II and III only

    e. I, II, and III

12. A CFP® professional must have and use a written disclosure form that includes which of the following?

    a. A statement of philosophy the professional adopts when working with clients.

    b. A statement identifying conflicts of interest.

    c. A statement disclosing how the professional receives compensation.

    d. All of the above.

13. CFP Board *Practice Standards and Code of Ethics* state that a CFP® professional must always make timely disclosures of all material information to clients. Which of the following forms will meet this requirement?

    a. SEC Form ADV, Part II.

    b. Form FPD—Disclosure Form—provided by CFP Board.

    c. A statement of the planners' life and business philosophy.

    d. All of the above.

    e. Only a and b.

14. In which of the following situations is it impermissible to reveal personal information about a client?

    a. To establish a brokerage account for a client.

    b. While the planner is being audited for his or her own tax return.

    c. To defend the CFP® professional against charges of wrongdoing.

    d. In a civil dispute between the CFP® professional and the client.

15. After finding out what Ashley had done, Bill terminated his working relationship with her and requested that she return all documents about his account immediately. Is Ashley in violation of any rule under the Principle of Professionalism if one year goes by and she fails to return Bill's original documents used in the financial planning process?

    a. Yes, because she is not allowed under the rules to hold original client documents.

    b. No, CFP Board gives planners at least two years to return files to terminated clients.

    c. Yes, because principles and rules require that she return the documents in a timely fashion.

    e. No, a CFP® professional is under no legal, moral, or ethical responsibility to return client data. In fact, this information must be retained by the planner in case of an audit.

16. Which of the following statements is true?

    I.    According to the Principle of Professionalism, a CFP® professional is not allowed to practice any profession unless a license is required by law.

    II.    The Principle of Confidentiality states that the same standards of confidentiality must be held between the CFP® professional, employers, and clients.

    III.    The Principle of Diligence states that a planner must make only recommendations that are suitable for each client.

    a.    I only

    b.    II only

    c.    II and III only

    d.    I, II, and III

17. Ashley, as a CFP® professional, is required to properly supervise subordinates when dealing with the subordinate's delivery of financial planning services. Which of the following would be considered properly supervised?

    a.    An intern makes recommendations that have not been reviewed by Ashley to a client.

    b.    Ashley's office manager, Marge, who is not licensed, is asked to research and suggest stocks to be included in a client's portfolio.

    c.    A licensed intern, before making a client recommendation, reviews the recommendation with Ashley.

    d.    An intern, who is not licensed, makes a trade, with Ashley's permission, in a client's account while Ashley is at lunch.

18. Which of the following statements is true?

    a.    When Ashley contacted Jane about Bill's divorce plans, she was also required by CFP Board *Practice Standards and Code of Ethics* to disclose conflicts of interest in writing.

    b.    Instructing the broker to purchase penny stocks was a violation of the CFP Board *Practice Standards and Code of Ethics*, which require implementing strategies suitable for the client.

    c.    Sharing information about Bill and Jane with Phil Rheem is a direct violation of CFP Board *Practice Standards and Code of Ethics*.

    d.    All of the above are true.

    e.    Only a and c are true.

19. Which of the following statements is true in relation to Ashley's reallocation of Bill Jackson's investment assets?

    a.  FINRA would find that these investments were unsuitable for Bill.

    b.  Ashley would be held harmless against a claim of unsuitability because she, in fact, conducted some research on the stocks before making the purchases.

    c.  Her actions are a prime example of churning.

    d.  If Ashley had discretion over Bill's account, she was entirely within her rights to make the penny stock purchases.

20. CFP Board *Practice Standards and Code of Ethics* rules state that a CFP® professional must offer advice only in the areas in which he or she is competent to do so. Ashley has obviously broken rules related to Principle 3. Why? Choose the best possible answer.

    a.  Ashley did not gain enough information from Bill before entering into the relationship with Jane.

    b.  Jane should have recognized Ashley's conflict of interest.

    c.  Ashley was unable to meet Bill's needs and objectives adequately.

    d.  Ashley was unable to provide competent services because of the conflict of interest concerning her friendship with Jane.

# Index

# M

## Q